TEXTBOOK ON

EC LAW

Seventh Edition

Josephine Steiner, BA, LLB

and

Lorna Woods, LLB, LLM, Solicitor

Blackstone Press

Published by
Blackstone Press Limited
Aldine Place
London W12 8AA
United Kingdom

Sales enquiries and orders
Telephone +44-(0)-20-8740-2277
Facsimile +44-(0)-20 8743-2292
e-mail: sales@blackstone.demon.co.uk
website: www.blackstonepress.com

ISBN 1-84174-023-3
© Josephine Steiner, Lorna Woods, 2000

First edition 1988
Second edition 1990
Reprinted 1991 twice
Third edition 1992
Reprinted 1993 twice
Fourth edition 1994
Reprinted 1995
Fifth edition 1996
Reprinted 1997
Sixth edition 1998
Reprinted 1999
Seventh edition 2000
Reprinted 2001, 2002

British Library Cataloguing in Publication Data
A CIP cataloguing record for this book is available from the British Library

Typeset in 10/11 Plantin by Style Photosetting Limited,
Mayfield, East Sussex
Printed and bound in Great Britain by Ashford Colour Press Limited,
Gosport, Hampshire

CONTENTS

PART ONE   SOURCES, NATURE AND EFFECT OF EC LAW

Development of the Union — Changes to the EC Treaty made by the TEU —
The other two pillars of the Union — Impact of the Treaty of Amsterdam —
Conflicting attitudes towards the Union — Expansion of membership —
Beyond Amsterdam — Further reading

Parliament (Articles 189–201 (ex 137–144) EC) — Council (Articles 202–210
(ex 145–154) EC) — Commission (Articles 211–219 (ex 155–163) EC) —
Budgetary procedures — Court of Justice (Articles 220–245 (ex 164–168) EC)
— Court of Auditors — Economic and Social Committee (Articles 257–262
(ex 193–198) EC) — Committee of the Regions — Impact of enlargement —
Further reading

3   Scope of the EC Treaty: laws and law-making   32
in the Community

Scope of EC Treaty — Law-making process — Subsidiarity — Problems in the
law-making process: proposed reforms — Legislative acts — Soft law —
Sources of EC law — Further reading

4   Principles of direct applicability and direct effects: 50
State liability under *Francovich*

Treaty Articles — Regulations — Directives — Principle of indirect effects —
Principle of State liability under *Francovich* v *Italy* — Decisions — Recommendations and opinions — International agreements to which the EC is a party —
Exclusions from the principle of direct effects — Conclusions — Further
reading

5   Principle of supremacy of EC law   85

The problem of priorities — The Court of Justice's contribution — The
Member States' response — Conclusions — Further reading

6   General principles of law   108

Rationale for the introduction of general principles of law — Development of
general principles — Rules of administrative justice — Equality — Subsidiarity
— General principles applied to national legislation — Relationship between
the EC/EU and the ECHR in the protection of human rights — Conclusions
— Further reading

PART TWO   ECONOMIC AND SOCIAL LAW OF THE EC:
ASPECTS OF THE INTERNAL MARKET

Section A   Free movement of goods

7   Introduction   135

Further reading

8   Customs union   139

Common customs tariff — Prohibition between Member States of customs
duties on imports and exports and of all charges of equivalent effect

9   Prohibition of discriminatory taxation   146

'Similar' products — Taxation affording indirect protection to domestic
products — Harmonisation of indirect taxation — Further reading

10   Elimination of quantitative restrictions on imports   151
and exports and all measures having equivalent effect

Prohibition, as between member States, of quantitative restrictions on
IMPORTS and of all measures having equivalent effect (Article 28 (ex 30)) —

apportionment — Payment of benefits to persons resident outside the competent State: special provisions — Evaluation — Further reading

Introduction — Equal pay for equal work: Article 141 (ex 119) EC — Pay — Discrimination — Objective justification — Equal work — Equal pay for work of equal value (Directive 75/117) — Principle of equal treatment for men and women (Directive 76/207) — Derogation from the equal treatment principle (Articles 2(2), 2(3) and 2(4)) — Sex as determining factor (Article 2(2)) — Pregnancy and maternity (Article 2(3)) — Positive discrimination (Article 2(4)) — Direct effects of Directive 76/207 — Principle of equal treatment in matters of social security (Directive 79/7) — Principle of equal treatment in occupational pension schemes (Directive 86/378) — Equal treatment in self-employment (Directive 86/613) — Remedies — Further reading

PART THREE
REMEDIES AND ENFORCEMENT OF EC LAW

Action before the European courts — Action before national courts — Conclusions — Further reading

Section A Action before national courts

Introduction — The procedure — Jurisdiction of the Court of Justice — Limitations on the Court's jurisdiction — Jurisdiction of national courts — Mandatory jurisdiction — Discretionary or 'permissive' jurisdiction — When will a decision be necessary? — *Acte clair* — Exercise of discretion — Exercise of mandatory jurisdiction — Effect of a ruling — Interim measures — Impact of the Treaty of Amsterdam — Conclusions on the preliminary rulings procedure to date — The future: impact of enlargement — Further reading

Section B Action before the Court of Justice against
Member States

Action by the Commission (Article 226 (ex 169) EC) — Failure to fulfil an obligation — Procedure — Defences — Effects of a ruling — Action by Member States (Article 227 (ex 170) EC) — Special enforcement procedures: State aids, breach of Article 95(4) (ex 100a(4)) procedures and measures to prevent serious internal disturbances — Further reading

Section C Action before the Court of Justice against
Community institutions

30   Direct action for annulment   506

31   Action for failure to act   532

32   Indirect review before the Court of Justice   544

33   Community liability in tort, action for damages   549

PREFACE

Many important changes have occurred in the European Union during the twelve years which have elapsed since this book was first published in 1988. Membership of the Union, originally called the European Economic Community, has risen to fifteen. The goal of the internal market, set down in the 1986 Single European Act, has been largely achieved. Nineteen ninety-two saw the signing at Maastricht of the Treaty on European Union, committing members to new Community goals, not least to economic and monetary union, and increasing governmental cooperation in the fields of foreign and security policy and justice and home affairs: the concept of Citizenship of the Union was born. The first stage of economic and monetary union came into effect in 1992; the final stage for participating Member States occurred on 1 January 1999. The Treaty of Amsterdam, signed in 1997, added significantly to the EC Treaty, renumbering most of its Articles, and effected radical changes to the institutional structures and decision-making processes of the Union, paving the way for a larger, more flexible Union. Applications for full membership by a number of European states were accepted in 1998. Thus the Union is committed to further enlargement. Despite disagreement both within and between Member States over the nature and pace of future developments, there are no doubts as to the need for the Union's continued existence.

The purpose of this seventh edition is not however to chart these developments, except in outline (although the changes introduced by the Treaty of Amsterdam are discussed in some detail), but to build on the framework laid down in previous editions. There is still a need for a single textbook of manageable size, concise but not simplistic, covering the major areas of EC law – constitutional, institutional and administrative as well as substantive – to cater for the growing body of students (and not only lawyers) from around the world who wish to study EC law, and for practitioners who realise that they can no longer afford to ignore it. The advent of the internal market and the continuing expansion of the Union has simply reinforced that need.

A book of this type cannot of necessity provide an in-depth account of the EC institutions (although this section has again been expanded in the current edition), nor can it cover all areas of substantive law. Much EC law, for example in the field of company or commercial or environmental law, or the law relating to employment or consumer protection, is increasingly, and more appropriately, incorporated into the general textbooks on these subjects. Some topics, such as agriculture or monetary union are too large or too specialised for inclusion. Others, such as transport, are still in the process of development. Thus, the book continues to concentrate on the more highly developed areas of EC law, what one might describe as fundamental Community law, the law relating to the free movement of goods, persons and services, competition law and sex discrimination, and on the remedies available for breaches of Community law.

There are a number of changes to this edition. The section on institutions and law-making have been expanded and amended in the light of both the Treaty of Amsterdam and the proposed enlargement of the Union. A new chapter on free movement under the citizenship rights and the Schengen provisions respectively has also been included. The chapters relating to remedies have, again, been substantially rewritten in the light of the Court of Justice's recent case law, particularly its development of the principle of State (and indirectly, Community) liability in damages following *Brasserie du Pêcheur* and *Factortame*. As before, the book aims to provide sufficient insight into the principles of EC law, including its current difficulties, and the processes of the European institutions, to enable the reader to pursue studies, resolve problems and enforce rights in areas of law whether or not covered by the book, as and when the need arises. The principal sources of EC law and a selection of textbooks are listed at the end of the book. Each chapter provides a list of further reading.

Our thanks go to all of those who helped in the preparation of this book: to colleagues in various institutions for their helpful comments and suggestions, especially Alan Riley, Jeremy Scholes and Fiona Smith; and finally to our husbands and families for their unflinching support, and for providing a welcome distraction from the demands of academic research.

Jo Steiner
Lorna Woods

September 2000

ABBREVIATIONS

Bull. EC	*Bulletin of the European Communities*
CAP	Common Agricultural Policy
CCT	Common Customs Tariff
CDE	*Cahiers de Droit Européen*
CET	Common External Tariff
CFI	Court of First Instance
CMLR	*Common Market Law Reports*
CML Rev	*Common Market Law Review*
COREPER	Committee of Permanent Representatives
D/G	Directorate-General
EAGGF	European Agriculture Guidance and Guarantee Fund
EC	European Community/Communities, Treaty Establishing the European Community
ECB	European Central Bank
EC Bull	*Bulletin of the European Communities*
EEA	European Economic Area
ECHR	European Convention for the Protection of Human Rights and Fundamental Freedoms 1950
ECJ	European Court of Justice
ECLR	*European Competition Law Review*
ECR	*European Court Reports* (official reports of the judgments of the European Court, English version)
ECSC	European Coal and Steel Community
EEC	European Economic Community
EFTA	European Free Trade Association
EIPR	European Intellectual Property Review
EL Rev	*European Law Review*
EPL	European Public Law
ESCB	European System of Central Banks
Euratom	European Atomic Energy Community
FSP	foreign and security policy
GATT	General Agreement on Tariffs and Trade
ICLQ	*International and Comparative Law Quarterly*

IGC	Intergovernmental Conference
JHA	justice and home affairs
JO	*Journal Officiel* (French version of OJ)
LIEI	*Legal Issues of European Integration*
LQR	*Law Quarterly Review*
MCA	Monetary Compensatory Amount
MLR	*Modern Law Review*
OJ	*Official Journal* (of the European Communities)
PL	*Public Law*
qmv	qualified majority voting
RPM	relevant product market
SEA	Single European Act
TCN	third country national
TEU	Treaty on European Union
ToA	Treaty of Amsterdam
WashLRev	Washington Law Review
WTO	World Trade Organization
YEL	*Yearbook of European Law*

Unless otherwise stated, cases cited were decided by the ECJ and Articles cited are Articles of the EC Treaty.

TABLE OF CASES

Court of Justice of the European Communities — Chronological List

Cases have been arranged in chronological order by case number and year. See page xlii for alphabetical list of Court of Justice of the European Communities cases.

Court of Justice of the European Communities — Alphabetical List

Cases have been arranged in alphabetical order. See page xv for chronological list of Court of Justice of the European Communities cases.

Belgian Courts

Danish Courts

French Courts

German Courts

Italian Courts

United Kingdom Courts

United States Courts

European Court of Human Rights

TABLE OF COMMISSION DECISIONS

TABLE OF UK STATUTES

TABLE OF EUROPEAN
COMMUNITY TREATIES

TABLE OF
EUROPEAN COMMUNITY
SECONDARY LEGISLATION

PART ONE

Sources, Nature and Effect of EC Law

ONE

From EEC to EU: a brief history of the development of the Union

Development of the Union

The European Economic Community (EEC) came into existence following the signing of the Treaty of Rome in 1957 by the six original Member States, France, Germany, Italy, Belgium, The Netherlands and Luxembourg. A second Rome Treaty signed by the same six States created Euratom (the European Atomic Energy Community) on the same day. These treaties, but particularly the EEC Treaty, represented the culmination of a movement towards international cooperation which had been growing throughout the 20th century, and which was given particular impetus in Europe following the devastation inflicted by the Second World War.

The institutional model for the EEC had already been provided by the European Coal and Steel Community (ECSC) set up in 1951 with the Treaty of Paris by the same six States. However, the scope of the EEC was altogether wider. The ECSC was concerned only with creating a single market in coal and steel; the EEC was designed to create an economic community. Although its aims were primarily economic, to create a single 'common' market in Europe, they were not exclusively so. The founder members of the EEC were fired by ideals as well as economic practicalities. As stated in the preamble to the EEC Treaty, its signatories were 'Determined to lay the foundations of an ever closer union among the peoples of Europe', 'Resolved by thus pooling their resources to preserve and strengthen peace and liberty'.

These words were not pious platitudes; they represented the spirit and purpose underlying the Treaty, and, in interpreting the Treaty and legislation enacted thereunder, the Court of Justice (ECJ), the original court of the EC, has never lost sight of these aims.

Although the institutional framework of the EEC, as of Euratom, was modelled on that of the ECSC, the three communities at the outset held only two institutions in common, the Assembly (subsequently renamed the Parliament) and the ECJ. It was not until the Merger Treaty 1965 that the other two main institutions merged. The High Authority, the executive body of the ECSC, merged with the EEC and Euratom Commission to form what is now the Commission, and the Council of Ministers of the ECSC with that of the EEC and Euratom to become a single Council. Henceforth the three communities continued to function as separate entities, but with shared institutions.

The United Kingdom, together with Denmark and the Republic of Ireland, finally joined the Communities in 1973 with the Treaty of Accession under a Conservative government led by Edward Heath. Incorporation of the Treaties into UK law was achieved by the European Communities Act 1972. (Norway joined at the same time but subsequently withdrew following a referendum which came out against membership.)

There were many reasons for our remaining outside the Community for so long. We were reluctant to loosen our existing ties with the Commonwealth, which membership of the EEC would clearly entail; we wished to retain our (perceived) 'special relationship' with the USA; and, as an island nation which had not been subject to enemy occupation during the First and Second World Wars, we no doubt lacked the sense of urgency which inspired our Continental neighbours. Suspicious that membership of the EEC would involve an unacceptable loss of sovereignty, we preferred the looser ties of the European Free Trade Association (EFTA) which we entered on its creation in 1959. When we did seek to join the EEC, persuaded by its clear economic success, our entry was blocked for some years, largely due to the efforts of the French President, General de Gaulle. Even after accession in 1973 public opinion in the UK was divided; it was only following a referendum in favour of membership conducted in 1975 under the government of the Labour Party that our membership was fully and finally confirmed.

In 1979 Greece, and in 1986 Spain and Portugal, signed acts of accession to join the Communities, bringing the then total membership to 12. Membership increased again with the accession of Austria, Finland and Sweden on 1 January, 1995. Norway held a referendum which again resulted in a vote against membership. Thus, membership currently comprises 15 States, although further enlargement is now proposed.

An important development in 1986 was the signing by the then 12 Member States of the Single European Act (SEA). A White Paper issued by the Commission in 1985 had revealed that despite the Community's long existence, many barriers still existed to the achievement of the single internal market. If the Community were to achieve the full economic benefits of the single market and meet the challenge of world competition further progress had to be made. The result was a new treaty, the SEA. The principal purpose of the SEA was to eliminate the remaining barriers to the single internal market within the deadline of 31 December 1992, to be achieved by a massive programme of harmonisation (see chapters 7, 10, 21). In addition, the SEA extended the sphere of community competence and introduced a number of procedural changes designed to accelerate the community decision-making process. The SEA, incorporated in the UK by the European Communities

(Amendment) Act 1986, undoubtedly injected a new dynamism into Community affairs. By February 1992, 218 of the 282 proposals forming the complete programme for the completion of the internal market had been adopted.

The late 1980s saw a growing movement within the Community towards closer European Union. In December 1989, two intergovermental conferences were convened pursuant to cooperation procedures introduced by the SEA to consider the questions of (a) economic and monetary and (b) political union. The conferences, which lasted for a year, resulted in the signing, at Maastricht, on 7 February 1992, of the Treaty on European Union (TEU).

The TEU comprised two distinct parts. One part (Article G, renumbered Article 8 following the ratification of the 1997 Amsterdam Treaty ('ToA') which, in pursuit of greater coherence, renumbered most of the articles of both the EC Treaty and the TEU), consisting of 86 paragraphs, introduced substantial amendments to the EEC Treaty, and renamed it the European Community (EC) Treaty, reflecting its wider purposes.

The second part of the TEU (Articles 1–7 and 9–53 — Articles A–F and H–S respectively as originally provided in the TEU), representing the political pillar of the Treaty, stood as a separate Treaty establishing the European Union (Article 1 (ex A)). It set out a number of general principles (Articles 1–7 (ex A–F)) and provided specifically for cooperation, with a view to adopting joint action, in the field of foreign and security policy (FSP), and eventually defence (Articles 11–28 (ex J)) and for cooperation and the framing of common policies in justice and home affairs (JHA) (Articles 29–45 (ex K)). These two areas of cooperation came to be referred to as the second and third pillars respectively of the European Union. The remaining pillar is the EC, together with ECSC and Euratom. The three communities comprising this pillar, referred to as the first pillar of the Union, are together called the European Communities.

The TEU was due to come into effect on 1 January 1993, following ratification as required by all Member States. As a result of difficulties, political and legal, causing delay in ratification in some Member States (notably the UK, Denmark and Germany), the Treaty did not enter into force until 1 November 1993. From that date the EEC Treaty became the EC Treaty, and will henceforth be referred to as such in this book, except where the term EEC is needed for reasons of historical accuracy. The term European Union (EU), introduced in Article 1 (ex A) of the TEU to describe the union of Member States as comprised under the European Community treaties and the TEU, is not strictly applicable to matters of law relating to the EC Treaty, although it is widely misused in that context. Therefore, although there are occasions when it might properly be used, for example to describe 'the EU' or 'EU countries' or 'EU citizens', the term EC will continue to be used throughout this book in order to avoid confusion.

Changes to the EC Treaty made by the TEU

Monetary union   Like the SEA, the TEU extended the scope of Community competence and strengthened its institutional machinery; in particular, the powers of the European Parliament. Perhaps one of the most politically sensitive issues was the introduction of provisions designed to lead to full economic and monetary union by 1999. The fact that both Britain and Denmark negotiated provisions allowing them to opt out of this process indicates the importance of this issue. Even Germany, which has been one of the driving forces behind monetary union, has experienced difficulties: the validity of Germany's entry into the single currency was challenged, albeit unsuccessfully, before the German Constitutional Court.

The road to monetary union fell into three stages (Articles 98–124 (ex 102a–109m) EC). Stage one consisted of the completion of the internal market and the removal of controls on the movement of capital. This stage has been completed. Stage two began on 1 January 1994. It aimed to ensure the convergence of the economies of the Member States, measured by criteria set out in the EC Treaty. These are commonly referred to as the 'convergence criteria'. Only countries which satisfy the convergence criteria will be able to join the single currency. The Member States joining economic and monetary union in the first wave were identified in a Commission recommendation based on its Convergence Report of 25 March 1998 on the state of the Member States' economies. Eleven States were identified as having satisfied the convergence criteria: Belgium, Germany, Spain, France, Ireland, Italy, Luxembourg, The Netherlands, Austria, Portugal and Finland (the UK and Denmark having, for the time being, opted out of monetary union). This recommendation was confirmed by the European Council meeting in May 1998. The final stage was the irrevocable locking of the exchange rates of the Member States' currencies and the introduction of a common currency, the euro. The date set for the introduction of the single currency was 1 January 1999, although euro coins and notes will not be issued in all the participating States until 2002. Following the introduction of the single currency, a new exchange rate mechanism was introduced between the euro and the currencies of those Member States which have not yet joined the single currency. In addition to this, the Treaty contains provisions detailing the institutions necessary to run the single currency (Articles 112–115 (ex 109a–109d) EC). These are the European Central Bank and a committee to determine economic policy, the Council of Economic and Finance Ministers (ECOFIN).

Union citizenship   The TEU also introduced the notion of citizenship of the Union (Article 17 (ex 8)). On the face of it, citizenship seems a relatively straightforward notion. It entitles EC nationals to certain rights such as freedom of movement throughout the Community (see chapters 19 and 23) and the right to vote and to stand in municipal elections or elections to the European Parliament in any Member State in which they are resident. The precise extent of the rights to be granted to citizens, however, is not clear. Will citizenship incorporate rights contained elsewhere in the EC Treaty hitherto granted to EC workers, the self-employed and their families (see chapters 19–22)? Does it include rights and duties found in the TEU provisions relating to the other pillars (e.g. Article 6(2) (ex F(2)) TEU)?

There has been much debate about the significance of European citizenship. Some see it as the beginning of the development of a common European identity or as a means to ameliorate the democratic deficit (see chapter 3) within the Union. Others have criticised it for being no more than a label for the rights of free movement already incorporated in the EC Treaty. The Treaty does allow the Member States to increase the rights attaching to the notion of citizenship, but it is still too early to tell how, if at all, citizenship will develop.

The other two pillars of the Union

Articles 11–28 (ex J) (FSP) and 29–42 (ex K) (JHA) of the TEU constitute the second and third pillars respectively of the European Union. Although they can be seen as extending the powers transferred to the European level, they can also be seen as maintaining the autonomy of the nation State. Decision-making within these pillars was, under the TEU, predominantly in the hands of the Council representing the Member States, and, although these two pillars share the institutions of the EC, the other Community institutions were limited in the role they played in both policy-making and enforcement. In addition, all decisions were required to be made unanimously and consequently progress towards effective policies within these areas would inevitably be slow. The TEU contained provisions whereby some of the policies in JHA could be transferred to the EC (former Article K.9 TEU). A comparison between the decision-making processes within these two pillars and those of the EC (chapter 3) would suggest that such a transfer must surely increase the speed of common policy-making in those areas. This was recognised and, following the ratification of the Treaty of Amsterdam, several policy areas originally dealt with under JHA (e.g., immigration and asylum of third-country (non-EU) nationals) are now dealt with under the EC Treaty (see further chapter 23). The decision-making procedures under JHA have also been amended following Amsterdam, specifying in limited circumstances the use of qualified majority voting (qmv).

Impact of the Treaty of Amsterdam

Former Article N(2) TEU provided that an intergovernmental conference (IGC) should be held in 1996 to examine the provisions which the TEU required to be reviewed. Other issues could also be included on the agenda (Article N(1) TEU). The purpose of the review was to revise the policies and institutional structure of the Union to ensure its effectiveness (Article 2 (ex B) TEU). This was an issue gaining ever more relevance with the increase of Union competence under the TEU and the proposed further expansion of Union membership. As the IGC discussions progressed, it became clear that the issues to be decided coalesced round three broad, interlinked themes: democracy, transparency and efficiency (discussed further in chapters 2 and 3). The review process continued through into June 1997, when a draft treaty was agreed at Amsterdam. This treaty, the Treaty of Amsterdam (ToA), was signed on 2 October 1997 and came into force on 1 May 1999. Since the

ToA renumbered all treaty articles, the new numbers of the treaty articles will henceforth throughout this book be used with the former numbers bracketed alongside them (e.g. Article 30 (ex Article 36) EC), save where reasons of historical accuracy (such as articles cited in the context of cases) dictate that only the original article number be shown.

The ToA, when compared with the ambitious TEU, may seem to achieve little; indeed, when one considers the stresses to which the EU will increasingly find its decision-making subject once membership is enlarged, the ToA could be criticised for failing to deal adequately with the difficult institutional questions involved. Nonetheless, the ToA can still be seen as constituting a cautious but significant expansion of the Community's scope. The first (EC) pillar has been strengthened by streamlining its decision-making powers and by the allocation of new competences (see chapter 3). Certain provisions, for example, those relating to the admission of third-country nationals, have been moved from the third pillar (JHA) to the EC pillar. In addition, the Schengen Agreement on the application of frontier checks on internal borders (an agreement outside the EC/EU framework between a number of the EU Member States) and its associated decisions have, in effect, been incorporated into the EC Treaty. All of these have been combined to form a new Title in Part Three of the EC Treaty, Title IV. These are discussed further in chapter 3. Some completely new provisions have also been introduced into the EC Treaty, such as those relating to unemployment. The Protocol on Social Policy, originally annexed to the EC Treaty by the TEU, has now been incorporated into the main body of the EC Treaty, replacing the existing social policy provisions (for further discussion of all these matters, and their significance, see chapter 19).

These changes reflect a shift of emphasis away from the mainly economic conception of the EC to a more political idea, founded on fundamental rights and principles. In particular, the provision prohibiting discrimination on grounds of nationality (Article 12 (ex Article 6) EC) has been developed by the insertion of a new clause (new Article 13 EC) authorising the Council to 'take appropriate action to combat discrimination based on sex, racial or ethnic origin, religion or belief, disability, age or sexual orientation'. Although not phrased in the absolute terms of Article 12 EC, it reinforces the idea of non-discrimination as a fundamental principle which the ECJ has invoked and used to significant effect in its case law (see chapters 20, 21 and 25).

This concern with fundamental principles is also evidenced by amended Article 7 (ex Article F) TEU. This provides that any Member State found to have committed a persistent and serious breach of the fundamental principles listed in Article 6 TEU may be suspended from voting in the Council of Ministers, although it will remain subject to obligations arising out of the Union membership, such as compliance with EC legislation. The principles listed in Article 6 TEU are: liberty, democracy, respect for human rights and fundamental freedoms, and the rule of law. Respect for the rule of law, in particular, is evidenced by the expansion of the ECJ's jurisdiction in relation to the new Part Three Title IV of the EC Treaty and to the JHA provisions remaining in the TEU. In both these cases, however, the jurisdiction of the

ECJ is subject to serious limitations (to be discussed further in chapters 23 and 27). Nevertheless, the ToA has extended the scope of Union competence under the EC Treaty and effected significant changes in the TEU. These clauses will be discussed further in subsequent chapters.

The last main change introduced by the ToA was the introduction of provisions allowing for 'closer cooperation' by Member States. This is often referred to as an example of the principle of 'flexibility', described as the leitmotif of the ToA. It allows differing conceptions of the European ideal and different degrees of commitment to coexist within the Union framework. As such, it is a variant of the concepts variously described as 'multi-speed Europe', 'Europe of variable geometry' and 'Europe of concentric circles' prior to the 1996 IGC. The ToA allows Member States which wish to cooperate more closely in specific areas within the general scope of the treaties, but which are not yet subject to Community legislation, to do so. Although the Union had, in effect, accepted this approach in specific policy areas, for example, the UK and Danish opt-out of monetary union under the TEU and the UK opt-out of the Protocol on Social Policy in the TEU, this is the first time that a *general* provision (new Article 11 EC and, in respect of JHA, new Article 40, subject in both cases to new Articles 43 and 44 TEU) allowing for such separate development within the Union framework, has been incorporated.

Cooperation is limited to the matters within the scope of the treaties and cannot in any way conflict with Community law (see new Article 11 EC). New Article 11 limits the circumstances in which closer cooperation may operate; in particular, a majority of the Member States must be involved, the action must be in the furtherance of the Union's objectives and closer cooperation must not affect the rights and obligations of Member States not involved. The provisions in relation to closer cooperation within the JHA provisions of the TEU are couched in similar terms (new Article 43 TEU).

This provision for closer cooperation may bring some advantages, notably by preventing the frustration of the integrationist aims of the majority of Member States by the minority, thus relieving the tensions between the Member States which disagree about the depth of European integration and allowing compromise within the Union. It also carries disadvantages. In particular, the boundary between matters falling only within the sphere of EC law proper and areas permitting closer cooperation may be unclear. Furthermore, is it possible in the context of the internal market for some Member States to become involved in closer cooperation without affecting the position of other Member States? In which case, should the other Member States be involved in the discussions leading to the adoption of closer cooperation measures even though they will not be bound by them? This problem has already surfaced in the context of the UK's role in the introduction of monetary union. On the other hand, if the ECJ interprets the provisions set out in new Article 11 EC strictly so as to preserve and even stretch the boundaries of Community law, then the opportunities for such cooperation will be severely curtailed. In any event, the very fact that the Community is contemplating an approach where some Member States go ahead regardless of the wishes of others will undermine the ideas of community and solidarity which are fundamental to the creation of both the internal market and an ever closer union. Unless benefits and burdens are equally shared, there is a danger that the achievements of the past 43 years could be undone.

Conflicting attitudes towards the Union

The difference between the European Communities and the other two pillars created by the TEU and largely retained by the ToA is illustrative of the conflicting attitudes held by Member States and individuals towards the Community (and now the Union) since its inception, as exemplified by the divergent views expressed by politicians. The problem is that there are two main competing visions of Europe: the intergovernmental and the federal. An intergovernmental approach characterised the original JHA and FSP provisions of the TEU: decision-making was firmly within the control of the Member States, and the agreement of *all* Member States was required before policies could be adopted. This is the approach commonly used in treaty organisations such as the World Trade Organisation. Contrast that with the position under the EC Treaty, which contains a number of unusual factors:

(a)　The creation of autonomous bodies which have the power to develop policies independently, to a degree, of Member States (see chapters 2 and 3). The ECJ has also played a significant role in the development of policies.

(b)　The width of the policy areas on which the European bodies can operate. Within these areas the Member States have limited their freedom of independent action.

(c)　The system for approving legislation: in some areas Member States can be outvoted, even within the Council of Ministers, resulting in the possibility of a Member State having to implement policies with which it does not agree.

(d)　The degree to which EC law permeates the national legal systems, creating rights and obligations enforceable by individuals within national courts. Again the ECJ has played a crucial role here (see chapter 4).

The ToA, in transferring matters from the JHA provisions of the TEU to the EC Treaty (thereby reducing the scope for purely intergovernmental action), has shifted the balance in favour of the supranational. It has also reduced the scope for an intergovernmental approach to decision-making retained in the TEU. Some would see this as continuing the movement begun in the TEU in the direction of a federal superstate. In *Brunner* v *European Union Treaty* [1994] 1 CMLR 57 Germany's power to ratify the TEU was challenged as being contrary to the German constitution. It was argued that in transferring further powers and competence to the EC institutions, the TEU was seeking to create a Euro-State. The German Constitutional Court found, it is submitted correctly, that the EC was a federation of States not a Euro-State. Nevertheless, the loss of autonomy of action of the Member States consequent on membership of the EC has certainly been considerable.

This has increased during the life of the EC as more and more powers have been transferred to the Community in the SEA, the TEU and now the ToA. Some integrationists approve of this as part of the process of achieving an 'ever closer union'. Others fear the loss of sovereignty and see the EC as having grown beyond the loose association of States within a free trade area that the EC was intended to be. This problem is not new, an early example being the disagreement leading to the Luxembourg Accords (see chapter 3).

Sometimes these differing views of the EU result in Member States being characterised as either Euro-sceptic or pro-Europe, but a degree of caution must be exercised about such generalisations. There is a difference between political rhetoric and legal reality. For example, Denmark, often seen as a reluctant Member State, has one of the better records for implementation of and compliance with Community law. By contrast, in the 1998 review of implementation of Community law, the Commission commented that France, often perceived as pro-European, has the worst record as far as enforcement actions (Article 226 EC (ex 169), see chapter 28) is concerned. Furthermore, there is a tendency for Member States' representatives to put national interest — or national political pressures — over the Community interest. This is not just the case with France (see its recent ban on British beef in defiance of the Community position) or the UK (veto on introduction of Community tax on interest income, thought to threaten the UK bond market), but with all Member States (see the impact of the Greek position on the accession of Turkey; Portugal on the diversion of Community funding to proposed new Member States).

With the introduction of monetary union, the transfer of further competence to the EC and the proposed expansion in membership the question, 'where next?' assumes a new significance as Member States try to fight for their own view on the future of Europe. The ToA has sought to solve the problem by the principle of 'flexibility'; but the danger is that a flexible Europe could become a fragmented Europe.

Expansion of membership

The prospect of a free internal market within the EC and ever-closer union between its members, together with a fear of a 'fortress', protectionist Europe, has led to a growing demand from European States outside the EC either to seek special trading agreements with, or to join, the Community. Following its liberation from Communist rule in 1989, East Germany, reunited in October 1990 with West Germany, was absorbed into the Community. In October 1991 the European Economic Area (EEA) was created. It was to have comprised the EC and the seven EFTA States, but three of the EFTA States have now joined the EU and Switzerland failed to ratify the EEA agreement. Under the EEA agreement, which entered into force on 1 January 1994, these States are subject to the existing body of Community law (the *acquis communautaire*) relating to the internal market and competition and all future rules in these areas, but they are not represented in the EC institutions. Thus, although they may participate in the

EC law-making process, they have no real power in the shaping of Community law. A customs union between the EU and Turkey came into force on 31 December 1995.

Applications for full membership of the EU have now been received from 13 countries. All have signed association agreements opening themselves to free trade and preparing themselves for membership. Treaty negotiations with Cyprus, Hungary, Poland, Estonia, the Czech Republic and Slovenia started in spring 1998, and in 1999 the Helsinki Council Meeting agreed to start negotiations with the remaining applicants, so by the year 2010 the EU could comprise as many as 28 members. Agenda 2000 has been established by the Commission with, amongst other aims, the purpose of easing the path of States hoping to join the Union.

Beyond Amsterdam

With the ink hardly dry on the ToA, the possible expansion of the Union has triggered yet another round of treaty negotiations, as the EC institutions seek to introduce changes that will allow the institutions to function effectively with so many Member States. (See further chapter 2.) The intention is to have treaty amendments agreed by the end of 2000, so as to allow the accessions of the applicant States to commence from 2002 onwards. Although these changes to the constitutions and working methods of the institutions are, perhaps, the most obvious problems that the Union will have to deal with, enlargement itself has further implications and the ongoing tensions within the Union will have to be addressed.

Each enlargement has meant that the new Member States need to bring their legal systems in line with the requirements of existing Community law and practice — the Community 'acquis'. This has tended to result in transitional periods for the new Member States, with the consequence that the full requirements of Community law are not immediately applied. This will be even more the case for the former Eastern bloc countries, 'whose democracies are hardly less fragile than their economies'. Thus, as well as there being Amsterdam-style flexibility in the system, more Member States means the application of differing standards, albeit for a limited period.

Some Member States, and the UK is seen as one, have welcomed further enlargement on this basis. This view is based on the argument that the integration process in the existing Member States will be held up to allow the new Member States to catch up. Further, wider membership means that the Union becomes increasingly heterogeneous, and consequently it becomes more difficult to agree policies. Power then remains with the individual Member States. On this view, wider Europe is incompatible with deeper (or more integrated) Europe. Conversely, others take the view that it is precisely because of these difficulties that greater control needs to be handed over to the institutions to make decision-making more effective. (See further chapters 2 and 3.) This approach would see a greater reliance on qualified majority voting and possibly an extension of the Parliament's powers, suggesting a more federal (or supranational) approach than an intergovernmental one.

Against this background, it is interesting to note proposals to extend Union action in certain areas. The Helsinki Council Meeting, which approved further applicants to membership, also approved a new model of defence cooperation and plans for a common European policy on asylum seekers. Although these issues are already within the Union competence, these proposals actually seek to take action in what have broadly been moribund or ineffective policy areas. The proposals have not been popular, being seen by some States as representing a further erosion of national sovereignty or likely to create a 'Fortress Europe'. Others have been concerned that the changes will undermine individual civil liberties.

Quite apart from new policies and institutional questions, the expansion in membership may have an impact on current EC policies. Although minimum standards have been set as prerequisites to membership, the fact remains that EU funding will be required to improve the applicant States' infrastructures. Thus, unless the current Member States agree to increase their contributions to the Community budget, the existing budget will have to be diverted from current beneficiaries to the new States. Equally, the Common Agricultural Policy, which consumes a significant proportion of the annual Community budget, will have to be reconsidered in the light of the new States' situation. All these questions are highly sensitive and will affect many of the Member States' own national interests. How these issues will be resolved, given the current difficulties with Member States putting national political consider-ations over the Community interest, is not clear.

In view of the disputes within the Union about its future, the continuing enthusiasm for membership may seem surprising, but it cannot be denied that the EC has achieved a great deal. It is an important market, responsible for in excess of 20 per cent of all world trade and 31 per cent of global output; it thus constitutes a trading block which has the potential significantly to influence world affairs. Membership of the EU gives States the opportunity to be part of this. Also, for some countries, it will indicate that they have achieved democratic respectability in the eyes of other nations. In addition to being a European State (Article 59 (ex O) TEU), the EU requires that all Member States have democratic systems of government and respect human rights (Article 6 (ex F)). Last, but by no means least, during the past 50 years the EC has enjoyed an era of unprecedented peace. It is easy to overlook the fact that one of the underlying aims of the European communities was, in the words of the preamble to the ECSC Treaty:

> . . . to substitute for age-old rivalries the merging of their essential interests; to create . . . the basis for a broader and deeper community among peoples long divided by bloody conflicts.

Further reading

Curtin, D., 'The Constitutional Structure of the Union: A Europe of Bits and Pieces' (1993) 30 CML Rev 17.

Curtin, D. and Decker 'The EU as a "layered" International Organisation: Institutional Unity in Disguise' in Craig, P. and de Burca, G. (eds), *The Evolution of EU Law* (Oxford University Press, 1999).

De Burca, G., 'The Institutional Development of the EC: A Constitutional Analysis' in Craig, P. and de Burca, G. (eds), *The Evolution of EU Law* (Oxford University Press, 1999).

Douglas-Scott, 'In Search of Union Citizenship' (1998) 18 YEL 29.

Edwards, D., 'The Impact of the Single Market' (1987) 24 CML Rev 19.

Gormley, L., 'Reflection on the Architecture of the EU after the Treaty of Amsterdam' in O'Keeffe, D. and Twomey, P. (eds), *Legal Issues of the Amsterdam Treaty* (Hart Publishing, 1999).

Harmser, R., 'A European Union of Variable Geometry' (1994) 45 NILQ 109.

Langrish, S., 'The Treaty of Amsterdam: Selected Highlights' (1998) 23 EL Rev 3.

Meyring, B., 'Intergovernmentalism and Supranationality: Two Stereotypes of a Complex Reality' (1997) 22 EL Rev 221.

Schilling, T., 'The Autonomy of the Community Legal Order: An Analysis of Possible Foundations' (1996) 37 Hav Int'l LJ 307.

Usher, J., 'Variable Geometry or Concentric Circles: Patterns for the European Union' (1997) 46 ICLQ 243.

Weiler, J.H.H., 'The Transformation of Europe' (1991) 100 Yale LJ 2403.

Weiler, J.H.H. and Haltern, U.R., 'Response: The Autonomy of the Community Legal Order — Through the Looking Glass' (1996) 37 Harv Int'l LJ 411.

Editorial: Comment on the ToA (1997) 34 CML Rev 767.

TWO

Institutions of the EC: composition and powers

The principal institutions as set up by the original EEC Treaty (Article 7 (ex 4) EC) to carry out the Community's tasks comprised:

(a) the Assembly or Parliament,
(b) the Council,
(c) the Commission, and
(d) the Court of Justice.

In addition, Article 7 (ex 4) provided for the setting up of an Economic and Social Committee and a Court of Auditors, and the Merger Treaty 1965 (Article 4) for the creation of a Committee of Permanent Representatives of the Member States (COREPER). As a result of the SEA a new Court of First Instance was set up in October 1988 (Decision 88/591 OJ C215/1, 1989). Under the TEU the Court of Auditors has now been added to the institutions listed in Article 7 (ex 4), a European Investment Bank has been created (Article 9 (ex 4b) EC), and provision made for the creation of a Committee of the Regions and the setting up of the European System of Central Banks (ESCB) and a European Central Bank (ECB) (Article 8 (ex 4a) EC).

Parliament (Articles new 189–201 (ex 137–44) EC)

Composition As created by the Treaty of Rome in 1957, the European Parliament, called in that Treaty the Assembly (but since the SEA called the Parliament), was not a democratic body, although the Treaty provided for the eventual introduction of direct elections. It consisted of representatives of Member States who were required to be members of a national parliament. The introduction of direct elections, which occurred in 1979, resulted in increased democracy and increased concentration and expertise, since members are responsible to their electorate, and, as anyone is now eligible to stand, many are no longer subject to the rigorous demands of the 'dual mandate' at home and in Europe. Parliament at present consists of 626 members, with Germany having 99, France, Great Britain and Italy each having 87 representatives, Spain 64, The Netherlands 31, Belgium, Greece and Portugal 25, Sweden 21, Austria 20, Denmark and Finland 16, Ireland 15 and Luxembourg 6. Following Amsterdam, the maximum number of MEPs was increased to 700. Members meet in plenary sessions of approximately one week per month in Strasbourg, although the majority of Parliament's Committee meetings, where much important work is done, are held in Brussels. The rest take place in Strasbourg or, occasionally, Luxembourg. Members, who are drawn from 75 political parties, sit in 11 broad multinational political groupings, the largest being the Socialist group; they are required to vote 'on an individual and personal basis' and 'They shall not be bound by any instructions and shall not receive a binding mandate' (Act Concerning Direct Elections, Article 4(1)). They are elected for five years. A perennial complaint is that, despite the introduction of direct elections, the uniform system of election envisaged by Article 190(3) (ex 138(3)) EC has not yet been introduced.

Functions   As befitted a non-elected body, the original Parliament had few powers. Its functions were advisory and supervisory. It was not intended as a legislative body. However, it did over the years acquire some legislative powers, particularly over the budget. Following the introduction of direct elections, Parliament has played an increasingly important consultative role in the legislative process and has been given the final say over certain aspects of the budget. The TEU and ToA have further and substantially increased its powers.

In its advisory role, Parliament was originally required by the Treaty to be consulted by the Council of Ministers where legislation is proposed in a number of specific (and important) areas, e.g., Articles 52, 83 and 308 (ex 63, 87 and 235 EC respectively), but contrast Article 40 (ex 49) (workers). In these areas the Council must seek, and is obliged to consider, Parliament's opinion, although there is no obligation to follow it. This is an essential procedural requirement. Legislation has been successfully challenged when, although the Parliament had been consulted on an initial draft of the legislation, it was not consulted following substantial amendment to the draft (*Parliament* v *Council* (case C–21/94) (road taxes); by contrast *Germany* v *Council* (case C–280/93) (banana quotas) was unsuccessful). In *Roquette Frères SA* v *Council* (case 138/79) and *Maizena GmbH* v *Council* (case 139/79) a Regulation of the Council was annulled because, although Parliament's opinion had been sought, the Regulation had been passed by the Council before that opinion had been obtained. Nonetheless, in *Parliament* v *Council* (case C–65/93), where the Parliament's opinion was clearly required as a matter of some urgency, the Council made all efforts to obtain that opinion in time. In failing to meet the deadline, the Parliament, according to the Court, had failed in its duty of cooperation. The Court, as a consequence, refused to annul the Regulation. How far the Parliament's duty of cooperation extends is not clear. The Advocate General in this case was clearly unhappy about the effect such a decision would have on the institutional balance and thought that any changes to it would be more appropriately dealt with by treaty amendment.

The requirement for consultation and cooperation by Parliament, and consequently Parliament's influence, was strengthened by the introduction of conciliation procedures in 1977 (Joint Declaration of the European Parliament, the Council and the Commission, OJ C89/1, 22.4.75) and the cooperation procedures introduced by the SEA. The SEA also greatly extended the range of matters on which Parliament had to be consulted. The SEA also gave Parliament the power of (final) assent in respect of the admission of new members and the conclusion of association agreements with non-member countries. The TEU gave Parliament certain rights to be consulted in respect of the JHA and CFSP provisions. What was then Article K.6 (now Article 34) TEU provided that Parliament was to be consulted on the principal aspects of activities within JHA provisions. This provision also ensured that the Parliament's views were duly to be taken into consideration. Similar provisions existed in respect of the CFSP provisions (Article 21 (ex J.7) TEU). Parliament's right to be consulted and informed has increased under the ToA, but it still has no real powers over the second and third pillars of the TEU.

As well as a right to be *consulted*, and to participate in *conciliation* and *cooperation* procedures, the TEU introduced for Parliament, in a new Article 251 (ex 189b) EC, a right of *co-decision* with the Council in certain defined areas. Thus, under this procedure, the European Parliament now has a significant power of veto in matters subject to the new procedures. The co-decision procedure was to apply in a number of areas previously governed by the less onerous cooperation procedures (e.g., Articles 40, 44, 46 and 94 (ex 49, 54(2), 56(2), 100a) EC) and in some new spheres of activity (e.g., culture, health, consumer protection). In other areas, the consultation or cooperation procedures (the latter now laid down in Article 252 (ex 189c) EC) were to continue to apply. In cases of doubt it will be necessary to consult the Treaty to ascertain which procedure is applicable, although the ToA has greatly extended the areas to which co-decision applies with the result that the cooperation procedures in future will largely disappear. These procedures will be examined further in chapter 3.

In its supervisory role, Parliament exercises direct political control over the Commission. Commissioners must reply orally or in writing to its questions. The Commission must publish a general report which is discussed in Parliament in open session. Parliament meets members of the Commission in committees, and in practice, though this is not required by law, members of Parliament are consulted by the Commission at the pre-legislative stage. Parliament also has the power to dismiss the Commission, by passing a vote of censure (Article 201 (ex 144) EC). Such a motion must be carried by a two-thirds majority of the votes cast, which must represent a majority of the members of Parliament. A particular weakness of this sanction is the fact that the existing Commissioners will remain in office until their replacements are appointed. Furthermore, there is nothing to prevent the Member States from suggesting the same Commissioners be reappointed. Nonetheless, it was the Parliament's dissatisfaction with the conduct of the Commission that resulted in the Commissioners resigning in 1999. Some, but not all, of the Commissioners were re-appointed. Prior to Maastricht Parliament had no say in the appointment of new Commissioners. This has now been remedied; under Article 214(2) (ex 158(2)) EC, Parliament must be consulted on the nomination of the President and the appointment of Commissioners and the Commission as a whole has to be approved by Parliament.

The Council is not subject to the control of Parliament, but is subject to extensive supervision. Parliament reports on the activities of the Council three times a year, and the President of the Council must present an address to Parliament at the beginning of every year. This is followed by a general debate. The incoming President also presents a survey of the previous six months' presidency, and the chairman of the conference of foreign ministers reports to Parliament once a year on the progress of European political cooperation. Unlike proceedings in the Council and the Commission, proceedings in Parliament are published in the *Official Journal*.

Although the original EEC Treaty did not give Parliament *locus standi* to challenge acts of the Council or the Commission, Parliament was held to be allowed to intervene in such cases before the ECJ in *Roquette Frères SA* v *Council* (case 138/79). Moreover, since it has *locus standi* to bring an action against these institutions for failure to act (under Article 232 (ex 175) EC, see chapter 31), and succeeded in doing so in *Parliament* v *Council* (case 13/83), it was thought that it must have *locus standi* to bring a complementary action for annulment of acts of the Council and the Commission under Article 230 (ex 173) EC (see chapter 30). The ECJ has now decided that it does not have a general power to challenge such acts (*Parliament* v *Council (Comitology)* (case 302/87)) but that it may bring an action under Article 230 (ex 173) in order to protect its own prerogative powers (*Parliament* v *Council (Chernobyl)* (case C–70/88); see chapter 30). This position has now been confirmed in an amendment to Article 230 (ex 173) introduced by the TEU. It is through Article 230 (ex 173) EC challenges that Parliament enforces its rights and seeks to ensure that the correct treaty base is used for legislative measures. This is important because the treaty base affects the degree of parliamentary involvement in the legislative process. Judicial review under Article 230 (ex 173) EC has been used vigorously for these purposes (see further chapter 30).

In order further to broaden Parliament's role it was given power under the TEU to set up a temporary committee of inquiry to investigate alleged contraventions or maladministration in the implementation of Community law (except where the alleged facts are being examined before a court or subject to legal proceedings) (Article 193 (ex 138c) EC) and has been required to appoint an Ombudsman to receive and enquire into complaints of maladministration in the activities of the EC institutions or bodies (with the exception of the Court of Justice and the Court of First Instance acting in their judicial capacity) (Article 195 (ex 138e) EC). Draft Regulations governing the role of the Ombudsman were produced by the Parliament in 1993 and confirmed by the Council in 1994 (Council Decision 94/114 OJ L54/25, 1994). According to Article 6(2) of those Regulations, the Parliament appointed its first Ombudsman (OJ L225, 1995). At the end of an investigation, the Ombudsman is under an obligation to produce a report to the Parliament and to the institution under investigation. The original complainant is also notified of the result. The Ombudsman has also to produce an annual report to Parliament. In addition, any natural or legal person residing or having its registered office in a Member State is to be given the right to address a petition to the European Parliament on a matter which comes within the Community's fields of activity, and which affects him, her or it directly (Article 194 (ex 138d) EC).

Parliament was also given a new power of initiative by the TEU. Under Article 192 (ex 138b) EC it may, acting by a majority of its members, request the Commission to submit any appropriate proposals on matters on which it considers that a Community act is required for the purpose of implementing the Treaty. It has been suggested that, provided Parliament stays within the guidelines set out in its rules of procedure, these requests are likely to be considered sympathetically by the Commission.

One area of the Parliament's activities which is sometimes overlooked is the work that it does in promoting human rights. We will see when looking at the role of general principles of community law (chapter 6) that the Parliament was instrumental in persuading the other institutions to recognise the importance of human rights and, in particular, the European Convention on the Protection of Human Rights. The Parliament is not concerned only with human rights protection within the Union. The European Parliament also established a subcommittee to identify urgent cases of human rights abuse throughout the world, and the facts surrounding each case. In appropriate circumstances it will put forward resolutions on specific cases to the whole Parliament. The passing of such resolutions can raise the profile of certain issues and can therefore play a useful role in generating pressure to remedy the problem. The subcommittee also produces an annual report and the degree of reaction that it provokes in countries criticised by it is indicative of its influence.

The powers given to the European Parliament at Maastricht went some way to redress the institutional balance in the Community, in which national interests as represented by the Council of Ministers have predominated, and to remedy the much-criticised 'democratic deficit' in the decision-making process. Critics suggested these changes did not go far enough and that the Parliament should have more powers following the 1996 IGC. The ToA has improved the situation by extending Parliament's powers of co-decision within a more streamlined co-decision procedure (new Article 251 EC — see further in chapter 3). It is only where particularly sensitive issues (for example, taxation) are concerned that the co-decision procedure will not apply, leaving the Council with the whip hand.

Council (Articles 202–210 (ex 145-154) EC)

Composition   The Council, following the TEU now called 'The Council of the European Union', consists of representatives of the Member States, one from each Member State, who must be 'at ministerial level, authorised to commit the government of that Member State' (Article 203 (ex 146) EC).

The Council is not a fixed body. Although it is limited to one voting delegate from each State, membership may fluctuate depending on the topic under discussion. For example, where matters of agriculture are at stake, the Ministers of Agriculture will normally participate; if the matters relate to general economic policy the Chancellors may be present; where high-level policy matters are to be discussed, the Council may consist of Heads of State. This has led to criticism that the Council of Ministers lacks coherency: there is no one who is responsible for co-ordinating policies. Where Heads of State come together in a specially constituted body, acting on matters of both EC law and political cooperation, the body is termed the European Council. Although it had been in existence from 1974 it was not recognised in the EC Treaty until the Single European Act. Article 2 SEA provided:

> The European Council shall bring together Heads of State or of government of the Member States and the President of the Commission of the European Communities. They shall be assisted by a Minister for Foreign Affairs and by a member of the Commission. They shall meet at least twice a year.

This provision has been further amplified by Article 4 (ex D) TEU.

Functions   The Council's task is 'to ensure that the objectives set out in this Treaty are attained' (Article 202 (ex 145) EC). To this end it 'shall . . . ensure coordination of the general economic policies of the Member States; have power to take decisions . . . and confer on the Commission, in the acts which the Council adopts, powers for the implementation of those rules which the Council lays down'. The degree to which ministers can comply with this requirement and satisfy their domestic obligations is, however, debatable.

Since the Council has the final power of decision on most secondary legislation some control by the Member States is thus assured. However, in most cases it can only act on the basis of a proposal from the Commission. Furthermore, other institutions are involved in the decision-making process to an increasing degree. Under the procedures introduced by the SEA, if it wishes to override Parliament's opposition to a measure it must do so by unanimous vote. Similarly it may amend the Commission's proposals provided it does so unanimously. Following the entry into force of the TEU it now shares decision-making with Parliament in some areas. The ToA increased the number of these areas. Nonetheless, since legislation (even under the co-decision procedure) cannot be enacted without the consent of the Council, its methods of voting are crucial. The Treaty (Article 205 (ex 148) EC as amended) provides that voting may be by a simple majority (which is rare), by qualified majority, or unanimity.

Unaniminity Originally, some more sensitive areas of the Treaty were required to be implemented only by unanimous vote (e.g., Article 94 (ex 100) EC on the approximation of laws). It was, however, intended that once the period of adjustment to membership, known as the transitional period, provided by the Treaty had expired, Member States would be required to move towards qualified majority voting. This did not happen. A crisis in the Council in 1962 resulted, at the insistence of the French, in the Luxembourg Accords (1966). Under the Accords, where vital national interests are at stake, States may insist on a unanimous vote. The Accords noted 'a divergence of views on what should be done in the event of a failure to reach agreement'. It has been suggested that this approach is partly a reaction against the judicial activism of the time.

The Luxembourg Accords did not have the force of law, but they were followed in practice, with the result that in many cases the Council sought unanimity where the Treaty would not have required it. In only one case, in 1982, was a measure passed by the Council by qualified majority vote against the wishes of the UK government, in a situation in which it was suggested that the UK was abusing its veto by attempting to force the Council's hand in a matter unrelated to the measure under discussion.

Qualified majority voting Qualified majority voting is a system of weighted voting. Clearly from the Community standpoint it makes for more rapid and effective decision-making than unanimity as the consent of all parties is not required. It is, however, controversial because it runs contrary to the idea that a nation State is a sovereign entity and the government (or ruler) of that entity has freedom to choose which policies to implement within that State. With qualified majority voting (and also with simple majority voting) a Member State could be put in the position of being under a Treaty obligation to put in place a policy for which it had not voted.

The recent accession of the new Member States revived difficulties with regard to qualified majority voting. Spain and the UK objected to what they saw as the dilution of their voting strength. Prior to the accession of Austria, Finland and Sweden, the big four States carried 10 votes apiece, Spain 8, Belgium, Greece, The Netherlands and Portugal 5, Denmark and Ireland 3 and Luxembourg 2 (total 76). The required minimum vote for a qualified majority was 54. Thus two big or up to six small States could be out-voted. The proposal on the accession of Austria, Finland and Sweden was that their votes be added to the total number of votes available and that the blocking minority would constitute the same percentage of the new total as the previous blocking minority had of the old total: approximately 71 per cent being required to constitute a majority. Clearly, this meant that the number of States required to block a proposal went up, and consequently Member States could more easily be out-voted. The UK and Spain suggested that the old number of votes required to block a proposal (23) should remain in place. Eventually, the Ioannina Compromise (1994) was agreed with the result that the blocking minority increased to 71 per cent of the new total, but if States carrying together 23 to 25 votes intend to vote against the proposal then negotiations will continue in an attempt to satisfy their concerns.

The Ioannina Compromise has raised concerns that the attitudes of Member States have not changed since the Luxembourg Accords. A contrary view has also been suggested. Although clearly there are difficulties, the Ioannina Compromise does represent some progress because under its terms the Member States are committed to trying to come to some form of compromise acceptable to all. Contrast this with the Luxembourg Accords, where Member States merely agreed to disagree.

The ToA looked at the question of qualified majority voting, as required by the Ioannina Compromise. The result is new Article 205 EC, which sets out the numbers of votes each Member State shall have as follows: Belgium 5; Denmark 3; Germany 10; Greece 5; Spain 8; France 10; Ireland 3; Italy 10; Luxembourg 2; The Netherlands 5; Austria 4; Portugal 5; Finland 3; Sweden 4; and UK 10. To adopt a measure, 62 votes are required, approximately 71 per cent of the votes. If the act is not based on a proposal from the Commission then, in addition, the approval of 10 Member States is required. One might argue that this has not really solved the problem of the dilution of Member States' voting rights, and that the issue will merely resurface at the next enlargement; indeed this is one of the issues to be discussed at the next round of treaty amendments in 2000.

In the light of the above perhaps the most significant innovation of the SEA was to increase the number of areas in which voting was to be by qualified majority. The majority of legislation required to complete the internal market was enacted by qualified majority. Only fiscal measures, measures relating to the free movement of persons and to the rights and interests of employed persons (Article 95(2) (ex 100a(2)) and measures relating to professional training and standards (Article 47(2) (ex 57(2)) now require a unanimous vote. The TEU further increased the scope for qualified majority voting (e.g., Article 130s (new 175) EC (environment)) as did the ToA (e.g., Article 46(2) (ex 56(2)) regarding the right of establishment and Article 141(3) (ex 119(3)) on equal pay). The more sensitive areas however remain subject to unanimous approval. As a result Member States have so far been prepared to accede to a qualified majority vote in the areas in which it has been required, although in some cases they have challenged the appropriateness of the legal basis of a measure demanding such a vote. But, 'as a last resort, the Luxembourg compromise remains in place untouched and unaffected by the SEA' (the Foreign Secretary, HC Parl. Deb. vol. 96, col. 320, 23 April 1986). Furthermore, the principle has been reinforced in the ToA in respect of the new 'flexibility' provisions of both the EC and EU Treaties (new Articles 11 EC and 43 TEU).

Since the Council is not a permanent body, meeting only a few days a month, and its members have full-time responsibilities at home, either as ministers or civil servants (civil servants have no power to vote), much of its work has been taken over by the Committee of Permanent Representatives (COREPER) (see Article 207 (ex 151) EC). COREPER is a permanent and full-time body, also consisting of representatives of Member States, whose main task is to scrutinise and sift proposals coming from the Commission prior to a final decision being made by the Council. COREPER is assisted in turn by a number of working groups, similarly represented, operating at different levels and in specialised areas. This sifting process, from working group to COREPER to Council, enables the more straightforward issues to be decided at the appropriate level, leaving the Council to focus on the more difficult or controversial decisions. Indeed, the amendments inserted by the ToA expressly recognise the power of COREPER to make procedural decisions where provided for by the Council's Rules of Procedure (see new Article 107(1) EC).

Commission (Articles 211-219 (ex 155-163) EC)

Composition The Commission has been described as the 'guardian of the Treaties'. The present Commission consists of 20 members (two from each of the big four and Spain, and one from each of the other States), chosen on the grounds of their general competence and 'whose independence is beyond doubt' (Article 213 (ex 157) EC). Appointed by 'common accord of the governments of the Member States' (Article 214(2) (ex 158(2)) EC), they must, in the performance of their duties, 'neither seek nor take instructions from any government or from any other body' (Article 213(2) (ex 157(2)) EC). Originally appointed for a four-year term, the period was increased to five years under the Maastricht Treaty (Article 214 (ex 158) EC), and is renewable.

The Commission is headed by a President appointed from among the Commissioners 'by common accord of the Member States' for a renewable term of two years (Article 213(2) (ex 158(2)) EC). Following Maastricht, the consent of Parliament is also required. It is divided into 23 directorates-general, each one responsible for certain aspects of Community policy (e.g., D/G competition), and headed by a director-general. Commissioners are given responsibility for particular directorates (a 'portfolio'). Portfolios vary considerably in size and prestige.

Functions The functions of the Commission are threefold. First, it acts as initiator or 'motor' of Community action. All important decisions made by the Council must be made on the basis of proposals from the Commission (subject to the Council's power to 'request the Commission to undertake any studies which the Council considers desirable for the attainment of the common objectives, and to submit to it any appropriate proposals' (Article 208 (ex 152) EC) and the Parliament's new powers to request the Commission to submit proposals (Article 192 (ex 138b) EC). Using the EC Treaty as its brief, the Commission may formulate proposals on any matter provided for under the Treaty, either where the power is specifically granted or under the more general power provided by Article 308 (ex 235) EC. Clearly, as long as a policy of unanimous voting was pursued by the Council the Commission's power of initiative was limited to what was politically acceptable; measures must of necessity be diluted for common consumption. Nevertheless, although the Council may limit the Commission's power of initiative, the importance of this power should not be underestimated. The power of

initiative allows the Commission to frame the terms of the debate in Council
and Parliament through the way it drafts the proposals. Furthermore, the
Commission has responsibilities which also give it control: it sets the legislative timetable for the year; and it formulates more general policy guidance
through its white papers.

Secondly, the Commission acts as the Community watchdog. Member
States are obliged under Article 10 (ex 5) EC to: 'take all appropriate
measures . . . to ensure fulfilment of the obligations arising out of this Treaty
or resulting from action taken by the institutions of the Community. . . . They
shall abstain from any measure which could jeopardise the attainment of the
objectives of this Treaty.' It is the Commission's task to seek out and bring
to an end any infringements of EC law by Member States, if necessary by
proceedings under Article 226 (ex 169) EC (see chapter 28) before the ECJ.
(See also similar provisions for the enforcement of the law relating to State
aids, Article 88 (ex 93) EC.) The Commission has a complete discretion in
this matter (see *Alfons Lütticke GmbH* v *Commission* (case 48/65) noted in
chapter 28). The Commission is also entrusted with administering and
enforcing EC competition policy and has the power to impose sanctions in
the form of fines and penalties on individuals in breach of EC competition
law (see chapter 17).

In order to carry out its role as watchdog it has extensive investigative
powers (see e.g., Regulation 17/62, Article 14), and Member States and
individuals (e.g., under Regulation 17/62) may be required to furnish any
information required pursuant to these powers.

Thirdly, the Commission functions as the executive of the Community.
Once a policy decision has been taken by the Council, the detailed implementation of that policy, often requiring further legislation, falls to the
Commission, acting under powers delegated by the Council. In exercising its
powers of implementation the Commission is subject to the supervision of a
range of advisory, management and regulatory committees, comprising national civil servants and appointed by the Council for that purpose. This
process is referred to as 'comitology'. It has been suggested that this system,
together with the Council's power under Article 202 (ex 145) (3rd indent) to
reserve the right 'to exercise directly implementing powers itself' alone, or on
the advice of its committees, tends to undermine the Commission's authority.

The Commission has in addition 'its (own) power of decision' (Article 211
(ex 155) EC). Competition policy is enforced solely by the Commission.
Similarly Regulations enacted, for example, in the field of agriculture to
implement Community rules may provide for decisions of an executive nature
to be taken by the Commission alone.

Lastly, in pursuit of the Community's external policies, the Commission is
required to act as negotiator, leaving agreements to be concluded by the
Council (Articles 300 and 133) (ex 228 and 113) EC). Certain agreements
can only be concluded after the assent of the European Parliament has been
obtained (Article 300(3)) (ex 228(3)). It has been suggested that the role of
the Council under the FSP provisions may in time overshadow this aspect of
the Commission's role.

Budgetary procedures

These are laid down by Article 272 (ex 203) EC. As might be expected, the Commission is responsible for drawing up a preliminary draft budget. The Commission thus sets the parameters, and fixes the 'maximum rate of increase' for 'non-compulsory items' of expenditure, which neither the Council nor the Parliament is free to exceed. The preliminary draft is forwarded to the Council, which establishes the draft budget and forwards it to Parliament. At this stage Parliament may approve the budget within 45 days, in which case it stands adopted. Alternatively Parliament may suggest 'modifications' or 'amendments'. 'Modifications' may be proposed to items of 'compulsory' expenditure — expenditure already accounted for by Community rules, principally the amount (around 70 per cent) allocated to the common agricultural policy. 'Amendments' refer to non-compulsory expenditure, principally concerned with regional or social policy. In this case the draft is returned to the Council, Parliament's 'modifications' may then be rejected by the Council acting by a qualified majority. Its 'amendments' too may be subject to 'modification' by the Council within a 15-day time-limit. However, on return to Parliament that body may reject the Council's 'modifications' within a 15-day time-limit, acting by a majority of its members and three fifths of the votes cast. Parliament may then adopt the budget.

Thus Parliament is responsible for adopting the budget and has the final say over 'non-compulsory' expenditure. It does too have one further weapon. If it is not satisfied with the budget overall it may reject it, and in 1979 and 1984 it did not hesitate to do so.

Court of Justice (Articles 220–245 (ex 164-168) EC)

Composition   The Court consists of 15 judges, one from each Member State, who elect a president from among themselves. The judges are assisted by eight advocates-general. They must be 'chosen from persons whose independence is beyond doubt' (Article 223 (ex 167) EC). An advocate-general's function is to assist the Court by presenting his 'submissions' — a detailed analysis of all the relevant issues of fact and law together with his recommendations to the Court. Although his recommendations are not always followed, where they are they are useful as a means of ascertaining the reasoning behind the Court's decision. The judgment itself, which is a single collegiate decision, is, to English eyes, terse, cryptic, with little indication of the reasoning on which it is based. Even where the advocate-general's recommendations are not followed they may still be invoked as persuasive authority in a subsequent case. Although the ECJ seeks to achieve consistency in its judgments, its precedents are not binding in the English sense; it always remains free to depart from previous decisions in the light of new facts. All cases before the ECJ are allocated a number, the last two digits of which refer to the year in which the action was started. Since the setting up of the CFI in 1988, all ECJ cases start with the letter 'C'. Cases with the suffix 'P' are appeals from the CFI, and those followed by 'R' are applications for interim relief.

In order to meet its increasing workload, the court may sit in chambers of three or five judges (Article 221 (ex 165) EC), a facility of which it has often taken advantage. The only category of cases which cannot be heard by the ECJ sitting in chambers are those which involve either a Member State or an institution which has requested that it be heard by the plenary session (Article 221(3) (ex 165(3))).

Functions The task of the ECJ is to 'ensure that in the interpretation and application of this Treaty the law is observed' (Article 220 (ex 164) EC). It is the supreme authority on all matters of Community law, and in this capacity may be required to decide matters of constitutional law (see e.g., chapters 5 and 6), administrative law (see chapters 30-32), social law (chapters 19-25) and economic law (chapters 7-18) in matters brought directly before it or on application from national courts. Its jurisdiction is principally over the acts of the institutions and Member States within the Communities' sphere of activity. It thus does not have jurisdiction over the actions of the European Council (*Roujansky* v *Council* (case T-584/93) and Article 46 (ex L) TEU excluded the ECJ's jurisidiction as regards the majority of the TEU provisions (see also *Grau Gomis* (case C-167/94)). The ECJ's jurisdiction in relation to instruments made under the JHA has been extended under the ToA: new Article 35 TEU provides that the ECJ may have jurisdiction in this area subject to the agreement of the Member States (discussed further below).

In its practices and procedures the ECJ draws on Continental models; in developing the substantive law it draws on principles and traditions from all the Member States. Since the EC Treaty is a framework treaty the Court has been extremely influential in 'filling the gaps', and in doing so has created law in bold, and, to those accustomed to English methods of interpretation, often surprising ways.

As Lord Diplock pointed out in *R* v *Henn* [1981] AC 850:

The European Court, in contrast to English courts, applies teleological rather than historical methods to the interpretation of the Treaties and other Community legislation. It seeks to give effect to what it conceives to be the spirit rather than the letter of the Treaties; sometimes, indeed, to an English judge, it may seem to the exclusion of the letter. It views the Communities as living and expanding organisms and the interpretation of the provisions of the Treaties as changing to match their growth.

The Court has on occasion been criticised for its activism. Others have argued that such boldness was necessary to carry the Community forward at a time, during the 1970s and early 1980s, when progress was blocked by political inertia. Whether in response to criticism, or as a result of the increased dynamism of the other institutions following the SEA, more recent judgments of the Court show signs of a new conservatism, although in certain areas, for example, sex discrimination, it continues to surprise, (see e.g., *Barber* v *Guardian Royal Exchange Assurance Group* (case C-262/88); see chapter 25). It has been this dynamism, or the consequences thereof, which has led to the suggestion that the jurisdiction of the Court be limited at the 1996 IGC. This suggestion was not taken up in the ToA. Indeed following the ToA, there is now the possibility that the ECJ's jurisdiction will be extended. Prior to the ToA, it had no power to rule on matters under the TEU. Following the ToA, it has the power to rule on decisions made under JHA provisions of the TEU, subject to agreement by individual Member States. Also, the transfer of competence over some of the JHA provisions to the EC Treaty will bring more policy areas under the ECJ's jurisdiction: it is here, however, that we find some limitations creeping in. Within these policy areas, only the courts of last instance may make a reference to the ECJ (new Article 68 EC), compared with the usual 'any court or tribunal' empowered to refer under Article 234 (ex 177) EC in respect of all other areas of the EC Treaty (see chapter 27). Furthermore, there are significant exceptions to the jurisdiction of the ECJ where a measure concerns national security (new Article 68(2) EC). These are worrying developments as they undermine the homogeneity of the ECJ's jurisdiction and reduce the scope for the protection of individuals.

Court of First Instance   In 1986 the SEA provided for the setting up of a new Court of First Instance (CFI). Approval for this court was obtained in October 1988 (OJ C215/1, 1989). The court commenced proceedings on 1 September 1989. There are now 15 judges who, as in the ECJ, may sit in chambers. Its jurisdiction includes disputes between the Community and its servants ('staff cases'), and applications for judicial review and damages by 'natural and legal persons', under Articles 230 and 232 (ex 173 and 175) respectively). There is a right of appeal on matters of law from this court to the ECJ. An applicant cannot appeal against a decision of the ECJ unless new facts come to light. (*ISAE/VP v Commission* (case C-130/91); see further chapters 26 and 29). Cases before the CFI are allocated numbers which are prefixed with the letter 'T'.

Court of Auditors

The Court of Auditors was established in 1975 under the Budgetary Powers Treaty (OJ L359/1, 31.12.1977). Its function is to exercise control and supervision over the implementation of the budget. Its creation represents an important step forward in the accountability of the institutions, particularly the Commission. Its annual report is published in the *Official Journal*. As a sign of its importance it was added to the list of Community institutions in Article 7 (ex 4) of the EC Treaty by the TEU. This change may be seen as purely symbolic. A more concrete change is the requirement that it must provide both the Parliament and the Council with a statement of assurance as to the reliability of the Community accounts and the legality of the underlying transactions (Article 248 (ex 188c(1)) EC) which, following the ToA, will be published in the *Official Journal*. New Article 248 EC also requires the Court of Auditors to report any cases of irregularity. It is, however, limited in its effectiveness because there seems to be no one conception amongst the Member States of what it is intended to do. Secondly, there is no one body to respond to the Court of Auditors' reports to ensure that the Community is getting value for the money it spends. This is worrying in a time where there is increased public concern about the amounts of public spending and potential fraud within the Community.

Economic and Social Committee (Articles 257–262 (ex 193–198 EC)

The Economic and Social Committee plays a consultative role in the Community decision-making process. Its members are appointed by the Council in their personal capacity, and represent a variety of sectional interests such as farmers, workers, trade unionists, or merely members of the general public. Where consultation is provided for by the Treaty this is an essential procedural requirement: such consultation must also be referred to in any resulting legislation. The Committee may also be consulted by the Council and the Commission whenever they consider it appropriate. In addition it is entitled to advise the Community institutions on its own initiative on all questions affecting Community law (summit declaration 1972, Bull. EEC 10-72, 23).

Committee of the Regions

This Committee was established by the TEU in order to represent regional interests, and to act, like the Economic and Social Committee, in an advisory capacity in specified circumstances, as provided by the EC Treaty (e.g., Article 149(4) (ex 126(4)) education; 151(5) (ex 128(5)) culture; 161 (ex 130d) and 162 (ex 130e) regional development).

Impact of enlargement

The current institutional structure of the Communities was established for a system with a more limited membership; originally there were only six Member States. Since 1957 membership of the Communities (and then the Union) has nearly trebled and significant policy areas, such as monetary union, have been added to the Community's remit, not to mention the impact of the introduction of the Union itself and the issues included in the other two 'pillars' (FSP and JHA). It is now generally accepted that the current institutional structure is unable to function effectively in the modern Union and that institutional problems will only be exacerbated by further enlargement. Obviously, expanding the Community's competence itself increases the number of tasks the Community institutions have to perform, but increased membership brings further problems. It will be more difficult to reach agreement within the institutions: not only is it more difficult to reach agreement between a greater number of representatives, but with eastward expansion the Member States will reflect a greater diversity of interests, traditions and languages. Thus, in addition to the sheer weight of numbers, there will be a risk of fragmentation as the Union becomes less cohesive. The current Member States were aware of this problem even before the ToA, resulting in a Protocol being annexed to the ToA regarding proposed institutional reform. This document envisaged a two-stage approach to reform. The first stage was to be a limited reform to be carried out prior to the next wave of enlargement, the second stage was to be a more comprehensive reform to be undertaken when EU membership exceeded 20. Given the decision of the Helsinki European Council, negotiations are now underway for the accession of sufficient candidate countries (assuming those negotiations are successful) to take membership well beyond the 20 required for significant institutional reform. As a result, the Member States decided that the next IGC should be aimed at carrying out the comprehensive institutional reform foreseen by the second stage of the ToA Protocol. The Cologne European Council decided that, in order not to cause unnecessary delay in enlargement, the IGC should be concluded by the end of 2000. There are three main areas which need reform: the size and composition of the institutions, especially the Commission; the weighting of votes in Council; and the extension of qualified majority voting. The main problems affecting the four main institutions — the Commission, Council, Parliament and ECJ — are set out below, although it is still too soon to know what solutions, if any, have been found for these questions.

Commission   With each successive enlargement, the number of Commissioners has also increased, as each new Member State is allowed a representative within the Commission. It is implicit in the ToA that this process will continue, although this may ultimately result in an unwieldy Commission. The Report of the Wise Men on the Institutional Implications of Enlargement (18 October 1999) suggested that, in addition to considering the size and composition of the Commission, the 2000 IGC should further strengthen the authority of the President of the Commission, in particular by giving him the authority to organise, coordinate and guide the working of the Commission. In the light of a number of scandals, ranging from gross mismanagement to corruption scandals involving the Commission, exposed in 1999, this Report also suggested that the individual responsibility of each Commissioner should be clarified, so as to allow for the removal of individual Commissioners in the case of dereliction of duty. It is intended, however, that the collegiate system of collective responsibility should, in general, remain.

Council   The reform of the Council focuses on two main issues, both of which have already proved to be problematic: qualified majority voting and the weighting of votes between Member States in the Council. It is important to address both these issues as otherwise, with the diversity of interests represented in the Council, individual Member States could easily block the adoption of measures, ultimately leading to a stagnation in the Union which would threaten the integration process.

As noted earlier, qualified majority voting is a more effective means of decision-making than relying on unanimity. It has therefore been suggested that the policy areas in which qualified majority voting is used for decision-making should be extended, as it progressively already had been under the SEA, TEU and ToA. The Commission, in its paper on enlargement, suggested that following enlargement, qualified majority voting should be the rule, with a presumption against the use of unanimity. Unanimous voting should be restricted to the most sensitive of issues. The Commission proposed that this be the case not only in the EC pillar but also within JHA. This is of course a sensitive issue, impinging as it does on national sovereignty and state autonomy, and the extent to which this will prove acceptable to all Member States is therefore debatable.

The question of the weighting of votes is closely linked to qualified majority voting, as the number of votes a Member State has and the total number of votes required to pass a measure under a qualified majority voting system determines how easily a Member State may be outvoted. Further, the increased number of Member States makes it more likely that groups of smaller Member States could outvote the larger Member States, meaning that potentially Member States with a small proportion of the Union's population could dictate policy. Not only does this mean that the autonomy of individual Member States is under threat, but also there are concerns about democracy were some Member States to end up with disproportionate power. The Commission has noted that, with the current membership of 15, a decision can be blocked by a group of Member States representing just 12 per cent of the EU's population and a decision can be passed by Member States representing 58 per cent of the EU's population. The new Article 205 EC confirmed the respective voting rights of the Member States in the light of the current membership following the last round of enlargement, but clearly this was only a stop-gap measure and it is questionable whether the current balance is right. With the probable increase in membership, the issue clearly will need addressing once again. At the time of writing no specific proposals had been advanced.

European Parliament   The ToA limited the size of the European Parliament to 700 members (Article 189 EC). The representatives from the present candidate countries will increase the size of the Parliament to beyond that figure. Some mechanism will need to be found for the allocation of seats between the Member States once the upper limit is reached.

The European Court of Justice   Enlargement will have an impact on the ECJ in two main ways. Enlargement will mean an increased number of cases coming before the ECJ, especially in the years immediately following enlargement as the new Member States' legal systems seek to adapt to Community *acquis*. One mechanism to deal with the increased workload is greater use of chambers of the Court, a development made more likely by the difficulty of operating the plenary court with an increased number of judges. The ECJ has commented that enlargement would mean the ECJ 'would cross the invisible boundary between a collegiate court and a deliberative assembly'. A move toward chambers or a devolved system of justice, however, may cause problems in ensuring uniformity between the different chambers, especially given the different legal traditions in which each judge will be grounded.

Although the institutions are all aware of the need for reform, and some are already carrying out internal organisational reviews on issues that do not require treaty amendment, the task facing the IGC is still large and many of the questions to be discussed are politically sensitive. It therefore remains to be seen if a new treaty can be agreed by the December 2000 deadline set by the Cologne European Council. If enlargement goes ahead, significant changes will have to be agreed if the need for constant treaty amendments is to be avoided.

Further reading

Arnull, A., 'The European Court and Judicial Objectivity: a Reply to Professor Hartley' (1996) 112 LQR 411.

Arnull, A., 'Taming the Beast? The Treaty of Amsterdam and the Court of Justice' in O'Keeffe, D. and Twomey, P. (eds), *Legal Issues of the Amsterdam Treaty* (Hart Publishing, 1999).

Bradley, K., 'The European Parliament and Treaty Reform: Building Blocks and Stumbling Blocks' in O'Keeffe, D. and Twomey, P. (eds), *Legal Issues of the Amsterdam Treaty* (Hart Publishing, 1999).

Capelletti, M., *The Judicial Process in Comparative Perspective* (Oxford: Clarendon Press, 1989).

Fennelly, N., 'The Area of "Freedom, Security and Justice" and the European Court of Justice — A Personal View' (2000) 29 ICLQ 1.

Harden, I., and Donnelly, K., 'The Court of Auditors and Financial Control and Accountability in the European community' [1995] EPL 599.

Hartley, T., 'Constitutional and Institutional Aspects of the Maastricht Treaty' (1993) 42 ICLQ 213.

Hartley, T., 'Federalism, Courts and Legal Systems: The Emerging Constitutions of the European Community' (1986) 34 Am J Comp L 229.

Hartley, T.C., 'The European Court, Judicial Objectivity and the Constitution of the European Union' (1996) 112 LQR 95.

Rasmussen, H., 'Between Self-Restraint and Activism: A Judicial Policy for the European Court' 13 EL Rev 28.

Skiadis, D.V., 'European Court of Auditors and European Investment Bank: An Uneasy Relationship' (1999) 5 EPL 215.

Slynn, G., 'The Court of Justice of the European Communities' (1984) 33 ICLQ 409.

Tridimas, T., 'The Court of Justice and Judicial Activism' (1996) 21 EL Rev 199.

THREE

Scope of the EC Treaty: laws and law-making in the Community

Scope of the EC Treaty

Although primarily an economic treaty, concerned with creating a single market in Europe, the original EEC Treaty extended far beyond the traditional free-trading agreement such as we find in GATT and EFTA, to cover a wide range of matters only peripherally economic, and expressly included a number of purely social goals. The Single European Act (SEA) further extended the scope of Community competence into new areas which had hitherto been dealt with only on a piecemeal basis. It also provided a formal framework for political cooperation by Member States which was absent from the original Treaty. This led at Maastricht, and to a lesser extent in Amsterdam, to a further and significant extension of Community goals. Since this book is concerned primarily with EC law, discussion of those elements of the TEU which do not affect EC law is outside the scope of this book.

The EC Treaty is essentially a 'framework' treaty (*traité cadre*); that is, it sets out as broad general principles the aims to be achieved, leaving its institutions, in the form of the Commission and the Council, with increasing consultation and sometimes in co-decision with Parliament, to fill the gaps by means of secondary legislation.

The general aims of the Treaty, as variously amended, are set out in Article 2:

The Community shall have as its task, by establishing a common market and an economic and monetary union and by implementing policies or activities referred to in Articles 3 and 4, to promote throughout the Community a harmonious, balanced and sustainable development of economic activities, *a high level of employment and of social protection*, equality between men and women, sustainable and non-inflationary growth, a high degree of competitiveness and convergence of economic performance, *a high level of protection and improvement of the quality of the environment,* the raising of the standard of living and quality of life, and economic and social cohesion and solidarity among Member States.

Article 3 provides:

For the purposes set out in Article 2, the activities of the Community shall include, as provided by this Treaty and in accordance with the timetable set out therein:

(a) the prohibition as between Member States, of customs duties and quantitative restrictions on the import and export of goods, and of all other measures having equivalent effect;

(b) a common commercial policy;

(c) an internal market characterised by the abolition, as between Member States, of obstacles to the free movement of goods, persons, services and capital;

(d) measures concerning the entry and movement of persons as provided for in Title IV;

(e) a common policy in the sphere of agriculture and fisheries;

(f) a common policy in the sphere of transport;

(g) a system ensuring that competition in the common market is not distorted;

(h) the approximation of the laws of the Member States to the extent required for the functioning of the common market;

(i) the promotion of coordination between employment policies of the Member States with a view to enhancing their effectiveness by developing a coordinated strategy for employment;

(j) a policy in the social sphere comprising the creation of a European Social Fund;

(k) the strengthening of economic and social cohesion;

(l) a policy in the sphere of the environment;

(m) the strengthening of the competitiveness of Community industry;

(n) the promotion of research and technology development;

(o) encouragement for the establishment and development of trans-European networks;

(p) a contribution to the attainment of a high level of health protection;

(q) a contribution to education and training of quality and to the flowering of the cultures of the Member States;

(r) a policy in the sphere of development cooperation;

(s) the association of the overseas countries and territories in order to increase trade and promote jointly economic and social development;

(t) a contribution to the strengthening of consumer protection;

(u) measures in the spheres of energy, civil protection and tourism.

Article 4 (ex 3a), introduced by the TEU, sets out the Community's policies in the field of economic and monetary union, including the creation of the single currency.

Although Article 3 was greatly extended by the TEU, it must be noted that Article 3(a)-(h), (j) and (s) as currently numbered were all present in the original EEC Treaty, albeit differently numbered and with some differences in wording. The remaining provisions were new to Article 3, but most of the activities listed had already been subject to some Community legislation, even before the SEA, and a number of these (Article 3(k), (l), (n)) had been incorporated into the Treaty by the SEA, if not in Article 3. Their incorporation into Article 3 thus merely reflected, and gave greater legitimacy to, existing practice. Only the provision for economic and monetary union in Article 4 (ex 3A) represented a genuine new departure for the EC. The ToA further amended Articles 2 and 3 EC, reflecting the increased emphasis to be put on both employment and environmental concerns (see italicised provisions of Article 2).

The principles of Article 3 are fleshed out in further more specific provisions of the Treaty. We have already noted the introduction of provisions relating to monetary union (chapter 1). In addition, and as a supplement to the activities listed in Article 3, the EC Treaty provided for the harmonisation of indirect taxation (Articles 90–93 (ex 95–99) EC); it laid down a principle of non-discrimination on the grounds of nationality (Article 12 (ex 6), formerly Article 7). As noted in chapter 1, this principle of non-discrimination has been extended by the ToA with the insertion of a new Article (new Article 13 EC) to cover discrimination on grounds of sex, race and ethnic origin, religion or belief, disability, age or sexual orientation. Unlike the provision on discrimination on grounds of nationality, the Treaty does not expressly state that such discrimination is prohibited, instead it merely permits the Member States, acting unanimously, to take action to combat such discrimination. A number of proposals are already under discussion.

The EC Treaty also provided for action in the field of social policy, requiring Member States to promote improved working conditions and living standards (Article 136 (ex 117)) and to harmonise conditions of health and safety (Article 138 (ex 118a)) for workers, and to observe a principle of equal pay for equal work for men and women (Article 139 (ex 119)). A Protocol on Social Policy was attached to the TEU. It further committed all Member States except the UK to a range of actions designed to protect the interests of workers. The social policy provisions in the EC Treaty were substantially amended as the ToA incorporated this Protocol on Social Policy into the main body of the Treaty (new Articles 136–145 EC), replacing and augmenting the existing provisions. This has the advantage of removing the potential for disputes over the borderline between social measures permissible under the EC Treaty and those which, hitherto, should have been made under the Protocol. In addition, following the ToA, the EC Treaty also includes a new chapter on employment (new Articles 125–130 EC). These provisions are not aimed at giving individuals rights to a job; rather, they aim at coordinating the Member States' employment policies so as to reduce unemployment. Thus, these policies may be seen as a form of economic management, an approach which is reinforced by these provisions' location within the Treaty, which is between monetary union and common commercial policy, rather than next to social policy.

Following the ToA, the Treaty also incorporated new measures (new Part Three Title IV, Articles 61–69 EC) to attain the free movement of individuals within the EC (see chapter 23). These have broadly based on the measures taken under the 1990 Schengen Agreement on the abolition of frontier controls between the signatory States, an agreement outside the Union framework but which most of the EU Member States have joined. A protocol annexed to the ToA states that on ratification of the ToA, the Schengen *acquis* (that is, all binding decisions made under the Schengen Agreement) will apply to the Member States and that these decisions will be treated as though they were measures made in accordance with procedures of the EC Treaty. The UK and Ireland have opted out of this chapter of the Treaty (although either of them may opt in to individual measures), and consequently the Schengen *acquis* and measures made under the new chapter in the EC Treaty will not necessarily apply to them. The Danes have also expressed reservations about these provisions. Thus, although the inequalities and the uncertainties concerning the scope of the social policy provisions of the EC Treaty will have been removed by the ToA, new but similar problems will replace them in relation to the free movement of persons.

External competence In order to enable the Community to carry out its policies towards third countries the EC Treaty provides that 'The Community shall have legal personality' (Article 281) (ex 210) EC), and Article 300 (ex 228) EC empowers the Commission to negotiate, and the Council to conclude, in most cases following consultation with Parliament, agreements between the Community and one or more States or an international organisation. The EC Treaty also contains a provision (Article 310 (ex 238) EC) allowing the Community to conclude association agreements. Many agreements have been concluded in the field of trade and aid under these provisions.

In addition, Article 133 (ex 113) EC allows the Commission, under the guidance of the Council, to enter into negotiations to make agreements necessary to implement the Common Commercial Policy. It was on this basis that representation for Member States at GATT meetings was developed. The line between Community competence and that of the Member States is not, however, clear-cut as *Opinion 1/94* shows. The Court in this opinion determined that not all the issues covered by the WTO fall within Community competence and therefore not only must the EC be a member of the WTO, but so must the Member States. This may lead to difficulties in the administration of the WTO as far as the Member States are concerned, as their membership, to a certain extent, is duplicated.

Such then, in outline, is the framework provided by the EC Treaty. The three main institutions of the Community — the Commission, the Council and the European Parliament — are empowered to legislate (subject to review by the European Court) on any of the matters within this framework. Many of the Treaty provisions, for example, the articles relating to free movement of goods and workers (Articles 25, 28 and 39 (ex 12, 30 and 48) respectively) contain obligations which are sufficiently precise to be applicable as they stand. Others provide for, and often require, further measures of implementation before they can take full legal effect. Article 94 (ex 100) EC provides for the 'approximation' (i.e. harmonisation) of such laws as directly affect the establishment or functioning of the common market by unanimous vote. Article 95 (ex 100a) makes similar provision for measures which have as their object the establishing or functioning of the internal market, in most cases, by qualified majority vote (see Article 95(4) and chapter 11). Even where the institutions are not specifically empowered to act, Article 308 (ex 235) provides:

> If action by the Community should prove necessary to attain, in the course of the operation of the common market, one of the objectives of the Community and this Treaty has not provided the necessary powers, the Council shall, acting unanimously on a proposal from the Commission and after consulting the European Parliament, take the appropriate measures.

This blanket power had been used as a basis for legislation on matters of regional or social policy (e.g., equal treatment for men and women) which fell within the broad aims of the Community as expressed in the preamble, but which were not spelt out specifically in the Treaty. Many of these matters have now been incorporated expressly into the EC Treaty by the SEA and TEU. As explained below, it is unlikely that Article 308 (ex 235) EC will be used as extensively as hitherto.

Implied powers   The Court has also determined that the Community has implied powers, so that when powers which are not specifically enumerated in the Treaty are required to achieve a Community goal, the Community is deemed to have the necessary powers. There are two possible formulations of this doctrine. The narrow approach states that the existence of a power implies the existence of any other power that is reasonably necessary for the exercise of the original power. This was the approach taken by the Court in *Fédération Charbonnière de Belgique* v *High Authority* (case 8/55). A wider approach was taken in *Germany* v *Commission* (cases 281, 283–5 & 287/85) where the powers of the Commission arising out of original Article 118 (which has been amended significantly and renumbered as 137 EC by the ToA) were the subject of dispute. The article provided the Commission with a task, that of promoting close cooperation between Member States in the social field, but did not give the Commission any specific legislative powers. Germany therefore argued that the proposed legislative act of the Commission was outside the Treaty. The Court commented that to avoid rendering provisions such as the then Article 118 totally ineffective, the powers necessary for carrying out the task must be inferred. This is a significant decision because there are many instances where the Commission has been allocated a task but not been given legislative power.

It is not just internally that the Court has deduced Community competence. Following *Commission* v *Council* (case 22/70) (the *ERTA* case) and
Opinion 1/76 it was thought that the EC would have implied powers to act in
the international sphere in relation to matters with respect to which the EC
has power to act within the Union under the EC Treaty. In addition, the
ERTA case appeared to suggest that the competence of the Community, in
this regard, was exclusive: Member States were precluded from acting. The
degree, however, to which this is still the case is now unclear following
Opinion 1/94, in which the Court held that, although the EC had exclusive
competence under Article 113 (now Article 133) to act in some spheres, with
respect to other areas (such as intellectual property) the Member States also
have competence. In more and more spheres the Court has acknowledged
that Member States and the Community have concurrent competence (e.g.,
Commission v *Council* (case C–25/94) (FAO Fishery Agreement)). Following
the German Constitutional Court's decision in *Brunner* v *European Union
Treaty* [1994] 1 CMLR 57 (see further below and chapter 5), it is likely that
the national courts will keep a watchful eye on all Community activities in
the internal and external field to ensure that the Community institutions do
not exceed their powers.

The degree to which the framework provided by the Treaty has been filled
in will form the subject-matter of later chapters of this book. Suffice it to say
that all the main areas of activity outlined above, in both the internal and
external fields, have been subject to some measures of implementation. In
some cases, such as agriculture and competition policy, implementation has
been extensive. In others, such as the free movement of capital, transport, and
freedom to provide services, progress was, initially, slow. As a result of the
SEA there has been substantial progress in these areas during the last few
years, as well as in the 'new' areas of health and safety, environmental and
consumer protection and research and technological development. The TEU
ensured continuing activity in these fields as well as in the newer field of
education and training, culture and the development of trans-European
networks and tourism. As noted above, the changes to be introduced by the
ToA, especially to Articles 2 and 3, indicate an increased emphasis to be
placed on environmental and employment policies.

From the foregoing outline two matters will be clear:

(a)   The framework provided by the Treaty, both originally and as amended by subsequent treaties (SEA, TEU, ToA), is extremely broad, embracing
many areas of economic and social activity which had hitherto been within
the sole competence of Member States.

(b)   Within that framework there is almost unlimited (though not uncon-
trolled) scope for legislation by the Community institutions.

Since, under Article 10 (ex 5) of the EC Treaty, Member States are
required to 'take all appropriate measures, whether general or particular, to
ensure fulfilment of the obligations arising out of this Treaty or resulting from

action taken by the institutions of the Community' and 'shall abstain from any measure which could jeopardise the attainment of the objectives of this Treaty' perhaps it is not surprising that Lord Denning MR was moved to say, in *H.P. Bulmer Ltd* v *J. Bollinger SA* [1974] Ch 401: ' . . . the Treaty is like an incoming tide. It flows into the estuaries and up the rivers. It cannot be held back'.

It is no doubt to stem that tide that the principle of subsidiarity was incorporated as a general principle into the EC Treaty by the TEU, in Article 5 (ex 3b) EC (discussed further below). It is with subsidiarity in mind that the German Constitutional Court delivered its landmark judgment in *Brunner* v *European Union Treaty* [1994] 1 CMLR 57. In upholding the powers of the German Parliament to ratify the Maastricht Treaty, it sounded a number of warnings about the extent of the powers of the Community and its institutions. Any further transfer of powers to Community level will need express democratic approval to be binding. Furthermore, the future use of Articles 95 and 308 (ex 100a and 235) EC will be curtailed as that court is not prepared to accept these articles alone as a basis for action. As it commented in the judgment (at para. 33):

> . . . because the principle of limited powers is adhered to, no power to extend its powers is conferred on the European Union, and the claiming of further functions and powers by the European Union and the Communities is made dependent on supplementation and amendment of the Treaty and is therefore subject to the affirmative decision of the national parliaments.

Law-making process

As we have seen, the legislative process involves three out of the five institutions: the Commission as initiator, the Council and the Parliament. The relative importance of the Parliament's role varies according to the nature of the legislation and whether the legislation is to be made according to the consultation, the cooperation or the codecision procedures.

Consultation procedure   This procedure requires that the Council consult the European Parliament before it adopts an act. Parliament's views must be considered but have no binding effect on the Council (see *Roquette Frères SA* v *Council* (case 138/79) discussed in chapter 2).

Cooperation procedure (Article 252 (ex 189c) EC)   This requires that the European Parliament be given the opportunity to propose amendments to the draft legislation.

First, the proposal is sent to both the Parliament and the Council. The Council agrees a common position on the proposal, after taking into account the opinion of the Parliament. Parliament then has a second opportunity to consider the draft proposal. It may agree with the common position of the Council. If this is the case, the Council may adopt the common position acting by qualified majority vote.

Alternatively, Parliament may propose amendments to the common position or reject it. Either way, the proposal is then returned to the Commission, to re-examine. The Commission produces a new draft adopting all, some, or none of Parliament's proposed amendments. The document is then sent to the Council. If the Council wishes to adopt the proposal in its new form, it may do so by qualified majority vote. If, however, it wishes to amend the proposal further (or even adopt the original agreed common position), it needs to act by unanimity. Thus, although the Council ultimately has the final say, it can only overrule Parliament (and the Commission) if it acts unanimously.

Co-decision procedure (Article 251 (ex 189b) EC)   This procedure, which was introduced by the TEU, improved the bargaining power of Parliament. Here, Parliament, as with the cooperation procedure, has two opportunities to view the proposal. If Parliament approves the common position, the act is adopted (usually by qualified majority vote in the Council). Parliament may reject the common position or propose amendments. The document is re-examined by the Commission, which may include or reject any or all of the Parliament's amendments in a new draft. The Council may accept the new form of document acting by qualified majority. If it wished to accept some of the Parliament's proposals which the Commission, in re-examining the document, has rejected then it may do so, but only by acting unanimously (Article 251(3)).

If the Council does not adopt the new form of the proposal then the Conciliation Committee, made up of the members of the Council or their representatives and an equal number of representatives of the Parliament, meets to try to reach a compromise. If the Conciliation Committee approves a joint text, it is then sent to the Council and the Parliament. Both institutions must approve the text for it to be adopted; either (or both) may reject it.

Thus, although the Council's common position may be affirmed, ultimately Parliament may veto a piece of legislation. It is also more difficult to ignore the Commission's views on the form of the amended proposal; if it wishes to do so, the Council must act unanimously. In giving the Parliament more power, the procedure might be seen as improving the democratic credentials of the Community, but the procedure is not only long-winded and complex, it also only applies within specified policy areas.

The amendments introduced by the ToA go some way to improving this situation. The list of areas in which co-decision may be used have been increased; indeed, the cooperation procedure has virtually ceased to exist. Perhaps more importantly, the co-decision procedure has been streamlined and in such a way as to tilt the balance of power a little more in the direction of the Parliament. Prior to the ToA, in the event of the Parliament rejecting the Council's common position entirely at its second reading, the Conciliation Committee was convened at that stage to try to reach a solution. Now, in such an event, the act shall be deemed not to be adopted. Further, the power of the Council to reaffirm its common position in the absence of agreement in the Conciliation Committee (albeit subject to rejection by Parliament), originally granted under TEU, has been removed by the ToA. If the institutions fail to reach an agreement through the Conciliation Committee, the proposed legislation will fall.

In each case where the institutions have the power to enact legislation, the Treaty specifies the type of legislation to be made and which sort of procedures must be used. The Treaty provision itself, or the procedure chosen, will specify whether the Council must act unanimously, by qualified majority voting or by simple majority voting. A failure to abide by these procedural requirements may give rise to an action for the annulment of the measure. The various combinations arising out of the possible permutations of the different voting procedures in Council, types of Community act and degrees of involvement of Parliament make the legislative process very complex. Despite attempts to do so, the ToA has done little to improve this situation. In addition to encouraging challenges to the correct legal base or procedural requirements likely, this complexity has been criticised as making the Community legal order impenetrable to the average lay person.

There are further restrictions on the making of Community acts. The institutions can only act within the scope of the powers conferred on them. Community acts must make their legal basis within the Treaty clear. This is done in the preamble to the legislation. Although the scope of the Treaty has been expanded, and Articles 308 (ex 235) and new 95 (ex 100a) are widely drafted, the freedom of the institutions to legislate is now counterbalanced by the notion of subsidiarity (Article 5 (ex 3b) EC).

Subsidiarity

Subsidiarity is, following the Maastricht Treaty, a well-known word. Its meaning is, however, not clear. The first paragraph of Article 5 (ex 3b) EC is not contentious: it merely restates what was common ground, that the Community can only act within the powers conferred on it by the Treaty. The difficulties start with the second paragraph. This states that:

> In areas which do not fall within its exclusive competence, the Community shall take action, in accordance with the principle of subsidiarity, only if and insofar as the objectives of the proposed action cannot be sufficiently achieved by the Member States and can therefore, by reason of the scale or effects of the proposed action, be better achieved by the Community.

Clearly, subsidiarity will not apply where the Community has exclusive competence. Therefore, to determine whether subsidiarity applies, we must distinguish between areas where the Community has exclusive competence and areas where it does not. Unfortunately, this is not clear: there are no provisions in the Treaty which identify the exclusive (or non-exclusive) powers of the Community. The Commission has argued that the Community has exclusive competence in areas relating to the creation of the internal market, for example, in free movement of goods, persons and services; in the

Common Commercial Policy; and in relation to the Common Agricultural Policy. This wide conception is not unchallenged, and the precise meaning of subsidiarity will not be identified until either the Treaty is amended or the ECJ gives a ruling on the matter. Although the ToA has a protocol on subsidiarity annexed to it, the protocol does not clarify where the boundary of exclusive Community competence lies. Nonetheless, it is perhaps as a result of the principle of subsidiarity that the ECJ seems to have taken a more restrictive view of the notion of exclusive competence in recent years (for example Opinion 1/94, *Commission v Council* (case 25/94)).

Looking now at the principle of subsidiarity itself, it can be seen that the idea in the second paragraph of Article 5 can be broken down into two further blocks:

(a)   that no Community action should be taken unless the action cannot be sufficiently achieved by the Member States; and

(b)   that because of the proposed scale or effects of the measure, the Community can better achieve the end result desired.

This test raises several issues: it is a test of comparative efficiency ('Commission Communication to the Council and the European Parliament', Bull EC 10–1992, 116) which might, in the context of achieving goals such as common trading rules throughout the Union, be seen to favour action at Community level. How this fits in with the definition of subsidiarity given in the preamble to the TEU (which, therefore, is of interpretative value) is not clear, as that version states that the principle of subsidiarity requires that decision-making should be made as close to the citizen as possible. Further, when will 'sufficiently' be satisfied? Will these questions relate to the scale or the effect of the proposed action? Although the protocol annexed to the ToA is aimed at clarifying the meaning of subsidiarity it does not answer these questions. It puts forward three criteria which reflect the two-stage test above:

(a)   the issue has transnational aspects which cannot be satisfactorily regulated by other Member States;

(b)   actions by Member States alone would conflict with requirements of the Treaty such as the internal market provisions;

(c)   action at Community level would produce clear benefits by reason of its scale or effects.

It is submitted that these criteria do no more than restate the problem; indeed they may even add to the difficulties because it is not even clear whether these criteria are cumulative or alternative. These problems are likely to lead to frequent litigation to obtain clarification of these points. Some writers have suggested that, in any event, these issues are not appropriately decided by the Court because of their political nature. In view of the fact that at least two cases have already been referred to the Court on this issue (e.g., *UK v Council* (case C–84/94) and *Germany v Parliament* (case C–233/94)), it seems that the Court has not, so far, refused jurisdiction.

The final element of subsidiarity is that contained in the third paragraph of Article 5. It states:

Any action by the Community shall not go beyond what is necessary to achieve the objective of this Treaty.

This requirement, an expression of the proportionality principle which permeates EC law (see chapters 6, 10, 21, 25), may have an impact on the type of action proposed by the Community. Rather than adopting an approach which prescribes the obligations of the Member States in minute detail, this would require the Community simply to provide the outline, leaving the Member States to fill in the detail. This would follow the 'new' approach to harmonisation already adopted by the institutions to ensure the completion of the internal market. Article 149 (ex 126) EC, for example, also embodies this approach which requires the Community to support and supplement Member State action rather than prescribing rules with which Member States must comply.

Problems in the law-making process: proposed reforms

Article N TEU required that the Treaty on European Union be revised in 1996 at an intergovernmental conference (IGC). Certain provisions of the Treaty stated expressly that they were to be revised, but other issues were also put forward for review. A committee, the Reflection Group, was established by the Council to consider issues to be on the agenda. We have already considered some of the issues discussed in the 1996 IGC, but the reports of the Reflection Group revealed that the central issues which the IGC had to tackle were democracy, transparency and, as already discussed in chapter 2, efficiency. We will look mainly at the first two of these issues, identifying the problem as presented at the IGC and then assessing what the ToA has done to improve the position.

Democracy   The EC decision-making process has often been criticised for its lack of democratic legitimacy. This is frequently referred to as the 'democratic deficit'. One of the main concerns is the lack of democratic accountability of the institutions. The Commission is not elected at all, the Commissioners being political appointments. Although the Council of Ministers is usually constituted of members of the national parliaments, those members tend not to have been elected for the purpose of serving as a member of the Council of Ministers. Any control is therefore indirect and only over the individual members rather than the Council as a body. The Belgian people will only have control over the Belgian ministers and not, for example, the Danish ministers. It is therefore possible for ministers to avoid taking responsibility, by passing the responsibility for a decision on to ministers of the other Member States. Furthermore, the quality of democratic control will rest with each of the national parliaments, and therefore its standard may well vary throughout the Union.

Another concern is the use of non-elected bodies in the decision-making process. There are many of these, for example, ECOSOC and the Committee of the Regions. These fulfil an advisory role only. Of more concern here is COREPER, which plays an important role in filtering out the non-contentious issues. It has been argued that in so doing, although technically the final decision is the Council's, in effect COREPER is functioning as a decision-making body. In deciding whether issues are contentious or not, COREPER frames the terms of the debate in Council, potentially having the effect of discouraging debate on certain issues.

The only directly elected body, the Parliament, has traditionally been the weakest of the institutions involved in the decision-making process. Admittedly, the TEU improved the position by increasing the control of Parliament over the Commission, introducing the Ombudsman and introducing the co-decision procedure. This latter, however, operated only in limited areas. We have seen that the ToA has now increased the areas in which co-decision is used and amended the procedure so as to limit further the Council's power under this procedure. Both of these moves can be seen as improving the democratic legitimacy of the Community. The transfer of the powers formerly contained in the TEU or the Schengen Agreement to the Community also brings issues which were dealt with in an intergovernmental and therefore undemocratic manner within the comparatively democratic system of the EC. The incorporation of Schengen brings its own problems, however. The protocol incorporating the Schengen *acquis* gives the force of law to decisions made under Schengen. Not only does the protocol not identify a full list of such texts, but also some of these decisions were made, following the old Schengen procedures, in secret by unelected bureaucrats rather than by politicians. This gives rise to concerns about the democratic accountability of the people who made these decisions; it also raises questions about respect for the rule of law within the Union. Finally, the changes to the articles relating to COREPER confirm that it may make procedural decisions, although it remains unaccountable. The ECJ has no jurisdiction to review acts of COREPER. Furthermore, its jurisdiction in relation to the new free movement of persons provision is limited and is subject to an exception in the interests of 'national security'.

Transparency   The complexity of the legislative procedures means that decision-making is not transparent. Consequently, it is difficult for individuals to become involved in the process and to hold the decision-makers accountable. The suggestion was to simplify these procedures, without altering the institutional balance. Similarly, improvements could be made in the way documents are drafted and made available. A Council resolution on plain language was passed in 1993 (OJ C166, 1993), but the position did not improve much. ECOSOC subsequently made an own-initiative resolution on plain language, requesting that the Commission make attempts actually to comply with the 1993 Council resolution on the same subject, arguably to as little effect.

The availability of documents is another part of the overall problem revolving round the way the decision-making process, particularly at Council level, operates. The complaint is that, because the Council operates behind closed doors, it is not possible for the citizen to identify who is agreeing to which proposals or the basis on which this is done. The counter-argument that has always been raised is that if Council meetings were completely open to the public gaze, it would make it difficult for the Ministers to reach decisions as many of the compromises made are politically sensitive. In 1993, a Code of Conduct regarding public access to Council and Commission documents was published (93/730/EC; see also Council Decision 93/731/EC, OJ L340, 1993). The significance of this was emphasised by *Carvel* v *Council* (case T–194/94). This case relied on the Code of Practice to seek the annulment of a Council decision refusing to reveal Council meeting minutes to the applicant. The CFI held that although the Code might permit the withholding of documents when certain specified interests would be threatened by their disclosure, this is not automatic. The rights of citizens to see documents must be balanced against the other interests. In this case the Council had *automatically* refused to reveal the minutes on the basis that all minutes are confidential. Since there was no attempt to take the claims of the applicant into account, the Council was therefore held to be in breach of the Code. Although this did not mean that citizens have an automatic right to see all documents, it was a step forward in that the Council has to consider whether it is proper to refuse access, arguably changing the attitude of ministers towards the release of non-controversial information. In addition, the Council agreed, amongst other points, that the outcome of votes on legislative acts should be made public, that debates on issues of public significance will be broadcast; and that access to the minutes of meetings will be facilitated (Bull 5–1995, 1.9.5).

Again, there has been some progress in this area following the ToA, but equally, some difficulties arise. Looking at the progress first, the streamlining of the co-decision procedure and the virtual removal of the cooperation procedure (this remains in monetary policy areas only) makes the legislative process simpler and, as a consequence, more transparent. A declaration annexed to the Amsterdam Treaty re-emphasises the points made in the Council resolution on plain language referred to above. It goes on to state that the institutions ought to establish by common accord guidelines for improving the drafting of Community legislation. Whether such guidelines will have much impact in practice is another question, although the declaration also obliges the institutions to take the internal organisational measures necessary to make sure the guidelines are properly carried out. Clarifying and codifying Community legislation will, it is to be hoped, improve transparency.

A new Article 255 EC provides that 'any citizen, and any natural or legal person residing or having its registered office in a Member State, shall have a right of access to European Parliament, Council and Commission documents'. Thus, all the institutions must amend their own rules of procedure to allow access to documents. Access to Council documents is particularly important. New Article 207 EC provides that, within the limits set down by the needs of efficient decision-making, documents involved in the legislative process should be accessible to the public and that, in any event, the results of the vote, explanations of the vote together with any statements in the minutes, shall be made public. Although it does not clarify what the needs of 'efficient decision-making' are, it is still to be hoped that this provision will increase the accountability of the ministers in the Council to their national parliaments, as individuals will be able to identify how the individual representatives of the Member States voted. The right to access documents is, however, subject to limitation in the public or private interest (new Article 255(2) EC). Although there have been a significant number of references on the question of access to information, what this means in practice is to be determined by the Council. It is too soon to tell how this will be interpreted. In view of the Council's past approach to the release of documents, one might assume that it will allow reasonably generous exceptions to the general right to information. A further limitation is set out in a declaration attached to the ToA which makes it clear that a document originating from a Member State will not be released to a third party without the prior consent of the relevant Member State.

Efficiency The institutions have also been criticised for being inefficient, especially as regards the time-consuming need to reach unanimity. This problem can only get worse with enlargement of the Community. The Commission will be pressing for an extension of qualified majority voting at the 2000 IGC, but, as noted in chapter 2, the issue is contentious. Furthermore, the Community law-making processes remain extremely complex, inevitably taking considerable time to reach agreement. This is compounded by the need to work in all 11 official languages. The number of languages will rise with enlargement and, although it is likely that not all documents will be translated into all languages, all legally binding documents of general application, as the situation currently stands, will be.

Although the majority of the issues to be dealt with at the next IGC in 2000 relate to enlargement and its impact on decision-making and efficiency within each of the institutions, there have also been suggestions that questions of democracy and transparency still need further attention. The Report of the Three Wise Men on Enlargement suggested that the use of the co-decision procedure should be extended still further. The Report, referring to the Millennium Declaration of the Helsinki European Council, suggested that more work also needs to be done on demystifying why and how the institutions work and how they are accountable. How this could be achieved in practice is another question.

Legislative acts

The legislative powers of the Community institutions are laid down in Article 249 (ex 189) EC:

In order to carry out their task the Council and the Commission shall, in accordance with the provisions of this Treaty, make regulations, issue directives, take decisions, make recommendations or deliver opinions.

Article 249 (ex 189) was amended by the TEU to take into account Parliament's power of co-decision.

These measures, described as 'acts', are defined as follows:

A regulation shall have general application. It shall be binding in its entirety and directly applicable in all Member States.

A directive shall be binding, as to the result to be achieved, upon each Member State to which it is addressed, but shall leave to the national authorities the choice of form and methods.

A decision shall be binding in its entirety upon those to whom it is addressed.

Recommendations and opinions shall have no binding force.

Thus there is a division between binding and non-binding acts. Only the first three are binding.

The principal feature of a *Regulation* is its general application. A Regulation is a normative rather than an individual act, designed to apply to situations in the abstract. Since it is 'binding in its entirety and directly applicable in all Member States' it does not require further implementation in order to take effect. Thus it may give rise to rights and obligations for States and individuals as it stands. Indeed, it has been held *(Leonesio v Ministero dell' Agricoltura e delle Foreste* (case 93/71)) that the rights bestowed by a Regulation cannot be subjected, at the national level, to implementing provisions diverging from those laid down by the Regulation itself.

A *Directive* is binding 'as to the result to be achieved, upon each Member State to which it is addressed', but allows States a discretion as to the form and method of implementation. Thus it is a measure intended to be addressed to, and binding on *States,* either individually or collectively, but apparently requiring implementation by States before it can be fully effective in law.

A *Decision* is an individual act designed to be addressed to a specified person or persons. As a 'binding' act it has the force of law and does not therefore require implementation in order to take effect. Decisions may be addressed to States or individuals.

Regulations, Directives and Decisions are subject to certain procedural safeguards — they must 'state the reasons on which they are based and shall refer to any proposals or opinions which were required to be obtained pursuant to this Treaty' (Article 253 (ex 190) EC).

These are essential procedural requirements. Any act which does not comply with these requirements will be subject to annulment (see chapter 30, Article 230 (ex 173) EC, chapter 27, Article 234 (ex 177) EC). Community legislation must now also comply with the principle of subsidiarity as laid down in Article 5 (ex 3b) EC. Further, any secondary legislation must be compatible with the Treaty (see, e.g., *Kohll,* case C-158/96, discussed further in chapters 21 and 24).

Recommendations and *Opinions,* since they have no binding force, are ineffective in law, although clearly of persuasive authority (see *Grimaldi* (case C–322/88) noted in chapter 4).

With regard to publication, Article 254 (ex 191) EC provides:

1. Regulations, directives and decisions adopted in accordance with the procedure referred to in Article 251 [ex 189b] shall be signed by the President of the European Parliament and by the President of the Council and shall be published in the *Official Journal* of the Community. They shall enter into force on the date specified in them or, in the absence thereof, on the twentieth day following that of their publication.
2. Regulations of the Council and of the Commission, as well as directives of those institutions which are addressed to all Member States shall be published in the *Official Journal* of the Community. They shall enter into force on the date specified in them or, in the absence thereof, on the twentieth day following that of their publication.
3. Other directives and decisions shall be notified to those to whom they are addressed and shall take effect upon such notification.

Thus the majority of EC legislation now requires publication in the *Official Journal*.

The line between these acts is not as clear-cut as Article 249 (ex 189) would suggest. It was held in *Confédération Nationale des Producteurs de Fruits et Légumes* v *Council* (cases 16 & 17/62) that the true nature of an act is determined not by its form but by its content and object. Thus the label attached to the measure is not decisive, and in the case of *International Fruit Co. NV* v *Commission (No. 1)* (cases 41-4/70) what was termed a Regulation was found to comprise a 'bundle of decisions'. Measures have been found to be hybrid; to contain some parts in the nature of a Regulation, and other parts in the nature of Decisions (see Advocate-General Warner's submissions in *NTN Toyo Bearing Co. Ltd* v *Council* (case 113/77)). In ascertaining the true nature of the act, the essential distinction seems to be between a Regulation, which is normative, applicable not to a limited identifiable number of designees but rather to categories of persons envisaged both in the abstract and as a whole, and a Decision, which concerns designated persons individually (*Confédération Nationale des Producteurs de Fruits et Légumes* v *Council*). The nature of a Directive has not been called into question, but considerable controversy has arisen over its effects. These will be discussed in chapter 4.

Soft law

In addition to the above types of law specified in Article 249 (ex 189) EC, the Commission has, in recent years, used new ways of developing policy, for example, by issuing guidelines (for example, in the State aid field, see chapter 12). In the area of competition law, the Commission has issued notices and had frequent recourse to 'comfort letters'. A notice provides guidance on the Commission's policy in particular fields. Comfort letters are assurances that the competition rules will not be enforced against an entity (see chapters 14–17). Both are non-binding and therein lies the difficulty: while these documents are often of great importance and are relied on by individuals, as non-binding instruments they are not open to challenge before the CFI, although they have been challenged before national courts (see chapters 16, 30 and 31). Furthermore, their creation is informal and ad hoc and not subject to the rules laid down in the Treaty for the enactment of other Community legislation. Thus, it is difficult to hold the policy-makers to account and this has further implications for democracy.

Sources of EC law

The sources of EC law comprise the following:

(a) The EC Treaty and Protocols, as amended by the succeeding Treaties: Merger Treaty 1965; Acts of Accession 1972 (UK, Ireland, Denmark), 1979 (Greece), 1985 (Spain, Portugal), 1995 (Austria, Finland, Sweden); Budgetary Treaties 1970, 1975; Single European Act 1986; Treaty on European Union 1992; Treaty of Amsterdam 1998.

(b) EC secondary legislation in the form of Regulations, Directives and Decisions. Recommendations and Opinions are of persuasive force only.

(c) Such international agreements as are entered into by Community institutions on behalf of the Community pursuant to their powers under the EC Treaty. These agreements may result from accession by the Community to existing agreements, such as GATT, or from new agreements such as the Lomé Convention. Conventions entered into by *Member States,* on the other hand, even though entered into pursuant to the EC Treaty, Article 293 (ex 220) EC, cannot be considered as forming part of Community law.

(d) Judicial legislation. This comprises the entire jurisprudence of the European Courts, embracing not only decisions, but general principles and even expressions of opinion, provided they concern matters of *Community law.* The importance and the extent of the Court of Justice's contribution to the corpus of EC law will become apparent in the course of this book.

As a matter of international law, the law arising from all these sources is binding on Member States which are obliged under Article 10 (ex 5) EC, to 'take all appropriate measures, whether general or particular, to ensure fulfilment' of all these obligations. Special provision was made for certain provisions of the EC Treaty to apply to countries linked to Member States by particular association agreements (Article 229 and Annex II (ex 227 and Annex IV)).

Since we in the UK are dualist in our approach to international law, that is, we do not regard international law as part of our own legal system unless it is incorporated by an Act of Parliament, EC law did not become binding on us as a matter of *internal* law until incorporated by the European Communities Act 1972.

Further reading

Bradley, K. St Clair, 'Comitology and the Law: through a Glass Darkly' (1992) 29 CML Rev 693.

Dashwood, A., 'The Limits of European Community Powers' (1996) 21 EL Rev 113.

Dashwood, A., 'States in the European Union' (1998) 23 EL Rev 201.

De Burca, G., 'The Quest for Legitimacy in the European Union' (1996) 59 MLR 349.

Dryberg, P., 'Current Issues in the Debate on Public Access to Documents' (1999) 24 EL Rev 3.

Duff, A., *Subsidiarity within the European Community* (Federal Trust Report).

Emilou, N., 'Subsidiarity; an Effective Barrier Against Enterprises of Ambition' (1992) 29 CML Rev 383.

Koopmans, T., 'The Role of Law in the Next Stage of European Integration' (1986) 35 ICLQ 925.

Lane, R., 'New Competences and the Maastricht Treaty' (1993) 30 CML Rev 939.

Lodge, J. (ed.), *The European Community and the Challenge of the Future*, 2nd ed. (Pinter, 1994).

Mackenzie Stuart, Lord, 'Problems of the European Community; Some Transatlantic Parallels' (1987) 36 ICLQ 183.

Mancini, G.F. 'The Making of a Constitution for Europe' (1989) 26 CML Rev 594.

Obradovic, D., 'Repatriation of Powers in the European Community' (1997) 34 CML Rev 59.

O'Keeffe, D., and Twomey, P., (eds), *Legal Issues of the Maastricht Treaty* (Wiley Chancery Law, 1994).

Peers, S., 'Justice and Home Affairs: Decision-making after Amsterdam' (2000) 23 EL Rev 183.

Rasmussen, H., 'On Law and Policy-making in the European Communities' (1986) Nijhoff Publications.

Swaine, E.T., 'Subsidiarity and Self Interest: Federalism at the European Court of Justice' (2000) 41 Harvard International LJ 1.

Usher, J., 'Variable Geometry or Concentric Circles: Patterns for the European Union' (1997) 46 ICLQ 243.

Wilke, M., and Wallace, H., 'Subsidiarity: Approaches to Power sharing in the EEC' (Royal Institute of International Affairs Discussion Paper No. 27) (1990).

Zuleeg, M., 'Cohesion and Democracy in the US and EC' (1997) 45 Am J Comp L 505.

Editorial: Comment on the ToA (1997) 34 CML Rev 767.

FOUR

Principles of direct applicability and direct effects: State liability under *Francovich*

As was noted in chapter 3, the European Community Treaties were incorporated into UK law by the European Communities Act 1972. With the passing of this Act all Community law became, in the language of international law, directly applicable, that is, applicable as part of our own internal system. Henceforth, 'Any rights or obligations created by the Treaty are to be given legal effect in England without more ado' (per Lord Denning MR in *H.P. Bulmer Ltd* v *J. Bollinger SA* [1974] Ch 401). As directly applicable law, EC law thus became capable of forming the basis of rights and obligations enforceable by individuals before their national courts.

Provisions of international law which are found to be capable of application by national courts *at the suit of individuals* are also termed 'directly applicable'. This ambiguity (the same ambiguity is found in the alternative expression 'self-executing') has given rise to much uncertainty in the context of EC law. For this reason it was suggested by Winter that the term 'directly effective' be used to convey this secondary meaning. Although this term has generally found favour amongst British academic writers the ECJ as well as our own courts tend to use the two concepts of direct applicability and direct effects interchangeably. However, for purposes of clarity it is proposed to use the term 'directly effective' or 'capable of direct effects' in this secondary meaning, to denote those provisions of EC law which give rise to rights or obligations which individuals may enforce before their national courts.

Not all provisions of directly applicable international law are capable of direct effects. Some provisions are regarded as binding on, and enforceable by States alone; others are too vague to form the basis of rights or obligations for individuals; others are too incomplete and require further measures of implementation before they can be fully effective in law. Whether a particular provision is directly effective is a matter of construction, depending on its language and purpose as well as the terms on which the Treaty has been incorporated into domestic law. Although most States apply similar criteria of clarity and completeness, specific rules and attitudes inevitably differ, and since the application of the criteria often conceals an underlying policy decision, the results are by no means uniform from State to State.

The question of the direct effects of Community law is of paramount concern to EC lawyers. If a provision of EC law is directly effective, domestic courts must not only apply it, but, following the principle of primacy of EC law (this principle will be discussed in full in chapter 5), must do so in priority over any conflicting provisions of national law. Since the scope of the EC Treaty is wide, the more generous the approach to the question of direct effects, the greater the potential for conflict.

Which provisions of EC law will then be capable of direct effect? The European Communities Act, s. 2(1), provides that:

> All such rights, powers, liabilities, obligations and restrictions from time to time created or arising by or under the Treaties, and all such remedies and procedures from time to time provided for by or under the Treaties, as in accordance with the Treaties are without further enactment to be given legal effect or used in the United Kingdom shall be recognised and available in law, and be enforced, allowed and followed accordingly; and the expression 'enforceable Community right' and similar expressions shall be read as referring to one to which this subsection applies.

This section thus provides for the direct application of Community law but offers no guidance as to which provisions of EC law are to be directly effective.

The EC Treaty merely provides in Article 249 (ex 189) that Regulations (but only Regulations) are 'directly applicable'.

Since, as has been suggested, direct applicability is a necessary precondition for direct effects this would seem to imply that only Regulations are capable of direct effects.

This has not proved to be the case. In a series of landmark decisions, the ECJ, principally in its jurisdiction under Article 234 (ex 177) EC to give preliminary rulings on matters of interpretation of EC law on reference from national courts, has extended the principle of direct effects to Treaty Articles, Directives, Decisions, and even to provisions of international agreements to which the EC is a party.

Treaty Articles

The question of the direct effect of a Treaty Article was first raised in *Van Gend en Loos* v *Nederlandse Administratie der Belastingen* (case 26/62). The Dutch administrative tribunal, in a reference under the then Article 177 (now 234), asked the ECJ:

Whether Article 12 of the EEC Treaty has an internal effect . . . in other words, whether the nationals of Member States may, on the basis of the Article in question, enforce rights which the judge should protect?

Article 12 EEC (now 25 EC) prohibits States from:

> . . . introducing between themselves any new customs duties on imports or exports or any charges having equivalent effect.

It was argued on behalf of the defendant customs authorities that the obligation in the then Article 12 was addressed to States and was intended to govern rights and obligations between States. Such obligations were not normally enforceable at the suit of individuals. Moreover the Treaty had expressly provided enforcement procedures under Articles 169 (now 226) and 170 (now 227) (see chapter 28) at the suit of the Commission or Member States. Advocate-General Roemer suggested that Article 12 was too complex to be enforced by national courts; if such courts were to enforce Article 12 directly there would be no uniformity of application.

Despite these persuasive arguments the ECJ held that the then Article 12 was directly effective. The Court held:

> . . . this Treaty is more than an agreement creating only mutual obligations between the contracting parties . . . Community law . . . not only imposes obligations on individuals but also confers on them legal rights.

These rights would arise:

> . . . not only when an explicit grant is made by the Treaty, but also through obligations imposed, in a clearly defined manner, by the Treaty on individuals as well as on Member States and the Community institutions.
>
> . . . The text of Article 12 sets out a clear and unconditional prohibition, which is not a duty to act but a duty not to act. This duty is imposed without any power in the States to subordinate its application to a positive act of internal law. The prohibition is perfectly suited by its nature to produce direct effects in the legal relations between the Member States and their citizens.

And further:

> The vigilance of individuals interested in protecting their rights creates an effective control additional to that entrusted by Articles 169 to 170 to the diligence of the Commission and the Member States.

Apart from its desire to enable individuals to invoke the protection of EC law the Court clearly saw the principle of direct effects as a valuable means of ensuring that EC law was enforced uniformly in all Member States even when States had not themselves complied with their obligations.

It was originally thought that, as the Court suggested in *Van Gend*, only prohibitions such as Article 12 (now 25) ('standstill' provisions) would qualify for direct effects; this was found in *Alfons Lütticke GmbH* v *Hauptzollamt Saarlouis* (case 57/65) not to be so. The Article under consideration in this case was Article 95(1) and (3) (now 90); this Article contains a prohibition on States introducing discriminatory taxation; Article 95(3) contained a positive obligation that:

> Member States shall, not later than at the beginning of the second stage, repeal or amend any provisions existing when this Treaty enters into force which conflict with the preceding rules.

The ECJ found that the then Article 95(1) was directly effective; Article 95(3), which was subject to compliance within a specified time-limit, would, the Court implied, become directly effective once that time-limit had expired.

The Court has subsequently found a large number of Treaty provisions to be directly effective. All the basic principles relating to free movement of goods and persons, competition law, discrimination on the grounds of sex and nationality may now be invoked by individuals before their national courts. In deciding whether a particular provision is directly effective certain criteria are applied; the provision must be sufficiently clear and precise; it must be unconditional, and leave no room for the exercise of discretion in implementation by Member States or Community institutions. The criteria are, however, applied generously, with the result that many provisions which are not particularly clear or precise, especially with regard to their scope and application, have been found to produce direct effects. Even where they are conditional and subject to further implementation they have been held to be directly effective once the date for implementation is past. The Court reasons that while there may be discretion as to the means of implementation, there is no discretion as to ends.

In *Van Gend* the principle of direct effects operated to confer rights on Van Gend exercisable against the Dutch customs authorities. Thus the obligation fell on an organ of the State, to whom Article 12 (now 25) was addressed. (This is known as a 'vertical' direct effect, reflecting the relationship between individual and State.) But Treaty obligations, even when addressed to States, may fall on individuals too. May they be invoked by individuals against individuals? (This is known as a 'horizontal effect', reflecting the relationship between individual and individual.)

Van Gend implies so, and this was confirmed in *Defrenne* v *Sabena (No. 2)* (case 43/75). Ms Defrenne was an air hostess employed by Sabena, a Belgian airline company. She brought an action against Sabena based on Article 119 (now 141 EC) of the EEC Treaty. It provided that:

> Each Member State shall during the first stage ensure and subsequently maintain the application of the principle that men and women should receive equal pay for equal work.

Ms Defrenne claimed, *inter alia,* that in paying their male stewards more than their air hostesses, when they performed identical tasks, Sabena was in breach of the then Article 119. The gist of the questions referred to the ECJ was whether, and in what context, Article 119 was directly effective. Sabena argued that the Treaty articles so far found directly effective, such as Article 12 (now 25), concerned the relationship between the State and its subjects, whereas Article 119 was primarily concerned with relationships between individuals. It was thus not suited to produce direct effects. The Court, following Advocate-General Trabucci, disagreed, holding that:

> . . . the prohibition on discrimination between men and women applies not only to the action of public authorities, but also extends to all agreements which are intended to regulate paid labour collectively, as well as to contracts between individuals.

This same principle was applied in *Walrave v Association Union Cycliste Internationale* (case 36/74) to Article 7 of the EEC Treaty (now Article 12 EC) which provides that:

> Within the scope of application of this Treaty, and without prejudice to any special provisions contained therein, any discrimination on grounds of nationality shall be prohibited.

The claimants, Walrave and Koch, sought to invoke Article 7 EEC in order to challenge the rules of the defendant association which they claimed were discriminatory.

The ECJ held that the prohibition of any discrimination on grounds of nationality

> . . . does not only apply to the action of public authorities but extends likewise to rules of any other nature aimed at regulating in a collective manner gainful employment and the provision of services.

To limit the prohibition in question to acts of a public authority would risk creating inequality in their application.

As will become evident in the chapters of this book devoted to the substantive law of the Community many Treaty provisions have now been successfully invoked vertically and horizontally. The fact of their being addressed to, and imposing obligations on, States has been no bar to their horizontal effect.

Regulations

A Regulation is described in Article 249 (ex 189) EC as of 'general application. . . binding in its entirety and directly applicable in all Member States'. It is clearly intended to take immediate effect without the need for further implementation.

Regulations are thus by their very nature apt to produce direct effects. However, even for Regulations direct effects are not automatic. There may be cases where a provision in a Regulation is conditional, or insufficiently precise, or requires further implementation before it can take full legal effect. But since a Regulation is of 'general application', where the criteria for direct effects are satisfied, it may be invoked vertically or horizontally.

Directives

A Directive is (Article 249 (ex 189) EC):

> . . . binding, as to the result to be achieved, upon each Member State to which it is addressed, but shall leave to the national authorities the choice of form and methods.

Because Directives are not described as 'directly applicable' it was originally thought that they could not produce direct effects. Moreover the obligation in a Directive is addressed to States, and gives the State some discretion as to the form and method of implementation; its effect thus appeared to be conditional on the implementation by the State. This was not the conclusion reached by the ECJ, which found, in *Grad* v *Finanzamt Traunstein* (case 9/70) that a Directive could be directly effective. The claimant in *Grad* was a haulage company seeking to challenge a tax levied by the German authorities which the claimant claimed was in breach of an EC Directive and Decision. The Directive required States to amend their VAT systems to comply with a common EC system. The Decision required states to apply this new VAT system to, *inter alia*, freight transport from the date of the Directive's entry into force. The German government argued that only Regulations were directly applicable. Directives and Decisions took effect internally only via national implementing measures. As evidence they pointed out that only Regulations were required to be published in the *Official Journal*. The ECJ disagreed. The fact that only Regulations were described as directly applicable did not mean that other binding acts were incapable of such effects:

> It would be incompatible with the binding effect attributed to Decisions by Article 189 to exclude in principle the possibility that persons affected may invoke the obligation imposed by a Decision. . . . the effectiveness of such a measure would be weakened if the nationals of that State could not invoke it in the courts and the national courts could not take it into consideration as part of Community law.

Although expressed in terms of a Decision, it was implied in the judgment that the same principle applied in the case of Directives. This was established beyond doubt in a claim based on a free-standing Directive in *Van Duyn* v *Home Office* (case 41/74). Here the claimant sought to invoke Article 3 of Directive 64/221 to challenge the Home Office's refusal to allow her to enter to take up work with the Church of Scientology. Under EC law Member States are allowed to deny EC nationals rights of entry and residence only on the grounds of public policy, public security and public health (see chapter 22). Article 3 of Directive 64/221 provides that measures taken on the grounds of public policy must be based exclusively on the personal conduct of the person concerned. Despite the lack of clarity as to the scope of the concept of 'personal conduct' the ECJ held that Mrs Van Duyn was entitled to invoke the Directive directly before her national court. It suggested that even if the provision in question was not clear the matter could be referred to the ECJ for interpretation under Article 177 (now 234) EC.

So both Directives and Decisions may be directly effective. Whether they will in fact be so will depend on whether they satisfy the criteria for direct effects — they must be sufficiently clear and precise, unconditional, leaving no room for discretion in implementation. These conditions were satisfied in *Grad*. Although the Directive was not unconditional in that it required action to be taken by the State, and gave a time-limit for implementation, once the time-limit expired the obligation became absolute. At this stage there was no discretion left. *Van Duyn* demonstrates that it is not necessary for a provision to be particularly precise for it to be deemed 'sufficiently' clear.

The reasoning in *Grad* was followed in *Van Duyn* and has been repeated on many occasions to justify the direct effect of Directives once the time-limit for implementation has expired. A more recent formulation of the test for direct effects is that the provision in question should be 'sufficiently clear and precise and unconditional'.

A Directive cannot, however, be directly effective before the time-limit for implementation has expired. It was tried unsuccessfully in the case of *Pubblico Ministero* v *Ratti* (case 148/78). Mr Ratti, a solvent manufacturer, sought to invoke two EC harmonisation Directives on the labelling of dangerous preparations in order to defend a criminal charge based on his own labelling practices. These practices, he claimed, were not illegal according to the Directive. The ECJ held that since the time-limit for the implementation of one of the Directives had not expired it was not directly effective. He could, however, rely on the other Directive for which the implementation date had passed.

Even when a State has implemented a Directive it may still be directly effective. The ECJ held this to be the case in *Verbond van Nederlandse Ondernemingen (VNO)* v *Inspecteur der Invoerrechten en Accijnzen* (case 51/76), thereby allowing the Federation of Dutch Manufacturers to invoke the Second VAT Directive despite implementation of the provision by the Dutch authorities. The grounds for the decision were that the useful effect of the Directive would be weakened if individuals could not invoke it before national courts. By allowing individuals to invoke the Directive the Community can ensure that national authorities have kept within the limits of their discretion. Arguably this principle could apply to enable an individual to invoke a 'parent' Directive even before the expiry of the time-limit, where domestic measures have been introduced for the purpose of complying with the Directive (see *Officier van Justitie* v *Kolpinghuis Nijmegen* (case 80/86)). This view gains some support from the case of *Inter-Environment Wallonie*

ASBL v *Region Wallonie* (case C–129/96). Here the ECJ held that even within the implementation period Member States are not entitled to take any measures which could seriously compromise the result required by the Directive.

Initially national courts were reluctant to concede that Directives could be directly effective. The Conseil d'État, the supreme French administrative court, in *Minister of the Interior* v *Cohn-Bendit* [1980] 1 CMLR 543, refused to follow *Van Duyn* v *Home Office* and allow the claimant to invoke Directive 64/221. The English Court of Appeal in *O'Brien* v *Sim-Chem Ltd* [1980] ICR 429 found the Equal Pay Directive (75/117) not to be directly effective on the grounds that it had purportedly been implemented in the Equal Pay Act 1970 (as amended 1975). *VNO* was apparently not cited before the court. The German federal tax court, the Bundesfinanzhof, in *Re VAT Directives* [1982] 1 CMLR 527 took the same view on the direct effects of the Sixth VAT Directive, despite the fact that the time-limit for implementation had expired and existing German law appeared to run counter to the Directive. The courts' reasoning in all these cases ran on similar lines. Article 249 (ex 189) expressly distinguishes Regulations and Directives; only Regulations are described as 'directly applicable'; Directives are intended to take effect within the national order via national implementing measures.

On a strict interpretation of Article 249 (ex 189) EC this is no doubt correct. On the other hand the reasoning advanced by the ECJ is compelling. The obligation in a Directive is 'binding "on Member States" as to the result to be achieved'; the useful effects of Directives would be weakened if States were free to ignore their obligations and enforcement of EC law were left to direct action by the Commission or Member States under Article 226 (ex 169) or Article 227 (ex 170). Moreover States are obliged under Article 10 (ex 5) to 'take all appropriate measures . . . to ensure fulfilment of the obligations arising out of this Treaty or resulting from action taken by the institutions of the Community'.

If they have failed in these obligations why should they not be answerable to individual litigants?

Vertical and horizontal direct effects: a necessary distinction   The reasoning of the ECJ is persuasive where an individual seeks to invoke a Directive against the State on which the obligation to achieve the desired results has been imposed. In cases such as *VNO, Van Duyn,* and *Ratti,* the claimant sought to invoke a Directive against a public body, an arm of the State. This is known as *vertical* direct effect, reflecting the relationship between the individual and the State. Yet as with Treaty Articles, there are a number of Directives, impinging on labour, company or consumer law for example, which a claimant may wish to invoke against a private person. Is the Court's reasoning in favour of direct effects adequate as a basis for the enforcement of Directives against individuals? This is known as *horizontal* direct effect, reflecting the relationship between individuals.

The arguments for and against horizontal effects are finely balanced. Against horizontal effects is the fact of uncertainty. Prior to the entry into force of the TEU, Directives were not required to be published. More compelling, the obligation in a Directive is addressed to the State. In *Becker* v *Finanzamt Munster-Innenstadt* (case 8/81) the Court, following *dicta* in *Pubblico Ministero* v *Ratti* (case 148/78), had justified the direct application of the Sixth VAT Directive against the German tax authorities on the grounds that the obligation to implement the Directive had been placed on the State. It followed that 'a Member State which has not adopted, within the specified time limit, the implementing measures prescribed in the Directive, cannot raise the objection, as against individuals, that it has not fulfilled the obligations arising from the Directive'. This reasoning is clearly inapplicable in the case of an action against a private person. In favour of horizontal effects is the fact that Directives have always in fact been published; that Treaty provisions addressed to, and imposing obligations on, Member States have been held to be horizontally effective; that it would be anomalous, and offend against the principles of equality, if an individual's rights to invoke a Directive were to depend on the status, public or private, of the party against whom he wished to invoke it; that the useful effect of Community law would be weakened if individuals were not free to invoke the protection of Community law against *all* parties.

Although a number of references were made in which the issue of the horizontal effects of Directives was raised, the ECJ for many years avoided the question, either by declaring that the claimant's action lay outside the scope of the Directive, as in *Burton* v *British Railways Board* (case 19/81) (Equal Treatment Directive 76/207) or by falling back on a directly effective Treaty provision, as in *Worringham* v *Lloyds Bank Ltd* (case 69/80) in which Article 119 (now 141) was applied instead of Directive 75/117, the Equal Pay Directive.

The nettle was finally grasped in *Marshall* v *Southampton & South West Hampshire Area Health Authority (Teaching)* (case 152/84). Here Mrs Marshall was seeking to challenge the health authority's compulsory retirement age of 65 for men and 60 for women as discriminatory, in breach of the Equal Treatment Directive 76/207. The difference in age was permissible under the Sex Discrimination Act 1975, which expressly excludes 'provisions relating to death or retirement' from its ambit. The Court of Appeal referred two questions to the ECJ:

(a)   Whether a different retirement age for men and women was in breach of Directive 76/207?

(b)   If so, whether Directive 76/207 could be relied on by Mrs Marshall in the circumstances of the case?

The relevant circumstances were that the area health authority, though a 'public' body, was acting in its capacity as employer.

The question of vertical and horizontal effects was fully argued. The Court, following a strong submission from Advocate-General Slynn, held that the compulsory different retirement age was in breach of Directive 76/207 and could be invoked against a public body such as the health authority. Moreover:

. . . where a person involved in legal proceedings is able to rely on a Directive as against the State he may do so regardless of the capacity in which the latter is acting, whether employer or public authority.

On the other hand, following the reasoning of *Becker*, since a Directive is, according to Article 189 (now 249), binding only on 'each Member State to which it is addressed':

It follows that a Directive may not of itself impose obligations on an individual and that a provision of a Directive may not be relied upon as such against such a person.

If this distinction was arbitrary and unfair:

Such a distinction may easily be avoided if the Member State concerned has correctly implemented the Directive in national law.

So, with *Marshall* v *Southampton & South West Hampshire Area Health Authority (Teaching)* the issue of the horizontal effect of Directives was, it seemed, finally laid to rest (albeit in an *obiter* statement, since the health authority was arguably a public body at the time). By denying their horizontal effect on the basis of the then Article 189 the Court strengthened the case for their vertical effect. The decision undoubtedly served to gain acceptance for the principle of vertical direct effects by national courts (see, e.g., *R* v *London Boroughs Transport Committee, ex parte Freight Transport Association Ltd* [1990] 3 CMLR 495). But problems remain, both with respect to vertical and horizontal direct effects.

Vertical direct effects First, the concept of a 'public' body, or an 'agency of the State', against whom a Directive may be invoked, is unclear. In *Fratelli Costanzo SPA* v *Comune di Milano* (case 103/88), in a claim against the Milan Comune based on the Comune's alleged breach of Public Procurement Directive 71/305, the Court held that since the reason for which an individual may rely on the provisions of a Directive in proceedings before the national courts is that the obligation is binding on all the authorities of the Member States, where the conditions for direct effect were met, 'all organs of the administration, including decentralised authorities such as municipalities, are obliged to apply these provisions.' The area health authority in *Marshall* was deemed a 'public' body, as was the Royal Ulster Constabulary in *Johnston* v *RUC* (case 222/84). But what of the status of publicly-owned or publicly-run enterprises such as the former British Rail or British Coal? Or semi-public bodies? Are universities 'public' bodies?

These issues arose for consideration in *Foster* v *British Gas plc* (case C–188/89). In a claim against the British Gas Corporation in respect of different retirement ages for men and women, based on Equal Treatment Directive 76/207, the English Court of Appeal had held that British Gas, a statutory corporation carrying out statutory duties under the Gas Act 1972 at the relevant time, was not a public body against which the Directive could be enforced. On appeal the House of Lords sought clarification on this issue from the ECJ. That court refused to accept British Gas's argument that there was a distinction between a nationalised undertaking and a State agency and ruled (at para. 18) that a Directive might be relied on against organisations or bodies which were 'subject to the authority or control of the State or had special powers beyond those which result from the normal relations between individuals'. Applying this principle to the specific facts of *Foster* v *British Gas plc* it ruled (at para. 20) that a Directive might be invoked against 'a body, whatever its legal form, which has been made responsible, pursuant to a measure adopted by the State, for providing a public service under the control of the State and has for that purpose special powers beyond those which result from the normal rules applicable in relations between individuals'. On this interpretation a nationalised undertaking such as the then British Gas would be a 'public' body against which a Directive might be enforced, as the House of Lords subsequently decided in *Foster* v *British Gas plc* [1991] 2 AC 306.

It may be noted that the principle expressed in para. 18 is wider than that of para. 20, the criteria of 'control' and 'powers' being expressed as alternative, not cumulative; as such it is wide enough to embrace any nationalised undertaking, and even bodies such as universities with a more tenuous public element, but which are subject to *some* State authority or control. However, in *Rolls-Royce plc* v *Doughty* [1992] ICR 538, the Court of Appeal, applying the 'formal ruling' of para. 20 of *Foster*, found that Rolls-Royce, a nationalised undertaking at the relevant time, although 'under the control of the State', had not been 'made responsible pursuant to a measure adopted by the State for providing a public service'. The public services which it provided, for example, in the defence of the realm, were provided to the *State* and not to the *public* for the purposes of benefit to the State: nor did the company possess or exercise any special powers of the type enjoyed by British Gas. Mustill LJ suggested that the test provided in para. 18 was 'not an authoritative exposition of the way in which cases like *Foster* should be approached': it simply represented a 'summary of the (Court's) jurisprudence to date'.

There is little evidence to support such a conclusion. The Court has never distinguished between its 'formal' rulings (i.e. on the specific issue raised) and its more general statements of principle. Indeed such general statements often provide a basis for future rulings in different factual situations. A restrictive approach to the Court's rulings, as taken in *Rolls Royce plc* v *Doughty*, is inconsistent with the purpose of the ECJ, namely to ensure the effective implementation of Community law and the protection of individuals' rights under that law by giving the concept of a public body the widest possible scope. This was acknowledged by the Court of Appeal in *National Union of Teachers* v *Governing Body of St Mary's Church of England (Aided) Junior School* [1997] 3 CMLR 630 when it suggested that the concept of an emanation of the state should be a 'broad one': the definition provided in para. 20 of *Foster* should not be regarded as a statutory definition: it was, in the words of para. 20, simply *'included among* those bodies against which the provisions of a Directive can be applied'.

Thus the British courts' approach to, and the outcome of the enquiry as to whether a particular body is an 'emanation of the state' for the purpose of enforcement of EC Directives is unpredictable. It is not altogether surprising that they fail to take a generous view when the result would be to impose liability on bodies which are in no way responsible for the non-implementation of Directives, a factor which was undoubtedly influential in *Rolls-Royce plc* v *Doughty*. But even if national courts were to adopt a generous approach, no matter how generously the concept of a 'public' body is defined, as long as the public/private distinction exists there can be no uniformity in the application of Directives as between one State and another. Neither will it remove the anomaly as between individuals. Where a State has failed to fulfil its obligations in regard to Directives, whether by non-implementation or inadequate implementation, an individual would, it appeared, following *Marshall*, be powerless to invoke a Directive in the context of a 'private' claim.

Horizontal direct effects In 1993, in the case of *Dori* v *Recreb Srl* (case C–91/92), the Court was invited to change its mind on the issue of horizontal direct effects in a claim based on EC Directive 85/577 on Consumer Protection, which had not at the time been implemented by the Italian authorities, against a private party. Advocate-General Lenz, urged the Court to reconsider its position in *Marshall* and extend the principle of direct effects to allow for the enforcement of Directives against *all* parties, public and private, in the interest of the uniform and effective application of Community law. This departure from its previous case law was, he suggested, justified in the light of the completion of the internal market and the entry into force of the Treaty on European Union, in order to meet the legitimate expectations of citizens of the Union seeking to rely on Community law. In the interests of legal certainty such a ruling should however not be retrospective in its effect (on the effect of Article 234 (ex 177) rulings see chapter 27).

The Court, no doubt mindful of national courts' past resistance to the principle of direct effects, and the reasons for that resistance, declined to follow the Advocate-General's advice and affirmed its position in *Marshall*: Article 189 (now 249) distinguished between Regulations and Directives; the case law establishing vertical direct effects was based on the need to prevent States from taking advantage of their own wrong; to extend this case law and allow Directives to be enforced against individuals 'would be to recognise a power to enact obligations for individuals with immediate effect, whereas (the Community) has competence to do so only where it is empowered to adopt Regulations'. This decision was followed in two cases decided in 1996, *El Corte Inglés SA* v *Rivero* (case C–192/94) and *Arcaro* (case C–168/95).

However, in denying horizontal effects to Directives in *Dori*, the Court was at pains to point out that alternative remedies might be available based on principles introduced by the Court prior to *Dori*, namely the principle of indirect effects and the principle of State liability introduced in *Francovich* v *Italy* (cases C–6 & 9/90). *Francovich* was also suggested as providing an alternative remedy in *El Corte Inglés SA* v *Rivero*.

Principle of indirect effects

The principle of indirect effects was introduced in a pair of cases decided shortly before *Marshall*, *von Colson* v *Land Nordrhein-Westfalen* (case 14/83) and *Harz* v *Deutsche Tradax GmbH* (case 79/83).

Both cases were based on Article 6 of Equal Treatment Directive 76/207. Article 6 provides that:

> Member States shall introduce into their national legal systems such measures as are necessary to enable all persons who consider themselves wronged by failure to apply to them the principle of equal treatment . . . to pursue their claims by judicial process after possible recourse to other competent authorities.

The claimants had applied for jobs with their respective defendants. Both had been rejected. It was found by the German court that the rejection had been based on their sex, but it was justifiable. Under German law they were entitled to compensation only in the form of travelling expenses. This they claimed did not meet the requirements of Article 6. Ms von Colson was claiming against the prison service; Ms Harz against Deutsche Tradax GmbH, a private company. So the vertical/horizontal, public/private anomaly was openly raised and argued in Article 177 (now 234) proceedings before the ECJ.

The Court's solution was ingenious. Instead of focusing on the vertical or horizontal effects of the Directive it turned to the then Article 5 of the EC Treaty. Article 5 (now 10) requires States to 'take all appropriate measures' to ensure fulfilment of their Community obligations.

This obligation, the Court said, applies to *all* the authorities of Member States, including the courts. It thus falls on the courts of Member States to interpret national law in such a way as to ensure that the objectives of the Directive are achieved. It was for the German courts to interpret German law in such a way as to ensure an effective remedy as required by Article 6 of the Directive. The result of this approach is that although Community law is not applied directly — it is not 'directly effective' — it may still be applied indirectly as domestic law by means of interpretation.

The success of the *von Colson* principle of indirect effect depended on the extent to which national courts perceived themselves as having a discretion, under their own constitutional rules, to interpret domestic law to comply with Community law. Courts in the UK are constrained by the terms of the European Communities Act. It was thought by some commentators that s. 2(1) of this Act, which provides for the direct application of Community law within the UK, only applied to directly effective Community law. If such were the case it would leave little room for the application of the *von Colson* principle. This was the view taken by the House of Lords in *Duke* v *GEC Reliance Ltd* [1988] AC 618. However, special facts obtained in that case. The House of Lords was being asked to construe s. 6(4) of the Sex Discrimination Act 1975 to comply with EC Equal Treatment Directive

76/207, as interpreted in *Marshall*. The Sex Discrimination Act had been amended to comply with the Court's ruling in *Marshall,* but it had not been made retrospective. The claimant's claim for damages, based on unequal treatment (different retirement ages for men and women), was in respect of the period prior to the amendment of the Sex Discrimination Act. The House of Lords clearly felt that it would be most unfair to penalise the defendant, a 'private' party, by interpreting the section against its literal meaning in order to comply with the 'oblique language' of the Directive, *a fortiori* when Parliament had clearly chosen *not* to amend the Act retrospectively.

A similarly constituted House of Lords took a different view in *Litster* v *Forth Dry Dock & Engineering Co. Ltd* [1990] 1 AC 546. Here, in a 'private' claim against an employer based on EC Directive 77/187 (safeguarding employees' rights in the event of transfer of undertakings), the House was prepared to interpret a domestic Regulation contrary to its prima facie meaning in order to comply with the Directive as interpreted by the ECJ in the case of *Bork* (case 101/87). The reason for its so doing was that the domestic Regulation in question had been introduced *for the purpose of* complying with the Directive.

The House of Lords' approach in *Litster* clearly represented an advance on *Duke* v *GEC Reliance Ltd.* However, it could not ensure that the *von Colson* principle would be applied to give Directives an indirect effect where, either deliberately or inadvertently, legislation has not been introduced for the purpose of complying with a Directive; nor where the question of whether legislation which has been introduced, either before or after the EC Directive, was intended to comply with community law, is unclear.

In *Finnegan* v *Clowney Youth Training Programme Ltd* [1990] 2 AC 407, in a claim under the Sex Discrimination (Northern Ireland) Order 1976 (SI 1976/1042), on facts very similar to those of *Duke* v *GEC Reliance Ltd,* concerning different retirement ages for men and women, the House of Lords refused to interpret art. 8(4) of the order to comply with Directive 76/207, as interpreted in *Marshall, even though the order had been made after the ECJ's decision in Marshall.* Their lordships' reason for so doing was that the provision in question, an exclusion from the non-discrimination principle for provision 'in relation to death or retirement' was enacted in terms identical to the parallel provision (s. 6(4)) of the Sex Discrimination Act 1975 which had been considered in *Duke* v *GEC Reliance Ltd,* and 'must have been intended to' have the same meaning as in that Act.

The ECJ considered these matters in *Marleasing SA* v *La Comercial Internacional de Alimentación SA* (case C–106/89). In this case, which was referred to the ECJ by the Court of First Instance, Oviedo, the claimant company was seeking a declaration that the contracts setting up the defendant companies were void on the grounds of 'lack of cause', the contracts being a sham transaction carried out in order to defraud their creditors. This was a valid basis for nullity under Spanish law. The defendants argued that this question was now governed by EC Directive 68/151. The purpose of Directive 68/151 was to protect the members of a company and third parties from, *inter alia,* the adverse effects of the doctrine of nullity. Article 11 of the

Directive provides an exhaustive list of situations in which nullity may be invoked. It does not include 'lack of cause'. The Directive should have been in force in Spain from the date of accession in 1986, but it had not been implemented. The Spanish judge sought a ruling from the ECJ on whether, in these circumstances, Article 11 of the Directive was directly effective.

The ECJ reiterated the view it expressed in *Marshall* that a Directive cannot of itself 'impose obligations on private parties'. It reaffirmed its position in *von Colson* that national courts must *as far as possible* interpret national law in the light of the wording and purpose of the Directive in order to achieve the result pursued by the Directive (para. 8). And it added that this obligation applied *whether the national provisions in question were adopted before or after the Directive*. It concluded by ruling specifically, and without qualification, that national courts were 'required' to interpret domestic law in such a way as to ensure that the objectives of the Directive were achieved (para. 13).

Given that in *Marleasing* no legislation had been passed, either before or after the issuing of the Directive, to comply with the Directive, and given the ECJ's suggestion that the Spanish court must nonetheless strive to interpret domestic law to comply with the Directive, it seems that, according to the ECJ, it is not necessary to the application of the *von Colson* principle that the relevant national measure should have been introduced for the purpose of complying with the Directive, nor even that a national measure should have been specifically introduced at all.

The strict line taken in *Marleasing* was modified in *Wagner Miret* v *Fondo de Garantía Salaria* (case C–334/92), in a claim against a private party based on Directive 80/987. This Directive is an employee protection measure designed, *inter alia*, to guarantee employees arrears of pay in the event of their employer's insolvency. Citing its ruling in *Marleasing* the Court suggested that, in interpreting national law to conform with the objectives of a Directive, national courts must *presume* that the State intended to comply with Community law. They must strive '*as far as possible*' to interpret domestic law to achieve the result pursued by the Directive. But if the provisions of domestic law cannot be interpreted in such a way (as was found to be the case in *Wagner Miret*) the State may be obliged to make good the claimant's loss on the principles of State liability laid down in *Francovich* v *Italy* (cases 6 & 9/90).

Wagner Miret thus represents a tacit acknowledgment on the part of the Court that national courts will not always feel able to 'construe' domestic law to comply with an EC Directive, particularly when the provisions of domestic law are clearly at odds with an EC Directive, and there is no evidence that the national legislature intended national law to comply with its provisions, or with a ruling on its provisions by the ECJ. In *Webb* v *EMO Air Cargo (UK) Ltd* [1993] 1 WLR 49, HL, Lord Keith of Kinkel noted that the ECJ in *Marleasing* had required national courts to construe domestic law to accord with the Directive 'only if it was possible to do so'. Invoking his own remarks in *Duke* v *GEC Reliance Ltd* [1988] AC 618 he suggested that this would only be possible if it could be done without 'distorting' the meaning of domestic legislation, that is, where a domestic law was 'open to an interpretation consistent with the Directive whether or not it is also open to an interpretation inconsistent with it'. Happily, in its final decision (*Webb* v *EMO Air Cargo Ltd (UK) (No. 2)* [1995] 1 WLR 1454, the House found, contrary to its original view (but it is submitted legitimately), that it was able to interpret the relevant sections of the Sex Discrimination Act to accord with the ECJ's ruling on the substance of the claim (see chapter 25). On the other hand in *R* v *British Coal Corporation, ex parte Vardy* [1993] ICR 720, a case decided after, but without reference to, *Marleasing*, the English High Court adverted to the House of Lords judgment in *Litster* but found that it was 'not possible' to interpret a particular provision of the Trade Union and Labour Relations Act 1992 to produce the same meaning as was required by EC Directive (see also *Re Hartlebury Printers Ltd* [1993] 1 All ER 470 at p. 478b, ChD). Similarly, in *Re a Rehabilitation Centre* [1992] 2 CMLR 21, in a claim for damages based on Equal Treatment Directive 76/207, against a private party, the German Federal Supreme Labour Court refused to 'construe' certain sections of the German Civil Code to comply with the Directive. It held that:

> even an interpretation of statutes by reference to conformity with the Constitution reaches its limits when it could come into conflict with the wording and evident intention of the legislature. The position can be no different as regards the interpretation of national law in the light of the wording and purpose of a Directive under Article 189(3) [now 249(3)] EEC.

Although the case was decided before *Marleasing* it is doubtful whether the court would depart from this view, so strongly stated, to give effect, albeit indirect, to a Directive which was not directly effective.

Thus the indirect application of EC Directives by national courts cannot be guaranteed. This reluctance on the part of national courts to comply with the *von Colson* principle, particularly as applied in *Marleasing*, is hardly surprising. It may be argued that in extending the principle of indirect effect in this way the ECJ is attempting to give horizontal effect to Directives by the back door, and impose obligations, addressed to Member States, on private parties, contrary to their understanding of domestic law. Where such is the case, as the House of Lords remarked in *Duke* v *GEC Reliance Ltd* (see also *Finnegan* v *Clowney Youth Training Programme Ltd*), this could be 'most unfair'.

However in the case of *Kolpinghuis Nijmegen* (case 80/86) the ECJ had suggested a limitation to the *von Colson* principle which might meet this objection. Here, in the context of criminal proceedings against Kolpinghuis for breach of EC Directive 80/777 on water purity, which at the relevant time had not been implemented by the Dutch authorities, the Court held that national courts' obligation to interpret domestic law to comply with EC law was 'limited by the general principles of law which form part of community law [see chapter 6] and in particular the principles of legal certainty and non-retroactivity'. Although expressed in the context of criminal liability, to which these principles were 'especially applicable', it was not suggested that the limitation should be confined to such situations. Thus, where an interpretation of domestic law would run counter to the legitimate expectations of individuals *a fortiori* where the State is seeking to invoke a Directive against an individual in order to determine or aggravate his criminal liability, as was the case in *Arcaro* (case C–168/95, see further below), the *von Colson* principle will not apply. The decision in *Duke* v *GEC Reliance Ltd* could be justified on this basis; that of *Finnegan* v *Clowney Youth Training Programme Ltd*, concerning, as it did, an order made after *Marshall*, and capable of interpretation in compliance with *Marshall*, could not. Where domestic legislation has been introduced in order to comply with a Community Directive, it is legitimate to expect that domestic law will be interpreted in conformity with Community law, provided that it is capable of such an interpretation. Where legislation has not been introduced with a view to compliance domestic law may still be interpreted in the light of the aims of the Directive as long as the domestic provision is reasonably capable of the meaning contended for. But in either case an interpretation which conflicts with the clear words and intentions of domestic law is unlikely to be acceptable to national courts. This has now been acknowledged by the Court in *Wagner Miret* (case C–334/92) and *Arcaro* (case C–168/95). In such a situation, as the Court suggested in *Wagner Miret*, it will be necessary to pursue the alternative remedy of a claim in damages against the State under the principles laid down in *Francovich* v *Italy* (cases C–6 & 9/90). It may be significant that in *El Corte Inglés SA* v *Rivero* (case C–192/94) the Court, in following the *Dori* ruling that a Directive could not be invoked directly against private parties, did not suggest a remedy based on indirect effect, as it had in *Dori*, but focused only on the possibility of a claim against the State under *Francovich*.

Principle of State liability under *Francovich* v *Italy*

The shortcomings of the principles of direct and indirect effects, particularly in the context of enforcement of Directives, as outlined above, led the Court to develop a third and separate principle in *Francovich* v *Italy* (cases C–6 & 9/90), the principle of State liability. Here the claimants, a group of ex-employees, were seeking arrears of wages following their employers' insolvency. Their claim (like that in the subsequent case of *Wagner Miret* (case C–334/92)) was based on Directive 80/987, which required Member States, *inter alia*, to provide for a guarantee fund to ensure the payment of employees' arrears of wages in the event of their employers' insolvency. Since a claim against their former employers would have been fruitless (they being insolvent and 'private' parties), they brought their claim for compensation against the State. There were two aspects to their claim. The first was based on the State's breach of the claimants' (alleged) substantive rights contained in the Directive, which they claimed were directly effective. The second was based on the State's primary failure to implement the Directive, as it was required to do under Article 189 (now 249) and Article 5 (now 10) of the EC Treaty. The Court had already held, in Article 169 (now 226) proceedings, that Italy was in breach of its Community obligations in failing to implement the Directive (*Commission* v *Italy* (case 22/87)).

With regard to the first claim, the Court found that the provisions in question were not sufficiently clear, precise and unconditional to be directly effective. Although the content of the right, and the class of intended beneficiaries, was clear, the State had a discretion as to the appointment of the guarantee institution; it would not necessarily itself be liable under the Directive. The claimants were, however, entitled in principle to succeed in their second claim. The Court held that where, as here, a State had failed to implement an EC Directive it would be obliged to compensate individuals for damage suffered as a result of its failure to implement the Directive if certain conditions were satisfied. That is, where:

(a) the Directive involved rights conferred on individuals,

(b) the content of those rights could be identified on the basis of the provisions of the Directive, and

(c) there was a causal link between the State's failure and the damage suffered by the persons affected.

The Court's reasoning was based on Member States' obligation to implement Directives under the then Article 189 (now 249) and their general obligation under Article 5 (now 10) EC to 'take all appropriate measures ... to ensure fulfilment of' their obligations under Community law; on its jurisprudence in *Van Gend en Loos* (case 26/62) and *Costa v ENEL* (case 6/64) that certain provisions of EC law are intended to give rise to rights for individuals, and that national courts are obliged to provide effective protection for those rights, as established in *Amministrazione delle Finanze dello Stato v Simmenthal SpA* (case 106/77) and *Factortame* (case C–213/89), see further chapters 5 and 26). It concluded that 'a principle of State liability for damage to individuals caused by a breach of Community law for which it is responsible is inherent in the scheme of the Treaty'.

Thus, where the three conditions of *Francovich* are fulfilled, individuals seeking compensation as a result of activities and practices which are inconsistent with EC Directives may proceed directly against the State. There will be no need to rely on the principles of direct or indirect effects. Responsibility for the non-implementation of the Directive will be placed not on the employer, 'public' or 'private', but squarely on the shoulders of the State, arguably, where it should always have been.

The reasoning in *Francovich* is compelling; its implications for Member States, however, remained unclear. Although expressed in terms of a State's liability for the non-implementation of a Directive, *Francovich* appeared to lay down a wider principle of liability for all breaches of Community law 'for which the State is responsible'. Would it then apply to legislative or administrative acts and omissions in breach of Treaty Articles or other provisions of EC law? Would it be an additional remedy, or available only in the absence of other remedies based on direct or indirect effects? Apart from the three conditions for liability, which are themselves open to interpretation, what other conditions would have to be fulfilled? Would liability be strict or dependent on culpability, even serious culpability, as was the case with actions for damages against Community institutions under Article 288 (ex 215(2)) (see chapter 33)? In the case of non-implementation of Directives, as in *Francovich* itself, the State's failure is clear; *a fortiori* when established by the Court under Article 226 (ex 169). But in cases of faulty or inadequate implementation it is not. The State's 'failure' may only become apparent following an interpretation of the Directive by the Court (see, e.g., the sex discrimination cases such as *Marshall* and *Barber* in chapter 25). Here the case for imposing liability in damages on the State is less convincing.

Many of these questions were referred to the Court of Justice for interpretation in *Brasserie du Pêcheur SA* v *Germany* and *R* v *Secretary of State for Transport, ex parte Factortame* (cases C–46 & 48/93). Advocate-General Tesauro suggested, in response to the questions referred, that:

(a)   The principle of State liability should not be confined to failure to implement EC Directives: it should attach to other failures to comply with Community law, including legislative failures.

(b)   A remedy under *Francovich* should be available whether or not there were other means by which Community rights might be enforced, that is, on the principles of direct or indirect effects.

(c)   As regards the conditions for liability, apart from the three conditions laid down in *Francovich*, the principles of State liability should be brought into line with the principles governing the Community's non-contractual liability under the then Article 215(2) (now 288). A State should only be liable for 'manifest and serious breaches' of Community law. In order for the breach to be 'manifest and serious' the content of the obligation breached must be clear and precise in every respect, or the national authority's interpretation 'manifestly wrong'. If the provision allegedly breached is not in itself clear and precise, the Court's case law must have provided sufficient clarification as regards its meaning and scope in identical or similar situations. If these conditions are fulfilled there is no need to add a further criterion of fault in the subjective sense, requiring actual knowledge or a deliberate breach of EC law.

The Court's decision was broadly in line with the Advocate-General's submissions on most of these issues. It held that the principle of State liability is applicable to *all* domestic acts and omissions, legislative, executive and judicial, in breach of Community law. Provided the conditions for liability are fulfilled it applies to breaches of *all* Community law, whether or not directly effective. However, arguing from the principles applicable to the Community's non-contractual liability under Article 215(2) (now 288(2)), the Court held that where a State is faced with situations involving choices comparable to those made by Community institutions when they adopt measures pursuant to a Community policy it will be liable only where three conditions are met (see paras 50 and 51 of the judgment):

(a)   the rule of law infringed must be intended to confer rights on individuals;

(b)   the breach must be sufficiently serious; and

(c)   there must be a direct causal link between the breach of the obligation resting on the State and the damage sustained by the injured parties.

The 'decisive test' for whether a breach is sufficiently serious is whether the institution concerned has 'manifestly and gravely exceeded the limits of its discretion' (para. 55). The factors to be taken into account in assessing this question included 'the clarity and precision of the rule breached, the measure of discretion left by that rule to the national or Community authorities, whether the infringement and the damage caused was intentional or voluntary, whether any error of law was excusable or inexcusable, the fact that the position taken by a Community institution may have contributed towards the omission, and the adoption or retention of national measures or practices contrary to Community law' (para. 56). For liability to arise it is not necessary for the infringement of Community law to have been established by the Court under Article 226 (ex 169) or 234 (ex 177); nor is it necessary to prove fault on the part of the national institution concerned *going beyond that of a sufficiently serious breach of Community law*. Thus in *Brasserie du Pêcheur* the Court rephrased the three conditions laid down in *Francovich* and incorporated a requirement that the breach be sufficiently serious. Condition (b) of *Francovich* (the content of the right infringed must be sufficiently clear) may now be regarded as contained within the definition of 'sufficiently serious'.

The Court based its decision on its past case law, particularly its reasoning in *Francovich*: States are obliged under Articles 189 (now 249) and 5 (now 10) EC to provide effective protection for individuals' Community rights and ensure the full effect of Community law. As regards its own jurisdiction to rule on the matter of States' liability in damages, challenged by the German government, it reasoned that, since the EC Treaty had failed to provide expressly for the consequences of breaches of Community law, it fell to the Court, pursuant to its duty under Article 164 (now 220) EC, to ensure that 'in the interpretation and application of this Treaty the law is observed'. The application of the Court's ruling and questions of damages and causation will be discussed further in chapters 5 and 26.

Despite the hostility with which this decision was greeted in anti-European quarters, it is submitted that the Court's ruling on the question of, and conditions for, liability is prima facie consistent with existing principles and, provided that the multiple test in para. 56 of what will constitute a 'sufficiently serious' breach is rigorously applied, strikes a fair balance between the interests of the Community in enforcing Community law and the interests of Member States in restricting liability to culpable breaches of Community law. For liability to arise, the institution concerned must have 'manifestly and gravely exceeded the limits of its discretion': the breach must be 'inexcusable'. If there is to be equality of *responsibility* as between the liability of the Community under Article 288(2) (ex 215(2)) EC and Member States under *Francovich*, the criterion of a 'sufficiently serious' breach laid down in *Brasserie du Pêcheur* should be interpreted strictly. The question remaining was whether the Court would apply the 'sufficiently serious' test to *all* claims based on *Francovich,* including claims for damage resulting from breaches of Community law which do *not* involve legislative 'choices' analogous to those made by Community institutions when implementing policy. Alternatively it might continue to 'interpret' Member States' actions as involving such choices, as it did, surprisingly, in *Brasserie du Pêcheur.* To limit the application of the sufficiently serious test to situations in which Member States are involved in 'legislative choices', by analogy with the position of Community institutions under Article 228(2) (ex 215(2)) (see chapter 33), as was suggested in *Brasserie du Pêcheur,* would be to ignore the essential difference between the position of Member States, when *implementing* Community law, and that of Community institutions when *making* Community law. Since liability depends on the breach by a Member State of a Community obligation, liability should in all cases depend on whether the breach is sufficiently serious. This is reflected in the multiple test laid down in para. 56. Given the lack of clarity of much EC law, and that Member States have no 'choice' to act in breach of Community law, it is submitted that the crucial element in para. 56 will often be the clarity and precision of the rule breached, as suggested by Advocate-General Tesauro in *Brasserie du Pêcheur.*

This view obtained some support in *R v Her Majesty's Treasury, ex parte British Telecommunications plc* (case C–392/93), a case decided shortly after *Brasserie du Pêcheur.* The case, brought by BT, concerned the alleged improper implementation of Council Directive 90/351 on public procurement in the water, energy, transport and telecommunication sectors (OJ L297/1, 1990). BT, which claimed to have been financially disadvantaged as a result of this wrongful implementation, was claiming damages based on *Francovich.* The Court, appearing to presume that the other conditions for liability were met, focused on the question whether the alleged breach was sufficiently serious. It applied the test of para. 56 of *Brasserie du Pêcheur.* Although it found that the UK implementing regulations were contrary to the requirements of the Directive, it suggested that the relevant provisions of the Directive were sufficiently unclear as to render the UK's error excusable. At para. 43 of its judgment the Court said that the Article in question (Article 8(1)) was:

. . . imprecisely worded and was reasonably capable of bearing, as well as the construction applied to it [by the ECJ] the interpretation given to it by the United Kingdom in good faith and on the basis of arguments which are not entirely void of substance. The interpretation, which was also shared by other Member States, was not manifestly contrary to the wording of the Directive or to the objective pursued by it.

This interpretation was, it is submitted, generous to the UK. Furthermore the Court held that in the context of the transposition of Directives, 'a restrictive approach to State liability is justified' for the same reasons as apply to Community liability in respect of legislative measures, namely, 'to ensure that the exercise of legislative functions is not hindered by the prospect of actions for damages whenever the general interest requires the institutions or Member States to adopt measures which may adversely affect individual interests' (para. 40).

The Court adopted a rather different approach in *R v Ministry of Agriculture, Fisheries and Food, ex parte Hedley Lomas (Ireland) Ltd* (case C–5/94). This case concerned a claim for damages by an exporter, Hedley Lomas, for losses suffered as a result of a UK ban on the export of live sheep to Spain. The ban was imposed following complaints from animal welfare groups that Spanish slaughterhouses did not comply with the requirements of Council Directive 74/577 on the stunning of animals before slaughter (OJ L316 10, 1974). The Spanish authorities had implemented the Directive, but had made no provision for monitoring compliance or providing sanctions for non-compliance. The UK raised the matter with the Commission, which, following discussion with the Spanish authorities, decided not to take action against Spain under the then Article 169. Although the UK ban was clearly in breach of the then Article 34 (now 29) of the EC Treaty, the UK argued that it was justified on the grounds of the protection of health of animals under Article 36 (now 30) (for further discussion of the substantive issues see chapter 11). However, the UK provided no evidence that the Directive had in fact been breached, either by particular slaughterhouses or generally.

The Court found that the ban was in breach of Article 34 (now 29), and was not justified under Article 36 (now 30). The fact that the Spanish authorities had not provided procedures for monitoring compliance with the Directive or penalties for non-compliance was irrelevant. 'Member States must rely on trust in each other to carry out inspections in their respective territories' (para. 19). Furthermore, the breach was 'sufficiently serious' to give rise to liability under *Francovich*. The Court suggested (at para. 28) that:

> where, at the time when it committed the infringement, the Member State in question was not called upon to make any legislative choices and had only considerably reduced, or even no, discretion, the mere infringement of Community law may be sufficient to establish the existence of a sufficiently serious breach.

This ruling, delivered two months after *R v Her Majesty's Treasury, ex parte British Telecommunications plc*, was surprising. While a finding that the UK would in principle be liable in damages was justified on the facts, the UK having produced no evidence of breach of the Directive constituting a threat to animal health to justify the ban under Article 36 (now 30), the suggestion that a 'mere infringement' of Community law might be sufficient to create liability where the State is not 'called upon to make any legislative choices' or has 'considerably reduced, or no, discretion' is questionable. While a State may have a choice as to the 'form and method of implementation' of Directives, and some discretion under the Treaty to derogate from basic Treaty rules, its discretion is strictly circumscribed, and it has no discretion to act in breach of Community law. The UK had no more 'legislative' discretion in implementing Directive 90/531 in *BT*, indeed possibly less, than it had under Article 36 (now 30) in *Hedley Lomas*. Indeed, prior to the Court's decision in *Hedley Lomas*, it was thought that a Member State *would* have a discretion to derogate from the prohibition of Article 34 (now 29) where this was necessary to protect a genuine public interest (see chapter 11). To pursue the analogy between the Community's liability for 'legislative choices involving choices of economic policy' and Member States' liability under *Francovich*, as the Court has done in all these cases, is to disguise the fact that *the two situations are not similar*. The principal reason for limiting liability under *Francovich* is not because Member States' 'discretion' in implementing Community law must not be fettered, but because the rules of Community law are often not clear. To hold them liable in damages for 'mere infringements' of such rules, thereby introducing a principle akin to strict liability, would not only be politically dangerous, it would be contrary to the principle of legal certainty, itself a respected principle of Community law (for further analysis see chapter 33).

Nevertheless the principle of liability for a 'mere infringement' of Community law in situations in which Member States are not required to make legislative choices was invoked by the ECJ in *Dillenkofer* v *Germany* (cases C–178, 179, 188, 189 and 190/94) in a situation in which Germany's failure, on all fours with that of the Italian government in *Francovich*, was clearly 'inexcusable' and therefore, as the Court acknowledged, 'sufficiently serious' to warrant liability. In neither *Hedley Lomas* nor *Dillenkofer* did the Court attempt to apply the multiple test laid down in para. 56 of *Brasserie du Pêcheur*.

However, in *Denkavit International BV* v *Bundesamt für Finanzen* (cases C–283, 291 & 292/94), which were cases involving claims for damages resulting from the faulty implementation of a Directive decided shortly after *Dillenkofer*, the Court reverted to its approach in *BT*. Following a strong submission from Advocate-General Jacobs it applied the criteria of para. 56 of *Brasserie du Pêcheur* and concluded that, as a result of the lack of clarity and precision of the relevant provisions of the Directive, and the lack of clear guidance from the Court's previous case law, Germany's breach of Community law could not be regarded as sufficiently serious to justify liability. Significantly, the Court did not draw a distinction, for the purposes of liability, between acts of Member States involving 'choices of economic policy' and 'mere infringements' of Community law.

In 1997 the ECJ's ruling in *Brasserie du Pêcheur* and *R* v *Secretary of State for Transport, ex parte Factortame Ltd* (cases C–46 and 48/93) was applied in the English High Court with a view to ascertaining whether the UK's action in introducing the Merchant Shipping Act 1988 in fact constituted a sufficiently serious breach of Community law (*R* v *Secretary of State for Transport, ex parte Factortame Ltd (No. 5)* [1998] 1 CMLR 1353. Hobhouse LJ considered the ECJ's case law on State liability and concluded that whether or not a Member State's action involved the exercise of discretion (i.e., 'legislative choices') the same test, requiring proof of a sufficiently serious breach of Community law, applied. That test, requiring a 'manifest and grave disregard of whatever discretion the Member State might possess', was based on the same principles as applied to Community liability under Article 215(2) (now 288), and was a relatively difficult one to meet. Having reasoned impeccably thus far he concluded that the UK's breach as regards the Merchant Shipping Act 1988 was sufficiently serious to warrant liability and referred the case back to the Divisional Court to decide the question of causation. Two factors in particular were cited by Hobhouse L as rendering the breach of Community law (Article 52 (now 43) EC) sufficiently serious: (a) the UK had introduced the measures in question in primary legislation in order to ensure that the implementation would not be delayed by legal challenge (at the time it was thought that primary legislation could not be challenged, but see now *R v Secretary of State for Transport, ex parte Factortame Ltd* (case C–213/89), noted in chapter 5); and (b) the Commission had from the start been opposed to the legislation on the grounds that it was (in its opinion) contrary to Community law.

Both the Court of Appeal and the House of Lords agreed with Hobhouse J that the UK's breach of Community law was sufficiently serious to warrant liability. Both courts applied the multiple test laid down in para. 56 of *Brasserie du Pêcheur* (cases C–46 and 48/93) (although they suggested that the list was 'not exhaustive') and found that the balance tipped in favour of the respondents. In pressing ahead with its legislation, against the advice of the Commission, despite its clear adverse impact on the respondents, and in a form (statute) which it was thought could not be challenged, the UK government was clearly taking a 'calculated risk'. Lord Slynn did, however, express the opinion, contrary to the view of Hobhouse J and the Court of Appeal, that the considered views of the Commission, although of importance, could not be regarded as conclusive proof as to:

(a) whether there had been a breach of Community law, and

(b) whether the breach was sufficiently serious to justify an award of damages.

Lords Hoffmann and Clyde expressed a similar view; the position taken by the Commission was 'a relevant factor to be taken into account' in deciding whether a breach was sufficiently serious, but it was not conclusive.

Following the House of Lords' decision in *Factortame*, Sullivan J in the English High Court, in assessing the seriousness of the Department of Social Security's breach of Article 7(1) of Sex Discrimination Directive 79/7 in *R v Department of Social Security, ex parte Scullion* [1999] 3 CMLR 798, also applied the multiple test of para. 56 of *Brasserie du Pêcheur*, which he described as the 'global' or 'basket' approach, and decided that, since there the scope of Article 7(1) was not clear at the relevant time, and there was no evidence that the Department had sought legal advice on the matter either from the Commission or from its own legal advisers, the breach was sufficiently serious.

Nevertheless, the ECJ's approach to the assessment of the matter of a 'sufficiently serious' breach remains inconsistent. In *Brinkman Tabakfabriken GmH v Skatteministeriet* (case C–319/96), it followed the more moderate line it had taken in *BT* (case C–392/93), and found that the Danish authorities' failure properly to implement Directive 79/30 on taxes other than turnover taxes affecting the consumption of manufactured tobacco was not sufficiently serious to incur liability. The classification adopted by the authorities, which resulted in the applicant having to pay the higher rates of taxes, was not 'manifestly contrary' to the wording and aim of the Directive. It was not clear from the Directive whether the tobacco rolls imported by the applicant, which had to be wrapped in paper in order to be smoked, constituted 'cigarette tobacco' or 'cigarettes'. Significantly, both the Commission and the Finnish government supported the classification adopted by the Danish authorities. The question of liability was in fact decided by the Court on the basis of causation. The Directive in question had not been implemented in Denmark by legislative decree, although the authorities had given immediate (albeit imperfect) effect to its provisions. There was therefore no direct causal link between that former (legislative) failure and the damage suffered by the applicant. It is implicit in the decisions that, contrary to the view of some commentators, provided that the requirements of a Directive are complied with in practice, a failure to implement a Directive by legislative means will not necessarily constitute a sufficiently serious breach to warrant liability.

Rechberger and Greindle v *Austria* (case C–140/97) concerned a claim for damages for losses suffered as a result of Austria's alleged imperfect implementation of Directive 90/314, designed to protect consumers in the event of travel organisers' insolvency. The ECJ found that the implementing measures, which failed to provide the level of protection required under the Directive, and which set the period for the commencement of claims at a date some months later than the time-limit for implementation of the Directive, were 'manifestly' incompatible with the Directive, and thus sufficiently serious to attract liability.

Thus in both *Brinkman* and *Rechberger*, the assessment as to whether the breach was sufficiently serious depended primarily on the clarity and precision of the provisions breached. However, in *Norbrook Laboratories Ltd* v *Minister of Agriculture, Fisheries and Food* (case C–127/95), a case involving a claim for damages for wrongful implementation of EC Directives on the authorisation of veterinary products, the ECJ, following an extensive examination of the provisions of the Directive allegedly breached, which revealed a number of clear breaches, invoked the *Hedley Lomas/Dillenkofer* mantra: 'Where . . . the Member State was not called upon to make legislative choices, and had considerably reduced, if no discretion, the mere infringement of Community law may be sufficient to establish the existence of a sufficiently serious breach'. It was left to the national court to assess whether the conditions for the award of damages based on *Francovich* were fulfilled.

Lastly, in *Klaus Konle* v *Austria* (case C–302/97), in a claim for damages for losses suffered as a result of laws of the Tyrol governing land transactions, allegedly contrary to Article 56 EC (now 46) and Article 70 of the Act of Accession, the Court, having examined these provisions for their compatibility with Community law, and finding some (but not all) of the laws 'precluded' by Community law, left it to the national court 'to apply the criteria to establish the liability of Member States for damage caused to individuals by breaches of Community law in accordance with the guidelines laid down by the Court of Justice'. Thus the national court was required to decide whether Austria's breach of Community law was sufficiently serious. The ECJ took a similar approach in *Haim v KLV* (case C-424/97).

If national courts are to assess this crucial question of the seriousness of the breach, as was required in *Klaus Konle* (and as, in principle, given the nature of the ECJ's jurisdiction under Article 234 (ex 177), they should, see chapter 27), it is essential that these guidelines be clear. The multiple criteria laid down in para. 56 of *Brasserie du Pêcheur* are clear and comprehensive. The *Hedley Lomas* requirement, that in some circumstances a 'mere infringement' of Community law will suffice to establish liability, clouds the issue. It is submitted that if it is to be invoked, it will be applicable only *following* an examination of the Community law allegedly breached under the multiple test in para. 56; for only then will the issue of whether the State has any 'discretion' in the exercise of its legislative powers be resolved. If the aim, and the substance, of the Community obligation allegedly infringed is 'manifest', the State will have no discretion to act in its breach. If it is not, the breach will not be sufficiently serious. Thus the *Hedley Lomas* mantra is, it is submitted, superfluous. Nevertheless, it was invoked in *Haim v KLV* alongside the multiple test of paragraph 56. This case also made it clear that legally independant public bodies may also be liable under *Francovich*.

Impact of the principle of State liability under Francovich   It remains to be seen whether, or the extent to which, the principle of State liability will have an impact on the principles of direct and indirect effects, particularly in the context of enforcement of Directives. If it is necessary to prove in all cases the existence of a sufficiently serious breach — and this is a difficult test to satisfy — there will still be a need for individuals to rely on these principles. Until now, liability under the principles of both direct and indirect effect has been strict (this was confirmed in *Draehmpaehl v Urania Immobilienservice OHG* (case C–180/95)); there has been no need to consider whether the alleged breach of Community law is 'sufficiently serious'. For direct effects, the criteria have in the past been loosely applied; sometimes, in the case of indirect effects (and sometimes in the case of direct effects), they have not been applied at all. On the other hand national courts' reluctance to apply these principles in some cases (e.g., *Duke v GEC Reliance Ltd*; *Rolls-Royce plc v Doughty*) appears to have stemmed in part from the perceived injustice of imposing liability, retrospectively, on parties, public or private, when the precise nature of their obligations under Community law at the relevant time was not clear. The existence of a remedy under *Francovich* could lead to a more rigorous application of the criteria for direct effects, especially following the denial by the Court of the direct effects of the relevant provisions of Directive 80/987 in *Francovich* itself. This latter fact was noted by, and appeared to be influential on, Blackburne J in *Griffin v South West Water Services Ltd* [1995] IRLR 15. In *Three Rivers District Council v Bank of England (No. 3)* [1996] 3 All ER 558, a case involving a claim for damages based on the defendants' breach of statutory duty in failing to supervise the credit institutions in the BCCI affair, Clarke J in the English High Court construed the EC Directive which the defendants had allegedly breached, and on which the claimants based their claim, as *not intended to give rise to rights for individuals* and therefore not directly effective. Does this represent an attempt on the part of the Court to limit the direct effect of Directives? If so, is it legitimate?

The ECJ's test for direct effects (the provision must be sufficiently clear, precise and unconditional) has never expressly included a requirement that the Directive should be intended to give rise to rights for the individual seeking to invoke its provisions. However, the justification for giving direct effect to EC law has always been the need to ensure effective protection for individuals' Community rights. Furthermore, the ECJ has, in a number of recent cases, suggested that an individual's right to invoke a Directive may be confined to situations in which he can show a particular interest in that Directive. In *Becker* v *Finanzamt Munster-Innenstadt* (case 8/81), in confirming and clarifying the principle of direct effects as applied to Directives, the Court held that 'provisions of Directives can be invoked by individuals *insofar as they define rights which individuals are able to assert against the state*'. Drawing on this statement in *Verholen* (cases C-87–C-89/90), the Court suggested that only a person with a direct interest in the application of the Directive could invoke its provisions: this was held in *Verholen* to include a third party who was directly affected by the Directive. Thus in *Verholen*, the husband of a woman suffering sex discrimination as regards the granting of a social security benefit, contrary to Directive 79/7, was able to bring a claim based on the Directive in respect of disadvantage to himself consequential on the discriminatory treatment of his wife.

In most recent cases in which an individual seeks to invoke a Directive directly, the existence of a direct interest is clear. The question of his or her standing has not therefore been in issue. Normally the rights he or she seeks to invoke, be it for example a right to equal treatment, or to employment protection, are contained in the Directive. Its provisions are clearly, if not explicitly, designed to benefit persons such as the individual. But there have been cases in which individuals have sought to exploit the principle of direct effects not for the purposes of claiming Community rights denied them under national law, but simply in order to establish the illegality of a national law and thereby prevent its application to them. This may occur in a two-party situation, in which an individual is seeking to invoke a Directive, whether as a sword or a shield, against the State. It presents particular problems in a three-cornered situation, in which a successful challenge based on an EC Directive by an individual to a domestic law or practice, although directed at action by the State, may adversely affect third parties. In this case the effect of the Directive would be felt horizontally. To give the Directive direct effects in these cases would seem to go against the Court's stance on horizontal direct effects in the line of cases beginning with *Dori* v *Recreb Srl*, and the reasoning in these cases. Two cases, with contrasting outcomes, *CIA Security International SA* v *Signalson SA* (case C–194/94) and *Lemmens* (case C–226/

97), illustrate the difficulty. Both cases involve Directive 83/189. The Directive, which is designed to facilitate the operation of the single market, lays down procedures for the provision of information by Member States to the Commission in the field of technical standards and regulations. Article 8 prescribes detailed procedures requiring Member States to notify, and obtain clearance from, the Commission in respect of any proposed regulatory measures in the areas covered by the Directive. In *CIA Security International SA v Signalson SA*, the defendants, CIA Security, sought to rely on Article 8 of Directive 83/189 as a defence to an action, brought by Signalson, a competitor, for unfair trading practices in the marketing of security systems. The defendants claimed that the Belgian regulations governing security, which the defendants had allegedly breached, had not been notified as required by the Directive: they were therefore inapplicable. Contrary to its finding in the earlier case of *Enichem Base v Comune di Cinsello Balsamo* (case C–380/87), involving very similar facts and the same Directive, the ECJ accepted this argument, distinguishing *Enichem* on the slenderest of grounds. Thus the effects of the Directive fell horizontally on the claimant, whose actions, based on national law, failed.

Article 8 of Directive 83/189 was again invoked as a defence in *Lemmens* (case C–226/97). Lemmens was charged in Belgium with driving above the alcohol limit. Evidence as to his alcohol level at the relevant time had been provided by a breath analysis machine. Invoking *CIA Security International SA v Signalson SA*, he argued that the Belgian regulations with which breath analysis machines in Belgian were required to conform had not been notified to the Commission, as required by Article 8 of Directive 83/189. He argued that the consequent inapplicability of the Belgian regulations regarding breath analysis machines impinged on the evidence obtained by using those machines; it could not be used in a case against him. The ECJ refused to accept this argument. It looked to the purpose of the Directive, which was designed to protect the interest of free movement of goods. The Court concluded:

> Although breach of an obligation (contained in the Directive) rendered a (domestic) regulations inapplicable inasmuch as they hindered the marketing of a product which did not conform with its provisions, it did not have the effect of rendering unlawful any use of the product which conformed with the unnotified regulations. Thus the breach (of Article 8) did not make it impossible for evidence obtained by means of such regulations, authorized in accordance with the regulations, to be relied on against an individual.

This distinction, between a breach affecting the marketing of a product, as in *CIA Security International SA v Signalson SA,* and one affecting its use, as in *Lemmens*, is fine, and hardly satisfactory. The decision in *CIA Security International SA v Signalson SA* had been criticised because the burden imposed by the breach (by the State) of Article 8, the non-application of the State's unfair practice laws, would have fallen on an individual, in this case the claimant. This was seen as a horizontal application in all but name. In two other cases decided, like *CIA Security International SA* v *Signalson SA*, in 1996, *Ruiz Bernaldez* (case C–129/94) and *Panagis Parfitis* (case C–441/93), individuals were permitted to invoke Directives in order to challenge national law, despite their adverse impact on third parties. *Lemmens*, on the other hand, did not involve a third party situation. The invocation by the defendant of Article 8 of Directive 83/189 did, however, smack of abuse. The refinement introduced in *Lemmens* may thus be seen as an attempt by the ECJ to impose some limits on the principle of direct effects as applied to Directives. Individuals seeking to base their claim on a breach of a Directive by the State will now need to establish that the breach interfered with a right or interest intended to be conferred on them. However, where this right or interest can be proved, the problem of adverse horizontal effects in cases involving third party situations, such as *CIA Security International SA* v *Signalson SA*, *Panagis Parfitis* and *Ruiz Bernaldez*, remains. Where individuals suffer damage in these situations, their only possible remedy lies in a claim under *Francovich*.

It is worthy of note that in *Three Rivers DC* v *Bank of England* (No. 3) (noted above), Clarke J invoked the same reasoning as he applied to the question of direct effects to the applicants' claim for damages under *Francovich*. He found that the Directive allegedly breached contained no right intended to benefit the claimant. If they had no sufficient right or interest for direct effects, they had no claim under *Francovich*, because 'here too it is necessary to establish the same right or interest' (at para. 66). The cases from the ECJ considered above suggest that it too may be moving towards the same approach, thereby achieving some sort of consistency between the rules relating to individual standing in claims based on the principle of direct effect and claims under *Francovich*. This approach was also adopted by Beldam J in the English Court of Appeal in *Bowden* v *South West Water Services* [1999] 3 CMLR 180. In examining the Environmental Directive 79/903, he found it to confer rights on the claimant for the purposes of a claim for damages based on direct effects and under *Francovich*.

Decisions

A decision is 'binding in its entirety upon those to whom it is addressed' (Article 249 (ex 189) EC).

Decisions may be addressed to Member States, singly or collectively, or individuals. Although, like Directives, they are not described as 'directly applicable', they may, as was established in *Grad* v *Finanzamt Traustein* (case 9/70), be directly effective provided the criteria for direct effects are satisfied. The direct application of Decisions does not pose the same theoretical problems as Directives, since they will only be invoked against the addressee of the Decision. If the obligation has been addressed to him and is 'binding in its entirety', there seems no reason why it should not be invoked against him. Although it has not so far arisen it might be permissible for an individual to invoke a decision against a 'public' party who is not the addressee of the Decision, but not against a 'private' (third) party, for the same reasons as apply in the case of Directives.

Recommendations and opinions

Since recommendations and opinions have no binding force and are not 'enforceable Community rights' within s. 2(1) of the European Communities Act 1972 it would appear that they cannot be invoked by individuals, directly or indirectly, before national courts. However, in *Grimaldi* v *Fonds des Maladies Professionnelles* (case C–322/88), in the context of a claim by a migrant worker for benefit in respect of occupational diseases, in which he sought to invoke a Commission recommendation concerning the conditions for granting such benefit, the ECJ held that national courts were 'bound to take Community recommendations into consideration in deciding disputes submitted to them, in particular where they clarify the interpretation of national provisions adopted in order to implement them or where they are designed to supplement binding EEC measures'. Such a view is open to question. It may be argued that recommendations, as non-binding measures, can at the most only be taken into account in order to resolve ambiguities in domestic law.

International agreements to which the EC is a party

There are three types of international agreements capable of being invoked in the context of EC law arising from the Community's powers under Articles 281, 300, 133 and 310 (ex 210, 228, 113 and 238) EC respectively) (see chapter 1). First, agreements concluded by the Community institutions falling within the treaty-making jurisdiction of the EC; secondly, 'hybrid' agreements, such as the WTO agreements, in which the subject-matter lies partly within the jurisdiction of Member States and partly within that of the EC; and thirdly, agreements concluded prior to the EC Treaty, such as GATT, which the EC has assumed as being within its jurisdiction, by way of succession. There is no indication in the EC Treaty that such agreements may be directly effective.

The ECJ's case law on the direct effect of these agreements has not been wholly consistent. It purports to apply similar principles to those which it applies in matters of 'internal' law. A provision of an association agreement will be directly effective when 'having regard to its wording and the purpose and nature of the agreement itself, the provision contains a clear and precise obligation which is not subject, in its implementation or effects, to the adoption of any subsequent measure'. Applying these principles in some cases, such as *International Fruit Co. NV* v *Produktschap voor Groenten en Fruit (No. 3)* (cases 21 & 22/72), the Court, in response to an enquiry as to the direct effects of Article XI of GATT, held, following an examination of the agreement as a whole, that the Article was not directly effective. In others, such as *Bresciani* (case 87/75) and *Kupferberg* (case 104/81), Article 2(1) of the Yaoundé Convention and Article 21 of the EC–Portugal trade agreement were examined respectively on their individual merits and found to be directly effective. The reasons for these differences are at not at first sight obvious, particularly since the provisions in all three cases were almost identical in wording to EC Treaty Articles already found directly effective. The suggested reason (see Hartley (1983) 8 EL Rev 383) for this inconsistency is the conflict between the ECJ's desire to provide an effective means of enforcement of international agreements against Member States and the lack of a solid legal basis on which to do so. The Court justifies divergencies in interpretation by reference to the scope and purpose of the agreement in question, which are clearly different from, and less ambitious than, those of the EC Treaty (*Opinion 1/91* (on the draft EEA Treaty)). As a result, the criteria for direct effects tend to be applied more strictly in the context of international agreements entered into by the EC.

Since the *International Fruit Co.* cases the Court has maintained consistently that GATT rules cannot be relied upon to challenge the lawfulness of a Community act except in the special case where the Community provisions have been adopted to implement obligations entered into within the framework of GATT. Because GATT rules are not unconditional, and are characterised by 'great flexibility', direct effects cannot be inferred from the 'spirit, general scheme and wording of the Treaty'. This principle was held in *Germany* v *Council* (case C–280/93) to apply not only to claims by individuals but also to actions brought by Member States. As a result the opportunity to challenge Community law for infringement of GATT rules is seriously curtailed. Despite strong arguments in favour of the direct applicability of WTO provisions from Advocate-General Tesauro in *T Hermes International* v *FH Marketing Choice BV* (case C–53/96), the Court has not been willing to change its mind. It appears that there is near-unanimous political opposition to the direct application of WTO law (see case note (1999) 36 CML Rev 663).

However, where the agreement or legislation issued under the agreement confers clear rights on *individuals* the ECJ has not hesitated to find direct effects (e.g., *Sevince* (case C–192/89); *Bahia Kziber* (case C–18/90)).

Thus, paradoxically, an individual in a dualist State such as the UK will be in a stronger position than he would normally be *vis-à-vis* international law, which is not as a rule incorporated into domestic law.

Exclusions from the principle of direct effects

In extending the jurisdiction of the ECJ to matters within the third (JHA) pillar of the TEU to encompass decisions and framework decisions in the field of political and judicial cooperation in criminal matters taken under Title VI TEU, the ToA expressly denied direct effects to these provisions (Article 34(2) TEU). Similarly, although areas within the third pillar of the TEU, relating to visas, asylum, immigration and judicial cooperation in civil matters, were incorporated into the EC Treaty (new Title IV), the ToA excluded the ECJ's jurisdiction to rule on any measure or decision taken pursuant to Article 62(1) 'relating to the maintenance of law and order and the safeguarding of internal security' (Article 68(2) EC), thus access to the ECJ via a claim before their national court was denied to individuals in areas in which they may be significantly and adversely affected.

Although not an express exclusion from the principle of direct effects, a situation in which an individual will not be able to rely on Community law arose in the case of *Rechberger and Greindle v Austria* (case C–140/97). The case, a claim based on *Francovich*, concerned Austria's alleged breaches of Directive 90/134 on package travel both before Austria's accession, under the EEA Agreement, and, following accession, under the EC Treaty. The ECJ held that where the obligation to implement the Directive arose under the EEA Agreement, it had no jurisdiction to rule on whether a Member State was liable under that agreement prior to its accession to the European Union (see also *Ulla-Brith Andersson v Swedish State* (case C–321/97)).

Conclusions

The principle of direct effects, together with its twin principle of supremacy of EC law, to be discussed in chapter 5, has played a crucial part in securing the application and integration of Community law within national legal systems. By giving individuals and national courts a role in the enforcement of Community law it has ensured that EC law is applied, and Community rights enforced, even though Member States have failed, deliberately or inadvertently, to bring national law and practice into line with Community law. Thus, as the Court suggested in *Van Gend* (case 26/62), the principle of direct effects has provided a means of control over Member States additional to that entrusted to the Commission under Article 226 (ex 169) and Member States under Article 227 (ex 170) (see further chapter 28). This control has now been reinforced by the rights which may be claimed by individuals under the principles of indirect effect and *Francovich*. But there is no doubt that the ECJ has extended the concept of direct effects well beyond its apparent scope as envisaged by the EC Treaty. Furthermore, although the criteria applied by the ECJ for assessing the question of direct effects appear straightforward, in reality they have in the past been applied loosely, and any provision which is justiciable has, until recently, been found to be directly effective, no matter what difficulties may be faced by national courts in its application, or what impact it may have on the parties, public or private, against whom it is enforced. Thus the principle of direct effects created problems for national courts, particularly in its application to Directives.

In recent years there have been signs that the ECJ, having, with a few exceptions, won acceptance from Member States of the principle of direct effects, or at least in the case of Directives of vertical effects (but see the Conseil d'État's decision in *Compagnie Générale des Eaux* [1994] 2 CMLR 373, noted in chapter 5), had become aware of the problems faced by national courts and was prepared to apply the principles of direct and indirect effect with greater caution. Its more cautious approach to the question of standing, demonstrated in *Lemmens* (case C–226/97), has been noted above. Its decision in *Francovich* (cases C–6 & 9/90), that the relevant articles of Directive 80/987 were not sufficiently clear and precise for direct effects, appeared significant. While it is likely that it wished in that case to establish a separate principle of State liability to remedy the inadequacies of the principles of direct and (particularly) indirect effects, it is possible that *Francovich* was seen by the Court as providing a more legitimate remedy. In *Comitato di Coordinamento per la Difesa della Cava* v *Regione Lombardia* (case C–236/92), the Court found that Article 4 of Directive 75/442 on the Disposal of Waste, which required States to 'take the necessary measures to ensure that waste is disposed of without endangering human health and without harming the environment', was not unconditional or sufficiently precise to be relied on by individuals before their national courts. It 'merely indicated a programme to be followed and provided a framework for action' by the Member States. The Court suggested that in order to be directly effective the obligation imposed by the Directive must be 'set out in unequivocal terms'. In *R* v *Secretary of State for Social Security, ex parte Sutton* (case C–66/95) the Court refused to admit a claim for the award of interest on arrears of social security benefit on the basis of Article 6 of EC Directive 79/7 on Equal Treatment for Men and Women in Social Security, although in *Marshall (No 2)* (case C–271/91) it had upheld a claim for compensation for discriminatory treatment based on an identically worded Article 6 of Equal Treatment Directive 76/207. The Court's attempts to distinguish between the two claims ('amounts payable by way of social security are not compensatory') were unconvincing. In *El Corte Inglés SA* v *Rivero* (case C–192/94) it found the then Article 129a of the EC Treaty requiring the Community to take action to achieve a high level of consumer protection insufficiently clear and precise and unconditional to be relied on as between individuals. This may be contrasted with its earlier approach to the former Article 128 EC, which required the Community institutions to lay down general principles for the implementation of a vocational training policy, which was found, albeit together with the non-discrimination principle of (the then) Article 7 EEC, to be directly effective (see *Gravier* v *City of Liège* (case 293/83), discussed in chapter 21). Thus a Directive may be denied direct effects on the grounds that:

(a)   the right or interest claimed in the Directive is not sufficiently clear, precise and unconditional; or

(b)   the individual seeking to invoke the Directive did not have a direct interest in the provisions invoked (*Verholen*, cases C-87–9/90); or

(c)   the obligation allegedly breached was not intended for the benefit of the individual seeking to invoke its provisions (*Lemmens*).

In the area of indirect effects, in *Dori* v *Recreb Srl* (case C–91/92), the ECJ, following its lead in *Marshall* (case 152/84), declared unequivocally that Directives could not be invoked horizontally. This view was endorsed in *El Corte Inglés SA* v *Rivero* and in *Arcaro* (case C–168/95). In *Wagner Miret* (case C–334/92) the ECJ acknowledged that national courts might not feel able to give indirect effect to Community Directives by means of 'interpretation' of domestic law. This was also approved in *Arcaro*. In almost all of these cases, decided after *Francovich*, the Court pointed out the possibility of an alternative remedy based on *Francovich*.

However, as subsequent case law on State liability has shown, *Francovich* is not a universal panacea. In order to succeed in a claim for damages the applicant must establish that the law infringed was intended to confer rights on individuals and that the breach is sufficiently serious (as well as the requisite damage and causation). In cases of non-implementation of Directives, as in *Francovich* or *Dillenkofer*, where there is no doubt about the nature of the Community obligation, the breach is likely to be sufficiently serious. However, where the Community obligation allegedly breached is less clear, the breach may well be found to be excusable. Thus it will still be necessary to rely on the principles of direct and even indirect effects. In doubtful situations all possible remedies should be pursued.

Further reading

Bebr, G., 'Agreements concluded by the Community and their possible direct effects; from International Fruit Company to Kupferberg' (1983) 20 CML Rev 35.

Bebr, G., 'Casenote on *Francovich*' (1992) CML Rev 557.

Caranta, R., 'Learning from our Neighbours: Public Law Remedies Homogenisation from Bottom Up' (1997) MJ 220.

Craig, P., 'Directives: Direct Effect, Indirect Effect and the Construction of National Legislation' (1997) 22 EL Rev 519.

Coppel, J., 'Rights, Duties and the end of *Marshall*' (1994) 57 MLR 859.

Craig, P., 'Once upon a Time in the West: Direct Effect and the Federalisation of EEC Law' (1992) 12 Oxford J Legal Stud 453.

Craig, P., '*Francovich*, Remedies and the Scope of Damages Liability' (1993) 109 LQR 595.

Craig, P., 'Once more unto the Breach: The Community, the State and Damages Liability' (1997) 113 LQR 67.

Curtin, D., 'The Province of government; Delimiting the Direct Effect of Directives' (1990) 15 EL Rev 195.

Curtin, D., 'The Effectiveness of Judicial Protection of Individual Rights' (1990) 27 CML Rev 209.

De Búrca, G., 'Giving Effect to European Community Directives' (1992) 55 MLR 215.

Green, N., 'Directives, Equity and the Protection of Individual Rights' (1984) 9 EL Rev 295.

Hartley, T., 'International agreements and the Community Legal System; some recent developments' (1983) 8 EL Rev 383.

Hartley, T., *Constitutional Problems of the European Union* (Hart Publishing, 1999).

Hilson, C. and Downes, T., 'Making Sense of Rights: The Place of Discretion' (1997) 46 ICLQ 941.

Lackoff, K. and Nyssens, H., 'Direct Effect of Directives in Triangular Situations' (1998) 23 EL Rev 397.

Lewis, C., and Moore, S., 'Duties, Directives and Damages in European Community Law' [1993] PL 151.

Mastoianni, R., 'On the Distinction between Vertical and Horizontal Direct Effects of Community Directives: What Role for the Principle of Equality?' (1999) 5 EPL 417.

Pescatore, P., 'The Doctrine of Direct Effect; an Infant Disease of Community Law' (1983) 8 EL Rev 155.

Plaza, M., 'Furthering the Effectiveness of EC Directives' (1994) 43 ICLQ 26.

Prechal, S. 'Remedies after *Marshall*' (1990) 27 CML Rev 451.

Prechal, S., *Directives in European Community Law* (Oxford: Clarendon Press, 1995), ch. 8.

Ross, M., 'Beyond *Francovich*' (1993) 56 MLR 55.

Ruffert, M., 'Rights and Remedies: European Community Law: a Comparative View' (1997) 34 CML Rev 307.

Shaw, J., 'European Community Judicial Method: its Application to Sex Discrimination Law' (1990) 19 ILJ 228.

Steiner, J., 'Coming to Terms with EEC Directives' (1990) 106 LQR 144.

Steiner, J., 'From Direct Effects to *Francovich*: Shifting Means of Enforcement of Community Law' (1993) 18 EL Rev 3.

Steiner, J., 'The Limits of State Liability for Breach of European Community Law' [1998] EPL 69.

Szyszczak, E., 'European Community Law: New Remedies, New Directions?' (1992) 55 MLR 690.

Szyczak, E., 'Making Europe more Relevant to its Citizens' (1996) 21 EL Rev 351.

Van den Berg, R., and Schafer, H.B., 'State Liability for Infringements of the EC Treaty' (1998) 23 EL Rev 552.

Van Gerven, W., 'The Horizontal Effect of Directive Provisions Revisited: the Reality of Catch-words' Institute of Public Law Lecture Series, University of Hull (1993).

Winter, T.A., 'Direct Applicability and Direct Effects' (1972) 9 CML Rev 425.

Wyatt, D., 'Direct Effects of Community Law, not forgetting Directives' (1983) 8 EL Rev 241.

FIVE

Principle of supremacy of EC law

The problem of priorities

The extended application by the ECJ of the principle of direct effects, together with the wide scope of the EC Treaty, covering a number of areas normally reserved to national law alone, led inevitably to a situation of conflict between national and EC law. In such a case, which law was to prevail? The way in which that conflict was resolved was of crucial importance to the Community legal order; it was a constitutional problem of some magnitude for Member States.

The EC Treaty is silent on the question of priorities. Perhaps this was a diplomatic omission; perhaps it was not thought necessary to make the matter explicit, since the extent to which Community law might be directly effective was not envisaged at the time of signing the Treaty. In the absence of guidance, the matter has been left to be decided by the courts of Member States, assisted by the ECJ in its jurisdiction under Article 234 (ex 177) EC (see chapter 27). As with the concept of direct effects, the Court has proved extremely influential in developing the law.

The question of priorities between directly effective international law and domestic law is normally seen as a matter of national law, to be determined according to the constitutional rules of the State concerned. It will depend on a number of factors. Primarily it will depend on the terms on which international law has been incorporated into domestic law. This in turn will depend on whether the State is monist or dualist in its approach to international law. If monist, it will be received automatically into national law from the moment of its ratification, without the need for further measures of incorporation. If dualist, international law will not become binding internally, as part of domestic law, until it is incorporated by a domestic statute. In the EC, France, for example, is monist; Germany, Belgium, Italy and the UK are dualist. But whether received automatically, by process of 'adoption', or whether incorporated by statute, by way of 'transformation', this does not settle the question of priorities. This will depend on the extent to which the State has provided for this, either in its constitution, where it has a written constitution, or, where it has no written constitution, in its statute of incorporation.

There is wide variation in the way in which, and the extent to which, Member States of the EC have provided for this question of priorities. Where States have a written constitution, provision may range from the whole-hearted acceptance of international law of the Dutch constitution (Article 66), which accords supremacy to *all* forms of international law, whether prior or subsequent to domestic law, to Article 55 of the French constitution, which, at the time of French accession to the Community, provided that treaties or agreements duly ratified 'have authority superior to that of laws' (thus leaving open the question of secondary legislation), to Article 24 of the German constitution, which provided, rather loosely, that the State 'may transfer sovereign powers' to international organisations (although Article 23 has been introduced to deal specifically with the EU); or Article 11 of the Italian constitution whereby the State 'consents, on conditions of reciprocity with other States, to limitations of sovereignty necessary for an arrangement which may ensure peace and justice between the nations'. (Under the principle of reciprocity, if one party to an agreement breaches his obligations, the other contracting parties may regard themselves as entitled to be relieved of theirs.)

A State which does not have a written constitution, and which is dualist, such as the UK, must provide for priorities in the statute of incorporation itself. This statute will have the same status as any other statute. As such it will be vulnerable to the doctrine of implied repeal, or *'lex posterior derogat priori'*, whereby any inconsistency between an earlier and a later statute is resolved in favour of the latter. The later statute is deemed to have impliedly repealed the earlier one (see *Ellen Street Estates Ltd* v *Minister of Health* [1934] 1 KB 590).

On a strict application of this doctrine, any provision of a domestic statute passed subsequent to the statute incorporating EC law, in our case the European Communities Act 1972, which was inconsistent with EC law, would take priority.

Given the differences from State to State it is clear that if national courts were to apply their own constitutional rules to the question of priorities between domestic law and EC law, there would be no uniformity of application, and the primacy of EC law could not be guaranteed throughout the Community. This was the principal reason advanced by Advocate-General Roemer in *Van Gend en Loos* (case 26/62) for denying the direct effects of Article 12 of the EEC Treaty (now 25 EC). Not only would this weaken the effect of Community law, it would undermine solidarity among the Member States, and in the end threaten the Community itself.

It is no doubt reasons such as these which led the ECJ to develop its own constitutional rules to deal with the problem, in particular the principle of supremacy, or primacy, of EC law.

The Court of Justice's contribution

The first cautious statement of the principle of supremacy of EC law came in the case of *Van Gend en Loos* (case 26/62). The principal question in the case was the question of the direct effects of Article 12 (now 25 EC). The conflict, assuming that Article were found directly effective, was between the then Article 12 and an *earlier* Dutch law. Under Dutch law, if Article 12 were directly effective it would, under the Dutch constitution, take precedence over domestic law. So the questions referred to the ECJ under Article 177 (now 234) did not raise the issue of sovereignty directly. Nevertheless, in addition to declaring that Article 12 (now 25) was directly effective, the Court went on to say that:

> . . . the Community constitutes a new legal order in international law, for whose benefit the States have limited their sovereign rights, albeit within limited fields.

The conflict in *Costa* v *ENEL* (case 6/64) posed a more difficult problem for the Italian courts. This case too involved an alleged conflict between a number of Treaty provisions and an Italian statute nationalising the electricity company of which the defendant, Signor Costa, was a shareholder, but here the Italian law was later in time. On being brought before the Milan *tribunale* for refusing to pay his bill (the princely sum of L1,925, or approximately £1.10), Signor Costa argued that the company was in breach of EC law. They argued *'lex posterior'*; the Italian Act nationalising the electricity company was later in time than the Italian Ratification Act, the Act incorporating EC law. Therefore it took priority. The Italian court referred this question of priorities to the ECJ. It also referred the matter to its own constitutional court. This time the principle of supremacy was clearly affirmed by the Court. It cited *Van Gend*; the States had 'limited their sovereign rights'. It went further. It looked to the Treaty; it noted that Article 189 (now 249) indicated that there had been a transfer of powers to the Community institutions; Article 5 (now 10) underlined States' commitment to observe Community law. The Court concluded:

> The reception, within the laws of each Member State, of provisions having a Community source, and more particularly of the terms and of the spirit of the Treaty, has as a corollary the impossibility, for the Member State, to give preference to a unilateral and *subsequent* measure against a legal order accepted by them on a basis of reciprocity. . . .
>
> The transfer, by Member States, from their national orders in favour of the Community order of the rights and obligations arising from the Treaty, carries with it a clear limitation of their sovereign right upon which a *subsequent* unilateral law, incompatible with the aims of the Community, cannot prevail. (Emphasis added.)

In the case of *Internationale Handelsgesellschaft mbH* (case 11/70) the Court went even further. Here, the conflict was between not a Treaty provision and a domestic statute, but between an EC Regulation and provisions of the German constitution. The claimant argued that the Regulation infringed, *inter alia*, the principle of proportionality enshrined in the German constitution and sought to nullify the Regulation on those grounds. Normally, any ordinary law in breach of the constitution is invalid, since the constitution is superior in the hierarchy of legal rules to statute law. EC law had been incorporated into German law by statute, the Act of ratification. There was no provision in the constitution that the constitution could be overridden by EC law. Article 24 merely provided for 'the transfer of sovereign powers to intergovernmental institutions'. So the question before the German administrative court (Verwaltungsgericht, Frankfurt) was: If there were a conflict between the Regulation and the German constitution, which law should prevail? As in *Costa*, the German judge referred the question to the ECJ and his own federal constitutional court (Bundesverfassungsgericht).

The ruling from the ECJ was in the strongest terms. The legality of a Community act cannot be judged in the light of national law:

> . . . the law born from the Treaty [cannot] have the courts opposing to it rules of national law *of any nature whatever*. . . . the validity of a Community instrument or its effect within a Member State cannot be affected by allegations that it strikes at either the fundamental rights as formulated in that State's constitution or the principles of a national constitutional structure. (Emphasis added.)

If the Court's ruling seems harsh in the light of the importance of the rights protected in a State's constitution, many of which are regarded as fundamental human rights, it is worth adding that the Court went on to say that respect for such rights was one of the principal aims of the Community and as such it was part of its own (albeit unwritten) law (see chapter 6).

The principle of supremacy of Community law applies not only to internal domestic laws, but also to obligations entered into with third countries, that is, countries outside the EU. In the *ERTA* case (case 22/70) the ECJ held, in the context of a challenge to an international road transport agreement to which the Community was a party, that once the Community, in implementing a common policy, lays down common rules, Member States no longer have the right, individually or collectively, to contract obligations towards non–Member States affecting these common rules. And where the Community concludes a treaty in pursuance of a common policy, this excludes the possibility of a concurrent authority on the part of the Member States. This means that where a State attempts to exercise concurrent authority it will be overridden to the extent that it conflicts with Community law. This principle does not, however, appear to apply to Member States' pre-accession agreements with third countries. Where such agreements are 'not compatible' with the EC Treaty, Member States are required to 'take all appropriate steps to eliminate the incompatibilities established' (Article 234 (now 307) EC). In *R v Secretary of State for Home the Department, ex parte Evans Medical Ltd* (case C–324/93), the Court conceded that provisions of such an agreement contrary to Community law may continue to be applied where the performance of that agreement may still be required by non–Member States which are parties to it. The Court has, however, urged national courts to give effect to such provisions only to the extent that it is necessary to meet the demands of that agreement (*Minne* (case C–13/93)). Thus, subject to this exception, as far as the ECJ is concerned *all* EC law, whatever its nature, must take priority over *all* conflicting domestic law, whether it be prior or subsequent to Community law. Given the fact that the Court was approaching the matter *tabula rasa*, there being no provision in the Treaty to this effect, on what basis did the Court justify its position?

The Court's reasoning is pragmatic, based on the purpose, the general aims and spirit of the Treaty. States freely signed the Treaty; they agreed to take all appropriate measures to comply with EC law (Article 5 (now 10) EC); the Treaty created its own institutions, and gave those institutions power to make laws binding on Member States (Article 189 (now 249) EC). They agreed to set up an institutionalised form of control by the Commission (under Article 169 (now 226), see chapter 28) and the Court. The Community would not survive if States were free to act unilaterally in breach of their obligations. If the aims of the Community are to be achieved, there must be uniformity of application. This will not occur unless all States accord priority to EC law.

The reasoning is convincing. Nonetheless national courts were understandably reluctant to disregard their own constitutional rules and the Italian and German constitutional courts in *Costa* v *ENEL* [1964] CMLR 425 at p. 430 and *Internationale Handelsgesellschaft mbH (Solange I)* [1974] 2 CMLR 540, adhering to their own traditional view, refused to acknowledge the absolute supremacy of EC law.

There were other problems too for national courts — problems of application. Even if the principle of primacy of EC law were accepted in theory, what was a national judge to do in practice when faced with a conflict? No English judge can declare a statute void or unlawful; in countries with a written constitution only the constitutional court has power to declare a domestic law invalid for breach of the constitution. Must the national judge wait for the offending national law to be repealed or legally annulled before he can give precedence to EC law?

The ECJ suggested a solution to this problem in *Simmenthal SpA* (case 106/77). This case involved a conflict between a Treaty provision, Article 30 (now 28) EC on the free movement of goods, and an Italian law passed *subsequent* to the Italian Act incorporating EC law, a similar clash to the one in *Costa* v *ENEL* (case 6/64). Following *Costa*, the Italian constitutional court had revised its view and declared that it would be prepared to declare any national law conflicting with EC law invalid. When the problem arose in *Simmenthal* the Italian judge, the Pretore di Susa, was perplexed. Should he apply EC law at once to the case before him, or should he wait until his own constitutional court had declared the national law invalid? He referred this question to the ECJ. The Court's reply was predictable:

. . . any recognition that national legislative measures which encroach upon the field within which the Community exercises its legislative power or which are otherwise incompatible with the provisions of Community law had any legal effect would amount to a corresponding denial of the effectiveness of obligations undertaken unconditionally and irrevocably by Member States pursuant to the Treaty and would thus imperil the very foundations of the Community (para. 18).

. . . a national court which is called upon . . . to apply provisions of Community law is under a duty to give full effect to those provisions, if necessary refusing . . . to apply any conflicting provision of national legislation, even if adopted subsequently, and it is not necessary for the court to request or await the prior setting aside of such provision by legislative or other constitutional means (para. 24).

The reasoning behind the judgment is clear. Unless Community law is given priority over conflicting national law at once, from the moment of its entry into force, there can be no uniformity of application throughout the Community. Community law will be ineffective. Thus, according to the ECJ, national judges faced with a conflict between national law, whatever its nature, and Community law, must ignore, must shut their eyes to national law; they need not, indeed must not, wait for the law to be changed. Any incompatible national law is automatically inapplicable.

The principles expressed in *Simmenthal SpA* were applied by the Court in *R v Secretary of State for Transport, ex parte Factortame Ltd* (case C–213/89), in the context of a claim before the English courts by a group of Spanish fishermen for an interim injunction to prevent the application of certain sections of the Merchant Shipping Act 1988, which denied them the right to register their boats in the UK, and which the claimants alleged were in breach of EC law. The question of the 'legality' of the British provisions under Community law had yet to be decided, following a separate reference to the Court of Justice. Thus the British courts were being asked to give primacy to a *putative* Community right over an allegedly conflicting national law, and to grant an interim injunction against the Crown, something which they considered they were not permitted to do under national law. Following a reference by the House of Lords asking whether they were obliged to grant the relief in question as a matter of Community law, the ECJ pointed out that national courts were obliged, by Article 5 (now 10) EC, to ensure the legal protection which persons derive from the direct effect of provisions of Community law. Moreover:

The full effectiveness of Community law would be . . . impaired if a rule of national law could prevent a court seised of a dispute governed by Community law from granting interim relief in order to ensure the full effectiveness of the judgment to be given on the existence of the rights claimed under Community law. It follows that a court which in those circumstances would grant interim relief, if it were not for a rule of national law, is obliged to set aside that rule (para. 21).

Thus the obligation on Member States to ensure the full effectiveness of Community law requires national courts not only to 'disapply' the offending national law but also to supply a remedy which is not available under national law.

A finding that a provision of national law is 'inapplicable' because of its incompatibility with Community law does not, however, result in its annulment, or even prevent its application in situations falling outside the scope of Community law. In *IN. CO. GE. '90* (cases C–10 & 22/97) the Court held that 'it does not follow from *Simmenthal* that a domestic rule which is incompatible with EC law is non-existent'. Similarly in *Arcaro* (case C–168/95) it made it clear that there was 'no method or procedure in Community law allowing national courts to eliminate national provisions contrary to a Directive which has not been transposed where that provision may not be relied on before the national court'. In *ICI* v *Colmer* (case C–264/96) the ECJ found a system of tax relief for holding companies with a seat in the EU discriminatory, and therefore contrary to EC law, when applied to subsidiary companies in other Member States, but lawful in a situation where holding companies control subsidiaries in non-Member States. Thus, despite its inapplicability in the former context, the national court was under no obligation to disapply national law in the latter situation, since that lay outside the scope of Community law. However:

> Where the same legislation must be disapplied as contrary to EC law in a situation covered by Community law it is for the competent body of the Member State concerned to remove that legal uncertainty insofar as it might affect rights deriving from Community rules.

It may be noted that all the earlier landmark rulings of the Court, up to and including *Simmenthal* (case 106/77), were expressed in terms of directly effective Community law. Until the Court introduced the principle of indirect effects in *von Colson* (case 14/83) and the principle of State liability in *Francovich* (cases C–6 & 9/90), it was thought that national courts would only be required to apply, and give priority to, EC law which was directly effective. This proved not to be the case. The obligation on national courts to interpret domestic law to comply with EC Directives which are not directly effective (because invoked horizontally), as extended in *Marleasing*, impliedly requires those courts to give priority to EC law. Similarly, although the granting of a remedy in damages against the State under *Francovich* does not require the *application* of Community law, the remedy, based on Member States' obligation to guarantee full and effective protection for individuals' rights under Community law, is premised on the supremacy of EC law. This obligation was held in *Francovich* (at para. 42) to apply to all rights 'which parties enjoy under Community law'. That protection cannot be achieved unless those rights prevail over conflicting provisions of national law. As *Brasserie du Pêcheur* and *R* v *Secretary of State for Transport, ex parte Factortame* (cases C–46 & 48/93) have now made clear, individuals' Community rights, including the right to damages, must prevail over *all* acts of Member States, legislative, executive or judicial, which are contrary to Community law.

The Member States' response

After a shaky start (we have already noted the Italian and German constitutional courts' response in *Costa* and *Internationale Handelsgesellschaft mbH*) the courts of Member States have now broadly accepted the principle of supremacy of EC law *provided they regard it as directly effective*. They have done so in a variety of ways: in some cases by bending and adapting their own constitutional rules; in others by devising new constitutional rules to meet the new situation.

Great Britain   As a dualist State without a written constitution the status of Community law in the UK derives from the European Communities Act 1972. To what extent does that Act enable our courts to give effect to the principle of supremacy of EC law?

The most important provisions are ss. 2 and 3.

Section 2(1) provides for the direct applicability of EC law in the UK:

All such rights, powers, liabilities, obligations and restrictions from time to time created or arising by or under the Treaties, and all such remedies and procedures from time to time provided for by or under the Treaties, as in accordance with the Treaties are without further enactment to be given legal effect or used in the United Kingdom shall be recognised and available in law, and be enforced, allowed and followed accordingly; and the expression 'enforceable Community right' and similar expressions shall be read as referring to one to which this subsection applies.

Section 2(2) provides a general power for the further implementation of Community obligations by means of secondary legislation.

This is subject to sch. 2. Schedule 2 lists the 'forbidden' areas, such as the power to increase taxation, to introduce retrospective measures or to create new criminal offences. These areas apart, s. 2(2) thus allows for ongoing domestic legislation over the whole field of objectives of the Treaty.

Section 2(4) is the section relevant to the question of primacy. It does not expressly say EC law is supreme. Section 2(4) provides (emphasis added):

The provision that may be made under subsection (2) above includes, subject to schedule 2 to this Act, any such provision (of any such extent) as might be made by Act of Parliament, and *any enactment passed or to be passed*, other than one contained in this part of this Act [i.e., an enactment of a non-Community nature], *shall be construed and have effect subject to the foregoing provisions of this section* [i.e., obligations of a Community nature].

Effect of the European Communities Act 1972, s. 2(1) and (4)

Directly effective EC law   The first question to arise is whether the combined effect of s. 2(1) and (particularly) s. 2(4) of the European Communities Act 1972 is sufficient to enable our courts to give priority to EC law, on

Simmenthal (case 106/77) principles, as the ECJ would require. Or does it merely lay down a rule of construction, whereby domestic law must be *construed,* so far as possible, to conform with EC law? The traditional constitutional view is that our doctrine of parliamentary sovereignty, and particularly the principle of implied repeal, makes entrenchment of EC law impossible. Parliament is not free to bind its successors. Therefore priority for EC law cannot be guaranteed, and s. 2(4) can only provide a rule of construction.

An approach based on the jurisprudence of the ECJ, particularly *Simmenthal,* would involve a departure from that view.

There was considerable wavering in the early years on the question of primacy. Lord Denning MR in *H. P. Bulmer Ltd* v *J. Bollinger SA* [1974] Ch 401 claimed that the Treaty 'is equal in force to any statute'. In *Felixstowe Dock & Railway Co.* v *British Transport Docks Board* [1976] 2 CMLR 655 he said in the context of an alleged conflict between an imminent statute and Article 86 (now 82) of the EC Treaty:

> It seems to me that once the Bill is passed by Parliament and becomes a statute, that will dispose of all this discussion about the Treaty. These courts will then have to abide by the statute without regard to the Treaty at all.

In 1979 the Court of Appeal in *Macarthys Ltd* v *Smith* [1979] ICR 785, a landmark case, took the 'European' view. Cumming-Bruce and Lawton LJJ, invoking the ECJ in *Costa* (case 6/64) and *Simmenthal* (case 106/77), were prepared, on the basis of the European Communities Act 1972, s. 2(4), to give European law 'priority'. Lord Denning MR preferred to use s. 2(4) as a rule of construction and construed the relevant English legislation (Equal Pay Act 1970) to conform with the principle of equal pay for equal work in Article 119 (now 141) EC. However, in doing so he took a rather broader view of 'construction' than is usually taken in construing international agreements. In construing our statutes, he said, 'we are entitled to look to the Treaty as an aid to its construction: and even more, not only as an aid but as an overriding force'. He went on to say that 'If . . . our legislation is deficient — or is inconsistent with Community law . . . then it is our bounden duty to give priority to Community law'.

The House of Lords in *Garland* v *British Rail Engineering Ltd* [1983] 2 AC 751 adopted the 'rule of construction' approach to s. 2(4). The case involved a conflict, as in *Macarthys Ltd* v *Smith,* between our own Equal Pay Act 1970 and the then Article 119 of the EC Treaty. The relevant section of the Equal Pay Act 1970, s. 6(4), which exempts from the equal pay principle provisions relating to death and retirement, had been broadly construed by the Court of Appeal to the detriment of the claimant. He sought therefore to rely directly on former Article 119. The House of Lords held that s. 6(4) must be construed to conform with Article 119 (now 141).

However, in *Garland* it was possible to construe the relevant English legislation to conform with EC law 'without any undue straining of the words'. The matter would be more difficult were a court to be faced with a clear and patently irreconcilable conflict. What should it do in such a situation? According to Lord Denning in *Macarthys Ltd* v *Smith,* it is its 'bounden duty' to give 'priority' to EC law. In *Garland* Lord Diplock suggested, while refusing to commit himself outright, that national courts must still construe domestic law to conform, 'no matter how wide a departure from the prima facie meaning may be needed to achieve consistency'. This approach was approved and applied in *Pickstone* v *Freemans plc* [1989] AC 66. Here the House of Lords, in contrast to the Court of Appeal, which had been prepared to apply EC law directly, chose to 'interpret' certain Regulations amending the Equal Pay Act 1970 against their literal meaning, even to the extent of reading certain words into the Regulations in order to achieve a result compatible with EC law. The provisions, said Lord Keith 'must be construed purposively in order to give effect to the manifest broad intentions of Parliament'. In this case it was clear, from evidence from House of Commons debates on the matter, that the Regulations had been introduced specifically in order to give effect to Community law.

In *Factortame Ltd* v *Secretary of State for Transport* [1990] 2 AC 85 the House of Lords was prepared to go further. Lord Bridge suggested that the combined effect of subsections (1) and (4) of the European Communities Act 1972, s. 2, was 'as if a section were incorporated in Part II [the impugned part] of the Merchant Shipping Act 1988 which in terms enacted that the provisions with respect to registration of British fishing vessels were to be without prejudice to the directly enforceable Community rights of nationals of any Member State of the EEC'. He suggested that if it were to be found that the British Act was in breach of the claimants' directly effective Community rights the latter rights would 'prevail' over the contrary provisions of the 1988 Act.

Subsequently, in applying the ECJ's ruling (in case C–213/89 noted above) that national courts must grant interim relief against the Crown where this was necessary to protect individuals' Community rights, the House of Lords, unanimously, granted that relief (*R* v *Secretary of State for Transport, ex parte Factortame Ltd* [1991] 1 AC 603 at 645). Here clearly no question of 'interpretation' of national law was possible; the House simply gave 'priority' to Community law. In justification, Lord Bridge pointed out that the principle of supremacy of Community law, if it was not always inherent in the Treaty, was 'well established in the jurisprudence of the Court long before the United Kingdom joined the Community. Thus, whatever limitation of its sovereignty Parliament accepted when it enacted the European Communities Act was entirely voluntary'.

As will be seen when we examine the question of remedies, the principle of primacy of Community law, together with obligation imposed by Article 10 (ex 5) EC on national courts to provide effective protection for individuals' Community rights (the 'effectiveness' principle), has resulted in remedies being granted which were not at the time available under national law (see further chapter 26).

The limits of primacy   As the above cases demonstrate, our courts, led by the House of Lords, have shown a clear willingness to accord supremacy to directly effective Community law, either by a (fictional) 'construction' of domestic law, or, where necessary, by applying EC law directly, in priority over national law. Their willingness to do so, as suggested by Lord Bridge in *Factortame*, appears to rest on the implied intentions of Parliament. However, both Lord Denning in *Macarthys Ltd* v *Smith* and Lord Diplock in *Garland* have made it clear that if Parliament were expressly to attempt to repudiate its EC obligations our courts would be obliged to give effect to Parliament's wishes.

> If the time should come when our Parliament deliberately passes an Act —
> with the intention of repudiating the Treaty or any provision in it — or
> intentionally of acting inconsistently with it — and says so in express terms
> — then . . . it would be the duty of our courts to follow the statute of our
> Parliament (per Lord Denning in *Macarthys Ltd* v *Smith* [1979] ICR 785
> at p. 789)

While this is unlikely to happen as long as we remain members of the Community, it was perhaps seen as important that it should remain a theoretical possibility. If our courts have changed in their approach to statutory interpretation in the context of Community law, the principle of parliamentary sovereignty remains intact.

This was borne out in *R* v *Secretary of State for Foreign and Commonwealth Affairs, ex parte Rees-Mogg* [1994] QB 552, QBD. Here the applicant, Lord Rees-Mogg, sought to challenge and prevent the ratification by Parliament of the Treaty on European Union (1992) on a number of grounds. One of his arguments ('the most interesting . . . jurisprudentially' per Lloyd LJ) was that in ratifying Title V of the Treaty, on foreign and security policy, the government would be transferring part of the Royal prerogative to Community institutions without statutory authority, as was required under British constitutional rules. Title V, as an inter-governmental agreement, was not part of the EC Treaty and therefore not properly included in the proposed act of ratification. The argument failed. Lloyd LJ held that Title V did not entail an abandonment or transfer of prerogative powers, but an exercise of those powers. 'In the last resort . . . it would presumably be open to the government to denounce the Treaty, or at least fail to comply with its international obligations under Title V.'

EC law which is not directly effective   In *Garland*, *Pickstone* and *Factortame* their Lordships' views on the European Communities Act 1972, s. 2(4), were expressed in the context of a conflict between domestic law and *directly effective* Community law. Is it possible to achieve primacy for EC law for provisions of EC Directives which, although sufficiently clear and precise for direct effects, are not directly effective because they are being invoked against a private party? In other words, does s. 2(4) of the Act enable our courts to follow *von Colson* (case 14/83) and *Marleasing* (case C–106/89) (see chapter

4) and interpret domestic law to comply with EC law, even when it is not directly effective? In *Duke* v *GEC Reliance Ltd* [1988] AC 618 the House of Lords thought not. The European Communities Act 1972, s. 2(1) and (4), said Lord Templeman, applied, and only applied, to EC law which was directly effective. 'Section 2(4) of the European Communities Act 1972 does not . . . enable or constrain a British court to distort the meaning of a British statute in order to enforce against an individual a Community Directive which has no direct effect between individuals'. However, as was suggested in chapter 4, a refusal to interpret the Sex Discrimination Act 1975 to comply with Equal Treatment Directive 76/207 was understandable on the particular facts of the case. In *Litster* v *Forth Dry Dock & Engineering Co. Ltd* [1990] 1 AC 546, in the context of a claim against a 'private' party, the House of Lords interpreted certain UK regulations to comply with EC Directive 80/777, citing and approving *Pickstone*, and suggesting that where legislation had been introduced specifically in order to implement an EC Directive, UK courts must interpret domestic law to comply with the Directive, if necessary 'supplying the necessary words by implication' in order to achieve a result compatible with EC law. No reference was made to *Duke* v *GEC Reliance Ltd*, nor to the fact that the Directive in question was not directly effective.

Thus, in the absence of evidence, such as was adduced in *Duke* v *GEC Reliance Ltd*, that Parliament did not intend to comply with Community law, *Litster* suggests that even where EC law is not directly effective, 'priority' for EC law should be ensured by way of interpretation of national law. However, there is no guarantee that *Litster* will be followed. In *Webb* v *EMO Air Cargo (UK) Ltd* [1992] 2 All ER 43 Lord Templeman's dicta in *Duke* v *GEC Reliance Ltd* were cited by the Court of Appeal and the House of Lords ([1993] 1 WLR 49). However, following a ruling from the ECJ on the interpretation of Directive 76/207, the House of Lords found that it was possible to construe s. 5(3) of the Sex Discrimination Act 1975 to comply with the Court's ruling without 'distorting' the meaning of the section. The Court of Appeal's decision had been based on a different, if equally legitimate, interpretation of s. 5(3), and past case law. On the other hand in *R* v *British Coal Corporation, ex parte Vardy* [1993] ICR 720, Glidewell J found that it was 'not possible' to follow the House of Lords' example in *Litster* and interpret certain provisions of the Trade Union and Labour Relations Act 1992 to comply with EC (Collective Redundancies) Directive 75/129 since they were clearly at odds with the Directive. Thus in the absence of ambiguity or evidence that Parliament intended UK law to have the meaning contended for or where there is a clear conflict between domestic and EC law, our courts will be reluctant to apply the *von Colson* principle, particularly as extended by the ECJ in *Marleasing*. This appears to have been acknowledged by the ECJ in *Wagner Miret* (case C–334/92). Arguably this approach, which respects the principles of legal certainty and non-retroactivity, is consistent with the principles of EC law expressed by the ECJ in *Officier van Justitie* v *Kolpinghuis Nijmegen* (case 80/86, noted chapter 4). Where it is not possible for national courts to give indirect effect to Community Directives, enforcement of EC law should perhaps be left to the Commission under Article 226 (ex 169), or, now, to an action against the State under *Francovich* (cases C–6 & 9/90), as suggested by the Court in *Dori* (case C–91/92) and *Wagner Miret*.

State liability in damages   The UK courts have had little difficulty in applying the principle of State liability following the ECJ's rulings in *Francovich* (cases C–6 & 9/90) and *Brasserie du Pêcheur* (cases C–46 & 48/93) They have accepted that the State may be liable for *legislative* breaches of Community law. In *R v Secretary of State for Transport, ex parte Factortame Ltd (No. 2)* [1991] 1 AC 603 the House of Lords demonstrated its willingness to grant an interim injunction to prevent the application of a British statute (allegedly) in breach of EC law in order effectively to protect the claimants' directly effective Community rights. In *R v Secretary of State for Employment, ex parte Equal Opportunities Commission* [1995] 1 AC 1, the House of Lords, following the 'precedent' set by *Factortame*, was prepared to grant a declaration that certain provisions of the Employment Protection (Consolidation) Act 1978, which imposed a two-year threshold for protection against unfair dismissal and redundancy, were incompatible with the then Article 119 EC (now 141). Lord Keith suggested that it was not necessary for the purposes of the case to declare the United Kingdom *in breach* of its obligations under Community law. A declaration establishing the *incompatibility* of domestic law with EC law would be sufficient to establish a State's 'failure' for the purposes of a claim under *Francovich*. It could be argued that as long as incompatibility was established, a formal declaration to that effect would not be necessary.

From these cases it was but a small step for our courts to accept a principle of liability in damages for legislative breaches of Community law. This step was taken by the Court of Appeal in *R v Secretary of State for the Home Department, ex parte Gallagher* [1996] 2 CMLR 951. Here Lord Bingham of Cornhill CJ, invoking the ECJ's ruling in *Francovich*, said, at para. 10.

> It is a cardinal principle of Community law that the laws of Member States should provide effective and adequate redress for violations of Community law by Member States where these result in the infringement of specific individual rights conferred by the law of the Community.

However, while accepting that the UK might be liable in principle for a British statute (the Prevention of Terrorism (Temporary Provisions) Act 1989) contrary to EC Directive 64/221, he rejected the applicant's claim. The applicant had failed to establish the requisite causal link between the alleged breach and the damage sustained. Even without the breach, a breach of the applicant's procedural rights under the Directive, the result, the applicant's removal from the UK, would have been the same. Nor was the breach of Community law sufficiently serious to warrant liability. Although the UK's transposition of the Directive was wrong, the error did not constitute a 'manifest and grave breach' of EC law.

In applying the ECJ's ruling on the damages claim in *Factortame* (case C–48/93) [1998] 1 CMLR 1353, the Court of Appeal [1998] 3 CMLR 192 and the House of Lords [1999] 3 CMLR 597 accepted the principle of State liability for damage resulting from a British statute, the Merchant Shipping Act 1988, found by the ECJ to be contrary to Article 52 (now 43) EC. Basing their reasoning on the Court's rulings in *Francovich* (cases C–6 & 9/90) and *Brasserie du Pêcheur* (cases C–46 & 48/93) they found that the UK's breach constituted a sufficiently serious breach of Community law, for which the UK might be liable in damages, subject to the applicants' establishing the requisite damage and causation.

Following the UK courts' example in *Factortame (No. 5)*, the High Court in *Bowden* v *South West Water Services* [1999] 3 CMLR 180 and *R* v *Dept of Social Security, ex parte Scullion* [1999] 3 CMLR 798 likewise dealt without demur with claims for damages based on *Francovich*. Thus our courts have had no problem in applying the principle of State liability, even when the breach of Community law is contained in a British statute. It interesting to note that the courts' decisions in all of these cases were based on the ECJ's jurisprudence: they did not seek to justify their decisions on the basis of the European Communities Act 1972. Had they thought it to be necessary, it is submitted that it would have been possible to do so. The rights recognised and incorporated into domestic law by the European Communities Act 1972, s. 2(1), are sufficiently widely expressed to embrace not only directly effective and indirectly effective Community rights but also rights based on *Francovich*. Furthermore, support for the primacy of all EC rights may be provided by the European Communities Act 1972, s. 3(1), which provides that:

> For the purposes of all legal proceedings any question as to the meaning or effect of any of the Treaties, or as to the validity, meaning or effect of any Community instrument, shall be treated as a question of law (and, if not referred to the European Court, be for determination as such in accordance with the principles laid down by and any relevant decision of the European Court or any court attached thereto).

The relevant decisions of the ECJ for the purposes of State liability, as has been acknowledged by the English High Court and the Court of Appeal, are clearly *Francovich* (cases C–6 & 9/90) and *Brasserie du Pêcheur* (cases C–46 & 48/93).

France   After some early resistance, the French courts at all levels now seem prepared to give primacy to EC law, provided it is found to be directly effective. They have done so in some of the cases by applying Article 55 of the French constitution (e.g., *Vabre* [1975] 2 CMLR 336, Cour de Cassation), in others by invoking the reasoning and case law of the ECJ (see *Von Kempis* v *Geldof* [1976] 2 CMLR 152, Cour de Cassation, and Procureur Général Touffait in *Vabre*). The Versailles Cour d'Appel in *Rossi di Montalera* v *Procureur Général* [1984] 1 CMLR 489 declared EC law to be 'top of the hierarchy of sources of law'. The Conseil d'État, the supreme French administrative court, has been the most reluctant of the French courts to concede the supremacy of EC law. In *Semoules* [1970] CMLR 395 it refused outright to do so. However, in *Nicolo* [1990] 1 CMLR 17 and *Boisdet* [1991]

1 CMLR 3, following a powerful submission from the Commissaire du Gouvernement, it recognised implicitly that Treaty Articles (*Nicolo*) and EC Regulations (*Boisdet*) must take precedence over (even subsequent) national laws, by examining the latter for their compatibility with Community law. Its judgment in *Boisdet*, unlike that in the earlier case of *Nicolo*, was based neither on the EC Treaty nor the French constitution but on the case law of the ECJ. In *Arizona Tobacco Products GmbH Export KG* [1993] 1 CMLR 253, the Conseil d'État awarded damages under *Francovich* (cases C–6 & 9/90) for losses suffered as a result of a *ministerial* order in breach of an EC Directive. In *Dangeville* damages were awarded by the Paris Cour Administratif d'Appel for losses resulting from the application of a French *statute* in breach of EC law. The basis for its decision was Article 5 (now 10) EC. It may be noted that in both cases the breach of EC law was clearly culpable, and had been established in a prior ruling by the ECJ under Article 169 (now 226). Also, although damages are available under French law in respect of unlawful *ministerial* action, they are not normally available in respect of unlawful *legislative* acts, except under principles pertaining to strict liability (*égalité devant les charges publics*).

Before the TEU was ratified the Conseil Constitutionel was asked to consider its compatibility with the French Constitution. Although the Constitution made no specific reference to the EU, the Conseil Constitutionel was prepared to infer from Article 55 (together with Article 46) of the Constitution that 'Community treaties cannot be called into question'. It held that powers could be transferred to permanent international organisations having legal personality and powers of decision. The Conseil was satisfied that the guarantees provided by Community law would suffice to ensure respect for individual rights and freedoms. However, the Constitution would have to be amended to allow for the transfer of sovereignty in the 'new areas' concerning economic and monetary union, the rights of EU nationals in local elections, and immigration into the Union of third-country nationals. This was done in 1992 with the introduction of a new Article 88(1–4), subject to the principle of reciprocity. Thus the European Community was mentioned for the first time in the French constitution. As Oliver has noted, 'the Conseil Constitutionel has now endorsed the increasingly liberal approach of the French judiciary to Community law'.

The only remaining problem area appears to be that of Directives. The Conseil d'État has consistently failed to give full effect to EC Directives. Whilst it has been prepared to allow individuals to invoke Directives against *general* administrative acts, it refuses to concede that a Directive can be relied on in support of an action for the annulment of an *individual* administrative act. It refused to do so in *Compagnie Générale des Eaux* [1994] 2 CMLR 373. The case concerned an appeal by Compagnie Générale des Eaux (CGE) against a decision of the Tribunal Administratif invalidating a contract between the Municipal Council of Reunion and CGE for breach of Public Procurement Directive 90/531. The original suit had been brought by a third party, M. Lachat, who had been denied an opportunity to tender as a result of the Council's alleged failure to follow the procedures laid down in the

Directive. The appeal succeeded. The Conseil d'État held that the Tribunal should never have entertained the original application. Following a line of authority starting with *Cohn-Bendit* [1980] 1 CMLR 543 (see chapter 4), it held that since, following Article 189 (now 249):

> national authorities alone remain competent to decide on the form in which Directives are to be implemented and to determine, under the supervision of national courts, suitable means for giving effect to them in internal law ... Directives cannot be relied upon by nationals of those States in support of an action against an administrative act which does not consist in delegated legislation.

Italy In Italy the constitutional court has moved far from its position in *Costa v ENEL* [1964] CMLR 425, and in *Frontini v Ministero delle Finanze* [1974] 2 CMLR 372, applying Article 11 of the Italian constitution, in a judgment based almost entirely on the reasoning of the ECJ, held that any question concerning the legality under the Constitution of incorporating Article 189 (now 249) of the EC Treaty into the Italian Act of ratification 'must be dismissed'. However, limitations of sovereignty permitted under Article 11 were 'solely for the purposes indicated' under the EEC Treaty; Article 189 (now 249) EC did not give the organs of the EEC power to violate fundamental principles of the Italian Constitution. The Constitutional Court would therefore continue to control the compatibility of measures taken under Article 189 with these principles. Since then the court has been unequivocal in its support for the principle of the supremacy of EC law, sometimes advocating the route-by-construction of domestic law (*SpA Comavicola*, noted (1982) 19 CML Rev 455), sometimes following the case law of the ECJ (*Granital SPA v Amministrazione Finanze dello Stato* Giur It 1984 I, 1, 1521; *BECA SpA* Giur It 1986 I, 1, 128).

However, in *SpA Fragd v Amministrazione delle Finanze* (Dec 232 of 21 April 1989 (1989) 72 RDI) the Constitutional Court reiterated its concern for fundamental human rights expressed in *Frontini*. The case involved a challenge to the legality under the Italian Constitution of a ruling from the ECJ under Article 177 (now 234) EC limiting the temporal effect of a declaration that certain provisions of Community law were invalid. The ruling was to apply only as regards the future: it was not applicable to the case in hand. It was argued that such a restriction would violate the individual's fundamental right to judicial protection protected under the Italian Constitution. The Constitutional Court found that a decision on the legality of the ECJ's ruling was not in fact relevant to the case before the national court: but it held that it would in principle be prepared to declare inapplicable a rule of Community law which infringed fundamental constitutional rights. As the subsequent case of *Roquette Frères SA v Hauptzollamt Geldern* (case C–228/92) indicates, this warning did not go unheeded by the ECJ (see further chapter 30).

Germany The German federal constitutional court too modified its original view in *Internationale Handelsgesellschaft (Solange I)* [1974] 2 CMLR 540. In

Steinike und Weinleg [1980] 2 CMLR 531 it suggested that any challenge to the constitutionality under German law of EC law could only be brought by way of challenge to the German Act of ratification itself, and in October 1986, in *Application of Wünsche Handelsgesellschaft (Solange II)* [1987] 3 CMLR 225 its position in *Internationale Handelsgesellschaft* was finally reversed. As long as EC law itself ensured the effective protection of fundamental rights, a ruling from the ECJ under Article 177 (now 234) would not, the court held, be subject to review. Similarly, in *Re Kloppenberg* [1988] 3 CMLR 1, in the context of a successful challenge to the Bundesfinanzhof's decision on the direct effect of Directives (see *Re VAT Directives* [1982] 1 CMLR 527, noted in chapter 4), it affirmed the principle of the supremacy of Community law in the strongest terms. In 1992, as in France, the constitution was amended to provide specifically for the transfer of sovereign powers to the EU (see new Article 23, Basic Law).

However, the case of *Brunner v The European Union Treaty (Eurocontrol)* [1994] 1 CMLR 57 indicates that the German federal constitutional court (Bundesverfassungsgericht), while respecting the supremacy of Community law in matters within the sphere of Community competence, will itself reserve the right:

(a) to ensure the protection of fundamental human rights guaranteed under the German constitution; and

(b) to decide whether the Union institutions have acted within their powers under the EC and EU Treaties.

The case involved a challenge to the German Federal Parliament's power to ratify the TEU. It was argued that the transfer via the proposed Act of Ratification of further powers and competences to the European Union would threaten human rights and democratic principles protected under the German constitution. The Bundesverfassungsgericht found these allegations unfounded. The TEU did not, as was suggested, establish a European State but a federation of States. It equipped the Union only with specific competences and powers in accordance with the principle of limited individual competences and established a principle of subsidiarity for the Union. It would permit no further extension of Community competence under Article 235 (now 308, see chapter 3). If the Union institutions or organisations were to develop the Treaty in a way not covered by the Treaty in the form that was the basis for the Act of Accession the resultant legislative instruments would not be binding within the sphere of German sovereignty. If parts of the Community legal order were to breach fundamental rights protected under the German Constitution it would declare those provisions inapplicable. Accordingly the court would review legal instruments of European institutions and agencies to see whether they remained within the sovereign rights conferred on them or transgressed them. Germany was one of the masters of the Treaty with the intention of long-term membership: but it could ultimately revoke its adherence by a contrary act.

Thus, according to the federal constitutional court, German sovereignty remains intact, and that court will itself decide whether the institutions of the Union have acted within their powers under the EC and EU Treaties.

The unequivocal stance of the federal constitutional court in *Brunner* has emboldened the German courts to take a stand in a series of cases concerning the Community's banana regime. The regime, which was set up in 1993 by EC Regulation 404/93, and which operated to the serious disadvantage of German importers, was challenged by Germany on the grounds that it breached the Community's international obligations (*inter alia* GATT) and violated vested property rights protected under the German Constitution. Despite strong arguments, acknowledged by Advocate-General Gulmann, that there were 'circumstances which might provide a basis for a finding that the Regulation was invalid' the ECJ found that there was no illegality in the Community's market organisation of bananas (*Germany* v *Council* (case C–280/93), see further chapter 6).

This case, which was extremely thin in its reasoning, for which it was roundly criticised, even by a former judge of the ECJ (see article by Everling noted below), did little to stem the flood of actions before the German (and not only German) courts seeking to suspend the application of the contested Regulation and/or to obtain compensation for damage suffered as a result of its application. Following *Germany* v *Council* the legality of the Banana Regulation was again questioned before the Frankfurt administrative court (Verwaltungsgericht), and further questions referred to the ECJ (*Atlanta* (case C–465/93)). While affirming national courts' power to award interim relief, even positive relief in the form of the grant of import licences, pending a ruling from the ECJ on validity, the ECJ confirmed its finding in *Germany* v *Council* on the legality of the Regulation, pointing out that in deciding whether or not to grant interim relief national courts were 'obliged to respect what the Community Court has decided on this issue' (*Atlanta* (case C–465/93)). This did not prevent further claims before the German courts raising the issue of the compatibility of the Regulation with the German Constitution, and questioning its applicability in Germany on the basis of *Brunner*. In one case, following rejection of the claimants' application for relief by the Kassel Verwaltungsgerichtshof, which followed the ECJ's ruling in *Germany* v *Council*, the claimants took their case to the federal constitutional court, which ordered a re-examination of the case, basing its decision on Article 19(4) of the German Basic Law. Article 19(4) enshrines the right to effective judicial protection. Significantly the constitutional court did not seek a ruling from the ECJ. On re-examination, the referring court granted the requested interim relief and referred further questions to the ECJ on the interpretation and validity of the Regulation. In another case, the federal finance court (Bundesfinanzhof) accepted the finding of the Finanzgericht Hamburg that parts of the Banana Regulation might be incompatible with GATT, and suggested that if they were, the German courts might be prevented from applying them following principles established in *Brunner*. Again further questions on the compatibility of the Regulation with GATT were referred to the ECJ (*T. Port GmbH & Co.* v *Hauptzollamt Hamburg-Jonas* (case C–364 and 365/95)). Thus although the courts have not openly contradicted the ECJ's judgment in *Germany* v *Council* (case C–280/93) they have been prepared to question its applicability and even refrain from applying it. As Everling points out, the German courts 'are deeply concerned about the extremely unjust effects of the Banana Regulation and insufficiency of the judicial control by the ECJ in this case'. So far they have avoided open conflict by awarding provisional relief and submitting further questions to the ECJ in the hope that the Court will reconsider its decision in case C–280/93. It appeared to have done so (albeit to a limited extent) in *T. Port GmbH & Co.* v *Hauptzollamt Hamburg-Jonas* (cases C–364 and 365/95) when it found that certain aspects of the banana regime were invalid for breach of the principle of non-discrimination. However, it has denied national courts' power to award interim relief in the context of the EC institutions' (allegedly unlawful) *failure to act*, holding that any challenge to such a failure could only be brought before the ECJ under Articles 173 and 175 (now 230 and 232 respectively) (*T. Port GmbH & Co. KG* (case C–68/95), judgment of 6 November 1996). As will be seen in chapters 30 and 31, this represents a weakness in the system of judicial control of the EC institutions.

However, as long as Community law does not threaten German constitutional rights or make unwarranted intrusions into areas within the legislative jurisdiction of Member States, the German courts are prepared fully to comply with the principle of primacy of EC law. In applying the ECJ's ruling in *Brasserie du Pêcheur SA* v *Germany* [1997] 1 CMLR 971, the German Federal Supreme Court held that, even though there was no basis for the applicants' claim for damages in these circumstances for legislative breaches of Community law under German law, liability in respect of such breaches 'flowed directly from that [Community] law itself'. Nevertheless, although the State might be liable in principle for such breaches, Germany was found on the facts not to be liable, since the breach of Community law which caused the applicants' damage (the prohibition on the use of additives in the manufacture of beer) was, as the ECJ itself had suggested, not sufficiently serious to give rise to liability.

Like the UK courts the German courts have had difficulty with the principle of direct effects, and particularly indirect effects, in the context of the application of EC Directives. In *Re a Rehabilitation Centre* [1992] 2 CMLR 21 the German Federal Supreme Court refused to 'interpret' the German Legal Code against its clear meaning, to comply with EC Equal Treatment Directive 76/207. The court held:

> even an interpretation of statutes by reference to conformity with the constitution reaches its limits when it comes into conflict with the wording and evident intention of the legislature. The position can be no different as regards the interpretation of national law in the light of the wording and purpose of a Directive.

As was suggested in chapter 4, it is likely that these difficulties and this resistance caused the ECJ to turn to the alternative remedy of State liability in damages in *Francovich* v *Italy* (case 9/90).

Denmark The Danish Supreme Court's response to the principle of primacy has been similar to that of the German constitutional court. In *Carlsen and*

Others v *Rasmussen* [1999] 3 CMLR 854 it was faced with a challenge to the legality of Denmark's Acts of Accession to the EC and Maastricht Treaties (1972 and 1993 respectively). These Acts were alleged to be contrary to s. 20 of the Danish Constitutional Act, which provides that the powers of the State can, 'to the extent permitted by statute', be delegated to international authorities according to a specified procedure. The challenge focused principally on the EC institutions' law-making powers under Article 235 (now 308) EC, Article 173 (now 230) and Article 177 (now 234). It was argued that the transfer of powers under these Articles was inconsistent with the constitution's premise of a democratic government. The Supreme Court found that the Acts of Accession were compatible with s. 20. Section 20 was of necessity loosely worded: since it was impossible to predict the extent of any future international cooperation, no detailed specification of the powers which could be delegated was provided. However, an international organisation could not be given the power to enact legislation or take decisions which were contrary to the Danish constitution. It was limited by s. 20 both in its area of responsibility and the extent of its powers. The powers given to the EC institutions under Article 235 were compatible with s. 20, since these institutions can act only within the powers conferred by the Treaty. The EC Treaty gave the ECJ the power to review the legality of Community law under Article 173 (now 230) and Article 177 (now 234). Nevertheless, a Danish court could itself rule a community act inapplicable in the extraordinary situation that such an act had been upheld by the ECJ but went beyond the surrender of sovereignty pursuant to the Act of Accession:

> The Danish courts cannot be deprived of the right to try questions as to whether an act of EC law exceeds the limits for the surrender of sovereignty made by the Act of Accession. If they find a Community act beyond the limits allowed by Article 20 Danish courts must rule that act inapplicable.

Belgium   The approach of the Belgian courts was novel, and perhaps closest of all in spirit to that of the ECJ. As a dualist state, EC law was incorporated into Belgian law by statute, but the constitution contained no provision (such as Article 55 of the French constitution) giving supremacy to international law. Thus EC law was particularly vulnerable to the doctrine of *lex posterior*. Nevertheless the Cour de Cassation in the case of *Le Ski* [1972] CMLR 330 refused to accept this argument in the context of a conflict between EC law and a later Belgian law. Even though EC law was incorporated by statute the court held that the normal *lex posterior* rule would not apply. That rule was based on the presumption that the legislature in passing a statute wished to amend any earlier conflicting statute. That presumption would not apply in the case of a treaty. A treaty represented a higher legal norm. Because of the nature of international treaty law, in the case of a conflict the treaty must prevail. Similar reasoning was applied by the magistrates' court of Antwerp, in the *Social Funds for Diamond Workers* case [1969] CMLR 315.

Conclusions

In a relatively short space of time the courts of Member States, despite their different constitutional rules and traditions, have adapted to the principle of supremacy of EC law where it is found to be directly effective. Their application of Directives, particularly their indirect application, remains uncertain. Their reaction to *Francovich*, as refined in *Brasserie du Pêcheur* (cases C–46 & 48/93) has been positive. Credit for national courts' acceptance of the principle of supremacy of EC law must go to the ECJ, which has supplied persuasive reasons for doing so. However, equal credit must go to the courts of Member States, which have contrived to embrace the principle of primacy of Community law while at the same time insisting that ultimate political and judicial control remains within the Member States. As *Fragd*, *Brunner* and *Carlsen* v *Rasmussen* indicate, the courts of Member States, particularly their supreme courts, will be vigilant, and use all the means at their disposal, to ensure that the EU institutions do not exceed their powers or transgress fundamental constitutional rights, particularly in the new post-Maastricht political climate, with its emphasis on subsidiarity. As Kumm suggests, 'they need to keep a handle on the emergency brake'; but they would disapply a Community act or a ruling from the ECJ only where that act or that ruling was manifestly and gravely erroneous. So far they have stopped short of outright defiance, thereby avoiding the unthinkable, a claim for damages against the State in respect of judicial breaches of Community law, as could in theory be brought following the ECJ's ruling in *Brasserie du Pêcheur*.

Further reading

See also the reading list at the end of chapter 4.

Bebr, G., 'Agreements Concluded by the Community and their Possible Direct Effects: from International Fruit Company to Kupferberg' (1983) 20 CML Rev 35.

Coppel, J. and O'Neill, A., 'The European Court of Justice: Taking Rights Seriously?' (1992) 29 CML Rev 669.

Craig, P., 'UK Sovereignty after *Factortame*' (1991) 11 YEL 221.

de Noriega, E., 'A Dissident Voice: The Spanish Constitutional Case Law on European Integration' (1999) 5 EPL 269.

De Witte, B., 'Community Law and National Constitutional Values' (1991) 2 LIEI 1.

Everling, U., 'Will Europe Slip on Bananas? The Bananas Judgment of the European Court and National Courts' (1996) 33 CML Rev 401.

Gaja, G., 'New Developments in a Continuing Story: the Relationship between EEC Law and Italian Law' (1990) 27 CML Rev 83.

Green, N., 'Directives, Equity and the Protection of Individual Rights' (1984) 9 EL Rev 295.

Hartley, T., 'International Agreements and the Community Legal System: Some Recent Developments' (1983) 8 EL Rev 383.

Herdegen, M., 'Maastricht and the German Constitutional Court: Constitutional Restraints for an Ever Closer Union' (1994) 31 CML Rev 235.

Hoskins, M., 'Tilting the Balance: Supremacy and National Procedural Rules' (1996) 21 EL Rev 365.

Kumm, M., 'Who is the Arbiter of Constitutionality in Europe?' (1999) 36 CML Rev 351.

Lang, J. T., 'The Community Constitutional Law: Article 5 EEC Treaty' (1990) 27 CML Rev 645.

Marshall, G., 'Parliamentary Sovereignty — the New Horizons' [1997] PL 1.

Obradovic, D., 'Aspects of European Constitutionalism' (1996) 21 EL Rev 32.

Obradovic, D., 'Repatriation of Powers in the European Community' (1997) 34 CML Rev 59.

Oliver, P., 'The French Constitution and the Treaty of Maastricht' (1994) 43 ICLQ 1.

Peers, S., 'Taking Supremacy Seriously' (1998) 23 EL Rev 146.

Pescatore, P., 'The Doctrine of Direct Effect: an Infant Disease of Community Law' (1983) 8 EL Rev 155.

Pollard, D., 'The Conseil d'État is European — Official' (1990) 15 EL Rev 267.

Reich, 'Judge-made Europe à la Carte: Some Remarks on Recent Conflicts between European and German Constitutional Law Provoked by the Bananas Litigation' (1996) 7 EJIL 103.

Roseren, P., 'The Application of Community Law by French Courts from 1982 to 1993' (1994) 31 CML Rev 315.

Roth, W., 'The Application of Community Law in West Germany: 1980–1990' (1991) 28 CML Rev 137.

Schermans, H., 'The Scales in Balance: National Constitutional Court v Court of Justice' (1990) 27 CML Rev 97.

Soakes, A.G., 'Pre-emption, Conflict of Powers and Subsidiarity (1998) 23 EL Rev 132.

Steiner, J., 'Coming to Terms with EEC Directives' (1990) 106 LQR 144.

Tatham, A., 'The Effect of European Community Directives in France' (1991) 40 ICLQ 907.

Weiler, J., 'The Community System: the Dual Character of Supranationalism' (1981) 1 YEL 267.

Weiler, J., 'The Transformation of Europe' (1991) 100 Yale Law Journal 2403.

Weiler, J., 'The Reformulation of German Constitutionalism' (1997) 35 JCMS 597.

Weiler, J. and Lockhart, '"Taking Rights Seriously" Seriously'? (1995) 32 CML Rev 51 and 579.

Winter, T. A., 'Direct Applicability and Direct Effects' (1972) 9 CML Rev 425.

Wyatt, D., 'Direct Effects of Community Law, not forgetting Directives' (1983) 8 EL Rev 241.

Wyatt, D., 'New Legal Order, or Old?' (1982) 7 EL Rev 147.

Zuleeg, M., 'The European Constitution under European Constraints: the German Scenario' (1997) 22 EL Rev 19.

SIX

General principles of law

After the concept of direct effects and the principle of supremacy of EC law the third major contribution of the ECJ has been the introduction into the corpus of EC law of general principles of law. Although primarily relevant to the final section of this book, to the question of remedies and enforcement of EC law, a discussion of the role of general principles of law is appropriate at this stage in view of their fundamental importance in the jurisprudence of the ECJ as compared with the relatively minor role they have played in English law to date. It is thus important at an early stage to appreciate their significance.

General principles of law are relevant in the context of EC law in a number of ways. First, they may be invoked as an aid to interpretation: EC law, including domestic law implementing EC law obligations, must be interpreted in such a way as not to conflict with general principles of law. Secondly, general principles of law may be invoked by both States and individuals in order to challenge Community action, either to annul or invalidate acts of the institutions (under Articles 230, 241, 234 and 236 (ex 173, 184, 177 and 179) EC), or to challenge inaction on the part of these institutions (under Articles 232 or 236 (ex 175 and 179) EC). Thirdly, as a logical consequence of its second role, but less generally acknowledged, general principles may also be invoked as a means of challenging action by a Member State, whether in the form of a legal or an administrative act, where the action is performed in the context of a right or obligation arising from *Community* law (see *Klensch* (cases 201 & 202/85); *Wachauf* v *Germany* (case 5/88); *Lageder* v *Amministrazione delle Finanze dello Stato* (case C–31/91); but *cf. R* v *Ministry of Agriculture, Fisheries and Food, ex parte Bostock* (case C–2/93)). This would follow in the UK from the incorporation into domestic law, by s. 2(1) of the European Communities Act 1972, of '*All* such rights, powers, liabilities, obligations and restrictions from time to time created or arising by or under the Treaties'. The degree to which general principles of law affect actions by Member States will be discussed in more detail later in this chapter. Lastly, general principles of law may be invoked to support a claim for damages against the Community (under Article 288(2) (ex 215(2))). Where damages are claimed as a result of an illegal act on the part of the Community institutions, it is necessary (but not sufficient) to prove that a sufficiently serious breach of a *superior rule of law for the protection of the individual* has occurred (*Aktien-Zuckerfabrik Schöppenstedt* v *Council* (case 5/71)) (see chapter 33).

General principles of law are not to be confused with the fundamental principles of Community law, as expressed in the EC Treaty, for example, the principles of free movement of goods and persons, of non-discrimination on the grounds of sex (Article 141 (ex 119) EC) or nationality (Article 12 (ex 6) EC). General principles of law constitute the 'unwritten' law of the Community.

The legal basis for the incorporation of general principles into community law is slim, resting precariously on three Articles. Article 230 (ex 173) gives the ECJ power to review the legality of Community acts on the basis of, *inter alia*, 'infringement of this Treaty', or '*any rule of law relating to its application*'. Article 288(2) (ex 215(2)), which governs Community liability in tort, provides that liability is to be determined '*in accordance with the general principles common to the laws of the Member States*'. And Article 220 (ex 164), governing the role of the ECJ, provides that the court 'shall ensure that in the interpretation and application of this Treaty *the law* is observed'.

In the absence of any indication as to the scope or content of these general principles, it has been left to the ECJ to put flesh on the bones provided by the Treaty. This function the Court has amply fulfilled, to the extent that general principles now form an important element of Community law.

Rationale for the introduction of general principles of law

One of the reasons for what has been described as the Court's 'naked law-making' in this area is best illustrated by the case of *Internationale Handelsgesellschaft mbH* (case 11/70). There the German courts were faced with a conflict between an EC Regulation requiring the forfeiture of deposits by exporters if export was not completed within an agreed time, and a number of principles of the German constitution, in particular, the principle of proportionality. It is in the nature of constitutional law that it embodies a State's most sacred and fundamental principles. Although these fundamental principles were of particular importance, for obvious reasons, in post-war Germany, other States of the Community too had written constitutions embodying fundamental rights. Clearly it would not have done for EC law to conflict with such principles. Indeed, as the German constitutional court made clear ([1974] 2 CMLR 540), were such a conflict to exist, national constitutional law would take precedence over EC law. This would have jeopardised not only the principle of primacy of EC law but also the uniformity of application so necessary to the success of the new legal order. So while the ECJ asserted the principle of primacy of EC law in *Internationale Handelsgesellschaft*, it was quick to point out that respect for fundamental rights was in any case part of EC law.

Another reason now given to justify the need for general principles is that the Community's powers have expanded to such a degree that some check on the exercise of the institutions' powers is needed. Furthermore, the expansion of Community competence means that the institutions' powers are now more likely to operate in policy areas in which human rights have an influence. Although those who wish to see sovereignty retained by the nation State may originally have been pleased to see the limitation of the EC institutions' powers, the development of human rights jurisprudence in this context can be seen as a double-edged sword, giving the ECJ increased power to impugn both acts of the Community institutions and implementing measures taken by Member States on grounds of infringement of general principles.

Development of general principles

The Court's first tentative recognition of fundamental human rights as part of EC law was prior to *Internationale Handelsgesellschaft*, in the case of *Stauder* v *City of Ulm* (case 29/69). Here the applicant was claiming entitlement to cheap butter provided under a Community scheme to persons in receipt of welfare benefits. He was required under German law to divulge his name and address on the coupon which he had to present in order to obtain the butter. He challenged this law as representating a violation of his fundamental human rights (namely, equality of treatment). The ECJ, on reference from the German court on the validity of the relevant Community Decision, held that on a proper interpretation the Community measure did not require the recipient's name to appear on the coupon. This interpretation, the Court held, contained nothing capable of prejudicing the fundamental human rights enshrined in the general principles of Community law and protected by the Court.

The ECJ went further in *Internationale Handelsgesellschaft*. There it asserted that respect for fundamental rights forms an integral part of the general principles of law protected by the Court — such rights are inspired by the constitutional traditions common to the Member States. One point to note here is that the ECJ is not comparing EC law with *national* law but with the principles of *international* law which are embodied in varying degrees in the national constitutions of Member States. A failure to make the distinction between general principles of international law (even if embodied in national laws) which the Community legal order respects and national law proper could erode the doctrine of supremacy of community law *vis-à-vis* national laws.

The *International Handelsgesellschaft* judgment can be taken as implying that only rights arising from traditions *common to* Member States can constitute part of EC law (the 'minimalist' approach). It may be argued that if the problem of conflict between Community law and national law is to be avoided in *all* Member States it is necessary for *any* human right upheld in the constitution of *any* Member State to be protected under EC law (the 'maximalist' approach). In *Hoechst* v *Commission* (cases 46/87, 227/88), in the context of a claim based on the fundamental right to the inviolability of the home, the Court, following a comprehensive review by Advocate-General Mischo of the laws of all the Member States on this question, distinguished between this right as applied to the 'private dwelling of physical persons', which was common to all Member States (and which would by implication be protected as part of Community law), and the protection offered to commercial premises against intervention by public authorities, which was subject to 'significant differences' in different Member States. In the latter case the only common protection, provided under various forms, was protection against arbitrary or disproportionate intervention on the part of public authorities. Similarly, but dealing with administrative law, in *Australian Mining & Smelting Europe Ltd* v *Commission* (case 155/79), in considering the principle of professional privilege, the Court found that the scope of protection for confidentiality for written communications between lawyers and their clients varied from State to State; only privilege as between independent (as opposed to in-house) lawyers and their clients was generally accepted, and would be upheld as a general principle of Community law.

These cases suggest that where certain rights are protected to differing degrees and in different ways in Member States, the Court will look for some *common* underlying principle to uphold as part of Community law. However, even if a particular right protected in a Member State is not universally protected, where there is an apparent conflict between that right and EC law the Court will strive to interpret Community law in such a way as to ensure that the substance of that right is not infringed. An exception to this approach can be seen in *Society for the Protection of the Unborn Child* v *Grogan* (case 159/90). This case concerned the officers of a students' union who provided information in Ireland about the availability of legal abortion in the UK. SPUC brought an action alleging that this was contrary to the Irish constitution. The officers' defence was based on the freedom to provide services within the Community and on the freedom of expression contained in the ECHR which also forms part of Community law as a general principle. The ECJ evaded this issue. Since the students' union did not have an economic link with the clinics whose services they advertised, the provision of information about the clinics was not an economic activity within the Treaty. As the issues fell outside the scope of EC law, the officers could not rely on either the provisions on freedom to provide services in the Treaty or on general principles of law. (See further chapter 21.)

Following *Internationale Handelsgesellschaft* the scope for human rights protection was further extended in the case of *J. Nold KG* v *Commission* (case 4/73). In this case J. Nold KG, a coal wholesaler, was seeking to challenge a Decision taken under the ECSC as being in breach of the company's fundamental right to the free pursuit of business activity. While the Court did not find for the company on the merits of the case, it asserted its commitment to fundamental rights in the strongest terms. As well as stating that fundamental rights form an integral part of the general principles of law, the observance of which it ensures, it went on to say:

> In safeguarding these rights, the Court is bound to draw inspiration from constitutional traditions common to the Member States, and it cannot

therefore uphold measures which are incompatible with fundamental rights recognised and protected by the constitutions of those States.

Similarly, international treaties for the protection of human rights on which the Member States have collaborated or of which they are signatories, can supply guidelines which should be followed within the framework of Community law.

The reasons for this inclusion of principles of certain international treaties as part of EC law are clearly the same as those upholding fundamental constitutional rights; it is the one certain way to guarantee the avoidance of conflict.

The most important international treaty concerned with the protection of human rights is the European Convention for the Protection of Human Rights and Fundamental Freedoms 1950 (ECHR), to which all Member States are now signatories. The Court has on a number of occasions confirmed its adherence to the rights protected therein, an approach to which the other institutions gave their support (Joint Declaration, OJ No. C103, 27.4.77, p. 1). In *R* v *Kirk* (case 63/83), in the context of criminal proceedings against Kirk, the captain of a Danish fishing vessel, for fishing in British waters (a matter subsequently covered by EC Regulations), the principle of non-retroactivity of penal measures, enshrined in Article 7 of the ECHR, was invoked by the Court and applied in Captain Kirk's favour. The EC Regulation, which would have legitimised the British rules under which Captain Kirk was charged, could not be applied to penalise him retrospectively. (See also *Johnston* v *Chief Constable of the Royal Ulster Constabulary* (case 222/84) (ECHR, Article 6, right to judicial process); *Hoechst* (cases 46/87, 227/88); *National Panasonic* v *Commission* (case 136/79) (ECHR Article 8, right to respect for private and family life, home and correspondence — not infringed).)

Thus it seems that any provision in the ECHR may be invoked, provided it is done in the context of a matter of EC law. In *Kaur* v *Lord Advocate* [1980] 3 CMLR 79, Court of Session of Scotland, an attempt was made to invoke the Convention (Article 8 'respect for family life') by an Indian immigrant seeking to challenge a deportation order made under the Immigration Act 1971. She failed on the grounds that the Convention had not been incorporated into British law. Its alleged incorporation via the European Communities Act 1972 did not enable a party to invoke the Convention before a Scottish court in a matter *wholly unrelated to EC law* (see also *SPUC* v *Grogan* (case 159/90) and *Kremzow* v *Austria* (case C–299/95)).

Other international treaties concerned with human rights referred to by the Court as constituting a possible source of general principles are the European Social Charter (1971) and Convention 111 of the International Labour Organisation (1958) (*Defrenne* v *Sabena (No. 3)* (case 149/77)). In *Ministère Public* v *Levy* (case C–158/91) the Court suggested that a Member State might even be obliged to apply a national law which conflicted with a ruling of its own on the interpretation of EC Directive 76/207 where this was necessary to ensure compliance with an international convention (in this case ILO Convention 89, 1948) concluded prior to that State's entry into the EC.

We saw at the beginning of this chapter that one of the central reasons for the introduction of fundamental rights into EC law was the resistance of some of the constitutional courts to giving effect to Community rules which conflicted with national constitutional principles. The ECJ's tactics to incorporate these principles and stave off rebellion were undoubtedly successful as exemplified by the *Wünsche* case ([1987] 3 CMLR 225), in which the German constitutional court resiled from its position in *Internationale Handelsgesellschaft* ([1974] 2 CMLR 540) (see chapter 5). This does not, however, mean that the ECJ can rest on its laurels in this regard. The Italian constitutional court in *Fragd (SpA Fragd v Amministrazione delle Finanze* Decision No. 232 of 21 April 1989) reaffirmed its right to test Community rules against national constitutional rules and stated that Community rules which, in its view, were incompatible with the Italian constitution would not be applied. Similarly, the German constitutional courts have reasserted the right to challenge Community legislation which is inconsistent with the German constitution (see, e.g., *Brunner v European Union Treaty* [1994] 1 CMLR 57; *M GmbH v Bundesregierung* (case 2 BvQ 3/89) [1990] 1 CMLR 570 (the tobacco advertising case) and the bananas cases — *Germany v Council* (Re Banana Regime) (case C–280/93), *Germany v Council* (Bananas II) (case C–122/95) and *T. Port GmbH v Hauptzollamt Hamburg-Jonas* (cases C–364 & 365/95) — discussed further in chapter 5). Although the supremacy of Community law *vis-à-vis* national law might not be threatened by the possibility of its review in accordance with provisions of national constitutions embodying general principles of international law, its uniformity and the supremacy of the ECJ might well be eroded if national courts seek themselves to interpret these broad and flexible principles, rather than referring for a Community ruling on these matters from the ECJ. Equally, a failure on the part of national courts to recognise fundamental principles, in conjunction with a failure to refer, may have a similar effect.

Deferring to the ECJ does, however, concentrate a significant degree of power in that Court, against whose rulings there is no appeal. One suggested safeguard for fundamental rights would be for the Community to accede to the ECHR. Questions of human rights and, in particular, interpretation of the ECHR, could then be taken to the European Court of Human Rights, a court which specialises in these issues. This would minimise the risk of the ECJ misinterpreting the ECHR and avoid the possibility of two conflicting lines of case law developing (e.g. *Orkem* (case 374/87) and *Funke v France* (case SA 256A)). The ECJ, however, has ruled that accession to the ECHR would not be within the present powers of the Community: Treaty amendment would be required before the Community could take this step (*Opinion 2/94* on the *Accession by the Community to the European Convention on Human Rights*). Treaty amendment requires the unanimous agreement of all Member States, which is sometimes difficult to obtain. Certainly, the 1996 IGC failed to incorporate any such reference into the ToA. These matters are again under review, as discussed below.

The ToA was not, however, entirely silent on the subject of the protection of fundamental rights. The TEU had included in the Union general provisions a reference to the ECHR to the effect that, 'The Union shall respect fundamental rights, as guaranteed by the European Convention for the Protection of Human Rights and Fundamental Freedoms . . . and as they result from the constitutional tradition common to the Member States, as general principles of Community law' (Article 6(2) (ex F(2) TEU)). Additionally, Article 6(1) (ex F(1)) TEU stated that the Union was founded on respect for 'liberty, democracy and respect for human rights'. However, by Article L TEU, as it then was (now amended and re-numbered as Article 46 TEU), the ECJ's jurisdiction as regards the general Union provisions was excluded. The ToA amended Article 46 (ex L) TEU to give the ECJ express competence in respect of Article 6(2) (ex F(2)) TEU with regard to action of the institutions 'insofar as the ECJ has jurisdiction either under the treaties establishing the Communities or under the TEU'. This would seem to be little more than a confirmation of the existing position, at least as far as the EC Treaty is concerned.

The ToA also inserted a new Article 7 into the TEU. This provided that where there has been a persistent and serious breach of a principle mentioned in new Article 6(1) TEU, the Council may suspend certain of the rights of the offending Member State, including its voting rights. Were this provision to be used, it could have serious consequences for the Member State in question; such a Member State would lose its opportunity to influence the content of Community legislation by which it would be bound, even in sensitive areas where otherwise it could have vetoed legislation. On this viewpoint, one might suggest that the need to comply with fundamental principles is being taken seriously indeed. It is likely, though, that this provision will be used only rarely given the severity of the breach needed to trigger the procedure which itself is long-winded, requiring unanimity (excluding the offending Member State) in the first instance. Given the potential consequences for Member States, however, the complexity of the procedure is perhaps appropriate. Nonetheless, it does detract from the effectiveness of the procedures.

Despite these difficulties, the general principles of Community law have been expanded through the case law of the ECJ to cover a wide variety of rights and principles developed from many sources. We will now look at some specific examples of those rights. The following is not, however, an exhaustive list, and there may be degrees of overlap between the categories mentioned.

Rules of administrative justice

Proportionality   This was the principle invoked in *Internationale Handelsgesellschaft mbH* (case 11/70). The principle, applied in the context of administrative law, requires that the means used to achieve a given end must be no more than that which is appropriate and necessary to achieve that end. The test thus puts the burden on an administrative authority to justify its actions and requires some consideration of possible alternatives. In this respect it is a more rigorous test than one based on reasonableness.

The principle has been invoked on many occasions as a basis of challenge to EC secondary legislation, often successfully (e.g., *Werner A. Bock KG* v

Commission (case 62/70); *Bela-Mühle Josef Bergmann KG* v *Grows-Farm GmbH & Co. KG* (case 114/76). It was applied in *R* v *Intervention Board for Agricultural Produce, ex parte E.D. & F. Man (Sugar) Ltd* (case 181/84) in the context of a claim by E.D. & F. Man (Sugar) Ltd before the English Divisional Court, on facts very similar to *Internationale Handelsgesellschaft.* Here the claimant, E.D. & F. Man (Sugar) Ltd, was seeking repayment of a security of £1,670,370 forfeited when it failed to comply with an obligation to submit licence applications to the Board within a specified time-limit. Due to an oversight they were a few hours late. The claimant's claim rested on the alleged illegality of the EC Regulations governing the common organisation of the sugar market. The Regulations appeared to require the full forfeiture of the deposit (lodged by the exporter at the time of the initial offer to export) in the event of a breach of both a *primary* obligation to export goods as agreed with the Commission and a *secondary* obligation to submit a licence application following the initial offer within a specified time-limit. The ECJ held, on a reference from the Divisional Court on the validity of the Regulations, that to require the same forfeiture for breach of the secondary obligation as for the primary obligation was disproportionate, and to the extent that the Regulation required such forfeiture, it was invalid. As a result of this ruling, the claimant was held entitled in the Divisional Court to a declaration that the forfeiture of its security was unlawful. A significant victory for the claimant.

The proportionality principle has also been applied in the context of the EC Treaty, for example, in the application of the provisions relating to freedom of movement for goods and persons. Under these provisions States are allowed some scope for derogation from the principle of free movement, but derogations must be 'justified' on one of the grounds provided (Articles 30 (ex 36) and 39(3) (ex 48(3))). This has been interpreted by the ECJ as meaning that the measure must be *no more than is necessary* to achieve the desired objective (see chapters 10 and 11 (goods), 20–23 (persons)).

In *Watson* (case 118/75) the proportionality principle was invoked in the sphere of the free movement of persons in order to challenge the legality of certain action by the Italian authorities. One of the defendants, Ms Watson, was claiming rights of residence in Italy. The right of free movement of workers expressed in Article 39 (ex 48) EC is regarded as a fundamental Community right, subject only to 'limitations' which are 'justified' on the grounds of public policy, public security or public health (Article 39(3) (ex 48(3)). The Italian authorities sought to invoke this derogation to expel Ms Watson from Italy. The reason for the defendants' expulsion was that they had failed to comply with certain administrative procedures, required under Italian law, to record and monitor their movements in Italy. The ECJ, on reference from the Italian court, held that, while States were entitled to impose penalties for non-compliance with their administrative formalities, these must not be disproportionate; and they must never provide a ground for deportation. Here, it is worth noting, it is a Member State's action which was deemed to be illegal for breach of the proportionality principle. Likewise, in *Wijsenbeek* (Case C–378/97) the ECJ held that, although Member States were still entitled to check the documentation of EC nationals moving from one Member State to another, any penalties imposed on those whose documentation was unsatisfactory must be proportionate: in this case, imprisonment for failure to carry a passport was disproportionate. (See further chapter 23.)

Similarly, in the context of goods, in a case brought against Germany in respect of its beer purity laws (case 178/84), a German law imposing an absolute ban on additives was found in breach of EC law (Article 30 (new 28 (ex 30) EC) and not 'justified' on public health grounds under Article 36 (new 30 (ex 36)). Since the same (public health) objective could have been achieved by other less restrictive means, the ban was not 'necessary'; it was disproportionate.

More recently, however, there seems to have been a refinement of the principle of proportionality. In the case of *Südzucker Mannheim/Ocshenfurt AG* v *Hauptzollamt Mannheim* (case C–161/96) the ECJ confirmed the distinction between primary and secondary (or administrative) obligations made in *R* v *Intervention Board for Agricultural Produce* (case 181/84). The breach of a secondary obligation should not be punished as severely as a breach of a primary obligation. On the facts of the case, the ECJ held that a failure to comply with customs formalities by not producing an export licence was a breach of a primary and not a secondary obligation. The ECJ stated that the production of the export licence was necessary to ensure compliance with export requirements and thus the production of the export licence was part of the primary obligation. On this reasoning, it may be difficult to distinguish between primary and secondary obligations.

Further, the ECJ has held that, where an institution has significant discretion in the implementation of policies, such as in CAP, the ECJ may only interfere if the 'measure is manifestly inappropriate having regard to the objectives which the competent institution is seeking to pursue' (*Germany* v *Council (Re Banana Regime)* (case C–280/93), para. 90). The same is also true of actions of Member States where they have a broad discretion in the implementation of Community policy (see *R* v *Minister of Agriculture, Fisheries and Food, ex parte National Federation of Fishermen's Organisations* (case C–44/94)). In these circumstances, the distinction between proportionality and *Wednesbury* reasonableness is not great.

Legal certainty   The principle of legal certainty was invoked by the Court of Justice in *Defrenne* v *Sabena (No. 2)* (case 43/75). The principle, which is one of the widest generality, has been applied in more specific terms as:

(a)   The principle of legitimate expectations.
(b)   The principle of non-retroactivity.

The principle of legitimate expectations, derived from German law, means that, in the absence of an overriding matter of public interest, Community measures must not violate the legitimate expectations of the parties concerned. A legitimate expectation is one which might be held by a reasonable person as to matters likely to occur in the normal course of his affairs. It does not extend to anticipated windfalls or speculative profits. In *Efisol SA* v *Commission* (case T-336/94) the CFI commented that an individual would have no legitimate expectations of a particular state of affairs existing where a 'prudent and discriminating' trader would have foreseen the development in question. Furthermore, in *Germany* v *Council (Re Banana Regime)* (case C–280/93), the ECJ held that no trader may have a legitimate expectation that an existing Community regime will be maintained. In that the principle requires the encouragement of a reasonable expectation, a reliance on that expectation, and some loss resulting from the breach of that expectation, it is similar to the principle of estoppel in English law.

The principle was applied in *August Töpfer & Co. GmbH* v *Commission* (case 112/77) (see chapter 30). August Töpfer & Co. GmbH was an exporter which had applied for, and been granted, a number of export licences for sugar. Under Community law, as part of the common organisation of the sugar market, certain refunds were to be payable on export, the amount of the refunds being fixed in advance. If the value of the refund fell, due to currency fluctuations, the licence holder could apply to have his licence cancelled. This scheme was suddenly altered by an EC Regulation, and the right to cancellation withdrawn, being substituted by provision for compensation. This operated to Töpfer's disadvantage, and it sought to have the Regulation annulled, for breach, *inter alia,* of the principle of legitimate expectations. Although it did not succeed on the merits, the principle of legitimate expectations was upheld by the Court. (See also *CNTA SA* v *Commission* (case 74/74), monetary compensation scheme ended suddenly and without warning: chapter 33.) In *Opel Austria GmbH* v *Council* (case T–115/94) the Court held that the principle of legitimate expectations was the corollary of the principle of good faith in public international law. Thus, where the Community had entered into an obligation and the date of entry into force of that obligation is known to traders, such traders may use the principle of legitimate expectations to challenge measures contrary to any provision of the international agreement having direct effect.

The principle of non-retroactivity, applied to Community secondary legislation, precludes a measure from taking effect before its publication. Retrospective application will only be permitted in exceptional circumstances, where it is necessary to achieve particular objectives and will not breach individuals' legitimate expectations. Such measures must also contain a statement of the reasons justifying the retroactive effect (*Diversinte SA* v *Administración Principal de Aduanos e Impuestos Especiales de la Junqueros* (case C–260/91)).

In *R* v *Kirk* (case 63/83) the principle of non-retroactivity of penal provisions (activated in this case by a Community Regulation) was invoked successfully. However, retroactivity may be acceptable where the retroactive operation of the rule in question improves an individual's position (see, for example, *Road Air BV* v *Inspecteur der Invoerrechten en Accijnzen* (case C–310/95)).

This principle also has relevance in the context of national courts' obligation to interpret domestic law to comply with Community law when it is not directly effective (the *Von Colson* principle, see chapter 4). In *Pretore di Salò* v *Persons Unknown* (case 14/86) in a reference from the Salò magistrates' court on the compatibility of certain Italian laws with EEC Water Purity Directive 78/659, which had been invoked against the defendants in criminal proceedings, the Court held that:

> A Directive cannot of itself have the effect of determining or aggravating the liability in criminal law of persons who act in contravention of the provisions of the Directive.

The Court went further in *Officier van Justitie* v *Kolpinghuis Nijmegen* (case 80/86). Here, in response to a question concerning the scope of national courts' obligation of interpretation under the *von Colson* principle, the Court held that that obligation was 'limited by the general principles of law which form part of Community law and in particular the principles of legal certainty and non-retroactivity'. Thus, where EC law is not directly effective national courts are not required to interpret domestic law to comply with EC law in violation of these principles.

Problems also arise over the temporal effects of ECJ rulings under Article 234 (ex 177). In *Defrenne* v *Sabena (No. 2)* (case 43/75) the Court held that, given the exceptional circumstances, 'important considerations of legal certainty' required that its ruling on the direct effects of the then Article 119 should apply prospectively only. Article 119 (now 141) could not be relied on to support claims concerning pay periods prior to the date of judgment, except as regards workers who had already brought legal proceedings or made an equivalent claim. However, in *Ariete SpA* (case 811/79) and *Meridionale Industria Salumi Srl* (cases 66, 127 & 128/79) the Court affirmed that *Defrenne* was an exceptional case. In a 'normal' case a ruling from the ECJ was retroactive; the Court merely declared the law as it always was. This view was approved in *Barra* (case 309/85). However, in *Blaizot* (case 24/86), a case decided the same day as *Barra,* 'important considerations of legal certainty' again led the Court to limit the effects of its judgment on the lines of *Defrenne.* It came to the same conclusion in *Barber* v *Guardian Royal Exchange Assurance Group* (case 262/88). These cases indicate that in exceptional cases, where the Court introduces some new principle, or where the judgment may have serious effects as regards the past, the Court will be prepared to limit the effects of its rulings. *Kolpinghuis Nijmegen* may now be invoked to support such a view. Nevertheless, the Court did not limit the effect of its judgment in *Francovich* (cases C–6, 9/90) contrary to Advocate-General Mischo's advice, despite the unexpectedness of the ruling and its 'extremely serious financial consequences' for Member States. Nor did it do so in *Marshall (No. 2)* (case C–271/91) when it declared that national courts were obliged, by Article 5 of Directive 76/207 and their general obligation under Article 5 (now 10) EC to ensure that the objectives of the Directives might be achieved, to provide full compensation to persons suffering loss as a result of infringements of the Directive, a matter which could not have been deduced either from the ECJ's case law or from the actual wording of the Directive (see further chapters 25 and 26).

The question of the temporal effect of a ruling from the ECJ under Article 234 (now 177) EC was considered by the Italian constitutional court in *Fragd (SpA Fragd v Amministrazione delle Finanze* Decision No. 232 of 21 April 1989) in the light of another general principle. Although the point did not arise out of the reference in question, the Italian court considered the effect that a ruling under Article 177 (now 234) holding a Community measure void should have on the referring court if the ECJ had held that the ruling would apply for future cases only, excluding the judgment in which it was given. The Italian constitutional court suggested that in the light of the right to judicial protection given under the Italian constitution, such a holding should have effect in the case in which the reference was made. A finding of invalidity with purely prospective effect would offend against this principle and would therefore be unacceptable.

Procedural rights   Where a person's rights are likely to be affected by EC law, EC secondary legislation normally provides for procedural safeguards (e.g., Regulation 17/62, competition law, chapter 17; Directive 64/221, free movement of workers, chapter 22; Directive 76/207, Article 6, equal treatment for men and women, chapter 25). However, where such provision does not exist, or where there are lacunae, general principles of law may be invoked to fill those gaps.

Natural justice: the right to a hearing   The right to natural justice, and in particular the right to a fair hearing, was invoked, this time from English law, in *Transocean Marine Paint Association* v *Commission* (case 17/74) by Advocate-General Warner. The case, which arose in the context of EC competition law (see chapter 17), was an action for annulment of the Commission's Decision, addressed to the claimant association, that their agreements were in breach of EC law. The Court, following Advocate-General Warner's submissions, asserted a general rule that a person whose interests are perceptibly affected by a decision taken by a public authority must be given the opportunity to make his views known. Since the Commission had failed to comply with this obligation its Decision was annulled. The principle was affirmed in *Hoffman-La Roche & Co. AG* v *Commission* (case 85/76), in which the Court held that observance of the right to be heard is, in all proceedings in which sanctions, in particular fines and periodic payments, may be imposed, a fundamental principle of Community law which must be respected even if the proceedings in question are administrative proceedings.

Another aspect of the right to a fair hearing is the notion of 'equality of arms'. This is exemplified in a series of cases against the Commission following a Commission investigation into alleged anti-competitive behaviour on the part of ICI and another company, Solvay. In the *Solvay* case (case T–30/91) the Court stated that the principle of equality of arms presupposed that both the Commission and the defendant company had equal knowledge of the files used in the proceeding. That was not the case here, as the Commission had not informed Solvay of the existence of certain documents. The Commission argued that this did not affect the proceedings because the documents would not be used in the company's defence. The Court took the view that this was not for the Commission to decide, as this would give the Commission more power *vis-à-vis* the defendant company because it had full knowledge of the file whereas the defendant did not. Equally, in the *ICI* cases (T–36 & 37/91) the Commission's refusal to grant ICI access to the file was deemed to infringe the rights of the defence.

There are, however, limits to the rights of the defence: in *Descom Scales Manufacturing Co. Ltd.* v *Council* (case T–171/94), the ECJ held that the rights of the defence do not require the Commission to provide a written record of every stage of the investigation detailing information which needed still to be verified. In this case, the Commission had notified the defendant company of the position although it had not provided a written record and the ECJ held that this was sufficient.

The right to a hearing within Article 6 ECHR also includes the right to a hearing within a reasonable period of time. The ECJ, basing its reasoning on Article 6 ECHR, thus held that, in respect of a case that had been pending before the CFI for five years and six months, the CFI had been in violation of its obligation to dispose of cases within a reasonable time (*Baustahlgewerbe* v *Commission* (case C–185/95 P)).

The duty to give reasons   The duty was affirmed in *Union Nationale des Entraîneurs et Cadres Techniques Professionels du Football (UNECTEF)* v *Heylens* (case 222/86). In this case, M. Heylens, a Belgian and a professional football trainer, was the defendant in a criminal action brought by the French football trainers' union, UNECTEF, as a result of his practising in Lille as a professional trainer without the necessary French diploma, or any qualifications recognised by the French government as equivalent. M. Heylens held a Belgian football trainers' diploma, but his application for recognition of this diploma by the French authorities had been rejected on the basis of an adverse opinion from a special committee, which gave no reasons for its decision. The ECJ, on a reference from the Tribunal de Grande Instance, Lille, held that the right of free movement of workers, granted by the then Article 48 (now 39) EC, required that a decision refusing to recognise the equivalence of a qualification issued in another Member State should be subject to legal redress which would enable the legality of that decision to be established with regard to Community law, and that the person concerned should be informed of the reasons upon which the decision was based.

Similarly in *Al-Jubail Fertiliser Company (SAMAD)* v *Council* (case C–49/88) in the context of a challenge to a Council Regulation imposing anti-dumping duties on the import of products manufactured by the applicants, the Court held that since the applicants had a right to a fair hearing the Community institutions were under a duty to supply them with all the information which would enable them effectively to defend their interests. Moreover if the information is supplied orally, as it may be, the Commission must be able to prove that it was in fact supplied.

The right to due process   As a corollary to the right to be informed of the reasons for a decision is the right, alluded to in *UNECTEF* v *Heylens* (case

222/86), to legal redress to enable such decisions and reasons to be challenged. This right was established in *Johnston v Chief Constable of the Royal Ulster Constabulary* (case 222/84). The case arose from a refusal by the RUC to renew its contracts with women members of the RUC Reserve. This decision had been taken as a result of a policy decision taken in 1980 that henceforth full-time RUC Reserve members engaged on general police duties should be fully armed. For some years women had not been issued with firearms nor trained in their use. Ms Johnston, who had been a full-time member of the Reserve for some years and wished to renew her contract, challenged the decision as discriminatory, in breach of EC Directive 76/207, which provides for equal treatment for men and women in all matters relating to employment. Although the measure was admittedly discriminatory, since it was taken solely on the grounds of sex, the Chief Constable claimed that it was justified, arguing from the 'public policy and public security' derogation of the then Articles 36 (now 30) (goods, see chapter 11) and 48 (now 39) (workers, see chapter 22), and from then Article 224 (now 297), which provides for the taking of measures in the event of, *inter alia,* 'serious internal disturbances affecting the maintenance of law and order'. As evidence that these grounds were made out the Chief Constable produced before the industrial tribunal a certificate issued by the Secretary of State certifying that the act refusing to offer Ms Johnston further employment in the RUC Reserve was done for the purpose of safeguarding national security and safeguarding public order. Under Article 53(2) of the Sex Discrimination (Northern Ireland) Order 1976 (SI 1976/1042) a certificate that an act was done for that purpose was 'conclusive evidence' that it was so done. A number of questions were referred to the ECJ by the industrial tribunal on the scope of the public order derogation and the compatibility of the Chief Constable's decision with Directive 76/207. The question of the Secretary of State's certificate and the possibility of judicial review were not directly raised. Nevertheless this was the first matter seized upon by the Court. The Court considered the requirement of judicial control, provided by Article 6 of Directive 76/207, which requires States to enable persons who 'consider themselves wronged' to 'pursue their claims by judicial process after possible recourse to the competent authorities'. This provision, the Court said, reflected:

> a general principle of law which underlies the constitutional traditions common to the Member States. That principle is also laid down in Articles 6 and 13 of the European Convention for the Protection of Human Rights and Fundamental Freedoms . . . .
>
> It is for the Member States to ensure effective judicial control as regards compliance with the applicable provisions of Community law and of national legislation intended to give effect to the rights for which the Directive provides.

The Court went on to say that Article 53(2) of the Sex Discrimination (Northern Ireland) Order 1976, in requiring the Secretary of State's certificate to be treated as conclusive evidence that the conditions for derogation are fulfilled, allowed the competent authority to deprive an individual of the possibility of asserting by judicial process the rights conferred by the Directive. Such a provision was contrary to the principle of effective judicial control laid down in Article 6 of the Directive. A similar approach has, in fact, been taken by the European Court of Human Rights in relation to such certificates issued in relation to a variety of substantive issues (e.g., *Tinnelly and Others* v *UK*, ECHR judgment, 10 July 1998).

Although the ECJ's decision was taken in the context of a right provided by the Directive it is submitted that the right to effective judicial control enshrined in the European Convention on Human Rights and endorsed in this case could be invoked in any case in which a person's Community rights have been infringed. The case of *UNECTEF* v *Heylens* (case 222/86) would serve to support this proposition. Further, the CFI has held that the Commission, in exercising its competition policy powers, must give reasons sufficient to allow the Court's review of the Commission's decision-making process, if that decision is challenged (e.g., *Ufex* v *Commission* (case C–119/97P)).

Thus general principles of law act as a curb not only on the institutions of the Community but also on Member States, which are required, in the context of EC law, to accommodate these principles alongside existing remedies and procedures within their own domestic systems of administrative law. This may result eventually in some modification in national law itself. In *Council of Civil Service Unions* v *Minister for the Civil Service* [1985] AC 374, HL, Lord Diplock, in considering the question of judicial review of the exercise of prerogative powers (resulting, in that case, in the exclusion of trade union membership), alluded to the question of 'legitimate expectations', and even 'the possible adoption in the future of the principle of "proportionality" which is recognised in the administrative law of several of our fellow members of the European Economic Community'. However, hopes that the principle of proportionality would be adopted as a principle of English administrative law were dashed in *R* v *Secretary of State for the Home Department, ex parte Brind* [1991] 1 AC 696, when the House of Lords (Lord Templeman excepted) refused to take 'the first step' in this direction. Lord Bridge and Lord Roskill did not, however, rule out the possibility of 'further development of the law in this respect'. To date, neither proportionality nor any other general principle of Community law has been accepted by British courts as applicable in the purely domestic context, although they have been applied in the context of claims involving Community law (see, e.g., Sedley J in *R* v *Ministry of Agriculture, Fisheries and Food, ex parte Hamble Fisheries (Offshore) Ltd* [1995] 1 CMLR 533, Laws J in *R* v *Ministry of Agriculture, Fisheries and Foods, ex parte First City Trading Ltd* [1997] 1 CMLR 250, and now Lords Slynn and Cooke in *R* v *Chief Constable of Sussex, ex parte International Traders Ferry Ltd* [1999] 2 CMLR 1320). There are, however, problems in determining the boundaries between matters of purely national law and matters of Community law (see further below).

Right to protection against self-incrimination   The right to a fair trial and the presumption of innocence of 'persons charged with a criminal offence' contained in Article 6 ECHR are undoubtedly rights which will be protected as general principles of law under Community law. However, in *Orkem* (case 374/87) and *Solvay* (case 27/88) the ECJ held that the right under Article 6 not to give evidence against oneself applied only to persons charged with an offence in criminal proceedings; it was not a principle which could be relied on in relation to infringements in the economic sphere, in order to resist a demand for information such as may be made by the EC Commission to establish a breach of EC competition law (see chapter 17). This view has now been placed in doubt following a ruling from the Court of Human Rights in the case of *Funke* v *France* (case SA 256A) [1993] 1 CMLR 897.

This case involved a claim, for breach of Article 6 ECHR, in respect of a demand by the French customs' authorities for information designed to obtain evidence of currency and capital transfer offences. Following the applicant's refusal to hand over such information fines and penalties were imposed. The European Court of Human Rights held that such action, undertaken as a 'fishing expedition' in order to obtain documents which, if found, might produce evidence for a prosecution, infringed the right, protected by Article 6(1) ECHR, of anyone charged with a criminal offence (within the autonomous meaning of that phrase in Article 6 ECHR), to remain silent and not incriminate himself. Thus it appears that Article 6, according to its 'autonomous meaning', is wide enough to apply to investigations conducted under the Commission's search and seizure powers under EC competition law, and that *Orkem* and *Solvay* may no longer be regarded as good law. This view, assimilating administrative penalties to criminal penalties, appears to have been taken by the ECJ in *Otto BV* v *Postbank NV* (case C-60/92).

Equality

The principle of equality means, in its broadest sense, that persons in similar situations are not to be treated differently unless the difference in treatment is objectively justified. This, of course, gives rise to the question of what are similar situations. Discrimination can only exist within a framework in which it is possible to draw comparisons, for example, the framework of race, sex, nationality, colour, religion. The equality principle will not apply in situations which are deemed to be 'objectively different' (see *Les Assurances du Crédit SA* v *Council* (case C-63/89) — public export credit insurance operations different from other export credit insurance operations). What situations are regarded as comparable, subject to the equality principle, is clearly a matter of political judgment. The EC Treaty expressly prohibits discrimination on the grounds of nationality (Article 12 (ex 6) EC) and, to a limited extent, sex (Article 141 (ex 119) EC provides for equal *pay* for men and women for equal work). In the field of agricultural policy, Article 34(3) (ex 40(3)) prohibits 'discrimination between producers or consumers within the Community'. The ToA introduced further provisions, giving the EC powers to regulate against discrimination on grounds of race, religion, sexual orientation or disability (Article 13 EC) and directives have been proposed under this article. However, a general principle of equality is clearly wider in scope than these provisions. In the first isoglucose case, *Royal Scholten-Honig (Holdings) Ltd* v *Intervention Board for Agricultural Produce* (cases 103 & 145/77), the claimants, who were glucose producers, together with other glucose producers, sought to challenge the legality of a system of production subsidies whereby sugar producers were receiving subsidies financed in part by levies on the production of glucose. Since glucose and sugar producers were in competition with each other the claimants argued that the Regulations implementing the system were discriminatory, i.e., in breach of the general principle of equality, and therefore invalid. The ECJ, on a reference on the validity of the Regulations from the English court, agreed. The Regulations were held invalid. (See also *Ruckdeschel* (case 117/76); *Pont-à-Mousson* (cases 124/76 & 20/77).)

Similarly, the principle of equality was invoked in the case of *Airola* (case 21/74) to challenge a rule which was discriminatory on grounds of sex (but not pay), and in *Prais* (case 130/75) to challenge alleged discrimination on the grounds of religion. Neither case at the time fell within the more specific provisions of Community law.

Subsidiarity

The principle of subsidiarity in its original philosophical meaning, as expressed by Pope Pius XI (Encyclical letter, 1931), that

> It is an injustice, a grave evil and disturbance of right order for a larger and higher association to arrogate to itself functions which can be performed efficiently by smaller and lower societies

was invoked in the Community context during the 1980s when the Community's competence was about to be extended under the Single European Act. It was incorporated into that Act, in rather different form, in respect of environmental measures, in the then Article 130r (now 174) EC, and introduced into the EC Treaty in Article 3b by the TEU. Article 3b (now 5) EC requires the Community to act:

> only if and so far as the objectives of the proposed action cannot be sufficiently achieved by the Member States, and can therefore, by reason of the scale or the effects of the proposed action, be better achieved by the Community.

Thus, as expressed in Article 5 (ex 3b) EC, subsidiarity appears to be a test of comparative efficiency; as such it lacks its original philosophical meaning, concerned with fostering social responsibility. This latter meaning has however been retained in Article A 1 (ex A) TEU, which provides that decisions of the European Union 'be taken as closely as possible to the people'. Although it has not been incorporated into the EC Treaty it is submitted that this version of the principle of subsidiarity could be invoked as a general principle of law if not as a basis to challenge EC law at least as an aid to the interpretation of Article 5 (ex 3b) EC (see chapter 3).

General principles applied to national legislation

It has been suggested that general principles of law, incorporated by the ECJ as part of Community law, also affect certain acts of the Member States. These fall into three broad categories:

(a)   when EC rights are enforced within national courts;
(b)   when the rules of a Member State are in (permitted) derogation from a fundamental principle of Community law, such as free movement of goods (Articles 25 and 28 (ex 12 and 30) EC) or persons (Articles 39 and 49 (ex 48 and 59)); and
(c)   when the Member State is acting as an agent of the Community in implementing Community law (e.g., *Klensch* v *Secrétaire d'État à l'Agriculture et à la Viticulture* (cases 201 & 202/85)).

Enforcement of Community law in national courts   The ECJ has repeatedly held that, in enforcing Community rights, national courts must respect procedural rights guaranteed in international law; for example, individuals must have a right of access to the appropriate court and the right to a fair hearing (see, e.g., *Johnston* v *RUC* (case 222/84) and *UNECTEF* v *Heylens* (case 222/86)). This applies, however, only where the rights which the individual seeks to enforce are derived from *Community* sources: Ms Johnston relied on the Equal Treatment Directive (Directive 76/207); M. Heylens on the right of freedom of movement for workers enshrined in the then Article 48 (now 39) EC. Likewise, any penalties imposed by national judicial bodies must be proportionate (e.g. *Watson and Belmann* (case 118/75)).

Derogation from fundamental principles   Most Treaty rules provide for some derogation in order to protect important public interests (e.g., Articles 30 (ex 36) and 39(3) (ex 48(3))). The ECJ has insisted that any derogation from the fundamental principles of Community law must be narrowly construed. When Member States do derogate, their rules may be reviewed in the light of general principles, as the question of whether the derogation is within permitted limits is one of Community law. Most, if not all, treaty derogations are subject to the principle of proportionality (e.g., *Watson* (case 118/75)). The *ERT* case (*Elliniki Radiophonia Tileorassi AE* v *Dimotiki Etairia Pliroforissis* (case C–260/89)) concerned the establishment by the Greek government of a monopoly broadcaster. The ECJ held that this would be contrary to the then Article 59 (now 49) regarding the freedom to provide services. Although the treaty provides for derogation from Article 49 (ex 59) in Articles 46 and 55 (ex 56 and 66), any justification provided for by Community law must be interpreted in the light of fundamental rights, in this case the principle of freedom of expression embodied in Article 10 ECHR. Similarly, in *Vereinigte Familiapress Zeitungsverlags- und vertriebs GmbH* v *Heinrich Bauer Verlag* (case

C–368/95), the need to ensure plurality of the media (based on Article 10 ECHR) was accepted as a possible reason justifying a measure (the prohibition of prize games and lotteries in magazines) which would otherwise breach the then Article 30 (now 28) EC.

State acting as Agent   When Member States implement Community rules, either by legislative act or as administrators for the Community, they must not infringe fundamental rights. Thus national rules may be challenged on this basis: for example, in *Commission* v *Germany* (case 249/86), the Commission challenged Germany' s rules enforcing Regulation 1612/86 which permitted the family of a migrant worker to install themselves with the worker in a host country provided that the worker has housing available for the family of a standard comparable with that of similarly employed national workers. Germany enforced this in such a way as to make the residence permit of the family conditional on the existence of appropriate housing for the duration of the stay. The ECJ interpreted the Regulation as requiring this only in respect of the beginning of their period of residence. Since the Regulation had to be interpreted in the light of Article 8 ECHR concerning respect for family life, a fundamental principle recognised by Community law, German law was incompatible with Community law. Thus when Member States are implementing obligations contained in Community law, they must do so without offending against any fundamental rights recognised by the Community. In *Wachauf* v *Germany* (case 5/88)) the ECJ held that:

> Since those requirements are also binding on the Member States when they implement Community rules, the Member States must, as far as possible, apply those rules in accordance with those requirements (para. 19).

In all three situations listed above, general principles have an impact because the situations fall *within the scope* of Community law. The ECJ has no power to examine the compatibility with the ECHR of national rules which do not fall therein (*Cinéthèque SA* v *Fédération Nationale des Cinémas Françaises* (cases 60 & 61/84)). The problem lies in defining the boundary between Community law and purely domestic law. The scope of Community law could be construed very widely, as evidenced by the approach of the Advocate-General in *Konstantinidis* v *Stadt Altensteig-Standesamt* (case C–168/91). There, he suggested that, as the applicant had exercised his right of free movement under the then Article 52 (now 43) EC, national provisions affecting him fell within the scope of Community law; therefore he was entitled to the protection of his human rights by the ECJ. The Court has not gone this far and seems, in recent cases, to be taking a more cautious approach than hitherto. This can be illustrated by contrasting two cases which arose out of similar circumstances: *Wachauf* v *Germany* (case 5/88) and *R* v *Ministry of Agriculture, Fisheries and Food, ex parte Bostock* (case C–2/93).

Wachauf was a tenant farmer who, upon the expiry of his tenancy, requested compensation arising out of the loss of 'reference quantities' on the discontinuance of milk production. When this was refused, he claimed that this was an infringement of his right to private property, protected under the German constitution. The German authorities claimed that the rules they applied were required by the Community Regulation, but the ECJ held that on its proper interpretation the Regulation required no such thing: although the Regulation did not itself provide the right to compensation, equally it did not preclude it. The discretion thereby given to the Member States by the Regulation should be exercised in accordance with fundamental rights, thus, in practice meaning that the applicant should receive the compensation.

Bostock similarly had been a tenant farmer. Following *Wachauf* (case 5/88) he argued that he too should be entitled to compensation for the value of the reference quantities on the expiry of his lease. Unlike the situation in Germany, though, this right was not protected by British law at the time when Bostock's lease ended. Bostock therefore sought to challenge that British law on the basis that the provisions breached general principles of non-discrimination and unjust enrichment. Despite its approach in *Wachauf*, the ECJ ruled that the right to property protected by the Community legal order did not include the right to dispose of the 'reference quantities' for profit. Furthermore, the ECJ held that the question of unjust enrichment, as part of the legal relations between lessor and lessee, was a matter for national law and therefore fell outside the scope of Community law.

It is difficult to reconcile these two cases. One clear message seems to be that there are limits to the circumstances when general principles will operate and that a challenge to national acts for breach of a general principle is likely to be successful only when national authorities are giving effect to clear obligations of *Community* law. In matters falling within the discretion of Member States, national authorities are not required to recognise general principles not protected by that State's national laws. With the incorporation of the ECHR into British law, as proposed by the current Labour government, these principles will become part of domestic law, but their impact will depend on the terms of their incorporation and their interpretation by the British courts.

Relationship between the EC/EU and the ECHR in the protection of human rights

All Member States of the EU have signed the ECHR, and in most Member States, the Convention has been incorporated into domestic law. (It was incorporated in the UK by the Human Rights Act 1998, which is due to come into force in October 2000.) When it is so incorporated, the Convention's provisions may be invoked before the domestic courts in order to challenge *national* rules or procedures which infringe the rights protected by the Convention. Even without the Convention being incorporated into domestic law, the Member States are bound by its terms and individuals, after they have exhausted national remedies, have a right of appeal under the Convention to the European Court of Human Rights.

As the preceding pages demonstrate, the ECJ has done a great deal to ensure the protection of human rights within the context of the application of Community law, whether by Community institutions or by Member States. But, as the ECHR has not so far been incorporated into *Community* law, its scope has been limited and the relationship between the ECHR and the Union legal system is somewhat unclear. The difficulties are illustrated by the decision of the European Court of Human Rights in the *Matthews* case (ECHR judgment, 18 February 1999).

Matthews concerned the rights of UK nationals resident in Gibraltar to vote in European Parliamentary elections. They were excluded from participating in the elections as a result of the 1979 agreement between the Member States which established direct elections in respect of the European Parliament. The applicants argued that this was contrary to Protocol 1, Article 3 of the ECHR, which provides that signatory States to the Convention are under an obligation 'to hold free elections at reasonable intervals by secret ballot, under conditions which will ensure the free expression of the opinion of the people in the choice of the legislature'. The British government argued that not only was Community law not within the jurisdiction of the ECHR (as the Community had not acceded to the Convention), but also that the UK government could not be held responsible for joint acts of the Member States. The European Court of Human Rights found, however, that there had been a violation of the Convention.

The Court held that States which are party to the ECHR retain residual obligations in respect of the rights protected by the Convention, even as regards areas of law-making which had been transferred to the Union. Such a transfer of power is permissible, provided Convention rights continue to be secured within the Community framework. In this context the Court of Human Rights noted the ECJ's jurisprudence in which the ECJ recognised and protected Convention rights. In this case, however, the existence of the direct elections was based on a *sui generis* international instrument entered into by the UK and the other Member States which could not be challenged before the ECJ, as it was not a normal Community act. Furthermore, the TEU, which extended the European Parliament's powers to include the right to co-decision thereby increasing the Parliament's claim to be considered a legislature and taking it within the terms of Protocol 1, Article 3 of the ECHR, was equally an act which could not be challenged before the ECJ. There could therefore be no protection of Convention rights in this regard by the ECJ. Arguing that the Convention is intended to guarantee rights that are not theoretical or illusory, the Court of Human Rights held that:

> The United Kingdom, together with all other parties to the Maastricht Treaty, is responsible *ratione materiae* under Article 1 of the Convention and, in particular, under Article 3 of Protocol 1, for the consequences of that Treaty. (para. 33)

It may be noted that it is implicit in the reasoning in this judgment that the EU is regarded by the Court of Human Rights as being the creature of the

Member States, which remain fundamentally responsible for the Community's actions — and those of the Union. This corresponds with the conception of the EU expressed by some of the Member States' constitutional courts (e.g., see the German constitutional court's reasoning in *Brunner* [1994] 1 CMLR 57).

Arguably, this judgment opens the way for the Member States to be held jointly responsible for those Community (or Union) acts that currently fall outside the jurisdiction of the ECJ, thus sealing lacunae in the protection offered to individual human rights within the Community legal order. The difficulty is, of course, that in this case only the UK was the defendant. The British government is thus dependent on the cooperation of the other Member States to enable it to fulfil its own obligations under the ECHR. It is possible that a case could be brought under the ECHR against all Member States jointly. Although this would not obviate the need for cooperation to remedy any violation found, this would avoid the situation where one Member State alone was carrying the responsibility for Union measures that were the choice of all Member States.

The implication that the Court of Human Rights will step in only where there is no effective means of securing human rights protection within an existing international body (i.e., that the ECJ has primary responsibility for these issues in the EU) is underlined by its approach in another case involving another European supranational organisation, Euratom (*Waite and Kennedy* v *Germany*, ECHR judgment 18 February 1999). There the Court emphasised the necessity for an independent review board which is capable of protecting fundamental rights to exist within the organisational structure.

The timing of these judgments is interesting, as the Member States are currently debating whether to introduce a Union Charter of Rights. As noted earlier, there has been some discussion as to whether the EC should accede to the ECHR. An alternative proposal is the creation of a Union Charter of Fundamental Rights. As well as seeking to enumerate European citizens' rights (and to protect them), the latter would represent a further step in the constitutionalisation of the Union. Although it was hoped that the Charter would be agreed in time for the 2000 IGC, there are some difficulties. In particular, it is not clear whether it is intended that the Charter should be legally binding or have merely declaratory status. Furthermore, will the ECJ have jurisdiction to rule on questions of interpretation? Lastly, how will the Charter interrelate with the ECHR itself? Unsurprisingly, different Member States, and different interest groups within the Union, take different stances on these issues, making agreement on anything but the most anodyne document unlikely.

Conclusions

The cases outlined above illustrate the importance of general principles of law in the judicial protection of individual rights. Member States' commitment to fundamental human rights has now been acknowledged in Article 6 (ex F) TEU. Nonetheless, certain points should be noted.

The fact that a particular principle is upheld by the ECJ and appears to be breached does not automatically lead to a decision in favour of the claimant. Fundamental rights are not absolute rights. As the Court pointed out in *J. Nold KG* v *Commission* (case 4/73), rights of this nature are always subject to limitations laid down in the public interest, and, in the Community context, limits justified by the overall objectives of the Community (e.g., *O'Dwyer* v *Council* (cases T–466, 469, 473–4 & 477/93)). The pursuit of these objectives can result in some hard decisions (e.g., *Dowling* v *Ireland* (case C–85/90), although the Court has held that it may not constitute a 'disproportionate and intolerable interference, impairing the very substance of those rights' (*Wachauf* (case 5/88) at para. 18). This principle was applied in *Germany* v *Commission (Re Banana Regime)* (case C–280/93), para. 78, another harsh decision.

Thus, where the objectives are seen from the Community standpoint to be essential, individual rights must yield to the common good. In *J. Nold KG* v *Commission* the system set up under an ECSC provision whereby Nold, as a small-scale wholesaler, would be deprived of the opportunity, previously enjoyed, to buy direct from the producer, to its commercial disadvantage, was held to be necessary in the light of the system's overall economic objectives. 'The disadvantages claimed by the applicant', held the Court, 'are in fact the result of economic change and not of the contested Decision'.

A similar example is provided in *Walter Rau Lebensmittelwerke* v *Commission* (case 279, 280, 285 & 286/84). Here the claimants were a group of margarine producers. They were seeking damages for losses suffered as a result of the Commission's 'Christmas butter' policy. This was an attempt to reduce the 'butter mountain' (surplus stocks acquired as a result of the Community's system of intervention buying under the common agricultural policy (CAP) by selling butter stocks at greatly reduced prices to certain groups of the population over the Christmas period. As a basis for their claim the claimants alleged that the Regulations implementing the Christmas butter policy were in breach of the principles of equality and proportionality. Since margarine and butter are clearly in competition with each other it might have been imagined that, following the first isoglucose cases (e.g., *Royal Scholten-Honig Holdings Ltd* v *Intervention Board for Agricultural Produce* (cases 103 & 145/77), they had a good chance of success. But they failed. The Court held that the measure must be assessed with regard to the general objectives of the organisation of the butter market:

> . . . taking into consideration the objective differences which characterised the legal mechanisms and the economic conditions of the market concerned, the producers of milk and butter on the one hand and the producers of oils and fats and margarine manufacturers on the other, are not in comparable situations.

The measures were no more than was necessary to achieve the desired objective.

This latitude shown to the Community institutions, particularly where they are exercising discretionary powers in pursuit of common Community policies (most notably the CAP) does not always extend to Member States in their implementation of Community law. Where Member States are permitted a certain discretion in implementation (and Member States have little discretion as regards the ends to be achieved), the Court will not substitute its own evaluation for that of the Member State: it will restrict itself solely to the question of whether there was a patent error in the Member State's action (*R* v *Minister of Agriculture, Fisheries and Food, ex parte National Federation of Fishermen's Organisations* (case C–44/94)). Otherwise, general principles of law are strictly enforced. Thus under the guise of the protection of individual rights general principles of law also serve as a useful (and concealed) instrument of policy. It is for this reason that some Member States may be reluctant to agree to a legally binding Union Charter of Fundamental Rights, since it would result in a significant enlargement of the ECJ's jurisdiction.

Further reading

Alston, P., *The EU and Human Rights* (OUP, 1999).

Canor, I., '*Primus inter pares*. Who is the Ultimate Guardian of Fundamental Rights in Europe?' (2000) 25 EL Rev 57.

De Búrca, G., 'Fundamental Human Rights and the Reach of EC Law' (1993) 13 Oxford J Legal Stud 283.

Jowell, J. and Lester, A., 'Beyond *Wednesbury*: Substantive Principles of Administrative Law' [1987] PL 368.

Krogsgaard, L., 'Fundamental Rights in the EC after Maastricht' [1993] LIEI 99.

Mancini, G. F. 'The Making of a Constitution for Europe' (1989) 26 CML Rev 594.

McGoldrick, D., 'The European Union after Amsterdam: An Organisation with General Human Rights Competence' in O'Keeffe, D. and Twomey, P. (eds), *Legal Issues of the Amsterdam Treaty* (Hart Publishing, 1999).

Mendelson, M., 'The European Court of Justice and Human Rights' (1981) 1 YEL 126.

Riley, A., '*Saunders* and the Power to Obtain Information in European Community and United Kingdom Competition Law' (2000) 25 EL Rev 264.

Schermers, H., 'The European Community Bound by Fundamental Human Rights' (1990) 27 CML Rev 249.

Schermers, H., 'The Scales in Balance: National Constitutional Court v Court of Justice' (1990) 27 CML Rev 97.

Schermers, H.G., *The Protection of Human Rights in the European Community* (Zentrum für Europäisches Wirtschaftsrecht, Vortäge und Berichte 36) (1994).

Schwarze, J., 'Tendencies towards a Common Administrative Law in Europe' (1991) 16 EL Rev 3.

Sharpston, E., 'Legitimate Expectations and Economic Reality' (1990) 15 EL Rev 103.

Twomey, P., 'The European Union: Three Pillars without a Human Rights Foundation' in D. O'Keeffe & P. Twomey (eds), *Legal Issues of the Maastricht Treaty* (Chancery Publications, 1993).

Usher, J.A., *General Principles of EC Law* (Longmans, 1998).

Weiler, J., 'Eurocracy and Distrust: Some Questions Concerning the Role of the European Court of Justice in the Protection of Fundamental Human Rights within the Legal Order of the European Communities' (1986) 61 Wash L Rev 1103.

Weiler, J.H.H., 'Fundamental Rights and Fundamental Boundaries: on Standards and Values in the Protection of Human Rights' in Neuwahl, N.A., *The European Union and Rights* (1995).

Weiler, J.H.H., and Lockhart, N. J. S., '"Taking Rights Seriously" Seriously?' (1995) 32 CML Rev 51, 579.

PART TWO

Economic and Social Law of the EC: Aspects of The Internal Market

SEVEN

Introduction

The law relating to the free movement of goods is one of the principal pillars of the internal market, defined in Article 14 (ex 7a) EC, originally Article 8a of the EEC Treaty, as:

> an area without internal frontiers in which the free movement of goods, persons, services and capital is ensured in accordance with the provisions of this Treaty.

The concept of the internal market, introduced by the Single European Act 1986, replaced the popular term 'common market' coined for the original EEC.

The principle of freedom of movement of goods has been described as a fundamental freedom, the 'corner-stone' of the Community. For most Member States the opportunity of access for their goods to a single, Community-wide market was, and remains, a primary reason for membership. The aim of the free movement provisions of the Treaty was to create within the Member States of the Community a single market, free of all internal restrictions on trade, based on a system of free competition. The free play of market forces within that larger market would increase economic efficiency, widen consumer choice, and enhance the Community's competitiveness in world markets. However, since the principle of freedom of movement was intended to apply to all goods, including goods imported from outside the Community, it was necessary to eliminate distortions of competition resulting from different national rules regulating trade with third countries by presenting a common commercial front to the outside world. To achieve these goals the Treaty sought:

(a)   To establish a *customs union* which shall involve (Article 23 (ex 9)) EC):

(i)   'the prohibition between Member States of customs duties on imports and exports and of all charges having equivalent effect', and

(ii) 'the adoption of a common customs tariff in their relations with third countries'.

(b) The elimination of quantitative restrictions on imports and exports and all measures having equivalent effect (Articles 28 and 29 (ex 30 and 34)) EC).

In addition States were required:

(c) To adjust any State monopolies of a commercial character so as to ensure that . . . no discrimination regarding the conditions under which goods are procured and marketed exists between nationals of Member States (Article 31 (ex 37) EC).

The provisions relating to the free movement of goods apply to both industrial and agricultural products (save, where agriculture is concerned, as otherwise provided in Articles 33–38 (ex 39–46) EC (Article 32(2) (ex 38(2)), whether originating in Member States or coming from third countries which are in free circulation in Member States, even where, in the latter case, the goods have been admitted to the original State of import under special dispensation from the Commission under Article 134 (ex 115) EC (*Levy* (case 212/88)). Products coming from third countries are regarded as in free circulation in a Member State 'if the import formalities have been complied with and any customs duties or charges having equivalent effect which are payable have been levied in that Member State, and if they have not benefited from a total or partial drawback of such duties or charges' (Article 24 (ex 10(1)) EC).

Though the terms are used interchangeably, 'goods' and 'products' are not defined in the Treaty. They were interpreted by the ECJ in *Commission v Italy (re Export Tax on Art Treasures)* (case 7/68) as anything capable of money valuation and of being the object of commercial transactions. In *R v Thompson* (case 7/78) they were held to include collectors' coins in gold and silver, provided they were not coins in circulation as legal tender. The latter are covered by the provisions of the Treaty relating to capital (new Article 56 (ex 73) EC, see *Bordessa* (cases C–358 & 416/93)). In *Commission v Ireland Re Dundalk Water Supply* (case 45/87) the concept of goods was held to apply not only to the sale of goods *per se* but to goods and materials supplied in the context of the provision of services. However, where goods are supplied in the context of the provision of services, in order to fall within the goods provisions of the Treaty, the importation or exportation of the goods in question must be an end in itself. Materials such as advertisements or tickets, supplied simply as an adjunct to a service, for example, a lottery, will fall within the provisions governing services, namely Articles 49 and 50 (ex 59 and 60) EC (*Her Majesty's Customs and Excise v Schindler* (case C 275/92), see chapter 21). The cases involving advertising of goods, especially those concerning broadcast advertising, illustrate the narrow boundary between goods and services (see, e.g., *de Agostini*, cases C–34–36/94, discussed further in chapters 10 and 21). In cases of doubt it is advisable to invoke both goods and services provisions.

Although the free movement provisions are addressed to Member States all the main Articles have been found to be directly effective and thus may be invoked by individuals, whether in dispute with the State or with another individual.

Because of the fundamental importance of the principle of free movement of goods the Treaty rules in this area have been strictly enforced, and exceptions, where provided, have been given the narrowest scope. In interpreting the rules the ECJ looks not to the name of a particular national measure, nor the motive for its introduction, but to its *effect* in the light of the aims of the Treaty; does it create an obstacle to the free movement of goods within the single internal market?

Interpreted in this way, many national measures, not overtly or intentionally protectionist, designed to achieve the most worthy objectives, have been found to be capable of hindering trade between Member States, prima facie in breach of Community law. Such measures, as will be seen, have nevertheless been permitted by the Court on an *ad hoc* basis where they could be proved to be 'objectively justified' as necessary to safeguard vital interests ('mandatory requirements'), such as the protection of health, or the environment, or the consumer. Such derogations clearly jeopardised the functioning of the single market. Nor was the problem confined to goods; it also applied to the other elements of the internal market. It thus became clear that if important public interests were to be protected without impairing the functioning of the internal market, action would have to be taken at Community level. Following the publication by the Commission in 1985 of a White Paper on the Completion of the Internal Market Member States agreed to embark on a massive harmonisation programme, designed to provide common standards of protection, to be completed by 31 December 1992. This was enshrined in the Single European Act 1996 (Article 14 (ex 7a) EC). In order to speed up the legislative process, a new Article 95 (ex 100a) was introduced into the EC Treaty, providing for the 'approximation' (i.e., harmonisation) of the 'provisions laid down by law, regulation or administrative action in Member States which have as their object the establishing and functioning of the internal market' (subject to some exceptions in Article 95(2) (ex 100a(2)) by measures to be enacted by qualified majority vote, instead of as heretofore, under Article 94 (ex 100), by unanimity. This programme, an example of 'positive integration' (as opposed to the 'negative integration' achieved by decisions of the ECJ rendering 'inapplicable' domestic measures contrary to EC law), has been largely successful. Although not all of the Commission's proposals were approved within the deadline, the vast majority of measures, particularly those relating to the free movement of goods, are now in place. By the end of 1994, 89 per cent of Community legislation relating to the internal market had been transposed into national law. Legislative activity has, of course, not ceased with the passing of 1992. Not only has Community competence extended since then, but legislation also needs to be reviewed and updated in the light of changing circumstances (see below). For example, the development of electronic commerce has generated directives on electronic signatures and on contracts concluded via electronic means.

Also relevant to the goods provisions, although not contained in the free movement of goods section of the Treaty, but in the competition section, are Article 90 (ex 95), which prohibits States from applying discriminatory taxation, and Article 87 (ex 92), which prohibits, subject to exceptions, the granting of State aids which threaten or distort competition. Since the principal purpose of the single market is to achieve the economic benefits of free competition within that market, and since these Articles relate to, and overlap with the goods provisions, as measures taken by Member States which threaten to undermine that competition, it seemed appropriate to consider Articles 90 and 87 (ex 95 and 92) in the context of the provisions of the Treaty relating to goods rather than under the heading of tax provisions or competition policy. Thus EC law affecting the free movement of goods will be seen to comprise the whole network of provisions designed to achieve the free movement of goods and free competition in the provision of goods within the Community.

If the pace of Community legislation was hectic in the run-up to 1992, it has slowed considerably in the post-Maastricht years, in the light of a changed political climate and the new principle of subsidiarity. The power ceded by Member States under Article 95 (ex 100a) EC proved wider than was anticipated, and more controversial. Although harmonisation measures have been passed in areas regarded as essential to the internal market, such as technical standards and industrial property, the Commission has sought to increase the effectiveness of existing legislation by assisting and encouraging businesses, particularly small businesses, to take advantage of the single market, and by monitoring Member States' implementation of Community Directives. The more recent emphasis in the internal market programme is that of simplifying legislation (SLIM), with the aim of increasing transparency and making cross-border transactions easier. Nevertheless, if Member States have in recent years been reluctant to commit themselves to further harmonisation, *a fortiori* by qualified majority vote, or dilatory in implementing EC legislation, they remain fully committed to the principle of the single market. The Heads of State, meeting in 1993 in the European Council, affirmed their commitment to the single market as being the main instrument for achieving the objectives of competitiveness, growth and employment. It is argued by many that economic and monetary union and a single currency, in eliminating the monetary barriers to the single market, will contribute significantly to the realisation of these objectives, although they will clearly involve a further loss of national sovereignty.

Further reading

Commission's White Paper on the Internal Market (COM Doc).
Commission's Annual Report on the Internal Market: from 1993.
Mortelmans, K., 'The Common Market, the Internal Market and the Single Market: What's in a Market?' (1998) 35 CML Rev 101.

EIGHT

Customs union

This is to be achieved by:

(a) the adoption of a common customs tariff towards third countries, and
(b) the prohibition between Member States of customs duties on imports and exports and of all charges having equivalent effect (Article 23 (ex 9) EC).

Allied to these provisions are Articles 3(b) and 131–134 (ex 110–115) EC, which provide for the establishment of a common commercial policy towards third countries.

Common customs tariff

As part of its common commercial policy, and in order to ensure equal treatment in all Member States for goods imported into the EC from third countries, thereby enabling *all* goods in circulation within the Community to benefit equally from the free movement provisions, the Treaty provided for the introduction of the common customs tariff (CCT), sometimes known as the common external tariff (CET). The CCT applies to all products imported into the Community from outside the EC, thus erecting a single tariff wall which no individual State is free to breach.

The operation of the CCT is governed by Articles 26–27 (ex 18–29) EC, and is enacted by directly applicable Regulations. Under the CCT goods are classified according to a common nomenclature, and are subject to common Community rules as to value and origin. Products are divided into lists, the classifications being derived from the Brussels Convention on Nomenclature for the Classification of Goods. The lists, and the applicable tariff rates, are set out in Annexe I to the EC Treaty. The CCT is published by the Commission and is regularly updated. The Council, acting by qualified majority on a proposal from the Commission, is empowered to alter or suspend duties within certain limits (Article 26 (ex 28)). Once goods are imported into the Community, that is, they have complied with import formalities and paid the relevant customs duties, the free movement provisions of the Treaty apply. Even where goods are imported into a Member State under a special tariff quota the ECJ has held that a State cannot deny the application of the free movement provisions to the import and export of such goods within the Community unless the Commission has, under Article 134 (ex 115) EC, authorised derogation in order to avoid a deflection of trade or economic difficulties in one or more Member States (see *Criel, nee Donckerwolcke* (case 41/76) and note by J. Usher (1986) 11 EL Rev 210).

Thus the Commission, subject to the Council's approval, has a central role in establishing and administering the CCT. In carrying out its task it is required to balance a number of (often conflicting) economic needs set out in Article 27 (ex 29), in the light of the general aims of the Community. Duties raised under the CCT are payable to the Community and form part of the Community's 'own resources'.

Prohibition between Member States of customs duties on imports and exports and of all charges of equivalent effect

This is governed by Articles 23 (ex 9) and 25 (ex 12–17). Article 25 (ex 12) is the 'standstill' provision, prohibiting the introduction between Member States of any new customs duties on imports and exports or any charges having equivalent effect; Articles 13–15 (as originally numbered) provided for the abolition of existing duties (or their equivalent) on *imports* within certain time limit, known as the transitional period. This period has now expired for all Member States and these provisions have been deleted by the ToA.

The prohibition applies to all duties, whether applied directly or indirectly. In *Van Gend en Loos* (case 26/62) the product in question had been reclassified under Dutch law, with the result that it became subject to a higher rate of duty. The ECJ held that this would constitute a breach of the then Article 12. Article 25 (ex 12) has also been held to apply to a charge on imports and exports into a *region* of a Member State, not only insofar as it is levied on goods entering that region from other Member States, but also when it is levied on goods entering that region from another part of the same State (*Simitzi* v *Kos* (cases C–485 & 486/93), re *ad valorem* municipality tax imposed on imports into and exports from the Dodecanese (Greece)). This obligation was held to derive from the 'absolute nature' of the prohibition of all customs duties applicable to goods moving between Member States. This also applies to additional charges levied on goods imported into a region which originated from a third country (*Société Cadi Surgélés* v *Ministre des Finances* (case C–126/94)).

If the meaning of 'custom duties' is clear, what are 'charges having equivalent effect' to a customs duty? It was held by the ECJ in the case of *Sociaal Fonds voor de Diamantarbeiders* (cases 2 & 3/69), in the context of a challenge to a 'tax' imposed on imported diamonds, that it included any pecuniary charge, however slight, imposed on goods by reason of the fact that they cross frontiers. The charge need not be levied at the frontier; it can be imposed at any stage of production or marketing; but provided it is levied *by reason of importation* it will breach Article 25 (ex 12) (*Steinike und Weinleg* v *Germany* (case 78/76)).

A charge of equivalent effect to a customs duty may come in many guises, and is often disguised as a 'tax'. Since genuine taxes fall to be considered under Article 90 (ex 95) EC, it is necessary at the outset to distinguish between a charge, falling within Articles 23 (ex 9) and 25 (ex 12), and a genuine tax. A genuine tax was defined in *Commission* v *France (Re Levy on Reprographic Machines)* (case 90/79) as one relating 'to a general system of internal dues applied systematically to categories of products in accordance with objective criteria irrespective of the origin of the products'. Thus to ascertain whether a 'tax' is genuine it must be examined to see whether it fits into an overall system of taxation or whether it has been superimposed on the system with a particular purpose in mind. Provided the tax is genuine, it may be imposed on imports even where the importing State produces no identical or similar product (*Commission* v *France*). In such a case it will not breach Article 25 (ex 12) but may be examined for its compatibility with Article 90 (ex 95).

A charge, in order to breach Article 25 (ex 12), need not be introduced for protectionist reasons. It was pointed out in the *Sociaal Fonds* case that there existed no diamond-mining industry in Belgium, and the proceeds of the charge were used for a most worthy purpose, to provide a social fund for workers in the diamond industry. These factors were held by the ECJ to be irrelevant. Such duties are forbidden independently of the purpose for which they are levied and the destination of the charge. In reaching its decision the Court looked at the effect of the measure: any pecuniary charge imposed on goods by reason of the fact that they cross frontiers is an obstacle to the free movement of goods.

A similar conclusion was reached by the ECJ in *Commission* v *Luxembourg (Re Import on Gingerbread)* (cases 2 & 3/62) in the context of a compensatory 'tax' on imported gingerbread. The governments claimed the 'tax' was introduced merely to compensate for the competitive disadvantage resulting from a high rate of domestic tax on rye, an ingredient of gingerbread. The purpose of the prohibition on measures of equivalent effect to customs duties, the Court held, was to prohibit not only measures ostensibly clothed with the classic nature of a customs duty but also those which, presented under other names or introduced by the indirect means of other procedures, would lead to the same discriminatory or protective *results* as customs duties. If compensatory 'taxes' of this type were allowed, States would be able to make up for all sorts of taxes at home by imposing a so-called balancing charge on imports. This would ensure that imported goods would lose any competitive advantage they might have as against the equivalent domestic product and thereby frustrate the objectives of the single market.

Even when the charge is levied in order to benefit the importer it may still breach Article 25 (ex 12). In *Commission* v *Italy (Re Statistical Levy)* (case 24/68) a levy, applied to all imports and exports, regardless of source, the proceeds of which were used to finance an export statistical service for the benefit of importers and exporters, was found to be in breach of the then Articles 9–16 (now 23–25) EC. The ECJ held that the advantage to importers was so general and uncertain that it could not be considered a payment for service rendered (see also *W. Cadsky SpA* (case 63/74), in relation to charges on the *export* of goods).

This implies that a charge levied for a service rendered to the importer and which is not too general and uncertain would be permissible. This principle has, however, been given the narrowest possible scope. The ECJ has held that where an inspection service is imposed in the general interest, for example, for health or safety purposes, or quality control, this cannot be regarded as a service rendered to the importer or exporter to justify the imposition of a charge *(Rewe-Zentralfinanz eGmbH v Landwirtschaftskammer Westfalen-Lippe* (case 39/73)). This principle applies regardless of the nature of the agency, public or private, providing the service, and whether or not the charge is borne by virtue of a unilateral measure adopted by the authorities or as a result of a series of private contracts (*Édouard Dubois et Fils SA v Garonor Exploitation SA* (case C–16/94)). Even when such inspections are expressly *permitted* under EC law, as in *Commission v Belgium (Re Health Inspection Service)* (case 314/82), the Court held that a charge for such a service cannot be regarded as a service rendered for the benefit of the importer. It is only when such services are mandatory, as part of a common Community regime, or arising from an international agreement into which the EC has entered (*Bakker Hillegom* (case C–111/89)), that Member States are entitled to recover the cost, and no more than the cost, of the service (*Bauhuis v Netherlands* (case 46/76)).

Thus, unless a service is required under Community law, it appears that only a service which gives a tangible benefit to the importer, or the imported goods, for example, a finishing or packaging service, will be regarded as sufficient to justify a charge, and even then it will not be permissible if the 'service' is one imposed on the importer in the general interest. Where a genuine service is provided for the benefit of the importer the ECJ has held that the charge must not exceed the value or the cost of the service (*Rewe-Zentralfinanz eGmbH* (case 39/73)), or a sum proportionate to the service provided (*Commission v Denmark* (case 158/82)). A charge based on the value of the goods is not permissible (*Ford España SA v Spain* (case 170/88)). In *Donner* (case 39/82) the Court suggested that a charge by the Dutch Post Office for dealing with the payment of VAT on imported books on behalf of the claimant might be regarded as a payment for services rendered but left the national court to decide whether on the facts it was, and if so whether it was proportionate.

Where a charge is imposed only upon domestically produced goods, the ECJ appears to take a more lenient view. In *Apple & Pear Development Council v K. J. Lewis Ltd* (case 222/82) a number of growers challenged a compulsory levy imposed on growers of apples and pears in the UK. The proceeds of the levy went to finance the Apple and Pear Development Council, a semi-public body whose functions included research, the compilation of statistics, provision of information, publicity and promotion. The ECJ held that since the levy did not apply to imported products there was no breach of the then Articles 9–16 (now 23–25). The charge would only be illegal if it served to finance activities which were incompatible with EC law.

All the cases considered so far have concerned unilateral charges, charges imposed only upon imported or exported products and not on the comparable domestic product (or vice versa). Clearly such charges undermine the principle of free trade and free competition within the common market. What about a non-discriminatory charge, applied to a particular product regardless of source? Will this be capable of infringing Articles 23 (ex 9) and 25 (ex 12) EC? This calls for a more subtle enquiry into:

(a)   the nature of the charge and its mode of calculation, and
(b)   the destination of the charge, i.e., who receives the benefit.

Three situations may be considered:

(a)   If the charge is identical in every respect and levied as part of a general system of taxation it will not fall within Article 25 (ex 12) and will be treated as a fiscal measure, and examined for its compatibility with Article 90 (ex 95) (prohibition on discriminatory taxation).

(b)   If the same charge is levied on a particular product, regardless of source, it will nonetheless breach Article 25 (ex 12) if the charge on the imported or exported product is not imposed in the same way and determined according to the same criteria as apply to the domestic product. This point was made by the ECJ in *Marimex SpA* v *Italian Minister of Finance (No. 2)* (case 29/72) in the context of a challenge to a 'veterinary inspection tax' imposed on imported meat, live and dead, to ensure that it conformed to Italian health standards. Similar domestic products were subject to corresponding inspections which were also 'taxed', but they were conducted by different bodies according to different criteria. The ECJ held that such a tax on imports would be in breach of the then Article 9 (now 23).

(c)   Even if the charge is levied at the same rate and according to identical criteria it may still breach Articles 23 (ex 9) and 25 (ex 12–17) if the proceeds of the charge are applied to benefit the domestic product *exclusively*. This point was first made in *Capolongo* v *Azienda Agricola Maya* (case 77/72). In this case the Italians had introduced a charge on imported egg boxes, as part of an overall charge on cellulose products, the aim being to finance the production of paper and cardboard in Italy. Although the charge was imposed on all egg boxes, domestic and imported, the Court held it was in breach of the then Article 13 (deleted by ToA). Although applied to domestic and imported goods alike, it was discriminatory if it was intended exclusively to support activities which specifically benefited the domestic product.

The scope of *Capolongo* was restricted in the subsequent case of *Fratelli Cucchi* v *Avez SpA* (case 77/76). Here a dispute arose concerning the legality of a levy on imported sugar. Domestically produced sugar was subject to the same levy. The proceeds of the levy went to finance the sugar industry, to benefit two groups, the beet producers and the sugar-processing industry.

The ECJ held that such a charge would be of equivalent effect to a customs duty if three conditions were fulfilled:

(a)   if it has the *sole* purpose of financing activities for the specific advantage of the domestic product;
(b)   if the taxed domestic product and the domestic product to benefit are the same; and
(c)   if the charges imposed on the domestic product are made up *in full*.

If these conditions are not fulfilled the charge will not breach Article 25 (ex 12) EC. However, where the same tax, levied on domestic and imported products alike, gives only *partial* benefit to the domestic product, it may be deemed a discriminatory tax, in breach of Article 90 (ex 95) EC (*Commission v Italy (Re Reimbursement of Sugar Storage Costs)* (case 73/79); *Cooperative Co-Frutta* (case 193/85)). A grant to a particular industry may be adjudged a State aid in breach of Article 87 (ex 92) EC.

Thus, the rules concerning charges of equivalent effect to a customs duty are strictly applied by the ECJ. Indeed, in its anxiety to ensure that no pecuniary restriction, however small, shall create obstacles to trade, particularly to imports, the Court is even prepared to countenance a degree of reverse discrimination, since Member States are required themselves to finance measures such as health inspections which may be fully justified in the public interest (see *Rewe-Zentralfinanz eGmbH* (case 39/73)). Nor does the Treaty or the Court provide for any exceptions in this field. In *Commission v Italy (Re Export Tax on Art Treasures)* (case 7/68) the Italians argued that the tax was justified in order to protect their artistic heritage. Under Article 30 (ex 36) States are entitled to derogate from the prohibition on imposing quantitative restrictions on imports (Article 28 (ex 30) EC) or exports (Article 29 (ex 34) EC), or measures of equivalent effect, on the grounds of *inter alia*, 'the protection of national treasures possessing artistic, historic or archaeological value'. The Court held that the then Article 36 (now 30) could never be invoked to justify a charge (see also *Marimex SpA* (case 29/72)).

Since Articles 23 and 25 (ex 9 and 12) are directly effective, any sums paid under an illegal charge are recoverable. Although repayment must be sought within the framework, and according to the rules, of national law, conditions must not be so framed as to render it excessively difficult or impossible in practice to exercise the rights conferred by Community law (*SpA San Giorgio* (case 199/82)). The principle of unjust enrichment may be invoked to deny a claim for repayment where the charge has been incorporated into the price of goods and passed on to purchasers *(SpA San Giorgio)*. However, national authorities may not impose the burden of proving that a charge has *not* been passed on to those persons seeking reimbursement, nor may restrictive or onerous evidential requirements (such as documentary evidence alone) be imposed. Member States are not entitled to presume that illegal taxes have been passed on (*Commission v Italy Re Repayment of Illegal Taxes* (case 104/86)). In *Just v Danish Ministry for Fiscal Affairs* (case 68/79), in a claim based on the then Article 95 (now 90), the Court held that national courts may take into account damage suffered by the person liable to pay the charge by reason of the restrictive effect of the charge on imports from other Member States. This principle should also apply to damage suffered as a result of a charge in breach of Article 25 (ex 12) EC (concerning remedies, see further chapter 26).

NINE

Prohibition of discriminatory taxation

Although the prohibition of discriminatory taxation is contained in the tax provisions of the Treaty, Article 90 (ex 95) may best be considered in the context of the free movement of goods, in particular Articles 23 and 25 (ex 9 and 12). In examining those provisions it was pointed out that the Court draws a distinction between a charge having equivalent effect to a customs duty and a genuine tax. A genuine tax is a measure relating to a system of internal dues applied systematically to categories of products in accordance with objective criteria irrespective of the origin of the products (*Commission* v *France (Re Levy on Reprographic Machines)* (case 90/79)). Even what may appear a genuine tax may be treated as a charge if it is earmarked to benefit only the domestic product subject to the tax (see *Fratelli Cucchi* v *Avez SpA* (case 77/76)). However, the fact that it is levied by a body other than the State, or is collected for its own benefit and is a charge which is special or appropriate for a specific purpose, cannot prevent it from falling within the field of application of Article 90 (ex 95) (*Ianelli & Volpi* v *Meroni* (case 74/76)).

Since the line between a charge and a genuine tax may be hard to draw, and since the Court has held (*Fratelli Cucchi* v *Avez SpA*) that the prohibition of customs duties and charges having equivalent effect and of discriminatory internal taxation are mutually exclusive, it is safer in case of doubt to invoke both Article 25 and Article 90 (ex 12 and 95 respectively) and leave the Court to define the boundaries.

A 'genuine' tax must comply with Article 90 (ex 95). It provides that:

No Member State shall impose, directly or indirectly, on the products of other Member States any internal taxation of any kind in excess of that imposed directly or indirectly on similar domestic products.

Furthermore, no Member State shall impose on the products of other Member States any internal taxation of such a nature as to afford indirect protection to other products.

Thus while States are free to decide on the rate of taxation to be applied to a particular product and discriminate between different types of product (for example *Outokumpu Oy* (case C–213/96), different sources of fuel) (subject to certain overriding provisions of EC law (see further below)), they are not free to apply rates which discriminate, directly or indirectly, as between domestic and imported products which are similar or which afford indirect protection to the former. To do so would give a competitive advantage to the less highly taxed product and thereby distort competition within the single market.

A measure will be indirectly discriminatory if, although applicable to all goods, regardless of origin, it falls more heavily on the imported product. For example in *Humblot* v *Directeur des Services Fiscaux* (case 112/84) a French car tax, calculated according to the power rating of the car, which imposed a disproportionately heavy burden on the more powerful cars, *all of which were imported*, was found to breach the then Article 95 (now 90). There was no apparent justification for the excessive difference between the rates charged on the different categories of car.

In assessing the question of discrimination it is necessary to take into account not only the rate of direct and indirect internal taxation on domestic and imported products but also the basis of assessment and the detailed rules for its collection. Where differences result in the imported product being taxed, *at the same stage of production or marketing*, more heavily than the similar domestic product, Article 90 (ex 95) is infringed (*Ianelli & Volpi* v *Meroni*). It may also be necessary to have regard to taxation levied at earlier stages of manufacture and marketing, particularly to ensure that goods are not taxed twice (*FOR* v *VKS* (case 54/72)). Thus the Court insists on strict equality, rather than broad equivalence, in order to ensure 'transparency'. It has even applied Article 90 (ex 95) to penalties. In *Commission* v *France* (case 276/91) a provision of the French customs code, which provided for more severe penalties for VAT offences in relation to imported goods than for similar offences related to domestic transactions, was found to breach the then Article 95 (now 90). Although some difference in treatment might be justified for administrative reasons, in that VAT offences committed outside the importing State were not as easily discoverable as those committed in the home State, this could not justify a manifest disproportion in the severity of the two categories of offences. It has been suggested that this decision, no doubt correct as to its result, would have been better based on Article 28 (ex 30), or Article 12 (ex 6), the general prohibition of discrimination on the grounds of nationality.

The Court has held that internal tax may be imposed on imported products even if there is no domestic production of a similar or competing product as long as it applies to the product as a class, irrespective of origin (*Fink-Frucht GmbH* (case 27/67), applied in *Commission* v *France* (case 90/79)). However, if in this case the 'tax' is set at such a level as to compromise the free circulation of trade within the Community it cannot be deemed part of a general system of taxation (*Commission* v *Denmark* (case 47/88)). It may, however, fall within other provisions of the Treaty.

Although Article 90 (ex 95) is expressed as applying to the 'products of other Member States', the Court has held (*Cooperative Co-Frutta SLR v Amministrazione delle Finanze dello Stato* (case 193/85)), arguing from *Criel, nee Donckerwolcke v Procureur de la République* (case 41/76), that the prohibition of discriminatory taxation must apply, by analogy with the free movement of goods provisions, to goods from third countries in free circulation within the Member States. Similarly, although the reference to 'products of other Member States' would seem to imply that Article 90 (ex 95) only applies to taxes which discriminate against imports, the Court has held that in order to guarantee the neutrality of national systems of taxation Article 90 (ex 95) will also apply to exports (*Statenskontrol v Larsen* (case 142/77)).

'Similar' products

It is clear that products need not be identical to fall within Article 90 (ex 95). What then is a 'similar' product? In the course of a number of judgments, mostly infringement proceedings against Member States under Article 226 (ex 169) EC (see chapter 27), in respect of allegedly discriminatory taxation of alcoholic drinks (e.g., *Commission v France (Re French Taxation of Spirits)* (case 168/78)), the Court has held that 'similar' must be interpreted widely. In assessing the question of similarity, classification of the product under the same heading in the CCT will weigh heavily, but it is not conclusive. The important factor is whether the products 'have similar characteristics and meet the same needs from the point of view of consumers . . . not according to whether they are strictly identical but whether their use is similar or comparable' (*Commission v Denmark* (case 106/84)). The concept of similarity is thus analogous to that of the relevant product market in EC competition law (see chapter 16).

In order to decide whether the products meet the same consumer needs the Court has held (*Commission v UK (Re Excise Duties on Wine)* (case 170/78)) that it is necessary to look not only at the present state of the market but also possible developments, i.e., the possibility of substituting one product for another. Taxation policy must not be allowed to crystallise consumer habits. Thus beer and wine, which were subject to different rates of tax in the UK (not surprisingly wine being more highly taxed!) might be regarded as 'similar' products. In its final judgment in this case the Court held that the decisive competitive relationship was between beer and the more 'accessible' wines, i.e., the lightest and cheapest varieties. The increasing popularity of wine bars in the UK over recent years testifies to the change in consumer habits anticipated by the Court.

Different rates of taxation may, however, be applied to what appear to be 'similar' products provided they are based on objective criteria, designed to achieve economic policy objectives which are compatible with EC law, and are applied in such a way as to avoid discrimination against imports or afford indirect protection to domestic products. This reasoning was applied in *Commission v France* (case 196/85) in the context of infringement proceedings in respect of a system of differential taxation in which certain wines known as natural sweet wines or liqueur wines, production of which is 'traditional or customary', attracted more favourable tax rates than ordinary wine. The purpose of the special rate was to bolster the economy in areas largely dependent on the production of these wines, to compensate for the relatively rigorous conditions under which they are produced. The Court found the economic policy objectives pursued by the French to be justified. Such rules, it said, may not be regarded as contrary to Community law merely because they may be applied in a discriminatory manner if it is not proved that they have in fact been applied in such a manner. Clearly in this case it felt that neither discrimination nor protectionist motives had been proved (see also *Chemial Farmaceutici SpA* v *DAF SpA* (case 140/79)). Where a system involving different rates of taxation, although prima facie objectively justified, in effect discriminates against the imported product or affords indirect protection to domestic products, it will not be permissible (*Bobie* v *HZA Aachen Nord* (case 127/75)). Reverse discrimination on the other hand will be permitted (*Peureux* v *Directeur des Services Fiscaux* (case 86/78)).

Taxation affording indirect protection to domestic products

Article 90(2) (ex 95(2)) may render it unnecessary to decide whether the products in question are 'similar'. Internal taxation will be contrary to Article 90 (ex 95) if it affords indirect protection to domestic products. Article 90(2) (ex 95(2)) is intended to cover 'all forms of indirect tax protection in the case of products which, without being similar within the meaning of Article 95(1) [now 90(1)], are nevertheless in competition, even partial, indirect or potential competition, with each other' (*Cooperative Co-Frutta SRL* (case 193/85)). It is thus wider than Article 90(1) (ex 95(1)), and wider than the concept of the relevant product market in EC competition law. This may be demonstrated by comparing *Cooperative Co-Frutta* with the case of *United Brands* v *Commission* (case 27/76, see chapter 16). In *Co-Frutta* a consumer tax, imposed on both domestic and imported bananas but which in practice applied almost exclusively to imported products (domestic production being extremely small), and which was not applied to other fresh (principally home produced) fruit was found to afford indirect protection to domestic production, in breach of the then Article 95(2) (now 90(2)). In *United Brands* on the other hand bananas were found to constitute a separate product market; the relevant product market did not include other fresh fruit. Clearly a more generous approach to the question of competition is justified in the context of Article 90(2) (ex 95(2)), in order to safeguard the Community against fiscal protectionism on the part of Member States.

Since Article 90(2) (ex 95(2)) does not depend on 'similarity' between the domestic and imported products, it will be necessary, in a claim based on this Article, to demonstrate that the domestic and imported products, while not being similar, are in fact in competition with each other, and that the effect of the impugned tax regime is to afford indirect protection to the domestic product (*Commission* v *UK* (case 170/78)). Clearly, in the case of discriminatory treatment of similar goods, a protective effect will be presumed.

Harmonisation of indirect taxation

Although the Community has the power to harmonise laws relating to indirect taxation to the extent that it is necessary to ensure the establishment and functioning of the internal market (Articles 93 and 94 (ex 99 and 100)) and has made considerable progress in this area in the case of VAT, excise duties and corporation tax, Member States have understandably been reluctant to cede competence to the Community outside these areas. Proposals to approximate rates of indirect taxation within broad tax bands, introduced under the internal market programme, have not so far met with success. Since different tax regimes clearly have an adverse impact on the functioning of the internal market by distorting the 'normal' flow of trade and competition within the Community the Commission has expressed its intention to continue to seek progress in this area. However, since fiscal measures remain subject to a requirement of unanimity, as an exception to the principle of qualified majority voting introduced by Article 95 (ex 100a), it is likely that progress will be slow. As Weatherill and Beaumont suggest, 'tax equalisation is not a serious prospect and is in any event scarcely conceivable in the absence of a single currency'. This position may, of course, now change with the advent of the Euro.

Further reading

Barents, R., 'Recent Case Law on the Prohibition of Fiscal Discrimination under Article 95' (1986) 23 CML Rev 641.

Danusso, M., and Denton, R., 'Does the European Court of Justice Look for a Protectionist Motive under Article 95?' (1991) 1 LIEI 67.

Easson, A., 'Fiscal Discrimination: New Perspectives on Article 95 of the EC Treaty' (1981) 18 CML Rev 521.

Grabitz, E., and Zacher, C., 'Scope for Action by Member States for the Improvement of Environmental Protection under EEC Law: the Example of Environmental Taxes and Subsidies' (1989) 26 CML Rev 423.

Schwartze. J., 'The Member States' Discretionary Powers under the Tax Provisions of the EEC Treaty' in J. Schwartze (ed.), *Discretionary Powers of the Member States in the Field of Economic Policies and their Limits under the EEC Treaty* (Baden-Baden: Nomos, 1988).

TEN

Elimination of quantitative restrictions on imports and exports and all measures having equivalent effect

The abolition of customs duties and charges of equivalent effect and prohibition on discriminatory taxation would not have been sufficient to guarantee the free movement of goods within the common market. In addition to pecuniary restrictions there are other barriers to trade of a non-pecuniary nature, usually in the form of administrative rules and practices, protectionist and otherwise, equally capable of hindering the free flow of goods from State to State. Articles 28 and 29 (ex 30–34) EC are designed to eliminate these barriers.

As will be apparent, Articles 28 and 29 EC cover a much wider range of measures than Articles 23 (ex 9) and 25 (ex 12), but unlike these latter articles provision is made for derogation under Article 30 (ex 36).

The principal provisions are:

(a) Article 28 (ex 30), which prohibits quantitative restrictions, and all measures having equivalent effect, on *imports*.

(b) Article 29 (ex 34), which contains a similar prohibition on *exports*.

Original Articles 31–33 which provided for the gradual abolition of import restrictions during the transitional period were deleted by the ToA.

Article 30 (ex 36) provides that the prohibitions in Articles 28 and 30 (ex 30–34) will not apply to restrictions on imports and exports which are *justified* on a number of specified grounds.

These Articles are addressed to, and relate to measures taken by, Member States. However, 'measures taken by Member States' have been interpreted in the widest sense to include the activities of any public body, legislative, executive or judicial, or even semi-public body, such as a quango, exercising powers derived from public law (e.g., *Apple & Pear Development Council* v *K.*

J. Lewis Ltd (case 222/82)). In *R* v *Royal Pharmaceutical Society of Great Britain* (cases 266, 267/87) the Court held that measures adopted by professional bodies, such as the Royal Pharmaceutical Society, on which national legislation has conferred regulatory or disciplinary powers were 'measures taken by Member States' subject to the then Article 30 (now 28). Nor need the 'measures' concerned be binding measures. This was expressly provided by the Commission in the preamble to its Directive 70/50, and confirmed by the ECJ in *Commission* v *Ireland (Re 'Buy Irish' Campaign)* (case 249/81). In this case certain activities of the Irish Goods Council, a govern-ment-sponsored body charged with promoting Irish goods by, *inter alia,* advertising, principally on the basis of their Irish origin, were held to be in breach of the then Article 30. Even though no binding measures were involved, the Board's actions were capable of influencing the behaviour of traders and thereby frustrating the aims of the Community.

Although Articles 28 and 29 (ex 30–34) are addressed to Member States, neither Community institutions nor individuals are free to act in breach of these articles. In *Commission* v *France* (case C–265/95), it became clear that the Member States' duties were more far-reaching than may have previously been thought. The problem in this case did not concern actions by the French State but rather its failure to take action to prevent private individuals from impeding the cross-border flow of goods. According to the Commission, the French government should have taken action to stop the blockade of imported agricultural produce and demonstrations in which property was damaged. The ECJ agreed, stressing the fundamental nature of the then Article 30 (now 28) and then referring to Article 5 (now 10) EC which puts Member States under an obligation 'to take all necessary and appropriate measures' to ensure that Community fundamental freedoms are respected in their territory. This ruling makes it clear that Member States' obligations extend to positive measures as well as refraining from taking action incom-patible with the EC Treaty. The precise extent of this obligation remains uncertain; the ECJ emphasised the duration and severity of the incidents in France and the passivity of the French authorities in this case. Note also that a Member State is only obliged to take 'necessary and proportionate' measures. Member States thus still retain some discretion in determining, for example, their policing policy, and would certainly not be obliged to quell every public demonstration. The question then is when does the Member State's obligation arise? In *R* v *Chief Constable of Sussex, ex parte International Trader's Ferry Ltd* [1997] 3 WLR 132, [1999] 1 CMLR 1320 a similar argument to that advanced by the ECJ in *Commission* v *France* was accepted by the English courts in relation to the then Articles 34 and 5 (now 29 and 10) EC. In the English case, the authorities had taken some action, providing policing of demonstrations by animal rights protestors against the export of live animals on three days a week, but this was not enough to eliminate the effects of the demonstrations on the export of live animals by the applicant. The House of Lords found for the authorities, but would the UK be seen as being in breach of its obligations had the question been referred to the ECJ? Certainly a majority of their Lordships suggested that, were the case to turn on the question of whether the Chief Constable's decision as to the appropriate level of policing constituted a measure having equivalent effect or not, that question should be referred. Furthermore, the view was expressed that, given the wide discretion in the field of internal security which Member States enjoy, the positive obligations imposed on a Member State by the then Article 5 (now 10) in conjunction with the then Article 34 (now 29) would not be sufficiently precise to be directly effective. These issues were not decisively resolved, as their Lordships held the Chief Constable's decision to limit policing of Shoreham Harbour to be justified under former Article 36 (now 30) on the grounds of public policy, in the sense of the need to maintain law and order. Further, the Chief Constable's decision, given the resources available, was not disproportionate. It is submitted that this ruling was, on the facts, correct. (This case is discussed further below and in Chapters 11 and 28). The question of the extent of Member States' obligations to take measures becomes ever more important in the light of the possibility of a claim for damages under the doctrine of State liability in respect of public authorities' liability for omissions (see chapter 4).

Community institutions may derogate from the provisions of Articles 28 and 29 (ex 30–34) where they are expressly authorised to do so by other provisions of the Treaty, for example in implementing the common agricultural policy (Articles 33–38 (ex 39–46) EC) (*Rewe Zentrale AG* v *Direktor der Landwirtschaftskammer Rheinland* (case 37/83)). But even where a particular activity falls within other provisions of the Treaty, such as the 'Services' provisions, it may still fall foul of Article 28 (ex 30) (*Commission* v *Ireland (Re Dundalk Water Supply)* (case 45/87); requirement that pipes required under a contract for the supply of services must comply with Irish specifications held in breach of the then Article 30).

Prohibition, as between Member States, of quantitative restrictions on IMPORTS and of all measures having equivalent effect (Article 28 (ex 30))

The prohibition is twofold, embracing:

(a) quantitative restrictions, and
(b) measures of equivalent effect to quantitative restrictions.

Quantitative restrictions   These were interpreted in *Riseria Luigi Geddo* v *Ente Nazionale Risi* (case 2/73) as any measures which amount to a total or partial restraint on imports, exports or goods in transit. They would clearly include a ban, as was found to be the case in *Commission* v *Italy (Re Ban on Pork Imports)* (case 7/61) and *R* v *Henn* (case 34/79) (ban on import of pornographic materials). They would also include a quota system, as in *Salgoil SpA* v *Italian Ministry for Foreign Trade* (case 13/68). The *Ditlev Bluhme* case (case C–67/97) confirms that a ban on imports operates as a quantitative restriction even if the prohibition extends to part only of a Member State's territory. This case concerned the Danish prohibition on the import onto the island of

Læsø of live domestic bees or reproductive material for them, the aim of which was to protect the Læsø brown bee. This, the ECJ held, was a quantitative restriction although it applied only to a small part of Denmark.

A covert quota system might operate by means of an import (or export) licence requirement. A licensing system might in itself amount to a quantitative restriction, or, alternatively, a measure of equivalent effect to a quantitative restriction. It was held in *International Fruit Co. NV v Produktschap voor Groenten en Fruit* (cases 51–4/71) that even if the granting of a licence were a pure formality the requirement of such a licence to import would amount to a breach of the then Article 30 (now 28). In that case it was deemed to be a measure of equivalent effect to a quantitative restriction.

Measures having equivalent effect to quantitative restrictions The concept of measures having equivalent effect to quantitative restrictions is altogether wider in scope than that of quantitative restrictions. Perhaps to the surprise of Member States, it has been interpreted very generously by both the Commission and the ECJ, to include not merely overtly protective measures or measures applicable only to imports or exports ('distinctly applicable' measures), but measures applicable to imports (or exports) and domestic goods alike ('indistinctly applicable' measures), often introduced (seemingly) for the most worthy purpose. Such measures have included regulatory measures designed to enforce minimum standards, for example, of size, weight, quality, price or content, to tests and inspections or certification requirements to ensure that goods conform to these standards, to any activity capable of influencing the behaviour of traders such as promoting goods by reason of their national origin, as was the case in *Apple & Pear Development Council v K.J. Lewis Ltd* (case 222/82) and *Commission v Ireland (Re 'Buy Irish' Campaign)* (case 249/81). Even if not designed to be protectionist, such measures, by imposing extra burdens on imported products, already required to comply with different standards in their home State, or simply by prejudicing consumer choice, clearly give domestic products an advantage over imported goods, thereby distorting competition in the single market.

To offer States guidance as to the meaning and scope of 'measures having equivalent effect' to quantitative restrictions, the Commission passed Directive 70/50. Although passed under the then Article 33(7) (which itself was deleted by the ToA) and therefore applicable only to measures to be abolished during the transitional period, it has been suggested that the Directive may still serve to provide non-binding guidelines to the interpretation of Article 28 (ex 30). Article 2(3) of the Directive provides a non-exhaustive list of measures capable of having equivalent effect to quantitative restrictions. These are divided into:

(a) 'measures, *other than those applicable equally to domestic or imported products*', i.e., 'distinctly applicable' measures, 'which hinder imports which could otherwise take place, including measures which make importation more difficult or costly than the disposal of domestic production' (Article 2(1)), and

(b)   measures *'which are equally applicable to domestic and imported products'*, i.e., 'indistinctly applicable' measures (Article 3). These measures are only contrary to Article 28 (ex 30) 'where the restrictive effect of such measures on the free movement of goods exceeds the effects intrinsic to trade rules', that is where 'the restrictive effects on the free movement of goods are out of proportion to their purpose', or where 'the same objective cannot be attained by other measures which are less of a hindrance to trade' (Article 3). Thus, indistinctly applicable rules appear to be acceptable provided that they comply with the principle of proportionality.

The ECJ, in 1974, in the case of *Procureur du Roi* v *Dassonville* (case 8/74), introduced its own definition of measures having equivalent effect to quantitative restrictions. This definition, now known as the *'Dassonville* formula', has since been applied consistently, almost verbatim, by the ECJ. According to the formula:

> All trading rules enacted by Member States which are capable of hindering, directly or indirectly, actually or potentially, intra-Community trade are to be considered as measures having an effect equivalent to quantitative restrictions.

Thus it is not necessary to show an actual hindrance to trade between Member States as long as the measure is capable of such effects. Unlike the competition provisions of Articles 81 and 82 (ex 85 and 86), which require an *'appreciable effect'* on trade and competition between Member States, the ECJ has in the past held that Article 28 (ex 30) is not subject to a *de minimis* rule (*van de Haar* (case 177/82)). It does, however, require proof of a *hindrance* to trade. A measure which is not capable of hindering trade between Member States, which merely affects the flow of trade *within* a Member State, will not breach Article 28 (ex 30). In *Oebel* (case 155/80) a Belgian law banning the production and delivery to consumers and retail outlets of bakery products during the night hours, designed to protect workers in small and medium-sized bakeries, was held not to breach the then Article 30 (now 28), because, although delivery of imported products through some outlets was precluded, 'trade within the Community remained possible at all times' (see also *Blesgen* (case 75/81)). In *Quietlynne Ltd* v *Southend Borough Council* (case C–23/89) a licensing requirement for the sale of sex appliances by sex shops was held not to breach Article 30 (now 28), since the goods in question, which included imported goods, 'could be marketed through other channels'. However, the case law of the Court has not been consistent on this point. In *Torfaen Borough Council* v *B & Q plc* (case 145/88) the Court found that a ban on Sunday trading in England and Wales under the Shops Act 1950, the effect of which was to restrict the volume of imports to the shops trading in breach of the rules, was prima facie contrary to the then Article 30 (now 28), even though alternative outlets for the sale of these goods existed during the working week (see also *Conforama* (case C–312/89) and *Marchandise* (case C–332/89)). Following a change in the Court's approach in recent years, these latter cases involving Sunday trading would be decided on a different basis today (see *Keck* (cases C–267 & 268/91) and subsequent cases to be discussed below).

A measure falling within the *Dassonville* formula but which operates solely to the disadvantage of domestic production will not fall foul of Community law. The ban in *Oebel* on the production of bakery products during the night, which prevented Belgian bakers from benefiting from the early morning trade in adjacent Member States, was found not to breach the then Articles 7 (now 12, ex 6 EC), 30 or 34 EEC (now 28 and 29 EC). The Court held that it was not contrary to the principle of non-discrimination on grounds of nationality for States to apply national rules where other States apply less strict rules to similar products.

The ECJ took the same view of a Dutch regulation concerning the permitted ingredients of cheese, which was only applicable to cheese produced in Holland (*Jongeneel Kaas BV* v *Netherlands* (case 237/82)) and of a French law requiring French retailers to adhere to a minimum selling price for books, provided it was not applied to books which, having been exported, were reimported into France *(Association des Centres Distributeurs Edouard Leclerc* v *'Au Blé Vert' Sàrl* (case 229/83)). In this respect, as in other areas (e.g., free movement of workers), the Court is prepared to accept a measure of reverse discrimination. While Member States must be compelled, in the interests of the single market, not to discriminate against, or in any way prejudice, imports, it seems that they may be safely left to act themselves in order to protect their own interests. There is now a consistent line of authority from the ECJ to this effect.

The measure in issue in *Dassonville* was a requirement, under Belgian law, that imported goods should carry a certificate of origin issued by the State in which the goods were manufactured. Dassonville imported a consignment of Scotch whisky from France. Since the seller was unable to supply the required certificate he attached a home-made certificate of origin to the goods and appeared before the Belgian court on a forgery charge. In his defence, he claimed that the Belgian regulation was contrary to EC law. On a reference from the Belgian court, the ECJ, applying the *Dassonville* formula, found the measure was capable of breaching the then Article 30 (now 28).

In the cases of *Tasca* (case 65/75) and *van Tiggele* (case 82/77) the *Dassonville* test was applied in the context of a domestic law imposing maximum and minimum selling prices respectively. The laws were indistinctly applicable. In both cases the issue of the then Article 30 (now 28) arose in criminal proceedings against the defendants for breach of these laws. Tasca was accused in Italy of selling sugar above the permitted national maximum price; van Tiggele in Holland of selling gin below the national minimum price. Both pleaded that the measures were in breach of EC law. Applying the *Dassonville* test the ECJ found that both measures were capable of breaching the then Article 30. Regarding the maximum price, the Court held a maximum price does not in itself constitute a measure equivalent in effect to a quantitative restriction. It becomes so when fixed at a level such that the sale of imported products becomes if not impossible more difficult. The maximum price in *Tasca* could have that effect, in that importers of more highly priced goods might have to cut their profit margins or even be forced to sell at a loss. In *van Tiggele* the minimum price also acted as a hindrance to imports, since it would prevent the (possibly) lower price of imported goods from being reflected in the retail selling price. The Court suggested, however, that a prohibition on selling below cost price, or a minimum profit margin, would be acceptable, since it would have no adverse effect on trade between Member States (principle applied in *Commission* v *Italy (Re Fixing of Trading Margins)* (case 78/82)).

In applying the *Dassonville* formula in these three cases, the Court did not distinguish between distinctly and indistinctly applicable measures, and ignored the proportionality test laid down for the latter in Directive 70/50. The breadth of the formula, especially when applied 'mechanically', looking to the *effect* of the measure on intra-Community trade rather than to the question of *hindrance*, bore harshly on Member States, particularly where the measure was indistinctly applicable and might be justified as in the public interest.

Indistinctly applicable measures: the *Cassis de Dijon* test

Perhaps taking heed of criticisms arising from its application of the *Dassonville* formula in these last three cases discussed above, the Court took a decisive step in the case of *'Cassis de Dijon' (Rewe-Zentral AG* v *Bundesmonopolverwaltung für Branntwein* (case 120/78) and paved the way for a distinction between distinctly and indistinctly applicable measures. The question before the ECJ in *Cassis* concerned the legality under EC law of a German law laying down a minimum alcohol level of 25 per cent for certain spirits, which included cassis, a blackcurrant-flavoured liqueur. German cassis complied with this minimum, but French cassis, with an alcohol content of 15–20 per cent, did not. Thus although the German regulation was indistinctly applicable, the result of the measure was effectively to ban French cassis from the German market. A number of German importers contested the measure, and the German court referred a number of questions to the ECJ.

The ECJ applied the *Dassonville* formula, but, developing a suggestion of the Court in *Dassonville* that State measures falling within the formula might be acceptable where the restrictions on intra-Community trade were 'reasonable', went on to state that:

> Obstacles to movement within the Community resulting from disparities between the national laws relating to the marketing of the products in question must be accepted insofar as those provisions may be recognised as being necessary in order to satisfy mandatory requirements relating in particular to the effectiveness of fiscal supervision, the protection of public health, the fairness of commercial transactions and the defence of the consumer.

This principle ('the first *Cassis* principle'), that certain measures, though within the *Dassonville* formula, will not breach Article 28 (ex 30) if they are necessary to satisfy mandatory requirements, has come to be known as the 'rule of reason', a concept borrowed from American anti-trust law and occasionally applied in EC competition law (see chapter 15).

Prior to *Cassis*, it was assumed that any measure falling within the *Dassonville* formula would breach Article 28 (ex 30) and could be justified only on the grounds provided by Article 30 (ex 36). Since *Cassis*, at least where indistinctly applicable measures are concerned, courts may apply a rule of reason to Article 28 (ex 30). If the measure is necessary in order to protect mandatory requirements, it will not breach Article 28 (ex 30) at all. Distinctly applicable measures on the other hand will normally breach Article 28 (ex 30), but may be justified under Article 30 (ex 36).

This distinction is significant, since the mandatory requirements permitted under *Cassis* are wider than the grounds provided under Article 30 (ex 36), and, unlike Article 30 (ex 36), are non-exhaustive. In *Oebel* (case 155/80) it was not disputed that the improvement of working conditions could consti-tute a mandatory requirement, although it was not necessary to the judgment, since the Court found the rules in any case compatible with the then Article 30 (now 28). In *Cinéthèque SA* (cases 60 & 61/84) Advocate-General Slynn suggested — in the context of a non-discriminatory French law prohibiting the marketing of videograms of films within 12 months of first showing, designed to protect the cinema industry — that cultural activities could constitute a mandatory requirement. Without expressly endorsing that state-ment the Court found that the rule, designed to encourage the creation of cinematographic works, was justified on *Cassis* principles and did not breach the then Article 30 (now 28). In *Commission* v *Denmark (Re disposable Beer Cans)* (case 302/86) the protection of the environment was held to constitute a mandatory requirement, and in *Torfaen Borough Council* v *B & Q plc* (case 145/88) measures such as the English and Welsh Sunday trading rules, designed to protect 'national or regional socio-cultural characteristics' were held to be justifiable under the rule of reason. More recently, in the *Vereinigte Familiapress* case (case C–368/95), the ECJ held that diversity of the press could constitute a mandatory requirement. The ECJ has, however, refused to contemplate a justification based on purely economic grounds (see, e.g., *Duphar BV* v *Netherlands* (case 238/82) and, more recently, *Decker* (case C-120/95)).

It should be noted that the rule of reason as laid down in *Cassis* was not in terms confined to indistinctly applicable measures. Although shortly after *Cassis* in *Gilli* (case 788/79) (Italian cider vinegar case) the Court suggested (para. 14) that the principle applied only where national rules apply *without discrimination* to both domestic and imported products, it has not insisted on this distinction, and, perhaps because the line between the two is not always clear, has not infrequently considered the question of justification of indis-tinctly applicable measures not on *Cassis* principles but under Article 30 (ex 36) (see *Sandoz BV* (case 174/82)). There appear to be two possible reasons for this approach: in some cases the Court is merely responding to questions submitted by national courts under Article 234 (ex 177); in others, where the 'mandatory requirement' falls under one of the specific heads of derogation provided by Article 30 (ex 36), the Court may prefer to rely on the express provisions of that Article (see e.g. *Commission* v *Germany (Re German Sausages)* (case 274/87) (health justification) and *Ditlev Bluhme* (case C–67/97) (protection of biodiversity and the environment/health and life of animals)).

In applying the rule of reason to the facts in *Cassis* the Court found that the German law was in breach of Article 30 (now 28). Although the measure fell within the categories suggested, being allegedly enacted in the interests of public health (to prevent increased consumption resulting from lowering the alcoholic content of cassis) and the fairness of commercial transactions (to avoid giving the weak imported cassis an unfair advantage over its stronger, hence more expensive, German rival), the measure was not *necessary* to achieve these ends. Other means, such as labelling, which would have been less of a hindrance to trade, could have been used to achieve the same ends. Thus the word 'necessary' has been interpreted to mean no more than is necessary, i.e., subject to the principle of proportionality. With *Cassis* the ECJ appears finally to have fallen in line with Directive 70/50, albeit adding a 'mandatory requirement' test to the principle of proportionality.

The Court established a second important principle in *Cassis* ('the second *Cassis* principle'). It suggested that there was no valid reason why 'provided that [goods] have been lawfully produced and marketed in one of the Member States, [they] should not be introduced into any other Member State' (para. 14).

Is this principle, known as the principle of 'mutual recognition', not in conflict with its *first* principle, the rule of reason? It is submitted that it is not. It merely gives rise to a presumption that goods which have been lawfully marketed in another State will comply with the 'mandatory requirements' of the importing State. This can be rebutted by evidence that further measures are *necessary* to protect the interest concerned.

That presumption will however be hard to rebut; the burden of proving that a measure is necessary is a heavy one, particularly when, although justifiable in principle, it clearly operates as a hindrance to intra-Community trade.

In *Prantl* (case 16/83) Article 30 (now 28) was invoked in the context of criminal proceedings against Prantl for breach of a German law designed to prevent unfair competition. He had imported wine from Italy in bulbous-shaped bottles which closely resembled a German bottle known as a '*Bocksbeutel*'. The *Bocksbeutel* was protected under German law as denoting a quality wine from a particular region of Germany. The Italian bottle was a bottle traditional to Italy. Although the measure was arguably justifiable under *Cassis* in the interests of fair trading ('the fairness of commercial transactions') and consumer protection, the Court held that as long as the Italian wine was in accord with fair and traditional practice in its State of origin there was no justification for its exclusion from Germany (but see now *Deutsche Renault AG* v *Audi AG* (case C–317/91), noted chapter 11).

Similarly in *Miro BV* (case 182/84) it was held that a generic name such as '*jenever*', reserved in Holland for gin with a minimum alcohol content of 35 per cent, could not be restricted to one national variety provided the imported product, in this case Belgian *jenever,* with a 30 per cent alcohol content, had been lawfully produced and marketed in the exporting State. This was despite the fact that Dutch *jenever* was subject to a higher rate of tax because of its high alcohol content and would be at a competitive disadvantage *vis-à-vis* the imported product. (See also *Ministère Public* v *Deserbais* (case 286/86) re minimum fat content for Edam cheese.)

Although, where a domestic measure is challenged before a national court it is for the national court to apply the proportionality principle, the ECJ has often, in interpreting Community law at the request of national courts, offered guidance as to the specific application of that principle. In doing so it has applied the principle rigorously, excluding all measures that go beyond what is strictly necessary to achieve the desired end. In *Walter Rau Lebensmittelwerke* v *De Smedt PVBA* (case 261/81) a Belgian law requiring margarine to be packed in cube-shaped boxes, allegedly introduced in the interests of consumers, to enable them to distinguish margarine from butter, was held to be in breach of Article 30 (now 28). The same objective could have been achieved by other means, such as labelling, which would be less of a hindrance to trade. Similar arguments have been used successfully to challenge national rules, allegedly in the interest of public health and consumer protection, concerning the permitted ingredients of pasta (*Drei Glöcken* (case 407/85)) and sausages (*Commission* v *Germany* (case 274/87)). More recently, in *Schutzverband gegen Unwesen in der Wirtschaft* v *Rocher* (case C–126/91) a German law prohibiting 'eye-catching' price comparisons in advertisements, designed to prevent consumers from being misled, was held to be disproportionate on the grounds that such advertisements were forbidden *whether they misled the public or not.* It was implied that a ban on *misleading* price comparisons would have been acceptable.

Where a defence is based on the rule of reason the genuineness of the justification proffered by Member States as well as the proportionality of the measure adopted will be closely scrutinised by the Court in the light of existing knowledge. This occurred in *Commission* v *Germany* (case 178/84). The case involved a challenge to the German beer purity laws. According to these laws, only beer brewed from specific approved ingredients could be designated 'beer'. The law also imposed an absolute ban on the use of additives. The Court examined the evidence scrupulously, and found that, having regard to the results of international scientific research, in particular the work of the FAO (Food and Agriculture Organisation) and WHO (World Health Organisation), and to eating habits in the Member State of importation, that the additives used did not constitute a danger to public health and met a real need, in particular a technological need. Although the drinking habits of the German population might have justified a selective exclusion of certain additives the exclusion of all additives was found on the evidence to be disproportionate.

By comparison, in the earlier case of *Sandoz BV* (case 174/82) the existing state of scientific knowledge was not such as to undermine a justification for a measure prohibiting, on public health grounds, the use of certain vitamin additives in food without prior authority. Provided the national authorities could prove a 'real need' for the measure, it would be permitted under Article 36 (now 30).

The extent to which Member States are now limited, in the interests of the single market, in their ability to introduce indistinctly applicable and seemingly justifiable measures is illustrated by the case of *Commission v UK (Re Origin Marking of Retail Goods)* (case 207/83). Here the Commission claimed that a British regulation requiring certain goods (e.g., clothing, textiles) sold retail to indicate their country of origin was in breach of Article 30 (now 28). The British government argued that the measure was justified on *Cassis* principles in the interest of consumers, who regarded the origin of goods as an indication of their quality. The Court refused to accept this argument. It held that the regulation merely enabled consumers to assert their prejudices, thereby slowing down the economic interpenetration of the Community. The quality of goods could as well be indicated on the goods themselves or their packaging, and the protection of consumers sufficiently guaranteed by rules which enabled the use of false indications of origin to be prohibited. Whilst manufacturers remained free to indicate their own national origin it was not necessary to compel them to do so. The regulation was in breach of the then Article 30 (now 28).

This judgment, initially surprising, demonstrates the Commission's and the Court's overriding concern to promote market integration by striking down national rules which tend to compartmentalise the market, particularly along national lines. In a single market, based on free competition, products must be allowed to compete on their merits, not on the basis of national origin. (See also *Apple & Pear Development Council v Lewis* (case 222/82); *Commission v Ireland (Re 'Buy Irish' Campaign)* (case 249/81) and chapters 14-16 on competition law.) There has, however, in recent years been some softening of the rules in respect of local or regional designations of origin of goods.

In *Exportur SA v LOR SA et Confiserie du Tech* (case C–3/91) the Court held that rules protecting indications of provenance and designations of origin laid down by a bilateral Convention between Member States were permissible under Community law provided that the protected designations had not acquired a generic connotation in their country of origin. A Regulation has now been enacted (Regulation 1107/96 ([1996] OJ L 148/1) under the procedure set down in Article 17, Regulation 2081/92 ([1992] OJ L 208/1) providing for the protection of designations of origin and geographic indications for in excess of 300 named products, such as Stilton cheese and Hereford beef. This Regulation protects registered designations of origin against all use, including 'evocations'. An evocation is a designation so evocative of the protected designation that, when a consumer is confronted with the product, the image that is triggered in the consumer's mind is that of the product the designation of which is protected. Thus, a soft cheese manufactured in Germany and called 'Cambozola' is an evocation of 'Gorgonzola' (*Consorzio per la Tutela del Formaggio Gorgonzola v Käserei Champignon Hormeister GmbH & Co. KG, Eduard Bracharz GmbH* (case C–87/97)). There are limitations to the protection granted. For example, since Cambozola had been made and registered as a trademark long before the introduction of the Regulation, the ECJ also held that notwithstanding the prima facie prohibition of the use of the evocation, the trade mark 'Cambozola' could still be used were its initial registration to have been made in good faith and its continued use not likely to deceive the public. Community law will not, however, allow Member States to protect generic names, such as Cheddar cheese, which are not tied to a particular geographical area. Thus the principles of *Miro BV* (case 182/84) and *Ministère Public* v *Deserbais* (case 286/86) remain good law.

Indistinctly applicable measures: a change of direction?

Although the rule of reason has allowed States some latitude to enact or maintain indistinctly applicable measures which are capable of hindering trade between Member States in order to protect important national interests, whilst ensuring that such measures are subject to judicial control as to their proportionality, the rule has not been without its problems. These have arisen from a tendency to a lax, 'mechanical' application of the *Dassonville* formula, requiring measures which might affect the volume of imports overall, but with little potential to *hinder* imports, to be justified under the rule of reason. Defence lawyers in Member States have been quick to exploit the 'Euro-defence' of Article 28 (ex 30) to charges involving a wide range of regulatory offences. Examples of such defences include challenges to Dutch laws restricting the use of free gifts for promotional purposes (*Oosthoek's Uitgever-smaatschappij BV* (case 286/81)); to French laws prohibiting the door-to-door selling of educational materials (*Buet* v *Ministère Public* (case 382/87)); to English laws requiring the licensing of sex shops for the sale of sexual appliances (*Quietlynn Ltd* v *Southend Borough Council* (case C–23/89)); to laws prohibiting 'eye-catching' price comparisons as in *Rocher* (case C–126/91); and a number of cases such as *Torfaen Borough Council* v *B & Q plc* (case 145/88) pleading the illegality under the then Article 30 (now 28) of national rules limiting Sunday trading. In all of these cases the legality of these measures under EC law was ultimately upheld, sometimes (e.g., *Quietlynn*), on the grounds that Article 28 (ex 30) was not applicable at all, more often following the application of the rule of reason. As was noted above, the case law has not been consistent here. Moreover, as the Sunday trading cases demonstrate, national courts face great difficulties in applying a rule of reason, particularly when there exist a number of possible justifications for the measure challenged and its harmful effect on trade between *Member States* (as opposed to between particular undertakings) is minimal. In these circumstances a national judge may be reluctant to entertain a challenge to domestic legislation, duly enacted by Parliament, based on its lack of proportionality (see e.g., Hoffmann J in *Stoke-on-Trent City Council* v *B & Q plc* [1991] Ch 48). These problems surfaced in the Sunday trading cases. In *Torfaen Borough Council* v *B & Q plc*, the ECJ had held that the rules in question, which prohibited large multiple shops such as the defendant's from opening on Sunday, might be justified to ensure that working hours be arranged to accord with 'national or regional socio-cultural characteristics', and directed the referring magistrates' court to examine the rules in the light of their proportionality. Unfortunately the precise grounds of justification permitted to protect such socio-cultural characteristics were not spelt out; nor was any guidance offered on the question of proportionality. Thus different British courts in different cases came to different conclusions. Courts which concluded that the socio-cultural purpose of the rules was to protect workers who did not want to work on Sunday not surprisingly concluded that the rules were disproportionate (e.g., *B & Q Ltd* v *Shrewsbury & Atcham Borough Council* [1990] 3 CMLR 535); those which saw the rules as designed to 'preserve the traditional character of the British Sunday' legitimately concluded otherwise: the rules were not more than was necessary to achieve that end (e.g., *Wellingborough Borough Council* v *Payless DIY Ltd* [1990] 1 CMLR 773). Despite a clear ruling from the Court in two cases subsequent to *Torfaen Borough Council* v *B & Q plc* (*Conforama* (case C–312/89); *Marchandise* (case C–332/89)) that similar rules would be permissible under the rule of reason, the question of the legality of the English Sunday trading rules was only decided conclusively when the ECJ, following a reference from the House of Lords in *Stoke-on-Trent City Council* v *B & Q plc* (case C–169/91), applying the (first) *Cassis* principle, found that the rules were justified and not disproportionate.

Whether as a result of these problems and the uncertainty surrounding the scope of Article 28 (ex 30) in the case of non-discriminatory national rules with a minimal impact (in terms of hindrance) on intra-Community trade, resulting in some exploitation of Community rules, or of a new post-Maastricht commitment to the principle of subsidiarity, the Court, in *Keck and Mithouard* (cases C–267 & 268/91), signalled an important change of direction.

These cases concerned the legality under EC law of a French law prohibiting the resale of goods in an unaltered state at prices lower than their actual purchase price, in the interests of fair trading, to prevent 'predatory pricing' (see chapter 16). Keck and Mithouard, who had been prosecuted for breach of this law, claimed that it was incompatible with EC law. Although the then Article 30 was not expressly invoked, the reference being made for interpretation of Articles 3 and the then 7 EEC (now 12, ex 6 EC), the Court, in order to provide the French court with a 'useful' reply, focused on Article 30 (now 28), which was clearly the relevant article. It cited the *Dassonville* test. It pointed out that legislation such as the French law in question:

> may restrict the volume of sales, and hence the volume of sales of products from other Member States, insofar as it deprives traders of a method of sales promotion. But the question remains whether such a possibility is sufficient to characterise the legislation in question as a measure having equivalent effect to a quantitative restriction on imports.

It went on to suggest:

in view of the increasing tendency of traders to invoke Article 30 [now 28] of the Treaty as a means of challenging any rules whose effect is to limit their commercial freedom even where such rules are not aimed at products of other Member States, the Court considers it necessary to re-examine and clarify its case law on this matter.

Citing the (first) *Cassis de Dijon* principle it drew a distinction between rules which lay down 'requirements to be met' by goods, such as those relating to designation, size, weight, composition, presentation, labelling and packaging, and rules relating to 'selling arrangements'. Rules governing 'requirements to be met' falling within the *Dassonville* formula remained subject to the (first) *Cassis* principle. However, 'contrary to what [had] previously been decided':

> the application to products from other Member States of national provisions restricting or prohibiting certain selling arrangements is not such as to hinder, directly or indirectly, actually or potentially, trade between Member States within the meaning of the *Dassonville* judgment, provided that those provisions apply to all affected traders operating within the national territory and provided that they affect in the same manner, in law and in fact, the marketing of domestic products and of those from other Member States.
>
> Where these conditions are fulfilled, the application of such rules to the sale of products from another Member State meeting the requirements laid down by that State is not by nature such as to prevent their access to the market or to impede access any more than it impedes the access of domestic products. Such rules therefore fall outside the scope of Article 30 [now 28] of the Treaty.

This new approach to Article 28 (ex 30) was affirmed, on the same grounds, shortly after *Keck*, in *Hünermund* (case C–292/92) in the context of a challenge to a rule of the Baden-Württemberg pharmacists' ruling body, prohibiting pharmacists from advertising, outside pharmacy premises, pharmaceutical products which they are authorised to sell. Without applying the *Cassis* test the rule was held not to breach Article 30 (now 28). It adopted the same approach, invoking the principle laid down in *Keck* relating to 'selling arrangements', in *Commission* v *Greece* (case C–391/92) and *Belgapom* (case C–63/94). Here it found that rules which required processed milk for infants to be sold only in pharmacies (*Commission* v *Greece*) and rules prohibiting sales yielding very low profit margins (*Belgapom*) were permissible under Article 30 (now 28) without resort to the rule of reason. Similarly in *Banchero* (case C–387/93), in a case involving an ingenious 'Euro-defence' to a smuggling charge, the Court found that Italian rules reserving the retail sale of tobacco to authorised distributors were compatible *per se* with Article 30 (now 28) even though the retailers were authorised to trade by a national body holding a monopoly over tobacco production in Italy. It was important to the judgment that the system did not impede access to the national market and showed no evidence of discrimination: the monopoly did not intervene in the procurement choices of retailers.

By contrast with these cases involving 'selling arrangements', measures constituting 'requirements to be met', such as a Dutch law prohibiting dealings in gold and silver products not bearing a Dutch, Belgian or Luxembourg hallmark (*Houtwipper* (case C–293/93)) and German rules requiring the labelling of the contents of certain foods additional to that which was required under Community law (*Commission* v *Germany* (case C–51/94) were examined, as *Keck* suggested, under the rule of reason and found not to be justified.

Nevertheless, the full scope of the Court's ruling in *Keck*, and the extent to which it has supplanted the need for the application of a rule of reason in the case of indistinctly applicable measures, remains to be seen. The move towards a more 'formalistic' approach towards Article 28 (ex 30) initiated in *Keck* has been both criticised as 'lacking in principle' and acclaimed for its 'tendency to cut back on unnecessary intrusions into the laws of the Member States in cases where access to the relevant national market is not at stake' (see the articles by Reich and Roth respectively, listed in the further reading). Roth argues, persuasively, that the focus of Article 28 (ex 30) should be on access to the (national) market, its purpose to promote interstate trade in goods, not to ensure commercial freedom as such. It is arguable that the more recent post-*Keck* cases see the ECJ responding to some of these criticisms and, at least, considering questions such as the impact of a measure on access to the market. Perhaps a more appropriate way to view *Keck* is, as the Advocate-General in *Volker Graf* (case C–190/98) suggested, to consider the view that selling arrangements are harmless in internal market terms as a rebuttable presumption rather than as a rule. Thus, even now, nearly a decade after the decision, the jury seems still to be out on *Keck*.

There is no doubt that the 'formalistic' approach introduced in *Keck* creates uncertainty. The ambit of the phrase 'certain selling arrangements' is unclear. One particular problem area in this context is that of advertising. One might argue that it falls within the ambit of 'selling arrangement' rather than 'requirements to be met'; indeed in *Leclerc-Siplec* (case C–412/93) the ECJ held that legislation which prohibits television advertising in a particular sector concerns selling arrangements for the products in that particular sector. Therefore, as the ECJ suggested in *Komsummentombudsmannen* v *De Agostini* (cases C–34–6/95), even an outright ban on the advertising of certain products — here toys — will not fall within the then Article 30 (now 28) provided always that such measures apply to domestically produced and imported products equally in law and in fact. In *De Agostini*, the prohibition did operate equally in law. The difficult question of whether it operated equally in fact was left by the ECJ to the national court, although the ECJ did note that in some circumstances the only practicable way to break into a new market will be through such advertising. The boundary between the two situations — sales promotion/advertising constituting a 'selling arrangement' on the one hand and product characteristics (including packaging) on the other — will not always be easy to identify. With the development of new television services, such as television shopping and 'infomercials', it will become increasingly difficult to identify where broadcasting (a service) ends and selling arrangements start.

There are in any event circumstances when advertising and mechanisms for increasing volume of sales will not fall within 'selling arrangements'. One example of this occurred in *Vereinigte Familiapress Zeitungsverlags- und Vertriebs GmbH* v *Heinrich Bauer Verlag* (case C–368/95), which concerned the Austrian prohibition on prize draws or competitions in periodicals. Although the ECJ accepted that publishers would include such games in publications with the hope of increasing circulation, this was not enough to bring the rule within *Keck*: the prohibition concerned the content of a magazine and therefore was a requirement to be met. Since it was an indistinctly applicable measure, it could, however, be justified under the *Cassis* rule of reason.

The ECJ itself undertook the assessment of the equal operation of the selling arrangement in law and in fact in *Schutzverband gegen unlauteren Wettbewerb* v *TK-Heimdienst Sass GmbH* (case C–254/98). Under Austrian legislation bakers, butchers and grocers may offer goods for sale on rounds from door to door, provided such sales are made by traders who have a permanent establishment in that district or in a municipality adjacent to it and the sales relate to the type of goods sold at that establishment. This rule became the subject of proceedings and the question as to whether the rule was compatible with Article 28 (ex 30) was referred. The ECJ found that the rules constituted a selling arrangement: it then went on to consider whether the rules applied equally in law and in fact. The fact that traders established in one part of Austria would also be affected in respect of home delivery services in other areas of Austria does not change this assessment. What is important is that 'the national legislation impedes access to the market of the Member State of importation for products from other Member States more than it impedes access for domestic products'. Given that many selling arrangements may not operate equally in fact, the *Keck* solution to the over-extension of Article 28 (ex 30) will be of limited utility.

It is submitted that a more principled approach, focusing on the question of whether a measure impedes access to a national market, subject to a *de minimis* rule, would provide a more workable rule. A test of 'substantial' hindrance was suggested by Advocate-General Jacobs in *Leclerc-Siplec* (case C–412/93), although the Court chose to apply *Keck*. An approach which considers the impact of a measure, however, seems to have been favoured by the ECJ in a number of cases recently. In *BASF AG* v *Präsident des Deutschen Patentamts* (case C–44/98), BASF tried to challenge a German law which, as permitted by the European Patent Convention, required patents that were granted by the European Patent Office in respect of Germany to be translated, at the patent proprietor's cost, into German. BASF argued that because of high translation costs, patent proprietors would be forced into choosing the countries in which to have patent protection as they would not be able to afford the translation costs for the entire Community. This, in turn, would affect patent proprietors' decisions about the Member States in which the patented product would be marketed, thus partitioning the internal market contrary to Article 28 (ex 30). In *ED Srl* v *Fenocchio* (case C–412/97), ED argued that Italian rules which precluded the obtaining of summary judgments against debtors who resided outside Italy would dissuade those resident in Italy from contracting with those who resided elsewhere, as debt recovery would be more difficult in respect of non-Italian residents. On this basis, it was argued that the rule should be regarded as incompatible with Article 29 (ex 34) as it would discourage exports. In both cases the ECJ gave these convoluted arguments short shrift, holding in both instances that the effect on Community law was too uncertain and indirect to constitute a measure having equivalent effect. A similar approach has also been used in the context of freedom of establishment (see chapter 21). These cases are unlikely to constitute a significant shift in the ECJ's approach to the scope of Article 28 (ex 30) in which access to markets is clearly impeded. (Contrast *Schutzverband gegen unlauteren Wettbewerb* v *TK-Heimdienst Sass GmbH* (case C–254/98) in which the Austrian government unsuccessfully tried to argue that the impact of the legislation there would be too uncertain.)

The ECJ's approach in *BASF* and *ED Srl* was similar to that in the earlier case of *DIP SpA* (cases C–140–2/94), although with a different result. *DIP SpA* concerned a challenge to an Italian law permitting the opening of new shops in particular areas only on receipt of a licence, to be issued by municipal authorities on the recommendation of a local committee. The committee, which represented a variety of interest groups, made its recommendations according to specific criteria. Perhaps because the rule did not fall clearly within the category of either 'requirements to be met' or 'selling arrangements' the Court did not apply the *Keck* formulae. Instead it looked at the effect of the measure, and found its restrictive effect 'too uncertain and too indirect' for the obligation which it imposed to be regarded as hindering trade between Member States. It was thus compatible with Article 30 (now 28). *Decker* (case C-120/95) is another case in which the ECJ did not consider the *Keck* formula, instead looking at the impact of the rules. The case concerned national rules which required an individual to obtain prior authorisation before incurring medical expenses in another Member State if the individual wanted those expenses reimbursed under health insurance cover. Here, the cost was related to the purchase of spectacles. In this case, the ECJ simply applied the *Dassonville* test and held that these rules 'must be categorised as a barrier to the free movement of goods, since they encourage insured persons to purchase those products in Luxembourg rather than in other Member States' (para. 36) and that the rules were not justified under the public health exception.

Whether the Court continues to apply *Dassonville*, as it did in *Decker*, or to operate on the basis of the distinction drawn in *Keck* or focuses on the question of hindrance to imports, subject to the application of a *de minimis* rule, as it appeared to do in *DIP SpA*, there will still be a need in many cases for courts to apply a rule of reason, since national regulatory rules more often than not constitute a real hindrance to imports. The *Cassis* judgment thus remains of supreme importance in the application of Article 28 (ex 30) to indistinctly applicable rules. Its twin principles formed the basis for the Commission's new approach to the freeing of the internal market within the 31 December 1992 deadline, outlined in its White Paper of 1985. Relying on the principle of mutual recognition, the presumption that goods lawfully marketed in one State are to be freely admitted into other Member States, the Commission proposed to concentrate its efforts on harmonisation measures designed to provide *essential* guarantees to safeguard the 'mandatory requirements' of Member States. As a result of this new approach, and greatly assisted by the change from unanimity to qualified majority voting under Article 95 (ex 100a) EC, introduced by the SEA, a large number of measures in the field of health and safety and environmental and consumer protection have been adopted in this area in recent years. These areas were expressly incorporated into the EC Treaty by the SEA. However, following Maastricht, any new proposals in these areas (as in any other areas) will need to be justifiable under the subsidiarity principle of Article 5 (ex 3b), to demonstrate that 'the objectives of the proposed action cannot be sufficiently achieved by the Member States and can . . . by reason of the scale or effects of the proposed action, be better achieved by the Community . . .'. Both the Commission and the Court appear to have taken heed of this principle. Following Maastricht the Commission has sought to restrict EC harmonising legislation to the minimum necessary for the purposes of the internal market. It has undertaken to review past legislation in the light of Article 5 (ex 3b). The Court in *Keck* and subsequent cases appears to be prepared to give more latitude to Member States in the enactment of indistinctly applicable measures which do not in fact impede access to national markets. If it seemed necessary in 1984, in *van de Haar* (case 177/82), to reject a *de minimis* rule, in the interests of the (burgeoning) single market, arguably that market is now sufficiently established for the Court to permit national rules where their burden on imports and exports is minimal, thereby bringing the rules in relation to goods into line with EC competition law (see chapter 15).

Prohibition, as between Member States, of quantitative restrictions on EXPORTS and of all measures having equivalent effect (Article 29 (ex 34))

All the principles relating to imports under Article 28 (ex 30) will also apply to exports under Article 29 (ex 34), including, as seems to have been accepted by the English courts in *R* v *Chief Constable of Sussex, ex parte International Trader's Ferry Limited* [1996] QB 197 (QBD), [1997] 3 WLR 132 (CA), [1999] 1 CMLR 1320, the possibility of Member States being under positive obligations by virtue of Article 29 (ex 34) in conjunction with Article 10 (ex 5), with one important exception. Measures which are *indistinctly applicable* will not breach Article 29 (ex 34) merely because they are capable of hindering, directly or indirectly, actually or potentially, intra-Community trade. The *Dassonville* test does not apply. To breach Article 29 (ex 34) such measures must have as their specific object or effect the restriction of patterns of exports and thereby the establishment of a difference in treatment between the domestic trade of a Member State and its export trade in such a way as to provide a particular advantage for national production or for the domestic market of the State in question, at the expense of the production or of the trade of other Member States. In other words, they must be overtly or covertly protectionist.

This principle was established in *P.B. Groenveld BV* (case 15/79). Here, a national law prohibiting the large-scale manufacture of horsemeat sausages and limiting the sale of such sausages by small specialist butchers to consumers only, designed to safeguard exports of such products to countries which prohibit the sale of horseflesh, was found, applying the above test, not to breach Article 34 (now 29), although, as Advocate-General Capotorti pointed out, it presented an almost insuperable obstacle to exports. The Court's judgment represented a clear departure from the opinion of the Advocate-General. He had approached the matter along the lines of Article 30 (now 28); he applied the *Dassonville* test, and *Cassis,* and found that the measure was not justified since other, less restrictive measures, such as labelling, could have been used to achieve the same ends.

In *Oebel* (case 155/80) the restriction on night working and delivery hours for bakery products, although undoubtedly a barrier to exports, since it precluded Belgian bakers from selling bread in adjacent Member States in time for breakfast, was found, following *P. B. Groenveld BV,* not to breach the then Article 34 (now 29).

On the other hand measures which are *distinctly applicable* and which discriminate against exports *will* be subject to the *Dassonville* test, and will normally breach Article 29 (ex 34). In *Bouhelier* (case 53/76) the requirement in France of an export licence, following a quality inspection, for watches destined for export was held to breach former Article 34 (now 29) since the same inspection and licences were not required for watches sold on the domestic market.

The principles of both *P.B. Groenveld BV* and *Bouhelier* were applied in *Jongeneel Kaas BV* (case 237/82). Here Dutch rules, indistinctly applicable, regulating the quality and content of cheese produced in The Netherlands were found not to breach the then Article 34 (now 29), even though domestic producers were thereby at a competitive disadvantage *vis-à-vis* producers from other States not bound by the same standard of quality, since they did not fall within the *P.B. Groenveld BV* criteria, whereas a distinctly applicable rule requiring inspection documents for exports alone was, following *Bouhelier,* in breach of the then Article 34 (now 29).

The Court's tolerance towards indistinctly applicable, non-protective restrictions on exports introduced in *P.B. Groenveld BV* is in line with the Court's attitude, noted above, towards reverse discrimination. Clearly where there is no danger of protectionism the Court can afford to take a more lenient view. Restrictions on imports, on the other hand, will always raise a suspicion of protectionism.

Since only protective or discriminatory measures will breach Article 29 (ex 34) it is submitted that a rule of reason will not be applied and justification can only be sought under Article 30 (ex 36). This will be discussed in the next chapter.

Further reading

Arnull, A., 'What Shall We Do on Sunday?' (1991) 16 EL Rev 112.

Barents, R., 'New Developments in Measures Having Equivalent Effect' (1981) 18 CML Rev 271.

Diamond, P., 'Dishonourable Defences: the Use of Injunctions and the EEC Treaty: Case Study of the Shops Act 1950' (1991) 54 MLR 72.

Gormley, L., 'Actually or Potentially, Directly or Indirectly? Obstacles to the Free Movement of Goods' (1989) 9 YEL 197.

Krämer, L., 'Environmental Protection and Article 30 EEC Treaty' (1993) 30 CML Rev 111.

Mortelmans, K., 'Article 30 of the EEC Treaty and Legislation Relating to Market Circumstances: Time to Consider a New Definition?' (1991) 28 CML Rev 115.

Oliver, P., 'Measures of Equivalent Effect: a Reappraisal' (1982) 19 CML Rev 217.

Quinn, M., and McGowan, N., 'Can Article 30 Impose Obligations on Individuals?' (1987) 12 EL Rev 163.

Reich, N., 'The November Revolution: *Keck, Meng, Audi* Revisited' (1994) 31 CML Rev 459.

Roth, W.H., Casenote on *Keck* and *Hünermund* (1994) 31 CML Rev 845.

Steiner, J., 'Drawing the Line: Uses and Abuses of Article 30 EEC' (1992) 29 CML Rev 749.

Weatherill, S., 'After *Keck*: Some Thoughts on how to Clarify the Clarification' (1996) 33 CML Rev 885.

White, E., 'In Search of Limits to Article 30 of the EEC Treaty' (1989) 26 CML Rev 235.

Wils, W.P.J., 'The Search for the Rule in Article 30: Much Ado about Nothing?' (1993) 18 EL Rev 475.

ELEVEN

Derogation from the elimination of quantitative restrictions

The principal provision for derogation from Articles 28 and 29 (ex 30–34) EC is Article 30 (ex 36) EC, which provides:

> The provisions of Articles 28 and 29 shall not preclude prohibitions or restrictions on imports, exports or goods in transit justified on grounds of public morality, public policy or public security; the protection of health and life of humans, animals or plants; the protection of national treasures possessing artistic, historic or archaeological value; or the protection of industrial and commercial property. Such prohibitions or restrictions shall not, however, constitute a means of arbitrary discrimination or a disguised restriction on trade between Member States.

Since indistinctly applicable measures restricting imports from Member States will now be subject to the rule of reason under *Cassis* (case 120/78), it will normally only be necessary to apply Article 30 (ex 36) EC to distinctly applicable measures in breach of Articles 28 and 29 (ex 30 and 34) EC. However, where indistinctly applicable measures are clearly discriminatory in their effect on imports or fall within one of the heads of derogation of Article 30 (ex 36) EC, the Court may consider the question of justification under Article 30 EC. (See *R* v *Royal Pharmaceutical Society of Great Britain* (cases 266, 267/87); *Commission* v *UK (Re UHT Milk)* (case 124/81) to be discussed later.) Distinctly applicable measures, on the other hand, can never be justified under *Cassis*.

This was tried in *Commission* v *Ireland (Re Restrictions on Importation of Souvenirs)* (case 113/80). Here the Irish government sought to justify, on *Cassis* principles, an Order requiring that imported souvenirs be marked 'foreign', or with their country of origin, arguing that the measure was necessary in the interests of consumers and fair trading — to enable consumers to distinguish the 'genuine' (home-produced) souvenirs from the (imported) 'fakes'. The Court held that since the measure applied only to imported souvenirs it could not be judged on *Cassis* principles. It could only be justified on the grounds provided by the then Article 36 (now 30). Since that Article created an exception to the principle of free movement of goods it could not be extended to situations other than those specifically laid down. Thus the measure could not be justified in the interests of consumer protection.

Although the grounds listed in Article 30 (ex 36) EC appear extensive they have been narrowly construed. The Court has held on many occasions that the purpose of this Article is not to reserve certain matters to the exclusive jurisdiction of the Member States; it merely allows national legislation to derogate from the principle of free movement of goods to the extent to which this is and remains justified in order to achieve the objectives set out there (*Commission* v *Germany (Re Health Control on Imported Meat)* (case 153/78)). A measure is 'justified' if it is necessary, and no more than is necessary, to achieve the desired result (the proportionality principle). Moreover, Article 30 (ex 36) EC cannot be relied on to justify rules or practices which, though beneficial, are designed primarily to lighten the administrative burden or reduce public expenditure, unless in the absence of such rules or practices the burden or expenditure would exceed the limits of what can reasonably be required (*Officier van Justitie* v *de Peijper* (case 104/75)).

As well as being necessary, measures must comply with the second sentence of Article 30 (ex 36); they must not 'constitute a means of arbitrary discrimination or a disguised restriction on trade between Member States'. Discrimination will be regarded as arbitrary if it is not justified on objective grounds. Thus, the enquiry under Article 30 (ex 36) is very similar to that conducted in applying the rule of reason and, as with the application of that rule, the presumption in favour of goods lawfully marketed in one of the Member States of the Community means that a State seeking to rebut that presumption must itself prove that the conditions for the application of Article 30 (ex 36) are satisfied.

Public morality

The public morality ground was considered in two English cases, *R* v *Henn* (case 34/79) and *Conegate Ltd* v *Customs and Excise Commissioners* (case 121/85). In *R* v *Henn,* the then Article 36 (now 30) was invoked to justify a ban on the import of pornographic materials. To a certain extent the ban was discriminatory, since not all pornographic material of the kind subject to the ban was illegal in the UK. In the UK it was illegal only if likely to 'deprave or corrupt', whereas under UK customs legislation, import was prohibited if the goods were 'indecent or obscene'. On a reference from the House of Lords the ECJ found that the ban was in breach of the then Article 30 (now 28) but was justified under former Article 36 (now 30). Although it was discriminatory, the discrimination was not arbitrary; nor was it a disguised restriction on trade between Member States; there was no lawful trade in such goods in the UK. The measure was genuinely applied for the protection of public morality, not for the protection of national products. It was for each State to determine in accordance with its own scale of values the requirements of public morality in its territory.

The court took a stricter view in *Conegate Ltd* v *Customs and Excise Commissioners*. Here Article 36 (now 30) was invoked to justify the seizure by HM Customs and Excise of a number of inflatable rubber dolls euphemistically described as 'love dolls' together with other exotic and erotic articles imported from Germany, on the grounds that they were 'indecent and obscene'. The importers claimed the seizure was in breach of the then Article 30 (now 28), and, since there was no ban on the manufacture and sale of such items in the UK (the sale was merely restricted), it was discriminatory. Their argument succeeded before the ECJ. The Court held that the seizure was not justified under the then Article 36 (now 30), since, unlike *R* v *Henn*, there was no general prohibition on the manufacture and marketing of such goods in the UK; nor had the State adopted serious and effective measures to prevent the distribution of such goods in its territory. (Similar reasoning has been applied in the sphere of free movement of persons, see chapter 22.)

Public policy

This ground, potentially wide, has been strictly construed, and has rarely succeeded as a basis for derogation under Article 30 (ex 36). However, in *R* v *Thompson* (case 7/78) a restriction on the import and export of gold collectors' coins was held to be justified on the grounds of public policy, since the need to protect the right to mint coinage was one of the fundamental interests of the State.

A similar principle has been applied to the public policy exception to the principle of freedom of movement of persons (see *Rutili* v *Ministre de l'Intérieure* (case 36/75) and chapter 22). However, the Court has repeatedly stated that public policy cannot provide a clause of general safeguard (*Commission* v *Italy (Re Ban on Pork Imports)* (case 7/61)) and can never be invoked to serve purely economic ends (*Commission* v *Italy* (case 95/81)). In *R* v *Secretary of State for the Home Department, ex parte Evans Medical Ltd* (case C–324/93) it found that a prohibition against the importation into the UK without a licence of the drug diamorphine could not be justified by the need to maintain the economic viability of the sole licensed manufacturer of the drug in the UK, although it might be permitted on public health grounds to ensure that a country has reliable supplies for essential medical purposes.

The interrelationship between public funding, in which economic considerations might play a part, and public policy underlay the debate in *R* v *Chief Constable of Sussex, ex parte International Trader's Ferry Ltd* [1997] 3 WLR 132, CA, [1999] 1 CMLR 1320 HL. The case arose in the context of widespread demonstrations by animal rights supporters against the transporting of live animals for slaughter. Demonstrations were centred in docks and airports around the UK. Extensive and expensive policing had been in force to ensure that the traffic in these animals, which was lawful, might not be prevented. The action arose from the Chief Constable's decision to restrict his force's services in policing demonstrations at particular ports to three days a week, in order to save resources. As a result, International Trader's Ferry Ltd was prevented by the protesters from transporting loads on the days on which policing had been withdrawn. The company sued the Chief Constable for the resultant losses under both English and EC law. The House of Lords' decision, confirming the legality of the Chief Constable's decision to withdraw policing of animal rights demonstrators on public policy grounds, was firmly based on the need to protect public order. Financial factors, such as the need to balance scarce resources, were relevant only to the reasonableness and proportionality of the Chief Constable's decision.

This case which, it is submitted, is on its facts correct, may be compared with *Commission* v *France* (case C–265/95). Here, in the context of widespread public demonstrations in France to prevent foreign produce from reaching local markets, the ECJ found that the French authorities, in failing to take any significant action against these demonstrations, despite repeated requests from the Commission, had failed in their obligations under the EC Treaty. Since they had adduced no evidence justifying this failure, they could not rely on the public policy derogation under Article 30 (ex 36).

Even where a public policy justification appears to be legitimate, as in *Campus Oil Ltd* (case 72/83) (see below), in which Advocate-General Slynn was prepared to accept a public policy justification, the Court has in the past preferred to base its judgment on other grounds. It seems that public policy will be an exception of last resort.

Public policy cannot be invoked on the grounds that the activity which the impugned national measure seeks to curb carries criminal sanctions (*Prantl* (case 16/83)). Indeed, in many cases, as in *Prantl* itself, Article 28 (ex 30) EC has proved a valid defence to a criminal charge.

Public security

This ground was successfully invoked in *Campus Oil Ltd* to justify an Irish order requiring importers of petroleum oils to buy up to 35 per cent of their requirements of petroleum products from the Irish National Petroleum Co. (INPC), at prices to be fixed by the minister. The measure was clearly discriminatory and protective. The Irish government argued that it was justified, on public policy and public security grounds, to maintain a viable national refinery which would meet essential needs in times of crisis. The Court found it in breach of the then Article 30 (now 28) but, contrary to the view of the Commission, justifiable on public security grounds, since its purpose was to maintain the continuity of essential oil supplies. Petroleum products, the Court held, are of fundamental importance to the country's existence, since they are needed not only for the economy, but for the country's institutions, its vital services, and the survival of its inhabitants. The Court stressed that purely economic objectives would not provide justification under the then Article 36 (now 30), but provided the measure was justified on other grounds the fact that it might secure economic objectives did not exclude the application of that Article. As to whether the measures were necessary, the Court held that a compulsory purchase requirement would be justified only if the output of the INPC refinery could not be freely disposed of at competitive prices, and the compulsory prices only if they were competitive in the market concerned; if not the financial loss must be borne by the State, subject to the application of Articles 87 and 88 (ex 92 and 93) (prohibition on State aids, see chapter 13).

Protection of the health and life of humans, animals and plants

Discriminatory measures for which justification may be sought on health grounds may include bans, tests and inspections of imports to ensure that domestic standards are met, and licensing or documentary requirements to provide evidence of this fact. To succeed on this ground it is necessary to prove a real health risk (see also *Duphar BV* (case 238/82)). This will not be the case where the exporting State maintains equivalent standards and those standards are adequate to meet that risk. Thus, in *Commission* v *UK (Re UHT Milk)* (case 124/81) the Court found that a requirement that UHT Milk should be marketed only by approved dairies or distributors (allegedly to ensure that milk was free from bacterial or viral infections) which necessitated the repacking and retreating of imported milk, was not justified, since there was evidence that milk in all Member States was of similar quality and subject to equivalent controls. (Although the measure was prima facie indistinctly applicable the Court considered it to be discriminatory in effect and examined it for its compatibility with Article 36 (now 30).) (See also *Decker* (case C–120/95) regarding the need to maintain the quality of medical products.)

By contrast, in *Rewe-Zentralfinanz eGmbH* (case 4/75) a plant health inspection applied only to imported apples, designed to control a pest called San Jose scale, which was clearly in breach of Article 28 (ex 30), was found to be justified on health grounds, since the imported apples constituted a real risk which was not present in domestic apples. Although discriminatory, the discrimination was not arbitrary. (Although the inspection was justified it will be remembered from chapter 8 that the charge for the inspection was not, since Article 30 (ex 36) is not available to justify a charge: *Rewe-Zentralfinanze GmbH* (case 39/73).)

More recently in *Ditlev Bluhme* (case C–67/97), a prohibition on the import onto the island of Læsø of Danish domestic bees and reproductive material for them was held to be justified under Article 30 (ex 36). The aim of the measure was to protect an indigenous population that was in danger of disappearance as a result of cross-breeding with other bee species. The ECJ held that by seeking to protect biodiversity through ensuring the survival of a distinct indigenous species, the measures protect the life of those animals.

The health justification has often failed on proportionality grounds, or because it constitutes 'arbitrary discrimination or a disguised restriction on trade between Member States'. In the *UHT Milk* (case 124/81), in addition to the marketing restrictions, UHT milk coming into the UK required a specific import licence. The Court found both requirements disproportionate; it was not necessary to market the products in that way, and the information gleaned from processing the licensing applications could have been obtained by other less restrictive means, for example, by declarations from importers, accompanied if necessary by the appropriate certificates. For similar reasons in *Commission v UK (Re Imports of Poultry Meat)* (case 40/82) a specific import licence requirement for poultry and eggs, allegedly designed to prevent the spread of Newcastle disease, was found not to be justified. Yet in *Commission v Ireland (Re Protection of Animal Health)* (case 74/82), which also concerned Newcastle disease, a similar import licence requirement was permitted under the then Article 36 (now 30) on account of the exceptionally high health standards of Irish poultry, a standard which was not matched by British flocks. The Court said it was necessary in each case to weigh the inconvenience caused by the administrative and financial burden against the dangers and risks to animal health. Thus it may be difficult to predict when a specific import licence requirement will or will not be justified.

In the first Newcastle disease case, *Commission v UK* (case 40/82) the same licensing system was found to result in a total ban on imports from six Member States. The Court found that the measure did not form part of a seriously considered health policy and operated as a disguised restriction on trade between Member States.

Similar protectionist motives were discovered in *Commission v France (Re Italian Table Wines)* (case 42/82). Here the Court found excessive delays in customs clearance of wine imported from Italy into France, pending analysis of the wine to ensure it complied with French quality standards. While it conceded that some analysis in the form of random checks, resulting in minor delays, might be justified, the measures taken by the French, which involved systematic checks greatly in excess of those made on domestically produced wine, were both discriminatory and disproportionate.

More recent cases have shown a greater leniency on the part of the Court, especially when the public health justification is convincing and there is no evidence of a protectionist motive. In *R v Royal Pharmaceutical Society of Great Britain* (cases 266, 267/87) the Court found that the rules of the Society prohibiting the substitution by pharmacists of other equivalent drugs for proprietary brands prescribed by doctors, although clearly discriminatory in the effect on imports, were justified to maintain patients' confidence and to avoid the 'anxiety factor' associated with product substitution (see also *Lucien Ortscheit GmbH v Eurim-Pharm Arzneimittel GmbH* (case C–320/93)).

The prohibition in the Danish bee case (*Ditlev Bluhme* (case C–67/97)) was also found to be proportionate. In that case, as well as there being no protectionist motive, the ECJ highlighted the fact that the measures formed the basis of a mechanism recognised in international law for the protection of species — the establishment of a conservation area.

Protection of national treasures possessing artistic, historic or archaeological value

So far these grounds have not been used to provide a basis for derogation under Article 30 (ex 36), but it was suggested in *Commission v Italy (Re Export*

Tax on Art Treasures) (case 7/68) that a desire to prevent art treasures leaving the country would have justified a quantitative restriction, even though it could not justify a charge. It is thought that it would normally apply to restrictions on exports. There is also now a Directive governing the export of cultural property (Directive 93/7/EC).

Protection of industrial and commercial property

The exception provided by Article 30 (ex 36) for industrial and commercial property must be read in conjunction with Article 295 (ex 222) EC, which provides that:

> This Treaty shall in no way prejudice the rules in Member States governing the system of property ownership.

Together these provisions would appear to ensure that national laws governing industrial property remain intact. However, since industrial property law by its very nature tends to contribute to a partitioning of the market, usually along national lines, its exercise inevitably restricts the free movement of goods and conflicts with the principle of market integration so fundamental to the Community. The competition provisions of the Treaty, Articles 81 and 82 (ex 85 and 86) EC (see chapters 15–18), may be invoked to prevent this partitioning, but they are not in themselves sufficient to deal with all the situations in which industrial property law may be used to compartmentalise the market. So the Commission, and more particularly the Court, since the Commission has no power, as it has under Articles 81 and 82 (ex 85 and 86) EC, to enforce the free movement of goods provisions against individuals, have solved the problem by the application of Articles 28 and 30 (ex 30 and 36). As a result, despite the prima facie protection offered to industrial property rights by Articles 30 and 295 (ex 36 and 222) EC, these rights, protected under national law, have undoubtedly been curtailed.

The scope of Article 30 (ex 36) was considered in *Deutsche Grammophon Gesellschaft mbH* v *Metro–SB–Grossmärkte GmbH & Co. KG* (case 78/70). Here Deutsche Grammophon (DG) were seeking to invoke German copyright law to prevent the defendant wholesalers from selling DG's Polydor records, previously exported to France, in Germany. Since a prohibition on reimport would clearly breach Article 28 (ex 30), the matter fell to be decided under the then Article 36 (now 30). Arguing from the second sentence of that Article, that 'prohibitions or restrictions shall not . . . constitute a means of arbitrary discrimination or a disguised restriction on trade between Member States' the Court concluded that the then Article 36 (now 30) permitted prohibitions or restrictions on the free movement of goods only to the extent that they were justified for the protection of the rights that form the *specific subject-matter of the property.* The Court drew a distinction between the *existence* of industrial property rights, which remains unaffected by Community law, and their *exercise*, which may come within the prohibition of the Treaty. If copyright protection is used to prohibit, in one Member State, the marketing of goods brought on to the market by the holder of the rights, or with his consent, in the territory of the other Member State (i.e., to prevent what are known as 'parallel' imports) *solely* because the marketing has not occurred in the domestic market, such a prohibition, maintaining the isolation of the national markets, conflicts with the essential aim of the Treaty, the integration of the national markets into one uniform market. Thus it would constitute an improper *exercise* of the property right in question and would not be justified under the then Article 36 (now 30).

The specific subject-matter of the property, to protect which property rights may be legitimately exercised under EC law, was expressed in *Centrafarm BV* v *Sterling Drug Inc.* (case 15/74) and *Centrafarm BV* v *Winthrop BV* (case 16/74), in the context of a claim for infringement of patents and trade marks respectively, as a guarantee that the owner of the trade mark or patent has the exclusive right to use that trade mark or patent, for the purposes of putting into circulation in the EC products protected by the trade mark or patent *for the first time;* either directly, or by the grant of licences to third parties. Once the protected product has been put on the market in a particular Member State by or with the consent of the owner, or by a person economically or legally dependent on him, such as a licensee, a subsidiary, a parent company or an exclusive distributor (but not an assignee of trade mark rights, see further *IHT* (case C–9/93)), he can no longer rely on national property rights to prevent its import from that State into other Member States. His rights have been exhausted.

This doctrine of 'exhaustion of rights' has been applied by the Court to trade marks (*Centrafarm BV* v *Winthrop BV* (case 16/74)), patents (*Centrafarm BV* v *Sterling Drug Inc.* (case 15/74)), industrial designs (*Keurkoop BV* v *Nancy Kean Gifts BV* (case 144/81)) and, subject to some qualification due to its special nature (see *Warner Brothers Inc.* v *Cristiansen* (case 158/86); *Coditel* v *Cine Vog Films* (case 62/79)), copyright (*Musik-Vertrieb Membran GmbH* v *GEMA* (cases 55 & 57/80)). It is thought that plant breeders' rights too would be subject to the principle, since they were held in *L. C. Nungesser KG* v *Commission* (case 258/78) to fall within the concept of industrial and commercial property.

In *Merck & Co. Inc.* v *Stephar BV* (case 187/80) the exhaustion principle was applied where the patent owner had sold his product in Italy, where there existed no system of patent protection. The Court held that having allowed the goods to be sold in Italy he must accept the consequences as regards free circulation in the Community.

However, where a product has been sold under a compulsory licence, without the consent of the owner, the latter is entitled under Article 30 (ex 36) EC to rely on his property right to prevent the marketing in a third Member State of that product resulting from the exploitation of the compulsory licence, since, not having consented to its use, he is still entitled to enjoy the substance of his exclusive licence *(Pharmon BV* v *Hoechst AG* (case 19/84). See also *Thetford Corp.* v *Fiamma SpA* (case 35/87)). Similarly, where the manufacturing or marketing of a product is lawful in a Member State, *not* through the owner's consent but because of the expiry of the protection period provided for industrial property rights under the law of that Member State, a person with exclusive rights in that product in another Member State may prevent the import of the protected product into the Member State in which he holds these rights (*EMI Electrola GmbH* v *Patricia* (case 341/87), re rights of reproduction and distribution of musical works).

Where a product has been put lawfully on the market in a particular Member State with the owner's consent and the period of protection permitted under national law in that State has *not* expired, its import into another Member State may not be restrained, even though the purpose of an attempt to prevent importation is to prevent parties taking advantage of different price levels in different Member States, whether the reason for the price differences be government policy, legislation, or ordinary market forces (*Centrafarm; GEMA*).

There have been a number of cases involving pharmaceuticals in which importers have sought to take advantage of these price differences and the exhaustion principle, but, because the same product has been marketed in different Member States under different guises, they have needed to repackage or relabel the goods to establish their identity in the Member State of import. The Court has held that persons may rely on trade-mark rights to prevent the import of such goods in order to avoid confusion as to the identity of the product, and to ensure that the consumer can be certain that the trademarked product has not been subject to interference by a third party. However, it was decided in *Hoffman-La Roche & Co. AG* v *Centrafarm* (case 102/77) that an attempt to prevent the import of the trade-marked goods would constitute a disguised restriction on trade between Member States (thus bringing it outside the then Article 36 (now 30)) where:

(a)   the marketing system for the products adopted by the owner of the trade-mark rights involves an artificial partitioning of the market; and where

(b)   the repackaging cannot adversely affect the condition of the product,

(c)   the proprietor receives prior notice of the marketing of the repackaged product, and

(d)   it is stated on the new package that the product has been repackaged.

The Court added that these principles were not confined to medical products.

Similar reasoning underlay the decision in *Centrafarm BV* v *American Home Products Corporation* (AHPC) (case 3/78) about whether the importer, Centrafarm (again!), could change the name of the product it was seeking to import from the UK into Holland from Serenid D, under which it was marketed in the UK, to Seresta, the name under which a near-identical drug from the same manufacturer (AHPC) was marketed in Holland. The Court held that the proprietor of a trade mark was entitled to rely on his property rights to prevent the unauthorised fixing of trade marks on to the goods. However, while it might be lawful for a manufacturer to use different trade marks in different Member States, where a trade-mark system is used in order to partition the market along national lines a prohibition on the unauthorised fixing of labels would constitute a disguised restriction on trade between Member States, thereby falling outside Article 30 (ex 36).

The importer in *Pfizer Inc.* v *Eurim-Pharm GmbH* (case 1/81) did its homework. Prior to importing Vibramycin tablets, manufactured by Pfizer Ltd in the UK, into Germany, Eurim-Pharm repackaged the tablets in packets resembling those used for Vibramycin tablets of German manufacture without tampering with the individual tablets; the new packages had windows through which the trade names 'Vibramycin' and 'Pfizer' could be seen. The pack stated that the tablets had been produced by Pfizer Ltd of Great Britain and had been repackaged and imported by Eurim-Pharm. And they had informed the claimant, Pfizer Inc. (USA), the parent company which owned the Vibramycin and Pfizer trade marks in Europe, in advance of what they were intending to do. The Court held that the claimant could not rely on its trade-mark rights and Article 36 (now 30) to prevent the import of the tablets into Germany under those circumstances. These rulings have been reaffirmed in *Merck and Co. Inc.* v *Primecrown Ltd* (cases C–267 & 268/95), *Bristol-Myers Squibb* v *Paranova A/S* (cases C–427, 429 & 436/93) and *Pharmacia & Upjohn SA* v *Paranova A/S* (case C–379/97).

The free movement of goods has, at least until relatively recently, taken precedence over national industrial property rights by reason of another doctrine introduced by the Court — the doctrine of common origin, introduced in the case of *Van Zuylen Frères* v *Hag AG* (case 192/73). This doctrine, now discredited, is thought to have applied only to trade-mark rights. The *Van Zuylen* case ('Hag I') arose from an attempt by Van Zuylen Frères, who owned the trade mark for Hag coffee in Belgium and Luxembourg, to prevent the import into Luxembourg of 'Hag' decaffeinated coffee made by Hag AG in Germany. The trade mark 'Hag' had been owned originally by a German company, Hag AG, which had operated in Luxembourg and Belgium through its subsidiary company, Hag Belgium. After the Second World War Hag Belgium was sequestrated and sold to a Belgian family. Its Hag trade mark was eventually transferred to Van Zuylen Frères. Thus Hag AG and Van Zuylen Frères legitimately owned the same mark. Could Van Zuylen Frères invoke their rights to prevent Hag AG from exercising its? There was no question of exhaustion of rights, since Hag AG had clearly not consented to the original transfer of its trade mark. The Court held that they could not. Drawing a distinction between the existence of trade-mark rights and their exercise the Court concluded that it was not possible to rely on a trade mark to prohibit, in one Member State, goods lawfully produced in another Member State under an identified mark which has the same origin.

The ruling in *Van Zuylen Frères* was reconsidered by the Court in a second case, *SA CNL-SUCAL* v *Hag GF AG* (case C–10/89) ('Hag II') in a reverse fact situation, Hag (Belgium) having changed hands and Hag (Germany) seeking to restrain import of the former's coffee into Germany. Following its ruling in *Pharmon BV* v *Hoechst AG* (case 19/84) the Court held that in the absence of an element of *consent* on the part of the trade-mark owner to the product being manufactured or marketed in another Member State the owner was entitled to protect his product against imported goods which could be confused with his but for which he was not responsible. The decision, which was carefully reasoned, was based on the purpose of trade-mark protection, which is to guarantee the identity and origin of the marked products to the consumer and ultimate user, and avoid the possibility of confusion. As Advocate-General Jacobs had pointed out, the word 'origin' did not refer to historical origin, but to the commercial origin of the goods, as a guarantee of uniform quality. The determining factor, as the Court pointed out (at para. 15), was the absence of consent on the part of the proprietor to the putting into circulation in another Member State of similar products bearing an identical mark or one leading to confusion, manufactured by an undertaking which is legally and economically independent of the proprietor.

Hag II concerned a situation in which a trade-mark right, originally in common ownership, had been divided *involuntarily*, without the consent of the original owner. In *IHT Internationale Heiztechnik GmbH v Ideal-Standard GmbH* (case C–9/93) the Court had to decide whether a *voluntary* assignment to an independent undertaking of trade-mark rights in Ideal-Standard products in Germany, originating from a French subsidiary of IHT (USA), would exhaust the rights of the owner of the same trade-mark rights in Germany, which was also a subsidiary of IHT (USA). Would the assignment of such rights by one member of the IHT group, *without the consent of the other*, exhaust the rights of the whole group?

The Court held that it would not. The principle of exhaustion of rights only applied where the owner of the trade mark in the importing State and the owner of the trade mark in the exporting State were the same, or where, even if they are separate persons, they are economically linked, for example, as licensee, or parent company, or subsidiary, or exclusive distributor. It did not apply where trade-mark rights have been assigned to an unrelated enterprise such that the assignor and related enterprises no longer have control.

Thus, in the absence of consent, the essential concept for the purposes of exhaustion of rights, replacing the concept of common origin, is unitary control. In the absence of consent, or unitary control, guaranteeing uniform standards, there will be no exhaustion of rights.

Where goods have no common origin but have been manufactured and marketed independently it has always been possible to invoke trade-mark rights to prevent imports of goods with the same or similar trade marks where this might lead to the confusion of the customer, even though marketing of these goods under their respective marks may be quite lawful and even protected in their country of origin. In *Terrapin (Overseas) Ltd v Terranova Industrie C.A. Kapferer & Co.* (case 119/75) a German firm, proprietors of the trade name Terranova, sought to prevent an English company from registering its trade name Terrapin in Germany, since the products of both firms (building materials) were similar, and would, the German company argued, lead to confusion amongst consumers. The ECJ held that the then Article 36 (now 30) could be invoked to prevent the import of goods marketed under a name giving rise to confusion where these rights have been acquired by different proprietors under different national laws as long as they do not operate as a means of arbitrary discrimination or disguised restriction on trade between Member States.

A similar situation, involving not trade marks but a registered design, arose in *Keurkoop BV* v *Nancy Keane Gifts BV* (case 144/81). Here Keurkoop BV, the proprietor in Holland of a registered design for a particular style of handbag, sought to prevent the import into Holland of an identical bag, manufactured in France to a design registered in France by a different owner. The ECJ held that it would be entitled under the then Article 36 (now 30) to exercise its property rights in order to prevent the bags being imported from France, since these bags had not been marketed in France by it or with its consent; the rights had arisen independently of each other. The Court did, however, suggest that the matter should be examined to ensure that there was no agreement or concerted practice between the parties concerned which might infringe Article 85 (now 81) (competition law, see chapter 15).

Keurkoop v *Nancy Keane* was followed in *Consorzio Italiano della Componentistica de Ricambio per Autoveicoli* v *Régie Nationale des Usines Renault* (case 53/87). Here Renault was held entitled under the then Article 36 (now 30) to invoke its registered patent rights in ornamental designs for car body parts to prevent the claimant association's members from manufacturing copies of Renault's parts in Italy, or marketing such parts following their manufacture in other Member States, *without Renault's consent* (see also *AB Volvo* v *Eric Veng* (case 238/87)).

In *Deutsche Renault AG* v *Audi AG* (case C–317/91) Audi was held entitled under the then Article 36 (now 30), as the owner of a registered and protected trade mark in Germany, the 'Quattro' mark, to prohibit the use in Germany by a Renault subsidiary established in Germany of the designation 'Espace Quadra' for a four-wheel drive vehicle marketed in France and elsewhere under that name, where the use of the name might cause confusion. It was left to the national court to decide whether the use of the name Espace Quadra would cause confusion, according to the meaning of the term in national (German) trade-mark law. The Court did, however, suggest that Community law 'did not lay down any strict interpretative criterion for the concept of the risk of confusion'. Following this judgment it may be doubted whether *Prantl* (case 16/83, see chapter 10) remains good law.

In the last four cases, property rights were being invoked in order to protect the owner's legitimate property in his *product*. Where the owner seeks to invoke his rights to prevent the import of goods solely because the public *may be misled as to their national origin* the Court has held (*Theodor Kohl KG* v *Ringelhan and Rennett SA* (case 177/83)) that national trade-mark law may not be relied upon in the absence of evidence of unfair competition. Similarly national measures which seek to employ industrial or commercial property rights in order to encourage or protect domestic production at the expense of imports from other Member States will breach Article 28 (ex 30) and will not be permitted under Article 30 (ex 36) (e.g., *Generics UK* v *Smith Kline* (case C–191/90) (re licences of right); *Commission* v *UK* (case C–30/90) (re compulsory patent licences)).

The principles outlined above will only apply to trade within the Community. Where parties seek to assert their property rights to prevent goods from third countries from entering the Community the free movement provisions of Articles 28 and 30 (ex 30 and 36) do not apply (*EMI Records Ltd* v *CBS United Kingdom Ltd* (case 51/75), *Generics UK Ltd* v *Smith Kline and French* (case C–191/90), *Silhouette International Schmied GmbH & Co. KG* v *Hartlaner Handelsgesellschaft mbH* (case C–355/96) — this last case concerned the Trade Marks Directive, discussed further below).

Because of the wide disparity in national trade-mark rules and its resulting adverse impact on the internal market, harmonisation at Community level was clearly required. In the field of *trade marks*, Directive 89/104 was passed in 1989 ((1989) OJ L 40/1). Its aim was to approximate those aspects of trade-mark law which most directly affect the functioning of the common market, to ensure that the conditions for obtaining and continuing to hold a registered trade mark right are the same in all Member States. The Directive defines trade-mark rights and the rights attached to trade-mark ownership, as well as its limitations. It provides common grounds for refusal of registration, invalidity and loss or exhaustion of rights. The effect of the measure, implemented in the UK in the Trade Marks Act 1994, is to broaden the scope of what may be registered as a trade mark and extend the rights conferred by trade mark registration, thereby reducing the need for reliance on the unpredictable remedy of passing off. However, as the Court pointed out in *IHT* (case C–9/93), the Directive does not change the essential character of national trade-mark law, which remains essentially territorial and independent.

The Trade Marks Directive has not been without its critics. One particular area of concern is the scope of the exhaustion doctrine in relation to goods from outside the EU, the case law on which parallels that in relation to similar cases brought under Article 30 (ex 36). In *Silhouette,* the ECJ held that national rules of an EU Member State providing for exhaustion of trade-mark rights for products put on the market outside the EEA with the consent of the trade mark proprietor were incompatible with the terms of the Trade Mark Directive. From the wording of Article 7(1), exhaustion would take place only if the goods had been put on the market within the EEA. The Court took the opportunity to refine the scope of this ruling in *Sebago Inc.* v *GB-Unic* (case C–173/98). Sebago was the owner of trademarks for shoes, registered in Benelux. GB-Unic sold some Sebago shoes which had been manufactured in El Salvador and imported into the EU via a supplier in Belgium. Sebago claimed that this violated its rights, as it had not consented to the sale of those shoes in the Community. GB-Unic argued that it is sufficient for consent (thereby triggering the exhaustion doctrine) if the proprietor of the trade mark has consented to the marketing in the EC of similar goods bearing the same trade mark. Having reaffirmed its judgment in *Silhouette,* the ECJ then went on to take a narrow view of consent, stating that consent must relate to the specific goods in respect of which exhaustion was claimed. This narrow interpretation of the Trade Mark Directive has been the subject of some adverse comment, as, by limiting the scope of the exhaustion doctrine, it allows companies to partition markets and maintain high prices. A report comparing prices between the EU and the USA showed that prices in the USA tend to be between 40–50 per cent of those in the EU.

As a result of this report, the Community institutions are proposing to revise the Trade Mark Directive.

In the absence of full harmonisation of national trade mark law, Regulation 90/94 (OJ L11, 14.1.94) was introduced. The Regulation provided for the introduction of a Community trade mark, covering all the Member States, to be obtained by a single application. Proposals are also under way for a Directive on the legal protection of designs (OJ C 287/157 30.10.95 amended [1996] OJ C 142), and the Commission has issued a green paper with a view to introducing a common system of rapid and inexpensive legal protection for 'low level' inventions, known as 'utility models' (COM (97) 691).

In the field of *copyright*, Directive 93/83 provided for the coordination of certain rules relating to copyright and rights relating to copyright applicable to satellite broadcasting (OJ L 246, 2.10.93), and Directive 93/98 provided for the harmonisation of the terms of protection of copyright and related rights (OJ L 290, 24.11.93). In 1995 the Commission adopted a green paper on copyright and related rights in the information society (COM (95) 382) on the basis of which arose a proposal for a Directive (COM (97) 628). A Directive has also been proposed to deal with artists' resale rights ([1996] OJ C 178). Specific Directives apply to copyright in the broadcasting area (e.g., the Lending Rights Directive 92/100/EEC ([1992] OJ L 346/61) and Satellite Broadcasting and Cable Retransmission Directive 93/83/EEC ([1993] OJ L 248/15)).

The case law of the ECJ, as examined above, represents an uneasy compromise between the single market principle and the need to safeguard legitimate industrial and commercial property rights protected under national law. A similar tension arises in the field of competition law (see chapters 16 and 18). The Court's more recent decisions indicate a greater willingness to safeguard the interests of creativity, originality and goodwill protected by intellectual property law, and to encourage and reward the taking of commercial risks. This is evidenced by a more generous approach to the question of the permitted *exercise* of property rights protected under national law (e.g. *EMI Electrola* v *Patricia* (case 341/87); *Deutsche Renault AG* v *Audi AG* (case C–317/91)) and by limiting the scope of the exhaustion principle (*Hag II* (case C–10/89); *IHT* (case C–9/93); but cf. *Silhouette* (case 355/96) and *Sebago* (case C–173/98)), although the difficulties with patents, especially pharmaceuticals, remain (e.g., *Merck* v *Primecrown* (cases C–267 & 268/95)). In the area of copyright law the Court has refused to apply the exhaustion principle to the showing of films and hiring of video cassettes (as opposed to their sale), recognising the owners' legitimate claim to benefit from repeated use (*Coditel* v *SA, Ciné Vog Films,* (case 62/79); *Warner Brothers Inc.* v *Cristiansen* (case 158/86)). Community legislation has supplemented the work of the Court and now provides a framework for the protection of industrial property rights in the Community. Thus a start has been made, and progress, if slow, is steady. Member States have clearly recognised industrial and commercial property law as an area in which, under the subsidiarity principle of Article 5 (ex 3b) EC, the objectives 'cannot be sufficiently achieved by the Member States' without endangering the single market and can be 'better achieved by the Community'.

It may be noted that any discrimination, direct or indirect, in relation to industrial and commercial property rights will fall foul of Article 12 (ex 6) EC (formerly Article 7 EEC), which prohibits 'any discrimination on the grounds of nationality' (*Collins* v *Imtrat* (cases C–92/92, 328/92)).

Article 30 (ex 36) EC and the harmonisation of Community rules

The EC Treaty provided from the beginning for the creation of common Community rules, not only in the areas marked out for common organisation, such as agriculture, but in all the areas of activity outlined in the Treaty, or falling within the broader objectives of the Community (see Article 308 (ex 235) EC and chapter 3). A huge body of rules is now in place. Many of these rules, particularly, but by no means exclusively, those enacted under Articles 94 and 95 (ex 100 and 100a) EC, for the purposes of the internal market, seek to harmonise national laws, normally by means of Directives. Although Directives require implementation at national level, and leave national authorities some choice as to 'the form and method of implementation' (Article 250 (ex 189) EC), once the period allowed for implementation has expired, Member States are not free to enact or maintain domestic measures inconsistent with their obligations under the Directive or with the general purposes of the Directive. Where there is a conflict between provisions of national and Community law, Community law must prevail (see chapter 5). The question arises, once harmonisation has taken place, to what extent are national authorities free to derogate from their obligations under the Treaty either under the *Cassis* rule of reason or Article 30 (ex 36) EC, or to enact more stringent rules? Does the existence of Community legislation pre-empt the field?

The general rule, applied initially in the field of agriculture, is that once a common Community organisation for a particular product has been set up, Member States are no longer entitled to maintain in force provisions or adopt practices which are incompatible with the scheme of common organisation or which jeopardise its aims or functioning (*Tasca* (case 65/75)). Clearly in an area such as agriculture subject to common and comprehensive organisation there will be little scope for unilateral action by Member States. But this is not to say that Community law, even here, pre-empts the field. There are different views on whether Community competence in a particular area is exclusive or concurrent with that of Member States. The Commission, unsurprisingly, takes the more generous view of the Community's exclusive competence. However, there is general agreement that in most areas of activity competence is concurrent, but the degree to which Member States are free to act varies according to whether harmonisation is comprehensive (as in areas subject to common organisation) or minimal, supporting and supplementing Member States' actions, as in education and vocational training (Article 149 (ex 126) EC) and culture (Article 151 (ex 128) EC). Even where there is full harmonisation, it is submitted that Member States are not wholly powerless to act in an emergency, in order to protect genuine and important national interests. Thus in each case it is necessary to examine the common provision to ascertain whether the field is occupied. If so, any national measure conflicting with the common provision will be illegal. If not, national measures are permissible provided they do not impair the effective functioning of the common organisation or run counter to Article 28 (ex 30) EC. In this case derogation may still be permissible under Article 30 (ex 36) EC.

It was originally thought that, once the Community had legislated in a particular field, States were no longer free to enact legislation in that field or resort to Article 30 (ex 36) EC (the 'strict' 'total' or 'classic' pre-emption theory). This view derived support from the Court's ruling in *Tedeschi* v *Denkavit Commerciale Srl* (case 5/77). Here in the context of a dispute concerning a Community Directive regulating the use of food additives, the Court held that where in the application of the then Article 100, Community Directives provide for harmonisation of the measures necessary to the free movement of goods, recourse to former Article 36 (now 30) was no longer justified. The Court appeared to take the same view in a case involving Solvents Directive 73/173 in *Ratti* (case 148/78). However, in both cases, the Directives contained 'market access' clauses, expressly prohibiting domestic restrictions on imports which complied with the requirements of the Directives, and, more importantly, provided safeguard procedures (requiring notification to, and approval by, the Commission) should Member States need to adopt 'protective measures' in the public interest. Where EC legislation did not provide such procedures it appeared to be possible for States to take emergency action based on Article 30 (ex 36) provided a *genuine* justification could be proved. In *van Bennekom* (case 227/82) the Court held (at para. 35):

It is only when Community Directives . . . make provision for the *full* harmonisation of all the measures needed to ensure the protection of [in this case] human and animal life and *institute Community procedures to monitor compliance therewith* that recourse to Article 36 [now 30] ceases to be justified. (Emphasis added.)

See also *van der Veldt* (case C–17/93). This view was modified in *R* v *Ministry of Agriculture, Fisheries and Food, ex parte Hedley Lomas (Ireland) Ltd* (case C–5/94), discussed in chapter 4. The case concerned a claim for damages against the UK for losses resulting from a ban on the export of live sheep to Spain on the grounds that Spain had failed to comply with Council Directive 74/557. The Directive, an animal welfare measure, required Member States to provide for the stunning of animals before slaughter. It did not expressly require Member States to monitor its implementation or provide penalties for non-compliance. The Directive was implemented by the Spanish authorities but without providing for monitoring procedures or penalties for non-compliance. Although the ban was clearly contrary to Article 34 (now 29), the UK argued that it was justified under Article 36 (now 30), as a measure designed for the protection of the health of animals. The Court found that it was not. The UK had failed to adduce any evidence that Spanish slaughter-houses were not fulfilling their obligations under the Directive.

This finding was no doubt correct on the facts: the necessity for a ban was not proved, and it was in any case disproportionate. Also, to the extent that the Directive provided for harmonisation of the measures necessary to achieve the *specific objective* required by the UK government (i.e., the stunning of animals before slaughter) the matter was covered by Community law. However, since Community law failed to prescribe procedures to monitor compliance, Member States might have thought they were entitled to resort to Article 30 (ex 36) EC when there was evidence that the Directive had been breached. This was suggested in *van Bennekom* (case 227/82). In *Hedley Lomas* the Court found otherwise.

> . . . recourse to Article 36 [now 30] is no longer possible where Community Directives provide for harmonisation of the measures necessary to achieve the *specific objective which would be furthered by reliance upon this provision.*
>
> This exclusion of recourse to Article 36 [now 30] cannot be affected by the fact that . . . the Directive does not lay down any Community procedure for monitoring compliance nor any penalties in the event of breach of its provisions. . . . Member States are obliged, in accordance with the first paragraph of Article 5 [now 10] and the third paragraph of Article 189 [now 250] of the Treaty, to take all measures necessary to guarantee the application and effectiveness of Community law. . . . In this regard, the Member States must rely on trust in each other to carry out inspections on their respective territories. (Paragraphs 18 and 19, emphasis added.)

This ruling was clearly designed to prevent Member States from taking reciprocal action contrary to the Treaty in the face of alleged breaches of Community law in order *to protect an interest which is already protected by community rules.* However, it does not mean that States are powerless to protect such an interest in the face of a breach of those rules. They may persuade the Commission to act under Article 226 (ex 169) EC. If the Commission refuses to act, they may themselves take action under Article 227 (ex 170) EC, if necessary seeking interim relief. Arguably they may now claim damages on the basis of *Francovich* v *Italy* (cases 6 & 9/90) (see chapter 3). But they will not be allowed to act unilaterally in breach of Articles 28 or 29 (ex 30 or 34) EC on the basis of Article 30 (ex 36). This is consistent with the Court's rejection of the defence of reciprocity in actions under Article 226 (ex 169) EC (see chapter 28).

Paragraphs 18 and 19 of *Hedley Lomas*, quoted above, were invoked in *R* v *Minister of Agriculture, Fisheries and Food, ex parte Compassion in World Farming Ltd* (case C–1/96). Here a British animal welfare group was seeking to prevent the export of live calves to other Member States which permitted the rearing of calves in crates, a practice prohibited by the UK (and a Council of Europe Convention). EC Directive 91/629, a harmonisation measure relating to the health of animals, laid down minimum common standards for the protection of live calves, but specifically allowed Member States to apply, within their own territory, stricter rules. In this way, as the ECJ pointed out, the Directive aimed to strike a balance between the interests of animal protection and the smooth functioning of the organisation of the market in calves and derived products. It followed that 'a Member State cannot rely on Article 36 [now 30] of the Treaty in order to restrict the export of calves to other Member States for reasons relating to the protection of the health of animals, which constitutes the specific objective of the harmonisation undertaken by the Directive'.

Where derogation may legitimately be sought from harmonisation measures enacted under Article 95(1) (ex 100(1)), this will now be governed by Article 95(4) (ex 100a(4)). This Article, introduced by the SEA in 1986, provides that where harmonising legislation has been passed by qualified majority, Member States seeking to 'apply national provisions on grounds of major needs referred to in Article 30 [ex 36], or relating to the protection of the environment or the working environment' must notify the Commission. The Commission may then 'confirm' the provisions after having verified that they do not constitute a means of 'arbitrary discrimination or disguised restriction on trade between Member States'. The Commission or any other Member State may bring the matter before the ECJ if it considers that a State is making improper use of these powers.

The ToA has now tightened up on these provisions. In notifying the Commission of its proposed national measures a Member State must also notify the grounds for maintaining them (new Article 95(4) EC). Furthermore, if a Member State deems it necessary to introduce national provisions based on scientific evidence relating to the protection of the environment or the working environment on grounds of a problem specific to that Member State arising after the adoption of a harmonisation measure, it must notify the Commission of the envisaged provisions as well as the grounds for introducing them (new Article 95(5) EC). The Commission will then be required to approve or reject these provisions within six months after having verified whether or not they constitute an obstacle to the functioning of the internal market. In the absence of a decision by the Commission within this period the (proposed) national provisions shall be deemed to have been approved (new Article 95(6) EC).

Thus Member States are not free to act unilaterally in breach of this Article; any derogation will now be subject to the Commission's approval, or, ultimately, the consent of the Court.

Although expressed to apply only where harmonisation measures have been enacted by qualified majority, it has been suggested that the same procedure should be available where legislation has been passed unanimously; the Article 95(4) (ex 100a(4)) procedure is not in terms limited to States which have *not* agreed to the measure in question, and some scope for derogation should be available to meet emergencies not foreseen at the time when the legislation was passed. Moreover, in an emergency, arguably it should not be necessary for a State to obtain *prior* approval for its actions from the Commission, provided that the need for action is genuine and urgent and the Commission is notified at the earliest possible time.

Minimum harmonisation

The trend, since the SEA, and particularly since Maastricht, to minimum harmonisation has created problems. Where harmonisation is minimal, Member States are theoretically free to lay down more stringent domestic standards. Such domestic measures, imposing extra burdens on producers, if applied to imported as well as domestic products, are likely to create barriers to the single market. If they do so, actually or potentially, will they be permitted to apply only to domestically produced goods, or may they be applied to all goods? If applicable only to domestic production, domestic producers will be disadvantaged. If applicable to all goods, when, and in what circumstances, will they be permitted?

The answer depends on the terms of the Directive. Confusingly, EC harmonisation measures do not follow a single pattern. Some contain 'market access' clauses. Member States are (expressly or impliedly) free to adopt more stringent measures than those laid down in the Directive as long as they do not prohibit or restrict the import of goods which satisfy the requirements of the Directive. Some contain no market access clause. In this case domestic measures over and above those required by the Directive which restrict interstate trade will be permissible provided they are justified under the rule of reason or Article 30 (ex 36). Where the Directive provides procedures for derogation, as in *Tedeschi* and *Ratti*, or, in the case of measures enacted under Article 95 (ex 100a) EC, under Article 95(4) (ex 100a(4)), those procedures must be followed.

What was not fully clear until *R v Secretary of State for Health, ex parte Gallaher Ltd* (case C–11/92) was whether domestic producers could invoke a market access clause in order to challenge national rules which applied only to domestic production. The case concerned a challenge by three leading UK cigarette producers to UK regulations implementing Tobacco Directive 89/622. The Directive required Member States to provide *inter alia* for health warnings on cigarettes to cover 'at least' 4 per cent of the packet (Article 4(4)). It contained a market access clause. Member States were not to prohibit or restrict the sale of products which complied with the Directive (Article 8(1)). The UK regulations provided for more extensive health warnings, to cover 6 per cent of the packet, but these were applicable only to domestic production. The applicants claimed that the rules, which imposed an extra burden on them as domestic producers, jeopardised the free movement of tobacco products and was contrary to the Directive and past case law. They invoked *Tedeschi* and *Ratti*. The Court disagreed. These cases were distinguishable. Although the UK regulations discriminated against domestic production, they were consistent with the scheme of harmonisation provided under EC law.

Thus, if *Gallaher* is followed (and always depending on the wording of the Directive), where there is minimum harmonisation and a market access clause, EC law will permit reverse discrimination, as it has done in other areas. This was confirmed in *R v Minister of Agriculture, Fisheries and Food, ex parte Compassion in World Farming Ltd* (case C–1/96), where the ECJ held unequivocally that where a Community Directive providing for minimum standards of harmonisation allows Member States to maintain stricter standards these can only be applied in their own territory. They will of course only apply to the State's own products. A similar approach seems now to be being taken in the fields of services and establishment (see chapter 21).

Gallaher has been criticised as tending to undermine competition in the single market and discourage experiment and diversity. It is argued that Member States are unlikely to enact legislation in the interest of higher standards where this will result in a competitive disadvantage for domestic products. However, in the light of the current trend favouring minimum Community harmonisation, based on the principle of subsidiarity, a system permitting reverse discrimination may be a more practical way of regulating Member States' freedom to supplement Community provision than ad hoc assessment by the Court under Article 30 (ex 36) EC or the rule of reason. Higher standards may even prove more attractive to consumers. Nevertheless, as Weatherill comments, the process of minimum harmonisation 'does not solve the specific problem of which market-partitioning national measures are justified and which are not'.

Derogation provisions other than Article 30 (ex 36) EC

In addition to the rule of reason and Article 30 (ex 36) EC there are further specific provisions of the Treaty allowing for derogation from the principles of Articles 28 and 29 (ex 30 and 34) EC, mainly in the field of economic and commercial policy; hence the Court's refusal to allow Article 30 (ex 36) to justify purely economic measures. These comprise:

(a)   measures to meet *short-term economic difficulties* ('conjunctural policy') (Article 99 (ex 103) EC),

(b)   measures to meet *balance of payment difficulties* (Articles 108–111 (ex 107, 108 and 109) EC), and most important of all,

(c)   measures to meet:

(i)   *deflections of trade* which might obstruct the execution of Community commercial policy, or

(ii)   *economic difficulties in any Member State* resulting from the implementation of commercial policy (Article 134 (ex 115) (see *Criel, nee Donckerwolcke* v *Procureur de la République* (case 41/76)).

Article 134 (ex 115) EC applies only in the context of the common commercial policy, i.e., to goods originating from third countries which are in free circulation within the EC, and is necessary, since deflections of trade or economic difficulties may well arise as a result of differences in regimes between Member States, permitted under the Community's common commercial policy.

Measures taken under the above Articles are required to be taken either by the Commission or the Council (on a proposal from the Commission), or, if taken by Member States, subject to authorisation or approval by the

Commission. They are thus subject to strict Community control. As with measures taken under Article 30 (ex 36), they must comply with the proportionality principle.

Derogation is also permitted *in the interests of national security* (Articles 296–7 (ex 223 and 224) EC). Under Article 296 (ex 223), a State 'may take such measures as it considers necessary for the protection of the essential interests of its security which are connected with the production of or trade in arms, munitions and war material', provided that such measures do not adversely affect competition within the common market regarding products which are not intended for military purposes. Under Article 297 (ex 224) EC, States may consult with each other and take steps to counteract measures taken by a Member State in the event of war or the threat of war or serious internal disturbances, or to carry out obligations undertaken for the purpose of maintaining peace or international security. Should the Commission or a Member State consider that a State is making improper use of its powers under Articles 296 and 297 (ex 223 and 224) they may bring that State before the Court under Article 298 (ex 225) EC. It would seem that for these provisions, as for Article 30 (ex 36), where there is a Community measure covering the specific subject, a Member State cannot rely on the derogation provided in the Treaty itself. In *R v HM Treasury, ex parte Centro-Com Srl* (case C–124/95), for example, the UK sought, on the basis of the UN sanctions against Serbia and Montenegro, to prevent the payments of sums held in a London bank account held by a Montenegrin to an Italian company. The ECJ, however, pointed out that this issue was dealt with by an EC Regulation and that the UK could thus not rely on the national security exception in the then Article 224 (now 297) EC.

Further reading

Alexander, W., 'IP and the Free Movement of Goods — 1996 Caselaw of the ECJ' [1998] 29 IIC 16.

Castillo de la Torre, F., 'Trade Marks and Free Movement of Pharmaceuticals in the European Community: To Partition or not to Partition' [1997] 6 EIPR 304.

Falke, J., and Joerges, C., *Traditional Harmonisation Policy* (Florence EUI Working Paper 91/13).

Flynn, J., 'How Well Will Article 100a(4) Work? A Comparison with Article 93' (1987) 24 CML Rev 689.

Roberts, G., Casenote on *Gallaher* (1994) 31 CML Rev 165.

Slot, P.J., 'Harmonisation' (1996) 21 EL Rev 378.

Waelbroek, M., 'The Emergent Doctrine of Community Pre-emption', in Sandalow, T., and Stein, E., (eds) *Courts and Free Markets* (Oxford: Clarendon, 1982).

Weatherill, S., 'Regulating the Internal Market: Result Orientation in the House of Lords' (1992) 17 EL Rev 299.

Weatherill, S., Casenote on *Gallaher* (1994) 19 EL Rev 55.

TWELVE

State monopolies of a commercial character

Complementary to Articles 28 and 29 (ex 30 and 34) EC is Article 31 (ex 37), which requires Member States to 'adjust any State monopolies of a commercial character so as to ensure that when the transitional period has ended no discrimination regarding the conditions under which goods are procured and marketed exists between nationals of Member States'.

States must also refrain from introducing any new measure contrary to the above paragraph or which restricts the scope of Articles 25, 28 and 29 (ex 12, 30 and 34) (Article 31(2)).

State monopolies are clearly capable of obstructing the free movement of goods since their position in a particular market enables them to control the flow of goods in and out of the country as well as the conditions under which trade in such goods takes place.

To qualify as a monopoly it is not necessary to exert total control of the market in particular goods; it is sufficient if the bodies concerned have as their object transactions regarding a commercial product capable of being the subject of trade between Member States, and play an *effective* part in such trade (*Costa* v *ENEL* (case 6/64)).

The aim of Article 31 (ex 37) is not to abolish monopolies *per se* but to ensure that they do not operate in a discriminatory manner, thereby obstructing the free movement of goods and distorting competition within the Community. In *Banchero* (case C–387/93), the ECJ held that the then Article 37(1) did not apply to a situation in which the Member State authorises the retailers permitted to sell a product, in this case, tobacco, provided that the State does not interfere with the *supply* of those goods to be sold, leaving the retailers free to choose the source of the product (see further chapter 10). Even if the rules of a commercial monopoly are not on their face discriminatory they will be condemned if they are liable in fact to have a discriminatory effect and to distort competition between Member States.

Article 31 (ex 37) only applies to State monopolies in the provision of goods. It does not apply to services. However, discrimination in the monopoly provision of services may be caught by Article 12 (ex 6) EC, together with the services provisions of the Treaty (Articles 49–56 (ex 59–66)), or by Article 82 (ex 86) (competition provision — abuse of a dominant position).

Although not expressly stated in the Article the Court has held that an exclusive right to import or export particular goods falls within the scope of Article 31 (ex 37) (*Manghera* (case 59/75)).

However, the Article only applies to activities which are intrinsically connected with the specific business of the monopoly (*SA des Grandes Distilleries Peureux* (case 119/78)). The activities must be capable of affecting trade between Member States.

THIRTEEN

Restrictions on State aid

Introduction

State aid, like State monopolies, poses a threat to the free movement of goods, since by conferring a benefit on a particular (normally domestic) undertaking or industry, it distorts competition between Member States and interferes with the functioning of the single market. With the completion of the internal market, and the intensification of competition likely to result therefrom, it is even more important that State aid to industry be strictly controlled. Indeed, in a document produced prior to the ToA (CSE (97) 1 final), the Commission identified the need to scrutinise aid as being one of the key actions for the future of the internal market, especially as levels of aid remain high. The line between State aid, discriminatory taxation and measures equivalent to charges or quantitative restrictions is often a fine one. Therefore, although included under the competition provisions of the Treaty and logically belonging there, for practical purposes it may more usefully be considered in advance, alongside and in conjunction with the provisions relating to the free movement of goods.

Even if it poses a threat to the Community interest, State aid represents for Member States a vital instrument of economic and social policy, necessary to the economic health of a region or to whole sectors of the economy, particularly in times of economic difficulty and high unemployment. The regulation of State aid is thus a sensitive area, requiring a balancing of the interests of Member States and of the Community and recent treaty amendments re-emphasise the tension between Member States' interests and the creation of the internal market. On the one hand, the industrial provision introduced by the TEU highlights the importance of not distorting competition (Article 157 (ex 130) EC). On the other hand, new Article 16 EC highlights the importance of public services and the need to ensure that those who are entrusted with such public services are capable of carrying out their mission. This provision may thus imply that competition concerns are not the only factors to be taken into account but that other considerations, such as social cohesion, also have a value.

Structure of State aid provisions

The EC Treaty attempts to achieve a balance between Member States and the Community by laying down a broad prohibition on the granting of State aid 'which distorts or threatens to distort competition by favouring certain undertakings or the production of certain goods' insofar as it affects trade between Member States (Article 87(1) (ex 92(1))), subject to express and extensive derogation to protect a number of legitimate economic and social goals (Article 87(2) and (3) (ex 92(2) and (3))). Article 87(2) (ex 92(2)) lays down the categories of aid that *'shall* be compatible with the common market'; these comprise:

(a)   aid having a social character, granted to individual consumers, provided that such aid is granted without discrimination related to the origin of the products concerned;

(b)   aid to make good the damage caused by natural disasters or exceptional occurrences;

(c)   aid granted to the economy of certain areas of the Federal Republic of Germany affected by the division of Germany, insofar as such aid is required in order to compensate for the economic disadvantages caused by that division.

Article 87(3) (ex 92(3)) lists those aids which *may* be compatible with the common market. These comprise:

(a)   aid to promote the economic development of areas where the standard of living is abnormally low or where there is serious underemployment;

(b)   aid to promote the execution of an important project of common European interest or to remedy a serious disturbance in the economy of a Member State;

(c)   aid to facilitate the development of certain economic activities or of certain economic areas, where such aid does not adversely affect trading conditions to an extent contrary to the common interest;

(d)   aid to promote culture and heritage conservation where such aid does not affect trading conditions and competition in the Community to an extent that is contrary to the common interest;

(e)   such other categories of aid as may be specified by decision of the Council acting by a qualified majority on a proposal by the Commission.

Machinery for the application of Article 87 (ex 92) is provided by Articles 88 (ex 93) and 89 (ex 94). Under Article 88(1) (ex 93(1)) the Commission is required, 'in cooperation with Member States', to 'keep under constant review all systems of aid existing in those States ["existing aid"]'. Under Article 88(3) (ex 93(3)) the Commission must 'be informed, in sufficient time to enable it to submit its comments, of any plans to grant or alter aid ["new aids"]'.

Whether acting in relation to existing aids or in response to plans for new aids, where the Commission considers State aid to be incompatible with the common market, it must act according to the procedure laid down in Article 88(2) (ex 93(2)):

> If, after giving notice to the parties concerned to submit their comments, the Commission finds that aid granted (or proposed) by a State or through State resources is not compatible with the common market having regard to Article 87 [ex 93], or that such aid is being misused, it shall decide that the State concerned shall abolish or alter such aid within a period of time to be determined by the Commission. (para. 1)
>
> If the State concerned does not comply with this decision within the prescribed time, the Commission or any other interested State may, in derogation from the provisions of Articles 226 and 227 [ex 169 and 170], refer the matter to the Court of Justice direct. (para. 2)

Where the Commission fails to impose a time limit for the abolition or amendment of existing aid the Court has held that a two-month time limit will normally be appropriate (*Gebrüder Lorenz GmbH* v *Germany* (case 120/73)).

The procedures laid down in Article 88(2) (ex 93(2)) must be followed and procedural guarantees such as the duty to give reasons and the right to a hearing, as general principles of Community law (see chapter 6), must be observed. The Commission's Decision must contain sufficient facts and figures to support its conclusions. Decisions issued in breach of any of these requirements may be annulled (see e.g., *William Cook* v *Commission* (case C–198/91)). The Court may however refuse to annul a Decision where the outcome would have been the same in the absence of the irregularity (*Commission* v *France* (case 259/85)).

In exceptional circumstances a Member State may apply to the Council for a Decision, which must be unanimous, that in derogation from Article 87 or 89 (ex 92 or 94), an aid which it is granting (existing aid) or intends to grant (new aid) is compatible with the common market. In this case where proceedings have already been initiated by the Commission under Article 88(2) (ex 93(2)) they will be suspended until the Council has made its attitude known (Article 88(2) (ex 93(2)), paras 3 and 4). It may be noted that under Article 87(3)(d) (ex 92(3)(d)) the Council has the power to extend the categories of aid for which dispensation is allowed.

Lastly, under Article 89 (ex 94) the Council, acting by qualified majority on a proposal from the Commission, is empowered to make Regulations concerning the application of Articles 87 and 88 (ex 92 and 93 respectively). A Regulation was adopted in May 1998 to facilitate the operation of the State aid system. It provides for the use of a block exemption system for certain categories of aid. So far three such block exemptions have been proposed: in respect of small and medium-sized enterprises; for small amounts of aid (*de minimis*); and in respect of aid for training ([2000] OJ C89). A second regulation (Regulation 659/99) has also been enacted which codifies the existing procedural practice of the Commission together with the rulings of the ECJ ([1999] OJ L83/1). It also provides for certain enforcement powers for the Commission. These provisions include a requirement on Member States to provide an annual report on all existing aid schemes.

The Commission insists on strict compliance by Member States with their obligation under Article 88(3) (ex 93(3)) to inform the Commission of plans to grant or alter aid. Since Member States not infrequently flouted this requirement, or, having notified the Commission, went ahead without giving the Commission time to respond, the Commission, in a practice note issued in November 1983 (OJ No. C318, 24.11.83, p. 3) expressed its intention to 'use all the measures at its disposal' to ensure compliance by Member States with Article 88(3) (ex 93(3)). Henceforth Member States which had granted aid illegally, i.e., without informing the Commission, or precipitately, would be required to recover such aid from recipients, and, in the agricultural sector, would be refused advance payments from the EAGGF (European Agriculture Guidance and Guarantee Funds). Since then the Commission has taken many decisions requiring the repayment of aid. In July 1990 British Aerospace was required to repay £44.4 million worth of 'sweeteners' it received when acquiring the Rover car group in 1988 (decision successfully challenged on procedural grounds in January 1992: new decision issued in March 1993 (EC Bull 3 1993 1.2.50)).

Recipient businesses are required to make repayments even if the business has changed hands and the new owners have never received aid from the State (*Re aid to ENI Lanerossi* (case C–303/88)). Repayment must be made even if it will cause the recipient of aid to be wound up (*Commission* v *Belgium* (case 52/84)). Even where the Member State argues that repayment is impossible, this argument cannot be raised without prior warning (*Commission* v *Italy* (case C–349/93)). The Member State, under its duty of cooperation in Article 10 (ex 5) EC, on encountering difficulties in obtaining repayment should inform the Commission of them together with suggestions for amendments to the decision requiring repayment so as to solve the problem. Further, in *TWD Textilwerke Deggendorf GmbH* v *Commission* (cases T–244 & 486/93), the Court of First Instance approved the Commission's stance according to which implementation of a decision approving the payment of lawful aid was conditional on repayment of earlier illegal aid. This strengthens the Commission's hand, but weaknesses remain in the system for recovery of aid. Most notably, there is the problem that the recipient of unlawful aid retains the benefit of that aid until the decision is made requiring repayment. The decision-making process can take a considerable time and so the benefit illicitly obtained can be considerable. To counterbalance this benefit, however, the Commission may request the payment of interest running from the date the enterprise received the aid (e.g., *Siemens SA* v *Commission* (case T–459/93)). The Commission has also issued a communication to the Member States warning that, in appropriate cases, it will adopt provisional decisions ordering repayment pending completion of the full investigation (OJ 22.6.1995 C 156/5).

In a number of cases a decision requiring repayment has been challenged on the grounds of breach of the claimant's legitimate expectations. In *RSV*

Maschinefabrieken & Scheepswerven NV v *Commission* (case 223/85) a Commission Decision ordering repayment of aid granted to RSV to write off financial losses was annulled at the suit of the recipient, since the Decision was issued, without justification for the delay, some 26 months after the aid had been granted. However, in *Commission* v *Germany* (case C–5/89), the Court, endorsing its decision in *Commission* v *Germany* (case 94/87), held that save in exceptional circumstances firms in receipt of State aid could not have legitimate expectations concerning the lawfulness of aid unless it had been granted in accordance with the procedures of the then Article 93 (now 88). The diligent recipient of aid would make sure that these procedures had been complied with. Nor could the Member State plead the legitimate expectations of recipients in order to evade its obligation to comply with the Commission's decision requiring the recovery of aid. To ensure 'transparency' the Commission now publishes an annual survey of its aid proceedings in the *Official Journal*, and warns potential recipients of the legal consequences of repayment decisions. It also publishes a section on State aids in its annual report on competition policy. In the light of these practices a defence based on legitimate expectations is only likely to succeed in exceptional circumstances such as those obtaining in *RSV* (case 223/85).

Thus all aids granted by Member States are subject either to the dispensation of the Council, or, more normally, the strict supervision and control of the Commission, with ultimate recourse to the Court, either in annulment proceedings under Article 230 (ex 173) EC (see chapter 30) or in proceedings under Article 88(2) (ex 93(2)).

Meaning of State aid

No definition of State aid is given in the Treaty but it has been broadly construed by the Commission and the European courts. State aid has been held to comprise any advantages granted directly or indirectly through State resources. As the Commission has noted in its Reports on Competition Policy, four cumulative elements must be shown to satisfy the test for State aid:

(a)   the measure must be specific rather than general in nature;
(b)   it must grant an advantage to an undertaking;
(c)   the aid must come from State resources; and
(d)   the advantage must distort competition and have an effect on inter-State trade.

Specificity   For a measure to be classified as State aid, it must assist only certain firms or sectors: general economic policy remains a matter for the Member States. Thus the concept does not include a system of minimum prices, since this is not an advantage granted to favour an undertaking or to benefit certain goods and will normally be applied to all goods irrespective of origin. (The latter will, however, be judged under Article 28 (ex 30) — see *van Tiggele* (case 82/77), discussed in chapter 10.) State aid also does not include special treatment for small enterprises in the form of exemption from obligations arising from social protection (*Kirsammer-Hack* v *Nurhan Sidal* (case C–189/91)). It follows that, although certain measures of tax or social policy could give a competitive edge to undertakings established in a given Member State (for example, by lower employment costs), they do not fall within the State aid rules.

It is, however, sometimes difficult to identify the boundary between the two categories. In the *Maribel bis/ter case* (*Belgium* v *Commission* (case C–75/97)), for example, the Commission decided that a Belgian law which provided for additional reductions in social security costs constituted aid because it benefited firms most exposed to international competition. Further, for a measure to be considered general, the Member State should have no discretionary power enabling it to vary the application of a measure depending on who was the beneficiary of the measure, even when the criteria to be taken into consideration were objective factors defined by law (*France* v *Commission (Kimberly Clark Sopalin)* (case C–241/94)). Thus, in the *DMT* case (case C–256/97), the ECJ held that the degree of discretion given to the body which had responsibility for chasing up social security payments from employers and employees meant that, although the policy was phrased in general terms, in practice it turned into aid aimed at specific companies.

Advantage to a firm   To constitute State aid, a benefit must be conferred. Aid falling within the terms of Article 87(1) (ex 92(1)) may be 'in any form whatsoever'. Thus aid can include, as well as actual payments, preferential tax treatment, preferential interest rates, grants to cover redundancy costs, investment grants and subsidies, financial incentives to privatisation (e.g., British Aerospace), or special prices for land, plant or power (e.g., *Kwkerij Gebroeders van der Kooy* (cases 67, 68 and 70/85) — power company supplying natural gas at special reduced prices to the horticulture industry). In *Syndicat Français de l'Express International* v *La Poste* (case C–39/94), the ECJ defined a State aid as including not only benefits such as subsidies, but also interventions which might mitigate the charges normally included in the budgets of an undertaking and which are therefore of the same character and have the same effect as subsidies. When determining whether State aid exists, the question relates not to the causes or aims of State intervention; instead the test is an objective one, concerned with the effects of such an intervention (see, e.g., *Italy* v *Commission* (*Re Aid to the Textile Industry*) (case 173/73), *Banco de Credito Industrial SA* v *Ayuntamiento de Valencia* (case C–387/92) and *Ladbroke Racing Ltd* v *Commission* (case T–67/94)).

To constitute State aid, the advantage must be granted for no consideration or countervailing benefit (*Denkavit* (case 61/79)). It will include injections of capital by a public investor which disregard any prospect of profitability (*Re aid to ENI Lanerosse* (case C–303/88)). The Court has also described aid as existing when State support has no objective commercial justification. The test of commercial justification is sometimes referred to as the hypothetical investor test. Its use is not entirely unproblematic, as it does raise the question of what normal investor behaviour would be. If commercial justification does, however, exist then the fact that the support also fulfils a political purpose will not render it 'aid' within Article 87 (ex 92) (*Belgium* v *Commission* (case C–56/93) — special tariff rates to large Dutch industrial producers of ammonia by a company in which The Netherlands government had a 50 per cent holding justified on commercial grounds).

Origin of resources   To fall within the State aid rules, the resources benefiting the undertaking must come from State resources, whether directly or indirectly. Aid may be granted through any central or local government body, or any agency subject to the control of the State. No distinction is made between aid granted directly by the State or by public or even private bodies established and operated by it to administer that aid (*Steinike und Weinleg* (case 78/76)). It is not necessary that the aid be paid directly out of public funds as long as the State plays a part in initiating or approving the aid. In *Kwekerij Gebroeders van der Kooy BV* v *Commission* (cases 67, 68 and 70/85), a power company created under private law but controlled by the State through a 50 per cent shareholding, and whose prices were subject to government control, was held to be equivalent to the State for the purpose of establishing State aid. In *Syndicat Français de l'Express (SFEI)* v *La Poste* (case C–39/94), the ECJ held that the provision of logistical or commercial support by a public undertaking (La Poste) to a private subsidiary which was engaged in an activity open to free competition, when that subsidiary gave no counter consideration, constituted aid. By contrast, in *Firma Sloma Neptun Schiffahrts AG* v *Seebetriebsrat Bodo Ziesemer of Sloman Neptun Schiffahrts AG* (cases C–72 and 73/91), the ECJ held that rules which permitted wages lower than the German minimum to be paid to foreign seamen did not constitute State aid. Although the lower wages costs resulting from the German rules benefited the boat companies, this was not aid for these purposes, as the advantage did not originate from State resources.

Distortion of competition   To constitute State aid in breach of Article 87 (ex 92), the benefit must distort or threaten competition by favouring certain undertakings or the production of certain goods. Given the tendency to use the hypothetical market investor test, i.e. identify whether a firm receives a benefit by reference to what a normal market operator would not do, if an advantage is found then it will, almost by definition, distort competition. Further, in *Vlaams Gewest* v *Commission* (case T–214/95), the CFI held that even small amounts of aid would distort competition for the purposes of this provision. Although the courts have taken this stringent view, the Commission seems to have taken a more generous approach. It issued a Notice on the *de minimis* rule for State aid in 1996 ([1996] OJ C–68/9), according to which small amounts of aid would not fall foul of the State aid rules. Furthermore, the Commission, under its powers in Regulation 659/99, has recently suggested a *de minimis* exception for small amounts of aid, thus giving a legislative basis for its approach to small amounts of aid contained in its Notice, the legal basis for which had hitherto been somewhat uncertain.

Impact on inter-State trade   Aid must be capable of affecting trade between Member States. Many of the considerations under this heading are similar to those which relate to assessing distortion of competition. State aid will be deemed to affect trade between Member States if the beneficiary of aid competes with enterprises in other Member States, even if it does not export to those States. The argument is that where aid is given in a Member State to an undertaking, the aid might make it harder for a competitor in another Member State to break into the national market. Thus, the courts are focusing on the potential impact rather than any actual quantified impact. Even a small amount of aid may affect trade between Member States if there is strong competition in the relevant sector (*ENI Lanerossi* (case C–303/88), see also *Vlaams Gewest* v *Commission* (case T–214/95)). Again, the introduction of the *de minimis* exception may ease the tension between the Commission's approach and that of the courts.

Exemptions and guidelines   The Commission has issued a number of Guidelines regarding the application of the State aid rules, for example the Guidelines on State Aid for Small and Medium-sized Enterprises ([1991] OJ C213/4) and the Guidelines on State Aid for Environmental Protection ([1994] OJ C72/3). As noted above, the Commission also adopted a Notice concerning small amounts of aid. It has now proposed the adoption of a *de minimis* block exemption. It seems likely that the adoption of the block exemption under enabling Regulation 659/99 will increase the amount of aid that will fall within the *de minimis* limit. A block exemption regarding aid to be used for training purposes has also been put forward.

Policy of the Commission

Whether aid is new or existing, whether it falls allegedly within Article 87(2) and (3) (ex 92(2) or (3)), apart from the exceptional case under Articles 87(3)(d) and 88(2) (ex 92(3)(d) and 93(2)), which will be decided by the Council, it is the Commission, subject to final adjudication by the Court, which decides whether it is in fact compatible with Community law. Applicants may thus challenge the Commission's decision that a particular payment or subsidy did (or did not) constitute State aid (see, e.g., *Ladbroke Racing Ltd* v *Commission* (case T–67/94)); or whether it falls within any exception. Clearly if it falls squarely within Article 87(2) (ex 92(2)) it must be allowed. If it falls within the permitted exceptions of Article 87(3)(a) to (c) (ex 92(3)(a) to (c)) the Commission has a discretion, both in permitting the exemption and in determining its scope (*Exécutif régional wallon* v *Commission* (case 67/87); modernisation aid granted to Glaverbel (Belgian glass manufacturers) not an important project of common European interest under the then Article 92(3)(b); to constitute the latter must form part of a transnational European programme).

The exercise of this discretion, as the Court commented in *Philip Morris Holland BV* v *Commission* (case 730/79) involves economic, political and social assessments which must be made in the Community context, the determining factor being the Community interest. As a general rule aid will only be allowed if it promotes recognised Community as opposed to national objectives and does not frustrate progress towards the single market (*20th Report on Competition Policy*). The Court will question the exercise of the Commission's discretion only in extreme cases.

In permitting *regional* aid under Article 87(3)(a) (ex 92(3)) (to counter underemployment and to assist development), the Commission looks not to national levels of employment and income but to the standard of the Community as a whole. As a result eligibility for such benefit will depend on the State's position relative to the Community average. The Commission has also, in the interests of transparency, recently issued guidelines on national regional aid ([1998] OJ C74/9), in which it outlines circumstances in which aid will be considered to be in the Community interest. In so doing, it replaces a significant number of heterogeneous documents previously covering this area.

In allowing *sectoral aid* (e.g., to agriculture, transport, particular industries) under Article 87(3)(c) (ex 92(3)(c) the Commission's main concern is to prevent the grant of State aid from exacerbating existing problems or from transferring them from one State to another. The Commission will not allow aid which strengthens the power of an undertaking compared with other undertakings competing in intra-Community trade. Thus, in *Philip Morris* the claimant failed to obtain the annulment of a Commission Decision refusing to allow the Dutch government to grant aid to increase the production capacity of a Dutch cigarette manufacturer, who was in competition in Europe with a number of other manufacturers.

Nor will the Commission allow Member States to 'shore up obsolete structures' *(16th General Report,* 1982, 104), to grant relief to rescue firms which are incapable of adjusting to conditions of competition *(15th Report on Competition Policy,* 1981, 103). Aid will only be permitted which will lead to sound economic structures to enable an industry to become competitive, to resolve underlying problems, not to postpone or shift the solution.

The majority of aids, notably regional and sectoral aids, for example, aids to the textile industry, to shipbuilding and (prior to the TEU) to the film industry, have been granted under Article 87(3)(c) (ex 92(3)(c)) — 'to facilitate the development of certain economic activities or of certain economic areas'. Regional aids, i.e., national as opposed to Community aid granted pursuant to its regional policy, have been subject to progressive coordination since the first formal guidelines were adopted in 1971 (First Resolution on Regional Aids, (1971) JO C111/1).

Exceptions under Article 87(3)(b) (ex 92(3)(b)) must relate to projects of common *European,* as opposed to national interest. Aid has been permitted under this head to enable firms to bring their plant into line with environmental standards (see Commission Guidelines on State Aid for Environmental Protection (OJ C72/3, 1994) at the time of writing extended to June 2000). Article 87(3)(d) (ex 92(3)(d)), which provides for the granting of aid to promote culture and heritage conservation, was introduced by the TEU 1992. The film industry, a former beneficiary under sub-para. (3) (c), has since the TEU been dealt with under this provision. In addition, an amendment to Article 159 (ex 130b) EC, also introduced by the TEU, will require decisions on State aid to take greater account of the need to strengthen economic and social cohesion (see Commission's Report on Competition Policy 1992 and ECOSOC resolution on 24th Report on Competition (OJ C39/79), 1996)).

Since German unification there is no longer any justification for continuing to subsidise areas of East Germany under Article 87(2)(c) (new 92(2)(c)) although the Commission has recognised that some State aid will be necessary to ease East Germany's transition to a market economy.

General aids as opposed to 'special' aids normally fall outside Article 87 (ex 92). General schemes may exceptionally be permitted for short periods to counter 'a serious disturbance in the economy of a Member State' (Article 87(3)(b) (ex 92(3)(b))).

The Commission has taken the view that the provisions on State aids apply to aid granted to both private and public undertakings. It has issued Directives (Directive 80/723 (OJ L 195/35), amended by Directive 85/43 (OJ L 229/20)) on the transparency of relations between Member States and public undertakings, requiring Member States to ensure that information regarding financial relations between public authorities and Member States be kept at the disposal of the Commission for a five-year period and to supply such information where the Commission 'considers it necessary so to request' (Article 5). In a communication based on these Directives issued in 1991 (OJ C 273/2) it expressed its concern at the volume of aid granted by States to public undertakings which had not been notified under the then Article 93(3) (£3.5 billion between 1985 and 1990). It stressed the need for the development of a policy for public undertakings, which had not hitherto been sufficiently subject to State aid disciplines. Aid granted to public undertakings in the manufacturing sector *must* be notified in advance to the Commission. This communication was annulled on procedural grounds in 1993, but, on the Court's recommendation, the Commission has now amended Directive 80/273 to require States to submit an annual report and has reduced the scope of the communication, which now simply describes its policy on aid to public undertakings (EC Bull 7/8 1993 1.2.80). In 1993 the Commission also introduced a system of standard notification of State aids (EC Bull 3 1993 1.2.39).

Relationship between State aid and other provisions of the Treaty

Article 28 (ex 30) EC   State aid that is permitted under Article 87 (ex 92) cannot in itself fall within Article 28 (ex 30). To that extent the provisions are mutually exclusive. However, some aspects of State aid, not necessary for the attainment of its object, may be incompatible with other provisions of the Treaty, even though they may not invalidate the aid as a whole (*Ianelli & Volpi SpA* v *Ditta Paola Meroni* (case 74/76)). Therefore, if the aid goes beyond what is necessary to achieve a particular legitimate objective it may infringe Article 28 (ex 30). Similarly, if it is applied to activities which are incompatible with Article 28 (ex 30) (e.g., 'Buy Irish' campaign sponsored by the Irish Goods Council: *Commission* v *Ireland* (case 249/81)).

Article 31 (ex 37) EC   On the same principle the operations of a State-owned monopoly are not exempt from Article 31 (ex 37) by reason of the fact that they may classify as aids. Even when the activities of a State monopoly are linked with a grant to producers subject to the monopoly they must still comply with the non-discrimination requirements of Article 31 (ex 37) (*Ianelli & Volpi SpA* v *Ditta Paolo Meroni* (case 74/76)).

Article 81 (ex 85) EC   Assessment under Article 88 (ex 93(2)) EC to determine the compatibility of aid with the common market and the exemption from liability under the competition provisions of Article 81(1) (ex 85(1)) provided by Article 81(3) (ex 85(3)) are separate procedures. A favourable determination under one will therefore not preclude an unfavourable decision under the other.

Article 86 (ex 90)   As will be seen in chapter 14, this provision prohibits rules contrary to the provisions of the Treaty, especially the competition provisions, being maintained in force in respect of 'public undertakings and those to which Member States have granted special or exclusive rights' (Article 86(1) (ex 90(1))). Article 86(2) (ex 90(2)), however, provides an exception to this general statement for 'Undertakings entrusted with the operation of services of general economic interest or having the character of a revenue-producing monopoly', which shall be subject to the Treaty rules only insofar as their application 'does not obstruct the performance . . . of the particular tasks assigned to them'. The development of trade, however, must not be affected to such an extent as would be contrary to the interests of the Community (Article 86(2) (ex 90(2)). This exception in Article 86(2) could overlap with the State aid rules thereby exempting those undertakings falling within Article 86(2) from State aid rules, but the precise limits of the two provisions are currently not clear. Although the question was raised in *Banco de Crédito Industrial SA* v *Ayuntamiento de Valencia* (case C–387/92), the ECJ did not address the issue.

Enforcement by individuals

Articles 87 and 89 (ex 92 and 94 respectively), both being dependent on the exercise of discretion by Community institutions, are not directly effective (*Ianelli & Volpi SpA* v *Ditta Paola Meroni* (case 74/76)). So, in the absence of a Decision from the Commission or ECJ, a national court has no power to decide whether a State aid is compatible with Article 87 (ex 92). However, the procedural obligations of Article 88(3) (ex 93(3)) are directly effective, and as such, as the Commission pointed out in its practice note of 1983, are amenable to assessment by national courts. Thus an individual, provided he has *locus standi* under national law, may challenge in his domestic courts a grant of aid by national authorites in breach of Article 88(3) (ex 93(3)). The

Commission issued a Notice on Cooperation between National Courts and the Commission in the State Aid Field (OJ C312/7, 23.11.1995). This establishes a machinery whereby national courts faced with a potential State aid may seek assistance from the Commission on whether it should be characterised as such. Further, the Commission has also issued guidelines concerning aid in certain sectors, such as the environment (OJ C72/3 1994) and employment (OJ C334, 1995). Also, as the ECJ noted in *Ianelli & Volpi SpA* v *Ditta Paolo Meroni,* if Article 87 (ex 92) is invoked before domestic courts in the context of directly effective provisions such as Article 28 (ex 30) and Article 31 (ex 37), questions relating to State aid may, along with other questions, be referred to the ECJ for preliminary ruling.

The case of *Syndicat Français de l'Express International* v *La Poste* (case C–39/94) illustrates the subtle relationship between Articles 87 and 88(3) (ex 92 and 93(3) respectively). The case concerned a claim for compensation for losses suffered by the applicant, a competitor in the provision of postal services, resulting from alleged State aid granted to La Poste without notification to the Commission, in breach of the then Article 93(3). The matter had been under consideration by the Commission for two years, following a complaint by SFEI, during which time the Commission had neither adopted a position nor taken a final decision. Hence SFEI's action before the French courts seeking, *inter alia,* compensation in respect of the alleged breach. The French court sought clarification on a number of questions:

(a)   whether the recovery of State aid was the only way of guaranteeing the effectiveness of Article 93(3) (now 88(3)) or whether parties such as the applicant who had suffered loss as a result of the alleged aid could recover compensation in their national court in respect of breaches of that Article, and

(b)   whether, when the matter is under investigation by the Commission, a national court is under an obligation to declare its lack of jurisdiction, or

(c)   if it has declared jurisdiction, it is obliged to stay proceedings until the Commission takes a decision.

The ECJ's reply was unequivocal. The involvement of national courts is the result of the direct effects of the then Article 93(3) (now 88(3)). The initiation of procedures before the Commission cannot release national courts from their duty to safeguard the rights of individuals in the event of a breach of the notification requirement. Faced with an alleged breach a national court may have to interpret the concept of aid contained in former Article 92 (now 87) in order to determine whether a State measure introduced without notification ought to have been subject to that procedure. In doing so it may refer to the ECJ for an interpretation of that Article. Where there is a lapse of time it will be for the national court to decide whether it is necessary to order interim relief such as the suspension of measures in order to safeguard the interest of parties. Although the ECJ did not rule specifically on the question of damages it is submitted that where it is necessary to award damages in order to safeguard individuals' rights under Article 88(3) (ex 93(3)) a national court may do so. Arguably, it may even, following *Antonissen* (case C–393/96 P(R)), order interim compensation (see further chapter 26).

In proceedings before national courts, actions by national authorities taken in breach of Article 88(3) (ex 98(3)) cannot be legalised by a subsequent finding by the Commission that the aid is compatible with EC law (*Fédération Nationale du Commerce Extérieur des Produits Alimentaires* v *France* (case C–354/90)). However, a failure to notify the granting of aid does not automatically lead to nullity (*France* v *Commission* (case C–301/87)).

Once a Decision in respect of State aid has been issued, a recipient or potential recipient may challenge that Decision before the ECJ under Article 230 (ex 173) EC; however, where a Decision affects a whole industry the Court has held that individual members have no standing to sue, although an organisation created to represent those members, if it took part in the proceedings relating to the granting of aid, may (*Kwekerij Gebruders van der Kooy* (cases 67, 68 & 70/85)). In addition, any interested party who suspects that aid is being granted in breach of Article 87 (ex 92) may complain to the Commission and request the Commission to act, and, provided he acts in time, may challenge any action or inaction on the part of the Commission resulting from his complaint (*Irish Cement Ltd* v *Commission* (case 166/86), see chapters 30 and 31). It is not just the originator of the complaint who can have standing to bring an action under these articles. The ECJ has held that, because of the lack of transparency and the lack of a role for third parties under Article 88(3) (ex 93(3)), it is not necessary for third parties to show participation in the Commission investigation or to have been substantially effected by the measure to have standing to challenge a Commission Decision concerning State aid. A competitor of the recipient of the aid could have standing (*William Cook plc* v *Commission* (case C–198/91); *Matra SA* v *Commission* (case C–225/91R)). In *ASPEC* v *Commission* (case T–435/93), the CFI held that the impact of a decision on the competitive environment of a market together with the small number of producers in that market would give the competing producers sufficient standing to challenge that Decision (see further chapters 30 and 31).

Any person seeking to challenge a decision concerning State aid, whether to himself or to another party, would be wise, where he has *locus standi*, to proceed quickly under Article 230 (ex 173) since following the decision of the Court in *TWD Textilwerke Deggendorf GmbH* v *Germany* (case C–188/92) there may be difficulties in obtaining relief under the alternative route to annulment provided by Article 234 (ex 177) (see further chapters 27 and 30).

Where repayment of aid is ordered, recovery will be governed by the domestic law of the State in question, provided that the rules do not render recovery excessively difficult or impossible in practice (*Commission* v *Germany* (case 94/87)). As noted earlier, interest will be payable from the date on which the unlawful aid was paid. Since the Court has decided that undertakings in receipt of State aid must be deemed to be aware of the rules regarding the recovery of illegally granted aid it is unlikely that a person in receipt of such aid can claim damages against the State, either on the basis of tort (see *Bourgoin SA* v *Ministry of Agriculture, Fisheries & Food* [1986] QB 716 in chapter 26) or under *Francovich* v *Italy* (cases C–6 & 9/90) (see chapters 4, and 28); arguably, in a 'normal' case he could be seen as having caused his own loss.

Further reading

Abbamonte, G.B., 'Competitors' Right to Challenge Illegally Granted Aid and the Problem of the Conflicting Decisions in the Field of Competition Law' [1997] ECLR 87.

Bacon, 'State aids and General Measures' (1997) 17 YEL 269.

Commission's Annual Reports on Competition Policy.

Cownie, F., 'State Aids in the Eighties' (1986) 11 EL Rev 247.

Evans, A., and Martin, M., 'Socially Acceptable Distortions of Competition: Community Policy on State Aid' (1991) 16 EL Rev 79.

Flynn, J., 'How Well Will Article 100a(4) Work? A Comparison with Article 93' (1987) 24 CML Rev 689.

Hellingman, K., 'State Participation as State Aid under Article 92 of the EEC Treaty: the Commission's Guidelines' (1986) 23 CML Rev 111.

Quigley, C., 'The Notion of a State Aid in the EEC' (1988) 13 EL Rev 242.

Rodger 'State aid — a fully level playing field' [1999] ECLR 251.

Ross, M., 'State Aids and National Courts: Definitions and Other Problems — a Case of Premature Emancipation?' (2000) 37 CMLR 401.

Ross, M., 'Challenging State Aids — the Effect of Recent Developments' (1986) 23 CML Rev 867.

Slot Piet, Jan, 'Procedural Aspects of State Aids: the Guardians of Competition versus the Subsidy Villains' (1990) 27 CML Rev 741.

Slotboom, M.M., 'State Aid in Community Law: a Broad or Narrow Definition?' (1995) 20 EL Rev 289.

Winter, J.A., 'Supervision of State Aid' (1993) 30 CML Rev 311.

FOURTEEN

Introduction

The structure of EC competition provisions

The competition policy of the Community is based on Article 3(g) EC, requiring: 'a system ensuring that competition in the common market is not distorted', and Articles 81-99 (ex 85–94) EC. The competition provisions can, broadly speaking, be divided into those which focus primarily on the activities of governments and those which deal with the actions of private (and some public) undertakings. The former consist of the rules on State aid (Articles 87–89 (ex 92–94) EC), although the other competition rules may also affect governments' policies. The rules on State aid are discussed in chapter 13. The second group of provisions consist of the rules concerning anticompetitive agreements or concerted practices between undertakings (Article 81 (ex 85)), the prohibition on abuse of a dominant position on the part of individual undertakings or groups of undertakings (Article 82 (ex 86)), the rules relating to public undertakings granted special or exclusive rights (Article 86 (ex 90) EC) and anti-dumping rules (former Article 91). The following chapters will focus on Article 81 (chapter 15), Article 82 (chapter 16), their enforcement (chapter 17) and the interrelationship between competition and intellectual property rights (chapter 18). Although the rules in Article 86 (ex 90) are becoming increasingly important with the dismantling of state monopolies, especially regarding the provision of utilities, this book will look more closely at this provision only insofar as it affects the operation of State aid rules or Article 82 (ex 86). The provisions concerned with the adverse effects on competition of dumping, the exporting of goods to the Community by third countries at prices which are less than the 'comparable' price of the like product on the domestic market (formerly dealt with by Article 91 EC and Regulation 3283/94, Article 1(2)), must regrettably fall outside the scope of this book.

After agriculture, competition policy is perhaps the most highly developed of the Community's common policies, with the greatest impact on undertakings situated both inside and outside the common market. It is an essential complement to the fundamental provisions of the Treaty designed to create the single market. The obligations imposed on Member States to ensure the free movement of goods and services and freedom of establishment within the Community would be of little effect if parties were free to engage in restrictive practices such as concerted price fixing or market sharing which inhibit the free play of market forces within the single market, particularly when such practices tend to partition the market along national lines.

Broadly speaking, the purposes of EC competition policy, which is spelt out in detail in the Commission's annual reports on competition policy, is to encourage economic activity and maximise efficiency by enabling goods and resources to flow freely amongst Member States according to the operation of normal market forces. The concentration of resources resulting from such activity functioning on a Community, rather than a national, scale is intended to increase the competitiveness of European industry in a world market. In addition to this primary goal, and sometimes conflicting with it, Community competition policy seeks to protect and encourage small and medium-sized enterprises so that they too may play their full part in the competitive process.

In order to understand and evaluate the policies pursued by the Commission it is necessary briefly to examine the economic theory underlying competition policy.

The theory of competition

The original concept of competition, dating from the 18th century, and Adam Smith's *Wealth of Nations* (1776), merely meant the absence of legal restraints on trade. Modern economic theory, however, which stems from the late 19th century, and led to the first antitrust legislation, the Sherman Act, in the USA in 1890, is based on the model of 'perfect competition'. This is an idealised concept, based on a number of assumptions. It assumes that there are in the market a large number of buyers and sellers, the latter all producing identical or homogeneous products; that consumers have perfect information, and always act in order to maximise utility; that resources flow freely from one area of economic activity to another, and that there are no impediments to the emergence of new competition ('barriers to entry'); and that business people always maximise profits. A system of 'pure' or 'perfect' competition guarantees the maximum efficiency, the optimum allocation of resources. It is the polar opposite to the monopoly.

The 'traditional' view, adopted by the early economists, was that the real world did not correspond to this model of perfect competition. Rival undertakings might choose to cooperate rather than compete. Markets could be divided. Such practices which stood in the way of the achievement of perfect competition, which restricted the freedom of buyers and sellers, must therefore be curtailed. It was necessary to regulate the market in order to bring it closer to the ideal. Intervention was also seen as necessary to keep open opportunities for competitive activity, particularly for small and medium-sized firms, and to preserve real choice for consumers.

Early antitrust law, e.g., the Sherman Act (1890, USA), was thus designed to make capitalism work more effectively.

Antitrust law in Western Europe, which only became widespread after the Second World War, was based on this traditional view. The influence of this view was particularly strong in Germany, where concentrations of industrial power in pre-war Germany were seen as having contributed to a concentration of political power. It was this German inheritance, together with the appeal of the traditional view following the Second World War, that shaped EC competition law. French law too, though in much smaller degree, influenced EC law, particularly in its concern to protect the small trader.

Opposed to the traditional view is the view of the Chicago school of economists. Although implicit in the *laissez-faire* view of the early 19th century it has only recently emerged and has been rapidly gaining ground over the traditional view, particularly in the USA. According to the Chicago school the real world approximates quite well to the model of perfect competition; even monopolies are not in themselves anti-competitive as long as there are no barriers to entry, i.e., as long as other business people are not prevented from entering the field as competitors. This will only occur if the minimum efficient scale of the operation is such as to make entry virtually impossible. Thus the Chicago school believes that only the minimum intervention is needed, and then only to curb the most blatant forms of anti-competitive activity since the market will regulate itself.

EC competition policy

The basic principles of EC competition policy, as adopted in the original EEC Treaty, were drafted in the broadest terms, leaving the Commission, subject to the supervision of the Court, to interpret these provisions and to develop detailed rules. In interpreting the Treaty the Commission was heavily influenced by the traditional school. It has been criticised as being excessively interventionist, at least in the early years.

In its concern to strike down all restrictions on competition it has been said that the Commission failed explicitly to distinguish between 'vertical' agreements (agreements between parties at different levels in the chain of distribution, e.g., between manufacturer and his selected dealer, or between dealer and retailer) which carry many economic advantages, and 'horizontal' agreements (agreements between parties at the same level in the economic chain, e.g., cartels between manufacturer and manufacturer, between dealer and dealer), which are potentially much more damaging to competition. Nor did it distinguish sufficiently between *ancillary restraints,* i.e., restraints which are attached to some pro-competitive transaction, and *naked restrictions* on competition, clothed with no desirable transaction at all. Whilst the latter are never justifiable, the former may be judged according to whether they are necessary in order to make the (desirable) transaction viable.

The Commission was also criticised for subordinating other goals, such as overall economic efficiency, to the supreme goal of market integration. Thus, in order to protect the single market, *intra-brand* competition (competition between undertakings dealing in the *same* product, e.g., between rival Ford car dealers) is protected at the expense of *inter-brand* competition (competition between undertakings dealing in *competing* products, e.g., between Ford dealers (or manufacturers) and Citroën dealers (or manufacturers)). The effect of this may be to reduce the competitiveness of the industry as a whole. These criticisms are less valid today, although the principal prohibition in Article 81(1) (ex 85(1)) continues to be interpreted broadly. The Commission now grants exemption to whole categories of agreements which, although in themselves restrictive of competition and prima facie in breach of Article 81(1) (ex 85(1)), are beneficial overall. Over the years, it has steadily extended the scope of these exemptions. A similar relaxation of the rules is seen in the Commission's approach to Article 82 (ex 88) and merger control. Of late, with the change in economic conditions (slowdown in growth, increased unemployment, increased competition worldwide), mergers have been allowed to proceed which would have been unlikely to have been accepted earlier.

It has also been suggested that by elevating the single market principle above all other considerations the Commission and the Court (which rarely departs from the view of the Commission in broad matters of policy) have failed to take into account other Community objectives relevant to the application of competition law, such as the need to counter regional or structural imbalances and to safeguard employment and the environment. The increasing integration of the internal market will clearly have regional, social and environmental repercussions which may necessitate the weighing of other wider policy considerations within the context of the application of Community competition rules. This was recognised by the Commission in a statement issued in 1993, in which it stressed the need 'to ensure that the natural and logical linkages between the Community's competition, research, environmental and social policies are fully taken into account in the Commission's approach to competition policy' (ISEC B 21/93). It was acknowledged by the Commission in its *23rd Report on Competition Policy* that the changes brought in by the Maastricht Treaty, such as the need to protect cultural diversity (Article 151 (ex 128) EC) and the environment (Article 174 (ex 130r(2)) EC), now require the Commission to balance more and more competing interests. This has been recognised in the State aid provisions. The Merger Regulation specifically requires the Commission, when considering whether to approve a merger, to take into account social factors such as the impact of the deal on employees' jobs (e.g., *Comité Central d'Entreprise de la Société Générale des Grandes Sources* v *Commission* (case T–96/92); *Comité Central d'Entreprise de la SA Vittel* v *Commission* (case T–12/93)). Concern for the environment was a factor in the favourable Commission decision on the *Philips/Osram* joint venture [1994] 5 CMLR 491, in which the Commission took note of the existence of equipment to reduce emissions at the factory in which the joint venture company was to operate. The new Article 16 EC, introduced by the ToA, which requires Member States providing 'services of general economic interest' to have regard to the 'shared values of the Union as well as their role in promoting social and territorial cohesion', illustrates

Member States' concerns regarding the impact of privatisation on the provision of public services. (See also the Protocol on Public Service Broadcasting annexed to the ToA.) Other changes following the ToA, notably the emphasis on environmental policy and concern about high levels of unemployment, also reflect this trend. The Commission has, however, noted that environmental protection programmes could also be used to partition markets or to disguise other anticompetitive practices (see *23rd Report on Competition Policy*). No doubt other policy objectives could also be so used.

These factors and criticisms may be kept in mind when specific cases fall to be examined. Approval or disapproval of Community policies will ultimately depend on one's view of its economic, social and political priorities. No doubt it was essential that market integration should come first during the Community's formative years. Equally it is not surprising that as the Community has become more closely integrated there has been a greater recognition on the part of the Commission and the Court of the need to promote economic efficiency, to enable European industry to compete more effectively in the world market. Indeed the Commission has pointed out the necessity, in a climate of slow economic growth and fierce competition, for distinguishing, in the application of its competition policy, between behaviour which leads to the development and restructuring of European industry and behaviour which holds back that process by partitioning markets and strengthening domestic positions.

Enforcement of EC competition law

Enforcement of EC competition law has been entrusted to the Commission under Regulation 17/62, the principal Regulation concerned with competition policy. Decisions of the Commission made pursuant to its policy may, however, be challenged under Article 230 (ex 173) EC (see chapter 30) and a failure to take such a decision may be challenged under Article 232 (ex 175) EC (see chapter 31). These matters are now dealt with by the Court of First Instance subject to appeal on points of law to the ECJ. Since Articles 81 and 82 (ex 85 and 86) EC) respectively) have been declared directly effective (*BRT* v *SABAM* (case 127/73)), Member States' courts may be called upon to apply EC competition law. In 1992 the Commission announced its intention actively to promote the application of Community competition law by national courts, pursuant to the principle of subsidiarity. To this end it issued a Notice in 1993 on cooperation between national courts and the Commission which is likely to result in a significantly enhanced role for national courts in this area (OJ C39/6, 1993), a development which has been mirrored in the State aid field. It has been proposed in the Commission's recent Modernisation White Paper ([1999] OJ C–132/1) that this approach of involving national competition authorities and courts be taken still further. As will be seen in chapter 17, this development will not be without its problems.

Unlike the provisions considered so far, a breach of Articles 81 and 82 (ex 85 and 86 respectively) may give rise to sanctions imposed by the Commission in the form of heavy fines and penalties. This is rare in EC law. Since companies in breach of competition rules may be subject to substantial fines, the European courts have been vigilant in ensuring that the companies' procedural rights are not infringed. For example, in *BASF AG* v *Commission* (cases T–80 et al./89), a decision was impugned because the decision was not properly adopted in all relevant official languages. In the Soda Ash cases, the CFI quashed Commission decisions because the companies' right of access to the file had been denied (*Solvay* v *Commission* (cases T–30–2/91); *ICI* v *Commission* (cases T–36 & 37/91)) (see further chapter 16).

Public undertakings

Although the obligations of Articles 81 and 82 (ex 85 and 86) are imposed on 'undertakings' and do not prima facie concern the activities of public authorities, Article 86(1) (ex 90(1)) expressly provides that EC competition law applies to 'public undertakings and undertakings to which Member States grant special or exclusive rights', subject to exception for undertakings 'entrusted with the operation of services of general economic interest or having the character of a revenue-producing monopoly' insofar as the application of the rules may 'obstruct the performance of the particular tasks assigned to them' (Article 86(2) (ex 90(2))). This exception has been strictly construed. Derogation will be permitted only to the extent that it is necessary to the performance of the particular tasks assigned to such undertakings and to the economic equilibrium of the service operated in the general economic interest, for example by providing a set-off between profitable and unprofitable activities (*Corbeau* (case C–320/91) re Belgian postal monopoly). Outside these exempted areas:

> The legal framework within which agreements are made or decisions are taken and the classification (i.e. public or private) given to that framework are irrelevant as far as the applicability of Community rules on competition are concerned. (*BNIC* v *Clair* (case 123/83))

With the current trend towards privatisation of 'services of general economic interest', in the interests of greater efficiency, it is unlikely that these rules, particularly those governing exemptions, will be relaxed. Even the new Article 16, which emphasises the importance of public services, states that it operates 'without prejudice' to Articles 73 (public transport), 86 (public undertakings) and 87 (State aid) and presumably therefore does not disturb the existing case law on these articles.

Even where there is no agreement or behaviour on the part of a public (or semi-public) body such as to give rise to liability under Articles 81 and 82 (ex 85 and 86), a State may not adopt or maintain in force any measures which deprive these articles of their effectiveness. Any public measure which endorses or encourages action in breach of Articles 81 and 82 (ex 85 and 86) will be deemed unlawful (*GB-INNO* v *ATAB* (case 13/77)). Thus a public body, depending on its actions and the measures concerned, may, in the context of anti-competitive action, incur liability under other articles of the Treaty (e.g. Articles 10 (ex 5), 28 and 29 (ex 30–34) (goods), 49 (ex 59) (services)) *or* Articles 81 and 82 (ex 85 and 86). Where doubt exists as to which articles are appropriate, all relevant articles should be pleaded.

A number of areas, such as transport, were originally excluded from EC competition law. As has been noted, there has been scope under Article 86(2) (ex 90(2)) for exemption for public undertakings. The scope of these exclusions has been considerably reduced in recent years, as the Commission has introduced liberalising measures in the field of communications, postal services, transport, energy, insurance and audiovisual media, with a view to further increasing competition in these spheres. Also, in order to achieve the benefits of free competition within the single market in the important field of public procurement, the Community has issued Directives governing the award of public supply and public works contracts, laying down detailed procedures for the advertising (in the *Official Journal*) and award of such contracts, including the payment of damages by authorities acting in breach of these procedures (see Directive 89/665 OJ No. L 395, 30.12.1989, p. 33).

Competition and third countries

In the external sphere the Commission has stepped up its attempts to secure the acceptance and adoption of EC competition policy by the Community's main trading partners by means of bilateral or multilateral negotiation (for example, the revised form of the EU/US Cooperation Agreement has now been adopted (OJ L94/47, 1995 and L13/38, 1995)), with a view to overcoming the adverse effects for EC traders of anti-competitive practices in non-EC markets.

Further reading

Commission's Annual Reports on Competition Policy.
European Competition Law Review.
Flynn, L., 'Competition Policy and Public Services in EC Law after the Maastricht and Amsterdam Treaties' in O'Keeffe, D. and Twomey, P. (eds) *Legal Issues of the Amsterdam Treaties*, (1999, Hart Publishing).
Gerber, D. J., 'The Transformation of European Community Competition Law?' (1994) 35 Harv Int'l LJ 97.
Gyselen, L., 'State Action and the Effectiveness of the EEC's Competition Provisions' (1989) 26 CML Rev 33.
Hancher, L., 'Community, State and Market' in Craig, P. and De Burca, G. (eds), *The Evolution of EU Law* (1999, Oxford University Press).
Hornsby, S., 'Competition Policy in the 80s: More Policy Less Competition?' (1987) 12 EL Rev 79.
Korah, V., 'EEC Competition Policy: Legal Form or Economic Efficiency' (1986) 39 Current Legal Problems 85.
Ross, M. 'Article 16 EC and services of general interest: from derogation to obligation?' (2000) 25 EL Rev 22.

Snyder, F., 'Ideologies of Competition in European Community Law' (1989) 52 MLR 149.

Whish, R., *Competition Law*, 3rd ed. (London: Butterworths, 1993), especially pp. 1–47.

Wesseling, 'Subsidiarity in Community Antitrust Law: Setting the Right Agenda' (1997) 22 EL Rev 35.

FIFTEEN

Anti-competitive agreements, decisions and concerted practices

The general scheme

Article 81(1) (ex 85(1)) prohibits:

> all agreements between undertakings, decisions by associations of under-takings and concerted practices which may affect trade between Member States and which have as their object or effect the prevention, restriction or distortion of competition within the common market.

A number of examples of the types of agreements covered by this article are provided in para. (1)(a) to (e).

Article 81(2) (ex 85(2)) provides that any agreement or decision in breach of Article 81(2) 'shall be automatically void'.

Under Article 81(3) (ex 85(3)), Article 81(1) may, however, be declared 'inapplicable' to agreements or decisions fulfilling a number of specified criteria.

Thus, Article 81(1) (ex 85(1)) provides a very broad base of liability subject to the possibility of exemption under Article 81(3) (ex 85(3)).

Under Regulation 17/62 (Article 9(1)) the Commission has the *sole* power to grant exemption under Article 81(3) (ex 85(3)). The Commission has, however, proposed that the power to grant exemption under Article 81(3) be extended to national authorities. This proposal is discussed further in chapter 17.

In order to obtain exemption, parties must notify their agreements or decisions to the Commission (Regulation 17/62, Article 4). Once notified, even if the agreement is subsequently found in breach of Article 81(1) (ex 85(1)) and not eligible for exemption, parties obtain immunity from fines (Article 15(5)(a) of the Regulation). However, except in the case of 'old' agreements (pre-accession, or those entered into prior to the entry into force of Regulation 17/62) which have provisional validity during the notification period, notification cannot prevent agreements from being void *ab initio* should the Commission eventually decide that they infringe Article 81(1) (ex 85(1)) and do not merit exemption under Article 81(3) (ex 85(3)) *(Brasserie de Haecht* v *Wilkin (No.2)* (case 48/72)). It is possible for an agreement to be held void in part only, if the offending clauses can be severed and are not sufficiently serious to vitiate the whole.

As an alternative to exemption, parties can seek 'negative clearance' from the Commission, i.e., a Decision that their agreement or decision does not infringe Article 81(1) (ex 85(1)) at all (Regulation 17/62, Article 2). It is possible, and common, for undertakings to apply for both negative clearance and exemption on the same form A/B.

The breadth of Article 81(1) (ex 85(1)) and the severity of the consequences of breach inevitably led to uncertainty. There was a risk that many desirable, pro-competitive agreements would fall foul of its provisions; certainly many would require exemption under Article 81(3) (ex 85(3)). There was thus a strong incentive for business people to play safe and notify. This resulted in an increasing work-load for the Commission which in turn resulted in long delays. It might take years before a final Decision was taken by the Commission. A Decision that an agreement was void could have disastrous consequences for all the parties concerned. There was thus a fear that businesses might be deterred from entering into beneficial, pro-competitive agreements for fear of the consequences.

In order to solve these problems the Commission has, over the years, issued a number of 'notices' and 'block exemptions'. The notices merely provide non-binding guidelines concerning the Commission's policy, principally as to the kinds of agreement which will *not* breach Article 81(1) (ex 85(1)) (e.g., Notice concerning minor agreements (1986) OJ No. C 231/02 as amended). The block exemptions, which are enacted by Regulation, apply to agreements which *do* breach Article 85(1) (new 81(1)) but, because of their beneficial nature, are exempt 'en bloc' on the grounds of Article 81(3) (ex 85(3)). Agreements falling within these notices and block exemptions need not be notified. However, notices, as non-binding measures, cannot guarantee immunity, and, to obtain the benefit of a block exemption, an agreement must contain *no* anti-competitive clauses additional to those allowed under the exemption, even though they may seem to be justifiable.

Elements of an infringement

Article 81(1) (ex 85(1)) contains three essential elements. There must be:

(a)   an agreement between undertakings, or a decision by an association of undertakings or a concerted practice,

(b)   which may affect trade between Member States, and

(c)   which must have as its object or effect the prevention, restriction or distortion of competition within the common market.

Agreements between undertakings, decisions by associations of undertakings and concerted practices

Undertakings   In the absence of a definition, the word 'undertaking' has been interpreted in the widest possible sense to include any legal or natural person engaged in some form of economic or commercial activity, whether in the provision of goods or services, including cultural or sporting activities (*9th Report on Competition Policy*, 116; *Bosman* (case C–415/93)), banking (*Züchner v Bayerische Vereinsbank AG* (case 172/80)), insurance (*Verband der Sachversicherer eV v Commission* (case 45/85)) (*13th Report on Competition Policy*) and transport (*Commission v Belgium* (case 156/77)). It is not necessary that the activity be pursued with a view to profit (e.g., *Fédération Française des Sociétés d'Assurance v Ministère de l'Agriculture et de la Pêche* (case C–244/94); see also *COAPI Decision* [1995] 5 CMLR 468 discussed below).

Although air and sea transport were treated as special cases and excluded from the enforcement provisions of Regulation 17/62, legislation has been introduced with a view to achieving full and free competition in these areas by 1 January 1993.

Article 81(1) (ex 85(1)) also applies in the sphere of agriculture (*The Community v Milchförderungs fonds* [1985] 3 CMLR 101, Commission Decision), coal and steel, and atomic energy, provided the matter falls outside the scope of existing provision in these areas. It applies to undertakings in the public as well as the private sphere (Article 86(1) (ex 90(1)) and *Re British Telecom*, Commission Decision 82/861 [1983] 1 CMLR 457, upheld by ECJ in *Italy v Commission* (case 41/83)) but, as regards undertakings falling within Article 86 (ex 90) EC, only insofar as the application of these rules 'does not obstruct the performance, in law or in fact, of the particular tasks assigned to them'. Lastly, in *Re UNITEL* [1978] 3 CMLR 306 an individual, in the form of an opera singer, was found to be an undertaking!

Agreements   Agreements are not confined to binding agreements or to those which are written down. A 'gentleman's agreement' will suffice. Often where competition authorities fail to show an agreement they will be able to prove the existence of concerted practices. In view of the wide scope of 'concerted practices' the precise extent of the concept of 'agreement' is of less significance.

Decisions by associations of undertakings   Clearly the effect of such decisions, i.e., of trade associations, may be to coordinate behaviour amongst undertakings with anti-competitive effects, without any need for actual agreement; hence their inclusion in Article 81(1) (ex 85(1)).

This provision has been widely interpreted, and is not confined to binding decisions. It was held in *NV IAZ International Belgium v Commission* (case 96/82) that even a non-binding recommendation from a trade association which was normally complied with could constitute a decision within Article 81(1) (ex 85(1)). In *Re the Application of the Publishers' Association* [1989] 4 CMLR 825 the Association's Code of Conduct was found by the Commission to have the character of a recommendation to its members and customers, and as such was to be considered as a decision of an association of undertakings, despite its non-binding character. As well as the association itself, its members may be liable for fines if they comply, even unwillingly, with a decision in breach of Article 81(1) (ex 85(1)).

Article 81(1) (ex 85(1)) also applies to decisions by associations of associations (*NV IAZ International Belgium* v *Commission*).

Concerted practices   These are altogether wider than 'agreements' and 'decisions by associations of undertakings'. The concept of a concerted practice was borrowed from US anti-trust law; when the original EEC Treaty was signed the competition rules of the Member States contained no rules against such practices. A concerted practice was defined in *Imperial Chemical Industries Ltd* v *Commission* (case 48/69) (Dyestuffs) as a form of cooperation between undertakings which, without having reached the stage where an agreement properly so-called has been concluded, knowingly substitutes practical cooperation between them for the risks of competition.

To constitute a concerted practice, it is not necessary to have a concerted plan. It is enough that each party should have informed the other of the attitude they intended to take so that each could regulate his conduct safe in the knowledge that his competitors would act in the same way. Similarly, in a series of cases, the CFI has held that meeting to exchange information about pricing structures also constitutes a concerted practice as the participants cannot fail to take this information into account when devising their own market strategies (e.g., *Shell International Chemical Co. Ltd* v *Commission* (case T–11/89)).

Clearly such practices can be just as damaging to competition as agreements or decisions by associations, and are much harder to prove.

Imperial Chemical Industries Ltd v *Commission* centred on three uniform price increases introduced by a number of leading producers (including ICI) of aniline dyes, almost simultaneously, in 1964, 1965 and 1967. The increases covered the same products. Between 7 and 10 January 1964 there was a 10 per cent increase; between 14 October and 28 December 1964 a 10-15 per cent increase was announced, to come into effect on 1 January 1965. At a meeting in Basle in August 1967 one of the producers announced an 8 per cent increase to take effect from 16 October. Two other producers subsequently announced a similar increase of 8 per cent. The Commission issued a Decision that they were engaged in concerted practices in the fixing of price increases, and imposed heavy fines on them (*Re Aniline Dyes Cartel* JO (1969) L195/11, [1969] CMLR D23). ICI sought annulment of that Decision, arguing that the price increases were merely examples of parallel increases common in oligopolistic situations (an oligopoly exists where the market is dominated by a small number of large independent concerns). The argument failed. The Court held that whilst parallel behaviour does not in itself constitute a concerted practice it provides strong evidence of such a practice if it leads to conditions of competition which do not correspond to the normal conditions of the market. This aspect of the decision has been criticised. While a finding of concerted practices was acceptable on the facts (the market was found to be divided on national lines; the prior meetings and announcements eliminated all uncertainty between the parties; the increases were general and uniform and covering the same products), it is submitted that a decision based solely on the 'normal conditions of the market' would be incapable of proof, and could render oligopolies highly vulnerable to a charge of concerted practices in the event of quite 'normal' parallel price increases.

Imperial Chemical Industries Ltd v *Commission* concerned the concerted practices of oligopolies. Oligopolies were also examined in *A. Ahlström OY* v *Commission (Re Wood Pulp)* (cases C–89, 104, 114, 116–7 & 125–9/85), in which the ECJ took a more cautious approach. In an action for the annulment of a Commission Decision fining a number of the world's leading wood pulp producers, which together held a two-thirds share of the Community market in wood pulp, for concerted practices in announcing quarterly simultaneous and identical price increases, the Court held that these factors did not provide evidence of concerted practices where the system of price announcements represented a 'rational response to the need to limit commercial risk in a long-term market'. It found that the similarity was the result of a high degree of market transparency, and the parallelism of the price increases could be satisfactorily explained by the oligopolistic tendencies of the market. On the other hand the parties' agreement, at meetings within their trade association, to fix recommended prices and to notify members in advance of any proposed deviation from these prices was held to restrict competition within the then Article 85(1) (now 81(1)).

Unilateral action: refusal to supply   Although Article 81(1) (ex 85(1)) appears to require some form of agreement or concertation on the part of two or more undertakings, there are circumstances when what appears to be a unilateral act may be found to breach it.

In *AEG-Telefunken* (case 107/82) the parties had notified their distribution agreements for AEG products and obtained negative clearance from the Commission. AEG was subsequently found in breach of the then Article 85(1) (now 81(1)) for having *operated* the agreements in such a way as to restrict competition by systematically refusing to allow dealers into its network who did not comply with the (unofficial) pricing policy apparently observed by existing members. Moreover, since AEG had acted outside the framework of its agreement as notified, notification did not bring it immunity from fines.

Similarly, in *Ford Werke AG* v *Commission* (case 25/84) the Court approved the Commission's refusal to grant clearance for what appeared to be a perfectly acceptable standard distribution agreement because Ford was refusing to supply existing distributors in Germany with right-hand-drive cars for export in England, apparently in order to maintain an artificial partitioning of the market and thereby different price levels in different Member States. Although there was no clear evidence of concerted action, certainly none of any agreement, the Court held that Ford's decision to cease supplies formed part of the contractual relations between Ford Werke AG and its dealers. Admission to Ford's dealer network implied acceptance by the contracting parties of the policies pursued by Ford. These cases demonstrate that the Commission and the Court, in applying Article 81(1) (ex 85(1)), will take into account the context in which a particular action operates, and will interpret the article against its literal meaning if that is necessary to suppress practices which are against the spirit, even if they seem to be within the letter, of EC competition law. *AEG–Telefunken* and *Ford Werke* were followed in *Sandoz* (1987) OJ No. L 222/28 and *Tipp-Ex* (1987) OJ No. L 222/1 (decision confirmed by the Court: *Tipp-Ex GmbH & Co. KG* v *Commission* (case C–279/87)).

Public authorities

Where public bodies are concerned, a distinction must be drawn between agreements or concerted practices entered into in the course of commercial activities, which are clearly capable of falling within Article 81(1) (ex 85(1)), and executive measures which merely permit or encourage such action which, although illegal under other provisions of the Treaty such as Articles 28 and 29 (ex 30–34) EC (see e.g. *GB–INNO* v *ATAB* (case 13/77)), will not in themselves breach this Article. In *Bodson* v *Pompes Funèbres* (case 30/87) a licensing arrangement, whereby the local authority granted exclusive rights in respect of certain funeral services to the Société des Pompes Funèbres, was held not to constitute an 'agreement between undertakings' within the then Article 85(1); but had the municipality imposed a certain level of prices on the licensees the Court suggested it would have been subject to EC competition rules.

In the *COAPI Decision* [1995] 5 CMLR 468, the Commission determined that the Spanish official association of industrial agents fell within the ambit of former Article 85, despite COAPI's argument that it was a public service body since it was established by government regulations, as was its scale of charges. The Commission, however, found that the agents were 'undertakings' and that the regulations constituted an agreement completely separate from the Spanish legislation. As the scale of charges, which set a minimum charge to be applied to foreign clients, affected trade between Member States COAPI was in breach of the then Article 85(1). This decision also makes it clear that associations offering international services with minimum or fixed rates of charges may be caught by Article 81 (ex 85), even if the association and its scale of charges is approved by a Member State.

Field of application of Article 81(1) (ex 85(1)) EC

Article 81(1) (ex 85(1)) applies to agreements or decisions of associations or concerted practices on a vertical level (e.g., between manufacturer and dealer) as well as a horizontal level (e.g., between manufacturer and manufacturer) (*Établissements Consten SA* v *Commission* (cases 56 & 58/64)). The undertakings must, however, be independent of each other. An agreement between a parent and its subsidiary will not breach Article 81(1) (ex 85(1)) unless the subsidiary enjoys full independence of action, the reason being that competition between them cannot be restricted by the agreement, since they were never in competition with each other (e.g., *Viho Europe BV* v *Commission* (case T–102/92)). However, a parent as well as its subsidiary may be liable for acts of the subsidiary *vis-à-vis* third parties in breach of Article 81(1) (ex 85(1)) where the subsidiary has acted as a result of the parent's promptings; and an agreement between parent and (non-independent) subsidiary may fall within Article 82 (ex 86) if it constitutes an abuse of a dominant position (*Béguelin Import Co.* v *GL Import-Export SA* (case 22/71)). Similarly members of an 'economic unit' comprising bodies with identical interests and subject to common control may be liable under Article 81 or 82 (ex 85 and 86 respectively) (*Hydrotherm* v *Compact* (case 170/83)). The same principles as apply to parents and subsidiaries apply to agreements between principal and agent. However, the Commission will scrutinize the relationship between the parties to ascertain its true nature (see e.g. *Pittsburg Corning Europe* [1973] CMLR D2; description of concession agreement as a commercial agency 'mere colouring').

An undertaking situated outside the EC may be liable under Article 81(1) (ex 85(1)) provided that the agreements or practices are implemented inside the common market. In *Imperial Chemical Industries Ltd* v *Commission* (case 48/69), ICI (UK) was held liable for the acts of its subsidiary in Holland although the UK was not yet a member of the EC. In *Woodpulp* [1985] 3 CMLR 474, Commission Decision, a number of firms, all from outside the EC , who were not acting through subsidiaries in the EC but who supplied two thirds of the EC consumption of wood pulp, were fined for concerted practices in breach of the then Article 85(1) on the grounds that the *effects* of their practices were felt in the Community. Although the Court, in *A. Ahlström & OY* v *Commission* (cases C–89, 104, 114, 116-7, 125-9/85), annulled the Decision in part and reduced the fines, since not all the concerted practices were proved, it held that the applicant firms could be liable, even though they were situated outside the EC, as long as their agreement or practices were *implemented* in the Community.

'Which may affect trade between Member States'

The agreement or decision by associations of undertakings or concerted practice must be one which may affect trade between Member States to breach Article 81(1) (ex 85(1)). In the absence of an effect on inter-State trade any restriction on competition is a matter for national law alone. However, the question of whether trade between Member States may be affected has been broadly interpreted by the Commission and the Court. In *Société Technique Minière* v *Maschinenbau Ulm GmbH* (case 56/65), the Court held that an agreement was capable of affecting trade between Member States if, on the basis of objective legal or factual criteria, it allows one to expect that it will exercise a direct or indirect, actual or potential effect on the flow of trade between Member States. The test is thus very similar to the *Dassonville* test applied in the context of Article 28 (ex 30) EC, but broader, since it requires simply an *effect* on, not a *hindrance* to, trade between Member States (see chapter 10). Clearly the most obvious effect on trade between Member States occurs when parties attempt to partition the market along national lines by means of restrictions on 'parallel' imports or exports (i.e., restrictions, usually agreed between manufacturers and appointed dealers, on dealers' powers to import or export goods across internal EC frontiers). But an effect on trade between Member States can occur even when an agreement takes place wholly within a Member State and appears to concern only trade within that State. This is so particularly in the case of decisions of associations of national agreements which are intended to operate across the whole national market. As the court pointed out in *Vereeniging van Cementhandelaren v Commission* (case 8/72) — in the context of a challenge to a Commission Decision that cement dealers' price-fixing scheme, limited to the Dutch market, infringed the then Article 85(1) (now 81(1)) — an agreement extending over the whole of the territory of a Member State by its very nature has the effect of reinforcing the compartmentalisation of markets on a national basis, thereby holding up the economic interpenetration which the Treaty is designed to bring about and protecting domestic production. The Court has on several occasions held that this provision applies to agreements between undertakings in the same State. For example in *Re Vacuum Interrupters Ltd* [1977] 1 CMLR D67, a joint venture agreement between three UK manufacturers to design and develop switch-gear apparatus in the UK was held capable of affecting trade between Member States, since in the absence of such agreement they would have attempted to develop the apparatus independently and to market it in other Member States. (See also *Re Italian Flat Glass* [1982] 3 CMLR 366 (agreement between Italian producers and wholesalers of glass representing more than half of the Italian market); *Salonia v Poidomani* (case 126/80) (national selective distribution system for newspapers capable of affecting trade between Member States).)

In the case of a domestic agreement between individual traders it may be necessary to examine the agreement in the context of other similar agreements, to ascertain whether, taken as a whole, they are capable of affecting trade between Member States (*Brasserie de Haecht SA v Wilkin (No. 1)* (case 23/67) (Belgian tied-house agreement part of a network of similar agreements)). The question to be asked is whether the agreements taken as a whole make a significant contribution to the sealing-off of national markets from competition from undertakings situated in other Member States (*Delimitis v Henninger Bräu* (case C–234/89)).

Since only a *potential* effect of trade need be proved the enquiry is not limited to existing patterns of trade; the Commission is prepared to speculate as to possible future patterns of trade. Thus in *Pronuptia* (case 161/84) the Court accepted the Commission's finding that a franchising agreement between Pronuptia in France (the franchisor) and its franchisee in Germany, which restricted the franchisee's power to operate outside a particular territory, was capable of affecting inter-State trade even though there was no evidence, and indeed it seemed highly unlikely, that the franchisee had any intention of extending its activities to other Member States.

The question of effect on trade between Member States is not concerned with the increase or decrease of trade which might result from an agreement; all that is required to be shown is a deviation (actual or potential) from the 'normal' pattern of trade which might exist between Member States (*Établissements Consten SA* v *Commission* (cases 56 & 58/64)). In assessing this question it is not necessary to examine every clause in the agreement as long as the agreement as a whole is capable of affecting trade between Member States (*Windsurfing International Inc.* v *Commission* (case 193/83)).

'Which have as their object or effect the prevention, restriction or distortion of competition within the common market'

As with the question of effect on trade between Member States, EC competition law is not concerned with the question of increase in trade between Member States but with whether there is a distortion of the 'normal' competition which should exist within the common market. Moreover, it is concerned not only with 'horizontal' agreements (i.e., between competing manufacturers, or competing wholesalers — the 'classic' cartel), which clearly restrict competition, but also with 'vertical' agreements (i.e., between manufacturer and distributor, between distributor and retailers, parties not competing with each other) which are often economically beneficial, since they streamline the distribution process and concentrate promotional activity, to the eventual benefit of consumers. These principles were established in *Établissements Consten SA* v *Commission* (cases 56 & 58/64).

This case concerned an exclusive dealership agreement between Grundig, a German company manufacturing electronic equipment, and Consten SA in France. Under the agreement Consten was appointed Grundig's sole distributor in France and granted exclusive rights to Grundig's trade mark, GINT, in France. Consten agreed not to re-export Grundig's products to any other EC country; Grundig agreed to obtain similar assurances from its dealers in other Member States. There was thus a total ban on parallel imports and exports in Grundig products, reinforced by the GINT trade mark. Consten discovered that another French firm, UNEF, had bought Grundig products from German traders and was selling them in France at prices below those charged by Consten. Consten brought an action against UNEF for infringement of its trade mark; UNEF applied to the Commission for a decision that the Consten-Grundig agreement was in breach of the then Article 85(1) (now 81(1)) and the Commission subsequently issued a Decision to that effect (*Re Grundig's Agreement* [1964] CMLR 489). In cases 56 & 58/64 the parties sought to annul that Decision. The claimants argued that the effect of their agreement was not to reduce trade between Member States but to increase it. The agreement served to concentrate and streamline the distribution of Grundig products in France, and trade in Grundig products had in fact increased. Moreover, Grundig faced lively competition from other rival producers. The Court rejected these arguments. The fact that trade in Grundig products had increased was irrelevant; the agreement might nonetheless affect trade between Member States and harm the object of the Treaty, namely the creation of the single market. Competition law was concerned not only with agreements which restricted competition amongst competing manufacturers (inter-brand competition). The object of the agreement was to eliminate competition in Grundig products at the wholesale level (intra-brand competition). Moreover, the parties could not rely on their trade-mark rights in these circumstances. To use them merely in order to partition the market constituted an abuse of such rights. However the Court was not prepared, as was the Commission, to declare the whole agreement void. Only the offending clauses were severed.

The decision in *Établissements Consten SA* v *Commission* has been criticised, but it must be acknowledged that restrictions on intra-brand competition, contained in vertical agreements, while they may carry economic benefits, are often used, as they were in the Consten-Grundig agreement, to partition the market, usually along national lines, in order to insulate the distributor in each State from competition from parallel imports from States where price levels are low. Artificially high price levels may thus be maintained. As has been noted in chapter 11, industrial property rights have been used to the same purpose.

Because of these dangers the Commission has preferred to maintain the prohibition under Article 81(1) (ex 85(1)) on these agreements, with the possibility of block exemption.

'Object or effect'   If the object of an agreement is to prevent or restrict or distort competition, for example, a naked price-fixing or market-sharing agreement between competing manufacturers, there is no need to prove its effect. Unless the agreement is clearly incapable of affecting competition, an anti-competitive effect will be presumed. Where the agreement is not designed to restrict competition, for example, a standard distribution agreement, a detailed economic analysis of its effects on the particular market will be necessary before a breach of Article 81(1) (ex 85(1)) can be proved.

The scope of the analysis required was considered in *Société Technique Minière* v *Maschinenbau Ulm GmbH* (case 56/65). The case involved an exclusive distribution agreement between a German manufacturer of heavy earth-moving equipment, Maschinenbau Ulm GmbH (MU), and a French distributor, Société Technique Minière (STM), similar to the Consten-Grundig agreement, but without its undesirable features. It contained no restrictions on parallel imports or exports, and no abusive use of trade marks. STM sought to resile on its agreement, claiming it was in breach of the then Article 85(1). On a reference from the Paris Cour d'Appel, the ECJ held that in order to ascertain whether an agreement is capable of preventing, restricting or distorting competition a number of factors must be examined, i.e.:

(a) *The nature and quantity of the products concerned* (i.e., the product market, and the parties' combined share in that market). The greater the market share held by the parties, the more damaging its impact on competition.

(b) *The position and size of the parties concerned* (i.e., their position in the market). The bigger they are, in terms of turnover and *relative* market share, the more likely it is that competition will be restricted.

(c) *The isolated nature of the agreement or its position in a series* (see also *Brasserie de Haecht SA* v *Wilkin (No. 1)* (case 23/67)). This is particularly relevant in the case of distribution agreements, which in themselves may appear insignificant, but which often form part of a network of similar agreements.

(d) *The severity of the clauses.* The more severe the clauses the more likely they will be deemed in breach of Article 81(1) (ex 85(1)). However, any clause that is more than is necessary to achieve the desired (beneficial) result will risk infringing Article 81(1) (ex 81(1)) (*L'Oréal NV* v *De Nieuwe AMCK PVBA* (case 31/80)).

(e) *The possibility of other commercial currents acting on the same products* by means of reimports and re-exports (i.e., parallel imports or exports). Thus any agreement which attempts to ban or even limit parallel imports or exports will normally breach Article 81(1) (ex 85(1)): *L. C. Nungesser KG* v *Commission* (case 258/78)).

The agreement between STM and MU was found on the facts not to breach the then Article 85(1) (now 81(1)).

Thus the enquiry needed to ascertain whether an agreement has the potential to prevent, restrict or distort competition within the common market is a wide-ranging one, often involving all the factors outlined above, *always* involving the first two. Such is the importance of the question of market definition that the Commission issued a Notice on the Definition of the Relevant Market for the purposes of Community competition law (([1997] OJ C 372/5) discussed in chapter 16). As will be seen, the Commission is equipped with wide investigative powers to undertake this analysis. National courts, on the other hand, particularly those with an accusatorial system such as ours, *a fortiori* our lower courts (e.g., *Potato Marketing Board* v *Robertsons* [1983] 1 CMLR 93, Oxford County Court) will have more difficulty in fulfilling this task (see *BEMIM* (cases T–114/92 and 5/93) discussed in chapter 17).

The *de minimis* principle

All agreements between business people curtail to some extent each other's freedom of action in the market-place. Clearly not all such agreements are capable of preventing, restricting or distorting competition to any noticeable extent. Always it is a question of size and scale, as the criteria of *Société Technique Minière* v *Maschinenbau Ulm GmbH,* particularly points (a) and (b), indicate, whether in fact they do so. Hence the importance in competition law of the *de minimis* principle.

The principle was introduced in the case of *Völk* v *Établissements Vervaecke Sprl* (case 5/69), which concerned an exclusive distribution agreement between Völk, a small-scale manufacturer of washing machines in Germany, and Vervaecke, a Dutch distributor of electrical goods. Völk agreed, *inter alia,* to block all sales of his machines into Vervaecke's territory by third parties (i.e., parallel imports). They were thus seeking absolute territorial protection for Vervaecke in relation to Völk's machines in Belgium and Luxembourg.

On a reference concerning the agreement's legality in the light of EC law, the Court ruled that in order to come within the then Article 85(1) (now 81(1)) competition must be affected to a noticeable extent; there must be a sufficient degree of harmfulness. Therefore it was necessary to take into account the position of the parties on the market for the product in question. In this case the effect of Völk-Vervaecke's agreement on the washing machine market in Belgium and Luxembourg was insignificant. (In fact Völk's production of washing machines was between 0.2 and 0.5 per cent of the German market, and his share in the Belgian and Luxembourg market was minute.)

Thus the size of the parties, and even more important, their share in the relevant product market, will be an essential factor in determining liability. However, if the parties are powerful in a particular market (e.g., alcoholic drinks), they cannot rely on the *de minimis* rule for any of their products within that market (e.g., Pimms (No. 1)) even though they may represent a negligible share of the market in other Member States (*Distillers Co. Ltd* v *Commission* (case 30/78)).

If an agreement falls within the *de minimis* principle, even if it contains the most blatantly anti-competitive clauses (e.g., price-fixing), even if the parties *intend* to restrict competition (clearly the aim of the territorial protection clause in *Völk* v *Vervaecke)* there will be no breach of Article 81(1) (ex 85(1)). Thus, in assessing the question of breach of Article 81(1) (ex 85(1)), some economic and market assessment will have to be made in every case, although agreements which do not have the object of restricting competition will require a more thorough analysis to prove that they are capable of that effect.

The principle of *Völk* v *Vervaecke* can at its best only provide a guideline serving to exclude agreements whose effect on competition is negligible. No figures were suggested as to the size of the market share needed to bring the principle into play. In *Miller International Schallplatten GmbH* v *Commission* (case 19/77) the Court held that a 5 per cent share in the product market did *not* come within the *de minimis* principle. A notice issued by the Commission in 1986 on agreements of minor importance (OJ C231/2, 1986, amended OJ C368/20, 1994) provided that, as a general rule, agreements between undertakings engaged in the production and distribution of goods and services which do not represent more than 5 per cent of the total market for such goods and services in the area affected by the agreement, and with an aggregate turnover of no more than 300 million ecus, would not fall within the then Article 85(1). The Commission replaced this with a new notice on agreements of minor importance ([1997] OJ C 372/1). This provides that an agreement will be *de minimis* where the total market share of all businesses involved is not more than 5 per cent in the case of a horizontal agreement or 10 per cent in the case of a vertical agreement. The Commission has indicated that it will revise its *de minimis* notice during 2000, although at the time of writing no proposals have been advanced. Further, agreements between small and medium-sized enterprises (as defined in Commission Recommendation 96/280 ([1996] OJ L 107/4)) will be treated as *de minimis* even if over the market threshold (para. 19). The Commission will not usually take action against such agreements (note para. 20 though). Where an agreement is not notified, because the parties in good faith believe it to be *de minimis*, but the Commission subsequently disagrees, the Commission will not impose fines. Certain types of sensitive agreements, such as resale price maintenance or price fixing, may still be found to violate Article 81(1) (ex 85(1)) EC even if below the market share thresholds. The Commission indicated in para. 11 of the Notice that, in general, it would leave the national authorities to take action against these infringements. The aim of the Commission in issuing the new Notice was to increase certainly about when an agreement would be *de minimis*. In the light of the exceptions to the general rules included in the notice and the possibility of differing interpretations of the thresholds by national authorities the boundaries are not always clear-cut. Nonetheless, in assessing the question of breach of this Article, the first question which should be asked is does the *de minimis* principle apply?

Agreements capable of preventing, restricting or distorting competition

Examples of agreements likely to breach Article 81(1) (ex 85(1)) are provided in subparas (a) to (e). Any agreement falling within these categories will raise a prima facie case of breach of this article, provided that it does not fall within the *de minimis* principle and that competition within the common market is affected. The Community dimension is essential, but, since it is subject to the same principles as the question of 'effect on trade between Member States', not hard to prove.

Although it is always a question of size and scale whether or not a breach of Article 81(1) (ex 85(1)) has occurred, it is possible from the approach of the Commission and the Court to the types of agreement listed in the article to distinguish between 'excusable' and 'inexcusable' restrictions. The inexcusable restrictions will breach the Article and are unlikely to obtain exemption under Article 81(3) (ex 85(3)). Excusable restrictions fall into one of two categories. *Either* they are found not to breach Article 81(1) (ex 85(1)) at all, or they are found in breach of the Article but eligible for exemption under Article 81(3) (ex 85(3)). The distinction is significant.

Article 81(1)(a) (ex 85(1)(a)): Agreements which directly or indirectly fix purchase or selling prices or other trading conditions

(a) *Price fixing.* Price-fixing agreements, because of their obvious anti-competitive effects, are almost always inexcusable. The ECJ was, in *Centres-Leclerc* v *'Au Blé Vert' Sàrl* (case 229/83), prepared to accept that French legislation allowing a system of retail price maintenance for books, the prices to be fixed by publishers, was compatible with the then Article 85(1). The government had claimed that the measure was indispensable to protect books as a cultural medium against the negative effects of fierce price competition and to maintain the existence of specialist bookshops. Evidence was adduced that most Member States operated some form of price maintenance for books. In the absence of common Community provision in the area, clearly a sensitive one, the Court was prepared to let these arguments prevail. However, in *Re the Application of the Publishers Association* [1989] 4 CMLR 825 the Commission found that the Publishers Association's Code of Conduct, which laid down standard conditions for the sale of books at fixed prices ('net book' prices) and which applied to books sold throughout the UK as well as to exports and reimports, and which provided, *inter alia*, for a system of *collective* price maintenance, was in breach of Article 85(1) (now 81(1)) and not eligible for exemption under Article 85(3) (now 81(3)). The CFI (case T–66/89) agreed with the Commission's decision because the agreement restricted competition within the single Community market, *even though it might produce beneficial effects within a national market*. The ECJ, however, overturned this ruling (*Publishers Association v Commission* (case C–360/92P)). The net book agreement was distinguished from the agreement in the Dutch books case (*VBVB v Commission* (cases 43 & 63/82)) to which the CFI had referred. That agreement was held to contravene the then Article 85(1) as it applied to all books and all publishers and was not capable of exemption under the then Article 85(3). The net book agreement, by contrast, applied only to some publishers and to those books which fell within the definition of a net book. Furthermore, the ECJ held that the Commission and CFI had failed to appreciate that the benefit to the book trade arising out of the agreement was not restricted to the UK but included the Irish market also, as both countries are primarily English speaking. Shortly after the ECJ's ruling the agreement collapsed. The impact of this change in the specialised book market remains to be seen.

Minimum prices are regarded in the same light as fixed prices. In *Hennessy/ Henkell* [1981] 1 CMLR 601, Commission Decision, a clause in an exclusive distribution agreement between Hennessy, the producer, in France, and Henkell, the distributor in Germany, setting maximum and minimum price limits for Hennessy's products, was found by the Commission to be in breach of the then Article 85(1) (now 81(1)), and not eligible for exemption under former Article 85(3) (now 81(3)). A similar finding was made and approved by the Court, in the case of recommended prices circulated amongst dealers in *AEG-Telefunken* (case 107/82). However, it was clear in *AEG-Telefunken* that the recommended prices were used to enable the parties to engage in concerted pricing policies. In *Pronuptia v Schillgalis* (case 161/84) the Court ruled that recommended prices issued in the context of a distribution franchising system would not breach Article 85(1) (now 81(1)) as long as they did not lead to concerted practices and the franchisee remained free to fix his own selling prices. In this area parallel pricing will provide strong evidence of concerted practices, although following *A. Ahlström OY* (cases C–89, 104, 116–17, 125–9/85), it will not be conclusive. In its subsequent Decision on the *Pronuptia* agreement ([1989] 4 CMLR 355) the Commission found the provision for recommended *maximum* prices to be acceptable.

(b) *Other trading conditions.* A manufacturer will often seek to impose trading conditions on his distributors (or retailers) in order to ensure that the premises are suitable, or that adequate after-sales service is provided. He may insist that his distributor holds minimum stocks or that he engages in specific promotional activities. In return for his efforts, a distributor may seek to safeguard his investment through protection from competition within his particular territory. To what extent are these arrangements compatible with EC law?

The first principle, laid down in *Metro-SB-Grossmärkte GmbH & Co. KG* v *Commission* (case 26/76), is that selective distribution systems will not breach Article 81(1) (ex 85(1)) provided that dealers are chosen on the basis of objective criteria of a *qualitative* nature relating to the technical qualifications of the dealer and his staff and the suitability of his trading premises, and that such conditions are laid down uniformly and not applied in a discriminatory manner.

In *L'Oréal* (case 31/80) the ECJ followed *Metro*, adding that the qualitative criteria must not go beyond what is necessary. What is regarded as necessary will depend on the nature of the product. In *Re Ideal/Standard Agreement* [1988] 4 CMLR 627 the Commission found that the characteristics of plumbing fittings were not sufficiently technically advanced to necessitate a selective distribution system in which wholesalers were required to be specialists in the sale of plumbing fittings and sanitary ware and to have a department specialising in the sale of such products. The products were too 'banal' to warrant such a system. With regard to *quantitative* criteria, such as, in *L'Oréal*, requirements that the distributor should guarantee a minimum turnover and hold minimum stocks, these were held to exceed the require-ments of a selective distribution system, and were thus in breach of the then Article 85(1), although it was suggested that they might be exemptible under what was Article 85(3). However, in *Pronuptia* v *Schillgalis*, in addition to a number of qualitative restrictions relating to layout, shop fittings, advertising and promotion, the Court did allow, as compatible with Article 85(1) (now 81(1)), a requirement that the franchisee should buy 80 per cent of its wedding dresses from Pronuptia and the remainder only from suppliers approved by Pronuptia. This requirement, like the qualitative requirements, was found essential in a franchising agreement to protect the know-how and reputation of the franchisor. The Commission confirmed in its Decision on *Pronuptia* that certain quantitative restrictions, including an obligation to hold minimum stocks, were permissible as essential to a franchising agreement, at the same time stressing that retail franchising agreements were different in kind from distribution agreements. It is submitted that apart from franchising agreements, quantitative restrictions will still require individual exemption.

Conditions in the form of import and export restrictions, designed to partition the market and to protect the distributor from (intra-brand) com-petition within his particular territory, as in *Consten/Grundig*, will always breach Article 81(1) (ex 85(1)) (unless it falls within the *de minimis* excep-tions discussed above) and will rarely qualify for exemption under Article 81(3) (ex 85(3)). The hard line taken by the Commission, with the qualified approval of the Court, is illustrated by its attitude to patent licensing agreements. In *L.C. Nungesser KG* v *Commission* (case 258/78), in the context of a licensing agreement assigning plant breeder's rights, the Court drew a distinction between an 'open' exclusive licence (restricting the grantor's right to grant other licences to the licensee's territory or to compete there himself), which was compatible with the then Article 85(1) (now 81(1)), and a 'closed' exclusive licence (restricting the rights of third-party importers or licensees in other territories to import into the licensee's territory), which was not. Nor did the latter qualify for exemption under Article 85(3) (now 81(3)), since the condition was not regarded as indispensable to the agreement. In *Hennessy/Henkell* a covert attempt by Jas. Hennessy & Co. to protect Sektellereien Henkell & Co. from competition from parallel imports by means of lowering their selling prices when 'infiltration' was threatened resulted in the striking down of the agreement as a whole. More recently, in *Herlitz AG* v *Commission* (case T–66/92), the CFI held that the fact that an export ban had not been implemented did not remove its offensive qualities: the mere existence of such a provision would still have, 'visual and psychological' effect (see also *Parker Ltd* v *Commission* (case T–77/92)). However, in *Pronuptia* there was a suggestion by the Court that a restriction on franchisees' rights to open up on other franchisees' territory, although in breach of Article 85(1) (now 81(1)), might be justified in order to protect franchisees' investment in the business. This has now been confirmed in the *Pronuptia* Decision, and followed in a Decision on the *Computerland Europe SA* franchising agreement [1989] 4 CMLR 259. Thus, a degree of territorial protection has been permitted in franchising agreements. This has now been incorporated in the Block Exemption on franchising agreements.

Article 81(1)(b) (ex 85(1)(b)): Agreements which control production, markets, technical developments or investments   These agreements, which are normally horizontal agreements, will invariably breach Article 81(1) (ex 85(1)). 'Naked' restrictions of this nature will rarely, if ever, qualify for exemption. However, where the restriction is ancillary to some desirable, pro-competitive agreement, such as a specialisation agreement between small and medium-sized firms, or a research and development agreement, it is likely to qualify for exemption — either block exemption or individual exemption. In *Re Vacuum Interrupters Ltd* [1977] 1 CMLR D67 the parties obtained individual exemption for such an agreement (research and development). (See also *Clima Chapée/Buderus* [1970] CMLR D7; *ACEC/Berliet* [1968] CMLR D35.)

Article 81(1)(c) (ex 85(1)(c)): Agreements to share markets or sources of supply   These too will normally be horizontal agreements in breach of Article 81(1) (ex 85(1)). A market sharing agreement may qualify for exemption if ancillary to some beneficial agreement on the same principles as apply to Article 81(1)(b) (ex 85(1)(b)), provided it does not attempt to establish absolute territorial protection for the product in question in the markets concerned. An agreement to share sources of supply would require exemption, and would be difficult to justify.

Article 81(1)(d) (ex 85(1)(d)): Agreements which apply dissimilar conditions to equivalent transactions with other trading parties, thereby placing them at a competitive disadvantage   Concerted discriminatory treatment will always breach Article 81(1) (ex 85(1)) and will rarely if ever be eligible for exemption. However, agreements imposing dissimilar conditions will only breach the Article 81(1) (ex 85(1)) if the transactions are 'equivalent'; there will be no breach if the difference in treatment is objectively justified (see *Metro-SB-Grossmärkte GmbH & Co. KG* v *Commission* (case 26/76)). Thus an agreement to charge different (but not fixed) prices to different customers would be permissible if the prices charged genuinely reflected different (e.g., transport) costs; it would not if they were based on what the market would bear. Similarly, 'quantity' discounts (discounts for bulk purchases), if they genuinely reflect cost savings, are permissible, whilst 'fidelity' or 'loyalty' rebates, which are tied to the volume of business transacted, are not.

Article 81(1)(e) (ex 85(1)(e)): Agreements which make the conclusion of contracts subject to acceptance by other parties of supplementary obligations which, by their nature and/or according to commercial usage, have no connection with the subject-matter of such contracts Such agreements, or, rather, such clauses in an agreement, will always breach Article 81(1) (ex 85(1)) and will require individual exemption under Article 81(3) (ex 85(3)). However, it is a matter of judgment whether an obligation is deemed to have the requisite connection with the subject-matter of the contract. Agreements guaranteeing exclusivity, such as exclusive supply agreements (*Hennessy/Henkell, Pronuptia*) or exclusive licensing agreements (*Nungesser*) are seen as essential to the subject-matter of the contract; attempts at territorial protection are not. Trading conditions based on necessary objective qualitative criteria are essential, those based on quantitative criteria are not (*Metro, L'Oréal*), although certain 'essential' quantitative restrictions may be imposed in franchising agreements (*Pronuptia*) at least if expressed in percentage terms. In *Hennessy/Henkell* a clause prohibiting Henkell & Co. from dealing in products competing with Hennessy's was found acceptable as essential to the exclusive distribution agreement; a clause prohibiting them from dealing in any other products at all was not, nor was it justifiable under the then Article 85(3). 'Non-competition' clauses, i.e., restraint of trade clauses attached on the sale of a business have been found by the Commission to be essential to the main contract, since the know-how and goodwill of a business protected by a non-competition clause are seen to constitute a substantial part of the assets transferred (*Reuter/BASF AG* [1976] 2 CMLR D44; approved by the court in *Remia BV* v *Commission* (case 42/84). However, the restraints must be no more than is necessary to preserve the value of the bargain. Thus in *Reuter/BASF AG* a non-competition clause of eight years' duration and extending to non-commercial research was found excessive, and not justifiable under Article 85(3) (now 81(3)), and in *Remia BV* a 10-year restriction on competition was reduced to four.

Other agreements The above list of agreements capable of preventing, restricting or distorting competition is not exhaustive. In *AEG-Telefunken* (case 107/82) and *Ford Werke AG* (case 25/84) a refusal to supply was found in breach of Article 85(1) (now 81(1)) where that refusal was made in the context of existing agreements in order to enable anti-competitive practices to continue. In *British American Tobacco (B.A.T.) and Reynolds v Commission* (cases 142 and 156/84) the ECJ held for the first time that the then Article 85(1) applied to mergers. The case arose from a proposed merger between Philip Morris Inc. and Rembrandt Ltd, which would have given Philip Morris a controlling interest in one of its principal competitors, Rothmans Tobacco (Holding) Ltd, in the EC cigarette market. The Commission had been alerted to the proposed merger by the parties' competitors, B.A.T. and Reynolds. Subsequently the agreement was modified by a Decision from the Commission reducing Philip Morris's shareholding in Rothmans Ltd, and thereby ensuring that the relationship between them remained competitive. The Decision was challenged by B.A.T. and Reynolds. While the Decision was upheld by the Court, the Court affirmed that Article 85(1) (now 81(1)) could apply in principle to mergers. Although the acquisition of an equity interest in a competitor did not in itself restrict competition, it might serve as an instrument to that end.

This Decision paved the way for the acceptance by Member States of a Regulation on merger control which had been languishing for many years. The final version of the Regulation, Regulation 4064/89 (corrected version OJ No. L 257, 21.9.90, p. 13) was adopted in December 1989, after much debate amongst Member States on the appropriate turnover and market share thresholds required to bring the Regulation into operation. It requires notification to and approval by the Commission of proposed mergers above certain combined turnover thresholds. The Merger Regulation has recently been amended. Previously, it distinguished between cooperative and concentrative joint ventures, concerning itself only with the latter. It now includes full-function joint ventures even where the joint venture is cooperative. The notices relating to the previous version of the Regulation, that is the notices on the Distinction between Concentrative and Cooperative Joint Ventures (OJ C385/1, 1994), on the notion of undertakings concerned (OJ C385/12, 1994) on the notion of concentration (OJ C385/5, 1994) and on the calculation of turnover (OJ C385/21, 1994), have all been amended to take account of the changes to the Regulation ([1997] OJ C66). Most notably, there is a definition of 'full-function' merger. The changes will mean that more mergers will be caught by the Merger Regulation, thus allowing for greater control by the Commission, and avoiding the need for the companies concerned to deal with the competition authorities in each Member State affected by the merger. (For further details of the Merger Regulation see chapter 16.)

Although neither the Commission nor the Court expressly distinguishes between naked and ancillary restrictions on competition, it is safe to say that naked restrictions in any of the above categories will breach Article 81(1) (ex 85(1)) and will be unlikely to obtain exemption under Article 81(3) (ex 85(3)).

Where ancillary restrictions are concerned, the approach of the Commission and the Court is not entirely consistent. Certain restrictions, contained in exclusive distribution agreements (*Metro-SB-Grossmärkte, L'Oréal,*

Hennessy/Henkell), or exclusive licensing agreements (*Nungesser*) or franchising agreements (*Pronuptia, Computerland*), or attached to the sale of a business (*Reuter/BASF, Remia BV*), although apparently falling within the wide words of Article 81(1) (ex 85(1)), have been construed as essential to the main agreement, and as such not in breach of the Article at all. Similarly, in *Bayer AG* v *Süllhöfer* (case 65/86) Advocate-General Darmon suggested that a no-challenge clause in a licensing agreement would be acceptable if it was *crucial* to the equilibrium of the licensing agreement, the object and effect of which is not shown to be specifically restrictive of competition. The Court confined itself to stating more narrowly that a no-challenge clause would not breach what was then Article 85(1) (now 81(1)) where the licence was granted for no consideration or, although granted for consideration, it related to some outdated procedure. Other restrictions in these same types of agreement, although not blatantly anti-competitive, and arguably regarded by one, if not both, of the parties as necessary to the transaction as a whole, have been found in breach of Article 81(1) (ex 85(1)) although possibly exemptible under Article 81(3) (ex 85(3)). And in other kinds of agreement, for example, research and development or specialisation agreements, restrictions (e.g., within Article 81(1)(b)) which are clearly justifiable in the context of the agreement as a whole have rarely been regarded by the Commission as acceptable *per se*; they must be given exemption under Article 81(3) (ex 85(3)). However, in *Elopak/Metal Box-Odin* (OJ L 209/15 1990), the Commission was prepared to grant negative clearance to a joint venture between Elopak/Metal Box and Odin for the purposes of research and development.

The former approach, where clauses which are to a certain extent restrictive of competition are permitted under Article 81(1) (ex 85(1)) as necessary to the agreement as a whole, is said to be an application of the rule of reason.

The rule of reason

The concept of 'rule of reason' originated in US anti-trust law, where it was applied in interpreting s.1 of the Sherman Act 1890. This section, which condemns every contract in restraint of trade, does not contain any definition of restraint of trade or any provision for exemption for beneficial agreements on the lines of Article 81(3) (ex 85(3) EC). It was left to the courts to decide whether or not a restraint of trade had occurred. In 1911 the US Supreme Court held, in *United States* v *American Tobacco* (1911) 221 US 106 at p. 179, that not every contract in restraint of trade was illegal; it would only be illegal if it was unreasonable in that it operated to the prejudice of the public interest by *unduly* restricting competition. Thus, in applying this 'rule of reason', the US courts attempt to balance the pro and anti-competitive effects of an agreement in order to assess whether a breach of s. 1 has occurred.

The structure of Article 81 (ex 85) is quite different. It was clearly intended that this weighing of the pro- and anti-competitive effects of an agreement was to take place not under Article 81(1) (ex 85(1)) but under Article 81(3) (ex 85(3)), the Commission alone having exclusive power to grant exemption under Article 81(3) (ex 85(3)) (Regulation 17/62, Article 9(1)). In this way uniformity of interpretation, and the maximum supervision and control by the Commission, would be guaranteed.

This scheme, however, had its drawbacks. The need to notify agreements to obtain exemption and the resulting work-load on the Commission led to long delays. If this created uncertainty for business people, it created even greater difficulties for national courts, since they were required to apply Article 81(1) (ex 85(1)) but not empowered to grant exemption under Article 81(3) (ex 85(3)). Nor could Article 234 (ex 177) EC help here, since in the absence of a Decision from the Commission the ECJ has no power to declare an agreement exempt under Article 81(3) (ex 85(3)).

One solution to this problem, adopted by the Commission, was to pass block exemptions. If parties structured their agreements to comply with the exemptions they would be free of risk. Another possible solution lay in the application of a rule of reason. Under the 'European' rule of reason, which is undoubtedly narrower than its US progenitor, only restrictions which constitute an *essential* element of the agreement, without which the agreement would be emptied of its substance, and which pose no real threat to competition or to the functioning of the single market, are deemed compatible with Article 81(1) (ex 85(1)). Non-essential restrictions, or restrictions which might interfere with the functioning of the common market, are left to be decided under Article 81(3) (ex 81(5)). Many of the agreements discussed above (e.g., *Metro-SB-Grossmärkte, L'Oréal, Hennessy/Henkell, Nungesser, Pronuptia, Reuter/BASF AG, Remia BV*) provide examples of both essential and non-essential restrictions. A similar two-tiered approach has already been noted in the Court's interpretation of quantitative restrictions under Articles 28 (ex 30) and 30 (ex 36), although in the case of Article 30 (new 28) justification under the *Cassis* rule of reason is more explicit (see chapter 10).

However, a continued reliance on Article 81(3) (ex 85(3)) for non-essential restrictions which are nonetheless justifiable, for example, in research and development agreements, ignores the central structural weakness of the exemption procedure, namely, the inability of national courts to apply Article 81(3). Even the ECJ overlooked this problem when it suggested in *Pronuptia* that the clauses seeking territorial protection for the franchisees could be examined in the light of Article 81(3) (ex 85(3)). (See also *L'Oréal*, Court's comments regarding quantitative restrictions.)

There is no doubt that the Commission and, more particularly, the Court (in *Nungesser* the Commission regarded even the open exclusive licence as in breach of the then Article 85(1), although exemptible under former Article 85(3)) have been moving tentatively towards a rule of reason approach, although neither has acknowledged the rule as such. However, rather than endorsing such a rule, and risking its unequal application by national courts, the Commission has sought to increase legal certainty and encourage agreements which are beneficial overall by issuing Notices indicating the types of agreement which will be acceptable under Article 81(1) (ex 85(1)) and introducing or extending block exemptions for those categories of agreement, which, although restrictive of competition, are clearly justified. Thus where an agreement appears to fall within Article 81(1) (ex 85(1)), is not covered by a Notice and has not been subjected to a rule of reason, it would be wise to structure the agreement to fit within a block exemption or to seek negative clearance or individual exemption under Article 81(3) (ex 85(3)). Following the Commission's Notice on Cooperation between the Commission and national courts in applying Articles 85 and 86 (now 81 and 82) (OJ No. C 39 13.2.93) national courts will be able to obtain assistance from the Commission in applying these Articles, and even on the question of exemption under Article 81(3) (ex 85(3)).

Article 81(3) (ex 85(3)): exemption

Under Article 81(3) (ex 85(3)), Article 81(1) (ex 85(1)) may be declared inapplicable to any agreement or category of agreement between undertakings, or any decision or category of decision by associations of undertakings:

. . . which contributes to improving the production or distribution of goods or to promoting technical or economic progress, while allowing consumers a fair share of the resulting benefit, and which does not:

(a)   impose on the undertakings concerned restrictions which are not indispensable to the attainment of these objectives;
(b)   afford such undertakings the possibility of eliminating competition in respect of a substantial part of the products in question.

In order to take advantage of these provisions, agreements other than agreements falling within the terms of the block exemptions (below) *must* be notified (Regulation 17/62, Article 4(1)). In the absence of notification exemption will not be granted (*Distillers Co. Ltd* v *Commission* (case 30/78)). Once the Commission has decided whether an agreement as notified is eligible for exemption or not it will issue a Decision to the parties to that effect. This Decision must be published in the *Official Journal* (Regulation 17/62, Article 21) and as a binding act it may be challenged before the Court of First Instance under Article 230 (ex 173) EC (see chapter 30). The parties concerned must be given an opportunity to be heard before a Decision is taken (Regulation 17/62, Article 19(1)), as may persons who can show a 'sufficient interest' (Article 19(2)). A Decision may be annulled if these essential procedural requirements are breached.

To obtain exemption under Article 81(3) (ex 85(3)) the agreement or decision must satisfy four essential criteria.

It must contribute to improving the production or distribution of goods or to promoting technical or economic progress   Thus the agreement as a whole must show positive benefits. These are expressed in the alternative, although the more benefits that are proved the greater the likelihood of exemption. Different kinds of agreement will produce different benefits.

(a)   *Production.*   Benefits in production are most likely to accrue from specialisation agreements. Specialisation enables each party to concentrate its efforts and achieve the benefits of scale; it avoids wasteful duplication. In *Clima Chappée/Buderus* [1970] CMLR D7 the Commission granted exemption to a specialisation and reciprocal supply agreement between Clima Chappée in France and Buderus in Germany. Both were engaged in the manufacture of air-conditioning and ventilation systems and central-heating apparatus in their own countries. They agreed each to manufacture a certain range of products exclusively, and to supply the other exclusively with these products in the other's own country. Clearly there was some reduction in competition in the common market since they were potential competitors. Nonetheless the gains in production and distribution were clear, and the agreement contributed to both technical and economic progress. The other elements of the then Article 85(3) (now 81(3)) too were satisfied. The agreement would result in fair shares for consumers because there was sufficient inter-brand competition to ensure that the parties would pass on the benefit of their agreement to the consumers. Nor had they imposed on each other restrictions which were not indispensable; they were not obliged to purchase the other's products unless they were competitive. And there was no possibility of eliminating competition in respect of a substantial part of the products in question. Even combined, the parties were subject to strong inter-brand competition for the products in question.

(b) *Distribution.* Benefits in distribution occur principally through vertical agreements in the form of exclusive supply or dealership or distribution agreements. The benefits result from the streamlining of the distribution process and the concentration of activity on the part of the distributor, whether it be in the provision of publicity, technical expertise, after-sales service, or simply the maintenance of adequate stocks. These factors were important in the *Transocean Marine Paint Association* Decision [1967] CMLR D9. The agreement here was between a number of small and medium-sized manufacturers and distributors of marine paint from inside and outside the EC. The purpose of their collaboration was to produce and market marine paints to identical standards and to organise the sale of these products on a world-wide basis. They hoped thereby to compete with the giants of the paint world. The paints were sold under a single trade mark, though members were free to add their own name and mark. Markets were to be divided up on national lines, and members were free to sell in each other's territory only on payment of a commission. There was thus a degree of territorial protection. (Their original plan to prohibit sales on each other's territory was dropped at the request of the Commission.) The advantage claimed for the agreement was the achievement of a world-wide distribution network for the same interchangeable product. Alone each manufacturer would be too small to offer adequate stocks and expertise.

Exemption was granted. The Commission agreed that the system did improve distribution; it streamlined the service to customers and led to a specialised knowledge of the market. Even the clauses granting limited territorial protection were permitted since they avoided fragmentation of the market, especially important during the launching period. Whilst competition between members was restricted, on an international scale it was greatly increased. The use of the trade mark too was permitted, since it was used in order to identify the product, not to partition the market.

(c) *Technical progress.* Technical progress is most likely to result from specialisation agreements, particularly those concerned with research and development. The *ACEC/Berliet* Decision [1968] CMLR D35 concerned an agreement between ACEC, who were manufacturers, *inter alia,* of electrical transmission systems for commercial vehicles, and Berliet, who manufactured buses in France. They wished to collaborate to produce a new prototype bus. ACEC was to develop a new transmission system for the bus; Berliet agreed to buy the system only from ACEC; ACEC to supply only Berliet in France and not more than one outlet in any other Member State. ACEC also undertook to give Berliet 'most favoured treatment', and agreed not to reveal to any other manufacturer information acquired from Berliet. Despite these many restrictions the Commission granted them exemption. There were clear gains in production and technical progress.

In *Re Vacuum Interrupters (No. 2)* [1981] 2 CMLR 217 an agreement in the form of a joint venture between the three leading British companies engaged in the manufacture of switch gear for research and the development of vacuum interrupters was exempted. It was found to lead to benefits on all four fronts, but particularly technical progress (see also *I.C.I./B.P.* [1985] 2 CMLR 330).

(d) *Economic progress.* Rather surprisingly economic progress has received scant attention in Decisions concerning exemption. It is normally presumed if improvements in production or distribution or technical progress are achieved. However, it did form the basis of a Decision granting exemption to an agreement regulating the holding of trade fairs in *Cecimo* [1969] CMLR D1 on the grounds that it tended to rationalise the operation and avoided wasteful duplication of time and effort.

The agreement must allow consumers a fair share in the resulting benefit   Provided there is sufficient (inter-brand) competition from other producers in the relevant market the improvements achieved will inevitably enure to the benefit of consumers, either in the form of a better product, or a better service, or greater availability of supplies or lower prices. If the parties fail to pass on the benefits to consumers they risk losing out to their competitors. Thus the parties' market share, both in absolute terms and in relation to their competitors, will be crucial. In all the cases considered above where exemption was granted the parties faced lively competition.

The agreement must not impose on the undertakings concerned restrictions which are not indispensable   This is the familiar proportionality principle, the downfall of many an otherwise-exemptible agreement, a trap to catch the greedy. The Commission will examine each clause in an agreement to see if it is necessary to the agreement as a whole. Fixed prices, even fixed maximum and minimum price limits, as in *Hennessy/Henkell* will rarely be indispensable, nor will clauses seeking absolute territorial protection (*Consten/Grundig* (cases 56 & 58/64), *Hennessy/Henkell, Nungesser* (case 258/78)). But even these restric-

within one or other of the block exemptions, which was not always appropriate, or apply for individual exemption. Following a consultation exercise in 1997, the Commission has now replaced these three block exemptions with a single block exemption (Regulation 2790/1999, [1999] OJ L 326/21) applying to *vertical restraints* (although special rules continue to apply to some sectors such as petrol distribution). This new block exemption came into force on 1 June 2000. It will apply to all agreements containing vertical restraints. It is wider than the previous block exemptions, as it will cover unfinished goods ('intermediate goods') and agreements between multiple parties.

The block exemption, unlike earlier block exemptions in the field, is based on a market share test; where the parties to the agreement have a combined market share of up to 30 per cent, the agreement will enter a 'safe harbour' where the agreement will automatically be exempt from the Article 81(1) (ex 85(1)) prohibition, unless it contains what are described as 'hard-core restrictions'. Market share will be determined by assessing the relevant geographical and product markets. The definition of these markets is discussed further in chapter 16. Agreements which exceed the safe harbour limit are not necessarily contrary to Article 81 (ex 85) but may need further examination.

Most of the original Regulations followed a similar pattern. First, they lay down the kinds of restrictions which are permitted, the 'white' list, the restrictions which are deemed 'essential' to the agreement in question; this is followed by the 'black' list — the kind of clauses which will not be permitted. With the *patent licensing* Regulation the Commission introduced a third category, the 'grey' restrictions. These are subject to a special procedure, known as the 'opposition' procedure. Under this procedure the grey restrictions must be notified to the Commission, but if they are not opposed within a specified period, they are deemed to be exempt. This procedure was incorporated into the *research and development* Regulation (418/85), and the *specialisation* Regulation (417/85), although it was applied here in a rather different context, only where the turnover ceiling limiting the application of the Regulation was exceeded. The procedure has also been incorporated in the franchising and technology transfer Regulations. Most of the Regulations, save the Technology Transfer Regulation which specifies four months, allow the Commission six months to act under the opposition procedure.

Exemption under the *specialisation* Regulation depends on the parties' combined turnover and their market share in the goods covered by the agreement. These figures have been raised each time the Regulation has been renewed. The current turnover limit is 1,000 million ecu (raised from 500 million by Regulation 151/93), with a market share of 20 per cent (10 per cent in the case of joint ventures). The opposition procedure may be applied where this turnover limit is exceeded.

Exemption under the *research and development* Regulation is also limited to parties with a combined market share of 20 per cent, this figure too having been regularly increased. There is no turnover limit. Following the adoption of Regulation 151/93, joint ventures are now covered by this exemption, which includes the joint exploitation of results.

The former *franchising* Regulation applied to distribution and servicing, but not to manufacturing franchises. The franchise system is described as based on the exploitation of intangible property rights such as trade marks or names and know-how, for the purpose of selling goods or providing services in premises of uniform appearances and with the same business methods (Article 1(2)).

The new *vertical restraints* block exemption similarly identifies certain types of clauses which will not be permissible. These are non-compete clauses in excess of five years; clauses which prevent a buyer from manufacturing or selling certain goods after the agreement has terminated (save where innovative products are concerned, in which a one-year prohibition would be acceptable); and 'hard-core restrictions'. Hard-core restrictions include minimum and fixed resale price maintenance; restrictions on resale outside exclusive and selective distribution networks; and restrictions on active or passive selling by members of a selective distribution network.

In selecting its white and black lists, the Commission has drawn on its earlier Decisions and the jurisprudence of the Court. Thus in exclusive distribution and purchasing agreements exclusivity is permitted, but absolute territorial protection is not. Distributors may be required not to seek business outside their territory actively, but they may not be prohibited from selling there. However, concessions have been made in the field of technology transfers, in that a five-year ban of 'passive' sales (i.e., licensee may not *respond* to unsolicited orders from other territories) is allowed. Time will run from the date when the goods in question were first put on the market in the common market.

Along with the introduction of the new block exemption on vertical restraints (and the provision of guidelines on vertical restraints), the Commission has fundamentally changed the current system of notification as regards vertical agreements by the enactment of Regulation 1216/99 ([1999] OJ L 148). The Commission has suggested that companies need no longer notify their agreements from the outset. Instead, companies could apply for exemption at a later date, with any exemption granted being backdated to the date of the agreement. It would seem that the Commission hopes that this reform will allow the Commission the time to concentrate on agreements which are problematic in competition terms, rather than having to spend its limited resources in approving harmless agreements.

Although it is still too soon to assess how the new regime for vertical restraints will work in practice, it has generated criticism from industry. The legal certainty, which the other block exemptions provide, has been sacrificed. In particular, the determination of market share is not an exact science, and industry will be even more reliant on its legal and economic advisers (who are bound to take a cautious view) as to whether it satisfies the market test or not. Arguably the change in notification procedures will not lessen the Commission's burden, as companies will try to get all the guidance and comfort that they can about the acceptability of their agreements.

As part of its plans to modernise competition law, the Commission has recently put forward another draft proposal regarding competition rules and horizontal cooperation agreements ([2000] OJ C 118/3). As the Commission's 1999 Report on Competition Policy noted, companies need to respond to increasing competitive pressure and changes in the market-place driven by globalisation and the speed of technological progress. In this context, the Commission does not want to discourage cooperation as it can be a means of sharing risk, saving costs, pooling know-how and consequently facilitating the launch of innovative products. The approach the Commission has proposed seems similar to that adopted in respect of vertical agreements, consisting as it does of a safe harbour clause for agreements under a certain market share. Again, the main thrust of the reforms is to free the Commission from considering cases which are no significant threat to competition, thus allowing the Commission to concentrate on more important cases. Although a market share approach for horizontal agreements is likely to run into similar criticisms to those encountered by the new block exemption on vertical restraints, action by the Commission in this area must be seen as a positive step, as the reform of the existing regime for horizontal restraints seems long overdue.

Comfort letters

Apart from introducing block exemptions and Notices, and a limited application of the rule of reason, the Commission has further attempted to reduce its work-load, and at the same time speed up its decision-making processes, by the issuing of 'comfort' letters. Originally issued in response to applications for negative clearance, their scope was expanded in 1983 (OJ No. C295, 2.11.83, p. 6) to cover applications for exemption under Article 85(3) (now 81(1)). A comfort letter is a communication from the Commission to the effect that, in its opinion, the agreement *either* does not infringe Article 81(1) (ex 85(1)) at all ('soft' negative clearance), *or* that it infringes that Article but is of a type that qualifies for exemption ('soft' exemption). Following this, the file is normally closed.

Unlike a formal Decision, which will only be issued following procedures laid down in Regulation 17/62, after lengthy investigation and consultation with all the parties concerned, a comfort letter represents a quick, informal way of providing assurance for the parties concerned. However, it may be 'cold comfort', since, as the ECJ pointed out in the *Perfume cases* (case 253/78; case 99/79), comfort letters are merely 'administrative letters' issued outside the framework of Regulation 17/62, and as such are not binding on national courts. Moreover, as non-binding measures, they cannot be challenged before the ECJ in annulment proceedings, either by the parties concerned or by a third party who is directly and individually concerned (see chapter 30). It has been suggested that, since the practice is an evasion of the procedures laid down in Regulation 17/62 it is itself *ultra vires*. The same shortcomings and criticisms apply to the Commission's new opposition procedures. Although the Commission has attempted to remedy the procedural deficiencies of comfort letters by publishing a notice of its intentions, in order to give third parties an opportunity to comment prior to its issuing a final letter, the non-binding status of the letter still gives rise to uncertainty. This problem has increased following the publication of the Commission's Notice on cooperation between national courts and the Commission in applying Articles 85 and 86 (now 81 and 82 respectively) (OJ No. C39 13.2.93). Here the Commission announced its intention in the future to concentrate its investigations on cases of particular political, economic or legal significance for the Community. Unless such issues were raised, notifications, whether for the purposes of negative clearance or exemption, would in future be dealt with by comfort letter. Complaints by parties with a legitimate interest (see further chapter 17) would no longer be sufficient, as heretofore, to trigger an enquiry if the complainant could secure adequate protection for his rights before his national courts. The CFI held in *BEUC* v *Commission* (case T–37/92) that a Commission decision that a complaint does not trigger Community interests may be reviewed under Article 173 (now 230) EC. This, however, still means that national courts will be required, in accordance with the principle of subsidiarity, to play an increasingly important role in the enforcement of EC competition law. In carrying out that task they could be guided by decisions of the Commission and the Court, and by opinions and official statements of the Commission. With the Commission's proposals to modernise the application of Articles 81 and 82 (ex 85 and 86), the role of the national authorities may be extended still further. As regards comfort letters, the Notice provides that they constitute 'a factor which national courts may take into account in examining whether the agreement or conduct in question are in accordance with the provisions of Article 85 [now 81]' (para. 20).

Since with a reduction in the number of formal decisions issued by the Commission national courts will be forced to rely increasingly on comfort letters, it is regrettable that the Commission was not more precise as to the effect of these letters. Faced with a problem a national court may under the Notice apply to the Commission for clarification. Any response must itself take the form of an informal decision. In the absence of evidence not placed before the Commission or good grounds for doubting the applicability of a comfort letter, or the Commission's clarification, the national court should be entitled to rely on such a letter, whether this results in a finding that an agreement is cleared under Article 81(1) (ex 85(1)) or exempted under Article 81(3) (ex 85(3)). If the Commission's letter were subsequently revised (by the Commission) or invalidated (by the CFI) which in either case is theoretically possible, arguably the principle of legitimate expectations could be invoked to shield the parties concerned from any adverse consequences, provided they had acted in good faith in reliance on the letter.

Further reading

See reading for chapter 14 and:

Barr, F., 'The New Commission Notice on Agreements of Minor Importance: Is Appreciability a Useful Measure?' [1997] ECLR 207.

Forrester, I. and Norall, C., 'The Laicization of Community Law: Self-help and the Rule of Reason' (1984) 21 CML Rev 11.

Green, N., 'Article 85 in Perspective: Stretching Jurisdiction, Narrowing the Concept of a Restriction and Plugging a Few Gaps' [1988] ECLR 190.

Steindorff, E., 'Article 85 and the Rule of Reason' (1984) 21 CML Rev 639.

Whish, R. and Sufrin, B., 'Article 85 and the Rule of Reason' (1987) 7 YEL 1.

SIXTEEN

Abuse of a dominant position

The prohibition

Article 82 (ex 86) EC provides that:

Any abuse by one or more undertakings of a dominant position within the common market or in a substantial part of it shall be prohibited as incompatible with the common market insofar as it may affect trade between Member States.

The prohibition is followed by a list of examples of abuse.

Whereas Article 81 (ex 85) is concerned with the dangers to competition arising from the grouping together of otherwise independent organisations, Article 82 (ex 86) is aimed at individual undertakings and the special problems raised by market power. If an agreement between independent undertakings which is merely capable of restricting or distorting competition is prohibited, *a fortiori* this must apply to abusive behaviour on the part of a dominant undertaking, which will have a much more profound effect on competition; indeed its very position may enable it to eliminate competition altogether.

As its wording makes clear, the scope of Article 82 (ex 86) is not limited to monopolies or single organisations enjoying substantial market power. It applies also to undertakings within the same corporate or economic group which, when combined, together create a position of dominance. Where parent companies are acting in close conjunction with their subsidiaries they will often be treated as a single undertaking (see *Eurofix & Bauco* v *Hilti AG* [1989] 4 CMLR 677).

It was thought originally that Article 86 (now 82) did not apply to undertakings which were independent of each other, and could not therefore be used to control oligopolies. This has not proved to be the case. In *Re Italian Flat Glass* ((1989) OJ L33/44) the Commission held that three Italian producers of flat glass, who between them held a 79 per cent to 95 per cent share of the Italian market in flat glass, had a *collective* dominant position in these markets and had abused that position. While the decision was annulled in part in *SIV* v *Commission* (cases T–68/89, T 77/89, T 78/89) for lack of proof of dominance, the application of the then Article 86 to oligopolies was not disputed by the CFI. The potential application of Article 82 (ex 86) to oligopolies has, however, since been affirmed, notably by the ECJ in *Municipality of Almelo* v *Energiededrifj IJsselmij NV* (case C–393/92). In that case, the ECJ stated that a collective dominant position would exist when 'the undertakings in question were linked in such a way that they adopt the same conduct on the market.' In *Irish Sugar* (case T–288/97), the CFI accepted the possibility that Irish Sugar, which produced sugar, and its distributor were together dominant, thus raising the possibility of vertical collective dominance as well as horizontal collective dominance. Nevertheless the implications of these decisions for oligopolies are not clear. In *Re Italian Flat Glass* the parties were engaged in concerted price-fixing and market-sharing practices in breach of the then Article 85(1). It remains to be seen whether Article 82 (ex 86) could be invoked to control oligopolistic practices which are not in breach of Article 81(1) (ex 85(1)), but which nevertheless undermine the competitive structure in a particular market. Nonetheless, it seems that Articles 81 and 82 (ex 85 and 86) are not mutually exclusive; where doubt exists as to which Article is applicable, both should be pleaded.

Undertakings

The term 'undertakings' is subject to the same broad interpretation as is applied to Article 81 (ex 85) EC, and covers the same activities, both public and private. As the Court held in *Italy* v *Commission* (case 41/83), in the context of a challenge to a Commission Decision that certain activities of British Telecom were in breach of the then Article 86 (now 82), the fact that the enterprise has statutory rule-making powers does not prevent EC competition law from applying to such powers. Similarly, the Commission pointed out in the *Belgian Telemarketing* Decision [1986] 2 CMLR 558 that the fact the dominant (in this case monopoly) position is brought about or encouraged by provisions laid down by law is no bar to the application of former Article 86 (now 82).

Like Article 81 (ex 85), Article 82 (ex 86) applies to undertakings engaged in the provision of goods or services, and can apply to any undertaking in the world as long as the abusive practices take effect inside the common market. The most vulnerable under Article 82 are the large multinationals. The Commission will not hesitate to take into account the economic strength of other members of a group or to fix them with liability if they are implicated in the abusive behaviour. The most obvious example is the case of *Europemballage Corp. and Continental Can Co. Inc.* v *Commission* (case 6/72). However, the scope of Article 82 (ex 86) is not limited, as will be seen, to very large concerns.

Article 82 (ex 86) contains three essential ingredients. There must be:

(a)   a dominant position,
(b)   an abuse of that position, and
(c)   the abuse must affect trade between Member States.

The principle of dominance

Dominance was defined in *United Brands Co.* v *Commission* (case 27/76), at para. 65, as:

> a position of economic strength enjoyed by an undertaking which enables it to prevent effective competition being maintained on the relevant market by giving it the power to behave to an appreciable extent independently of its competitors, customers, and ultimately of its consumers.

To this the Commission added in *AKZO Chemie BV* [1986] 3 CMLR 273 at para. 67 that:

> The power to exclude effective competition is not . . . in all cases coterminous with independence from competitive factors but may also involve the ability to eliminate or seriously weaken existing competitors or to prevent potential competitors from entering the market.

In order to assess whether an undertaking has sufficient economic strength to behave independently of, or even exclude, competitors, it is necessary first to ascertain the relevant market in which competition is said to exist. As the Court pointed out in *Europemballage Corp. and Continental Can Co. Inc.* v *Commission* (case 6/72), a position can be dominant within the meaning of Article 82 (ex 86) only if it is dominant in a relevant product market.

The relevant product market (RPM)

This is defined by the Commission in its Notice on the Definition of the Relevant Market (OJ [1997] C 372) and the Court in terms of product substitution. The relevant product market is one in which products are substantially interchangeable (*Istituto Chemioterapico Italiano SpA* v *Commission* (cases 6 & 7/73)). It includes identical products, or products considered by consumers to be similar by reason of their characteristics, price or use. Two questions are central to this enquiry:

(a)   To what extent is the customer, or importer, or wholesaler, able to buy goods *similar* to those supplied by the dominant firm, or *acceptable as substitutes?* This is known as cross-elasticity of demand.
(b)   To what extent are other firms *able to supply, or capable of producing* acceptable substitutes? This is known as cross-elasticity of supply.

These questions may be assessed by reference to the characteristics of the product, its price, or the use to which it is to be put. Although the principles are expressed in terms of goods or products they apply equally in the context of services.

Ascertaining the relevant product market is no easy matter. Its difficulties are illustrated in the case of *Europemballage Corp. and Continental Can Co. Inc.* (case 6/72). This case involved the proposed takeover of a large Dutch packaging firm, Thomassen & Drijver-Verblifa NV (TDV) by Europemballage Corporation, a company registered in the USA, held and controlled by another US company, Continental Can Co. Inc. Continental Can was a powerful organisation engaged in packaging operations throughout the world. It held an 86 per cent share in a German packaging company, Schmalbach--Lubeca-Werke AG (SLW), prominent in Germany in the manufacture of, *inter alia,* light metal containers for meat and fish and bottle-sealing machines. Continental Can proposed to transfer its interest in SLW to Europemballage. Thus the whole deal would result in Europemballage and, indirectly, Continental Can, holding significant market power in Europe. The Commission issued a Decision that the takeover of TDV by Continental Can via Europemballage constituted a breach of the then Article 86 (now 82).

Continental Can, through its holding in SLW, was alleged to be dominant in Germany in three separate product markets:

(a)   light metal containers for meat products,
(b)   light metal containers for fish products, and
(c)   metal closures for glass containers.

The acquisition of TDV by Europemballage would have further increased its dominance in these markets, since it would have removed an important potential competitor to SLW. Continental Can and Europemballage sought to annul the Commission's Decision. Although the Court agreed with the Commission in principle that the takeover could constitute an abuse, it found that the Commission had failed to prove the claimants' dominance in the relevant product market. The Commission had failed to explore the question of product substitution. In order to be regarded as a distinct market, the Court held, the products in question must be individualised not only by the mere fact that they are used for packing certain products, but by particular characteristics of production which make them *specifically suitable for this purpose*. The Commission had also failed to consider the question of substitution on the supply side, i.e., whether other potential competitors might not be able to enter the market by simple adaptation.

The Commission was more thorough in *United Brands Co.* v *Commission* (case 27/76). In this case the Commission claimed that United Brands, one of the world's largest banana empires, producer of 'Chiquita' bananas, was abusing its dominant position in a number of ways. The question was whether the relevant product market was bananas, branded and unbranded, as the Commission claimed, or fresh fruit, as United Brands claimed. Clearly it was in the Commisson's interest to define the market as narrowly, and in the interest of United Brands to define it as widely, as possible. The Commission produced research from the Food and Agriculture Organisation which revealed that the existence of other fruit had very little influence on the price and consumption of bananas. Moreover, bananas occupied a special place in the diet of the very young, the sick, and the old. For them other fruits were not acceptable as substitutes. This time the Court accepted the Commission's view of the relevant product market.

It has been argued that the relevant product market could have been defined even more narrowly, either as branded bananas, or as bananas bought for the old, the sick or the very young, since there was evidence that customers continued to buy branded bananas even when they were considerably more expensive than unbranded bananas, thus showing little cross-elasticity of demand, while for the old, the sick and the very young, there was practically no cross-elasticity at all.

A more recent example of a very narrow product market concerned the distribution of tickets for the World Cup football matches held in France ([2000] OJ L–5/55), which was the responsibility of a non profit-making organisation set up under French law for the purpose. The dispute concerned the tickets that were to be made available to the general public, as sale was subject to the proviso that those buying the tickets could provide an address in France. In finding that the World Cup tickets constituted a separate product market, the Commission took into account the popularity of football and the fact that one sport cannot be substituted for another. Within the football sphere, the Commission noted the significance of the tournament itself in contrast with other football tournaments, such as national cup finals, and the fact that the tournament does not take place every year. Lastly, it noted the huge demand for tickets, leading the Commission to suggest that even an increase of 10 per cent in the ticket price would have little effect on consumer demand. The Commission then went on to distinguish even between the types of tickets available, that is, between those tickets that were sold for particular games so that supporters would know which teams would be playing, and the tickets and passes which were for a number of games but which were sold before it was known which teams were playing in a given match. Further, the Commission determined that, as it was important to take into account the circumstances in which the sale took place, blind sales which took place in 1997 were not substitutable by ticket sales at a later date.

On the question of cross-elasticity, both the Commission and the Court will scrutinize the evidence with care, and will not necessarily agree with the experts. In *Eurofix & Bauco* v *Hilti AG* [1989] 4 CMLR 677, in the context of a finding of abuse against Hilti, a firm dominant in the market for cartridge strips and nails compatible with Hilti nail guns, the Commission rejected an econometric study produced by Hilti which purported to show significant cross-elasticity between nail guns and power drills, finding that the methodology of the study 'needed further refinement'. Moreover, the findings of the study were inconsistent with the way in which the market operated. The decision in *Hilti* was approved by the Court (*Hilti* v *Commission* (case 98/88)).

The relevant product market, and the question of substitutability, is not necessarily defined by reference to consumers. In *Istituto Chemioterapico Italiano SpA* v *Commission* (cases 6 & 7/73) the abuse alleged against Commercial Solvents Corporation (CSC), an American company, and its Italian subsidiary, Istituto Chemicoterapico Italiano SpA (ICI), was a refusal to supply an Italian company, Zoja, with a particular chemical, aminobutanol, which CSC had supplied to Zoja in the past through ICI. The chemical was required for processing into ethambutol, a drug used for the treatment of tuberculosis. CSC had a near monopoly in aminobutanol, which was widely used as the best, and cheapest, for the manufacture of ethambutol. CSC refused to supply Zoja with aminobutanol in order that it might itself manufacture ethambutol in Italy through ICI. However, ethambutol was not the only drug suitable for treating tuberculosis. There existed a number of others, based on different raw materials. Thus there was a substitutable end product. Moreover, ethambutol could be made from other raw materials. So was the relevant product market aminobutanol, CSC's raw material, as the Commission decided — in which case CSC was undoubtedly dominant — or was it raw materials for making ethambutol — in which case CSC was probably not dominant — or was it, as CSC claimed, the end product, a drug for the treatment of tuberculosis — in which case CSC was undoubtedly not dominant? In an action before the Court for annulment of the Commission's decision, CSC argued that what mattered was whether consumers had a choice of drugs for tuberculosis. Article 86 (now 82) was aimed at abuses which prejudiced the interests of consumers. The Court disagreed. The Article was concerned not only with abuses which prejudiced consumers directly. It was also aimed at abuses which prejudiced consumers indirectly by impairing the competitive structure. The effect of CSC's refusal to supply Zoja was to eliminate one of the principal manufacturers of ethambutol in the common market. Nor was the Court prepared to accept that Zoja could switch to other raw materials for the manufacture of ethambutol. The Court found that it was not feasible for Zoja to adapt its production in this way. Only if other raw materials could be substituted *without difficulty* for aminobutanol could they be regarded as acceptable substitutes. Since they could not the relevant product market was aminobutanol.

The hard line taken in this case illustrates that the Commission and the Court are not concerned merely with the immediate protection of the consumer; they are concerned to protect competition at the manufacturing level and in particular to prevent the smaller firm from suffering at the hands of its more powerful competitors. Similar thinking lay behind the Commission and the Court's approach in *Établissements Consten SA* v *Commission* (cases 56 & 58/64). Both reflect the influence of French and German competition policy on EC law.

In the above cases the relevant product market was a substantial one and the parties alleged to be dominant in that market wielded considerable power. But the relevant market, whether in goods or services, can be quite small, and provided an undertaking is dominant in that market it does not need to be generally powerful to fall foul of Article 82 (ex 86) EC. In *Hugin Kassaregister AB* v *Commission* (case 22/78) a Swedish firm, Hugin, which manufactured cash registers, supplying them to Liptons Cash Registers and Business Equipment Ltd in the UK through its British subsidiary, Hugin Cash Registers Ltd, was found to be dominant in the supply of spare parts for Hugin machines to independent repair businesses. (See also *AB Volvo* v *Erik*

Veng (case 238/87).) In *British Brass Band Instruments* v *Boosey & Hawkes Interim measures* [1988] 4 CMLR 67 the relevant product market, in which Boosey & Hawkes held a 90 per cent share, was held to be instruments for *British style* brass bands. The fact that the market, or in this case the sub-market, was defined in narrow terms, did not, the Court said, exclude the application of the then Article 86. 'The essential question is whether the sub-market is sufficiently distinct in commercial reality.' Similarly certain activities of a firm which seem quite insignificant may constitute a relevant market in which that firm may be dominant. In *General Motors Continental NV* [1975] 1 CMLR D20 the issuing of test certificates for second-hand imports of Opel cars, carried out exclusively by General Motors in Belgium, constituted the relevant market, even though in one year (1973) only five cars were involved; and in *British Leyland plc* [1984] 3 CMLR 92, BL was found to be dominant in the provision of national type-approval certificates for its vehicles since it alone had the right to issue these certificates. The decision was approved by the Court in *British Leyland plc* v *Commisson* (case 226/84).

Dominance in fact

Once the relevant market is established it is necessary to ascertain whether the parties concerned are dominant within that market. When will an undertaking be regarded as dominant? The Commission suggested in *United Brands Co.* [1976] 1 CMLR D28 that:

Undertakings are in a dominant position when they have the power to behave independently without taking into account, to any substantial extent, their competitors, purchasers and suppliers. Such is the case where an undertaking's market share, either in itself or when combined with its know-how, access to raw materials, capital or other major advantage such as trade-mark ownership, enables it to determine the prices or to control the production or distribution of a significant part of the relevant goods. It is not necessary for the undertaking to have total dominance such as would deprive all other market participants of their commercial freedom, as long as it is strong enough in general terms to devise its own strategy as it wishes, even if there are differences in the extent to which it dominates individual submarkets.

Thus the question of dominance requires a wide-ranging economic analysis of the undertaking concerned and of the market in which it operates. According to the Commission the significant factors will be:

(a) *Market share.* This will be of the first importance. In *Istituto Chemioterapico Italiano SpA* (cases 6 & 7/73), CSC (according to the Commisson; this was not found proved by the Court) held a virtual monopoly in aminobutanol. In *Europemballage Corp. and Continental Can Co. Inc.* (case 6/72) SLW, owned by Continental Can, held a 70-80 per cent share in the RPM in Germany. In *Tetra Pak International SA* v *Commission* (case T–83/91) the CFI remarked that a market share of 90 per cent would be regarded as dominant save in exceptional circumstances. But such a high figure is not essential. United Brands held only a 40-45 per cent share in the banana market in a substantial part of Europe. Where the share is less than 50 per cent, the structure of the market will be important, particularly the market share held by the next largest competitor. In *United Brands* (case 27/76) the nearest competitors held 16 per cent and 10 per cent shares in the market. Where the market is highly fragmented the Commission has even suggested that a share of 20-40 per cent could constitute dominance (*10th Report on Competition Policy*). The Court has held that the existence of lively competition does not rule out a dominant position (*United Brands*).

(b) The *length of time* during which a firm has held its position in the relevant product market. This point was stressed in *Instituto Chemicoterapico Italiano* and *United Brands*. The firm cannot be dominant unless it is dominant *over time*. Clearly the longer a firm has been dominant, the greater the barriers to entry for potential competitors.

(c) *Financial and technological resources.* A firm with large financial and technological resources will be in a position to adapt its market strategy in order to meet and drive out competitors. It may indulge in predatory pricing, selling below cost if necessary to undercut rivals (see *AKZO Chemie BV* Decision [1986] 3 CMLR 273); it can maintain demand for its product by heavy advertising, thereby reducing cross-elasticity of demand, as was clearly the case in *United Brands*. Technological resources will enable a firm to keep ahead of potential competitors.

(d) *Access to raw materials and outlets.* The greater the degree of vertical integration (i.e., control over businesses up and downstream in the marketing process) the greater a firm's power to act independently. However powerful Zoja may have been as a manufacturer of ethambutol, it was dependent on CSC for its raw materials. CSC on the other hand controlled both raw materials and outlets via ICI. United Brands enjoyed an even greater degree of vertical integration. Its empire extended virtually from the plantation to the table. They owned plantations, fleets of refrigerated vessels and refrigerated warehouses in key ports throughout Europe.

(e) *Behaviour.* The Commission suggested in *United Brands* that an undertaking's behaviour can in itself provide evidence of dominance. In *United Brands* the firm's discriminatory rebate system was taken, inter alia, as an indicium of independence. In *Eurofix & Bauco* v *Hilti* the Commission regarded Hilti's discriminatory treatment of its customers as 'witness to its ability to act independently and without due regard to other competitors or customers'.

Economists have questioned the validity in economic terms of some of these criteria, and even more so their application by the Commission in particular cases. For example, although United Brands had large financial and technological resources and enjoyed a high degree of vertical integration there was evidence that it faced fierce competition from time to time and its share of the market was falling. Moreover its banana operations were not showing steady profits. These factors would not seem to indicate a power to behave independently of competitors.

Barriers to entry   In assessing dominance it is not enough to examine the allegedly dominant undertaking's position in the existing state of the market; the question of *potential* competition must be assessed. This requires an examination into the whole range of barriers, geographical, financial, technical and temporal, to entry into that market. The Commission's decision in *Continental Can* was annulled for a failure to explore the possibility of product substitution. Both the Commission and the Court have been criticised for giving undue weight to such barriers, and particularly for failing to take a long-term view as to the prospects of market entry. This may result in a finding of dominance when the market is, in the longer term, contestable (see e.g., *Michelin* v *Commission* (case 322/81)).

Associated markets   Proof of dominance in a particular market need not always be required. Where two markets are deemed to be associated, and a company is dominant on one of them, proof of dominance on the other does not need to be illustrated. In *Tetra Pak International SA* v *Commission* (case T–83/91) the CFI held that associative links between two product markets could be shown because the key products were the same in both markets and because many of the manufacturers and consumers in the two markets were also the same. Thus, for a company dominant in one market to be in breach of Article 82 (ex 86) EC in respect of an associated market, only abusive behaviour need be shown. The decision of the CFI has been confirmed by the ECJ (*Tetra Pak International SA* v *Commission* (case C–333/94P)).

The relevant geographical market

To fall within Article 82 (ex 86) an undertaking must be dominant 'within the common market or in a substantial part of it'. Thus the question of dominance must be assessed also in the context of the relevant geographical market. The relevant geographical market is the one in which the 'objective conditions of competition are the same for all traders' (*United Brands Co.* v *Commission* (case 27/76)). It is the market in which available and acceptable substitutes exist, described, helpfully, by Overbury as 'the area in which consumers are willing to shop around for substitute supplies or in which manufacturers are willing to deliver'. This will depend on the cost and feasibility of transportation as well as consumer habits and preferences. Where goods are homogeneous and easily and cheaply transportable the relevant geographical market may be large. The Commission suggested in the *AKZO Chemie BV* Decision [1986] 3 CMLR 273 that in certain circumstances the whole of the common market may constitute the relevant geographical market. In *Eurofix & Hilti* the whole of the EC was found to constitute the relevant geographical market in the nail cartridge market. Where goods are differentiated, or where consumer tastes are inflexible, or where transportation is difficult or costly, a single State or even part of a State may constitute the relevant market. Where a service is only needed within one particular State, as in *General Motors Continental NV* [1975] 1 CMLR D20 or *British Leyland plc* v *Commission* (case 226/84) clearly that State will represent the relevant market. As the Court commented in *United Brands,* in order to ascertain whether a particular territory is large enough to amount to a substantial part of the market, the pattern and volume of the production and consumption of the products as well as the habits and economic opportunities of vendors and purchasers (and the users of services) must be considered. In *B&I/Sealink* the Commission decided that a port or airport, even if not itself a substantial part of the common market, may be considered such insofar as reasonable access to the facility is indispensable for the exploitation of a transport route which is substantial for the purposes of Article 82 (ex 86). Thus Sealink's action as port authority in Holyhead in altering its own ferry times, thereby limiting access to the post by B&I's ships, was found to breach the then Article 86.

In determining the relevant geographic market, the cost of transport is particularly important. In deciding in *Hilti* that the relevant market was the whole of the EC, the Commission took into account the fact that nail cartridges could be transported throughout the Community at relatively little cost. Clearly geographical markets have been growing and will continue to grow as the barriers to the single internal market are removed.

In considering the relevant geographical market the Commission has been criticised for failing adequately to take into account the possibility of countries outside the EC forming part of the market, even though in the case of certain products (e.g., vitamins) a world market may exist. For this reason a firm may be treated as dominant even though it is subject to substantial competition world-wide. However, in *SIV* v *Commission Re Italian Flat Glass* (cases T–68, 77 & 78/89) the Commission's Decision was annulled in part on the grounds, *inter alia,* that the Commission had failed to take into account imports of flat glass from non-Member States.

The Commission, in its Notice on the Definition of the Relevant Market, suggests that a starting point in determining the extent of the relevant market, both in respect of the product market and the geographic market, is to postulate a small, non-transitory change in prices and then to evaluate the likely reaction of customers to that change. The question is, would the consumer switch to readily available substitutes? If such an increase were to result in a loss of profits as consumers switched to alternatives, clearly there are other suppliers or alternative products in the market. This test would then be reapplied, decreasing the relevant products or areas until there is no such change.

The temporal market

In assessing the question of dominance the temporal aspect of the market should also be considered. It has been suggested that the Commission in *United Brands* should have defined the relevant product market by reference to the particular time of the year (e.g. the winter months), when there was little opportunity for product substitution. The Commission did take the temporal element into account in *Re ABG Oil* [1977] 2 CMLR D1 in limiting the market for oil to the period of crisis following the OPEC action in the early 1970s.

Abuse

It is not dominance *per se* but the abuse of a dominant position that brings Article 82 (ex 86) into play. Examples of abuse are provided by the Article. They comprise:

(a)   directly or indirectly imposing unfair purchase or selling prices or unfair trading conditions;

(b)   limiting production, markets, or technical development to the prejudice of consumers,

(c)   applying dissimilar conditions to equivalent transactions with other trading parties, thereby placing them at a competitive disadvantage,

(d)   making the conclusion of contracts subject to acceptance by the other parties of supplementary obligations which, by their nature or commercial usage, have no connection with the subject of such contracts.

These are merely examples; the list is not exhaustive.

A glance back to Article 81 (ex 85) will reveal that the kinds of abuse prohibited under Article 82 (ex 86) run in close parallel to the examples of concerted behaviour likely to breach Article 81(1). As far as most forms of behaviour are concerned, the difference between Article 81 and Article 82 (ex 85 and 86) is a difference in degree rather than in kind. The existence of a dominant position merely makes the conduct more dangerous; thus there is no possibility of exemption for a breach of Article 82 (ex 86).

Abuses prohibited under Article 82 (ex 86) have been divided into two categories, the exploitative abuses and the anti-competitive abuses. Exploitative abuses occur when an undertaking seeks to take advantage of its position of dominance by imposing oppressive or unfair conditions on its trading partners. Examples of these are provided under (a), (c) and (d) above, and some behaviour under (b). Anti-competitive abuses are those which, while not in themselves unfair or oppressive, are damaging because they reduce or eliminate competition. Such behaviour would arise under paragraph (b) above, and certain practices falling under paragraph (d). Many kinds of behaviour fall into both categories (e.g., *Istituto Chemioterapico Italiano SpA* (cases 6 & 7/73)).

For the abusive behaviour to fall within Article 82 (ex 86), it is not necessary that the dominant undertaking reaps financial or commercial benefit from the behaviour the subject of complaint. In the World Cup case ([1999] OJ L5/55), the non profit-making organisation with the responsibility for organising the distribution of tickets put forward the argument that it had not benefited from the limitation it had imposed on ticket sales, an argument the Commission dismissed as irrelevant.

Exploitative abuses

United Brands Co. v *Commission* (case 27/76) provides a number of such abuses.

(a) *Unfair prices.* According to the Commission, United Brands Co. was charging excessively high prices for its branded bananas. Although this point was not found proved by the Court, the Court agreed with the Commission on the matter of principle. An excessive price was defined by the Court as one which bears no reasonable relation to the economic value of the product. This test was applied in *General Motors Continental NV* [1975] 1 CMLR D20 to prices charged by General Motors for its exclusive inspection service for second-hand Opel cars imported into Belgium. The Commission decided that it had charged excessive rates on the service for five Opel cars in 1973. The Court, in annulment proceedings (case 26/75), applying the 'reasonable relation to economic value' test, found that GM's charges were excessive. The charge of abuse was, however, not sustained, as GM had amended its charges and reimbursed the five customers for the excessive charge.

In *British Leyland plc* v *Commission* (case 226/84) the fees charged for the type-approval certificates for left-hand drive cars (when issued) were found to be excessive and discriminatory.

Problems arise over the question of 'economic value'. Deciding the economic value of a product or a service is a complex accounting exercise which leaves ample scope for differences of opinion. Economists would disagree as to what constituted the economic value of a product, and indeed, whether it can be accurately ascertained at all. What uniformity, then, can be hoped for from national courts when called upon to apply Article 82 (ex 86)?

(b) *Unfair trading conditions.* United Brands was found to be imposing unfair conditions by refusing to allow importers to resell bananas while they were still green. This meant that only wholesalers with the correct storage and ripening facilities were able to handle the bananas. The fact that the consumer might thereby be assured of obtaining a better, more standardised product did not prevent the Commission and the Court from finding that this requirement constituted an abuse. Again we find EC competition law protecting the 'middleman'.

In the World Cup Decision ([1999] OJ L 5/55), the Commission, citing the ECJ in *Tetra Pak II* (case C–333/94P), held that restrictions which in effect distinguished between different nationalities and which consequently limited the market choice for the consumer, were unfair trading conditions. This type of abuse also runs contrary to the central Community principle of non-discrimination on grounds of nationality.

(c) *Discriminatory treatment.* United Brands was charging prices with a difference of, in some cases, more than 100 per cent in different common market countries, not, apparently, according to objective criteria, but according to what the market would bear. This constituted discriminatory treatment. Similarly *British Leyland* (case 226/84) charged different prices for type-approval certificates for left-hand drive cars, without objective justification.

(d) *Refusal to supply.* United Brands refused to supply one of its most important wholesalers, who had constructed special facilities to store and ripen the bananas, in retaliation for his taking part in an advertising campaign for a competitor. This was found to be an abuse. A refusal to supply which is not retaliatory would fall into the category of anti-competitive abuses, to be discussed next.

Anti-competitive abuse

This kind of abuse is less easy to detect than the exploitative abuse. Here the dominant firm uses its position in such a way as to undermine or even eliminate existing competitors, thereby reinforcing or increasing its dominance. A number of examples may be considered:

(a) *Tying-in.* A good example of tying-in practices is provided by the case of *Hoffman-La Roche & Co. AG* v *Commission* (case 85/76). La Roche was the largest pharmaceutical company in the world, with a dominant position in seven separate vitamin markets. The alleged abuses lay in a number of tying-in practices. Customers undertook to buy all or most of their requirements from La Roche ('requirements contracts'); as a reward they were entitled to 'fidelity' rebates (discounts). The agreement also contained 'English' clauses. These provided that if customers found other suppliers offering similar products at cheaper prices they should ask La Roche to 'adjust' their prices. If La Roche failed to respond they were free to buy elsewhere. None of these clauses was oppressive as far as La Roche's customers were concerned. But the Commission (approved by the Court) found the practices to be abusive. The tying-in system limited their customers' freedom to buy from competing suppliers; the English clauses were unacceptable because they enabled La Roche to identify competitors and take pre-emptive action, e.g., by dropping its prices to its competitors' levels, thereby nipping potential rivals in the bud. Similar tying-in practices were condemned in *Hilti*.

(b) *Predatory pricing.* This is a strategy whereby prices are reduced, below cost if necessary, in order to drive potential competitors out of the market. In *AKZO Chemie BV* [1986] 3 CMLR 273, Commission Decision, AKZO, a firm dominant world-wide in the production of organic peroxides, was found to be engaged in such practices. However, as the Commisson pointed out, it may be necessary to examine a firm's costs and motives in order to ascertain whether its low prices are predatory or merely the result of efficiency. Where low pricing is susceptible of several explanations evidence of an anti-competitive intent may be needed. Indeed, the lowering of prices may even be evidence of weakness. In *Hoffman-La Roche* the Court suggested that the fact that an undertaking is compelled by the pressure of its competitors' price reductions to lower its prices is in general incompatible with that independence which is the hallmark of dominance. The Court, in its first decision on predatory pricing (*AKZO Chemie* v *Commission* (case 62/86)), agreed with the Commission. There was a distinction, in competition law terms, between lowering prices in order to win new customers and trying to eliminate a competitor. In the case of *AKZO* the firm's 'avowed intention' had been to eliminate one of its competitors. In the more recent case of *Compagnie Maritime Belge Transports SA* v *Commission* (case T–24–6 & 28/93) the CFI emphasised the need to show intent. In this case, it was not clear that the dominant undertakings (this was a case involving collective dominance) had actually traded at a loss: certainly the Commission in its investigation did not carry out an analysis of costs and prices. There was, however, evidence to show that the motive behind the practice complained of was to drive the only existing competition out of the market. In this circumstance, the CFI seemed to place the burden on the dominant undertakings to show that their behaviour was not anti-competitive. Although the ECJ reduced the fines imposed in this case on appeal, the Court did confirm this aspect of the CFI's ruling (*Compagnie Maritime Belge Transports* v *Dafra Lines* (case C–395–6/96P)). In the case of an allegation of abuse, though, how does the dominant undertaking show that its behaviour was normal in the circumstances? The danger is that normal price competition (for example, the reaction of a dominant undertaking to the news that one of its customers has been offered a lower price by a competitor) may be confused with predatory pricing.

(c) *Refusal to supply.* Where supplies (or services) are refused in order to reduce or eliminate competition, such a refusal will constitute abuse. This appeared to be the case in *Istituto Chemioterapico Italiano SpA* (cases 6 & 7/73) where it was intended that CSC's subsidiary, ICI, would take over production of ethambutol previously undertaken by Zoja (see also *Hugin Kassaregister AB* v *Commission* (case 22/78)). Boosey & Hawkes' cessation of supplies to BBI was designed deliberately to prevent them entering into the market as competitors. Similarly BL's covert purpose in refusing type-approval to imports of left-hand drive cars was to keep imports out, thus maintaining an artificial partitioning of the market. However, a refusal to supply either an existing or a new customer will not necessarily be abusive. Arguing from *Metro-SB-Grossmärkte GmbH & Co. KG* v *Commission* (case 26/76), a refusal may be permissible if it is non-discriminatory and objectively justified. However, a refusal of supplies, particularly to an existing customer, will require cogent justification, and any signs of an anti-competitive motive will be fatal. In *Radio Telefis Eireann* v *Commission* (case T–69/89), *British Broadcasting Corporation* v *Commission* (case T–70/89) and *Independent Television Publications Ltd* v *Commission* (case T–76/89) the Court of First Instance upheld a decision of the Commission which condemned, for the first time, a refusal to supply a party with whom it had no pre-existing commercial relationship. Here the applicant TV companies were seeking to exploit their copyright in TV programme listings to prevent competitors from publishing TV programme guides in competition with their own publications, to the detriment of consumers. The ECJ upheld this decision on appeal (*Radio Telefis Eireann* v *Commission* (cases C–241 & 242/91P) (*Magill* case)). The ECJ focused on the fact that the television companies were the sole source of the information which is needed to produce weekly listings guides for all channels, that there was a market for such a product and the product was not being produced because of the behaviour of the television companies, and that the television companies were therefore *without objective justification* seeking to reserve a secondary market (television guide publishing) to themselves.

Some have seen this as indicating the development of an 'essential facilities' doctrine. By this we mean that an undertaking which owns or controls a facility that is necessary for a business, but which could not practically be reproduced by a competing entity or a potential competing entity, has an essential facility. This must, in the absence of objective justification, be made available to the competitor on reasonable terms. Thus, in the *Magill* case, the television companies were required to give the information about their programmes to rival publishers, and, in the case of access to a port, the ferry company controlling access to the port was not permitted to deny access or schedule departures to the detriment of rival companies providing ferry services out of that port without objective justification (*Sealink* case [1992] 5 CMLR 255). Where there is no objective justification such behaviour is a prima facie breach of Article 82 (ex 86).

Although the essential facilities doctrine is likely to become increasingly important with the demolition of State monopolies in the provision of utilities, for example, gas and electricity supply, it must be approached with caution. In the case of intellectual property rights in particular, it could prove to operate against innovation and investment in research and development if ultimately companies were compelled to give away the results of their own efforts and expense. Thus, the question of objective justification for the withholding of an essential facility will be crucial.

(d) *Exclusive reservation of activities.* Similar principles to those applicable to a refusal to supply will apply where a dominant undertaking reserves certain activities to itself. This occurred in *Italy* v *Commission* (*Re British Telecommunications* (case 41/83)) where BT reserved for itself exclusive rights to its telex forwarding services, and in *Belgian Telemarketing* (case 311/84), in which a telephone marketing service was channelled exclusively through RTL's agent. The Court pointed out in *Belgian Telemarketing* that there was no 'objective necessity' for its so doing. This implies, in line with *Metro,* that the exclusive reservation of certain activities by a dominant undertaking, whether for itself or for an appointed agent, might be permissible if it were necessary and objectively justified. However the Court was not prepared to accept that the preservation of RTL's image constituted a 'necessity'.

(e) *Import and export bans.* In view of the hard line of the Commission and the Court over such restrictions under Article 81 (ex 85) it is no surprise that import and export bans have been held to constitute abuse under Article 82 (ex 86) (*Suiker Unie* v *Commission* (case 40/73)). Apart from when industrial property rights are legitimately exercised to this end it is hard to imagine a situation in which such a ban would not be deemed an abuse.

(f) *Mergers and takeovers.* In all the examples of anti-competitive behaviour considered so far, there has existed an element of exploitation; the parties have used their dominance, if not unfairly or oppressively, in order to reduce or eliminate competition. Perhaps the most surprising development came in the case of *Continental Can* (*Europemballage Corp. and Continental Can Co. Inc.* v *Commission* (case 6/72)). Here the Commission had applied the then Article 86 in the context of a proposed merger, namely, the proposed takeover by Continental Can, which owned an 86 per cent share in SLW in Germany, of TDV in Holland, the entire package to be held by Continental Can's subsidiary Europemballage. The Commission issued a Decision that the proposed takeover constituted an abuse of their dominant position within the common market (*viz.* Germany). In annulment proceedings Continental Can argued that such action could not be regarded as an abuse. Article 86 (now 82) was concerned only with behaviour detrimental to consumers. Moreover, it required some causative link between the position of dominance and abuse. Neither Continental Can nor Europemballage had used their power to effect the merger. The Court, in annulment proceedings, disagreed. Article 86 (now 82), the Court said, cannot allow mergers which eliminate competition. Prejudice under that Article does not mean affecting consumers directly but also prejudice through interference with the structure of competition itself. Nor was it necessary to prove a causal link between the dominance and the abuse. The mere fact of dominance rendered the proposed takeover an abuse. Although the Court annulled the Commission's Decision on the grounds that the relevant product markets had not been fully proved, the principle was established. Following *Continental Can* in *Tetra Pak* (case T–51/89) the take-over by Tetra Pak of a company holding an exclusive licence to new technology for sterilising milk cartons was held to constitute a breach of the then Article 86. Although the acquisition of an exclusive licence was not *per se* abusive, Tetra Pak's acquisition of that licence had the practical effect of precluding all competition in the relevant market. The existence of an exemption under the Exclusive Licence Block Exemption Regulation (2349/84) did not release a dominant undertaking from its obligation to comply with former Article 86 (now 82).

Continental Can and Article 82 (ex 86) remained the basis on which the Commission exercised control over mergers until the Court decided for the first time, in *BAT & Reynolds* v *Commission* (cases 142, 156/84), that mergers could also fall within Article 81(1) (ex 85(1)) (see chapter 15). This widened the scope of the Commission's control, since its jurisdiction no longer depended on the need to prove dominance. *BAT & Reynolds* v *Commission* provided the impetus for the passing of the Merger Regulation, Regulation 4064/89 (corrected version OJ No. L 257 21.9.90), proposals for which had been circulating for many years.

The Merger Regulation

Regulation 4064/89 (most recently amended by Regulation 1310/97 [1997] OJ L 180/1), which came into effect on 30 October 1990, applies to mergers, acquisitions and certain joint ventures, between firms with a combined worldwide turnover of more than 5,000 million ecus, where at least two of the firms have a combined turnover of more than 250 million ecus in the EC but do not earn more than two-thirds of their turnover in a single Member

State (Article 1). A new Article 1(3) introduced by Regulation 1310/97, provides that where a concentration does not meet these thresholds, it may still have a Community dimension if:

(a) the combined aggregate worldwide turnover of all the undertakings is more than ECU 2,500 million,

(b) in each of at least three Member States, the combined aggregate turnover of all the undertakings is more than ECU 100 million;

(c) in each of at least three Member States, the aggregate turnover of each of at least two of the undertakings concerned is more than ECU 25 million; and

(d) the aggregate Community-wide turnover of each of at least two of the undertakings concerned is more than ECU 100 million

unless each of the undertakings concerned achieves more than two-thirds of its aggregate Community-wide turnover within one Member State. A joint venture will be concentrative if it performs on a lasting basis all the functions of an autonomous economic entity. The Commission has issued guidance on the concept of a concentration, calculation of turnover and the definition of a full-function joint venture ([1997] OJ C 66). This latter notice replaces the Commission notice on the distinction between concentrative and cooperative joint ventures ([1994] OJ C 385/1).

The principle underlying the Regulation is that of the 'one-stop shop'. Concentrations falling within the Regulation will be subject to the exclusive jurisdiction of the Commission (Article 21) and must be notified to the Commission (Article 4). A failure to notify or to supply correct or exact information may result in fines of from 1,000 to 50,000 ecus (Article 14). Concentrations falling outside the Regulation's thresholds will be subject to control by the relevant national authority. However, a Member State or Member States jointly may ask the Commission to intervene in respect of a concentration falling outside the Regulation which will 'significantly impede' competition within its own territory (Article 22(3)). Similarly the Commission may refer a matter notified to it to the relevant national authority where it is thought to be appropriate. In this context, the Commission has set out its policy for determining which cases should be dealt with by Member States in a Notice on Cooperation between National Competition Authorities and the Commission ([1997] OJ C 313/1).

A concentration will be permitted if it does not 'create or strengthen a dominant position as a result of which effective competition would be impeded in the common market or a substantial part of it' (Article 2(2)). In making its decision the Commission must take into account the 'need to preserve and develop effective competition within the common market' (Article 2(1)). The Commission has one month in which to decide whether to investigate the matter and four months from the date on which proceedings are initiated in which to reach a final Decision (Article 10).

Procedures governing notification and detailed provision in respect of hearings and time limit are laid down in Regulation 447/98. This Regulation replaces Regulation 17/62 in respect of *all* concentrations (Article 22(2)). As a result the Commission's competence to apply Articles 81 and 82 (ex 85 and 86) to concentrations is significantly reduced, and individuals' right to complain to the Commission under Article 3 of Regulation 17/62 in respect of these matters is excluded. These factors, and the high thresholds originally set by Regulation 4064/89, whereby a concentration is deemed to have a 'community dimension', have been criticised as introducing a weakness into EC competition law. The recent changes to the Merger Regulation mean that more mergers may now fall within it. This is, it is suggested, an advantage for cross-border mergers as the companies involved will no longer have to deal with the national competition authority in every Member State affected by the merger but will instead only have to make one application for clearance to the Commission. It will have the additional advantage of facilitating the application of a uniform merger policy.

Since Articles 81 and 82 (ex 85 and 86) are directly effective individuals remain free despite the Regulation to raise questions concerning *any* concentration, whatever its dimensions, before their national courts. Thus it cannot be guaranteed that concentrations falling outside the Regulation will not be found to breach these Articles. This problem apart, the Regulation has introduced a welcome degree of certainty in an area likely to be subject to ever-increasing activity as firms both within and outside the Community seek to take advantage of the opportunities offered by the single EC market. In order to increase 'transparency' the Commission publishes a detailed analysis of its decisions under the Merger Control Regulation in its annual reports on Competition Policy.

The abuse must affect trade between Member States

As with Article 81 (ex 85), there must be some effect on trade between Member States for Article 82 (ex 86) to apply, but such an effect is not hard to establish. The Court held in *British Leyland plc* v *Commission* (case 226/84) that it was not necessary to establish any specific effects, as long as there was evidence that a particular activity *might* affect trade between Member States. Thus a theoretical possibility will be sufficient.

However, in *Hugin Kassaregister AB* v *Commission* (case 22/78) the Court annulled the Commission's Decision ([1978] 1 CMLR D19) that Hugin had acted in breach of the then Article 86. Although it agreed with the Commission on the questions of the relevant product market and abuse, it found that Hugin's refusal to supply Liptons with spares did not affect trade between States. Hugin was a Swedish firm and thus outside the common market, and Liptons was functioning in London on a purely local scale.

An effect on trade between Member States was held in *Istituto Chemioterapico Italiano SpA* (cases 6 & 7/73) to include repercussions on the competitive structure within the common market. This was approved and followed by the Court in *Bodson* v *Pompes Funèbres* (case 30/87) and an effect on trade between Member States found despite the Commission's view that a monopoly in funeral services granted to Pompes Funèbres by the municipality of Charleville-Mèziéres did not affect trade between Member States.

Article 82 (ex 86) is directly effective, and gives rise to rights and obligations for individuals. Thus, provided the matter is seen to have the requisite Community dimension, an individual may challenge behaviour, and obtain remedies, in a situation in which he would have no remedy under national law (see chapter 17).

Negative clearance and exemption

There is no provision for exemption from liability under Article 82 (ex 86). Thus a party cannot notify and obtain exemption from fines. However, parties may apply for negative clearance under Article 2 of Regulation 17/62 in order to obtain a Decision that their proposed action provides no ground for action under Article 82 (ex 86).

Relationship with Article 86(2) (ex 90(2)) EC

Some public undertakings (such as utility companies) defending a claim of alleged abuse under Article 82 (ex 86) may seek to rely on Article 86(2) (ex 90(2)). This provides that undertakings entrusted with the operation of services of general economic interest or which have the character of a revenue-producing monopoly are subject to the rules in the Treaty (including competition rules) unless the performance of the tasks assigned to them would be obstructed by the application of those rules. This exception is subject to the proviso that the 'development of trade must not be affected to such an extent as would be contrary to the interests of the Community'.

Thus this is a three-stage test. To be able to rely on this exception, not only must the entity show, first, that it is the requisite type of undertaking, but, secondly, that it cannot perform the tasks assigned to it without relying on provisions or behaviour which would normally be in breach of competition provisions, in particular, Article 82 (ex 86). In *Corbeau* (case C–320/91), Corbeau was prevented from running a postal service because the Belgian postal service had a monopoly. Potentially this could have breached the then Article 86 (now 82) unless the Belgian postal service could rely on former Article 90(2) (now 86(2)). The ECJ accepted that the Belgian postal service was an undertaking within the then Article 90(2) and also that a certain amount of restriction of competition was necessary to enable it to remain economically viable. The postal service is required to perform some services which can only be carried out at a loss (for example, delivery to outlying areas) and it funds these activities from profit-making activities. Unrestricted competition would allow other companies to 'cream off' the profitable services without having to carry out the non-profitable activities, leaving the Belgian postal service with the obligation but not the means of paying for it. This does not mean, however, that all competition can be excluded: in deciding if a case falls within Article 86(2) (ex 90(2)) the authorities must identify the extent of restriction necessary to enable the undertaking to perform its tasks, taking into account, 'the economic conditions in which the undertaking operates, the costs which it has to bear and the legislation, particularly concerning the environment, to which it is subject' (*Municipality of Almelo* v *Energiebedrijf IJsselmij NV* (case C–393/92), para. 49).

The Community interest must also be taken into account. Although it is not clear what precisely this element of Article 86(2) (ex 90(2)) requires, it will clearly curtail the scope of the exception provided under this Article. It has been suggested from the terms of the *Almelo* judgment that, broadly speaking, the same assessment will be made as is made under Article 81(1) (ex 85(1)) (see further chapter 14), entailing a balancing of the needs of the undertaking with other Community goals. It is not clear what impact the new Article 16, which obliges Member States to ensure that services of general economic interest 'operate on the basis of principles and conditions which enable them to fulfil their missions', will have, as on the one hand both the Community and Member States are required to take into account the 'shared values of the Union as well as their role in promoting social and territorial cohesion' and, on the other hand, this provision is expressed to be without prejudice to certain treaty articles including Article 86 (ex 90).

Further reading

Andrews, P., 'Is Meeting Competition a Defence to Predatory Pricing? The Irish Sugar Decision Suggests a New Approach' [1998] ECLR 49.

De Jong, H., 'Unfair and Discriminatory Pricing under Article 86' [1980] ECLR 297.

Elland, W., 'The Mergers Control Regulation and its Effect on National Merger Control and the Residual Application of Articles 85 and 86' [1991] ECLR 19.

Flint, J., 'Abuse of a Collective Dominant Position' [1978] 2 LIEI 21.

Fuller Baden, 'Economic Analysis of a Dominant Position: Article 86 of the Treaty' (1979) 4 EL Rev 423.

James, S.M., 'The Concept of Abuse in EEC Competition Law: an American View' (1976) 92 LQR 242.

Korah, V., 'Concept of a dominant Position within the Meaning of Article 86' (1980) 17 CML Rev 395.

Lang, J. Temple, 'Defining Legitimate Competition: Companies' Duties to Supply Competitors and Access to Essential Facilities' (1994) 18 Fordham Int'l LJ 437.

Overbury, C., 'First Experiences of European Merger Control', (1991) European Law Review Competition Law Checklist 1990 p. 79.

Pathak, 'EEC Concentration Control: the Foreseeable Uncertainties' [1990] ECLR 119.

Rodger, B.J., 'Market Intregration and the Devepment of European Competition Policy to Meet New Demands. A Study of Oligopolistic Markets and the Concept of a Collective Dominant Position under Article 86 of the Treaty' [1994] 2 LIEI 1.

Schödermeier, M., 'Collective Dominance Revisited: An Analysis of the EC Commission's New Concepts of Oligopoly Control' [1990] ECLR 28.

Sharpe, T., 'Predation' [1987] ECLR 53.

Siragusa, M., and Subiotto, R., 'The EEC Merger Control Regulation: the Commission's Evolving Case Law' (1991) 28 CML Rev 877.

Smith, P., 'The Wolf in Wolf's Clothing; the Problem of Predatory Pricing' (1989) 14 EL Rev 209.

Soames, T., 'An Analysis of the Principles of Concerted Dominance: A Distinction without a Difference?' [1996] ECLR 24.

Tillotson, J., and MacCulloch, A., 'EC Competition Rules, Collective Dominance and Maritime Transport' (1997) 21 World Competition (Law and Economics Review, Geneva) No. 1, 57.

Vajda, C., 'Article 86 and a Refusal to Supply' [1981] ECLR 97.

Vogelenganz, P., 'Abuse of a Dominant Position in Article 86: the Problem of Causality and some Applications' (1976) 13 CML Rev 61.

SEVENTEEN

Enforcement of the competition provisions: powers and procedures

In all matters except concentrations, as defined in the Merger Control Regulation 4064/89, Article 3, which are governed by Regulation 2367/90, the powers and procedures governing EC competition law are laid down in Regulation 17/62. It is the Commission which has the central role in enforcing Articles 81 and 82 (ex 85 and 86) EC, through the Directorate-General responsible for competition policy, although national courts, and even individuals, have an increasing part to play. The involvement of national competition authorities and courts will extend still further should the proposals in the Commission's White Paper on the Application of Articles 85 and 86 [now 81 and 82] ([1999] OJ C–132/1), known as the Modernisation White Paper, be introduced.

In order to fulfil its tasks the Commission enjoys substantial powers; at the same time it is subject to strict procedural requirements under Regulation 17/62 and to a general duty of confidentiality (*AKZO Chemie BV* v *Commission* (case 53/85)). It must also respect general principles of law (see chapter 6). A breach of these obligations can result in the annulment of its Decision by the CFI, subject to appeal on points of law to the ECJ, and even a successful action for damages (*Adams* v *Commission (No. 1)* (case 145/83)). Both the Commission and the Court may order interim measures pending its final decision, the Commission pursuant to a ruling from the Court, the Court under Articles 242, 243 (ex 185 and 186) EC.

Powers and duties of the Commission

Powers of dispensation   As has already been noted, it is the Commission's task under Regulation 17/62 to monitor agreements with a view to granting negative clearance or exemption. While national courts may apply Article 81(1) and Article 82 (ex 85 and 86 respectively), subject to the special rules applying to vertical restraints (Regulation 1216/99, [1999] OJ L 148), only the Commission can grant exemption under Article 81(3) (ex 85(3)), and individual exemption can only be granted following notification of the parties' agreements (or proposed course of action) in the prescribed manner (form A/B). Although notification cannot prevent an illegal agreement from being declared void (under Article 81(2) (ex 85(2))), except in the case of 'old' (pre-accession) agreements (see chapter 15), it can result in immunity from fines (Regulation 17/62, Article 15(5)(a)). However, under Article 15(6) the Commission may withdraw that immunity by Decision if after a preliminary examination the agreement is found in breach of Article 81(1) (ex 85(1)) and not eligible for exemption under Article 81(3) (ex 85(3)).

Before taking a final Decision *adverse to* the applicant the Commission must give him an opportunity to be heard on the matters to which he objects (Regulation 17/62, Article 19(1)). There are certain rights of access to the Commission's file so as to assist defendants in the preparation of their defence (Commission Notice on Internal Rules of Procedure for Access to the File [1997] OJ C 23/3). Applications for a hearing by persons who show a 'sufficient interest' must also be granted (Regulation 17/62, Article 19(2)).

Before taking a Decision *favourable* to the applicant the Commission must publish a summary of the relevant application or notification and all interested parties must be invited to submit their comments (Regulation 17/62, Article 19(3)).

All final Decisions granting or refusing negative clearance or exemption must be published in the *Official Journal* (Regulation 17/62, Article 21).

Since a final decision concerning negative clearance or exemption may require an extensive analysis of the economic context in which the agreement operates in order to assess its effect on competition within the single market, some years may elapse before such a Decision is issued. Because of this, and because of the volume of notifications received, and a lack of resources to deal formally with all the cases brought to its attention, the Commission has resorted to a number of short cuts (see chapter 15). Many cases are now settled informally; block exemptions have been issued, thus obviating the need for notification. Vertical agreements covered by the new Block Exemption on Vertical Restraints (Regulation 2790/1999, [1999] OJ L 326/21) need not now be notified. Where agreements are notified, comfort letters may be issued giving soft clearance or exemption, after only brief investigation and enquiry, following which the Commission will close the file. The extension of the opposition procedure has increasingly relieved the Commission of the need to issue even an informal reply. These developments have no doubt speeded up the decision-making process, and given some security to the parties concerned; they have reduced the backlog of cases, but they have been criticised as lacking the essential safeguards of the prescribed procedures. Although the Commission has tightened up its procedures in recent years, publicising its intentions in respect of a particular practice or agreement, and giving third parties an opportunity to comment before issuing a final comfort letter, the lack of a formal Decision from the Commission has deprived interested parties of both the procedural safeguards to which they were entitled under Regulation 17/62 and the chance of judicial review by the

Court, since only binding Decisions are capable of annulment. As was noted in chapter 15, the Commission, in its Notice on Cooperation between National Courts and the Commission in applying Articles 85 and 86 [now 81 and 82] EC ([1993] OJ C 39/6), and its further Notice on Cooperation with National Competition Authorities ([1997] OJ C 313/3), has now expressed its intention to concentrate its resources on notifications, complaints and own-initiative proceedings which have particular political, economic or legal significance for the Community, thus suggesting that more cases will be dealt with informally or, given both the Notice on Cooperation and the Modern-isation White Paper, by national authorities.

Investigative powers   If the Commission is to undertake a market analysis adequate to enable it to make a Decision concerning negative clearance or exemption, it must be able to obtain the necessary information. *A fortiori* if it is to fulfil its main task, carried out through D/G IV, of rooting out agreements or practices in breach of Article 81 and 82 (ex 85 and 86) EC which have not been notified, with a view to bringing them to an end by formal Decision (Regulation 17/62, Article 3). To these ends it has been given extensive powers:

(a)   *Requests for information* (Regulation 17/62, Article 11). The Commission may obtain from the governments of Member States and competent authorities of Member States, and from undertakings and associations of undertakings, all information which is 'necessary' to enable it to carry out its task of enforcing Articles 81 and 82 (ex 85 and 86) EC.

(b)   *Inquiry into sectors of the economy* (Regulation 17/62, Article 12). The Commission may conduct general inquiries into whole sectors of the economy if economic trends suggest that competition in the common market is being restricted or distorted. To achieve this task it may request every undertaking in the sector concerned to supply details of agreements, decisions or concerted practices considered exempt, and undertakings or groups of undertakings which may be dominant to supply information concerning their structure and practices.

(c)   *Investigations by the Commission* (Regulation 17/62, Article 14). The Commission may undertake all necessary on-the-spot investigations.

These include the power to enter premises, to examine books or business records, to take copies of such records, and to conduct oral examinations. Investigations may be 'voluntary', under Article 11(2), or 'compulsory', under Article 11(3). Before undertaking such investigations Commission officials are required to produce written authorisation in the form of a Decision specifying the subject-matter and purpose of the investigation (Article 14(3)). The Decision 'shall appoint the date on which the investigation is to be made'. In *National Panasonic (UK) Ltd* v *Commission* (case 136/79) National Panasonic sought to annul the Commission's Decision of authorisation required by Article 14. The Commission's officials had arrived at dawn, unannounced but bearing their authorisation, and had conducted their search and seizure operations before Panasonic could summon its lawyers to the scene. Panasonic argued that Article 14(3) required that some prior warning should have been given, as required for a request for information under Article 11. The Court disagreed; looking for support to the preamble to Regulation 17/62 (eighth recital) it found the Commission was entitled to undertake 'such investigations as are necessary' to bring to light any breaches of the then Article 85 or 86 (now 81 and 82).

As a result of its investigations the Commission discovered that National Panasonic and its distributors were engaged in concerted practices in breach of former Article 85(1) (see [1983] 1 CMLR 497).

In *Hoechst* v *Commission* (cases 46/87, 227/88) Hoechst sought likewise to challenge the legality of the Commission's 'dawn raid'. Hoechst claimed that the search breached the fundamental principle of the inviolability of the home, and that the Commission's Decision of authorisation under Article 14(3) lacked precision, as a result of which they had been deprived of their right to a fair hearing. The ECJ held that while EC law provided protection against arbitrary or disproportionate intervention on the part of public authorities (see chapter 6), there was no evidence that these principles had been breached. Moreover, it was for the Commission (subject to the control of the Court), and not for national courts, to decide on the necessity of the investigation, although the Commission must respect the procedural guarantees provided under national law for the purposes of such investigations. As to the lack of precision of the grounds of the Commission's Decision, the Court held that the Commission is not required to provide the addressee with 'all the information at its disposal with regard to the alleged infringement or to provide a rigorous classification of those infringements', as long as it 'clearly indicates the suspicions which it is seeking to verify'. The Court found that although the Commission's statement of reasons was drafted in very general terms, it contained the essential information required by Article 14(3). The reasoning in *Hoechst* was followed in *Dow Benelux NV* v *Commission* (case 85/87) and *Dow Chemical Ibérica SA* v *Commission* (cases 97–9/87).

(d) *Investigations by the authorities of Member States* (Regulation 17/62, Article 13). The Commission may request the competent authorities of the Member States to undertake the investigations which it considers necessary under Article 14(1) or which it has ordered under Article 14(3). In the latter case they too must produce written authorisation. Normally officials of the competent authority in the Member State where the investigation takes place will accompany the Commission's officials.

Undertakings are bound to comply with the (legitimate) demands of the Commisson under Articles 11, 12 and 14. If they fail to do so, or give false or misleading information, they are liable to penalties (Regulation 17/62, Articles 15 and 16 and Article 14 of the Merger Regulation). The Commission imposed a periodic penalty of 1,000 ecus per day on Hoechst as a result of their refusal to submit to the Commission's searches. This too was found by the Court to be legitimate. More recently, fines have been imposed on a number of companies for supplying misleading information: fines of 50,000 Euros were imposed in respect of each of two occasions when misleading information was supplied by Deutsche Post; and KLM was fined 40,000 Euros. By contrast, Anheuser Busch and Scottish and Newcastle were each fined 3,000 Euros. The relatively low level of fine reflects intent — or rather lack of it — on the part of the last two companies. Deutsche Post's and KLM's actions, by contrast, were seen as deliberate attempts to mislead.

It was originally thought, on the basis of Advocate-General Warner's comments in *Australian Mining & Smelting Europe Ltd* v *Commission* (case 155/79), that information cannot be withheld even if it is self-incriminating. However, in *Orkem* v *Commission* (case 374/87) the Court held that the Commission, although entitled under Article 11 of Regulation 17/62 to compel an undertaking to provide all necessary information relating to facts of which it might have knowledge, could not compel the undertaking to incriminate itself by admitting to infringements of competition rules. To do so would infringe the undertaking's right to a fair hearing, which was a fundamental principle of Community law. It was for the Commission to prove that a breach of Article 85 or 86 (now 81 and 82) had occurred (see also *Solvay & Cie* v *Commission* (case 27/88) decided on the same day).

Confidentiality

The Commission is subject to a duty of confidentiality. Regulation 17/62, Article 20(1) provides that 'information acquired as a result of the application of Articles 11, 12, 13 and 14 shall be used only for the purpose of the relevant request for information'. Article 21, which is concerned with publication of decisions, provides that publication 'shall have regard to the legitimate interests of undertakings in the protection of their business secrets' (Article 21(2)).

The scope of Article 20(1) arose for decision in *Dirección General de Defensa de la Competencia* v *Asociación Española de Banca Privada* (case C–67/91), when the Court was asked to rule on the legitimacy of the use, by national authorities responsible for the enforcement of national competition law, of information received from the Commission pursuant to its requests for information under Article 11 or supplied in requests or notifications (for the purposes of obtaining negative clearance and exemption) under Articles 2, 4 and 5. Under Article 10(1) the Commission is required to transmit to the competent authorities of the Member States copies of applications and notifications together with copies of the most important documents lodged with the Commission for the purposes of establishing the existence of infringements of Articles 81 and 82 (ex 85 and 86) or of obtaining negative clearance or a decision in application of Article 81(3) (ex 85(3)). The Court held that the obligation imposed on the Commission and the competent authorities of the Member States by Article 20(2) not to disclose 'information acquired by them as a result of the application of this Regulation and of the kind covered by professional secrecy' implied not only a prohibition on the disclosure of confidential information but also the impossibility for authorities holding the information to use it for a purpose other than that for which it had been acquired. The same applied to information notified under Articles

2, 4 and 5, even though it was not expressly subject to the obligations of Article 20(2). The use of such information had to respect the legal context in which such information had been acquired. However, national authorities were not obliged to suffer 'acute amnesia', although information acquired under all these Articles was to remain within the internal ambit of national authorities, it could be used to assess whether it was appropriate to open *national* procedures.

With regard to the 'protection of business secrets' under Article 21(2), the Court held in *AKZO Chemie BV v Commission* (case 53/85) that it was for the Commisson to decide whether a particular document contained business secrets. However, before communicating documents allegedly containing business secrets to third parties the Commission must, by Decision, inform the undertaking whose alleged secrets are to be revealed, and give it an opportunity to challenge that Decision before the ECJ. Furthermore, the Commission, basing its position on the judgment of the ECJ in *BPB Industries plc v Commission* (case C–310/93P), now suggests, in its Notice on Access to the File, that the rights of allegedly abusive dominant undertakings to documents on the file which emanate from third parties may be greatly limited. This may have unfortunate consequences for the defendant company, as it would seem that its rights are being reduced on the basis of an unproven allegation.

Confidential communications between lawyer and client receive limited protection. According to *Australian Mining & Smelting Europe Ltd* certain correspondence between a client and an independent lawyer based in the EC or with an establishment in the EC , principally correspondence dealing with the defence of the client after the initiation of proceedings by the Commission, is privileged, while similar dealings with an in-house lawyer are not.

In addition to the specific duties imposed by Regulation 17/62, the Commission is under a general duty 'not to disclose information of the kind covered by the obligation of professional secrecy' imposed by Article 287 (ex 214) EC. In *Adams v Commission (No. 1)* (case 145/83) the applicant, Mr Adams, obtained damages for breach of this duty, in exceptional, and tragic, circumstances. As a senior executive working for Hoffman-La-Roche in Switzerland, he had secretly and voluntarily passed to the Commission documents about La Roche's business activities, as a result of which La Roche was eventually fined 300,000 ecus for breach of the then Article 86 ((case 85/76) fine reduced to 200,000 ecus by Court). Adams had asked for his identity to be kept secret. The Commisson did not reveal his identity, but in the course of its investigations it passed the documents to La Roche, albeit doctored, and as a result Adam's identity as informer was discovered. La Roche subsequently brought criminal proceedings against Adams, who was found guilty of industrial espionage under Swiss law and sentenced to one year's imprisonment. During this time his wife committed suicide. In his subsequent claim against the Commission for damages the Court held that the Commission's duty of confidentiality under the then Article 214 (now 287) applied to information supplied even on a voluntary basis. It was in breach of that duty since it had not taken care to prevent his identity becoming known, and had not taken steps to warn Adams when it learned that La Roche was contemplating criminal action against him. However, damages were reduced by 50 per cent on account of Adams's contributory negligence. (He had failed to give the Commisson his precise address; failed to warn it that the documents might give a clue to his identity, and had returned to Switzerland knowing that in doing so he risked arrest.) A cautionary tale.

Sanctions

Fines and penalties   The Commission has power to impose fines for breaches of Articles 85 or 86 (ex 81 or 82) of up to 1 million euros (the value of the euro is normally around 66 pence) on an undertaking, or 10 per cent of its turnover, whichever is the greater (Regulation 17/62, Article 15(2)). In the latter case, fines are calculated on the basis of group turnover in the relevant sector, not only in the countries where the offence took place but globally (*Re Benelux Flat Glass Cartel* [1985] 2 CMLR 350). The size of the fine will depend on a number of criteria (see *Re Benelux Flat Glass Cartel*). These are:

(a)   The nature of the infringement. It is the 'classic' type — e.g., market sharing, price fixing?

(b)   The economic importance of the undertakings and their share of the relevant market.

(c)   The duration of the infringements.

(d)   Whether the infringements are deliberate, i.e., intended to restrict competition, or inadvertent.

(e)   Whether the party has already been found to have infringed Articles 85 or 86.

(f)   Whether the behaviour is open or underhand. In *Re Benelux Flat Glass Cartel* the parties had observed the letter of their written undertaking to the Commission, but indulged in practices against its spirit.

Where it is clear that the parent companies in a group are the main culprits they will be fined more heavily than their subsidiaries. The Commission adopted guidelines on calculating fines, according to which a base sum, defined with reference to the duration and the gravity of the infraction, will be calculated without reference to turnover ([1998] OJ C–9/3). This sum will be increased when aggravating circumstances exist or reduced to take account of extenuating circumstances. The guidelines divide infringements into minor, serious and very serious infringements. Fines for infringements will, for each category of infringement, be in the range of ECU 1,000 to ECU 1 million; ECU 1 million to ECU 20 million; and above ECU 20 million respectively, although since the advent of monetary union fines are levied in euros. Fines will be increased by up to 50 per cent for infringements of medium duration (in general, one to five years); and by up to 10 per cent per year for infringements of long duration (in general, more than five years). These figures may be further amended in the light of specific circumstances of the case, although the Commission may not exceed the upper limit for fines set out in Article 15 of Regulation 17/62.

The adoption of the guidelines will make the calculation of fines more transparent and coherent. It may be, however, that informing business people of the basis of calculation will make it easier for them to judge when it will be economically viable to contravene competition rules. It is perhaps to counter this that recent fines imposed by the Commission have been heavy. For example, in January 1998 the Commission imposed a fine of 102 million ecus on Volkswagen, as its Italian subsidiaries and distributors had been refusing to sell VW and Audi cars to German and Austrian customers. Fines of over 90 million euros were imposed on 10 companies following the District Heating Pipe Cartel investigation.

Even before the introduction of the guidelines, the Commisson did not hesitate to use its powers to the full. In *Re 'Pioneer' Hi-Fi Equipment* [1980] 1 CMLR 457 it imposed fines of almost 7 million ecus on four firms for concerted market-sharing practices in breach of the then Article 85(1) (now 81(1)). *Pioneer* was approved by the ECJ in annulment proceedings (cases 100-3/80), although the fines were reduced by approximately 2,500,000 ecus overall, due to an incorrect assessment on the part of the Commission as to the duration of the offences. In *Re Peroxygen Cartel* [1985] 1 CMLR 481 fines totalling 9 million ecus were imposed for breach of the then Article 85(1) on a number of companies, all major producers world-wide of peroxide products, in respect of a market-sharing and price-fixing cartel of extreme gravity and long duration. In *Re Polyethylene* (OJ L 74/21 1989) 17 undertakings were fined a total of 60 million ecus for similar concerted price-fixing and market sharing practices in the low density polyethylene industry. (See also *Re Polypropylene Cartel;* and *Community* v *ICI* [1988] 4 CMLR 347.) And in *Tetra Pak* (1991) the Commission fined the Swiss-based packaging company Tetra Pak 75 million ecus in respect of pricing policies (including predatory pricing) and market-sharing practices which were deliberately designed to eliminate actual or potential competitors in the aseptic and non-aseptic markets in machinery and cartons. The CFI upheld the Commission's decision (case T–83/91) including the amount of the fine, as did the ECJ (case C–333/94 P) on Tetra Pak's appeal from the CFI's decision.

As has been noted, the Commission also has power to fine undertakings from 100 to 5,000 ecus for intentionally or negligently failing to supply the information required under Article 11, 12 or 14 of Regulation 17/62, or for supplying false or misleading information (Regulation 17/62, Article 15(1)).

In addition the Commission may impose periodic penalty payments of from 50 to 1,000 ecus per day for a failure to comply with a Commission Decision requiring parties to end infringements under Article 81 or 82 (ex 85 or 86) EC or for failure to cooperate in enquiries and investigations under Article 11(5) or Article 14(3) (Article 16). Hoechst was fined 1,000 ecus per day under these provisions.

The ECJ, under Article 229 (ex 172), and now the CFI, has unlimited jurisdiction in regard to fines. It will not, however, substitute its discretion for that of the Commission. The matter will normally be determined in the context of proceedings for annulment under Article 230 (ex 173), and according to the same principles (see chapter 30).

As many of the cases examined in the context of Articles 81 and 82 (ex 85 and 86) EC indicate, it is not uncommon for undertakings to seek annulment of the Commission's Decisions. While annulment is rare, fines are frequently reduced. Until the case of *AEG-Telefunken* (case 107/82), there had been further incentive to try for annulment. Unsure of the extent of its powers in this area the Commission had not charged interest on fines for the period prior to commencement of review proceedings. There was some evidence that parties were embarking on annulment actions as a tactical manoeuvre. Any possibility of doing so came to an end with *AEG-Telefunken,* when the Court held that the Commission had power to demand interest from the date of the Decision itself.

Other orders   Article 3 of Regulation 17 deals with termination of infringements. Paragraph 1 states that in the case of an infringement of Article 81(1) or 82 (ex 85(1) or 86) EC, the Commission 'may by decision require the undertakings concerned to bring such infringement to an end'. Paragraph 3 provides that the Commission may address 'recommendations for the termination of the infringement' to the undertakings concerned.

In *Radio Telefis Eireann* v *Commission* (cases C–241 & 242/91P) (the *Magill* case) the ECJ held that the Commission has the power under Article 3 to require positive measures (such as the licensing of intellectual property) from undertakings as well as requiring them to desist from certain behaviour.

Interim measures   Although Regulation 17/62 gives the Commission no express power to issue interim measures, the ECJ in *Camera Care Ltd* v *Commission* (case 792/79R) decided that the Commission does have that power, implied in Article 3 of Regulation 17/62. The case came before the Court as a result of the Commission's Decision refusing to make an interim order at the request of Camera Care, a retail photographic business, requiring Hasselblad to supply Camera Care with its cameras. The Commission believed it had no power to do so. On a very broad interpretation of Article 3 of Regulation 17/62, the Court, borrowing from the principles applicable to its own jurisdiction under Articles 242 and 243 (ex 185 and 186, held that the Commission could take interim measures provided they were:

(a)   indispensable,
(b)   urgent,
(c)   to avoid serious or irreparable damage to the party seeking its adoption *or* in a situation which is intolerable to the public interest.

In exercising this power the Commission must observe the essential procedural safeguards of Article 19 of Regulation 17/62 (hearings of parties and third parties), *and* the interim measure must be open to challenge before the ECJ. The Court has held that damage is not serious and irreparable if it is purely financial and can, in the event of success in the main action, be wholly recouped (*Cargill* v *Commission; interim measures* (case 229/88R)).

The scope of *Camera Care* was reduced somewhat in *Ford of Europe Inc.* v *Commission* (cases 228 & 229/82). Here the Court held that an interim order can be granted only if it falls within the framework of the final Decision. As with the European Court's jurisdiction under Articles 81 and 82 (ex 85 and 86) EC, interim relief can be granted only if it 'relates to' the principal application before the court. Thus the Commission's interim order requiring that Ford Germany continue to supply right-hand drive cars to German distributors was annulled, since the final Decision was to be a Decision in response to its application for negative clearance or exemption.

Concentrations

As noted in chapter 16, the Merger Control Regulation 4064/89 repealed Regulation 17/62 in respect of *all* concentrations. Concentrations falling within the Merger Regulation will be subject to the powers and procedures laid down in Regulations 4064/89 and 2367/90, which are broadly similar in scope to those of Regulation 17/62. The Commission now has no power to act in respect of concentrations falling outside the Merger Regulation, unless it is requested to do so by a Member State (see chapter 16).

The role of national authorities

Article 84 (ex 88) EC gave the 'authorities in Member States' the power to administer the competition provisions of the Treaty until these powers were taken over by the Commission in Regulation 17/62. The Commission is currently reviewing the procedures for the application of Articles 81 and 82 (ex 85 and 86). These proposals are outlined below. For the time being, the role of the national authorities is defined by Regulation 17/62 as follows.
According to Article 9(3) of Regulation 17/62:

As long as the Commission has not initiated any procedure under Articles 2 [negative clearance], 3 [investigation either on application of third parties or on own initiative], or 6 [exemption], the authorities of the Member States shall remain competent to apply Article 85(1) [now 81(1)] and Article 86 [now 82].

Initial uncertainties as to the meaning of, 'authorities in Member States' and the limitations of Article 9(3) were dispelled in *BRT* v *SABAM* (case 127/73). Here the Court held that the competence of national courts to apply the then Articles 85 and 86 (now 81 and 82 respectively) derived from the direct effects of those provisions, and not from the then Article 88 or Regulation 17. Thus, Article 9(3) of Regulation 17 could not operate to deprive individuals of rights held under the Treaty itself. Where the Commission has instituted parallel proceedings, a national court faced with a problem of Article 81 or 82 (ex 85 and 86) EC may stay proceedings until a Decision has been made; but it is not obliged to do so.
Since Articles 81 and 82 (ex 85 and 86) EC are directly effective, they can be invoked before any domestic court in matters to which they are relevant. Both the Commission and the ECJ have encouraged national courts to apply

EC competition law, no doubt in the hope of lessening the Commission's administrative burden. In the *Perfume* cases (e.g., *Lancôme* (case 99/79)) the Court held that even the issuing of a comfort letter could not deprive national courts of their freedom to apply the then Articles 85 and 86. Despite the passing of the Merger Regulation and the principle of one-stop shopping, national courts remain competent to apply Articles 81 and 82 (ex 85 and 86) EC to *all* concentrations. The Commission's Notice on Cooperation (1993 OJ No. C39/6), has now made it clear that national courts will be required to play the principal role in safeguarding the directly effective rights of individuals under EC competition law.

Yet allowing, indeed requiring, national courts to apply these Articles raises formidable problems.

Exemptions National courts, at all levels, are free to make a finding of infringement of Articles 81 and 82 (ex 85 and 86) EC or no infringement. In doing so they may be guided by decisions of the Commission and the Court. They may also rely on comfort letters indicating that the agreement or practice does or does not appear to fall within Article 81(1) (ex 85(1)) (although following the *Perfume* cases they are not obliged to do so). They may find that an agreement is exempt under a block exemption. But currently they have no express power to grant individual exemption under Article 81(3) (ex 85(3)), even if it might appear to be justified on existing authority. Nor can they obtain assistance on this matter from the Court, since the Court has no power to grant exemption. Where the Commission has instituted parallel proceedings, the national court may stay proceedings until a Decision is made. Pending that decision it may grant interim relief. If the Commission exempts the agreement in question under Article 81(3) (ex 85(3)) it may then apply that decision. But what if the Commission has not instituted proceedings?

In *Delimitis v Henninger Bräu AG* (case C–234/89) the Court suggested a number of ways in which the Commission might assist national courts in applying the then Articles 85 and 86, based on their obligation of mutual assistance derived (according to the Court in *Zwartveld*, case C–2/88 Imm) from Article 5 (now 10) EC. These suggestions were approved in *Automec v Commission* (case T–24/90). These cases provided the spur and the model for the Commission's Notice on Cooperation (1993). The Notice outlines a variety of ways in which the Commission may help national courts in applying EC competition law, also based on its duty of cooperation under Article 10 (ex 5) EC. In addition to established sources of guidance such as official decisions of the Commission and the Court, and opinions and official statements of the Commission, the Notice suggests that national courts may consider and apply 'substantive provisions of individual exemptions' (para. 8) and comfort letters, whether in the form of 'soft' negative clearance or 'soft' exemptions. These constitute 'factual elements' which the national court may 'take into account' in examining whether the agreement or conduct examined is in accordance with the provisions of Article 81 or 82 (ex 85 or 86) EC. If, having considered these factors, a national court is unable to take a decision, it may stay proceedings and ask the Commission ('within the limits of its national procedural law') for information as to:

(a) *whether the agreement has been notified.* If it has not there is no possibility of obtaining an exemption, no matter how compelling the case for justification under Article 81(3) (ex 85(3)). This strict rule provides the incentive for notification. If the agreement has been notified the national court may ask the Commission;

(b) *whether a decision has been issued or comfort letter sent;* or

(c) *when a decision or comfort letter is likely to be sent.*

It may also seek:

(d) *an interim opinion on whether the agreement is likely to obtain negative clearance or exemption.*

Although opinions and letters obtained pursuant to these procedures are not strictly binding on national courts, and are expressed as being given in order to provide 'useful guidance for resolving disputes', it may be presumed that such guidance is given on the understanding that it will be followed. Thus it appears that national courts, despite their inability to grant exemptions, are encouraged by the Notice to approve, even if this means 'exempting' agreements on the basis not only of formal decisions (which include individual exemption decisions) but of comfort letters and opinions comprising 'soft' negative clearance and exemption from the Commission. Desirable though these developments may be their legitimacy is dubious. Nor are they conducive to certainty, since, in the absence of a full enquiry, resulting in a formal decision from the Commission, whether of negative clearance or exemption, an agreement or practice, even if approved by a national court, is always open to challenge.

Remedies Where a national court finds an agreement in breach of Article 81(1) or Article 82 (ex 85(1) and 86) it may declare that agreement void, but it has no power to order fines. What remedies should it provide? In the absence of common Community provision the ECJ has held that Member States must make available the same remedies as are available for comparable breaches of national law (*Rewe-Zentralfinanz* v *Landwirtschaftskammer für das Saarland* (case 33/76)), and that the remedies must be real and effective, both to protect individuals' Community rights and to deter breaches of Community law (*Harz* v *Deutsche Tradax GmbH* (case 79/83)). These principles were affirmed in the Commission's Notice on Cooperation (1993), in which it suggested that national courts, in their task of safeguarding the subjective rights of private individuals under the then Articles 85 and 86 (now 81 and 82), must make available all the legal means capable of contributing to the effective protection of individuals' rights, including interim relief, injunctions and compensation for damage suffered as a result of infringement of these rights 'where such remedies are available in proceedings relating to similar national law' (para. 11). However, it may not be clear in this context which national law remedy is 'similar' since EC law is *sui generis*.

It is submitted that the courts of Member States should approach the question of damages with caution, since, in the absence of common Community provision, unequal treatment as between competing undertakings could undermine the very principles of free and fair competition which Articles 81 and 82 (ex 85 and 86) EC seek to uphold. It was hoped that some of these issues would be addressed by the Court when it ruled on a number of questions relating to the award of damages under English law referred by the High Court (in the context of provisions equivalent to Articles 81 and 82 (ex 85 and 86) in the ECSC Treaty) in *H.J. Banks & Co. Ltd* v *British Coal Corporation* (case C–128/92). Regrettably, and surprisingly, the Court avoided the issue and decided that the provisions in question were not directly effective. The question of remedies has recently arisen again in the UK in the context of beer supply agreements; these issues have been referred to the ECJ, but it will be some time before a ruling is handed down (*Courage* v *Creehan*, judgment 27 May 1999 (CA)). (For further discussion of remedies see chapter 26.)

Application of Articles 81 and 82 (ex 85 and 86) EC   Although the legal principles applicable to Articles 81 and 82 (ex 85 and 86) are reasonably clear, their application to the facts involve what is primarily an economic assessment. Questions of market size and structure, of the relevant product market, the relevant geographical market, of the effect of an agreement on competition or on trade between Member States, or whether prices or trading conditions are 'unfair', or, in the case of concentrations, whether they may undermine or impede effective competition within the common market, require the analysis of an extensive array of economic data, and the application by lawyers of complex economic criteria. The relevant information and expertise will not always be available to national courts, and if they are there is ample scope for differences of opinion in their application. The problem is particularly acute in adversarial systems such as that of the UK, where the gathering of evidence and the conduct of the investigation lies in the hands of the parties. A ruling from the ECJ under Article 234 (ex 177) will merely provide guidance on the law; it will not assist in its application to the facts. In *Bureau Européen des Médias de l'Industrie Musicale (BEMIM)* v *Commission* (cases T–114/92 & 5/93) the CFI conceded that, because of the complexity of the case or the lack of factual information, a national court might not be able to provide sufficient protection for individuals' rights under Articles 81 or 82 (ex 85 or 86).

The Commission's Notice on Cooperation (1993) has attempted to alleviate some of these problems by suggesting that national courts may apply to the Commission for factual information in the form of statistics, market studies and economic analyses, which the Commission will seek to supply (subject to the normal obligations of confidentiality) in the shortest possible time. In *Postbank NV* v *Commission* (case T–353/94) the CFI suggested that, given the difficulty for Member States' courts in assessing economic questions even in the light of such reports, the Commission was under a positive obligation to assist the courts. Nevertheless it is submitted that even with this assistance the complexity of the task is such that, unless individuals' rights under Articles 81 and 82 (ex 85 and 86) are enforced by specialised national courts or tribunals, working in close cooperation with their counterparts in other Member States, within a framework of common Community rules, there is unlikely to be uniformity of application either from court to court or from Member State to Member State. The result could be to endanger rather than advance the cause of competition.

The Commission has suggested increasing the involvement of the national competition authorities in the enforcement of EC competition law and recently introduced a Cooperation Notice ([1997] OJ C 313/3) to parallel that already in existence in respect of national courts. The Commission has, however, acknowledged that not all cases involving EC competition law are suited to application by national enforcement authorities. The Notice on Cooperation gives guidance on when a case should be dealt with by the national competition authorities, which is where three conditions are met:

(a)   the case essentially involves a single Member State;
(b)   there is a clear infringement of Community rules;
(c)   the infringement has no chance of being exempted by the Commission on grounds which are provided for in Community law and for whose implementation the Commission is solely responsible. In practice this means an infringement of Article 81(1) (ex 85(1)) is unlikely to be exempted under Article 81(3) (ex 85(3)), or an abuse falling within Article 82 (ex 86), for which there is no exemption (see chapter 15 for a discussion of the impact of Article 83(2) (ex 90(2)) EC).

Cases which satisfy the above requirements may still be dealt with by the Commission if it considers them to be of sufficient Community interest. Examples include where the case concerns a point of law not yet considered either by the ECJ or CFI; or where the case concerns anti-competitive behaviour by a public undertaking falling within the definition in Article 86(1) (ex 90(1)) EC. The economic magnitude of a case is not normally enough on its own to warrant it being dealt with by the Commission. The ECJ and CFI have laid down conditions to be taken into consideration by the Commission when determining whether or not there is sufficient Community interest for the Commission to act. (See *Automec* v *Commission* (case T–24/90), *BENIM* (case T–114/92) and *Union Française de l'Express (Ufex)* v *Commission* (case C–119/97P) discussed below.)

To aid the national authorities in their application of Articles 81(1) and 82 (ex 85(1) and 86 respectively), the Commission has called on those Member States, which have not yet done so, to adopt national legislation enabling the authorities in their implementation of Community competition principles. Although the UK has recently amended its competition regime by the entry into force of the Competition Act 1998, which mirrors the approach taken under Articles 81 and 82 (ex 85 and 86), there are still a number of Member

States in which the competition authorities seem not to have the necessary powers to apply these provisions.

Whether EC competition law is enforced by national courts or by other national authorities, it seems that, as the CFI held in *BEMIM* (Case T–5/93), the rights of the complainant must be adequately safeguarded. This will require access to all necessary information as well as respect for the parties' procedural rights (see below and chapter 6).

Conflict between national and Community competition law   There are occasions when agreements or practices are subject to both national and EC competition law. What is a national judge to do if faced with a conflict between these rules? Clearly national competition law cannot be applied to legalise action which is prohibited under Community law. Here, as elsewhere, Community law must take priority. But what if the national law is stricter than Community law? Can national law declare illegal action (for example an exempted agreement) which is permitted under Community law? In *Wilhelm v Bundeskartellampt* (case 14/68) the Court made it clear that the then Article 85 (now 81) did not prevent restrictive agreements being examined under national law, although undertakings may not be liable twice in respect of the same infringement. However, parallel application of national rules was only permissible insofar as it did not prejudice the uniform application of Community competition law or compromise the useful effect of the EC Treaty. Thus it appears that national rules which are stricter than Community rules may be applied provided that they do not undermine Articles 81 and 82 (ex 85 and 86) EC or breach other provisions of the EC Treaty, for example Article 28 (ex 30) or Article 49 (ex 59) EC. Similar principles would apply to provisions introduced by the TEU, which permit Member States in certain areas (health and safety of workers, Article 138 (ex 118a) EC, consumer protection, Article 153 (ex 129a) EC, environment, Article 176 (ex 130t) EC) to adopt 'more stringent measures' than those applied under Community law.

The role of individuals

Since Articles 81 and 82 (ex 85 and 86) EC are directly effective, vertically and horizontally, individuals are free to invoke these provisions either as a sword or a shield before their national courts. They should thus be able to obtain an injunction to prevent a breach of these Articles, or damages in lieu of an injunction, or a declaration, or the appropriate interim relief. If a definitive tort can be proved damages may be obtained. As shown in *Viho Europe BV v Commission* (case T–102/92), however, the individual must adduce sufficient evidence to enable the court, whether national or European, to decide the case. In this case, the CFI refused to consider the claim under the then Article 86 (now 82) since the applicant gave no precise particulars on which a claim of abuse of a dominant position might be based.

In addition to these rights, individuals have been given a special place in the enforcement of EC competiton law under Regulation 17/62. Under Article 3(2) any natural or legal person who can claim a 'legitimate interest' may apply to the Commission to investigate and terminate alleged infringements of Article 81 or 82 (ex 85 and 86). The question of 'legitimate interest' has been widely interpreted. It would certainly include any trader who feels he has been unfairly treated or excluded in breach of these Articles. Furthermore, 'legitimate interest' is not restricted to individuals. An association of individuals may claim a legitimate interest in lodging a complaint provided that it is entitled to represent the interests of its members and the conduct complained of is likely to affect their interests (e.g., *BEUC* v *Commission* (case T–37/92); *BEMIM* v *Commission* (cases T–114/92 & 5/93)). In the case of concentrations, with the repeal of Regulation 17/62, this right under Article 3(2) has now been removed.

Following the approach announced in its Notice on Cooperation (1993), the Commission may refuse to consider complaints submitted to it on the grounds that the matter lacks the requisite political, economic or legal significance for the Community. In *Automec* v *Commission* (case T–24/90) ('*Automec II*'), the CFI identified conditions the Commission should take into account were it to reject a complaint for lack of Community interest: the significance of the alleged infringement as regards the functioning of the common market; the probability of establishing the existence of the infringement; and the scope of the investigation required. The question of whether these factors were the only factors that could be taken into account, or indeed constituted factors the Commission must take into account, arose in *Union Française de l'Express (Ufex)* v *Commission* (case C–119/97P). There, the ECJ held that in view of the fact the assessment of Community interest varies from case to case, 'the number of criteria of assessment the Commission may refer to should not be limited, nor conversely should it be required to have recourse exclusively to certain criteria' (para. 79). If the Commission were to decline to continue an examination of a complaint, whether for lack of Community interest or otherwise, it must state reasons for so doing which must be sufficiently precise and detailed to enable the CFI to review that decision. Thus, the Commission must set out the facts justifying the decision and the legal considerations on the basis of which it was adopted. In the context of lack of Community interest, the ECJ stated that the Commission is required to assess in every case how serious the alleged interference with competition is and how persistent its consequences are. The fact that the behaviour complained of has ceased does not necessarily mean that there is no Community interest, especially if the anti-competitive effects of that behaviour continue. In *BEMIM* v *Commission* (cases T–114/92 & 5/93), the CFI held that the Commission was entitled to reject a complaint on the basis of lack of Community interest provided the rights of the complainant would be adequately protected, in particular, by the national courts. In *BEUC* v *Commission* (case T–37/92), however, the CFI held that it could review a decision of the Commission rejecting a complaint on these grounds and, as the ECJ subsequently reiterated in *Ufex*, that any such decision must be properly reasoned. Since the Community interest, or lack of it, could be used to argue for or against an issue being dealt with by national authorities, it is incumbent on complainants seeking to persuade the Commission to act against alleged infringements of Articles 81 and 82 (ex 85 and 86) to appeal against a rejection by the Commission and adduce convincing evidence that their interests will not be sufficiently safeguarded by action before their national courts or competition authorities. This was something which the applicant failed to do in *BEMIM*.

Because a person with sufficient interest has a right to request action from the Commission under Article 3(2) he also has a right to be heard (Article 19(2)). The Court has held that this does not entitle the complainant to an oral hearing; written observations may be sufficient (*British American Tobacco Co. Ltd* v *Commission* (cases 142 & 156/84)). A complainant also has limited rights of discovery, subject to the Commission's duty to protect business secrets. In *AKZO Chemie BV* v *Commission* (case 53/85) the Court held that the obligation of professional secrecy is mitigated in regard to third parties on whom Article 19(2) confers a right to be heard, although such third parties' rights of access are more constrained than those of a defendant company. The Commission may communicate to such a party certain information covered by the obligation of professional secrecy insofar as it is necessary to do so for the proper conduct of the investigation. However, the Court drew a distinction between 'obligations of professional secrecy' and 'business secrets'. Business secrets require exceptional protection. Third parties may not in any circumstances be given access to documents containing business secrets. How and where the Commission is, in its discretion, to draw the line between 'obligations of professional secrecy' and 'business secrets' is not clear.

An individual may request the Commission to act under Article 3(2) of Regulation 17, but he cannot compel it to do so. However, if the Commission issues a Decision as a result of an application under Article 3(2), the complainant may challenge that Decision before the CFI whether or not the Decision is addressed to himself (*Metro-SB-Grossmärkte GmbH & Co. KG* v *Commission* (case 26/76) (see chapter 30)).

The right of individuals to apply to the Commission under Article 3(2) is a valuable means of enforcement of EC competition law; many infringements have come to light via this route. Clearly for individuals this route is cheaper than a direct action before a national court, since the Commission shoulders the burden of enquiry. It may too be more effective, since the threat of fines may act as a deterrent to wrongdoers. *Camera Care* (case 792/79R) has opened up the possibility of obtaining interim orders from the Commission to prevent damage occurring. In *British Brass Band Instruments* v *Boosey & Hawkes; interim measures* (case iv/32.279) British Brass Band Instruments were successful in obtaining such an order, requiring Boosey & Hawkes to continue supplying them with brass band instruments, thereby avoiding irreparable damage. On the other hand, as Sir Neil Lawson observed in *Cutsforth* v *Mansfield Inns Ltd* [1986] 1 CMLR 1, English High Court, 'the mills of Brussels [can] grind very slowly indeed'. The claimants in *Cutsforth* v *Mansfield Inns Ltd* were suppliers of pin-tables and gaming machines to pubs and clubs in the Humberside area of England. The defendants were brewers who had taken over a group of tied houses in that area. Under their new tenancy agreements tenants were required to install in their pubs only pin-tables and gaming machines on the defendants' approved list. The claimants, who had supplied the pubs in the past, were not on that list. They complained to the Commission. They also applied for an interim injunction in the English High Court to prevent the defendants from enforcing their agreements. Sir Neil Lawson considered there was a serious case to be tried, and granted them the injunction. There was no time to wait for Brussels to decide.

By contrast, Lord Jauncey (in *Argyll Group plc* v *Distillers Co. plc* [1986] 1 CMLR 764, Outer House of the Court of Session) refused to grant an interim interdict to prevent a merger between Distillers and Guinness. He was not convinced (it is submitted correctly) that a prima facie case had been made out.

Thus it appears that if the case is reasonably clear, and urgent, an action seeking interim relief before domestic courts may produce the best results. A fortiori if the claimant seeks damages, since the Commission has no power to award compensation to those injured as a result of breaches of EC competition law. But if there is no urgency, and little prospect of a successful claim for damages, and certainly if the case is a complex or difficult or doubtful one, a complaint to the Commission would be preferable. Where substantial sums are at stake firms would be advised to hedge their bets and proceed both ways.

Following the Commission's Notice on Cooperation (1993), individuals may no longer have a choice between complaining to the Commission, under Article 3(2), and proceeding before their national court. As noted above, where a complainant is able to secure adequate protection for his directly effective Community rights in an action before his national court, the Commission will not itself investigate the complaint but will simply 'close the file'. This development, clearly designed to deter would-be complainants and divert them towards their domestic courts, will deprive individuals of an important source of protection. It also risks depriving the Commission of a valuable source of information, since many infringements of Articles 81 and 82 (ex 85 and 86) EC have come to light as a result of complaints under Article 3(2). It remains to be seen, but is open to doubt, whether national courts, even with the assistance of the cooperation procedures outlined in the Notice, will prove an adequate substitute for action under Article 3(2) and provide effective (and it is hoped uniform) protection for individuals' rights under Articles 81 and 82 (ex 85 and 86) EC. The problems arising from the Commission's new approach and its limitations have, as mentioned earlier, now been recognised both by the Commission in its 24th Report on Competition Policy and its Notice on Cooperation between National Authorities and the Commission; and by the CFI (*BEUC* v *Commission* (case T–37/92); *BEMIM* v *Commission* (cases T–114/92 & 5/93)).

Reform of the application of competition policy

As noted earlier, the Commission has undertaken a review of the application of competition policy (see the Modernisation White Paper, [1999] OJ L

132/1). The review has been driven by the pressure of work the Commission is under and the concern that, in spending time reviewing all the notified agreements, many of which are relatively harmless in competition terms, the Commission does not have resources enough to investigate and discover serious breaches of competition rules, such as cartels and bid-rigging. As with the other institutions, the Commission is also aware that enlargement can only stretch its resources further.

A fundamental overhaul of the competition system seemed necessary. To this end, the Commission has put forward a number of proposals. The review of the vertical restraints block exemption, which removed the notification obligation (Regulation 1216/99), flagged up the change in emphasis and can perhaps been seen as the first stage in the modernisation process (see further chapter 15). The Modernisation White Paper develops the approach to enforcement by proposing three linked changes.

The first of these proposals is the removal of the Commission's monopoly on granting exemptions under Article 81(3) (ex 85(3)) and, with limited exceptions, the notification procedure. Instead, businesses will be reliant on their own legal and economic advice to assess for themselves whether the proposed deal infringes Article 81(1) and if so, whether an exemption can be obtained under Article 81(3). The Commission proposes to issue guidelines to assist companies and their legal advisers in making this assessment. Also, in novel circumstances the Commission can still review the case.

The national competition authorities and courts will be involved in the application of Article 81(1) and (3), as well as Article 82 (ex 86). Although the application of competition policy is to be decentralised, the determination of the policy itself remains the preserve of the Commission. Thus it will still be the Commission that issues guidance notices and determines the terms of future block exemptions.

The corollary of these changes is that there will need to be greater cooperation between the Commission and the national authorities (and between the national authorities themselves). The cooperation mechanism includes the right of the Commission to intervene in a case pending before a national court or competition authority and impose its own decision before a final decision at national level is made. In addition, the national authorities are under an obligation to supply information to the Commission regarding their application of the EC competition rules.

Questions have been raised about the desirability of these proposals. In particular, businesses are concerned that the changes would result in a fragmentation of the single market and hold up cross-border deals. UNICE, the confederation of European employers' groups, has expressed the concern that there will be inconsistencies between Member States, leading to companies looking to structure deals within the most favourable national jurisdiction. Additionally, the removal of the notification system will result in a lack of certainty for businesses about the legality of their arrangements. The Commission, therefore, seems to have an uphill struggle before it to persuade businesses and Member States that its proposals are an improvement on the existing system.

Further reading

Davidson, J., 'Action for Damages in the English Courts for Breach of EEC Competition Law' (1985) 34 ICLQ 178.

Harris, B., 'Problems of Procedure in EEC Competition Cases' (1989) 139 NLJ 1452.

House of Lords Select Committee on the European Communities, *1st Report. Enforcement of Community Competition Rules* (House of Lords Papers, Session 1993–94, 7) (London: HMSO, 1993).

House of Lords Select Committee on the European Union, *Reforming EC Competition Procedures*, 29 February 2000 (House of Lords Paper 33, Session 1999–2000) (London: HMSO, 2000).

Hunnings, N., 'The Stanley Adams Affair: the Biter Bit' (1987) 24 CML Rev 65.

Jacobs, F., 'Damages for Breach of Article 86' (1983) 8 EL Rev 353.

Klimisch, A. and Krueger, B., 'Decentralised Application of EC Competition Law: Current Practice and Future Prospects' (1999) 24 EL Rev 463.

Kon, S., 'Article 85(3): A Case for Application by National Courts' (1982) 19 CML Rev 541.

Levitt, M., 'Access to the File: The Commission's Administrative Procedures under Articles 85 and 86' (1997) 34 CML Rev 1413.

Maitland-Walker, J., 'Have English Courts gone too far in Challenging the Effectiveness of EC Competition Law?' [1999] ECLR 1.

Riley, A., '*Saunders* and the Power to Obtain Information in European Community and United Kingdom Competition Law' (2000) 25 EL Rev 264.

Shaw, J., 'Decentralization and Law Enforcement in EC Competition Law' (1995) 15 LS 128.

Steiner, J., 'How to Make the Action Fit the Case: Domestic Remedies for Breach of EEC Law' (1987) 12 EL Rev 102.

Wesseling, R., 'Subsidiarity in Community Antitrust Law: Setting the Right Agenda' (1997) 22 EL Rev 35.

Whish, R., 'The Enforcement of EC Competition Law in the Domestic Courts of Member States' [1994] ECLR 60.

Zinsmeister, U., Rikkers, E. and Jones, J., 'The Application of Articles 85 and 86 by national Competition Authorities' [1999] ECLR 275.

See also further reading for chapter 26.

EIGHTEEN

Competition law and industrial property rights

The exercise of industrial and commercial property rights such as trade marks, patents and copyright must inevitably restrict competition; indeed their very purpose is to give their owner some protection against competition by giving him monopoly rights for a certain period of time as a reward for his creative endeavour or acquired goodwill in his product. These rights are recognised in Articles 30 and 295 (ex 36 and 222) EC (see chapter 11). But, as was pointed out in chapter 11, the ECJ has drawn a distinction between the *existence* of industrial property rights and their *exercise*. The mere existence of industrial property rights cannot infringe Articles 81 or 82 (ex 85 or 86) EC; an improper or abusive exercise of these rights can. Thus in *Établissements Consten SA* v *Commission* (cases 56 & 58/64) Consten could not rely on its trade mark rights to prevent parallel imports of Grundig products from other Member States. The purpose of the GINT trade mark was not to protect the owner's legitimate rights in his product, for example, to prevent other goods being passed off as Grundig's, but to partition the market and ensure absolute territorial protection for Grundig products in France. Thus its exercise in the context of Grundig's dealer agreement was in breach of the then Article 85(1) (now 81(1)).

The same principle has been applied to patents and copyright. In *Parke, Davis & Co.* v *Probel* (case 24/67) the Court held that an 'improper exploitation' of patent rights in the context of agreements, decisions of undertakings or concerted practices or by firms in a dominant position could breach EC competition law.

In *Re GEMA* [1971] CMLR D35 the Commission found that GEMA, an authors' rights society holding a dominant position in authors' copyright in Germany, was improperly exploiting its rights in breach of the then Article 86 (now 82).

The exploitation of industrial or commercial property rights will be improper if these rights are used in order to defeat Community law on restrictive practices (*Consten*). Any concerted attempt or attempt by a dominant undertaking to use these rights to partition markets, or to maintain artificial price levels, or to impose discriminatory or unfair conditions on trading partners is liable to fall foul of Articles 81 or 82 (ex 85 and 86) EC. In *Re GEMA*, GEMA was exploiting its copyrights by discriminatory practices; it was discriminating against nationals from other Member States, who could not become full members; it paid supplementary fees, 'loyalty bonuses', only to some of its members from a fund to which all had contributed, without objective justification. It was imposing unfair conditions on its members, by extending its contractual rights to non-copyright works, and claiming rights to future works. All these practices went beyond what was necessary to protect GEMA's legitimate property rights.

Similarly, in *Windsurfing International Inc.* v *Commission* (case 193/83) WSI, the owner of patent licences in a special sail rig (comprising mast, mast foot, sail and pair of curved booms) for use with windsurfing boards, was seeking in its licensing agreements to impose unnecessary restrictions on its licensees in breach of the then Article 85(1) (now 81(1)). For example, licensees were required to exploit the patents (for the rigs) *only* for the manufacture of sailboards using hulls which had been given WSI's prior approval; to pay royalties for rigs made under the patent on the basis of the selling price of the *complete* sailboard; to manufacture only in a specified manufacturing plant; and they were not permitted to challenge the licensed patents. These provisions were all found to constitute improper exploitation.

Thus in placing limitations on the exercise of industrial property rights the Commission, supported by the Court, has curtailed the very substance of these rights. These rights can now only be exercised to protect what the Commission regards as the 'specific subject-matter' of the property concerned.

The specific subject-matter of the property, to protect which industrial property rights may legitimately be exercised, has been narrowly defined. For patents, it is to ensure, to the holder, so as to recompense the creative effort of the inventor, the exclusive right to use an invention (*Centrafarm BV* v *Sterling Drug Inc.* (case 15/74)). Patent rights clearly merit protection if the Community wishes to encourage creative endeavour. Thus while patent licensing agreements have generally been held in breach of Article 81(1) (ex 85(1)) the Commission has been prepared to grant exemption under Article 81(3) (ex 85(3)) (e.g., *Davidson Rubber Co.* [1972] CMLR D52). The Commission's attitude to these agreements has been embodied in its block exemption on patent licensing (Regulation 2349/84) now replaced by the Technology Transfer Regulation (Regulation 240/96, OJ L31/2, 1996). However, the block exemption contains an extensive black list in Article 3, and has drawn the line at allowing licensees full territorial protection. *Windsurfing International Inc.* v *Commission* (case 193/83) and *L.C. Nungesser KG* v *Commission* (case 258/78) would still fall outside its protection.

The specific subject-matter of a trade-mark right is to protect the owner from competitors who would profit, deliberately or accidentally, from the reputation and goodwill attached to the mark by selling goods with the same mark, or one which was sufficiently similar to cause confusion in the mind of the consumer (see e.g., *Deutsche Renault AG v Audi AG* (case C–317/91)). Thus, trade-mark rights cannot be used simply to prevent parallel imports within the EC of the trade-marked product, which may be cheaper than the same product sold in the importing State, even to protect a distributor's investment in a particular territory from 'free riders' (i.e., parallel importers who seek to take advantage of the product's goodwill, built up by the promotional efforts of others). It is only rights *in the product* which are protected.

The specific subject-matter or purpose of copyright protection was held in *Radio Telefis Eireann v Commission* (case T–69/89) to be to protect the owner's moral rights in the work and ensure a reward for creative endeavour, which entitles the holder to exclusive rights of performance and reproduction of the protected work (para. 71). Thus RTE could not take advantage of its legitimate monopoly in radio and TV broadcasts by refusing to grant licences for the reproduction of its advance programme listings to potential competitors, thereby retaining an 'unlawful monopoly downstream'. Such an exercise of copyright did not correspond to its essential function of copyright protection but pursued an aim 'manifestly contrary to Article 86 [now 82]'. On appeal (*Radio Telefis Eireann v Commission* (cases C–241 & 242/91P)), the ECJ upheld the CFI's judgment, but without ruling explicitly on the purpose of copyright. In *Re GEMA* the Commission suggested that any conditions embodied in an agreement or practice or imposed by a dominant undertaking which go beyond what is necessary to protect the owners' *existing* property, and certainly any discriminatory treatment, risk infringing Articles 81 or 82 (ex 85 or 86). In *Ministre Public v Tournier* (case 395/87), in the context of a reference concerning the compatibility of reciprocal arrangements between copyright management societies with the then Articles 30, 85 and 86 (now 28, 81 and 82), the Court held that contracts entered into with users would not infringe the then Article 85 (now 81) unless the practices at issue exceeded the limits absolutely necessary for the attainment of the legitimate copyright objective of safeguarding the rights and interests of their members *vis-à-vis* users of the protected property, in this case recorded music.

It must be emphasised that such protection as is offered to protect the specific subject-matter of the property concerned has been significantly reduced by the doctrine of exhaustion of rights discussed at length in chapter 11. Any rights claimed in the context of agreements or practices within Articles 81 or 82 (ex 85 and 86) EC which are not permitted under this doctrine will risk infringing EC competition law. Furthermore since *Radio Telefis Eireann v Commission* (cases C–241 & 242/91P), it is clear that, where exceptional circumstances exist, the holder of an intellectual property right will not be permitted to refuse to license it (see chapter 16 for further discussion).

Lastly, the fact that an industrial property right such as an exclusive licence falls within a block exemption cannot protect an undertaking from liability under Article 82 (ex 86) EC if that right is abused, even where the abuse consists only in increasing an already dominant position, thereby eliminating effective competition in a substantial part of the common market (*Tetra Pak* (case T–51/89)).

NINETEEN

Introduction: an outline of EC social policy

The EC began life as an organisation concerned primarily with economic issues. In creating a common market, the original EEC Treaty needed to ensure that the factors of production, that is, economically active individuals, were able to circulate freely within the Community in the same way as goods or capital. This basic principle, enshrined in what is now Article 3(c) EC, sought to establish, in the interests of economic efficiency, 'an internal market, characterised by the abolition, as between Member States, of obstacles to the free movement of goods, *persons, services* and capital'. This was reinforced by provisions for the enactment of 'flanking' measures to ensure more uniform standards of worker protection (then Articles 117–122, now replaced by Articles 136–145) and by the principle of equal pay for equal work for men and women (then Article 119 EEC, now 141 EC), the principal purpose of which was to create a more level playing field within the single internal market. But these ancillary provisions and the ECJ's jurisprudence demonstrate that the Community was from the beginning also concerned with humanitarian goals. As Advocate-General Trabucci commented in *F v Belgium* (case 7/75), 'the migrant worker is to be regarded not as a mere source of labour but as a human being' (see also *Defrenne v Sabena (No. 2)* (case 43/75)). This approach has been reinforced by successive Treaty amendments. The TEU (1992) notably extended Article 2 to pledge the Community to a 'high level of employment and of social protection, the raising of the standard of living and quality of life, and economic and social cohesion and solidarity among Member States'. Likewise, the introduction of European citizenship in the TEU (Part 2 of the EC Treaty) emphasised the move away from the notion of the individual as a purely economic actor. Citizenship rights, set out in Articles 18–21 (ex 8a–8d) EC, comprise the right 'to move and reside freely within the territory of the Member States', the right to stand and vote in municipal and European Parliament elections, and the right to petition the Ombudsman and the European Parliament. The introduction of the concept of citizenship raises questions as to what rights citizens should expect, and has fuelled the debate on whether the Community should do more to protect the individual citizen. This question, for example, was addressed by the Commission in *Modernising and Improving Social Protection in the EU* (COM (97) 102 of 13 March 1997). Despite the opportunity to amend the citizenship provisions that the ToA (1997) provided, nothing was done expressly to expand the rights attaching to citizenship, although it did introduce the so-called area of freedom, security and justice (Article 62(1) EC). Nonetheless, when considering the provisions relating to the free movement of persons and to provisions on social policy in general, it is important to remember the dual imperatives, economic and social, affecting the development of these provisions and their interpretation.

Freedom of movement: fundamental Community rights

The basic principles relating to the free movement of persons are contained in Articles 39–42 (ex 48–51) EC (workers), and Articles 43–48 (ex 52–58) EC (freedom of establishment). The freedom to provide services is contained in Articles 49–55 (ex 59–66) EC. These freedoms have been further substantiated by secondary legislation. Although the ECSC and Euratom Treaties contain their own specific provisions for workers in the industries they cover, EC law relating to the free movement of persons will apply to those workers insofar as their position is not covered by those Treaties. The rules apply throughout the territories of the Member States of the Community.

The basic rights enshrined in these provisions, granted to EU nationals (defined according to the law of each Member State) and companies and firms formed in accordance with the law of one of the Member States (Article 48 (ex 58)), comprise the right freely to leave, or enter and reside in a Member State for the purposes of work, or establishment, or the provision of services, and the right to be treated in the host Member State free from discrimination on the grounds of nationality. In *Tilmant* v *Groupement des ASSEDIC de la Région Parisienne* [1991] 2 CMLR 317 the French Cour de Cassation held, no doubt correctly, that the principle of non-discrimination applied also to workers working outside the EU where the legal relationship of employer and employee is situated in the Community, whether by reason of the place where it is established or by reason of the place where it takes effect. These basic Community rights are not absolute. Rights of entry and residence are subject to derogation on the grounds of public policy, public security and public health (Articles 39(3) (ex 48(3)) and 46 (ex 56); Directive 64/221). Exceptions from the non-discrimination principle are provided for 'employment in the public service' (Article 39(4) (ex 48(4)) and 'activities connected with the exercise of official authority' (Article 45 (ex 55)).

Although the rights contained in the Treaty were originally expressed to be limited to those who are economically active, that is, workers or persons, natural or legal, exercising rights of establishment or providing services in the host State, broad definitions of the relevant terms, in particular the definition of worker, and generous interpretation on the part of the Court, have extended the scope of their protection. Furthermore, secondary legislation enacted in 1968 and 1970 extended these rights to the families of migrant workers. Unlike the worker, members of the family are not required to be nationals of a Member State to claim Community rights. Similar rights have now been extended to a wider category of persons, firstly by the enactment of three directives (90/364, 90/365, 90/366 (amended and re-enacted as Directive 93/96) OJ L180, 13.7.90) granting rights of entry and residence to retired persons, to persons of independent means and to students (provided they are EU nationals) 'insofar as they do not enjoy these rights under other provisions of Community law' and then by provision for the introduction of citizenship rights under Articles 18 et seq (ex 8a–e), introduced by the TEU. The Schengen Agreement signed in 1990 (see further below) already allowed for the free movement of EU citizens between its signatory States. Under the ToA all existing Schengen provisions will be incorporated into the EC Treaty and apply to most Member States.

Despite the wide protection offered to EU citizens and their families there are limits to the protection offered by Community law. First, in order to invoke the non-discrimination principle there must exist a cross-border element. An individual who has never sought to exercise his or her right to freedom of movement will not be able to rely on EC law rights. The matter will be regarded as 'wholly internal' (see, e.g., *R* v *Saunders* (case 175/78); *Ministère Public* v *Gauchard* (case 20/87)). This principle, that EC law has no application to purely internal matters, can operate harshly. In *Morson* v *Netherlands* (cases 35 & 36/82), two mothers from Surinam wished to join their children in The Netherlands. Since they were not entitled to do so under Dutch law they sought to rely on EC law, which permits family members to join EC migrants. In this case the applicants were unsuccessful: since their children had never exercised their right to freedom of movement in the Community there was no factor connecting them with Community law. Equally in *Sloman* (cases C–72 & 73/91) the ECJ held that it was not contrary to Community law to discriminate against migrant workers from third countries (that is, countries outside the EU) in the absence of factors connecting them with Community law. Once a connecting factor has been established, however, migrants will be able to rely on EC rights on returning to their own Member State (*R* v *Immigration Appeal Tribunal, ex parte Secretary of State for the Home Department* (case C–370/90)).

Secondly, at least in the earlier years of the Community, in order to invoke the non-discrimination principle it was necessary for the migrant claimant to be or have been engaged in some form of economic activity in the host State. In *Walrave* v *Association Union Cycliste Internationale* (case 36/74), in the context of a challenge to the cycling association's rules relating to 'pacemaker' cyclists, which were clearly discriminatory, it was held that the prohibition of discrimination on the grounds of nationality contained in former Article 7 EEC (currently Article 12 (ex 6) EC) does not apply to sports teams which have nothing to do with economic activity. The practice of sport is subject to Community law *only insofar as it constitutes an economic activity* within Article 2 of the Treaty. Thus, just as the rights of free movement are only granted to workers and the self-employed and their families (albeit, as will be seen, very liberally interpreted), so, in order to invoke the principle of non-discrimination of Article 12 (ex 6) EC in this context, there must be some economic nexus.

This principle has been considerably eroded over the past 26 years, as the European Economic Community has been transformed into the European Union. In *Gravier* v *City of Liège* (case 293/83) and *Cowan* v *French Treasury* (case 186/87) the Court held that students (*Gravier*) and tourists (*Cowan*), temporarily resident in a Member State as recipients of services, were entitled to invoke the then Article 7 EEC (now 12 EC) in order to claim equality of treatment in respect of certain financial benefits available under national law only to nationals of the host State (see also *Commission* v *Spain* (case C–45/93)). Similarly the Directives extending free movement rights to persons of independent means, to retired persons and to students also appeared to dilute the need for an economic link. Nevertheless, persons claiming under these Directives must be covered by medical insurance and must have sufficient financial resources to avoid becoming a burden on the Member State. This suggests that such persons may not be able to claim publicly-funded welfare benefits on a basis of equality with nationals of the host State. Likewise, although European citizenship is not limited to the economically active, it is 'subject to the limitations and conditions laid down in this Treaty and by the measures adopted to give it effect' (Article 18(1) (ex 8a(1)) EC). A more recent decision of the ECJ now suggests that Union citizens who are not economically active but who enjoy or acquire rights to enter and reside in another Member State may invoke the non-discrimination principle to claim rights currently accorded to that State's nationals or to migrant workers and their families, although the extent to which they may do so remains unclear (*Maria Martinez Sala* v *Freistaat Bayern* (case C–85/96)). Thus important questions regarding the scope of application of the non-discrimination principle remain to be resolved, either by secondary legislation or by the Court. On the Court's past record it is unlikely that it would tolerate discriminatory treatment of EU migrants and their families or deny *settled* immigrants the right of residence when their resources are exhausted.

Principle of non-discrimination   This basic right contained in Articles 39, 43 and 49 (ex 48, 52 and 59) is that migrant workers should not be discriminated against on grounds of nationality. This is reinforced by Article 12 (ex 6) EC (originally 7 EEC) which provides that 'Within the scope of application of this Treaty, and without prejudice to any special provisions contained therein, any discrimination on grounds of nationality shall be prohibited'. This provision has been important in ensuring that the migrant individual and his family, once legally resident in the host Member State, receives parity of treatment with nationals of the host State in respect not only of employment rights but of social rights in general.

The prohibition of discrimination on the grounds of nationality applies to all forms of discrimination, both overt and covert. It will often take the form of a residence or length of residence requirement. In *Sotgiu* v *Deutsche*

Bundespost (case 152/73) the claimant was an Italian national employed by the German post office in Germany. His family lived in Italy. Following the issue of a circular, post office workers separated from their families in Germany were to be paid an increased 'separation' allowance while workers who were living abroad at the time of recruitment would continue to be paid at the same rate. Thus the rule was not overtly discriminatory, since it applied to all workers, regardless of nationality. But clearly its effects could fall more heavily on foreigners. The Court, on a reference from the Bundesarbeits-gericht held that the prohibition of discrimination (expressed here in Article 7(1) of Regulation 1612/68, but equally applicable to Article 12 (ex 6) EC) prohibited all covert forms of discrimination which, by the application of criteria other than nationality nevertheless led to the same result. A residence criterion thus *could* have a discriminatory effect, prohibited by the Treaty and the Regulation. The same reasoning has been applied in the context of the provision of services and establishment (as well as to workers), to professional rules and codes of practices or even professional qualifications. Such rules may be indirectly discriminatory, since by imposing conditions additional to those required in the worker's home State, and which may be more difficult or burdensome for the migrant worker to satisfy, they create obstacles to the free movement of persons in the same way as indistinctly applicable rules applied to goods (see chapter 10). As in the case of goods, such measures may be permitted if they are objectively justified, that is, if they are not disproportionate and pursue legitimate ends. The extent to which these principles applicable to goods can be applied in the context of workers, establishment and services has been raised in a number of cases. (See, for example, the comments of the Advocates-General in *Bosman* (case C–415/93) and *Volker Graf* (case C–190/98). See chapter 20). Certain differences in approach remain, as illustrated by the case of *Alpine Investments* (case C–384/93) (see further chapter 21).

Whether direct or indirect, a difference in treatment may be permitted if it takes into account objective differences in the situation of workers, such as the extent of their qualifications (provided they are not nationality based) or experience. However, it is not always easy to decide whether there are 'objective differences' in the situation of workers, or whether their position is in fact comparable. The question was considered in the case of *Finanzamt Köln-Altstadt* v *Schumacker* (case C–279/93). The case involved a challenge by Schumacker, a Belgian working in Germany but resident in Belgium, to the German tax regime, which he claimed was indirectly discriminatory. The scheme refused certain tax benefits to non-resident workers. The Court held that a regime which denied non-residents benefits accorded to residents would be permissible where the worker earned the bulk of his income (and therefore was taxed) in his State of residence, since that State was in a better position, in assessing his overall tax liability, to take into account the personal and family circumstances of the worker. In this situation the two categories of taxpayer, resident and non-resident, were not comparable. Discrimination can arise 'only through the application of different rules to comparable situations or the application of the same rules to different situations'.

However, where, as in *Schumacker's* case, the worker earned all or at least 90 per cent of his income in another Member State, and the Member State of residence was unable to take into account the taxpayer's personal and family circumstances (because of the absence of income in that State), a tax regime such as the German regime in question would in effect be discriminatory, contrary to EC law. (Further examples of the Court's approach to indirect discrimination and objective justification are provided in chapters 20, 21 and 25.)

All the original EC Treaty provisions and most of the secondary legislation concerning freedom of movement of persons, as well as Article 12 (ex 6) EC itself, have been held to be directly effective. They thus form a fertile source of rights for individuals. Although many of the obligations contained in the secondary legislation will fall on the authorities of Member States, some of them (e.g., Regulation 1612/68) will be vertically and horizontally effective, and all the main Treaty provisions, including Article 12 (ex 6), will be vertically and horizontally effective.

The growing social dimension

In addition to the rights conferred on those seeking to exercise their right to free movement, the Treaty seeks to increase social protection in areas such as employment and education. Where not already included, these goals were explicitly incorporated into the EC Treaty by the TEU (see Article 3(i), (o) and (p)). The purpose of EC *employment* legislation is to harmonise national laws, normally by Directive, in order to provide common standards of protection throughout the Community, in the interest both of the worker and the more effective functioning of the single market. Harmonised standards are intended to create a level playing field, and avoid social dumping. It is thought that disparity between the laws of Member States as regards standards of employment protection will give a competitive advantage to States with lower standards. EC action in the field of *social rights* aims to promote and encourage the well-being of Union citizens, by action in the field of public health, or education, or to benefit the disabled, the deprived ('victims of social exclusion') or the elderly, or victims of disaster. Measures here are designed to stimulate and complement rather than replace national provision, according to the principle of subsidiarity.

Although the TEU re-emphasised the need for increased social protection, both by extending the Community's goals and by introducing a more rounded conception of the individual in the Community, the Member States were by no means in agreement about the extent of the rights to be granted by Community law, particularly in relation to employment legislation. In the field of employment rights 11 of the then 12 Member States (the UK excepted) signed an Agreement on Social Policy in a protocol attached to the Maastricht Treaty, with a view to 'continuing along the path laid down in the 1989 Social Charter'. The agreement had as its objectives: 'the promotion of employment, improved living and working conditions, proper social protection, dialogue between management and labour, the development of human resources with a view to lasting high employment and the combating of exclusion' (Article 1). The signatory States were required to take implementing measures in respect of these policy areas, but this has turned out to be problematic. Difficult questions arose as to where the boundary between the Protocol and the EC Treaty's pre-existing social provisions lay. These difficulties are now, as far as social policy is concerned, at an end. Following the change in UK government, the UK agreed to have the provisions of the Agreement on Social Policy incorporated into the EC Treaty by the ToA, replacing the social chapter provisions currently there, to give a more extensive set of rights to workers. The few measures agreed under the Agreement were extended to the UK in advance of the ratification of the ToA. It is arguable that the removal of the UK's long-standing opposition to the social policy will prove to be a catalyst in enacting secondary legislation to give European citizens some of the social rights they currently lack. However, the new social protection provisions introduced by the ToA (Articles 136–141 EC) are, in keeping with the spirit of the ToA, extremely cautious, and voting will continue to be required to be unanimous in the more sensitive areas (e.g., Article 137(3)). Although Member States which wish to provide more extensive employment protection may do so by means of the new cooperation agreements (see chapter 2), they may be reluctant to impair their competitive position by doing so.

Schengen, Justice and Home Affairs and third-country nationals

The EC Treaty has always envisaged the possibility of a frontier-free Europe. This was re-emphasised by the insertion by the SEA of Article 14 (ex 7a) EC (originally 8a EEC), which provides for 'an area without internal frontiers in which the free movement of goods, persons, services and capital is ensured'. Progress on achieving an internal market in persons, by abolishing the barriers existing at the frontiers of Member States, was slow, partly because of the sensitivity of the area and partly because Member States were not agreed on whether the internal market in persons should include third-country nationals (TCNs) or be limited to EC nationals. The result was that certain Member States concluded an agreement outside the framework of the EC/EU to achieve such an area. Under an agreement signed at Schengen in 1990, five Member States (Germany, France and the Benelux countries, later joined by Italy, Spain, Portugal and Greece) agreed to remove all checks on the movement of people across their borders.

With the changes introduced by the TEU, the Union began to develop, under the Justice and Home Affairs pillar (JHA) of the TEU, the beginnings of a policy as regards TCNs. However, although some decisions were made under JHA, progress in this area was slow. Therefore, the need to reform the JHA was an important issue to be resolved at Amsterdam.

Prior to Amsterdam, the majority of Member States had signed, if not ratified, the Schengen Agreement. The majority thus agreed at the 1996 IGC in effect to incorporate the terms of the Schengen Agreement into the EC Treaty (the UK and Ireland opting out, and the Danish being undecided).

The result was a new Title IV in Part Three of the EC Treaty. When in force, individuals lawfully resident within the EU will be able to travel between Member States which have agreed to Title IV without being stopped at internal borders. Member States are also to develop common immigration and visa policies under these new provisions. (See chapter 23 for further detail.) These changes, especially the ability to move freely between Member States, will benefit third-country nationals as well as EU citizens.

With the advent of the concept of European citizenship and the development of common immigration and asylum policies, as now envisaged under the ToA, there will be further pressure to extend the rights currently granted to EU workers and their families to all persons legitimately resident in the European Union. Although the concept of citizenship under Article 17 (ex 8) EC comprises only limited political rights, it provides for the granting of rights 'to move and reside freely within the territory of the Member States'. These provisions are likely to lead, at least in the long run, to more extensive social rights for EU citizens. It remains to be seen how far TCNs (who are not members of the family of EU nationals) legitimately resident in the Community will be able to claim equality of treatment with EU nationals once a common immigration policy is in place. So far, the emphasis under JHA as regards TCNs seems to have been directed more at keeping them out of the EU, rather than integrating them into the Community and, once admitted, giving them rights such as those enjoyed by EU nationals. TCNs should enjoy rights of free movement throughout the single market and equality of access to, and conditions of, employment. Although the Commission has put forward a number of proposals in this area, obtaining agreement on such measures will take time. At the moment TCNs may only challenge discriminatory measures when they breach provisions of EC law (e.g., *Rush Portuguesa Lda* v *Office National d'Immigration* (case C–113/89), work permit requirement for third-country nationals legitimately employed in the EC incompatible with the then Article 59 EC; see also *Vander Elst* v *Office des Migrations Intenationales* (case C–43/93)), or where they can claim rights under directly effective provisions of international treaties entered into by the Community (e.g., *Sevince* (case C–192/89); *Bahia Kziber* (case C–18/90)) or by the Member State in which they are employed. Otherwise, even where they are legitimately resident, or indeed have been born in the European Union, TCNs cannot claim the same rights of EU citizenship as EU nationals: nor are they entitled to rights granted under EC secondary legislation. The ToA, although it does re-emphasise the importance of human rights and the rule of law (see Articles 6 and 7 TEU) and introduce an area of freedom, security and justice (Article 61 EC), does not change this. As Weiler comments:

It would be ironic that an ethos which rejected the nationalism of the Member States gave birth to a new European nation and European nationalism. . . . We have made little progress if the Us becomes European (instead of German or French or British) and the Them becomes those outside the Community or those inside who do not enjoy the privileges of citizenship.

The above represents a broad outline of Community social policy. Due to limits of time and space the focus of this book is on the law relating to the free movement of persons, employed and self-employed, and sex discrimination, which is included because it is already highly developed and has had a significant impact on UK employment law. Regrettably, much EC social law must remain outside the scope of this book.

Further reading

'Are European Values Being Hoovered Away?' (editorial comment) (1993) 30 CML Rev 445.

Closa, C., 'The Concept of Citizenship in the Treaty on European Union' (1992) 29 CML Rev 1137.

Curtin, D., and Meijers, H., 'The Principle of Open government in Schengen and the European Union: Democratic Retrogression?' (1995) 32 CML Rev 391.

Curtin, D., and O'Keeffe, D. (eds), *Constitutional Adjudication in European Community and National Law* (1992), p. 67.

d'Oliveira, H., 'Expanding External and Shrinking Internal Borders: Europe's Defence Mechanism in the Areas of Free Movement, Immigration and Asylum', in O'Keeffe, D., and Twomey, P. (eds), *Legal Issues of the Maastricht Treaty* (1994, Wiley Chancery Law), p. 261.

d'Olivera, H., 'Nationality and the European Union after Amsterdam' in O'Keeffe, D. and Twomey, P. (eds), *Legal Issues of the Amsterdam Treaty* (1999, Hart Publishing).

Fitzpatrick, B., 'Community Social Law after Maastricht' (1992) 21 ILJ 199.

O'Higgins, T.F., 'The Family and European Law' (1990) 140 NLJ 1643.

O'Keeffe, D., 'The Free Movement of Persons and the Single Market' (1992) 17 EL Rev 3.

O'Keeffe, D., 'Trends in Free Movement of Persons' in O'Reilly, J. (ed.), *Human Rights and Constitutional Law*' (1992), p. 262.

O'Keeffe, D., 'Union Citizenship' in O'Keeffe, D., and Twomey, P. (eds), *Legal Issues of the Maastricht Treaty* (1994, Wiley Chancery Law).

Peers, S., 'Towards Equality: Actual and Potential Rights of Third-country Nationals in the European Union' (1996) 33 CML Rev 7.

Pickup, D., 'Reverse Discrimination and Freedom of Movement for Workers' (1989) 23 CML Rev 135.

Shaw, J., 'Twin-track Social Europe — the Inside Track' in O'Keeffe, D., and Twomey, P. (eds), *Legal Issues of the Maastricht Treaty* (1994, Wiley Chancery Law).

Watson, P., 'The Community Social Charter' (1991) 28 CML Rev 37.

Watson, P., 'Social Policy after Maastricht' (1993) 30 CML Rev 481.

Weiler, J. H. H., 'The Transformation of Europe' (1991) 100 Yale LJ 2403.

For EC social legislation generally see *Directory of Community Legislation in Force*, ch. 05.

TWENTY

Free movement of workers

Fundamental Community rights

The principal Treaty provision governing the free movement of workers is Article 39 (ex 48) EC:

> 1. Freedom of movement for workers shall be secured within the Community by the end of the transitional period at the latest.
> 2. Such freedom of movement shall entail the abolition of any discrimination based on nationality between workers of the Member States as regards employment, remuneration and other conditions of work and employment.
> 3. It shall entail the right, subject to limitations justified on grounds of public policy, public security or public health:
> (a) to accept offers of employment actually made;
> (b) to move freely within the territory of Member States for this purpose;
> (c) to stay in a Member State for the purpose of employment in accordance with the provisions governing the employment of nationals of that State laid down by law, regulation or administrative action;
> (d) to remain in the territory of a Member State after having been employed in that State, subject to conditions which shall be embodied in implementing Regulations to be drawn up by the Commission.
> 4. The provisions of this Article shall not apply to employment in the public service.

As required under Articles 39(3)(d) (ex 43(3)(d)) and 40 (ex 49), secondary legislation was introduced to give further substance to the above principles. The principal measures are:

(a) Directive 68/360, governing rights of entry and residence.

(b)   Regulation 1612/68, governing access to, and conditions of, employment.

(c)   Regulation 1251/70, governing rights to remain in the territory of a Member State after having been employed there.

(d)   Directive 64/221, governing Member States' right to derogate from the free movement provisions on the grounds of public policy, public security or public health.

These measures, as the Court held in *Procureur du Roi* v *Royer* (case 48/75), merely determine the scope and detailed rules for the exercise of rights conferred directly by the Treaty. Article 39 (ex 48) may thus be relied on by individuals in their national courts. Clearly, an individual may enforce the rights contained in Article 39 against public bodies. Further, as the ECJ, drawing on its previous case law (*Walrave* (case 36/74), see chapter 21 and *Bosman* (case C–415/93) discussed further below), recently stated in its judgment in *Angonese* v *Cassa di Risparmio di Bolzano SpA* (case C–281/98), 'limiting application of the prohibition of discrimination based on nationality to acts of a public authority risks creating inequality in its application' (para. 33). Therefore the prohibition on discrimination set out in Article 39 applies to private persons as well as to public bodies (para. 36).

Personal scope

The rights granted under Article 39 (ex 48) and the secondary legislation implementing it are granted to workers and their families. The fact of employment provides the requisite economic nexus to bring these provisions into play. The families' rights derive from their relationship with the worker.

Workers   As the ECJ held in *Levin* v *Staatssecretaris van Justitie* (case 53/81), the concept of 'worker' is a Community concept, not dependent for its meaning on the laws of Member States. In *Lawrie-Blum* v *Land Baden-Württemberg* (case 66/85), the ECJ suggested that the 'essential characteristic' of a worker is that during a certain period of time he performs services for and under the direction of another in return for remuneration. He or she must be a national of one of the Member States. Nationality is determined according to the domestic law of the Member State concerned. Where a state has acceded to the EC but is still subject to transitional arrangements, a national of that State may claim rights as a 'favoured EC national' only insofar as that status ensues from the transitional provisions, unless he has been lawfully employed in the territory of one of the old Member States (*Lopes da Veiga* (case 9/88)).

The term 'worker' has been generously construed. In *Hoekstra* v *BBDA* (case 75/63) the Court held that it extended not merely to the present worker, but to one who, having lost his job, is capable of taking another. As will be seen, Directive 68/360 expressly provides that a worker's right of residence cannot be withdrawn merely because he is temporarily incapable of work, either as a result of illness or accident or involuntary unemployment (Article 7(1)).

In *Levin* (case 53/81) the ECJ held, in response to a request for a preliminary ruling from the Dutch Raad van State, that the term 'worker' applied even to those who worked to a limited extent (i.e., part-time), provided that the work was 'real' work, and not nominal or minimal. The rights only attach to those who perform or wish to perform an activity of an economic nature. The Court went on to say that this principle applied whether the worker was self-supporting or whether he wished to make do with less than the national minimum income. Thus it was able to side-step the problem of the part-time worker who relies on public funds for his support.

This issue was squarely faced in *Kempf* v *Staatssecretaris van Justitie* (case 139/85). Kempf was a German, a part-time music teacher working in The Netherlands from 1981 to 1982. During this time he was in receipt of Dutch supplementary benefit, both sickness benefit and general assistance. In November 1981 he applied for a Dutch residence permit. He was refused on the grounds that he was not a 'favoured EC citizen', since his income from his work was not sufficient to meet his needs. He challenged that decision before the Dutch courts. The Raad van State referred to the ECJ the question whether a part-time worker such as Kempf, whose income was below subsistence level and who did not have sufficient means of support, was a 'worker' entitled to benefit under Community law. The Court replied that he was. Freedom of movement of workers was, it held, one of the fundamental freedoms and must, as such, be defined broadly; a person who pursued a genuine and effective activity as an employed person, even on a part-time basis, could not be excluded from the scope of Community rules merely because he sought to supplement his income, which was lower than the means of subsistence, by other lawful means of subsistence. It was irrelevant whether the income was supplemented out of a private income or from public funds.

The boldness of this judgment will be more apparent when the full extent of the rights flowing from the status of 'worker' or 'favoured Community citizen' is appreciated. The Court has, however, held that the duration of the activity concerned was a factor which might be taken into account in assessing whether the employment was effective and genuine or so limited as to be marginal or ancillary (*Raulin* (case C–357/89)).

Following *Kempf,* in *Steymann* v *Staatssecretaris van Justitie* (case 196/87) the Court held that the claimant's occupation as part of a religious community, entitling him to his 'keep' and pocket money, but not to formal wages, constituted a genuine and effective activity where commercial activity is an inherent part of membership of that community. By contrast, in *Bettray* v *Staatssecretaris van Justitie* (case 344/87) paid activity provided by the State as part of a drug rehabilitation programme under its social employment law was held by the Court not to represent 'real and genuine economic activity'. Thus, in order to give rise to the status of 'worker', the work performed must fulfil, or derive from, some *economic* purpose. It has been suggested, however, that the principle of *Bettray* does not apply to 'ordinary' sheltered employment. The undertaking in *Bettray* existed solely for the purpose of rehabilitation and re-education of the persons employed therein.

Families   Families are defined in Regulation 1612/68 (Article 10(1)) as a worker's 'spouse and their descendants who are under the age of 21 years or are dependants', and 'dependent relatives in the ascending line of the worker and his spouse'.

(a)   *'Spouse'.*   In *Netherlands* v *Reed* (case 59/85) the ECJ, on a reference from the Dutch Supreme Court, was asked whether the term 'spouse' included a cohabitee. The case concerned Ms Reed's right to reside in Holland with her English cohabitee of five years' standing, who was working in Holland. Ms Reed, who was also English, was not herself a worker. The Court held that in the present state of Community law the term spouse referred to marital relationships only. However, this did not mean that Ms Reed was not entitled to remain in Holland. Since her cohabitee was a worker in Holland, and since aliens with stable relationships with *Dutch* nationals were entitled in similar circumstances to reside in Holland, it would be discriminatory, in breach of what is now Article 12 (ex 6) EC and 39 (ex 48) (also Article 7(2) of Regulation 1612/68), not to accord him the same treatment as national workers. Thus Ms Reed was not entitled to remain as a 'spouse' but she was entitled to remain on account of her cohabitee's rights under EC law.

Another question which arises, and has yet to be decided by the ECJ, is whether a divorced spouse is entitled to claim rights as a 'spouse' under EC law. In *Diatta* v *Land Berlin* (case 267/83) the Court held that a separated spouse (in this case a Senegalese national), who intended to obtain a divorce and who was living apart from her husband, a worker in Germany, did not lose her rights of residence in Germany merely because she did not live under the same roof as her husband. The marital relationship is not dissolved, the Court held, when spouses live separately. Since the matter came before the Court on a reference for interpretation under the then Article 177 (now 234), it was not necessary for the Court to decide on the effect of divorce on a spouse's rights.

In *R* v *Secretary of State for the Home Department, ex parte Sandhu* [1982] 2 CMLR 553 Comyn J in the English High Court took the view that separation and divorce did not automatically put an end to non-EC spouse's rights. In this case Sandhu, an Indian, had married a German lady and settled with her in England, where they produced a son. He obtained a steady job. Subsequently the marriage broke down, and his wife returned to Germany with their son. In 1976 he went to visit them in Germany. When he returned to England he was informed that he was no longer entitled to remain in England. His rights had come to an end on the departure from England of his wife. He appealed against the decision.

In a remarkable judgment, very close to the ECJ in its approach and reasoning, Comyn J pointed out that if an EC worker could remove the 'cloak of protection' from a non-EC spouse by deserting or divorcing him, or by leaving the country, 'this would add a new terror to marriage'. Arguing from the purpose of EC provisions of freedom of movement for workers, and from Regulation 1251/70, by analogy with the family's right to remain after the death of the worker (see below) and taking into account Sandhu's steady job, his son in Europe, and his duties of maintenance towards him, Comyn J concluded that he was entitled to remain. Unfortunately for Mr Sandhu neither the Court of Appeal ([1983] 3 CMLR 131) nor the House of Lords (*The Times*, 10 May 1985) agreed. On a literal interpretation of the relevant EC legislation and following an earlier Immigration Appeal Tribunal case (*Grewal* v *Secretary of State for the Home Department* [1979-80] Imm AR 119), the Court of Appeal concluded that Sandhu's right of residence ceased when his wife returned to Germany. The court refrained from considering the effect of separation or divorce in a case where the EC worker remains in the same country as his spouse (or ex-spouse). The House of Lords agreed with the Court of Appeal and refused to seek an interpretation on the matter from the ECJ. Their Lordships considered that the matter had already been covered, to Sandhu's detriment, by *Diatta* (case 267/83).

Yet, as has been demonstrated, the questions considered by the ECJ in *Diatta* were quite different, and were resolved in the separated spouse's favour. Were the Court to be faced with the problem in *Sandhu*, its conclusions, it is submitted, would be closer to Comyn J's than those of the Court of Appeal or House of Lords. The policy reasons in favour of giving some security of residence to divorced or abandoned spouses of a bona fide marriage, especially when there may be children of the marriage who will still remain members of the worker's family surely require that the law be construed to ensure that a spouse's EC rights do not necessarily cease on divorce or when the worker leaves the country.

The problem is particularly acute where the spouse is not a national of a Member State, as in *Sandhu* and *Diatta*. A spouse who has EC nationality can always become a worker in her own right, and, after *Kempf* (case 139/85), even for a spouse with family responsibilities this should not prove too daunting a prospect.

A situation not unlike that of Mr Sandhu arose in the case of *R* v *Immigration Appeal Tribunal, ex parte Secretary of State for Home Department* (case C–370/90). Mr Singh was an Indian who had married an English national in 1982. He and his wife subsequently went to work in Germany, returning in 1985 to open a business in the UK. Their marriage broke down in 1988. Following the issue of a decree nisi but before the decree became absolute, the UK authorities sought to deport Mr Singh. His appeal against the deportation order was successful before the Immigration Appeal Tribunal. In an action for judicial review of that decision by the Secretary of State certain questions were referred to the ECJ. Unfortunately the questions concerned Mr Singh's right, under EC law, to enter and reside in the UK when he and his wife returned from Germany. The Secretary of State claimed that since Mr Singh's wife returned not as an EC migrant, but pursuant to her rights as a British citizen, Mr Singh could not claim the benefit of his rights as a spouse under EC law. The question of the effect of the subsequent divorce was not an issue before the Court (although the fact of divorce was known), since the parties were not divorced at the relevant time. The ECJ held that as the spouse of an EC national who had exercised her rights to work in Germany he was entitled on their return to claim his rights as a spouse under EC law. It is perhaps of some significance that the Court, in finding in favour of Mr Singh, refrained from considering the effect of his divorce; also, as Advocate-General Grévisse pointed out, there was no evidence before the Court that the marriage had not been genuine. This could indicate that a generous view might be taken of the rights of a divorced spouse, *a fortiori* one who was not an EC national, provided that the marriage was genuine. Despite this ruling and the time that has passed since the *Sandhu* ruling, it has to be noted that the English Court of Appeal still interprets the rights of the divorced spouse restrictively. In *Secretary of State for Social Security* v *Remilien* [1996] All ER (EC) 850 two EC nationals, divorced from UK nationals but still living in the UK with their children, were held, after their entitlement to income support expired, no longer to be entitled to live in the UK. It is unfortunate that the case was decided on English law points without being referred to the ECJ for a ruling on the extent of these individuals' EC law rights.

(b) *Dependants and descendants*   Similar problems as arose in *Sandhu* could arise for a spouse's dependent relatives. If they, like the spouse, are not EC nationals, they too risk losing their status as 'favoured Community citizens' on the separation or divorce of their relative.

For the children of the marriage, or the worker's dependent relatives, problems should not arise. Even after divorce they will remain members of the worker's family.

Although families are expressed in terms of 'descendants' it would be in keeping with the ECJ's approach to take a broad view of the rights of children of the family. It would not be likely to deny favoured EC citizen status to children who had been treated as children of the family even though they were not, strictly speaking, descendants.

A family member threatened with loss of EC rights in a case such as *Sandhu's* could invoke the principle of respect for the right to family life expressed in Article 8 of the European Convention of Human Rights, which in the context of the application of Community law must be respected by the authorities of Member States (see *Commission* v *Germany* (case 249/86) and chapter 6). Unfortunately, this issue was not considered in the *Remilien* case.

It may be, however, that in future the position of TCNs whose relationship with an EC national has terminated will be dealt with by secondary legislation. The Commission has proposed an amendment to Regulation 1612/68 to this effect (COM (1998) 394 final), but it has not yet been agreed by the Council and the European Parliament.

Material scope

Rights of entry and residence (Directive 68/360)   These rights are regulated by Directive 68/360: they comprise, for the worker and his family (as defined above: Regulation 1612/68, Article 10(1)(a)), the right:

(a) To leave their home State in order for the worker to pursue activities as an employed person in another member State (Directive 68/360, Article 2).

(b) To enter the territory of another Member State 'simply on production of a valid identity card or passport' (Article 3(1)). Entry visas (or their equivalent) may not be demanded except for members of the family who are not nationals of a Member State. Member States are required to accord to such persons every facility for obtaining the necessary visas (Article 3(2)).

(c) To obtain a residence permit, on production of, for the worker:

(i)   the document with which he entered the territory, and
(ii) a confirmation of engagement from the employer or a certificate of employment (Article 4(3)(a) and (b));

and, for members of the family:

(i)   their documents of entry,
(ii) a document proving their relationship with the worker, to be issued by the competent authority of the State of origin or the State whence they came and, if they are dependent on the worker,
(iii) a document issued by the same authorities testifying that they are dependent on the worker or that they live under his roof in that country (Article 4(3)(c), (d) and (e)).

The residence permit must be valid throughout the territory of the Member State which issued it; it must be valid for at least five years from the date of issue; and it must be automatically renewable (Article 6(1)). This may be described as the right to 'settled' or 'lawful' residence.

Breaks in residence not exceeding six consecutive months and absence on military service shall not affect the validity of a residence permit (Article 6(2)).

A valid residence permit may not be withdrawn from a worker solely on the grounds that he is no longer in employment, either because he is temporarily incapable of work as a result of illness or accident, or because he is involuntarily unemployed (Article 7(1)). When the residence permit is renewed for the first time the period of residence may be restricted (but not to less than 12 months) if the worker has been involuntarily unemployed for more than 12 consecutive months (Article 7(2)).

Temporary workers (working from three to 12 months) are entitled to a temporary residence permit for the duration of their employment (Article 6(3)). Seasonal workers and those working for less than three months are entitled to reside during the period of their employment without a residence permit (Article 8).

These provisions are generous, and have been even more generously interpreted by ECJ. In *Procureur du Roi* v *Royer* (case 48/75) the Court held that the right of entry granted by Article 3 included the right to enter *in search of work*. The Court did not suggest the length of time appropriate to such a search, but it had been thought that a period of three months would be allowed, since EC legislation on social security (Regulation 1408/71, Article 69) allows for the payment of unemployment benefit for up to three months in another Member State while the claimant is looking for work. In *R v Immigration Appeal Tribunal, ex parte Antonissen* (case C–292/89), the ECJ was asked to rule on the legality of English immigration rules which permit the deportation of migrants after six months if they have failed to find employment. The Court held that there was 'no necessary link' between the right to unemployment benefit under Regulation 1408/71 and the right to stay in a Member State for the purpose of seeking work. A Member State could, however, deport an EC migrant if he had not found employment after six months unless he provided evidence that he was continuing to seek employment and that he has a genuine chance of being engaged. Significantly the Court chose not to impose a specific time-limit. More recently, it was held that Belgian legislation which, in effect, excluded those seeking work after three months was in contravention of Community law (*Commission v Belgium* (case C–344/95)). Thus, it seems that, at the least, those genuinely seeking work are entitled to stay in the host Member State for longer than three months.

If the right to enter a Member State in search of work is available to all EC citizens, the right to a residence permit is, it seems, conditional on the finding of employment. However, once in employment, the Court has held (*Royer*) that a worker's right to reside in the State where he is employed is not dependent on his possession of a residence permit. The right of residence is a fundamental right, derived from the Treaty itself (Article 39 (ex 48) EC) and not from implementing legislation nor from documents issued by national authorities. Thus neither a worker nor his family can be denied entry to, or be deported from, a Member State merely because they do not possess a valid residence permit (see also *R v Pieck* (case 157/79)). As long as the worker has a right of residence as a worker, he will be entitled to reside as long as he would have been entitled had he been in possession of a residence permit, i.e., in normal circumstances, five years plus a minimum of one further year. And as long as he is entitled to stay, his family will also be entitled to stay.

A Member State is, however, entitled to demand that migrant workers and their families comply with its administrative formalities on immigration, and can even impose penalties in the form of fines for non-compliance, provided that the penalties are not disproportionate. In *Messner* (case C–265/88) a time-limit of three days from crossing the frontier in which aliens were required to register their presence with the Italian police, sanctioned by criminal penalties, was found to be unreasonable. A failure to comply with such formalities can never be a ground for deportation (see also *Watson* (case 118/75); *Commission v Belgium* (case 321/87)).

Although Directive 68/360, Article 7(1), specifically provides that a valid residence permit cannot be withdrawn if the worker becomes incapable of work through illness or accident or involuntary unemployment, Article 7(1) implies that that right will be lost if he is *voluntarily* unemployed. The question of whether unemployment is voluntary or involuntary may be confirmed by the 'competent employment office' (Article 7(1)).

This distinction between voluntary and involuntary unemployment was described as 'critical' by the Immigration Appeal Tribunal in *Giangregorio* v *Secretary of State for the Home Department* [1983] 3 CMLR 472. It was suggested in that case that whilst the Secretary of State might rely on evidence as to whether the unemployment was voluntary or involuntary, a worker seeking to establish that his unemployment was involuntary must himself prove it to be so. However, an unemployed worker, even if involuntarily unemployed, must have attained the status of EC worker in the host State before becoming unemployed in order to qualify for residence under Directive 68/360. In *Tsiotras* (case C–171/91) an unemployed Greek who had worked in Germany prior to Greece's accession to the EC, but who was unemployed at the time of accession and subsequently, and had no reasonable prospect of obtaining employment in Germany, was held by the ECJ not to have acquired a right to reside in Germany.

Since the rights of the family are 'parasitic', in that they depend on their relationship with the worker, their rights of residence will be coterminous with his, unless the family members are EC citizens who qualify in their own right as workers, or have acquired the right to remain as his survivors under Regulation 1251/70.

All the above rights may be denied to a worker, whether temporary or long-term, and to a member of his family, on the grounds of public policy, public security and public health (Article 10; see chapter 22).

The question of whether a worker or a member of his family is entitled to 'settled' residence in a Member State is of fundamental importance because, as will be seen, their right to equal treatment in the host State, and all that that involves, has been held to flow not so much from the claimant's status as a worker, although it originates there, as from the worker's, and his family's, 'lawful residence' in a Member State.

Access to employment; equality of treatment (Regulation 1612/68) Regulation 1612/68 was passed to implement the then Articles 48(2) and 48(3)(a) and (b) (now 39(2) and 39(3)(a) and (b)) of the EC Treaty. As stated in the preamble to Regulation 1612/68, the attainment of the objective of freedom of movement for workers requires, in addition to rights of entry and residence, 'the abolition of any discrimination based on nationality between workers of the Member States as regards employment, remuneration and other conditions of work and employment' (first recital). It also requires, in order that the right of freedom of movement may be exercised 'in freedom and dignity', equality of treatment in 'all matters relating to the actual pursuit of activities as employed persons' and that 'obstacles to the mobility of workers shall be eliminated, in particular as regards the worker's right to be joined by his family and the conditions for the integration of that family into the host country' (fifth recital). The ECJ has drawn heavily on this preamble in interpreting this Regulation and other measures in this field.

Regulation 1612/68 is divided into several parts. Part I, which is of principal concern here, is entitled 'Employment and workers' families'. Title I, 'Eligibility for employment' covers a worker's rights of access to employment; Title II, 'Employment and equality of treatment', covers his right to equality of treatment not only in all matters relating to employment, but also to 'social advantages', including matters of housing. Title III, 'Workers' families' deals with families' rights. The remaining parts of the Regulation provide for the setting up of machinery and institutions for the clearance and coordination of vacancies and applications for employment.

Eligibility for employment (Articles 1-6) Any national of a Member State has the right to take up activity as an employed person, and pursue such activity, in the territory of another Member State under the same conditions as nationals of that state (Article 1).

A Member State may not discriminate, overtly or covertly, against non-nationals, by limiting applications and offers of employment (Article 3(1)), or by prescribing special recruitment procedures or limiting advertising or in any other way impeding recruitment of non-resident workers (Article 3(2)). Member States must not restrict by number or percentage the number of foreign nationals to be employed in any activity or area of activity (Article 4; see *Commission* v *France (Re French Merchant Seamen)* (case 167/73) — ratio of three French to one non-French imposed under Code du Travail Maritime 1926 on crew of French merchant ships held in breach of EC law).

Member States must offer non-national applicants the same assistance in seeking employment as are available to nationals (Article 5).

States are, however, entitled to permit the imposition on non-nationals of conditions 'relating to linguistic knowledge required by reason of the nature of the post to be filled' (Article 3(1)). In *Groener* v *Minister for Education* (case 379/87) the ECJ held that a requirement of Irish law that teachers in vocational schools in Ireland should be proficient in the Irish language would be permissible under Article 3(1) in view of the clear policy of national law to maintain and promote the use of the Irish language as a means of expressing national identity and culture. The Irish language was the national language and the first official language of Ireland. Such a requirement must not, however, be disproportionate to the objectives pursued. A similar approach to the non-discrimination Treaty provision of the then Article 48(2) (now 39(2)) was taken, albeit with a different result, in *Spotti* v *Freistaat Bayern* (case C–272/92), in the context of a challenge to a German law permitting contracts of limited duration for foreign language teaching assistants. The Court held that such contracts, prima facie in breach of former Article 48(2), would only be permitted if they were objectively justified. Since the principal justification for the rules was that they ensured up-to-date tuition it is not surprising that the Court found them not to be justified (see also *Alluè* v *Università degli Studi di Venezia* (cases C–259, 331 & 332/91); *Commission* v *Luxembourg* (case C–111/91)). The burden of proving justification for discriminatory rules will always be heavy: the rules must be designed to achieve legitimate ends, and must be both appropriate and necessary to achieve those ends.

In all these cases, treated by the Court as examples of covert or concealed discrimination, the Court appears to be moving towards a test similar to the

Bilka Kaufhaus test as applied to cases of indirect sex discrimination (see chapter 25) and the first *Cassis* principle applied to indistinctly applicable measures affecting goods (see chapter 10). A similar trend will be seen in the context of the rules relating to services and establishment (see chapter 21). This approach as regards workers was clarified in the *Bosman* case (case C–415/93), which raised the question of whether former Article 48 (now 39) would apply to rules which were not overtly discriminatory but which still had an adverse impact on individuals' ability to exercise their free movement rights. The case centred on Belgian football transfer rules, which accorded with international football rules. These rules provided that a club which sought to engage a player must pay a specified, sometimes considerable sum to the player's existing club. The rules applied irrespective of the nationality of the player and whether the player was going to be playing for a Belgian team or not. Further, there were limits on how many non-nationals a club could employ. In Bosman's case, he was signed up to play for a Belgian team and the rules effectively stopped him from moving to play for a French team. After a lengthy legal dispute, the matter was referred to the ECJ. Bosman argued that the rules were, *inter alia*, contrary to the then Article 48 (now 39). The ECJ held that, although the rules were not discriminatory, they still 'directly affect[ed] players' access to the employment market in other Member States and are thus capable of impeding freedom of movement of workers'. In principle, therefore, the rules were incompatible with the then Article 48 (now 39) unless they pursued a legitimate aim compatible with the Treaty, were justified by pressing reasons of public interest and were proportionate. In *Bosman*, therefore, the ECJ was not concerned with discrimination but with the question of whether cross-border access to the job market of each Member State was safeguarded. In this approach we clearly see parallels to that taken by the ECJ in relation to the free movement of goods and 'indistinctly applicable' measures.

The *Bosman* ruling, like the *Dassonville* and *Cassis de Dijon* judgments as regards free movement of goods, potentially could affect many national rules. The ECJ took the opportunity to refine the scope of *Bosman*, and consequently the scope of Article 39 (ex 48) as regards non-discriminatory rules which nonetheless might affect the functioning of the internal market, in *Volker Graf* v *Filzmoser Maschinenbau* (case C–190/98). The rules challenged in this case concerned Austrian employment legislation which required employers to make certain payments to employees on the termination of an employment contract, when the employee was not leaving the job voluntarily. Graf handed in his notice to go to work in Germany. He claimed the payments, but Filzmoser Maschinenbau refused to make the payments as Graf was leaving voluntarily. He argued that the rules which excluded him from receiving the payments were likely adversely to affect those who sought to move from Austria to another Member State more than those who were leaving employment but staying in Austria. Arguing from the ECJ's approach in *Bosman*, Graf claimed that the Austrian rules were incompatible with what is now Article 39 EC. The question as to whether this was incompatible with the requirements of the free movement of workers was referred. The ECJ confirmed that Article 39 (ex 48) not only applies to discriminatory rules but also to rules which, although they are expressed to apply without distinction, impede the exercise of free movement rights. It went on to say, however, that for such rules to constitute an obstacle prohibited under Article 39 (ex 48), the provisions 'must affect access of the workers to the labour market'. In this case, the entitlement was only contingent on certain events happening — basically the unfair dismissal of an employee — and therefore any effect on the internal market of this sort of rule was too uncertain and indirect to fall within the prohibition. Thus, although the ECJ's test of measures affecting access to the host market would seem on the face of it to be very broad, the latter part of the judgment clearly focuses on the need for an obstacle to accessing that market to exist. A similar approach can be seen, as regards goods, in *Dip Spa* (cases C–140–2/94) (discussed in chapter 10).

An employer may require a non-national to undergo a vocational test provided he expressly requests this when making his offer of employment (Article 6(2)). These provisions may not however be used as a means of covert discrimination.

Employment and equality of treatment (Articles 7-9)   These rights are expressly granted to workers. However, as will be seen, some of these rights have now been extended to benefit the families of workers.

(a)   *Conditions of work.* Article 7(1) provides that:

A worker who is a national of a Member State may not, in the territory of another Member State, be treated differently from national workers by reason of his nationality in respect of any conditions of employment and work, in particular as regards remuneration, dismissal, and should he become unemployed, reinstatement or re-employment.

This Article covers all forms of discrimination, direct and indirect. In *Ugliola* (case 15/69) a condition whereby a German employer took into account, for the purposes of calculating seniority, employees' periods of national service *in Germany,* thereby prejudicing an employee such as Ugliola, who was required to perform his national service in Italy, was held unlawful under this Article. Similarly in *Sotgiu* v *Deutsche Bundespost* (case 152/73) the German post office's decision to pay increased separation allowances only to workers living away from home in Germany, was held to be *capable* of breaching Article 7(1) (see chapter 19). More recently, in *Schöning-Kougebetopoulou* v *Freie und Hansestadt Hamburg* (case C–15/96), the ECJ held that a collective wage agreement which provided for promotion on grounds of seniority after eight years' employment in any given group, excluding periods of comparable employment in the public service of another Member State, was contrary to the Treaty. The terms of the agreement manifestly worked to the disadvantage of migrant workers as they are less likely, or it is harder for them, to satisfy the eight-year rule.

(b)   *Social and tax advantages.* Article 7(2) packs perhaps the largest punch of all EC secondary legislation in this area. It entitles the migrant worker to 'the same social and tax advantages as national workers'. The term 'social advantages' has been interpreted in the widest sense.

(i) *Social advantages.* In *Fiorini* v *SNCF* (case 32/75) the Court was faced with a claim by an Italian lady living in France, the widow of an Italian who had worked in France, for a special fare reduction card issued by the French railways to parents of large families. Her husband had claimed it while he was alive. She had been refused the card on the grounds that she was not of French nationality. She claimed discrimination in breach of Article 7 of the EEC Treaty (now Article 12 (ex 6) EC) and Article 7(2) of Regulation 1612/68. The French tribunal took the view that Article 7(2) was not applicable, since it was concerned only with advantages granted to citizens within the ambit of work or by virtue of work as employed persons. On a reference by the Paris Cour d'Appel the ECJ took a different view. It held that, although certain provisions of Article 7(1) refer to relationships deriving from the contract of employment, there are others which have nothing to do with such relationships. Article 7(2) covers all social and tax advantages, whether or not attached to contracts of employment. Moreover, these rights continue even if the advantages are sought after the worker's death to benefit the family remaining. Since the family had a right under Community law (Regulation 1251/70) to remain in France, they were entitled under Article 7(2) to equal 'social advantages'.

Subsequently, in *Even* (case 207/78), the Court held, following *Fiorini,* that the social advantages covered by Article 7(2) were 'those which, whether or not linked to a contract of employment, are generally granted to national workers primarily because of their objective status as workers *or by virtue of the mere fact of their residence on national territory*' (emphasis added). This formula, the *'Even'* formula, has since been applied in a number of cases in the context of claims by both workers and the members of their families to a wide range of social benefits.

In *Reina* v *Landeskreditbank Baden-Württemberg* (case 65/81) an Italian couple living in Germany, the husband being a worker in Germany, invoked Article 7(2) to claim a special childbirth loan, State-financed, from the defendant bank. The loan was payable under German law only to German nationals living in Germany. The bank argued that the loan was not a 'social advantage' within Article 7(2), since the loan was granted not as a social right, but rather in the field of political rights, for demographic purposes, i.e., to increase the birth rate in Germany. Granting of the loan was, moreover, discretionary. It argued also that the difference in treatment was justified on account of the practical difficulties of recovering loans from workers who return to their own countries. Despite these persuasive arguments the ECJ found, on a reference from the Stuttgart Verwaltungsgericht, that since the loan was granted by reason of the claimant's objective status as a worker or by virtue of the mere fact of residence it was a 'social advantage' within Article 7(2). Social advantages covered not only benefits granted as of right but also those granted on a discretionary basis.

In *Castelli* v *ONPTS* (case 261/83), on similar reasoning, an Italian mother, who, on being widowed, went to live with her son in Belgium (the son having been a worker and retired there), was held entitled to claim a guaranteed income (not a social security benefit) paid to all old people in Belgium. Since she had a right under Article 10 of Regulation 1612/68 to install herself with her son, she was entitled to the same social and tax advantages as Belgian workers and ex-workers. The Court again applied the *Even* formula; the old-age benefit was one granted to national workers primarily because of their objective status as workers or by virtue of their residence of national territory.

The same reasoning was applied in *Hoeckx* (case 249/83), and *Scrivner* (case 122/84), to claims in Belgium for a minimum income allowance, the 'minimex', by a member of the family of a worker and an unemployed worker respectively. (See also *Frascogna* (case 256/86); *Deak* (case 94/84), 'tiding over' allowance paid to young job-seekers a 'social advantage'; *Schmid* (case 310/91), allowance for handicapped child of a retired worker; *Commission* v *Luxembourg* (case 111/91), childbirth allowance.) Similarly in *Matteucci* v *Communauté Française de Belgique* (case 235/87) a scholarship to study abroad arising under a reciprocal arrangement between Belgium and Germany was held to constitute a social advantage to which the child of an Italian, established as a worker in Belgium, was entitled. (See also *Meeusen* (case C–337/97).)

The benefit claimed must however constitute a social advantage for the State's own nationals. In *Belgium* v *Taghavi* (case C–243/91) the Iranian wife of an Italian national residing as a worker in Belgium was held not entitled to a benefit for handicapped persons, described as a 'personal' right and not a social security benefit, on the grounds that the benefit was not available to spouses of *Belgian* nationals who were not themselves EC nationals.

Thus the right to the same social advantages as nationals of the host State has come to depend not so much on the claimant's status as a worker or even as a member of the family of a worker, but on his lawful residence in that State. Hence the crucial importance, stressed in the context of Directive 68/360 (see above), of the initial enquiry as to whether the claimant is entitled under Directive 68/360, or Regulation 1251/70 (see below) or under the parallel provision for the self-employed (see chapter 21) to reside there.

However, the right to equal social advantages cannot be claimed by all EC nationals and their families who are lawfully resident in the host State. An important limitation was placed on Article 7(2) in *Centre Public d'Aide Sociale de Courcelles* v *Lebon* (case 316/85), in the context of a claim by a French national, Ms Lebon, for the Belgian minimex. She was living in Belgium and her claim was based, *inter alia*, on the fact that she was looking for work in Belgium. The ECJ held, in answer to one of several questions referred, that the right to equality of treatment in the field of social and tax advantages granted by Article 7(2) enured for the benefit only of workers and not for nationals of Member States who migrate in search of employment.

Thus in *Lebon*, for the first time, the Court drew a distinction between those who are lawfully entitled to 'settled' residence as a result of obtaining employment, and those who are permitted temporary rights of residence in order to search for work. Only the former will be entitled to equality of treatment in respect of all social advantages. Likewise, EC nationals (and their families) who move within the Community in order to receive services will not be entitled to full equality of treatment as regards social benefits provided by the host State. On the other hand, EC nationals claiming rights of establishment, who are also entitled to 'settled residence' of at least five years, should be able to claim equal social advantages under Article 12 (ex 6) EC by analogy with Article 7(2) of Regulation 1612/68 (see chapter 21 and Directive 73/148).

A second important limitation was placed on Article 7(2) in the cases of *Brown* (case 197/86) and *Lair* (case 39/86). These will be discussed shortly.

In this area, as with discrimination in other areas, indirect discrimination may be permitted as 'objectively justified' if the legislation pursues a legitimate end and the measure is no more than is necessary to achieve that end. (For an example of the ECJ's reasoning see *O'Flynn* v *Adjudication Officer* (case C–237/94).)

(ii)   *Tax advantages*   Although migrant workers are entitled under Article 7(2) of Regulation 1612/68 to the same tax advantages as nationals of the host State, this is an area where a measure such as a residence requirement, which is covertly discretionary, may be objectively justified, or where the situations of the national worker and the migrant worker will not be regarded as comparable. Such may be the case, as was conceded in *Schumacker* (case C–279/93) (see chapter 19) where the worker's residence and principal place of work (and therefore of income) is in another Member State, in which the taxing authorities are better able to take into account his personal and family circumstances (see also *Wielockx* v *Inspector der Directe Belstingen* (case C–80/94)). In *Bachmann* v *Belgium* (case C–204/90) the Court found that a Belgian rule, which allowed the deduction from income tax of contributions to health and life insurance policies only if they were paid in Belgium, although indirectly indiscriminatory, was justified as necessary to ensure the coherence of the tax system. Under this system, tax deductions in respect of insurance contributions could be offset by taxes levied from insurers in Belgium. This would not be possible where insurance was effected in another Member State. This case may be contrasted with *Asscher* (case C–107/94), a case involving the right of establishment where differential taxation rates were found to be indirectly discriminatory but unjustified. This case can be seen as an example of the ECJ seeking to limit the circumstances in which a Member State may rely on the coherence of the tax system justification. (See more recently *Verkooijen* (case C–35/98) — rebates for income tax limited to residents — unjustified.) As in other areas involving indirect discrimination, the Court will in each case scrutinise the justification offered and ensure that the measures adopted are not disproportionate.

(c)   *Access to training in vocational schools and retraining centres.* Article 7(3) entitles workers to access, under the same conditions as national workers, to training in vocational schools and retraining centres.

Although Article 7(3) is expressed in terms of access, it seems likely that the ECJ will take a broad view of what is meant by access. In *Casagrande* v *Landeshauptstadt München* (case 9/74) the Court held, in the context of a claim by a child, under Article 12 of Regulation 1612/68, that the right to be *admitted* to the host State's educational, apprenticeship and vocational training courses included not only admission but 'general measures to facilitate attendance', which in Casagrande's case, included a grant. Since grants and loans would now appear to be included in the category of 'social advantages' under Article 7(2) there is perhaps no need for special pleading for their inclusion in Article 7(3). This was the view taken by the Court in *Brown* and *Lair*. In a claim for a university maintenance grant based on Article 7(2) and 7(3), the Court opted for a restrictive interpretation of Article 7(3), holding that the term 'vocational school' applied only to institutions offering sandwich or apprenticeship courses, whilst pointing out that the claim could constitute a 'social advantage' under Article 7(2). Article 7(2) and 7(3) were not mutually exclusive.

This question of equal rights to grants to pursue educational, apprenticeship or vocational training courses had given rise to particular anxiety in Member States. Although the rights are only available to migrant workers and their families who are legitimately resident in the host Member State, it seemed that all that might be necessary to obtain 'legitimate residence' was initially to secure a job: following *Levin* (case 53/81) and *Kempf* (case 139/85), it need not be full-time, as long as it was a real job. If the worker then lost his job, or gave it up, was he then to be entitled to equal access to any course, and any grant of his choice, either because it constituted 'vocational training' within Article 7(3) or a 'social advantage' under Article 7(2)? If this were the case, would not Member States, particularly those which were generous in their social provision, be vulnerable to exploitation?

There existed no authoritative ruling from the ECJ on this important question until the matter was raised in *Brown* (case 197/86) and *Lair* (case 39/86). In both these cases the parties, having obtained a place at university, Brown at Cambridge, to study engineering, and Ms Lair at the University of Hanover, to study languages, were claiming maintenance grants from the UK and German authorities respectively. Although Brown had dual French/English nationality, he and his family had for many years been domiciled in France; Lair was a Frenchwoman. Prior to taking up his place at Cambridge, Brown had obtained university sponsorship from, and worked for, Ferranti in Scotland. The job was clearly intended as a preparation for his university studies, and had lasted for eight months. Lair had worked intermittently in Germany for over five years, with spells of involuntary unemployment. Both parties were refused a grant and sought to challenge that refusal on the basis of, *inter alia*, Regulation 1612/68, Articles 7(2) and 7(3) (their claim based on the original Article 7 of the EEC Treaty (now Article 12 (ex 6) EC) and 'vocational training' will be discussed in chapter 21, in the context of *Gravier* (case 293/83)).

Advocate-General Sir Gordon Slynn submitted that both courses were capable of constituting vocational training within Article 7(3); if not, they would in any case fall under Article 7(2), as 'social advantages'. The crucial question, therefore, was whether Brown and Lair were 'workers', entitled to claim under these provisions. Brown had come to the UK primarily to prepare for his engineering studies at Cambridge; he had obtained his place at Cambridge prior to taking up work in the UK. Lair on the other hand had undoubtedly come to Germany many years before, intending to work. The Advocate-General suggested that a distinction might be drawn between persons who migrate genuinely in the capacity of a worker and those who move to another State for other purposes, e.g., in order to become a student, or to gain some work experience before their studies begin. Only the former, he suggested, could invoke Article 7(2) and (3) of Regulation 1612/68. While he did not think States could prescribe a minimum residence period before entitlement to benefits under the Article could arise (under German law five years' continuous employment was required for foreigners), the length of time during which a claimant had been in residence in a Member State, as well as what he was doing during that time, could be taken into account in deciding whether he was there in the capacity of a genuine worker. He suggested that a year's residence might provide a guideline as to the genuineness of the work, although even this would not be a watertight test.

The Court, which delivered judgments in both cases on the same day, took a rather different approach. As has been noted, it chose to interpret Article 7(3) narrowly, with the result that neither course would constitute 'training in vocational schools'. If the parties were to succeed it could only be on the basis of Article 7(2). A grant to cover university education was undoubtedly a 'social advantage'. But were the applicants 'workers'? The Court did not agree with the Advocate-General that the grant of social advantages might be subject to a minimum residence period, as a measure of the genuineness of the claimant's status as a worker. The concept of worker, the Court held, must have a community meaning. Nevertheless, in Brown's case, although he might be regarded as a worker, he was not entitled to claim the grant as a social advantage because he had acquired the status of worker exclusively as a result of his having been accepted for admission to university. The employment was merely ancillary to the studies to be financed by the grant. With regard to Lair's claim, the Court draw a distinction between a claim by a migrant worker who was *in*voluntarily unemployed, who, if legitimately resident, was entitled to the same treatment as regards reinstatement or re-employment as national workers, and one who gave up his work in order to undertake further training in the host Member State. In the latter case, he might only claim a grant for such a course if there was some link between the studies to be pursued and his previous work activity.

Thus the Court chose to base its decision in both cases on fine factual distinctions rather than on the 'genuineness' of the claimant's status as a worker, although it did add in *Lair,* in response to the expressed worries of Member States as to the possibility of abuse, that 'insofar as a worker has entered a Member State for the sole purpose of enjoying, after a very short period of work activity, the benefit of the student assistance system in that State, it should be observed that such abuses are not covered by the community provisions (i.e. Article 7(2) and 7(3)) in question' (para. 43). It is regrettable that in its concern to appease the anxiety of Member States it chose in *Lair* to limit the scope of Article 7(2) by denying a right to 'social advantages' in the form of grants to migrant workers who have not become unemployed but who genuinely want to improve their prospects by retraining in a *new* field of activity. In an era of rapid technological and economic change such as will inevitably occur if the single internal market becomes a reality, flexibility in the workforce is surely to be encouraged. In *Raulin* (case C–357/89), in a claim by a French national for a grant to pursue a full-time course in the plastic arts in the Netherlands, following 60 hours work as a waitress there, the Court followed *Brown* and *Lair*, adding only that in assessing whether the work undertaken was 'effective and genuine' for the purpose of acquiring the status of worker, both the length of time of employment and all the activities undertaken in the host State might be taken into account, but not the activities conducted elsewhere in the Community.

(d) *Trade union rights; rights of respresentation and management.* Under Article 8 of Regulation 1612/68 a migrant worker is entitled to equality of treatment as regards 'membership of trade unions and the exercise of rights attaching thereto, including the right to vote and to be eligible for the administration and management of bodies governed by public law and from holding office governed by public law'.

(e) *Housing.* A migrant worker is entitled to enjoy 'all the rights and benefits accorded to national workers in matters of housing, including ownership of the housing he needs' (Article 9; see *Commission* v *Greece* (case 305/87), restrictions on foreigners' right to acquire property held unlawful). The right extends to public and private housing. It is submitted that all statutory protection in this field must apply equally to 'favoured EC citizens', i.e., those who are lawfully resident. These rights would also constitute 'social advantages' under Article 7(2).

Workers' families (Articles 10–12)

(a) *Residence.* Members of a workers' family are defined as:

(i)   the worker's spouse and their descendants who are under the age of 21 or are dependants; and
(ii) dependent relatives in the ascending line of the worker and his spouse.

Members of a worker's family have a right to install themselves with the migrant worker (who must be an EC national) 'irrespective of their nationality' (Article 10(1)).

States are required to facilitate the admission of any member of the family not falling within the above definition if they are 'dependent on the worker ... or living under his roof in the country whence he comes' (Article 10(2)). Once admitted and installed it is submitted that such members attain the status of favoured EC citizens. In *Lebon* (case 316/85) the Court held, in the context of a claim for the Belgian minimex by the adult child of a retired French worker living in Belgium, that the status of dependency resulted from a purely factual situation, i.e., support provided by the worker; it did not depend on objective factors indicative of a need for support.

However, *Lebon* also established that once a worker's children reach the age of 21 they will cease to be 'members of the family' unless they are still dependent on the worker. They will thus lose their rights as favoured community citizens until they themselves become 'workers'. The High-level Panel Report on the Free Movement of Workers (1997) has suggested that the upper age limit be removed, although no action has, as yet, been taken.

In order that the family may install themselves with the worker he must have available for his family 'housing considered as normal for national workers in the region where he is employed' (Article 10(3)). The Court has held (*Commission* v *Germany* (case 249/86)) that as long as the family is living in appropriate housing conditions when the worker begins his working life in the host State, Member States may not require this condition to be satisfied throughout the entire duration of their residence. To do so would infringe the fundamental principle of respect for family life enshrined in Article 8 of the Convention for the Protection of Human Rights and protected as part of Community law. Thus a German law which made the granting of a residence permit conditional on the worker's continuing compliance with Article 10(3) was in breach of Community law.

(b)   *Employment.* By Article 11:

> Where a national of a Member State is pursuing an activity as an employed or self-employed person in the territory of another Member State, his spouse and those of the children who are under the age of 21 years or dependent on him shall have the rights to take up any activity as an employed person throughout the territory of that same state, even if they are not nationals of any Member State.

This Article was invoked in *Gül* (case 131/85) by the Turkish-Cypriot husband of an English woman working as a hairdresser in Germany. He had qualified as a doctor of medicine at Istanbul University, and taken further qualifications in anaesthetics in Germany. He had worked there on a temporary basis for some years. When he applied for permanent authorisation to practise in Germany he was refused on account of his nationality. He sought to annul this decision as in breach of EC law. The ECJ, in response to a request for a preliminary ruling, held that as long as he had the qualifications and diplomas necessary for the pursuit of the occupation in question in accordance with the legislation of the host State, and observed the specific rules governing the pursuit of that occupation, he was entitled under Article 11, as the spouse of an EC worker, to practise his profession in that State, even though he did not have EC nationality. Thus in the case of a spouse seeking to practise a profession it will be necessary to establish whether the spouse's qualifications are recognised as equivalent, which in Gül's case they were. (For a fuller discussion of this matter see chapter 21.)

In *Diatta* (case 267/83) the Court held that a spouse's right under Article 11 to take up employment in the host State gave her the right to install herself in that State even under a separate roof from her husband, since it might be necessary to live apart from her husband in order to exercise her right to work. Article 11 did not, however, itself give rise to a right of residence independent of her position as a spouse.

(c)   *Children: access to educational apprenticeship or vocational training courses* (Article 12). As was mentioned in the context of workers' rights under Article 7(3), the case of *Casagrande* (case 9/74) established that this Article entitled children not merely to admission to such courses but also to general measures to facilitate attendance, including grants. This right has been held to extend to a grant to study abroad provided it is available to nationals of the host State (case C–308/89)). In *Commission* v *Belgium* (case 42/87) the Court held that the children of migrant EC workers are entitled to full national treatment as regards *all* forms of State education, even if the working parent has retired or died in that State. The Court went further in *Moritz* v *Netherlands Minister for Education* (case 390/87). This case involved a claim for an educational allowance from the Dutch authorities by the child of a migrant worker, a German, who had left Holland and returned to his native country. His son sought to return to Holland to complete his studies there since he could not do so in Germany, there being no coordination of school-leaving certification as between the two countries. The Court held that in such a case, having regard to the need to ensure the integration of migrant workers in the host State, and the need for continuity in their children's education, a child was not to be regarded as having lost its status as a 'child of the family' benefiting from the provisions of Regulation 1612/68 merely because his family had moved back to its State of origin. It may be presumed that his rights under Regulation 1612/68 would cease when the course was concluded. A similarly generous approach was taken in *Gaal* (case C–7/94). Here it held that an orphaned child of a (deceased) migrant worker, a Belgian national (legitimately) living in Germany, who was over the age of 21 and not dependent on his remaining parent, was entitled to claim equality with nationals under Article 12 in order to obtain finance for studies in Scotland from the German authorities. The Court held that the definition of family in Article 10 could not be invoked to limit financial assistance to students by age or dependency.

Despite the fact that Article 12 does not give a spouse the right to equal access to educational, apprenticeship or vocational training courses, a spouse was successful in claiming such a right in *Forcheri* v *Belgium* (case 152/82). Mrs Forcheri was the wife of an Italian working as a Community official in Brussels. She applied for admission to a social work training course in Brussels. She was accepted, but required to pay a special fee, the *'minerval'*, required of all students who were not Belgian nationals. She claimed that the fee was discriminatory, in breach of Articles 7 (now 12 (ex 6) EC) and 48 EEC (now 39 EC) and Article 12 of Regulation 1612/68. The ECJ, on a reference from the Brussels Juge de Paix, drawing support from the fifth recital in the preamble to Regulation 1612/68, held that to require of a national of another Member State, *lawfully established* in the first Member State, an enrolment fee which is not required of its own nationals constitutes discrimination by reason of nationality which is prohibited by Article 7 (now 12 (ex 6)) of the Treaty.

Thus, in Mrs Forcheri's case, the right was deemed to arise not from Article 12 of Regulation 1612/68, from which she was clearly excluded, but from Article 7 of the EEC Treaty (now Article 12, (ex 6) EC). Her position as a favoured EC citizen, as the spouse of a worker, brought her 'within the scope of application of this Treaty'.

In the light of developments in the past few years it would now be permitted to base such a claim for fees levied at the lower, Belgian rate on Article 7(2), as a social advantage.

However, it should be borne in mind, as was made clear in *Lebon* (case 316/85), that members of the worker's family are only *indirect* beneficiaries of the right to equal treatment accorded to the worker under Article 7(2) of Regulation 1612/68; social advantages can only be granted to members of the family under Article 7(2) as advantages to the *worker*. This is a subtle distinction, but an important one.

Rights to remain in the territory of a Member State after having been employed in that State (Regulation 1251/70) This Regulation implements Article 39(3)(d) (ex 48(3)(d) EC. As stated in the preamble to Regulation 1251/70, 'the right of residence acquired by workers in active employment has as a corollary the right . . . to remain in the territory of a Member State after having been employed in that State' (first recital); moreover, 'the exercise by the worker of the right to remain entails that such right shall be extended to members of his family; [and], in the case of the death of the worker during his working life, maintenance of the right of residence of the members of his family must also be recognised' (seventh recital).

Regulation 1251/70 thus provides for the right of the worker and his family to remain permanently in the State in which he has worked on retirement, incapacity, or, in the case of the family, the death of the worker. It also makes special provision for the 'frontier' worker, i.e., one who lives in one, and works in an adjacent, state.

Members of the family are defined as in Regulation 1612/68, Article 10.

(a) *Workers* (Article 2(1)). Article 2(1) provides that:

The following shall have the right to remain permanently in the territory of a Member State:

(i) *Retirement* — a worker who, at the time of termination of his activity, has reached the age laid down by the law of that Member State for entitlement to an old-age pension and who has been employed in that State for at least the last 12 months and has resided there continuously for more than three years.

(ii) *Incapacity* — a worker who, having resided continuously in the territory of that State for more than two years, ceases to work there as an employed person as a result of permanent incapacity to work. If such incapacity is the result of an accident at work or an occupational disease entitling him to a pension for which an institution of that State is entirely or partially responsible, no condition shall be imposed as to length of residence.

(iii)   *Frontier workers* — a worker who, after three years' continuous employment and residence in the territory of that State, works as an employed person in the territory of another Member State, while retaining his residence in the territory of the first State, to which he returns, as a rule, each day or at least once a week.

Periods of time spent working in another Member State are to be considered as spent working in the State of residence for the purposes of satisfying the employment requirements of subparagraphs (a) and (b).

If the worker's spouse is a national of the State concerned, or has lost her nationality through marriage to the worker, the residence and employment requirements of subparagraphs (a) and (b) will not apply (Article 2(2)).

(b)   *Members of the family* (Article 3). Members of the worker's family will be entitled to remain permanently under two sets of circumstances:

(i)   If the worker has himself acquired the right to remain (Article 3(1)).

(ii)   If the worker dies during his working life before having acquired the right to remain and either:

(1)   the worker has resided continuously in that State for at least two years, or

(2)   his death resulted from an accident at work or an occupational disease, or

(3)   the surviving spouse is a national of that State of residence or has lost the nationality of that State by marriage to the worker (Article 3(2)).

Article 4 provides that continuity of residence as required under Article 2 and 3 will not be affected by temporary absences not exceeding three months per year, nor longer absences due to compliance with obligations of military service: and periods of involuntary unemployment, duly recorded by the competent employment office, and absences due to illness or accident, are to be considered as periods of employment for the purposes of Article 2 (Article 4(2)).

Thus, provision is generous, and designed to provide the maximum security for the migrant worker and his family.

The beneficiaries of these rights are given two years, from the time when they first became entitled, to exercise them. During this time they may leave the territory concerned without forfeiting their rights (Article 5).

Persons exercising their right to remain are entitled to a residence permit which must be valid (throughout the territory of the State concerned) for at least five years, and must be automatically renewable (Article 6). As stated in *Royer* (case 48/75), their right of residence will not depend on the residence permit; the permit will merely provide proof of their right of residence.

Persons exercising their rights to remain in a Member State under Regulation 1251/70 will be entitled to equality of treatment as established by Regulation 1612/68 (Article 7). Thus they may claim all 'social advantages' provided by that State on the same basis as nationals.

Regulation 1251/70, Article 3(2), was invoked, *inter alia,* in the case of *R v Secretary of State for the Home Department, ex parte Sandhu* [1982] 2 CMLR 553 in order to argue for a right of permanent residence in the UK for Mr Sandhu when his EC wife left him to return to Germany. It was argued that separation and divorce could be regarded in the same light as the death of the worker. To deny a spouse security of residence in the case of separation or divorce would equally create an obstacle to the free movement of workers. The argument succeeded before Comyn J, but not before the Court of Appeal ([1983] 3 CMLR 131) or the House of Lords (*The Times,* 10 May 1985). It is a convincing argument which deserves to be revived. As noted earlier, the Commission has put forward a proposal which, if enacted, would remedy some of the current defects in TCNs' position under EC law (COM (1998) 394 final).

The harshness of Community law in relation to third-country workers is illustrated in the case of *Bozkurt* (case C–434/93). Bozkurt was a Turkish national who had worked and lived in the Netherlands for nine years. He became incapacitated following an accident at work. Following the accident the Dutch authorities refused to renew his residence permit. He sought to challenge their decision under provisions of an association agreement between the EC and Turkey, arguing for an interpretation along the lines of Regulation 1251/70. He failed. In the absence of an express provision in the EEC–Turkey agreement he had no right to remain in his State of employment on retirement or incapacity. *Bozkurt* may be contrasted with *Tetik* v *Land Berlin* (case C–171/95). Here, in the case of a Turkish worker who was still able and willing to work, the ECJ found that such an individual remains within the definition of 'worker' for the purpose of the EC–Turkey agreement and was therefore entitled to rely on the rights in that agreement to remain. Turkey is, of course, now in the process of accession to the EU, and therefore the position of Turkish workers may well change. It should be noted that workers from other countries which have signed cooperation agreements with the EU will not necessarily have the same favourable position as regards the right to work in the EU as Tetik did. In *Nour Eddline El-Yassini* v *Secretary of State for the Home Department* (case C–416/96), a question was referred to the ECJ concerning the extent of the protection granted by Article 40 of the EEC–Morocco cooperation agreement, which provided that Moroccans were not to be discriminated against as regards access to jobs and working conditions on the grounds of nationality. El-Yassini had been granted leave to remain in the UK on the basis of his marriage to a UK national. When his marriage broke down, he applied to remain in the UK on the basis of Article 40: he was employed and the right to work has been held, under a similarly worded provision in the Turkish cooperation agreement, to include the right to reside. The ECJ held, however, that the approach taken as regards the Turkish agreement did not apply to the Moroccan agreement. The UK was therefore free to refuse to renew El-Yassini's residence permit, although he had a permanent job, when the reason for granting him residence in the first place (i.e., his marriage) ceased to exist. Thus, the outcome in each case will depend on the wording of each agreement as well as on the ECJ's approach to its interpretation.

'Employment in the public service'

In the field of employment rights, Member States are entitled under Article 39(4) (ex 48(4)) EC to deny or restrict access to 'employment in the public service' on the basis of a worker's nationality. Given the potential breadth of this provision, it is not surprising that it has been exploited by Member States nor that the ECJ has given it the narrowest scope.

The German post office sought to rely on this exclusion in *Sotgiu* v *Deutsche Bundespost* (case 152/73) to counter Sotgiu's allegations that the post office's rules granting extra allowances to workers living apart from their families in Germany were discriminatory. On a reference from the Bundesarbeitsgericht the ECJ held that the exception provided by the then Article 48(4) (now 39(4)) did not apply to all employment in the public service. It applied only to 'certain activities' in the public service, connected with the exercise of official authority. Moreover, it applied only to conditions of *access;* it did not permit discriminatory conditions of employment once access had been granted.

The matter was further clarified in *Commission* v *Belgium (Re Public Employees)* (case 149/79). This was an infringement action against Belgium for breach of the then Article 48 (now 39). Under Belgian law, posts in the 'public service' could be limited to Belgian nationals. This was applied to all kinds of posts: unskilled workers, railwaymen, nurses, plumbers, electricians and architects, employed by both central and local government. The city of Brussels (seat of the EC Commission!) was one of the chief offenders. The Belgian government (supported by France and Germany intervening) argued that all these jobs were 'in the public service' within the then Article 48(4). The ECJ disagreed. The concept of public service was a Community concept; it applied only to the exercise of official authority, and was intended to apply only to employees *safeguarding the general interests of the State.* The fact that higher levels of a post might involve the exercise of official authority would not justify assimilating the junior levels to that status. Belgium was in breach of EC law.

Similar proceedings were brought, and upheld, against France in *Commission* v *France (Re French Nurses)* (case 307/84) against a French law limiting the appointment of nurses in public hospitals to French nationals.

When a particular job will involve 'the exercise of official authority' is not altogether clear. It certainly does not apply to civil servants generally. In *Lawrie-Blum* v *Land Baden-Württemberg* (case 66/85) the Court held that access to certain posts could not be limited by reason of the fact that in a given Member State persons appointed to such posts have the status of civil servants. To make the application of Article 39(4) (ex 48(4)) dependent on the legal nature of the relationship between the employer and the administration would enable Member States to determine at will the posts covered by the exception laid down in that provision. To constitute employment in the public service, employees must be charged with the exercise of powers conferred by public law or must be responsible for *safeguarding the general interests of the State* . In *Bleis* v *Ministère de l'Education Nationale* (case C–4/91) the Court held that the concept of public service 'presumes on the part of those occupying such posts the existence of a special relationship of allegiance to the State and reciprocity of rights and duties which form the foundation of the bond of nationality'. This approach by the ECJ might be termed a 'functional' approach to the determination of whether the 'exercise of official authority' is involved, as it considers the responsibilities of each job individually.

On these criteria it seems that the derogation provided by Article 39(4) (ex 48(4)) will be of limited use, confined to occupations such as the judiciary and the higher echelons of the civil service, the armed forces and the police. Article 39(4) needs to be viewed in conjunction with Article 45 (ex 55), which provides that the freedom of establishment permitted under EC law 'shall not apply, so far as any given Member State is concerned, to activities which in that State are connected, even occasionally, with the exercise of official authority'. Identical principles will apply to the interpretation of both provisions.

Since most of the posts in the above cases may not be denied to non-nationals, access to these posts by way of examination or training must be open, on equal terms, to workers (or their families) who are non-nationals. Thus in *Lawrie-Blum* (case 66/85) a practical training scheme for teachers, organised in Baden-Württemberg within the framework of the civil serivce, was not within the then Article 48(4) (now 39(4)) and could not be confined to German nationals.

In view of the widespread practice among Member States of excluding non-nationals from a wide range of occupations in the public service on the basis of Article 39(4) (ex 48(4)) the Commission published a Notice in 1988 (OJ No.C 72/2) announcing that it proposed to review certain sectors of employment which it considered to be for the most part 'sufficiently remote from the specific activities of the public sphere as defined by the European Court that they would only in rare cases be covered by the exception of Article 48(4) [now 39(4)]'. These comprise:

(a) public health care services,
(b) teaching in State educational establishments,
(c) research for non-military purposes in public establishments, and
(d) public bodies responsible for administering commercial services.

Furthermore, the Commission has brought Article 226 (ex 169) EC actions against certain Member States for failure to take action following the communication (for example, *Commission* v *Belgium* (case C–173/94); *Commission* v *Greece* (case C–290/94); *Commission* v *Luxembourg* (case C–473/93)). In its judgments given on the same day, the ECJ confirmed the Commission's approach of identifying types of work which would rarely fall within Article 59(4) (ex 39(4)) EC. In these circumstances, it is still open to the national authorities to show, on a functional basis, that specified jobs within such sections do fall within the public service exception. It has been suggested that the review should result in the opening up of many posts which in many

Member States are currently reserved for nationals, representing a 'tremendous leap forward in the attainment of a true community-wide labour market' (see Watson, noted below). In the light of the case law, it seems that this has yet to happen.

Derogation on grounds of public policy, public security or public health

The rights of entry and residence and the right of permanent residence granted by the Treaty to migrant workers and their families are not absolute. States remain free to deny these rights to migrant workers or their families on grounds of 'public policy, public security or public health'. Because of the importance of this principle and the fact that Directive 64/221, passed to implement the principle, applies to all categories of migrant workers, employed and self-employed, it will be dealt with separately in chapter 22.

Non-workers

The legislation described above only applies to workers and their families, albeit generously interpreted by the ECJ. The extent and impact of the treaty amendments introduced by the TEU and ToA regarding the freedom of non-workers to move throughout the Union will be discussed in chapter 23.

Further reading

See also further reading for chapter 19.

Daniele, L., 'Restrictions to the Free Movement of Persons' (1997) 22 EL Rev 191.

Hartley, T., 'Free Movement of Students in European Community Law' (1989) Cahiers de Droit Européen.

O'Keeffe, D., 'Judicial Interpretation of the Public Exception to the Free Movement of Workers', Curtin, D., and O'Keeffe, D., (eds), *Constitutional Adjudication in European Community Law and National Law* (1992), p. 89.

Peers, S., 'Social Advantages and Discrimination in Employment Caselaw Confirmed' (1997) 22 EL Rev 157.

Steiner, J., 'The Right to Welfare: Equality and Equity under Community Law' (1985) 10 EL Rev 21.

Watson, P., 'Free Movement of Workers: a One way Ticket?' (1993) 22 ILJ 68.

Woods, L., 'Family Rights in the EU — disadvantaging the disadvantaged?' (1999) 11 Child & Family Law Quarterly 17.

TWENTY ONE

Freedom of establishment; freedom to provide services; freedom to receive services

The freedoms granted to workers under Article 39 (ex 48) were also granted by the Treaty to the self-employed in the form of a right of establishment (Articles 43–48 (ex 52–58) EC) and a right to provide services (Articles 49–55 (ex 59–66) EC). The principal Articles are Article 43 (ex 52) (establishment) and Articles 49 and 50(3) (ex 59 and 60(3)) EC (services).

Establishment

Article 43 (ex 52) in its original form provided:

> Within the framework of the provisions set out below, restrictions on the freedom of establishment of nationals of a Member State in the territory of another Member State shall be abolished by progressive stages in the course of the transitional period. Such progressive abolition shall also apply to restrictions on the setting up of agencies, branches or subsidiaries by nationals of any Member State established in the territory of any Member State.
>
> Freedom of establishment shall include the right to take up and pursue activities as self-employed persons and to set up and manage undertakings, in particular companies and firms within the meaning of the second paragraph of Article 58 [now 48], under the conditions laid down for its own nationals by the law of the country where such establishment is effected, subject to the provisions of the Chapter relating to capital [Chapter 4].

The ToA removed the reference to the progressive abolition of restrictions during the transitional period, this period having long since expired. Instead, the obligation is expressed as having taken effect.

'Companies or firms' means 'companies or firms constituted under civil or commercial law, including cooperative societies, and other legal persons governed by public or private law, save for those which are non-profit-making' (Article 48(2) (ex 58(2)) EC).

Companies or firms formed in accordance with the law of a Member State and having their registered office, central administration or principal place of business within the Community shall, for the purposes of this Chapter, be treated in the same way as natural persons who are nationals of Member States (Article 48(1) (ex 45(1)) EC).

Services

Articles 49 (ex 59) and 50(3) (ex 60(3)) in their original form provided:

Within the framework of the provisions set out below, restrictions on freedom to provide services within the Community shall be progressively abolished during the transitional period in respect of nationals of Member States who are established in a State of the Community other than that of the person for whom the services are provided (Article 59 [now 49]).

Without prejudice to the provisions of the Chapter relating to the right of establishment [Chapter 2], the person providing a service may, in order to do so, temporarily pursue his activity in the State where the service is provided, under the same conditions as are imposed by that State on its own nationals (Article 60(3) [now 50(3)]).

Again the ToA removed the reference to the transitional period.

These rights too are granted to companies or firms formed in accordance with the law of a Member State (Article 56 (ex 66) EC).

'Services' are defined as those 'normally provided for remuneration, insofar as they are not governed by the provisions relating to freedom of movement for goods, capital and persons' (Article 50(1) (ex 60(1)) EC). Services in the field of transport are 'governed by the provisions of the Title [Part Two, Title IV] relating to transport' (Article 51 (ex 61) EC). The liberalisation of banking and insurance services connected with movements of capital was to be effected 'step by step with the progressive liberalisation of movement of capital' although the ToA removed the word 'progressive' from this article. Article 50 (new 60) EC provides a non-exhaustive list of examples of services.

Note the economic element required by this definition. In *Deliege* (joined cases C–51/96 and C–191/97), the ECJ borrowed the tests from *Levin* (case 53/81) and *Steymann* (case 196/87) in relation to workers (see chapter 20) to clarify the concept of economic activity. That is, the services performed must be genuine and effective and not marginal and ancillary.

Although the ECJ has repeatedly held that the basic Treaty freedoms must be interpreted widely, there are limits. In *Society for the Protection of Unborn Children Ltd* v *Grogan* (case C–159/90), the provision of information, contrary to the Irish constitution, about abortion clinics in other Member States by officers of a students' union was held not to receive the protection of the then Article 59 (now 49). Although abortion (where legal in the Member State in which the procedure took place) could constitute a service within the Treaty, the link between the provision of an information service about the clinics and the clinics themselves was too tenuous to be considered a restriction on the freedom to provide services. Some have suggested that this judgment is an isolated decision and that the ECJ's reasoning in this case was motivated by a desire to avoid a sensitive political issue. The Irish position as regards abortion was formalised by a Protocol annexed to the TEU.

Where goods are supplied in the context of the provision of services they will be governed by the provisions relating to services as long as the goods are ancillary to the services provided. Thus in *Her Majesty's Customs and Excise* v *Schindler* (case C–275/92) a lottery service which involved, *inter alia*, the provision of tickets and advertising material fell to be examined exclusively under the then Article 59 (now 49) EC.

Because of the special nature of services, lending themselves to promotion and even provision via modern 'distance' methods of communication, a service can be deemed to 'move' within the Community without either the provider or the recipient moving across national borders. Thus, Article 49 (ex 59) can be used to regulate either the provider, or the service itself. In *Alpine Investments BV* v *Minister van Financiën* (case C–384/93) a Dutch prohibition on 'cold calling' (the soliciting of business by telephone), by providers of financial advice established in The Netherlands, was held to constitute a barrier to the free provision of services contrary to the then Article 59 (now 49) EC (although it was found on the facts to be justified). Restrictions on cross-border advertising relating to the distribution of goods will be dealt with under the free movement of goods provisions of Article 28 (ex 30) (*Leclerc-Siplec* v *TF1 Publicité SA* (case C–412/93), decided on *Keck* principles, see chapter 10).

The right of establishment and the right to provide services are accorded under the Treaty to EC nationals and to companies formed according to the law of one of the Member States. Where in the latter case the central management or principal place of business lies outside the Community the company's activities must have an 'effective and continuous link with the economy of a Member State, excluding the possibility that this link might depend on nationality, particularly the nationality of the partners or the members of the managing or supervisory bodies, or of persons holding the capital stock' ('General programme for the abolition of restrictions on freedom to provide services', *Common Market Reporter*, para. 1546; JO 1962, 32). This link is the price exacted for valuable access to the Community market. To benefit from the freedom to provide services, an EC national must be established in a Member State.

Distinction between establishment and services

The difference between the right of establishment and the right to provide services is one of degree rather than of kind. Both apply to business or professional activity pursued for 'profit' or 'remuneration'. A right of establishment is a right to install oneself, to 'set up shop' in another Member State, permanently or semi-permanently, whether as an individual, a partnership or a company, for the purpose of performing a particular activity there. In the German insurance case (*Commission* v *Germany (Re Insurance Services)* (case 205/84)) the Court suggested that an enterprise would fall within the concept of 'establishment' even if its presence is not in the form of a branch or agency but consists merely of an office managed by the enterprise's own staff or by a person who is independent but is authorised to act on a permanent basis for the enterprise. The concept of establishment has been held to be 'a broad one, allowing a Community national to participate on a stable and continuous basis in the economic life of a Member State other than his own' (*Gebhard* v *Consiglio dell'Ordine degli Avvocati e Procuratori di Milano* (case C–55/94)). The right to provide services, on the other hand, connotes the provision of services in one Member State, on a temporary or spasmodic basis, by a person established in another Member State. In the latter case it is not necessary to reside, even temporarily, in the Member State in which the service is provided. The temporary nature of the activities in question should be determined in the light not only of the duration of the service but of its regularity, periodicity and continuity (*Gebhard* (case C–55/94)). Applying these principles in *Gebhard* the Court found that the setting up of chambers in Italy by a German barrister, a practising member of the Stuttgart Bar, was held to fall within the concept of establishment. A person could be established, within the meaning of the Treaty, in more than one Member State, in particular, in the case of companies, through the setting up of branches or subsidiaries, and, in the case of members of the professions, by establishing a second professional base. The Court suggested that the Treaty provisions relating to workers, establishment and services were mutually exclusive. Therefore, in case of doubt, all should be pleaded. However, in view of the fine line between 'establishment' and 'provision of services', and the fact that the general principles applicable to both are the same (as they are to workers, see *Royer* (case 48/75) discussed in chapter 20), too much emphasis should not be placed on the difference between the two. Despite dicta by the Court purporting to distinguish between the two, interpretation of both provisions appears to be moving towards convergence. *Gebhard* is significant in this respect.

Fundamental Community rights

In addition to the Treaty, secondary legislation has now been enacted granting rights of entry and residence to the self-employed in near-identical terms to those applicable to workers. The legislation comprises:

(a)   Directive 73/148 (rights of entry and residence; equivalent to Directive 68/360).

(b)   Directive 75/34 (right to remain permanently in a Member State after having been self-employed there; equivalent to Regulation 1251/70).

Those who establish themselves are entitled, like workers, to a residence permit to be valid for not less than five years from the date of issue, and automatically renewable (Directive 73/148, Article 4(1)).

In the case of services the right of residence is 'of equal duration with the period during which the services are provided' (Directive 73/148, Article 4(2)).

Regulation 1612/68, being expressed in terms of the situation of employment, has no parallel for the self-employed. Hence the special importance in this area of the principle of non-discrimination on the grounds of nationality. Where the self-employed or their families are 'lawfully resident' in a Member State, Article 12 (ex 6) may, in certain circumstances, be invoked to ensure that they receive equal treatment in the form of 'social' or any other advantages with nationals of the host Member State. Certainly this would apply to persons or businesses established in the host Member State. In the case of the provider of services, the matter is less clear. While he is undoubtedly able to claim full equality as regards access to, and conditions of, work within the host Member State it is unlikely that he can claim for himself and his family benefits in the form of social assistance, especially when they are ongoing, such as may be claimed as social advantages under Article 7(2) of Regulation 1612/68. It is submitted, although it has yet to be decided by the Court, that these should be claimed from the Member State in which the applicant is permanently established. An analogy could perhaps be drawn here with the person migrating in search of employment, who, according to *Lebon* (case 316/85) has no entitlement to the social advantages provided by the host Member State (see chapter 20).

Both the right of establishment and the freedom to provide services are subject to derogation on the grounds of 'public policy, public security or public health' (Articles 46 and 56 (ex 56 and 66) EC). Under these Articles Member States 'may provide for special treatment for foreign nationals'. This is implemented in terms of 'measures concerning the movement and residence of foreign nationals' by Directive 64/221 (see chapter 22). Both freedom of establishment and freedom to provide services are expressed not to apply to 'activities which in that State are connected, even occasionally, with the exercise of official authority' (Articles 46 and 56 (ex 55 and 66) EC).

The right of establishment and the right to provide services have been described by the ECJ as 'fundamental Community rights'. The principle on which these rights are based is the principle of non-discrimination on grounds of nationality, whether arising from legislation, regulation or administrative practice. The principle is binding on all competent authorities as well as legally recognised professional bodies (*Steinhauser* v *City of Biarritz* (case 197/84) (Article 43 (ex 52) EC); *Walrave* v *Association Union Cycliste Internationale* (case 36/74) (Article 49 (ex 59) EC)).

Discrimination: personal and professional Community law on establishment and services, although concerned with the same rights and based on the same principles as the law relating to workers, also has much in common with the law concerning the free movement of goods. The provisions have a twofold purpose: to the extent that they confer on EC nationals who are self-employed *personal* rights, in the form of a right to enter and reside in a Member State and pursue activities, on a temporary or permanent basis, free from discrimination on the grounds of nationality, their purpose is akin to that of Article 39 (ex 48) EC; inasmuch as they seek to achieve freedom of establishment and the free movement of services in a single, Community-wide market and pertain to the practice of a particular profession their goals are economic, more like those of Article 28 (ex 30) EC. While infringements of the former 'personal' rights normally take the form of discrimination on the grounds of nationality, which can rarely be justified, measures which interfere with the functioning of the single market by impeding the free movement of services and freedom of establishment will not necessarily be discriminatory. Where they apply equally to all persons who establish themselves or provide services in a particular Member State and are designed to protect some public interest, they may more readily be justified.

The early case law of the ECJ on Articles 43, 49 and 50 (ex 52, 59 and 60) tended to focus on personal rights and broad principles of discrimination on the grounds of nationality. The concept of discrimination was extended to include measures which discriminated indirectly against non-nationals such as the residence requirement in *Sotgiu* (case 152/73), which the Court had suggested might be 'objectively justified'. Direct discrimination, as established in *Bond van Adverteerders* v *Netherlands* (case 352/85), could only be justified under Articles 45 and 55 (new 56 and 66) EC. These provisions, expressed in terms of *personal* rights, allowing Member States to provide for 'special treatment' for foreign nationals, were very strictly construed.

It was thought initially that national regulatory rules and professional practices which were not discriminatory, which applied 'without distinction' to all persons providing services or established in a particular Member State, and which clearly served a useful purpose, could not be challenged under the Treaty (e.g., *Koestler* (case 15/78)). The rights granted to EC nationals under Articles 43, 49 and 50 (ex 52, 59 and 60) EC were to establish themselves and provide services in other Member States 'under the same conditions' as applied to the State's own nationals. Although national regulatory rules might create barriers to the free movement of services and freedom of establishment they could only be removed by harmonisation, as provided under Articles 46 and 47 (ex 56 and 57) EC. Since harmonisation proved slow to achieve, some of these measures came to be challenged as 'discriminatory' and it was suggested that they would be permissible provided they could be objectively justified (see, e.g., *van Binsbergen* (case 33/74); *Commission* v *Germany, re Insurance Services* (case 205/84)). But the case law was slow to develop and the principles were unclear. It was not until 1991 with *Säger* v *Dennemeyer and Co. Ltd* (case C-76/90) that the Court established a coherent approach to indistinctly applicable rules in the field of services parallel to that pioneered in the sphere of goods in the 1970s in *Dassonville* (case 8/74) and *Cassis de Dijon* (case 120/78). In doing so it undoubtedly opened up the possibility for further claims under Article 49 (ex 59), and with it, as with any easing of the rules, some abuse (see, e.g., *TV 10 SA* v *Commissariaat voor de Media* (case

C–23/93)). The principles introduced in *Säger* were applied in *Gebhard* (case C–55/94) to establishment under the then Article 52 (now 43). These matters will be discussed further below.

Limitations on the freedoms

The right of establishment and the freedom to provide services provided under Articles 43 and 49 (ex 52 and 59) EC are not absolute. Apart from the express derogations of Articles 45, 46 and 55 (ex 55, 56 and 66) EC, they are subject to one important limitation. The right to equality of opportunity provided by Articles 43(2) and 50(3) (ex 52(2) and 60(3)) can only be exercised 'under the conditions laid down for its own nationals by the law of the country where such establishment is effected' (Article 43(2) (ex 52(2)) EC or 'under the same conditions as are imposed by that State on its own nationals' (Article 50(3) (ex 60(3)) EC).

The difficulty for non-nationals seeking to establish themselves or provide services in another Member State is that they may not be able to satisfy the conditions laid down in that Member State for the practice of the particular trade or profession which they wish to exercise. The relevant conditions are those prescribed by trade or professional bodies, normally reinforced by law, relating to:

(a)   the education and training required for qualification for the job, and
(b)   rules of professional conduct.

Both of these vary greatly in scope and content and quality from Member State to Member State. The need to comply with these conditions thus provided a potent barrier to freedom of movement for the self-employed; it also hindered the free movement of workers, since they too may wish to work as employees in a trade or profession which is subject to regulation at national level.

Because of these difficulties the Treaty provided for the abolition of existing restrictions on freedom of establishment and freedom to provide services to be achieved in progressive stages during a transitional period. During the first stage the Council, acting on a proposal from the Commission, was to draw up a general programme on the abolition of restrictions on freedom of establishment (former Article 53, which was deleted by the ToA) and on the freedom to provide services (Article 52 (ex 63) EC). In addition these institutions were required, during the first stage, to 'issue Directives for the mutual recognition of diplomas, certificates and other evidence of formal qualifications' (Article 47(1) (ex 57(1)) EC) and to 'issue Directives for the coordination of the provisions laid down by law, regulation or administrative action in Member States concerning the taking up and pursuit of activities as self-employed persons' (Article 47 (ex 57(2))).

The general programmes were adopted in 1961 (*Common Market Reporter* paras 1335 and 1546; JO 1962, 36, 32). Although not binding, they provide valuable guidelines in the interpretation of the Treaty, and have been invoked on a number of occasions by the Court (e.g., *Steinhauser* (case 197/84) and *Gravier* (case 293/83) both to be discussed later in this chapter). The issuing of Directives under Article 47(1) and (2) (ex 57(1) and (2)) proved a more difficult task. National professional bodies were understandably reluctant to compromise on long-established principles and practices, and although many Directives passed (for full range see *Encyclopedia of European Community Law*, vol. C, part C12) in areas ranging from wholesaling to hairdressing to medicine, progress was slow. The architects' Directive alone took 17 years to pass.

Since the right of establishment and the right to provide services provided under Articles 43 and 49 (ex 52 and 59) appeared to be conditional on the issuing of Directives under Article 47(1) and (2) (ex 57(1) and (2)) it was thought that these rights could not be invoked by individuals until such Directives had been passed. This matter was tested in *Reyners* v *Belgium* (case 2/74). Reyners was a Dutchman, born, educated and resident in Belgium, and a doctor of Belgian law. He was refused admission to the Belgian Bar since he was not of Belgian nationality. He challenged this decision, claiming that it was in breach of the then Article 52 (now 43). The Belgian government argued that this Article was not directly effective, since it depended for its effect on the issuing of Directives under Article 57 (now 47). On a reference for interpretation from the Belgian Conseil d'État on this point, the ECJ held that Article 52 (now 43) was directly effective from the end of the transitional period. The provisions of Article 57 (now 47) were complementary to Article 52 (now 43); they were not a necessary precondition. The purpose of Article 57 was merely to facilitate the increase of freedom of establishment; that Article, together with the then Article 7 EEC (now 12 (ex 6) EC), required that the actual conditions imposed could not be stricter than those imposed on the State's own nationals. The same principle was applied in the context of services in *van Binsbergen* (case 33/74).

Thus even though recognition and harmonisation have not been achieved in a particular profession by the issuing of Directives under Article 47 (ex 57), once the transitional period had expired Articles 43, 49 and 50 (ex 52, 59 and 60) EC, together with Article 12 (ex 6) EC, may be invoked to challenge a national rule, whether in the form of a nationality or a residence requirement, which is discriminatory. This principle applies to both direct and indirect discrimination, and relates not only to the taking up of an activity but to pursuit of that activity in the widest sense. This principle was confirmed in *Steinhauser* v *City of Biarritz* (case 197/84). Steinhauser was a German, a professional artist resident in Biarritz. He applied to the Biarritz authorities to rent a *'crampotte'*, a fisherman's hut of a type used locally for the exhibition and sale of works of art. He was refused on the grounds of his nationality; under the city's regulations *crampottes* could only be rented by persons of French nationality. He challenged that decision, and the ECJ, on reference from the Pau administrative tribunal, held that freedom of establishment provided under the then Article 52 (now 43) related not only to the taking up of an activity as a self-employed person but also the pursuit of that activity in the widest sense.

Thus, citing the general programme on the abolition of restrictions on freedom of establishment (1962 JO 36), the right to equal treatment was held to include, *inter alia*, the right to rent premises, to tender, and to qualify for licences and concessions. More recently, in *Hayes* v *Kronenberger GmbH* (case C–323/95), the requirement for non-national claimants to pay an amount into court as security for costs was held to be in breach of Article 12 (ex 6) EC as nationals of that Member State would not have to do so. (A similar determination has been made in respect of services; see below.)

The Court went further in *Commission* v *Italy (re Housing Aid)* (case 63/86). Here it held that a cheap mortgage facility, available under Italian law only to Italian nationals, was in breach of the then Article 7 EEC (now Article 12 (ex 6) EC), even where such provision was an aspect of social law, and thus (it was implied) should be available on a basis of equality in Italy to EC nationals providing services *as long as the nature of the services provided was such as to require a permanent dwelling there.*

Where access to property by non-nationals involves the investment of capital, it may also, or perhaps only, fall under Article 56 (ex 73b) regarding the free movement of capital. (See, e.g., *Konle* v *Austria* (case C–302/97).) Regrettably, discussion of the Treaty's provision concerning capital fall outside the scope of this book.

Professional qualifications

Even though Directives have not been passed ensuring mutual recognition of diplomas, certificates and other evidence of formal qualifications in a particular trade or profession, it will be discriminatory, in breach of Articles 43, 49 and 50 (ex 52 or 59 and 60) together with Article 6 (new 12) EC to refuse permission to practise to a person whose qualifications have been recognised as equivalent to those required in the State in which he seeks to practise.

In *Thieffry* v *Conseil de l'Ordre des Advocats à la Cour de Paris* (case 71/76) the Court held that the French Bar Council could not refuse to allow Thieffry, a Belgian national with a Belgian law degree, to undertake practical training for the French bar, since his Belgian degree had been recognised by the University of Paris and he had acquired a qualifying certificate in France for the profession of *avocat*. Similarly, in *Patrick* v *Ministre des Affaires Culturelles* (case 11/77) the Court held that Patrick, an Englishman, who had trained as an architect in England, was entitled to invoke the then Articles 52 and 7 (now Articles 43 and 12 (ex 6) EC) in order to practise architecture in France, since, although no diplomatic convention ensuring recognition had been agreed, as was required by French law, and no EC Directives relating to architects had at that time been passed, his English qualifications had been recognised as equivalent to the corresponding French degree under a Ministerial Decree of 1964.

Where a Directive has been issued for the mutual recognition or harmonization of qualifications in a particular profession that profession may no longer insist on compliance with its own requirements by persons who have qualified in another Member State according to the terms of the Directive.

Thus in *Broekmeulen* (case 246/80) the Dutch General Practitioners' Committee was unable to refuse Broekmeulen permission to practise as a GP in Holland even though he had qualified as a GP in Belgium, where it was not necessary to complete the three years' specialised training required for GPs in Holland. The EC Directive 75/362 relating to training for GPs did not require GPs to undergo training additional to their original (three-year) qualification. Parties may not, however, claim freedom of establishment under Article 43 (ex 52) EC or freedom to provide services under Article 49 (ex 59) in reliance on a Directive issued under Article 47 (ex 57) until the period provided for its implementation has expired (*Auer* (case 136/78), or, *a fortiori*, where they do not fall within the terms of the Directive (*Dreessen* v *Conseil National de l'Ordre des Architectes* (case C–447/93)).

Where a person is entitled to claim rights of establishment or freedom to provide services as a result of possessing recognised or equivalent qualifications (whether recognised by Directive or otherwise) he may do so even though he possesses the nationality, but not the qualifications, of the Member State in which he seeks to pursue his activities (*Knoors* (case 115/78); *Broekmeulen* (case 246/80); *Auer* (case 136/78)). Here there is a clear cross-border element, and therefore the matter is not regarded as purely internal (*cf. Moser* v *Land Baden-Württemberg* (case 180/83), discussed in chapter 19).

Until recently, where qualifications obtained in a particular Member State have *not* been subject to harmonisation or recognised in another Member State, it would not have been discriminatory, and therefore not prima facie in breach of EC law, for a State or a professional body to refuse a person possessing these qualifications permission to practise. In *Arantis* v *Land Berlin* (case C–164/94), however, the ECJ held that where a profession was not regulated by an EC directive, the then Articles 6 and 52 (now 12 and 43) EC required the authorities in a host Member State to take into account an individual's qualifications and other relevant experience acquired in the home State. In doing so, the ECJ extended its ruling in *Vlassopoulou* (case C–340/89), which is discussed below in relation to regulated professions, to unregulated professions. This will have a significant effect in blocking any gaps in the protection afforded to those with EC qualifications which are not covered by an EC Directive.

Mutual recognition

Because of the problems outlined above, and because progress on harmonisation for the purpose of mutual recognition of qualifications had been so slow, the Community decided on a new approach. Instead of attempting to harmonise by profession, known as the sectoral or 'vertical' aproach, the Commission was henceforth to adopt a general or 'horizontal' approach, based not on harmonisation but on the mutual recognition of qualifications, and applicable not to individual professions but to all areas of activity for which a higher education diploma was required. Directive 89/48 ((1989) OJ No.L 19/16), based on these principles, was approved in December 1988.

The Directive applies only to regulated professional activities, although it is sufficient if they are regulated in only one State in the Community. It does not attempt to modify the rules applicable to particular professions in individual Member States, nor does it apply to professions which were already subject to separate Directives providing for the mutual recognition of diplomas. Like the prior harmonisation Directives it will apply to workers as well as the self-employed.

The starting-point for the principle of mutual recognition is a higher education diploma awarded on completion of professional education and training of at least three years' duration, or the equivalent period part time. Where, in the host State, the taking up and pursuit of a regulated profession is subject to the possession of a diploma, the competent authority of that State may not refuse to authorise a national of a Member State to take up and pursue that profession on the same conditions as apply to its own nationals, provided the applicant holds a diploma required in another State for the pursuit of the profession in question, *or* has pursued that profession for at least two years in a State which does not regulate that profession (Article 3).

Where the applicant's education and training is at least one year shorter than that which is required by the host State, or where there is a shortfall in the period of supervised practice required by the host State, the applicant may be required to provide *evidence of professional experience*. This may not exceed the shortfall in supervised practice, nor twice the shortfall in duration of education and training, required by the host State; in any event, it may not exceed four years (Article 4(1)(a)).

The host State may also require an *adaptation period* not exceeding three years:

(a)   where matters covered by the applicant's education and training differ substantially from those covered by that of the State; or

(b)   where the activities regulated in the host State are not regulated in the applicant's State of origin; or

(c)   where the profession regulated in the host State comprises activities which are not pursued in the State from which the applicant originates,

provided, in the latter two situations, the difference corresponds to *specific* education and training required in the host State and covers matters which differ *substantially* from those covered by the evidence of formal qualification (Article 4(1)(b)).

Instead of the adaptation period the applicant may opt for an aptitude test. However, for professions whose practice requires precise knowledge of national law and in which the giving of advice on national law is an essential and constant aspect of that activity, a State may stipulate either an adaptation period or an aptitude test (Article 4(1)(b)).

The requirements of periods of professional experience *and* adaptation cannot be applied cumulatively. Thus the total period cannot exceed four years.

In addition, the host Member State may allow an applicant to undertake in the host State, on a basis of equivalence, that part of his training which consists of supervised professional practice (Article 5).

Member States were required to implement the Directive by 4 January 1991. Thus provisions which are sufficiently clear, precise and unconditional, were directly effective from that date, at least against a 'public' body, an agency of the State (see chapter 4). Since professional bodies normally operate subject to statutory authorisation and control, it is submitted that this factor should constitute a sufficiently 'public' element for the purposes of the enforcement of the Directive. The Directive thus represents a significant breakthrough, removing many of the existing and substantial barriers to the free movement of the employed and the self-employed.

Directive 89/48 has now been supplemented by Directive 92/51, which applies the same principle of mutual recognition to diplomas and certificates awarded after a post secondary education course of at least one year's duration, whether or not they are complemented by professional training and experience. The Directive was due to be implemented by 18 July 1994. However, even in areas not covered, or not yet covered, by these Directives, the Court has held 'that professional bodies of a Member State, in deciding whether to allow persons who do not satisfy their own State's professional requirements, must take into account the applicant's qualification and compare them with the 'home' requirements, in order to assess whether they are in fact equivalent. Applicants are entitled to be given reasons for decisions, and must have an opportunity to challenge them in judicial proceedings (*Vlassopoulou* v *Ministerium für Justiz* (case C–340/89)). There is now a consistent line of authority to this effect.

A person who has qualified in a non-Member State cannot invoke either the Directives or the Community principle of mutual recognition even though the qualification is recognised in a *particular* Member State and the person has been practising the profession *within that State*: the only entitlement is to practise *in that State* (*Tawil-Albertini* v *Ministre des Affaires Sociales* (case C–154/93)). However, if a Member State chooses to recognise such a qualification, it must take into account practical training or professional experience obtained in other Member States in order to determine whether the requisite national training period has been fulfilled (*Haim* v *Kassenzah-närtzliche Vereinigung Nordrhein* (cases C–319/92; C–424/97)). The Council has issued a recommendation encouraging Member States to recognise diplomas and other evidence of formal qualifications obtained by Community nationals in non-Member States (OJ L19/24, 1989).

The impact of professional rules

As well as rules relating to qualifications and training, professional bodies lay down rules governing the conduct of the profession in question, relating both to access to the profession and practice within it. Practice of a profession may be subject to a licensing or registration requirement. Such rules are often reinforced by legislation. These rules are normally justified as in the public good. They do, however, constitute barriers to the free movement of persons, since, as in the case where national standards are applied to imported goods, compliance by persons who have qualified and practised according to the rules of another Member State may be both difficult and expensive. Such rules place a particular burden on the providers of services since they will in all likelihood be subject to professional regulation, providing equivalent standards and safeguards, in the Member State in which they are established. They also fetter freedom of establishment. In some cases, where national rules restrict the categories of persons entitled to practise certain professions the practice of a profession in which a person is fully qualified in his home State may be impossible (e.g. in Italy and France, certain forms of 'alternative' medicine may only be practised by medical doctors: *Nino* (cases C–54 & 91/88 & 14/89) (biotherapy, pranotherapy); *Bouchoucha* (case C–61/89) (osteopathy)).

It is no doubt with these problems in mind that the ECJ has sought to impose some limits on a Member State's powers to demand observance of its own professional rules by persons providing services and even by those seeking establishment in its territory.

In *van Binsbergen* (case 33/74) it was acknowledged, in the context of a challenge to a residence requirement imposed by the Dutch Bar on those seeking to provide certain legal services in Holland, that specific requirements imposed on a person providing services would not infringe the then Articles 59 and 60 (now 49 and 50) where they have as their purpose the application of professional rules justified by the general good — in particular, rules relating to organisation, ethics, qualifications, supervision and liability, which are binding on any person established in the territory of the Member State in which the service is provided. The person providing the service cannot take advantage of his right to provide services to avoid the professional rules of conduct which would be applied to him if he were established in that State. Thus, even a permanent residence requirement for persons engaged in certain activities (e.g., administration of justice) would be permissible where it was objectively justified by the need to ensure the observance of professional rules of conduct.

However, a residence requirement could not be imposed if the desired ends could be achieved by less restrictive means. Professional rules which inhibit the free provision of services would only be permissible if they were:

(a) non-discriminatory,
(b) objectively justified, and
(c) not disproportionate.

These principles were subsequently applied in *Webb* (case 279/80) in the context of the provision of manpower services. The Court added in *Webb* that, in ascertaining whether its own rules are justified, the host Member State must take into account the justifications and safeguards already provided by the applicant in order to pursue the activity in question in his State of establishment (approved in *Commission* v *Germany (Re Lawyers' Services)* (case 427/85)).

The principles expressed in *van Binsbergen* and *Webb* were refined and developed in 1986 in the 'insurance' cases (*Commission* v *Germany (Re Insurance Services)* (case 205/84), *Commission* v *Ireland (Re Co-insurance Services)* (case 206/84), *Commission* v *France* (case 220/83), *Commission* v *Denmark (Re Insurance Services)* (case 252/83)). These actions were based on alleged infringements of the then Articles 59 and 60 (now 49 and 50) and Directive 78/473 (insurance directive) by the defendant Member States in their rules regulating the provision of insurance services. The rules and the breaches alleged in each State were similar. In *Commission* v *Germany,* the rules required, *inter alia,* that a person providing direct insurance must be established and authorised to practise in the State in which the service is provided. In giving judgment the Court first distinguished between establishment and the provision of services, defining establishment broadly, as noted above.

With regard to the provision of services, the Court held that the then Articles 59 and 60 (now 49 and 50) require the removal not only of all discrimination based on nationality but also *all restrictions on his freedom to provide services imposed by reason of the fact that he is established in a Member State other than that in which the services are provided.*

Because of this, the Court held that not *all* the legislation applicable to nationals or those engaged in permanent activities could be applied to the *temporary* activities of enterprises established in another Member State. It could be applied only if three criteria were satisfied:

(a)   it is justified by imperative reasons relating to the public interest;
(b)   the public interest is not already protected by the rules of the State of establishment; and
(c)   the same result cannot be obtained by less restrictive means.

Thus, in the field of services, the Court has moved towards a test for professional rules not unlike the *Cassis de Dijon* (case 120/78) test applied to goods (see chapter 10). As with that test, it is likely that the criteria will be strictly applied to ensure that each rule is necessary and genuinely justified. If not, it will breach Articles 49 and 50 (ex 59 and 60). In *Commission* v *Germany* the Court found that the establishment requirement was not justified; indeed, it was the very negation of the freedom to provide services and would only be permissible if indispensable. The authorisation requirement, on the other hand, at least as related to the rules concerning technical reserves, might be justified for the protection of policyholders and insured persons. Thus the Commission's action failed in this respect. Applying the same approach in *Commission* v *Luxembourg* (case C–351/90) the Court found that a 'single surgery' rule applied in Luxembourg, the effect of which was to prohibit doctors, dentists and veterinary surgeons established outside Luxembourg from opening surgeries in Luxembourg, was not justified, as was argued, in the interest of good professional practice (to ensure proximity to patients). Such a general prohibition (which in any case was applied more strictly to professionals established in other Member States) was found to be 'unduly restrictive', 'too absolute and too general'.

The move towards an approach based on *Cassis*-type principles was confirmed in *Säger* v *Dennemeyer and Co. Ltd* (case C–76/90). Dennemeyer was a specialist in patent renewal services based in the UK. He provided these services in Germany, without the licence which German law requires for persons attending to the legal affairs of third parties. Such licences were not normally granted to patent renewal agents. Dennemeyer's right to provide such services in Germany was challenged by Säger, a German patent agent operating in Germany. Dennemeyer argued that the German rules were a hindrance to the freedom of movement of services, contrary to the then Articles 59 and 60(3) (now 49 and 50(3)). A number of questions were referred to the Court. As Advocate-General Jacobs pointed out, while it was clear that Article 59 (now 49) applied to discriminatory rules, it was not yet clear whether it applied to rules which were applicable to all providers of services, whether established in the Member State in which the service was provided or not. The principles laid down in *van Binsbergen* and the insurance cases had proceeded on the basis that the rules in question were discriminatory. While it was not unreasonable to expect compliance with the rules of the Member State by any person established in that State, there was less justification for demanding compliance by those providing services there. In these circumstances he suggested an approach based on the Court's jurisprudence on the then Article 30 (now 28) in relation to indistinctly applicable rules.

The Court endorsed his suggestion. While asserting that:

> Article 59 [now 49] requires not only the abolition of all discrimination against a person providing services on the ground of his nationality but also the abolition of any restriction, even if applied without distinction to national providers of services and to those of other Member States, when it is liable to prohibit or otherwise impede the activities of a provider of services established in another Member State where he lawfully provides similar services (para. 12)

it held that:

> Having regard to the particular characteristics of certain specific provisions of services, specific requirements imposed on the provider cannot be regarded as incompatible with the Treaty.

However:

> The freedom to provide services may be limited only by rules which are justified by imperative reasons relating to the public interest and which apply to all persons and undertakings pursuing an activity in the State of destination insofar as that interest is not protected by rules to which the person providing the service is subject in the State in which he is established. In particular, these requirements must be objectively necessary in order to ensure compliance with professional rules and must not exceed what is necessary to attain those objectives.

It may be noted that, to establish a prima facie breach of Article 49 (ex 59), the rule challenged must be 'liable to prohibit or otherwise impede' the provision of services. This is a stricter test than the *Dassonville* test applied to goods. On the other hand, the criteria relating to justification, embracing the principles of proportionality and mutual recognition, are substantially the same as the twin principles laid down in *Cassis*, albeit lacking examples as to what will constitute 'imperative reasons relating to the public interest'.

The principles laid down in *Säger* v *Dennemeyer and Co. Ltd* have been followed in a succession of cases in which national or professional rules likely to 'prohibit or otherwise impede' the free provision of services have been tested for their compatibility with Article 49 (ex 59). Thus in *Commission* v *France* (case C–154/89) a requirement of French law that tourist guides must obtain a licence by examination, although justifiable in principle in the interest of consumers as contributing to a 'proper appreciation of places and things of interest', was found to be disproportionate. The licence requirement went further than was necessary in order to protect this interest. In *Vander Elst* v *Office des Migrations Internationales* (case C–43/93) the requirement of a French work permit for third-country nationals seeking to work in France was held not to be justified by 'overriding reasons in the general interest' (to regulate access to the national labour market), since these workers were already in possession of a work permit obtained in Belgium. On the other hand, in *Ramrath* v *Ministre de la Justice* (case C–106/91) rules governing the conditions for the provision of auditing services in Luxembourg were found on the facts to be justified and not disproportionate. Similarly in *Alpine Investments BV* v *Minister van Financiën* (case C–384/93) a Dutch prohibition on 'cold calling' by providers of financial advice established in The Netherlands was found to be justified in order to protect consumers and the reputation of The Netherlands' security market and was not disproportionate. Thus in each case the measure in question and its alleged justification were tested on their merits.

In the more recent case of *Kohll* (case C-158/96 — prior authorisation of medical expenses by home State required), the ECJ citing *Commission* v *France* (case C-381/93) applied a slightly different test from that used in *Säger*. It held that what is now Article 49 (ex 59) 'precludes the application of any national rules which have the effect of making the provision of services between Member States *more difficult* than the provision of services purely within one Member State' (para. 33, authors' emphasis). It is not clear whether the use of this test will become generalized within Article 49 case law nor, indeed, what difference in practice the use of this test would make. In any event, as with other services case, the measure in question must be examined to identify if it is objectively justified.

In all these cases except *Vander Elst* and *Kohll* (which, involving third-country workers and social security respectively, may be regarded as 'special') the rules applied equally to all providers of services in the Member State in question, that is, they were 'indistinctly applicable'. Although some of the measures could have been described as 'discriminatory' to the extent that they imposed an extra burden on non-national providers, the Court did not approach the matter as one of discrimination. It is submitted that this is a more satisfactory approach to indistinctly applicable measures than one based on the slippery (and often artificial) concept of discrimination. Only distinctly applicable or overtly discriminatory measures should now breach Article 49 (ex 59) *per se*, capable of justification only under Article 46 (ex 56).

The principles established in *Säger* v *Dennemeyer and Co. Ltd* appeared to apply only to the provision of services. Paragraph 13, suggested that:

a Member State may not make the provision of services in its territory subject to the conditions required for establishment . . . and thereby deprive of all practical effectiveness the provisions of the Treaty whose object is, primarily, to provide services.

This implied that persons who established themselves in a Member State must comply with the conditions laid down in that State for its own nationals. Following *Gebhard* v *Consiglio dell'Ordine degli Avvocati e Procuratori di Milano* (case C–55/94) this appears not now to be the case. *Gebhard* involved a challenge by a German lawyer, a member of the Stuttgart Bar, to a decision by the Milan Bar Council prohibiting him from practising from chambers set up in Italy under the title 'avvocato'. He claimed the rules of the Milan Bar breached the then Articles 59 and/or 52 (now 49 and 43). As noted above, his situation was found to fall within the concept of establishment, and therefore outside the scope of Lawyers' Directive 77/249 concerning services. Directive 89/48 on mutual recognition did not apply. To what extent, then, could the rules relating to qualifications and professional practice at the Italian Bar be enforced against him?

The Court held that the possibility for a national of a Member State to exercise his right of establishment, and the conditions for the exercise of that right, had to be determined in the light of the activities which he intended to pursue on the territory of the host Member State. Where an activity was not subject to any rules in the host State, a national of another Member State was entitled to establish himself on the territory of the first State and pursue his activities there. On the other hand, 'Where the taking up and pursuit of a particular activity was subject to certain conditions in the host State a national of another Member State intending to pursue that activity must in principle comply with them'. However:

National measures which hinder or make less attractive the exercise of fundamental freedoms guaranteed by the Treaty must fulfil four conditions:
(i)   they must be applied in a non-discriminatory manner;
(ii)   they must be justified by imperative requirements in the general interest;
(iii)   they must be suitable for securing the attainment of the objective which they pursue;
(iv)   they must not go beyond what is necessary in order to attain it.
Member states must take into account the equivalence of diplomas and if necessary proceed to a comparison of the knowledge and qualifications required by their national rules and those of the person concerned.

It was left to the national court to decide whether the rules in question were in fact justified.

Thus *Gebhard* squares the circle by bringing the rules relating to establishment into line with those relating to services. The difference between them is now one of fact and possibly result but not of principle. Indeed, since the emphasis in both cases is on justification for the rules in terms of the *activity undertaken* rather than on the burden imposed on the 'guest' undertaking, it is possible that the result in both cases will be the same. It is worthy of note that conditions which simply 'hinder or make less attractive' the fundamental freedoms provided by the Treaty will now require justification. This is less strict than the 'prohibit or otherwise impede' threshold introduced in *Säger* v *Dennemeyer and Co. Ltd*. Whether this test is now to be applied to both establishment and services is not clear. In *Gebhard* the ECJ noted that both constitute 'fundamental freedoms provided by the Treaty'. It would thus make sense that the same test is applied to both Articles. Nonetheless in recent case law on Article 49 (ex 59) EC, the ECJ has in the main applied the *Säger* test and has not adopted that set out in *Gebhard*. In any event, the Court has turned its back on an earlier suggestion from Advocate-General Jacobs (delivered in the context of claims based on the then Article 59 and Article 30 (now 49 and 28 respectively), see *Alpine Investments* (case C–384/93) and *Leclerc-Siplec* (case C–412/93)) that the Court adopt a *de minimis* rule, and only rules which 'substantially impede' the freedom to provide services will be deemed prima facie in breach of Community law. The trend as regards Article 43 (ex 52) EC (and to a lesser degree Articles 49 and 50 (ex 59 and 60)) seems to be towards a weaker *Dassonville*-type test. Ironically this is occurring a time when the Court in *Keck* (cases C–267 & 268/91) and subsequent cases appears to be adopting a more lenient approach to indistinctly applicable rules in the context of claims concerning goods under Article 28 (ex 30) EC (see *De Agostini* (cases C–34–6/98) and chapter 10.

As is the case for qualifications, where Directives have been passed harmonising or recognising professional rules the provisions of the Directive will be conclusive on the matter. However, in each case it will be necessary to decide whether the rule in question has been covered by the Directive. For example, the Lawyers Directive (Directive 77/249) gave limited rights to provide services: it did not give rights of establishment. This position will be changed by the new Lawyers Directive (Directive 98/5 [1998] OJ L77/36), to be implemented by 14 March 2000. In *Commission* v *Germany* (case 205/84) the insurance Directive was found to be designed to ensure that undertakings were solvent; it did not attempt to harmonise national rules concerning technical reserves. Thus the rules protecting this interest fell to be judged according to the threefold criteria laid down by the Court.

A new approach to harmonisation

As with the area of professional qualifications and training, the Commisson, in its White Paper of 1985, determined on a new approach to professional rules and standards with a view to the completion of the internal market in services by January 1992. In place of the 'endless fruitless search for common rules and standards', the Commission was to adopt an approach similar to that which it was to apply to goods (see chapter 10). This was to be based on:

(a)   the harmonisation of *essential* safeguards and standards applicable to activities as a whole; and
(b)   within that framework, acceptance of the standards of other Member States on a basis of mutual trust and recognition, on the principle of home country control and supervision.

Essential to the effective functioning of these principles would be the concept of the single licence known as home country regulation. This would allow an institution licensed in one Member State to offer its services to another Member State, either by establishing a branch or agency in that State or by supplying its services there.

These principles have formed the basis for important legislation in the field of banking, insurance, investment and postal services. Substantial progress in all these areas has now been made (for details see *Directory of Community Legislation in Force*, ch. 06). In the absence of legislation, or where provision is incomplete, the principles of *Säger* (case C–76/90) and *Gebhard* (case C–55/94) may now be invoked to fill lacunae.

Other barriers to freedom

In addition to rules governing qualifications and standards of practice there may be other measures taken by Member States capable of hindering the freedom of establishment or the freedom to provide services. Rules which discriminate against non-nationals will clearly breach Articles 43, 49 and 50 (ex 52, 59 and 60) EC, and require justification under Article 46 (ex 56). It might have been expected that rules which were not discriminatory, which applied without distinction to all persons providing services or establishing themselves in a Member State, might have been treated by analogy with the principles of *Dassonville* (case 8/74) and *Cassis* (case 120/78) in the sphere of goods. Once a hindrance to cross-border provision of services or establishment had been established the measure might be justified on the ground of imperative reasons of public interest, provided that it was suitable and necessary to achieve its purpose. This was not initially the case.

It was only with *Her Majesty's Customs and Excise* v *Schindler* (case C–275/92) that the Court unequivocally adopted the *Säger* (case C–76/90) line of reasoning to indistinctly applicable measures outside the sphere of professional qualifications and rules. The case arose when HM Customs confiscated invitations and application forms sent by Schindler from The Netherlands, inviting participation in a lottery organised by the German Länder. Schindler, who acted on behalf of the organisers, sought to prevent the invitations being confiscated under UK legislation. He claimed that the UK rules infringed his freedom to provide services, contrary to the then Articles 59 and 60 (now 49 and 50). This time the Court followed the

Advocate-General's advice. It found that the organisation of lotteries such as the one in question constituted an economic activity within the then Article 59 (now 49). Although it was applicable without distinction to British as well as non-British lotteries, it was likely to 'prohibit or otherwise impede' the provision of lottery services. It was, however, justified by 'overriding considerations of public interest', in this case the protection of consumers and the maintenance of order in society, and it was not disproportionate, since such activities involved a high risk of crime and fraud. Unlike Advocate-General Gulman the Court did not consider the relevance or scope of the then Article 56 (now 46).

It may be hoped that this exemplary approach to indistinctly applicable rules will be applied to all measures which 'prohibit or otherwise impede' the free provision of services. As regards establishment, it seems that the ECJ is also taking the *Gebhard* approach in circumstances other than those relating to professional conduct or qualifications. In *Sodemare SA* v *Regione Lombardia* (case C–70/95) the ECJ adopted a similar approach, although, on the facts, it found that the Italian authorities were entitled to limit the involvement of the private sector in old people's homes to non profit-making bodies. Thus the trend towards harmonisation of the rules relating to goods, establishment and services is continuing. As with claims involving the free movement of goods, there is a case for the adoption of a *de minimis* rule, in order to prevent abuses (see Advocate-General Jacobs in *Alpine Investments* (case C–384/93) and *Leclerc-Siplec* (case C–412/93) and chapter 10) and this approach seems to have been taken in the context of workers in *Graf* (case C–150/98). Overtly discriminatory measures will continue to be justifiable only under Article 46 (ex 56) EC, just as discriminatory measures affecting the free movement of goods can only be justified under Article 30 (ex 36) EC.

Home country regulation and abuse of freedom of establishment and the right to provide services

There has been a concern that the exercise of free movement rights in certain contexts may give rise to a dilution of national standards as businesses establish themselves in the Member State with the most favourable regime and then rely on Articles 43 (ex 52) or 49 (ex 59) to trade in Member States with more stringent regulatory regimes.

In both the field of education and training and professional rules, and whether or not the activity in question is subject to EC Regulation, the Court has made it clear that Community law may not be used (or abused) in order to undermine the legitimate rules and standards of Member States. For example, in *van de Bijl* v *Staatssecretaris van Economische Zaken* (case 130/88), the Court was asked to rule on a claim by a Dutch decorator, based on EC Directive 64/427, which provides, *inter alia*, for the mutual recognition of qualifications for self-employed persons in small craft industries. Under the Directive States are required to accept a certification of competence and work experience provided by the appropriate authorities of another Member State in respect of work performed in that State. It was suggested in van de Bijl's case that the certificate issued by the UK authorities, which the Dutch authorities had refused to accept as a basis for registration in Holland, was based on questionable evidence. The Court held that the host (i.e. Dutch) State was entitled to take steps (e.g. verification of evidence) to prevent the relevant Community rules being used for the purpose of circumventing the rules relating to particular occupations applicable to its nationals (see also *van Binsbergen* (case 33/74)).

Another case involving deliberate manipulation of EC rules is *TV10* (case C–23/93), in which a company established itself in one Member State and broadcast into another Member State, The Netherlands, thus hoping to avoid the Dutch limitations on broadcast advertising. When challenged it was argued that the Dutch rules constituted a barrier to the freedom to provide broadcasting services. Arguably, this case could have been decided on the basis that the Dutch rules were indistinctly applicable and justifiable (the Dutch rules were aimed at protecting pluralism in the media). The ECJ approached the issue differently. It adopted a broad interpretation of the concept of establishment and decided that the company involved was actually established in The Netherlands. On this basis, the Dutch rules were applicable to the broadcaster.

The extent to which this is good law now is debatable. The argument that VT4 Ltd, a company established under the laws of England and Wales, was actually established in Belgium as that was the Member State to which its broadcasts were directed was put forward, but discounted, in another broadcasting case: *VT4 Ltd v Vlaamse Gemeenschap* (case C–56/96). More recently, in *Centros v Erhvervs- og Selskabsstyrelsen* (case C–212/97), the ECJ had to consider an attempt to exploit the difference in national rules relating to company formation. Under English law there is no minimum share capital requirement, whereas in Danish law there is a minimum capital requirement of DKK 200,000. Two Danish nationals incorporated a company in the UK (which had a capital on £100, only £2 of which was paid up) and then sought to rely on freedom of establishment to trade in Denmark. They made no attempt to trade in the UK. The Danish authorities refused to register the establishment of a branch office of the company in Denmark, since to do so would constitute a way of avoiding the Danish rules on the provision for and the paying-up of minimum share capital. The ECJ referred in its judgment to previous cases involving abuse of Community law and distinguished between situations where the rules avoided related to provision of a service (as in *TV10*) and the current situation, which related to the establishment of a company. The ECJ then commented that the very purpose of the Treaty is to allow companies to set up subsidiaries and branches throughout the Community. It then concluded:

That being so, the fact that a national of a Member State who wishes to set up a company chooses to form it in the Member State whose rules of company law seem to him the least restrictive and to set up branches in other Member States cannot, in itself, constitute an abuse of the right of establishment. The right to form a company in accordance with the law of a Member State and to set up branches in other Member States is inherent in the exercise, in a single market, of the freedom of establishment guaranteed by the Treaty. (para. 27)

The Court then concluded that the objectives pursued by the Danish regulations (the protection of creditors) did not fall within the derogation provided by the then Article 56 (now 46). The Court's approach would seem, then, to be an attempt to narrow the possible use of the 'abuse' exception to the free movement principle, although the precise scope of the *Centros* ruling is, as yet, not clear.

Problems with a perceived downward spiral of standards may also arise when policy areas have been harmonised by Directive. Minimum harmonisation allows Member States to set different standards, higher than those set out in the Directive. These rules must of course be compatible with general treaty objectives. The difficulty in this context arises when there is a market access clause. This will mean that a Member State may require those established within its jurisdiction to comply with the higher standards but cannot impose these requirements on those established elsewhere in the Community. This is often referred to as negative or reverse discrimination. As is the case with goods (see chapter 10), this is permissible under Community law. It is also open to abuse, but it would seem that the same general rules apply as do to the Treaty articles. The ECJ, in some cases, seems to have avoided this difficulty by re-characterising the legal issue in question, so as to allow the host Member State some control. In *De Agostini* (case C–34–6/98), the question of broadcasting aimed at children in Sweden would seem to fall under the Television without Frontiers Directive (89/552, as subsequently amended by 97/36), which contained a market access clause. The broadcaster was established in the UK, which does not prohibit such broadcasts. On this assessment, given the market access clause and the rules of the Member State in which the broadcaster was established, the Swedish could do nothing to stop the broadcasts. The ECJ, however, took the view that the advertisements should be seen as relating to the sale of the goods they were advertising rather than the service of broadcasting, thereby removing regulation away from the British and allowing the Swedes to maintain their rules (provided such rules operate equally in law and in fact). (See also chapter 10.)

This area of law is problematic. It highlights the ever-present tension between the need to create and to facilitate the functioning of the internal market and the competence of the Member States and their legitimate concerns. As with the pre-*Keck* case law on the scope of Article 28 (ex 30), the Court seems to be encountering some difficulty in distinguishing between legitimate exploitation of rules and their abuse. It is indeed unfortunate that the ECJ has not developed a unified principle to deal with cases in this area.

Activities connected with the exercise of official authority

Article 45 (ex 55) EC provides that:

The provisions of this Chapter [right of establishment] shall not apply, so far as any given Member State is concerned, to activities which in that State are connected, even occasionally, with the exercise of official authority.

This provision also applies to the provision of services (Article 55 (ex 66) EC).

This derogation has been considered in some detail in chapter 20 in the context of Article 39(4) (ex 48(4)) relating to workers. The principles applicable to workers will apply equally to the establishment and services provisions. As in the case of workers, the derogation has been given the narrowest scope.

It was invoked in *Reyners* v *Belgium* (case 2/74). One of the arguments raised by the Belgian government in defending the Belgian Bar's rule restricting the profession of *avocat* to Belgian nationals was that the profession of *avocat* fell within the then Article 55 (now 45); it was connected with official authority. The Court disagreed. Article 55 (now 45) applied only to 'activities' connected with the exercise of official authority; it did not apply to professions or occupations as a whole. The derogation, the Court held, was aimed at the exercise of *prerogative power*. While the exercise of judicial power would represent an exercise of official authority, the activities of an *avocat* would not.

In *Thijssen* v *Controladienst voor de Verzekeringen* (case C–42/92) the Court found that the post of Approved Commissioner, subject to appointment as an adviser by insurance undertakings from a list compiled by the Belgian Office de Contrôle des Assurances, and who had a duty to assist that Office in an auxiliary and preparatory role, could not be considered to involve 'direct and specific participation in the exercise of official authority within the meaning of Article 55(1) [now 45(1)]'. Thus eligibility for such a post could not be confined to Belgian nationals.

Freedom to provide services and the exercise of industrial property rights

It was held in *Coditel* v *Ciné Vog* (case 62/79) that the freedom to provide services granted by the then Article 59 (now 49) could not be invoked to prevent the legitimate exercise of industrial property rights. Here, SA Ciné Vog Films, a Belgian film distribution company owning performing rights in certain films in Belgium, including a film called *Le Boucher,* sought to prevent Coditel, which operated a cable television service in Belgium, from picking up *Le Boucher* from German television and transmitting it in Belgium, in breach of Ciné Vog's copyright. Coditel argued that to prevent it from so doing would constitute an interference with its freedom to provide services, in breach of the then Article 59 (now 49). On a reference from the Tribunal de Première Instance, Brussels, the ECJ held that that Article does not encompass limits on the exercise of certain economic activities which have their origin in the application of national legislation for the protection of intellectual property, save where such application constitutes a means of arbitrary discrimination or a disguised restriction on trade between Member States. Such would be the case if that application enabled parties to an assignment of copyright to create artificial barriers to trade between Member States. This was not found to be the case with Ciné Vog.

Thus, as with the application of Article 30 (ex 36) EC in the context of goods (see chapter 11) the legitimate use of industrial property rights is protected; its misuse is not.

Freedom to receive services

The freedom provided by Articles 49 and 50 (ex 59 and 60) is expressed in terms of the freedom to *provide* services. It has now been extended by the ECJ to embrace the freedom to *receive* services.

The point was originally raised in *Watson* (case 118/75), where the Commission suggested that the freedom to move within the Community to receive services was the necessary corollary to the freedom to provide services. This was approved by the Court in *Luisi* v *Ministero del Tesoro* (case 286/82) in the context of criminal proceedings in Italy against Luisi and Carbone for breach of Italian currency regulations. They were accused of taking foreign currency out of the country in excess of the maximum permitted under Italian law. They had taken the money out for the purposes of tourism and medical treatment. The question referred to the ECJ was whether payment for such services represented movements of capital, within the then Articles 67–73 of the EC Treaty (provisions which will be deleted by the ToA), or payments for the provision of services; if the latter, was it governed by the then Articles 59–66 (now 49–55)?

Advocate-General Mancini, arguing from *Watson* (case 118/75) suggested that Article 59 (now 49) was concerned with the receipt of services as well as their provision. In support of this view he cited the general programme for the abolition of restrictions on the freedom to provide services (*Common Market Reporter*, para. 1545, JO 1962, 32), Directive 64/221, which expressly refers in Article 1(1) to 'freedom of movement for employed or self-employed persons or the *recipients* of services' and Directive 73/148, Article 1(1)(b), which requires Member States to abolish restrictions on the movement and residence of 'nationals of Member States wishing to go to another Member State as *recipients* of services'.

The Court, following Advocate-General Mancini, found the money to be payment for services and held that freedom to provide services, as provided by Article 59 (now 49), includes the freedom, for recipients of services, to go to another Member State, without restriction, in order to receive a service there. Recipients of services were held to include tourists, persons receiving medical treatment and persons travelling for the purposes of education and business.

Thus the right to enter and remain in another Member State for the purpose of receiving services is established. In *Commission* v *Netherlands (Re Entry into Dutch Territory)* (case C–68/89) the Court held that nationals of one EC State were entitled to enter another Member State simply on production of a valid identity card or passport. National immigration authorities were not entitled to question EC nationals seeking to enter a Member State except in order to query the validity of the identity card or passport. On the other hand, when applying for a residence permit national authorities may require proof of the applicant's status as a provider or recipient of services. Recipients of services are entitled to residence for the period during which the service is provided (Directive 73/148, Article 4(2)). Any restrictions on these freedoms will prima facie breach Articles 49 and 50 (ex 59 and 60), subject to limitation on the grounds of public policy, public security and public health (Articles 46 and 55 (ex 56 and 66) EC). The question remains whether the recipient of services, by reason of his status or his right of residence, can invoke these Articles, together with Article 12 (ex 6) EC, to claim equality of treatment with nationals of the host State. A number of services, such as education and medicine, are publicly funded and provided not so much as a commercial activity but as a public service. Are these to be available to nationals of the Member States on the same basis as to the States' own citizens?

Education: vocational training

This matter was considered in the context of educational services in *Gravier* v *City of Liège* (case 293/83). The applicant in this case was a young French woman who had applied to and been accepted by the Liège Académie des Beaux-Arts for a four-year course in the art of strip cartoons. As a foreign student she was charged a special fee, known as a *'minerval'*, for the course. This was not payable by Belgian citizens, whether or not they lived or paid taxes in Belgium, nor by EC nationals working in Belgium, or members of their families. She brought an action before the Belgian Courts, claiming the fee was discriminatory. Her case rested on two arguments.

First, she suggested that the *minerval* constituted an obstacle to her freedom of movement to receive services as established in *Luisi* v *Ministero del Tesoro* (case 286/82) in breach of Article 59 (now 49). Her second argument was based on the vocational nature of the course. Vocational education fell within the scope of the Treaty; as a matter covered by EC law it was discriminatory, in breach of the original Article 7 EEC (now 12) (ex 6) EC), to charge higher prices to EC nationals who were not Belgian citizens or resident in Belgium. This argument was based primarily on *Forcheri's* case (case 152/82), see chapter 20. Here Ms Forcheri, the wife of an Italian working in Brussels, had succeeded in challenging the higher fees demanded of her as a non-national, to attend a social work course in Brussels. Although her success was based primarily on her lawful residence in Belgium as the wife of an EC worker, which brought her 'within the scope and application of this Treaty' and thus former Article 7 EEC (now Article 12 EC), it rested in part on the fact that the course for which she subscribed was vocational. Vocational training, the Court held, was one of the matters covered by Community law; covered in general terms by the then Article 128 EEC ('The Council shall, acting on a proposal from the Commission and after consulting the

Economic and Social Committee, lay down general principles for implementing a common vocational training policy') and specifically, at least for workers and their children, in Regulation 1612/68 (Articles 7(3) and 12, see chapter 20). Therefore provision of vocational training was subject to former Article 7 of the EEC Treaty (now Article 12 EC).

The ECJ, following Advocate-General Sir Gordon Slynn, found in Ms Gravier's favour on this second ground. Access to vocational training was a matter covered by Community law; moreover, it was an essential element in promoting freedom of movement for persons throughout the Community. The Court expressly dissociated itself from the wider issues involved, discussed at length by Sir Gordon Slynn, concerning the organisation and financing of such courses, and confined its judgment merely to conditions of access to a course affecting foreign students alone, and relating to a particular kind of course, namely vocational education. However, its definition of vocational education was very wide. It was held to include all forms of teaching which prepares for and leads directly to a particular profession, trade or employment, or which provides the necessary skills for such profession, trade or employment, even if the programme of instruction includes an element of general education.

The decision in *Gravier* caused considerable concern amongst Member States. This decision, with its wide definition of vocational training, meant that many courses, including perhaps university courses, often entailing substantial contributions from public funds (the Belgians pointed out that the *minerval* itself only covered 50 per cent of the cost of the education provided), would have to be offered on equal terms to all EC nationals. Moreover, the precise scope of the term 'vocational training' was unclear. Subsequent cases have provided some answers to these questions.

In *Blaizot* v *University of Liège* (case 24/86), in the context of a claim by university students of veterinary science for reimbursement of the *minerval,* based on *Gravier,* the Court applied the *Gravier* definition of vocational training and held that university education could constitute vocational training:

> not only where the final exam directly provides the required qualification but also insofar as the studies provide specific training (i.e. where the student needs the knowledge so acquired for the pursuit of his trade or profession), even if no legislative or administrative provisions make the acquisition of such knowledge a prerequisite.

In general university courses would meet these criteria. The only exception would be courses designed for persons seeking to 'improve their general knowledge rather than prepare themselves for an occupation'. Even where, as in veterinary or medical science, the training comprises two stages, the second representing the practical stage, the first, academic stage must be regarded as vocational. The two stages must be viewed as a single unit.

Similar reasoning informed the Court's decision in *Belgium* v *Humbel* (case 263/86). This case concerned a claim by the Belgian authorities for the payment of the *minerval* in respect of *secondary* education received in Belgium by the son of a French national living in Luxembourg. Although the course as a whole appeared to be vocational, the fees giving rise to the dispute concerned one year within that course of general education. The Court held that such a course of general education must none the less be treated as 'vocational' if it forms an integral part of an overall programme of vocational education.

Finally, on the same day as the decision in *Humbel*, the Court, in a case brought by the Commission against Belgium (*Commission* v *Belgium* (case 42/87)) challenging its rules on access to higher education, revised in the light of *Gravier*, allowing access, *inter alia*, to only 2 per cent of 'outsiders', held that inasmuch as the rules related to vocational training they were in breach of Article 7 EEC (now Article 12 EC).

Thus, where educational courses are concerned, provided they are found *overall* to be vocational, according to the generous interpretation provided by the Court, EC nationals who are neither migrant workers nor the children of migrant workers living in the State in which the education is provided may claim equal access under equal conditions to nationals of the home State, even if the courses are financed or subsidised by the State as a matter of social policy.

Gravier was indeed a landmark case, an example of the Court in activist mood. The legal basis for the decision, resting on (what was at the time) Article 128 EEC, is slender. While Article 128 EEC may have provided a sufficient legal basis for the issuing of Directives in the field of vocational training (as the Court found in *UK* v *Commission* (case 56/88)), it may be doubted that it was sufficiently clear, precise and unconditional to give rise to direct effects. Article 128 EEC was replaced in the Maastricht Treaty by Article 127 (now 150) EC, which requires the Community to implement a vocational training policy which will 'support and supplement the action of Member States while fully respecting the responsibility of the Member States for the content and organisation of vocational training'. This Article represents one of several specific examples of the subsidiarity principle introduced by the TEU. The TEU also introduced a specific provision relating to education, Article 149 EC (ex 126), although the precise relationship between Article 149 and the new Article 150 is not clear.

Scholarships and grants

The Court in *Gravier* (case 293/83) refrained from considering whether the right of EC nationals to vocational training carried with it a right to grants and scholarships from the host State to enable them to take up these courses. Advocate-General Sir Gordon Slynn was clearly of the opinion that such a right was not included in the right to receive services. In this same context the Belgian, Danish and British governments regarded such a result as unthinkable in view of the differences which exist between the number of students moving, for educational purposes, into different Member States. The matter was resolved in *Brown* and *Lair* (cases 197/86, 39/86: for detailed discussion of these cases see chapter 20). Both *Brown* and *Lair* involved claims for maintenance grants for university courses. In both cases their entitlement to the grants as 'workers', or the 'children of migrant workers', was doubtful. So they sought also to rely on *Gravier,* arguing that the course in question constituted vocational training, to which the then Article 7 EEC applied. Thus they were entitled to be treated on a footing of equality with nationals.

The Court, no doubt anxious to quell the anxieties of Member States on this issue, disagreed. Although university courses (following *Blaizot*) were capable of constituting vocational training, to which they were entitled to equal access in respect of fees, Article 7 EEC (now Article 12 (ex 6) EC) did not apply to maintenance grants. Assistance in the form of maintenance grants, the Court held, fell outside the scope of the EC Treaty. It was a matter of educational policy, and, as such, had not been entrusted to the Community institutions; it was also a matter of social policy, which fell within the competence of Member States insofar as it was not covered by the provisions of the EC Treaty.

Whilst there is little logic in the distinction between fees, which relate to conditions of access to vocational training, and maintenance grants, which do not, it is clear that the judgments in *Brown* and *Lair* reflected the Court's desire, on grounds of policy, to call a halt to the development of a Community educational policy by means of judicial decision. The judgments were greeted with relief by Member States.

The specific right of students to residence lasting for the duration of their course of studies was enacted in Directive 90/366 (Article 2) (OJ L 180, 13.7.90, p. 30), as reintroduced in 1993 following its annulment by the Court (see chapter 19). Families' rights are confined to spouses and dependent children. The Directive expressly provides that it 'shall not establish any entitlement to the payment of maintenance grants by the host Member State on the part of students benefiting from the right of residence (Article 3).

More recently, in an October 1996 Green Paper entitled *Obstacles to Mobility,* the Commission identified that the position of those seeking to move for educational or training purposes was still relatively weak compared to those who moved to work. Amongst its nine main proposals, it suggested in particular that measures be taken to ensure 'social protection' for anyone wanting to travel in the Union as part of training or studying, this facility already being accorded to people moving in the EU for the purposes of employment. It further suggested the creation of a European area of qualifications through mutual recognition of studies and training courses in another Member State; and the abolition of the 'territoriality' of grants, thereby allowing the least privileged to train or study in another Member State. Lastly, it proposed that a legal framework be established to deal with the situation of 'student/trainees' and volunteers in the Union, to solve the problems of social security and taxation. No action has yet been taken on these proposals.

Cross-border medical care

Similar issues concerning the inter-relationship between the public provision of services and the scope of the freedom of provide (and receive) services that arose in the field of education have also arisen in the context of cross-border medical care.

Kohll (case C-158/96) concerned the Luxembourgoise requirement that, if an individual wanted to be able to reclaim the cost of medical treatment outside Luxembourg back from the medical insurance company, then prior authorisation granted only in limited circumstances would be required. Kohll sought to challenge this rule on the basis of what was then Article 59 (now 49). The Luxembourg government argued that the rule complied with Article 22 of Regulation 1408/71 concerning social security. The ECJ agreed that in principle it is for Member States to organise their own social security systems, including the right or duty to be insured with a social security scheme and the benefits available under any such scheme, it held that in doing so Member States must comply with Community law, including the right to provide and receive services. The ECJ held that the orthodontist's treatment in Germany in issue in this case was to be considered 'services' for the purposes of the EC Treaty as the treatment was provided for remuneration and constituted a professional activity. Thus the Luxembourg social security rules regarding medical treatment had to be considered in the light of Article 49 (ex 59). They were found to constitute a barrier to the freedom to provide services and were not objectively justified either for the protection of the financial equilibrium of the social security system or for reasons of national health.

This judgment (and *Decker* (case C-120/95), handed down the same day concerning the provision of spectacles and therefore considered under Article 28 (ex 30); see chapter 10), which caused some concern among many Member States, raised many questions about the scope of the Treaty freedoms in the context of public health care and the congruence between the case law regarding medical care and the existing case law on public services.

In this context it should be noted that the *Kohll* situation is different from the cases on education. In those cases, the host Member State bore the cost the individuals moving to receive services; here, the cost is repatriated. Concern has arisen as to whether the *Kohll* approach will be adopted in regard to health care systems which operate by providing the service free rather than by reimbursing the cost, a question which has been referred to the ECJ in the as-yet not decided cases of *Geraets-Smits v Stichting Ziekenfonds* and *H.T.M. Peerbooms v Stichting CZ Groep Zorgverzekeringen* (case C-157/99). The Advocate General in this case has, however, adopted the reasoning in *Humbel* and *Wirth* (discussed below) to suggest that the provision of health care in such systems does not fall within Article 50 (ex 60) EC, constituting instead part of the Member State's obligation towards its population (para. 47).

Scope of equality principle

One further question, raised but not answered in *Gravier* (case 293/83), was whether the equality principle could be applied as an adjunct to the right, established in *Luisi* (case 286/82) to move within the Community to *receive* services under Article 59 (now 49). In considering the question in *Gravier*, Advocate-General Sir Gordon Slynn suggested that in the sphere of education a distinction should be drawn between education which was provided by private finance, with a view to profit, and education as a public service, financed wholly or partly by the State, as an aspect of social policy. Similar reasoning was adopted by the Court in *Humbel* (case 263/86). Here, the claimant, a French youth, living with his family in Luxembourg, sought to resist the payment of the *minerval* in respect of his secondary education in Belgium on the basis of his right to receive services under the then Article 59. (His claim under former Article 7 EEC and vocational training has been noted above.) The Court pointed out that Article 59 (now 49) applies to 'services provided for remuneration'. The essential characteristic of remuneration is that it 'constitutes the countervailing financial advantage for the services in question and is normally fixed between the supplier and the recipient of the services' (para. 17). This characteristic is not present in the case of a course of study provided in the framework of a national educational system. In providing such a system the State is fulfilling its duty to its people in the social, cultural, or educational field. These principles were affirmed by the Court in *Wirth* v *Landeshaupt Hannover* (case C–109/92).

Thus apart from the area of vocational training (access and fees) which is governed by *Gravier*, services such as health and education provided by the State for the benefit of its citizens, and not for commercial reasons, with a view to profit, cannot be claimed on a basis of equality by EC nationals who have temporary residence as recipients of services but do not enjoy 'lawful residence' on a 'settled' or permanent basis as 'favoured Community citizens', that is, those who are or have been, employed and self-employed migrants and their families (see chapter 19) in the State providing the services.

The equality principle was applied to benefit a recipient of services in rather different circumstances in *Cowan* v *French Treasury* (case 186/87). Here the claimant, an English citizen on holiday in Paris, was claiming compensation for personal injuries sustained as a result of a mugging in the Paris Metro. Under French law compensation in respect of such injuries was provided out of public funds and payable only to French nationals. Cowan claimed that since he was claiming as a tourist, exercising his freedom to receive services, this rule was in breach of former Article 7 EEC (now Article 12 (ex 6) EC. The ECJ held that as a recipient of services he was entitled to equal protection against, and compensation for, the risks of assault. This right was a corollary of his right to receive services.

Since the judgment was expressed in narrow, specific terms, it remains to be seen what rights are to be regarded as a 'corollary' to the right to receive services.

In *Commission* v *Spain* (case C–45/93) the Court found that in charging discriminatory entrance fees to national museums (lower fees being charged for Spanish citizens and residents and EC nationals under 21 years) Spain was acting in breach of Article 6 (now 12) EC (at the time Article 7 EEC) and Article 59 (now 49) EC. The freedom to provide services recognised by Article 59 included the freedom for recipients of services, including tourists, to go to another Member State in order to enjoy those services under the same conditions as nationals. Since visiting museums was one of the determining reasons for which tourists decide to go to another Member State, any discrimination with regard to admission would influence some persons' decisions to visit the country. The fact that a museum service was a public service financed by the State was not raised by the Spanish government and thus not considered by the Court.

In a rather different context, in *Hubbard* v *Hamburger* (case C–20/92), a provision of German law requiring a national of another Member State who, in the capacity of executor of a will, had brought proceedings before one of its courts, to lodge security for costs, something which was not required of German nationals, was held to constitute discrimination on grounds of nationality, prohibited by the then Articles 59 and 60 (now 49 and 50) EC. Although in this case both the provider (the executor) and the recipient (the beneficiary) of services were established outside German territory (in the UK), the rule was clearly a barrier to the free provision of services.

Thus the scope of application of the non-discrimination principle as applied to recipients of services remains unclear, although recent cases indicate that it will not be ungenerously applied. It is submitted that with the espousal by the Community of the concept of European citizenship the Court will seek to prohibit discrimination against EC nationals and their families in all areas except where the State is fulfilling its duty to its people in the social, cultural or educational field and where reciprocity cannot be guaranteed, particularly where a substantial outlay of public funds may be involved.

Further reading

See also reading for chapters 18 and 19.

Art J., 'Legislative Lacunae; the Court of Justice and Freedom to Provide Services', in Curtin, D., and O'Keeffe, D. (eds), *Constitutional Adjudication in European Community Law and National Law* (Butterworths Ireland, 1992), p. 121.

Cabral, P., 'Cross-border medical care in the European Union — bringing down a first wall' (1999) 24 EL Rev 387.

Daniele, L., 'Non-discriminatory Restrictions to the Free Movement of Persons' (1997) 22 EL Rev 191.

Dine, J., 'The Harmonization of Companyy Law in the European Community' (1989) 9 YEL 93.

Edward, D., 'Establishment and Services: an Analysis of the Insurance Cases' (1987) 12 EL Rev 231.

Lonbay, J., 'Education and Law: the Community Context' (1989) 14 EL Rev 363.

Looijestijn-Clearie, A., '*Centros Ltd* — A complete U-Turn in the Right of Establishment for Companies?' (2000) 49 ICLQ 621.

Mei, A. P., 'Cross-Border Access to Medical Care within the European Union — Some Reflections on the Judgments in *Decker* and *Kohll*' [1998] *Maastricht Journal of European and Comparative Law* 277.

Pertek, J., 'Free Movement of Professionals and Recognition of Higher Education Diplomas' (1992) 12 YEL 293.

Roth, W. H., 'The European Community's Law on Services: Harmonisation' (1988) 25 CML Rev 35.

Van der Woude, M., and Meade, P., 'Free Movement of the Tourist in Community Law' (1988) 25 CML Rev 117.

TWENTY TWO

Free movement of persons: limitation on grounds of public policy, public security or public health (Directive 64/221)

The exception provided by Articles 39(3) and 46 (ex 48(3) and 56) EC was implemented in Directive 64/221 to give substance to the rather vague and potentially catch-all provisions of the Treaty. It allows for 'special measures concerning the movement and residence of foreign nationals which are justified on the grounds of public policy, public security and public health'. The scope of the Directive is twofold. First it lays down the principles on which a State may refuse entry or residence to those who would otherwise be eligible, on the grounds of public policy, public security or public health; and secondly it lays down stringent procedural safeguards which must be followed by the relevant authorities when they are seeking to exclude non-nationals on one of the permitted grounds. The Directive applies to all those who come within the freedom of movement provisions of the Treaty, both employed or self-employed, as well as to their families; it also extends to those who move within the Community as 'recipients of services' (first recital) and to those entitled to free movement under Directives 90/364 (persons of independent means); 90/365 (retired persons) and 90/366 (students) (Article 2). It applies, however, only to restrictions on the *movement* and *residence* of *natural* persons. It does not allow for discrimination as regards access to or conditions of employment, nor does it apply to legal persons. The former will be subject to the derogation provided under Article 2(2) of Regulation 1612/68 (linguistic knowledge) or Articles 39(4) (ex 48(4)) (public services) or 45 (ex 55) (activities connected with official authority): discrimination as regards the latter will be governed by Articles 46 and 50 (ex 56 and 60) EC. Because of these limitations in Directive 64/221, interpretations of the concept of public policy delivered under its provisions, and which relate to the personal factors justifying discrimination, will not necessarily be appropriate to the public policy exception applicable to undertakings under Article 46 (ex 56) EC. This has not yet been recognised by the Court, which tends to interpret Article 46 (ex 56) by reference to cases decided under Directive 64/221 (see, e.g., Advocate-General Mancini's opinion and the Court's judgment in *Bond van Adverteerders* (case 352/85) noted in chapter 21). Nevertheless, the Directive provides a rich source of substantive and procedural rights for individuals, since all its main provisions are directly effective.

The Directive seeks to lay down the circumstances in which measures taken by Member States on the grounds of public policy, public security or public health, may, and may not, be permitted.

'Measures' taken on the grounds of public policy, public security or public health were defined in *R* v *Bouchereau* (case 30/77) as any action affecting the rights of persons coming within the field of application of Article 39 (ex 48) EC to enter and reside freely in a Member State on the same conditions as apply to nationals of the host State.

Directive 64/221 does not at present apply to third-country nationals (save those of EEA countries) since they are not yet allowed rights of free movement and residence in the EU. Once common immigration and asylum rules have been adopted under the new post-ToA free movement provisions of the EC Treaty (and this will no doubt take time), and third-country nationals are given rights of free movement and residence throughout the EU, Directive 64/221, as it is expressed in terms of 'foreign nationals', could be applied to third-country nationals.

The Commission has recently issued a Communication on the rights contained in this Directive (COM (1999) 372) clarifying and amplifying the ECJ's case law. The Commission claimed that the Communication was necessary given the age of the Directive, the importance of the rights contained within it and, with the introduction of European citizenship, the new context in which it will need to be interpreted.

Public policy, public security, public health

While public security and public health are self-explanatory, the meaning and scope of the public policy derogation are less clear. In *Van Duyn* v *Home Office* (case 41/74) the Court held, on a reference from the English High Court, that the concept of public policy must be interpreted strictly; its scope cannot be determined unilaterally by Member States without being subject to control by the institutions of the Community. However, the Court conceded that the concept of public policy must vary from State to State; States must have an area of discretion within the limits defined by the Treaty. As the European integration project progresses, Member States' individual area of discretion will get narrower. Thus, the Court took a rather stricter view in *Rutili* v *Ministre de l'Intérieur* (case 36/75), in the context of an action by Rutili, an Italian and a noted political agitator, to annul a decision from the Minister which restricted his activities to certain regions of France. The Court held that restrictions cannot be imposed on the right of a national of a Member

State to enter the territory of another Member State, to stay there and to move within it, unless his presence constitutes a *genuine and sufficiently serious threat to public policy* ('*une menace réelle et suffisamment grave pour l'ordre public*'). This principle, the Court added, was an embodiment of the principles contained in the European Convention on Human Rights that no restrictions in the interests of national security or public safety shall be placed on the rights secured by Articles 8 to 11 of the Convention other than such as are *necessary* for the protection of those interests in a democratic society. All restrictions are thus subject to the proportionality principle.

The concept was narrowed even further in *R v Bouchereau* (case 30/77) where the Court added that the concept of public policy must always presuppose a genuine and sufficiently serious threat to the requirements of public policy *affecting one of the fundamental interests of society*.

Directive 64/221 lays down a number of circumstances in which measures taken on the grounds of public policy or public security will *not* be justified:

(a) They 'shall not be invoked to service economic ends' (Article 2(2)). Here the Directive makes explicit what was found to be implicit in Article 30 (ex 36) EC, in the context of goods. To allow an economic justification would clearly run counter to the fundamental aims of the Treaty.

(b) 'Previous criminal convictions shall not *in themselves* constitute grounds for the taking of such measures' (Article 3(2), emphasis added). Thus under certain circumstances past criminal convictions may constitute sufficient grounds, but they will not necessarily do so. (See *R v Bouchereau* (case 30/77) and *Donatella Calfa* (case C–348/96), to be discussed below.)

(c) 'Expiry of the identity card or passport used by the person concerned to enter the host country and to obtain a residence permit shall not justify expulsion from the territory' (Article 3(3)). As was noted in *Procureur du Roi v Royer* (case 48/75), the right of residence does not depend on the possession of a residence permit, it merely provides proof of such a right, which derives from the Treaty itself. The same principle applies to identity cards and passports. As was established in *Watson* (case 118/75), a State may impose penalties for failure to comply with administrative formalities, provided the penalties are not disproportionate, but a failure to comply with such formalities can never provide grounds for deportation. (See also *Wysenbeel* (case C–378/97), discussed in chapter 23.)

Where public health is concerned, the only diseases or disabilities justifying refusal of entry or refusal to issue a first residence permit are those groups listed in the Annex to Directive 64/221 (highly infectious or contagious diseases, e.g., tuberculosis and syphilis; drug addiction; profound mental disturbance), Article 4(1). In its Communication (COM (1999) 372), the Commission makes the point that all the Community institutions have clearly stated that the free movement of persons with HIV/AIDS must be safeguarded. Moreover, diseases or disabilities occurring *after* a first residence permit has been issued 'shall not justify refusal to renew the residence permit or expulsion from the territory' (Article 4(2)).

What kind of measures, then, will be justified on public policy or public security grounds?

Measures taken on the grounds of public policy or public security must be based *exclusively* on the *personal conduct* of the individual concerned (Article 3(1)).

Personal conduct

To justify exclusion, the personal conduct does not have to be illegal. In *Van Duyn* v *Home Office* (case 41/74) the claimant Ms Van Duyn, a Dutch national, was refused entry into the UK on the grounds of public policy. She was seeking to enter the UK to take up employment with the Church of Scientology. The practice of scientology was not illegal in the UK but it was regarded as socially undesirable. The refusal was claimed to be on the basis of her personal conduct. Two questions were referred, *inter alia,* to the ECJ. First, can membership of an organisation count as 'personal conduct' within the meaning of Article 3(1)? Secondly, if it can, must such conduct be illegal in order to provide grounds for exclusion on public policy grounds?

In reply to the first question, the Court distinguished between past and present association; past association cannot count as personal conduct; present association, being a voluntary act of the person concerned, can.

With regard to the second question, the Court held that the conduct does not have to be illegal to justify exclusion of non-nationals, as long as the State has made it clear that it considers the activities in question to be 'socially harmful', and has taken administrative measures to counteract the activities. *Van Duyn* must now be read in the light of the more restrictive test advanced in *R* v *Bouchereau* (case 30/77); the activities in question must be sufficiently socially harmful to pose a genuine and sufficiently serious threat to the requirements of public policy affecting one of the fundamental interests of society.

The kind of evidence needed to prove that a particular activity is considered by the State to be sufficiently harmful to justify exclusion on the grounds of public policy was considered by the ECJ, in the context of many questions referred by the Liège District Court, in the case of *Adoui and Cornuaille* v *Belgium* (cases 115 & 116/81). Here two prostitutes were appealing against the Belgian authorities' refusal to grant them a residence permit in Belgium, where they were seeking to practise their arts. The Court held that Member States could not deny residence to non-nationals by reason of conduct which, when attributable to a State's own nationals, did not give rise to repressive measures or other genuine and effective measures to combat such conduct. Thus, evidence of measures of this nature will have to be adduced to prove that the public policy justification is genuine.

Article 3(2) expressly provides that previous criminal convictions shall not in themselves constitute grounds for measures taken on public policy grounds. The same principle applies to current criminal convictions. In *Bonsignore* v *Oberstadtdirektor of the City of Cologne* (case 67/74), Bonsignore, an Italian worker living in Germany, bought a pistol in breach of German firearms law, and accidentally shot his brother. The action against his brother carried no punishment, but he was fined for unlawful possession of a firearm, and his deportation was ordered. On a reference on appeal from the Vervaltungsgericht, the German authorities argued that his deportation was necessary as a general preventive measure, to deter other immigrants from committing similar offences. The ECJ rejected this argument, holding that the concept of personal conduct expresses the requirement that a deportation order may only be made for breaches of the peace and public security which might be committed by the individual concerned. Thus deportation could not be based on reasons of a general preventive nature.

It should be noted that certain circumstances do permit Member States to take general preventative measures, notably measures connected with gatherings attended by large numbers of people, especially when the people come from different Member States. In a Communication, the Commission suggests examples of such events: large sports events, rock concerts and political demonstrations. The violence at football matches in particular has led Member States to take measures to ensure safety and public order, some of which have been adopted under the Justice and Home Affairs pillar (Joint Action with regard to Cooperation on Law and Order and Security, [1997] OJ L 147, 5/6/97).

The conduct in *R v Bouchereau* (case 30/77) was more serious than in *Bonsignore*. Mr Bouchereau was a French national who took up employment in the UK in 1975. In June 1976 he was found guilty of unlawful possession of drugs. He had already pleaded guilty to a similar offence in January 1976, and had received a 12-month conditional discharge. In June 1976 the court (Marlborough Street Magistrates) wished to make a deportation order against him. He claimed this was contrary to the then Article 48 (now 39) EC and Directive 64/221. One of the questions referred to the ECJ concerned Article 3(2) of the Directive and 'previous criminal convictions'. If they could not 'in themselves' constitute grounds for exclusion, when could they be taken into account? Were they relevant only insofar as they manifested a propensity to act in such a manner, contrary to public policy or public security? The Court held that the existence of previous convictions could only be taken into account as evidence of personal conduct constituting a *present* threat to the requirements of public policy, as showing a propensity to act in the same way again. However, past conduct alone *could* constitute a threat to the requirements of public policy. Thus, it would depend on the gravity of the conduct, past or present, whether it would in fact constitute a present threat to the requirements of public policy. This point was re-emphasised in *Donatella Calfa* (case C–348/96), concerning a Greek rule which automatically required the expulsion of non-nationals who had been convicted of certain offences, for life. Calfa was an Italian tourist who was convicted of offences relating to the possession of drugs. She appealed against her sentence on the basis that it was incompatible with her right to receive services under what is now Article 49 (ex 59). The ECJ held that her expulsion could only be based on personal conduct *besides* the commission of the offence. It seems that national authorities must thus look at the individual's conduct in addition to that which gave rise to the criminal offence. In any event, all rules must be proportionate, which an automatic life ban is not.

Since a denial of residence must be based exclusively on personal conduct, it follows that a worker who is entitled to residence cannot be refused entry or deported merely because the worker is involuntarily unemployed or unable to work through incapacity, even if the worker becomes a charge on public funds (see *Lubbersen* v *Secretary of State for the Home Department* [1984] 3 CMLR 77, Immigration Appeal Tribunal). The same applies to the worker's family. This accords with Directive 68/360.

The ECJ held in *Rutili* (case 36/75) that derogation on the grounds of public policy, public security or public health can only apply to a *total* ban on residence in a Member State; partial restrictions on the right of residence of non-nationals cannot be imposed unless such measures are also applied to nationals. This aspect of the decision has been criticised as an unnecessary restriction on Articles 39(3) and 46 (ex 48(3) and 56) of the EC Treaty. The derogation exists precisely in order to enable Member States to discriminate against non-nationals on limited and specific grounds. As the ECJ pointed out in *Van Duyn* (case 41/74), it is a principle of international law that States cannot deny rights of residence to their own nationals. To require a total ban where a partial ban would suffice is surely to impose on non-nationals greater restrictions than are necessary to protect the particular interest concerned.

Procedural rights

Directive 64/221 provides extensive procedural safeguards for parties seeking to assert rights of entry or residence in Member States. Since these rights are directly effective, any decision issued in violation of these rights may be challenged as contrary to EC law.

(a) *Temporary residence.* Where a person's identity card or passport has expired or the nationality of the holder is in dispute the State which issued that identity card or passport must allow its holder to re-enter its territory without formalities (Article 3(4)).

A person awaiting a decision to grant or refuse a first residence permit in a Member State must be allowed to remain temporarily in that State pending that decision. The decision must be taken as soon as possible and not more than six months from the date of application (Article 5(1)).

In the event of a decision to refuse the issue of a residence permit or to expel a person from the territory of a Member State that person shall be allowed, 'save in cases of urgency', not less than 15 days (if he has not yet been granted a residence permit), or one month (in all other cases), in which to leave the country (Article 7).

(b) *Reasons for decisions.* 'The person concerned shall be informed of the grounds of public policy, public security or public health upon which the decision taken in his case is based, unless this is contrary to the interests of the security of the State involved' (Article 6). The Court held in *Rutili* (case 36/75) that the authority making the decision must give the applicant a precise and comprehensive statement of the ground for the decision, to enable the applicant to take effective steps to prepare his or her defence.

The Commission in its Communication also made the point that the duty to give reasons applies also to decisions regarding the applications for visas by family members who are third country nationals.

(c) *Remedies: rights of defence.* By Article 8:

> The person concerned shall have the same legal remedies in respect of any decision concerning entry, or refusing the issue or renewal of a residence permit, or ordering expulsion from the territory, as are available to nationals of the State concerned in respect of acts of the administration.

Thus all domestic public law remedies must be made available. The extent of this obligation was considered in a recent case, *R v Secretary of State for the Home Department, ex parte Shingara* (cases C–65 & 111/95), which concerned two EC nationals, both of whom were refused entry to the UK on public policy grounds. The relevant UK legislation provided that individuals objecting to a decision under that legislation could appeal to a special tribunal, save where the exclusion had been ordered on grounds of the public good. In this circumstance, most likely to affect non-nationals, the only recourse was to general administrative law remedies, that is, judicial review. The applicants queried whether this satisfied the requirement in Article 8 to have the 'same legal remedies'. The ECJ held that this requirement was satisfied because the remedies available to the non-nationals were the same as those available to UK nationals in respect of administrative law generally. It pointed out, following its reasoning in *Adoui and Cornuaille v Belgium* (cases 115 and 116/81) and *Van Duyn* (case 41/74), that, as far as refusal of entry and deportation were concerned, Member States were not permitted under international law to refuse their own nationals entry and residence as they were in the case of non-nationals, thus the distinction was justified.

By Article 9:

> (1) Where there is no right of appeal to a court of law, or where such an appeal may be only in respect of the legal validity of the decision, or where the appeal cannot have suspensory effect, a decision refusing renewal of a residence permit or ordering the expulsion of the holder of a residence permit from the territory shall not be taken by the administrative authority, save in cases of urgency, until an opinion has been obtained from a competent authority of the host country before which the person concerned enjoys such rights of defence and of assistance or representation as the domestic law of that country provides for.
>
> This authority shall not be the same as that empowered to take the decision refusing renewal of the residence permit or ordering expulsion.
>
> (2) Any decision refusing the issue of a first residence permit or ordering expulsion of the person concerned before the issue of the permit shall, where that person so requests, be referred for consideration to the authority whose prior opinion is required under paragraph 1. The person

concerned shall then be entitled to submit his defence in person, except where this would be contrary to the interests of national security.

Where the remedies under Article 8 are insufficient, Article 9 provides a safety net, incorporating the minimum requirements of natural justice. Under this Article, as the Court pointed out in *Rutili* (case 36/75), the person concerned must at the very least be able to exercise his or her rights of defence before a competent authority, which must not be the same as that which adopted the measure which restricted the person's freedom.

Questions concerning the scope of Article 9(1) were raised before the Court of Justice in *R v Secretary of State for the Home Department, ex parte Santillo* (case 131/79). Santillo, an Italian, had been convicted in the UK of a number of crimes of violence including rape, buggery and indecent assault. He was sentenced to eight years in gaol, with a recommendation for deportation at the end of his sentence. Nearly five years later the Home Secretary made a deportation order against him. He applied for judicial review to quash this decision. Two issues were raised in the proceedings. First, whether the trial judge's recommendation was an 'opinion from a competent authority', as required by Article 9(1); and secondly, if so, whether a lapse of time between the issuing of this 'opinion' and the making of the order could deprive the judge's recommendation of its status as an 'opinion' under Article 9(1). The ECJ, on a reference for interpretation from the English High Court, held that the trial judge's recommendation did amount to an 'opinion' within Article 9(1); but that the safeguard provided by Article 9 could only be a real one if that opinion were sufficiently proximate in time to the decision recommending deportation, to ensure that the factors justifying deportation still existed at the time when the order was made. A change of heart or political climate could mean that the public policy justification had ceased to exist.

Following the ruling from the ECJ, Donaldson LJ in the Queen's Bench Divisional Court ([1980] 1 CMLR 1) found that the trial judge's 'opinion' was still valid, since there was no evidence that the position had changed since the time when the original recommendation was made.

In *Monteil v Secretary of State for the Home Department* [1984] 1 CMLR 264, the applicant was more fortunate. M Monteil was a French national, who had been convicted in the UK of a number of offences, including importuning and indecency, and sentenced to 12 months' imprisonment. At the end of his sentence the authorities sought to deport him. He appealed against the deportation order, claiming that he was a 'new man'. His crimes had been the result of alcoholism of which he now claimed he was cured. His arguments and his evidence succeeded before the Immigration Appeal Tribunal. Citing *Santillo* (case 131/79) and *Bouchereau* (case 30/77), the tribunal concluded the deportation would only be justified if he showed a propensity to commit the same crimes again. This would not be the case if he were cured.

Similar arguments succeeded in *Proll v Entry Clearance Officer, Düsseldorf* [1988] 2 CMLR 387. The appellant, Ms Proll, a German citizen, had been a member of a terrorist organisation, the Bader Meinhof gang, and had been convicted of a number of offences for her activities in the group. She had applied for permission to enter the UK in 1980, 1981, and 1985, on the last occasion in order to carry out photographic work for a German magazine. Her application was rejected on each occasion. On appeal, the Immigration Appeal Tribunal found that, even in 1979 when she was convicted, the German court had found that she had undergone a 'change of heart' in respect of her political beliefs and activities, as a result of which it had imposed a minimum 12–month sentence. There was no evidence before the Immigration Appeal Tribunal that she had undergone further change since that time. Thus, since her conduct presented no present threat to the requirements of public policy or public security, UK rules (para. 83 of HC 169), which allowed deportation to be ordered in respect of *past* offences, could have had 'no application' to Ms Proll.

Paragraphs (1) and (2) of Article 9 deal with slightly different situations: paragraph (1) deals with the situation of the person who has not yet entered the country; paragraph (2) with someone who has. In *R* v *Secretary of State for the Home Department, ex parte Shingara* (cases C–65 & 111/95) the ECJ confirmed that the limitation of the rights in Article 9(1) to situations where the addressee has 'no right of appeal to a court of law, or where such an appeal may be only in respect of the legal validity of the decision, or where the appeal cannot have suspensory effect' also applies to the rights set down in Article 9(2). Otherwise the two categories of persons would have different rights when such a difference was not objectively justified.

The scope of Article 9(2) was considered prior to *Shingara* in *R* v *Secretary of State for the Home Department, ex parte Gallagher* (case C–175/94). Gallagher had been convicted in Ireland for the possession of rifles for unlawful purposes. He subsequently went to Engand and took up employment there. He was arrested and deported. On arrival in Ireland he challenged the deportation decision as unlawful, and was interviewed in Dublin. His interviewer gave no name and no information concerning the grounds for his expulsion. At his request his case was reconsidered by the Home Secretary, but the deportation decision was not reversed. He challenged those decisions under Article 9 of Directive 64/221, questioning the status of these bodies as 'competent authorities'. The ECJ found that the matter fell within Article 9(2), which provided for challenge before a competent authority *after* the deportation decision had been made, and only at the request of the person concerned. The Directive did not specify how the competent authority should be appointed, nor what its composition should be. It was nonetheless essential that it should be independent of the authority empowered to take the measure concerning deportation, and that the person concerned should be able to submit his or her defence. There was no need to notify the claimant of the identity of the authority as long as the national court was in a position to determine whether it was impartial. These questions were left to the national court to decide.

It seems, following the *Shingara* case, that where an individual who has been refused admission to a Member State, reapplies for admission to a country after a reasonable length of time (in *Shingara* approximately three years), the procedural safeguards in Articles 8 and 9 would apply anew to that reapplication.

Further reading

Connor, T.C., 'Migrant Community Nationals: Remedies for Refusal of Entry by Member States' (1998) 28 EL Rev 157.

Furse, M. and Nash, S., 'Free Movement, Criminal Law and Fundamental Rights in the European Community' [1997] JR 148.

Hall, S., 'The European Convention on Human Rights and Public Policy Exceptions to the Free Movement of Workers under the EEC Treaty' (1991) 16 EL Rev 466.

Handoll, J., *Free Movement of Persons in the European Union* (1995, J. Wiley and Son), ch. 7.

O'Keeffe, D., 'Practical Difficulties in the Application of Article 48 of the EEC Treaty' (1982) 19 CML Rev 35.

Van Overbeek, P. M., 'Aids/HIV Infection and the Free Movement of Persons in the European Economic Community' (1990) 27 CML Rev 791.

Vincenzi, C., 'Deportation in Disarray: the Case of EC Nationals' [1994] Crim LR 163.

TWENTY THREE

Completion of the internal market: extending free movement rights

The EC Treaty has always contained provisions granting free movement rights to workers and those seeking to establish themselves or provide (or receive) services. As the preceding chapters show, these rights, although broadly interpreted by the ECJ, have previously been aimed primarily at those who are economically active and are EC nationals, although special rules apply to their families. Even following the SEA, which introduced a number of changes including Article 14 EC (ex 7a), the EC Treaty did not create an internal market allowing the free movement of persons throughout the Community, as not all EC nationals would enjoy all free movement rights under the Treaty. The position of 'third country nationals' (TCNs) was even more restricted as, unless they were family members of an EU national, they would fall outside the protection of EC law. Another difficulty, as far as the creation of the internal market was concerned, was the fact that the Member States continued to maintain some form of border or passport control. Thus, even when EU nationals sought to exercise their rights of free movement under the Treaty, they would still have to stop at borders between Member States to show their identification. The emphasis on border control arises because there are strong links between the creation of an area without internal frontiers and a common immigration policy. As Member States scale down or eliminate their own controls on immigration, stringent external control, particularly as regards TCNs, needs to exist to replace national controls before an area without internal borders would be acceptable to the Member States.

Recent treaties have changed the position as regards both the need for an economic nexus between the EU national and the host Member State, and the exclusion, except to the extent that TCNs are an EU national's family members, of TCNs from basic Community rights. The TEU introduced the idea of European citizenship, and one of the primary citizenship rights is the right of free movement throughout the Community. The ToA took a further step towards creating an area without passport controls by introducing a new title to the EC Treaty, Title IV (Articles 61–69 EC), which deals with visas, asylum, immigration and other policies relating to the free movement of persons. These provisions take the Community further towards the completion of the internal market as regards persons. The new provisions do, however, raise certain questions. Clearly one needs to define the scope of the new rights; but, in addition, difficult issues regarding the relationship between the original free movement rights (workers, establishment and services) and the new rights arise, particularly as regards the operation of any derogation from these rights.

The citizen's right of free movement

Article 18 (ex 8a) EC provides:

> 1.   Every citizen of the Union shall have the right to move and reside freely within the territory of the Member States, subject to the limitations and conditions laid down in this Treaty and by the measures adopted to give it effect.

A second paragraph gives the Community institutions the power to enact legislation to facilitate the exercise of the rights granted. As with other free movement of persons provisions, secondary legislation can be enacted only if the Council unanimously agrees to the proposal. The European Parliament's role in the enactment of any such legislation is limited; the Council need only consult it.

Who benefits from the right?   The rights in Article 18 (ex 8a) are granted to all European citizens. Article 17 (ex 8) defines European citizens as: 'Every person holding the nationality of a Member State'. On the face of it, this is broader than the pre-existing free movement rights, as there is no need to show any economic activity on the part of the individual seeking to move from one Member State to another.

As a Protocol to the TEU made clear, it is for each Member State to decide for itself who is to be considered a national of that Member State. Thus, Member States may only require that an individual provide appropriate identity documents and may not criticise the decision of another Member State to recognise an individual as having the nationality of that Member State. This approach pre-dates the introduction of European citizenship. In *Micheletti* (case C–369/90), for example, the ECJ held that the Spanish could not challenge the claim of Micheletti — who had the nationality of both Italy and Argentina — to be Italian on the grounds that the Spanish did not recognise the concept of dual nationality. According to the ECJ, the important point was whether the Italians recognised his claim (see more recently *Stephen Saldanha and MTS Securities Corporation* v *Hiross Holding AG* (case C–122/96)). On this basis, the viewpoint of the Member State is determinative. Note, however, that the English High Court has recently referred to the ECJ certain questions concerning the extent of the freedom of Member States to define citizenship and, in particular, the limitations imposed on this freedom by the need to respect individuals' fundamental rights (*R v Secretary of State for the Home Department, ex parte Manjit Kaur*, judgment 11 December 1998).

Leaving the determination of citizenship to the Member States may have a number of consequences. In contrast to the definition of 'workers' (see chapter 20), the notion of European citizen would seem not to be a Community concept. Thus, the fact that the Member States themselves take radically different approaches to the question of determining nationality may introduce inequalities as to the type of person who benefits from citizenship rights across the Community. Furthermore, the decision of one Member State on this point can have a significant impact on the composition of Union citizens as a whole, but, despite the fact that this decision may consequently affect other Member States, it is a decision that the other Member States cannot influence at all.

Scope of the rights   The rights which may be granted under Article 18 (ex 8a) include not just the right to travel throughout the Community, but also the right to set up residence anywhere within the Community. Although the wording of the provision might suggest that Article 18 gives the right of free movement within a Member State, it seems that purely internal situations remain outside the scope of Community law.

It is not yet clear whether Article 18 has direct effect. Many Member States, such as the UK, think it does not, whereas the Commission believes that it does. It should be noted that the mere fact that secondary legislation is envisaged in a policy area, as here, does not automatically preclude the Treaty provision itself from having direct effect, as the ECJ itself ruled in the context of freedom of establishment and freedom to provide services (see *Reyners* (case 2/74); *Van Binsbergen* (case 33/74) discussed in chapter 21). The ECJ has, however, not yet ruled on whether Article 18 has direct effect. Indeed, although a number of cases have been referred on this point, the ECJ has managed to deal with the references on other grounds (e.g., *Wijsenbeek* (case C–378/97)). The English courts in *Kaur* have now referred the question of whether the right to reside contained in Article 18 (ex 8a) has direct effect (similar questions arose in *R v Secretary of State for the Home Department, ex parte Flynn* [1997] 3 CMLR 888 (CA) but were not referred). It remains to be seen whether the ECJ will finally address this somewhat controversial issue.

Whether the rights contained in Article 18 (ex 8a) EC are broad-ranging enough to achieve a free market in persons is debatable. To a certain extent, it depends on whether a broad or narrow view of the internal market is taken, i.e. whether the creation of an area without internal frontiers is seen as being intended to benefit only EU nationals or whether it should include TCNs. Clearly, citizenship rights will benefit only EU nationals. Further, in *Wijsenbeek* (case C–378/97), the ECJ had to consider whether the introduction of

European citizenship rendered border controls illegal. In this case the ECJ held that Member States were still entitled to check the identity documents (in this case the passport) of EU nationals travelling between Member States, despite the fact the all EU nationals are now European citizens. The ECJ then went on to hold, however, that any penalties for failure to comply with such rules must be proportionate in the light of European citizenship and the right to move from one Member State to another. In this, the ECJ made a distinction between the right to move between Member States and the ability to do so without having to prove one's identity or nationality. Thus, this ruling would suggest that citizenship on its own is not enough to create an area without internal frontiers even if it is a lot easier, as an EU national, to cross those borders.

In general, the relationship between the rights in Article 18 and the original free movement rights is not clear. Some commentators have suggested that the rights in Article 18 (ex 8a) are no more than a re-statement and consolidation of the pre-existing situation, especially given the enactment of three Directives to allow the free movement of students, the retired and other persons (Directives 93/96, 90/365 and 90/364 respectively). Since the right in Article 18 is 'subject to the limitations and conditions laid down in this Treaty', this view would mean that Article 18 (ex 8a) continues to exclude those who would not have been able to rely on the original free movement rights. Certainly, this would seem to have been the view of some of the English courts. In *R v Secretary of State for the Home Department, ex parte Vitale* [1996] All ER (EC) 461, for example, Vitale sought entry to the UK although he did not have a job and was not looking for one. The English courts rejected his claim to entry into the UK on the basis that he was not a worker. They did not accept that he might have a right of entry as a European citizen. Further, even Directive 90/364, which is described as giving rights of entry and residence to all categories of persons who cannot claim such a right under any other provision, is itself limited by the requirement that individuals must not be a financial burden on the host Member State. Similar restrictions arise in the Directives for students and the retired. Thus, the rights of free movement in these Directives are not available to all, but only to the affluent. Seeing citizenship as providing no more than the existing free movement rights would mean that certain classes of individual (the unemployed poor) would be excluded from exercising these rights. The Commission, in a recent Communication on Directive 64/221/EEC (COM (1999) 372), would seem not to agree with this approach. Following the approach it has taken in its reports on European citizenship (COM (97) 203), the Commission emphasised instead the 'fundamental and personal' nature of the right conferred by Article 18 (ex 8a). Further, the Advocates-General have suggested that a wider view of the scope of citizenship rights should be taken. (See, for example, the Opinions of the Advocate-General in *Wijsenbeek* (case C–378/97) and *Martinez Sala* (case C–85/96).)

The Commission Communication on Directive 64/221/EEC makes it clear that in the Commission's opinion, citizenship rights are subject to limitations for reasons of public policy, public security or public health, as provided in that Directive. This must be right. Nonetheless, in interpreting this Directive,

Member States must take into account the existence and nature of citizenship and limit any action to what is strictly necessary and proportional. Directive 64/221/EEC is discussed further in chapter 22.

The exercise of the rights in Article 18 (ex 8a) may be facilitated or subject to limitations imposed by secondary Community legislation. To date, no proposals have been put forward on this treaty base, although there have been calls for provisions, for example in the Action Plan for the Internal Market (CSE (98) 1 final, 4 June 1997) which was endorsed by the Amsterdam European Council.

Impact of the ToA: the new free movement rights

The position prior to ToA   As well as introducing European citizenship, the TEU created the Justice and Home Affairs (JHA) pillar of the Union, which dealt with, amongst other issues, asylum policy, rules regarding the crossing of borders (either between Member States or with third countries) and immigration and treatment of TCNs. As this took place within the JHA Pillar, which operated on an intergovernmental basis, the intention was for Member States to coordinate their policies and to adopt common positions or conventions. Any such decisions were to be decided on a unanimous basis between the Member States, with the EC institutions occupying only a peripheral role. The Commission was described in the original Article K.4 TEU as being 'fully associated' with the work under the JHA Pillar (whatever that might mean), and the Parliament was merely to be kept informed. Thus, the JHA did not have the impetus towards law-making that the EC does, either in terms of the type of measure which could enacted within its purview, or as regards its decision-making processes. Although progress was consequently slow, some agreements were reached, such as the Recommendation on harmonising means of combating illegal immigration ([1996] OJ C–5/1) and the Recommendation on the combating illegal employment of third country nationals ([1996] OJ C–304/1). A proposed Convention on the Admission of Third Country Nationals was never adopted, however.

As a general proposition, TCNs were outside the scope of the EC Treaty (as opposed to Union competence under JHA). The only EC provision which dealt expressly with their position was the former Article 100c EC (which was deleted by the ToA), which provided for the adoption of a common visa policy. This in itself created the possibility of overlap with the provisions in the JHA, potentially resulting in disputes as to the appropriate treaty base for action. Other attempts to extend the EC competence to cover TCNs were limited and tended to view these individuals in a somewhat inhuman light (see, e.g., *Vander Elst* v *Office des Migrations Internationales* (case C–43/93) discussed in chapters 19 and 21). Any attempt to progress towards an internal market which included TCNs was blocked through political difficulties, in particular divergences in views as to whether the internal market was intended to benefit only the nationals of the Member States or not.

With regard to EU nationals, the difficulties experienced in completing the internal market, and indeed the different views of what this concept entailed,

led to some Member States forming a separate agreement outside the Community framework. This was the Schengen Agreement 1985, which subsequently led to an implementing Convention in 1990. Schengen aimed to remove passport controls between Member States and to strengthen controls at the external borders. An Executive Committee was set up to take any detailed decisions necessary to implement the Schengen Agreement. The Agreement was eventually signed by the majority of Member States (and also some non-Member States), although implementation of the Convention was patchy, with political problems being exacerbated by technical difficulties. One particular problem was that travel between Member States was now possible on the Schengen basis (i.e., without frontier controls) for Schengen State nationals, or on the EC basis (with passport controls) for those Member States which had not signed up. This came perilously close to institutionalising discrimination between nationals of the two groups of Member States.

Changes introduced by Amsterdam The ToA in effect moved the immigration, free movement and asylum element of the JHA Pillar into a new Title IV of the EC Treaty (Articles 61–69 EC) and deleted the former Article 100c EC. Note that not all Member States have agreed to the new section of the Treaty; the UK, Ireland and Denmark have all refused to sign up to its provisions. The position of these Member States is dealt with through protocols attached to the ToA.

The new Article 61 EC provides that the Council is to adopt measures aimed at 'ensuring the free movement of persons in accordance with Article 14, in conjunction with directly related flanking measures with respect to external border controls, asylum and immigration'. The two following articles, Articles 62 and 63, provide more detail on the measures to be taken, dealing with internal and external borders on the one hand and asylum seekers on the other. Furthermore, Article 61 also provides for the possibility of measures being taken 'to prevent and combat crime', although any such measures must be compatible with the provisions in the JHA Pillar (Article 31(e) TEU), which deal with similar issues. A detailed discussion of the asylum provisions and those relating to crime prevention and judicial cooperation are outside the scope of this work: the remainder of the chapter will focus on the creation of an area without internal frontiers. In all the areas covered by Article 61 EC, however, the Council has to take legislative action within five years. Failure to do so could, in principle, open the way for an action under Article 232 (ex 175) EC for failure to act (see chapter 31). The Council and Commission adopted an action plan (3 December 1998) which lays down a timetable of measures to be adopted to achieve the objectives specified in this title within the next five years, including the establishment of a high level working group on asylum and immigration.

The principal provision relevant to the present chapter is Article 62. Article 62 can be broken down into three distinct areas:

(a)   the creation of the internal market in persons (Article 62(1));
(b)   the standards and procedures to be followed by Member States in respect of persons crossing external borders, including rules on uniform visa

policy in respect of stays of more than no more than three months (Article 62(2)); and

(c)   the granting to TCNs of the right to travel within the territory of the Member States for up to three months (Article 62(3)).

In achieving the above-mentioned aims of Article 61, this title of the Treaty relies heavily on the approach adopted under the Schengen Agreement. A Protocol attached to the EC Treaty, as amended by the ToA, states that from the coming into force of the ToA, the Schengen *acquis* shall immediately apply to the Member States who have not opted out of this section of the Treaty. The Schengen *acquis* is described as including the Schengen Agreement and Convention together with decisions and declarations adopted under Schengen. The decisions made will be divided between the new Title IV in the EC 'pillar' and the remaining JHA provisions as appropriate, depending on the decision's subject-matter. Unfortunately, as many of these decisions were not made by transparent legal process, it is hard to identify a complete list of the decisions making up the Schengen *acquis*. Nonetheless, the Member States (all 15 of them) managed to identify the relevant decisions, defined in a Council Decision of 20 May 1999. At the same time, the Council divided these measures between the EC provisions and the JHA, so that each decision was awarded retrospectively an appropriate treaty base. The decisions on the removal of internal frontiers, the right to circulate for nationals of third countries, control of external borders and visa policy are now based within the EC Treaty. Future measures will, of course, be made in accordance with the procedures set out in the EC Treaty.

Note that the Protocol dealing with the position of Ireland and the UK permitted these countries to opt in to the Schengen *acquis* should they so wish. As the UK and Ireland did so wish, a Council Decision was passed identifying the decisions within the Schengen *acquis* that are to apply to the UK and Ireland (Decision 2000/29 of 26 June 1999, [2000] OJ L 15/1).

Who benefits from the creation of the area without internal frontiers?   Unlike the other provisions of the EC Treaty, it would seem that the provisions in this title apply to everyone, whether they be a national of a Member State who has signed up to this title of the EC Treaty or not. Article 62(1) EC specifically states that measures for eliminating controls on persons crossing borders between Member States shall benefit all individuals, 'be they citizens of the Union or nationals of third countries'. Other provisions, such as those relating to visas, are specifically aimed at the position of TCNs.

Scope of Article 62   A preliminary question is whether these are provisions that are capable of having direct effect. Since the ToA has been in force only for a relatively short time, the ECJ has not yet had the opportunity to comment on this issue. The nature of the Article's objectives — the establishment of common policies and the enactment of legislation — means that the Article is unlikely to give rise to rights on which individuals may rely, thus rendering the possibility of Article 62 having direct effect unlikely. Furthermore, the fact that the Treaty envisages the Council having a space of five years in which to take action may mean in any event that until that time, the obligations in these provisions could not be unconditional.

Another point to note here is that this Article is all about crossing borders. By contrast to the other free movement rights (Articles 18, 39 and 43 EC), except those relating to the provision of services, this Article does not give the right of residence. Nonetheless, with the introduction of these provisions, we see the position of TCNs coming within the scope of EC law, and also the beginnings of an EC immigration policy. This would imply that individuals immigrating into the Union on the basis of this provision might also be granted a right to reside in the relevant Member State.

No legislation has as yet been made under the new Treaty provisions, although some pre-existing drafts based either on the old JHA provisions or other EC Treaty provisions may be amended. In particular, a Convention on the Crossing of External Borders (COM (97) 387 final [1997] OJ C 337), which would develop a common approach between the Member States to entry by TCNs, had been proposed prior to the ToA. Under consideration since 1993, the draft Convention foundered on a dispute between the UK and Spain, which still continues, as to the status of Gibraltar. Despite this political difficulty, the Commission, on the suggestion of the European Parliament ([1999] OJ C 150) is proposing to convert the draft convention into a proposal for a Directive.

Assessment of the new provisions   It is likely that reaction to the new Treaty provisions will be mixed. On the one hand, the Community has assumed responsibility for a new area of law, hitherto outside Community competence. It is to be hoped that with this will come more efficient, transparent decision-making which is subject to some judicial scrutiny. On the other hand, there are some serious difficulties with these provisions. For the first five years at least, Council decision-making within this title will require unanimity which might be difficult to attain. Further, the involvement of the other institutions, especially the Parliament, is limited to consultation only, giving rise to concerns about democratic accountability.

Although the ECJ does have jurisdiction within the new Title IV of the Treaty, this is subject to special arrangements undermining the development and homogeneity of Community law both in this area and generally. Any measure or decision based on Article 62(1) concerning internal law and order or national security falls outside the ECJ's competence (Article 68(2) EC). Article 62(1) includes measures which are aimed at ensuring the free movement of persons within the internal market. Quite apart from difficulties determining the scope of the exception in Article 68(2), there is a question as to how this will relate (as far as EU nationals and their families are concerned) to the grounds of derogation from the original free movement rights under Articles 39 (ex 48), 43 (ex 52) and 49 (ex 59) and Directive 64/221/EEC, all of which do fall within the jurisdiction of the ECJ. Those who are workers, seeking to establish themselves or to provide services, will presumably be able to rely on a number of treaty provisions to move between

Member States. In addition to Articles 39 (ex 48), 43 (ex 52) or 49 (ex 59), such individuals will be able to rely on Article 18 (ex 8a) and the rights in the new title. Should a Member State wish to refuse an individual entry under the establishment, services or free movement of workers provisions, it can do so only for reasons of public policy, public security and health. The derogation by Member States from the original free movement provisions is subject to judicial scrutiny by the ECJ. Although these grounds for derogation are not exactly the same areas listed in Article 68(2), there will be some overlap between the two, for example in the case of criminals or terrorists. In this instance, the individual may find that there are EC rules which the ECJ has jurisdiction to apply under the original freedom of movement provisions at the same time as a Member State may try to claim that the issue is outside the ECJ's jurisdiction because of the operation of Article 68(2) EC. Although the matter has not yet been decided, a commonsense approach must be to look at the most specific rules (i.e., the original free movement rules) first and use the new provisions as a fall-back where appropriate. This would give the maximum opportunity for judicial scrutiny by the ECJ in this area and limit Article 68(2) to situations involving TCNs and in which there is a real need to take account of concerns for internal security. Further, homogeneity of EC law is also undermined by limited access to the ECJ under Article 234 (ex 177) introduced by Article 68 and the opt-outs. The adverse impact on EC law would be minimised were the proposed circumscribed approach to Article 68(2) taken.

Overlap may well occur in other areas too. The Treaty itself foresees that there is some connection between this new title of the Treaty and the JHA pillar of the TEU. Thus, the ECJ may well be called on — as it was in *Commission* v *Council (Air Transport Arrangements)* (case C–170/96), a case concerning the appropriate legal basis for action harmonising Member States' policies on airport transit visas — to determine the boundaries between the two treaties. In this case the Member States had taken joint action under former Article K.3 TEU (now as amended Article 31 TEU), whereas the Commission argued (unsuccessfully) that the appropriate basis for action should have been former Article 100c EC (now deleted by ToA). Although the precise scope of the relevant provisions in that case has changed, there is still considerable room for confusion as to where the boundary between Title IV to the EC Treaty and the JHA 'pillar' of the TEU properly lies.

One final concern relates to the incorporation of the Schengen *acquis* into the Union structure. The decisions made by a non-elected and unaccountable committee in relative secrecy have been turned into binding Community law. This surely offends against the principles, such as democracy and respect for the rule of law, upon which the Community is built. Nonetheless, as Curtin commented in regard to the changes introduced in this area by the ToA:

> By virtue of this move and of the fact that the 'single institutional framework' will henceforth be used, a quantum leap takes place in terms of democratic accountability and judicial control. The leap is from none to some. The result may be imperfect but it is definitely a move in the right direction.

Further reading

Curtin, D. and Meijers H., 'The Principle of Open government in Schengen and the EU' (1995) 32 CMLR 391.

Kuijper, P.J., 'Some legal problems associated with the communitization of policy on visas, asylum and immigration under the Treaty of Amsterdam and incorporation of Schengen *acquis*' (2000) 37 CML Rev 345.

'Schengen: the Pros and Cons' (1995) 32 CML Rev 7 (editorial comment).

Schutte, J., 'Schengen: its Meaning for the Free Movement of Persons in Europe' (1991) 29 CML Rev 549.

Simpson, G., 'Asylum and Immigration in the European Union after the Treaty of Amsterdam' (1999) 5 EPL 91.

TWENTY FOUR

Social security

The freedom of movement granted by the Treaty to workers and the self-employed and their families would have been deprived of much of its effect if persons, in exercising these rights, risked losing out on social security benefits acquired in their home State. Under the laws of Member States, both eligibility for benefit and the amount of benefit paid may depend on the number and extent of contributions made to the institution responsible for social security in the relevant state. Eligibility may also be conditional on the claimant's residence in the State responsible for payment and benefits.

It was to meet these problems that Article 42 (ex 51) of the EC Treaty provided for measures to be adopted in the field of social security to secure for migrant workers and their dependants the implementation of two fundamental principles:

(a) aggregation, for the purpose of acquiring and retaining the right to benefit and of calculating the amount of benefit, of all periods taken into account under the laws of the several countries;

(b) payment of benefits to persons resident in the territories of Member States.

To this end, Regulation 1408/71 was passed, replacing the earlier Regulation 3/58. Regulation 1408/71 was implemented and supplemented by Regulation 574/72. Initially applying only to workers and their families these Regulations were amended to include the self-employed by Regulations 1390/81 and 3795/81.

The aim of EC legislation on social security is not to harmonise Member States' social security legislation but to *coordinate* their provision in order to secure the objectives of Article 42 (new 51); to ensure that claimants' contributions in different Member States are *aggregated* for the purpose outlined in Article 42(a) (new 51(a)) of the EC Treaty, and that persons entitled to benefits may *collect* them wherever they are resident in the Community. The system is designed to abolish as far as possible the territorial limitations on the application of the different social security schemes within the Community (*Hessische Knappschaft* v *Maison Singer et Fils* (case 44/65)). However, in securing these objectives, clearly Member States' social security laws will be modified. Where States have not amended their laws to comply with EC law, EC law, on the principle of the supremacy of EC law, should prevail (see chapter 5, and *Costa* v *ENEL* (case 6/64); inconsistent provisions of national law should simply not be applied (*Simmenthal SpA* (case 106/77)). National legislation affected by Regulation 1408/71 does not include conventions on social security concluded between one Member State and a non-Member State, even when the convention has been incorporated into national law. Thus in *Grana Novoa* v *Landesversicherungsanstalt* (case C–23/92) the applicant, a Spanish national who had never worked in Spain but had worked in Switzerland and then in Germany and who was seeking invalidity benefit in Germany, was unable to invoke Regulation 1408/71 in order to challenge an exclusion in a convention on social security concluded between Germany and Switzerland and claim aggregation of social security rights acquired in Switzerland.

Regulation 1408/71, as supplemented by Regulation 574/72, is long and complex. It is not possible in a book of this nature to examine each substantive provision in detail. Instead it is proposed to examine its general scope, both in terms of the *persons* and the *kind of benefits* covered, and the *principles* on which the detailed provisions are based. An understanding of these principles will often provide a better basis for the interpretation of specific provisions than a detailed study of those provisions themselves. As with other EC secondary legislation, the preamble provides a vital key to interpretation.

The complexity of Regulations 1408/71 and 574/72, and the difficulty of reconciling the autonomous systems of Member States with the demands of Community law, have inevitably resulted in loopholes and anomalies, some remedied by the Court, some beyond the power of the ECJ to resolve. Where this has occurred Regulations amending Regulations 1408/71 and 574/72 have been passed. The principal amending Regulations are Regulation 2001/83 (OJ L 230/6, 1983), and Regulation 1248/92 (OJ L 136/7, 1992).

Personal scope

Regulation 1408/71 covers the same groups as are covered by the other legislation relating to free movement of persons: workers, the self-employed and their families and survivors. The workers and self-employed must be nationals of one of the Member States. It also covers survivors who are EC nationals irrespective of the nationality of the worker, and stateless persons and refugees (Article 2).

However, the definition of the employed and self-employed and of members of the family is different.

Employed and self-employed The employed and self-employed to whom the Regulation applies are defined as '. . . any person who is *insured*, compulsorily or on an optional continued basis, for *one or more* of the contingencies covered by the branches of a social security scheme for employed or self-employed persons' (Article 1(a)(i) as amended by Regulation 1390/81, Article 1(2)(a)).

As the Court held in *Hoekstra* (case 75/63), the concepts of worker (and self-employed) in the context of social security have a Community meaning, referring to all those who, as such, and under whatever description, are covered by different national schemes of social security. The scheme may be compulsory or optional; contributory or non-contributory; it may cover different kinds of benefit. These factors are irrelevant. As long as the employed or self-employed person is covered by some national scheme for insured persons in one of the Member States he will be covered by the Regulation, even, it seems, if he is or has been working outside the Community (see *Laborero* (cases 82 & 103/86) — claimants working in Belgian Congo). Nor need the worker be currently insured; provided he *has been* insured under such a scheme the Regulation will apply to him (Regulation 1408/71, Article 2(1); *Hoekstra* (case 75/63)).

Also by contrast with other legislation relating to workers, EC law on social security is not confined to those who move within the Community in the context of employment. It may apply to persons who move as recipients of services (e.g., *Kohll* (case C-158/96)). In *Hessische Knappschaft* v *Maison Singer et Fils* (case 44/65) a German worker was killed in a road accident while on holiday in France. His dependants were paid by the German social security authorities who then sought to sue the driver of the vehicle responsible for the accident in France. To do so they needed to rely on their rights of subrogation under Regulation 3/58 (now Regulation 1408/71, Article 93(1)). It was argued that the rights arising under the then Article 51 (now 42) of the EC Treaty were such as to promote freedom of movement for workers *as* workers, not *qua* holidaymakers. The Court disagreed, holding that nothing in the then Article 51 required that the concept of worker be limited solely to migrant workers *sensu stricto,* or to workers required to move for the purpose of their employment.

Thus in the case of social security the economic nexus rests on the fact of insurance and not on the fact of employment. It follows that the part-time worker will only benefit from EC legislation in this area if he is or has been insured under a national insurance scheme. However, inasmuch as a difference in treatment between part and full-time workers as regards access to social security schemes and levels of benefit may constitute indirect sex discrimination, part-time workers may acquire social security rights under Directive 79/7, which provides for the equal treatment of men and women in matters of social security (see chapter 25).

Members of the family 'Member of the family' is defined in Article 1(f) as 'any person defined or recognised as a member of the family or designated as a member of the household by the legislation under which benefits are provided', and 'where . . . the said legislations regard as a member of the family or a member of the household only a person living under the same roof as the worker, this condition shall be considered satisfied if the worker in question is mainly dependent on that worker'. Clearly the definition of member of the family will differ from State to State, as it may also differ, depending on the benefit claimed, even within a State. Given that national laws on social security continue to be applied (although in modified form), a definition by reference to the laws of Member States was perhaps the only feasible solution. But it was bound to lead to anomalies. The ECJ has not hesitated, by reverting to the general principles expressed in the preamble to Regulation 1408/71, or by arguing from Regulation 1612/68, to extend a State's definition of family where it was necessary to promote freedom of movement for workers (e.g., *F* v *Belgium* (case 7/75); *Piscitello* (case 139/82)).

Both families' and survivors' benefits under EC social security legislation derive from the worker's insurance, unless they are or have been themselves insured under the appropriate scheme. The Court has not infrequently made exceptions to this principle (e.g., *F* v *Belgium* to be discussed later in this chapter). In its earlier case law, the ECJ distinguished between social security benefits which were granted as a personal right and those acquired solely through the claimant's status as a member of the family of a worker. Only the latter could be claimed, on a basis of equality with national claimants, under Regulation 1408/71 (*Kermaschek* (case 40/76)). However, in *Bestuur van de Sociale Verzekeringsbank* v *Cabanis-Issarte* (case C–308/93), the ECJ departed from *Kermaschek*. Here it held that the claimant, a French woman who had lived with her French husband in Holland while he worked there, and who had never herself been a worker, could, on their return to France following his retirement, invoke the non-discrimination principle of Article 3 of Regulation 1408/71 in order to claim equality of contribution to a Dutch voluntary personal pension scheme to which she had contributed while she was living in the Netherlands. To maintain a distinction between rights in person and derived rights would, the Court held, 'undermine the fundamental Community law requirement that its rules should be applied uniformly, by making their applicability to individuals depend on whether the national law relating to the benefits question treats the rights concerned as rights in person or derived rights, in the light of the specific features of the domestic social security scheme'.

Cababanis-Issarte and *Kermaschek* concerned rights which were undisputedly social security rights. Social benefits which are not strictly speaking social security rights covered by Regulation 1408/71 should now be claimed alternatively or additionally under Regulation 1612/68, Article 7(2), as a 'social advantage'. This seems to accord with the Court's jurisprudence dating from the mid-1970s and *Fiorini* (case 32/75) (see chapter 20).

Despite the ECJ's attempts to close the gaps in the protection afforded to migrant workers and their families, lacunae still exist, as noted by the High-level Panel Report on the Free Movement of People. In particular, the Regulation (with the exception of Article 22) does not apply to Community nationals who are not economically active or their families, nor does it apply to third-country nationals legally resident in a Member State and who are not part of a migrant EC worker's family. Some proposals to limit these discrepancies have been put forward by the Commission, notably a proposal to extend the protection offered by Regulation 1408/71 to third-country nationals. Whether the political will exists to enact such legislation is, however, another question.

Principles

The general principles underlying Regulation 1408/71 are stated in the preamble; they are laid down in more detailed form in the Regulation itself. Most of these principles are designed to secure one further overriding goal, that the migrant worker and his family should suffer no disadvantage as a result of moving within the Community.

Non-discrimination on grounds of nationality   This is perhaps the most important principle. It has certainly been the most frequently invoked. Article 3(1) of Regulation 1408/71 provides that:

> Subject to the special provisions of this Regulation, persons resident in the territory of one of the Member States to whom this Regulation applies shall be subject to the same obligations and enjoy the same benefits under the legislation of any Member State as the nationals of that State.

Article 3(1) is thus a specific application of the general principle of non-discrimination expressed in Article 12 (ex 6) EC, and like that provision it applies to all forms of discrimination, direct and indirect. Discrimination will often take the form of a residence or length of residence requirement. A benefit covered by the Regulation cannot be refused in breach of Article 3. Unlike other areas of EC law it appears that in its social security rules reverse discrimination is not permitted. The Court held in *Kenny v Insurance Officer* (case 1/78):

> . . . it is for the national legislation to lay down the conditions for the acquisition, retention, loss or suspension of the right to social security benefits so long as those conditions apply without discrimination to *the nationals of the Member State concerned* and to those of other Member States (para. 16, emphasis added).

Payment regardless of residence   This principle derives from Article 42(b) (ex 51(b)) of the EC Treaty. Article 10(1) of Regulation 1408/71 provides that:

> Save as otherwise provided in this Regulation, invalidity, old-age or survivors' cash benefits, pensions for accidents at work or occupational diseases and death grants acquired under the legislation of one or more Member States shall not be subject to any reduction, modification, suspension, withdrawal or confiscation by reason of the fact that the recipient resides in the territory of a Member State other than that in which the institution responsible for payment is situated.

It will be noted that this principle, known as the 'exportability' principle, is not expressed to apply to *all* social security benefits; sickness benefits and family benefits, for example, are subject to special provision in Regulation 1408/71 and Regulation 574/72. Article 10 is expressed to apply only 'save as otherwise provided'.

No overlapping of benefits   Article 12(1) of Regulation 1408/71 provides that:

> This Regulation can neither confer nor maintain the right to several benefits of the same kind for one and the same period of compulsory insurance.

In *Schmidt* v *Rijksdienst voor Pensioenen* (case C–98/94) the Court held that benefits will be of the 'same kind' when the purpose and object as well as the basis on which they are calculated and the conditions for granting them are identical. On the other hand characteristics which are purely formal are not relevant criteria for the classification of benefits. Benefits calculated or produced on the basis of periods of employment of two different persons cannot be treated as benefits of the same kind. Thus in *Schmidt* a retirement pension for a divorcee, designed to ensure for that person adequate means of support, was not of the same kind as a personal retirement pension.

Where a worker has contributed to social security schemes in two or more Member States, he may have become entitled to benefit in respect of the same contingency from more than one State. Article 12 operates to prevent him receiving double benefit. However, since entitlement is subject to the single State principle (see below), and the 'competent' State is determined according to Community law, Article 12 could result in the claimant receiving a lesser sum from the competent State than that to which he would be entitled under the law of another State. Where this occurs the Court has held he is entitled to receive the difference between the smaller and the larger sum, the difference payable by the competent institution in the more 'generous' State. 'A worker cannot be deprived of more favourable allowances by substituting the benefits available from one Member State for the benefits due from another Member State' (see e.g. *Baldi* (case 1/88), family allowances; *Di Felice* (case 128/88), retirement pension; *Georges* (case 24/88), family allowances).

The Court has held that in applying national rules against overlapping of benefits it is for the national court to classify the benefits in question in accordance with the applicable national legislation, taking into account the rules relating to conflcit of laws, since Community rules are not relevant here (*Union Nationale des Mutualités Socialistes* v *Del Grosso* (case C–325/93)).

Article 12(1) does not apply to benefits in respect of invalidity, old age, death (pensions) or occupational disease, for which there is special provision for apportionment amongst Member States (Article 12(1)).

Aggregation   This principle, derived from Article 42(a) (ex 51(a)) of the EC Treaty, is spelt out specifically with regard to each type of benefit covered.

Article 18(1) for example, relating to sickness and maternity benefit, provides (as amended by Regulation 2864/72, Article 1(3)) that:

> The competent institution of a Member State whose legislation makes the acquisition, retention or recovery of the right to benefits conditional upon the completion of insurance periods or periods of employment or residence shall, to the extent necessary, take account of insurance periods or periods of employment or residence completed under the legislation of any other Member State as if they were periods completed under the legislation which it administers.

In *Klaus* v *Bestuur van de Nieuwe Algemene Bedrijfsvereniging* (case C–482/93), in the context of a claim for sickness benefit, the Court held that where the grant of benefit is subject to a condition that the claimant was not already unfit for work at the time of becoming insured (as is permissible under EC law), the competent institution must take into account periods of insurance completed in another Member State. The starting point for 'becoming insured' will thus be when the claimant first became insured. The fact that the person was for a short period neither employed nor seeking work in the competent Member State does not interrupt the continuity of periods of insurance completed by that person or preclude the application of the aggregation principle.

Other Articles provide in similar terms for each specific benefit, e.g., Article 38, invalidity benefit; Article 45, old age and death pensions; Article 64, death grants; Article 67, unemployment benefits; Article 72, family benefits.

Thus, *where necessary,* account must be taken of periods of *contribution, employment* and *residence* in all the Member States in which the insured person has worked in order to ascertain:

(a)   his eligibility for benefit, and
(b)   the amount of benefit to which he may be entitled.

The single State principle   This is provided by Article 13, which states as a general rule that:

> A worker to whom this Regulation applies shall be subject to the legislation of a single Member State only.

The specific rules for determining which legislation is applicable are contained in Articles 14-17 which will be discussed later in this chapter.

No disadvantage   As noted above, the Court has held that a worker may not be allowed to suffer disadvantage as a result of the application of Community rules. EC rules against overlapping cannot result in a loss of advantages for a migrant worker. Where the worker is doubly entitled, he or she may choose the more advantageous benefit (*Iacobelli* v *I.N.A.M.I.* (case C–275/91)). The worker cannot as a result of moving from one Member State to another be put in a worse position than workers who have not availed themselves of their right of free movement (*Masgio* (case C–10/90)). There appear, however, to be certain exceptions to this principle. Where the disadvantage results from national rules concerning conditions of *affiliation* to a social security scheme, Community law cannot be applied to remedy this deficiency; such rules are regarded as a matter of national law alone (see *Schmitt* (case 29/88); *Coonan* (case 110/79)). In *Bastos Moriana* v *Bundesanstalt für Arbeit* (case C–59/95) various EC migrant workers (or their widows) who had spent time working in Germany returned to their respective home States. Following the aggregation principle they received an invalidity pension set at the level payable in Germany to take account of the contributions made whilst resident in Germany. They subsequently applied for a supplementary benefit to make up the difference between the level of the German dependent child allowance and the smaller dependent child allowances paid by their home States. Since their right to the German pension arose only as a result of the aggregation principle of Article 45, they were unsuccessful. They would only be entitled to the supplementary benefit if their entitlement to the supplementary pension had been acquired solely by virtue of insurance periods completed in Germany. Similarly, the Court has held that it is for Member States to determine the *temporal effect* of its social security rules: where new rules are introduced without retrospective effects, Community law cannot be invoked to allow these rules to be applied to remedy inequalities suffered prior to their introduction (*Jordan* (case 141/88); see also *Steenhorst Neerings* (case C–338/91)).

Thus the Court has been forced to acknowledge that some disadvantage to migrant workers will inevitably result from the fact that Article 42 (ex 51) is not designed to create a common social security scheme but simply to coordinate national social security schemes (see *McLachlan* v *CNAVTS* (case C–146/93)).

Material scope

Article 4(1) of Regulation 1408/71 provides that:

This Regulation shall apply to all legislation concerning the following branches of social security, reflecting the nine official categories recognised by the ILO:

(a) sickness and maternity benefits;
(b) invalidity benefits, including those intended for the maintenance or improvement of working capacity;
(c) old-age benefits;
(d) survivors' benefits;
(e) benefits in respect of accidents at work and occupational diseases;
(f) death grants;
(g) unemployment benefits;
(h) family benefits.

Article 4(2) provides that the Regulation shall apply 'to all general and special social security schemes, whether contributory or non-contributory'.

However, the Regulation does *not* apply to 'social and medical assistance, to benefit schemes for victims of war or its consequences, or to special schemes for civil servants and persons treated as such' (Article 4(4)).

Thus, provided a person is or has been insured under a general scheme for the whole population covering 'one or more' (Article 2(1)) of the contingencies provided for under Article 4(1), that person, or a person claiming through that person, may invoke the principles and detailed rules of the Regulation (and Regulation 574/72 where appropriate) to support a claim for any of these benefits or to challenge a refusal to grant such benefits in breach of these Regulations. Only the benefits listed in Article 4(4) lie outside the scope of the Regulations, the most important exclusion being benefits in the form of 'social assistance'.

Social assistance

Since the term 'social assistance' is not a term of art, is not defined in Regulation 1408/71, and will be subject to different interpretations in different Member States, interpretation has been left to the ECJ, largely on reference from national courts seised with the problem. Not surprisingly the Court has given the term the narrowest scope.

In a series of cases, starting with *Frilli* v *Belgium* (case 1/72), the Court, in assessing whether a particular benefit, which may look like social assistance, qualifies as social security, has applied a 'double function' test. Some kinds of benefit, the Court reasons, perform a double function; they are akin to social assistance, since need is the essential criterion, and eligibility is not dependent on employment; yet they are akin to social security since they confer on the beneficiary a legally defined position. Since such difficulties must not be allowed to prejudice the rights of workers, such benefits must be deemed to be social security benefits, and assimilated where possible to the social security benefits listed in Article 4(1). Applying this test in *Frilli,* a non-contributory guaranteed minimum income, unrelated to insurance, payable in Belgium to Belgian citizens or those resident for a minimum period of five years, was assimilated to the old age pension and deemed to be social security; as such it could not be denied to Frilli in breach of Regulation 1408/71, Article 3. Similarly in *Callemeyn* v *Belgium* (case 187/73) a special payment to the handicapped, unrelated to either employment or contributions (the claimant being the wife of a migrant worker), refused by the Belgian authorities on the grounds of her nationality, was assimilated to invalidity benefit and held, applying the same test, to constitute social security.

In *F* v *Belgium* (case 7/75) the claimant was the 14-year old handicapped son of an Italian worker in Belgium. He had been refused a special grant for handicapped persons, again because he could not fulfil the (Belgian) nationality or (15-year) residence requirement. Prima facie the benefit was social assistance; it was not a 'family' benefit, nor a workers' invalidity benefit; it was not related to contributions and was available to the whole (handicapped) population. Nevertheless, applying the double function test the Court found it to be social security within Regulation 1408/71. In a remarkable judgment, the Court, arguing from the general aims of the Treaty, as expressed in Articles 2, 7 EEC (now Article 12 (ex 6) EC) and 51 (now 42), from the preamble to Regulation 1408/71, and from Regulation 1251/70, concluded that a dependent person such as Mr and Mrs F's son was entitled to equality of treatment as long as his parents were resident in a Member State. Even when he ceased to be a minor his right to equality of treatment would not cease. The migrant worker, as Advocate-General Trabucchi suggested, must be treated not just as a source of labour but as a human being.

These cases were followed by many others (e.g., *Inzirillo* (case 63/76); *Vigier* (case 70/80); *Piscitello* (case 139/82)) in which benefits of extremely dubious status as social security benefits were upheld as such, whether or not they were claimed as supplements to existing benefits (as was the case in *Frilli* (case 1/72) and *Callemeyn* (case 187/73)), and even when they could not be assimilated to any of the existing categories of social security benefits (e.g., *Palermo* (case 237/78) — special non-contributory allowance to elderly mothers of large families designed to increase the birth rate in France). The only criterion by which a claim might still be excluded as constituting 'social assistance', applied by the Court in *Fossi* (case 79/76) and *Tinelli* (case 144/78), was if the benefit involved a discretionary assessment of need or personal circumstances. Needless to say this test did not serve to exclude many claims (*Fossi* and *Tinelli* were claiming as 'victims of war' and as such in any case within Regulation 1408/71, Article 4(4)).

The Court's desire to extend the principle of equality of treatment to *all* social benefits is understandable. To allow Member States to discriminate against migrant workers in the provision of social assistance would undoubtedly create barriers to the free movement of workers and to their and their families' integration into the host State. But if its aims were wholly legitimate, in interpreting the social assistance exclusion of Article 4(4) virtually out of existence, the same cannot be said of the means chosen to achieve its ends.

Perhaps sensing that it had gone too far, the Court switched its approach in the 1980s. Instead of stretching Regulation 1408/71 to encompass 'social assistance' type claims the Court chose an alternative route, treating the benefits as 'social advantages' under Article 7(2) of Regulation 1612/68, the scope of which was being expanded following the introduction of the 'lawful residence' test in *Even* (case 207/78) (the *Even* formula; see chapter 20 and cases such as *Reina* (case 65/81) and *Forcheri* (case 152/82)). In *Reina*, it will be recalled, the Court held that Article 7(2) of Regulation 1612/68 applied even to benefits granted on a discretionary basis, the one remaining acknowledged indicium of 'social assistance'.

As a result of its new approach, in *Castelli* (case 261/83) an Italian mother, legitimately resident with her son (who was also a pensioner, having worked and retired in Belgium), was found entitled to a guaranteed income (not a pension) paid in Belgium to all elderly people, and in *Hoeckx* (case 249/83) and *Scrivner* (case 122/84) the claimants were held entitled to the Belgian minimum income allowance, the 'minimex', not, as previously in *Frilli* (case 1/72), on the basis of Regulation 1408/71, but on the basis of Article 7(2) of Regulation 1612/68. Since in all cases the claimants were 'lawfully resident' in Belgium, they were entitled to be treated equally with Belgian nationals. The nationality and residence requirement required for eligibility for the benefits would not be enforced against them. On similar reasoning, in *Frascogna (No. 1)* (case 157/84) and *(No. 2)* (case 256/86), an Italian widow who went to live with her son, who was a worker in France, was held entitled under Article 7(2) of Regulation 1612/68 to a special old-age allowance granted by the French authorities. The 15-year residence qualification required of foreigners under French law could not be applied to Ms Frascogna to deprive her of her rights. It is interesting to note that Ms Frascogna's claim under Regulation 1408/71 was rejected.

Following these cases it seems that the doubtful claims, i.e., those which do not obviously qualify as social security, will now be more likely to succeed under Regulation 1612/68 than under Regulation 1408/71 (see e.g., *Schmid v Belgium* (case C–310/91)). *A fortiori* claims by those such as part-time workers, who are often not insured under a general social security scheme.

Regulation 1408/71 will, of course, continue to apply, and apply alone, to 'genuine' social security benefits, and, if a claimant wishes to 'export' a benefit this can only be achieved under the specific provisions of that Regulation. 'Social advantages' under Regulation 1612/68 cannot be exported unless the benefits are exportable as a matter of *national* law (e.g., *Carmina di Leo* (case 308/89)). In *Piscitello* (case 139/82) Ms Piscitello's claim for an Italian 'social aid pension' to be exported and paid to her in Belgium, where she went to live with her daughter, was assimilated to the category of 'old-age pension' and export was permitted under Article 10 of Regulation 1408/71. It has been argued that it was legitimate to do so in this case since she was entitled to the pension in her own right as an Italian citizen; but as a general rule it is undesirable that benefits which are not strictly speaking social security benefits should be exported, since 'assistance'-type benefits usually require an on-the-spot assessment of need and are tied to national standards of living. Unlike the social security provision set up by Regulation 1408/71, there exists within Member States no reciprocal machinery for the processing of such claims. As the law has now developed it is submitted that Ms Piscitello's claim could now equally be brought against the Belgian authorities for the equivalent Belgian provision under Regulation 1612/68, on the same basis as *Frascogna*. On the principle of no overlapping of benefits she would clearly not be entitled to both.

A claimant who wishes to invoke the aggregation principle will likewise have to show that his claim falls within Regulation 1408/71. In *Campana* (case 375/85) the Court held that a special (contributory) benefit providing aid for vocational training for unemployed workers was included within the benefits covered by Regulation 1408/71, Article 4(1); therefore the claimant was entitled to invoke the aggregation principle in order to qualify for the benefit. It seems that the benefit was assimilated to unemployment benefit even though the claimant was employed at the time of applying for the aid; it was held to be justified as designed to prevent *future* unemployment. In *Newton* v *Chief Adjudication Officer* (case C–356/89) a mobility allowance, payable under British law, which as the Court acknowledged had 'much in common' with social assistance, was assimilated to an invalidity allowance and held to be claimable in France, where the claimant had gone to retire. However, in this case the claimant had been employed in France. The Court suggested that the allowance in question could not be claimed as a social security benefit outside national territory by persons who had been subject, as employed or self-employed persons, to the *exclusive* legislation of the Member State from which they were claiming.

From the above cases it is clear that the ECJ will use all the means at its disposal to ensure that migrant workers and their families are in no way disadvantaged as a result of moving within the Community. In order to achieve its ends the Court will not be deterred by apparent shortcomings in EC legislation.

Operation of the system

The principles on which EC law are based have already been considered. It remains to examine the operation of the system in practice, concluding with a brief reference, by way of example, to certain more detailed provisions relating to specific benefits.

If benefits are to be governed by the single State principle (Regulation 1408/71, Article 13(1)) and each Member State is to continue to apply its own rules as to:

(a)   the kind of benefits to be provided, and
(b)   the conditions for eligibility for these benefits,

the crucial question for the migrant worker, who may have lived and worked in a number of Member States, or who may reside in one Member State and work in another, is which social security law will apply in his case?

Applicable law: *lex laboris*

The general rule is simple: the applicable law is the law of the State in which a person works — *lex laboris*. This is governed by Regulation 1408/71, Article 13(2)(a), as amended by Regulation 1390/81, which provides that:

a person employed in the territory of one Member State shall be subject to the legislation of that State even if he resides in the territory of another Member State or if the registered office or place of business of the undertaking or individual employing him is situated in the territory of another Member State.

Furthermore, Article 13(2)(b) provides that:

a person who is self-employed in the territory of one Member State shall be subject to the legislation of that State even if he resides in the territory of another Member State.

If the applicable law is the law of the State in which a person works, then that is the State with which the person is currently insured, and the institution responsible in that State for such insurance will be responsible for payment of benefits. The *lex laboris* principle applies from the moment when the person takes up employment.

The institution with which the worker is insured at the time of application for benefits, and which is thus responsible for payment of benefits, is known as the 'competent institution' (Article 1(o)).

The State in whose territory the competent institution is situated is known as the 'competent State' (Article 1(q)).

There is special provision in Article 13 for civil servants (13(2)(d)), the armed forces (13(2)(e)), and seamen on board a vessel flying the flag of a Member State (13(1)(c)).

Article 14 provides a number of exceptions to the *lex laboris* principle. These exceptions relate to:

(a)   the temporary worker;
(b)   the worker who is employed in two or more Member States, and
(c)   the frontier worker.

(a)   *The temporary worker.* Article 14(1)(a) as amended by Regulation 1390/81 provides that:

A person employed in the territory of a Member State by an undertaking to which he is normally attached who is posted by that undertaking to the territory of another Member State to perform work there for that undertaking shall continue to be subject to the legislation of the *first* Member State, provided that the anticipated duration of that work does not exceed 12 months and that he is not sent to replace another person who has completed his term of posting.

Scope for extension of the 12-month period is provided by Article 14(1)(b).

In *Manpower Sàrl* (case 35/70) the Court held that a worker, provided on a temporary basis by a German company providing staffing services, would fall within these provisions as long as the worker remained paid by, and answerable to, the company providing the services. By contrast, in *Hakenberg* (case 13/73) a commercial traveller, paid by commission, representing an undertaking in one Member State, and spending nine months of each year canvassing for orders in other Member States, did not fall within Article 14(1)(a) (originally Article 13(1)(a) or Regulation 3).

(b)   *The worker employed in two or more Member States* (Article 14(2)). This category embraces (i) the worker in international transport (Article 14(2)(a)) and (ii) 'others' (Article 14(2)(b)). In these cases the order of priority will be:

(1) The law of his State of residence if he is employed there either principally (Article 14(2)(a)(ii), worker in international transport) or partly (Article 14(2)(b)(i), 'other').

(2) The law of the State where he is employed by a permanent branch or agency.

(3) The law of the State where the registered office or place of business of the undertaking with which he is employed is situated.

(c) *The frontier worker* (Article 14(3)). The frontier worker is defined as a person 'employed in the territory of one Member State by an undertaking which has its registered office or place of business in the territory of another Member State and which straddles the common frontier of these States'. Here the applicable law is the law of the State in which the undertaking has its registered office or place of business.

Article 14 is enacted in similar terms for the self-employed in Article 14a, which was added by Regulation 1390/81.

Once the applicable law has been determined, depending on whether the normal (*lex laboris*) principle or one of the exceptions applies, the competent institution within that Member State must, on an application for benefit, apply the aggregation principle. In order to ascertain the question of the applicant's eligibility and the extent of his entitlement, insurance periods and periods of employment or residence *completed under the legislation of any other Member State* must be taken into account to the extent that this is necessary under the law of the competent State. Once this has been ascertained, the person eligible for benefit is entitled (pursuant to Article 10(1) of Regulation 1408/71 and subject to the reservations contained therein) to *receive* these benefits wherever he may be resident in the Community on the following terms:

(a) *benefits in cash* according to the law of the competent State, and
(b) *benefits in kind* according to the law of the State of residence.

This principle is spelt out in general terms in Article 19 and in specific terms throughout the Regulation, e.g., Article 22 (sickness benefit), Article 25 (unemployment benefit), Article 55 (industrial injury benefit). Benefits in kind can include certain cash payments, for example, to cover medical expenses payable by way of reimbursement. The distinction between payments in cash and payment in kind is made purely for practical, administrative purposes. Although the host Member State provides the benefits through the appropriate national agencies, it is the competent institution which is ultimately responsible for payment, whether the benefit is in the form of cash or kind (Article 19; see also *Kohll* (case C–158/96) and *Decker* (case C–120/95) re payment for medical 'treatment' outside competent State). Thus claims will be processed and reimbursement provided on a reciprocal basis, under machinery provided by Regulations 1408/71 and 574/72. No such provision exists for benefits in the form of 'social advantages' claimed under Article 7(2) of Regulation 1612/68.

Since the competent institution is ultimately responsible for the financing of benefits both in cash and in kind it is no surprise that the Court has held, in the context of a claim for benefits in kind in respect of sickness benefit for members of the family, that a claimant may be entitled to a benefit in kind according to the law of the State of employment where members of the family are not entitled to those benefits under the legislation of their State of residence (*Delavant* v *Allegemeine Ortskrankenkasse für das Saarland* (case C–451/93)). It is unlikely that the principle would be confined to benefits for members of the family.

Principle of apportionment

Where certain social security benefits are concerned, one further principle may apply, the principle of apportionment. This principle, which applies to what may be called the substantial or long-term benefits, the invalidity, old-age and survivors' pensions, means that the financial burden may, if beneficial to the claimant, be divided between the competent institutions in Member States in which a person has worked and contributed throughout his working life in proportion to the length of time he has worked in each Member State. In this way each institution will bear its own share of the burden and the worker will receive in benefit a share appropriate to his or her contributions in each Member State in which the worker has worked (for details see Article 46). In order that the worker should not lose out under this system, provision is made that a worker cannot receive as a total sum less than he or she would have been entitled to had the worker received his or her entire pension according to the law of the worker's State of residence (Article 50).

Despite these provisions, situations can arise where, as a result of the splitting of benefits, claimants will not receive as much as they would have received had the benefit been provided according to the legislation of a single Member State. This was acknowledged by the Court in *McLachlan* (case C–146/93) as inevitable given the differences in Member States social security rules.

There exists no similar provision for apportionment of liability for benefits received as 'social advantages' under Regulation 1612/68.

Payment of benefits to persons resident
outside the competent State: special provisions

Unemployment benefits Since the right to unemployment benefit normally depends on the claimant being available for work in the competent State, specific provision was made in Regulation 1408/71 to enable unemployed persons to go to another Member State in order to seek employment without losing their entitlement to benefit from the competent institution. Under Article 69, a person wishing to retain his or her entitlement must:

(a)   register with the employment services of the competent State as a person seeking work, and remain available for at least four weeks after

becoming unemployed. The competent institution may authorise his departure before such time has expired (Article 69(1)(a)). He must then

(b)   register as a person seeking work with the employment services of
each of the Member States to which he goes within seven days of the day
when he ceased to be available to the employment services of the State he left
(Article 69(1)(b)).

If the person complies with these requirements, his or her entitlement to
benefits from the competent State (which may be paid in the person's State
of residence: Article 70) will continue for up to three months, provided the
person is eligible for benefits of this duration.

If a person does not find work, and returns to the competent State before
the expiry of the three-month limit, his or her entitlement to benefits from
the competent State will continue; if the person does not return within that
period he or she will 'lose all entitlement to benefits under the legislation of
the competent State' (Article 69(2)). In exceptional cases, the time-limit may
be extended by the competent institution. The Court has encouraged
Member States to be generous in their approach to these provisions. In
Perotta v *Allgemeine Ortskrankenkasse München* (case C–391/93) it suggested
that in the case of illness it is not necessary that a formal application for
extension should be made; it may be inferred from the claimant's application
for sickness benefit shortly before the expiry of the period in respect of which
sickness benefit may be paid. The state of the claimant's health may be
regarded as *force majeure*, justifying a waiving of the time limit. It will be
regarded as *force majeure* if it prevents the claimant returning to the competent
State. The concept is not to be limited to the 'absolute impossibility' of
returning but must be understood as designating 'abnormal and unforeseeable circumstances outside the control of the unemployed person', the
consequences of which could not have been avoided except at the cost of
excessive sacrifice. The Court is clearly conscious of the need, particularly in
times of high unemployment, to avoid a rigid application of the rules where
they are likely to deter the unemployed from moving within the Community
in order to find work.

The Commission too is concerned to assist job hunters by easing the social
security rules. In February 1996 it introduced proposals for two Regulations
designed to ensure that people who move between Member States should not
be penalised by losing their entitlement to social security benefits. Under one
proposal, citizens who move to another Member State in search of work
would be entitled, under certain conditions, to continue receiving unemployment benefits. The other proposal would allow the limited transfer of
pre-retirement benefits between Member States. A Europe-wide employment
body, EURES, was launched by the Commission in November 1994.
EURES operates as a network of 450 advisers who can access European
databases listing job vacancies and living and working conditions. It handled
180,000 contacts with job seekers in its first 10 months.

As a general rule, the competent State in the case of unemployment benefit
is the State in which the claimant was last employed and insured. The

claimant must, however, remain available for work in that State, subject to the provisions of Article 69. Should the claimant return to reside in his or her 'home' State, responsibility for unemployment benefit will transfer to that State provided the claimant registers as available for work there. However, an unemployed worker resident in a State other than that in which he or she was last employed is entitled to invoke the exportability principle of Article 19 in order to claim from the competent institution in the latter State other benefits, such as sickness or invalidity benefit, without restriction on time, since these provisions were intended to be payable to workers residing, even permanently, outside the competent State (*Chief Adjudication Officer* v *Twomey* (case C–215/90)). Only when the worker obtains work in another Member State will responsibility for social security benefits transfer to the competent institution in that State.

Family benefits   In accordance with the principle of payment regardless of residence, Article 73(1) as amended by Regulation 1390/81 provides that:

> An employed person subject to the legislation of a Member State other than France shall be entitled to the family benefits provided for by the legislation of the first Member State for members of his family residing in the territory of another Member State, as though they were residing in the territory of the first State.

Applying these provisions in *Martinez* v *Bundesanstalt für Arbeit* (case C–321/ 93), the Court held that a State cannot, under its tax regime, link entitlement to and the amount of family benefit to the family's residence on its territory. For the purposes of determining these matters, all the relevant tax legislation must be applied on the basis that the spouse resides notionally in the Member State providing the benefits.

Where family benefit is claimed under this Article a worker cannot be refused benefit on the grounds that he or she only works part-time, nor can the worker's rights depend on having been insured on particular calendar days (*Bestuur der Sociale Verzekeringsbank* v *Kits van Heijningen* (case C–2/ 89)).

Article 73(2) provided an exception to the rule in Article 73(1) in the case of France, to the effect that an employed person subject to French legislation shall be entitled:

> in respect of members of his family residing in the territory of a Member State other than France, to the family allowances provided by the legislation of the Member State in whose territory those members of the family reside . . . .

This exception, which was included on the insistence of the French, whose family benefits at the time were more substantial than those provided in other Member States, was challenged, successfully, in *Pinna* (case 41/84). The Court held that since disparities already existed as a result of the application of the different national systems of social security law, Community law could not be allowed to add to these disparities. Although the exception applied to all EC claimants, including the French, it was in breach of the general principle of non-discrimination since its *effects* would be more likely to fall on migrant workers. Thus the general principle of exportability, as provided by Article 73(1), applied.

Article 74 provides for unemployed persons on the same terms as Article 73. Where family benefits are payable under Article 74 for dependent children under 21 it is not permitted to require children who are unemployed to be available for employment in the competent State as a condition for the award of benefit. The condition of availability for work must be regarded as fulfilled where the child is at the disposal of the employment office of the Member State in which he resides (*Bronzino* (case C–228/88); *Gatto* (case C–12/89)).

In order to avoid overlapping of benefits, Article 10(1) of Regulation 574/72 provides that where entitlement to family benefits in a particular Member State is *not* subject to conditions of insurance of employment they shall be suspended where benefits are due in pursuance of Article 73. *However,* if the spouse of the worker or unemployed person referred to in Article 73(1) *exercises a trade or professional activity* in the territory of the said Member State, the right to family benefits or family allowances due in pursuance of Article 73(1) 'shall be suspended; and only those family benefits or family allowances of the Member State in whose territory the member of the family is residing shall be paid, the cost to be borne by that Member State' (Article 10(1)(a)).

Thus, where the spouse looking after the family is herself economically active, responsibility shifts from the originally competent institution to the institution of the family's State of residence. However, in order that the family should not lose out by moving, where in the latter case the sum received is lower than that which would have been received as a result of the application of Article 73, entitlement under Article 73(1) is suspended only up to the amount received in respect of the same period and the same member of the family in the State of residence of the spouse pursuing a professional or trade activity in that State (*Beeck* (case 104/80); see also *Georges* (case 24/88), noted above; *Dammer* (case C–168/88), parents working in State A and B, family residing in State C).

These cases demonstrate that the Court will always interpret against the literal meaning of a specific provision where a literal interpretation would conflict with the principles and purpose behind the legislation, particularly when to do otherwise would create a barrier to the free movement of workers.

Evaluation

EC law on social security has been criticised as being over-complicated, poorly understood, and not appropriate to current economic and social realities. Complication is inevitable in a system which seeks to coordinate 15 different sets of different and already extremely complex rules. Lack of understanding follows. High unemployment and a growing and ageing population throughout Europe are placing heavy demands on national social security systems. EC social security rules, intended to assist and encourage the free movement of workers, including the unemployed, within the single market, are not adequate to this task. Limited in scope to *national statutory* social security schemes, EC law fails to meet the need of the new, white-collar unemployed for transferability of benefits acquired under private social insurance schemes. Yet the trend towards such schemes is growing. Existing rules, or the absence of rules, provide a potent, indeed a growing, barrier to the freedom of movement of persons, ironically at a time when other barriers are collapsing. There is no doubt a real need for a thorough overhaul of the rules.

The Commission is aware of the problem but has acknowledged that in the present climate, when all Member States are facing problems in financing their social security systems, there is little prospect of moving, at least in the short term, towards a harmonised system of European social security law. Such a move would have to be approved unanimously. In 15 States of differing political colours and different priorities, consensus over the content of social security law would be unlikely. Proposals have been made for a social 'snake', akin to the monetary 'snake', designed to bring the provision of national benefits within a permitted European 'band', to be exceeded only with the approval of Member States, and for a separate sixteenth European system as an optional alternative to a private or national insurance scheme (see the article by Laske listed in the further reading). But the time does not seem ripe for radical change in this sphere. The Commission has introduced some measures to assist the unemployed, as indicated above; in the post-Maastricht spirit of subsidiarity it has urged Member States to increase cooperation at Community level by regular meetings of senior national officials, with a view to greater coordination of social security laws and, eventually, harmonisation. This could be seen as an opportunity for restructuring and reform: hopefully it will not be used as a means of levelling down social protection throughout the Community. The Community is committed under Article 2 of the EC Treaty to a 'high level of employment and social protection'. This should apply *a fortiori* to its most vulnerable citizens.

Further reading

Cobral, P., 'Cross-border medical care in the European Union' (1999) 24 ELR 587.

Cornelissen, R., 'The Principle of Territoriality and the Community Regulations on Social Security' (1996) 33 CML Rev 436.

Eichenhoffer, E., 'Co-ordination of Social Security and Equal Treatment of Men and Women in Employment: Recent Social Security Judgments of the Court of Justice' (1993) 30 CML Rev 1021.

Laske, C., 'The Impact of the Single European Market on Social Protection for Migrant Workers' (1993) 30 CML Rev 515.

Mei, A.P., 'Cross-Border Access to Medical Care within the European Union — Some Reflections on the Judgment in *Decker* and *Kohll*' (1998) *Maastricht Journal of European and Comparative Law* 277.

Steiner, J., 'The Right to Welfare: Equality and Equity under Community Law' (1985) 10 EL Rev 21.

Vershueren, H., 'EC Social Security Coordination Excluding Third Country Nationals: Still in Line with Fundamental Rights after the *Gaygusuz* Judgment?' (1997) 34 CML Rev 991.

Watson, P., 'Minimum Income Benefits: Social Security or Social Assistance?' (1985) 10 EL Rev 335.

TWENTY FIVE

Sex discrimination

Introduction

Prior to the ToA, EC law on sex discrimination comprised:

(a)   Article 119 of the EC Treaty, which laid down a general principle of *equal pay for equal work* for men and women.

(b)   Directive 75/117, which implements the principle of equal pay in more specific terms, to include equal pay for work of *equal value*.

(c)   Directive 76/207, which provides for *equal treatment* for men and women in the context of employment.

(d)   Directive 79/7, which applies the equal treatment principle to matters of social security.

(e)   Directive 86/378, which extends the equal treatment principle to occupational pension schemes.

(f)   Directive 86/613, which provides for equal treatment in self-employment.

The ToA incorporated into the main body of the EC Treaty, as Chapter 1 to new Title XI of the Treaty, the provisions of the Protocol on the Social Chapter, which had been annexed by the TEU to the EC Treaty, some of which also have a bearing on sex discrimination. The incorporation of the terms of the Protocol on the Social Chapter not only means that legislation enacted under these provisions will now extend to the UK (which had hitherto opted out of the extended social policy provisions) as well as to the other Member States, but that the social protection provisions contained within the EC Treaty will be extended significantly. Still central to the Social Chapter, however, is the original EC provision prohibiting sex discrimination, now amended and renumbered as Article 141 EC (ex 119).

Linked closely to the question of sex discrimination are a number of issues: the position of part-time workers, and the impact of pregnancy and maternity on the working woman. During recent years, the Community has developed the political will to enact certain Directives in these areas: the Part-Time Workers Directive (Directive 97/81); the Pregnancy and Maternity Directive (Directive 92/85); the Parental Leave Directive (Directive 96/34); and, more generally, the Burden of Proof in Sex Discrimination Directive (Directive 97/80). The implementation date in respect of all these Directives has now passed. Despite this legislative activity, the case law of the ECJ in this area remains important, as the Directives must be understood in the context of the Court's rulings on both Article 141 (ex 119) and the equality Directives. Thus in assessing the compatibility of national implementing measures with Community law, the Directives and the ECJ's case law should both be examined.

The equality principle, which applies equally to both sexes, applies only in the context of employment. It has been described as one of the 'foundations of the Community', designed, according to the ECJ in *Defrenne* v *Sabena (No. 2)* (case 43/75), apropos the then Article 119 (now 141), to achieve a 'double objective', economic and social. It seeks as an economic goal to ensure that States which have implemented the equality principle do not suffer a competitive disadvantage *vis-à-vis* those which have not; and as a social goal to achieve 'social progress', the 'improvement of the living and working conditions of their peoples', as required by the Treaty (preamble, 2nd and 3rd Recital).

No doubt because of this double objective, EC law on sex discrimination, unlike the fundamental Treaty provisions relating to goods and workers, is not limited in its application to migrant workers. Its application may be, and invariably is, 'wholly internal'. It is, however, confined strictly within the economic context; it was not designed to settle questions concerned with the organisation of the family or to alter the division of responsibility between parents. Nor is the prohibition on discrimination absolute; a difference in treatment as between men and women may be permitted if it falls within the specified exceptions set out in the Directives or, in the case of indirect discrimination, where it is 'objectively justified'.

Since Article 141 (ex 119) EC and, to a more limited extent, the Directives on sex discrimination have been declared directly effective (see chapter 4), EC law has been invoked on a number of occasions by individuals seeking to challenge allegedly discriminatory practices which are nonetheless permissible under domestic law. Although Member States have altered their laws to comply with EC requirements, domestic implementation has frequently been found inadequate. Furthermore, the case law in this area has had a significant impact on each Member State's national procedures and remedies (discussed further in chapter 26).

Equal pay for equal work: Article 141 (ex 119) EC

Prior to the ToA, the then Article 119 provided:

Each Member State shall during the first stage ensure and subsequently maintain the application of the principle that men and women should receive equal pay for equal work.

For the purpose of this Article, 'pay' means the ordinary basic or minimum wage or salary and any other consideration, whether in cash or in kind, which the worker receives, directly or indirectly, in respect of his employment from his employer.

What is now Article 141 was amended by the ToA to include a fourth paragraph which permits positive discrimination. This will be discussed further below.

Pay

What constitutes pay? If the concept of pay is generously defined in Article 141 (ex 119), it has been even more generously construed. It was applied in *Garland* v *British Rail Engineering Ltd* (case 12/81) to cover the grant of special travel facilities to ex-employees after retirement, even though the benefit was received following termination of employment and was not granted pursuant to any contractual entitlement. The Court held that the argument that the facilities are not related to a contractual obligation is immaterial. The legal nature of the facilities is not important for the purposes of the application of Article 141 (ex 119) provided that they are granted in respect of the applicant's employment. On similar reasoning in *Worringham* v *Lloyds Bank Ltd* (case 69/80) a supplementary payment made by employers to male employees under the age of 25, for the purpose of contribution to the employees' occupational pension scheme, was held to be pay. Sums which are included in the calculation of the gross salary payable to the employee and which directly determine the calculation of other advantages linked to the salary, such as redundancy payments, unemployment benefits, family allowances and credit facilities, form part of the worker's pay. Since the payment was not made to female employees under the age of 25 the scheme was in breach of the then Article 119.

New questions about the scope of 'pay' for the purposes of Article 141 (ex 119) continue to arise. In *Hill and Stapleton* (case C–143/95) a pay scale which discriminated between full- and part-time workers regarding the calculation of annual pay increments was considered to fall within Article 141 (ex 119), as the scale determined the progression of the workers' pay. *Abdoulage* v *Regie Nationale des Usines Renault* (case C–218/98) concerned a measure which provided that women going on maternity leave, as well as continuing to receive full pay, should also receive a lump sum of FFR 7,500. The ECJ agreed that the lump sum could be considered to fall within pay for the purposes of Article 141 (ex 119). In *R* v *Secretary of State for Employment, ex parte Seymour-Smith* (case C–167/99) the ECJ held that redundancy payments also constituted pay.

Pensions and social security benefits The precise extent to which employers' contributions to pensions and other social security benefits fall within the scope of Article 141 (ex 119) has been much litigated.

Worringham v *Lloyds Bank Ltd* (above) was followed in *Bilka-Kaufhaus GmbH* v *Weber von Hartz* (case 170/84) in the context of a claim by a female part-time worker, Ms Weber, who was seeking to challenge her employer's occupational pension scheme. The scheme was non-contributory, financed solely by the employer. Under the scheme part-timers were entitled to benefit only if they had worked with the firm for at least 15 out of a total of 20 years. No such limitation was imposed on full-timers. Ms Weber alleged that the scheme was indirectly discriminatory, in breach of the then Article 119 (now 141), since the majority of part-time workers were women. The Court agreed that it was *capable* of falling within this Article, since the scheme was contractual, not statutory, in origin; it originated from an agreement made between Bilka and the works council representing the employees, and the benefits were financed solely by the employer as a supplement to existing social security schemes. The benefit thus constituted consideration paid by the employer to the employee in respect of his employment.

The reasoning in *Bilka-Kaufhaus GmbH* (case 170/84) seemed to imply that benefits paid by an employer pursuant to or in lieu of a *statutory* scheme might not constitute pay. In *Defrenne v Belgium (No. 1)* (case 80/70) the Court had held that although payment in the nature of social security benefits was not excluded in principle from the concept of pay, it was not possible to include in this concept, as defined in Article 119 (now 141), social security schemes and benefits, especially retirement pensions, which were directly settled by law without reference to any element of consultation within the undertaking or industry concerned, and which covered without exception all workers in general. Thus although Ms Defrenne (an air hostess) was entitled to invoke the then Article 119 against her employer to claim equal pay to that of her male counterparts (cabin stewards) (*Defrenne v Sabena (No. 2)* (case 43/75)), she was unable to challenge a Belgian law requiring different contributions in respect of male and female employees, made by the employer, to a social security scheme directly imposed by law. Such benefits are, the Court held, 'no more emoluments paid directly by the employer than are roads, canals, or water drains'.

However, the ambit of statutory social security schemes excluded from Article 141 (ex 119) in *Defrenne* has been whittled down by subsequent decisions of the Court. In *Liefting* (case 23/83) a statutory pension scheme applicable to a *particular group* of workers, namely civil servants, was found to be within the scope of the then Article 119. The Court held that sums which public authorities are required to pay, though not in themselves pay, become pay if they are included in calculating their employees' gross pay used in the calculation of other salary benefits. If, as a result, the salary-related benefits are not the same for men as for women, Article 141 (ex 119) is infringed.

Article 141 (ex 119) was again held applicable to a statutory social security benefit in *Rinner-Kühn v FWW Spezial Gebäudereinigung GmbH & Co KG* (case 171/88). The case concerned a claim by a part-time worker, an office cleaner, against her employer, involving a challenge to German legislation permitting employers to exclude part-time workers (defined as persons working 10 hours or less a week) from entitlement to sick pay. Prima facie the claim appeared analogous to the statutory social security scheme held in

Defrenne to be outside the scope of the then Article 119. Nevertheless, the Court found that the continued payment of wages to a worker in the event of illness fell within the definition of pay; therefore national legislation such as the legislation in question, which *allowed* employers to maintain a global difference in pay between the two categories of workers (one of which was predominantly female) must be regarded as contrary to the objectives pursued in Article 119. Being indirectly discriminatory, it would be acceptable only if objectively justified.

In *Barber* v *Guardian Royal Exchange Assurance Group* (case C–262/88), the Court found, in a claim by a group of male employees who were seeking to challenge payments made by their employer under a contracted-out pension scheme, which operated as a substitute for the statutory social security scheme, and under a statutory redundancy scheme, both of which were payable at different ages for men (65) and women (60), that such payments also constituted 'pay' since the worker received these benefits, albeit indirectly, from his employer in respect of his employment.

> Although it is true that many advantages granted by an employer also reflect considerations of social policy, the fact that a benefit is in the nature of pay cannot be called into question where the worker is entitled to receive the benefit in question from his employer *by reason of the existence of the employment relationship* (para.18).

This point was re-emphasised in *Beune* (case C–7/93), which concerned civil service pensions. The Court held that, even where the pension scheme was affected by considerations of social policy, State organisation, ethics or budgetary concerns (factors usually indicative of a social security scheme), the pension scheme of a public employer would still constitute pay where (a) it concerned only a certain category of workers rather than general categories; (b) it was directly related to the period of service; and (c) it was calculated by reference to the employee's last salary (para. 45).

Thus, as was suggested in *Barber*, the only statutory social security schemes which appear now to fall outside Article 141 (ex 119) are statutory social security pension schemes provided for workers in general as a matter of social policy and funded from the public purse. The precise ambit of the statutory social schemes outside Article 141 (ex 119) is, despite numerous cases on this issue, still unclear.

While the application of Article 141 (ex 119) in a clear case of discrimination in respect of employers' *contribution* to an occupational pension scheme, as in *Worringham* v *Lloyds Bank Ltd* (case 69/80), causes few problems, its extension in *Barber* to the *award* of pensions hitherto tied to a permitted difference in pension age for men and women, in which actuarial factors also play a part, has created problems and led to great complexity.

Because the ruling in *Barber* was likely seriously to affect the financial balance of contracted-out pension schemes, contributions and calculations for which had been based on different retirement ages for men and women, and because, as the Court conceded, both Member States and the parties concerned were reasonably entitled to consider that this provision did not apply to pensions paid under contracted-out pension schemes, the Court held that its ruling as regards such schemes could not be applied retrospectively. Article 119 (now 141) might not be relied on to claim entitlement to a pension with effect prior to the date of judgment, except in the case of workers, or those claiming under them, who had before that date initiated legal proceedings or raised an equivalent claim under the applicable national law (para. 45). Following dispute over the scope of this ruling, as to whether Article 141 (ex 119) applies to all claims for *pensions arising* after the date of judgment or only to claims based on *benefits earned* after this date, the matter was finally resolved by a protocol issued at Maastricht in favour of the latter, more restrictive view. According to the Protocol:

> For the purposes of Article 119 [now 141] of [the Treaty establishing the European Community], benefits under occupational social security schemes shall not be considered as remuneration if and insofar as they are attributable to periods of employment prior to 17 May 1990, except in the case of workers or those claiming under them who have before that date initiated legal proceedings or introduced an equivalent claim under the applicable national law.

This interpretation of *Barber* has since been applied by the Court in many cases including *Ten Oever* (case C–109/91, survivors' benefit); *Coloroll Pension Trustees Ltd* v *Russell* (case C–200/91); *Moroni* (case C–110/91, supplementary pension scheme, early retirement); *Neath* v *Hugh Steeper Ltd* (case C–152/91, supplementary pension scheme, early retirement); and *Defreyn* (case C–166/99, additional pre-retirement payment). However, in *Vroege* (case C–57/93), and *Fisscher* (case C–128/93) the Court held that the limit on retrospectivity of its ruling in *Barber* did not apply where it should have been clear to the employer that the terms fell within Article 119 (now 141). In these cases, the provisions related to *access* to pension schemes, which, following *Bilka-Kaufhaus* (case 170/84), should be considered pay. Thus, provided the female employees were prepared to pay the requisite contributions to a pension scheme for any period between *Defrenne* and *Barber*, employers were also obliged to make the relevant employer's contributions to such schemes retrospectively. This principle was affirmed in *Preston* and *Fletcher* (case C–78/98).

Further problems arising from the application of Article 141 (ex 119) to the award of occupational pensions are illustrated in *Neath* v *Hugh Steeper Ltd* (case C–152/91). The case concerned a contracted-out pension scheme in which men were treated less favourably than women in respect of early retirement and lump-sum payments in lieu of pension payments. Neath claimed that, following *Barber*, this was contrary to the then Article 119. The Court, however, distinguished between the *accrual of the right* to receive benefits and the *funding* of those benefits. Both the pension payments themselves and the employees' contributions to a pension scheme fell within 'pay', therefore neither should distinguish between the sexes. The funding arrangements established by the employer, however, fall outside the scope of Article 141 (ex 119) because the purpose of those arrangements is to ensure that there are adequate resources to make the pension payments when due. An employer, when calculating its contribution to funding, may therefore rely on actuarial factors which, for example, take into account differing average life expectancies of the sexes and thus may make different payments in respect of men and women (para. 22). A corollary to this argument is that capital sum or transfer benefits such as lump-sum payments that are based on the method and amount of funding also do not fall within Article 141 (ex 119) (para. 33). The full implications of the judgment in *Neath* are still not yet known. It is clear, however, that *Neath* is a retreat from the position in *Barber*, and has made the boundaries between pay and pensions even less certain.

The Court's judgment in *Neath* does not affect a further principle established in *Barber*, that, in order to comply with Article 141 (ex 119), it is not enough that the overall package of remuneration received by men and women be equal. Each element of the consideration paid to both sexes must be equal. The system of pay must be 'transparent', in order that clear comparisons as between men and women may be made.

This broad interpretation of pay to include benefits relating in the widest sense to retirement or even death (provided they are not social security benefits *sensu stricto*) is important, since it provides an opportunity for individuals to challenge as 'pay' matters, relating for example to different retirement ages for men and women, which might otherwise fall under the Equal Treatment Directive (Directive 76/207) (see further below) and Occupational Pensions Directive (Directive 86/378) and even Directive 79/7 on Equal Treatment in Matters of Social Security (discussed in greater detail below). In doing so the Court can often sidestep the limitations of these Directives as well as the problems of horizontal direct effect.

Discrimination

Discrimination, in breach of Article 141 (ex 119), can be direct or indirect.

Direct discrimination   Direct discrimination occurs when men and women are treated differently by virtue of their sex. In these cases, a difference in pay can never be justified. However, a difference in treatment as between men and women, even doing the same work or of equal value, will not necessarily constitute discrimination. In *Birds Eye Walls Ltd* v *Roberts* (case C–132/92) the Court found that a bridging pension, paid *ex gratia* to employees compelled on the grounds of ill health to take early retirement, and calculated to bridge the gap between the sum received under their occupational pension scheme and the State pension they would receive on reaching the statutory age of retirement, although less for the applicant woman than it would have been for a man, was not discriminatory on the grounds of sex. The mechanisms used for calculating the bridging pension were sexually neutral; the applicant's lower bridging pension corresponded to her lower input into the State pension scheme, *for which she had freely opted*. Thus the applicant and the men with whom she sought to compare herself were not in comparable situations. For similar reasons different rates of pay may be awarded according to employees' qualifications, provided they are relevant to the job undertaken.

The Court has also accepted that when Member States seek to amend national laws to achieve parity between the sexes, economic considerations may result in both sexes being treated at the level of the disadvantaged group, rather than improving the position of the disadvantaged group to the level of the advantaged group. In *de Weerd* (case C–343/92, discussed below), the Court commented that Member States, in order to control public spending, may remove benefits from certain categories of persons, provided that this was not done in a discriminatory manner. In *Smith* v *Avdel Systems Ltd* (case C–408/92) the ECJ was faced with a claim based on the changes made to pension schemes following *Barber*. The Court held that where discrimination is found, the disadvantaged class should, in the absence of domestic measures rectifying the position, be treated in the same way as the advantaged class. This did not, however, prevent the Member State from introducing measures which 'levelled down' benefits: in this case raising the statutory retirement age to 65. Sex equality, it would seem, does not always benefit women.

Indirect discrimination   Indirect discrimination occurs where rules which seemingly apply to both sexes, adversely affect a significant proportion of one sex more than the other. Unlike direct discrimination, indirect discrimination may be 'objectively justified'. In *Jenkins* v *Kingsgate (Clothing Productions) Ltd* (Case 96/80) the ECJ was asked whether a difference in pay (in this case 10 per cent) between part-time and full-time workers could constitute discrimination when the category of part-time workers was exclusively or predominantly female (only one, exceptional male was employed part-time). The Court held that such a difference would not infringe Article 119 (now 141) provided that the difference in pay was 'objectively justified' and in no way related to discrimination based on sex. However, such inequality of pay would breach this Article where, having regard to the difficulties encountered by women in arranging to work the minimum (full-time) number of hours a week, the pay policy of the undertaking cannot be explained by factors other than discrimination based on sex.

In *Bilka-Kaufhaus GmbH* v *Weber von Harz* (case 170/84) the Court was faced again with a claim by a part-time worker, this time challenging her employer's occupational pension scheme, which discriminated overtly against part-time workers. Here both full- and part-time workforces comprised both men and women, but of the men employed (28 per cent of the total workforce), only 10 per cent worked part-time, as against 27.7 per cent of the female work-force. Overall, male part-time workers comprised only 2.8 per cent of the total workforce. The disadvantage suffered by part-timers thus fell disproportionately on the women. The ECJ was asked whether such a scheme might breach Article 119 (now 141). Citing para. 13 of the judgment in *Jenkins* v *Kingsgate (Clothing Productions) Ltd* almost verbatim, the Court held (at para. 29) that if it was found that a considerably smaller percentage of men than of women worked part-time, and if the difference in treatment could not be explained by any other factor than sex, the exclusion of part-time workers from the occupational scheme would be contrary to Article 119 (now 141). The difference in treatment would, however, be permissible if it were explained by objectively justified factors which were unrelated to discrimination based on sex. It would be for the employer to prove, and for national courts to decide, on the facts, whether the difference in treatment was in fact objectively justified.

Although many circumstances where part-time employees have been disadvantaged have been found to constitute indirect discrimination by virtue of the larger number of female part-time workers, not all claims succeed: there is a boundary between being paid less because of working less and being discriminated against. In *Stadt Lengerich* v *Helmig* (cases C–399/92 et al.) part-time workers alleged indirect discrimination because they did not receive overtime payments for working in excess of their normal working hours. Overtime only became payable when they worked longer than the full-time workers' normal hours. The ECJ held that this was not discrimination because part-timers and those who worked full-time received payment on the same basis for the hours worked. By contrast, *Kuratorium für Dialyse und Nierentransplantation eV* v *Lewark* (case C–457/93) dealt with a part-time worker who took part in a training course arranged within full-time working hours but in excess of her normal working hours. She was compensated for the loss of her normal part-time wages but did not receive payment in respect of all the hours she spent at the course. The Court held that this was discrimination because the overall pay she received in respect of the course was less per hour than that received by her full-time colleagues. It is hoped that the EC Directive on part-time workers will clarify the extent of such workers' rights ([1998] OJ L 14/9).

Having identified a difference in treatment, is the difference automatically discriminatory? In *Enderby* v *Frenchay Health Authority* (case 127/92) the ECJ commented that a difference in treatment between men and women would give rise to a presumption that discrimination existed. It would then fall to the employer to try to justify the difference in treatment. In the *Royal Copenhagen* case (case C–400/93), however, both men and women worked on a piecework basis under which their wages consisted of a fixed base payment plus a variable amount determined by reference to the work produced. The Court held that here a difference in pay between groups did not necessarily raise an inference of discrimination: the difference in pay might reflect differences in output. The national court must decide if the difference results from differences in output or from unacceptable differences in the amount the worker is paid per item. The Court's approach in this case is clearly more cautious than in *Enderby* as it moves away from the position that a purely statistical difference between groups of men and women creates a presumption of discrimination. Further, it is arguable that in *Royal Copenhagen* the Court is mixing together questions which should be asked when determining justification of indirect discrimination with those that determine discrimination in the first place.

A similarly cautious approach can be discerned in *Angestellten Betriebsrat der Wiener Gebietskrankenkasse* v *Wiener Gebietskrankenkasse* (case C–309/97). The case concerned the difference in pay between two groups of psychotherapists. One group had been trained as doctors; the other, predominantly female group, which received lower pay, comprised graduate psychologists. This group argued, following *Enderby*, that as they were involved in the same work as the doctors they should be on the same pay scale. The ECJ rejected this argument, accepting instead the argument that the difference in training could mean that the two groups of psychotherapists would be required to perform different duties and therefore could not be said to be performing the same work. Thus the approach in *Enderby* was not so much overruled as side-stepped in this case, the ECJ turning the issue into one of equal work rather than discrimination.

It is clear, however, from both *Jenkins* and *Bilka-Kaufhaus GmbH* that the fact that the group adversely affected by a particular measure comprises both sexes does not prevent that measure being discriminatory on the grounds of sex, as long as it affects one sex to *a disproportionate extent*. If this were not so, as Nicholls LJ pointed out in the Court of Appeal in *Pickstone* v *Freemans plc* [1989] AC 66, as long as there is a man there doing the same work, 'which in some cases might be wholly fortuitous or even, possibly, a situation contrived by an unscrupulous employer', the woman cannot make the comparison, even if the difference in pay is attributable solely to grounds of sex. The criteria to identify when disproportionate discrimination occurs have not been precisely delineated. Further, the question of whether discrimination exists might vary over time as statistical evidence and working patterns changed (*R* v *Secretary of State for Employment, ex parte Seymour-Smith* [1995] ICR 889). Thus a regulation which disadvantages part-time workers will be discriminatory only for as long as a disproportionate number of workers are of one sex. Ultimately, unless one sex is disproportionately affected, a claim under Article 141 (ex 119) of discrimination *based on sex* will not succeed.

Pregnancy Clearly, pregnancy may have an adverse impact on a woman's pay which, since only women become pregnant, is not easily categorised as direct or indirect discrimination. The difficulties pregnant women encounter have thus given rise to a specific jurisprudence on pregnancy, discussed later.

Objective justification

As noted above, differences in pay (or treatment) which discriminate indirectly against women or men will be permissible if they are objectively justified. Guidelines as to what might constitute objective justification were laid down in *Bilka-Kaufhaus GmbH* v *Weber von Harz* (case 170/84). There the Court held that in order to prove that a measure is objectively justified the employer must prove that the measures giving rise to the difference in treatment:

(a)   correspond to a 'genuine need of the enterprise',
(b)   are suitable for obtaining the objective pursued by the enterprise, and

(c)   are necessary for that purpose.

These principles, reminiscent of *Cassis de Dijon* (see chapter 10), have been consistently applied by the Court. Requirements (b) and (c) together represent the familiar proportionality principle. What factors, then, will be regarded by the Court as providing 'objective justification' meeting a 'genuine need of the enterprise'?

Arguments based on economic factors and market forces   *Jenkins* v *Kingsgate (Clothing Productions) Ltd* (case 96/80) and *Bilka-Kaufhaus GmbH* (case 170/84) suggest that economic factors would prove acceptable justification. In *Bilka-Kaufhaus GmbH* the defendants argued that part-time workers were less economic; they were less ready to work on Saturdays and in the evening; that it was necessary to pay more to attract full-timers. Justification on these grounds was not disputed in principle. Whether it would in fact be accepted would depend on whether the need for the difference in pay could be proved, and if so whether the proportionality principle were satisfied. In applying this ruling the German court found that it was not.

Although the Court has been sympathetic to the Member States' concern to control budgetary expenditure (e.g., limitations imposed in *Barber* (case C–262/88); *Steenhorst-Neerings* (case C–338/91)), a *purely* economic justification of discrimination is unlikely to be successful. In *de Weerd* (case C–343/92) concerning Directive 79/7, the Court stated that to allow budgetary considerations to justify discrimination between men and women would be tantamount to agreeing that the fundamental principle of equality could vary over time and throughout the Community depending on the state of the Member States' public finances (paras 35 and 36) (see also *R* v *Secretary of State for Health, ex parte Richardson* (case C–137/94).

Administrative convenience   In *Kirsammer-Hack* v *Sidal* (case C–189/91), in a claim based on Equal Treatment Directive 76/207, the Court was prepared to concede that an exclusion from employment protection provided under German legislation for employees of firms comprising fewer than five employees, excluding employees working less than 10 hours a week or 45 hours per month, even if indirectly discriminatory against women, would be objectively justified on the grounds of the need to lighten the administrative, financial and legal burdens on small enterprises, acknowledged by the Community in the then Article 118a EC and its Directives on health and safety of workers.

Social policy objectives   In *Rinner-Kühn* (case 171/88) the Court suggested that a justification based on a 'genuine objective of social policy' might be acceptable, provided that the means selected were appropriate and necessary to the attainment of that objective. However, it firmly rejected an argument that the difference in treatment as regards sick pay between part and full-time workers was justified on the grounds that part-timers were not integrated into the business in the same way as full-time workers. 'These considerations', the

Court said, 'only represent generalised statements concerning certain categories of workers and do not admit the conclusion of objective justification
unrelated to any discrimination on the grounds of sex'. Since women form
the majority of the part-time workforce, it is they, as the Commission pointed
out in *Rinner-Kuhn,* who are most vulnerable and in need of protection; thus
a social policy objective resulting in discrimination against part-time workers
is unlikely to be seen as valid justification. A justification on the grounds of
social policy has, however, been accepted in a number of social security cases
not involving part-time workers (e.g., *Teuling* (case 30/85); *Commission* v
Belgium (case C–229/89)).

Proportionality It is likely that, as with the *Cassis de Dijon* principle applied
to the free movement of goods (see chapter 10), the Court will seek to ensure
that the proportionality principle is rigorously applied, and will not hesitate
to pass judgment on whether a purported 'objective justification' is suitable
and necessary to achieve its desired and legitimate end. It did not prove
necessary to do so in *R* v *Secretary of State for Employment, ex parte Equal
Opportunities Commission* [1995] 1 AC 1. Here the House of Lords, in an
exemplary judgment, examined the justification for certain provisions of the
British Employment Protection (Consolidation) Act 1978, which discriminated against part-time workers, and found, contrary to the views of the
Court of Appeal, that the alleged increase in the availability of part-time work
likely to result from the difference in treatment (encouraging employers to
employ part-time workers) was, on the facts, simply not proved. Moreover,
legislation permitting such discrimination against part-time workers 'would
surely constitute a gross breach of the principle of equal pay and could not
possibly be regarded as a suitable means of achieving an increase in part-time
employment' (per Lord Keith). The judgment contained a suggestion (contained in the Commission's then draft Directive on part-time workers, OJ
C224/4, 1990) that the elimination of disproportionate administrative costs
might justify some discrimination in the case of those working for less than
eight hours per week; but there was no objective justification for the
thresholds established by the British legislation.
   It is to be hoped that national courts and tribunals, charged with assessing
this crucial question of objective justification, will evaluate the genuineness of
the justification offered, and its necessity, with the same analytical rigour as
the House of Lords. Where a justification is proved by the defendant to be
genuine and necessary it will be permitted.

Equal work

Equal work has been defined in Directive 75/117 as the 'same work' or 'work
to which equal value has been attributed'.

Same work In *Macarthys Ltd* v *Smith* (case 129/79) Advocate-General
Capotorti suggested that 'same work' is not confined to identical work; it
should include jobs which display a high degree of similarity the one to the

other, even if there is not total identity between them. Since 'similar' work will shade into work 'of equal value', which is also subject to the equality principle, a precise definition of 'same' work is unnecessary.

Work of equal value This concept was introduced into EC law by Directive 75/117. However, since the Court has held (*Jenkins* v *Kingsgate (Clothing Productions) Ltd* (case 96/80)) that Directive 75/117 is merely confined to restating the principle of equal pay as set out in Article 141 (ex 119), and in no way alters its content and scope, a claim for equal pay for work of equal value may be brought under Article 141 (ex 119) as well as under Directive 75/117. Indeed, a claim under Article 141 (ex 119) is advisable since it avoids possible problems over the direct effects of the Directive. The concept of work of equal value will be further discussed in the context of Directive 75/117.

Any comparisons made for the purpose of deciding whether a man and a woman are engaged on the same work, or work of equal value, must be confined to parallels which may be drawn on the basis of concrete appraisals of the work actually performed by employees of different sex within the same establishment or service (*Macarthys Ltd* v *Smith* (case 129/79)). Thus comparisons cannot be made with the 'hypothetical male'. Further, comparisons must be made with groups picked on an objective basis and not those chosen solely with the aim of maximising the final amount received by the complainants. For example, in *Royal Copenhagen* (case C–400/93) the applicants sought to compare three groups each with different average pay. The lowest-paid group (female) sought to be upgraded first to the pay rate of the middle, male group and then to argue that the discrimination between the middle group (still mainly male) and the highest group (female) was also unjustified sex discrimination, thus raising all workers in the compared groups to that of the highest-paid group. The ECJ took the view that choosing comparator groups to allow 'leapfrogging' was not acceptable.

Comparisons are, however, not necessarily limited to the same establishment or service. In *Defrenne* v *Sabena (No. 2)* (case 43/75), the ECJ held that the then Article 119 applied to discrimination which has its origin in legislative provisions ('general' social security provision excepted) or in collective labour agreements and which may be detected on a purely legal analysis of the situation. Moreover, where the employer is the same the fact that the pay of different groups of workers has been determined under separate collective bargaining agreements does not necessarily prevent the application of Article 141 (ex 119) (see *Enderby* v *Frenchay Health Authority* (case C–127/92); compare with *Royal Copenhagen* (case C–400/93) and *Angestellten Betriebsrat der Wiener Gebietskrankenkasse* v *Wiener Gebietskrankenkasse* (case C–309/97)). However, in the absence of collective agreements or job evaluation schemes affecting undertakings or industries at a national level, it is submitted that comparisons cannot be made *across* undertakings or industries.

As is clear from *Macarthys Ltd* v *Smith* comparisons are not limited to men and women engaged in contemporaneous employment. Nor is it necessary that the employment should be in the same Member State.

Equal pay for work of equal value (Directive 75/117)

As has been noted, Directive 75/117, which was based on Article 119 (now 141), was introduced merely to implement and supplement that Article. Article 1 provides:

> The principle of equal pay for men and women outlined in Article 119 of the Treaty, hereinafter called 'principle of equal pay', means, for the same work or for work to which equal value is attributed, the elimination of all discrimination on grounds of sex with regard to all aspects and conditions of remuneration.
>
> In particular, where a job classification system is used for determining pay, it must be based on the same criteria for both men and women and so drawn up as to exclude any discrimination on grounds of sex.

Article 2 requires Member States to:

> introduce into their national legal systems such measures as are necessary to enable all employees who consider themselves wronged by failure to apply the principle of equal pay to pursue their claims by judicial process after possible recourse to other competent authorities.

In addition, Article 6 requires Member States, in accordance with their national circumstances and legal systems, to:

> take the measures necessary to ensure that the principle of equal pay is applied. They shall see that effective means are available to take care that this principle is observed.

In *Commission* v *United Kingdom (Re Equal Pay for Equal Work)* (case 61/81) the UK was found to have failed, in breach of Directive 75/117 (Articles 1 and 6), to provide a means whereby claims of equal value might be assessed in the absence of a job evaluation scheme having been implemented by the employer.

Neither Articles 1 or 6 of Directive 75/117 nor *Commission* v *United Kingdom* (case 61/81) require that a claim to equal value must be assessed pursuant to a job evaluation study; indeed, the Court pointed out in *Commission* v *United Kingdom* that a system of job classification is only one of several possible methods for determining pay for work to which equal value is attributed. All that seems to be required under EC law is that where a prima facie claim to equal value exists, either as a result of a job evaluation study, as in *O'Brien* v *Sim-Chem Ltd* [1980] ICR 573, House of Lords, or otherwise, an assessment must be made, if necessary in adversarial proceedings, by a body with the requisite power to decide whether work has the same value, after obtaining such information as may be needed.

It is regrettable that the Court in *Commission* v *United Kingdom* did not spell out in greater detail the scope of Member States' obligations in this field.

Clearly some comparability must exist before a legitimate claim to equal value can arise. But how 'like' must two different jobs be for them to be deemed to be comparable? And if they are 'broadly' comparable, how, and in what detail, are they to be assessed in order to decide whether they are equal value? Will a 'felt fair' order of jobs, depending on the general level of expectation as to the value of the job, be adequate, as the Employment Appeal Tribunal suggested in *Bromley* v *H & J Quick Ltd* [1987] IRLR 456, or should not, as the Court of Appeal decided, a full analytical study be made? If such a study is undertaken, what criteria are to be applied? Clearly the answers to all these questions, and the solutions adopted, will vary from State to State, as will their cost to the State. Moreover, a finding of equal value will have serious repercussions on costs, both for the individual concerned and possibly for an entire industry. This in turn will affect its competitiveness within the common market. Thus unless the rules relating to the application of the principle of equal value are determined and applied in a uniform manner throughout the Community they are likely to defeat the very 'economic objectives' which they were designed, in part, to achieve.

Where a job classification scheme is devised as a means of determining comparability, some general guidance as to its content was provided by the ECJ in *Rummler* v *Dato-Druck GmbH* (case 237/85). Here a woman packer, classified under wage group III under a job evaluation scheme implemented by her employers, and not, as she considered appropriate, under group IV, was seeking to challenge the criteria on which the scheme was based. These criteria included the muscular effort, fatigue and physical hardship attached to the job. She claimed this was discriminatory. The ECJ held that a job classification scheme based on the strength required to carry out the work or the degree of physical hardship which the work entailed was not in breach of Directive 75/117 as long as:

(a) the system as a whole precluded discrimination on grounds of sex; and

(b) the criteria employed were objectively justified. To be objectively justified they must:
    (i) be appropriate to the tasks to be carried out, and
    (ii) correspond to a genuine need of the undertaking.

In addition, the classification scheme as a whole, if not to be discriminatory, must take into account the criteria for which each sex has a particular aptitude. Criteria based exclusively on the values of one sex contain, the Court suggested, 'a risk of discrimination'.

The principles of *Rummler* v *Dato-Druck* were extended significantly in *Handels- og Kontorfunktionærernes Forbund i Danmark* v *Dansk Arbejdsgiverforening for Danfoss* (case 109/88), in the context of a challenge by the Danish Employees' Union to the criteria agreed by the Danish Employers Association and applied by the firm of Danfoss. These included, *inter alia*, the criteria of 'flexibility' and 'seniority'. While the minimum pay for each grade was the same for men and women, it was found that the average pay *within* each grade was lower for women than for men. The applicants alleged that the criteria were indirectly discriminatory. The ECJ held that where the application of neutral criteria, such as the criterion of quality (one element of 'flexibility'), was shown to *result* in systematic discrimination against female workers, this could only be because the employer applied it in an abusive manner. The criteria applied must be 'of importance for the specific duties entrusted to the workers concerned'. Where a pay system is characterised by a 'total lack of "transparency"', that is, when the criteria for determining pay increments are not explicit, and where a female worker establishes, by comparison with a relatively large number of employees, that the average pay of female workers is lower than that of male workers, the onus is on the employer to prove that the criteria employed are justified. Moreover, in view of the greater difficulties faced by women in organising their time in a flexible manner, the criterion of adaptability (another element of 'flexibility'), which was prima facie capable of justification, would also require proof of justification from the employer. The criterion of seniority was found by the Court to be sufficiently transparent not to require justification by the employer. Thus, where the criteria employed are not transparent, or where they operate to the patent disadvantage of women, the employer must carry the burden of justification. Note that the question of burden of proof in sex discrimination cases will, in most Member States, now be dealt with under the Burden of Proof Directive (Directive 97/80), although the UK has a longer period in which to implement it.

Lastly, under Article 4 of Directive 75/117, States are required to ensure that provisions of collective agreements, wage scales, wage agreements or individual contracts of employment contrary to the principle of equal value 'shall be, or may be declared, null and void or may be amended'.

States must also, under Article 5, ensure full protection for employees against dismissal as a reaction to a complaint or to legal proceedings 'aimed at enforcing compliance with the principle of equal pay'.

Since the provisions of Directive 75/117 merely define the scope and substance of Article 141 (ex 119) EC they may be invoked, vertically or horizontally, in the context of a claim under that Article. As *Defrenne* v *Sabena (No. 2)* (case 43/75) established, Article 141 (ex 119) is effective against *all* parties. Following *Marshall* v *Southampton and South West Hampshire Area Health Authority (Teaching)* (case 152/84), Directive 75/117, as a Directive, will not *in itself* be horizontally effective (see chapter 4).

Principle of equal treatment for men and women (Directive 76/207)

Directive 76/207, which is based not on Article 141 (ex 119) of the EC Treaty but on the institutions' general powers under Article 308 (ex 235), lays down the principle of equal treatment for men and women in Article 1(1):

> as regards access to employment, including promotion, and to vocational training and as regards working conditions and, on the conditions referred to in paragraph 2, social security.

'Working conditions' are defined to include 'conditions governing dismissal' (Article 5).

Article 1, paragraph 2, provides for further action to implement the principle of equal treatment in matters of social security. This has now been achieved with Directives 79/7 (statutory schemes) and 86/378 (occupational schemes). The principle of equal treatment is defined in Article 2 as meaning that:

there shall be no discrimination whatsoever on grounds of sex either directly or indirectly by reference in particular to marital or family status.

For the purposes of this Directive, 'sex' has been held to have a wide meaning, not limited to issues of gender discrimination. In *P v S* (case C–13/94), P's contract of employment was terminated because of P's proposed sex change. The question referred to the ECJ related to Article 5 of the Directive: did the Directive preclude dismissal of a transsexual for a reason related to his or her gender reassignment? The Court held that the meaning of the Directive, in view of the fundamental principle of equality which it represented, could not be interpreted so as to limit the protection to discrimination on grounds of gender. In the light of the broad terms of this judgment, the ECJ's more recent ruling in *Grant v South-West Trains Ltd* (case C–249/96) seems a somewhat surprising retreat. The case concerned a claim by a female employee with a female partner for rail benefits to which married couples were entitled. The ECJ rejected this, stating that the reference to 'sex discrimination' was not a reference to gender orientation. Thus the present state of protection with regard to gender discrimination is unclear, but not promising. Presumably, it will in future, be for the Member States to take action under new Article 13 EC, which provides that the Member States, acting unanimously, may take appropriate action to combat discrimination based on, *inter alia*, sexual orientation. In this context it should be noted that the Commission has recently been consulting on three Directives, to be enacted under Article 13 EC, to combat discrimination both generally and in the workplace.

Derogation from the equal treatment principle is provided under Article 2(2)–(4) (discussed below).

The principal context in which the equal treatment Directive has been invoked in the UK has been to challenge different retirement ages as between men and women, since both the Equal Pay Act 1970 and the Sex Discrimination Act 1975 excluded from their scope 'provisions' in relation to death or retirement'. Directive 76/207 contains no such exclusion, but Directive 79/7, Article 7(1), governing equal treatment in matters of social security, allows Member States to exclude from the scope of the equal treatment principle 'the determination of pensionable age for the purposes of granting old-age and retirement pensions and the possible consequences thereof for other benefits'. Directive 86/378 (Article 9) provided a parallel exclusion in respect of occupational pension schemes. It was therefore thought, it is submitted with some justification, that different retirement ages for men and women were permissible under EC law, especially since they were tied to the statutory pensionable age, which in the UK was 60 for women and 65 for men.

The scope of these provisions was considered by the Court in *Burton* v *British Railways Board* (case 19/81) in the context of a challenge by a railway worker, Mr Burton, to a voluntary redundancy scheme operated by British Rail. Under the scheme women were entitled to apply for voluntary redundancy at 55, and men at 60. Mr Burton, who, at 58, wished to take early retirement, alleged that the scheme was discriminatory. Since it fell within the exemption of the Sex Discrimination Act 1975, s. 6(4), as interpreted by the Court of Appeal in *Garland* v *British Rail Engineering Ltd* [1979] ICR 558 and *Worringham* v *Lloyds Bank Ltd* [1982] ICR 299, Directive 76/207 offered him his only chance of success. On reference from the Employment Appeal Tribunal for an interpretation on the scope and application of Directive 76/207 the ECJ held that the Directive applied in principle to conditions of access to voluntary redundancy schemes. Moreover, the word 'dismissal', brought within the equality principle by Article 5, must be widely construed to cover termination of the employment relationship, even as part of a redundancy scheme. However, since in this case the ages for voluntary retirement were calculated by reference to, and tied to, the statutory retirement age (60 for women, 65 for men), Article 7 of Directive 79/7, which permitted States to exclude from the equal treatment principle 'the determination of pensionable age', applied. Thus his claim under Directive 76/207 must fail.

Undeterred by *Burton* v *British Railways Board,* the applicant in *Marshall* v *Southampton and South West Hampshire Area Health Authority (Teaching)* (case 152/84) brought a similar claim under Directive 76/207. Ms Marshall, an employee of the AHA, was seeking to challenge its compulsory retirement policy, under which women employees were required to retire at 60, and men at 65. On a reference from the Employment Appeal Tribunal the ECJ, following *Burton* v *British Railways Board,* interpreted the retirement scheme as a 'condition governing dismissal' within Article 5 of Directive 76/207. However, distinguishing *Burton,* on the slenderest grounds (benefits *tied to* a national scheme which lays down a different minimum pensionable age for men and women) the Court found that her case was *not* within the exclusion of Article 7 of Directive 79/7. This Article allowed Member States to exclude from the equal treatment principle the determination of pensionable age *'for the purposes of granting old-age and retirement pensions and the possible consequences thereof for other benefits'.* Where pensionable age was being determined *for other purposes,* e.g., as in *Marshall,* for the purpose of *retirement* the equal treatment principle would apply.

The ECJ took the same line, on the same reasoning, in *Roberts* v *Tate & Lyle Industries Ltd* (case 151/84). This time the applicant failed in her challenge to her employer's compulsory early retirement scheme. Although the scheme entitled those retiring to an accelerated pension under the firm's occupational pension scheme, it was held to fall within the scope of Directive 76/207 as a condition governing dismissal, and not Directive 79/7. However, in this case it was not discriminatory, since the age for retirement was fixed at 55 for both men and women (see also *Beets-Proper* v *F. van Landschot Bankiers NV* (case 262/84)).

Thus Member States' power under Article 7 of Directive 79/7 to exclude from the equal treatment principle 'the determination of pensionable age' has, in view of the fundamental importance of the principle of equal treatment, been given the narrowest scope. It seems it will only apply where the difference in age is *for the purpose* of the granting of old-age and retirement *pensions* and the possible consequences thereof for other benefits 'falling within the statutory [or occupational] social security schemes' (*Marshall*, para. 35, see further below). Moreover, the exclusion from the equal treatment principle only applies to the determination of pensionable age for the purposes of granting *statutory* social security pensions. Despite the express exclusion in respect of the 'determination of pensionable age for the purposes of granting old-age or retirement pensions' as regards *occupational* pension schemes, contained in Directive 86/378, the Court held in *Barber* (case C–262/88) that the setting of different retirement ages for men and women for the granting of such pensions was in breach of Article 119 (now 141), since the difference in age *resulted* in a difference in pay. On similar reasoning different ages of access to statutory redundancy benefit for men and women were also held in breach of the then Article 119. *Burton* v *British Railways Board* (case 19/81) appears to have been distinguished out of existence. As was noted above, a difference in the employer's contribution to funded, defined-benefit schemes, affecting the transfer of pension rights and lump sum payments to employees was held in *Neath* v *Hugh Steeper Ltd* (case C–152/91) to fall outside Article 119 (now 141); it may thus be presumed that it will also fall outside Directive 76/207.

Although the main discussion about the scope of the Equal Treatment Directive has concerned equal retirement ages and pensions, that is not the only area where its boundaries are unclear. *Meyers* v *Adjudication Officer* (case C–116/94) concerned family credit, which, at first glance, might fall within social security, Directive 79/7. Ms Meyers, however, brought an action under the Equal Treatment Directive claiming that rules precluding her from deducting child-minding expenses from her income and thus preventing her from claiming family credit were indirectly discriminatory because the rules had a disproportionate adverse effect on single mothers. The Court held that since family credit provided a top-up income to low-income workers and therefore provided both assistance and an incentive for them to accept work, the scheme fell within the Equal Treatment Directive as it concerned both 'access to employment' and 'conditions of employment'. It would seem that the case was not brought under Directive 79/7 following *Jackson* v *Chief Adjudication Officer* (cases C–63 & 64/91) (discussed in more detail below), which held that supplementary benefits did not fall within the terms of that Directive.

Like Directive 75/117, Directive 76/207 requires States to 'take the necessary measures to ensure that any laws, regulations and administrative provisions contrary to the principle of equal treatment be abolished' (Article

3(2)(a)) and 'any provisions contrary to the principle of equal treatment . . . in collective agreements, individual contracts of employment, internal rules of undertakings or in rules governing the independendent occupations and professions shall be, or may be declared, null and void or may be amended' (Article 3(2)(b)). The UK was found in breach of these provisions in *Commission* v *United Kingdom (Re Equal Treatment for Men and Women)* (case 165/82).

Derogation from the equal treatment principle (Articles 2(2), 2(3) and 2(4))

Article 2(2) and (3) of Directive 76/207, which provides for exemption from the equal treatment principle for 'activities . . . for which . . . the sex of the worker constitutes a determining factor' (Article 2(2)), and for 'provisions concerning the protection of women, particularly as regards pregnancy and maternity' (Article 2(3)), may be seen as a specific implementation of the principle of 'objective justification' considered in the context of equal pay. In addition, Article 2(4) provides some scope for positive discrimination, by allowing for 'measures to promote equal opportunities for men and women, in particular by removing existing inequalities which affect women's opportunities in the areas referred to in Article 1(1)'. These Articles provide for derogation from the equal treatment principle in the case of *direct* discrimination, based on the sex of the worker. However, Articles 2(2) and 2(3), which could be invoked to the detriment of women, have been given the narrowest scope. Despite its potential to benefit women, Article 2(4) has also been construed narrowly.

Sex as a determining factor (Article 2(2))

Article 2(2) was considered by the ECJ in the Commission's second action against the UK (*Commission* v *United Kingdom (Re Equal Treatment for Men and Women)* (case 165/82)) for failure to comply with the equal treatment Directive. One of the failures alleged was the exemption from the equal treatment principle, provided under the Sex Discrimination Act 1975, for employment in a private household (s. 6(3)(a)) and for firms employing less than six staff (s. 6(3)(b)). The UK argued that these provisions were justifiable under Article 2(2) of Directive 76/207. The Court disagreed. Whilst exemption under Article 2(2) might be available in the *individual* case under such circumstances, where the sex of the worker was a determining factor, Article 2(2) did not justify a blanket exclusion. It did, however, provide a valid defence to a charge against the UK in respect of its restriction, under the Sex Discrimination Act 1975, s. 20, on male access to the profession of midwifery. The Court found that this was an activity for which the sex of the worker was a determining factor.

In *Stoeckel* (case C–345/89) a general ban on night work for women, provided for under German law, allegedly to protect women, was held by the Court not permissible under Article 2(2). However, in *Ministère Public* v *Levy* (case C–158/91) faced with a question of the compatibility of *Stoeckel* with French law imposing restrictions on night work in industry for women, designed to give effect to a provision of the ILO 1948, the Court suggested that national courts must not apply provisions of national law contrary to Article 5 of Directive 76/207 'unless the application of national law is necessary to ensure compliance with international obligations' resulting from a convention concluded with third countries 'before the entry into force of the EC Treaty'. (See also *Office Nationale de l'Emploi* v *Minne* (case C–13/93) and *Habermann-Beltermann* (case C–421/92).) The point came before the ECJ again in the case of *Commission* v *Italy* (case C–207/96). In this case, Italy prohibited women from working overnight in accordance with the ILO Convention. Italy had, however, following the ECJ's previous ruling, denounced the Convention. The ECJ thus held that it could not rely on the Convention and that the prohibition was contrary to EC law.

Article 2(2) was also raised as a defence in the case of *Johnston* v *Chief Constable of the Royal Ulster Constabulary* (case 222/84) (see chapter 6). This action was brought by a female member of the Royal Ulster Constabulary (RUC) against a decision by the RUC refusing to renew her contract of employment. The RUC had decided as a matter of policy not to employ women as full-time members of the RUC reserve, since they were not trained in the use of firearms nor permitted to use them. In proceedings before the ECJ concerning the interpretation of Directive 76/207, and in particular the scope for derogation from the equal treatment principle available under EC law, the RUC argued, by analogy with Article 48(3) (now 39) EC (see chapter 22), that in view of the political situation in Northern Ireland derogation was justified on public safety or public security grounds; it was also justified under Article 2(2) of Directive 76/207. To allow women to carry and use firearms, the RUC claimed, increased the risk of their becoming targets for assassination. The Court held that there was no general public safety exception to the equal treatment principle available under the EC Treaty. A claim for exemption could *only* be examined in the light of the provisions of Directive 76/207. With regard to Article 2(2), the Court held that:

(a) The derogation provided under Article 2(2) could be applied only to specific *duties*, not to activities in general. Nonetheless, it was permissible to take into account the *context* in which the activity takes place.

(b) Where derogation is justified in the light of (a) the situation must be reviewed periodically to ensure that the justification still exists.

(c) Derogation must be subject to the principle of proportionality.

It was for national courts to decide whether these conditions are satisfied.

Similar principles were applied, if somewhat leniently, in *Commission* v *France* (case 318/86). The Commission's action was in respect of recruitment practices in the French civil service, in particular the prison service and the police. Under the system in force men and women were subject to different recruitment procedures, with a fixed percentage of posts being allocated according to sex. The complaint concerning the prison service centred on access to the post of head warder (in male prisons), which was not accessible to women. The complaint regarding the police concerned recruitment to certain police corps generally.

In the case of the prison service the Court found that it was justifiable to discriminate on the grounds of Article 2(2) in respect of the post of *warder*. Since professional experience acquired as a warder was desirable for the performance of the duties of a prison governor (a post for which head warders were eligible), and since it was desirable to provide promotion opportunities for those in the lower (warders') posts, it was acceptable to treat the *head* warder's post in the same way. The recruitment practices were justified under Article 2(2). The recruitment practices of the police, on the other hand, were not permissible under Article 2(2). The exclusion provided by Article 2(2), the Court held, allows exceptions to the non discrimination principle only in relation to specific *activities,* and these exceptions must be sufficiently transparent to permit effective scrutiny. The fact that certain police functions cannot be performed by men and women does not justify discriminatory treatment in admission to the police force in general.

The scope of Article 2(2) has more recently come under consideration in *Sirdar* v *The Army Board* (case C–273/97). The army board refused to transfer a female chef (who would otherwise be made redundant) to the Royal Marines because of her sex. She argued that this was contrary to the approach set down in *Johnston.* The ECJ, however, took a different view. It confirmed that Member States have a discretion regarding measures necessary for ensuring public security, although it further noted that any derogation from fundamental Treaty rights (such as equality) must be narrowly construed and be proportionate to its aims. In this case, the ECJ focused on the special nature of the Marines, who are, in effect, front-line troops and in respect of whom an absolute rule provides that *all* Marines must be combat ready, irrespective of their normal role. It seems that it was the particularly dangerous nature of the Marines' role that, according to the ECJ, justified the UK's decision that the Marines should remain exclusively male. By contrast, in *Kreil* v *Germany* (case C–285/98) a German rule of more general ambit which precluded women from occupying posts which would involve the use of firearms constituted sex discrimination, even taking into account Member States' discretion regarding the organisation of their armed forces. Arguably, then, these rulings continue the approach to Article 2(2) which requires a *specific* assessment of the *specific* duties to be performed in individual cases.

Pregnancy and maternity (Article 2(3))

In *Johnston* v *Chief Constable of the RUC,* the RUC also sought to justify its action under Article 2(3), as 'concerning the protection of women, particularly as regards pregnancy and maternity'. The Court found that the risks to policewomen arising from the situation in Northern Ireland were not within the scope of Article 2(3). Article 2(3) was intended to protect women's biological condition.

This interpretation of Article 2(3) had been supplied in *Hofmann* v *Barmer Ersatzkasse* (case 184/83) in response to a claim by a father to six months' leave following the birth of his child to look after the child while the mother went back to work. German law, which granted such leave only to the mother, was, he claimed, discriminatory, in breach of Directive 76/207. The Court disagreed. Special provision for maternity leave was, the Court held, permissible under Article 2(3), which was concerned to protect two types of female need. It protected:

(a) the biological condition of women during and after pregnancy; and
(b) the relationship between mother and child during the period following pregnancy and birth.

Directive 76/207 was not intended to cover matters relating to the organisation of the family or to change the division of responsibility between parents.

A second case brought by the Commission against France (*Commission* v *France* (case 312/86)) related to special privileges in the form of, *inter alia*, extended maternity leave, lower retirement age, extra time off to allow for children's illness and holidays, and extra allowances to meet the cost of nursery schools and child minders, awarded under French law to married women. The French sought to justify these privileges under Article 2(3) and 2(4). The Court, citing *Hofmann*, found that such measures fell outside the limits of Article 2(3); nor was there any indication that the rights claimed corresponded to the situation envisaged under Article 2(4). Thus, if such privileges are to be justified, they can only be justified on objective grounds *unrelated to sex*, such as the need to assist persons who carry primary responsibility for the welfare of the family, and particularly of children. As the Court pointed out in *Commission* v *France*, such responsibility may be undertaken by men. (As an example of the application of 'neutral' criteria, see *Teuling* (case 30/85), which is discussed later in this chapter.)

Contrast *Commission* v *France* with *Abdoulage* v *Regie Nationale des Usines Renault* (case C–218/98), albeit a case based on the then Article 119 (now 141) rather than the Equal Treatment Directive. In *Abdoulage* a group of men sought to challenge the payment, in addition to their maternity pay, of a lump sum to women going on pregnancy leave. The men argued that a recent father was not entitled to the same amount and that therefore the measure discriminated against men. The ECJ held the payment of the lump sum to be compatible with Community law as it was intended to compensate woman for the problems inherent in having to take time off work for maternity leave, and which are consequently specific to women.

The precise extent to which, and circumstances in which, a dismissal or refusal to employ a woman for reasons connected with pregnancy and childbirth will breach Directive 76/207 remains unclear. In *Dekker* v *VJV-Centrum* (case C–177/88) the defendant employer had withdrawn his offer of employment to the claimant when he discovered she was pregnant. He argued that his action was justified; her absence during maternity leave would not on the facts be covered by insurance, and he could not afford to pay for a replacement worker. The ECJ held that a refusal to employ a woman on the grounds of pregnancy constituted direct discrimination on the grounds of sex; as such it could not be justified on the basis of financial detriment to the employer.

The effect of this ruling was undermined in the Court's judgment in *Handels- og Kontorfunktionærernes Forbund i Danmark v Dansk Arbejdsgiver-forening (Hertz)* (case C–179/88) delivered on the same day. This case concerned a claim by a female employee against dismissal on the grounds of her extended absence from work as a result of illness which, though connected with pregnancy and childbirth, was suffered some time *after* the end of her maternity leave. The Court held that in this case there was no need to distinguish between illness resulting from pregnancy and maternity and any other illness such as might be suffered by a man. The dismissal was thus not directly discriminatory and could be justified. The reason for the distinction between *Dekker* and *Hertz*, suggested in *Hertz*, lay in Article 2(3) of Directive 76/207 which provides for measures concerning the protection of women, particularly as regards pregnancy and maternity.

Hertz was seized upon by the English Court of Appeal in *Webb v EMO Air Cargo (UK) Ltd* [1992] 2 All ER 43, in the context of a claim at first sight closer to *Dekker*, for discrimination on the grounds of pregnancy. The claimant had been engaged to replace another employee who had become pregnant. Two weeks after accepting the post she discovered she too was pregnant. When she informed the employer of this fact she was dismissed. Glidewell LJ, following counsel for the employer's advice, chose to read *Dekker* and *Hertz* together. Dismissal on the grounds of pregnancy might under *some* circumstances constitute direct discrimination. But on these facts, where the claimant had been employed specifically to replace another pregnant worker, the situation should rather be compared with that of a man in a similar situation, for example, a man with an arthritic hip, who found, shortly after taking up employment, that he was soon to be called for a hip replacement operation necessitating a long absence from work. Since an employer would have been justified in dismissing a man under these circumstances, the claimant's dismissal was not discriminatory on the grounds of sex.

Following the applicant's appeal to the House of Lords questions as to the legality of dismissal on the grounds of pregnancy in these particular circumstances were referred by that court to the ECJ ([1992] 4 All ER 929) and the dismissal was found to be illegal (case C–32/93). In this ruling, the Advocate-General and the ECJ rejected the idea that a pregnant woman should be compared with a sick man (see also *Habermann-Beltermann* (case C–421/92)).

The ECJ's judgment raises some questions, not the least of which concerns where the boundary lies between being dismissed for pregnancy which is unacceptable; and being dismissed for being ill, albeit because of pregnancy, which, provided it occurs outside the normal maternity leave, is acceptable (see *Hertz*). In *Handels- og Kontorfunktionærernes Forbund i Danmark acting on behalf of Larsson v Dansk Handel & Service acting on behalf of Føtex Supermarket*

A/S (case C–400/95), the ECJ held that a woman could be dismissed for absences other than maternity leave caused by pregnancy-related illnesses occurring both prior to and after the birth of the child. In a subsequent case, *Brown* v *Rentokil* (case C–394/96), it held that a woman could not be dismissed at any time during her pregnancy for absences arising from pregnancy-related illnesses. The uncertainty created by these conflicting rulings may lessen as the Pregnancy Directive will in future protect women as regards pregnancy-related illnesses suffered during pregnancy or prior to the end of maternity leave.

Another question arising in *Webb* concerned whether availability for work constitutes a fundamental condition of the employment contract. The ECJ rejected this contention, but on the basis that the time that the woman would be unavailable for work constitutes only a small proportion of the contract time in an indefinite contract. This does, however, undermine the position of women on short-term contracts. Can they be dismissed on the basis that their pregnancy constitutes too large a proportion of the contract? Fortunately, the Pregnancy Directive provides core maternity rights including periods of maternity leave and protection from dismissal during such leave, whether the worker is on a short-term or indefinite contract, and will thus protect workers in this position. The Pregnancy Directive does not, though, deal with the position of the woman who is not appointed because she is pregnant. Presumably, this could still fall within the Equal Treatment Directive following *Dekker*. Certainly, the ECJ held in *Mahlburg* v *Land Mecklenburg-Vorpommern* (case C–207/98), that a hospital could not refuse to appoint a pregnant woman to a permanent post as a theatre nurse on the basis that she would not be able to carry out her duties while she was pregnant. In this case German legislation prohibited expectant mothers from being exposed to chemicals with which the applicant would have come into contact as part of her job. This demonstrates that where a permanent post is in issue, temporary absence or incapacity (even from the commencement date of the appointment) will not be a legitimate ground for refusal of employment.

The Pregnancy Directive also specifies that women on maternity leave are entitled to an 'adequate allowance'. Ironically, this provision weakened the applicants' arguments in *Gillespie* v *Northern Health and Social Services Board* (case C–342/93) that equal pay requires full pay. The ECJ followed the Directive (although the actual situation in *Gillespie* predated it) holding that maternity pay did not need to be full pay, provided it was adequate. The Court also held, however, that maternity pay must take account of any pay increases during the maternity leave or during the period with reference to which the maternity pay is calculated. The ECJ has also ruled on the impact of maternity leave (in conjunction with sick leave) on a woman's entitlement to be considered for a 'merit increase' (*Caisse Nationale D'Assurance Vieillesse des Travailleurs Salaries (NAVTS)* v *Thibault* (case C–136/95)). As far as the applicant was concerned, the difficulty arose because she did not satisfy the prerequisite of six months' work because of the time she had had off, and was therefore ineligible for the pay rise. The ECJ agreed that this was contrary to the requirements of the Equal Treatment Directive. It stated that if a woman continued to be bound by her contract of employment, she should not be deprived of benefits which apply to men and other women by virtue of the employment relationship. The ECJ, in so holding, emphasised that the Equal Treatment Directive was intended to promote substantive equality. (See also *Gillespie* (case C–342/93).) Whether this desire to safeguard substantive equality is respected in all the ECJ's judgments relating to pregnancy issues is, however, another matter. The precise scope of the rights under the Pregnancy Directive will no doubt continue to be the subject of further litigation.

Positive discrimination (Article 2(4))

The third exception to the principle of equal treatment is that of positive discrimination, which permits schemes to enable women to compete equally with men. Article 2(4) of the Equal Treatment Directive provides that:

> This Directive shall be without prejudice to measures to promote equal opportunity for men and women, in particular by removing existing inequalities which affect women's opportunities.

The Court has seen this as another derogation from the principle of equal treatment, rather than a means of achieving that goal and has, therefore, regrettably, construed the provision narrowly. In *Kalanke* v *Freie Hansestadt Bremen* (case C–450/93), the ECJ held that a rule requiring the appointment of the female candidate when applicants were equally qualified and there was an under-representation of women at the level of the position for which the applicants were applying did not fall within Article 2(4). The Court stated that the purpose of the provision was to allow measures intended to eliminate or reduce actual instances of inequality so as to allow women to compete equally. In giving women 'absolute and unconditional' priority, the system overstepped the limits in Article 2(4).

This somewhat harsh decision caused outcry in certain quarters, including suggestions that Article 2(4) be broadened to allow positive discrimination. However, it may be that *Kalanke* is now of historical value only. The ToA amended the then Article 119 so as to strengthen the provision for positive discrimination.

The new para. (4) to Article 141 (ex 119) EC provides that:

> With a view to ensuring full equality in practice between men and women in working life, the principle of equal treatment shall not prevent any Member State from maintaining or adopting measures providing for specific advantages in order to make it easier for the under-represented sex to pursue a vocational activity or to prevent or compensate for disadvantages in professional careers.

The ECJ started to interpret the existing provisions in the light of this change even prior to the entry into force of the ToA (*Marschall* (case C–409/95)).

See also *Badeck* (case C–158/97), decided after the ToA came into force. It seems that the crucial difference between these two cases and *Kalanke* is the existence of what the ECJ has termed a 'saving clause'. This means that the legislation which provides for the preferential treatment of women is not automatic, instead containing a clause that permits the appointment of a man if other societal reasons specific to that man apply. One example of such a factor is a policy designed to ensure the appointment of appropriately qualified handicapped people. (Compare *Abrahamsson and Anderson* v *Fogalqvist* (case C–407/98).)

The above cases involving exemption from the equal treatment principle all concern direct discrimination. Where the discrimination is indirect the same principles apply as apply in the field of pay; a difference in treatment as between one group of workers and another which *affects* one sex disproportionately will require objective justification. Here the justification need not be brought within Article 2 of Directive 76/207, since the difference in treatment for which justification is required is not between men and women, but between one group of workers (e.g. part-timers) and another (e.g. full-timers). Following *Danfoss* (case 109/88) the onus of proving justification will fall on the employer. *Kirsammer-Hack* v *Sidal* (case C–189/91) provides an example of a successful defence of objective justification to a claim of indirect discrimination, based on the need to protect small undertakings against excessive administrative, financial and legal burdens.

Direct effects of Directive 76/207

As we have seen, one of the central problems with the equal treatment Directive has been the extent to which it may be directly effective. While a claim for equal pay under Directive 75/117 may be brought under Article 141 (ex 119) EC, and, where possible, pay has been interpreted broadly to remedy this deficiency, no such option exists for a claim to equal treatment per se, since the Directive is based on the general law-making powers of Article 308 (ex 235) EC. The problems arising from this and the potential alternative means of obtaining a remedy (through either indirect effect or the doctrine of State liability) are discussed further in chapters 4 and 26.

Principle of equal treatment in matters of social security (Directive 79/7)

Directive 79/7, which implements the principle of equal treatment for men and women in matters of social security, became directly effective once the date for its implementation by Member States had expired, on 23 December 1984 (see *Netherlands* v *Federatie Nederlandse Vakbeweging* (case 71/85); *McDermott* v *Minister for Social Welfare* (case 286/85); *Clarke* v *Chief Adjudication Officer* (case 384/85)). No extension of time is permitted for transitional arrangements (*Dik* v *College van Burgemeester en Wethouders* (case 80/87)). Since Directive 79/7 applies only to *statutory* social security schemes its effects must inevitably be vertical. Also, since Directive 79/7 merely implements the principle of equal treatment in the field of social security expressed in Directive 76/207 (Article 1(1)) there is, as *Burton v British Railways Board* (case 19/81) illustrates, some overlap between the two Directives. There is also considerable uncertainty as to where the boundary between Article 141 EC (ex 119) and Directive 79/7 lies (*Beune* (case C–7/93)).

Personal and material scope   Directive 79/7 applies to the working population, defined broadly to include 'self-employed persons, workers and self-employed persons whose activity is interrupted by illness, accident or involuntary unemployment and persons seeking employment', and to 'retired or invalided workers and self-employed persons' (Article 2). In *Drake v Chief Adjudication Officer* (case 150/85) the Court held that the term 'working population' must be defined broadly, to include persons who have been working but whose work has been interrupted. Thus Mrs Drake, who had given up work to look after her invalid mother, was entitled to claim a right to equal treatment under Directive 79/7. Directive 79/7 may also be invoked by the spouse of a person falling within Article 2, provided that the benefit claimed is within the scope of the Directive; 'others too may have an interest in seeing the principle of non-discrimination respected on behalf of the person protected' (*Verholen* (cases C–87, 88 and 89/90)). However, Article 2 cannot be invoked by persons who have not been employed and are not seeking work, or by those who have worked but whose work has not been interrupted by one of the risks referred to in Article 3(1) (*Achterberg-te Riele and Others v Sociale Verzekeringsbank* (cases 48, 106, 107/88)). This approach was followed in *Johnson v Chief Adjudication Officer* (case C–31/90), in which the ECJ held that a woman who had voluntarily given up work to care for her children would not be within the scope of the Directive unless she was looking for work when one of the risks outlined in the Directive occurred.

The principle of equal treatment under Directive 79/7 applies to:

(a)   statutory schemes providing protection againt sickness, invalidity, old age, accidents at work or occupational diseases and unemployment; and

(b)   social assistance, insofar as it is intended to supplement or replace these schemes (Article 3(1)).

In *Drake* the Court held that the benefits covered by the Directive must constitute whole or part of a statutory scheme providing protection against one of the specified risks or a form of social assistance having the same objective. It appears that the statutory scheme must be one for workers in general, and not one, as in *Liefting* (case 23/83), relating to persons employed by the State. A contracted-out scheme operating as a substitute for the statutory scheme will be treated as an occupational pension scheme, within Directive 86/378 (*Newstead v Department of Transport* (case 192/85)).

In an uncharacteristically restrictive interpretation the Court, contrary to Advocate-General Tesauro's recommendations, in *R v Secretary of State for Social Security, ex parte Smithson* (case C–243/90), denied the claimant's right to equality of treatment in respect of housing benefit under Directive 79/7 on the grounds that it was not within the scope of the Directive. Although eligibility for the benefit, and the amount of benefit, was ascertained, *inter alia*, by reference to a (discriminatory) invalidity pension, the benefit was not 'directly and effectively' linked to the protection provided against one of the risks specified in Article 3(1); a similarly restrictive approach was adopted in *Jackson* v *Chief Adjudication Officer* (cases C–63, 64/91). Here, in a claim by two single mothers, one engaged in vocational training, one in part-time work, in respect of supplementary allowance and income support, the Court held that these benefits, which might be granted in a variety of situations to persons whose means were insufficient to meet their needs, did not relate to any of the risks listed in Article 3(1). Nor did they fall within Directive 76/207. Although the benefits in question might affect the single parent's ability to undertake vocational training or part-time employment, they did not relate to the subject matter of the Directive, which was *access* to employment, including vocational training and promotion and working conditions.

The Court's attitude in these cases stands in stark contrast to its previous approach to the 'social assistance' exemption in Social Security Regulation 1408/71 and to the concept of 'social advantage' under Regulation 1612/68 (see chapters 21 and 22). *Jackson* v *Chief Adjudication Officer* may be contrasted with the more recent case of *Meyers* v *Adjudication Officer* (case C–116/94). In *Meyers*, the ECJ held that family credit, by enabling a single mother to go out to work, concerned access to employment and therefore fell within the ambit of the Equal Treatment Directive 76/207. *R* v *Secretary of State for Health, ex parte Richardson* (case C–137/94) concerned UK regulations dealing with exemptions from prescription charges which were linked to retirement age and were therefore discriminatory. The ECJ held that such rules fell within Article 3(1) because they formed part of the statutory scheme providing protection against one of the risks covered by the Directive, namely, sickness. These cases indicate that the ECJ may have had second thoughts about its earlier case law. Nonetheless, there must still be some links with the risks listed in Article 3(1): in *Atkins* v *Wrekin District Council* (case C–228/94) concessionary travel passes awarded to old age pensioners were held not to fall within the terms of the Directive.

Survivors' benefits, and family benefits not granted by way of increases to the benefits covered by the Directive, are excluded from Directive 79/7 (Article 3(2)).

Provided that the benefit in question is covered by Directive 79/7, the fact that it may be payable under national legislation to a third party does not take it outside the scope of the Directive. Otherwise, as the Court pointed out in *Drake*, it would be possible, by making formal changes to existing benefits covered by the Directive, to remove them from its scope. On this reasoning Mrs Drake was held entitled herself to invoke Directive 79/7 in respect of an invalidity allowance payable on behalf of her mother.

Scope of the equal treatment principle   The principle of equal treatment means, according to Directive 79/7, Article 4(1), that:

there shall be no discrimination whatsoever on grounds of sex either directly, or indirectly by reference in particular to marital or family status, in particular as concerns:

— the scope of [social security] schemes and the conditions of access thereto,
— the obligation to contribute and the calculation of contributions,
— the calculation of benefits including increases due in respect of a spouse and for dependants, and
— the conditions governing the duration and retention of entitlement to benefits.

Thus in *Drake* an invalidity allowance payable to a married man but not to a married woman was found in breach of Article 4(1).

Where a provision is indirectly discriminatory, it may be found to be objectively justified (see the earlier discussion on objective justification). In *Teuling* (case 30/85) an invalidity benefit, the amount of which was determined by marital status and either the (low) income derived from the spouse's occupation or the existence of a dependent child, designed to compensate for the 'greater burden' borne by persons in these categories, although indirectly discriminatory against women, was held to be objectively justified (see also *Commission* v *Belgium* (case C–229/89)). Such benefits, sexually neutral and designed to meet objective needs such as the need to support dependants, happen to benefit men more than women because the former are still, if to a diminishing degree, more likely to be responsible for dependants. Similarly, benefits to aid the long-term unemployed are acceptable because they are designed for gender-neutral policy purposes which, although they may benefit men more than women, are still justified (*Posthuma-van Damme* v *Bestuur van de Bedrijfsverenigung voor Detailhandel, Ambachten en Huisvrouwen* (case C–280/94)). In this case the ECJ also emphasised the wide margin of discretion Member States have in choosing their social policies.

Supplementary benefits payable in respect of a spouse or persons deemed to be dependent on the claimant are payable under Article 4(1) irrespective of the sex of the claimant. This applies even if it results in double payment, for example, payment to both spouses in respect of the same dependants. In response to the Irish government's argument in *Cotter* v *Minister for Social Welfare* (case C–377/89) that this would result in unjust enrichment the Court held that a defence based on this principle would enable the authorities to use their own unlawful conduct as a ground for depriving Article 4(1) of the Directive of its full effect.

In *Ruzius-Wilbrink* (case 102/88) the ECJ held that the principle of equal treatment expressed in Article 4(1) was capable of being applied to part-time workers. The claim concerned invalidity benefits provided under the Dutch social security system. Under the scheme the amount payable to part-timers was linked to the claimant's previous income; full-time workers, regardless of the size of their previous income, were entitled to a guaranteed 'minimum subsistence income'. The claimant, who had been a part-time worker, claimed that the system was indirectly discriminatory against women, since the part-time workforce in the Netherlands contained a much smaller percentage of men than women. The Court held that in these circumstances the difference in treatment would breach Article 4(1) of Directive 79/7 unless it could be justified by objective factors unrelated to sex. The fact that it would be unfair, as was argued by the Netherlands Social Insurance Board, to grant part-time workers an allowance higher than the wages they had previously received in employment was held not to amount to objective justification, since in a substantial number of cases the amount granted to those entitled to a minimum subsistence income also was higher than their previous income.

The principle of equal treatment is 'without prejudice to the provisions relating to the protection of women on the grounds of maternity' (Article 4(2)). These provisions are likely to be interpreted according to the same principles as apply to Article 2(3) of Directive 76/207.

Exclusions Article 7(1) expressly allows Member States to exclude certain matters from the scope of the equal treatment principle. These are:

(a)   the determination of pensionable age for the purposes of old-age and retirement pensions and possible consequences thereof for other benefits;
(b)   benefits or entitlements granted to persons who have brought up children;
(c)   wives' derived old-age or invalidity benefits, and
(d)   increases granted in respect of dependent wives related to long-term invalidity, old-age, accidents at work and occupational disease benefits.

Article 7 must now be read in the light of the Court's case law under Directive 76/207, and in particular *Marshall* (case 152/84), *Roberts* (case 151/84) and *Beets-Proper* (case 262/84). The exemption for the determination of pensionable age will apply *only* for the purposes of old-age and retirement pensions and possible consequences thereof for other social security benefits. In *R v Secretary of State for Social Security, ex parte Equal Opportunities Commission* (case C–9/91), in an action brought by the EOC for a declaration that the British Social Security Act 1965, in maintaining different periods of contribution by men and women towards social security benefits, the men's being longer, tied to the difference in pensionable age, was in breach of Directive 79/7, the Court held that the derogation provided by Article 7(1)(a) applied to any forms of discrimination 'necessarily linked' to the different statutory pensionable age. This would include the maintenance of different contribution periods for male and female workers. Such a scheme reflected the purpose of the derogation, which was to:

allow Member States to maintain temporarily the advantages accorded to women with respect to retirement in order to enable them progressively to adapt their pension systems . . . without disrupting the complex financial equilibrium of those systems, the importance of which could not be ignored.

The scope of Article 7(1)(a) was further tested in *Secretary of State for Social Security* v *Thomas* (case C–328/91) in a claim by a number of women for severe disablement allowances and invalid care allowances. Under British law these benefits were not payable to those who had reached pensionable age (60 for women, 65 for men) unless at that age they were already in receipt of the benefits. The applicants had not received these benefits before attaining pensionable age, nor had they, on reaching that age, been in receipt of an old age pension. They argued that the tying of benefits to pensionable age (save in the case of those already in receipt of benefits) was discriminatory, particularly since they were entitled, following *Marshall*, to continue working until the age of 65. The central question was whether the benefits in question fell within the exception provided by Article 7(1)(a).

Citing *R* v *Secretary of State for Social Security, ex parte Equal Opportunities Commission* (case C–9/91), that the permitted derogation of Article 7(1)(a), as regards the 'possible consequences thereof for other benefits' was confined to 'forms of discrimination existing under other benefit schemes which are *necessarily and objectively* linked to the difference in retirement age', the Court held that discrimination in respect of other benefits would only be necessary 'to avoid disrupting the complex financial equilibrium of the social security system or to ensure consistency between retirement pension schemes and other benefit schemes' (para. 12). Since the benefits in question were non-contributory there was no question in this case of disruption of the financial equilibrium of the UK social security system; nor was discrimination necessary to avoid inconsistency between different benefit schemes. Since, as the UK had argued, the benefits were intended to replace income in the event of materialisation of the risk, the principle of consistency required that they should be available in cases such as the applicants', where claimants were unable to work and were not in receipt of an old age pension. In any event, national rules against overlapping would prevent double recovery by those in receipt of a pension.

By contrast, in *Secretary of State for Social Security* v *Graham* (case C–92/94), a case concerning discrimination in respect of contributory invalidity pensions, the ECJ held that the difference in treatment was necessarily and objectively linked to the permitted difference in retirement ages for men and women. To interfere with the ability to set retirement ages would encroach on the rights of the Member States under Article 7(1)(a) and would also introduce inconsistencies in the treatment of able-bodied women who had retired at 60 and their disabled counterparts. Although the Court identified the purpose of the provisions as replacing income from employment, it did not conclude that, as women are entitled to remain in employment until 65 (*Marshall* (case 152/84)) they should be entitled to a replacement income for that period should they be prevented by illness from being able to work. This somewhat circumspect decision may well have been driven, in part, by the need to allay Member States' fears about the reduced scope for exemption under Article 7(1)(a). The ECJ in general has taken a very restrictive view of Article 7(1)(a)'s scope, as it does of all derogations from fundamental Community rights. *Graham* therefore indicates a slightly broader approach, but whether it will constitute the basis of a new approach is another question. In *Taylor* (case C–382/98), which concerned winter fuel payments, the ECJ took an approach similar to that in the *Equal Opportunities Case* (case C–9/91). By contrast, in *Hepple* (case C–196/98, which concerned a reduced earnings allowance, the ECJ held that the scheme fell within Article 7(1)(a), and therefore unequal age conditions linked to different pensionable ages for men and women could be imposed. Although the difference in treatment was not necessary to maintain the financial equilibrium of the scheme — as had been the case in *Thomas* and *Graham* — the ECJ accepted that the rules were designed to achieve a coherence between the allowance and the pension scheme and were objectively necessary for that purpose. It is equally uncertain whether the other exceptions will be narrowly or generously construed.

States are required under Article 7(2) periodically to examine matters excluded under Article 7(1) to ascertain whether they are still justified.

Principle of equal treatment in occupational pension schemes (Directive 86/378)

Directive 86/378, which is complementary to Directive 79/7, implements the equal treatment principle in the field of occupational, as opposed to statutory, pension schemes. The Directive was subject to a three-year implementation period, which expired on 31 July 1989 (Article 12). However, under Article 8, States were given until 1 January 1993 to take 'all necessary steps to ensure that the provisions of occupational [pension] schemes contrary to the principle of equal treatment are revised'. This implies that while States might be liable for failure to implement the Directive from 1 August 1989, the Directive did not become *fully* effective until January 1993. However, where the difference in treatment arises from the employer's contribution, direct or indirect, to the pension scheme, by way of consideration paid by the employer to the employee in respect of his employment, as in *Worringham* v *Lloyds Bank Ltd* (case 69/80), *Bilka-Kaufhaus GmbH* v *Weber von Harz* (case 170/84) and *Barber* (case 262/88), it may fall to be treated under Article 141 (ex 119) as 'pay', subject to the temporal limitations of *Barber* and the substantive limits imposed by *Neath* v *Hugh Steeper Ltd* (case C–152/91). Following *Bilka-Kaufhaus* such benefits can even be claimed by part-time workers where the discriminatory effects fall disproportionately on one sex, provided that the difference in treatment is not objectively justified. Where the matter falls within Article 141 (ex 119) any problems concerning the direct effects of the Directive will be avoided.

With a few important exceptions Directive 86/378 is enacted in near-identical terms to Directive 79/7. It applies to occupational schemes 'not governed by Directive 79/7 whose purpose is to provide workers . . . with benefits intended to supplement the benefits provided by statutory social security schemes or to replace them' (Article 2). It applies to the same categories of persons (Article 3) in respect of the same risks (Article 4). Directive 86/378, however, contains no exclusions for survivors' and family benefits parallel to that of Article 3(2) of Directive 79/7, *provided* these benefits form part of the consideration paid by the employer by reason of the employee's employment (Article 4).

Article 6 gives a list of examples of provisions contrary to the equal treatment principle. Article 6(f) prohibits the fixing of different retirement ages for men and women, and Article 6(j) the laying down of different standards or standards applicable only to a specified sex. Article 6(h) prohibits the setting of different levels of benefit 'except insofar as it may be necessary to take account of actuarial calculation factors which differ according to sex in the case of benefits designated as contribution-defined'. Similarly although different levels of employee contribution are prohibited in principle (Article 6(i)) they *may* be set 'to take account of the different actuarial calculation factors' (Article 9(c)). Thus differences in treatment may be objectively justified. Different levels of employer contribution may also be permitted if they are set 'with a view to making the amount of [contribution-defined] benefits more equal' (Article 6(i)).

Article 9, like Article 7 of Directive 79/7, enables Member States to exempt from the equal treatment principle the 'determination of pensionable age for the purposes of granting old-age or retirement pensions, and the possible implications for other benefits'. This provision was construed seemingly out of existence in *Barber* (case C–262/88): hence the Court's decision that its ruling on this issue should not be retrospective.

Article 9(b) provides that 'survivors' pensions which do not constitute consideration paid by the employer are exempt from the equal treatment principle until the date on which equality is achieved in statutory schemes, or at the latest, until equality is required by a Directive'. Following *Barber* such benefits, being paid by the employer as a result of the employment relationship, are likely to be construed as consideration and thus will not be exempt under Article 9(b). *Newstead* (case 192/85), which had decided otherwise, thereby excluding the employer's provision for survivors from the equality principle under Article 9(b), is unlikely to be followed. Survivors' pensions which do *not* constitute consideration paid by the employer are also exempt from the equal treatment principle *either* until the date on which equality is achieved in statutory schemes, *or,* at the latest, until equality is required by a Directive (Article 9(b)).

Following the decision in *Barber* (case 262/88), much of this Directive is redundant. It has relevance only in regard to occupational schemes for the self-employed and to schemes which the Court has held to be outside Article 141 (ex 119) (*Neath* v *Hugh Steeper Ltd* (case C–152/91); *Coloroll Pension Trustees Ltd* v *Russell* (case C–200/91)). As a result, the Commission is proposing to amend the Directive.

Equal treatment in self-employment (Directive 86/613)

Directive 86/613 is designed to ensure the application of the equal treatment principle 'as between men and women engaged in an activity in a self-employed capacity, or contributing to the pursuit of such an activity, as regards those aspects not covered by Directives 76/207 and 79/7 (Article 1). It is thus complementary to Directive 76/207.

The Directive applies to 'all persons pursuing a gainful activity for their own account . . . including farmers and members of the liberal professions' and to 'their spouses, not being employees or partners, where they habitually . . . participate in the activities of the self-employed worker and perform the same tasks or ancillary tasks' (Article 2).

The principle of equal treatment implies 'the absence of discrimination on the grounds of sex, either directly or indirectly, by reference in particular to marital or family status' (Article 3). This is without prejudice to measures concerning the protection of women during pregnancy and motherhood (preamble, ninth recital).

Under Article 4 Member States are required to take all necessary measures to ensure the elimination of all provisions which are contrary to the principle of equal treatment as defined in Directive 76/207, especially in respect of the establishment, equipment or extension of a business or the launching or extension of any other form of self-employed activity including financial facilities.

Member States are also required: 'Without prejudice to the specific conditions for access to certain activities which apply equally to both sexes' to take the measures necessary to ensure that the conditions for the formation of a company between spouses are not more restrictive than the conditions for the formation of a company between unmarried persons (Article 5).

Where a contributory social security scheme exists for self-employed workers in a Member State, the States must take the necessary measures to enable those spouses who participate in the activities of the self-employed worker, and who are not protected under the self-employed worker's social security scheme, to join a contributory social security scheme voluntarily (Article 6).

States are required to introduce 'such measures as are necessary to enable all persons who consider themselves wronged by failure to apply the principle of equal treatment in self-employed activities to pursue their claims by judicial process, possibly after recourse to other competent authorities' (Article 9).

Member States were required to bring into force the measures necessary to comply with the Directives by 30 June 1989. The date for compliance was extended to 30 June 1991 for States which had to amend their legislation on matrimonial rights and obligations in order to secure the principle of equal treatment in the formation of companies (Article 12). The Directive became directly effective as against the State on the expiry of the applicable time-limit. Since the date for implementation has passed it may now be invoked as an aid to interpretation against private parties (*von Colson* (case 14/83) and *Harz* (case 79/83)).

Remedies

Directive 76/207, Directive 75/117 and the Pregnancy Directive all require States to 'introduce into their national legal systems such measures as are

necessary to enable all persons who consider themselves wronged by failure
to apply the principle of equal treatment . . . to pursue their claims by judicial
process after possible recourse to other competent authorities'. In *von Colson*
v *Land Nordrhein-Westfalen* (case 14/83) and *Harz* v *Deutsche Tradax GmbH*
(case 79/83) the Court held that this imposes a duty on national courts to
provide remedies which ensure 'real and effective' protection for individuals'
Community rights and have a real deterrent effect on the employer. These
requirements, together with the principles of direct effects and the retroactivity of rulings under Article 234 (ex 177), have had a profound influence on
the legal systems of the Member States. *Marshall* v *Southampton and South
West Hampshire Health Authority (Teaching) (No. 2)* (case C–271/91) decided
that States could not impose statutory limits on damages. This ruling, which
was retroactive, has had significant effects with huge financial consequences
for 'public' employers. The Ministry of Defence alone was subject to claims
in excess of one million pounds. It has been suggested that in seeking to
ensure the effective enforcement of its sex discrimination laws the ECJ in
Marshall (No. 2) went a step too far. Given that Directive 76/207 did not
itself provide a clear and precise directly effective remedy, and that the
damages available under the Equal Pay and Sex Discrimination Acts were not
so low as to be considered either nominal or ineffective it is submitted that
the Court should at least have tempered the effect of its ruling by limiting it
along the lines laid down in *Barber*. It now seems, however, that the ECJ,
although not departing from the principles of *von Colson and Harz*, is
prepared to accept some limits on the effects of *Marshall (No. 2)* (see further
R v *Secretary of State for Social Security, ex parte Sutton* (case C–66/95),
Draehmpaehl (case C–180/95) and *Magorrian* (case C–246/96) discussed in
chapter 26).

Further reading

Arnull, A., 'Article 119 and the Principle of Equal Pay for Work of Equal
Value' (1986) 11 EL Rev 200.
Curtin, D., 'Effective Sanctions and the Equal Treatment Directive: the *Von
Colson* and *Harz* cases' (1985) 22 CML Rev 505.
Curtin, D., 'Scalping the Community Legislator: Occupational Pensions and
Barber' (1990) 27 CML Rev 475.
Docksey, C., 'The Principle of Equality between Men and Women: a
Fundamental Right under Community Law' (1991) 20 ILJ 258.
Hervey, T., and O'Keeffe, D. (eds), *Sex Equality Law in the European Union*
(Wiley, 1996).
Honeyball, S., 'Pregnancy and Sex Discrimination' (2000) 29 ILJ 43.
Mancine, G.F. and O'Leary, S., 'The New Frontiers of Sex Equality Law in
the European Union' (1999) 24 EL Rev 331.
McCrudden, C., 'The Effectiveness of European Equality Law: National
Mechanisms for Enforcing Gender Equality Law in the Light of European
Requirements' (1993) 13 Oxford J Legal Stud 320.
Prechel, S., 'Remedies after *Marshall*' (1990) 21 CML Rev 451.

Shaw, J., 'European Community Judicial Method: its Application to Sex Discrimination Law' (1990) 19 ILJ 228.

Steiner, J., 'Sex Discrimination under UK and EEC law: Two plus Four Equals One' (1983) 32 ICLQ 399.

Szyszczak, E., 'Pay Inequalities and Equal Value Claims' (1985) 48 MLR 139.

Whiteford, E., 'Social Policy after Maastricht' (1993) 18 EL Rev 202.

Wyatt, D., 'Enforcing EEC Social Rights in the United Kingdom' (1989) 18 ILJ 197.

PART THREE

Remedies and Enforcement of EC Law

TWENTY SIX

Introduction

The foregoing chapters, which by no means cover the whole range of Community law, should be sufficient to illustrate the extent to which EC law now permeates our lives. In addition to the law stemming from the Treaty, a wealth of secondary legislation has been, and is in the constant process of being, enacted, covering a wide and ever-increasing range of activities. Much of this law is directly effective (see chapter 4), and will, under the principle of primacy of EC law (see chapter 5), take precedence over any conflicting rules of national law. It thus forms an important source of *rights* and *obligations* for both States and individuals.

An effective system of enforcement requires that the rights arising under EC law may be enforced against three groups of people:

(a) *The institutions of the Community*, who in their law-making or administrative capacity may have acted or failed to act in breach of EC law.

(b) *Member States*, which in carrying out or failing to carry out their obligations under the Treaty or secondary legislation may have acted in breach of EC law.

(c) *Individuals*, who in failing to comply with their obligations under the Treaty or secondary legislation may have acted in breach of EC law.

The EC Treaty itself provides an extensive range of remedies. It provides, by way of *direct* action before the European Courts, for actions against the institutions of the Community and against Member States.

Action before the European courts

Actions against the institutions of the Community comprise:

(a) Actions for judicial review, in the form of actions to 'review the legality of acts of the Council and the Commission other than recommendations or opinions' (Article 230 (ex 173), the 'annulment action', and Article 241 (ex 184), the 'plea of illegality'), and an action for 'failure to act' (Article 232 (ex 175));

(b)   Actions for damages (Articles 234 and 288(2) (ex 178 and 215(2)); and

(c)   Actions in respect of disputes between the Community and its servants ('staff cases' (Article 236 (ex 179)).

All claims by natural and legal persons under (a) and (b), including the new areas introduced in Regulation 4064/89 (control of concentrations between undertakings), Regulation 40/94 (Community trade mark) and Regulation 2100/94 (Community plant variety rights) and all claims under (c) are now dealt with by the Court of First Instance (CFI), with a right of appeal to the ECJ (Article 225 (ex 168a) EC). Appeal is limited to points of law and must be based on the grounds of lack of competence of the CFI, breach of procedure before it which adversely affects the interests of the appellant, or infringement of Community law by the CFI (Article 51 of the Statutes of the Court of Justice). An appeal must contain the pleas in law and legal arguments relied on (Article 112(1)(c), Court of Justice's rules of procedure). It must indicate precisely the contested elements of the judgment which the appellant seeks to have set aside and also the legal arguments specifically advanced in support of the appeal. That requirement is not satisfied by an appeal confined to repeating the pleas and arguments previously submitted to the CFI. The CFI has exclusive jurisdiction to establish the facts, except where the substantive inaccuracy of its findings is apparent from the documents submitted to it, and to assess these facts (*John Deere* v *Commission* (case C–7/95P), discussed further in chapter 29). The CFI also has jurisdiction to hear and determine actions brought by natural and legal persons relating to the European Central Bank (see Council Decisions 93/350 (OJ L144/21, 1993) and 94/149 (OJ L66/29, 1994)).

The European Courts have no jurisdiction over acts of the European Council (*Roujansky* v *Council* (case T–584/93)) nor, prior to the ToA, over matters governed by the TEU. Following the transfer by the ToA (new Article 46 TEU) to the (new Title IV) EC Treaty of matters within the third pillar of the TEU relating to visas, asylum, immigration and judicial cooperation in civil affairs, the ECJ will assume a limited jurisdiction over these matters (Article 68 EC), as well as over framework decisions and decisions concerning police and judicial cooperation in criminal matters remaining within the third pillar of the TEU, subject to agreement, both as to the jurisdiction itself and its extent, by individual Member States (new Article 35 TEU). The ToA also gave the Court jurisdiction over the new 'flexibility' clauses providing for 'closer cooperation' agreements to be established under the new Articles 11 EC and 40 TEU and, for the first time, express power to rule on the conformity of action of the EC institutions with fundamental human rights in those areas where the Court has jurisdiction under the EU Treaties (new Article 46(1)(d) TEU). Matters within the second pillar of the TEU (Foreign and Security Policy) remain wholly outside the jurisdiction of the ECJ.

Actions against Member States comprise:

(a)   Action by the Commission against a Member State for failure 'to fulfil an obligation under this Treaty' (Article 226 (ex 169) EC);

(b)   Action by a Member State against another Member State for failure 'to fulfil an obligation under this Treaty' (Article 227 (ex 170) EC);

(c)   Action by the Commission against a Member State, via accelerated procedures similar to those provided under Article 226 (ex 169), for breach of its obligation to notify the Commission under Article 88(2)(b) (ex 93(2)(b)) (State aids) and Article 95(4) (ex 100a(4)) (unilateral restrictions on free movement of goods);

(d)   Similar accelerated proceedings brought by the Commission under Article 298 (ex 225) where emergency measures taken by Member States under Articles 272 (ex 203) (to protect essential security interests) and 272 (ex 204) (in the event of serious internal disturbances) distort conditions of competition within the Community.

These actions are brought directly before the ECJ.

Right to intervene   Under Article 37 of the Protocol on the statute of the Court of Justice, Member States and Community institutions have a right to intervene in cases before the Court. This right is also open to 'any other person establishing an interest in the result of any case submitted to the Court', except in cases between institutions of the Community or between Member States and institutions of the Community. In *British Coal Corporation v Commission* (case T–367/94), a case based on the parallel provisions of the statutes of the ECSC, the Court held that an applicant must establish a 'direct, existing interest in the grant by the Court of the order as sought and not purely an interest in relation to the plea in law advanced'. The fact that representative associations have a right to intervene in order to protect their members in cases raising questions of principle liable to affect those members cannot be relied on in support of an individual application to intervene (see also *Dorsch Consult Ingenieurgesellschaft mbH* v *Council & Commission* (case T–184/95)).

Interim relief   Although actions before the Courts do not have suspensory effect the Courts may, 'if [they] consider that the circumstances so require it, order that the application of the contested act be suspended' (Article 242 (ex 185)). They may also order 'any necessary interim measures in any of the above proceedings' (Article 243 (ex 186)). However, action under Article 242 (ex 185) is admissible only if the applicant is challenging that measure 'in proceedings before the Court'. Similarly action under Article 243 (ex 186) will be admitted only if it is made 'by a party to the case before the Court and relates to that case' (Rules of Procedure, Article 83(1); Rules of Procedure of the CFI, Article 104(2)). Interim measures may not be ordered 'unless there are circumstances giving rise to urgency and factual and legal grounds establishing a prima facie case for the measures applied for'. The urgency of the application will be assessed according to the necessity for such an order in order to prevent serious and irreparable damage (Rules of Procedure, Article 83). Parties wishing to establish the existence of 'serious and irreparable damage' for the purpose of obtaining the suspension of a Community act must provide documentary evidence both as regards the specific damage suffered or likely to be suffered and the causative link between that damage and the contested act (*Descom Scales Manufacturing Co. Ltd* v *Council* (case C–6/94R), application for suspension of anti-dumping Regulation rejected for lack of evidence). Purely financial damage cannot in principle be regarded as irreparable (*Cargill* v *Commission* (case 229/88R)). The interim measures requested must be of such a nature as to prevent the alleged damage (*Commission* v *United Kingdom (Re Merchant Shipping Rules)* (case 246/89R)). In such proceedings relief can be very speedy. In *Commission* v *Ireland (Re Dundalk Water Scheme)* (case 45/87R) an interim injunction was granted *ex parte* within three days of application.

The case of *Antonissen* (case C–393/96 P/R) concerned a claim for an interim award of damages. The case came on appeal to the President of the ECJ from the President of the CFI, who had rejected the applicant's request. The applicant sought provisional damages, pending a final ruling in a claim for compensation against the Community. The applicant, a dairy farmer, had been refused a milk quota on the basis of an allegedly invalid EC Regulation. As a result he had received a request for payment of a substantial supplementary levy, threatening to cause him severe financial distress. The President of the ECJ allowed his appeal. He held that if an interim order is justified, prima facie, in law and in fact, and it is urgent, in order to avoid serious and irreparable damage, it must be made before a decision is reached in the main proceedings. An absolute prohibition on obtaining, in interim proceedings, part of the compensation claimed in the main proceedings, and seeking to protect the applicant's interest, would not be compatible with the individual's right to effective judicial protection. Such payment may be necessary to ensure the practical effect of the judgment in the main application. However, before ordering such payment the Court must examine the applicant's assets to assess whether it would be possible to recover any payment by way of advance when the final judgment is delivered. Recourse to such a remedy must be restricted to situations in which the prima facie case is strong and the urgency is undeniable.

Action against individuals   There is no provision in the EC Treaty for direct action before the ECJ *against individuals*. Individuals may however be vulnerable to fines and penalties under EC secondary legislation (e.g. Regulation 17/62, see chapter 17), which may be challenged before the CFI. Under Article 229 (ex 172) the ECJ has unlimited jurisdiction in regard to the penalties provided in such Regulations.

Action before national courts

Basic principles   In addition to these direct remedies before the European Courts, questions of infringement of EC law by Community institutions and

Member States may also be raised before national courts. In describing Regulations as 'directly applicable' (Article 249 (ex 189) EC) and in providing a means whereby national courts might refer questions of interpretation and validity of EC law to the ECJ (Article 234 (ex 177) EC) the Treaty clearly envisaged a role for national courts in the enforcement of EC law. This role has been greatly enlarged by the development by the ECJ of the principle of direct effects and, more recently, the principles of indirect effects and State liability under *Francovich* v *Italy* (cases C–6 & 9/90) (see chapter 4). A ruling on the interpretation of Community law may reveal that a national law or practice is inconsistent with Community law; a ruling that a provision of an EC Regulation, or a Directive or a Decision is invalid renders it unenforceable against the individual concerned. In both cases it may provide the basis for a claim in damages.

This possibility of an alternative remedy via their national courts is of particular importance for individuals, since they have no *locus standi* to bring a direct action before the ECJ in respect of infringements of EC law by Member States, nor any power to compel the Commission to bring such an action (see *Alfons Lütticke GmbH* v *Commission* (case 48/65), chapters 29 and 30). Also their *locus standi* in direct actions against the EC institutions for judicial review is limited. Moreover, national courts remain the only forums in which action can be brought *by* individuals in respect of infringements of EC law *against* individuals.

Where individuals seek to assert their Community rights before national courts or tribunals, they may do so in the context of any proceedings of national law, public or private, in which EC rights are relevant, in pursuit of any remedy, interim or final, available under national law. The ECJ has laid down a number of principles which must be observed by national courts in claims involving Community law. It has held consistently that:

> In the absence of Community rules it is for the domestic systems of each Member State to designate the courts having jurisdiction and the procedural conditions governing actions at law intended to ensure the protection of the rights which subjects derive from the direct effects of Community law, it being understood that such conditions cannot be less favourable than those relating to similar actions of a domestic nature nor render virtually impossible or excessively difficult the exercise of rights conferred by Community law.

(See *Rewe Zentralfinanz* v *Landwirtschaftskammer Saarland* (case 33/76), *Comet BV* v *Productschap voor Siergevassen* (case 45/76), *Express Dairy Foods Ltd* v *Intervention Board for Agricultural Produce* (case 130/79), *Peterbroeck* (case C–312/93), *Van Schijndel* (cases C–430 & C–431/93).)

This statement may be seen to embody three separate principles:

(a)   The principle of national treatment ('it is for the domestic systems of each Member State to designate . . . effects of Community law').

(b)   The principle of non-discrimination ('conditions cannot be less favourable than those . . . of a domestic nature').

(c)   The principle of effectiveness ('nor render impossible or excessively difficult the exercise of rights conferred').

Since the national remedy provided for a claim based on domestic law may not be exactly comparable to a claim based on EC law, or, although seemingly comparable, may operate to the detriment of the party relying on EC law, commentators, and even the Court, have tended to merge the first and second principles into a single principle of *equivalence*.

Another version of the effectiveness principle, enunciated in *Harz* v *Deutsche Tradax GmbH* (case 79/83) requires that the remedies and sanctions provided for breach of Community law must have a real deterrent effect and must be 'such as to guarantee full and effective protection' for individuals' Community rights.

The rights which individuals may claim under Community law are no longer confined to rights under directly effective Community law; they now include rights based on the principles of indirect effect and State liability under *Francovich*. Thus EC law may be invoked as a defence to a criminal charge (e.g., *Ratti* (case 148/78)) or to resist payment of a charge exacted, or support a claim for the return of money withheld, in breach of EC law (e.g., *Van Gend en Loos* (case 26/62)). It may provide a basis for an injunction, to prevent or put an end to action in breach of EC law (e.g., *Garden Cottage Foods Ltd* v *Milk Marketing Board* [1982] QB 1114, Court of Appeal; [1984] AC 130, House of Lords) or a declaration, e.g., that a particular national measure is illegal, being based on an invalid EC Regulation (e.g., *Royal Scholten-Honig* v *Intervention Board for Agricultural Produce* (cases 103 & 145/77). It may also provide the basis for a claim in damages, either on the principles of direct or indirect effect, against parties acting in breach of substantive provisions of EC law, or, under *Francovich*, v *Italy* (cases C–6 & 9/90), against the State itself for its failure to comply with its obligation under Article 10 (ex 5) EC to 'take all appropriate measures . . . to ensure fulfilment of the obligations arising out of this Treaty or resulting from action taken by the institutions of the Community'. Thus acts of Member States or of Community institutions which are illegal under EC law may be challenged, and remedies provided. Whilst the illegal acts are not set aside as a result of the action, they cannot be enforced.

In order to assist national courts in their task of enforcing EC law, Article 234 (ex 177) gives the ECJ, and *only* the ECJ, jurisdiction to give preliminary rulings concerning the interpretation of EC law and the validity of acts of the institutions of the Community at the request of national courts. Although the ECJ has no power to *decide* the issue before the national court, an interpretation on the matter of Community law involved, or on the validity of the act in question, will normally be sufficient to establish whether an infringement of EC law has occurred. On this basis the national court may then supply the appropriate remedy. As noted above, the Court's jurisdiction to rule on these matters has been extended by the incorporation into the EC Treaty of areas previously governed by the TEU, and by a new jurisdiction over parts of the third pillar (police and judicial cooperation in criminal matters) remaining within the TEU, in provisions analogous to Article 234 (ex 177). Regrettably, these provisions are more limited in scope than Article 234 and, in allowing Member States a choice as to the extent and even the possibility of access to the ECJ, seriously undermine the uniformity of judicial protection for individuals under EU law (see further chapter 27).

Principles of equivalence and effectiveness The obligation to comply with the twin principles of equivalence and effectiveness has on occasions created problems for national courts. Clearly, a rule which discriminates, directly or indirectly, against claimants relying on EC law will be contrary to Community law. Such was the case in *Criminal Proceedings against Bickel and another* (case C–274/96). Here, rules of the Trento-Alto region of Italy, which provided that the German language was to have the same status as Italian in relations between *citizens of that area* and the judicial and administrative authorities, but which did not extend to persons of Austrian and German nationality and residence, were held to be discriminatory in their effect, contrary to the then Article 6 (now 12) EC. Similarly, rules that deny access to the courts altogether, such as a rule restricting payment of a duty held by the ECJ to be contrary to EC law to claimants who have brought an action for repayment before the delivery of that judgment, as was the situation in *Barra* v *Belgium* (case 309/85), will clearly be ineffective in protecting the Community rights of persons bringing their claim, based on that judgment, after the date of judgment (see also *Deville* v *Administration des Impôts* (case 240/87)). But there are many situations in which the position is not so clear. First, it may not be easy to assess what is an 'equivalent' national remedy. EC law is *sui generis*. It cuts across the boundaries and classifications of national law. Even where domestic law provides a remedy in the context of a similar claim, for example in restitution, or in the field of employment law, such claims may be dealt with in different courts, subject to different procedures and different limitations as to time or the award of damages. Some potential remedies may be more 'effective' than others. How, then, is equivalence to be assessed? Does the principle of effectiveness require that the most generous treatment be accorded to claims based on EC law? Secondly, there are circumstances in which an equivalent domestic remedy may not exist. EC law is supreme over all national law. Where an individual seeks to invoke his Community rights in order to challenge national law, he may do so against any law, whatever its nature. In most Member States concepts of sovereignty prohibit challenge to the legality of statute or, *a fortiori*, constitutional law. Furthermore, in most Member States there are lacunae, gaps in the legal protection of individuals, arising from traditional privileges and immunities. Sometimes these limitations are justified, sometimes they are not. What remedy or procedure is to be provided by national courts in these circumstances?

The ECJ, in its jurisdiction under Article 234 (ex 177), has provided guidance on these matters. Its approach to the principles of equivalence and effectiveness has developed over the years, from an absolutist, interventionist approach in cases such as *Marshall (No. 2)* (case C–271/91), *Emmott* (case C–208/90) and *Factortame (Nos 1 and 2)*, towards a more 'hands-off' approach, described by Tridimas as a policy of 'selective deference to national rules of procedure'. In *Dorsch Consult* (case C–54/96) it held:

> It is for the legal system of each Member State to determine which court or tribunal has jurisdiction to hear disputes involving individual rights derived from Community law. . . . It is not for the Court of Justice to involve itself in the resolution of questions of jurisdiction to which the classification of certain legal situations may give rise in the national legal system.

While in earlier judgments the Court was prepared to prescribe specific Community rules and express its views on the adequacy or effectiveness of particular domestic remedies or procedures, more recently it has emphasized that:

> . . . it is for national courts to ascertain whether the procedural rules intended to secure that the rights derived from Community law are safeguarded under national law and comply with the principle of equivalence (*Levez* v *Jennings (Harlow Pools) Ltd* (case C–326/96))

Likewise, having laid down basic guidelines to assist national courts in determining questions of effectiveness, it has left it to national courts to decide whether their rules are effective to safeguard individuals' Community rights.

The cases considered in this section, and the principles laid down in these cases, demonstrate this new, more deferential approach to matters of equivalence and effectiveness. *Palmisani* v *INPS* (case C–261/95) concerned a claim for damages for losses suffered as a result of the belated transposition of Directive 80/987 on the protection of employees in the event of their employers' insolvency. INPS was the agency responsible for managing the fund set up to guarantee employees' arrears of wages as required by the Directive. Following the ECJ's ruling in *Francovich* (cases C–6 & 9/90), the Directive had finally been implemented in Italy by legislative decree. Under the decree, claims for compensation from INPS were limited to not more than one year from the date of entry into force of the decree. The claimant's claim, having been brought outside this period, had been rejected by the Italian court. He argued before the ECJ that the one-year limitation period was unlawful, being contrary to the requirement of equivalence and effectiveness. On the question of equivalence, he pointed to other, more generous limitation rules governing claims for damages and to the 'manifest difference' between (for example) the five-year limitation period for reparation in general claims for non-contractual liability and the one-year period allowed for claims based on *Francovich*. The Court held that in order to ascertain comparability, 'the essential characteristics of the domestic system of reference must be examined'. Prior to the passing of the legislative decree there was no remedy in Italy for such a claim: 'If the domestic system [was] incapable of serving as a basis for a claim under *Francovich* no other relevant comparisons [could] be made'. The Member State must therefore make reparation for the consequences of the loss or damage caused to the claimant on the basis of national rules of liability, provided that they satisfy the requirement of effectiveness. On the question of the effectiveness of the remedy provided, with its one-year limitation rule, the Court held that although in principle reparation must be commensurate with the loss or damage sustained (see *Marshall (No. 2)* (case C–271–91) and *Brasserie du Pêcheur* (cases C–46 & 48/93)), 'reparation cannot always be ensured by the retroactive and proper application in full of the measures implementing the Directive'. The setting of 'reasonable' limitation periods was permitted under EC law. A one-year limitation period such as the one in question 'cannot be regarded as making it excessively difficult or *a fortiori* impossible to lodge a claim for compensation'. Thus the one-year limitation period would not be incompatible with EC law.

In *Levez* v *TH Jennings (Harlow Pools) Ltd* (case C–326/96), in a claim for damages in respect of sex discrimination brought under the then Article 119 EC (now 141) and Directive 75/117, the Court was asked to consider a two-year time limit on arrears of payment of damages under the UK Equal Pay Act in the light of the principles of equivalence and effectiveness. It was argued that the claim, brought before an industrial tribunal, could have been brought before a county court, by analogy with claims for unlawful deductions from wages or unlawful discrimination in terms of employment on grounds of race or disability, which were subject to more generous limitation rules. The Court held that it was 'for national courts to ascertain whether the procedural rules intended to safeguard rights derived from Community law were safeguarded under national law and complied with the principle of equivalence'. A rule of national law would be deemed equivalent 'where the purpose and cause of action are similar'. However, citing an earlier case of *EDIS* v *Ministero delle Finanze* (case C–231/96), it held that 'that principle is not to be interpreted as requiring Member States to extend their most favourable rules to all actions brought . . . in the field of employment law'. In assessing equivalence, the national court must consider 'the purpose and essential characteristics of allegedly similar domestic actions'. It must review the different procedures as a whole and weigh the relative advantages and disadvantages of each. On the facts it was found that the two-year period could not be enforced against the applicant, since, having been misled by her employer, she had no way of determining whether she was being discriminated against, or to what extent: 'To allow her employer to rely on the two-year rule would be to deprive his employee of the means provided by the Directive of enforcing the principle of equal pay before the court.' Thus, *in these particular circumstances* the remedy provided was ineffective. In applying the ECJ's ruling in *Levez*, the Employment Appeal Tribunal ([1999] 3 CMLR 715) found that the two-year limitation period provided under the Equal Pay Act did not satisfy the requirement of equivalence, since it had been introduced in order to give effect to Britain's EC obligations and it applied only to equal pay claims based on sex discrimination. This is, it is submitted, a somewhat stricter line than that taken by the ECJ in *Palmisani*.

One of the characteristics likely to be deemed 'essential' to the question of 'similarity' will be whether the action involves a public authority or is one between private parties. *EDIS* v *Ministero delle Finanze* (case C–231/96) was one of a number of claims for the recovery of a company registration charge which had been found in the case of *Ponente Carni* (cases C–71/91, C–178/91) to be contrary to EC law. Under the relevant Italian decree such an action was subject to a three-year limitation period, running from the date of payment of the charge. The claimants argued that the appropriate comparator for limitation purposes was the 10-year period applicable to actions for recovery of money between private individuals. The Court disagreed. There was no need for a Member State to extend its most favourable rules to claims based on EC law. Repayment of the charges in question could be claimed only if the substantive or formal conditions laid down by the various national laws were complied with.

'Community law does not in principle preclude the legislation of a Member State from laying down, alongside a limitation period applicable under the ordinary law to actions between individuals for the recovery of sums paid but not due, special detailed rules governing claims and legal proceedings to challenge the imposition of charges and other levies. The position would only be different if those detailed rules applied solely to actions based on community law for the repayment of such charges and levies' (para. 37).

This passage was cited verbatim in a similar claim for repayment of the Italian registration charge in *IN.CO.GE '90* (cases C–10 & 22/97). Here the Court held that 'any reclassification of the legal relationship between the tax authorities and certain companies in that state . . . in such circumstances . . . is a matter for national law'

Similarly, in *Criminal Proceedings against Nunes* (case C–186/98) the Court upheld the right of a Member State to impose criminal penalties for the improper use of the European Social Fund, even though the Regulation governing misuse of such funds provided only for civil remedies. The Court held that where a Community Regulation failed to provide specifically for any penalty for an infringement of Community law Article 10 (ex 5) of the EC Treaty required Member States to take all measures necessary to ensure the application and effectiveness of that law. The choice of penalties remained at Member States' discretion, provided that the penalty chosen complied with the principle of equivalence, and was 'effective, proportionate and dissuasive'.

As the Court pointed out in *EDIS*, this principle of national procedural autonomy is a necessary consequence of the diversity of national legal systems and the lack of Community rules. Although the Court has in the past been prepared to lay down some common rules, as will be seen from some of the cases examined below, it appears to have judged that the time is not ripe for further development in this field. However, there is little doubt that, given the opportunity, the Court will continue to monitor national rules and procedures to ensure that the rules applied to claims based on EC law are no less favourable than those applied to similar claims based on domestic law, and, whether or not a national comparator exists, they do not render impossible or excessively difficult the exercise of rights conferred by EC law or, if criminal sanctions are involved, they are effective, proportionate and dissuasive.

This view is borne out in the recent case of *Adidas AG* (Case C–223/98), decided in 1999. The case concerned the implementation by the Swedish authorities of EC Regulation 3295/94, designed to prevent trade in counterfeit goods. Under the Regulation implementation was left expressly to the national authorities. Following the seizure of counterfeit goods by the Swedish customs the owner of the original product sought to take action to enforce his rights against the consignee of these goods. The Swedish authorities, bound by their national confidentiality rules, refused to reveal his identity. In a reference for interpretation of the Regulation under Article 177 (now 234) the Court found that the system laid down by the Regulation depended directly for its effective application on the information supplied to the holder of the right. If the identity of the consignee could not be disclosed to him it was in practice impossible for him to proceed with his case. The Regulation could not therefore be understood as precluding disclosure to the holder of the right of the information which he needs.

Impact of EC law on national remedies

Although EC law does not in principle prescribe specific remedies and procedures to be adopted by national courts in actions based on EC law, the obligation to ensure that national remedies are effective, or sufficiently effective, to protect individuals' Community rights has on occasions required the modification of national law, even the provision of new remedies. These will now be considered, bearing in mind that some of the earlier cases might be decided differently today.

Interim relief In *R v Secretary of State for Transport, ex parte Factortame Ltd* (case C–213/89) the Court held that English courts were obliged to provide interim injunctions against the Crown where there was no other means of protecting individuals' Community rights, even though, as the House of Lords had found in that case ([1990] 2 AC 85), no such remedy was available as a matter of national law. Following the ECJ's ruling, the House of Lords granted the requested relief ([1991] 1 AC 603 at 645). In *Zuckerfabrik Süderdithmarschen AG* (cases C–143/88, 92/89) the ECJ laid down *Community* criteria for the granting of interim relief pending a ruling from the ECJ under Article 177 (now 234) on the validity of a Community Act, based on the principles applicable to the exercise of its own jurisdiction to grant such relief under Articles 185 and 186 (now 242 and 243) EC. Relief should be granted only if the facts and legal circumstances are such as to persuade the court that:

(a)   serious doubts exist about the validity of the Community measures on which the contested administrative decision is based,
(b)   in cases of urgency, and
(c)   to avoid serious and irreparable damage to the party seeking the relief.

Given that the granting of interim relief pending a ruling on the *validity* of Community law involved a new situation for national courts, and that the suspension of a Community act would have serious implications for the Community legal order, it is not surprising that the Court provided a common Community solution here. However, although it might have been desirable, in the interests of the coherence of legal remedies, to require national courts to apply the same criteria in a claim for interim relief pending a ruling on the *interpretation* of Community law, the Court is not now likely to do so. Thus, in this context, national procedural rules will continue to apply. It may be noted that in *R* v *Secretary of State for Health, ex parte Imperial Tobacco Ltd* (*The Times*, 16 November 1999, QBD) Turner J. considered it unnecessary to apply the criteria provided by the ECJ *in Zucherfabrik Suderdithmarschen AG* in a claim for an interim injunction to prevent the enactment of domestic regulations banning tobacco advertising pending a ruling from the ECJ on the validity of the Directive on which the regulations were based. He preferred to apply the domestic criteria applicable to claims for interim relief, thereby 'avoiding the problem of the applicant having to prove that the damage that he would suffer in the absence of the grant of suspensory relief would be irreparable'. However, his justification, on the facts perhaps acceptable, was that in this case the date for implementation of the Directive, 30 July 2001, had not yet been passed; thus an interim injunction would not have the effect of suspending the application of an *existing* EC obligation.

Zuckerfabrik Süderdithmarschen AG concerned the granting of *suspensory* measures pending a ruling on the validity of a Community measure under Article 177 (now 234). In *Atlanta Fruchthandelsgesellschaft mbH* (case C–465/93) the Court held, in the context of a claim for interim relief in the form of a grant of licences to import bananas from third countries pending a ruling on the validity of a Council Regulation setting up a common banana regime, that the principles laid down in *Zuckerfabrik Süderdithmarschen AG* also applied to the grant of *positive* measures. It was not possible to make a distinction between an order designed to preserve an existing position and an order intended to create a new legal position. In deciding whether to grant such relief, national courts must respect existing decisions from the ECJ on the matter in question whether under Article 177 (now 234) or Article 173 (now 230); they must take into account the Community interest, particularly the damage which the non-application of a Community Regulation may cause to an established Community regime. National courts may also consider the repercussions which an interim order may entail on important individual interests and even on national interests, economic and social. Furthermore, if the grant of interim relief represents a financial risk for the Community the national court must be in a position to require the applicant to provide adequate guarantees, such as the deposit of money or other security. Thus the decision whether or not to grant interim relief is a difficult one, not to be taken lightly, particularly when it involves the suspension of a normative act, a Community Regulation, as was the case in *Atlanta Fruchthandelsgesellschaft mbH*.

Zuckerfabrik Süderdithmarschen AG and *Atlanta Fruchthandelsgesellschaft mbH* concerned the national courts' powers to grant interim relief pending a ruling from the ECJ on the validity of a Community Act, a Regulation. In the more recent case of *T. Port GmbH & Co. KG v Bundesanstalt für Landwirtschaft und Ernährung* (case C–68/95), the CFI refused to take the next logical step when it held that national courts had no power to order interim measures pending a decision on the EC institutions' *failure to act*. Indeed the national courts had no jurisdiction to refer questions concerning such alleged failures to the ECJ. Judicial review of alleged failures on the part of the institutions could only be carried out by the Community courts. Given the limited access of individuals to the Community courts under Article 232 (ex 175) EC this decision appears to have left a gap in the judicial protection of individuals (see further chapter 31).

In the light of the ECJ's decision in *Antonissen* (case C–393/96 P/R) that an individual's right to effective judicial protection may on occasions only be guaranteed by an interim award of damages (albeit subject to rigorous criteria), and the principle of effective judicial protection, it may be questioned whether a rule of British law which altogether prevents our courts from requiring the Crown (see *R v Secretary of State for Transport, ex parte Factortame Ltd (No. 2)* [1991] 1 AC 603) or a local authority (*Kirklees Metropolitan Council Borough Council v Wickes Building Supplies Ltd* [1993] AC 227) to give cross-undertakings in damages as a condition for granting or refusing interim relief is compatible with EC law.

Challenge to statutory provisions   Claims based on Community law will often involve a challenge to legislative acts or omissions. In many cases the challenge is indirect, ancillary to the principal action based on Community law. If the national court finds the provisions of a national statute incompatible with Community law, it may grant the remedy requested and simply 'disapply' them, on the principles established in *Simmenthal SpA (No. 2)* (case 106/77, see chapter 5). The case of *R v Secretary of State for Employment, ex parte Equal Opportunities Commission* concerned a direct challenge to a domestic statute, something which is clearly not permitted in British law. The Equal Opportunities Commission applied for a declaration that certain provisions of the Employment Protection (Consolidation) Act 1978 were contrary to Community sex discrimination law and an order of mandamus requiring the Secretary of State to rectify the breach. A majority of the Court of Appeal thought that it would be 'wrong and unconstitutional for the Courts to grant a declaration or mandamus in an attempt to enforce obligations of Community law which, if they existed, did so only in international law' ([1993] 1 WLR 872). The House of Lords disagreed, and granted a declaration that the provisions in question were *incompatible* with EC law (the claim for mandamus was not pursued) ([1995] 1 AC 1). There was no need to declare that the UK or the Secretary of State were in *breach* of their obligations under Community law. A declaration of incompatibility would suffice for the purposes sought by the EOC and was capable of being granted consistently with the precedent afforded by *Factortame (No. 2)* [1991] AC 603.

Damages In *Marshall (No. 2)* (case C–271/91) the ECJ, applying the effectiveness principle in a claim for damages against an employer, based on Equal Treatment Directive 76/207, held that where damages were awarded for breaches of individuals' rights under the Directive national courts must provide 'full' compensation, including interest on the award from the date of judgment. A system in which compensation was subject to statutory limits, as provided under the UK Sex Discrimination Act 1975, would not be 'sufficiently effective to achieve the objectives of the Directive'. A principle of full compensation required that 'reparation be commensurate with the loss or damage sustained' (see also *Bonifaci*, cases C–94/95, C–95/95). Applying this principle in *Brasserie du Pêcheur*, cases C–46 & 48/93) the ECJ held that a 'total exclusion' of loss of profit as a head of damage would not be permissible. Even an award of exemplary damages 'could not be ruled out' if such damages could be awarded pursuant to a similar claim or action founded on domestic law (para. 89).

However, in recent years the Court has been prepared to accept some limits to the principle of full compensation. In *R v Secretary of State for Social Security, ex parte Sutton* (case C–66/95), in a claim based on EC Directive 79/7 on equal treatment for men and women in social security, it accepted a statutory bar on the payment of interest on an award of damages, even though the wording of the Directive on which the applicants sought to rely, requiring Member States to ensure that persons alleging discrimination are able to 'pursue their claims by judicial process', was virtually identical to that on which the applicants based their claim in *Marshall (No. 2)* (case C–271/91). *Marshall* was distinguished on the basis that there the award of interest was an 'essential component of compensation for the purpose of ensuring real equality of treatment'; By contrast, *Sutton* 'concerned social security benefits paid by the competent bodies which must . . . examine whether the conditions laid down in the relevant legislation were fulfilled'. The amounts paid 'in no way constituted reparation for loss or damage sustained'. The distinction is fine, and may be seen as an example of the Court's more cautious approach following criticisms of its activism expressed by some Member States in the period leading up to the ToA. The Court in *Sutton* was similarly reserved in its comments on the possibility of recovery of interest on arrears of payment in an alternative claim based on *Francovich*. It enunciated the principles governing state liability in damages but insisted that it was for the national court to assess, in the light of those principles, whether the claimant was entitled to reparation for the loss she had suffered.

However, *Marshall (No. 2)* was followed in *Draehmpaehl v Urania Immobilienservice OHG* (case C–180/95), a case decided on the same day as *Sutton*. Here, in a claim by a man, the Court held that a limit of three months' wages as compensation for sex discrimination as regards access to employment (the job advertisement requested female applicants), and a six-month aggregate limit where several applicants were involved, would not guarantee effective judicial protection for individuals' Community rights. A three-month limit would only be acceptable as reasonable if the employer could prove that the applicants would not have been given the job in the absence of discrimination. Clearly, if the applicant would have been given the job in the absence of discrimination, the limits on compensation in this case would not have been sufficient to compensate for the damage sustained.

Restitution There have been many claims before national courts for the return of money paid in breach of Community law. The EC Treaty prohibits the imposition of customs duties or charges having equivalent effect, and discriminatory taxation (see chapters 8 and 9). These charges are normally levied by national authorities. As early as 1960 the ECJ held, in the context of a claim for sums levied in breach of the ECSC treaty, that once a Member State had been found to have breached Community law it must take the necessary measures to make good the lawful effects of the breach, making restitution for sums wrongfully levied as a result of that breach (*Humblet* v *Belgium* (case 6/60)). There is now a consistent line of authority to this effect (see, e.g., *Express Dairy Foods Ltd* v *Intervention Board for Agricultural Produce* (case 130/79)). Prior to the House of Lords' decision in *Woolwich Equitable Building Society* v *Inland Revenue Commissioners* [1993] AC 70, it was thought that there was no general right under English law to the recovery of money paid under a mistake of law. Since sums paid in breach of Community law would normally be paid under a mistake of law, such a rule would not have been 'sufficiently effective' to protect individuals' Community rights. This factor undoubtedly coloured the House of Lords' finding in *Woolwich Equitable Building Society* v *Inland Revenue Commissioners*, in the context of a claim based on domestic law, that money paid under a mistake of law was in certain circumstances recoverable as a matter of British law. 'It would be strange,' said Lord Goff, 'if the right of the citizen to recover overpaid taxes were to be more restricted under domestic law than European law'.

Limitation periods: the rise and fall of Emmott The effectiveness principle has also been invoked to challenge national limitation rules. In *Express Dairy Foods Ltd* v *Intervention Board for Agricultural Produce* (case 130/79) the Court suggested that a 'reasonable' period of limitation would not make it 'impossible in practice' for national courts effectively to protect individuals' Community rights. This principle, consistently invoked, was put in doubt in by the Court's decision in *Emmott* v *Minister for Social Welfare* (case C–208/90), decided in 1991.

The case concerned a challenge to the Irish authorities' refusal to grant Ms Emmott disability benefit. She claimed that this was discriminatory, in breach of Directive 79/7 on equal treatment for men and women in matters of social security. At the time when her cause of action arose she was unaware that it was directly effective. When she became aware that it was, following a ruling from the Court in *McDermott* v *Minister for Social Welfare* (case 286/85) she applied to the Minister for her case to be reviewed. Her application was deferred pending a ruling from the ECJ in *Cotter* v *Minister for Social Welfare* (case C–377/89). When she was finally granted leave to institute proceedings, she was found to be out of time. The Irish judge referred to the ECJ to ascertain whether it was contrary to Community law for the authorities of a

Member State to rely on national procedural rules, in particular relating to time limits, in defending claims based on Community Directives. The Minister argued that, even though a Directive had not been implemented, or properly implemented, the principle of direct effects enabled the individual effectively to assert his Community rights, at least against a 'public' body. The Court disagreed. It held that the principle of direct effects provided only a minimum guarantee: as long as a Directive has not been properly implemented the individual is in a state of uncertainty; the individual is unaware of the full extent of his or her rights. Therefore the competent authorities of Member States cannot rely, in an action against them based on the Directive, on national procedural rules relating to time limits for bringing proceedings as long as that Member State has not properly implemented that Directive into national law.

This decision, expressed in the broadest terms, gave rise to some alarm in Member States. It might be acceptable in a case in which the State's failure to implement a Community Directive is clear, or when, as in *Emmott*'s case, it was 'excessively difficult', as a result of action by the national authorities, for the claimant to enforce her rights. But it was likely to cause injustice, contrary to the principle of legal certainty, when applied in cases of inadvertent failure on the part of the State and when it exposed public bodies, acting bona fide according to their legitimate understanding of the law, to a flood of retrospective claims. It might be years before a Directive was found not to have been 'properly' implemented into national law. Nor was it clear whether *Emmott* applied solely to the non or faulty implementation of Directives. The reasoning on which the decision was based might be applied to any breach of Community law, including claims under *Francovich* v *Italy* (cases C–6 & 9/90).

Perhaps recognising that it had gone too far, the Court distinguished *Emmott* in *Steenhorst-Neerings* (case C–338/91). Here it held that a statutory limit on the retrospective payment of invalidity benefit (thus not in itself a limitation period, although similar in its effect) was not contrary to EC law, being justified by the need to preserve the financial equilibrium of social security funds. There was a difference between national rules fixing time limits for bringing an action, as in *Emmott*, and rules which merely limited the retroactive effect of claims. *Steenhorst-Neerings* was followed, on similar facts, in *Johnson* v *Chief Adjudication Officer* (case C–410/92), in which the benefit in question was non-contributory, therefore posing no threat to the financial balance of social security funds (see also *Alonso-Pérez* v *Bundesanstat für Arbeit* (case C–394/93), three-month ceiling on the retrospective payment of family benefits did not render the exercise of Community rights impossible). *Emmott* was further narrowed in *Peterbroeck* (case C–312/93), in which a Belgian procedural rule, preventing litigants from raising new pleas more than 60 days after the lodging of an administrative decision, was found not to be objectionable *per se*, although on the facts it could not be accepted, since it prevented the national court from raising the question of the compatibility of the measure in question with Community law before the ECJ under the then Article 177 (now 234). The Court held that:

. . . each case which raises the question of whether a national procedural provision renders application of Community law impossible or excessively difficult must be analysed by reference to the role of that provision in the procedure, its progress and its special features, viewed as a whole, before the various national instances. In the light of that analysis the basic principles of the domestic legal system, such as protection of the *rights of the defence, the principle of legal certainty*, and the *proper conduct of procedure, must*, where appropriate, *be taken into consideration* (para. 14).

In the light of these principles, Advocate-General Jacobs suggested in *Denkavit International BV* v *Kamer van Koophandel en Fabrieken voor Midden-Gelderland* (case C–2/94) that a 30-day limitation period prescribed in Holland for challenge to a routine administrative decision, based on EC Directive 69/335, would be acceptable: it did not make reliance on Community law 'virtually impossible or excessively difficult'. He suggested that Community law did not preclude reliance on such limits, even where the relevant Directive had not been implemented in national law. He further suggested that *Emmott* should be confined to the 'particular circumstances of the case', where a Member State was in default both in failing to implement a Directive and in obstructing the exercise of a judicial remedy in reliance on it, or where the failure to meet the time limit was in some way due to the conduct of the national authorities. In the interests of legal certainty, the obligation to set aside time limits should be confined to 'wholly exceptional circumstances' such as obtained in *Emmott*. Regrettably, in view of its finding on the main issue, the ECJ did not find it necessary to rule on the legality of the 30-day limitation period. However, in *Fantask A/S* v *Industriministeriet* (case C–188/95) the ECJ accepted a Danish statutory five-year limitation period for the recovery of debts, running from the date on which the debt became payable, in the context of a challenge to the Ministry's refusal to reimburse company registration charges levied from the applicant in breach of EC Directive 69/335. The Court held (at para. 48) that it had:

acknowledged, in the interests of legal certainty, which protects the taxpayer and the authorities concerned, that the setting of reasonable limitation periods for bringing proceedings [was] compatible with Community law. Such periods cannot be regarded as rendering impossible or excessively difficult the exercise of rights conferred by Community law, even if the expiry of those periods necessarily entails the dismissal, in whole or in part, of the action brought.

This paragraph was cited by the Court in *Levez* (case C–326/96) and *EDIS* (case C–231/96).

The five-year limitation period was re-examined in *Fantask* and found to be neither discriminatory nor unreasonable. Distinguishing *Emmott*, the Court held that *Emmott* was 'justified on the particular facts of the case, in which the time bar had the result of *depriving the applicant of any opportunity whatsoever* to rely on her right to equal treatment under the Community Directive'.

Similar thinking, albeit to different effect, lay behind the Court's ruling in *Magorrian* v *Eastern Health and Social Services Board* (case C–246/96). This case concerned a claim for the retrospective payment of certain pension benefits to which the applicant, a female part-time worker, found she was entitled under Article 119 (now 141) EC following a ruling from the ECJ (see *Fisscher* (case C–128/93), chapter 25). Her claim, which related to the period from 1976 to 1990, was subject to a two-year limitation period running from the date of commencement of her action. The defendant Board opposed her claim, relying on *Steenhorst-Neerings* and *Johnson*. The Court distinguished these cases. The claim in this case was not, it held, for the retrospective award of certain additional benefits but for the recognition of entitlement to full membership of an occupational scheme through acquisition of MHO status, which confers entitlement to the additional benefits. The two-year limitation rule prevented the entire record of service from 1976 to 1990 being taken into account for the purposes of calculating the additional benefits which would be payable even after the date of the claim. It thus 'struck at the very essence' of the applicant's rights and would not be permissible under Community law. The ECJ took the same view of the same rule in *Preston* v *Wolverhampton NHS Healthcare Trust* (case C-78/98).

Thus it seems that reasonable limitation rules will be acceptable, since they do not render the exercise of Community rights impossible or excessively difficult; but where they 'deprive the applicant of any opportunity whatsoever' to rely on her rights, or 'strike at the very essence of those rights', or where the applicant has been misled as to her Community rights, as in *Levez*, they will not be permitted. The trend of case law since *Emmott* indicates that the Court will be slow to regard Member States' limitation rules as unreasonable. In *Preston* v *Wolverhampton NHS Healthcare Trust* (case C-78/98), in contrast to its finding on the two-year limitation rule, the ECJ found a six-month bar on proceedings (following termination of employment) acceptable under EC law. Nevertheless, the acceptance of reasonable limitation rules will inevitably operate to modify the principle of full compensation, as occurred in *Fantask* (case C–188/95), in which the applicant sought, unsuccessfully, to recover company registration charges levied in breach of Community law over a nine-year period, from 1983 to 1992. The limits of what will be regarded as reasonable remain unclear.

State non-contractual liability   *Francovich* (cases C–6 & 9/90) established the principle of State liability in damages for breaches of Community law, and laid down three basic conditions for liability. *Brasserie du Pêcheur* (cases C–46 & 48/93) clarified the scope of that principle and fleshed out these conditions. Member States were to be liable for *all* breaches of Community law, legislative, executive and judicial, whether the Community law breached was directly effective or not, provided that the three conditions for liability were met:

(a)   the rule of Community law infringed must be intended to confer rights on individuals;

(b)   the breach of Community law must be 'sufficiently serious'; and

(c)   there must be a direct causal link between the breach of the obligation resting on the state and the damage sustained by the injured parties.

Following *Brasserie du Pêcheur* it is clear that condition (b), the question of whether the breach of Community law is 'sufficiently serious', is a matter of *Community* law, to be decided by national courts according to the criteria laid down in *Brasserie du Pêcheur* (see further chapter 4). Although the ECJ has not been asked to rule on condition (a), its approach in the cases involving State liability, starting with *Francovich*, and the opinions of the Advocates-General in those cases, indicate that it will be interpreted by analogy with the Court's approach to individuals' rights under the principle of direct effects, as has occurred in the English courts (see e.g. *Three Rivers District Council* v *Bank of England* (1996) 3 All ER 558; *Bowden* v *S West Water Services* (1999) 3 CMLR 180 (CA)). However, until the Court rules specifically on this matter its scope as a principle of Community law is unclear. On the other hand it was made clear in *Brasserie du Pêcheur* that condition (c) 'requiring a causative link between the State's breach and the applicant's damage' continues to be determined according to the principles applicable to equivalent claims based on national law, although the Court suggested that the causal link should be 'direct'. The case of *Brinkman* (case C–319/96) was decided on the basis of causation. The case concerned a claim for damages for losses suffered as a result of the Danish authorities' allegedly wrongful implementation of Directive 79/32 on taxes affecting the consumption of manufactured tobacco. On importation the applicant's product (unwrapped tobacco rolls) had been classified as cigarettes rather than smoking tobacco, and as such subjected to a higher rate of duty. Although the Directive had not been implemented by ministerial decree the Danish authorities had given immediate effect to its relevant provisions. The Court found that the authorities had committed a breach of EC law, having interpreted the Directive incorrectly; but they would not be liable since there was no direct causal link between their breach and the damage suffered by the applicant. Denmark's failure to transpose the Directive had not caused the applicants damage. However the Court refrained from providing a Community definition of causation. It must therefore be assumed that questions of causation will continue to be determined on the basis of national law, subject to the requirement that the causal link be direct. This appears to have been presumed in *Rechberger* (case C–140/97). Here, in considering the Austrian government's liability for failing adequately to transpose Directive 90/314 EEC on package travel the ECJ pointed out that the Austrian court had found that there was a direct causal link between that failure and the damage suffered by the applicant. The government's argument that imprudent conduct on the part of the travel organiser or the occurrence of exceptional and unforeseeable events might break that causal link was not accepted. As the ECJ pointed out, it is submitted correctly, such circumstances would not have presented an obstacle to the refund of money paid over or the repatriation of consumers if the guarantee system had been put in place in accordance with the requirements of the Directive.

Thus the principle of State liability remains a hybrid, part national, part Community law. This has created problems for national courts. Prior to *Brasserie du Pêcheur* it was assumed, following *Francovich*, that a claim for damages against the State must be brought on the same basis, and according to the same rules, as the 'equivalent' claim based on national law. However, although the claim in English law would clearly be in the nature of a tort it was not clear which tort was appropriate. The nearest 'equivalent' actions available against a public authority, the torts of misfeasance in public office, of breach of statutory duty, or of negligence, were, as the Court found in *Brasserie du Pêcheur*, too restrictive to provide effective protection for individuals' Community rights under *Francovich*. A similar problem had arisen in the context of claims for damages based on the principle of direct effects (see, e.g., *Garden Cottage Foods Ltd* v *Milk Marketing Board* [1984] AC 130 (HL); *Bourgoin SA* v *Ministry of Agriculture, Fisheries and Food* [1986] QB 716 (CA)). Furthermore, English law admitted no claim for damages in respect of legislative or judicial acts. Thus the only way in which individuals' rights under *Francovich* might be effectively protected was either by 'modifying' (i.e. reinterpreting) the existing national remedies of misfeasance or breach of statutory duty (negligence having been rejected as clearly inappropriate), resulting in the possibility of a different standard of liability, depending on whether the claim was based on national or Community law, or by admitting that the Community principle of state liability was a new principle calling for the creation of a new *sui generis* 'Francovich' tort.

In applying the ECJ's ruling in *R* v *Secretary of State for Transport, ex parte Factortame Ltd (No. 5)* [1998] 1 CMLR 1353 Hobhouse LJ in the English High Court adopted a compromise position. He examined the question of breach, and the seriousness of the breach, according to the principles laid down by the ECJ in *Brasserie du Pêcheur*. He concluded that 'whilst it could be said that the cause of action was *sui generis*, it was of the character of a breach of statutory duty'. He could find no similarity between the applicants' claim in respect of the UK's breach of its Community obligations and a claim in respect of tortious misfeasance. Thus, if the English courts were to follow his lead and treat claims based on *Francovich* as breaches of statutory duty, they would do so on the understanding that such claims could be subject to different principles, and a different approach to interpretation, from those which apply to similar claims based on domestic law. Given that the ECJ has now laid down a number of precise conditions for State liability, it is submitted that it would be better to acknowledge the unique nature of such a claim, based on the breach of a higher legal norm, and treat it as a *sui generis* tort. This now appears to have occurred. Both the Court of Appeal and the House of Lords in *Factortame (No. 5)* dealt with the matter of liability simply by applying the principles of Community law laid down by the ECJ in *Brasserie du Pêcheur*. Likewise, shortly after the final decision in *Factortame (No. 5)*, Sullivan J in the English High Court, in assessing the seriousness of the public authorities' breach of Directive 79/7 in *R* v *Department of Social Security, ex parte Scullion* ([1999] 3 CMLR 798), adopted the 'basket' or 'global' approach laid down by the ECJ in para. 56 of *Brasserie du Pêcheur* (cases C–46 & 48/93) see chapter 4) and made no attempt to fit a claim for damages based on *Francovich* into the straight-jacket of the English law of torts.

However, regrettably, as noted above, the rules governing State liability laid down in *Brasserie du Pêcheur* were not comprehensive. It was left to national courts to decide, according to the principles applicable to equivalent claims based on national law, whether the Community law breached was intended to benefit persons such as the applicant (condition (a)); whether there existed the appropriate direct causal link between the State's breach and the applicant's damage (condition (c)); and whether the damage suffered was of a kind in respect of which damages might be awarded.

In *Three Rivers District Council v Bank of England* [1996] 3 All ER 558, a case decided shortly before *Factortame (No. 5)*, the English High Court was faced with a claim for damages based on breach of statutory duty for the Bank's failure to supervise the credit institutions (notably BCCI), resulting in damage to the investors. The applicant investors argued that the failure was in breach of EC Banking Directive 77/780. Their claim was based on the direct effects of the Directive or, in the alternative, *Francovich*. Clarke J, applying the English approach to construction in claims based on breach of statutory duty, found that the Directive in question was not intended to give rise to rights to individuals. Nor, for the same reason, did the applicants have a claim under *Francovich*. Whether their claim was based on the direct effects of Directive 77/780 or on *Francovich*, the applicants must establish the relevant Community rights required to be protected. The result required by the Directive did not extend to the compensation of savers for any breach of the duties imposed by the Directive. On appeal to the House of Lords, the appellants argued their claim for damages under the English tort of misfeasance in public office, as well as on Community law. Again they failed (*The Times*, 19 May 2000). The House found that the respondents did not have the requisite intention or recklessness for liability in misfeasance; nor were the obligations in the Directive allegedly breached sufficiently well defined to give rise to rights for individuals.

Like Clarke J in the High Court in the *Three Rivers* case, the English Court of Appeal in *Bowden v South West Water Services* [1999] 3 CMLR 180, focused on the first condition of *Francovich*, whether the Community law allegedly breached was intended to confer rights on the applicant. It construed Environmental Directive 79/903 as intended to benefit persons such as the claimant, whose living as a fisherman had been affected by the defendant's alleged failure properly to implement the Directive, and allowed his claim to proceed. It is submitted that an applicant who has suffered damage as a result of alleged breaches of Community law should not be turned away because of an over-restrictive approach to the question of individual rights, a notoriously slippery and subjective concept. Liability can always be restricted or excluded, where this is justified, under the second or third conditions of *Francovich*, on the basis of the seriousness of the breach or the directness of the damage.

It is a matter for regret that the ECJ, in laying down common Community rules concerning the nature of the breach required to give rise to liability, failed to provide some common rules or guidelines covering *all* aspects of liability, since, particularly in the area of non-contractual liability, the rules relating to breach and damage and causation are interrelated, and operate together as control mechanisms restricting or extending liability according to perceived requirements of policy. While the overall result may not differ greatly from State to State the individual elements vary considerably. Thus as long as the principle of national treatment applies in any of these areas there will be inequality in the application of the principle of State liability from State to State. There will also be uncertainty, since national rules are vulnerable to attack as being ineffective, or insufficiently effective, to protect individuals' rights. However, given the ECJ's unequivocal affirmation of the principle of national treatment in recent years, further judicial development of common Community rules appears unlikely.

Although a principle of State liability for executive acts, and judicial remedies in respect of such acts, already exists in all Member States, these claims will now also be subject to the rules laid down in *Brasserie du Pêcheur*. *Haim* v *Kassenzahnartzliche Vereinigung Nordrhein* (case C-424/97) has established that a legally independent body may be liable under *Francovich*, as well as the Member State itself. As with legislative acts, existing national remedies may need to be modified to ensure that they are effective in protecting individuals' rights; alternatively (and preferably) claims may be brought under a new *Francovich* tort.

A principle of liability for judicial acts in breach of Community law, as laid down in *Brasserie du Pêcheur*, clearly breaks new constitutional ground in most if not all Member States. If available in theory, it is unlikely to be applied freely in practice. If only for reasons of polity, neither the ECJ nor a national court is likely to find a judicial breach of Community law sufficiently serious to warrant liability.

Conclusions

The role played by the ECJ in securing the enforcement of Community law against both EC institutions and Member States cannot be overstated. Recognising and respecting the limitations of the remedies provided under the EC Treaty, it has provided, via the principles of direct effects, indirect effects, and State liability in damages, an extremely effective alternative means of enforcement of Community law by individuals, within the courts of Member States. It has insisted on the effective protection of individuals' Community rights by these courts, even when the rights have not been expressly, or even impliedly, granted to individuals. This principle of effective judicial protection has revealed the deficiencies in national legal systems and extended the scope of legal protection of individuals in matters of Community law. This has spilt, and will continue to spill, over into domestic law, raising the standard of judicial protection in matters of purely national law: national courts are rightly reluctant to apply a double standard. This process has resulted in some harmonisation of remedies in the legal systems of Member States.

However, the Court has on occasions gone too far. In requiring national courts to give effect to individuals' Community 'rights' it has imposed obligations on both Member States and individuals, even when the scope, and even the existence of these rights, is far from clear. For this reason sometimes its rulings under Article 234 (ex 177), as in *Marshall (No. 2)* and *Emmott*, have been criticised. Hence the threat by Member States to reduce the jurisdiction of the Court at Amsterdam. Fortunately this was not done. However, the Court has clearly taken heed of Member States' concerns and since that time proceeded, where it has proceeded, cautiously.

Further reading

Albors-Llorens, A., 'Changes in the Jurisdiction of the European Court of Justice under the Treaty of Amsterdam' (1998) 35 CML Rev 1273.

Barav, A., 'The Enforcement of Community Rights in the National Courts: the Case for Jurisdiction to Grant Interim Relief' (1989) 26 CML Rev 369.

Bebr, G., Casenote on *Francovich* (1992) 29 CML Rev 557.

Bell, 'Enforcing Community Rights before National Courts: Some Developments' (1994) LIEI 111.

Biondi, A., 'The ECJ and certain national procedural limitations: not such a tough relationship' (1999) 36 CML Rev 1271.

Bridge, D., 'Procedural Aspects of the Enforcement of EEC Law through the Legal Systems of the Member States' (1985) 10 EL Rev 28.

Caranta, R., 'Judicial Protection against Member States: a new Jus Commune takes shape' (1995) 32 CML Rev 679.

Caranta, R., 'Learning from our Neighbours: Public Law Remedies Homogenization from Bottom Up' (1997) MJ 220.

Convery, J., 'State Liability in the UK after *Brasserie du Pêcheur*' (1997) 34 CML Rev 603.

Coppell, J., 'Domestic Limitations on Recovery for Breach of EC Law' (1998) ILJ 259.

Craig, P., *Francovich*, Remedies and the Scope of Damages Liability' (1993) 109 LQR 595.

Craig, P., 'Once more unto the Breach: the Community, the State and Damages Liability' (1997) 113 LQR 67.

Fennelly, N., 'The Area of Freedom, Security and Justice and the European Court of Justice' (2000) 46 ICLQ 941.

Gravells, N., 'Disapplying an Act of Parliament: Constitutional Enormity or Community Law Right?' [1989] PL 568.

Himsworth, C., 'Things Fall Apart: the Harmonisation of Community Judicial Protection Revisited' (1997) 22 EL Rev 291.

Hoskins, M., 'Tilting the Balance: Supremacy and National Procedural Rules' (1996) 21 EL Rev 365.

Howe, Lord, (1996) 21 EL Rev 187.

Jacque, J. P., and Weiler, J., 'On the Road to European Union: a New Judicial Architecture: an Agenda for the Intergovernmental Conference' (1990) 27 CML Rev 185.

Lang, J.T., 'Community Constitutional Law: Article 5 EEC Treaty' (1990) 27 CML Rev 645.

Lang, J.T., 'The Duties of National Courts under Community Constitutional Law' (1997) 22 EL Rev 3.

Lang, J.T., 'The Duties of National Authorities under Community Law' (1998) 23 EL Rev 109.

Oliver, P., 'Enforcing Community Rights in English Courts' (1987) 50 MLR 881.

Prechal, S., 'Community Law in National Courts: The lessons from *Van Schijndel*' (1998) 35 CML Rev 681.

Ross, M., 'Refining Effective Enjoyment' (1990) 15 EL Rev 476.

Ross, M., 'Beyond *Francovich*' (1993) 56 MLR 55.

Ruffert, M., 'Rights and Remedies in EC Law: a Comparative View' (1997) 34 CML Rev 307.

Snyder, F., 'The Effectiveness of European Community Law' (1993) 56 MLR 19.

Steiner, J., 'How to Make the Action Fit the Case: Domestic Remedies for Breach of EEC Law' (1987) 12 EL Rev 102.

Steiner, J., 'From Direct Effects to *Francovich*' (1993) 18 EL Rev 3.

Steiner, J., *Enforcing EC Law* (1995, Blackstone Press).

Steiner, J., 'The Limits of State Liability for Breach of European Community Law' [1998] EPL 69.

Szyczak, E., 'Making Europe More Relevant to its Citizens' (1996) 21 EL Rev 351.

Tridimas, N., (1996) 21 EL Rev 199.

Tridimas, N., 'Enforcing Community Rights in National Courts: some recent developments' (2000) YEL Forthcoming.

Van Gerven, W., 'Bridging the Gap between Community and national law: towards a principle of homogeneity of legal remedies' (1995) 32 CML Rev 679.

Woods, L. and Smith, F., 'Causation in *Francovich*: The Neglected Problem' (1997) 46 ICLQ 925.

Wyatt, D., 'Enforcing EEC Social Rights in the UK' (1989) 18 ILJ 191.

TWENTY SEVEN

Article 234 (ex 177) EC and the preliminary rulings procedure

Introduction

A glance through the preceding chapters of this book will reveal that the majority of cases cited, and almost all the major principles established by the ECJ, were decided in the context of a reference to that court for a preliminary ruling under what was originally Article 177 (now 234) EC. Cases such as *Van Gend en Loos* (case 26/62), *Costa* v *ENEL* (case 6/64) and *Defrenne* v *Sabena (No. 2)* (case 43/75), concerned with questions of interpretation of EC law, enabled the ECJ to develop the crucial concepts of direct effects and the supremacy of EC law. *Internationale Handelsgesellschaft mbH* (case 11/70); *Stauder* v *City of Ulm* (case 29/69) and *Royal Scholten-Honig (Holdings) Ltd* (cases 103 & 145/77) (see chapters 6 and 29), which raised questions of the validity of EC law, led the way to the incorporation of general principles of law into EC law. The principle of State liability in damages was laid down in *Francovich* (cases C–6, 9/90) in Article 177 (now 234) proceedings. In all areas of EC law, the Article 234 (ex 177) procedure has played a major role in developing the substantive law. Staff cases apart (the ECJ has jurisdiction under Article 236 (ex 179) to decide disputes between the Community and its servants), the procedure accounts for over 50 per cent of all cases heard by the ECJ. This percentage has of course increased as the CFI has taken over responsibility for judicial review actions (chapters 30 and 31) and actions for damages (chapter 32). Nonetheless, the preliminary rulings procedure plays a central part in the development and enforcement of EC law.

If the procedure has been valuable from the point of view of the Community, as a means of developing and clarifying the law, it has been equally valuable to the individual, since it has provided him with a means of access to the ECJ when other, direct avenues have been closed. In this way he has been able indirectly to challenge action by Member States (e.g., *Van Gend en Loos* — import charge levied in breach of the then Article 12) or by Community institutions (e.g., *Royal Scholten-Honig* — EC Regulation invalid for breach of principle of equality) before the ECJ and obtain an appropriate remedy from his national court.

The importance of the Article 234 (ex 177) procedure, both in absolute terms and relative to other remedies, has been greatly increased by the development by the ECJ of the concept of direct effects. Where originally only 'directly applicable' Regulations might have been expected to be invoked before national courts, these courts may now be required to apply Treaty Articles, Decisions and even Directives. Even where EC law is not directly effective it may be invoked before national courts on the principles of indirect effects or State liability under *Francovich*. As a result, national courts now play a major role in the enforcement of EC law.

Although the preliminary rulings procedure has assumed such an importance in the ways outlined above, its primary and original purpose was to ensure, by means of authoritative rulings on the interpretation and validity of EC law, the correct and uniform application of EC law by the courts of Member States. In assessing its effectiveness, and the attitudes of national courts and the ECJ towards its use, this function, as well as its importance both for individuals and for the Community, should be borne in mind.

The procedure

Article 234 (ex 177) EC provides that:

> The Court of Justice shall have jurisdiction to give preliminary rulings concerning:
> (a)   the interpretation of this Treaty;
> (b)   the validity and interpretation of acts of the institutions of the Community;
> (c)   the interpretation of the statutes of bodies established by an act of the Council, where those statutes so provide.
>
> Where such a question is raised before any court or tribunal of a Member State, that court or tribunal may, if it considers that a decision on the question is necessary to enable it to give judgment, request the Court of Justice to give a ruling thereon.
>
> Where any such question is raised in a case pending before a court or tribunal of a Member State, against whose decisions there is no judicial remedy under national law, that court or tribunal shall bring the matter before the Court of Justice.

The preliminary rulings procedure is not an appeals procedure. It merely provides a means whereby national courts, when questions of EC law arise, may apply to the ECJ for a preliminary ruling on matters of interpretation or validity prior to themselves applying the law. It is an example of shared jurisdiction, depending for its success on mutual cooperation. As Advocate-

General Lagrange said in *De Geus en Uitdenbogerd* v *Robert Bosch GmbH* (case 13/61), the first case to reach the Court on an application under the then Article 177:

Applied judiciously — one is tempted to say loyally — the provisions of Article 177 [now 234] must lead to a real and fruitful collaboration between the municipal courts and the Court of Justice of the Communities with mutual regard for their respective jurisdiction.

In order to assess how this collaboration operates, in principle and in practice, it is necessary to examine the procedure from the point of view of: (a) the ECJ, and (b) national courts.

Jurisdiction of the Court of Justice

The jurisdiction of the ECJ is twofold. It has jurisdiction to give preliminary rulings concerning:

(a) interpretation, and
(b) validity.

Interpretation In its interpretative role, the Court may rule on the interpretation of the Treaty, of acts of the institutions, and of statutes of bodies established by an act of the Council, where those statutes so provide. Its jurisdiction with regard to interpretation is thus very wide. 'Interpretation of the Treaty' includes the EC Treaty and all treaties amending or supplementing it. It did not, however, pursuant to original Article L TEU, have jurisdiction to interpret Articles A–F, J and K TEU (save for the third subparagraph of Article K. 3(2)(c) Article K. 3(2)(c)(3)) (*Grau Gomis* (case C–167/94)). As noted in chapter 2, the ToA amended the original Article L (now 46) TEU giving the ECJ jurisdiction in relation to the JHA Pillar of the TEU (subject to the requirement in new Article 35 TEU that Member States must, by declaration, accept the ECJ's jurisdiction) and the TEU provisions on closer cooperation (now Articles 43–45 TEU). These changes will be discussed further below.

'Acts of the institutions' covers not only binding acts in the form of Regulations, Directives and Decisions, but even non-binding acts such as Recommendations and Opinions, since they may be relevant to the interpretation of domestic implementing measures. On the same reasoning the Court has held that an act need not be directly effective to be subject to interpretation under Article 234 (ex 177) (*Mazzalai* (case 111/75)), nor need the party concerned have relied on the act before his national court: that court can raise it before the ECJ of its own motion (*Verholen* (cases 87, 88 & 89/90)). The Court has also given rulings on the interpretation of international treaties entered into by the Community, on the basis that these constitute 'acts of the institutions' (see *R. & V. Haegeman Sprl* v *Belgium* (case 181/73)). This includes 'mixed agreements', such as the WTO agreement, where interpretation relates to obligations under-taken by the Community (*Hermes* (case C–53/96), noted (1999) 36 CML Rev 663). However, it has held in the context of a claim based on the Statute of the European School that it has no jurisdiction to rule on agreements which, although linked with the Community and to the functioning of its institu-tions, have been set up by agreement *between Member States* and not on the basis of the Treaty or EC secondary legislation (*Hurd* v *Jones* (case 44/84) — headmaster of European School unable to invoke Statute against HM Tax Inspectorate).

Validity   Here the Court's jurisdiction is confined to acts of the institutions. It has been suggested, by extension of the reasoning in *R. & V. Haegeman Sprl* v *Belgian State,* that 'acts of the institutions' would include international agreements entered into by the Community. Here, however, the ruling would be binding only on the Community members; it would be ineffective against third-party signatories. The grounds for invalidity are the same as in an action for annulment under Article 230 (ex 173) (see chapter 30).

As with interpretation, Article 46 (ex L) TEU excludes the majority of the TEU from the ECJ's jurisdiction. Although the ECJ has not had to consider the limits to its jurisdiction under Article 46 (ex L) TEU in respect of references for a preliminary ruling, it has had to consider these matters in the context of a judicial review action (*Commission* v *Council (Airport transit visas)* (case C–170/96)). The case concerned the appropriate Treaty base for airport transit visas, the Council arguing that the then Article K.3 TEU (which has been significantly amended by the ToA) was the appropriate base, the Commission (and the Parliament) considering that the then Article 100c EC (repealed by the ToA), which dealt with visas, was more appropriate. The Council claimed that the ECJ had no jurisdiction to hear the case as the then Article L (now 46) TEU applied to exclude the ECJ's jurisdiction. The ECJ emphasised that the then Article L was subject to Article M (now 47) TEU, which provides that nothing in the TEU shall affect the EC Treaty, which the ECJ has interpreted to include the *acquis* (i.e., the entire body of EC law). The ECJ from this basis argued that it had the duty to review measures made under TEU provisions to ensure that they did not erode Community law. Presumably, it would take a similar approach were a similar question to arise under an Article 234 (ex 177) EC reference on validity. This boundary may now be of less significance as the ToA, in amending Article 46 TEU, permitted the ECJ jurisdiction to interpret and review the validity of certain acts and agreements made under the JHA pillar, should the Member States agree thereto (see Article 35 TEU).

One important question in relation to the ECJ's jurisdiction under Article 234 (ex 177) and correspondingly the national courts' right to refer was identified in *T. Port GmbH & Co. KG* v *Bundesanstalt für Landwirtschaft und Ernährung* (case C–68/95). There the ECJ held that the EC Treaty did not, under the then Article 177 (now 234), give the Member States' courts the power to refer questions concerning an EC institution's alleged failure to act. Any such claim would have to be brought under Article 175 (now 232) EC.

Limitations on the Court's jurisdiction

Matters of Community law   The Court is only empowered to give rulings on matters of Community law. It has no jurisdiction to interpret domestic law, nor to pass judgment on the compatibility of domestic law with EC law. The Court has frequently been asked such questions (e.g., *Van Gend en Loos* (case 26/62); *Costa v ENEL* (case 6/64)), since it is often the central problem before the national court. But as the Court said in *Costa v ENEL*: 'a decision should be given by the Court not upon the validity of an Italian law in relation to the Treaty, but only upon the interpretation of the above-mentioned [Treaty] Articles in the context of the points of law stated by the Giudice Concili- atore'. Where the Court is asked to rule on such a matter it will merely reformulate the question and return an abstract interpretation on the point of EC law involved.

Interpretation, not application   The Court maintains a similarly strict dividing line in principle between interpretation and application. It has no jurisdiction to rule on the application of Community law by national courts. However, since the application of Community law often raises problems for national courts, the Court, in its concern to provide national courts with 'practical' or 'worthwhile' rulings, will sometimes, when interpreting Community law, also offer unequivocal guidance as to its application (see e.g., *Stoke-on-Trent City Council v B&Q* (case C–169/91); *R v Her Majesty's Treasury, ex parte British Telecommunications plc* (case C–392/93)).

Non-interference   The Court maintains a strict policy of non-interference over matters of what to refer, when to refer and how to refer. Such matters are left entirely to the discretion of the national judge. As the Court said in *De Geus en Uitdenbogerd v Robert Bosch GmbH* (case 13/61), its jurisdiction depends 'solely on the existence of a request from the national court'. However, it has no jurisdiction to give a ruling when, at the time when it is made, the procedure before the court making it has already been terminated (*Pardini* (case 338/85); *Grogan* (case C–159/90)).

No formal requirements are imposed on the framing of the questions. Where the questions are inappropriately phrased the Court will merely reformulate the questions, answering what it sees as the relevant issues. It may interpret what it regards as the relevant issues even if they are not raised by the referring court (e.g., *OTO SpA v Ministero delle Finanze* (case C–130/92)). Nor will it question the timing of a reference. However, since 'it is necessary for the national court to define the legal context in which the interpretation requested should be placed', the Court has suggested that it might be convenient for the facts of the case to be established and for questions of purely national law to be settled at the time when the reference is made, in order to enable the Court to take cognisance of all the features of fact and law which may be relevant to the interpretation of Community law which it is called upon to give (*Irish Creamery Milk Suppliers Association v Ireland* (cases 36 & 71/80); approved in *Pretore di Salò* (case 14/86)). In

Telemarsicabruzzo SpA v *Circostel* (cases C–320, 321, 322/90) it rejected an application for a ruling from an Italian magistrates' court on the grounds that the reference had provided no background factual information and only fragmentary observations on the case. The ECJ has since reaffirmed this approach in several cases (e.g., *Pretore di Genova* v *Banchero* (case C–157/92); *Monin Automobiles* v *France* (case C–386/92)). The ECJ has held, however, that the need for detailed factual background to a case is less pressing when the questions referred by the national court relate to technical points (*Vaneetveld* v *Le Foyer SA* (case C316/93)) or where the facts are clear, for example, because of a previous reference (*Crispoltoni* v *Fattoria Autonoma Tabacchi* (cases C–133, 300 & 362/92). The concern seems to be that not only must the ECJ know enough to give a useful ruling in the context, but that there is also enough information for affected parties to be able to make representations. This, according to the ECJ, is especially relevant in competition cases (*Deliege* (case C–191/97), paras 30 and 36). (See further chapter 17.) The Court has now issued 'Guidelines to National Courts Making References' (1996), consolidating its rulings in these cases.

The above limitations of the Court's jurisdiction are more apparent than real. The line between matters of Community law and matters of national law, between interpretation and application are more easily drawn in theory than in practice. An interpretation of EC law may leave little room for doubt as to the legality of a national law and little choice to the national judge in matters of application if he is to comply with his duty to give priority to EC law. The Court has on occasions, albeit in abstract terms, suggested that a particular national law is incompatible with EC law (e.g., *R* v *Secretary of State for Transport, ex parte Factortame Ltd* (case C–221/89); *Johnston* v *RUC* (case 222/84)). The Court may even offer specific guidance as to the application of its ruling. In the *BT* case (case C–392/93), for example, the ECJ commented:

> Whilst it is in principle for the national courts to verify whether or not the conditions of State liability for a breach of Community law are fulfilled, in the present case the Court has all the necessary information to assess whether the facts amount to a sufficiently serious breach of Community law.

The Court then went on to hold that there had been no breach. Further, in rephrasing and regrouping the questions the Court is able to select the issues which it regards as significant, without apparently interfering with the discretion of the national judge.

It may be argued that some encroachment by the ECJ onto the territory of national courts' jurisdiction is necessary to ensure the correct and uniform application of Community law. However, its very freedom of manoeuvre in preliminary rulings proceedings, combined with its teleological approach to interpretation, have resulted on occasions in the Court overstepping the line, laying down broad general (and sometimes unexpected) principles, with far-reaching consequences, in response to *particular* questions from national courts (e.g., *Barber* (case 262/88); *Marshall (No. 2)* (case C–271/91)). This has not been conducive to legal certainty. Such activism has not gone without criticism, as calculated to invite 'rebellion', even 'defiance' by national courts (see Rasmussen noted in chapter 2).

Although the ECJ has in a few, albeit increasing number of cases refused its jurisdiction, it has generally, despite a constantly growing workload, encouraged national courts to refer. One exception to this open door policy in the early years occurred in the cases of *Foglia* v *Novello (No. 1)* (case 104/79) and *Foglia* v *Novello (No. 2)* (case 244/80). Here for the first time the Court refused its jurisdiction to give a ruling in both a first and a second application in the same case. The questions, which were referred by an Italian judge, concerned the legality under EC law of an import duty imposed by the French on the import of wine from Italy. It arose in the context of litigation between two Italian parties. Foglia, a wine producer, had agreed to sell wine to Mrs Novello, an exporter. In making their contract the parties agreed that Foglia should not bear the cost of any duties levied by the French in breach of EC law. When duties were charged and eventually paid by Foglia, he sought to recover the money from Mrs Novello. In his action before the Italian court for recovery of the money that court sought a preliminary ruling on the legality under EC law of the duties imposed by the French. The ECJ refused its jurisdiction. The proceedings, it claimed, had been artificially created in order to question the legality of the French law; they were not 'genuine'.

The parties were no more successful the second time. In a somewhat peremptory judgment the Court declared that the function of what was then Article 177 (now 234) was to contribute to the administration of justice in the Member States; not to give advisory opinions on general or hypothetical questions.

The ECJ's decision has been criticised. Although the proceedings were to some extent artificial, in that the duty should ideally have been challenged at source, by the party from whom it was levied, the Italian judge called upon to decide the case was faced with a genuine problem, central to which was the issue of EC law. If, in his discretion, he sought guidance from the ECJ in this matter, surely it was not for that Court to deny it.

It has been suggested that the importance of this decision should not be exaggerated. No doubt political considerations and national (wine) rivalries played their part (the Court 'must display special vigilance when . . . a question is referred to it with a view to permitting the national court to decide whether the legislation of another Member State is in accordance with Community law': *Foglia* v *Novello (No. 2)*). Perhaps too, conscious of its increasing workload, the Court opted for this decision '*pour décourager les autres*'. *Foglia* v *Novello* may be contrasted with *Dzodzi* v *Belgium* (cases C–297/88 and C 197/89). Here the Court was prepared to provide a ruling on the interpretation of EC social security law in a purely 'internal' matter, for the purpose of clarifying provisions of Belgian law invoked by a *Togolese national*. The Court held that it was 'exclusively for national courts which were dealing with a case to assess, with regard to the specific features of each case, both the need for a preliminary ruling in order to enable it to give judgment, and the relevance of the question'. Following *Dzodzi*, in *Leur Bloem* (case C–28/95), the ECJ held that it has jurisdiction to interpret provisions of Community law where the facts of the case lie outside these provisions but are applicable to the case because the national law governing the main dispute has transposed the Community rule to a non-Community context ('spontaneous harmonisation'). This is subject to the proviso that national law does not expressly prohibit it (*Kleinwort Benson* (case C–346/93)).

The principles expressed in *Foglia v Novello* were, however, applied in *Meilicke v ADV/ORGA AG* (case C–83/91). Here the Court refused to answer a lengthy and complex series of question relating *inter alia*, to the interpretation of the second Company Law Directive. The dispute between the parties centred on a disagreement as to the interpretation of certain provisions of German company law. It appeared that the EC Directive was being invoked in order to prove one of the parties' (a legal academic's) theories. The Court held that it had no jurisdiction to give advisory opinions on hypothetical questions submitted by national courts. This case has been followed by others in which the ECJ declined jurisdiction either on the basis that the questions referred were not relevant to the dispute before the national court (e.g., *Dias v Director da Alfândega do Porto* (case C–343/90); *Corsica Ferries Italia Srl v Corpo dei Piloti del Porto di Genova* (case C–18/93)) or because the matter was purely internal (*Kleinwort Benson Ltd v City of Glasgow District Council* (case C–346/93); *cf. Dzodzi v Belgium* (cases C–297/88 & 197/89)). In *Monin Automobiles — Maison du Deux-Roues* (case C–428/93), the ECJ suggested that the questions referred must be 'objectively required' by the national court as 'necessary to enable that court to give judgment' in the proceedings before it as required under the then Article 177(2) (now 234(2)). This case concerned a company which was in the process of being wound up. It argued that it should not be finally wound up until certain questions relating to EC law had been answered. Conversely, the company's creditors thought that the company had been artificially kept in existence for too long already and should be wound up immediately. The national court referred the EC law questions to determine the strength of the company's argument. The ECJ held that, although there was a connection between the questions and the dispute, answers to the question would not be *applied* in the case. The ECJ therefore declined jurisdiction.

It is submitted that these cases should not be construed as constituting a new, restrictive approach on the part of the ECJ towards applications under Article 234 (ex 234). Admittedly, the ECJ has declined jurisdiction in a number of cases, but, looking at the facts of these cases, and of *Telemarsicabruzzo SpA v Circostel* (cases C–320–2/90) and similar cases, it can be argued that rejection was justified in the circumstances. This point is reinforced if we contrast the above cases with *Leclerc-Siplec v TF1 Publicité SA* (case C–412/93), which, in effect, concerned a challenge to French law. The Commission suggested that, in the light of the *Foglia* cases, there was no dispute before the national court because the parties were agreed about the outcome and that, therefore, the ECJ did not have jurisdiction to answer the question. The ECJ disagreed, holding that the parties' agreement did not render the dispute less real and that the question needed an answer because, without it, the referring court could not deal with the dispute before it. Furthermore, in *Leur-Bloem* (case C–28/95) the ECJ despite the opinion of the Advocate-General to the contrary, distinguished *Kleinwort Benson* and returned to its more generous approach in *Dzodzi*.

More worrying is the Court's decision, in March 1994, in *TWD Textilwerke GmbH* v *Germany* (case C–188/92). Here the Court refused to give a ruling on the validity of a Commission decision, addressed to the German government, demanding the recovery from the applicants of State aid granted by the government in breach of EC law. Its refusal was based on the fact that the applicants, having been informed by the government of the Commission's decision, and advised of their right to challenge it under the then Article 173 (now 230), had failed to do so within the two-month limitation period. Having allowed this period to expire the Court held that the applicants could not, in the interests of legal certainty, be permitted to attack the decision under former Article 177 (now 234). This decision, wholly out of line with its previous jurisprudence, which has been to encourage challenges to validity under Article 234 (ex 177) rather than (the more restrictive) Article 230 (ex 173), has caused concern, as calculated to drive parties, perhaps prematurely, into action under Article 230 (ex 173), for fear of being denied a later opportunity to challenge Community legislation under Article 234 (ex 177) (see further, chapter 28).

In a more recent judgment, the ECJ mitigated some of the effects of its judgment in *TWD*. In *R* v *Intervention Board for Agriculture, ex parte Accrington Beef Co. Ltd* (case C–241/95), the parties had not sought to bring an action for annulment within the time limits set out in the then Article 173 (now 230). Nonetheless, the ECJ was prepared to hear the preliminary ruling reference because it was not clear, as the parties were seeking to challenge a Regulation, that they would have had standing to bring an action under Article 173 (now 230). In addition it may be noted that while a national court is able to interpret Community law without recourse to the Court under Article 234 (ex 177), it has no power to declare a Community law invalid (*Zuckerfabrik Süderdithmarschen AG* v *Hauptzollamt Itzehoe* (cases C–143/88, C–92/89)).

Jurisdiction of national courts

Jurisdiction to refer to the ECJ under Article 234 (ex 177) is conferred on 'any court or tribunal'. With rare exceptions (e.g., *Nordsee Deutsche Hochseefischerei GmbH* (case 102/81) to be discussed below; *Corbiau* v *Administration des Contributions* (case C–24/92) (a fiscal authority is not a court or tribunal); *Victoria Film A/S* v *Riksskatteverket* (case C–134/97) (a court exercising its administrative duties is not a court or tribunal)), this has been interpreted in the widest sense. In *Pretore di Salò* v *Persons Unknown* (case 14/86), the ECJ held that this applied to any court acting in the general context of a duty to act, independently and in accordance with the law, upon cases in which the law has conferred jurisdiction upon it, even though its functions may not be of a judicial nature.

Thus the name of the body is irrelevant. Provided that it has the power to give binding determinations of the legal rights and obligations of individuals, it will be a court or tribunal within Article 234 (ex 177). Whether a particular body qualifies as a court or tribunal within that Article is a matter of *Community* law.

In *Broekmeulen* (case 246/80) the Court was faced with a reference from the appeal committee of the Dutch professional medical body. The claimant in the case, Mr Broekmeulen, was appealing against the Dutch GP's registration committee's refusal to register him as a GP. His appeal was based on EC law. One of the questions referred was whether the appeal committee was a 'court or tribunal' within the then Article 177 (now 234). The Court held that it was

> . . . in the practical absence of an effective means of redress before the ordinary courts, in a matter concerning the application of Community law, the appeal committee, which performs its duties with the approval of the public authorities and operates with their assistance, and whose decisions are accepted following contentious proceedings and are in fact recognised as final, must be deemed to be a court of a Member State for the purpose of Article 177 [now 234].

It was imperative to ensure the proper functioning of Community law that the ECJ should have the opportunity of ruling on issues of interpretation and validity.

More recently, the ECJ held that an individual immigration officer, an Immigration Adjudicator, could make a reference (*El-Yassini* v *Secretary of State for the Home Department* (case C–416/96)). In so finding, the ECJ applied the criteria developed in its previous judgments in this area, such as whether the body concerned is established by law, whether it is permanent, whether its jurisdiction is compulsory, whether its procedure is *inter partes*, whether it applies rules of law and, as in the case of *X* (cases C–74 and 129/95), whether it is independent (see also *Dorsch Consult* v *Bundesbaugesellschaft Berlin* (case C–54/96), para. 23). In this case, the office of Immigration Adjudicator was a permanent office, established by statute which gives the officer in question the power to hear and determine disputes in accordance with rules set down by statute. The ECJ further agreed with the Advocate-General, who had emphasised the *inter partes* nature of the procedure (para. 20) and the fact that the Adjudicators are required to give reasons for their decisions.

The Court had taken a less generous view in the earlier case of *Nordsee Deutsche Hochseefischerei GmbH* (case 102/81). The case arose from a joint shipbuilding project which involved the pooling of EC aid. The parties agreed that in the event of a dispute they would refer their differences to an independent arbitrator. Their agreement excluded the possibility of recourse to the ordinary courts. They fell into disagreement and a number of questions involving the interpretation of certain EC Regulations were raised before the arbitrator. He sought a ruling from the ECJ as to, *inter alia,* whether he was a 'court or tribunal' within the meaning of the then Article 177 (now 234). The Court held that he was not. The question, the Court held, depends on the nature of the arbitration. Here the public authorities of Member States were not involved in the decision to opt for arbitration, nor were they called upon to intervene automatically before the arbitrator. If questions of Community law were raised before such a body, the ordinary courts might be called upon to give them assistance, or to review the decision; it would be for *them* to refer questions of interpretation or validity of Community law to the ECJ.

The Court's decision ignored the fact that in this case recourse to the courts was excluded, and the arbitrator was thus required to interpret a difficult point of Community law, of central importance in the proceedings, unaided.

Since in *Nordsee Deutsche Hochseefischerei GmbH* there was no effective means of redress before the ordinary courts and the decisions of the arbitrator were accepted following contentious proceedings and recognised as final it seems that the only factor distinguishing it from *Broekmeulen* was the element of *public* participation or control. This, it seems, will be essential.

It is likely that the decision in *Nordsee Deutsche Hochseefischerei GmbH* (as in *Foglia* v *Novello (No. 1)* (case 104/79)), was dictated to some extent by a fear of the floodgates. While the ECJ was anxious in the early days of the Community to encourage referrals under the then Article 177 (now 234), its very success in this respect has led to an ever-increasing workload (delays in obtaining preliminary rulings have tripled, and now take an average of 18 months to two years) resulting in some attempts by the Court to shift some of the load on to national courts. Although there is much to be said for encouraging national courts, now more experienced in the application of EC law, to decide matters for themselves, there is no justification for a position whereby access to the ECJ is totally excluded. It is regrettable that the arbitrator in *Nordsee Deutsche Hochseefischerei GmbH* did not ask the Court whether the position would be the same if recourse to the ordinary courts had been excluded. Had he done so, the ECJ's stance on the need for public participation or control might in this case have been modified.

Another possible limitation on the ability of the national courts to refer questions to the ECJ concerns the degree to which national courts are free to refer an issue of Community law of their own motion. In *R* v *Secretary of State for the Environment, ex parte Greenpeace Ltd* [1994] 4 All ER 352, the English High Court took the approach that since the parties did not request a preliminary rulings reference, then, despite the fact that national rules expressly permit the court to refer of its own motion, the court should not make a reference. It is submitted that this approach is unduly restrictive. It ignores the underlying purpose of Article 234 (ex 177), which is to ensure correct and uniform interpretation of EC law throughout the Community, and it undermines the effectiveness of the Community law remedies. Although the ECJ has not discussed this point directly, it has itself assumed jurisdiction to rule on questions not referred (*OTO SpA* v *Ministero delle Finanze* (case C–130/92)) and it has more recently touched on these questions indirectly in *Peterbroeck Van Campenhout & Cie SCS* v *Belgium* (case C–312/93) and *van Schijndel* v *Stichting Pensioenfonds voor Fysiotherapeuten* (cases C–430 & 431/93). Unlike the British example cited above, the last two cases involved applications to amend pleadings to include a new point of Community law. In *Peterbroeck* the ECJ held that because the claimant had, in the circumstances, not had the opportunity of amending its pleadings before the time limit for so doing had expired, the effectiveness of Community law would preclude the application of national procedural rules preventing the court from considering an issue of Community law. In *Van Schijndel* the applicants sought to introduce the Community law point on appeal. The ECJ held that if one could include new points of national law on appeal, one could not treat Community rules less favourably, but the national court was otherwise not obliged to raise the issue of its own motion in civil cases where the Community law point was beyond the existing ambit of the dispute. In civil litigation, both parties to the dispute have the opportunity to define the issues relevant to their dispute, and to allow the introduction of new issues might endanger legal certainty and procedural fairness. Thus one may conclude that Community law does not *prevent* national courts from raising issues of their own motion and, where it is desirable to ensure effective protection of individuals' rights, it should be done, provided that both parties have an opportunity to put forward their cases.

Although any court or tribunal may refer questions to the ECJ under Article 234 (ex 177), a distinction must be drawn between those courts or tribunals which have a discretion to refer ('permissive' jurisdiction) and those for which referral is mandatory ('mandatory' jurisdiction). Under Article 234(3) (ex 177(3)), where a question concerning interpretation is raised 'in a case pending before a court or tribunal of a Member State, *against whose decisions there is no judicial remedy under national law*, that court or tribunal *shall* bring the matter before the Court of Justice' (emphasis added). For all courts other than those within Article 234(3) (ex 177(3)) referral is discretionary. Note that special rules apply to cases falling within the new Title IV to the EC Treaty, introduced by the ToA. These are discussed below. (See also chapter 23.)

Mandatory jurisdiction

The purpose of Article 234(3) (ex 177(3)) must be seen in the light of the function of Article 234 (ex 177) as a whole, which is to prevent a body of national case law not in accordance with the rules of Community law from coming into existence in any Member State (*Hoffman-La Roche AG* v *Centrafarm Vertiebsgesellschaft Pharmazeutischer Erzeugnisse mbH* (case 107/76)). To this end Article 234(3) (ex 177(3)) seeks to ensure that, when matters of EC law arise, there is an obligation to refer to the ECJ at some stage in the proceedings. This purpose should be kept in mind when questions of interpretation of Article 234(3) (ex 177(3)) arise.

The scope of Article 234(3) (ex 177(3)) is not entirely clear. While it clearly applies to courts or tribunals whose decisions are *never* subject to appeal (the 'abstract theory'), such as the House of Lords in England, or the Conseil d'État in France, it is less clear whether it applies also to courts whose decisions *in the case in question* are not subject to appeal (the 'concrete theory'), such as the Italian magistrates' court (*guidice conciliatore*) in *Costa* v *ENEL* (case 6/64) (no right of appeal because sum of money involved too small). And when leave to appeal from the Court of Appeal (or, in certain criminal matters, from the High Court) to the House of Lords is refused, or when the High Court refuses leave for judicial review from a tribunal decision, do these courts become courts 'against whose decisions there is no judicial remedy under national law'?

Lord Denning MR in *H.P. Bulmer Ltd* v *J. Bollinger SA* [1974] Ch 401, Court of Appeal, appeared to espouse the narrower 'abstract' theory when he said '. . . short of the House of Lords, no other English court is bound to refer a question to the European Court at Luxembourg'. Stephenson and Stamp LJJ expressly withheld comment on this point. In *Re a Holiday in Italy* [1975] 1 CMLR 184 the National Insurance Commissioner followed Lord Denning and refused to refer in the context of an application for judicial review.

The judgment of the ECJ in *Costa* v *ENEL* appears, albeit *obiter*, to support the wider, 'concrete' theory. In that case, in the context of a reference from the Italian magistrates' court, from which there was no appeal due to the small amount of money involved, the Court said, with reference to the then Article 177(3): 'By the terms of this Article . . . national courts against whose decisions, *as in the present case*, there is no judicial remedy, *must* refer the matter to the Court of Justice' (emphasis added). Taking into account the function of Article 234(3) (ex 177(3)) and particularly its importance for the individual, this would seem to be the better view.

It has been suggested that where the right of appeal or judicial review depends on the granting of leave, a lower court or tribunal from which a reference under Article 234 (ex 177) is sought must *either* grant leave or refer to the ECJ. Where this is not done, and leave depends on permission from a superior 'final' court, that latter court should be obliged to grant the requested leave. Any other course would frustrate the purpose of Article 234 (ex 177) and amount to a denial of the individual's Community rights.

This point was raised, but unfortunately not referred to the ECJ, in *SA Magnavision NV* v *General Optical Council (No. 2)* [1987] 2 CMLR 262, Queen's Bench Division. In this case the appellant company manufactured reading glasses in Belgium and had been prosecuted for selling its spectacles through concessionary outlets within shops in the UK, in breach of the rules of the General Optical Council. Under these rules the selling of spectacles in the UK was prohibited except under the supervision of a doctor or optician. The company was found guilty by Cardiff Magistrates and its appeal before

Macpherson J in the High Court (*Magnavision (No. 1)* [1987] 1 CMLR 887) failed. That court refused to grant the appellant leave to appeal to the House of Lords. The company subsequently applied to the Divisional Court for leave to appeal to the House of Lords on a point of general public importance; namely, if the Divisional Court refuses leave to appeal in such a case does it become a court of last resort within Article 177(3) (now 234(3))? Since judgment had already been given (although the order had not been drawn up) in the original case Watkins JL clearly thought it a 'most daring application'. Although he admitted that the refusal of leave to appeal from *Magnavision (No. 1)* had turned the Divisional Court into a 'final' court, representing 'the end of the road' for the claimant, he refused to grant the leave requested. There was no longer any point in referring, he said, 'We are *functus* in every sense'. Similar difficulties arose in the litigation between Chiron Corporation and Murex Diagnostics Ltd (*Chiron Corporation v Murex Diagnostics Ltd* (No. 2) [1994] 1 CMLR 410 and *Chiron Corporation v Murex Diagnostics Ltd* (No. 8) [1995] All ER (EC) 88) in which the English Court of Appeal refused to make a reference and also refused leave to appeal to the House of Lords. The House of Lords itself then refused leave to appeal. Thus the matter still awaits an authoritative ruling from the ECJ.

Although Watkins LJ's decision was no doubt correct, and consistent with the ECJ's view in *Pardini* (case 338/85) and *Grogan* (case C–159/90), it is submitted that a reference to the ECJ at some stage on the substantive issue in both *Magnavision (No. 1)* and the Chiron and Murex litigation would have been highly desirable, since, in each case, the point of law was not a simple one and was of considerable importance to one of the parties. The issue may finally be resolved by the ECJ. In *Lyckeshog* (case C–99/00), the question has been referred of whether national courts are 'final' courts for the purposes of Article 234(3) (ex 177(3)) if leave to appeal from their judgment is required. Some have suggested that, in the light of the recurring possibilities for review of the ECJ's jurisdiction which the repeated Treaty amendments constitute and the consequent threat of its jurisdiction's curtailment, the ECJ may take a narrow view of this question. Alternatively, the ECJ may find it politic to deal with the reference without answering this question.

Discretionary or 'permissive' jurisdiction

Courts or tribunals which do not fall within Article 234(3) (ex 177(3)) enjoy, according to the ECJ, an unfettered discretion in the matter of referrals. A court or tribunal at any level is free, 'if it considers that a decision on the question is necessary to enable it to give judgment', to refer to the ECJ in any kind of proceedings, including interim proceedings (*Hoffman-La Roche AG v Centrafarm Vertriebsgesellschaft Pharmazeutischer Erzeugnisse mbH* (case 107/76)), at any stage in the proceedings. In *De Geus en Uitdenbogerd v Robert Bosch GmbH* (case 13/61) the Court held that national courts have jurisdiction to refer whether or not an appeal is pending; the ECJ is not even concerned to discover whether the decision of the national judge has acquired the force of *res iudicata*. However, following *Pardini* (case 338/85) and *Grogan* (case C–159/90), if proceedings have been terminated and the Court is aware of this fact it may refuse jurisdiction on the grounds that its ruling is not necessary to enable the national court to give judgment.

Even if the ECJ has already ruled on a similar question, national courts are not precluded from requesting a further ruling. This point was made in *Da Costa en Schaake NV* (cases 28-30/62). There the Court held, in the context of a reference for interpretation of a question substantially the same as that referred in *Van Gend en Loos,* that the Court should retain a legal right to depart from its previous judgments. It may recognise its errors in the light of new facts. It ruled in similar terms in the context of a request concerning the effect of a prior ruling of validity in *International Chemical Corporation SpA* v *Amministrazione delle Finanze dello Stato* (case 66/80). Here it held that while national courts could assume from a prior declaration of invalidity that the Regulation was invalid, they should not be deprived of an opportunity to refer the same issue if they have a 'real interest' in making a further reference.

This discretion to refer is in no way affected by national rules of precedent. This important principle was established in the case of *Rheinmühlen-Düsseldorf* (case 166/73); (case 146/73). In this case, which concerned an attempt by a German cereal exporter to obtain an export rebate under Community law, the German federal tax court (the Bundesfinanzhof), hearing the case on appeal from the Hessian tax court (Hessische Finanzgericht), had quashed the Hessian court's judgment and remitted the case to that court for a decision on certain issues of fact. The Hessian court was not satisfied with the Bundesfinanzhof's ruling since questions of Community law were involved. It sought a ruling from the ECJ on the interpretation of the Community law, and also on the question of whether it was permissible for a lower court to refer in this way when its own superior court had already set aside its earlier judgment on appeal. On an appeal by Rheinmühlen-Düsseldorf to the Bundesfinanzhof challenging the Hessian court's right to refer to the ECJ, the Bundesfinanzhof itself referred certain questions to the Court of Justice. The principal question, raised in both cases, was whether the then Article 177 (now 234) gave national courts an unfettered right to refer or whether that right is subject to national provisions whereby lower courts are bound by the judgments of superior courts.

The Court's reply was in the strongest terms. The object of the then Article 177 procedure, the Court held, was to ensure that in all circumstances the law was the same in all Member States. No provision of domestic law can take away the power provided by Article 177 (now 234). The lower court must be free to make a reference if it considers that the superior court's ruling could lead it to give judgment contrary to Community law. It would only be otherwise if the question put by the lower court were substantially the same. The ECJ's view may be compared with that of Wood J in the Employment Appeal Tribunal in *Enderby* v *Frenchay Health Authority* [1991] ICR 382. Here he suggested that lower English Courts were bound even in matters of Community law by decisions of their superior courts; thus they should not make references to the ECJ but should leave it to the House of Lords, *a fortiori* when the House has decided on a particular issue that British law does not conflict with EC law. Wood J's observations are clearly at odds with Community law. It appears that *Rheinmühlen-Düsseldorf* was not cited before the tribunal. A reference to the ECJ was subsequently made in this case by the Court of Appeal ([1992] IRLR 15) resulting in a ruling (case C–127/92) and a decision on an important issue of equal pay for work of equal value contrary to that of Wood J and in the claimant's favour (see chapter 25).

If national courts have the widest discretion in matters of referral, when, and on what basis, should they exercise this discretion? Two aspects of this problem may be considered.

First, the national judge must consider that a decision on a question of Community law is *'necessary* to enable it to give judgment'; then, if it is necessary, he must decide whether, in his discretion, he should refer.

Guidelines on both these matters have been supplied by the ECJ and by national courts. It is submitted that as the ultimate arbiter on matters of Community law only the ECJ's rulings are fully authoritative on this point.

When will a decision be necessary?

The ECJ was asked to consider this matter in *CILFIT Srl* (case 283/81). The reference was from the Italian Supreme Court, the Cassazione, and concerned national courts' mandatory jurisdiction under what was then Article 177(3) (now 234(3)). On a literal reading of Article 234(2) and (3) (ex 177(2) and (3)) it would appear that the question of whether 'a decision on a matter of Community law if necessary' only applies to the national courts' discretionary jurisdiction under Article 234(2) (ex 177(2)). However, in *CILFIT* the ECJ held that:

> it followed from the relationship between Article 177(2) and (3) [now 234(2) and (3)] that the courts or tribunals referred to in Article 177(3) [now 234(3)] have the same discretion as any other national court or tribunal to ascertain whether a decision on a question of Community law is necessary to enable them to give judgment.

There would be no need to refer if:

(a) the question of EC law is irrelevant; or
(b) the provision has already been interpreted by the ECJ, even though the questions at issue are not strictly identical; or
(c) the correct application is so obvious as to leave no scope for reasonable doubt. This matter must be assessed in the light of the specific characteristics of Community law, the particular difficulties to which its interpretation gives rise, and the risk of divergences in judicial decisions within the Community.

These guidelines may be compared with Lord Denning's in *H.P. Bulmer Ltd* v *J. Bollinger SA* [1974] Ch 401, Court of Appeal. He suggested that a decision would only be 'necessary' if it was 'conclusive' to the judgment. Even then it would not be necessary if:

(a) the ECJ had already given judgment on the question, or
(b) the matter was reasonably clear and free from doubt.

Although the criteria in both cases are similar, the first and third *CILFIT Srl* criteria are clearly stricter; it would be easier under Lord Denning's guidelines to decide that a decision was not 'necessary'. Lord Denning's guidelines were applied by Taylor J in *R v Inner London Education Authority, ex parte Hinde* [1985] 1 CMLR 716 and he decided not to refer (see also *Brown v Rentokil Ltd* [1995] 2 CMLR 85, Scottish Court of Session). The issues at stake in the former case have proved to be both important and difficult, and were only finally resolved by the ECJ in the cases of *Brown* (case 197/86) and *Lair* (case 39/86) (for full discussion of the issues see chapter 20).

Acte clair

Criteria (b) and (c) of *CILFIT Srl* (case 238/81) and (a) and (b) of *H.P. Bulmer Ltd v J. Bollinger SA* [1974] Ch 401 could be described as versions of *acte clair*. *Acte clair* is a doctrine originating in French administrative law, whereby if the meaning of a provision is clear no 'question' of interpretation arises. The doctrine was introduced in the context of interpretation of treaties, in order to strengthen the powers of the Conseil d'État *vis-à-vis* the executive. If doubts existed concerning the interpretation of a treaty, the courts were obliged to refer to the government. If the provision was found to be *acte clair*, there was no need to refer. The utility of the doctrine, in that context, is clear.

The doctrine was first invoked in the sphere of EC law by Advocate-General Lagrange in *Da Costa en Schaake NV* (cases 28-30/62), in the context of a reference on a question of interpretation almost identical to a matter already decided by the Court in *Van Gend en Loos* (case 26/62). Like *CILFIT Srl*, it arose in a case concerning the court's mandatory jurisdiction under the then Article 177(3) (now 234(3)). While asserting that former Article 177(3) 'unqualifiedly' required national courts to submit to the ECJ 'every question of interpretation raised before the court' the Court added that this would not be necessary if the question was materially identical with a question which had already been the subject of a preliminary ruling in a similar case.

This case has been taken as an endorsement by the Court of *acte clair*, albeit interpreted in a very narrow sense. The principle was approved in *CILFIT Srl* and the ECJ's (1996) guidelines also incorporate these principles.

Acte clair was applied in a much wider sense, in very different circumstances, in the French case of *Re Société des Pétroles Shell-Berre* [1964] CMLR 462. This case involved a number of difficult questions of French and EC competition law. These questions had not been subject to prior rulings under the then Article 177 (now 234). Nevertheless the Conseil d'État, led by the Commissaire du Gouvernement, Madame Questiaux, took the view that only if the judge is not competent to determine the meaning of an act is he faced with a 'question of interpretation' and decided that there was no doubt as to the meaning and so there was no need to refer.

The dangers of *acte clair* were revealed in the Court of Appeal in the case of *R v Henn* [1978] 1 WLR 1031. There Lord Widgery suggested that it was clear from the case law of the Court of Justice that a ban on the import of pornographic books was not a quantitative restriction within the then Article 30 (now 28) of the EC Treaty. A subsequent referral on this matter by the House of Lords revealed that it undoubtedly was. Lord Diplock, giving judgment in the House of Lords ([1981] AC 850), warned English judges not to be too ready to hold that because the meaning of an English text seemed plain to them no question of interpretation was involved: the ECJ and the English courts have very different styles of interpretation and may ascribe different meanings to the same provision. He did, however, approve a version of *acte clair* consistent with that of the ECJ in *Da Costa en Schaake NV* and *CILFIT Srl* in *Garland v British Rail Engineering Ltd* [1983] 2 AC 751 when he suggested that where there was a 'considerable and consistent line of case law' from the ECJ the answer would be 'too obvious and inevitable' to be capable of giving rise to what could properly be called a question within the meaning of Article 234 (ex 177).

Although most of the above cases arose in the context of Article 234(3) (ex 177(3)) they have been discussed at this stage because they may equally be invoked in the context of national courts' discretionary jurisdiction, and they demonstrate that *acte clair* can be applied both in a narrow sense, as in *Da Costa en Schaake NV* ('provision materially identical') and *CILFIT Srl* ('so clear as to leave no room for doubt, taking into account' etc.) and in a looser, more subjective sense, as in *H.P. Bulmer Ltd v J. Bollinger SA* ('reasonably clear and free from doubt') and *Shell-Berre* ('no doubt'). Although a loose interpretation does not have such serious consequences in the context of a court's discretionary jurisdiction as in its mandatory jurisdiction, a narrow interpretation is preferable if the pitfalls of *R v Inner London Education Authority, ex parte Hinde* [1985] 1 CMLR 716 and *R v Henn* are to be avoided. Where a disappointed party does not have the means or the stamina to appeal it may result in a misapplication of EC law.

Exercise of discretion

If courts within the area of discretionary jurisdiction consider, applying the *CILFIT* criteria, that a decision from the ECJ is necessary, how should they exercise their discretion?

On the question of timing, the ECJ has suggested that the facts of the case should be established and questions of purely national law settled before a reference is made (*Irish Creamery Milk Suppliers Association v Ireland* (cases 36 & 71/80)). This would avoid precipitate referrals, and enable the Court to take cognisance of all the features of fact and law which may be relevant to the issue of Community law on which it is asked to rule. A similar point was made by Lord Denning MR in *H.P. Bulmer Ltd v J. Bollinger SA* [1974] Ch 401 ('Decide the facts first') and approved by the House of Lords in *R v Henn* [1981] AC 850. However, Lord Diplock did concede in *R v Henn* that in an urgent, e.g., interim matter, where important financial interests are concerned, it might be necessary to refer *before* all the facts were found.

With regard to other factors, Lord Denning suggested in *H.P. Bulmer Ltd v J. Bollinger SA* that time, cost, workload of the ECJ and the wishes of the parties should be taken into account by national courts in the exercise of their discretion.

Factors such as time and cost need to be treated with care, weighing the fact, as did Bingham J in *Commissioners of Customs and Excise v Samex ApS* [1983] 3 CMLR 194, that deferring a referral may in the end increase the time and cost to the parties: there may be cases where it is appropriate to refer at an early stage. The more difficult and uncertain the issue of EC law, the greater the likelihood of appeal, requiring, in the end, a referral to the ECJ under Article 234(3) (ex 177(3)).

The workload of the ECJ is an increasing problem and no doubt a reason for some modification in recent years of its open-door policy. However, whereas it may justify non-referral in a straightforward case, it should not prevent referral where the point of EC law is difficult or novel. The *CILFIT* criteria should operate to prevent unnecessary referrals.

The wishes of the parties also need to be treated with caution. If the point of EC law is relevant (which under *CILFIT* it must be) and difficult or uncertain, clearly *one* of the parties' interests will be better served by a referral. As Templeman LJ said in the Court of Appeal in *Polydor Ltd v Harlequin Record Shops Ltd* [1980] 2 CMLR 413 when he chose to refer a difficult point of EC law in proceedings for an interim injunction, 'it is the right of the plaintiff [claimant] to go to the European Court'. Furthermore, the ECJ has held that the question of referral is one for the national court and that a party to the proceedings in the context of which the reference is made cannot challenge a decision to refer, even if that party thinks that the national court's findings of fact are inaccurate (*SAT Fluggesellschaft mbH v European Organization for the Safety of Air Navigation* (case C–364/92)).

Another factor which might point to an early referral, advanced by Ormrod LJ in *Polydor Ltd v Harlequin Record Shops Ltd* is the wider implications of the ruling. In *Polydor Ltd v Harlequin Record Shops Ltd* there were a number of similar cases pending. The issue, which was a difficult one, concerned the protection of British copyright law in the context of an international agreement between the EC and Portugal, and affected not merely the parties to the case but the record industry as a whole.

Lastly, in *R v Henn* Lord Diplock suggested that in a criminal trial on indictment it might be better for the question to be decided by the national judge and reviewed if necessary through the hierarchy of the national courts. Although this statement could be invoked to counter spurious defences based on EC law, and unnecessary referrals, it is submitted that where a claim is genuinely based on EC law, and a ruling from the ECJ would be conclusive of the case, delay would serve no purpose. The time and cost of the proceedings would only be increased.

Where matters of validity are concerned special considerations apply. Although a national court may find a Community act to be valid, it has no power to make a finding of invalidity. Thus, despite the apparent permissive words of Article 234(2) (ex 177(2)), where a court has serious doubts as to the validity of the act in question, provided that a decision on the question of EC law is 'necessary', a referral to the ECJ should be made. A national court may, however, grant an interim injunction based on the (alleged) invalidity of Community law. These matters, hinted at in *Foto-Frost* v *Hauptzollamt Lübeck-Ost* (case 314/85), have now been confirmed in *Zuckerfabrik Süderdithmarschen AG* v *Hauptzollamt Itzehoe* (cases C–143/88 and C–92/89).

Exercise of mandatory jurisdiction

Which courts and tribunals fall within the mandatory jurisdiction of Article 234(3) (ex 177(3)) has already been discussed. It is submitted that the wider interpretation of Article 234(3) (ex 177(3)), the 'concrete theory', is more in accordance with the functions and purposes of Article 234 (ex 177) than the stricter 'abstract theory'. *Costa* v *ENEL* (case 6/64) may be invoked to support this view.

Where a court or tribunal falls within Article 234(3) (ex 177(3)), this creates, as the Court pointed out in *Da Costa en Schaake* (cases 28-30/62), an absolute obligation to refer. However, as the Court suggested in *CILFIT*, this obligation only arises if the court 'considers that a decision on the question is necessary to enable it to give judgment' (Article 234 (ex 177)).

While it is clearly not necessary for 'final' courts to refer questions of Community law in every case, a lax approach by such courts towards their need to refer, resulting in non-referral, may lead to an incorrect application of Community law and, for the individual concerned, a denial of justice. For him, this is the end of the road.

It is here that the doctrine of *acte clair* is of crucial significance. Under this doctrine, if the court is satisfied that the answer to the question of Community law, whether concerning interpretation or validity, is clear, then no decision on the question is 'necessary'. The judge is thus relieved of his obligation to refer.

As has been noted, the application of *acte clair* prevented the French Conseil d'État in *Shell-Berre* from referring to the ECJ when the matter of EC law seemed, to many eyes, far from clear. What seemed clear to Lord Widgery in *R* v *Henn* turned out to be incorrect. Moreover, the doctrine, depending as it does on a subjective assessment as to what is clear, can all too easily be used as a means of avoiding referral. This appears to have occurred in *Minister of the Interior* v *Cohn-Bendit* [1980] 1 CMLR 543. In this case, heard by the French Conseil d'État, the supreme administrative court, Cohn-Bendit sought to invoke an EC Directive (Directive 64/221, see chapter 22) to challenge a deportation order made by the French authorities. Certain provisions of the Directive had already been declared by the ECJ to be directly effective (*Van Duyn* v *Home Office* (case 41/74); see chapter 4). Despite urgings from the Commissaire du Gouvernement, M. Genevois, that in such a situation the Conseil d'État must either follow *Van Duyn* and apply the Directive or seek a ruling from the Court under the then Article 177(3) (now 234(3)), the Conseil d'État declined to do either. In its opinion, the law was clear. The Directive was not directly effective.

The role of *acte clair* in EC law was clarified by the ECJ in *CILFIT Srl* (case 283/81) in the context of a question from the Italian Cassazione (Supreme Court) concerning its obligation under the then Article 177(3), namely, did that Article create an absolute obligation to refer, or was referral conditional on a prior finding of a reasonable interpretative doubt? From the Court's response, that there was no need to refer if the matter was (a) irrelevant, (b) materially identical to a question already the subject of a preliminary ruling, or (c) so obvious as to leave no scope for reasonable doubt, the second and third criteria may be taken as endorsing a version, albeit a narrow one, of *acte clair*. On the second criterion, which was a reiteration of its position in *Da Costa en Schaake*, the Court held that the questions at issue need not be identical, as long as the Court has already dealt with the point in question. Of particular importance to its third criterion is the Court's rider that, in deciding whether a matter was free from doubt, account must be taken of the specific characteristics of Community law, its particular difficulties, and the risk of divergence in judicial interpretation. Similar points were made by Lord Diplock in *R* v *Henn* and Lord Denning MR in *H.P. Bulmer Ltd* v *J. Bollinger SA*. Henceforth, if *acte clair* is to be invoked in the context of EC law, it must be on the basis of the criteria supplied by *CILFIT Srl*. Nevertheless, the House of Lords did not make a reference on the direct effects of the provisions of the Banking Directive (Directive 77/780) in *Three Rivers DC* v *Bank of England* (*The Times*, 19 May 2000), simply declaring the matter to be *acte clair*.

However, the *CILFIT* criteria are not foolproof and have been criticised as providing national courts with an excuse not to refer, undermining the very purpose of Article 234(3) (ex 177(3)). In *R* v *Secretary of State for the Home Department, ex parte Sandhu, The Times*, 10 May 1985, the House of Lords was faced with a request for a ruling on the interpretation of certain provisions of Regulation 1612/68 (concerning rights of residence of members of the family of workers), in the context of a claim by an Indian, the divorced husband of an EC national, threatened with deportation from the UK as a result of his divorce. The *CILFIT* criteria were cited, as was *Diatta* v *Land Berlin* (case 267/83), a case dealing with the rights of residence of a *separated* wife living apart from her husband, which was decided in the wife's favour. The House of Lords applied the second *CILFIT* criterion, found that the matter had already been interpreted in *Diatta,* and, on the basis of certain statements delivered *obiter* in *Diatta*, decided not to refer. On their Lordships' interpretation Mr Sandhu was not entitled to remain in the UK. Thus a loophole in the *CILFIT* criteria was exploited with disastrous results for Mr Sandhu. (For further discussion of the case see chapter 20.)

A Court may avoid its obligations under Article 234(3) (ex 177(3)) by deciding the case before it without considering the possibility of referral (see, e.g., *Mees* v *Belgium* [1988] 3 CMLR 137, Belgian Conseil d'État). In *Wellcome Foundation Ltd* v *Secretary of State for Social Services* [1988] 1 WLR 635 the House of Lords, in considering the factors to be taken into account by a licensing authority in issuing a licence to parallel import a trade-mark medicine, thought it 'highly undesirable to embark on considerations of

Community law which might have necessitated a referral to the Court of Justice under Article 177'.

By contrast, the German Federal Constitutional Court has emphasised national courts' duty to refer under Article 234(3) (ex 177(3)), according to the *CILFIT* criteria, in the strongest terms. In quashing the German Bundesfinanzhof's decision on the direct effects of Directives in *Re VAT Directives* [1982] 1 CMLR 527, *Kloppenburg* v *Finanzamt Leer* [1989] 1 CMLR 873 (see chapter 4), it held that a court subject to Article 177(3) (now 234(3)) which deliberately departs from the case law of the ECJ and fails to make a reference under that Article is acting in breach of Article 101 of the German constitution. The principle of *acte clair* could not operate where there existed a ruling from the ECJ to the contrary (*Re VAT exemption* [1989] 1 CMLR 113). In *Re Patented Feedingstuffs* [1989] 2 CMLR 902 the same court declared that it would review an 'arbitrary' refusal by a court subject to the then Article 177(3) (now 234(3)) to refer to the ECJ. A refusal would be arbitrary:

(a)   where the national court gave no consideration at all to a reference in spite of the accepted relevance of Community law to the judgment and the court's doubt as to the correct answer;

(b)   where the law consciously departs in its judgment from the case law of the ECJ on the relevant questions, and nevertheless does not make a reference or a fresh reference; and

(c)   where there is not yet a decisive judgment of the ECJ on point, or such judgments may not have provided an exhaustive answer to the relevant questions or there is a more than remote possibility of the ECJ developing its case law further, and the national court exceeds to an indefensible extent the scope of its necessary judicial discretion, as where there may be contrary views of the relevant question of Community law which should obviously be given preference over the view of the national court.

These principles, applied in good faith, should ensure that a reference to the ECJ will be made, at least by the German courts, in the appropriate case. Perhaps other courts will be persuaded to follow the German Constitutional Court's example.

Effect of a ruling

Clearly a ruling from the ECJ under Article 234 (ex 177) is binding in the individual case. Given Member States' obligation under Article 10 (ex 5) EC to 'take all appropriate measures . . . to ensure fulfilment of the obligations arising out of this Treaty or resulting from action taken by the institutions of the Community' and, in the UK, under the European Communities Act 1972, s. 3(2), to take judicial notice of any decision of the ECJ, it should also be applied in all subsequent cases. This does not preclude national courts from seeking a further ruling on the same issue should they have a 'real interest' in making a reference (*Da Costa en Schaake* (cases 28-30/62) —

interpretation; *International Chemical Corporation SpA* (case 66/80) — validity).

The question of the temporal effect of a ruling, whether it should take effect retroactively (*'ex tunc'*, i.e., from the moment of entry into force of the provision subject to the ruling) or only from the date of judgment (*'ex nunc'*) is less clear. In *Defrenne* v *Sabena (No. 2)* (case 43/75) the Court was prepared to limit the effect of the then Article 119 (now 141) (see chapter 25) to future cases (including *Defrenne* itself) and claims lodged prior to the date of judgment. 'Important considerations of legal certainty' the Court held, 'affecting all the interests involved, both public and private, make it impossible to reopen the question as regards the past'. The Court was clearly swayed by the arguments of the British and Irish governments that a retrospective application of the equal pay principle would have serious economic repercussions on parties (i.e., employers) who had been led to believe they were acting within the law.

However, in *Ariete SpA* (case 811/79) and *Salumi Srl* (cases 66, 127 & 128/79) the Court made it clear that *Defrenne* was to be an exceptional case. As a general rule an interpretation under Article 234 (ex 177) of a rule of Community law 'clarifies and defines where necessary the meaning and scope of that rule as it must be or ought to be understood and applied *from the time of its coming into force*' (emphasis added). A ruling under that Article must therefore be applied to legal relationships arising prior to the date of the judgment provided that the conditions for its application by the national court are satisfied. 'It is only exceptionally', the Court said 'that the Court may, in the application of the principle of legal certainty inherent in the community legal order and in taking into account the serious effects which its judgments might have as regards the past, on legal relationships established in good faith, be moved to restrict for any person concerned the opportunity of relying on the provision as thus interpreted with a view to calling into question those legal relationships . . . '.

Moreover, 'such a restriction may be allowed *only* in the actual judgment ruling upon the interpretation sought' and 'it is for the Court of Justice *alone* to decide on the temporal restrictions as regards the effects of the interpretation which it gives'.

These principles were applied in *Blaizot* (case 24/86) and *Barra* (case 309/85). Both cases involved a claim for reimbursement of the Belgian minerval, based on *Gravier* (case 293/83, see chapter 21). In both cases the claims were in respect of periods prior to the ECJ's ruling in *Gravier*. In *Barra* it was not disputed that the course for which the minerval had been charged was vocational; but *Blaizot's* course, a university course in veterinary medicine, was, the defendant university argued, not vocational, thus not within the scope of the *Gravier* ruling.

Since *Barra's* case fell squarely within *Gravier* and the Court had imposed no temporal limits on the effect of its judgment in *Gravier* itself, that ruling was held to apply retrospectively in *Barra's* favour. *Blaizot* on the other hand raised new issues. In deciding that university education could, and a course in veterinary science did, constitute vocational training the Court, clearly conscious of the impact of such a ruling on Belgian universities if applied retroactively, decided that 'important considerations of legal certainty' required that the effects of its ruling should be limited on the same lines as *Defrenne*, that is, to future cases and those lodged prior to judgment.

Thus unless the Court can be persuaded to change its mind and reconsider the question of the temporal effect of a prior ruling in a subsequent case when *no* new issues are raised, the question of the temporal effect will need to be considered in every case in which a retrospective application may give rise to serious repercussions as regards the past. Yet it is in the nature of this kind of ruling that it, and therefore its consequences, are unpredictable. Should a party wish, subsequently, to limit the effects of an earlier ruling, it will be necessary to ensure, as in *Blaizot,* that some new issue of EC law is raised.

In *Barber* v *Guardian Royal Exchange Assurance Group* (case C–262/88) the court was again persuaded by 'overriding considerations of legal certainty' to limit the effects of its ruling that employers' contracted-out pension schemes fell within the then Article 119 (now 141) EC (see chapter 25). Unfortunately the precise scope of the non-retroactivity principle that 'Article 119 may not be relied upon in order to *claim entitlement* to a pension with effect prior to that of this judgment (except in the case of workers . . . who have initiated proceedings before this date or raised an equivalent claim under the applicable national law)' was disputed as being unclear. This lack of specificity, a characteristic of the Court's style of judgment, can create problems in the context of rulings on interpretation under Article 234 (ex 177). The Court's judgments can on occasions be too Delphic, leaving too much to be decided by national courts. It has taken a Protocol to the Maastricht Treaty and further cases to spell out the precise scope of the *Barber* ruling (see chapter 25). It is likely to be years before the *full* implications of the Court's rulings in *Francovich* (cases C–6, 9/90) and *Marshall (No. 2)* (case C–271/91) are revealed.

Despite its commitment to the principle of legal certainty the Court has chosen not to limit the effect of its rulings in a number of cases in which it has introduced new and unexpected principles with significant consequences for Member States and even (in the case of Treaty Articles) for individuals. It did not limit the effects of its judgment in *Francovich* despite Advocate-General Mischo's warnings as to the 'extremely serious' financial consequences for Member States if it were not so limited: nor did it do so when it laid down a principle of full compensation for breach of a directly effective Directive in *Marshall (No. 2)*. Thus, where a ruling is likely to result in serious consequences, whether for States or 'public' or private bodies, for example employers, Member States would be advised to take advantage of their opportunity to intervene in Article 234 (ex 177) proceedings (as they are entitled to do under Article 93, Protocol on the Statute of the Court of Justice) to argue against retroactivity, as they did successfully in *Defrenne* and *Barber*. Other 'interested parties' may also apply to intervene.

The effects of the ECJ's strict approach to retroactivity may be mitigated by its more recent approach to Member States' procedural rules. In a number of cases (*IN CO GE '90* (cases C–10 & 22/97) and *EDIS* (case C–231/96)), it has held that the principle of retroactivity should not prevent the application of detailed procedural rules (in these cases relating to limitation of actions) governing legal proceedings under national law, provided that these national rules do not make it 'impossible or excessively difficult' for individuals to exercise their Community rights (see further chapter 26).

The cases considered above relate to rulings on interpretation. Where matters of validity are concerned, the Court's approach is more flexible. It has assimilated the effects of a ruling of invalidity to those of a successful annulment action, as a result of which the illegal act is declared void. However, arguing from Article 231(2) (ex 174(2)), which enables the Court, in a successful annulment action, to limit the effects of a Regulation which it has declared void (see chapter 30), the Court has limited the effects of a finding of invalidity in a number of cases, sometimes holding the ruling to be purely prospective (i.e., for the future only, *excluding* the present case, e.g., *Roquette Frères* v *France* (case 145/79); policy doubted in *Roquette Frères SA* v *Hauptzollamt Geldern* (case C–228/92, see chapter 30); see also the Italian constitutional court in *SpA Fragd* v *Amministrazione delle Finanze* Decision No. 232 of 21 April 1989 (see chapters 5 and 6)), sometimes limiting its effects on the principles of *Defrenne* (e.g., *Pinna* (case 41/84)). The Court has not so far insisted that the effect of a ruling of invalidity can only be limited in the case in which the ruling itself is given.

The Court is more likely to be prepared to limit the effects of a ruling on validity than one on interpretation. Where matters of validity are concerned parties will have relied legitimately on the provision in question. A retrospective application of a ruling of invalidity may produce serious economic repercussions: thus it may not be desirable to reopen matters as regards the past. On the other hand too free a use of prospective rulings in matters of interpretation would seriously threaten the objectivity of the law, its application to all persons and all situations. Moreover, as the Court no doubt appreciates, a knowledge on the part of Member States and individuals that the law as interpreted may not be applied retrospectively could foster a dangerous spirit of non-compliance.

Interim measures

A national court may be requested to order interim measures pending a ruling from the ECJ under Article 234 (ex 177), either on interpretation or validity. *R* v *Secretary of State for Transport, ex parte Factortame Ltd* (case C–213/89) established that a national court must grant interim relief pending a ruling on the interpretation of Community law where this is necessary to protect individuals' directly effective Community rights, even where such a remedy is not available as a matter of national law. As a result of this ruling the House of Lords was prepared to grant an interim injunction against the Crown, preventing the application of the Merchant Shipping Act 1988. In *Zuckerfabrik* (cases C–143/88 & 92/89) the Court confirmed that national courts may also be obliged to grant interim relief pending a ruling from the ECJ on the validity of Community law, and set out the criteria to be applied by national courts in the exercise of their discretion as to whether or not to do so. It may be deduced from the terms of the Court's judgment that these criteria should be applied in all applications for interim relief, whether relating to matters of interpretation or validity. National courts' powers to grant interim relief pending a ruling under Article 234 (ex 177) have been held to include positive as well as suspensory measures (*Atlanta Fruchthandelsgesellschaft mbH* v *Bundesamt für Ernährung und Forstwirtschaft* (case C–465/93)) (see further chapter 26).

Contrary to the current position under British law, it is submitted that cross undertakings should be available against both local and central authorities in order effectively to protect the applicant who is refused interim relief but finally succeeds at trial. Alternatively, as the House of Lords suggested in *Kirklees Metropolitan Borough Council* v *Wickes Building Supplies Ltd* [1993] AC 227, he could in these circumstances claim damages against the State under *Francovich* (cases C–6 & 9/90). This would however require some relaxation of the existing threefold criteria governing eligibility (see chapter 4).

Impact of the Treaty of Amsterdam

Despite some suggestions prior to the 1996 IGC that the ECJ's jurisdiction under the preliminary ruling procedure be curtailed, the ToA has, to the contrary, increased the areas on which the ECJ may, in principle, rule. JHA and closer cooperation procedures of the TEU may now fall within its ambit. Additionally, the new Title IV in Part Three of the EC Treaty (on visas, asylum, immigration and other policies relating to free movement of persons), the subject matter of which was, prior to the ToA, mainly dealt with by the JHA Pillar and therefore outside the ECJ's competence, will in future fall within the ECJ's jurisdiction (Article 68 EC). This will have benefits in ensuring a respect for the rule of law and for access to justice.

Praise for the developments in the ToA cannot be unqualified, however; the provisions indeed raise some concerns. As noted earlier, the ECJ will have jurisdiction in relation to the JHA provisions of the TEU only in respect of 'framework decisions and decisions', and only insofar as each Member State accepts its jurisdiction (new Article 35 TEU). Even then, the Member States may not necessarily accept the ECJ's jurisdiction to the same degree. The Member States have the option of limiting the rights of the national courts to refer a question to the ECJ to courts against whose decision there is no judicial remedy under national law. This 'flexible' approach to jurisdiction will, at least, lead to confusion, but may also be criticised for the uncertainties and inequalities it introduces into the system: individuals' rights of access to the ECJ will vary depending on the Member State in which the action is brought. To a certain extent, one may still comment that this is better than the previous position under the TEU, where there was no such access.

The same is not true of the position of the new Title IV of the EC Treaty. Unlike any previous amendment to the EC Treaty, these new provisions have been subjected to a different regime as regards the jurisdiction of the ECJ.

Although Article 234 (ex 177) EC will, in principle, apply to these provisions, there are certain differences. Notably, only the courts against whose decisions there is no judicial remedy are required to ('shall') make a reference 'if they consider it necessary' to do so. Furthermore, the ECJ will not have jurisdiction in relation to measures taken under new Article 62(1) EC (concerning the crossing of external borders) relating to 'the maintenance of law and order and safeguarding of internal security'.

Thus the new provisions create holes in the judicial protection offered; unlike the JHA Pillar of the TEU, the ECJ's jurisdiction under former Article 177 (now 234) prior to the ToA applied to the whole of the EC Treaty. The ToA amendments undermine the homogeneity and generality of access to the ECJ. Many important references under Article 177 (now 234) came from the lower courts: now these courts will, in this new area, be precluded from making references. Consequently, individuals seeking a European ruling will be forced to litigate through their national appeal structure. The provision also creates uncertainty: when will circumstances necessitating the mainten- ance of law and order or safeguarding internal security arise? Indeed, who decides this question? It affects, in particular, those most in need of protec- tion: an asylum seeker, for example, may not be in a position to exhaust national remedies. Even if he does, he may then find he falls outside the ECJ's jurisdiction. The new approach, accepted with reluctance by the Commission on the insistence of Member States, hardly matches up with a Community which claims to be based on the rule of law and respect for human rights.

Conclusions on the preliminary rulings procedure to date

The success of the preliminary rulings procedure depends on a fruitful collaboration between the ECJ and the courts of Member States. Generally speaking both sides have played their part in this collaboration. The ECJ has rarely refused its jurisdiction or attempted to interfere with national courts' discretion in matters of referral and application of EC law. National courts have generally been ready to refer; cases in which they have unreasonably refused to do so are rare. Equally rare are the cases in which the ECJ has exceeded the bounds of its jurisdiction without justification.

However, this very separation of powers, the principal strength of Article 234 (ex 177), is responsible for some of its weaknesses. The decision whether to refer and what to refer rests entirely with the national judge. No matter how important referral may be to the individual concerned (e.g., *Sandhu*) he cannot compel referral; he can only seek to persuade. And although the ECJ will extract the essential matters of EC law from the questions referred it can only give judgment in the context of the questions referred (see *Hessische Knappschaft* v *Maison Singer et Fils* (case 44/65)). Thus it is essential for national courts to ask the right questions. In addition, since the relevance of the questions can only be assessed in the light of the factual and legal circumstances of the case in hand, these details too must be supplied. A failure to fulfil both these requirements may result in a wasted referral or a misapplication of EC law.

As the body of case law from the ECJ develops and national courts acquire greater confidence and expertise in applying EC law and ascertaining its relevance to the case before them, there will be less need to resort to Article 234 (ex 177). Thus the initial question, whether a decision on a question of EC law is 'necessary', will be crucial. *CILFIT Srl* (case 283/81) has supplied guidelines to enable national courts to answer this question; these guidelines, applied in the light of the rider added by the court, should ensure that references are made in the appropriate case and unnecessary referrals avoided. Where a lower court is in doubt as to whether a referral is necessary the matter may be left to be decided on appeal. On the other hand, where a final court has the slightest doubt as to whether a decision is necessary it should always refer, bearing in mind the purpose of Article 234(3) (ex 177(3)) and its particular importance for the individual litigant. These courts would do well to follow the lead provided by the German Constitutional Court. They will be more likely to do so if they are confident that the ECJ will not abuse its power in these proceedings by interpreting EC law too freely and failing to pay sufficient regard to 'important considerations of legal certainty'.

The significance of the ECJ's rulings and the Article 234 (ex 177) procedure have been well recognised by courts, commentators and Member States, as was evidenced by the suggestion made in the run-up to the 1996 IGC that the current jurisdiction of the ECJ should be curtailed. As noted above, the ECJ's jurisdiction was not in the end limited. The restrictions placed on its new jurisdiction, however, indicate not only that these areas are sensitive, but that the Member States wished to limit the opportunities for the ECJ to deliver one of its more far-reaching judgments in these areas. One point seems certain: the creation of a new approach to references to the ECJ indicates that both the Court and the procedure have been a victim of their own success, and the occasional excess.

The future: impact of enlargement

The current system governing preliminary rulings is under stress as, despite the *acte clair* doctrine, the number of references made to the ECJ remains high. With enlargement, the backlog can only get worse. There will be an increased number of referrals as an enlarged geographic jurisdiction will lead to a greater number of people (and courts) covered by EC law. The very fact that the current candidate countries are new to the EC legal system will mean that they are likely to create initially a disproportionate number of references. This arises from two linked points. The first is that there are more likely to be questions arising in the new Member States as their legal systems adjust to the Community legal order. Further, their courts are less likely to have the experience and confidence to deal with many EC law questions without guidance from the ECJ, especially given that many of the current candidate countries are relatively new to democracy and a market economy.

Not only does the likelihood of an increased workload and the current backlog of cases suggest that changes need to be made, but also the increased number and increasingly varied background of judges at the Court will make it more difficult for the ECJ to act effectively. Equally, consistency of approach between the different chambers may be hard to maintain. The ECJ is well aware of these problems and has put forward certain proposals to be considered by the 2000 IGC (Proceedings 08/00).

The first of these proposals is that both the ECJ and the CFI be given the power to amend their own rules of procedure, as in an enlarged Union obtaining the unanimous consent of the Council will be difficult and time-consuming. The Courts also approved two suggestions put forward by the Commission's working group. The first provides for the possibility of conferring on the CFI jurisdiction to answer questions referred for a preliminary ruling in certain matters falling within the ambit of 'special proceedings'. The second suggests that, in certain matters, for example industrial and commercial property, boards of appeal should be set up with judicial power to hear and determine disputes before such disputes can be brought before the ECJ and the CFI. Additionally, the Courts have suggested that recourse to the ECJ by way of appeal against decisions given by the CFI should be restricted.

The restriction of access to the ECJ may cut down that Court's workload and, subject to the CFI not being swamped by the cases diverted to it, may reduce the backlog in cases — especially the preliminary references. Nonetheless, this will constitute a significant change in the judicial architecture within the European Union, and it remains to be seen whether the political actors will find these proposals acceptable.

Further reading

Alexander, W., 'The Temporal Effects of Preliminary Rulings' (1988) 8 YEL 11.

Anderson, D., 'The Admissibility of Preliminary References' (1994) 14 YEL 179.

Barnard, C., and Sharpston, E., 'The Changing Face of Article 177 References' (1997) 34 CML Rev 1113.

Bebr, G., 'Preliminary Rulings of the Court of Justice — their Authority and Temporal Effect' (1981) 18 CML Rev 475.

Bebr, G., 'Arbitration Tribunals and Article 177' (1985) 22 CML Rev 498.

Bebr, G., 'The Reinforcement of the Constitutional Review of Community Acts under Article 177 EEC' (1988) 25 CML Rev 684.

Dashwood, A. and Arnull, A., 'English Courts and Article 177 of the EEC Treaty' (1984) 4 YEL 255.

Gray, C., 'Advisory Opinions and the European Court of Justice' (1983) 8 EL Rev 24.

Harding, C., 'The Impact of Article 177 of the EEC Treaty on the Review of Community Action' (1981) 1 YEL 93.

Koopmans, T., 'The Future of the Court of Justice of the European Communities' (1991) 11 YEL 15.

Maher, I., 'National Courts as European Community Courts' (1994) 14 LS 226.

O'Keeffe, D., 'Appeals against an Order to Refer under Article 177 of the EEC Treaty' (1984) 9 EL Rev 87.

O'Keeffe, D., 'Is the Spirit of Article 177 under Attack? Preliminary References and Admissibility' (1998) 23 ELR 509.

Pescatore, J., 'Interpretation of Community Law and the Doctrine of the *Acte Clair*' in Bathurst, M. E., et al. (eds), *Legal Problems of an Enlarged European Community* (London: Stevens, 1972).

Rasmussen, H., 'The European Court's *Acte Clair* Strategy in *CILFIT* (1984) 9 CML Rev 242.

Rasmussen, H., 'Between Self-Restraint and Activism; a Judicial Policy for the European Court' (1988) 13 EL Rev 28.

Toth, A., 'The Authority of Judgments of the European Court of Justice: Binding Force and Legal Effects' (1984) 4 YEL 1.

Tridimas, T., 'The Court of Justice and Judicial Activism' (1996) 21 EL Rev 199.

Waelbroeck, M., 'May the Court of Justice Limit the Retrospective Operation of its Judgments?' (1981) 1 YEL 115.

Watson, J., 'Experience and Problems in Applying Article 177 EEC' (1986) 23 CML Rev 207.

'*Quis Custodiet* the European Court of Justice?' Editorial (1993) 30 CML Rev 905.

TWENTY EIGHT

Enforcement actions

The principal remedy provided by the Treaty for infringements of EC law by Member States is the direct action before the ECJ under Article 226 (ex 169) EC, which provides:

> If the Commission considers that a Member State has failed to fulfil an obligation under this Treaty, it shall deliver a reasoned opinion on the matter after giving the State concerned the opportunity to submit its observations.
>
> If the State concerned does not comply with the opinion within the period laid down by the Commission the latter may bring the matter before the Court of Justice.

A similar procedure is provided for action by Member States under Article 227 (ex 170) EC.

Also, 'in derogation from the provisions of Articles 226 and 227', the Commission is empowered to bring a Member State before the Court under Article 88(2) (ex 93(2)) (infringement of Community rules on State aid provision, see chapter 13), Article 95(4) (ex 100a(4)), para. 3 (improper use of derogation procedure provided by Article 95(4) (ex 100a(4)), para. 1, see chapter 11) and Article 298 (ex 225) (measures taken to protect essential security interests or to prevent serious internal disturbances, see chapter 11).

The Commission's power under Article 226 (ex 169) applies to the whole of the EC Treaty (Article 46 TEU). By contrast to the position as regards the preliminary reference procedure (see chapter 27), this power, bringing with it the possibility of the ECJ's jurisdiction, has not been limited in regard to the new Title IV in the EC Treaty introduced by the ToA. Conversely, although the ECJ's jurisdiction to interpret the provisions of the JHA remaining within the TEU has been introduced by the ToA, the Commission has not been given the power to bring a Member State which has failed in its obligations under these provisions before the ECJ. This omission has been criticised (see article by Albors Llorens, noted in chapter 26).

Action by the Commission (Article 226 (ex 169) EC)

Article 226 (ex 169) EC, which gives the Commission power to bring Member States before the ECJ when they have failed to fulfil their obligations under Community law, is a specific example of the supranational nature of EC law. Because of the danger of non-compliance by Member States with their Community obligations, particularly in times of national or local difficulties, and because the success of the Community depends above all on solidarity and the uniform observance of its laws by all Member States, it was thought necessary to provide in the Treaty for a procedure whereby Member States suspected of infringing EC law might be called to account before the ECJ. The Commission, whose duty it is under Article 211 (ex 155) EC to 'ensure that the provisions of this Treaty and the measures taken by the institutions pursuant thereto are applied', was given the task of initiating and controlling this procedure.

The purpose of Article 226 (ex 169) EC is threefold. First, and primarily, it seeks to *ensure compliance* by Member States with their Community obligations. Secondly, it provides a valuable non-contentious *procedure for the resolution of disputes* between the Commission and Member States over matters of Community law: at least one-third of all Article 226 (ex 169) EC proceedings are settled at the preliminary informal stage. And finally, where cases do reach the ECJ they serve not only to bring particular breaches of EC law to light but also to *clarify* the law for the benefit of all Member States.

It is no doubt on account of the latter function that the Court has held that even if a State has complied with its obligations prior to the hearing before the Court, the Commission is entitled to judgment; it is not necessary for the Commission to show the existence of a 'legal interest' (*Commission* v *Italy (Re Ban on Pork Imports)* (case 7/61)).

Article 226 (ex 169) was not designed as a punitive measure. Until the passing of the TEU (1992) no sanction was provided against Member States found by the Court in breach of their obligations; they were merely required 'to take the necessary measures to comply with the judgment of the Court of Justice' (original Article 171 EC). Although normally no time limit was prescribed for Member States' compliance the Court had held (*Commission* v *Italy* (case 69/86)) that implementation of a judgment must be undertaken immediately and must be completed within the shortest possible time. Where a State failed to comply with these obligations the Commission could only seek to enforce the judgment by further proceedings for breach of original Article 171. While few such actions were taken in the early days of the Community, their number increased alarmingly in the course of the 1980s. As a result the then Article 171 (now 228) was amended by the TEU to allow the Commission, subject to the Court's approval, to impose fines and penalties on Member States which had failed to comply with a judgment against them in former Article 169 (now 226) proceedings. The Commission has now taken a number of decisions under this provision (see further below).

Failure to fulfil an obligation

Although national governments appear before the Court as defendants in an Article 226 (ex 169) action, proceedings are brought against the *State*. Thus they may be brought in respect of a failure on the part of *any* agency of that State, executive, legislative or judicial. The responsibility of the State is engaged 'whatever the organ of the State whose action or inaction constitutes a failure, even if it concerns an institution which is constitutionally independent' (*Commission* v *Belgium* (case 77/69)). So far no action has been taken in response to a judicial failure. Although national courts have on occasions clearly acted in breach of their obligations (e.g., *Minister of the Interior* v *Cohn-Bendit* [1980] 1 CMLR 543 — French Conseil d'État failed to comply with its obligation under former Article 177(3), see chapter 27) and action in respect of such infringements could have been undertaken in theory (per Advocate-General Warner in *Meyer-Burckhardt* v *Commission* (case 9/75)), the Commission, no doubt agreeing with Advocate-General Warner that such action should not be lightly undertaken, prefers to publicise national courts' failures in its annual reports on the monitoring and application of Community law. Following one such report, in which the Commission criticised both the Italian Consiglio di Stato and the French Conseil d'État for a number of failures, it noted with approval a 'major reversal' in the French Conseil d'État's attitude to the application of EC law (see Seventh Report (1990) OJ No. C232/1). Considerations of diplomacy could not, however, prevent an action before a domestic court against a national judicial failure based on *Francovich* v *Italy* (case C–6 & 9/90), which, following the ECJ's judgment in *Brasserie du Pêcheur* (cases C–46 & 48/93), remains a possibility.

A State's 'failure' may be in respect of any binding obligation arising from Community law. This would cover obligations arising from the EC Treaty and its amending and supplementing Treaties; from international agreements entered into by the Community and third countries where the obligation lies within the sphere of Community competence; from EC Regulations, Directives and Decisions; and even from general principles of law recognised as part of Community law where the breach of these principles occurs within the context of an obligation of EC law. 'Failure' can include any wrongful act or omission, ranging from non-implementation to partial implementation to faulty implementation of Community law, or simple maintaining in force national laws or practices incompatible with EC law. As the case of *Commission* v *France* (case C–265/95) also makes clear, the failure to fulfil an obligation may also arise in circumstances where the State has failed to take action to prevent other bodies from breaching EC law. In this case, the French authorities' failure to take action in the face of blockades of imported products was found, following an Article 169 (now 226) action by the Commission, to be a breach of Article 30 (now 28) in conjunction with Article 5 (now 10) (see further chapter 10).

Notices of Member States' failures may come as a result of the Commission's own enquiries, from (increasing) complaints from the public, or from the European Parliament. The Commission's Report on the Application of

Community Law for 1998 showed that the number of complaints from the public increased by 18 per cent from the 1997 figure to 1,128, whereas 396 cases in respect of the same period had been detected by the Commission. Although this figure constitutes approximately only one-quarter of the number of cases resulting from complaints, it is worth noting that the Commission inquiries for the previous year, 1997, had led to just 261 cases. The Commission, therefore, claims that it has become more effective in this regard.

Procedure

The sensitive nature of an action under Article 226 (ex 169) is reflected in its procedure. It follows a number of stages. The initial stages, both formal and informal, between the Commission and the Member State, are designed to achieve compliance by persuasion. Only if this fails is it necessary to proceed to the final, judicial stage before the ECJ.

Informal proceedings The Commission begins informally with a notification to the State concerned of its alleged failure, to which the State will respond. At least one-third of complaints are settled at this stage. Where they are not the Commission may proceed to the next, formal stage.

Formal proceedings: first stage The Commission opens proceedings by letters of formal notice, inviting the Member State concerned to submit its observations. In order that the State has a full opportunity to put its case the Commission must first inform the State of its grounds of complaint. The complaint need not at this stage be fully reasoned, but the State must be informed of *all* the charges which may be raised in an action before the Court. In *Commission* v *Italy (Re Payment of Export Rebates)* (case 31/69) the Commission alleged that Italy was in breach of its EC obligations in failing to pay certain export rebates to its farmers, required under EC Regulations; in opening the proceedings the Commission charged Italy with breaches up to 1967, but failed to mention a number of breaches committed after that date. When the matter came before the Court, the Court refused to consider the later breaches. The Court said that the Member States must be given an adequate and realistic opportunity to make observations on the alleged breach of Treaty obligations. In deciding whether a State has had such an opportunity the Court may take into account communications made by the Commission during the informal stage.

   Following the submission of the State's observations to the Commission the Commission issues a 'reasoned opinion'. Half of the cases which continue past the informal stage are resolved without the need for the Commission to issue this 'opinion'. The reasoned opinion will record the infringement and require the State to take action to end it, normally within a specified time-limit. Although it cannot introduce issues not mentioned in the formal notice, this does not mean that the reasoned opinion and the formal notice have to be exactly the same. In particular, the Commission may limit the scope of the enquiry (*Commission* v *Italy* (case C–279/94)). Further, although the opinion must be 'reasoned' it need not set out the Commission's case in full. In the case of *Commisson* v *Italy (Re Ban on Pork Imports)* (case 7/61) the Court held, in response to the Italian government's claim that the Commission's reasoned opinion was inadequate, that the reasoned opinion need only contain a coherent statement of the reasons which had convinced the Commission that the Italian government had failed to fulfil its obligations. No formalism was required. The only purpose of the reasoned opinion was to specify the point of view of the Commission in order to inform the government concerned, and, possibly, the Court. The reasoning behind the decision is clear. If the State refuses to accept the Commission's opinion, it may proceed to the second stage before the Court. It will then be for the Court to weigh in detail the merits of the case on both sides.

In *Commission* v *Germany* (case C–191/95) Germany challenged the admissibility of Article 226 (ex 169) proceedings on a number of grounds. The first of these related to the Commission's decision to issue the reasoned opinion for breach of the principle of collegiality. Germany argued that the Commissioners themselves at the time did not have all the facts to enable them to make such a decision; furthermore they had not seen the draft reasoned opinion. The ECJ held that the decision to issue a reasoned opinion could not be described as a measure of administration or management and could not be delegated by the Commissioners themselves to their officers. Nonetheless, this does not mean that the Commissioners have to agree the wording of the reasoned opinion; it is sufficient if they have the information on which the decision to send a reasoned opinion is based.

The ECJ has held (*Alfons Lütticke GmbH* v *Commission* (case 48/65)) that the reasoned opinion is merely a step in the proceedings; it is not a binding act capable of annulment under Article 230 (ex 173). Thus while the defendant State may choose to impugn the Commission's opinion in proceedings under Article 226 (ex 169) before the Court, where the Member State complies with the opinion, a third party, possibly adversely affected by the Commission's opinion, has no equivalent right. However, in *Amministrazione della Finanze dello Stato* v *Essevi SpA* (cases 142 & 143/80) the Court held that the Commission has no power in Article 169 (now 226) proceedings to determine conclusively the rights and duties of a Member State. These may only be determined, and their conduct appraised, by a judgment of the Court. The Commission may not, in the opinion which it is obliged to deliver under Article 226 (ex 169), exempt a Member State from compliance with its obligations under the Treaty or prevent individuals from relying, in legal proceedings, on the rights conferred on them by the Treaty to contest any legislative or administrative measure of a Member State which may be incompatible with Community law. Thus a third party, dissatisfied with the Commission's opinion, could raise the issue of the legality of the Member State's action indirectly before his national court and seek a referral on the relevant questions of interpretation to the ECJ under Article 234 (ex 177). This was done in *Essevi SpA* in a domestic action for the recovery of taxes levied allegedly in breach of the then Article 95 (now 90).

The same principle would apply where the Commission has decided in its discretion not to institute or pursue Article 226 (ex 169) proceedings. In *Alfons Lütticke GmbH* v *Commission* (case 48/65), Alfons Lütticke GmbH had complained to the Commission that its own (German) government was acting in breach of EC law by introducing a levy on imported powdered milk in breach of EC law. As an importer of powdered milk the levy affected it adversely. It asked the Commission to take action under the then Article 169 against Germany. The Commission refused. Germany had since withdrawn the levy and the Commission decided in its discretion not to take action. It was a political compromise. Lütticke, on the other hand, wished to establish the infringement in order to recover for losses suffered while the German law was in force. Since what was then Article 169 (now 226) gave the Commission a discretion in the matter there was no way in which its refusal to bring proceedings could be challenged either under the then Article 173 (now 230) (annulment action) or former Article 175 (now 232) (failure to act) (see chapters 30 and 31). However, in a parallel action before its national courts in *Alfons Lütticke GmbH* v *Hauptzollamt Saarlouis* (case 57/65), it succeeded in obtaining a ruling under the then Article 177 (now 234) from the ECJ on the direct effects of former Article 95 (now 90), the Article which it alleged the German government had breached. Since the Article was found directly effective, it could be applied in the company's favour.

While there are no time-limits in respect of the stages leading up to the reasoned opinion, thereby giving both parties time for negotiation, the Commission will normally impose in its reasoned opinion a time-limit for compliance. A Member State will not be deemed in breach of its obligations until that time-limit has expired. Where the Commission does not impose a time-limit the Court has held that a reasonable time must be allowed. A State cannot be relieved of its obligations merely because no time-limit has been imposed (*Commission* v *Italy (Re Premiums for Reducing Dairy Production)* (case 39/72)). The Commission has a complete discretion in the matter of time limit, subject to the possibility of review by the Court. The Court may dismiss an action under Article 226 (ex 169) on the grounds of inadequate time-limit. An action by the Commission against Belgium for its failure adequately to implement the *Gravier* Decision (case 293/83) was dismissed on the grounds that the 15 days compliance period prescribed by the Commission in its reasoned opinion did not give Belgium sufficient time to respond to its complaints, either before or after the issuing of its reasoned opinion (*Commission* v *Belgium (Re University Fees)* (case 293/85)). On the other hand, in *Commission* v *Belgium* (case 85/85) a compliance period of 15 days was held to be reasonable in the light of the extensive information provided by the Commission at the informal stage.

Formal proceedings: second stage If a Member State fails to comply with the Commission's reasoned opinion within the specified time-limit, proceedings move to the final, judicial stage before the Court. Again, the initiative rests with the Commission, which '*may* bring the matter before the Court of Justice' (Article 226 (ex 169)). No time-limits are imposed; the Commission is free to choose the most appropriate means of bringing the infringement to an end (*Commission v France (Re Euratom Supply Agency)* (case 7/71), proceedings brought under Euratom Treaty). Here the Commission is obliged to set out the subject matter of the dispute, the submissions and a brief statement of the grounds on which the application is based. With regard to the latter it is not enough simply to refer to all the reasons set out in the letter of formal notice and the reasoned opinion (*Commission v Germany* (case C–43/90)).

The judicial stage is not a review procedure, although at this stage the legality of the Commission's reasoned opinion may be reviewed (*Commission v Belgium* (case 293/85)). Here the Court, exercising plenary jurisdiction in contentious proceedings, conducts a full enquiry into the merits of the case and decides the matter *de novo*. Interested Member States (but not individuals: *Commission v Italy (Re Import of Foreign Motor Vehicles)* (case 154/85R)) are entitled to intervene in the proceedings. The Commission is entitled to request, and the Court to order, interim measures (e.g. *Commission v UK (Re Merchant Shipping Rules)* (case 246/89R); *Commission v Ireland (Re Dundalk Water Scheme)* (case 45/87R), see chapter 26). Application for interim relief may, however, only be made 'by a party to the case before the Court' and where it 'relates to' that case (Rules of Procedure, Article 83(1)).

Defences

Many defences to an action under Article 226 (ex 169) have been attempted; few have succeeded. The best defence is clearly to deny the obligation. It may be conditional, for example, on a time-limit which has not expired. Where a breach of secondary legislation is alleged, the legislation may be attacked for illegality. Otherwise, the traditional defences of international law offer little hope of success.

The defence of *reciprocity*, an accepted principle of international law, even entrenched in some Member States' constitutions (e.g., France, Article 55), whereby in the event of a breach of his obligations by one party the other party is likewise relieved of his, was rejected by the Court in *Commission v Luxembourg and Belgium (Re Import of Powdered Milk Products)* (cases 90 & 91/63). Here the governments argued that their alleged breach of what was then Article 12 of the EC Treaty (now 25) would have been legal but for the Commission's failure to introduce certain measures which they were authorised to enact. This argument, based on reciprocity, the Court held, was not applicable in the context of Community law. The Community was a new legal order; it was not limited to creating reciprocal obligations. Community law governed not only the powers, rights and obligations of Member States, but also the *procedures* necessary for finding and sanctioning all violations that might occur.

The defence of reciprocity was also rejected in the context of a failure by another Member State to comply with a similar obligation; it made no difference that Article 169 (now 226) proceedings had not been instituted against that State in respect of a similar breach (*Commission v France (Re*

Restrictions on Imports of Lamb) (case 232/78); *Steinike und Weinlig* (case 78/76)).

Similar reasoning to that advanced in *Commission* v *Luxembourg and Belgium* led to the rejection of a defence of *necessity* in *Commission* v *Italy (Re Ban on Pork Imports)* (case 7/61). The Treaty provided, in Article 226 (ex 169) , for procedures to be followed in cases of emergency. This precluded unilateral action on the part of Member States.

A defence based on *force majeure* was rejected in *Commission* v *Italy (Re Transport Statistics)* (case 101/84). Here Italy was charged with non-implementation of a Community Directive; the reason for its non-implementation was that the data-processing centre involved in the implementation of the Directive had been bombed. The Court held that while this might amount to *force majeure,* which could provide an excuse for non-implementation, a delay of four and a half years, as in this case, was inexcusable. As the Court said, 'time will erode the validity of the excuse'.

The concept of *force majeure* was considered in the case of *McNicholl* v *Ministry of Agriculture* (case 296/86), not in Article 226 (ex 169) proceedings, but in order to challenge via the preliminary rulings procedure the forfeiture of a deposit for failing to comply with an export undertaking as required by Community law. The Court held that:

> whilst the concept of *force majeure* does not presuppose an absolute impossibility of performance, it nevertheless requires that non-performance of the act in question be due to circumstances beyond the control of persons pleading *force majeure,* that the circumstances be abnormal and unforeseeable and that the consequences could not have been avoided through the exercise of all due care.

This definition should be equally applicable in Article 226 (ex 169) proceedings. Where it is clear that the fulfilment of a Community obligation will be impossible, a Member State should alert the Commission at the earliest opportunity in order to ascertain whether a compromise arrangement can be made (*Commission* v *Italy* (case C–349/93)).

Another defence, frequently raised and consistently rejected by the Court, is based on *constitutional, institutional or administrative difficulties* within a Member State. As the Court held in *Commission* v *Italy* (case 28/81), a Member State cannot plead the provisions, practices or circumstances existing in its own legal system in order to justify a failure to comply with obligations resulting from Community Directives. The same reasoning would apply to a failure to comply with any other Community obligations (e.g., *Commission* v *Italy (Re Premiums for Reducing Dairy Production)* (case 39/72 — Regulation).

Similarly in *Commission* v *United Kingdom (Re Tachographs)* (case 128/78) the Court refused to accept an argument based on *political* (i.e., trade union) difficulties, submitted as justification for a failure to implement a Community Regulation on the installation of tachographs.

Another popular but equally unsuccessful defence rests on the argument that while Community law may not be applied *de jure, administrative practices ensure that EC law is in fact applied.* This argument was advanced in *Commission* v *France (Re French Merchant Seamen)* (case 167/73), in an action based on the French Code Maritime. The code was clearly discriminatory, since it required a ratio of three Frenchmen to one foreigner in certain jobs. The French government's argument that the code was not enforced in practice was unsuccessful. Enforcement by administrative practices, the Court held, is not enough. The maintenance of national laws contrary to EC law gives rise to an ambiguous state of affairs, and leaves citizens of a Member State in a state of uncertainty (see also *Commission* v *Ireland* (case C–381/92)).

Similar reasons led to the rejection of another argument in the same case based on the *direct effects* of Community law. If the Community law in question, in this case what was then Article 7 of the EEC Treaty (now Article 12 (ex 6) EC), were directly effective, argued the French, this would be enough to ensure that the State fulfilled its obligations. The Court did not agree (see also *Commission* v *Belgium (Re Type Approval Directives)* (case 102/79)).

The Court took a (seemingly) more moderate line in *Commission* v *Germany (Re Nursing Directives)* (case 29/84). Here it conceded that a defence based on direct effects might succeed if the State's administrative practices guaranteed that the Directives would be applied fully and ensured that the legal position was clear and that all persons concerned were fully aware of their rights. These requirements were not, however, found to be satisfied in this case. It is submitted that they will rarely be satisfied. This seems to be borne out in the case of *Commission* v *Italy* (case 168/85), in which the Court held that the right of citizens to plead directly applicable provisions of the Treaty before national courts is only a minimum guarantee and insufficient in itself to ensure full and complete application of the Treaty.

Where there is a derogation from a Treaty obligation in the Treaty itself, provided the terms of that derogation are satisfied then it goes without saying that an Article 230 (ex 169) EC action would be unsuccessful. In *R* v *Chief Constable of Sussex, ex parte International Trader's Ferry Ltd* [1999] 1 CMLR 1320 the House of Lords was asked to consider whether a failure by the Sussex constabulary adequately to police animal rights protestors seeking to obstruct the export of live cattle from local ports was in breach of Community law. Faced with mounting and unsustainable costs, the Chief Constable had decided to reduce policing from five to three days per week. Although that failure might constitute a barrier to exports, in breach of the then Article 34 (now 29), it was argued that the breach was justified under Article 36 (now 30), on public policy grounds. Given that there was no likelihood of obtaining funds from the government, and that the police had a continuing obligation to protect the general public against crime and disorder, the restrictions on policing were neither unreasonable nor disproportionate. This argument was accepted by the House of Lords. The question is, would it have been accepted by the ECJ?

The ECJ faced a similar situation of civil disorder, this time by French farmers blocking imports of agricultural produce, contrary to the then Article 30 (now 28) EC, in *Commission* v *France* (case C–265/95). Here, despite complaints by the Commission, the French authorities had failed to take any significant action to prevent the demonstrations, arguing that more determined action might lead to more serious breaches of public order or even to social conflict. The ECJ refused to accept these arguments. 'Apprehension of internal difficulties', the Court held, 'could not justify a failure by a Member State to apply Community law correctly. . . . It was for a Member State to guarantee the full scope and effect of that law, to ensure its proper implementation, unless the State could show that action by it could have consequences for public order with which it could not cope.' The government had failed to adduce any evidence of the latter. Although a serious threat to public order might justify non-intervention by the police, that argument could only be adduced with regard to a specific incident, and not, as in the case in question, in a general way, covering all the incidents cited.

Thus the Court has conceded in principle, it is submitted correctly, that the need to preserve public order is, in an appropriate situation, a valid defence. Given the competing demands of public order in *R* v *Chief Constable of Sussex* and the necessity, in the face of finite public funds, to strike a balance between them, it may be argued that the House of Lords was right in concluding that the Chief Constable's decision, taken conscientiously, to reduce policing at the ports was justified, albeit on public policy or public order grounds rather than simply on the grounds of cost, and was not disproportionate.

Effects of a ruling

If the Court finds that the Member State has failed to fulfil its obligations under the EC Treaty the Member State is 'required to take the necessary measures to comply with the judgment of the Court of Justice' (Article 228 (ex 171) EC). Until the Maastricht Treaty the only sanction against a State which had failed to comply with a ruling from the Court under Article 226 (ex 169) was a second action under that Article for failure to comply with its obligations under Article 228 (ex 171). The number of such repeat actions had been steadily increasing. Although the ECJ had provided individuals with a means of enforcement of their Community rights via the principles of direct and indirect effects and State liability under *Francovich* (cases 6, 9/90), these remedies were uncertain and unequal in their application, and provided a remedy only in the individual case. Following its clarification in *Brasserie du Pêcheur* (cases C–46 & 48/93), a remedy under *Francovich* will only be available in circumstances where the State has 'manifestly and gravely' acted or failed to act in breach of EC law. A State will not be liable in damages for 'excusable' failures. Although excusable failures may be established in actions based on direct effects or indirect effects, in which liability has hitherto been strict, or under Articles 226 and 227 (ex 169 and 170), success in such actions will not *of itself* guarantee that States rectify their breaches of Community law. Thus at Maastricht a further weapon was added to the Court's armoury. Under a revised Article 228 (ex 171):

If the Commission considers that the Member State concerned has not taken such measures (to comply with the Court's judgment under Article 226) it shall, after giving the State an opportunity to submit its observations, issue a reasoned opinion specifying the points on which the Member State concerned has not complied with the judgment of the Court of Justice.

If the Member State concerned fails to take the necessary measures to comply with the Court's judgment within the time limit laid down by the Commission, the latter may bring the case before the Court of Justice. In so doing it shall specify the amount of the lump sum or penalty payment to be paid by the Member State concerned which it considers appropriate in the circumstances.

If the Court of Justice finds that the Member State concerned has not complied with its judgment it may impose a lump sum or penalty payment on it.

There is no Treaty limit to the level of fines that may be imposed by the Commission. Initially it was not clear how the Commission was going to calculate the fines, and it was only in November 1997 that the Commission published guidance on calculating the penalty payments ([1997] C 332 COM (97) 299). For the first few years after Maastricht, there were no actions involving the imposition of fines. In 1996 and 1997, the first fines were proposed. In one case, the Commission recommended that France be fined 105,500 ecus (approx £67,800) per day for non-compliance with a court ruling on the protection of wild birds handed down about two months previously. These sums are significant enough to act as a deterrent to offending Member States. As the Commission itself noted in its 1996 report on monitoring the application of Community law, the use of fines has led to a more uniform, complete and simultaneous application of Community law rules in all Member States. In its 1998 report, the Commission noted that it had suggested the use of fines in five cases in the year under review and that, in all bar two involving Greece, a solution had been quickly found after the fines had been proposed. Thus, it would seem that the amended Article 228 (ex 171) EC will at least go some way to persuade Member States that there is nothing to be gained and much to be lost by failing fully to comply with their obligations under Community law.

Action by Member States (Article 227 (ex 170) EC)

Article 227 (ex 170) provides:

A Member State which considers that another Member State has failed to fulfil an obligation under this Treaty may bring the matter before the Court of Justice.

Before a Member State brings an action against another Member State for an alleged infringement of an obligation under this Treaty, it shall bring the matter before the Commission.

The Commission shall deliver a reasoned opinion after each of the States concerned has been given the opportunity to submit its own case and its observations on the other party's case both orally and in writing.

If the Commission has not delivered an opinion within three months of the date on which the matter was brought before it, the absence of such opinion shall not prevent the matter from being brought before the Court of Justice.

The procedure is thus similar to that of Article 226 (ex 169) EC save that it is initiated by a Member State which, if the Commission fails to deliver a reasoned opinion within three months, is entitled to bring the matter before the ECJ. In addition, both parties are entitled to state their case and comment on the other's case both orally and in writing.

It has been suggested that since Article 227(1) (ex 170(1)) gives Member States a general right to bring proceedings, the issuing of a reasoned opinion cannot preclude the complainant State from bringing proceedings before the Court if it is dissatisfied with the opinion or if it wishes to obtain a final judgment from the Court. This latter occurred in *France* v *United Kingdom (Re Fishing Net Mesh Sizes)* (case 141/78).

The procedure provided under Article 227 (ex 170) has rarely been used; Member States seem cautious about bringing an action under this provision because, since no Member State has a perfect record for the implementation of Community law, there is a danger that a defendant State might bring a retaliatory action against its prosecutor. It is likely to be deemed more politic to bring the alleged infringement to the attention of the Commission, leaving the Commission to act under Article 226 (ex 169). Nonetheless, the Article 227 (ex 170) procedure was used in *Belgium* v *Spain* case (case C–388/95), concerning the rules regarding the application of the wine denomination, Rioja. It is interesting to note that the dispute brought in other Member States, which intervened in favour of one side or the other, revealing a split in opinion between the main wine growing States and others. The ECJ found in favour of Spain.

In case of dispute between Member States, the Treaty also provides a further, voluntary procedure. Under Article 239 (ex 182) EC, States may agree to submit to the ECJ any dispute relating to the subject-matter of the Treaty.

Special enforcement procedures: State aids, breach of Article 95(4) (ex 100a(4)) procedures and measures to prevent serious internal disturbances

These procedures, which apply only within the areas specified, operate 'in derogation from the provisions of Articles 226 and 227'. There are certain essential differences between these procedures and Articles 226 and 227 (ex 169 and 170). In the case of Article 88(2) (ex 93(2)) the Commission, after giving the parties concerned an opportunity to submit their comments, issues a *Decision* requiring the Member State concerned to alter or abolish the disputed aid within a specified time-limit. If the State concerned does not comply with the Decision within the prescribed time, the Commission or any other interested State may bring the matter to the ECJ. Since a *Decision*, unlike a reasoned opinion, is a binding act it will be subject to challenge under Article 230 (ex 173) EC (*Commission* v *Belgium* (case 156/77); see chapter 32).

Article 298 (ex 225) EC provides an accelerated procedure whereby the Commission can, without preliminaries, bring a Member State directly before the ECJ if it considers that that State is making improper use of its powers provided under Articles 296 and 297 (ex 223 and 224) EC. Under these provisions Member States are empowered to take emergency measures to protect essential security interests (Article 296 (ex 223)) or in the event of serious internal disturbances, war or threat of war, or for the purposes of maintaining peace and international security (Article 297 (ex 224)). A ruling of the Court under Article 298 (ex 225) is given in camera.

Article 95(4) (ex 100a(4)), para. 3, introduced by the Single European Act 1986, provides for the same accelerated procedure, whereby the Commission *or a* Member State may bring a State before the ECJ if it considers that the State is making improper use of the powers provided for in Article 95(4) (ex 100a(4)), para. 1 to 'apply national provisions on grounds of major needs referred to in Article 30 or relating to protection of the environment or the working environment' (see chapter 11).

Further reading

Barav, A., 'Failure of Member States to Fulfil their Obligations' (1975) 12 CML Rev 369.

Borschardt, G., 'The Award of Interim Measures by the European Court' (1985) 22 CML Rev 203.

Commission's Annual Reports on the Monitoring and Application of Community Law (OJ C editions).

Craig, P., 'Once upon a Time in the West: Direct Effect and the Federalisation of EEC Law' (1992) 12 Oxford J Legal Stud 453.

Dashwood, A., and White, R., 'Enforcement Actions and Articles 169 & 170' (1989) 14 EL Rev 388.

Evans, A., 'The Enforcement Procedure of Article 169 EEC: Commission Discretion' (1970) 4 EL Rev 442.

Everling, U., 'The Member States of the European Community before their Court of Justice' (1984) 9 EL Rev 215.

Gray, C., 'Interim Measures of Protection in the European Court' (1979) 4 EL Rev 80.

Snyder, F., 'The Effectiveness of European Community Law' (1993) 56 MLR 19.

TWENTY NINE

Judicial review: introduction

The institutions of the Community, in particular the Commission and the Council, have been given power under the Treaty to make laws binding on Member States and individuals. Their area of competence has been significantly extended by successive treaty amendments, the Single European Act, the Maastricht Treaty and, lastly, the Treaty of Amsterdam. As well as creating rights and obligations for States and individuals, secondary legislation may empower the Commission to impose substantial fines and penalties (e.g., Regulation 17/62 in the area of competition law, see chapter 17). It is therefore essential that the exercise of such powers be subject to review by the ECJ (or now the CFI), whose responsibility it is to see that 'the law is observed' (Article 220 (ex 164) EC).

As has already been noted (chapters 26 and 27), Community secondary legislation may be challenged *indirectly* before the courts of Member States, and questions of validity referred to the ECJ under Article 234 (ex 177) EC. Chapters 29–32 are concerned primarily with the means whereby States, and sometimes individuals, may challenge the institutions *directly* before the European Courts.

There are two ways in which control over the institutions needs to be exercised. First, it is necessary to ensure that the legislation issued by the institutions is valid; i.e., that the institution has the power to issue the act concerned, that it has been passed according to the correct procedures, and exercised for the right purposes. This constitutes a check on the institutions' *activities*. This is provided under Article 230 (ex 173), and, as an adjunct to that Article, Article 241 (ex 184). Secondly, there is a need to check on the institutions' *inactivity;* — to ensure that the institutions do not fail to act when they are under a legal duty to do so. This is provided by Article 232 (ex 175).

Judicial review under Articles 230 and 232 (ex 173 and 175) requires an examination of three separate questions. First there is the question of *locus standi*: does this applicant have the right, personally, to bring proceedings? Secondly, has he brought his action in time? These two questions relate to admissibility. And thirdly, if the first questions are answered in the affirmative, is he entitled to succeed on the merits?

Although the system of judicial review provided by the Treaty is modelled on French administrative law, many of the concepts will be familiar to English lawyers.

Originally, the court that had the jurisdiction to hear judicial review actions was the ECJ. Due to pressure of work, these types of actions now fall into the jurisdiction of the CFI, subject to appeal to the ECJ. There was a danger that applicants who had sufficient resources would, were the CFI to find against them, seek always to have the ECJ review the case. Thus, as with most appellate courts, there are limitations on appeals to the ECJ. The precise scope of the ECJ's power to review was summarised recently in *John Deere Limited* v *Commission* (case C–7/95P).

In determining this case, the ECJ started by referring to Article 255 (ex 168a) EC and Article 51 of the EC Statute of the Court of Justice, which state that an appeal is to be limited to points of law and must be based on the grounds of lack of competence of the CFI, breach of procedure before the CFI which adversely affects the interests of the appellant, or infringement of Community law by the CFI. Furthermore, Article 112(1)(c) of the Court's Rules of Procedure provides that an appeal must contain the pleas in law and the legal arguments relied on in the appeal; this means that an appeal must indicate *precisely* the contested elements of the judgment which the appellant seeks to have set aside, and also the legal arguments *specifically* advanced in support of the appeal. The ECJ also commented that this requirement, 'is not satisfied by an appeal confined to repeating or reproducing word for word pleas in law and arguments previously submitted to the Court of First Instance, including those based on facts expressly rejected by that court'. Such an approach would constitute no more than a re-examination by the ECJ of the application submitted to the CFI. The ECJ has no jurisdiction to do this. It also has no jurisdiction to establish facts of examined evidence. Thus, the appraisal by the CFI of the evidence does not constitute a point of law which is subject to review by the ECJ, unless the evidence has been fundamentally misconstrued (see also *Hilti* v *Commission* (case C–53/92P), para. 42).

These requirements clearly limit the scope for potential appeals; this does not, however, seem to have stopped some applicants from trying, especially in the competition field. Although the ECJ will refuse jurisdiction, these cases still impact on the ECJ's workload as in each case it still has to investigate the issue of the appeal's admissibility.

THIRTY

Direct action for annulment

Article 230 (ex 173) EC), provides:

The Court of Justice shall review the legality of acts adopted jointly by the European Parliament and the Council, of acts of the Council, of the Commission and of the [European Central Bank], other than recommendations and opinions, and of acts of the European Parliament intended to produce legal effects *vis-à-vis* third parties.

It shall for this purpose have jurisdiction in actions brought by a Member State, the Council or the Commission on grounds of lack of competence, infringement of an essential procedural requirement, infringement of this Treaty or of any rule of law relating to its application, or misuse of powers.

The Court shall have jurisdiction under the same conditions in actions brought by the European Parliament by the Court of Auditors and by the European Central Bank for the purpose of protecting their prerogatives.

Any natural or legal person may, under the same conditions, institute proceedings against a decision addressed to that person or against a decision which, although in the form of a regulation or a decision addressed to another person, is of direct and individual concern to the former.

The proceedings provided for in this Article shall be instituted within two months of the publication of the measure, or of its notification to the plaintiff, or, in the absence thereof, of the day on which it came to the knowledge of the latter, as the case may be.

Reviewable acts

Reviewable acts, defined as acts 'other than recommendations and opinions', are not confined, as they might appear to be, to Regulations, Directives or Decisions. The Court has held that they include all measures taken by the institutions designed to have legal effect, whatever their nature or form (*Commission* v *Council (Re European Road Transport Agreement)* (case 22/70)).

The measure in this case was a Council resolution setting out the position to be taken by the Council in the preparation of the road transport agreement. The Commission sought to challenge this resolution, since it considered that the matter lay outside the Council's sphere of competence. Applying the above test, the action was declared admissible.

Similarly in *Re Noordwijk's Cement Accoord* (cases 8–11/66), the act challenged was a registered letter sent by the Commission to the applicant in the context of EC competition policy, to the effect that the companies' immunity from fines was at an end. The letter was not called a 'decision'. Nevertheless it was held that since it produced legal effects for the companies concerned and brought about a change in their legal position it was an act capable of annulment under the then Article 173 (now 230) (see also *BEUC* v *Commission* (case T–37/92)). In *France* v *Commission (Re Pension Funds Communication)* (case C–57/95) the ECJ held that a communication, which was phrased in imperative language, was intended to have legal effects and therefore could be challenged. On the other hand, preliminary measures, designed simply to pave the way for a final decision, are not reviewable (see *Nashua Corporation* v *Commission* (cases C–133, 150/87)). Thus in *Dysan Magnetics Ltd* v *Commission* (case T–134/95), the opening by the Commission of a dumping investigation, a purely preparatory measure which preceded the adoption of definitive anti-dumping duties, and which did not have an immediate and irreversible effect on the legal situation of concerned undertakings, was held not to be open to challenge under the then Article 173 (now 230). On the other hand in *Air France* v *Commission* (case T–3/93) a mere statement by a Commission spokesman, not published but reported by the press agencies, that a proposed acquisition of Dan-Air by British Airways lay outside the scope of the Commission's competence under Regulation 4064/89, was held to be capable of annulment, since it confirmed the Commission's position 'beyond all doubt'. The fact that the statement was not addressed to a particular person and was given orally was not relevant: it was the content and legal effect of the measure which were crucial.

This principle, that it is the true nature and effect of a measure rather than its label which determines whether it may be reviewed under Article 230 (ex 173), is very important, since this provision is subject to a strict two-month time-limit. If the measure is not recognised as a binding act and challenged in time, the action will be declared inadmissible, whatever its merits (e.g., *Commission* v *Belgium* (case 156/77) — no success under Article 184 (now 241) because the original act (a letter) was not attacked in time; see chapter 32).

Although only acts of the Council and the Commission were expressed to be capable of challenge under the original Article 173, the Court had, prior to the passing of the TEU, admitted challenges to acts of the European Parliament having legal force with regard to third parties (see *Luxembourg* v *Parliament* (case 230/81); *Partie Ecologiste ('Les Verts')* v *Parliament* (case 294/83)). This was justified on the grounds that Parliament had over the years acquired powers to issue such acts. In *Luxembourg* v *Parliament*, Luxembourg was seeking to challenge Parliament's resolution to move its seat from Luxembourg to Strasbourg and Brussels. In *'Les Verts'* v *Parliament* the Green Party sought to challenge a decision of the Bureau of Parliament on the allocation of campaign funds for the 1984 European elections. Clearly Parliament's acts in these cases produced significant legal effects for both applicants (*cf. Les Verts* v *Parliament* (case 190/84)). These principles have now been incorporated into Article 230 (ex 173) EC. Also, reflecting Parliament's new powers of co-decision granted under the TEU, Article 230 (ex 173) now provides for challenge to acts adopted 'jointly by Parliament and the Council' under Article 251 (ex 189(b)) EC. Acts of the European Central Bank may also be challenged. Nevertheless, in order to be capable of challenge, the measure must proceed from a Community institution empowered under the Treaty to enact binding measures. Thus in *Commission* v *Council* (case C–25/94), a decision by the Committee of Permanent Representatives (COREPER), and in *Parliament* v *Council* (case C–181/91), a decision of the *Member States meeting in Council* (but not of the *Council* as such), could not be challenged.

The ECJ's jurisdiction under this provision is, of course, limited to Community acts. This does not mean that the actions of the Union will completely escape the ECJ's review. The ECJ has already held that it has the power to review actions taken under the JHA pillar of the TEU to ensure that such measures have been properly adopted thereunder and are not diluting the Community *acquis* (*Commission* v *Council (Air Transport Arrangements)* (case C–170/96)). Following the ToA, Article 35 TEU provides for judicial review of actions taken under the JHA pillar, albeit limited in terms of the measures which may be challenged (framework decisions and decisions) and the grounds of challenge. Furthermore, only the Commission and the Council can bring an action under these provisions. Parliament and 'natural or legal persons' have no *locus standi* to challenge action in this area.

Locus standi; who may bring an action?

Privileged applicants   Member States, the Council and the Commission are entitled to challenge *any* binding act under Article 230 (ex 173). A 'Member State' for the purposes of this Article does not include governments of regions or of autonomous communities (*Region Wallonie* v *Commission* (case C–95/97)). Further, the general right is not conferred expressly on Parliament. Clearly, as a body whose task it is to supervise the Council and the Commission it may have an interest in challenging the acts of those bodies. Its interest was patent in *Roquette Frères SA* v *Council* (case 138/79) and *Maizena GmbH* v *Council* (case 139/79) when it was permitted (on the basis of Article 37 of the Statute of the Court) to intervene before the Court in annulment proceedings brought by Roquette Frères SA under the then Article 173 (now 230), and thereby help to establish a failure on the part of the Council to consult Parliament.

Since Parliament has *locus standi* under Article 232 (ex 175) to bring an action against the institutions for failure to act, it had been suggested that it should have a parallel right under Article 230 (ex 173), especially since, as will be seen, an action under Article 232 (ex 175) may be blocked, leaving the applicant only to his remedy under Article 230 (ex 173). However, in *Parliament* v *Council (Comitology)* (case 302/87), a case in which Parliament was seeking to annul a Decision of the Council laying down procedures to be followed by the Commission in determining, *inter alia*, the composition of the Committee of Representatives of Member States, the Court held that this was not the case. It held, somewhat surprisingly, that there was 'no necessary link' between an action for failure to act and an action for annulment.

The Court modified its position in *Parliament* v *Council (Chernobyl)* (case C–70/88). Here it held, in the context of a challenge to a Decision taken by the Council, allegedly in breach of its obligation to consult Parliament, that Parliament did have *locus standi* to challenge acts of the Council or the Commission under the then Article 173 where this was necessary to protect its prerogative powers (applied *Parliament* v *Council* (case C–65/90)). This position was confirmed in the amendment to Article 173 (now 230) contained in the Maastricht Treaty. Regrettably the Heads of State at Maastricht chose not to grant Parliament a *general* right to challenge acts of the Council and the Commission, neither did they consider the matter at Amsterdam. Arguably, as the only democratically elected EC institution, with an express role in *supervising* Community activities, it should have been given this power.

The Court has been strict in its interpretation of the revised Article 230 (ex 173), and has been concerned to demonstrate its respect for the institutional balance prescribed by the Treaty. In *Parliament* v *Council (Re Aid to Bangladesh)* (cases C–181 & 248/91), while the Commission was found to have acted outside its authority in its handling of aid to Bangladesh, Parliament was held to have no standing to challenge such action. Since the Commission's error did not involve a modification to the Community budget (over which Parliament was required to be involved), no prerogative power of Parliament had been infringed. Similarly Parliament's claim was held inadmissible in *Parliament* v *Commission (Re Legislation on Organic Production)* (case C–156/93), on the grounds that Parliament had failed to show how its prerogatives had been infringed. However, in both proceedings the Court did examine the substantive issues raised, and in one case (C–248/91) found the illegality proved. Moreover, where Parliament's prerogatives are in issue the Court insists on strict compliance with form. Thus in *Parliament* v *Council (re European Development Fund)* (case C–316/91), in which an act of the Council had been challenged as enacted on the wrong legal basis, not requiring consultation with Parliament, whereas the allegedly correct legal basis required such consultation, it refused to accept the Council's argument that there had been no breach of Parliament's prerogatives since Parliament had in fact been consulted.

The ToA has now granted the Court of Auditors a similar right to bring actions to protect its prerogatives.

Non-privileged applicants   Compared with Member States and Community institutions, the *locus standi* of individuals under Article 230 (ex 173) is much more limited. A 'natural or legal person' is entitled only to challenge:

(a)   a decision addressed to *himself or herself,* or

(b)   a decision, in the form of a regulation or a decision addressed to another person, which is of direct and individual concern to himself or herself.

A 'natural or legal person' includes a State which is not a Member State of the EC (*Gibraltar* v *Council* (case C–298/89)).

All claims by natural or legal persons are now brought before the CFI with a right of appeal to the ECJ on points of law only (see chapter 28).

No problem exists where the decision is addressed to the applicant, with one minor exception (to be discussed in chapter 31). Provided the applicant brings the action within the two-month time-limit his or her claim will be admissible. Many such decisions have been successfully challenged (e.g., in competition law; see chapters 15 to 17).

Where the decision is addressed to another person, problems arise. 'Another person' has been held to include a Member State (*Plaumann & Co.* v *Commission* (case 25/62)). Despite dicta by the ECJ in *Plaumann,* that the provisions of the Treaty concerning the right to seek a legal remedy ought not to be interpreted strictly, the Court, and now the CFI, has adopted a very restrictive approach towards the individual seeking to challenge acts addressed to another person, although there has been some relaxation of the rules in recent years. For example, although the Court has been unwilling to entertain actions by trade or other associations under Article 230 (ex 173), maintaining that 'defence of a common interest is not enough to establish admissibility', the CFI held in *Associazione Italiana Tecnico Economica del Cemento (AITEC)* v *Commission* (cases T–447–9/93) that a trade association would be permitted to bring an action against a decision addressed to 'another person' where it represented the individual interests of some of its members whilst at the same time protecting the interests of the section as a whole. The CFI noted that 'in these circumstances collective action brings procedural advantages'. As a result Italian and British associations of cement producers were able to challenge a Commission decision addressed to the Greek government approving the grant of State aid to a Greek producer, Heracles, and succeeded in obtaining its annulment. Likewise a trade union and a works council, as 'recognised representatives' of employees affected by a proposed merger under Merger Regulation 4064/89, were held entitled to challenge a Commission decision approving Nestlé's takeover of Perrier SA (see *Comité Central d'Entreprise de la Société Générale des Grandes Sources* v *Commission* (case T–96/92)). In *Federolio* v *Commission* (case T–122/96), the CFI identified three situations when an association would be granted *locus standi:*

(a)   the trade association has been expressly granted procedural rights;

(b)   it represents the individuals or undertakings which themselves have standing; or

(c)   the trade association itself is affected — for example if its right to negotiate is affected.

This will still leave many associations or pressure groups without *locus standi* (see, for example, *Stichtling Greenpeace Council* v *Commission* (case C–585/93), the subject of an unsuccessful appeal (case C–321/95 P)). Perhaps this is not surprising, given the stringency of the test applied to individuals.

For a claim by a 'natural or legal person' against a decision addressed to 'another person' to be admissible, three criteria must be satisfied:

(a) the measure must be equivalent to a decision;
(b) it must be of direct concern to himself or herself; and
(c) it must be of individual concern to himself or herself.

Since *all* of these criteria must be fulfilled the question of admissibility may be decided, and the application rejected, on the basis of any one of them. In the order in which it examines the above requirements, and in its approach to all three criteria, the Court has not been consistent.

The measure must be, as far as the applicant is concerned, a Decision   Since many of the Commission's policies, for example in the highly regulated field of agriculture, are implemented by directly applicable Regulations, often with wide-ranging and adverse effects on individuals (e.g., withdrawal of subsidies, imposition of levies), many cases have arisen in which individual applicants have sought to challenge Regulations. Although it would have been open to the Court to interpret Article 230(2) (ex 173(2)) to enable them to do so provided that the applicant could prove 'direct and individual concern', the Court was originally insistent that a natural or legal person could not challenge a 'true' Regulation. For this reason in *Koninklijke Scholten-Honig NV* v *Council and Commission* (case 101/76) the applicant glucose producers' attempt to challenge certain Regulations requiring glucose producers to pay levies on the production of glucose, for the benefit of sugar producers, was held, despite the merits of the case, to be inadmissible. (See also *Calpak SpA* v *Commission* (cases 789 & 790/79) — attempt (failed) by Italian pear processors to challenge a Regulation fixing production aids for pear processors; *Alusuisse* (case 307/81).)

However, whether a measure is, as far as the applicant is concerned, a 'true' Regulation or not involves a very subtle enquiry, a fact underlying the decision of the ECJ in *R* v *Intervention Board for Agricultural Produce, ex parte Accrington Beef Co. Ltd* (case C–241/95). There, the ECJ acknowledged that an individual seeking to challenge a Regulation could not be sure whether or not he would have *locus standi* under the then Article 173 (now 230). In *Confédération Nationale des Producteurs de Fruits et Légumes* v *Council* (cases 16 & 17/62) the Court held that in order to determine the legal nature of an act it is necessary to consider the nature and content of an act rather than its form. It is the substance, not the label, which is crucial. A true Regulation is a measure of general application, i.e., normative; it applies to objectively determined situations and produces legal effects on categories of persons viewed abstractly and in their entirety. On the other hand the essential feature of a Decision, which is defined as 'binding upon those to whom it is addressed' (Article 249 (ex 189)) arises from the limitation of the persons to whom it is addressed; a Decision concerns designated persons individually.

In *International Fruit NV v Commission (No. 1)* (cases 41-4/70) the applicants, a group of fruit importers, were held entitled to challenge a Community 'Regulation' laying down the quantity of import licences to be issued for a certain period. The quantity of licences was calculated on the basis of applications from, *inter alia*, the applicants, received during the preceding week; thus it applied to a finite number of people and was issued in response to their applications. Although it appeared to be a general measure it was found in fact to be a disguised bundle of decisions addressed to each applicant (see also *Roquette Frères SA v Council* (case 138/79)).

The ECJ has also suggested that a measure may be 'hybrid' in nature, i.e., it may be a measure of general application which is, nonetheless, in the nature of a decision for certain 'designated individuals'. In the *Japanese ball-bearings* cases (cases 113 & 118–21/77) four major Japanese producers of ball-bearings were held entitled to challenge an EC anti-dumping Regulation. Although the measure was of general application some of its Articles specifically referred to the applicants. Therefore, for them, it was in the nature of a decision. In *Allied Corporation v Commission* (cases 239 & 275/82) some of the applicant companies seeking to annul an anti-dumping Regulation were charged with illegal dumping in the Regulation itself. The ECJ held that although measures involving anti-dumping duties were:

> as regards their nature and scope, of a legislative character, inasmuch as they apply to all traders concerned taken as a whole, the provision may nonetheless be of direct and individual concern to those producers and exporters who are charged with practising dumping.

On this basis the applicant producers' and exporters' claims were held to be admissible.

In *Timex Corporation v Council* (case 264/82) the applicant company, which succeeded in establishing *locus standi* to challenge another anti-dumping Regulation, was this time a complainant which, through its national trade association, had brought certain illegal dumping practices (concerning Russian watches and watch movements) to the Commission's attention. The Regulation had been issued as a result of enquiries following Timex's complaints. The ECJ held that although the measure was legislative (i.e., normative) in nature, it was a decision of direct and individual concern to Timex since it had been issued in response to Timex's complaint and the company had given evidence to the Commission during the anti-dumping proceedings.

It may be noted that in *Allied*, in admitting that the measures challenged were legislative in character, i.e. 'true' Regulations, the ECJ did not consider the question whether they were in the nature of a decision to the applicants. It appeared to be sufficient that the applicants had established direct and individual concern. This approach, although not followed in *Timex*, has since been adopted in a number of cases, principally, but not exclusively, in the context of challenge to Regulations imposing anti-dumping duties. Under EC anti-dumping rules such duties, which are normally levied on importation of the product concerned, can only be imposed by Regulation. Such Regulations may adversely affect undertakings such as producers and exporters situated outside the Union who have no opportunity to challenge the measures in an action before the courts of Member States. The Court has admitted a number of challenges to Regulations by producers or exporters who were able to establish that they were identified in the measures adopted by the Commission or the Council (as in *Timex*) or were concerned in the Commission's preliminary investigations (see *Nashua Corporation* v *Commission* (cases C–133, 150/87), *Neotype* v *Commission* (case C–305/86)): also by importers whose retail prices for the goods in question or whose business dealings with the manufacturer of those goods played a part in establishing the existence of dumping (*Enital* v *Commission* (case C–304/86); *Gestetner Holdings plc* v *Commission* (case C–156/87)). Such claims were admissible because (as well as the applicants being directly concerned) the factors cited above were deemed to constitute individual concern. In *Extramet Industrie SA* v *Council* (case C–358/89), the ECJ went further and admitted a challenge to a 'true' Regulation by an *independent* importer whose retail prices and business dealings in the goods in question were *not* taken into account in establishing the existence of dumping, simply because he was able to establish individual (as well as direct) concern.

Also, outside the area of anti-dumping, in *Sofrimport* v *Commission* (case C–152/88), the ECJ allowed an applicant importer to challenge a Regulation suspending imports into the EC of apples from certain third countries solely on the basis of direct and individual concern; the Court did not avert to the question of whether the measure was in the nature of a decision as regards the applicant.

In *Codorniu SA* v *Council* (case C–309/89) the principal producer in Spain of quality sparkling wine, and holder of graphic trade-mark rights in the title 'Gran Cremant di Codorniu' was allowed to challenge EC Regulations on the description of sparkling wines in which the word 'cremant' was to be reserved for certain quality sparkling wines produced in France and Luxembourg. Although the measures in question were legislative measures applicable to traders in general they were of individual concern to the applicant.

These cases suggest that in the context of a challenge to a Regulation, where the applicant can prove direct and (particularly) individual concern the Court may no longer require proof that the measure constitutes a decision as far as he is concerned. This approach, although prima facie contrary to the literal wording of Article 230 (ex 173) EC and the Court's earlier case law is, as Advocate-General Jacobs pointed out in *Extramet*, consistent with the general scheme and purpose of the Article and necessary to ensure effective judicial protection for those (such as manufacturers and exporters in countries outside the EC) who may be seriously affected by Regulations but who lack alternative or adequate means by which to challenge them. Since the concept of individual concern is very strictly interpreted by the Court it may be argued that it is sufficient in itself (together with the concept of direct concern) to restrict access to judicial review of Regulations by natural or legal persons. Moreover, since as will be seen the two questions of (a) whether a measure, although called a Regulation, is in fact in the nature of a decision to the applicant and (b) whether it is of individual concern to the applicant often involve the same enquiry: thus where the latter criterion is met, the need to prove the former becomes superfluous.

There have been few examples of challenge by natural or legal persons to Directives. Since Directives are addressed to Member States it might have been thought that they are closer to a decision than to a Regulation, and as such, more likely to be challengeable. However in *Gibraltar* v *Council* (case C–298/89) the Court refused to admit a challenge to an EC Directive by the government of Gibraltar (found to be a natural or legal person) on the grounds that Directives, being 'normally a form of indirect regulatory or legislative measure' were not open to challenge by such persons. Since the Directive in question, although affecting the applicants by excluding them from its territorial scope, applied to 'objectively determined situations' the applicants' claim was inadmissible. Here, however, unlike the applicants mentioned above who succeeded in establishing *locus standi* to challenge Regulations, the applicants were unable to prove individual concern. In *Salamander and others* v *European Parliament and Council* (joined cases T-172 and T-175-177/98), concerning a challenge to the tobacco advertising directive (Directive 98/43/EC), the CFI seemed to suggest that a directive could in principle be capable of challenge by individuals provided they could show direct and individual concern. In this case, however, the applicants were unable to show direct concern.

By contrast with the position taken in *Gibraltar* v *Council* in relation to Directives, where the measure in question is described as a Decision, provided it has a specific addressee, the Court presumes it to be a Decision, even though, as in the case of a Decision addressed to a Member State, it may lay down normative rules.

The measure must be of direct concern to the applicant   A measure will be of direct concern to the applicant if it leaves the Member State no real discretion in implementation. Often the Commission will issue a Decision to a State requiring, or authorising, the State to act in a particular manner. Whether the individual affected by such action may challenge the Community Decision will depend on whether the action affecting the applicant was within the area of the Member State's discretion or not. In *Eridania* v *Commission* (cases 10 & 18/68) an Italian sugar-refining company sought to challenge three Commission Decisions granting aid to its competitors. Its action under the then Article 173 (now 230) was declared inadmissible. Although the Commission's Decisions had authorised the granting of aid, and indeed named the companies concerned, those Decisions were not of direct concern to the applicants, since the decision regarding the *allocation* of the aid had been made by the Italian government. This was a matter within the government's discretion. Where the matter of which the applicant complains lies within the discretion of the State the appropriate challenge is to the national authority responsible for the relevant decision.

The question of whether a particular Community Decision leaves room for discretion on the part of a Member State is susceptible of different interpretations. Interpreted broadly, as in *Plaumann & Co.* v *Commission* (case 25/62) and *SA Alcan Aluminium Raeren* v *Commission* (case 69/69), it could mean that where the Commission merely *permits* or *authorises* a Member State to act the State still retains a discretion as to whether to act or not. In *Alcan* the Court agreed with Advocate-General Roemer's suggestion in *Plaumann* that even where the Commission *refuses* permission to act, the State, in its discretion, may choose to act in disregard of this refusal and face the consequences of an action under what was then Article 169 (now 226). On the other hand, interpreting the question of discretion narrowly, as in the *Japanese ball-bearings* case (cases 113 & 118–21/77), it could be said that where implementation of a Community Decision is *automatic* or a *foregone conclusion*, as can be presumed where permission or authorisation is sought, no real discretion exists on the part of the State, and the measure will be of direct concern to the applicant.

A number of cases in which the applicant has succeeded in establishing *locus standi*, such as *Alfred Toepfer KG* v *Commission* (cases 106 & 107/63) and *Werner A. Bock KG* v *Commission* (case 62/70) have involved Decisions of confirmation (*Toepfer*) or authorisation (*Bock*). In these cases it seems to have been presumed that the measures were of direct concern to the applicants. In the more recent case of *AE Piraiki-Patraiki* v *Commission* (case 11/82), in the context of a Commission Decision authorising the French to impose a quota system on imports of Greek yarn, Advocate-General VerLoren van Themaat suggested that a Community measure would be of direct concern if its legal effects on interested parties and their identity could 'with certainty or with a high degree of probability be inferred'. The Court considered that the possibility that the French government would not take advantage of the Commission's Decision was 'purely theoretical'. Thus the more recent dicta and the practice of the Court indicate that the more generous attitude to questions of direct concern — at least as far as the involvement of Member States is concerned — will be preferred to the restrictive approach of *Plaumann* and *Alcan*. Nonetheless on the question of direct concern *Plaumann* and *Alcan* still remain a trap for the unwary (see Commission's view in *Spijker Kwasten BV* v *Commission* (case 231/82)).

Decisions need not, of course, be addressed to Member States. Where Decisions have been addressed to natural or legal persons, the CFI has taken a narrow view of when these Decisions could be said to affect other persons directly. Thus, the Commission's decision to approve Nestlé's takeover of Perrier in *Comité Central d'Entreprise de la Société Générale des Grandes Sources* v *Commission* (case T-96/92) was found not to be of direct concern to the applicant employee representative bodies. Any disadvantage suffered by employees following the merger would result from action by the merged undertaking itself, subject to the protection provided for employees in these circumstances under national and Community law. It did not result directly from the Commission's decision. The applicants were only directly concerned by the decision to the extent that their procedural rights, granted to 'recognised representatives' under the Merger Regulation, might have been infringed. More recently, a supplier under a contract with the Ukraine, which received financial aid from the Community, was held not to be directly affected by a Commission Decision that its contracts did not satisfy the Community's criteria for release of payments to the Ukraine (*Richco Commodities Ltd* v *Commission* (case T–509/93)). The CFI pointed out that there was no legal relationship between the supplier and the Commission. The fact that the contract was expressed to be conditional on payment of the aid was irrelevant; standing under Article 230 (ex 173) cannot be dependent on decisions made in commercial negotiations. This ruling may now be open to question. In a series of cases on appeal from the CFI regarding the same point, the ECJ has held the individual to be directly concerned (see, e.g., case C–403 & 404/96 *Glencore Grain Ltd* v *Commission*).

The measure must be of individual concern to the applicant   The concept of individual concern has been construed very restrictively by the Court. Because it operates to exclude so many cases it is often the first criterion to be examined, as it was in *Plaumann & Co.* v *Commission* (case 25/62). Plaumann & Co. were importers of clementines who sought to annul a Commission Decision, addressed to the German government, refusing the government permission to reduce its customs duties on clementines imported from outside the EC. Plaumann & Co. claimed that as a large-scale importer of such clementines they were 'individually concerned'. The Court disagreed. The importing of clementines, the Court held, was an activity which could be carried out by anyone at any time. There was nothing in the Decision to distinguish Plaumann & Co. from any other importer of clementines. In order to establish individual concern, the applicant must prove that the Decision affects him or her because of:

> certain characteristics which are peculiarly relevant to him, or by reason of circumstances in which he is differentiated from all other persons, and not by the mere fact that he belongs to a class of persons who are affected.

The *'Plaumann'* test has become the classic test for individual concern. It is, however, more easily stated than applied, since it does not specify *what* characteristics 'peculiarly relevant to him' the applicant must prove to establish individual concern or what circumstances will differentiate him from all other persons.

It will *not* be sufficient to prove that his business interests have been adversely affected, as was clearly the case in *Plaumann & Co.* v *Commission*. *Nor* that they were affected in a different way, or more seriously, than other similar traders. These arguments were rejected in *Eridania* (cases 10 & 18/68), and in *Calpak* (cases 789 & 790/79), in which the applicant pear processors claimed that the Commission's mode of calculation of pear processing aids operated particularly unfairly on itself as a private company as compared with other pear producers such as public companies and cooperatives.

Nor is it sufficient that the applicant's identity is known to, or ascertainable by, the Commission when the measure is passed. In *UNICME* v *Council* (case 123/77) an association of Italian motorcycle importers was seeking to annul a Commission Regulation, authorising the Italian government to impose temporary quotas on motorcycles imported from Japan. The measure was in retaliation for the imposition by the Japanese of a quota on the import of Italian ski boots. Members of the association were the only persons concerned and they were all concerned. They were ascertainable and many had already applied for import licences. Their application was held inadmissable. The Court found it unnecessary to consider whether the contested measure was a true Regulation, since it was not of direct or individual concern to the applicants. It 'would only affect the interests of the applicants when their request for a licence was refused'. 'The possibility of determining more or less precisely the number or even the identity of the persons to whom the measure applies by no means implies that it must be regarded as being of individual concern to them.' While the former statement may be open to question as a ground for denying direct and individual concern, since it could be applied to *any* act addressed to a third party, such as the Decisions in *Bock* and *International Fruit Co. NV*, which were found to be of individual concern, the latter recurs consistently in the Court's case law on individual concern.

Will a measure be deemed of individual concern if a causal connection can be proved between a particular measure and the applicant's own case? This was not found to be the case in *Spijker Kwasten BV* v *Commission* (case 231/82). Here the Commission issued a Decision, at the request of the Dutch government, enabling the government to ban the import of Chinese brushes for a six-month period, from July to 31 December 1982. Prior to the above request being made the applicant had applied for a licence to import such brushes. There was no doubt a causal link between its application and the Dutch government's request. The request and the Commission's Decision were prompted by its application. Moreover the company was the only importer of these brushes in Holland, and the only one likely to want to import them during the six-month period in question. Yet it was held not to be individually concerned. The measure, the Court held, was of general application. There was nothing to stop others applying for licences during that same period.

This case also confirmed a point established earlier in *Glucoseries Réunies* v *Commission* (case 1/64), that the fact that the applicant (in this case the sole producer of glucose in Belgium and the principal exporter of glucose in France) is the *only* person likely to be affected by the measure is not a characteristic peculiarly relevant to him such as to give rise to individual concern, as long as there is a theoretical possibility that others can enter the field and be affected by the same measure.

What characteristic peculiarly relevant to him must the applicant then prove in order to establish individual concern?

Measure referable specifically to applicant's situation and affecting a closed class Although there is no single satisfactory test a common thread runs through most of the cases in which individual concern has been held to exist. In almost every case the measure which the applicant seeks to challenge, although addressed to another person, is referable specifically to his situation. Moreover, not only does it affect him as though he were the person addressed, but it affects him either *alone* or as a member of a fixed and *closed* class; no one else is capable of entering the field and being affected by the same measure.

For example, the measure may have been issued in response to a licence or tender application. In *Alfred Toepfer KG v Commission* (cases 106 & 107/63) Toepfer had, amongst others, requested a licence from the German government to import cereals from France. The Commission's Decision, made at the request of the German government, was a confirmation of the government's measure refusing to grant the import certificate. The only persons affected by the Decision were those who had already applied for licences. Thus they were individually concerned.

Similarly in *Werner A. Bock KG v Commission* (case 62/70), the firm of Bock had applied for a permit to import a consignment of Chinese mushrooms, for which it already had a firm offer. Since Chinese mushrooms at the time were in free circulation in the EC, the German government, if it wished to prohibit their import into Germany, needed authority from the Commission to do so. Following Bock's application, the German government, on 11 September, applied to the Commission for that authority, which the Commission granted by a Decision on 15 September. The Court held that Bock was individually concerned; the Decision was passed in response to its application. (See also *Simmenthal SpA v Commission* (case 92/78) — Decision issued in response to claimant's tender.)

A similar connection existed in *Philip Morris Holland BV v Commission* (case 730/79). Here the Decision in question, which was addressed to the Dutch government, requested the government to refrain from granting State aid to the applicant tobacco company, Philip Morris. The Court assumed without argument that the company was individually concerned. In *Consorzio Gruppo di Azione Locale 'Murgia Messapica' v Commission* (case T–465/93) the applicant consortium had applied for grants from the Community Leader programme: they were found to be individually concerned by the Commission's decision addressed to the Italian authorities rejecting their application for aid.

International Fruit Co. NV v Commission (No. 1) (cases 41 - 4/70) concerned a Commission 'Regulation', controlling the issue of import licences for apples from non-Member States. The Regulation was issued by the Commission on the basis of applications received during the preceding week, following an assessment of the overall situation. It applied *only* to those who had applied for licences during that week. It was held to be of individual concern to the applicants. On the same reasoning the measure was found not to be a true Regulation at all, but a bundle of Decisions.

However, even a 'true' Regulation can be of individual concern to *some* individuals, as it can be in the nature of a Decision to some individuals, if it is referable expressly or impliedly to their particular situation, either alone or as a member of a known and *closed* class (*Japanese ball-bearing case* (cases 113 & 118 — 21/77); *Allied Corporation* v *Commission* (cases 239 & 275/82); *CAM SA* v *Commission* (case 100/74), overruling *Compagnie Française Commerciale et Financière SA* v *Commission* (case 64/69)). Likewise in *Codorniu SA* v *Council* (case C–309/89) the applicant producers of sparkling wine were differentiated from all other producers of sparkling wine because they were prevented by the Regulation from exercising their registered trade-mark right in 'Gran Cremant di Codorniu'. *Sofrimport SARL* v *Commission* (case C–152/88) also concerned a successful challenge of this nature. The applicants, who were fruit importers, were seeking to annul a number of Commission Regulations suspending the issue of import licences for apples from Chile and fixing quantities of such imports from third countries. Under one of the Regulations (2702/72) the Commission was required under Article 3 to take into account, when exercising its powers under the Regulations, the 'special position of products in transit' when the Regulations come into force. The applicants had goods in transit when the contested Regulations came into force. The ECJ held that they were individually concerned. 'Such persons constituted a restricted group *which could not be extended* after the contested measure took effect.'

The reason why the applicant in *Spijker Kwasten* (case 231/82) failed to establish individual concern was that, although there was a causal link between its licence application and the Commission's Decision, the latter measure allowing the Dutch authorities to introduce a quota was deliberately designed to take effect for the period *subsequent* to that for which the applicant had applied for licences. The applications it had already lodged were not affected by the measure: it applied only to future transactions: thus there was a theoretical possibility that other traders could be equally affected.

Measure issued as a result of proceedings initiated by applicant or in which the applicant has played a legitimate part A rather different situation in which the necessary link has been held to exist between the applicant and the challenged act to constitute individual concern, is when the act is not 'directed at' him but issued as a result of proceedings in which the applicant has played a legitimate part. In *Metro-SB-Grossmärkte GmbH & Co. KG* v *Commission* (case 26/76) the applicant was seeking to challenge a Decision issued to another firm, SABA, in the context of EC competition policy. The Decision was issued following a complaint by Metro under Article 3 of Regulation 17/62 (see chapter 17) that SABA was acting in breach of the then Article 85. The Court held, on the question of admissibility, that since persons with a legitimate interest were entitled, under Article 3 of Regulation 17/62, to request the Commission to investigate the infringement they should be allowed to institute Article 173 (now 230) proceedings in order to protect that interest. Thus Metro was individually concerned.

On similar reasoning, in *Timex Corporation* v *Council* (case 264/82), Timex was deemed to be individually concerned and permitted to challenge an anti-dumping Regulation; the company had initiated the complaint (as it was entitled to do under a further anti-dumping Regulation) and had given evidence in the proceedings. (See also *COFAZ* v *Commission* (case 169/84) — applicants individually concerned in Commission Decision concerning State aids; they had initiated the complaint and taken part in the proceedings; see also *FEDIOL* v *Commission* (case 191/82); *Associazione Italiana Tecnico Economica del Cemento* v *Commission* (cases T–447–9/93); *Comité Central d'Entreprise de la Société Générale des Grandes Sources* v *Commission* (case T–96/92) (applicants were 'recognised representatives of employers' under Regulation 4064/89).)

Anti-dumping cases   It has been noted above that in considering whether the measure challenged is in the nature of a decision to the applicant, the Court appears to have moved towards a more liberal approach, particularly in the context of a challenge to anti-dumping duties, even when they are imposed in 'true' Regulations. It has also relaxed its approach to the question of individual concern in this area. Where the applicant is a complainant or has been concerned in the preliminary investigations he will be individually concerned on the principles outlined above. But he will also be deemed to be individually concerned where his retail prices or business dealings have been used as a basis for establishing the existence of dumping (see *Enital* (case C–304/86)). However, in the absence of these factors the ECJ was not in its earlier case law prepared to find individual concern. In *Allied*, independent importers (as opposed to manufacturers and exporters) who had not been involved in the preliminary proceedings and who were affected simply as members of a class failed to establish individual concern. However, in *Extramet* (case C–358/89) the ECJ, departing from its previous case law, was prepared to concede that an independent importer, who was not involved in the original proceedings and whose retail prices or dealings with manufacturers or exporters of the goods in question were not taken into account by the Commission in establishing the existence of dumping was individually concerned in a Regulation imposing definitive anti-dumping duties on imports of calcium metal from the People's Republic of China and the Soviet Union. The ECJ held that:

> the recognition of the right of certain categories of traders to bring an action for the annulment of certain anti-dumping Regulations cannot prevent other traders from also claiming to be individually concerned by reason of certain attributes which are peculiar to them and which differentiate them from all other persons.

The relevant attributes, satisfied in *Extramet* were:

(a)   they were the largest importer of the product forming the subject-matter of the anti-dumping measure and were the end users of the product;

(b)   their business activities depended to a very large extent on the imports in question and were seriously affected by the contested Regulation;

(c)   there was a limited number of manufacturers of the product concerned and the importers had difficulty in obtaining supplies from the sole

Community producer, who was its main competitor for the processed product (pure calcium for use in the metallurgy industry).

The judgment in *Extramet* extends, but does little to clarify the law in this difficult area; it does however indicate a possible trend towards a more liberal approach to the question of individual concern where the number of affected applicants is limited and the effect of the measure on the applicant severe. The principles stated were not expressly confined to anti-dumping cases.

In addition to the categories of cases outlined above in which individual concern may be found two further exceptional cases must be mentioned. In *Partie Écologiste 'Les Verts' v Parliament* (case 294/83) the ECJ found that the Green Party was individually concerned in Parliament's Decision, taken in 1983, allocating funds for the European election campaign of 1984, even though the Decision affected all the political parties, actual and potential, seeking election in 1984. The Green Party was thus only affected as a member of an indeterminate class. However, the Court's decision on this matter was clearly (and expressly) based on policy. It reasoned that the political parties represented on the Bureau making the Decision on the allocation of funds had themselves benefited from the allocation, and there was no way in which rival groupings might challenge this allocation in advance of the elections. The case was thus admissible and the applicants succeeded in their claim for annulment. As has been noted, the Court took a more restrictive view in the subsequent case of *Les Verts v Parliament* (case 190/84).

AE Piraiki-Patraiki v Commission (case 11/82) concerned rather different facts. The applicants were a group of Greek manufacturers and exporters of cotton yarn, who sought to challenge a Commission Decision addressed to the French government authorising the latter to impose a quota system on the import of Greek cotton yarn. Since the Decision applied generally and there were no factors linking it directly with the applicants' particular situation one might have imagined that individual concern would be lacking. This was not found to be the case. The Court found that for those who, prior to the Decision, had entered into contracts to be performed subsequently, the Decision was of individual concern. The Court's Decision was firmly based on Article 13(3) of the Act of Accession 1979, which imposes a duty on the Commission to consider those whose contracts may be affected by their measures. The Commission's Decision was held not to be of individual concern to manufacturers and exporters whose existing contracts were not affected by the measure.

In that the Act of Accession expressly required the Commission to take into account those manufacturers and exporters whose contracts might be affected by its measures the decision is consistent with *Sofrimport* (case C–152/88). Nevertheless, while such a class is closed it is potentially very wide. Thus *AE Piraiki-Patraiki* must be seen as a case resting on its own special facts, and not as giving rise to a general claim for individual concern based on interference with the applicants' existing contracts. EC legislation will frequently interfere with existing business contracts: this will not of itself be sufficient to constitute individual concern.

There is no doubt that it is fear of opening floodgates, together with a desire not unduly to hamper the institutions in their task of implementing Community policies, problems common to all administrative law systems, which has led the courts to interpret Article 230 (ex 173), particularly Article 230(2) (ex 173(2)) concerning the *locus standi* of individuals, restrictively. In closing the door to an application under this Article the courts have often adverted to the possibility of alternative means of challenge to the validity of Community law under Article 234 (ex 177), in an action before the applicant's national court (e.g., *Spijker Kwasten BV v Commission* (case 231/82); *UNICME* (case 123/77)). Any binding Community act can be challenged in preliminary rulings proceedings (see chapter 27). It has been suggested that this roundabout approach to matters of validity (which can only be decided authoritatively by the ECJ) is prompted by a desire to filter out unnecessary claims and ensure that only the claims of genuine merit reach the ECJ. One such claim was *Royal Scholten-Honig (Holdings) Ltd v Intervention Board for Agricultural Produce* (cases 103 & 145/77) in which the claimant finally succeeded in obtaining a declaration of invalidity on a reference under the then Article 177 (now 234), having failed to establish *locus standi* in an action under the then Article 173 (now 230) (*Koninklijke Scholten-Honig NV v Council and Commission* (case 101/76)) on the grounds that the disputed measure was a true Regulation. Thus where there is an appropriate issue of national law which a 'natural or legal person' may raise before his national court, to which he may attach a challenge to the validity of Community law, *a fortiori* where there may be difficulty in establishing individual concern, the safer course would be to raise the issue of invalidity before his national court and press for an early reference to the ECJ under Article 234 (ex 177). Where he has no claim under national law, and thus no alternative remedy, and is able to establish direct and individual concern, the courts' recent case law suggests that an application under Article 230 (ex 173) may be admissible even if the applicant seeks to challenge a true Regulation.

The above comments, based on the ECJ's past jurisprudence, have now to be considered in the light of *TWD Textilwerke Deggendorf GmbH v Germany* (case C–188/92), decided in 1994. Here the ECJ refused to exercise its jurisdiction under the then Article 177 (now 234) to declare on the validity of a Commission decision, addressed to the German government, requiring the government to recover State aids paid to the applicant in breach of the then Articles 92 and 93 (now 87 and 88) EC. The German government had informed the applicants of the existence of the decision and of their right to challenge it under what was then Article 173 (now 230), but the applicants took no action under this Article. Instead they sought to challenge the decision later, in the context of domestic proceedings for recovery of the aid wrongfully paid. When the German judge referred to the ECJ for a ruling on the validity of the Commission's decision the ECJ refused its jurisdiction on the grounds that the applicants could and should have challenged the decision directly under former Article 173. Since they had been informed of the decision and of their right to challenge it they could not circumvent the two-month limitation period of that Article by resorting to action under Article 177 (now 234).

The implications of this decision remain unclear, but are disturbing. Although the applicants were aware of the decision as soon as it was received and clearly would have had *locus standi* to challenge it under the then Article 173 (now 230), as being directly and individually concerned, it was not addressed to them. Nor had they been informed of its existence officially, by the Commission. Can and should a notification and advice to act by a national government be deemed sufficient notice of a party's rights and obligations, when he is not the addressee of the decision, such as to require that he move immediately to action under Article 230 (ex 173), or forfeit his right of challenge? Can this be deemed effective judicial protection for individuals' Community rights? Although the *TWD* ruling has been applied subsequently (for example, *Wiljo NV v Belgium* (case C–178/95)), the ECJ has also recognised the difficulties for an applicant unsure of his *locus standi*. In *R v Intervention Board for Agricultural Produce, ex parte Accrington Beef Co. Ltd* (case C–241/95) the ECJ held that a preliminary rulings reference challenging the validity of a Regulation was admissible despite the applicant's failure to bring a claim under former Article 173 (now 230) within the time limit, since it was not clear that the applicants would have had standing for a judicial review application. Given the difficulties of establishing clear rules in relation to *locus standi* for Article 230 (ex 173), the extent of this ruling is not clear, although the approach in *TWD* will undoubtedly continue to create uncertainty, and encourage pre-emptive and possibly inappropriate action under that Article by parties fearing rejection in preliminary rulings.

In a report issued in May 1995 for the IGC in 1996 on possible revisions of the provisions relating to the judicial system, the ECJ pointed out the limitations of direct action for annulment for natural or legal persons. It questioned whether the right to bring an action under this provision, which individuals enjoy only with regard to acts of direct and individual concern to them, was sufficient to guarantee for them effective protection against possible infringements of their fundamental rights from the legislative activity of the Community. Unfortunately, no action was taken at Amsterdam to guarantee that protection and it is not clear whether the matter will be addressed at the 2000 IGC.

Admissibility and interim relief   In an action for interim relief in a claim based on invalidity of a Community, measure, the court will not usually examine the question of admissibility, so as not to prejudice the substance of the case. However, where there is a contention that the claim is 'manifestly inadmissible', the judges hearing the application for interim relief must investigate whether there is a prima facie case for finding that the main application is inadmissible.

Time-limits

An applicant, whether an individual, a Member State or a Community institution, must bring a claim for annulment within two months of:

(a) the publication of the measure, or

(b) its notification to the claimant, or, in the absence thereof,

(c) the day on which it came to the knowledge of the latter, as the case may be (Article 230(3) (ex 173(3)) EC).

The Rules of Procedure of the Court of Justice 1985 provide that time runs from receipt by the person concerned of notification of the measure or, where the measure is published, from the 15th day after its publication in the *Official Journal* (Article 83(1)).

Since Regulations and, following the TEU, Directives and Decisions adopted under the co-decision procedure of Article 251 (ex 189b) EC and Directives of the Council and the Commission addressed to all Member States are required to be published, time will run for them from the date of their entry into force, which will be either the date specified in the provisions or on the twentieth day following that of their publication (Article 254(1) and (2) (ex 191(1) and (2)) EC). Other Directives and Decisions 'shall be notified to those to whom they are addressed and shall take effect upon such notification' (Article 254 (ex 191(3))). In the case of a measure addressed to a person other than the applicant, time will run from the date of the applicant's knowledge. This has been held to require 'precise knowledge' of both the contents of the measure in question and the grounds on which it is based. This is necessary to ensure that the applicant is able to exercise his right to initiate proceedings. Thus a summary of the measure will not suffice (*Commission* v *Socurte* (case C–143/95 P)). Once he is aware of the existence of the measure he must, however, ask for a full text within a reasonable period (*Consorzio Gruppo di Azione Locale 'Murgia Messapica'* v *Commission* (case T–465/93)).

The 'date of knowledge' is the date on which the applicant became aware of the precise content of the measure. It is not the date on which he realised it was challengeable. Hence the importance of recognising an act as a measure capable of annulment.

The limitation period may be extended to take into account the distance between the ECJ at Luxembourg and the applicant's place of residence (Rules of Procedure, Article 81(2)). In the UK 10 days are allowed. It may also be extended if the party concerned proves the existence of unforeseeable circumstances or *force majeure* (Article 42 of the Protocol on the Statute of the Court). In *Bayer AG* v *Commission* (case C–195/91 P) the ECJ held that in order to establish such grounds the applicant must show 'abnormal difficulties, independent of the will of the person concerned, and apparently inevitable, even if all due care is taken'. Likewise, the concept of 'excusable error', justifying derogation from time limits, can concern only 'exceptional circumstances' in which the conduct of the EC institution has given rise to a pardonable confusion on the part of the party concerned. The appplicant cannot rely on his or her own organisation's internal malfunctioning as an excuse for an error.

Once the two-month time-limit has expired a claimant cannot seek to challenge a measure by the back door, either by invoking Article 241 (ex 184) (*exception d'illégalité*, see *Commission* v *Belgium* (case 156/77)) or by alleging a failure to act when the institution concerned refuses by Decision to amend or withdraw the disputed measure (see *Eridania* v *Commission* (cases 10 & 18/68)) or take the requested action (*Irish Cement Ltd* v *Commission* (cases 166/86, 220/86), see chapter 31). Time limits will not be allowed to run afresh when the addressee objects to the EC institution's initial reasoning and that institution (normally the Commission) merely confirms its original decision (*Control Union Gesellschaft für Warenkontrolle mbH* v *Commission* (case C–250/90)).

An indirect challenge using the preliminary rulings procedure before the applicant's national court will, on the other hand, not be subject to the two-month limit. In actions before national courts national rules of limitation apply, provided they are adequate to ensure the effective protection of individuals' Community rights (see chapter 26). However, following *TWD Textilwerke Deggendorf GmbH* v *Germany* (case C–188/92) it is possible that an individual who has *locus standi* under Article 230 (ex 173) will not be allowed to circumvent the time limit imposed by that Article by challenging legislation outside those limits under Article 234 (ex 177). If this is the case access to the Court under Article 234 (ex 177) should only be denied when the applicant's *locus standi* under Article 230 (ex 173) is unequivocally clear.

The merits

Once the Court has decided that the claim is admissible, the case will be decided on the merits. Article 230 (ex 173) provides four grounds for annulment, drawn directly from French administrative law. These are:

(a) Lack of competence.
(b) Infringement of an essential procedural requirement.
(c) Infringement of the Treaty or any rule of law relating to its application.
(d) Misuse of powers.

Lack of competence   This is the equivalent to the English doctrine of substantive *ultra vires*. The institution responsible for adopting the measure in question must have the legal authority to do so. This may derive from the EC Treaty or from secondary legislation. In the *ERTA* case (case 22/70) the Commission challenged the Council's power to participate in the shaping of the road transport agreement, since under the Treaty (Article 300 (ex 228)) it is the Commission which is empowered to negotiate international agreements and the Council whose duty it is to conclude them. On the facts the Court found that the Council had not exceeded its powers. On a number of occasions Community law has been challenged as having been enacted under the wrong legal basis (see *Parliament* v *Council* (case C–295/90)). Clearly the choice of legal basis will be important, as it will determine the appropriate procedure to be followed and the vote required for the adoption of legislation (see chapters 2 and 3).

The Court allows the institutions some latitude in their choice of legal base and their scope for action under that base. In *Germany* v *Commission* (case

C–359/92) it held that the then Article 100a (now 95), which provides for the approximation of the provisions laid down by law, regulation or administrative action in Member States which have as their object the establishing and functioning of the internal market, was to be interpreted as 'encompassing the Council's power to lay down measures relating to a specific class of products and, if necessary, individual measures concerning those products'. Thus Germany's challenge to Article 9 of Council Directive 92/59 on product safety, based on former Article 100a, which empowered the Commission to adopt decisions requiring Member States to take temporary measures in the event of a serious and immediate risk to the health and safety of consumers, failed. In *Portugal* v *Council* (case C–268/94), the Portuguese government sought the annulment of a Decision on the basis that the wrong treaty base had been used. The decision referred to what were then Articles 113 and 130y (now 120 and 181) EC, dealing with commercial policy, which only required that the Decision be adopted by qualified majority vote. The Portuguese government claimed that the agreement to which the Decision related contained provisions aimed at protecting democracy and human rights in India, and therefore should have been made under former Article 235 (now 308) EC, which would have required unanimity. The ECJ held that on the facts of the case the provisions of the then Article 130y (now 181) were broad enough to encompass the complained-of clauses, and that to rule otherwise would be to deprive the specific clauses of their substance. The Court is stricter in its approach to questions concerning the allocation of competence between the EC institutions (see, e.g., *France, Netherlands and Spain* v *Commission* (case C–327/91)), and, as noted earlier, the ECJ's decisions have protected the procedural rights of the European Parliament (see, e.g., *Parliament* v *Council (Re European Development Fund)* (case C–316/91)).

Infringement of an essential procedural requirement   This is equivalent to procedural *ultra vires* in English law. Institutions, when enacting binding measures, must follow the correct procedures. These procedures may be laid down in the EC Treaty or secondary legislation (e.g., Regulation 17/62 on competition law, see chapter 17). For example, Article 253 (ex 190) of the EC Treaty requires that all secondary legislation must state the reasons on which it is based, and must refer to proposals and opinions which were required to be obtained. The Court has held that reasons must not be too vague or inconsistent; they must be coherent; they must mention figures and essential facts on which they rely. They must be adequate to indicate the conscientiousness of the Decision, and detailed enough to be scrutinised by the Court (*Germany* v *Commission (Re Tariff Quotas on Wine)* (case 24/62) — Commission Decision annulled; too vague, no facts and figures). The purpose of the requirement to give reasons is to enable those concerned to defend their rights and to enable the Court to exercise its supervisory jurisdiction. However, the Court will not annul an act for an insignificant defect. Nor will it annul an act on this ground unless the claimant can prove that, but for this defect, the result would have been different (*Distillers Co. Ltd* v *Commission* (case 30/78)).

In *Roquette Frères SA* v *Council* (case 138/79) and *Maizena GmbH* v *Council* (case 139/79) a Council Regulation was annulled on the grounds of the Council's failure to consult Parliament, as it was required to do under the then Article 43(2) (now 37) EC. Although the Council had consulted Parliament, it was held not to have given Parliament sufficient time to express an opinion on the measure in question. Where no time-limit is imposed it is presumed that Parliament must be given a reasonable time in which to express its opinion.

Infringement of the Treaty or any rule of law relating to its application Clearly, when an act is invalid for lack of competence or for an infringement of an essential procedural requirement, this may involve an infringement of the Treaty, but this ground of annulment is wider since it extends to *any* Treaty provision. In *Adams* v *Commission (No. 1)* (case 145/83), an action for non-contractual liability (see chapter 33), the Commission was found to have acted in breach of its duty of confidentiality under the then Article 214 (now 287).

Infringement of any rule of law relating to the Treaty's application is wider again, and certainly wider than any comparable rule of English law. This is where general principles of law, discussed at length in chapter 6, are relevant. A measure can be annulled if it is in breach not only of any general principle of law approved by the Court (e.g., equality, proportionality) but of any principle common to the constitutions of Member States (*Internationale Handelsgesellschaft mbH* (case 11/70)) and even principles of international treaties in the field of human rights on which Member States have collaborated (*J. Nold KG* v *Commission* (case 4/73)). In *Royal Scholten-Honig (Holdings) Ltd* v *Intervention Board for Agricultural Produce* (cases 103 & 145/77) a Community Regulation was held invalid for breach of the principle of equality. In *Transocean Marine Paint Association* v *Commission* (case 17/74) (see chapter 6) part of a Decision was annulled for breach of the principle of natural justice. In *August Töpfer & Co. GmbH* v *Commission* (case 112/77) a Decision was annulled for breach of the principle of legal certainty, for infringement of the applicant's legitimate expectations. Although the Court will not lightly set aside legislation for breach of this principle and will expect businessmen to anticipate and guard against foreseeable developments, within the bounds of 'normal' economic risks, this is a ground of some potential (see *Amylum* v *Council* (case 108/81); *Mulder* v *Council* (case C–104/89)). Note, however, that a trader is unlikely to have legitimate expectations that do not accord with existing Community rules (see, for example, *Efisol SA* (case T–336/94)). Thus, it is difficult to argue that a requirement to pay back illegally granted State aid would be in breach of legitimate expectations. In *Opel Austria GmbH* v *Council* (case T–115/94), the CFI held that the principle of legitimate expectations within the EC was the corollary of the principle of good faith in public international law. Therefore, where Community institutions have deposited their instruments of approval of an international agreement and the date of the entry into force of that agreement is known, any measures contrary to provisions of such agreements having direct effect, will be in breach of legitimate expectations. In *Racke* (case C–162/96), the ECJ held that the ECJ's jurisdiction to review the validity of a Community act could not be limited as regards the grounds on which it could find a measure invalid. In this case, it held that a Community measure, a Regulation, could be held to be invalid were it contrary to international law.

Although it has not yet been done successfully, legislation could in principle be challenged for breach of the principle of subsidiarity, either as a general principle or as now expressed in Article 5 (ex 3b) EC. The German government raised the question of subsidiarity, albeit in a different context, in *Germany* v *Parliament* (case C–233/94). It sought to challenge Directive 94/19, arguing that there had been a breach of the duty to state reasons for the legislation as required by the then Article 190, in that the Directive did not explain how it complied with the principle of subsidiarity set out in Article 3b (now 5) EC. The ECJ rejected this argument, stating that the necessary information could be inferred from the recitals to the Directive.

Because of the breadth of the concept of 'any rule of law relating to the [treaty's] application', the acts of the EC institutions are vulnerable to attack on this ground. Thus the ECJ has held that where the Community legislature has a discretion to act in a complex economic situation, such as the implementation of the Community's agricultural policy, both as regards the nature and scope of the measures to be taken and the finding of basic facts, the Court, in reviewing the exercise of such a power, 'must confine itself to examining whether it contains a manifest error or constitutes a misuse of power or whether the authority in question did not clearly exceed the bounds of its discretion' (*Commission* v *Council* (case C–122/94)). The ECJ's approach to the Community's liability in damages for legislative measures involving choices of economic policy, which the CFI adopts also, reflects a similar concern not to fetter the discretion of the EC institutions when they are implementing Community policy. In this context the Court may be accused of occasionally going too far to protect the Community institutions (see *Germany* v *Council* (case C–280/93), chapters 6 and 33).

Misuse of power   This concept stems from the French '*détournement de pouvoir*'. It means, broadly, the use of a power for purposes other than those for which it was granted, for example, where powers granted to help one group (e.g., producers) are used to benefit another (e.g., distributors) (see *Simmenthal SpA* v *Commission* case 92/78)). It has been defined by the ECJ as 'the adoption by a Community institution of a measure with the exclusive or main purpose of achieving an end other than that stated or evading a procedure specifically prescribed by the Treaty for dealing with the circumstances of the case' (*Parliament* v *Commission* (case C–156/93)). The concept is not confined to abuses of power, nor is an ulterior or improper motive essential; an improper or illegitimate use of power is all that is required. However, this provision has been narrowly interpreted. In *Fédération Charbonnière de Belgique* v *High Authority* (case 8/55), in interpreting the comparable provision (Article 33) of the ECSC Treaty, the Court held that a measure will not be annulled for misuse of power if the improper use had no effect on its substance; nor will it be annulled if the authority had acted from mixed motives, proper and improper, as long as the proper purpose was dominant. It is thus a difficult ground to establish.

The case of *Werner A. Bock KG* v *Commission* (case 62/70) was considered, but not decided, on this ground. Although there was no clear collusion between the German government and the Commission over the issuing of the Decision, there were definite signs of collaboration. The case was eventually decided, and the Decision annulled, for breach of the principle of proportionality. The Commission's action was more than was necessary in the circumstances, since the quantities of mushrooms at stake were so small as to be insignificant.

There is much overlap between the above grounds. The Court rarely examines each one precisely and is often vague as to which ground forms the basis of its decision. *BEUC* v *Commission* (case T–37/92) concerned the Commission's decision not to investigate the agreement between the British Society of Motor Manufacturers and the Japanese government limiting imports of Japanese cars to 11 per cent of total UK sales. This decision was prima facie contrary to the then Article 85(1) (now 81)), but was justified by the Commission, *inter alia*, because the agreement was permitted as a matter of UK policy. The CFI annulled the decision simply on the ground that it constituted an 'error of law'. Despite the Court's lack of precision in these matters it is wise to plead as many grounds as seem applicable.

The grounds apply equally to an examination of the validity of a measure on reference from national courts under Article 234 (ex 177). They also apply to an enquiry into the validity of Regulations under Article 241 (ex 184) (chapter 32) and to an application for damages under Article 288(2) (ex 215(2)) (chapter 33) where the action is based on an illegal act of the institutions.

Consequences of a successful action

If an annulment action under Article 230 (ex 173) is successful the act will be declared void under Article 231 (ex 174). A measure may be declared void in part only, provided that the offending part can be effectively severed. Under Article 231(2) (ex 174(2)), however, the Court may, following a successful action for annulment, 'state which of the effects of the Regulation which it has declared void shall be considered as definitive'. This has been done in the interests of legal certainty, to avoid upsetting past transactions based on a Regulation, a normative act. In *Roquette Frères SA* v *France* (case 145/79) a declaration of invalidity of a Community Regulation was held to be purely prospective in its effects. The wisdom of such a ruling has since been doubted, on the grounds that such a limitation would deprive the applicant of his right to effective judicial protection (*Roquette Frères SA* v *Hauptzollamt Geldern* (case C–228/92)). However, in *Parliament* v *Council* (case C–360/93) the ECJ annulled two Council decisions and, on the basis of the then Article 174(2) (now 231(2)), ordered that *all* the effects of the annulled decisions must be maintained in force. In *R* v *Ministry of Agriculture, Fisheries and Food, ex parte H. and R. Ecroyd Holdings Ltd* (case C–127/94) the ECJ held that, in a complex field, an individual may not rely on a ruling of invalidity, even in a situation arising *after* that ruling, until replacement legislation has been introduced. Nonetheless, it should be noted that in a subsequent case involving Ecroyd (*Ecroyd* v *Commission* (case T–220/97)), the CFI held that should a court find a measure invalid, it is not enough to repeal that measure; the position of the complainants must also be addressed so that they do not continue to suffer loss. A successful action for damages under Article 288(2) (ex 215(2)) could arise in these circumstances, as indeed it did in this case.

A slightly different point arose in *Commission* v *AssiDoman Kraft Products AB* (case C–310/97P). The case concerned certain fines imposed on a number of undertakings for breach of the competition rules. Some of the undertakings appealed against the Commission's decisions, resulting in the partial annulment of the Commission's decision and the reduction of the fines imposed on the appellant undertakings. Several other companies, which had also been fined but which had not been party to the appeal, then requested that the Commission reconsider their position in the light of the annulment ruling. The Commission refused, as it argued that the companies involved in the competition proceedings had each been addressed individually and therefore a finding of invalidity as regards a decision addressed to one company did not affect a similar decision addressed to another. The applicant companies sought to challenge before the European courts on the basis that the Commission was obliged to do this by virtue of Article 233 (ex 176). The matter finally came before the ECJ, the CFI having found in the companies' favour. The ECJ overturned the CFI's ruling, holding that the scope of Article 233 (ex 176) was limited in two ways. First, a ruling for annulment could not go further than the applicant requested, and thus the matter tried by the Community courts could relate only to aspects of the decision which affected the applicants. The ECJ then held that although the operative part of the judgment and its reasoning were binding *erga omnes*, this 'cannot entail annulment of an act not challenged before the Community judicature but alleged to be vitiated by the same illegality' (para. 54). The applicants in this case could not of course challenge the original Commission decision to fine them because the time limits for bringing a challenge had long expired. Although one might argue that the companies in this case could have challenged the Commission's decision earlier, the ruling in this case does lead to the anomalous position that some companies are treated less favourably than others in an equivalent situation.

Thus, as the above cases demonstrate, policy pulls both ways. Where individual rights are at stake and those rights are reasonably clear, it may be hoped that the principle of effective judicial protection wins, at least for the applicant and in respect of claims arising after the date of judgment.

Further reading

Arnull, A., 'Challenging EC Anti-dumping Regulations: the Problem of Admissibility' [1992] ECLR 73.

Arnull, A., 'Private Applicants and the Action for Annulment under Article 173 of the EC Treaty' (1995) 32 CMLR 7.

Bebr, G., 'The Standing of the European Parliament in the Community System of Legal Remedies: a Thorny Jurisprudential Development' (1990) 10 YEL 170.

Bradley, K. St. Clair, 'The Variable Evolution of the Standing of the European Parliament in Proceedings before the Court of Justice' (1988) 8 YEL 27.

Bradley, K. St Clair, 'Sense and Sensibility: *Parliament* v *Council* Continuing' (1991) 16 EL Rev 245.

Craig, P., 'Legality, Standing and Substantive Review in Community Law' (1994) 14 Oxford J Legal Stud 507.

de Wilmars, M. and Mertens, J., 'The Case Law of the ECJ in Relation to the Review of the Legality of Economic Policy in Mixed Economy Systems' (1982) 1 LIEI 1.

Greaves, R., '*Locus Standi* under Article 173 EEC when Seeking Annulment of a Regulation' (1986) 11 EL Rev 119.

Harding, C., 'The Private Interest in Challenging Community Action' (1980) 5 EL Rev 345.

Harlow, C., 'Towards a Theory of Access for the European Court of Justice' (1992) 12 YEL 213.

Hartley, T.C., *The Foundations of European Community Law,* 3rd ed. (1994, Clarendon Press).

Kerse, C.S., 'The Complainant in Competition Cases: A Progress Report' (1997) 34 CML Rev 213.

Neuwahl, N.A.E.M., 'Article 173 Paragraph 4 EC: Past, Present and Possible Future' (1996) 21 EL Rev 17.

Rasmussen, H., 'Why is Article 173 Interpreted against Private Plaintiffs?' (1980) 5 EL Rev 112.

Schermers, H.G. and Waelbroeck, D.F., *Judicial Protection in the European Communities,* 5th ed. (1992, Kluwer Law & Taxation Publishers).

THIRTY ONE

Action for failure to act

If the institutions of the Community are to operate according to the rule of law, as they are obliged to do under Article 7 (ex 4) of the EC Treaty, they must be answerable not only for their actions but for their failure to act in breach of EC law. This is provided for by Article 232 (ex 175), as follows:

> Should the European Parliament, the Council or the Commission, in infringement of this Treaty, fail to act, the Member States and the other institutions of the Community may bring an action before the Court of Justice to have the infringement established.
>
> The action shall be admissible only if the institution concerned has first been called upon to act. If, within two months of being so called upon, the institution concerned has not defined its position, the action may be brought within a further period of two months.
>
> Any natural or legal person may, under the conditions laid down in the preceding paragraphs, complain to the Court of Justice that an institution of the Community has failed to address to that person any act other than a recommendation or an opinion.
>
> The Court of Justice shall have jurisdiction under the same conditions in actions or proceedings brought by the European Central Bank in the areas falling within the latter's field of competence and in actions or proceedings brought against the latter.

Actions brought by a natural or legal person under Article 232 (ex 175) EC now fall within the jurisdiction of the CFI, although appeal on points of law may be made to the ECJ (see chapter 28).

Articles 232 and 230 (ex 175 and 173 respectively) are essentially complementary remedies. As the ECJ held in *Chevalley* v *Commission* (case 15/70) when confronted with the applicant's uncertainty as to whether the then Article 175 or Article 173 (now 232 and 230 respectively) was the appropriate form of action, it is not necessary to characterise the proceedings as being under one or the other Article, since both Articles merely prescribe one and the same method of recourse. They represent two aspects of the same legal remedy. For this reason it has been suggested that any inconsistency between the two provisions should be resolved by applying the same principles to both. This is known as the 'unity principle'. This is all the more important in the light of the Court's interpretation of Article 232 (ex 175), which may result in an action, begun under that Article, being concluded under Article 230 (ex 173). However, the unity principle appears to have been denied in *Parliament* v *Council (Comitology)* (case 302/87), at least in the context of *locus standi*, when, contrary to Advocate-General Darmon's Submissions, the Court refused to admit an action by Parliament under the then Article 173 (now 230), seeking to annul a Decision of the Council relating to the composition and role of Committees of Representatives of Member States, on the grounds that there was 'no necessary link' between an action for failure to act and an action for annulment. While the ECJ modified its position in *Parliament* v *Council (Chernobyl)* (case C–70/88) by allowing Parliament *locus standi* under former Article 173 in order to protect its own prerogative powers, the Heads of State at Maastricht were content to reflect this position and, in amending the Article, chose not to extend the unity principle to its logical conclusion. Despite the opportunity to review the position at the Amsterdam IGC, no change was made. Furthermore, unlike the provisions, albeit limited, for annulment of measures taken under the JHA pillar of the TEU (see chapter 30), Article 35 TEU does not provide for an action for failure to act in respect of measures in this area. Nonetheless, in cases arising under the EC Treaty, the CFI continues to refer to the unity principle, or to the coherence between the two principles, in its judgments (see, e.g., *Gestevision Telecinco* v *Commission* (case T–95/96)).

Reviewable omissions

The institution's failure to act must, first and foremost, be 'in infringement of this Treaty'. Since this would include legislation enacted under the Treaty it would apply to any failure on the part of the institution to act when it was under a legal duty to do so. In *Parliament* v *Council* (case 13/83), in an action by Parliament under the then Article 175 (now 232) alleging the Council's failure to implement a Community transport policy, the Court held that 'failure' can cover a failure to take a number of decisions; the nature of the acts which may be requested need not be clearly circumscribed as long as they are sufficiently identified. The failures alleged by Parliament in this case were:

(a)   failure to introduce a common transport policy, as required by the then Article 74, and
(b)   failure to introduce measures to secure freedom to provide transport services, as required by the then Articles 75, 59, 60 and 61.

The Court held that Parliament was entitled to succeed on the second allegation but not on the first. While the second obligation was complete and legally perfect, and should have been implemented by the Council within the

transitional period, the former obligation was insufficiently precise to constitute an enforceable obligation. This case, together with the Single European
Act, provided the momentum for the development of a Community transport
policy during the past few years.

Originally action under Article 175 (now 232) could be brought only
against the Council or the Commission. As amended by the TEU, action may
now be brought against the European Parliament, thereby acknowledging, as
did the new Article 230 (ex 173), Parliament's acquired powers to take
actions having legal force with regard to third parties. Omissions of the
European Central Bank will also be subject to review under Article 232 (ex
175). Although the Court of Auditors was awarded the power to bring actions
under Article 230 (ex 173) by the ToA, its actions are not subject to review
under Article 232 (ex 175). This is probably a consequence of their limited
and non-binding status.

Although only non-binding acts in the form of recommendations and
opinions are expressly excluded in the context of individual action under
Article 232(3) (ex 175(3)), the unity principle would suggest that a failure
under Article 232 (ex 175) would only cover a failure to issue a binding act.

Locus standi

Unlike the position under Article 230 (ex 173), Parliament, as one of the
'institutions' of the Community is, along with Member States and the other
institutions, a 'privileged applicant' under Article 232 (ex 175). Privileged
applicants enjoy a right to challenge *any* failure on the part of the Council
and the Commission, i.e., an omission to adopt *any* binding act which these
institutions have a duty to adopt. Parliament's (partial) success in *Parliament* v
Council (case 13/83) illustrates the potential, as yet largely untapped, of
Article 232 (ex 175) as a means of control of the two principal law-making
institutions by a directly elected and determined Parliament. Under the TEU
the European Central Bank was given *locus standi* to bring proceedings under
Article 232 (ex 175) 'in the areas falling within [its] field of competence'.

By comparison with Member States and Community institutions, individuals, as under Article 230 (ex 173), have a limited *locus standi* under Article
232 (ex 175(3)). Natural or legal persons may bring proceedings only where
the institution complained of has failed to address to that person any act other
than a recommendation or an opinion. Since an act which is addressed to a
designated person is in substance a Decision, this seems to mean that an
individual's *locus standi* is limited to a failure on the part of the Council or
Commission to adopt what is in essence a *Decision* addressed to *himself or
herself.* The individual has no express *locus standi* to challenge an omission to
address to *another person* a Decision of direct and individual concern to
himself or herself.

This apparent deficiency has been remedied by the Court. In *Nordgetreide
GmbH & Co. KG* v *Commission* (case 42/71), Advocate-General Roemer,
invoking the unity principle, suggested that since the then Articles 173 and
175 (now 230 and 232 respectively) constituted part of a coherent system, an

individual should have a right to demand a Decision *vis-à-vis* a third party in which the individual was directly and individually concerned. In *Bethell* v *Commission* (case 246/81) this right was implied when the Court, in rejecting Lord Bethell's claim as inadmissible, held that he had failed to show that the Commission had failed to adopt, in relation to him, a measure *which he was legally entitled to claim*. Thus, in the context of Article 232 (ex 175), the equivalent to a Decision of direct and individual concern under Article 230 (ex 173), was a Decision which the applicant is *legally entitled to claim*. This test was relaxed in *T. Port GmbH & Co. KG* v *Bundesanstalt für Landeswirtschaft und Ernährung* (case C–68/95)). Reasoning from the unity principle and the test of direct and individual concern used in respect of former Article 173 (now 230) actions, the ECJ stated that former Article 175(3) could be invoked where an institution has failed to act in respect of a measure which would have concerned the applicant in the same way (para. 59). This test was suggested in the context of the ECJ's refusal to allow a preliminary rulings reference in respect of an alleged failure to act. The CFI relied on the *T. Port* case, and adopted its reasoning, in the more recent cases involving challenges to the funding of public service broadcasters (e.g., *Gestevision Telecinco SA* v *Commission* (case T–95/96)), thus suggesting that this approach has now been consolidated into the courts' case law.

Many of the claims under former Article 175 (now 232), prior to case C–68/95, failed because the applicant was seeking the adoption of an act which he was not entitled to claim (e.g., *Bethell*; *Firma C. Mackprang Jr* v *Commission* (case 15/71) — claimant seeking amendment of a Decision addressed to the German government; *Star Fruit Company SA* v *Commission* (case 247/87); *J* v *Commission* (case T–5/94) — individual not entitled to demand action by Commission under the then Article 169; *Ladbroke Racing Ltd* v *Commission* (case T–32/93) — individual complainant no right to demand action by Commission under State aid provisions of the then Article 90(3)). *Ladbroke* may be compared with the more recent case of *Bundesverband der Bilanzbuchhalter eV* v *Commission* (case C–107/95 P) in which the ECJ accepted that in limited circumstances, details of which it did not elaborate, an applicant could demand action under Article 90(3) (now 86(3)) EC. In *Gestevision Telecinco SA* v *Commission* (case T–95/96), the CFI held that an individual could demand that the Commission make a decision at the end of the initial investigatory phase of State aid proceedings under the then Article 93(3) (now 88(3)). Further, where the Commission has difficulty in determining whether the funding in issue constitutes State aid or whether it is compatible with the common market, 'the institution has a duty to gather all necessary views and to that end initiate the procedure under 93(2) [now 86(3)]'. In both of these circumstances, Article 232 (ex 175) proceedings could therefore be brought against a failure on the Commission's part to act. It may be that the easing of the test here and in *T. Port* (case C–68/95) will result in an increase in the number of successful actions brought by non-privileged applicants. Arguably, a more generous approach to individuals' *locus standi* under Article 232 (ex 175) EC is justified if individuals are to be denied access to the ECJ to challenge an institution's failure to act under Article 234 (ex 177) EC.

On rather different reasoning in another failed claim in the earlier case of *Eridania* v *Commission* (cases 10 & 18/68), the Court held that the applicants could not invoke the then Article 175 (now 232) in order to obtain a revocation by the Commission of a Decision addressed to third parties, since other methods of recourse, namely, Article 173 (now 230), were provided by the Treaty; to allow parallel recourse via Article 175 (now 232) would enable applicants to avoid the conditions (i.e. time limit) laid down by the Treaty.

It is clear that the act demanded must be in substance a Decision. In *Nordgetreide GmbH & Co. KG* v *Commission* (case 42/71) the applicant company was seeking the amendment by the Commission of a Regulation. When the Commission rejected its request the company instituted two actions, one for failure to act, under the then Article 175 (now 232), and one under the then Article 173 (now 230) for annulment of the Commission's Decision refusing to act. The action under the then Article 175 (now 232) would in any case have failed because, as Advocate-General Roemer pointed out, the company was seeking from the Commission what would have amounted to a normative act; in fact the Court found its claim inadmissible on different grounds (to be discussed below). The claim under former Article 173 (now 230) was also held inadmissible. Although the contested Decision was addressed to the applicant, the Court held that a Decision refusing to act (a 'negative' Decision) would only be open to attack under Article 173 (now 230) if the *positive* measure being sought were open to attack (see also Advocate-General Gand in *Alfons Lütticke GmbH* v *Commission* (case 48/65)). Since the company was seeking to amend a Regulation, this would not be the case. This same reasoning would apply to a refusal by the Commission to issue a Decision to another person which the applicants were not entitled to claim. Thus, even though a Decision may have been addressed to the applicant, Article 230 (ex 173) cannot be invoked as an adjunct to Article 175 (new 232) to annul a decision not to act, in order to compel an institution to act *when it has no duty to do so at the behest of the applicant.* Although this has been attempted on a number of occasions (e.g., *Alfons Lütticke GmbH* v *Commission* (case 48/65); *Star Fruit Company SA* v *Commission*; *J* v *Commission* (case T–5/94) — applicants demanding action by the Commission under the then Article 169 against a Member State; *Bethell* v *Commission* (case 246/81) — applicant seeking to force Commission to take action under the then Article 89 against Member States' airlines), it has always failed.

A case in which the applicant was entitled to demand action from the Commission, but in which its claim was surprisingly held inadmissible, was *Deutscher Komponistenverbande* v *Commission* (case 8/71). Here the applicant alleged that the Commission had failed in its obligation under EC competition law (Regulation 17/62) to grant it, as a complainant under Article 3 of that Regulation, a hearing. Advocate-General Roemer suggested that acts susceptible of action under the then Article 175 (now 232) should cover any measures which give rise to legal effects for the applicant; they should then include measures of a procedural nature. The Court disagreed, holding that former Article 175(3) (now 232(3)) only applied to a failure to adopt a

Decision; it did not cover the promulgation of a formal act. Nevertheless the Court did examine the merits and concluded that since the applicant had had an opportunity to make its submissions in writing there had been no failure on the part of the Commission.

It is submitted that Advocate-General Roemer's view is to be preferred to that of the Court. Since there was no doubt that the applicant was entitled to a hearing any failure to grant it that hearing should have been actionable under the then Article 175 (now 232). And if it was refused such a hearing, as it was, it should have been entitled to challenge that refusal under former Article 173 (now 230), since the positive measure requested was one which it was entitled to demand. No such challenge was made in *Deutscher Komponisternerbande* v *Commission*.

This view seems to have been taken by the Court in *FEDIOL* v *Commission* (case 191/82). In this case an EC federation of seed crushers and oil processors was seeking to compel the Commission to take action against alleged dumping practices on the part of Brazil. As undertakings which considered themselves injured or threatened by subsidised imports, the applicants were entitled under Regulation 3017/79 (the principal anti-dumping Regulation) to lodge a complaint (Article 5), to be consulted (Article 6), and to receive information (Article 9). In April 1980 they lodged a complaint with the Commission. Following enquiries and negotiations with the Brazilian government the Commission decided to take no further action. In September 1981 FEDIOL instituted Article 175 (now 232) proceedings. Following further correspondence between FEDIOL and the Commission the Commission informed FEDIOL by letter in May 1982 that it intended to take no further action against Brazil. FEDIOL then brought Article 173 (now 230) proceedings to annul that letter. The Court held that since the Regulation under which they complained recognised specific rights on the applicants' part they were entitled to a review by the Court of any exercise of power by the Community institutions which might affect these rights. Thus the action was held admissible. Although the applicants could not compel the Commission to take action against Brazil, that being a matter within the Commission's discretion, they were entitled to a review by the Court of the Commission's letter of May 1982 to ensure that their procedural rights were respected.

It is submitted that this case can be reconciled with the earlier case of *GEMA* v *Commission* (case 125/78). Here GEMA initiated a complaint to the Commission under Article 3 of Regulation 17/62, alleging a breach by Radio Luxembourg of the then Articles 85 and 86 (now 81 and 82). In March 1978 the Commission wrote to GEMA saying that it had decided not to pursue the matter. In May 1978 GEMA instituted Article 175 (now 232) proceedings against this refusal to act. Subsequently, in March 1979 GEMA brought proceedings under Article 173 (now 230) to annul the letter of March 1978. The action under the then Article 175 (now 232) failed because the Commission was held to have defined its position in the letter of March 1978. The action under the then Article 173 (now 230) failed on the grounds that, assuming that the letter could be contested, this did not entitle the applicants to a *final Decision* on the existence of an infringement under Article 86 (now 82). In any case the letter had not been challenged in time and the parties' attempts to extend the limit on the grounds of fresh issues based on matters of fact and law (Rules of Procedure, Article 42(2)) failed. In the appeal in *Guérin Automobiles* v *Commission* (case C–282/95 P), the ECJ confirmed that a letter to a complainant was a definition of a position for the purposes of what was then Article 175 (now 232), but that it could not be challenged because the letter was a preparatory stage in proceedings. The applicants were entitled under competition procedural rules to make representations, after which the Commission must make a decision which would have legally binding effects. It would be at this stage that an applicant could challenge a failure to act although it still could not force the Commission to take a decision that was favourable to the applicants.

Thus in all of these cases the parties were only entitled in law to protection by way of review under former Articles 175 and 173 (now 232 and 230) in order to protect their procedural rights. They had no right to compel the Commission to institute proceedings against third parties; that was a matter within the Commission's discretion (see also *Ladbroke Racing Ltd* v *Commission* (case T–32/93)). Even in *Gestevision*, where the Commission seemed to be under an obligation to investigate the funding to State broadcasters further, this obligation arose out of the need to protect the procedural rights of all involved and did not entitle Gestevision to any particular finding on the question of State aid.

By comparison with these cases, the claimant in *Bethell* v *Commission* (case 246/81), was found to have no rights at all. In this case Lord Bethell, member of the House of Lords, Euro MP and veteran campaigner for the 'freedom of the skies', was attempting to force the Commission to take action against a number of European airlines for allegedly anti-competitive practices. Although air transport is subject in principle to EC competition rules it was excluded from the application of Regulation 17/62, being subject to enforcement under Article 89 (now 85) EC by the Commission. Under that Article, unlike Regulation 17/62, no right is granted to persons with a 'legitimate interest' to request the Commission to act in respect of suspected infringements. Lord Bethell complained to the Commission and requested action. The Commission wrote back to Lord Bethell, explaining in detail why it had decided not to take action in this matter. Lord Bethell then instituted Article 175 (now 232) proceedings against the Commission for its failure to act, and Article 173 (now 230) proceedings for the annulment of its letter of refusal to act. Both actions were declared inadmissible. In order for his claim to be admissible under the then Article 175 (now 232) it was necessary to prove that the Commission, having been called upon to act, had failed to adopt in relation to him a measure *which he was legally entitled to claim*. This he had clearly failed to prove. Nor was he entitled to challenge the Commission's negative refusal under former Article 173 (now 230) since he was not in the position of actual or potential addressee of a Decision which the Commission *had a duty to adopt* with regard to him.

Where an individual does have a right to complain and to request action, as in *FEDIOL, GEMA* and *Guérin*, should the Commission take action and issue a Decision to a third party, the complainant will be deemed to be directly and individually concerned, and will be entitled to a full review of the Decision under Article 230 (ex 173) EC (*Metro-SB-Grossmärkte GmbH & Co. KG* v *Commission* (case 26/76); *Timex Corporation* v *Council* (case 264/82), see chapter 30; *COFAZ* (case 169/84); *British American Tobacco Co. Ltd* v *Commission* (cases 142 & 156/84)).

Procedure

Where the applicant has a right to require an institution to act, and the institution is thus under a corresponding duty, the applicant must first call upon the institution to act. No time-limit is imposed in respect of the institution's alleged failure, but the Court has held that proceedings must be brought within a reasonable time of the institution's having demonstrated its intention not to act (*Netherlands* v *Commission* (case 59/70) case brought under Article 35 of the ECSC Treaty).

The institution then has two months within which it may either act in accordance with the request, or 'define its position'.

If the institution fails to act or to define its position the claimant has two months within which to bring his case before the ECJ, running from the date on which the institution should have defined its position. These limits are strictly enforced. In *Guérin Automobiles* v *Commission* (case T–195/95) the Commission, responding to a complaint by Guérin concerning an alleged breach by Nissan of the then Article 85(1) (now 81(1)), merely sent them a copy of Nissan's response to the complaint. When Guérin subsequently submitted their observations to the Commission in February 1995, the Commission failed to respond. In October 1995 they brought an action before the CFI under the then Article 175 (now 232). The Court found the action inadmissible. Even supposing that the letter sent by the applicants in February 1995 could be regarded as an invitation to act in the sense of the then Article 175, to which the Commission had failed to respond, the application to the CFI should have been introduced within four months of the date on which the letter was sent, as required by that Article. Guérin wrote to the Commission again, and then brought another action under former Article 175 (now 232), this time within four months from the date of this letter. Again, the company was unsuccessful, as the Commission had, by the time the matter came before the CFI, defined its position.

Article 232 (ex 175) is silent as to what happens if the institution concerned defines its position. Although it was not necessary so to construe this Article, the Court held in *Alfons Lütticke GmbH* v *Commission* (case 48/65) that a definition of position brought proceedings under Article 175 (now 232) to an end. The claimant in this case, it will be remembered, was attempting to persuade the Commission to bring an action under former Article 169 (now 226) against the German government for its alleged infringement of the then Article 95 (now 90). When the Commission refused to act Alfons Lütticke GmbH brought proceedings under the then Article 175 (now 232) for failure to act. The Commission defined its position in a letter to Lütticke, again refusing to act, and Lütticke brought proceedings under the then Article 173 (now 230) to annul that refusal.

There were a number of reasons, submitted by Advocate-General Gand, why both claims should fail. With regard to the action under former Article 175 (now 232):

(a)   The Commission's refusal to take action under Article 169 (now 226) was not an infringement of the Treaty; the decision as to whether or not to act was a matter within the Commission's discretion.

(b)   The act requested by Lütticke was not a decision addressed to itself, but one addressed to a third party (the German government) which it was not entitled to demand.

(c)   The Commission's refusal to act was a 'definition of position' within Article 175 (now 232); this definition of position ended the Commission's failure to act.

The Court, in the briefest of judgments, chose to rely on the third ground. Since the Commission had defined its position the action under the then Article 175 (now 232) was inadmissible.

With regard to the action under the then Article 173 (now 230), Advocate-General Gand's submissions were again convincing. The applicant would only be entitled to challenge the Commission's refusal to act (the 'negative decision'), he suggested, if it would have been entitled to challenge the positive act requested. This it would not, since it had no right to demand action from the Commission *vis-à-vis* the German government. The Court, on the other hand, chose to treat the Commission's refusal not as a definition of position but as a 'reasoned opinion' under former Article 169 (now 226), which, as a purely preliminary act, was not, the Court held, capable of annulment.

The Court did adopt reasoning similar to that of Advocate-General Gand in *Lütticke* in *Star Fruit Company SA* v *Commission* (case 247/87). Here, as in *Lütticke*, the applicants, a firm of banana importers, were seeking to compel the Commission to institute Article 169 (now 226) proceedings, this time against France in respect of the French regime regulating banana imports, which they considered was in breach of the then Article 30 (now 28) EC. They had complained to the Commission and the Commission had acknowledged their request. The applicants subsequently brought Article 175 (now 232) proceedings against the Commission for their failure to take action against France, and Article 173 (now 230) proceedings for the annulment of the Commission's letter of acknowledgment. On the claim for failure to act, the Court held that since the Commission was not required to instigate proceedings under Article 169 (now 226), but on the contrary had a discretionary power, 'individuals were not entitled to require that the institution adopt a particular position'.

On the claim under former Article 173 (now 230), the Court pointed out that by requesting the Commission to set in motion a procedure under the then Article 169 (now 226) the applicant was 'in reality requesting the adoption of acts which were not of direct and individual concern to it within the meaning of Article 173 [now 230], and which in any event it could not challenge by means of an action for annulment'.

The Court has, however, consistently followed its position in *Lütticke* and held that, in Article 232 (ex 175) proceedings, a definition of position by the defendant institution ends its failure to act. Thus it is not surprising that so few cases have reached the ECJ and now the CFI under that Article. However, this is not necessarily the end of the road for the applicant. In a *legitimate* case, *where he is entitled to demand action* from the institution concerned, he may challenge the definition of position, as a Decision addressed to himself, under Article 230 (ex 173), and provided that he does so in time, his application should be admissible. It is submitted that *Lütticke*, with its special facts (applicant not entitled to demand action), and its judgment cast in terms of Article 226 (ex 169), cannot be invoked to prevent such a challenge. *FEDIOL* (case 191/82) now exists to support this view. Although not described as such, the Commission's letter of May 1982, in which the Commission informed FEDIOL of its decision not to act, and which FEDIOL were held entitled to challenge under the then Article 173 (now 230), was undoubtedly a 'definition of position' within former Article 175 (now 232) (see *GEMA* (case 125/78)). Such an interpretation may also be implied from *Irish Cement Ltd* v *Commission* (case 166/86). Here the applicants, who had complained to the Commission of certain State aids granted by the Irish government to rival companies, which they alleged were in breach of the then Article 92 (now 87), had failed to challenge the Commission's definition of position in time. As a result it was not necessary for the Court to pursue the question of whether the applicants were 'directly and individually concerned' in (i.e. entitled to demand) the Commission's decision in respect of action under the then Article 93(2) (now 88(2)). (As noted earlier in the *Gestevision* case, the CFI has now held that in certain circumstances individuals can demand the Commission take action under Article 88(2) (ex 93(2)).)

Thus where an institution defines its position and refuses to act, an applicant who is not entitled to demand that action cannot challenge that refusal under Article 230 (ex 173); and even a legitimate claim under Article 232 (ex 175) is likely to result in an action to review that refusal under Article 230 (ex 173). In the latter case it is therefore essential that a definition of position be recognised as a Decision capable of challenge under Article 230 (ex 173), and that it be challenged in time (*cf. GEMA*; *Irish Cement Ltd*). The extent of the review conducted by the Court under Article 230 (ex 173) will depend on the extent of the applicant's rights. Since the institutions have wide discretionary powers in the pursuit of economic policy objectives, individuals' rights, at last where action *vis-à-vis* third parties are concerned, are likely to be limited, and mainly of a procedural nature. However, as has been demonstrated in *Parliament* v *Council* (case 13/83), Article 232 (ex 175) offers considerable scope for privileged applicants.

In *Parliament* v *Council* (case 13/83) Parliament's case was heard before the ECJ under former Article 175 (now 232), since the Council's 'definition of position' was found to be inadequate. Since it neither confirmed nor denied the alleged failure (implementation of transport policy), and failed to reveal the Council's position with regard to the measure which the Council intended to adopt, it was held not to amount to a definition of position at all. Thus the Court was able to entertain a case of important constitutional significance without having to decide whether Parliament would have had *locus standi* to challenge the Council's definition of position under the then Article 173 (now 230). Since, following this case, the institutions are likely to be more careful in defining their position, it is only a matter of time before this question arises before the Court. It had been thought that when the opportunity arose the Court would 'square the circle' and extend *locus standi* under Article 230 (ex 173) to Parliament. This opportunity was offered and denied in general terms in *Parliament* v *Council (Comitology)* (case 302/87). Although inroads were made by the ECJ in *Parliament* v *Council (Chernobyl)* (case C–70/88), when it declared that Parliament had a right to bring an action under the then Article 173 (now 230) in order to protect its prerogative powers, Parliament was not held to possess a *general* right of action. This position was affirmed when Article 230 (ex 173) was amended by the TEU. However in *Parliament* v *Council (Comitology)* (case 302/87) the Court suggested that in the case of an action by Parliament 'a refusal to act under Article 175 [now 232] could be brought before the Court on the basis of Article 175 [now 232] where it did not put an end to the failure to act'. Although this statement was obiter, and is inconsistent with the Court's view that a definition of position ends a failure to act (surely a refusal to act must constitute a definition of position?) it is to be hoped that it will be followed, since in the absence of *locus standi* under Article 230 (ex 173) an action before the Court in respect of an alleged failure to act is the only way in which Parliament's rights under Article 232 (ex 175) may be adequately protected.

Consequences of a successful action

Whether the action is admitted before the Court under Article 232 (ex 175), as a failure to act, or under Article 230 (ex 173), as a claim for annulment of a decision not to act, the consequences of a successful action are the same. Under Article 233 (ex 176):

> The institution whose act has been declared void or whose failure to act has been declared contrary to this Treaty shall be required to take the necessary measures to comply with the judgment of the Court of Justice.

Thus the institution will be required by the Court to take action to remedy its failure. It will not necessarily be the action required by the applicant. Should he wish to challenge the institution's implementation of the judgment he could do so under Article 230 (ex 173).

No sanctions beyond the possibility of further action under Article 232 (ex 175) are provided for non-compliance with the Court's judgment. Unlike Article 228 (ex 171), which was amended by the TEU to provide for the imposition of fines and penalties on Member States which fail to comply with a judgment of the Court under Article 226 (ex 169), Article 233 (ex 176) was not amended to provide for similar penalties against EC institutions in respect of their failures established under Article 232 (ex 175). Also, although Article 233(2) (ex 176(2)) provides that the obligation imposed by Article 233(1) (ex 176(1)) 'shall not affect any obligations which may result from the application of the second paragraph of Article 288' (governing the Community's non-contractual liability) the opportunity for individuals to obtain damages from the Community is, as will be seen, extremely limited (see chapter 33).

Further reading

Bradley, K. St Clair, 'The Variable Evolution of the Standing of the European Parliament in Proceedings before the Court of Justice' (1988) 8 YEL 27.

Bradley, K. St Clair, 'Sense and Sensibility: *Parliament* v *Council* Continuing' (1991) 16 EL Rev 245.

Hartley, T. C., *The Foundations of European Community Law*, 3rd ed. (Oxford: Clarendon Press, 1994).

Schermers, H. G., *Judicial Protection in the European Communities*, 5th ed. (London: Kluwer Law & Taxation Publishers, 1992).

THIRTY TWO

Indirect review before the Court of Justice

Article 241 (ex 184) EC provides:

> Notwithstanding the expiry of the period laid down in the fifth paragraph of Article 230, any party may, in proceedings in which a Regulation adopted jointly by the European Parliament and the Council, or a Regulation of the Council or of the Commission is in issue, plead the grounds specified in the second paragraph of Article 230, in order to invoke before the Court of Justice the inapplicability of that Regulation.

As with the other judicial review actions, Article 241 (ex 184) has been amended to reflect the ability of the European Parliament and the European Central Bank to adopt binding acts.

Although Article 241 (ex 184) entitles 'any party' to attack a Regulation 'notwithstanding the expiry' of the time-limit laid down in Article 230 (ex 173), it is not designed to provide a means of escaping the restrictions either of time or *locus standi* laid down in Article 230 (ex 173). No action can be brought *directly* against a Regulation under Article 241 (ex 184). As the Court held in *Milchwerke Heinz Wöhrmann & Sohn KG* v *Commission* (cases 31 & 33/62), in the context of an action brought under the then Article 184 to annul three Commission Decisions, a plea under Article 241 (ex 184) can be raised as an *incidental* matter *only* in the course of legal proceedings based on other provisions of the Treaty. In *Wöhrmann* the action was brought *solely* under the then Article 184 (now 241), since the time limit within which the Decisions should have been challenged under former Article 173 (now 230) had elapsed. Thus the application was rejected. (See also *Commission* v *Belgium* (case 156/77) and, more recently, *Comité des Salines de France* v *Commission* (case T–154/94).)

The purpose of Article 241 (ex 184), the 'plea of illegality', or *'exception d'illégalité'*, as it is called in French law, from which it is taken, is to allow a party to question the legality of a general act on which a subsequent act (e.g., a Decision), or failure to act, is based. A Decision is often, indeed normally, based on some general authorising act. Although the Decision may be challengeable under Article 230 (ex 173), it may in itself be unimpeachable. But it may be based on a general act that is not. A non-privileged applicant has no *locus standi* to challenge a general act under Article 230 (ex 173). And even a privileged applicant, a Member State or an institution may not be aware of the illegality of the general act until affected by some subsequent act issuing from that 'tainted' source. By this time the two months within which the original act should have been challenged may have elapsed. Article 241 (ex 184) thus provides a means whereby this underlying act may be challenged *indirectly*, free of time limit, before the ECJ in proceedings in which it is 'in issue', in much the same way as questions concerning the validity of EC law may be raised indirectly in the context of domestic proceedings before national courts.

Proceedings in which Article 241 (ex 184) may be invoked

In theory Article 241 (ex 184) may be invoked in the context of any proceedings brought directly before the ECJ in which it is relevant. In *Hessische Knappschaft* v *Maison Singer et Fils* (case 44/65) the Court was not prepared to consider a claim under the then Article 184 in the context of a reference from a national court under Article 177 (now 234). However, in that case the parties had attempted to raise the plea of illegality as a new issue; it had not been raised in the reference by the national court. Their attempt to raise it before the ECJ was thus seen by the Court as an interference with the national court's discretion, and, as such, unacceptable. Nevertheless, it would not be necessary to invoke Article 241 (ex 184) before a national court since these courts are free to refer to the ECJ under Article 234 (ex 177) questions of validity of *any* Community act, and are not constrained by the time limit applicable to a direct challenge under Article 230 (ex 173) (see chapter 27).

The main context in which Article 241 (ex 184) is likely to be invoked is to support a challenge under Article 230 (ex 173) to the validity of a measure based on the original, allegedly invalid, act. If the underlying act, challenged under Article 241 (ex 184), is found invalid, it will be declared 'inapplicable' and the subsequent act, affecting the claimant, will be void. Thus the principal object of the exercise will be achieved. Article 241 (ex 184) may also be relevant to an action under Article 232 (ex 175) for failure to act, where the failure (e.g., to issue a Decision to the claimant) is based on an invalid general act (see *SNUPAT* v *High Authority* (cases 32 & 33/58), action under the equivalent provision of the ECSC Treaty, Article 35). It may also, in theory, be invoked to support an action for damages under Articles 235 (ex 178) and 288(2) (ex 215(2)) EC, or arising out of contract under Article 238 (ex 181) (which gives the court 'jurisdiction to give judgment pursuant to any arbitration clause contained in a contract concluded by or on behalf of the Community') or in appeals against penalties under Article 229 (ex 172) EC. It is submitted that Article 184 (new 241) may also be invoked as a defence to an action against a Member State under Article 226 (ex 169) (but see *Commission* v *Belgium* (case 156/77)). A legitimate challenge under Article

241 (ex 184) may be brought by the applicant or the defendant. There must, however, always be a 'direct judicial link' between the act (or failure to act) affecting the applicant and the general underlying measure subject to challenge (*Italy* v *Council* (case 32/65)).

Since Article 241 (ex 184) is only a complementary remedy it is essential to its success that the time limit and *locus standi* requirements imposed in the principal action before the Court are observed. Article 241 (ex 184) does not provide a means of evading these limits (see *Wöhrmann* (cases 31 & 33/62); *Commission* v *Belgium* (case 156/77)).

Reviewable acts

Although Article 241 (ex 184) is expressed to apply only to Regulations, the Court, in keeping with its approach in Article 230 (ex 173) (it is the substance and effect of a measure, not its form, which determines its true nature), has held that Article 241 (ex 184) applies to any general act having binding force. In *Simmenthal SpA* v *Commission* (case 92/78) the claimant, a meat processing company, was seeking to annul, under the then Article 173 (now 230), a Decision addressed to the Italian government, in which the company was directly and individually concerned. The basis of its claim for annulment was that the 'parent' measure, a general notice of invitation to tender, on which the Decision was based, was invalid. The Court held that since the notice was a general act, which, although not in the form of a Regulation, produced similar effects, it could be challenged under Article 184 (now 241). The challenge was successful and resulted in the annulment of the Decision affecting the claimant.

Is the scope for challenge under Article 241 (ex 184) limited to general measures?

The principal reason for making an 'exception' for Regulations would appear to be to enable individuals, who are unable to challenge general acts under Article 230 (ex 173), to do so when they seek, legitimately, to rely on their invalidity in the context of other proceedings before the Court. A secondary reason would be that, since a Regulation is 'of general application' and is not addressed to anyone, its invalidity may not be apparent to the claimant until a subsequent individual measure, based on the general measure, brings it to his attention. Both reasons, i.e., lack of opportunity to challenge and absence of notification, would justify extending the scope of Article 241 (ex 184) to enable an individual to challenge, indirectly, any 'parent' act which was not addressed to him or in which he was not directly and individually concerned. The second reason would provide grounds for allowing a privileged applicant to challenge indirectly any 'parent' act which was not addressed to the applicant. This matter has yet to be decided by the Court.

Locus standi

Although *locus standi* under Article 241 (ex 184) appears to apply to 'any party', doubts have been expressed as to whether it extends to privileged applicants. It is argued that since Member States and institutions (but not Parliament) are entitled to seek annulment of *any* act under Article 230 (ex 173), to allow them to invoke Article 241 (ex 184) would be to enable them to challenge acts which they should have challenged, within the time limit, under Article 230 (ex 173). However, Advocate-General Roemer in *Italy* v *Council* (case 32/65) took the view that a Member State *should* have *locus standi* under Article 241 (ex 184), since the wording of the provision was in no way restrictive, and the illegality of the general provision might not become apparent until it was applied subsequently in a particular case. The Court did not comment on the matter, since it found that the Regulations in issue were not relevant to the case, but its silence could be read as consent. Advocate-General Roemer's reasoning is persuasive. Moreover, Article 241 (ex 184) can never be used *merely* to circumvent time limit; it can only be invoked as an incidental issue, when the claimant is affected by some subsequent act (or failure) arising from the original general act. This provides ample safeguard against abuse.

This is illustrated by *Commission* v *Belgium* (case 156/77). Here the then Article 184 was raised as a defence to an enforcement action against Belgium for infringement of Community law relating to State aids. The Belgians had failed to comply with a Commission Decision of May 1976, addressed to the Belgian government, requiring the Belgians to abolish certain State aids within a three-month period; neither had they attempted to challenge that Decision. In proceedings brought by the Commission in December 1977 for non-compliance with the Decision the Belgian government argued, invoking the them Article 184, that the Decision was invalid. The claim was held inadmissible. The Court found that the Belgians' claim was in essence a claim for the annulment of the Decision of May 1976. They had been free to contest this Decision under the then Article 173 (now 230), but had failed to do so within the time-limit. They could not allow this limit to elapse and then challenge the Decision's legality under former Article 184 (now 241).

This case, it is submitted, does not decide that Article 241 (ex 184) can never be raised in enforcement proceedings against Member States. The Belgians' claim under the then Article 184 was rejected on different and wholly legitimate grounds. They were not invoking the Article as a collateral issue; their defence was based *solely* on the legality of a Decision addressed to them which they had failed to challenge in time.

Grounds of review

The grounds on which Regulations may be challenged under Article 241 (ex 184) are the same as those provided under Article 230 (ex 173) (see chapter 30).

Simmenthal SpA v *Commission* (case 92/78) provides an interesting and rare example of a successful challenge based on Article 241 (ex 184). The general act challenged under the Article — the general notice of invitation to tender — was found to have been used for purposes other than those for which it had been granted. The power under which the notice was passed (contained in a prior Regulation) to set minimum purchase prices for beef, was *granted* in order to help processors; it was being *used* to help importers in general.

Consequences of a successful challenge

Where an action under Article 241 (ex 184) is successful, the Regulation is declared 'inapplicable'. Since there is no time-limit within which acts may be challenged under the Article, it is not, for reasons of legal certainty, void, but voidable. However, a declaration of inapplicability will render a subsequent act, based on that act, void. Thus, although action under Article 241 (ex 184) is an 'incidental matter', it will be conclusive of the principal action before the Court. A declaration of inapplicability under this Article may also be invoked to prevent the application of the invalid act in a subsequent case.

Further reading

Hartley, T.C., *The Foundations of European Community Law*, 4th ed. (1998, Clarendon Press).

Schermers, H.G., *Judicial Protection in the European Communities*, 5th ed. (1992, Kluwer Law & Taxation Publishers).

THIRTY THREE

Community liability in tort, action for damages

Community liability in tort, described as 'non-contractual liability', is governed by Article 235 (ex 178) and Article 288(2) (ex 215(2)). According to Article 235 (ex 178):

> The Court of Justice shall have jurisdiction in disputes relating to the compensation for damage provided for in the second paragraph of Article 288.

Article 288(2) (ex 215(2)) provides that:

> In the case of non-contractual liability, the Community shall, in accordance with the general principles common to the laws of the Member States, make good any damage caused by its institutions or by its servants in the performance of their duties.

Thus, the Community may be liable for both *'fautes de service'*, i.e., wrongful acts on the part of one of its institutions, and *'fautes personelles'*, wrongful acts on the part of its servants. Provided in both cases that the wrongful acts are committed in the performance of the perpetrator's Community functions, the responsible institution may be sued. Where more than one institution is concerned, or where there is doubt as to which institution is responsible, both (or all) may be sued. In the case of *faute personelle*, the Community is liable on the principle of vicarious liability, albeit interpreted in a slightly narrower sense than that in which it is understood under English law (see *Sayag* v *Leduc* (case 9/69), proceedings under Article 188(2) of the Euratom Treaty, in which it was held that the Community is only liable for those acts of its servants which, by virtue of an internal relationship, are the *necessary* extension of the tasks entrusted to the institutions).

In applying Article 288(2) (ex 215(2)) the Court is required to determine liability 'in accordance with the general principles common to the laws of Member States'. Where the principles of non-contractual liability, which embrace principles concerning the basis of liability (i.e. fault or non-fault), causation and damages are not 'common' to all Member States, the Court has drawn on the principles governing tortious liability in the Member States in order to develop its own specific principles of Community law. The process is thus different from its approach to the incorporation of general principles of law for the purposes of judicial review of Community law (see chapter 6).

As was the case with actions for failure to act under Article 232 (ex 175), following the ToA (Article 35 TEU) failed to provide for an action for damages in respect of measures taken under the JHA pillar of the TEU.

Locus standi

Unlike the position in the area of judicial review, there are no personal limitations on the right to bring an action under Article 288(2) (ex 215(2)). Moreover, a specific and generous limitation period of five years is provided (Article 43 of the Protocol on the Statute of the Court of Justice), running from the occurrence of the event giving rise to liability. The Court has held that the limitation period cannot begin until all the requirements for liability, particularly damage, have materialised (*Birra Wührer SpA* v *Council* (cases 256, 257, 265 & 267/80 & 5/81)). Thus, where the damage results from a legislative measure, time runs not necessarily from the date of enactment but from the date on which the injury occurs, or at least when the applicant becomes aware of it (see, e.g., *Buhring* v *Council* (case T–246/93)). These *locus standi* provisions are important, since, as will be seen, it may be possible to obtain a declaration of invalidity in the context of a claim for damages, thereby circumventing the *locus standi* limitations of Article 230 (ex 173) (see *Aktien-Zuckerfabrik Schöppenstedt* v *Council* (case 5/71)). The ECJ did, however, make the point in *Krohn & Co. Import-Export GmbH & Co. KG* v *Commission* (case 175/84) that a claim might not be admissible if the purpose of the then Article 215(2) (now 288(2)) action was purely to attain by another route the remedy provided by the then Article 173 (now 230), an approach reaffirmed by the CFI in declaring an action inadmissible in *Cobrecaf SA* v *Commission* (case T–514/93) and reflecting that taken by the ECJ regarding time limits on Article 234 (ex 177) references on the validity of Community acts (*TWD Textilwerk Deggendorf GmbH* v *Germany* (case C–188/92)) (see chapters 27 and 30).

Elements of non-contractual liability

The basic elements of non-contractual liability are familiar. They embrace:

(a)   a wrongful act (or omission) on the part of the institution (*faute de service*) or its servants (*faute personelle*),

(b)   damage to the claimant, and
(c)   a causative link between the two.

For liability to arise, all three elements must be proved. Although under certain Continental systems (e.g., France), a public body may be strictly liable where a claimant suffers exceptional or abnormal damage as a result of a public measure taken in the general interest, on the principle of *'égalité devant les charges publiques'* (equal apportionment of public burdens), neither the ECJ nor the CFI have yet endorsed a principle of liability without fault in EC law, despite the opportunity to rule specifically on this matter in *Atlanta* (case T–521/93) and *Édouard Dubois et Fils SA* v *Council* (case T–113/96). The ECJ has not, however, ruled out that possibility (see *Compagnie d'Approvisionnement* v *Commission* (cases 9 & 11/71); *Biovilac* v *Commission* (case 59/83)). In *Dorsch Consult* (case T–184/95), the CFI commented, without specifically ruling on the point of whether liability could arise for a lawful act, that a precondition for such liability would in any event be the existence of 'unusual' and 'special' damage, which in this case was not satisfied.

Wrongful acts or omissions

Although, following Continental traditions, non-contractual liability is not divided up into specific 'torts', wrongful acts and omissions may be grouped under three broad categories:

(a)   Failures of administration. Community institutions are under a duty of good administration. Failures of administration would include, for example, a failure to adopt satisfactory procedures, a failure to obtain the relevant facts before making the decision, the giving of misleading information or a failure to give the necessary information (e.g., *Odigitria AAE* v *Council* (case T–572/93) — but no liability because of lack of causal link). As with negligence, the decision taken or advice offered need not be right as long as it is adopted according to the correct procedures and the conclusions reached are reasonable in the light of the information to hand. This category would also include a single negligent act. For example, in *Grifoni* v *Euratom* (case C–308/87), a case concerning the Euratom Treaty, Euratom contracted with Mr Grifoni to have the roof of a building repaired. Whilst inspecting the roof, Grifoni fell off. The ECJ held that Euratom was at fault in not providing the necessary guard rails. Liability here thus approximates, loosely, to liability for 'operational' failures in negligence (see *Anns* v *Merton London Borough Council* [1978] AC 728, House of Lords).

(b)   Negligent acts by a servant in the performance of his duties (e.g., in English law, *Ministry of Housing and Local government* v *Sharp* [1970] 2 QB 223).

(c)   The adoption of wrongful (i.e., illegal or invalid) acts having legal effect, or the wrongful failure to adopt a binding act when under a duty to do so.

Since this latter is the most important area of non-contractual liability and is closely linked with the remedies considered so far relating to judicial review, the present chapter will focus principally on this issue.

Liability for wrongful acts having legal effect

It is perhaps self-evident that liability cannot arise from action taken under primary legislation, that is pursuant to the EC treaties themselves. This was confirmed in *Édouard Dubois et Fils SA* v *Council* (case T–113/96). Here the applicant, a customs agent, was seeking damages for losses arising from the completion of the single internal market. Following its completion on 1 January 1993 his business suffered 'an almost total and definitive cessation of its activities as a customs agent', resulting in material damage valued at FF112,339,703. He claimed compensation on the basis of strict liability or, alternatively, fault. The CFI held that the agreement to complete the single internal market contained in the SEA, as an agreement between Member States, could not give rise to non-contractual liability on the part of the Community. Articles 235 (ex 178) and 288(2) (ex 215(2)), being also primary Community law, cannot be brought to bear on instruments of an equivalent level where this is not expressly provided for. It was thus unnecessary to answer the question concerning strict liability.

As regards liability in respect of executive acts, there is some indication in the EC Treaty that damages may be recoverable as a result of unlawful action or a wrongful failure to act on the part of the EC institutions. Article 233(2) (ex 176(2)) provides that the obligation to remedy a failure to act 'shall not affect any obligation which may result from the application of the second paragraph of Article 288'. From this it may be deduced, applying the 'unity' principle (see chapters 30 and 31), that liability in damages for unlawful legislative acts exists and that liability under Article 288(2) (ex 215(2)) exists as a *separate* remedy from the remedies under Articles 230 and 232 (ex 173 and 175) for judicial review.

This was not the view taken originally by the ECJ in *Plaumann & Co.* v *Commission* (case 25/62)). Here, it held that, since Plaumann & Co. lacked *locus standi* to challenge the contested Decision under the then Article 173 (now 230) (see chapter 30), their claim for compensation, based on the illegality of that same decision, must fail. The Court cannot, by way of an action for compensation, take steps that would nullify the legal effects of a Decision which has not been annulled.

The Court changed its mind in *Alfons Lütticke GmbH* v *Commission* (case 4/69). In this case, Lütticke, having failed to establish the Commission's failure to act under Article 175 (now 232) (see chapter 31), sought damages from the Commission in a separate action under Article 215(2) (now 288(2)). The action was held admissible. The Court said that the action for damages provided for under the then Articles 178 and 215(2) was established as *an independent form of action with a particular purpose to fulfil*. It would be contrary to the independent nature of this action, as well as to the efficacy of the general system of forms of action created by the Treaty, to regard as a ground of inadmissibility the fact that, in certain circumstances, an action for damages might lead to a result similar to that of an action for failure to act under Article 175 (now 232).

Although *Lütticke* failed on the merits (there being no wrongful failure), an important principle was established.

It was confirmed in *Aktien-Zuckerfabrik Schöppenstedt* v *Council* (case 5/71). On the reasoning cited above the Court held that the claimant company could sue the Council for damages on the basis of an allegedly illegal Regulation even though as a 'natural or legal person' they would have no *locus standi* to seek its annulment under Article 173 (now 232). *Schöppenstedt* was subsequently approved and applied in *Krohn & Co. Import-Export GmbH & Co. KG* v *Commission* (case 175/84). Here the Court held that since an action for non-contractual liability was an autonomous form of action, the expiry of the time-limit for challenge under Article 173 (now 230) did not render an action for damages inadmissible.

Thus the principle expressed initially in *Lütticke* (case 4/69) that action for non-contractual liability is an independent form of action now seems firmly established, and it will not be necessary in a claim for damages based on an illegal act (or failure to act) to bring a prior action for annulment or failure to act, nor even to establish *locus standi* to bring such action.

However, the problem with an action for non-contractual liability lies not in establishing admissibility but in succeeding on the merits of the case. The ECJ has adopted a very restrictive approach towards Community liability in tort, particularly towards liability resulting from the adoption of wrongful acts (or the wrongful failure to adopt an act). Such an approach is common to most legal systems. And indeed there are strong policy reasons for limiting the non-contractual liability of public authorities. These bodies are charged by law to take decisions in the general interest over a wide range of activities. These decisions often involve the exercise of discretion and affect a substantial section of the public. Sometimes the decisions are unlawful. Whilst it is right that such decisions be subject to judicial review, it may be argued that to expose public bodies to liability in damages for unlawful acts in the absence of bad faith or an improper motive or (*quaere*) 'gross' negligence would unduly hamper the administrative process and impose an excessive burden on the public purse (see the 'policy' arguments expressed in *Rowling* v *Takaro Properties Ltd* [1988] AC 473, Privy Council), *a fortiori* in a community as large as the EC.

Thus it is not sufficient for Community liability to arise that the measure in question is unlawful, nor that the institution has unlawfully failed to act. Where the action concerns a legislative measure which involves choices of economic policy the Community incurs no liability unless a sufficiently serious breach of a superior rule of law for the protection of the individual has occurred. This formula, known as the '*Schöppenstedt*' formula (from *Aktien-Zuckerfabrik Schöppenstedt* v *Council* (case 5/71)), must be satisfied.

The *Schöppenstedt* formula

This contains three essential elements. It requires:

(a) *A legislative measure involving choices of economic policy.* Although the term 'legislative act' relates primarily to Regulations it will apply to any binding act which purports to lay down general rules. The Decision in *Firma E. Kampffmeyer* v *Commission* (cases 5, 7 & 13-24/66), addressed to the German government and authorising it to withhold import licences for maize during a certain period would, it is submitted, constitute a legislative measure. In *Gibraltar* v *Council* (case C–298/89) the Court suggested, albeit in the context of proceedings under former Article 173 (now 230), that Directives 'normally' constitute 'a form of indirect regulatory or legislative measure'. It was accepted in *Odigitria AAE* v *Council* (case T–572/93) that an international agreement dealing with fishing rights would be a legislative act involving economic policy because of its impact on the Community's fisheries policy. The majority of legislative measures will involve choices of economic policy, since the institutions enjoy wide discretionary powers in all areas of activity, and it is possible to construe many measures even of a social nature as economic in the context of the EC Treaty.

Of course, if there is no legislative act involving economic policy choices, this does not prevent an applicant from bringing a successful claim under Article 288(2) (ex 215(2)); it merely means that the *Schöppenstedt* formula is not applicable (see, e.g., *Grifoni* (case C–308/87)).

(b) *A breach of a superior rule of law for the protection of individuals.* Any general principle, such as equality or proportionality, accepted as part of Community law (see chapter 6) would constitute a superior law for the protection of individuals. A breach of the principle of legitimate expectations was argued successfully in a claim for damages in *Sofrimport SARL* v *Commission* (case C–152/88 see chapter 30). Here the Commission, in issuing Regulations suspending import licences for imported apples from Chile, and imposing quotas on fruits from third countries, had failed to take account of the applicants' interest as undertakings with 'goods in transit' when the Regulations were issued, as required under Community law (Regulation 2702/72, Article 3). Most general principles of *Community* law (e.g., freedom of movement for workers; non-discrimination between producers and consumers (Article 34(2) (ex 40(2)), agriculture) whether expressed in the EC Treaty or in secondary legislation could likewise form the basis of a claim for damages. In *Société Commerciale Antoine Vloeberghs SA* v *High Authority* (cases 9 & 12/60), (action under ECSC Treaty) the Court held, in the context of a claim for damages based on the High Authority's alleged infringement of the principle of free movement of goods (in this case coal), that this principle was not intended for the benefit of coal importers. However in *Firma E. Kampffmeyer* v *Commission* (cases 5, 7 & 13-24/66) a provision in an EC Regulation directed at ensuring 'appropriate support for agricultural markets' was construed as intending to benefit, *inter alia,* the interests of individual undertakings such as importers. The claimants, as importers, were thus entitled to claim damages as a result of the Commission's action in breach of these provisions. It seems therefore that as long as the rule of law can be construed as designed in part to benefit a particular class of people it may be deemed to be 'for the protection of individuals'.

(c) *The breach must be 'sufficiently serious'.* A breach of a superior rule of law, even a fundamental rule such as the principle of equality, is not in itself sufficient to give rise to a claim in damages. The claimant must prove that the breach is 'sufficiently serious'. This principle has been very narrowly construed. In *Bayerische HNL Vermehrungsbetriebe GmbH & Co. KG v Council* (cases 83 & 94/76, 4 15 & 40/77), the Court suggested that in a legislative field in which one of the chief features is the exercise of a wide discretion, the Community does not incur liability unless the institution concerned has *manifestly and gravely disregarded the limits on the exercise of its power.*

In interpreting this requirement two approaches may be noted. Sometimes the Court looks at the *effect* of the measure on the applicant, at the nature and extent of the harm to his interests. Sometimes it looks at the nature of the breach; in what way, and to what extent, is the institution *culpable*? It seems from the developing case law that both enquiries are relevant. The breach must be both serious as regards its effect on the applicant *and* inexcusable.

The effect of the measure In *HNL v Council* the Court adopted an approach based on the effect of the measure. The action, brought by a number of animal feed producers, was for damages for loss suffered as a result of an EC Regulation requiring animal feed producers to purchase skimmed milk powder instead of the cheaper and equally effective soya, as a means of disposing of surplus stocks of milk. This Regulation had been found by the Court in a prior preliminary ruling proceeding (*Bela-Mühle Josef Bergmann KG v Grows-Farm GmbH & Co. KG* (case 114/76); *Granaria BV v Hoofdproduktschap voor Akkerbouwprodukten (No. 1)* (case 116/76)) to be in breach of the principles of non-discrimination and proportionality. In deciding whether the breach was sufficiently serious, whether the Commission had manifestly and gravely disregarded the limits on the exercise of its powers, the Court looked at the effect of the breach. It had affected a wide group of persons (all buyers of protein for the production of animal feed); the difference in price between the skimmed milk and soya had only a limited effect on production costs, insignificant beside other factors such as world prices; and the effect of the Regulation on their profits did not exceed the normal level of risk inherent in such activities. Thus the breach was not sufficiently serious.

The same approach proved more successful for the applicants in the 'grits' and 'quellmehl' cases (e.g., *P. Dumortier Frères SA v Council* (cases 64 & 113/76, 167 & 239/78, 27, 28 & 45/79)). Here the claimants, a group of grits and quellmehl producers were seeking compensation for damage resulting from an EC Regulation, withdrawing subsidies for grits and quellmehl whilst retaining them for starch. All these products had previously benefited from subsidies, and all were to a certain extent in competition. As in *HNL* the Regulation had been held unlawful, in breach of the principle of equality, in preliminary ruling proceedings (see *Firma Albert Ruckdeschel & Co.* (case 117/76)). Following these proceedings the Commission restored the subsidies, but only from the date of the Court's judgment. The claimants claimed damages for losses suffered during the period prior to that judgment. And they succeeded. In this case they were a small, clearly defined group, and their loss went beyond the risks normally inherent in their business.

The case of *Sofrimport SARL* v *Commission* (case C–152/88) suggested that not only must the group affected be small and clearly defined but it must also be closed. In this case, in deciding that the applicant importers were entitled to damages the Court pointed out that undertakings such as the claimants, with goods in transit at the time when the Regulations were made, constituted a 'restricted group *which could not be extended* after the contested measures took effect'. A similar point was made by Advocate-General van Gerven in *Mulder* (cases C–104/89, C 37/90). *Mulder* involved a claim for damages by milk producers based on a number of EC Regulations which had previously been found invalid in two pairs of judgments of the Court, for breach of the principle of legitimate expectations (*Mulder* and *von Deetzen* (cases 120/86, 170/86); *Spagl* and *Pastätter* (cases C–189/89, C 217/89)). The challenge in the former claims was to two EC Regulations which, in increasing production levies on dairy products, had provided for exemption from the levies for quotas calculated by reference to undertakings in production during a particular year (the 'reference year'). Because of the choice of year the claimants, who had made no milk deliveries during the reference year, received no levy-free quota. The second challenge was to the Regulation which replaced the Regulations annulled in *Mulder* and *von Deetzen*. Under this Regulation the applicants were allocated specific 'reference quantities' for quota purposes, calculated at 60 per cent of the milk or milk equivalent produced in the year prior to their application. Having established the illegality of the Regulations in both pairs of cases the applicants sought damages for losses suffered as a result of both the original and the replacement Regulations.

The Court found for the applicants in their claim based on the original Regulations. Here the Community institutions had

> failed . . . to take account of the specific situation of a clearly defined group of economic agents, namely producers . . . The total exclusion of producers concerned from the allocation of the reference quantity could not be regarded as foreseeable or as falling within the economic risks inherent in producing milk.

On the other hand the breach committed by the Community institutions which formed the basis of their second damages claim, based on the replacement Regulation, although infringing the applicants' legitimate expectations, was not sufficiently serious. It was the result of an economic policy choice, necessary to give effect to the Court's prior judgments. It may thus be implied that the measure was deemed to be foreseeable and within the bounds of the economic risks inherent in milk production. It may be noted that in the successful claim the Court did not follow the Advocate-General's suggestion that the group, as well as being clearly defined, should be closed. It did however appear to adopt his suggestion that whether a particular policy was within the bounds of the normal economic risks inherent in a particular enterprise was related to the question of whether such a risk was foreseeable.

The nature of the breach In the 'Isoglucose' cases (*Koninklijke Scholten-Honig NV v Council* (case 143/77); *G.R. Amylum NV v Council* (cases 116 & 124/77)) the claimant glucose producers were seeking damages for losses suffered as a result of a Community Regulation which imposed levies on the production of glucose in order to increase consumption of Community sugar. Clearly there was some competition between glucose and sugar. The Regulation had been found invalid, in breach of the principle of equality, in a prior preliminary ruling reference in *Royal Scholten-Honig (Holdings) Ltd v Intervention Board for Agricultural Produce* (cases 103 & 145/77) (see chapter 27). The claimants were a small and closed group, and the damage which they suffered as a result of the Regulation was described as 'catastrophic'. One firm, the Dutch firm Koninklijke Scholten-Honig NV had been forced into liquidation. Yet they failed to obtain damages. Although the treatment of the glucose producers as compared with that of the sugar producers was 'manifestly unequal', the Court held that the defendants' errors were not of such gravity that their conduct could be regarded as 'verging on the arbitrary'.

Similarly, in *Roquette Frères SA v Commission* (case 20/88) Roquette failed in their claim for damages suffered as a result of a Regulation setting the level of monetary compensatory amounts (MCAs) which had been declared invalid in preliminary ruling proceedings in *Roquette Frères v France* (case 145/79) (see chapter 27). Since the ruling had been declared prospective only, Roquette had suffered loss by way of MCAs paid and profits lost prior to the date of judgment. The Court held that the Commission's fault in calculating MCAs was a purely 'technical error' which 'could not be regarded as amounting to a serious infringement of a superior rule of law or manifest and grave disregard by the Commission of the limits on the exercise of its powers'.

More recently in *Nölle v Council* (case T-167/94) the applicant claimed that the Community institutions in determining an anti-dumping case had not chosen an appropriate country as a reference point. The CFI agreed that, in not giving proper consideration to this suggestion, the Community had breached the 'principle of care', a rule for the protection of individuals but held that this was not a sufficiently serious breach. The CFI contrasted the insufficient investigation of the appropriate reference country which occurred in this case with a total failure to consider an alternative country. This latter could be conduct, 'which in the circumstances might well have constituted a serious failure to meet its obligations of proper administration . . .'.

The claimants in *Sofrimport SARL v Commission* (case C–152/88) on the other hand were successful. In *Sofrimport* the Court found that the Commission had 'failed completely' to take the claimants' interests into account, as it was required to do under the Regulations concerned. Similarly in the successful damages claim in *Mulder* it pointed out that the Council, in totally excluding the producers concerned from the allocation of a reference quantity, was held to have 'failed *completely*, without invoking any higher interest', to take account of the applicant milk producers' specific situation. In doing so they had 'gravely and manifestly disregarded the limits of their discretionary power'. On the other hand in adopting the replacement Regulation, the subject of the second claim, the institutions were engaged in necessary economic policy choices and were taking into account the higher public interest.

Thus to succeed in a claim for damages resulting from a wrongful act in a field in which the Community institutions exercise a wide discretion, it will probably be necessary to prove that:

(a) the measure has adversely affected a (quaere small and) clearly defined group,
(b) its effect goes beyond the normal level of risk inherent in the claimant's business i.e., is unforeseeable, and
(c) the institution's breach was a serious one, and was *without justification*.

Whether a particular risk is regarded as foreseeable will be determined according to the standard of the prudent and discriminating trader (see, e.g., *EFISOL SA* v *Commission* (case T–336/94)). A breach of an obligation designed to protect persons such as the claimant, as in *Sofrimport*, is likely to be regarded as sufficiently serious to ground a claim under Article 288(2) (ex 215(2)) in the absence of strong justification. It may also be argued that the institution has no discretion in such a matter; such a failure does not involve 'choices of economic policy' and should not be assessed under the *Schöppenstedt* formula. But even where the institution is clearly acting within the limits of its discretion, *Mulder* suggests that it cannot 'completely' ignore the interests of traders. Where choices are made which are likely to cause serious harm to certain groups they must be justified on the grounds of some overriding public or Community interest.

In view of the stringent nature of the *Schöppenstedt* formula it is not surprising that very few claimants succeed. As Advocate-General Tesauro pointed out in *Brasserie du Pêcheur* (cases C–46 & 48/93) on the date on which the opinion was approved (26 November 1995), only eight awards of damages against Community institutions had been made. Although there have been a small number of successful cases since then, these have tended to arise in the context of administrative failures rather than in circumstances involving economic policy (e.g., *New Europe Consulting and Brown* v *Commission* (case T–231/97) and *Embassy Limousines* v *European Parliament* (case T–203/96)).

Where the Court rejects a claim for damages, as in the isoglucose cases, it often points out that applicants are not without a remedy. The action must be assessed having regard to the whole system of legal protection of individuals set up by the Treaty. Where a person suffers, or is likely to suffer, damage as a result of an unlawful act he may challenge that measure before his national courts and seek a ruling under Article 234 (ex 177) on its validity. The Court has said that the existence of such an action is by itself of such a nature as to ensure the effective protection of the individuals concerned. Not all would agree with this view. There may be no issue of national law in which to raise questions of EC law. As is borne out in *Koninklijke Scholten-Honig NV v Council* (case 143/77), heavy, even irreparable losses may be incurred while proceedings before the national courts are pending. An action before a national court may be successful in obtaining interim relief (see, e.g., *Zuckerfabrik Süderdithmarschen AG v Hauptzollamt Itzehoe* (cases C–143/88 & 92/89); *Antonissen v Council* (case C–393/96 P/R), noted chapter 26), or, in time, a declaration of invalidity: but where damage has occurred a national court cannot award compensation for wrongs attributable to the Community (see *Krohn* (case 175/84), discussed below). Surely the most appropriate forum in which to challenge Community action (or inaction) would be before the European Courts under Article 230 (ex 173) EC (or Article 232 (ex 175) EC), alongside, or prior to, a claim for damages under Article 228(2) (ex 215(2)). Yet, as has been seen in chapter 30, the individual has no *locus standi* to challenge or demand genuine legislative measures under these Articles. Community institutions as well as Member States are bound by the European Convention on Human Rights and general principles of law to protect the individual's right to an effective judicial remedy (see Advocate-General Jacobs, *Extramet*, case C–358/89). Since the European Courts are understandably reluctant to expose the Community to unlimited claims, and, where the exercise of discretion by a Community institution is concerned, to fetter that discretion by the prospect of such exposure (for a similar approach towards matters of 'policy' see Lord Wilberforce in *Anns v Merton London Borough Council* [1978] AC 728, House of Lords), arguably the most effective protection for applicants would be speedy interim relief from the European Courts to forestall the application of unlawful measures and prevent damage occurring. Although this may be obtained in an action under Article 228(2) (ex 215(2)) (see *Kampffmeyer* (cases 56–60/74), considered below), it would seem more logical, in the absence of damage, to proceed under Article 230 (ex 173). Where damage is suffered as a result of lawful action on the part of the Community, perhaps the Courts could be persuaded, in exceptional cases, to accept some form of strict liability on the principle of *'égalité devant les charges publiques'*. It cannot be right that a few should bear a disproportionate burden as a result of measures enacted in the interest of the many.

Individual acts

It should be noted that the 'Schöppenstedt' formula only applies to legislative acts involving choices of economic policy; it does not apply to individual acts which do not involve the exercise of discretion. Since such acts affect only their addressees they do not raise the same floodgates problems, thus it is not necessary to subject them to such stringent criteria. The Court is not always mindful of this point (see Advocate-General Tesauro's criticism of the Court's application of Article 215(2) (now 288(2)) in *Brasserie du Pêcheur* (cases C–46 & 48/90)). Where an individual act is prima facie unlawful and threatens to cause damage to its addressee, it may be challenged under Article 230 (ex 173). Where he fails to challenge the measure in time he may still bring an independent action under Article 288(2) (ex 215(2)) where damage has occurred as a result of its application (*Krohn* (case 175/84)). To succeed, however, it may not be enough to establish the illegality of the measure. Although there is little authority on this point it is thought that fault must be proved, although what may be deemed to constitute fault in this context remains unclear. In *Grifoni* v *Euratom* (case C–308/87), for example, a failure to provide a guard rail despite clear guidelines requiring their provision provided the basis for community liability.

Damage

The ECJ (and now the CFI) is as restrictive in its approach to damages as it is to fault. Clearly the Court will award compensation for damage to person or property provided the damage is sufficiently direct. Although it will in principle award damages for economic loss, such losses must be specific, not speculative. Only actual, certain and concrete damages are recoverable (*Société Roquette Frères* v *Commission* (case 26/74) [1976] ECR 677). Thus in *Firma E. Kampffmeyer* v *Commission* (cases 5, 7 & 13-24/66) the Court was prepared to award damages for lost profits on contracts which had already been concluded, which applicants had had to cancel as a result of the illegal Decision, although these damages were reduced to only 10 per cent of the profits they might have expected to make, on account of the risks involved in the transactions in question. Applicants who had not concluded contracts prior to applying for import permits were awarded no damages at all. In *CNTA SA* v *Commission* (case 74/74) the Court found that the Commission had breached the principle of legitimate expectations when it introduced a Regulation, suddenly and without warning, which deprived the claimant of export refunds at a particular rate, fixed in advance. Although the Regulation was not in itself invalid, the Commission's mode of introduction of the measure was wrongful. Thus the Commission was liable in principle. However, although CNTA had entered into export contracts on the basis of its legitimate expectations, the Court held that it was only entitled to recover for losses actually suffered, not anticipated profits, and, since currency fluctuations at the time of import had resulted in its suffering no loss on the refunds themselves, it recovered no damages ([1976] ECR 797) (see also *Firma Gebrüder Dietz* v *Commission* (case 126/76)).

Where the loss has been passed on to third parties, or could have been passed on in higher prices, no damages will be recoverable (*Interquell Stärke-Chemie GmbH & Co. KG* v *Council* (cases 261 & 262/78), 'quellmehl' case). In *P. Dumortier Frères SA* v *Council* (cases 64 & 113/76, 167 & 239/78, 27, 28 & 45/79) the claimants satisfied the Court that the losses could not have been passed on without risk of losing valuable markets. An injured party is expected to show reasonable diligence in limiting the extent of his loss; otherwise he must bear the damage himself (*Mulder* (case C–104/89)). In *Antillean Rice Mills NV* v *Commission* (cases T–480 & 483/93), the CFI suggested that since the damage to the applicants was foreseeable they could have taken precautions against it. Since they did not, 'neither the fault nor the damage alleged by the applicants are such as to cause the Community to incur non-contractual liability'.

In *Dorsch Consult* (case T–184/95), the CFI held that the applicant had not shown actual and certain damage. The case concerned a contract for the provision of services in Iraq. The applicants had not been paid for the work done when the UN Security Council imposed a trade embargo on Iraq, which the European Community implemented within the EC. As a response to this, the Iraqi government froze all property, assets and income from them held at the material time by the governments, undertakings, companies and banks of those States which had adopted 'arbitrary decisions' against Iraq. The applicants claimed that the Community was liable for the damage it had suffered from not being able to obtain payment from Iraq. The CFI pointed out that the applicants had not tried to press for payment, even when the relevant Iraqi law was repealed.

In *Farrugia* (case T–230/94) the CFI considered a claim for compensation for the loss of a chance. The applicant claimed that an error on the part of the Commission concerning his nationality had deprived him of the opportunity of a fellowship in the field of research and technological development in the UK. The CFI found that although the Commission had made a mistake the applicant had failed to prove that, in the absence of that mistake, he would have had a 'strong chance' of being awarded the fellowship he sought. This implies that the Court would consider a claim for loss of a chance of success provided that the chance was proved to be sufficiently strong. The Court did not indicate what standard of proof would be necessary to establish a 'strong chance' of success.

Damages are payable in the applicant's national currency at the exchange rate applicable on the date of the judgment under Article 288(2) (ex 215(2)). Interest on that sum is payable from the date of judgment (*Dumortier*).

Causation

The Court is similarly restrictive in its approach to matters of causation. In *Dumortier* it said that the principles common to the laws of Member States cannot be relied on to deduce an obligation to make good every harmful consequence, even a remote one, of unlawful legislation. The damage must be a *sufficiently direct* consequence of the unlawful conduct of the institution concerned.

Thus in *Dumortier* the parties were entitled to recover the refunds which had been unlawfully withheld as a result of the invalid Regulation, but not for further alleged losses in the form of reduced sales or for general financial difficulties resulting in the closing of some factories. Even though these difficulties might have been exacerbated by the illegal Regulation they were not a sufficiently direct consequence of the unlawful act to render the Community liable (see also *Blackspur DIY Ltd* v *Council* (case T–168/94)). Other factors such as obsolescence and financial stringency were responsible. Similarly, where a party engages in activities designed to replace activities denied or restricted as a result of Community law any operating losses incurred as a result of these activities will be deemed too remote, and not attributed to the Community (*Mulder* (cases C–104/89, C 37/90)).

The ECJ (and now the CFI) has taken the view that the acts of the applicants, and sometimes even their failure to act, will break the chain of causation. Traders are expected to act as prudent business people. For example, in a claim based on misleading information the required causal link will be established only if the information would have caused an error in the mind of a reasonable person (*Compagnie Continentale France* v *Council* (case 169/73); see also *SA Oleifici Mediterranei* v *EEC* (case 26/81) and *Antillean Rice Mills NV* v *Commission* (cases T–480 & 483/93)). In *EFISOL SA* v *Commission* (case T–336/94) the CFI suggested that a legitimate expectation (as to a certain state of affairs) could not arise from conduct on the part of the (Community) administration which was inconsistent with Community rules. Thus it seems that the prudent trader is expected to know if a Community institution misapplies Community rules!

In *International Procurement Services SA* v *Commission* (case T–175/94) the applicant tenderer suffered loss in a contract with the Mozambique government. Following advice from the Commission the government reduced the payment originally agreed for the supply of steel billets by the applicant. Although the Commission was found to have indirectly influenced the Mozambique government' s decision to pay the lower price, the applicant's damage was held by the CFI to derive from two factors: the Mozambique government's refusal to pay the originally agreed price, and the applicant's failure to challenge that refusal in arbitration proceedings, as it was entitled to do. The fact that IPS had taken that course of action because it was 'in urgent need of liquid funds' would not have the effect of attaching responsibility for the damage to the defendants.

Thus where other factors can be seen as contributing to the claimant's loss the damage is normally seen as too remote. The CFI considered the nature of the causal link more recently in *Dorsch Consult* (case T–184/95). There, it commented that the applicant had not succeeded in showing that the adoption by the Iraqi government of a law freezing the applicants' assets in retaliation for the trade embargo imposed on Iraq was 'an objectively foreseeable consequence, in the normal course of events, of the adoption' of that Community's regulation implementing the embargo. Thus a requirement of foreseeability seems to have been introduced as a precondition to the finding of a causal link.

The Court does not as a general rule attempt to apportion blame on the basis of contributory negligence. It appears that apportionment is reserved for claims of particular merit. In *Adams* v *Commission (No. 1)* (case 145/83) Adams's damages for the Commission's breach of confidence, which had caused him irreparable financial and emotional damage, were reduced by 50 per cent to take into account Adams's contribution in failing to protect his own interests (see chapter 17). Similarly, in *Grifoni* v *Euratom* (case C–308/87), although Euratom was clearly at fault in not providing guard rails, equally Grifoni, an experienced contractor, should have known that he had to take some precautions himself. His damages were reduced, also by 50 per cent.

Relationship between Article 288(2) (ex 215(2)) and other remedies

If a claim for damages for non-contractual liability, particularly a claim based on an unlawful legislative act, is unlikely to succeed for the many reasons outlined above, its value in the overall scheme of remedies available against the Community should not be underrated. Since an action under Article 288(2) (ex 215(2)) is an independent form of action (*Lütticke* (case 4/69); *Schöppenstedt* (case 5/71); *Krohn* (case 175/84)), an action for damages based on invalidity or wrongful failure may be effective in obtaining a declaration of invalidity or failure to act notwithstanding that the applicant has no *locus standi,* either personal or temporal, to challenge that same act (or inaction) in proceedings under Article 230 (ex 173) or Article 232 (ex 175). Moreover, the Court has held (*Kurt Kampffmeyer Mühlenvereinigung KG* v *Council* (cases 56-60/74)) that where the damage to the claimant is imminent, or likely with a high degree of certainty to occur, the claimant may bring proceedings under Article 288(2) (ex 215(2)) *before* the damage has occurred. Although he may not be found entitled in principle to damages, he may obtain a declaration of invalidity or unlawful failure to act, including interim relief, in time to prevent the damage occurring.

It is submitted that the Court will admit such actions under Article 288(2) (ex 215(2)) only where a claim for damages is genuine; it will not allow this provision to be used solely as a means of evading the *locus standi* limitations of Articles 230 and 232 (ex 173 and 175) (see *Krohn* (case 175/84) and *Cobrecaf SA* v *Commission* (case T–514/93)).

Concurrent liability

Since Community law is to a large extent implemented by national authorities, there may be cases in which it is unclear whether the cause of action, for example, for the return of money paid under an invalid Regulation, or for a wrongful failure on the part of a national body to pay a subsidy to which the applicant feels he is entitled, lies against the national authority, in national courts, according to national law, or against a Community institution, before the Court of Justice, or against both. Motivated no doubt by a desire to reduce its work-load and/or its potential liability, the Court, as illustrated by *Koninklijke Scholten-Honig NV* (case 143/77) (and countless other cases), prefers to direct applicants to seek a remedy before their national courts, leaving questions of validity to be referred to the ECJ, if necessary, under Article 234 (ex 177).

Largely as a result, it is submitted, of this preference the case law on what might loosely be termed concurrent liability is both confusing the contradictory.

Initially, in cases such as *Firma E. Kampffmeyer* v *Commission* (cases 5, 7 & 13-24/66) and *R. & V. Haegeman Sprl* v *Commission* (case 96/71), the ECJ espoused a doctrine of 'exhaustion of national law remedies'. In *Kampffmeyer* the applicant grain dealers were seeking, before the ECJ:

(a) the return of levies paid to the German authorities, and
(b) compensation for contracts cancelled

as a result of an invalid EC Regulation. They had already begun parallel proceedings before the German courts, but those proceedings had been stayed pending the outcome of the Community proceedings.

The ECJ held that the German court should first be given the opportunity to decide whether the German authorities were liable. The proceedings were stayed accordingly.

In *Haegeman* the applicant was seeking the annulment of a Commission Decision refusing to return levies paid to the German authorities by the applicant as a result of an allegedly invalid Regulation. This time, unlike *Kampffmeyer*, the levies had been paid into Community funds, and Haegeman had not instituted parallel proceedings before its national courts. Again the Court refused to admit the action. Haegeman's claim should have been made against the national authorities to whom the refunds were originally paid.

There followed a series of cases in which claims before the ECJ:

(a)   for the return of *sums unlawfully levied* (e.g., *Société Roquette Frères* v *Commission* (case 26/74)), and

(b)   seeking payment of *sums unlawfully withheld* (*IBC* v *Commission* (case 46/75); *Lesieur Costelle et Associés SA* v *Commission* (cases 67–85/75)),

were held inadmissible on the grounds that the applicants should have brought their actions before their national courts.

On the other hand in *Compagnie d'Approvisionnement de Transport et de Crédit SA* v *Commission* (cases 9 & 11/71); *Merkur-Aussenhandels GmbH* v *Commission* (case 43/72); *Holtz & Willemsen GmbH* v *Council* (case 153/73); *CNTA SA* v *Commission* (case 74/74) the ECJ was prepared to admit claims seeking payment of *sums unlawfully withheld* without requiring claimants to proceed first before their national courts.

In *Firma Gebrüder Dietz* v *Commission* (case 126/76), and *CNTA* (case 74/74) the applicants were seeking damages for losses suffered as a result of the sudden introduction by the Commission of MCAs; they had not brought actions before their national courts. Their claims under the then Article 215(2) (now 288(2)) were held admissible.

In the second grits and quellmehl cases, and the isoglucose cases, admitted under former Article 215(2) (now 288(2)), proceedings had already been brought and the invalidity of the measures in question decided, before the applicants' national courts.

From the above cases the following tentative conclusions may be drawn:

(a)   A claim for the return of sums unlawfully paid to the relevant national authorities should always be brought before a national court, even though those sums may have been paid into Community funds (*Kampffmeyer, Haegeman; Roquette*; see also more recently *Industrie-en Handelsonderneming Vreugdenhil BV* v *Commission* (case C–282/90)).

(b)   A claim for sums unlawfully withheld, even when withheld by a national authority, may be brought *either* before national courts or the ECJ. The weight of authority (*Compagnie d'Approvisionnement; Merkur; Holtz &*

Willemsen; CNTA) leans towards this view. However, the existence of *IBC* and *Costelle* render it advisable to bring such a claim before a national court, *provided* that no further damages are required from the Community *and* payment of the sums involved was required to be channelled through the national authority.

(c) A claim for unliquidated damages for losses suffered as a result of illegal Community action (e.g., financial losses in *Dietz; CNTA; Dumortier*) can *only* be brought before the European Courts under Article 288(2) (ex 215(2)). In this respect it is submitted that *Kampffmeyer* was wrong. Therefore, if these losses result from sums unlawfully withheld, the appropriate forum for recovery of *both* sums would be at the European level.

Further support for principles (b) and (c) above may also be derived from *Krohn & Co. Import-Export GmbH & Co. KG* v *Commission* (case 175/84). Krohn & Co. was seeking compensation for financial losses suffered as a result of its national (German) authority's refusal to grant it licences to import manioc from Thailand. In rejecting its application the authorities were acting on mandatory instructions from the Commission. Krohn brought an action before the German courts seeking an annulment of the national authority's decision and an injunction requiring it to issue the licences, and a parallel action before the ECJ for compensation for losses suffered as a result of its action in denying him the licences. The Commission argued that the action under the then Article 215(2) (now 288(2)) was inadmissible, since:

(a) the refusal of the licence came from the national authority;

(b) the applicant should have exhausted its remedies before its national court; and

(c) to admit liability would be equivalent to nullifying the Commission's Decision, which the applicant had failed to challenge in time.

All three arguments were rejected by the Court. With regard to (a) the Court found that although the refusal emanated from the national authority the unlawful conduct was to be attributed not to the German authorities but to the Community itself. The Commission was the 'true author' of the Decision.

With regard to (b) the Court held that while admissibility may be dependent on national rights available to obtain the annulment of a national authority's decision, that would only be the case where national rights of action provide an *effective means of protection* for the individual concerned and are capable of resulting in compensation for the damage alleged.

Clearly, since the alleged 'tort' had been committed by the Community, only the Community would be liable to pay compensation.

The Court's response to (c) has already been noted. An action under the then Article 215(2) (now 288(2)) was an autonomous form of action with a particular purpose to fulfil (*Lütticke* (case 4/69)).

Thus, in deciding whether action should be brought before a national court or before the European Courts, the appropriate question is whether action before a national court can provide an *effective means of protection* for the claimant's interests. Where he merely seeks the return of money paid, or payment of money unlawfully withheld, or a declaration of invalidity or an injunction to prevent the application of the unlawful act, a *fortiori* when the wrongful act can be laid at the door of the national authorities (see *Société des Grands Moulins des Antilles* v *Commission* (case 99/74); *Krohn*, in which it was held that national courts retain sole jurisdiction to order compensation for damage caused by national institutions), he should proceed before his national courts. Where he seeks damage from the Community for injury suffered as a result of wrongful acts attributable to the Community, his action must be before the CFI (or ECJ). This is a right which cannot be 'exhausted' before a national court. Where remedies are required of both national authorities and the Community, it will be necessary to proceed against both. Clearly he cannot recover twice in respect of the same loss.

Relationship between Community liability and State liability under *Francovich*

In developing the principles of State liability in *Brasserie de Pêcheur* (cases C–46 & 48/93), the Court borrowed from the principles applicable to Community liability under Article 288(2) (ex 215(2)). The ECJ suggested that the conditions under which Member States incur liability must be the same as those which apply to the Community; the protection of individuals' rights cannot vary depending on whether a national authority or a Community authority is responsible for the act or omission which is the subject of complaint. We have seen that the ECJ has been very strict, some would say too strict, in its approach to Community liability, particularly in respect of legislative measures, adopting a stringent test for *each* element of liability, namely, fault, damage and causation. This has been justified by the Court's 'concern to ensure that the legislative function is not hindered by the prospect of actions for damages whenever the general interest requires the institutions . . . to adopt measures which may adversely affect individual interests' (*R* v *HM Treasury, ex parte BT* (case C–392/93), para. 40). In its anxiety to protect the EC institutions it has applied the restrictive *Schöppenstedt* test indiscriminately to claims arising from actions which do not involve legislative choices. For this it has been rightly criticised.

Although the ECJ suggested in *Brasserie du Pêcheur*, apropos Member States' liability, that the French and British governments' breaches of Community law (Articles 28 and 43 (ex 30 and 52)) occurred in an area in which they exercised a wide discretion, comparable to that enjoyed by EC institutions when making 'choices of economic policy', justifying the application of the restrictive *Schöppenstedt* 'sufficiently serious' test as the basis for liability, it is clear (and this was acknowleged by Advocate-General Tesauro and the Court in *Brasserie du Pêcheur*) that Member States often have little or no discretion in implementing Community law and no discretion to act in breach of Community law. On the other hand, Member States do have problems in implementing Community law arising from the lack of clarity and precision of much of that law, for which, as the Court acknowledged in *BT* and *Denkavit* (cases C–283, 291 & 292/94), allowances need to be made.

Thus the emergence of the principle of State liability served to highlight the limitations of Article 288(2) (ex 215(2)) and pointed to the need for a broader and more flexible test for liability capable of taking into account the different types of breach and the different situations of EC institutions and Member States.

This was provided in *Brasserie du Pêcheur*. Here the Court confirmed the concept of the 'sufficiently serious' breach as the basis for liability, but introduced, in para. 56, a wide range of criteria by which the question of whether the breach was sufficiently serious might be judged. These included 'the clarity and precision of the EC rule breached, the measure of discretion left by that rule to the national or Community authorities, whether the infringement and the damage caused was intentional or voluntary, whether [the] error of law was excusable or inexcusable' (see further chapter 4). This test was to apply to all breaches of Community law, whether by EC institutions or by Member States. It thus provided a more sophisticated tool than the former *Schöppenstedt* test, enabling the Court to decide, in a whole variety of circumstances, whether a breach of Community law, whether committed by an EC institution or by a Member State, was sufficiently serious to attract liability.

Following *Brasserie du Pêcheur* claims for damages under Article 288(2) (ex 215(2)) should now be approached in the same way as claims based on *Francovich* against Member States. Although the *Schöppenstedt* jurisprudence will continue to apply, albeit now as one of the factors subsumed under para. 56 of *Brasserie du Pêcheur*, in situations in which the defendant institution is acting pursuant to a wide discretion (and this will often be the case in claims under Article 288(2) (ex 215(2)) EC), the other factors listed in para. 56 can and should be taken into account in other situations, depending on the nature of the breach. This should result in a more discriminating approach to claims under Article 288(2) (ex 215(2)) (as well as under *Francovich*), and some widening of Community liability.

Nevertheless, the prospects for individuals seeking damages against the Community remain limited. Even if the applicant succeeds in establishing the existence of a sufficiently serious breach he must still clear the formidable hurdles of damage and causation. This may be less of a problem in claims against Member States, where the principle of national treatment and effectiveness will continue to apply. Although restrictive rules in relation to damages and causation, as well as to breach, may be necessary in order to protect the Community against liability 'unlimited in time, extent and class' (*Ultramares Corporation* v *Touche* (1931) 174 NE 441) in the context of claims by commercial undertakings for purely economic loss (and if so the same protections should be offered to Member States), it may be questioned whether the rules in total provide effective, or sufficiently effective, judicial protection for private persons. In any event, if there is to be coherence between the rules of Community and State liability, there should be equity as regards individuals' rights *vis-à-vis* the two levels of authority and as between the Member States and EC institutions themselves.

Further reading

Hartley, T.C., *The Foundations of European Community Law*, 4th ed. (1998, Clarendon Press).

Schermers, H.G., *Judicial Protection in the European Communities*, 5th ed. (1992, Kluwer Law & Taxation Publishers).

Schermers, H., Heukels, T., and Mead, P. (eds), *Non-contractual Liability of the European Communities* (1988, Nijhoff Publications).

Steiner, J., 'The limits of State Liability for Breach of European Community Law' (1998) EPL 69.

Wils, W., 'Concurrent Liability of the Community and a Member State' (1992) 17 EL Rev 191.

BIBLIOGRAPHY

PRINCIPAL SOURCES OF EC LAW

Encyclopedia of European Community Law, K.R. Simmonds (general ed.) (London: Sweet & Maxwell, looseleaf). Constitutional Treaties, together with annexes and protocols. Secondary legislation.

Official Journal (L series): Community secondary legislation.

Official Journal (C series): non-binding Community instruments; proposals, notices, opinions, resolutions, reports of proceedings in Parliament and the Court of Justice.

European Commercial Cases.

European Current Law.

European Court Reports: reports of cases from the Court of Justice.

Common Market Law Reports: reports of cases from the Court of Justice and national courts.

Bulletin of the European Union: reports on day-to-day activities of the Communities; supplements on specific topics.

Annual *General Report on the Activities of the European Communities.*

Annual *Report on Competition Policy.*

Halsbury's Laws of England, 4th ed., vols 51 and 52 (D. Vaughan, coordinating ed.) (London: Butterworths, 1986).

Databases:

CELEX — Official EEC database; full text of all primary and secondary legislation; ECJ and CFI case reports, legislative proposals and national measures implementing EEC Directives.

JUSTIS — provides access to CELEX (not full text).

LEXIS — commercial database containing European Court reports, European commercial cases, Commission competition decisions and access to

CELEX (not full text) (Butterworths).

Europa site: contains links to European legislation, cases, and preparatory documents and press releases. URL: http://europa.eu.int.

FURTHER READING

General introductory

Swann, D., *European Economic Integration* (Cheltenham: Edward Elgar, 1995).

Selected textbooks in specialised areas

(a) *Introductory*

Edwards, D., *European Community Law — an Introduction*, 2nd ed. (London: Butterworths, 1995).
Mathijsen, P., *A Guide to European Union Law*, 7th ed. (London: Sweet & Maxwell, 1999).
Slynn, G., *Introducing a New Legal Order* (London: Sweet & Maxwell, 1992).

(b) *General textbooks*

Craig, P., and De Búrca, G., *EC Law: Text, Cases and Materials*, 2nd ed. (Oxford: Clarendon Press, 1998).
Evans, A., *European Union Law* (Oxford: Hart Publishing, 1998).
Green, N., Hartley, T., and Usher, J., *The Legal Foundations of the Single European Market* (Oxford: OUP, 1991).
Kapteyn, P., and Ver Loren van Themaat, P., *Introduction to the Law of the European Communities*, 3rd ed. by L.W. Gormley (The Hague: Kluwer Law International, 1998).
Weatherill, S., and Beaumont, P., *EU Law*, 3rd ed. (London: Penguin, 1999).
Weatherill, S., *Cases and Materials on EC Law*, 5th ed. (London: Blackstone Press, 2000).
Wyatt, D., and Dashwood, A., *Substantive European Community Law*, 4th ed. (London: Sweet & Maxwell, 2000).

(c) *Constitutional, institutional and administrative law*

Brown, N., and Jacobs, F., *The Court of Justice of the European Communities*, 5th ed. (London: Sweet & Maxwell, 2000).
Ellis, E., *Public Law of the European Community: Text, Materials and Commentary* (London: Sweet & Maxwell, 1995).
Hartley, T.C., *The Foundations of European Community Law*, 4th ed. (Oxford: Clarendon Press, 1998).
Hartley, T. 'Constitutional Problems of the European Union' (Oxford: Hart Publishing, 1999).
Lasok, D., and Bridge, J., *Law and Institutions of the European Union*, 7th ed. (London: Butterworths, 2000).
Lenaerts, K., *Constitutional Law of the European Union* (London: Sweet & Maxwell, 1999).

Schermers, H.G., and Waelbroeck, D.F., *Judicial Protection in the European Communities,* 5th ed. (London: Kluwer Law & Taxation Publishers, 1992).

Usher, J.A., *EC Institutions and Legislation* (London: Longmans, 1998).

Weiler, J.H.H., *The Constitution of Europe* (Cambridge University Press, 1997).

(d) Substantive law

(i) *Agriculture*

Barents, R., *The Agricultural Law of the EC* (Deventer: Kluwer Law & Taxation, 1994).

Usher, J., *Legal Aspects of Agriculture in the European Community* (Oxford: Clarendon Press, 1988).

(ii) *Civil jurisdiction and enforcement of judgments*

Dashwood, A., Hacon, R.J., and White, R., *A Guide to the Civil Jurisdiction and Judgments Convention* (London: Kluwer Law and Taxation Publishers, 1987).

Kaye, P., *Civil Jurisdiction and Enforcement of Foreign Judgments* (Abingdon: Professional Books, 1987).

Plender, R., *European Contracts Convention: the Rome Convention on the Choice of Law for Contracts* (London: Sweet & Maxwell, 1991) (2nd edition due 2001).

(iii) *Company law*

Andenas, M., and Kenyan Slade, S., *Financial Market Regulation and Company Law* (London: Sweet & Maxwell, 1993).

Dine, J., *EC Company Law* (Chichester: Chancery Law Publishing, looseleaf).

Drury, R., and Zuereb, P., *Company Laws: a Comparative Approach* (Dartmouth, 1991).

Edwards, V., *EC Company Law* (Oxford: Clarendon Press, 1999).

Gleichman, K., *Perspectives on European Company Law* (European Edition, 1990).

Maitland-Walker, J. *Guide to European Company Laws,* 2nd ed. (London: Sweet & Maxwell, 1997).

Rider, B., *European Financial Services Law* (The Hague: Kluwer, 1998).

Tirard, J-M., *Corporate Taxation in EC Countries* (London: Sweet & Maxwell, 1994).

Usher, J., *Law of Money & Financial Services in the EC,* 2nd ed. (Oxford: OUP, 2000).

(iv) *Competition law*

Bellamy, C.W., and Child, G.D., Common Market Law of Competition, 4th ed. (London: Sweet & Maxwell, 1993).

Cook, J., and Kerse, C., *EC Merger Control,* 3rd ed. (London: Sweet & Maxwell, 1999).

Gilstra, D.J. (ed.), *Competition Law in Europe and the USA* (London: Kluwer, 1991).

Gormley, L.W. (ed.), *Current and Future Perspectives on EC Competition Law* (The Hague: Kluwer Law International, 1997).

Goyder, D., *EEC Competition Law*, 3rd ed. (Oxford: Clarendon Press, 1998).

Hancher, L., EC State Aids, 2nd ed. (London: Sweet & Maxwell, 1999).

Jones, C., Van der Woude, M., and Lewis, X., *EC Competition Law Handbook* (London: Sweet & Maxwell, annual).

Korah, V., An Introductory Guide to EC Competition Law and Practice (London: Sweet & Maxwell, 1994).

Stanbrook, C., and Bentley, P., *Dumping and Subsidies*, 3rd ed. (The Hague: Kluwer Law International, 1996).

Whish, R., *Competition Law,* 3rd ed. (London: Butterworths, 1993).

(v)   *Environment*

Krämer, L., *Focus on European Environment Law*, 2nd ed. (London: Sweet & Maxwell, 1997).

Krämer, L., *EC Treaty and Environmental Law*, 3rd ed. (London: Sweet & Maxwell, 1998).

(vi)   *Free movement of goods*

Oliver, P., *Free Movement of Goods in the EEC,* 3rd ed. (London: European Law Centre, 1995).

(vii)   *Remedies*

Brealey, M., and Hoskins, M., *Remedies in EC Law* (London: Longman, 1994).

Heukels, T., and McDonnell, A., *The Action for Damages in Community Law* (The Hague: Kluwer Law International, 1997).

Steiner, J., *Enforcing European Community Law* (London; Blackstone Press, 1996).

(viii)   *Tax*

Farmer, P., and Lyal, R., *EC Tax Law* (Oxford: Clarendon, 1995).

Meussan, G.T.K., *The Principle of Equality in European Taxation* (The Hague: Kluwer, 1999).

(ix)   *The social dimension*

Burrows, F., *Free Movement in European Community Law* (Oxford: Clarendon Press, 1987).

Dashwood, A., and O'Leary, S., *The Principle of Equal Treatment in EC Law* (London: Sweet & Maxwell, 1997).

Ellis, E., *European Community Sex Equality Law* (Oxford: OUP, 1991).

Handoll, J., *Free Movement of Persons in the European Union* (J. Wiley & Son, 1995).

Hervey, T., and O'Keeffe, D. (eds), *Sex Equality Law in the European Union* (Wiley, 1996).

Hervey, T., *European Social Law and Policy* (London: Longmans, 1998).

Nielsen, R., and Szyszczak, E., *The Social Dimension of the European Community*, 3rd ed. (Handelshøjskolens Forlag, 1997).

Prechal, S., and Burrows, N., *Gender Discrimination Law of the European Society* (Dartmouth: Gower, 1990).

Schermers, H.G., et. al. (eds), *Free Movement of Persons in Europe* (Dordrecht: Nijhoff, 1991).

Verwilghen, M., *Equality in Law between Men and Women in the European Community* (Louvain-la-Neuve: Presses Universitaires de Louvain, 1987).

(x) *Transport*

Balfour, *European Community Law* (London: Butterworths, 1995).

Greaves, R., *Transport Law of the European Community* (London: Athlone Press, 1991).

Articles, casenotes and reviews

American Journal of International Law.
Cahiers de Droit Européen.
Common Market Law Review.
European Business Law Review.
European Competition Law Review.
European Intellectual Property Review.
European Law Review.
European Public Law.
International and Comparative Law Quarterly.
Journal of Common Market Studies.
Journal of World Trade Law.
Legal Issues of European Integration.
Maastricht Journal.
Yearbook of European Law.

INFORMATION

Information Office of the European Commission, Jean Monnet House, 8 Storey's Gate, London SW1P 3AT. Tel: 0171-973 1992.

European Business Information (Small Firms' Service), 11 Belgrave Road, London SW1V 1RB. Tel: 0171-828 6201.

European Documentation Centres (in most major cities).

European Information Centres (in most major regional centres).

INDEX

sent to boarding school, an illness that had ended up with him being sent home to attend a small, family-run day school. There was a fragility about Sebastian Mayhew that sometimes perturbed Ellen; she was instinctively gentle with him, sensing the private battles he fought.

Well now, Riley. Ellen recalled with some embarrassment now a conversation they had had during those short, unreal weeks between Dr Redmond's death and her dismissal from Gildersleve Hall. She had been angry, and had accused him of not caring enough to find the truth about what had happened to Dr Redmond. Instead of sending her away with a flea in her ear, as she had deserved, he had offered to meet her in the Green Man in Copfield. It had been a generous gesture. He must have been busy with his work and his family, and yet he had made time for her.

She took her address book out of her briefcase and leafed through it. Yes, it was still there, neatly noted, the telephone number that Riley had given her in the Green Man. She wondered fleetingly why she had bothered to note it down – habit, she supposed.

Riley always got up at six so that he could wash and shave before getting Annie up. Mornings, they had a tight time-table. Quarter to seven, he woke her up and gave her a cup of milk. She complained about the milk, said that it tasted of vegetables (Annie disliked vegetables), but he coaxed her to drink it because it was good for her. Then the bathroom, where she washed her face and cleaned her teeth. After she had dressed, Annie ate her Rice Krispies while Riley grabbed some toast and made a shopping list.

When Annie's hair was done, he checked she had everything she needed for school (handkerchief, scarf and gloves, plimsolls), and then Renée, who took Annie to school in the mornings and collected her in the afternoon, arrived. Riley said goodbye to Annie and left the house. Renée, a young Swiss woman studying English at the Berlitz School, was a godsend, filling in the hours when he needed to be at work as well as doing some light housework. Annie got on well with Renée, and had accepted her company without too much fuss.

Riley spent the first hour at work with his superintendent, discussing their strategy for dealing with the various gangland bosses who were trying to carve up London between them. Riley advocated waiting and watching: jump in too soon and you rounded up only the small fry, the puppets, and not the men who pulled their strings or the financial network that supported them. Take the foot soldiers off the streets and more would instantly spring up in their place, while their masters went to ground.

The meeting was finished when a call came in about a body found in a warehouse on Great Dover Street. Needing some fresh air, Riley took Sergeant Davies and drove across the river. The warehouse was the only building left standing on a large bomb site. There had been a frost during the night and ice seamed the water in the puddles. To one side of the area, the pink, geometric shapes of brick walls were rising out of the ground. Near the warehouse, men in overalls leaned on picks and smoked cigarettes.

The victim was forty or so, thickset, with greying black curls. Riley took a good look at him, checking if he had seen him before, but if so, he had forgotten, and anyway, a man looked different with a pickaxe through his skull. He ordered photographs and fingerprints to be taken and spoke to the owner of the warehouse, a Mr Rossiter. Riley registered the Rolex watch on Mr Rossiter's wrist as well as his cashmere topcoat.

He remained at the warehouse until the body was taken away to the mortuary, and then he returned to Scotland Yard. He had Sergeant Davies search through the files for any references to Mr Rossiter. Something nagged at him; he stood at the window of his office, looking out to the grey, scarred streets of London, digging at the memory.

But his thoughts drifted, as they had numerous times since he had encountered Ellen Kingsley on the hospital steps. He recalled his sharp delight in recognizing her, the touch of her hand and her smile. He thought back to the first time he had seen her, at Gildersleve Hall – the fall of her red hair against her white face, and the way she had fought to remain composed in spite of the shock she had suffered.

He, more than most, had reason to distrust the lightning bolt, the *coup de foudre*. Pearl had taught him that first appearances could be deceptive, and that allowing yourself to act on your initial emotional response was dangerous. He would leave a polite note with a porter at the hospital, he decided, to check that Ellen was all right. To do anything more would be to risk dragging himself into the sort of morass he had only recently crawled out of.

The phone rang. Riley picked it up, said his name.

'Hello, Riley,' said Ellen.

Garrett and Clive were doing up a house in Kensington. Heading there after the art shop closed on Saturday lunch-time, India found the door slightly ajar and went inside. It was very cold in the house so she kept her coat and gloves on while she explored. Wreaths of plaster leaves surrounded high ceiling roses, and pale winter sunlight flooded through tall windows. Inside a room overlooking the garden at the back of the house she found an oil painting of three little girls in long dresses. She wondered what it would be like to live in a house like this, to be married and to have three daughters. She found it hard to imagine, had always found a happy marriage hard to imagine, but she liked babies and remembered clearly the day that Sebastian had been born. Her father had woken her up in the morning and told her that he had a surprise for her. He had taken her to the bedroom he shared with her mother, and India had seen the baby in the crib. She had never forgotten the perfection of Sebastian's tiny features or the pearly minuteness of his fingers and toes.

Though marriage and children had rarely seemed more than a fantasy to India, that morning, curled up together in bed, Garrett had told her he loved her. Did she love him? She had little experience of such things so she found it hard to tell.

She went outside. Sitting on a low wall at the edge of the terrace she ate a Wagon Wheel. Garrett came out, shivering, turning up the collar of his leather jacket.

'Give us some,' he said, and India broke the biscuit in half and handed him a piece.

'What's up with you?' she said. He was mooching sullenly round the garden.

'I'm just sick of bloody London.'

'Let's go away then.'

He gave her a sideways glance. 'Yeah, why not? We could go to Paris. Or the south of France, that would be better.'

'Rome,' she said, joining in. 'Or Venice. We could go on a gondola.'

'No, I mean it. You just hop on a train.' Garrett's expression, which had been moody until then, had become animated. 'There's a night train from Victoria.'

'A night train,' India repeated.

'You go to sleep and in the morning you wake up in the south of France. You can catch a boat to Africa from Marseilles. We could go to Casablanca. *Casablanca* – think of it, Indy!'

'I'll go and pack my bathing costume.'

'Will you? Cool!'

'Oh, don't be so stupid! Of course I won't!'

'If it's the money—'

'Feeling flush, are you, Garrett?' she said sarcastically.

'I could get some cash.'

'Get on with it, then.' She stood up, stuffing the empty Wagon Wheel packet into her pocket. 'Then I can go to the shops instead of standing out here in the freezing cold.'

'So if I get the money, you'll come abroad with me?'

'No, Garrett,' she said, with exaggerated patience. 'I won't. And I'll tell you why. Because it's too far away. Because I have to go to work next week. And because neither of us speak French or African or anything else.'

'I learned French at school.'

'Oh yes. *Je suis, tu es, il est.* Very handy. Do you really think that'll get us jobs?'

'Something'll turn up.'

'You haven't even got a proper job here, so why would anything miraculously turn up anywhere else? Why would some Frenchman want to employ someone as dim as you, Garrett?' She was shouting at him now.

'Shut up, Indy.' He looked angry. 'We could work in a café or something. Washing up. You don't need to speak French to wash up.'

She cried, 'Oh, you can be so *stupid!*' and ran through the house and out of the front door on to the pavement. When she looked back over her shoulder, she saw that Garrett was coming after her, his expression one of black fury, and she darted across the road so suddenly that cars hooted and swerved.

A bus was pulling up to a stop ahead; she hopped on

to it. Sitting on the bus, her anger died and she began to weep. It hadn't even seemed to occur to Garrett that she would mind leaving Sebastian, that she would not for one single moment consider leaving him. She and Garrett had been going out in an off-and-on way for more than a year, and yet he had not understood this most fundamental thing about her. Tears spilled over her lids, and the older woman sitting beside her clucked and said, 'They're not worth crying over, ducks. Me, all my kiddies died in a fire in the Blitz. I couldn't stop crying for a week and I've never cried since.'

India got off the bus after a couple of stops and made her way to Oxford Street. She worked methodically, going through the cluster of little dress shops around Great Marlborough Street until she found a beautiful frock, cream-coloured with a slightly dropped waist and a black grosgrain silk bow on the bust, in a shop with only one old lady serving, who sounded flustered when a customer came in to complain about a fallen hem. In the changing room, India folded up the dress and tucked it beneath her coat, then waited until the customer was on her high horse again before slipping out. 'It's too big round the hips,' she called out as she made for the door of the shop.

Outside, she walked smartly away, looking back over her shoulder a couple of times before losing herself in the crowds on Oxford Street. Then she thought of her friend, Michael Colebrook, and headed for his flat in Half Moon Street. She loved Michael's flat, which was cool and dark and orderly. There, she had a bath, did her hair and put on the new dress. When she came back into the sitting room, Michael smiled at her and told her she was beautiful.

They sat on the sofa and watched the television, and afterwards Michael took her to the Trocadero for dinner. Friends joined them, Ed and his wife, a sulky brunette, and Oliver and Vinnie and Justine. India, who loved to be part of a crowd, had a wonderful time. Afterwards, they went on to a nightclub in Leicester Square.

Between dances, wandering round the room, she saw him. He was sitting at a table by the dance floor with half a dozen other people. It took her a moment to place him, then she remembered that Ellen had introduced her to him at the science lecture. He had had a funny name: Pharoah.

He was looking at her. India pretended she hadn't seen him as she walked slowly past his table to the bar. Making out she was searching for something in her bag, she waited to see whether he had taken the bait.

A voice said, 'I do like coincidences,' and India looked up.

'Do you, Dr Pharoah?'

'Especially this sort of coincidence. How are you, Miss Mayhew?'

'I'm very well. I didn't imagine you a nightclub sort of person.'

'I'm delighted to hear that you have imagined me at all. Now, I wouldn't have imagined I'd meet someone like you in a lecture theatre.'

'Someone like me?'

'Someone as lovely as you. May I buy you a drink?'

India asked for a Martini. She was enjoying herself. She would make him fall in love with her, she decided, just for the fun of it. She smoothed down the cream-coloured folds of her frock and chinked her glass against his.

He said, 'I take it that you're not a scientist?'

'I work in an art shop.' She shrugged her shoulders. 'It's just to pass the time. I don't need to do it.'

'Pass the time until what?'

'Until I get married, I expect,' she said airily.

'Are you planning to get married?'

She gave him a teasing smile. 'I haven't decided yet. Maybe I won't. Are you here with your wife, Dr Pharoah?'

He didn't even blink. 'Marcus, you must call me Marcus. And no, I'm with friends. My wife is at home.'

'Doesn't she like nightclubs?'

'Not much, no.'

'But you do.'

'I like to feel that anything can happen. And sometimes, in places like this, they do.'

'What is it you'd like to happen?'

'Something unexpected. Something restorative.' A smile touched his eyes. 'An adventure.'

'I wouldn't have thought you needed adventures, Marcus. You must live a very exciting life, being famous.'

He said modestly, 'Not famous, I wouldn't say. Very few

scientists are truly *famous*. Einstein, Oppenheimer, James Watson perhaps, now . . . only a few.'

India speared the olive at the bottom of her Martini glass. 'How do you know Ellen?'

'Miss Kingsley?' Again, he didn't react. 'She used to work for me.'

'Why doesn't she like you?'

This time, a small frown. 'I'm not sure that—'

'I could tell, at the lecture.'

'A colleague of mine, Dr Redmond, died a couple of years ago. It was very sad, a loss both to Gildersleve Hall and to me personally – he was a friend of mine. Miss Kingsley was working for me at the time. Because the death was sudden, the police were called in. Miss Kingsley told them that she had overheard me quarrelling with Dr Redmond shortly before his death.' Pharoah swirled his drink round his glass, swallowed it, and signalled to the barman for another. 'I'm afraid I have a temper. I'm not proud of it. I was angry with Miss Kingsley because I thought she should have shown greater loyalty. I thought she should have shown *me* greater loyalty. So I dismissed her.'

'Ellen's a very honest person.'

'People like that, one must admire them, I suppose, but they seem to hardly notice the damage they do. It must be nice to have the luxury of such frankness. I had to protect Gildersleve Hall. I've worked damnably hard for it.' His gaze raked round the room. 'And you, Miss Mayhew, how do you know Miss Kingsley?'

'We were at school together. Ellen's my best friend. My oldest friend.'

'Woman are so much better at keeping friendships than we men are.'

'I expect that's because we're more faithful.'

'Do you admire faithfulness?'

'I should think so.'

'I wonder whether it can be an excuse for stagnating, for staying in a rut.'

India wondered whether his wife felt the same. 'Perhaps you're just easily bored.'

'Perhaps I am. But I'm not bored now, so you must tell me more about yourself, Miss Mayhew, and prevent my boredom returning. You work in an art shop, and you're not married. What else can I find out about you? What else do you do?'

'Oh, I have such a busy life. I go to all sorts of places. I've been to dozens of different countries, because of my parents. Daddy's in the Diplomatic Service. We've lived in Paris . . . Rome . . . Venice . . .'

'A diplomat – perhaps I know him.'

This was dangerous: India changed the subject. 'Of course,' she said dreamily, 'my absolute favourite place in the whole world is our home. It's called Applegarth. If you saw it, you'd think it was the most lovely old house you've ever seen. There's a meadow and an orchard and the most beautiful garden.'

'It sounds idyllic. Where is it?'

'In Devon.' India had been to Devon recently with Garrett, delivering a car, and had liked it a lot.

'Are you a close family?'

'Very.'

India could see in her mind's eye the kitchen at Applegarth. It was her favourite room in the house. She knew the furnishings intimately and felt just then a pang of longing for its familiar embrace. There was one of those big old iron ranges, which kept the room warm all the time, and a large pine table laid with blue and white striped china. The curtains were prettily faded florals and the old dresser was crammed with family treasures. Their housekeeper, a rosy-cheeked Devon woman, was washing up, and India's mother was baking scones. Her father looked up smiling from his newspaper as India came into the room. He said, 'And what would my favourite girl like to do today?'

Marcus Pharoah said, 'Don't you agree?'

India started. 'I beg your pardon?'

'I said that one must be thankful that you forsake the pleasures of Applegarth from time to time.'

In his eyes, there was a flicker of something. Perhaps greed, perhaps hunger. Or perhaps he was teasing her, perhaps he had seen through her and was laughing at her. He had somehow got the upper hand in the conversation, and the elation she had brought about that afternoon by stealing the dress collapsed like a burst bubble and was replaced by emptiness, and she discovered that she didn't want to talk to him any more.

The band struck up 'Try a Little Tenderness'. India searched through the crowds for Michael.

'Thank you so much for the drink, Marcus,' she said, politely offering him her hand. 'And now you must excuse me because I'm going to dance.'

Chapter Five

Ellen had rung to ask Riley and Annie to tea. Riley accepted, and the following Sunday he stowed Annie and the bunch of golden chrysanthemums he had bought the previous day in the car and drove to Islington.

There were seven of them to tea in the scruffy kitchen of the four-storey house. Joe Kingsley was a blond, boisterous, masculine version of Ellen, with the same grey, discerning eyes. Then there were the brother and sister, India and Sebastian Mayhew. Sebastian was very young, startlingly angelic-looking, quiet, and though Riley tried to chat to him pleasantly and put him at his ease, nervous. His sister India also looked angelic but you knew instinctively that she wasn't. India Mayhew had a neat, curvy figure, big blue eyes and a bee-stung mouth. Trouble with a capital T, Riley thought privately. Though her boyfriend, Garrett, was sitting beside her, she flirted indiscriminately with all the men, including Riley himself. Riley wasn't attracted to her; he had come across too many India Mayhews in other, darker, situations, girls who were pretty and spirited and vulnerable, to be attracted to her, but he liked her. She kept the conversation going and was generous with her smiles and good humour and kind to Annie, didn't talk down to her, and let her go through her huge, grubby make-up bag and even stick a finger in the pots and potions.

And anyway, why would he have looked at any other woman in the room when Ellen was there? He noted the easy, bantering relationship she had with her brother, and her relaxed gentleness with Annie. Now and then, he caught her eye. Sometimes her amused expression seemed to reflect his own thoughts about Miss Mayhew, to say, yes, I know she makes a lot of noise and flies about, but she's fun, isn't she? And sometimes he saw something else, some emotion he had become familiar with, having seen it on the faces of the women neighbours who had called round after Pearl had walked out, offering cakes and stews and occasionally rather more.

Pity.

Better sort that out, he thought.

After tea, the Mayhews and the boyfriend left, and Ellen got out her microscope and showed Annie how it worked. Half of Riley's mind was on his conversation with Joe Kingsley about rugby, but the other half watched Annie and Ellen. For a long time after Pearl's disappearance,

Annie had woken during the night with bad dreams. By day she had seemed to regress, to go back to the thumb-sucking and tantrums of babyhood, and there had been a few run-ins at school, where she had been disciplined for bad behaviour. However he himself might feel at Pearl's absence, and however much easier he might find it to look after his daughter now that he did not also have to look after Pearl, Annie missed her mother dreadfully, and his heart ached for her. It cheered him to see her smile and exclaim at what she saw through the microscope, her dark head close to Ellen's auburn one.

At the end of the afternoon, Ellen walked outside with him and Annie to where his car was parked. She thanked him for the flowers and he thanked her for the tea. And then, before she could say goodbye and return to the house, he asked her to supper the following weekend.

The phone rang. Thinking it might be Garrett, India rolled off the sofa and picked up the receiver.

'Miss Mayhew? It's Marcus Pharoah. I wondered whether I might buy you a drink.'

India considered Marcus Pharoah's request. Then she said, 'It's very kind of you to ask but I'm afraid I'm terribly busy at the moment.' She put the phone down.

The next night, he phoned again and India put him off again. The third time he phoned, he said, 'Why won't you have a drink with me?'

'Because you're too old,' she said. 'And because you think

too much of yourself, I can tell, and I'm tired of men like you.'

'I'm forty-three,' he said. 'How old are you?'

'Twenty-two.'

There was a silence. She pointed out, 'So you're almost twice as old as me.'

'So I am. I'd have thought you older.'

'I've lived hard,' she said sarcastically.

'You have a presence. So many young women seem unformed, as if their personality hasn't settled yet.'

'You're an expert, are you, Marcus?'

'I was merely making an observation. Do you think age matters?'

'I don't know. When you say "unformed", I expect you mean boring.'

'I find a great many people boring, but I don't believe age has much to do with it. It's more a question of attitude to life. I could point out to you all the advantages of being older. I know the best places to go and I can afford to go to them. I wouldn't expect a great deal of your attention or time.'

'And,' she said, 'you're married.'

'I am married, it's true, but I haven't been happily married for a long time.'

'Men always say that,' said India sceptically.

'Do we?'

'I'm sure you know that you do. You've done this before, haven't you?'

'It depends what you mean by "this".'

'Asking girls out for drinks. You're not going to tell me I'm the first, are you?'

'No. But this is different.'

'Oh dear. They all say that, too.'

'Alison and I have lived separate lives for many years. She has her interests, I have mine. We stay together for the sake of our daughter. You mustn't misinterpret what I'm asking of you, India. You gave me the pleasure of your company the other evening and I'd like to return the compliment, nothing more.'

Liar, she thought.

'I have to go back to Cambridge this evening,' he said. 'I'll be in Claridges's bar between six and seven. Do you know it?'

'Yes. But I won't come.'

He said, 'The thing is, I can't stop thinking about you.'

India smiled, a little sadly. 'That's another thing they all say, Marcus.'

Riley's house in Tufnell Park was pleasant and spacious and contained a great many books, prints and records – a mixture, Ellen saw, leafing through them while he was putting Annie to bed, of classical (lots of Mozart) and jazz. Pearl's presence still pervaded the house. It was there, surely, in the Daphne du Mauriers and Monica Dickenses on the bookshelves, and in the bright, colourful cushions and curtains, with their stylized representations of poppies and seedheads and kites – not Riley's taste, Ellen guessed – and in the photograph on the sideboard of a laughing and strikingly beautiful woman.

When he returned downstairs Riley asked her whether she minded eating in the kitchen; Ellen said no, of course not. It was a large, airy room, the table at one end of it beside French windows looking out to the garden. Annie's paintings and drawings were stuck on the walls and fridge. Ellen guessed that Riley had many memories of eating with Pearl in the dining room, which he found too painful to revive.

'I'm afraid I haven't much of a repertoire as a cook,' he said, but the lamb chops and vegetables were delicious, and she complimented him. He had had to teach himself to cook when he was in the army, he explained, army rations benefiting from some augmentation whenever possible. There followed a discussion about army life, during which they discovered that Riley, an ex-paratrooper, and Ellen's father, then a colonel in the Royal Engineers, must have been in northern France in 1944 at much the same time and not so many miles apart.

He cleared away their plates, topped up their wine glasses, and took a chocolate cake out of a tin. He said, as he filled the kettle to make coffee, 'It's good of you to come, Ellen. I appreciate you making the time.'

'It's a pleasure,' she said. 'Besides, it's helping me to hide from my ex-boyfriend.'

'Ex-boyfriend?' He looked amused.

'He keeps coming round to the house and begging me to come back to him. No, not begging – more pointing out the error of my ways, telling me how much he knows I must miss him.'

'And do you?'

'Not at all. Thus my need to go to ground.'

In the short silence that followed, she examined her words. If there was a fault her family had in common, she thought, it was their reluctance to acknowledge difficult emotional situations with seriousness. The truth was that her break-up with Simon had been unpleasant. She had hurt him and she shrank from that, disguising her reaction with jokes and mockery in a way that was oh, so English.

She said, 'How are you, Riley?'

'Fine.'

'Oh, come off it,' she said, giving him a hard look. 'Your wife walked out on you three months ago. You can hardly be fine.'

He was making coffee; he turned to face her. 'What should I tell you? One day in August Pearl left Annie with a friend, packed a bag and walked out. I've no idea where she's gone and I've no idea whether she's planning to come back.'

'That's awful, Riley.'

'I suppose it is.'

'You must miss her so much.'

'No.' His voice remained level. 'No, I feel relieved. I feel free. I don't miss her at all. I never loved her. There are rather a lot of people I'm having to lie to about this – Annie, of course, and Pearl's parents – but I'd prefer not to lie to you.' His lids dipped down, masking the bitterness in his eyes. 'Have I shocked you, Ellen?'

'Yes,' she said honestly. 'I thought – I suppose I just assumed . . .'

He put the coffee pot on the table. 'You're trying to decide whether it's polite to ask me any more about my marriage. Or whether to tactfully change the subject.'

'I don't want to be intrusive. But I don't want you to think I'm shying away from it either.'

Fleetingly, he put a hand on her shoulder. 'I know. Forgive me. I didn't invite you here to put you through some tortuous social situation.'

She studied him. Ex-paratrooper, policeman: he was probably tough enough to cope with a searching question or two. She said bluntly, 'You must have loved Pearl when you married her.'

'No.' He shook his head.

'You don't seem the sort of man to marry on a whim.' She searched his face for signs of anger or offence; finding none, a thought occurred to her, and she said, 'Oh.'

'Wrong again.' Riley was pouring the coffee. 'Annie was born eighteen months after we married, if that's what you're thinking. Actually, you're pretty much wrong on two counts. I might not have married on a whim, but I asked Pearl to marry me three weeks after we first met.'

She said, 'Was it wartime?'

211

He gave a grim smile and said, 'Yes.'

'My father believes it's an evolutionary imperative, the rush to find a partner before a man goes off to battle.'

'Does he? He may be right.'

'I saw the photograph. She's very beautiful, Riley.'

'I keep the picture there for Annie.' He handed her a cup of coffee. 'Beauty's not enough, desire's not enough, I learned that very quickly. I went away for two and a half years and when I came home, whatever I'd once felt for her had gone.'

'But you married her.'

'I was bound to her. She had no second thoughts.'

'That was honourable of you.'

'Was it?' He made an impatient gesture. 'I'm not so sure now. Perhaps I cheated Pearl as well as myself.' He was quiet for a moment. She did not interrupt him, sensing the care with which he chose his words.

'I could never make her happy,' he said. 'Not for any length of time. She was never content. And when she was unhappy, she'd pick quarrels about anything. My tone of voice or the expression on my face, or some failing or habit of mine. At first you try to change. Or you fight back. My God, the arguments we used to have. Sometimes they seemed to clear the air, other times they'd go on bruising us both for days. And then Annie came along and after that I fell into the habit of appeasing Pearl. It was easier, you see, less disruptive. I'd be understanding, I'd sympathize with whatever it was that was bothering her because it made for a quieter life. Or if that was impossible I'd try cautiously to make her see sense. But after a while, you start despising yourself. You know you're lying, and that you're acting a part. And I could see that she despised me as well. So I disengaged, I cut myself off from her emotionally. And yet that didn't work either. I ended up letting Pearl get away with things I never thought I'd tolerate in a friend, let alone a wife.' Another clear-eyed look. 'You must forgive me for inflicting this on you, but I need to be honest. I was telling you the truth when I said I felt free. Though I admit I feel a certain amount of guilt as well.'

'You did your best, I'm sure, Riley.'

He frowned, and she wondered whether he was going to comment on the banality of her statement. But he said only, 'Did I? Pearl was unhappy because she was ill, Ellen. I knew then that she was ill some of the time, but it's only now, when I look back, that I can see that she was ill all the time.'

'When you say ill . . .'

'She alternated constantly between depression and euphoria. She could be good company during the early stages of the euphoric phase, but then it always cranked up out of control. Eventually, it would be as if she'd fallen over a cliff. She'd slide into depression, into silence and weeping. She always tried so hard with Annie. I could see the effort it took her sometimes just to speak, and I admired her for that. What I'm telling you is that it took me a long time to

213

realize that the euphoria was part of the problem as well.' Frowning, he ran a hand over his face. 'After she left, I spoke to her psychiatrist. Perhaps if I'd realized sooner, something could have been done. Maybe not. But I couldn't give her what she wanted. And I think we wore each other out.'

'Riley.' She reached out across the table and touched his hand. 'We all muddle along, don't we? Oh dear,' she sighed and gave an apologetic smile, 'it seems to be my day for unoriginal remarks. But poor you.'

He shook his head. 'Poor Annie. And poor Pearl.'

'I think you're still in recovery, Riley.'

'Like an alcoholic, perhaps? You may be right.'

'I could say these things take time, but then I might have to go and shoot myself.'

'Then you'd better not. Ellen, I'm very fortunate – I have my beautiful daughter, I have a comfortable life, and I have my work.' His expression contained a measure of black humour. 'And my work teaches me that there are many lives far more chaotic than mine.'

'I suppose that's some consolation. Have you looked for Pearl?'

'Yes, for Annie's sake. But no trace so far. People disappear for a variety of reasons. Because they want to escape from their problems. Because they need a new start. Because they've started a new relationship.' He put up his palms, spreading out his fingers. 'It's possible. As I said, she wasn't happy.'

He picked up the wine bottle. There were a couple of

inches left and he shared it between them. Then he took the wine glasses and coffee things into the sitting room.

Ellen sat down in an armchair as Riley chose a record. 'I seemed to have talked endlessly about myself,' he said as he put the record on the turntable. 'How crashingly dull for you. How are you? How is your brother? And India – how is India?'

'I'm fine. Though I despair of myself slightly. And Joe's in love with India, the idiot.'

'Poor devil. Why do you despair of yourself?'

'Because I go to work, I come home, I see my friends.'

'It sounds perfectly pleasant to me.' Again, that half-smile. 'In fact I'd have thought it rather enviable.'

No, she thought, she fell too easily into routine, into cautiousness. She was twenty-four years old and sometimes it seemed to her that she might as well have been forty.

'Gildersleve was an adventure,' she said, 'even if it was a rather unpleasant one in the end. But what I do now is run-of-the-mill. You've obviously been through a rough time with Pearl, but at least you felt strongly about her once. I've never been in love with any of my boyfriends. I've never even . . .' She felt suddenly embarrassed, talking about such things with him, but she ploughed on. 'You talk about desire. I can't say I ever felt like that about Simon. Or Daniel, or either of his predecessors.'

'Give it time, Ellen.'

'Why do the wrong men always fall in love with me?' Unexpectedly, it came out as a heartfelt wail.

He said seriously, 'I expect that the others, the ones you might like, think you're unobtainable.'

'Me? Unobtainable?' She laughed, but then, remembering Gildersleve, didn't feel like laughing any more. 'No, it's me who falls in love with unobtainable men,' she muttered.

He was studying her. 'Is it possible,' he said, 'that you don't fall in love with anyone new because you're still thinking of him, the unobtainable one?'

Frowning, she looked away. 'I don't think so. I really don't think so. It was years ago, at Gildersleve. Actually, you must have met him. Do you remember Alec Hunter?'

'A little.' There was a short silence: piano music poured through the room, then Riley said, 'But it didn't come to anything?'

'No. Alec was in love with Andrée Fournier. Do you remember? We shared the lab.'

And as if it had been only yesterday, she found herself recalling the sharp coldness of the season and the equally piercing pain she had experienced on looking out of the window and seeing Alec and Andrée together.

'That was my only experience of unrequited love,' she said crisply, and swallowed the last of her wine. 'And the truth is, it wasn't much fun.'

Then she changed the subject.

India returned to the flat one evening to find Garrett sitting on a stool in the kitchen. He looked a sight, his lip swollen and puffy, a jagged cut on his eyebrow. Sebastian was dabbing at the cut with a flannel.

Garrett said, 'Fell off my bike.'

India peered at the cut. 'You should get that stitched.'

Garrett shuddered. 'Not likely.'

Sebastian dabbed on antiseptic and Garrett yelped. Then Sebastian stuck a piece of plaster over the cut.

'Poor old thing,' India said. 'You've an awful lot of bruises.' Tenderly, she kissed an undamaged part of his face.

Garrett snaked an arm round India's hips and pressed his head against her side. 'I need to talk to you, darlin',' he said.

'I'm very tired.'

'No, I really need to talk to you.'

He followed her into the bedroom and shut the door behind them. India unbuttoned her coat and Garrett said, 'Can I stay here the night, Indy?'

'I told you, I'm dead beat. And my head's splitting.'

'I don't want to go back to my flat.'

India dropped the coat on top of a heap of clothes on the floor. She looked at him suspiciously. 'What's going on?

He sat down on the bed. 'I didn't fall off the bike.'

'So what happened to your face?'

'It was one of Bernie's apes. Bloody Lee.'

She stared at him. 'Garrett, you're frightening me.'

'It wasn't my fault.' He clenched his fists. 'That stupid bastard, Clive.'

India's knees felt wobbly. She sat down at the dressing

217

table and blobbed cold cream on her face. 'What's Clive done? Where is he?'

'I don't know. I think he's scarpered.' Garrett sounded aggrieved. 'Typical bloody Clive, runs off when it was his idea in the first place.'

'His idea? What idea?' India swung round to face him. 'If you don't tell me what's going on, I'll black the other eye.'

'I told you, it wasn't my fault.' Reading India's expression, he added hastily, 'OK, OK. You know the houses Clive's been doing up for Bernie? Clive had this idea. Sometimes tenants want to move in before a place is finished. They can't find anywhere else, you see, and they see us working there and ask us. So Clive let them. Just a week or two early, while we were still putting the paint on.'

'But Clive told Bernie, didn't he?'

Garrett said miserably, 'No.' He dropped his head.

India felt cold inside. 'He didn't keep the rent? He didn't keep Bernie's rent?'

'It wasn't really Bernie's rent. They hadn't officially moved in.'

'And you knew?' Her voice rose. 'You should have told Clive not to be such an idiot! I suppose he gave you a cut?'

Garrett groaned. 'Just a few bob. Bernie found out somehow, and now Clive's done a bunk and Bernie blames me. When I went back to the flat, Lee was there. He's a brute. He'd have killed me if Ronnie hadn't turned up. I can't go back to the flat, Indy, I can't.'

'What did Lee want? Apart from the pleasure of beating your face to a pulp.'

'The money.' Garrett pulled down a window and flicked out his cigarette stub. 'He said I've got to pay Bernie back the money.'

'How much do you owe him?'

'About thirty quid.'

India stared at him, appalled. 'Thirty? Oh, Garrett!'

'I'll sell the motorbike.'

India thought that Garrett would make five pounds on the bike if he was lucky, but did not say so to spare his feelings.

'You shouldn't have come here,' she said. 'What if Lee had come after you? What about Sebastian?' She began to jab the pins back into her hair. 'I'll go and talk to Bernie.'

She stood up, smoothing down her dress, and inspected herself in the mirror. She was wearing her blue silk. She unpinned the waxed paper flowers and rummaged through her jewellery box until she found a brooch that was probably paste but might pass for diamonds. She pinned it on to the neckline of her frock, sprayed on some Yardley and reapplied face powder and lipstick.

She said to Garrett, 'You can stay here the night, if you like, but you're not to bother Sebastian. And if the doorbell rings, don't answer it.'

'Thanks, India,' he said, and planted his swollen lips on hers. 'Love you, darlin'.'

But he didn't, she thought, as she picked up her coat

219

and bag and let herself out of the flat, because if he had loved her, really, properly loved her, he would have stopped her going to Bernie.

India looked in on all Bernie's usual haunts and eventually found him in the Blue Duck nightclub in Piccadilly.

On a small stage to one side of the room, a girl in sequins was waving a couple of fans in a dispirited fashion. There was a drumroll and a tinkling of cymbals and the girl finished her number to a smattering of applause. Then the band struck up 'Mack the Knife' and couples took to the dance floor.

Bernie was sitting at a table with his entourage of women. He gave India a knowing stare.

'And what brings you here, India?'

'I'd like a word with you, please, Bernie.'

'Shove off,' said Bernie to the brunette sitting beside him. When she made an offended moue, he called out, 'Don, Gina wants to dance,' and a thickset, dark man came over to the table and yanked Gina out of her seat. Bernie smacked her bottom as they headed off to the dance floor.

Bernie said, 'Sit down, India.'

'Actually,' she said, 'I need to speak to you in private.'

His high-pitched voice squeaked up an octave. '"Actually",' he mimicked, '"I need to speak to you in private." Prissy little madam. Who d'you think you are? Maybe I've got better things to do.'

'Please, Bernie,' she said quietly.

He eyed her, then rose from his chair. She wondered whether he preferred to speak to people seated, a king at his court, because he was so short.

They found a corner away from the band, near the bar. Bernie said, 'I suppose you're here because of that toerag, Garrett Parker.'

'He'll pay you the money back.'

'Maybe that's not the point. Maybe I don't like to be cheated. Maybe I don't like to be made a fool of.'

'Garrett wasn't trying to make a fool of you, Bernie.'

'Ah, but it looks that way.' Bernie wrinkled up his nose. 'It's all about reputation in my line of work. I can't afford to look like I'm going soft. Bad for business. Everyone has to think about their reputation, don't they? You're just the same, India. That's why you turn up your nose at me. You think you're too good for me. You think you're better than those silly cows I go around with. You're thinking about your *reputation*.'

As he spoke, he stared down the front of her dress. Leaning forward, he pressed his lips into the hollow of her throat and murmured, 'I always get what I want in the end.'

India gripped her hands together, trying not to shudder. 'Garrett will give you the money in a couple of weeks,' she said steadily. 'Please, Bernie, as a favour to me.'

Another fish-eyed look, and then he shrugged. 'A week. Not a day longer. Tell your boyfriend he's got something I want. Tell him I'll have it like that,' Bernie clicked his fingers, 'if he tries to cheat me again.'

'Thank you, Bernie.'

'And don't you forget.' Slowly, as if he was sealing a bargain, his head inclined. 'You owe me, India.'

It was almost three in the morning when she got back to the flat. India let herself in quietly, so as not to wake Sebastian. Garrett was sprawled over two-thirds of the bed, snoring through his bloodied nose. India pulled off her clothes, pushed an arm and leg aside, and crawled in beside him. She lay for a long time in the darkness, kept awake by Garrett's snores and the thoughts that wouldn't stop churning through her head. She tried imagining the kitchen at Applegarth, the stove and the print curtains, the familiarity and warmth. She tried imagining her father saying to her, 'What's up, honey? You mustn't worry about anything. I'm here, it'll be all right.'

But she couldn't concentrate hard enough. Instead of the orchard at Applegarth, she saw the house in the woods, the overgrown lawns and the heavy tops of the trees, flopping back and forth in the wind, that second summer.

July 1942. Her mother hadn't left her bed for a week. India managed, just about. Sebastian hadn't been to school for ages and nor had she, but that was all right because everyone seemed to have forgotten about them.

When she took her mother a cup of tea in the morning, Cindy was asleep. India said, 'I've brought your tea, Mummy,' but her mother didn't say anything. She was lying on her side, the blanket pulled most of the way over her head, a fan of fair hair spilling over the pillow. India put the cup and saucer on the bedside table and went down-stairs to give Sebastian his breakfast.

It was a fine day, so in the morning they played in the garden. The house wasn't very nice inside by then, anyway. It had seemed to wriggle out of India's fragile control during the last few months, and there was a funny smell. They spent the morning making clay pots. India filled a bucket with water and Sebastian dug up clay with the little metal spade Daddy had bought for him, ages ago when they had gone to the seaside.

India made sandwiches for lunch, scraping out the last of a pot of jam. She made Sebastian wash his hands under the pump before he ate his lunch. She took a sandwich up to her mother, but she was still asleep. The cup of tea remained on the bedside table, undrunk, cold. She wondered whether she should wake her mother up, but she remem-bered Mummy saying she felt so much better after a good sleep, so in the end she just left the sandwich and carried the cup and saucer back downstairs.

In the afternoon, she and Sebastian went to the den that they had made in the woods. The den was in a box tree. The leaves made a dark green cloudy roof above the hollow inside, and they used the curving yellow branches for seats. Sebastian played with India's old tea set. He didn't seem to mind that there were only four saucers and one cracked cup left. India breathed in the dusty sharp scent of the box and watched the diamonds of light that filtered through the green cloud. She couldn't remember her mother sleeping so long before. She began to think she should go back to the house and wake her up.

Sebastian was filling up the cup with soil and holding it to the mouth of his toy giraffe. When India told him she was going back to the house, he whimpered. She told him he was to stay in the box tree and wait for her. 'I won't be two ticks,' she said. Neil had used to say this, before he went out to the pub to buy beer, though Neil was always more than two ticks. Sebastian started to cry. Hot with impatience, India said, 'I'll bring you back something nice,' and ran back through the woods.

It was very quiet in the house. She had been hoping that as soon as she opened the door she would hear her mother moving around, or the kettle purring, or 'My Funny Valentine' on the gramophone. She realized, as she went upstairs, that she was frightened, but she pushed that thought away.

Cindy was still asleep. She was lying in exactly the same position as she had been that morning, the blanket pulled up, her hair over the pillow. The sandwich was untouched.

India said, 'Mummy.' Then, louder, 'Shall I make you another cup of tea?'

Her mother didn't move. India felt angry with her. It wasn't fair that she was left to do everything, to keep Sebastian amused and think of things to eat when they hardly had any food. She gripped her mother's shoulder and shook it.

The blanket slipped back. Her hair had fallen over her

mother's face. Gently, India brushed it away. Cindy's skin felt cold, colder than it had in the winter when India had rubbed her feet for her. 'Mummy?' she whispered.

She took the sandwich for Sebastian instead and went back into the woodland. Sebastian wasn't in the box tree, which alarmed India. He might have got himself lost in the forest, like Hansel and Gretel. She ran around for a while, searching for him, calling out his name, and then she caught a glimpse of blue shirt behind a birch tree. He cried when she shouted at him but cheered up when she gave him the sandwich.

They spent the rest of the day in the garden. India didn't like being inside the house now. Sebastian wanted to kiss his mother goodnight before he went to bed, but India wouldn't let him because she had peeked into the bedroom at teatime and had seen that Cindy was still lying on her side, just the same. Sebastian cried again so India told him a story to cheer him up. She wondered whether Sebastian was crying a lot because he was hungry. She was hungry too. After Sebastian went to bed she searched the pantry for something to eat. There was no bread left, no butter, no jam. There were some crackers; she ate half a dozen, though she hated the way they stuck to her tongue and throat. Longing for sweetness, she tried eating a spoonful of cocoa powder but it was bitter and horrid. When it started to go dark, she crawled into bed with Sebastian. She knew that she should go and look at her mother again, but in the darkness she was afraid to. She lay curled up against Sebastian's warm little body, listening to the ghosts. There were ghosts in the house in the woods, she and Sebastian had both heard them. A tapping on a window, footsteps on the stairs when everyone was asleep. She thought she heard her mother walking round the house, a cold hand sliding along a banister, a door opening, the soft sigh of a cushion as Cindy lowered herself on to the sofa. India lay still and frozen in the darkness, waiting to hear the first few bars of 'My Funny Valentine'. Then she pulled the blanket over her head and stuffed her fingers into her ears.

She felt much better when she woke in the morning. Her mother would be all right now and would give her money so that she could buy some food at the shop. India padded along the corridor to Cindy's room.

But nothing had changed. Cindy's face now had an odd look, as if her skin was sinking back into her skull. India could hardly bear to touch her, but when she did, she still felt cold.

A voice said, 'Mummy?' and India, startling, looked up and saw Sebastian in the doorway.

'Go away!' she yelled at him. 'Don't come in!' and he ran off.

It took her ages to stop him crying this time, and he didn't seem right for the rest of the morning. After breakfast, she tried to coax him to have another tea party with his animals, but he shook his head and just sat on the grass, sucking his thumb and holding his giraffe. She wondered whether he was ill and, if so, whether her mother was ill too. The other possibility frightened her too much to think about; whenever it flickered into her head, her mind seemed to go blank.

In the end, she fetched Sebastian's story books and read to him. While she read, she tried to work out what to do. She thought of phoning the doctor and was cross with herself for not having thought of it before.

She let Sebastian make mud pies in the kitchen saucepans, something he was never normally allowed to do. Then she looked in the little notebook in the kitchen, where Cindy wrote lists of things, but the doctor's number wasn't there. She opened her mother's navy-blue handbag and searched for her address book among the clutter of handkerchieves and bottles of pills, lipstick and comb and powder compact.

India went upstairs. Cindy's bedroom was hot and fuggy, so she drew back the curtains and opened a window. She avoided looking at the bed and ran out of the room, closing the door behind her, as soon as she found the address book on the dressing table. Downstairs, she looked through the book. There was no one called 'Dr' anything. But Neil's phone number was there. She imagined Neil striding into the house in his navy uniform and saying, 'You have to think of those children, Lucinda,' and making everything right again.

For lunch, she put everything edible she could find on a tray and took it out to the garden. Sebastian pretended to make cakes out of very old glacé cherries and cream crackers. He wasn't crying so much now and he had stopped asking for Mummy, and when he wasn't eating, he sat with his thumb in his mouth. After lunch, India took him indoors and washed his face with a flannel. She couldn't find Sebastian's own hairbrush, so she teased out the tangles with the comb from Mummy's handbag. He looked better when she had finished with him, but not much. He had a bedraggled look; she saw, looking into the bathroom mirror, that she looked bedraggled too.

There were only a few pennies left in Mummy's purse. Searching round the house, India found a couple more down the back of the sofa. She had intended to cycle to the shop but Sebastian refused to ride his trike, just shook his head and wouldn't say anything when she asked him why not. She almost shouted at him again, but in the end lifted him on to the saddle of her own bike and told him to hold on to her as she pushed it up the road. It was very tiring pushing him all the way up the hill, and it was hard not to cry.

At the top of the hill, she propped the bicycle against a hedge and hauled open the heavy door of the phone box. Sebastian sat on the floor, watching an ant scuttle along the windowframe. India dialled the operator and asked to be put through to Neil's number. Eventually the operator said, 'Putting you through,' and a voice said, 'The Caird residence.' India asked for Neil. The voice said, 'He's not here, dear, he's at sea. Who's calling?'

India put the phone down. She gnawed her lip to stop herself crying. Of course Neil was on his ship – how stupid of her not to have thought of that! She took Sebastian's hand and dragged him out of the phone box. A black cat was walking along the path ahead of them, so she pointed it out to Sebastian, partly to cheer him up, and partly because she needed to distract herself.

Inside the shop, an old lady was talking to Mrs Day. The old lady was wearing a navy-blue beret, like the one India had worn at her London school, and a grey overcoat even though it was hot. When Mrs Day saw Sebastian, she said, 'How's my poppet, then?' Normally, India would have nudged him, because Mrs Day sometimes gave Sebastian a biscuit or an apple, but she knew that there was no point nudging today because Sebastian had stopped speaking even to her.

'Cat got his tongue, Mrs Matthews,' said Mrs Day to the old lady. Then, to India, 'What can I do you for?' She always said this; it was supposed to be a joke, though it wasn't funny at all.

India asked for a tin of pilchards. Mrs Day was very fat, and while she stretched, puffing heavily, to reach the pilchards from the topmost shelf, India stole a look at the old lady before stuffing an apple from the sack on the floor into the pocket of her dress. Mrs Day put the tin of pilchards on the counter and India asked how much it cost. One shilling and tuppence, Mrs Day said, and India said she only had fivepence.

'I don't do tick,' said Mrs Day.

'What have you got for fivepence?'

Mrs Day looked back at the shelves. 'I could do you a piece of cheese. Or some nice carrots.'

The old lady was looking through a cardboard box of old books that had been in the shop since the first time India had come there. As Mrs Day cut the cheese, India nudged a loaf of bread on the counter into her shopping bag.

India put the cheese in her bag and took Sebastian's hand. As she made for the door of the shop, the old lady said, 'Oh, no, you don't, miss.'

India tried to run for it, but the old lady, moving with surprising speed, got between her and the door. 'Look in her bag!' she crowed triumphantly as she grabbed India's arm. 'Go on, Irene, look in her bag!'

Mrs Day heaved her bulk out from behind the counter, and peered into India's shopping bag. 'Oh dearie me.'

'I was going to pay you next time.' India tried to shake off the old lady, but her grip was like iron.

'She's put an apple in her pocket as well. You want to call Constable Gilbert, Irene.'

A man came out of the back of the shop. He was wearing trousers held up with braces over a vest. 'What's all the noise about?'

The old lady said, 'This little madam's thieving.'

'Thieving?'

'I'll sort it out, Reg,' said Mrs Day.

Sebastian was crying. Mrs Day picked him up and made soothing noises. She said to India, 'Why did you do such a naughty thing? A big girl like you should know better. You've got yourself into a lot of trouble.'

'You want to call the constable,' said the old lady again.

'Thank you, Mrs Matthews,' said Mrs Day sharply.

'Thieving,' said Reg.

The policeman lived up the road. They would send her to prison and then who would look after Sebastian? It occurred to India that if Mrs Day felt sorry for her, she might not be so angry with her and then she might not be sent to prison. So she whispered to Mrs Day, 'My mother's dead.'

'Dead?' repeated Mrs Day. India nodded. Mrs Day looked shocked. 'I didn't know. You poor little things. When did she die, dear?'

'Yesterday, I think.'

'Yesterday?'

'She won't wake up.' India kept her voice low so that Sebastian couldn't hear. 'She's in bed and I brought her cups of tea and everything but she won't wake up. And she's gone all cold.'

With difficulty, Mrs Day stooped until she was level with India. Then she whispered, 'Dead? Surely not, dear.'

'I think so.'

'I expect she's just poorly. Reg can go and see if there's anything he can do to help.'

'She won't speak,' said India. 'She hasn't said anything since the day before yesterday. And there's nothing to eat.'

And because she knew that Mrs Day was fond of Sebastian, 'He's crying because he's hungry.'

'You're not fibbing, are you?' said Mrs Day, looking at India hard. 'You wouldn't fib about something like that?'

India pressed her lips together and shook her head.

She and Sebastian were taken into the back room, Mr Day's room, and sat down among the cardboard boxes and milk crates. The wireless was on, playing 'Music While You Work'. Mrs Day gave them glasses of milk and pieces of bread and butter while Mr Day, now wearing a shirt, went out. Sebastian gulped down the milk but India felt too sick to drink hers. When Mr Day came back, accompanied by the constable, India gave Mrs Day an agonized look, but Mrs Day ruffled her hair and murmured, 'We won't say any more about that. Don't fret, dear.'

The three adults talked for while. India tried to hear what they were saying, but couldn't. Sebastian clambered on to India's knee. She could feel him falling off to sleep, getting heavier in the way he had done when he had been a baby and had needed a nap every afternoon.

Through the side door, India could see a garden. Tall hollyhocks raised pink flowers the size of saucers to the sun. A chicken pecked in the dust. India imagined her and Sebastian living with Mrs Day. Sebastian could play in the garden and she could help in the shop. She could cut the cheese with the length of wire and measure out flour from the sack with the scoop and she could put the little brass weights on the scales, something she had always wanted to do.

Reg and the policeman left the shop. Much later, after the grown-ups came back, Mrs Day drew India aside and told her that her mother was indeed dead. She cried at last, though she had known it anyway.

The hard thing was telling Sebastian. He didn't really understand and kept on asking for his mother. India told him that Mummy was in heaven, that she was walking in meadows full of flowers beside a silver river. But he still cried and cried.

India drifted off as the birds sang their dawn chorus, slept through her alarm and slept through Sebastian bringing her a cup of tea. When, eventually, she woke, she looked at her wristwatch. It was half past ten. She screamed.

Garrett moved and said blurrily, 'What's wrong?'

She yelled at him, 'I'm late! I'm late for work and it's all your fault!'

India threw on some clothes, dragged a comb through her hair and ran to the Tube station. She put on a pair of dark glasses and told Miss Maloney she had a migraine, but Miss Maloney gave her a disbelieving sneer and sacked her anyway.

When she went back to the flat, Garrett had gone. India had a bath, washed her hair and lay on the sofa, leafing through a magazine. Another memory drifted through her mind, and she curled up on the sofa, trying not to think about it, but it was there, a shard of ice, and wouldn't be dislodged.

Back in the summer of 1942, India had assumed that she and Sebastian were to go on living at the grocer's shop. But one morning, Mrs Day had told them that they had a visitor. The visitor's name had been Miss Cassidy and she was going to take the two of them to live in a nice house in the countryside.

India, cutting to the quick, had asked Mrs Day whether they were to be Miss Cassidy's children.

Miss Cassidy had given a little laugh, and said, 'Oh, no, I'm just a children's nurse.'

Mrs Day had wheezily lowered her great bulk on to a low chair, looked India in the eye and explained that though she would have liked to have kept them, Reg wouldn't have it. Reg had never wanted kids. Miss Cassidy was going to take them to a lovely home and Mrs Day was sure they would be very happy.

India had said, 'We'll be together, won't we? We'll be able to sleep in the same room? He won't sleep if I'm not there.'

'Of course.'

'You promise?'

Miss Cassidy had promised. Then their things had been packed into their mother's old suitcase and they had left the shop with Miss Cassidy. A bus, two trains and another bus, and then a walk down a long, narrow road between stubble fields. Miss Cassidy had insisted on holding Sebastian's hand even though India had known he would have preferred to hold hers. 'It's the rules, young lady.' India knew that Miss

Cassidy had taken a dislike to her but she didn't seem to mind Sebastian, which was comforting.

It was a long day, and by the time they reached Charnwood, the sun was setting. Miss Cassidy hauled them through gates and down a gravel drive that led to a dusty courtyard on which prams were parked. Then they were taken through a side door and along corridors to a room in which a lady wearing a nurse's cap peered down their throats and inspected their hair for nits.

Eventually Miss Cassidy came back to the room. 'Where to, Matron?' she said.

'The girl to eleven, the boy to six.'

India said, 'We're sleeping in the same room.'

'Oh no, dear,' Matron said. 'Boys and girls never go in the same room.'

Miss Cassidy made to take Sebastian's hand. India grabbed him, hugging him to her tightly. Someone was called, and they prised Sebastian from her. Then they held her back, kicking and struggling, as Miss Cassidy had carried Sebastian screaming out of the room.

The clamour of the telephone seemed to mingle with the memory of Sebastian's screams.

India slid off the sofa and the magazine tumbled to the floor. Picking up the receiver, she said her name.

It was Marcus Pharoah. She was fed up with everything and sick of all of the people she went around with. She needed a change. When he asked her whether she was free for a drink, she said, 'Yes, if you like, I don't mind.' And in the small silence that followed, she wondered whether he felt triumphant or whether some part of him almost regretted the ending of the chase.

Christmas with her family in Wiltshire was for Ellen much as it always was, a pleasant mixture of delicious food, cooked by her mother, squabbles with Joe over boardgames, and long walks with her father over a snow-sprinkled Salisbury Plain.

Something had changed, though. It struck her, on the train back to London, that for the first time she felt that she was going home. Not *leaving* home, on this, her return to the capital, but *going* home.

She went to see her friends. A party put on by some of the men in the lab, with bread and cheese and bottles of beer from the pub. Supper with India and Sebastian, with crackers to pull and the cold remains of a Christmas pudding. And then the phone ringing and India darting out and shutting the sitting-room door while she took the call, and Sebastian raising his eyebrows as he and Ellen washed up, saying, 'Some new chap.'

Ellen wondered what had happened to dark, impudent Garrett, who had danced with her in the Mayhews' kitchen.

She and Riley went for a long walk over Hampstead Heath. Annie ran with the kite along a rough, grassy ridge and the kite thwacked and ducked and then leaped into the air, and Annie's coat flared bright red against the muted greys and browns of the trees.

* * *

India sold the Dresden shepherdess, the Clarice Cliff jug and the Venetian glass paperweight and gave the money to Garrett to pay Bernie. The sitting room of the flat looked bare without the ornaments. They had belonged to Rachel, and they had sat on the mantelpiece since the very first time India and Sebastian had arrived at her flat. Rachel had let India hold the shepherdess, a rosy-cheeked girl in a tight pink dress. It had seemed extraordinary to India that they should have come to live in a place that contained such things. Though she and Sebastian had been at the orphanage for only six weeks, its aridity had scratched her soul.

India put a vase on the mantelpiece and Sebastian put winter pansies in it, but it wasn't the same. She saw Garrett less often because that wasn't the same either. Bad things had a way of sliding off Garrett, but the scar over his eye hadn't healed well. She had been right, he should have got it stitched. She went to Christmas parties and sometimes Bernie was there and sometimes he was not, but she made sure never to be alone with him, always to be part of a crowd.

In January, she found a job waitressing in a café near the British Museum. It was OK, but it paid less than the art shop. In the evenings, Marcus Pharoah liked to drive her out to the countryside, where they dined in quiet restaurants beside rivers or in market towns. This, India supposed, was because he didn't want to run into any of his friends. He was married, after all. India didn't tell Ellen about Marcus Pharoah because she knew Ellen wouldn't approve. You told people only what they wanted to know: this was something she had learned a long time ago. As time passed, India sometimes felt guilty, but she could see how the conversation would go, and how hurt Ellen would feel that she, India, hadn't mentioned that she'd been seeing Marcus, whom Ellen disliked, for weeks. Why risk Ellen being cross with her for something that would never last?

Sometimes the tables in the smart restaurants were set up beside tall picture windows. Occasionally in the darkness, a rowboat would glide along the Thames, lit by a torch or lantern, a necklace of water tumbling from the oars. The restaurants were the sort where waiters moved silently to pick up your fork if you dropped it on the floor and to pull out your chair when you stood up or sat down. There was the chink of crystal glasses and the gleam of candlelight, and when you unfolded your napkin it was as thick and stiff as cardboard. It was all rather different to India's café in Bloomsbury, where the clientele, a bookish lot, turned pages while spraying cigarette ash on the floor and slopping coffee into their saucers.

She went along with it. A girl needed a good meal now and then, and times were hard. She wouldn't sleep with him because that only made complications. And she was tired of all that, needed a break from men wanting things from her, had begun to feel grubby with it all. India Mayhew, that fictitious creature, daughter of a diplomat, loving child of loving parents, as made-up and insubstantial as a unicorn in a forest, seemed to her almost threadbare, worn through. So she would sit in Marcus Pharoah's green sports car and go along to the smart restaurants in Henley and Newbury, for a while, at least. And then, a few months along the line, he would lose interest in her or she would break it off, and they would forget about each other, no harm done.

Chapter Six

A windy, rainswept Thursday evening in February. The seminar room at University College was already full when Ellen and Professor Malik arrived for a meeting of the Biochemical Society, so they sat in the back row. As an Oxford man stood up to give a talk on the chemical structure of enzymes, Ellen's gaze drifted idly over the audience, stopping as she reached a figure sitting several rows ahead of her.

The line of his shoulders and the mop of black curls seemed familiar to her, reminding her sharply and painfully of her autumn and winter at Gildersleve. Her view of him was partially blocked by his neighbour, a thickset gentleman who blew his nose repeatedly. But she thought – she could not be sure – that it was Alec Hunter.

If it was him, no matter. Hardly surprising that they should run into each other as the scientific community was small and self-selected. She had only to smile and say hello, how are you, and then walk away. It would get it over and done with, their first meeting after Gildersleve. Yet she felt the fast pulse of the blood through her veins as she scanned the room, searching for Andrée Fournier yet failing to find her.

The talk ended and the discussion began. An argument over the interpretation of data was soon under way, people adhering with great passion to different viewpoints. Alec – if it was Alec – said nothing at first, and Ellen remembered how he had liked to keep silent during the seminars at Gildersleve, letting the conversation flow before intervening to tell everyone else they were wrong. She felt a surge of annoyance, recalling his unwillingness to listen, his confidence in his own position, and then wanted to laugh at herself. She was not even sure that it was him. She might have taken an irrational dislike to some innocent stranger.

Then he turned to speak to the man beside her and she caught a glimpse of his profile. The straight nose, firm chin and those eyes, with their slight heaviness at the outer corners and the unlimited depth of their blueness: all these things had fascinated her, once.

He proceeded to demolish with ruthless efficiency the point made by the previous speaker. The discussion became hot-tempered, most of the audience joining in, talking over each other, their voices rising in pitch. Ellen noticed that Alec never interrupted and never allowed his enthusiasm

241

for his subject to inform his tone. These were his faults, a detachment that amounted to indifference, a hauteur that he employed to cut himself off from other people and an impatience with the perceived slowness of others. *Hunter's lord of the manor or some such back home*, Martin Finch's voice echoed, and Ellen found it all too easy to imagine Alec striding in a lordly fashion round the ancestral estates. He was a cold fish and that was the truth of it. She felt sorry for Andrée, crazy for such a man.

Now he was saying, 'If you would merely look at the evidence . . .' and Ellen spoke for the first time.

'The evidence is inconclusive. I'm afraid Dr Hunter is mistaken if he believes the argument to be clear-cut.'

Looking back at her, Alec scowled.

'It's all too easy to draw the wrong conclusions from imperfect data.' It was hard, with that fierce blue glare directed at her, not to fidget, to brush back an imaginary lock of hair or tug at the hem of her skirt. 'Unless you know the whole picture, you can't form a true judgement.'

'There's no judgement to be drawn. These are matters of fact.'

'I disagree. But perhaps it depends on your viewpoint.'

'Not at all. A fact is a fact.'

'But we can be misled, Dr Hunter. We can believe we're seeing all the evidence when some of it is closed off to us. Surely you'd agree with that?'

'There can be good reasons for holding back information,' Alec said curtly. 'Sometimes you have no choice.'

Ellen fell silent, pressing her hands together, stilling their tremor, running her tongue over her lips to moisten them. Her heart tripped as if she had drunk too much coffee, and she had the dull beginnings of a headache.

Neither she nor Alec spoke again during the final quarter of an hour of the discussion. As the seminar ended and the participants shuffled to their feet, Ellen glanced along the rows of chairs. Alec was gathering up briefcase and jacket and turning towards her. Then someone clapped him on the shoulder, engaging him in conversation.

She and Professor Malik left the room. Sherry was served in a common room along the corridor. Warm and overly sweet, it slid down the throat, taking the sting out of a day that had become unpleasantly complicated. Malik left her to speak to one of the University College professors and Ellen found herself on the fringes of a group. She knew that there were layers of inclusion and that she was on the perimeter. She was out of touch, no longer in the heart of things. Worse still, tonight she struggled to concentrate. Phrases – long chain molecules . . . Bragg diffraction . . . carbohydrate polymers – drifted by her but did not latch on. The back of her neck prickled, almost as if she could feel his gaze. Would he seek her out? Would he speak to her? Perhaps not. After all, what was she to him? A former colleague, from a brief time, years ago.

A voice said, 'Ellen,' and she turned.

'Hello, Alec. How are you?'

'Very well, thank you. And you?'

'Marvellous. Did you enjoy the seminar?'

'Not especially. Did you?'

'Very much. How's King's?'

'Good. It's good. I didn't know you were in London.'

Was that a thread or two of silver in the black hair round his temples? Had he put on a little weight, perhaps, in the intervening years? She told him about the hospital, then waited for him to say something patronizing.

But he said only, 'Sounds interesting. Useful, too. Good to know you're doing something of benefit to people.'

Was there condescension in his voice? No, to be fair, she did not think so. She said, 'How's Andrée?'

'Fine, I assume.'

'She wasn't able to come tonight?'

'Hardly. She's in Paris.'

'Oh. Visiting?'

'Working.'

'That must be difficult.'

'Difficult?' A touch of perplexity. 'I don't think so. It was a good move for her. She needed a new start and she never particularly liked England.'

It was her turn to feel confused. 'Do you mean that Andrée's living in Paris?'

'Yes. Has been for a couple of years.'

So, Andrée Fournier had returned to France two years ago. Alec had given no hint that he and Andrée were seeing each other at weekends or writing to each other or making plans for a future together. Did that mean that the relationship had broken up again – that he, Alec, had given Andrée the push again? His uninterested 'Fine, I assume' seemed to imply so, and her anger with him returned.

'Poor Andrée,' she said. 'We were never close, but I can't help feeling sorry for her.'

He seemed about to respond when the man who had been sitting beside him during the seminar heaved into view, breathing asthmatically. 'I meant to tell you, Hunter.' A painful wheeze. 'I was speaking to Bernal the other day . . .'

Ellen took the opportunity to move away. She could no longer see Professor Malik, and the other participants of the seminar had gathered themselves into little groups, sharing gossip or debating problems. She stood by a window that looked out on to a square of asphalt. The rain had got up; she watched the patterns it churned up on the surface of the puddles.

A woman from Birkbeck came to talk to her. A quick glance round the room showed Ellen that the asthmatic man had pinned Alec into a corner and that Professor Malik had gone. The Birkbeck woman was leaving too; talking of crystallography, she and Ellen snapped up their umbrellas as they came out of the building and on to the street.

The rain made a wall of noise that almost muffled the sound of the traffic. As they walked along the pavement, a couple stepped out of a taxi and made a dash for a front door. A delivery boy slung his bicycle with a clang against some railings and hurried down a set of basement steps.

Ellen looked back. There was Alec Hunter, coming towards her, she could see the bob of his black head as he threaded through the crowds. She felt a surge of annoyance. Why couldn't he leave her alone? They had said all that was needed to be said, had exchanged a few pleasantries and a few more barbed comments. Nothing further need pass between them.

Ellen shook hands with her friend, who walked off to her bus stop. Alec drew level with her.

'You seem to think me at fault in some way,' he said. 'I'd like to know why.'

Rain glued his hair to his scalp and she remembered from Gildersleve his habit of forgetting hat and gloves, not seeming to notice the weather. It was a sort of conceit, she thought, the pretension of a handsome man who knew his appeal to women.

She saw no point in holding back. She might as well say what she had been thinking for so long. Perhaps it would puncture his self-regard. Though she doubted it.

'Have you any idea how unhappy you made Andrée? Have you any idea how she felt all the time I was at Gildersleve?'

'Naturally I knew—'

'Then how could you do it? So cruel, Alec!'

'So that's it. You think it was me who made Andrée unhappy.' He gave a short laugh.

His laughter fuelled her anger. 'You have to take some responsibility. All those months of moping after you

246

finished with her the first time, and then you start the whole thing up again only to drop the poor woman once more! No wonder she's gone back to Paris!'

She began to walk fast along the pavement, winding between the girls in mackintoshes, who laughed as they ran arm in arm through the rain. Alec fell into step beside her. She waited, weary and disillusioned, for the inevitable justifications.

But all he said was, 'You're wrong, Ellen.'

'When I was at Gildersleve, I thought you had some kindness in you. I didn't think you were that sort of man.'

He caught her hand, halting her. 'That sort of man?'

'The sort of man who likes the chase but gets bored after the conquest.'

His grip slid away. They were standing in the shadow of a shop awning. Swollen drops of rain slid from the striped oilcloth, which cast channels of darkness on his features, blackening the narrowed lines of his eyes and chiselling sharp indentations round his mouth.

'No,' he said slowly. 'I told you, you've got it all wrong. You think you knew what was going on at Gildersleve, but you didn't, not at all.'

'Then tell me, Alec.'

'Not here.' He glanced at his watch. 'I have to get back to my lab, there's some work I need to finish tonight. Will you walk with me?'

She felt great reluctance. 'I don't think I want to.' Yet something in his expression, some unexpected vulnerability, made her explain, 'It was hard for me, leaving Gildersleve. It took me a long time to get over what happened there. I don't want to rake it all up again.'

'You spoke back there about not judging without knowing the true picture. I think you owe me the chance to explain.'

She met his eyes. 'I owe you nothing, Alec.'

'Ellen, please.'

Somehow she found herself continuing along Gower Street beside him. They were silent at first, keeping a distance between them, antagonistic, mutually repelling each other, their orbits never touching.

And then he said, 'Pharoah and Andrée were having an affair.'

Whatever she had expected him to say, it was not that. They were parted by a straggle of soldiers in khaki, who eyed her as she passed, but then, as they joined together once more, she said, 'Surely not.'

'It's true.'

She began to see, as they walked on, how such a thing might have been possible, how such a thing, Pharoah and Andrée, might have fitted into the silences and secrets of Gildersleve Hall.

'When?'

'It started before you came to the lab. You thought I was making her unhappy. I expect I did sometimes, though I never meant to, but Pharoah made her a damn sight more unhappy.'

It seemed to Ellen as if she had been threading through a labyrinth, confused, eyes half closed. 'I didn't know. I had no idea.'

'Andrée and I started dating not long after she arrived at the lab. At first, it was good, we were happy. But then, after a while, I noticed a change in her. Sometimes she seemed elated and sometimes she was touchy and moody. I began to wonder whether she wanted to break it off. When she told me she did, I was cut up, of course, but I accepted it. But then, one day, I found her crying in the lab. She wouldn't tell me what was troubling her at first, but eventually she admitted she'd been seeing Pharoah.'

'But he's married!' Her words, foolish and naive, seemed to echo.

Alec gave a sardonic smile. 'A wife and daughter. House in the country. The picture of the happy family. It's all false with Pharoah, smoke and mirrors. It took me a while to catch on. I was fooled by the façade, just like everyone else.'

She felt the suppressed rage in his voice, a vibration rather than an alteration in volume, like the first rumbles of thunder, a sound like stones rubbing together under the sea.

'Andrée wasn't the first,' he said. 'Pharoah had other girls at Gildersleve, before I started working there. I got Bill Farmborough drunk once and he spilled the beans.'

'Other girls?' she whispered.

'Yes.' That bitter half-smile. 'Perhaps he always has one

on the go. Perhaps he chooses them for their looks. They come to work at Gildersleve, Pharoah turns on the charm, tells the girl she has a great future, takes her along to meetings and conferences. Perhaps Andrée was flattered. Even after he'd finished with her she couldn't seem to see through him. She couldn't seem to see what he was really like, what a liar and hypocrite he was.'

A whirr, a scratch, as the pieces of the puzzle fell into place. Perhaps Pharoah had taken Andrée to a meeting at the Cavendish; perhaps Andrée, blinded by the bright light of his attention, had agreed to go for a drink with him afterwards. Perhaps they had gone on together to dinner somewhere. Andrée, a sophisticated Frenchwoman, would not have run away to the safety of the bus and her lodgings.

Perhaps Pharoah had invited Andrée to his house in Barton. Ellen remembered the Pharoahs' primrose-yellow drawing room, Marcus Pharoah's friends and family, his spoiled, beautiful daughter, and his wife, crying among her orchids. Had Alison Pharoah seen her, Ellen, as her next rival, the next insult? Had she wept because she dreaded the thought of enduring the same humiliation, the same hurt, over and over again?

There were memories she would have preferred to subdue, but they sprang at her now. The hotel in Cambridge on that strange, fogged winter evening, and Pharoah sitting opposite her.

Would you like Rowena to be a scientist, Marcus?

I should love her to be one, especially if she managed to do so while being as charming and attractive as you and Mademoiselle Fournier.

Alec said, 'I couldn't tell you about it when you were at Gildersleve, you must see that. For Andrée's sake.'

'Of course,' she murmured.

Cabs and buses were hurrying irritably along Oxford Street, hooting their horns, windscreen wipers thrashing. Alec saw a gap in the traffic, gave Ellen's hand a tug, and they dashed across the road.

As they reached the other side he spoke again. 'Andrée thought Pharoah would leave his wife and marry her. I don't suppose he considered it for a moment. It's Alison who has all the cash. Pharoah kept Gildersleve going with Alison's money. Alison would have destroyed him if it had come out into the open. She's not the sort to allow herself to be made a fool of publicly.'

Alison Pharoah had been both beautiful and glacial. Pharoah had implied that his wife was mentally ill, depressed perhaps, but maybe Alison Pharoah's depression had been a consquence of her husband's faithlessness.

'How long did it last?'

'Six months. Pharoah finished with her that autumn, a few weeks before Redmond died. He used her. He got her into his bed and then, when he was tired of her, he gave her the push.'

The crowds were being swallowed up into buses and Underground stations. Pharoah and Andrée Fournier, Pharoah dropping Andrée Fournier – and turning his attention

251

elsewhere? To her? Was it possible? Was that, in fact, why Pharoah had sacked her, and was that why he had written that vituperative letter to Professor Malik – not because of what had happened to Dr Redmond, and not because she had told the police about the two men's quarrel, but because she had not responded to his advances, had not become his mistress?

Another memory intruded: herself, looking out of the lab window, Martin standing at her side, as she watched Alec and Andrée kissing in the copse. She said, 'Why did you stay at Gildersleve?'

'Because I hoped she'd change her mind.' Alec sounded tired. 'I thought that if I hung on she'd realize the truth about Pharoah and come back to me. Stupid of me. People go on believing what they want to believe, in spite of all the evidence. She still thought she was in love with him. It took me a long time to accept that.'

'But you still loved her, didn't you?'

His brows snapped together, as black as the rain clouds. 'All those months I'd waited for her, I went on thinking so. When Pharoah dropped her, I was glad for her sake as well as mine. She was in a state, and she was worried about her job, of course. She was in a mess and I was there, and yes, it felt good. I suppose that's why she went along with it, why she said she'd come back to me, because she needed someone then, Perhaps she couldn't face having no one. But there was nothing left. It didn't take either of us long to find that out. It was like breathing oxygen into a dead

thing. You wonder, when you look back, whether it was love making you hang on or possessiveness.'

Who else might have known about Pharoah and Andrée Fournier? Not Martin: he, an inveterate gossip, would surely have passed it on to her. Could Dr Redmond have known? Could that have been what he had been referring to when he had threatened Pharoah after their quarrel? *I'll make sure everyone knows the truth about you.* Ellen dismissed the thought almost immediately. Dr Redmond had been uninterested in people. He wouldn't have noticed a love affair, such a thing would not have registered on his consciousness.

London shimmered, the light from the gas lamps fractured and pellucid. When the buildings parted, Ellen caught glimpses of the river ahead, dense and dark and oily. The wind tugged at her umbrella, turning it inside out. Alec took it from her, punching it back into shape, and now, as they walked, he held the umbrella, and they moved closer together, sheltering beneath it. When his sleeve brushed against her arm, it felt resonant, like electricity.

Reaching the Strand, they turned down towards King's. Inside, she noticed that though Alec's laboratory was larger than his one at Gildersleve, the equipment in it – X-ray apparatus, rotation camera, thermostat – gave it a familiarity. Compared to the streets outside, the room felt warm and comfortable.

Ellen draped her gloves and scarf over a radiator and squeezed the rainwater out of her hair, combing it with her fingers while Alec made coffee for both of them.

She said, 'Do you hear from Andrée at all?'

'She writes, now and then. She's working in a government lab in Paris. In her last letter she told me she'd become engaged. There was an old flame, someone she knew at school.'

'I hope she'll be happy.'

As she watched him work, she remembered doing the same at Gildersleve in the aftermath of Dr Redmond's death, sitting in his lab in the basement, letting herself be soothed by the familiar tasks, and by his presence.

'Someone told me Dr Kaminski had left Gildersleve,' she said.

'Jan left a few months after I did. I don't expect he much cared for what Pharoah did after Redmond died.'

'What do you mean?'

'Pharoah had the cottage and the woodland put up for sale. Some builder has bought it. Apparently there are plans to put up houses there.'

Ellen remembered walking in Peddar's Wood after the snow had fallen. The twisted shapes of the trees and the silence. You took pieces from the past and treasured them for ever.

'Poor Dr Redmond,' she said sadly. 'He would have hated that.'

'I think Kaminski resigned because he found it all too hard to swallow. Even good old Bill commented on the indecent haste. Now there's someone who'll stay at Gildersleve until they cart him off in a wooden box. Never

254

the sharpest knife in the drawer, old Bill, but he knows which side his bread's buttered on.' Alec's voice was acid. 'Pharoah got someone in to do your work after you left, Ellen. Some yes-man, dull as ditchwater Cambridge type who went home to his mother at the weekends. It's getting the mix of people that makes a place work and Gildersleve wasn't working by the time I left.' He put down the pen with which he was noting down figures. 'You were missed, Ellen.'

She remembered the first time she had seen Alec Hunter, when he had passed her on the stairs at Gildersleve. That image of him had remained with her, striped by shadows and sunshine and suffused with the tang of the chilly autumn air and the promise of the day.

'I should go,' she said.

'Must you?'

He swung round on his chair, then rose. He took her scarf from the radiator and, standing in front of her, looped it round her neck. Then, with his forefinger, he gently tucked back a loose lock of hair behind her ear.

'I must look a mess,' she murmured.

'No. You look beautiful.'

And then, standing on tiptoe, she brushed her lips against his mouth. He pulled her to him and their kiss was deep and long-lasting. She could feel the beat of his heart through the damp fabric of his shirt and the warm roughness of his face against hers. Her own heart beat out its rhythm, staccato and overemphatic, and she seemed to feel the fast

255

passage of blood through her veins. She needed him to touch every part of her, her skin cried out for him to do so. *Don't stop.* She was unsure whether she had spoken aloud or whether the words drummed inside her head. Their wet clothing caught and dragged, her hands against the flat musculature of his back, his fingertips connecting with the small bones at the top of her spine. She heard the ring of a telephone, the tick of a clock, and she wanted to consume him, and to be consumed.

India knew straight away that Marcus Pharoah was in a bad mood. He didn't get out of the car as he usually did, to hold open the door for her, but leaned across and opened it from the inside so that she could slide into the passenger seat beside him.

He said, 'You're over an hour late.'

'Am I? Darling, I'm so sorry, I've lost my watch.'

His fingers tapped the steering wheel. 'I thought you weren't going to turn up.'

'You could have come into the flat.'

She said this knowing that he felt awkward doing so. He had once, when she had been late before, done exactly this. He and Sebastian hadn't got on; Marcus had tried to talk to Sebastian, but Sebastian had been mutely terrified of Marcus.

He said, 'I don't mind ten, fifteen minutes late. It's a female prerogative, isn't it? But an hour and a quarter . . . we may have lost our table at the restaurant.'

'That's all right, I'm not hungry.' India picked up her bag and climbed out of the car.

He looked furious. 'I dislike impoliteness. Lack of consideration. It makes you look cheap.'

Cheap. Slowly, she turned to face him. 'I didn't forget and I wasn't busy. Maybe I didn't want to see you, Marcus. Maybe it's as simple as that.'

His eyes narrowed. 'Rather a change of heart. What's wrong? Haven't I come up with the cash quick enough?'

'I wouldn't touch your money!'

'Then why are you here?' He reached into a pocket, drew out a handful of change, and hurled it at her. Shillings and sixpences rolled over the pavement; she stepped back. He said, smiling, 'Go on, India, pick it up, you know you want to.'

'I might be cheap,' she yelled at him as she walked away, 'but you're a conceited pig!'

A bus had drawn into the road ahead of them. India ran along the pavement and jumped on to it. It was crowded and she had to stand on the platform. She was wearing a short black jacket with a fur collar over her blue silk; the conductor said, 'Where are you heading for, Cinderella?'

'Anywhere,' said India. She saw through the window Marcus Pharoah's car draw out from the kerb with a screech and a streak of green into the traffic.

After several stops she alighted and walked the rest of the way to Garrett's flat in Victoria. You knew where

you were with old friends, she thought. They knew what you were.

India climbed up three flights of stairs and knocked on a door. She called out, 'It's me, Garrett!'

A key turned in the lock. She saw, beyond Garrett, the open rucksack on the bed. He let her in, closed the door, then rammed home the bolt.

'Where are you going?'

'Back home for a while. Oliver's driving north tonight. He said he'd give me a lift.'

'Garrett, you can't. You'll hate it.'

'Clive isn't coming back and I haven't much work. And I don't like the way Lee looks at me.' He stuffed a crumpled shirt into the rucksack.

'Were you going to leave without telling me?'

'I thought you were fed up with me.'

'I am.' With her fingertip, she traced the red line of the scar above his eye. 'You're one of the most annoying people I know.'

He looked down at her, frowning. 'I'll miss you, Indy.'

She gave him a kiss and then left him to his packing. Not bad going, India, she said to herself as she walked along the street. Quarrel with one man, say goodbye to another, all in the same night. She told herself that it didn't matter, and that both men, in their different ways, were equally annoying, but it made her feel miserable to think how these things always went wrong for her, as though they had slithering, evasive lives of their own, and she

found herself longing for the sanctuary of the flat and Sebastian.

Two days had passed since the night Ellen and Alec had kissed. During that time, winter had returned, speckles of snow dancing in the grey, attenuated air. A blizzard was sweeping over the entire country, roads were blocked and vehicles abandoned, livestock stranded on hill pastures.

Alec did not call. She began to feel uneasy. She lay on the bed in her room, reading and writing letters, the radio on, waiting for the phone to ring, the knock on the door. She couldn't go out to see anyone, India or Riley or any of her other friends, because she needed the phone to ring. She found herself going through the events of the evening minutely, putting them in chronological order because that seemed to matter. He had touched her first – his finger, brushing back a lock of her hair, the memory of which even now, in its aftermath, made her shiver and squeeze her eyes shut – but it had been she who had initiated the kiss, she who had stood on tiptoe and touched her mouth to his.

Over and over, she ran it through her mind, slow motion. Perhaps he hadn't intended to kiss her. Perhaps that had been a friendly, brotherly gesture, that sweeping back of her hair. Perhaps she had taken him by surprise, kissing him, and his response had been automatic, what any man might do when a woman threw herself at him.

259

She phoned King's, left a message. At the hospital, she centrifuged blood samples and separated serum and waited. In the privacy of the ladies' cloakroom at lunchtime, she washed her hands and combed her hair and paused, looking at her reflection in the mirror. Her face was flushed and a film of sweat lay on her forehead. Had she been careless? Had she forgotten to wear her gloves, and brushed a finger against the contents of a test tube or petri dish and caught a fever? No, she knew she had not. It was only the memory of the shame of what had happened that brought the heat to her face. She had not merely kissed him, she had *clawed* at him. She had dug her fingers into his hair, had pressed her body against his. God knows what would have happened if she hadn't heard someone come to the door. She might have torn off their clothes, as wild as Bacchus's followers in the painting that Daniel had admired in the National Gallery, with their reaching, contorted limbs and dishevelled garments. She might have let him take her standing up against the wall, like a streetwalker. She had disgusted him. It was understandable that he hadn't called.

Snow pelted the pavements as she walked to work. She was becoming familiar with shame, with its twists and turns and its habit of tapping you on the shoulder in the middle of the night and keeping you awake with its sly, taunting grin. Alec might have a girlfriend. He might have been about to tell her about Andrée Fournier's successor when she had lunged at him. How would she bear it, if they were ever to meet again? She would have to leave the

hospital. She would have to leave London, just as she had begun to feel truly at home there.

Snowdrifts were trapping passengers in trains and the RAF had given up hunting Russian submarines and had turned instead to dropping fodder for stranded sheep. Professor Malik told her of a job going at University College; listlessly, she began to pull together a letter of application. She went to see India, but India was in an odd mood, talking and smoking too much, and her company grated. Riley suited her better; they shared a pot of coffee and listened to 'Blue Haze' and talked about not very much. The notes of the piano fell like the raindrops that had struck the pavements as she and Alec had walked along the Strand. Riley had once told her that men thought her unobtainable. He had been wrong, though. Not unobtainable at all, just desperate. But when the record was finished, she hurried back to Islington to see if anyone had left a message.

One evening, one of the lodgers took an overdose of sleeping pills and had to be rushed off by ambulance to hospital. Ellen and Joe sat in the waiting room as Dave's parents battled through a flooded East Anglia to their stricken son. They spoke in muted tones, looking up whenever they heard the clack of a nurse's shoes on the polished lino. A girl, suggested Ellen. Joe shook his head. He didn't think so. He'd always wondered whether poor old Dave batted for the other team. He shrugged. He wasn't sure, they'd never spoken about it. Perhaps Dave had thought

he would disapprove, chuck him out, call the police. Dave had mentioned a friend who'd recently been arrested on charges of indecency. Perhaps that had preyed on his mind. Joe didn't give a damn, had no interest in what other people did in bed. And anyway, you fell in love with whoever you fell in love with and there was nothing you could do about it. He sounded despondent; Ellen, looking at her brother, reached out and squeezed his hand, and thought of India, and what she did, almost without thinking, and was aware of resentment.

The next day, when she woke, the sky was a clear and flawless blue. Though the cold seared, a sharp frost made London glitter, as if made of crystal. How rarely did one act on impulse. How rarely did one allow oneself to be swept along by feelings, by passion. If she never saw Alec again, should she regret what had happened? No, because it had come from her true self. She had spoken with her true voice, had allowed her body to speak for her. When she was an old woman, when she was alone and her beauty gone, she would look back on that evening and smile.

Travelling home at six o'clock, she noticed that the intensity of the cold had ebbed a little. In the hallway of the Islington house, puddles had formed on the checkered tiles. She swept up the brown envelopes that lay muddying beneath the letter box. As she glanced through them, the telephone rang. She picked up the receiver.

The operator told her that she was putting through a

call from Nottingham. And then, on the other end of the line, she heard Alec's voice, greeting her.

Ellen sat down on the bottom stair. Thank God he had got through to her at last, Alec said, he'd been trying for days. He had been in Scotland: his mother had phoned late on the night he and Ellen had met. She had been taken ill and he had driven up through the night and the following day to be with her. But he had become stranded, marooned on Seil Island by the snow. The phone lines were down and even after his mother had recovered and he had made it back on to the mainland, many of the roads had been impassable.

Relief flooded through her like wine: she wanted to laugh. *Hoping to get home tonight — depends on the roads — snowdrifts as high as Colditz.* The line was breaking up, interspersed by crackles. The front door banged open and Ellen had to squeeze aside to allow one of the students to get past her. *Missed you*, he yelled, over the interference, and she yelled back into the receiver, *I missed you too*. He said, *When I get back—* and then the line went dead.

She put down the receiver, and sat for a while, prolonging the moment, and then she gathered up her gloves and scarf and bag and went upstairs.

The identity of the body in the Great Dover Street warehouse, the curly-haired man in the cheap suit, had been established after house-to-house inquiries. George Clancy had been a Dubliner who had lived at various addresses

during the nine months he had spent in London prior to his death. A phone call placed by Riley to the Garda in Dublin had established that Clancy had a cousin there as well as a criminal record – nothing major, but ugly little crimes: extortion, assault and battery and demanding money with menaces. The Garda spoke to the cousin, who grudgingly agreed to arrange a funeral.

It was always possible, of course, that one of Clancy's past misdeeds had come back to haunt him, that some Irishman with a long memory had thought it worth his while to get on the ferry and cross the Irish Sea and stick a pickaxe in Clancy's head. But Riley didn't think so. Forensic tests had confirmed that the Dubliner had died in the warehouse, which had been used, Riley was certain, to store contraband. So, Clancy had either had an unlucky accident, had made a bad choice of place to sleep the night, or he had been lured to the warehouse by his killer. Riley suspected the latter.

So now Riley and his team were combing back though Clancy's months in London, trying to work out what he had been up to and why he had come to die in the warehouse. In the weeks before his death, Clancy had lived in lodgings near Borough Market. A West Indian family had since moved into the room; not knowing what else to do with his belongings, they had packed them into a cardboard box which they handed over to the sergeant who interviewed them during the house-to-house. In the box was a notebook containing addresses, one of which was for a

house in Camden that Riley had been interested in for some time. The house was rented by a petty criminal called Terry Curran, who had served prison sentences in the past for handling stolen goods, and who went to the same drinking dens as Rex White, who ran a string of gambling houses and brothels in north London.

Riley had questioned Mr Rossiter, the owner of the warehouse, until Rossiter had brought in an expensive lawyer, who had accused the police of harassing his client. The expensive lawyer had, in the past, worked for Bernie Perlman, who was in much the same line of business as Rex White. Rossiter, his lawyer, and Perlman were sometimes to be seen sharing a table at the Blue Duck nightclub in Mayfair. Though White and Perlman had a great deal in common – greed, and a fondness for violence – they existed in competition. London gangsters each had their own patch of territory, their stake in an area which they enforced through protection rackets and brutality. Bernie Perlman's territory took in the Borough and a large area south of the river. Rivalries – someone's tame hoodlum trespassing on someone else's turf, for instance – could spark off a war to the death. It seemed probable to Riley that George Clancy had worked in some menial capacity for Rex White and had somehow stumbled upon the Great Dover Street warehouse and its contents. And that the warehouse itself was used by Bernie Perlman. Clancy's death, Riley suspected, had been intended as a warning.

He had Sergeant Davies and a detective constable watch

the Camden house, but Davies became over-enthusiastic one night, and, while the constable slipped off to buy chips, went to investigate a van parked outside the house. Davies appeared at the station the next day with a black eye and bruises. After Riley had reprimanded him for checking out the van on his own, he got Davies to describe the men who had attacked him. One had been small, bald-headed and stupid-looking, said Davies; the other – the bastard who had kicked him in the stomach – had short ginger hair and a pale, fleshy face. He looked . . . spectral, added Davies with a shudder. Riley, who hadn't suspected Davies of a poetic soul, sent him away to write up his report and help the police artist draw up a mugshot.

So far, there was nothing to link the various elements – the murder, the stolen goods, the gangland rivalries. Riley could see some of the spiders, but not the web. His desk was heaped with manilla files; more box files were stacked on the shelves and floor. Somewhere in the sheaves of paper might be the piece of evidence that he could use to bring Perlman and White to justice. Though Riley doubted it: the biggest spiders were always careful to place themselves – and their paper trail – out of reach. Words and figures jangled in front of his eyes; he slid the papers back into the file and closed it.

Riley rose and went to the window. Staring out at the sea of roofs and twists of smoke from chimneys, he let himself think of Ellen. It was over a fortnight since he had last seen her. Their careers, and Annie, and a certain

wariness on his part, meant that they met only infrequently. And yet he had grown closer to her. He had confided in her the true nature of his feelings for Pearl. He remembered the bitter taste of his jealousy when she had spoken to him of Alec Hunter.

In the immediate aftermath of Pearl's leaving home, Riley hadn't looked for close involvement with anyone. He had concentrated on giving Annie a stable upbringing and on his work. And then he had encountered Ellen on the steps of St Stephen's hospital. At first he had wondered whether there was in his instant attraction to Ellen a warning echo of his infatuation with Pearl, back in 1944. By now, such reservations had fallen away. Ellen was not Pearl. She was neither changeable nor unpredictable. She was intelligent, kind, generous, thoughtful and beautiful, and he loved her, loved her completely and utterly, loved the reality of her and not the illusion. He loved the small scar on her forehead, a relic of a fall from a tree when she had been a child, and he loved her grace and her economy of movement and the passionate flow of her hands as she talked.

Riley glanced at his watch. It was nearly seven o'clock. His in-laws, Vera and Basil, were staying over at his house to look after Annie. Easy enough to squeeze a free hour out of the evening.

He went into the adjacent office, where he borrowed an *Evening Standard* from a colleague. Running an eye over the Entertainments columns, he caught sight of an advertisement for a concert at the Wigmore Hall that Saturday. What

did she like, what were her tastes? He gathered his raincoat and briefcase, left Scotland Yard and drove to Islington.

One of the students let him into the lodging house. Riley went upstairs, skirting round the uncollected post, anoraks and muddy football boots scattered on the treads.

Ellen was in the kitchen. 'Riley,' she said, turning to him, kissing his cheek. 'How are you? Would you like some tea? How's Annie?'

While they talked, he noticed her smile and the way she darted around, making him tea, finding him a biscuit, removing a pile of books from a chair so that he could sit down. He found himself taking great pleasure in her response to him: it gave him optimism. You could run through a relationship like a balance sheet, totting up meetings and recollecting conversations. Or you could read the turn of a smile, a brightness of eye.

He explained about his in-laws staying over, then said, 'Are you free on Saturday?'

'I'm afraid not. What were you thinking of?'

He masked his disappointment. 'Nothing in particular.'

Ellen put the tea in front of him and dug a packet of sugar out of a cupboard. Then she said, 'Riley, I must tell you, the most wonderful thing has happened.'

A boy in a checked shirt came into the kitchen, yawning and opening cupboards. Ellen dropped her voice and sat down next to Riley.

'Do you remember I told you about Alec?' Her eyes were shining.

'Alec?' A slamming of doors, a crash, and another loud yawn as a cheese grater was unearthed.

'Alec Hunter. At Gildersleve.'

Yes, he remembered Alec Hunter. *Only a little*, he had said to Ellen when they had spoken of him before, but that had not been true. He remembered Hunter clearly enough. A little spoiled, Riley had thought, recalling how Hunter had hardly looked up from his work and had brushed off his questions with an obvious lack of interest. Clever, handsome, and – Riley had gleaned this from the remark of another Gildersleve scientist – well-off. A man who was used to the world dancing to his tune.

He said, 'What about him?'

'I saw him a couple of weeks ago, at a meeting. He was there. I knew he was in London, and then I saw him. I could hardly believe it was him at first.'

As she spoke, the words spilled over each other in joyful little phrases. The pleasure Riley had felt, seeing her, began to shrink, and he steeled himself for what he knew must come next.

'We're going to the theatre on Saturday,' she said. 'That's why I can't come to the concert. We just – well, we hit it off straight away.' She flung him another smile. 'Do you remember what I said to you about the wrong men falling in love with me, and me falling for the wrong men? Well, this is different, I know it is. It's so wonderful – and we both feel the same!'

A heavy awareness of his own capacity for self-deception

mixed with an uncontrollable flash of dislike for Hunter. He said, 'I thought you told me Hunter and Miss Fournier were together.'

'That was all a mistake. They were seeing each other for a few months and then they broke up.' Her voice dropped to a murmur. 'Alec told me that Andrée was having an affair with *Pharoah* when I was at Gildersleve. Isn't that extraordinary?'

He could smell her perfume; he moved away from her. Disillusion made him speak harshly. 'Good God, it sounds like a hotbed of intrigue. I suppose that's what happens in these places that are cut off from normal society.'

'It wasn't *Alec's* fault, Riley.'

'No?' He rose, abandoning his tea, which now seemed to taste sour. 'Miss Fournier . . . and now you . . . He has a knack of adapting to circumstances pretty quickly.'

'*Riley*.' She had flushed.

'You are sure that the affair with Miss Fournier is really over?'

'Andrée's been living in Paris for the past two years.' Ellen sounded angry. 'I can't think why you're being like this.'

'Because I don't want to see you hurt.'

'I won't be.' The words were hard and crisp.

The silence that fell on them was interrupted by the grating of cheese and the sawing of bread. Riley picked up his briefcase.

'I should go.'

270

He said goodbye, managed to paste some sort of smile on his face. Which slipped away as he walked to the car. Two things were plain to him. One was that Ellen was infatuated with Alec Hunter. The other was that there had never been a moment when she had considered him as anything other than a friend. He saw himself through her eyes now: older, staid, the father of a child.

A *husband*. However much he might feel his marriage to be at an end — and however drastically Pearl herself had finally ripped it in two — they were still tied in the eyes of the law. At any moment Pearl might return home, bringing with her a trail of emotion and drama. He would not live with her again as man and wife, but Annie's presence meant that there would always be a tie between them. Ellen must see this, even if he had not, until this moment, fully realized its implications. He might *feel* free, but he was not. No wonder she had thought Alec Hunter a better bet.

Parking the car outside his house, he sat for a moment, hands resting on the steering wheel. Stop fooling yourself, Riley, he thought wearily. Ellen wasn't with Hunter because she thought him a *better bet* — or because he was younger or more dashing. And nor was she *infatuated*. Ellen had chosen Hunter because she had fallen in love with him. It was as simple as that.

India didn't hear from Marcus Pharoah for a month. She thought he'd had enough, wondered whether she cared. Though she missed the dinners, the attention.

271

One evening, the phone rang.

'I was trying to see whether I could manage without you,' he said, 'but I don't seem to be able to.'

'You sound as though you mind about that.'

'It would be simpler if I felt otherwise.'

'Is that what you want, Marcus, a simple life?'

He laughed. 'No, of course not.' A pause, then he said, 'I'm phoning to apologize to you. What I said to you that evening was unforgivable. I'd had a bad day. I told you that I have a temper. I try to keep it under control, but sometimes I fail.'

She was feeling generous. 'It's all right. I was awfully late.'

'Did you miss me, India?'

'Enormously.'

'Liar. I know a wonderful place by a watermill. Famous people go there – actors and politicians. I've booked us a table.'

'Rather presumptuous of you, Marcus.'

'If you turn me down I shall have to ask some dry-as-dust colleague. I'm hoping you'll take pity on me.'

They dined in a glass conservatory at the back of the building. Palms in brass pots were dotted on the black and white tiles. Outside, lanterns lit a lawn that ran down to a millpond.

India was ravenous, eating every scrap of food, and would have licked her plate had she not been on her best behaviour. The waiter poured her a second cup of coffee

and at Marcus's request brought another plate of petits fours.

Marcus said, 'I was worried about you, all this time.'

'I don't believe you.' She smiled at him. 'I don't think you're the sort of person to worry about anything.'

'I worry about all sorts of things. Whether I can coax a grant out of this or that organization, whether I'll manage to stay awake through a particularly dull speech. And you, India. I worry about you. You need someone to look after you.'

'Mummy and Daddy do.' She put a miniature choux bun into her mouth whole. 'I told you.'

'Of course you did.' Pharoah took out his cigarette case and offered it to her. He flicked his lighter and India leaned forward, cupping her cigarette.

He said, 'What's the matter with your brother?'

'Sebastian?'

'I don't mean to pry, but there's something wrong, I can see that.'

She saw no reason not to say, 'Sebastian had a nervous breakdown. It was when we were children, when we were at boarding school.'

It had been wartime and Rachel had been working for the Ministry of Supply and had had to travel around the country. So, boarding schools. It must have seemed like a good idea at the time.

Pharoah slid the ashtray across the table to her. 'What happened?'

'Sebastian ran away but then they found him and brought him back to school. But in the end he had to go home to Aunt Rachel's.'

'Your parents—'

'They were busy,' she said quickly, covering herself.

'Did he see anyone?'

'A psychiatrist, you mean? Yes, lots of them. There was a nice one, Sebastian liked her, she seemed to help.'

'And—' He broke off, frowning, tapping the filter tip of his cigarette on the tabletop.

'What, Marcus?' She looked at him coolly. 'Sebastian isn't dangerous, anything like that, if that's what you're concerned about.'

'No, of course not. He seems a gentle soul.'

'He is. He's the nicest person in the world. I'd do anything for him.'

'Your loyalty does you credit. What I was going to ask you – and I hope you'll forgive my intrusion – is whether you've ever suffered similarly yourself.'

'Do you mean, have I ever had a breakdown?' She gave a loud peal of laughter and some of the other diners turned to stare at her. 'No, never.'

'Some doctors believe there's a genetic inheritance, that these things run in families, but I'm not convinced. I believe personal experience counts for a great deal. If your brother, for instance, found boarding-school life too difficult for him.'

Or if he had to play in the garden while his mother was

lying dead in the house, she thought, but said, 'Yes, I expect it was that.'

'And now? How is Sebastian now?'

'He's fine. Most of the time, anyway.'

'But you still worry about him.'

That he had noticed surprised and impressed her. 'I don't want him to be ill again, that's all. He gets upset about all kinds of things – beggars in the streets and whether there'll be a nuclear war. I never think about things like that. What's the point? I can't do anything about it so I may as well have fun now.'

'A very sensible philosophy.' He rested his cigarette on the edge of the ashtray, frowning, and said, 'It puzzles me, what I feel for you.'

'Puzzles you?'

'Yes, I think that's the word. I feel there should be a solution, an explanation. I feel I should be able to put my finger on it, to pinpoint exactly what it is that troubles me about you.'

'I hadn't thought of myself as troublesome.'

'Really, India?' His gaze seemed to dissect her. 'Is that true?'

She pouted her lips into the shape of a kiss. 'I expect you're drawn by my startling beauty.'

'Yes, it may well be that.'

'Or my cleverness, or my wonderful sense of humour.'

'I think it's because you like to put on this exterior. You make yourself look pretty and you laugh and you chatter.

And all the time you try not to give anything away. One longs to know what lies beneath.'

She had expected to see criticism in his eyes, or that expression of cynical perception that had disconcerted her before. Instead, to her surprise, she saw sadness.

When he spoke again, his voice was quiet, almost as if he was struggling to explain something to himself.

'Me, I like to know,' he said softly. 'I'm a scientist, after all. I like reasons, explanations. I like to understand. I don't like to feel *invaded*, taken over. I don't like to feel *touched*.'

Alec Hunter had seeped into every part of her life. His image was there, slotting itself into her mind as she worked in the lab, distracting her. It startled her to recall how, before, she had been so neat, so contained, so tidily complete. Now, her desire for him seemed to leak through her nerve endings, flowing into her world and colouring it. Her mouth was bruised with his kisses; as she looked down the microscope she ran the tip of her tongue over her lips, tasting them. She felt his touch, as if it, too, had left its mark, a bruise on her skin, invisible, painless. She had to sift him out of her thoughts or nothing would have got done.

Spring tumbled in, daffodils nodding in the lawns, blue skies showing between fleets of rainclouds. When the weather was fine, Alec waited for her outside the hospital at lunchtime. Sometimes they walked to a small park where dogs barked and sparrows flurried down from the trees

and then rose up again like a gust of brown leaves. Once, a child blew bubbles from out of a plastic pot, mouth pursed up, coaxing iridescent globes that bounced and bobbled and clung to each other. A stream of bubbles danced through the air, their colours shivering from pink to blue, swirling like oil on water in the moment before they burst.

Every four weeks Alec drove to Scotland for a long weekend, to visit his mother. He followed a routine established over many years, driving up on a Friday, stopping only for short breaks, reaching the island late in the evening. He took his mother into Oban for shopping and lunch and ferried her to visit friends, and headed back to London early on Monday morning. Rather an endurance test, he admitted.

In his absence, Ellen's days mislaid a dimension and what had once been solid and substantial became flat and featureless. She picked up her old life as if it was a duty, and it took an effort to find much to savour in it. How had she existed before, in such a wilderness? She caught herself sometimes boring her friends, Alec this and Alec that. But what could she do when she struggled to find meaning and delight in anything that had no connection with him?

In his basement flat in Clerkenwell, a waxed jacket hung on a hook and books were stacked on the shelves: Graham Greene and Aldous Huxley and Schrödinger's *What Is Life?* As the weeks passed, her belongings migrated to the flat

from the lodging house: a pair of socks, a paperback book, a lipstick and a bottle of shampoo.

Her clothing blotted the floor, white and navy-blue. A cream-coloured slip clung like a ghost to the back of a chair and nylons curled into question marks on the carpet. The mattress was lumpy and unforgiving, stuffed with horsehair which worked itself out in tufts through the striped ticking. The rises and falls of the mattress tried to push them together and pull them apart, but they clung on to each other, drowning sailors in a choppy sea. Afterwards, they lay between the sheets, peaceful, languorous, limbs too heavy to move, the flat of her palm on his chest, feeling the slowing pulse of his heart.

He would leave the bed and pull on a pair of trousers and wander into the kitchen. She would see the hollow of his spine and remember how she liked to place kisses along its length. She would see the sheen of sweat on his shoulders and would recall the scent of him, which was impressed on her own skin. She would watch him through the open door, filling the kettle, spooning out coffee, as he tossed phrases back to her like gifts: a word or two on the progress of his work, a remark about an acquaintance. Sometimes she wondered whether there wasn't something desperate about it, something diminishing in the urgency of their bodies, that dragged them into this room, tearing off their clothes as they fell on the bed.

Only sometimes. Mutely, their bodies spoke for them, an intimate language, a press of flesh on flesh or the touch

of a finger as feathery as a penstroke. *I love you, I love you. My love, my darling, my red, red rose.*

She was making coffee. *Any Questions* was rattling away on the radio and Alec was buttoning up his shirt, towelling his hair.

'I have these nightmares,' he said. 'I get to the end of the experimental process at last and finally I've got some decent results. I've almost wrapped it all up and then I hear that some chap at Cambridge or Edinburgh has done everything I have and more. Or – and this is worse – some colleague, some chatterer, comes into the lab when I'm working, runs an eye over my notes, and says yes, but what about the something-or-other?'

'Something-or-other?'

'Some vital point I've completely managed to overlook. A hole in the entire theory that I should have noticed but haven't and when it's pointed out to me, I realize that it's all going to fall apart, years of work down the drain and me looking a complete fool.'

She kissed him. 'Get your results written up, then forget about it. We could go away for a weekend as soon as you've finished.'

He ran his fingers through his damp hair. 'It's always the same at the end of a big project. There's a sort of dread attached to it. You've been chewing over the same thoughts for months or even years and they've worn thin. You can hardly remember what it was that excited you in the first

place and yet everyone's about to pick it over, looking for errors. I wonder if you ever get over it, the fear of failure.'

'Dr Pharoah once told me there were two different types of scientists. There's the single-minded and methodical, and the erratic but inspired. I'm single-minded and methodical, of course. That was why I minded so much when Pharoah said I was slovenly.'

They amused themselves, putting their mutual acquaintances into categories. Denis Padfield and Bill Farmborough had both been plodders, Alec said. He doubted if Farmborough had had an original idea in twenty years.

'Martin was erratic but inspired, obviously. Jan Kaminski had a good mind but Pharoah dumped all the administrative work on him so he didn't have the time to do original research. Pharoah might have liked to portray Gildersleve Hall as a breeding ground of genius, but there were only ever one or two people there of any real talent.' Alec swirled round the last half inch of coffee in his cup. 'Redmond was the one who had the reputation when Gildersleve first started up. Kaminski once told me that Redmond never forgot anything. He could refer word for word to a book he'd read ten years earlier.'

Alec put on his jacket and dropped his keys and wallet into a pocket. As they left the flat, he said, 'Perhaps Redmond was sidelined because he didn't fit in. He was a bit of a commie and I don't suppose that helped. There was an argument once, in the dining room. Some fellow from the Treasury came to dinner and Redmond had a go at him. He

still believed all that communist claptrap – the death of capitalism, common ownership of the means of production, the whole lot.'

They walked to the Tube station. Buses lumbered along the road; through their mud-flecked windows, Ellen saw the blurred shapes of tired people, slumped in their seats. It occurred to her that whatever discussions had taken place in the dining room of Gildersleve, she would not have been privy to them, because women had not been allowed to dine there. She was aware of a sudden distaste, along with a feeling of relief that she had left Gildersleve. Other scientific institutions might not have the same prestige but neither did they treat their female staff with such casual contempt.

'Kaminski disapproved of Redmond's communism,' said Alec. He held her hand as they headed down the steps into the ticket hall. 'After all, his country was pretty well torn apart by the Russians. In the war, Redmond's politics would have been overlooked because we were all supposed to be on the same side. Times have changed, though.'

Alec bought tickets; on the escalator Ellen stood one step in front of him. His hand rested lightly on her shoulder and she threaded her fingers between his. Alec was right: with the coming of the Cold War times had changed, and America in particular no longer welcomed those with left-wing leanings.

Waiting on the platform they stood face to face, her hands tucked into his jacket pockets. They talked of their

futures, which had, over the passing months, come to exist not in parallel but to converge.

A hot, rushing wind, and a train drew into the platform. The carriage was crowded and they had to stand by a door. His arms steadied her as the train rocked and screamed through the tunnels.

And she heard him say, 'I want you to come to Scotland with me, Ellen. I want you to meet my mother. And I wondered, would you marry me? Would you? I know we haven't been seeing each other all that long, but why wait? I knew after a week, didn't you?' She saw in his eyes a mixture of hope and anxiety. 'I don't know how we'll work it out, but it's what I want. Is it what you want too, Ellen?'

And she could only say with utter certainty, 'Yes, Alec. Oh yes.'

Chapter Seven

Michael's father had died. When he returned to London after the funeral, India went out for a drink with him, to keep him company. They went to the Colony Room, which Michael said was a good place for getting plastered.

He told her about the funeral. 'Awful. No grace or meaning. And no one could sing the hymns. We're a tune-less lot, the Colebrooks.'

'I've never been to a funeral. They didn't let Sebastian and me go to our mother's because they thought we were too young.'

His round black robin's eyes studied her. 'You haven't missed much. Dismal affairs.' He gave a cackle of laughter. 'I suppose that's the idea.' He took two cigarettes out of a case, lit them both and passed one to India. 'I sometimes

think I envy the Catholics. At least there's some *passion*. But I don't, not really. Sex I approve of, but passion's dangerous. It makes people act out of character.'

A naval rating with a sweet, smooth boy's face asked Michael for a light and Michael passed him his cigarette. Then he said to India, 'A little bird told me someone had seen you with Marcus Pharoah,' and she shot him a glance.

'Do you know him?'

'I wouldn't say that I *know* him.' The sailor handed back the cigarette and Michael smiled at him. 'I've met him at the odd dinner or reception. But of course, one knows who he is. Did you know that he's divorcing his wife? Or I think it may be the other way round, she's divorcing him. He has rather a reputation.'

'Are you warning me off, Michael?'

'I'm telling you to be careful, that's all. Pharoah has a public face. If it became known that you and he were having an affair—'

'We're not.'

'People will assume that you're having an affair, India,' said Michael gently. 'There'll be gossip. Actually, there already is.'

If it was not a love affair, this thing between her and Marcus, then what was it? It was not a friendship, that was for sure. They quarrelled as often as they were nice to each other, and though Marcus might not have so much as kissed her, she knew that he wanted to.

Sometimes she thought she should have tried harder

at school. Then she could have been a nurse or a teacher or something like that. Then she would have been respectable. She had always meant to be respectable, could never quite work out how it had turned out otherwise. Marcus Pharoah was cool, watchful, elegant and powerful. Though these qualities attracted her, they disquieted her as well. India acknowledged power but at the same time saw it as a threat. Confronted by it, naked and gleaming, she found herself compelled to wriggle out of its hold.

Coming out of Glasgow, Alec and Ellen headed north towards Loch Lomond. Their pace slowed to accommodate the winding road which ran along the foot of the mountains where the steep, rocky slopes were darkly wooded or dense with russet-coloured bracken. To the other side of the car, the houses and trees parted now and then to reveal an island or a castle and the shining black surface of the water.

At Ardlui they stopped to drink tea in a hotel on the north end of the loch. When they had finished they stretched their legs in the hotel garden, walking down to where shrubs with dark green leathery leaves walled a narrow path that led to the shore. A yacht, white sails belling in the wind, tacked in the breeze. Standing by the chill water, Ellen's touch went instinctively to the ring on the third finger of her left hand. She and Alec had chosen it together, three diamonds on a gold band.

Back to the car and then on and on, through Crianlaroch and Tyndrum, beside mountains that rose in gaunt grey peaks to the sky, their slopes scarred by falls of scree or forested by birch and rowan. Rivers meandered through flat-bottomed valleys that even in the afternoon sunshine seemed barren, bleak and ominous, or rushed and cascaded from the heights of rock and boulder, catching the light and fragmenting it to crystal.

On again, through the port of Oban, past its harbour and hotels, and then along a narrow road that rose and fell with the contours of the hills. When another vehicle came towards them, Alec had to tuck the car up on to the verge to allow it to pass. The shores of a sea loch, strewn with bladderwrack, glittered in the fading sunshine, and fir trees made a dense impenetrable mass that fell away suddenly, revealing a sea dotted with distant blue-green islands. In the garden of a white cottage, a woman unpegged washing from a line as a flurry of rain smudged the windscreen of the car. The sun came out from behind the clouds and a rainbow shimmered before dissolving into the air.

They drove over the arched stone bridge that spanned the distance between the mainland and Seil Island. It was nicknamed the bridge over the Atlantic, Alec told her, because the water that ran through the narrow channel flowed from the Atlantic Ocean. On the island, more low white buildings – a pub, a shop, a church – clustered round the far end of the bridge, and then the road headed

away from the small settlement, threading beside marsh-land where reeds swayed, feathery and fringed, and past derelict, roofless stone buildings, before winding up again into the hills. Sheep dotted the upper fields and the trees that grew on the windswept tops had bent and twisted, stooping low to keep their grip on the earth. And Ellen felt that sense of freedom that comes from the unearthli-ness of islands, from being cut off from solidity and the everyday.

As the car reached the summit of the hill, Alec braked and pulled into the side of the road. In the time it had taken them to drive from Oban, dusk had fallen. They looked down from the high ground to the coast, to a silken sea and the wide, inky sky beyond. Cliffs jutted, one behind the other, like wings on a stage set, enclosing a bay, and a strange landscape of fields and ponds and stone heaps scat-tered the shallow coastal plain. Ellen saw a dozen low, white houses as well as a few more substantial buildings. Some of the houses had small, square gardens, thickly walled, thrown like deckled grey playing cards over the undulating grass.

Where the land met the sea the sand appeared to have been scorched, burned to a band of black rubble which pushed itself up into jagged rocks on to which waves rushed and sprayed. In other places the shoreline had narrowed to a charcoal-coloured ribbon. Sheets of water, enclosed by black barricades, made glassy lakes, some square in shape, others circular or oblong. The last of the

sunlight trembled on the horizon, leaving behind it a streak of luminescence and an armada of islands, some sizeable, others little more than pinnacles of rock, a few huddled close to the coast of Seil, others evanescent fragments, almost lost in the distance.

She turned to Alec in delight. 'It's so glorious.'

'Isn't it? Nearly home now.' His hand ran along her thigh. 'I'm afraid we're going to have to be on our best behaviour for the next week.'

'No creeping through the corridors at night?'

'My mother's very conventional about such things.' They were kissing. 'She's a regular churchgoer.'

'I wouldn't dream of trespassing on her hospitality.'

'I shall dream about it every night.'

The hoot of a car horn; Alec pulled away, gave a wave to the driver of the vehicle. 'That's Bill Maclean,' he said. 'He rents land from my mother.'

He put the car into gear, pulled back on to the road and headed downhill. Ellen breathed in the salty sharpness of the sea. They followed the road round the perimeter of the bay, slowing as they reached a gate set between two tall hedges.

'Home at last,' said Alec, and swung the car up a steep driveway.

It was impossible in the dusk to tell the extent of the gardens that surrounded Kilmory House, but as they headed up the drive Ellen saw lawns and borders unfolding to either side of the car. And then the drive swung round in

a wide curve through trees, and there was the house itself, larger than the other houses Ellen had seen on the island, long, two-storeyed and white-walled, its roofs a series of slated gables.

Light shone through a front window and a lamp was lit in the gravel courtyard where a Land Rover was parked beside a pair of stone urns. Then the front door opened and a black Scottie dog shot out, yapping. A small, slim, dark-haired woman followed it.

'Hamish! *Heel*.'

Alec climbed out of the car. 'Hello, Mother.'

When they embraced, the top of his mother's head barely reached Alec's chin. Mrs Hunter reached out her fingertips to touch her son's face. 'Darling, I was so worried. Did you have a dreadful journey? I've been expecting you for hours. I was afraid there'd been an accident. Those roads . . .'

'There was some heavy traffic in Glasgow and we stopped at Ardlui for tea, that's all. Ellen needed a break.' Alec put his arm round Ellen's shoulders. 'Mother, meet Ellen.'

Mrs Hunter took Ellen's hand. 'Welcome to Kilmory House, dear. Alec's told me so much about you.'

'It's very kind of you to invite me to your home, Mrs Hunter.'

'Och, it's no trouble at all. Alec's friends are always welcome.' Mrs Hunter laughed and put a hand to her throat. 'So silly of me, sitting indoors all afternoon, waiting for

the pair of you! And on such a wonderful fine day! I didn't dare go out, because I was sure that the moment I so much as slipped through the door to buy a bottle of milk you'd turn up.'

Alec looked concerned. 'We wouldn't have minded. You shouldn't have stayed indoors because of us.'

'Dear, I wanted to be here to welcome you, that's all. And Catriona very kindly offered to fetch the milk.'

'Cat's here?'

'Yes, she came home for a wee break. I knew you'd want to see her so I asked her to supper. But we mustn't stand out here chatting, Ellen will catch cold.'

Alec carried the suitcases into the house. The hallway was tiled in slate and panelled with dark wood. On a side table stood a bowl of tulips and two photographs, one of Alec, dressed for hiking, against a background of hills and sky, the other a portrait of a man in naval uniform.

In the better light inside the house, Ellen was able to see Mrs Hunter more clearly. Her features were regular and finely cut, and her eyes were Alec's, dark blue and almond-shaped. Her wavy dark hair was streaked with iron-grey and her complexion was tanned and seamed with a cobweb of lines. She was wearing a tweed skirt and a blue woollen jersey, on the collar of which was pinned an agate brooch bordered with pearls.

Mrs Hunter showed Ellen upstairs. The room in which she was to stay for the next week was at the front of the

house. Ellen, who felt guilty, remembering the stop at Ardlui because she had wanted to see Loch Lomond properly instead of through a window of a car, as well as an earlier break to buy postcards, exclaimed about the freshness of the decor and the warmth of the fire in the grate.

'I'm afraid we still need a fire, even in May,' said Mrs Hunter. 'No doubt in London you'll be throwing windows open to let in the sun. Come down when you're ready, dear. Take your time. There's no need to rush for our sakes.' She left the room.

Ellen rushed. She unpacked her suitcase, shaking out clothes crumpled from their two-day journey, and hung them in the wardrobe. She would have loved to have soaked in a hot bath but instead quickly washed, cleaned her teeth, brushed her hair, and changed into a green and white striped blouse that seemed to have survived its incarceration in the case without too many creases. Then she powdered her nose and reapplied lipstick. She wondered who Catriona was. Alec had not mentioned her before. A schoolfriend, perhaps, or a neighbour's daughter.

A last quick glance in the mirror and then she left the room. On the landing, Chinese vases stood on the side tables, and oil paintings, seascapes mostly, hung on the walls. The corridor wound through the building, doors leading off it to more rooms, and there were unexpected steps as the floor changed level. The house had a settled look, as if what was contained inside it had been there for generations. The

hollows in the crimson-brown wood of the stair treads reinforced the impression of permanence.

She found Alec in the drawing room, talking to a tall, thin man with whitening fair hair and a weatherbeaten face. He was introduced to Ellen as Donald Frazer, a friend of the family.

Alec poured her a sherry. 'Cat's helping my mother with the supper,' he said.

The predominant feature of the room was a floor-to-ceiling, five-sided bay window. Chairs and sofas were arranged inside the window, which looked out over the bay, where a dull bronze light now delineated the horizon. Standing at the window, Alec told her the names of the islands, which were melting into the darkening sea and sky. On a fine day, he said, you could see as far as Islay.

The door opened and a tall, slim young woman came into the room. 'Marguerite's made far too much, as usual,' she announced. 'We shall all have to stuff ourselves silly.'

'Cat,' said Alec, 'come and meet Ellen, my fiancée. Ellen Kingsley, this is Catriona Campbell.'

Catriona's long, dark, curling hair was caught back in a ponytail and tied with a navy-blue ribbon. Her eyes were well-shaped and thickly lashed, and her pale complexion was flushed pink along the cheekbones. She was wearing a simple pleated kilt and an oatmeal-coloured jersey, no jewellery, and, so far as Ellen could tell, no make-up.

'Welcome to Seil Island, Miss Kingsley,' said Catriona,

taking Ellen's hand. 'We've all been dying to meet the girl who's captured Alec's cold heart at last.'

'Unfair,' said Alec, smiling.

'It's perfectly true and you know it. What's your secret, Miss Kingsley? I shall have to find out. Alec, you never alter a jot. So unfair to those of us who are growing grey.' Catriona's hands had come to rest on Alec's shoulders. Her lips pressed against his, then she spun away.

'I'm dying for a drink,' she said. 'Not that frightful muck, Donald.' Mr Frazer had opened the sherry bottle. 'A proper drink.'

Catriona flung herself on to a sofa. Frazer handed Catriona a whisky. 'Go away and leave us in peace, Alec,' said Catriona. 'I want to talk to Miss Kingsley.' She patted the seat beside her and Ellen sat down. 'You must be exhausted. Seil Island's a long enough trek from Glasgow. It must be an awful fag from London.'

'Do you live in Glasgow, Miss Campbell?'

'I'm a nurse at the Royal Infirmary. I share a flat in Garnet Hill Street with some other girls.'

'Do you enjoy nursing?'

'Well enough.' Catriona grimaced. 'There are no jobs here. All the young people work on the mainland. Alec tells me you work in a hospital too.'

'Yes, in a clinical laboratory.'

'I'm sure that's much more glamorous than nursing. I'm a staff nurse, so I can leave all the bedpans and bed baths to the juniors, thank goodness. There's a ward sister's

post going but I can't decide whether to apply. The pay would be better but all the ward sisters are old battleaxes. I can't help thinking it goes with the job, like a dark blue uniform.'

Ellen laughed. 'I can't imagine you a battleaxe, Miss Campbell.'

'Can't you?' Miss Campbell raised her eyebrows. 'I can. Sometimes, when it's been a hard day and I'm tired and I want to go home, I hear myself barking out orders to the pros in that tone of voice. You know – impatient, fed up with having to say the same thing twice. When I was a pro, I used to hate it when staff nurses spoke to me like that.' Catriona took a mouthful of her drink, closed her eyes and gave a satisfied smile. 'Mmm. I'll say this for Marguerite, she always keeps a good whisky in the house. But I promise I won't talk about work any more. It's such a relief not to have patients moaning at me for a day or two, so I'm not going to spoil my break by thinking about them for a moment.'

'Does your family still live on the island?'

Catriona nodded to the window. 'You see those lights over there on the far side of the bay? That's our house. My father was the doctor for the islands until he retired two years ago. If I look out my bedroom window when I wake up and can see Kilmory House, I know it's going to be a fine morning. If I can't see it then we're in for some lousy weather. But I don't mind the bad weather here. You can start the day in a rainstorm and by the end of it you'll be

sitting in the sun. In Glasgow, it can rain all day, never stops, such rain and greyness.'

'This is such a beautiful part of the world. You must miss it.'

'Oh, I wouldn't say that I particularly miss the *island*.' Catriona's eyes, hazel flecked with green, met Ellen's. 'When Marguerite told me you and Alec were driving up, I thought of trying to cadge a lift from Glasgow. But it seemed a bit of a nerve, asking you to put up with an old girlfriend in the back of the car.'

Old girlfriend. Well, that was something Alec hadn't thought to mention. Ellen said, 'We wouldn't have minded at all. Perhaps on our way home.'

'How long will you be here?'

'A week.'

'A *week*. Goodness, how brave of you. I'm only staying a couple of nights. I've become rather attached to civilization — cafés and cinemas and decent shops, things like that.' Catriona touched Ellen's hand. 'How dreadful of me. I haven't congratulated you on your engagement. I hope you and Alec will both be very happy.' She gave a sideways glance towards the door then lowered her voice. 'You must ask yourself, though, whether you and *Marguerite* can ever be happy.'

Before Ellen could swallow her surprise at the remark and respond, Catriona went on, 'I'm dying for a cigarette but Marguerite doesn't approve of women smoking. Do you think we dare nip out for a fag? No, better not, I can

hear a clanking of pots and pans, can't you? Supper must be nearly ready.'

Over a meal of Scotch broth followed by roast lamb and apple tart, Donald Frazer, tapping his plate for emphasis, told Ellen the history of the slate industry on the islands, from its modest beginnings in the late eighteenth century and its glory days in the mid-nineteenth, when the slate had been excavated from the deep quarries and taken by steamer all over the world, to its decline and eventual closure.

'You'll see the disused quarries on the island, Miss Kingsley,' he said. 'They've all been flooded for years. There was a tidal wave towards the end of the last century which drove the sea into them. They tried to get them working again, but it was the beginning of the end. They were buying slates more cheaply from other parts of the world by then anyway. That was the death knell for Seil and the other slate islands. When the industry died, the exodus of people began. It's when the young people leave,' he added, echoing what Catriona Campbell had said earlier that evening, 'that's when a place begins to die.'

'Nonsense, Donald,' Mrs Hunter said briskly. 'Dying, indeed. Stop your maundering and eat your dinner.'

The conversation moved on to some roof tiles that needed replacing, a storm-damaged tree that Alec must lop the branches from. Ellen took little part in the conversation and so was able to reflect on Catriona's earlier comment.

You must ask yourself, though, whether you and Marguerite can ever be happy. It seemed to her an extraordinary thing to say, especially on a first meeting. And it made little sense: it was Alec she was marrying, not Marguerite.

And yet she was troubled, because since she and Alec had arrived at Kilmory House, Mrs Hunter had not mentioned their engagement. It was of course possible that Alec and his mother had spoken of it while Ellen had been upstairs, changing, but it had been Catriona who had raised a glass of wine to them at the beginning of the meal. And although Mrs Hunter had joined in the toast, she had moved the conversation briskly on. 'Alec's friend', Mrs Hunter had called her, on their arrival, and for a strange, skewed moment Ellen had found herself questioning whether Alec had told his mother of the engagement – he had a habit, after all, of keeping his emotional cards close to his chest. But of course he had, she remembered him telling her that he had written, and the principal reason for this visit to Scotland had been to introduce his mother to his future wife. And yet it seemed odd that Mrs Hunter had not yet asked them about their wedding plans. Could it be that she disapproved of the engagement? No, far more likely that she was simply waiting for a quieter moment.

After they had dined, Mrs Hunter refused their offers of help with the clearing-up, though she permitted Mr Frazer to carry the dirty dishes into the kitchen and fetch logs for the fire. Alec suggested to Ellen they get a breath of

fresh air. Crossing the garden, holding his hand, the blades of grass brushed against her ankles and every nerve end tingled with anticipation of their kiss.

Moonlight sketched out the perimeter of a pond and the statue of a girl standing amid the slender white trunks of silver birches. Their leaves whispered, making a faint percussion.

Alec patted the stone girl's head. 'Meet wee Jeanie. Cat and I once put one of Donald's old pipes in her mouth and a box of matches in her hand. I thought my mother would go through the roof when she saw it, but fortunately she saw the funny side.'

'Catriona told me that you and she used to date.'

'Did she?' His gaze flicked back to the house. 'That was years ago. We were just wee bairns.' A smile curled his mouth. 'Come here.' They kissed, then he said, 'So what do you think of my island?'

'I like it very much.'

'I wondered whether you might find it . . .'

'What?'

'Too cut off. We are rather perched on the edge of the Atlantic.'

A voice called out, 'Dear me, caught out. I won't tell if you won't, Alec,' and they pulled apart. A pinpoint of bobbing orange light close to the house told Ellen that Catriona had succeeded in escaping outdoors for a smoke. As they walked back through the garden, Catriona detached herself from the wall against which she was leaning, scuffed

the cigarette stub beneath the sole of her shoe, and went back inside with them.

Her mind refused to settle, lying in bed that night. Images from the day darted through her head: the white-sailed yacht on Loch Lomond, the translucent waters of the shores of Loch Feochan. And Catriona, breezing into the sitting room of Kilmory House and kissing Alec. Had he not spoken of Miss Campbell because he had thought her unimportant? Or because they had at one time been close? In Catriona's teasing attitude to Alec Ellen thought she glimpsed something more than the ordinary fondness of friendship. Her imagination created a much younger Alec and Catriona, walking hand in hand along Seil's black beaches or embracing by a stormy sea.

And yet it was hard to picture Catriona capable of holding Alec's interest for long. Alec might come from a remote part of Scotland but his tastes were sophisticated. Catriona's simple clothing and freshly scrubbed face were in contrast to Andrée Fournier's cool elegance. And she had detected a hardness in Catriona that surely must eventually displease; it had shown itself in a fondness for mockery and the cynical manner with which she had spoken of her patients at the hospital.

A flurry of rain washed against the window. Ellen thought she heard from somewhere in the house light footsteps padding across floorboards. She listened, eyes open in the darkness. It must be the dog, Hamish. She rolled on to her

side, pulled the eiderdown over her head, and drifted off to sleep.

The next morning there were puddles in the courtyard, but the skies had cleared and the sea in the bay was calm. Looking out of her bedroom window, Ellen saw the garden, washed with rain, glittering in the sunlight. She breathed in the cool air, noticing the absence of traffic noise and fumes. Her eye was drawn to a mass of blood-red flowers, vivid against dark conifers. Above were paths and terraces and flower borders, but she found her gaze dropping back to that crimson smear over the hillside.

She glanced at her watch. It was half past nine. Quickly, she washed and dressed and then went downstairs. The house was silent. In the dining room she saw that the table had been cleared: she must have slept through breakfast. A lonely piece of toast cooled on a plate, so she ate it, then left the room. She paused in the hall, her eye caught by the two photographs on the side table. The snapshot of Alec showed him glancing back over his shoulder, one hand raised in salute, a smile touching the corners of his mouth, as if the photographer had taken him by surprise. She wondered who had taken it. Mrs Hunter, perhaps. Or Catriona.

She picked up the other photograph, of the man in naval uniform, and looked at it more closely. This picture was formal in character, a studio portrait, she guessed. The naval officer appeared to be older than Alec was now. Strikingly

good-looking, his piercing, direct gaze was searching, almost severe.

A voice said, 'He was a handsome man, don't you think?'

She looked up. Mrs Hunter was standing in the doorway. 'Is this Alec's father?' asked Ellen.

'That's my husband,' said Marguerite. 'That's Francis.'

'What was he like?'

'He was wonderful. Francis taught me everything. I was nothing before I met him, a silly wee creature who didn't know a thing about life. He told me what to wear and how to behave and what books to read. He was my whole life and I would have given my own life for him.' She took the photograph from Ellen, ran her handkerchief over the glass, then replaced the frame on the table.

'I'm sorry.' She wasn't sure why she was apologizing – for disrupting the arrangement of photographs or for Mrs Hunter's widowhood. 'I hope you'll forgive me for missing breakfast,' she said. 'I'm afraid I overslept. I don't know what happened, I hardly ever oversleep.'

Mrs Hunter smiled. 'No doubt you were tired after your journey. Shall I cook you some breakfast or would you like to see my garden first?'

'I'd love to see the garden. Where's Alec?'

'I've sent him to Oban for some messages. We didn't like to disturb you and I'm always so thankful when he's home with his car. It's a hard business for me, getting things from the shops. Mr Fleming comes round with his

van, but he doesn't stock everything. Our little shop does its best, of course.'

'Don't you drive, Mrs Hunter?'

'Oh no.' A tinkling laugh. 'Francis did all the driving. He was a wonderful man with a car, he kept it going whatever the weather. Donald Frazer put the car away in the garage for me after Francis died and, do you know, when Alec was old enough to learn, the motor started the first time he tried it.'

Ellen expressed suitable admiration.

Marguerite said, as they went outside, 'Are you a gardener yourself, Miss Kingsley?'

'I'm afraid not. Do please call me Ellen.'

'And you must call me Marguerite.'

The stone slabs in the courtyard had been sheened to a satiny purplish-grey by the night's rain. Prisms of light danced on the lawn. In the sunshine, Ellen's fears of the previous evening seemed groundless. She and Marguerite Hunter needed time to get to know each other, that was all. The relationship between future mother-in-law and daughter-in-law was bound to be a delicate one.

A movement caught her eye and Ellen saw the Scottie dog rush out from behind a thicket. 'Here, Hamish!' Mrs Hunter called. 'He likes to chase rabbits. He's never caught one yet, but he likes to try.'

'I thought I heard him last night, running about the house.'

'Oh, I think you were mistaken, Ellen.' Mrs Hunter picked

a browned bud from a shrub as she passed. 'I always shut Hamish in the kitchen at night. I don't believe in a dog having the run of a house.'

The lawns were bordered by rockeries and flower beds. Ellen saw, looking up, that paths and terraces had been cut into the steep hill that rose up behind Kilmory House. They were heading up the slope, beyond the silver birches, past the statue of the girl beside which she and Alec had kissed the previous night.

'The garden was quite neglected when Francis inherited the house,' explained Marguerite. 'Francis was a keen gardener, like myself. He dug out all the terraces himself. When there's heavy rain, the soil can slip down the hillside, so you have to shore up the terraces. Not one of Francis's terraces has ever fallen down.'

'It must have been hard work.'

'He was never afraid of that. He was a practical man. I admire a practical man.'

They were passing the banks of shrubs, with their dark red blooms, that Ellen had seen from her bedroom window. In the shade, pearls of dew still clung to the scarlet petals.

'What are these?' she asked.

'These? They are my pride and joy. You've chosen a good time to see my garden, Ellen. It's at its best at this time of year, when the rhododendrons and azaleas are out. Kilmory House is famous for them. You can see them in blossom from the far side of the bay, as clear as rubies.'

They continued to walk up the hillside. Moss-covered

stones lay at the sides of the path and the streams that rushed between the rocks were bordered by ferns. The path climbed steeply on, higher and higher, into the trees, narrowing so that they had to go in single file. Marguerite led the way. The older woman was quick and agile on the paths she must know so well, and she had a wiry strength that belied her age and slight figure. Ellen's indoor shoes, not bought for rough walking, struggled to gain purchase on the damp stones. When she glanced back over her shoulder, she saw the slate roof of the house below.

Beneath the covering of trees, the air was colder and the shadows darker. A brown blanket of needles had spread itself out beneath the red trunks of the pines and there was a woody, resinous scent. Pale green lichens frilled the branches. A bridge straddled a rocky gorge where a stream surged and bubbled.

High on the escarpment, a hedge of evergreens parted to reveal another terrace. Clay pots stood to either side of a paved area, some planted with spring bulbs. A small wooden summerhouse, its front open to the elements, sheltered a table and two chairs.

'This is Catriona's favourite place,' said Marguerite. 'She'll sit here for hours sometimes. I call it her hidey-hole.' Marguerite went to stand at the edge of the terrace. 'Come and see the view, Ellen.'

'I'll stay here, I think.'

'You mustn't worry. You'll be quite safe.'

Yet her heart was thudding. Was it because of the steep

climb up the hillside or was it her awareness of the abyss just a few yards away? Or could it be the implacability she sensed in Marguerite, a spirit that was relentless and unalterable?

'I'm afraid I dislike heights,' she said, and sat down on one of the chairs in the summerhouse. After a few minutes, Marguerite joined her.

'It must be difficult for you, managing on your own,' said Ellen.

'It is, sometimes. It's a big place for one person. But I wouldn't live anywhere else. Donald is a good sort and helps me with the heavy work. And Alec comes home every month.'

'And I'm sure we'll try our best to continue to do so after we're married.'

A jolt seem to run through the older woman's body, as if she had put her hand to a nettle. Ellen said gently, 'I love Alex very much, Mrs Hunter. And I intend to make him very happy.'

Marguerite's gaze, which had been fixed ahead of her, moved slowly across the vista before coming to rest on Ellen.

'Aye, I'm sure you mean well.'

The shock of those words did not have time to die away before Ellen heard a sound, footsteps and then the rustle of branches. Looking round, she saw Alec coming up the path through the trees towards them.

*   *   *

'Where are we going?'

Marcus Pharoah had been waiting outside the café after India finished work. This evening, he was driving a big black car instead of the green Austin-Healey.

'My flat,' he said as he put the car into gear.

'I didn't know you had a flat.'

'I don't care for hotels.'

'I'd rather go to a restaurant.'

'No.' His gaze flicked to her, then back to the traffic. 'I'm not in the mood for that.'

'But I'm hungry.' It came out as a whine.

He suppressed a sigh and said, with the exaggerated patience one might use when speaking to a difficult child, 'My housekeeper will have left a cold meal. And it's all right, you don't have to worry about your dubious virtue. I'm not in the mood for that sort of tussle tonight either.'

Dubious virtue. She wondered whether to be outraged. 'You don't sound as if you're in the mood for company at all, Marcus.'

'Most company, no. But if I were to spend the evening on my own then I would drink too much, and I dislike the thought of that.'

Through the windscreen, she watched Hampstead Road peel by. 'Why me?'

'I tried to think who I could tolerate and yours was the only name I came up with.' He gave a sour smile. 'I wonder whether it's because in some ways you remind me of

myself. You have a need to enhance the world, and you employ a certain economy with the truth.'

Something in his eyes, some knowledge or intimacy, made her look away. 'Stop it, Marcus.'

'That ridiculous cottage you've made up.' A wave of his hand. 'The meadow . . . the orchard.'

'Applegarth?'

'Yes, Applegarth. A tip for the future. If you're going to lie, don't over-elaborate. It's always more convincing if you don't stray too far from the truth.'

'Applegarth is true.'

'No, it isn't.' He sounded tired rather than angry. 'You might like Applegarth to exist, but it doesn't. Applegarth is a fantasy, as are the loving mother and the father in the diplomatic corps and the holidays abroad.'

She made a sound; he interrupted. 'I like to know what's going on. And I'm good at finding things out.'

So am I, she thought. You don't come from the sort of places I've come from without learning to watch your back.

She said, 'You didn't tell me you were getting divorced.'

'No, I didn't.'

'It's a big thing to leave out.'

'Yes, I suppose it is.'

He changed down gear to stop for a zebra crossing. A couple walked over it, the woman pushing a pram. India considered climbing out of the car and running away, as she had so often done before, but what then?

Instead she said, 'I'm a little tired, you see, Marcus, of being for amusement only.'

'I've never thought of you in that way. I don't know whether you're able to believe that, but it's the truth.'

He started up the car again, heading along Chalk Farm Road. They drove into Belsize Park. Outside a red-brick block of mansion flats, Pharoah slowed the car to a halt. It had rained earlier that day and puddles sheened the tarmac.

Inside the building, a porter greeted them and opened the lift for them. The flat was on the third floor. Pharoah unlocked the front door and they went inside.

In the sitting room, he took glasses from a sideboard and mixed drinks. The room was sparsely furnished in a masculine style: a shelf of books, a stack of records, architectural prints on the walls. Everything was polished and perfect. A plant in a shiny black bowl stood on the coffee table, its long, filigreed, lime-green petals reflecting in the polished surface.

'It's an orchid,' said Pharoah, following her gaze. 'I forget which type. Alison grows them, it's a hobby of hers. Perhaps I should send it back to her. I'll be living here from now on, you see. Alison insists.'

'Do you mind?'

'About losing the Barton house? No, not particularly.'

'I meant about the divorce. You look as if you mind.'

'Only for Rowena's sake.' He handed a glass to India. 'I mind that she should suffer because of me and I mind that

308

some of the mud will inevitably stick to her. Most of all, I mind a great deal that I shall inevitably see less of her.'

'I'm sorry, Marcus.'

He gave a shrug of acknowledgement. 'I spent the afternoon at my lawyer's. A dispiriting experience. I didn't think Alison would take it so far. She wants me to suffer and she knows what to do to make it hurt.' His gaze, dark and brooding, flicked in her direction. 'What is it? I'm boring you, aren't I? I expect you'd prefer me to be treating you to a good dinner and telling you how beautiful you are. I'll make it up to you, I promise. Though, come to think of it, perhaps I'm tired of being for amusement only too. We seem to have gone on like this for some time, don't we?'

'"Like this"?'

'Playing our respective games.'

'What would you prefer?'

'A greater degree of honesty between us. You know, you tell me about the skeletons in your cupboard and I'll admit to some of mine.' A flash of a humourless smile. 'A pact between thieves, if you like. A useful metaphor, wouldn't you agree?'

India, feeling suddenly wary, did not respond.

'Your first boarding school,' he said. 'You were expelled for stealing, weren't you?'

Her heart tripped. She put down the glass and made for the door. But he, too, moved quickly, intercepting her, the flat of his hand against the door, preventing her from opening it.

'I told you,' he said softly. 'I like to know.'

'Let me go!'

'I'm not judging you, India. I've taken a few things I shouldn't have in my time. Not sweets from shops – bigger things than that.'

Tears of humiliation stung behind her lids; she swung away and sat back down on the sofa. 'It was a long time ago,' she muttered. 'It's nothing to do with you.'

'I'd rather hoped it was by now.'

She scrabbled in her bag for her handkerchief; Pharoah offered her his own. She rubbed at her face with it, streaking it with mascara, and said harshly, 'You think you know everything about me, but you don't. You don't know anything at all. People like you, you haven't a clue.'

'Then tell me.'

She shook her head, took her cigarettes out of her bag, lit one, and went to stand at the window, smoking. It was nearly dark and she could see the headlamps of the cars on the road. She would like to go away, she thought, far, far away. But then, Sebastian.

She heard him say, 'Let me tell you what I know already. I know that your mother was called Lucinda Taylor and that she was a dancer. Your father, Ralph Mayhew, was killed in the Blitz and your mother died of heart disease a year and half after that. After she died, you and your brother were sent to an orphanage, but then your aunt, Rachel Taylor, took you in.'

A cyclist passed on the street below, light flicking

between the trees. London always looked melancholy at dusk, India thought.

She turned back to him. 'The way you say it, Marcus, you make it sound careless. And it was, in a way. We'd rather slipped through the cracks, Sebastian and I. But Rachel cared. She found us. She looked after us.'

'You loved her.'

'Yes, I did.' Looking back, India wondered whether Rachel had felt guilty for having lost contact with her younger sister, and for having been away, working in Scotland, when the police had called at the flat to tell her of Lucinda's death. They had left a note. It had been 1942 and a lot of people were dying.

'Rachel was lovely,' she said. 'She was kind and gentle and she was never cross with us, even when I was bad and even when Sebastian was ill. She had to travel a lot for her work, so Sebastian and I were sent to boarding schools.'

'But it didn't work out.'

'Not for Sebastian, no. And for me . . .' She shrugged. 'I didn't fit in. How could I have?'

'Was that why you stole? Because you disliked the school?'

'No, not at all. I told you you wouldn't understand.' She flicked ash on the carpet; irritably, Marcus slammed an ashtray on to the sill beside her. 'Now it's my turn to guess,' she said. 'I expect you had a family who loved you and looked after you. Being looked after is just as important as being loved, I know this. I don't suppose you ever went

hungry and I don't suppose you've ever known what it is to be completely alone. I'm sure you went to a good school and no doubt you were very clever. And then you probably went to Oxford or Cambridge, and I expect you were very clever there too.'

'Not a bad summary of my early career. I might add that I found my family stifling and that when I was fortunate enough to be encouraged by my chemistry teacher at school, I discovered what it was I wanted to do with my life.'

'How convenient, to have everything sorted out. Your brilliant career and your marriage to Alison. I shouldn't think you've ever had to worry about anything.'

'Not true,' he said. 'Actually.'

She sat down on the sofa beside him, tucking her feet beneath her. 'What?' she said scornfully. 'Maybe your cat was run over by a car. Maybe some girl you fell in love with was in love with someone else. It's a shame, but these things happen.'

'My first wife died a year after we were married.'

This shocked India. 'Oh. How awful. What happened?'

'An infection.' He gave a taut smile. 'No penicillin then. It was a long time ago, before the war.'

'You never said.'

'You and I, we don't exactly talk about the *substance* of life, do we, India? Rosanne and I were very young. I'd recently graduated from Cambridge and I was working in America at the time. We had that optimism that goes with

312

extreme youth, that absolute conviction that everything would work out well for us.' His mouth twisted. 'After it happened, I discovered that there is a glance that says *actually I'd rather not know*. People don't want to hear about such tragedies, it reminds them of the fragility of their own happiness. I returned to England as soon as I could. One or two good friends listened to me when I'd had too much to drink, but otherwise I never spoke about it. And do you know, soon enough it was almost as if it had never happened. As if it had been nothing more than a nightmare.'

India crawled a hand along the sofa and folded it over his. She felt the warmth of his hand in hers, a small connection that for the first time seemed to tie them together.

'I'm sorry about tonight.' He raised her hand and kissed it. 'I should have kept away from you. I'm in a foul mood, I'm afraid. I never loved Alison, I knew that when I married her. She was very beautiful – she still is – and I was very attracted to her, but I never loved her. I married her for several reasons, some good, some less so. At the time, I didn't think I was capable of loving any more. But I still wanted the other pleasures that marriage can bring – a home, a family. I've never liked living alone, I'm not made for it, and I hated the thought of spending the rest of my life a single man. I don't judge myself for that, and I don't think it was wrong of me, to want to wipe the slate clean and start again. Do you?'

She shook her head. 'What were the bad reasons?'

'Oh, money, what else?' He gave a wry smile. 'Money

and power – the two are inextricably linked. Alison comes from a wealthy family. By that time, I'd learned what money can do. And what I'd once thought would satisfy me – a position in some reputable university and the funds to pursue my own research – was no longer enough. I wanted more. I needed Alison's money to unlock my future. The Josephs are financiers and they had the social connections my own family lacked. You can only get so far through talent and hard work, I'd realized. You could say that I married Alison so that in the end I was able to have Gildersleve Hall.'

'Why is she divorcing you?'

'Because of my adultery. Do you want to know the gruesome details? There have been several affairs, I admit it. The first was during the war. Alison and Rowena spent the war years in the Lake District, in Alison's parents' country house, and celibacy has never much appealed to me. There have been others since. There was a girl a couple of years ago. Alison found out about her.'

'Does she know about us?'

'Not that I know, but it would make no difference if she did. She won't change her mind now. Alison is capable of great intransigence, she always has been.'

'You can't blame her, Marcus.'

'No.' He ran a hand across his eyes. 'Though it suited her, being Marcus Pharoah's wife. She has a lover, some City type she met on the hunting field. I thought of making it difficult for her, citing him in the divorce, but

my solicitor tells me it would be unwise. And besides, Rowena . . .'

She shuffled round to face him. 'What will you do now?'

'I shall try not to let her poison my daughter's mind against me. And I shall fight for Gildersleve.' He frowned. 'An occurrence can seem unfortunate, but if you take hold of it, take control, you can seize the advantage.'

'How confident you are, Marcus.' There was some mockery in her tone. 'Most of us lurch from one disaster to another, and here are you, like a captain of a ship.'

'Oh, I think you've learned to manipulate events very well, India. You know when to blow hot or cold. Clever women always do.' He scooped her up and sat her on his lap, studying her. 'I'm sorry, that sounded bitter. I wanted to avoid that. I suppose this will at least free us.'

'Us?'

'Yes. No need to hide away in corners any more. Perhaps I'll show you off.'

'Why?' she said coolly. 'For revenge?'

'Now, that would be cheap of me.' He brushed back her hair from her forehead.

'I thought it was me who was cheap, Marcus.'

'You? I don't think so.'

There was a heat in his voice, and as he touched his lips lightly against the curve of her neck he drew down the zip on the back of her dress. She closed her eyes, drawing in a breath, and he ran his hand down her back. He kissed her again, then eased first the sleeves of her dress over her

shoulders, and then the straps of her slip. 'No, I really don't think so,' he murmured. 'On the contrary, India, I've always had a feeling you might turn out to be rather costly.'

Riley and Ellen had, with reasonable speed, smoothed over the disagreement that had taken place after Ellen had told him that she was seeing Alec Hunter. Riley had made the running, phoning to apologize, knowing himself to be in the wrong. Ellen had forgiven him, he thought, because, intoxicated with love, she found it hard not to be happy.

They saw each other less frequently now. Ellen naturally spent most of her time with Alec. Emotionally, Riley had tried to take a few steps back. The news of her engagement to Alec Hunter had been a body blow and he had realized that a part of him had hoped that the relationship would not last. Which had been wrong of him. Ellen loved Alec Hunter. Forget her, he had told himself. Put her out of your mind, think about something else.

So he had thrown himself into his work. But that, also, frustrated him. Progress was painfully slow. Mr Rossiter still went around in his sharp suits and gold watch, and the two gangsters, White and Perlman, carried on their violent trade without hindrance. Among those of Riley's colleagues still investigating the death of George Clancy in the Great Dover Street warehouse, there was the feeling, sometimes voiced, that after almost six months they had reached a dead end.

Riley persevered, seeking out nuggets of fact and teasing

out connections. Though Clancy hadn't been an important man or an admirable man, nothing he had found out about him had suggested that he had deserved to die such a brutal, bloody death. The warehouse itself no longer existed. It had been demolished, and the land cleared to build houses and offices. The land was owned by a property company, of which David Rossiter was a director, but the gangster Bernie Perlman's name was also there on the title deeds.

Riley sat one evening at the bar of the Blue Duck night-club in Mayfair, spinning out a whisky, watching a skinny brunette in feathers and sequins bob around beneath a spotlight to the music of a three-piece band. The habitués of the nightclub, a mixture of businessmen and fading actors and the odd member of parliament, came and went. Two more evenings passed, and Bernie Perlman did not come to the club; two more evenings during which Riley acquired a headache from cheap whisky as well as a dislike of the song 'Blue Velvet', the skinny brunette's star number. Perhaps Perlman had gone on holiday and was sunning himself on some foreign beach. Perhaps his crimes had caught up with him and he was floating in the river, his feet encased in concrete, his short, fat corpse nibbled by whatever fish could cope with the Thames's poisonous brown water.

On Saturday night the Blue Duck was busy. Riley sat at a shady corner of the bar with a good view of the room. He chatted to a tough, vivacious woman in a shiny red

dress, who told him about her hair salons and her bad marriage. Then the woman in the red dress moved away and Riley's thoughts drifted, circling until they came to rest where they so often did, with Ellen.

Since her visit to Scotland, Riley had noticed an alteration in her mood. He had sensed for the first time reservations, doubts. 'I'm sure Marguerite would rather I wasn't a career woman, and I'm sure she'd prefer it if I were Scots,' she said to him one evening, when she called round. Her tone had been light, almost joking.

Give it time, he said to her. Mothers-in-law and daughters-in-law . . . Two women in love with the same man. She had smiled and changed the subject.

The skinny brunette had left the stage and the band was whipping up the first bars of 'That's Amore'. Half a dozen couples shuffled on to the dance floor. Riley's eye was caught by a flurry of people coming into the room. One of the larger tables had been kept clear by the nightclub staff and it was to here that the newcomers – half a dozen men and five young, dolled-up women – headed. Waiters hurried to pull out chairs, girls rushed off with drinks orders.

A short, plump man sat down in the chair with the best view of the dance floor. Riley recognized Bernie Perlman. One of Perlman's men hauled a blonde in a pink dress up to dance. Waitresses brought bottles of champagne to the table, and there was a popping of corks. The dark-haired girl sitting next to Perlman lolled her head on his shoulder,

closing her eyes. She looked, Riley thought, very young and very drunk.

Another man appeared in the doorway to the nightclub, then crossed the room to Bernie Perlman's table. As the spotlight circled and the newcomer was caught in its light, Riley saw his pale, pasty face, small, pink-lidded eyes and crew-cut ginger hair. *Like a spectre*: Sergeant Davies's words came back to him.

The man made his way to the table, then bent to murmur something in Bernie Perlman's ear. Perlman made an angry movement, dislodging the girl sleeping on his shoulder. With a shriek, she slid off the chair on to the floor, landing hard on her rear. The other guests roared with laughter.

Riley crossed the room to Perlman's table. He offered his hand to the girl sprawled on the floor and gave her a friendly smile as he helped her to her feet. Tears streaked sooty lines of mascara down her face. As she brushed herself down, Riley looked up and met the gaze of the ginger-haired man. Riley gave another smile, different in nature to the one he had given the girl, and then walked away.

India was dining at Le Caprice with Marcus Pharoah and his brother, Devlin.

Marcus said, 'Where's Louise?'

'She can't make it, I'm afraid.' Devlin Pharoah was reading the menu. 'She's not very well.'

'Liar,' said Marcus softly.

Devlin shrugged. 'You're asking a lot, Marc.'

The two men looked at each other. India wondered whether they were about to fight, and said, 'I'd like the fishcakes and a Bellini, please,' and Devlin Pharoah laughed and the moment passed.

'You have such immature tastes,' said Marcus. 'Nursery food and fizzy drinks.'

'Don't be grumpy. Anyway, if my tastes are immature, what does that say about you?'

'That I need to educate you.'

She made a derisive noise. 'Lots of people have tried to do that.'

'Have they? I had the impression you'd spent most of your life running wild.'

Devlin Pharoah said, 'I'm with Miss Mayhew. Nothing wrong with fishcakes and a Bellini. You hardly play by the rules yourself, Marcus,' he added pointedly.

'Unlike India, I like to give the impression of doing so.'

'I don't think so,' said Devlin. 'Not this time, anyway.'

Pharoah gave a smile. 'My little brother disapproves of you, India.'

'Not at all.' Devlin lounged in his chair, his dark eyes brimming with curiosity. 'I approve of Miss Mayhew completely. How could I not? She's utterly charming.'

'Thank you, Mr Pharoah.'

'Devlin, please.'

'Don't flirt, Dev. Disapproval I'll tolerate, but not that.'

The waiter came to take their order and the two brothers conferred over the wine list. Devlin Pharoah was slighter

and shorter than his elder brother and his arched brows and hooded eyes gave him the look of a genial demon, India thought.

A claret was ordered. When the waiter had gone, Marcus Pharoah said to Devlin, 'I'm surprised Louise has allowed you out with me.'

'I'm under strict instructions.'

'To do what?'

'To make you see sense, of course.' Devlin gave a wave of his hand. 'Don't worry, I've no intention of trying.'

'Has Alison been speaking to you?'

'To Louise. Thick as thieves those two, you know that.'

'She wouldn't have me back if I went down on bended knee and pleaded with her. Which I've no intention of doing. So why does she care what company I keep?'

Devlin said quietly, 'Because it humiliates her.'

Pharoah made an angry outbreath and looked away. Devlin turned to India and gave her an apologetic smile. 'I'm sorry, Miss Mayhew, to have this conversation in front of you. Marcus can be a difficult man to get hold of.'

'I don't mean,' explained India, 'to annoy anyone. Or to humiliate anyone.'

'I'm sure you don't.'

'We're just having fun, you know.'

Devlin's eyes glittered with amusement. 'Perhaps that's what gets people's backs up. It's a characteristic of the English, isn't it, resenting those who have fun. Our Puritan side.'

Marcus said, 'Rather ironic, you, Devlin, lecturing me on my morality.'

'As I said, I'm merely the messenger. Mercury, firing a warning shot across the bows.'

'Oh, I think I've already got the message. There must be half a dozen people here whom I would have said I knew reasonably well, and yet they've hardly acknowledged me.'

'You must do as you choose. But you'll pay a price for it.'

'One worth paying.' Reaching across the table, Pharoah took India's hand.

'So long as you're sure.'

'I am. Without reservation. How's that boy of yours?'

Devlin seemed to accept the change of subject. His expression soured. 'The school won't have him back next term.'

'What happened?'

'Some silly business with a girl. I've found a place in Scotland that'll take him. Miles from anywhere so no temptation in sight.'

'What does Rufus think of that?'

'He's refusing to go. I've told him it's either that or he comes to work for me.'

'And?'

Devlin shook his head. 'I don't know. We don't speak. He's out every night, God knows where he goes. He's a moody little bugger. I've stopped his allowance, that'll make him see sense. What about Rowena?'

'She's very well. Won a prize for her painting.'

'Clever girl.'

'I haven't seen her. Just letters and phone calls.' Pharoah's brooding gaze locked on to his brother's. 'Alison's making things difficult.'

'I told you, old boy, price to pay,' said Devlin softly.

'A couple of years' time and Rowena will be able to do as she likes. Anyway, she and Alison quarrel like cat and dog, they always have done.'

On the way back to the flat, in the taxi, they sat in silence, India's head against Marcus Pharoah's shoulder, his arm round her.

'Perhaps we should stop seeing each other,' she said.

'No.' His hand, which had been stroking her hair, paused.

'Just for a while.'

'Because some silly fools gossip?'

'Because,' she said, sitting up and twitching her frock into place, 'your wife won't let you see your daughter.'

'Even if you and I never saw each other again it would make no difference. Alison would still keep Rowena from me. She wants to punish me. No – she wants to destroy me.'

He fell silent, looking out of the taxi window, as the London streets slid by. India knew that he was deeply angry, that the conversation with his brother had angered him, and all this troubled her. She said, 'I should go home,' and he said more forcefully this time, 'No.'

'I haven't seen Sebastian for days.'

'I'm sure Sebastian will survive your absence for a few more hours. I need to talk to you, India, and I need some company for an hour or two. You can do what the hell you like afterwards.'

'Shall we have a drink somewhere?'

He shook his head.

'Or a dance?' she suggested.

'Now you're tormenting me.' He kissed her hand. 'I'd prefer to go back to the flat. I promise you a proper night out tomorrow to make up for it. Who knows, I might even attempt to steer you round the dance floor.'

In his flat, Pharoah made drinks. 'I may lose Gildersleve Hall,' he told her. 'I've fought against it, I've fought damned hard. But it eats money, has been doing so for years, and I simply don't have any more.'

'Because of the divorce?'

'Yes. I spent a long, dull morning with my accountant.' He loosened the knot of his tie. 'Lawyers and accountants, that's what my life has come to. I used to be able to borrow from Alison's family but, unsurprisingly, that source has dried up.'

'If you went to a bank—'

He gave a bitter laugh. 'If only it was that easy. They're like a coven of old witches, these City money men. A rumour goes round that you're short of cash and they won't give you the time of day. I've tried everything I can think of but I'm running out of ideas. I seem to have spent a great deal of the last ten years entertaining bores and

bureaucrats, trying to coax money out of them for Gildersleve, and now they slam doors in my face.'

He took a cigarette from a box on the sideboard. 'Alison's name is on the title deeds of Gildersleve Hall,' he said. 'Her father insisted when he helped me to buy the place.' He frowned. 'It's funny, I thought I'd mind more than I do. These things have a natural lifespan, perhaps. There was a time when I would have sold my soul for Gildersleve.' He gave a humourless laugh. 'Perhaps I did so.'

'What will you do?'

'I'm not sure yet. I've been offered a post at a university in America. But I've not given up on Gildersleve yet, damn them.' He struck his lighter. 'The Americans still believe in themselves. Look at us – we won the bloody war, but you wouldn't think so. We can't seem to shake off this wartime habit of cheeseparing economy. We have such small pleasures and small ambitions.'

'I don't think that's so bad,' she said. 'I used to long for a pair of proper nylons when I was at school. Just one pair. We had to wear black woolly stockings, you see.'

'The thought of you in black woolly stockings cheers me enormously, India.'

'Small pleasures . . . the restaurants, the sports car, the vintage wines . . . oh, and India.'

'You're mistaken, you know, in seeing yourself as a small pleasure.' As he spoke, he drew her to him, his hands on her bottom, pressing her against him. He said softly, 'It would mean giving up certain things, if I went away.'

'Your daughter.'

'Yes, Rowena.' His eyes were lit by dark flames. 'Perhaps it might not be such a bad idea to leave England for a few years. Let the fuss die down. But they haven't offered me enough money yet.' A smile played round the corners of his mouth. 'Not enough to tempt me away from certain small pleasures, anyway.'

Chapter Eight

In the middle of June, Ellen left the hospital to start a new job as a research assistant to a friend of Professor Malik's, Jerry Collins, a professor at London University. Jerry was American, a large man with wild, curly hair and an expansive good humour, whose big hands looked deceptively incapable of the delicate work that crystallography demanded. An expert in his field, his good humour and friendliness made him easy to get along with, and he and Ellen had hit it off from the interview.

Her task was to grow, mount and photograph crystals. She also supervised the young women who came into the lab to compute the immense and tedious calculations required for Professor Collins's work. Picking up her old occupations in the laboratory, making her solutions, examining her crystals under the microscope and noting down their flaws and measurements, she felt a deep sense of

peace, as if she had come back on course after being blown about by a storm.

At the end of June, Alec drove up to Seil Island. He went on his own; it had occurred to Ellen that if she held back and made sure that mother and son had time together, then Marguerite would have the chance to get used to their engagement. She had not told Alec of Marguerite's remark in Kilmory House's garden. *Aye, I'm sure you mean well.* It seemed better to keep it to herself. Indeed, returning to London, she had questioned whether she had misheard Mrs Hunter; whether, up there on the high terrace, the whine of the wind and the rustling of the trees had transformed an innocuous response into something more ominous.

They decided that theirs would be a long engagement, lasting at least two years. She had just started a new job and Alec was soon to embark on a new research project. During that time, she and Marguerite would get to know each other. She hoped that they would grow to love each other. Marguerite must be given the chance to get used to a changed situation, and she, Ellen, must look for common ground between them, some interest that they could share. Marguerite must surely want grandchildren. If their relationship could not at first be close, then the arrival of a baby must eventually bring them together. As for Catriona, the jealousy she had felt on Seil she now brushed aside. If Catriona still had feelings for Alec then she was to be pitied rather than feared.

But it was not only Margeurite who seemed less than wholeheartedly keen on the engagement. Earlier that summer, Ellen and Alec had driven down to Wiltshire to meet her parents. Her father had grilled Alec over the dinner table. What were his prospects? How old was he? Did he intend to remain in academia? What of his family, his background, his education, his politics? Afterwards, when her father had retired to his study, Ellen had murmured to Alec that her father expected everyone to plan their future like a military campaign. He mustn't mind.

What had disappointed her more was the conversation that had taken place one evening when she and her father had gone out for a walk on the chalk hills that rose up behind the village. 'He's a pleasant chap,' her father had said, 'but are you sure he's solid enough for you, Ellen?' By 'solid', he had meant reliable, straightforward, lasting. 'Of course he is,' she had answered, hurt, and her father, seeing that, had tucked her hand round his arm.

'So long as you're happy, darling. He's rather decorative, that's all, and I've a tendency to doubt decorative men. Your mother thinks he's the cat's whiskers.' But the conversation had left for the first time in her life a small distance between them that had not quite been repaired.

After her first month in her job, Ellen decided to give a dinner party to thank Professor Malik for helping her find the new position. As well as the professor, his wife and Alec, she also wanted to invite Riley. She looked forward to her friend meeting her fiancé properly. Not having seen

much of India for some time and needing another female guest, Ellen invited her too.

The only evening convenient for all the guests was a Friday. There was a heatwave, and there were meetings at the college that Ellen had to attend that day, so she had to rush out to the shops in her lunch hour and haul the groceries home on the Underground. There was a surprising amount of work involved in cooking for six people, and the shortcomings of the shared kitchen were soon brought home to her – the battered saucepans with their loose handles, the lack of matching cutlery or a fridge.

Riley was the first to arrive. Pulling off her apron, Ellen ran downstairs and let him in. He offered her a bunch of roses, tied up in brown paper.

'They're from my garden,' he said, following her upstairs. 'There may be the odd greenfly.'

'They smell gorgeous. And such a lovely pink. Thank you, Riley.'

'How's it going?'

'Awful. I'm worried that the fish is off. It's been sitting in my bag in the heat all afternoon. I don't want to poison everyone. And the jelly won't set.'

In the kitchen, Ellen unwrapped the package of sole and Riley sniffed it and judged it acceptable.

'And the jelly . . .' She fetched it from the windowsill.

Raspberries bobbed in a scarlet sea. Riley peered at it. 'It may be unsalvageable, I'm afraid. What are you making?'

'Trifle.'

'Have you any cream?'

Ellen nodded.

'I'll rescue the raspberries, if you like, and then we could have raspberries and cream for pudding.'

'Riley, thank goodness you're here. A cool head in a crisis. Do you mind if I leave you to it and go and get changed? I must look a fright.'

'Rubbish. You look lovely, as always.'

'Flatterer.' She dashed off to the bathroom.

When she returned upstairs, make-up applied and peppermint-green cotton frock on, she heard Riley's and Alec's voices from the kitchen.

Riley was saying, 'We met some years ago, very briefly, at Gildersleve Hall.'

Alec said, 'I'm afraid I don't remember. What on earth are you doing?'

'Fishing out raspberries.'

'How extraordinary. I'll take over, if you like.'

'There's no need, I've just about finished.'

'Riley, thank you.' Entering the room, Ellen kissed both men. 'Riley's just sorting out my rather disastrous pudding,' she explained to Alec.

'How admirably domestic,' said Alec.

'Darling, would you . . .?' She swept up her hair.

He tugged up her zip the last few inches, then drew her into his arms and brushed his mouth against hers. Ellen was aware of Riley moving away to inspect the view out of the window.

Then the doorbell rang, and she hurried downstairs again to find the Maliks and India introducing themselves to each other on the front step. Back in the kitchen, there was a flurry of introductions and wine pouring, then the tomato soup was warmed and the guests were seated. Ellen made sure everyone had bread and butter, wine and water, and was relieved that the soup was pronounced delicious.

At first the conversation was of crystallography.

Riley asked, 'When you say that the X-rays can reveal the structure of the crystal . . .'

Alec looked up from his soup. 'It's rather difficult to explain to the layman. Did you have any sort of a scientific education?'

'I struggled through the odd exam,' murmured Riley.

'I meant, a university education.'

'I'm afraid not. Wartime, you see.'

Professor Malik spoke. 'Were you in the services, Mr Riley?'

'The army.'

'I volunteered for a tank regiment,' said Malik wistfully. 'But I was turned down and told I must work in a government lab. I've always regretted that.'

'You wouldn't have liked it, dear.' Gita Malik patted her husband's arm. 'Too dark and enclosed. You know you hate even the Underground.'

'I suppose a policeman has little use for a university degree,' said Alec.

'Oh, come now, Hunter.' Malik tore a piece of bread in half. 'Detective work and scientific research must have certain elements in common. The search for the truth . . . the close scrutiny of evidence.'

Riley said, 'And a couple of years in a parachute regiment has had its uses.'

'I daresay one has to be physically fit in your line of work,' said Alec. 'All that chasing criminals and clobbering them with truncheons.'

'I try not to clobber people if I can help it.'

'But a certain amount of force must be required.'

'True, though as I said, I try to keep it to a minimum.'

'You hear stories . . .'

'You shouldn't believe everything you read in the papers, Hunter.'

What was wrong with them? thought Ellen, irritated, as she cleared away the soup bowls. Why on earth were they behaving like this? Two grown men, scrapping like schoolboys, when all she had wanted was for them to be friends. Hot and tired, she found the pair of them equally tiresome.

Then India said, 'I'm afraid I was *completely hopeless* at school. I didn't even pass the needlework exam. Our headmistress, Miss MacBeith – do you remember her, Ellen, she was absolutely terrifying – told me that if I didn't pull my socks up, I'd end up as a charlady or an adventuress.'

There was a ripple of laughter. Riley said, 'And what was your answer to that?'

333

India gave a demure little smile and lowered her lids. 'That I thought adventuress was a better career option. Nicer clothes, you see.'

India, too, found the dinner party rather an ordeal. Her affair with Marcus Pharoah weighed heavily on her mind throughout the evening. Though, rationally, it didn't seem likely that Ellen would find out about her and Marcus because Ellen didn't go to the sorts of places that Marcus liked, irrationally, she found herself imagining scenarios where some scientific colleague might have mentioned to Ellen that Marcus Pharoah was getting divorced from his wife and was having an affair with India Mayhew. She was afraid that if Ellen found out, she would be disapproving or furious or hurt, or all three. As both Devlin Pharoah and Michael had pointed out, there was already gossip. It would be impossible, after so many months, to pass the affair off to Ellen as temporary or unimportant, and equally unlikely that she could convince Ellen that she had not deliberately refrained from mentioning Marcus. The situation made her feel uneasy, and though she did not exactly avoid Ellen, she did not go out of her way to call on her either. Though she knew without doubt that Ellen was a nicer and better person than Marcus, there was something tiring about having to make a continual effort to make out that she herself was better than she really was. Marcus knew what she was. He didn't accept her – quite the opposite; she knew that he tried to change her, to mould her – but

perhaps that was preferable to trying to live up to Ellen's exacting standards.

Dining with Marcus one evening, he talked about America once more.

'Do you remember me telling you that Midhurst College, in Vermont, has offered me a post? They've been courting me for years. It's a small place and they want to build up a biochemistry department, create it from scratch. They've come up with a decent offer at last.'

He seemed to expect a response so she said obligingly, 'That's marvellous, Marcus.'

'Marvellous?' His lip curled. 'Not, *oh Marcus, please don't leave me*? Or, *oh Marcus, I'll miss you so much*? Who else will buy you expensive frocks, India?'

He had bought her the frock she was wearing that day, which was made of a greeny-gold jacquard silk. When, earlier, they had walked into the restaurant, she had seen the men turn to look at her.

She disliked it when he was sarcastic, and he had that mean look in his eye which she had learned to be wary of, which told her his mood could so easily tip over into censure of her. To distract him, she said, 'That place . . . your laboratory—'

'Gildersleve,' he said irritably. 'It's called Gildersleve Hall.' He shook his head. 'I've decided to close it down. I'd rather make something better elsewhere than go on fighting against fools. Have you ever been to America?'

'Never.'

'You'd love it. The air seems fresher. Everywhere feels new. It gives you hope.'

Yet he looked angry rather than hopeful. Stirring his coffee, the direction of his glance drifted over the tables in the restaurant. Disliking a silence, India said, 'I will miss you, Marcus, honestly.'

His gaze snapped back to her. 'But I'm not your only – oh, what would be the word? Admirer? No, too coy. Escort? Certain unfortunate connotations, don't you think? Lover, then, I suppose we shall have to settle for that. I'm not the only one, am I?'

'No,' she said calmly. 'Does that bother you?'

'It doesn't *surprise* me.'

She made to rise but he reached out a hand and gripped her wrist. 'Stop it,' he murmured. 'Stop running away from me.'

India sank back in her seat. 'I'm not sure what you want me to say.'

'Nothing you would want to say,' he said bitterly. 'I may as well tell you – I was wondering whether you'd like to come with me.'

She said, startled, 'To America?'

'Rather than Iceland or Siam? Yes, of course.'

'Marcus—'

'I realize that you would be concerned about your brother, about Sebastian. I would make provision for him.'

'*Provision*,' she repeated. 'What sort of provision?'

'Whatever is suitable, whatever you think best. Take that

expression off your face, India. You can be so quick to take offence – it's childish of you. I only meant that I understand you feel you have a responsibility towards him and that that might inhibit what choices you make.'

She softened. 'Sebastian needs me,' she said.

'Sebastian isn't a child any more. He's a grown man. He needs to learn how to stand up for himself.'

'He can't. He's not that sort of person.'

'India, you're not doing him any favours. Sebastian won't have any sort of life if he constantly shelters behind you. To be fulfilled, to be happy, he must learn to live apart from you. You need to let him grow up.'

A part of her knew this, but she said obstinately, 'I won't leave him, Marcus. *America*. Why should I want to go to America?'

'If we were to marry.'

She laughed. 'I can't possibly marry you, Marcus.'

'Why not?'

'Because you're married already, for one thing.'

'Not for much longer. My divorce will come through in a matter of months.'

'I don't want to marry anyone. I've never wanted to marry anyone.'

He lit cigarettes and handed one to her. 'So that you have something to fidget with,' he said.

'Marcus, *honestly*, it's quite impossible. And I think that if you thought about it properly, you'd see that it was a very bad idea.'

'I have thought about it. I told you, I don't care to live alone.'

'Then marry someone else.'

'I can't seem to think of anyone else I'd like to marry. And besides, I've fallen in love with you.'

She sidestepped this, saying, 'I don't think I'd be any good at being married. I don't think I'm the right sort of person.'

'Is there a right sort of person?'

'You know what I mean. There are women who become wives and women who become mistresses. I'm the second sort, aren't I?'

'And is that how you see your life going on? Is that what you want for yourself when you are thirty, forty . . . fifty?'

For some reason, India found herself thinking of Peachey, in her mouldering flapper dresses, surrounded by the portraits that had been painted in her pomp. Perhaps she would end up like that, she thought, living on her own with half a dozen smelly moggies, surrounded by past glories.

'I don't know,' she muttered.

'Do you have no ambitions at all?'

'I've never thought, oh, perhaps I should become a film star, or perhaps I should write a book, if that's what you mean.' She twisted a pleat of her frock round a finger. 'I don't know that I've ever known anyone who was *happily* married.'

'Some people manage it. A few people. My parents were happy enough.'

'I'm not sure that mine ever were. And anyway . . .'

'What is it?'

'Do you remember the lecture I went to with Ellen? Where we first met?'

'At the Royal Institution?'

'Yes. You talked about bad blood.'

'Did I? How unscientific of me. I expect I was trying to employ some term the layman might understand.'

'Do you believe in it?'

'I was speaking about hereditary diseases. *Belief* doesn't come into it.'

'I meant, do you think that bad blood can run in a family?'

'It can do, in a sense. Where there is evidence of disease, then you could say that bad blood runs in a family.'

'Do you think those sort of people should marry? Do you think they should have children?'

'I believe that it's irresponsible to knowingly breed defectives. They can't live useful lives and there's always the risk that they'll pass on their sickness to the next generation.'

India thought of the house in the woods, the shimmer and shadow of bluebells, and her mother dancing with Neil to 'My Funny Valentine'.

She said, 'I'm not sure my mother was the sort of person who should have had children.'

'Your mother died of heart disease brought on by a bout of rheumatic fever in her childhood.'

She raised her eyebrows. 'You checked?'

'Yes, I checked. It's on the death certificate. There's no reason to believe that her poor health should be passed on to you. India, you're worrying about nothing. You are the picture of health. I've always noticed this about you, your physical perfection. You have such symmetry and form. It's quite striking.'

'You're talking about me as if I were a dog in a show. You'll be admiring my glossy coat next.'

He smiled. 'I'm sorry, forgive me. But physical health is a powerful source of attraction. Inevitably, the beautiful tend to marry the beautiful. Genetically, it makes sense. The less fortunate are left to take what they can.'

'Do you think yourself beautiful, Marcus?'

'I wouldn't put it quite like that. But I've never had a day's illness in my life. I pity those who always seem to be ailing from one thing or another. India, what do you want in life? You must think about it. You won't believe me now but time rushes on. You can end up finding it is too late to take a step in a different direction.'

They parted not long afterwards. Back at the flat, Sebastian was asleep on the sitting-room sofa. India tiptoed into the kitchen and poured herself a glass of milk. She sat down on an armchair. Sebastian lay motionless under the blankets, one arm flung out, the light from the kitchen touching his tangled fair curls. Watching him sleeping, she felt an

immense tenderness for him. Marcus Pharoah might tell her that she needed to let Sebastian stand up for himself, but Pharoah did not have the memories she had, of Sebastian weeping for his mother, or Sebastian withdrawn and frightened at the orphanage or silent and uncommunicative in the aftermath of his breakdown, refusing to leave his bed, refusing to speak even to her. He did not know Sebastian's generosity and simplicity nor the fears that haunted him. Nor did he understand that she needed Sebastian as much as he needed her, because he was the one person who knew and understood her and who never, ever criticized her.

India went into her bedroom. There, she cold-creamed off her make-up, brushed out her hair and changed into her pyjamas. It was a warm night and she lay on the bed, thinking about Pharoah's offer. She had had proposals of marriage before, some serious, some less so, and had always turned them down. She didn't take Pharoah's proposal seriously. It had been made on a whim, she suspected, because he was angry about his divorce and losing his precious Gildersleve Hall. He was angry, in fact, that he had not been able to have everything his own way. Later on, he would regret the proposal. She doubted that he would ever repeat it.

But Pharoah had touched on a nerve when he had asked her what she pictured herself doing with her life. She remembered Aunt Rachel asking her the same thing, sitting at the kitchen table with her and discussing possible

careers – teaching, secretarial college, nursing. None of these futures had materialized; indeed, they had all seemed improbable at the time, though India had not said this to Rachel. Since she had left school she had had a series of jobs, none of which had lasted more than six months. She knew that she often struggled to concentrate, that her timekeeping was appalling and that when she was rattled, she made mistakes. It was, if you thought about it, dismaying that at the age of twenty-three and after an expensive education, she was still waiting on tables in a cheap café. And not even doing that very well.

She wanted to be safe. And to be safe, you had to have money. Though Marcus Pharoah might claim to be hard up, it was plain to India that he didn't know what he was talking about. Poor men didn't dine at Le Caprice or run sports cars. Marrying Marcus Pharoah would take her into a different world, a better world. A girl like her, a girl who was pretty rather than clever, fun rather than studious, could better herself by marrying well. Marriage could give her the security she longed for. It would give her a home; it would give her children.

Marcus Pharoah claimed to have fallen in love with her. Often people said they were in love when it seemed to India that what they were really talking of was desire or even fondness. Love, in her opinion, should be selfless. Love meant putting another person before yourself. Rachel had loved them and had given up a lot for them. Their mother had told her and Sebastian that she loved them,

and yet she had not noticed when they had gone hungry. She had talked of love while her daughter had taught herself to steal from shops and inside her son something had broken, perhaps for ever.

Love implied a certain carelessness with the emotions. Pharoah was capable of carelessness, certainly, or his wife would not be divorcing him. India herself avoided and distrusted love, was fearful of its messiness and its intemperate demands. People who loved, people who were in love, lost the capacity to see things clearly. They weren't wary, they didn't see the traps.

I've fallen in love with you. He had said it reluctantly, as if love was a disease that he had unwittingly contracted. He, Marcus Pharoah, who was never ill.

In late August, Alec and Ellen went back to Seil Island. They spent their first morning exploring the coast, following tracks that crossed fields of livestock and skirted beside beaches. Buttercups flecked the grass and rock plants in delicate miniature grew in crevices between the stones. On the beaches, waves spilled and sucked against a shoreline flecked with a mosaic of sea-smoothed slates and frilled green seaweed. Above the cliffs, a buzzard soared high in the sky, the black fingers of its wingtips outstretched to catch the air currents. Further out, crested white breakers smashed against angular rocks. The sea surrounded them, its colour constantly changing and its turbulent surface reflecting diamonds of light. The Lords of the Isles had

sailed through these seas; Campbells and MacDonalds had had ownership of the lands.

In the afternoon, Alec helped his mother with the estate paperwork. Ellen offered to help in the house or the garden but was told by Marguerite that she was not needed. Feeling at a loose end, she walked to the village of Ellenabeich, at the far end of the bay. Here, tall granite cliffs smeared with tumbling sheets of scree loomed high over rows of small, white single-storey cottages. A strip of grass divided the cottages from the rubble of stones on the beach. The houses seemed caught between the rocks and the sea. The scene was pretty enough now, but Ellen found that she almost shrank from imagining what it would be like in the dark of winter, on this precipice on the edge of the Atlantic.

She posted her cards and walked to the harbour. Boats clustered against a jetty made of tightly packed slate, bobbing up and down in a livening sea. The tiny island of Easdale lay across a short stretch of water. Ellen could see, over the dividing waves, its rumpled outline and small harbour.

Someone waved to her from an incoming boat. Ellen recognized Catriona Campbell and waved back, watching as Catriona skilfully steered the yacht into the harbour and tied it up to an iron stanchion on the jetty.

Catriona ran up the slipway. Drops of water streamed from her yellow oilskins and her face was flushed. A lock of dark curling hair had come loose from her ponytail; she swept it back with her hand.

'Hello, there! I heard you and Alec were back on the island. How are you?'

'I'm very well,' said Ellen. 'I didn't know you sailed, Miss Campbell.'

'Call me Catriona, please. "Miss Campbell" might do for stuffy suppers at Kilmory House but I was hoping we might be friends. You don't mind if I call you Ellen, do you?'

'Not at all, please do.'

'Do you sail, Ellen?'

'I'm afraid not. It looks so exhilarating.'

Catriona glanced back at the boat and smiled. 'It's one of the things I miss most when I'm away from home. If I'm feeling miserable or in a bad mood I take the yacht out and it always puts me right. I'll take you out sometime, if you like. We could go to Luing, or one of the uninhabited islands. Alec too, of course, though I find he likes to take over. Men do, don't they? Where is he, by the way? I shall scold him for leaving you on your own.'

'I don't mind at all. He's looking over some legal documents for his mother.'

'Marguerite's keeping his nose to the grindstone, then. She never gives up.'

This time, she had to ask. 'What do you mean?'

'Oh, nothing really. Mothers and sons, you know. Woe betide any of us who come between them.' Catriona glanced at her watch. 'I must dash, I'm afraid. I'd offer to keep you

company for the afternoon but my father wants me to come to Oban with him and I'm late already.'

Catriona had begun to walk away when she turned back to Ellen. 'How silly of me, I almost forgot. I wondered whether you and Alec would like to come to supper on Friday evening. Marguerite, too, of course.'

'That's very kind, but I don't know our plans yet, I'm afraid.'

'Oh, I'm sure it'll fit in. Eightish. Just an informal supper, no need to dress up.' With a wave of the hand, Catriona left the harbour.

On Friday, dressing for dinner at the Campbells' house, Ellen chose a cream wool skirt and a lilac jersey. When she was ready, she went downstairs. Alec and Marguerite were sitting in the drawing room. Alec was wearing a dark suit, Marguerite a full-length blue frock.

Seeing her, Ellen felt doubtful. 'Should I have dressed up more? Should I change?'

'Certainly not.' Alec kissed her. 'You look beautiful. Drink, darling?'

'You look sweetly pretty in that lilac,' said Marguerite. 'I've just the one going-out frock and I reach for it every time. So dreary of me.'

They had a gin and tonic, then put on their coats and left the house. The fine weather that had lasted since their arrival on the island had begun to break up and a wind whipped the trees in the garden. As Alec drove them along

the road beside the bay, Ellen saw the white horses that crested the waves crashing on to the black rocks, sending spray high into the air.

Outside the Campbells' house, half a dozen cars were parked along the narrow track. The building, though substantial, was smaller than Kilmory House. The lower windows were lit up and as they walked up the path to the front door they heard, beneath the wild roar of the wind and the sea, the sound of voices and laughter.

A tall, smiling man with a head of thick silver hair and heavy black eyebrows opened the door and greeted them, introducing himself to Ellen as Dr Campbell. A girl took their coats and they were shown into a drawing room. Crimson velvet curtains hung at the window and Persian rugs were scattered on the dark floorboards. Couples sat on sofas or stood in groups at the window and fireplace. A glance round the room told Ellen that all the women were wearing evening frocks. Some of the women's dresses were pre-war in style, cut on the bias, straining a little across the bust; others wore long tartan skirts and white blouses. Pearls gleamed at throats, gold bracelets jangled on wrists. Ellen felt a rush of dismay. She was the only woman present wearing a knee-length skirt, the only one wearing a jersey. Should she ask Alec to drive her back to Kilmory House so that she could quickly change? No – how foolish and vain that would look.

It took a moment to register that the young woman coming towards them was Catriona Campbell. The Catriona

of previous encounters, unremarkable in kilt and jersey or windswept in oilskins, had gone, replaced by a tall, slender young woman whose black velvet evening dress moulded to the curves of her body and whose upswept hair flattered the pale oval of her face. Emerald earrings and a skilful application of make-up brought out the green in her eyes.

Just an informal supper, no need to dress up. Had she misunderstood what Catriona had said to her? No, she did not think so. Or had Catriona changed her mind and had the party grown, as parties sometimes will, starting as one thing and ending up as another? This was possible, she supposed. After all, it had been she who had assumed that the five of them would be the only guests. Catriona had said nothing about numbers. Yet she counted fourteen in the room, including their own party, and it crossed her mind that occasions such as this took planning, especially on an island like Seil. Surely it would be hard to organize at the last moment food, drink, flowers and the hire of a girl from the village to pass around glasses of wine?

She felt awkward as Alec introduced her to the other guests. It seemed to her that in their gazes she saw perplexity and disappointment. She wondered whether they thought she let Alec down or whether they considered her too inept or too snobbishly English to dress up for a dinner in a remote part of Scotland. The tables had been turned: she, Ellen, was now the frumpy girl-next-door in the everyday skirt and jumper, while Catriona, vivid in black velvet and

emeralds, flared like a candle. Had Catriona deliberately manipulated the situation? And if so, why?

She gave herself a mental shake. She mustn't start imagining things. What did it matter if she was not wearing her party frock? She was here, with Alec, as his fiancée. Yet she was relieved when Catriona clapped her hands and announced that dinner was served.

'Sounds like a storm's getting up.'

The man sitting at the dining table to one side of Ellen – Gillis Maclean, red hair and blue eyes – had spoken.

'Damn,' said Catriona. 'I was planning to take the boat out tomorrow.'

They had almost finished the main course. 'Might be a touch rough, Cat,' said Gillis. 'Where were you thinking of heading for?'

'Only to Luing.' Catriona, seated at one end of the table, smiled at Ellen. 'I promised you and Alec a trip, didn't I?'

'Sounds fun,' said Alec.

Marguerite frowned. 'Not if the weather's bad, Catriona dear.'

'No, of course not.'

Ellen had noticed how the other guests deferred to Mrs Hunter. Though in Catriona's demure amiability, she thought she detected only a pretence of acquiescence.

'I hope you're a good sailor, Miss Kingsley,' said Gillis.

'I haven't had much opportunity to find out. Only a steamer to France and a few ferry trips to the Isle of Wight.

There isn't a great deal of opportunity for sailing in London. Just pleasure trips down the Thames. My hours at work can be long, so I don't have much time for hobbies.'

'What do you do?'

'I'm a scientist, a biochemist.'

'Like you, Hunter.' One of the Campbells' neighbours, a gaunt, freckled man, nodded at Alec.

'These career women,' said Marguerite, with a thin smile.

'Where did you meet?'

'At Gildersleve Hall, in Cambridgeshire. We were both working there.'

'Romance among the test tubes,' said the freckled man, and there was a ripple of laughter.

'Alec's such a clever lad.' This from an older woman, a Mrs Douglas, who was wearing a white blouse with a yellowing lace jabot. 'You must be so proud of him, Marguerite.'

'How's it going, Hunter?' asked Gillis Maclean. 'Split the atom yet?'

Alec smiled. 'I think you'll find someone got there before me. And atomic science isn't really my field.'

'I suppose you'll find it hard to give all that up.'

It was Donald Frazer who had spoken. 'Give it up?' said Ellen. 'Why should Alec want to give up his work?'

'When he comes back to the island.'

'Alec has told you, Ellen, hasn't he?'

Both Donald and Marguerite spoke at the same time. It was on the tip of Ellen's tongue to say, *told me what?* but she

managed not to. Across the table, she met Alec's eyes. A beat passed, she waited for him to speak, but instead he gave a quick frown and looked away.

'Alec's making a name for himself,' Ellen said, her voice level. 'It would be a terrible waste if he were to abandon his work.'

'Alec has a duty.' Marguerite's voice was clear and quiet. 'He's always known that.'

Mrs Douglas broke the uncomfortable silence that followed. 'I expect you were trying not to put Miss Kingsley off, weren't you, Alec? I daresay you were afraid that if she knew she was to live on such an outpost, she might have second thoughts.'

The remark was kindly meant but it fell flat. And shortly afterwards another discussion started up, this time about the price of land.

Because Marguerite felt tired and asked Alec to drive her back to Kilmory House straight after dinner, Ellen had no opportunity to talk to him in the bustle of movement as the party left the dinner table.

She, too, would have liked to have gone home. The evening had become stale and wearisome and the shock of the conversation that had taken place over the dinner table had not dissipated; she felt shaken, as if she had been struck by an ice-cold wave. As Catriona served coffee in the drawing room and Dr Campbell dispensed brandies, Ellen sat on a sofa, talking to Mrs Douglas. She was glad

of the older woman's garrulousness, and the rambling anecdotes about grandchildren provided a cloak for her own confusion. Was it true? What had Marguerite and Donald Frazer being referring to – a promise, or some ill-defined understanding, of more significance to mother, perhaps, than son? And if Alec had given any sort of undertaking to his mother, how could he have neglected to mention something so important to her? During their many conversations about their future, they had talked of houses and children – in general terms, nothing fixed so far, not even a wedding date.

When Alec returned to the house, he sat on the arm of the sofa beside her, his hand resting on her shoulder. Though his touch should have comforted, it did not. The turmoil of her thoughts was matched by a rising wind outside that rattled the windows in their frames and made the flames of the fire gutter and flare, and Ellen was relieved when there was a general movement to the front door, where the Campbells were thanked and kisses and handshakes exchanged.

As they walked down the path to the gate, the sound of the sea, not far away, was disturbing and insistent, fighting for attention against the screaming wind.

'I'm sorry,' said Alec. 'I put you on the spot, back there at dinner.'

'It's not true, is it, what Marguerite said? That you mean to leave London and come back here?'

'Nothing's settled.'

His words – his evasion – inflicted another shock.

'So you don't rule it out.'

'I can't.'

'And you didn't think to mention this to me?'

'I was going to talk to you about it.'

'When, Alec?'

His muttered, 'I was waiting for the right moment, that's all,' was almost lost in the howling gale.

They reached the car. As he started up the engine, Alec said, 'You're making it sound as if I've kept some guilty secret from you. My mother's lived here alone since my father died. It's hard for her, she's not young any more, and she could do with someone to help with the house and the land. I can't just walk away from it without a backward glance, surely you see that?'

'To have to learn at dinner, in front of strangers . . .' In front of your mother, she wanted to say.

'I should have said something, I realize that now.'

'Said something?' The inadequacy of this remark left her almost speechless. 'Alec, I felt such a fool!'

The windscreen wiper had jammed; he banged at the inside of the screen with his fist, trying to free it. 'I'm sure no one thought you were a fool, darling. They all thought you were perfectly delightful.'

'Alec, you can't just brush it away like that! It was utterly humiliating. I was apparently the only person in the room not to know where we're going to set up home!'

'You're getting it out of proportion.'

She snapped, 'It was hateful! Still, I'm sure Catriona took pleasure in it.'

His gaze flashed to her. 'What are you talking about?'

'Just another little thing you failed to mention, that's all.'

Cascades of rain dashed against the windscreen so that the road ahead was absorbed into the blackness of the landscape and the night. 'I can't see a damned thing.' Alec stabbed a foot on the brake, the car came to a halt and he climbed out. As he leaned across the bonnet, wrestling with the wiper blade, Ellen saw how, above the sea, clouds like strips of grey rag parted now and then to reveal a moon that shone on the writhing waves beneath.

He got back into the car, and they moved off. 'Catriona's gone out of her way to be welcoming to you,' Alec said tightly. 'She made a special effort to come to the house when you first visited the island, just to say hello to you, she told me so. She's offered to take you out in the yacht and she's invited you to dine at her home. What more could she do?'

'She resents me, Alec.'

'Why on earth should she do that?'

'It's obvious. Because she's in love with you.' There, it was out.

'That's nonsense.' He sounded furious.

'I was the only woman there not in evening dress. When I met Catriona at the harbour, she told me that the dinner was to be informal. She said there was no need to dress up.'

But even to her, it sounded weak, a silly fuss about not having worn the right frock.

'I expect you misheard her.' She could hear the irritation in his voice. 'Or she was trying to put you at your ease, so you didn't feel you had to go to too much effort. Does it matter so much?'

'It matters that she deliberately wrong-footed me.'

'Cat isn't like that.'

'What is she like, then, Alec?' The words ripped out of her, unbidden. 'You've hardly told me anything about her!'

They had reached Kilmory House. They headed up the drive. Alec parked in the courtyard. As the car headlamps flooded the paving stones, illuminating the leaves and twigs that danced across the terrace, she turned towards him.

'How long were you together?'

'Ellen, for heaven's sake—'

'How long, Alec?'

'About a year.' An angry shake of the head. 'Something like that. What does it matter?'

'I suspect it still matters to Catriona.'

'Nonsense. You're not jealous, are you? Not of Cat?'

'No, of course not.'

But she was. It was an emotion she had little experience of, and she disliked the fact that she was capable of it. She disliked most of all that Catriona's scheming and her own insecurity had ended in this, a quarrel with the man she loved.

Somewhere in the distance a gate or door banged open

and shut, an irregular cannonade. A sheet of newspaper jumped and leaped like an imp, wrapping itself around pots and shrubs before bounding on down the slope. Some of her anger died away and she was able to speak more calmly.

'Alec, you've known these people all your life. But I have to walk into their homes, a complete stranger. I want you to be proud of me, and I need to understand what they mean to you. I want to know your family and friends, to like them, and one day, I hope, to love them. That's important to me because I love you.'

'And I love you, too.' Letting out a breath, he crushed her hand in his. 'You know that, don't you, Ellen? Cat's an old friend, that's all. She's the nearest thing I've ever had to a sister. We went round together for a while, it's true, but it wasn't important. We were always in and out of each other's houses, Cat and I, and I suppose one day I noticed she wasn't a little girl with skinned knees any more.' He paused, looking out of the windscreen. 'There's a side to Cat that likes to stir, to make mischief. And after a while, it began to put my back up.'

Because she had noticed those same characteristics in Catriona, she felt comforted. She said, 'So you broke it off.'

'Yes, I did. We were going our separate ways anyway. There was never a chance of anything serious coming of it. I went off to Edinburgh to study, and Cat went off to train as a nurse, and that was the end of it. And since then, she's always had someone on the go. Every time I see her

there's a different boyfriend. No doubt she has this latest fellow running round after her like all the others.' He took her hand in his. 'Ellen, why are we wasting our time talking about Cat? She doesn't matter. It's you I love. Only you.'

She dropped her head on to his shoulder, closing her eyes. She heard him sigh. 'The truth is I've put off the decision for a long time and it makes me feel guilty.'

'Guilty?'

'It would have been much easier for my mother if I'd come back to the island years ago.'

'But you didn't want to?'

'No, I didn't.'

'Because of your work?'

'Among other things.' He gave a bitter laugh. 'I have become a master of prevarication. I'm not proud of it.'

Ellen had remembered something Alec had said to her on the night of Dr Redmond's death, as they had walked back to Copfield together. That sometimes he hated Seil Island, and that belonging somewhere meant that you had to keep going back. She felt a rush of sympathy for him. She, who was rootless, had no easy way of understanding what it was to be tied to a place, or how hard it might be to leave.

Now and then that night, she dozed off. Then the moan of the wind or a fusillade of rain against the windowpane jolted her awake. Lying in the darkness, she seemed to relive incidents from the evening. She had not misheard

Catriona, and no, Catriona had not been trying to put her at her ease. Quite the opposite. Of this she was certain.

It was easy to understand what, ten years ago, might have attracted Alec to Catriona. Her vividness and her athletic grace had an obvious appeal. But he, too, had noticed the dash of unkindness in her, as well as her sharpness of tongue. If Catriona had manipulated a situation in which she would make herself look good in front of Alec and Ellen would be overshadowed, the attempt had misfired.

No, she did not fear Catriona. Other memories troubled her far more: Marguerite at the dinner table, her expression touched with triumph as Donald Frazer let slip that Alec was expected to return to the island. And Marguerite in Kilmory House's sitting room, earlier that evening, dressed in the full-length evening frock that she claimed to wear for every social event. Coincidence, surely. Marguerite would not have planned to make her, Ellen, look a fool. Marguerite and Catriona would not have been in league together. No, surely not.

This, the dead heart of the night, allowed her thoughts to veer and stumble along paths she might not by daylight have ventured down. You could say that back in May, when she had first come to the island, the news of their future marriage had not been welcomed with open arms. Might you say more? That Mrs Hunter resented the engagement? Or that she would prefer Alec to marry Catriona, the island girl?

Marguerite's good opinion of her was vital. The fact of

Francis Hunter's early death had bound mother and son tightly together. There was the possibility that their bond might never allow admittance of another. That she might always feel an outsider, and that Marguerite might tolerate her but never like or love her.

Though they had repaired things before they went back into the house, her disagreement with Alec had left her feeling raw and despondent and she knew that out there, sitting in the car in the storm, nothing had been confronted and nothing had been decided. If Alec had promised his mother to return to the island some day, then she would have to live here with him – and with Marguerite. Could she adapt to such a different life? Could she give up all that had been so hard won?

If she and Alec were to have children, she had always known that she would have to give up work for a while. But not for any length of time, because she had seen too often how hard it was for a female scientist to have both a career and a family. Those women who took years off to bring up their children never returned to research. A little teaching, perhaps, was all that was left to them. The few exceptions employed nannies or nursemaids and came back to the laboratory as soon as their babies were weaned. To move to Seil Island would be to put an end to both their careers, Alec knew this, which was why he had put off the decision, and why, presumably, he had baulked at speaking of it to her. Her heart rebelled against it. A better way must be found.

She got out of bed and went to the bathroom to fetch a glass of water. Back in her room, she took two aspirins and opened *The Day of the Triffids*. Bill Mason's struggles, roaming through a London of blinded inhabitants, distracted her from the events of the evening. After a couple of chapters Ellen closed her book and switched off the light. Her mind had calmed and a feeling of certainty and confidence washed over her. Shared problems and shared solutions – didn't those things lie at the heart of a marriage? Dream images rose up into her unconscious like mermaids floating to the surface of the still water of the island's quarries, flickering between the memories as she felt her muscles relax and her heartbeat slow.

Something woke her. The wind had died down and she heard the sound clearly. A tap-tapping, a regular beat, a squeak of floorboard, the scuff of a shoe. She had heard the same sound on her first night on the island. Someone was walking along the corridor.

No. The footsteps came from above. This time she was sure of it, and she felt herself transfixed by a nameless and irrational fear. Something was wandering through the attics in the dark quiet of the early hours of the morning, free, untrammelled, able to roam at will. What was it?

She flicked on the light. There was a moment of sharp terror and then the items in the room resolved into reasonable, rational shapes – a wardrobe, a dressing table, her jersey hanging over the back of a chair.

The sound had stopped. It had been the dog, perhaps.

Marguerite must have thought she shut Hamish into the kitchen at night but maybe he knew a way out. Or she had been woken by the beat of her own heart, which her foolish imagination had transformed into a spectre.

Yet the wisps and shreds of fear remained and it was a long time before she was able to switch off the light and lie down and close her eyes once more.

She dreamed that she was standing on the edge of the high terrace that looked down over Kilmory House. The low wall was no longer there and her toes curled round the precipice. Far below her, scarlet petals had drifted over the garden, so that the grass and shrubs appeared to be bloodstained. She felt rather than saw the presence of someone behind her. A footstep, a light pressure on the small of her back, and she was falling . . .

Ellen woke, fighting for breath. A flare of light showed around the curtains and the clock told her that it was not quite seven in the morning. Her head ached and her eyes felt gritty with lack of sleep. Throwing on a pair of trousers and a jersey, she went downstairs and outside into the garden. Here, in the cool, fresh air, the alarms of the night slid away and the apparitions that had haunted her were dissolved into figments of the imagination by the sunshine.

She walked up the hillside. The grass was wet with dew and the scents of damp earth and new leaves were strong and fresh. Looking up, she saw ahead of her a smear of scarlet petals around the sides of the path. The petals of the

roses had been torn from the branches by the force of the wind. Her dream came back to her – that vertiginous drop, that endless fall – and she realized that her unsettled consciousness had dug up her memories of the death of Dr Redmond and impressed them on to the high terraces of Kilmory House.

A movement above her made her tilt her head, shading her eyes from the sun. Alec was coming out from beneath the trees. She ran to meet him and he took her in his arms. And she closed her eyes, burying her head in his shoulder, and the sweet, fierce longing she felt for him was mixed with both fear and relief.

He said, 'Let's get out, shall we?' and she nodded.

Arm in arm, they walked down the path. Reaching the courtyard, he said, 'Wait here,' and she stood in the sunshine until he returned, carrying a small knapsack.

'Breakfast,' he said with a smile.

They went out through the gates. With every step they took away from Kilmory House towards the harbour at Ellenabeich, her heart seemed to lift. There, Alec spoke to a fisherman, and they clambered into the small boat that pitched gently up and down beside the jetty.

Crossing the short strait of water that divided Seil from its much smaller neighbour of Easdale, it seemed to Ellen that the sea had become a different element from the previous night. A few boats were moored in Easdale's narrow harbour. Alec gave Ellen his hand to help her from the boat and thanked the fisherman. The rowing boat

headed back across the bay to Ellenabeich as Alec and Ellen walked from the harbour.

Their route took them over Easdale to its westernmost edge, where it faced out to the deserted island of Insh, and then beyond, across the Atlantic. This sweep of coast was a crumpled, jagged mass of sea walls. The beaches were formed of broken slates whose blue-grey sheen caught the early morning sun; the previous night's storm had cast up wreaths of glistening brown seaweed and driftwood and several beached jellyfish, which lay among the debris, their round gelatinous forms solidifying.

A narrow isthmus divided two quarries. Walking along it, Ellen saw in the still turquoise water a mass of shingled slate sloping down steeply, the stones blurring into the depths. Huge submerged rock formations, like underwater leviathans, were dimly discernible beneath the surface of the water. Old stone buildings, roofless and grown over with plants, lay in the shadow of the high land in the centre of the island, leftovers from a past that was long gone. Though the sea sparkled and a thousand flowers glittered like jewels cast into the grass, the place had a melancholy air.

They sat down on a rock overlooking the sea. Alec opened the knapsack. He took out apples, rolls, hard-boiled eggs and a thermos of coffee. He poured out the coffee and handed the cup to Ellen.

He said, 'About last night—'

'It doesn't matter.'

'I think it does. I wanted to talk to you about Cat. I wasn't fair to you, I wasn't honest. And I wouldn't want you to find out from anyone else.'

She felt a ripple of apprehension. She heard him say, 'I was nineteen, Cat was a couple of years younger. I suppose proximity had something to do with it.' He ran a hand over his jaw as he looked out to where the waves rose and fell. 'There was, back then, a kind of understanding between my mother and Dr Campbell. It was a joke, more than anything.'

'An understanding?'

'That Cat and I should marry one day. They used to tease us about it. My parents and the Campbells had always been friends, so you see it was . . .' He didn't finish his sentence. Instead, he said, 'I told you it wasn't important. It isn't now, but it was then. It lasted about a year. And then, as I said, we went our separate ways.'

It took a huge effort to hide the jolt of feeling inside her. But she had to know. 'Was Catriona your first love?'

'Yes.'

'And you were hers?'

'Yes, I suppose I was.'

Another question: *And were you lovers?* But she found she did not need to ask that – her answer was already there in Catriona's careless kiss, laden with intimacy and knowledge, as she had greeted Alec back in May, when Ellen had first come to Kilmory House. It was there, too, in the teasing way Catriona addressed him. The emotion that ran

through her was, Ellen knew, unreasonable – she, too, had had lovers – and she fought to suppress it.

Alec took her hand, pressing it against his face. 'Someone had to be first,' he said.

And yet, as she took an apple and began to eat, she wished bitterly that it hadn't been Catriona. Odd that she could stomach the memory of his romance with Andrée Fournier so much more easily than the discovery of an affair with Catriona. Perhaps it was because she and Andrée were not so dissimilar in type – scientists, intellectual, self-possessed, even a little reserved. Catriona was a different kind of woman. That Alec had been attracted to her, that he had fallen in love with her, showed a side of him she did not know. That only Catriona knew.

She said, 'Would your mother still prefer you to marry Catriona?'

He laughed. 'Good God, I shouldn't think so. Why would she? She knows it's long over with.'

'Catriona's from the island. It would be understandable if your mother would prefer you to marry a girl from the island.'

He turned towards her, smiling and frowning at the same time. 'You're not worrying about that, are you? Not really?'

'I'm not sure I'm the sort of woman your mother would have chosen for you.'

'You're worrying about nothing. My mother adores you. She told me so.'

'Really?'

'Yes.'

She let out a breath. 'I'm so glad. Silly of me to worry.'

'Darling, we just need to take it slowly. You don't mind, do you? We need to give my mother time to get used to it. It's been hard for her, since my father died.'

'What happened to him, Alec?' She knew only the barest details. She had been reluctant to make him dig up painful memories.

'He died of pneumonia.' He was looking out to sea, shading his eyes from the light. 'It was in the war.'

'Was it sudden?'

'Very. He had a cold but it was nothing serious. I was away at school when it happened. I didn't even get the chance to say goodbye to him.'

She had little experience of bereavement. A grandmother, a cousin who had been killed at the D-Day landings. She had known neither well.

'You poor thing,' she said. 'And so dreadful for your mother.'

'She invited a medium to the house.'

Startled, she said, 'A medium? Ectoplasm and ouija boards?'

'Pretty much. Pernicious nonsense. Loathsome woman, utter fraud. I remember her drifting around the room, saying these things – that she could feel my father's presence in some part of the house, or that she'd seen his boat in the bay at night. Nothing that could be proved or disproved, of course. I knew she was a fraud, even then, even though I

was a child, but she managed to convince my mother that my father was still there, on the island, in some sense. We've never talked about it. We talk about everything else, but not that.'

'Perhaps it gave her some comfort.'

'*False* comfort. Lazy answers and lies.'

She knew that his loathing of superstition was intractable, admitting no space for any other interpretation. She changed the subject.

'Has your mother never thought of marrying again?'

'Never, as far as I know.'

'I wondered whether Mr Frazer—'

'Donald?' Alec's expression lightened and he laughed. 'They're friends, that's all. Donald helps my mother with some of the estate work.'

'Poor Marguerite. It must be lonely.'

He picked up a slate and hurled it into the water. 'My father was the love of her life. She told me so once, not long after he died.'

There was something repellent, she thought, in the placing of such an emotional burden on a young child.

Alec climbed on to a jagged grey rock. 'All the young people know they'll probably have to leave the island. My mother won't admit it, but it's true. I had to leave and so did Cat. You go away to school and university or you go away to work. Some people return but most don't. They go to the mainland or to England or even to America. There's little work here, and anyway, island life's too hard

367

and it's too restricting. People won't put up with it these days. I help out whenever I come home, but most of the burden falls on my mother. At some point, I'm going to have to start pulling my weight. Mother's kept the place going since my father died and now she believes it's my turn. And she's right.' He looked back at her. 'You wouldn't want me to be the sort of man who'd leave his mother to cope with everything on her own, would you, Ellen? You couldn't love that sort of man?'

'No, perhaps not. But—'

'We'll work something out, I know we will. The thing that matters most to me is to be with you.' He came to sit beside her, putting his arm round her. 'Poor girl, you look tired. I'd meant this to be a holiday for you.'

'It is. I didn't sleep well last night, that's all. The storm . . .' She had been about to tell him about the footsteps she had heard in the night, but something made her reluctant to and she said instead, 'I dreamed about Dr Redmond. I wonder why.'

'Indigestion, probably, after that enormous meal.'

She laughed. 'Too much venison and red wine? Yes, I expect you're right.'

'What did you dream?'

'That I was falling.' The bleakness returned, tumbling over her like a shadow.

He hugged her. 'We'll go for a long walk this afternoon, work it off. Not here – you'd have to do several circuits of Easdale to make even a half-decent walk.'

Tentatively, she put to him an idea that had come to her during the night.

'Alec, why don't you ask your mother to come to London next month? Buy her a train ticket, book her into a nice hotel, give her a treat. We could take her round, show her the sights. I'm sure it would be good for her.'

'She won't come.' He looked out over the sea, frowning. 'I've asked her before, many times.'

'If you tried again . . . I thought that perhaps when we're married, if we were able to find a house in London – some lovely part of London, Hampstead or Richmond, somewhere like that – we could make one of the floors into a little flat for your mother. She might take a while to get used to the change, but who knows, she might love it. If we had children, it would mean she could be close to them. She wouldn't even need to sell this house if she didn't want to. Surely some tenant or factor could be found?'

'She wouldn't consider it.' He began to pack the remains of their breakfast into the knapsack. His voice was without timbre as he said, 'Ellen, my mother will never leave Kilmory House. She would never be happy anywhere else.'

And the thought occurred to her: and if I can never be happy here?

Chapter Nine

Marcus Pharoah was away for a fortnight in America. In his absence, India sought out the company of her old friends once more. There was a certain relief in being with Vinnie and Oliver and Simon, who didn't tell her off for failing to work out what to do with her life. In fact, some of her friends were far more aimless than she was, preferring to avoid work at all costs, sleeping on other people's sofas and pretending to be artists or writers, when really they stayed in bed all day and hung around pubs at night, now and then summoning up the energy to try and persuade someone to go to bed with them.

In their undemanding company, India spent an afternoon at Peachey's house, then dashed through the rain showers on to a pub. India was wearing the greeny-gold frock Marcus had bought her, a little damp because she hadn't brought a coat. She thought how happy she was to be

sitting with her friends, laughing and joking and fooling around. Ed and Justine joined them and they all wandered off to the West End. It was late, and a drizzle hung in the air, hazing the pavements, and only a few cars motored along the quiet streets.

Ed offered to pay their entrance to a nightclub. Ed was the only person who had enough money to buy drinks, and the others crowded round him at the bar, though India knew that away from him they often spoke of him as a figure of fun: Ed and his boring job in a bank and his wife who cheated on him. The room was dark and poky. India saw that the purple velvet curtains were marked with cigarette burns and the flocked wallpaper was peeling. The clientele sat at small, round tables draped with fringed cloth. India read in the faces that loomed out of the dim light expressions of boredom and envy and greed. She felt her buoyant mood of earlier in the evening start to slip away as she stood alone, smoking and listening to the three-piece band.

Then she saw him. Bernie, making his way towards her, cutting through the throng at the bar. She felt a rising panic, mixed with revulsion. Since she and Marcus Pharoah had become lovers, she had kept away from Bernie.

She dropped her cigarette on the floor and hurried out of the room. In the street, she took off her high heels and ran along the pavement until she saw a taxi. She hailed it and climbed into the back seat, where she sat, her shoes in her lap, catching her breath. Looking out of the rear

windscreen, she saw Bernie standing on the pavement, his short, plump form broken into smudged, glittering fragments by the street lamps and the raindrops on the glass.

Ellen went with Riley and Annie and Annie's friend, Kathleen, to Regent's Park. There was a chill in the air and the fallen leaves were piling up on the grass.

She said, 'I may have to give up my work and go and live on the island.'

Riley threw her a glance. 'You're not serious, are you?'

'Yes, I am. I didn't understand, you see, Riley.' Briefly, she told him about the dinner party at Catriona's house, and about her mortifyingly public discovery that she and Alec were expected to live on the island after they married.

He pointed out, 'That's not the same as *Alec* expecting it.'

'But I think it will happen.' Her voice was heavy.

'Only if you agree to it. What does Alec say?'

'Not much.' She scuffed leaves on the grass.

'You weren't aware of this before?'

'No, not properly.'

She thought back to their quarrel, while the storm had whipped up the breakers on the sea. Since then, they had discussed their future on numerous occasions but had come to no conclusions.

She said, 'Alec told me that he's been putting off returning to the island for years. And that makes him feel guilty, because he knows his mother needs him. I can see that he's in an impossible situation.'

'It's difficult for him, yes.'

She sensed something held back, and said quickly, 'It's not unreasonable, Riley. It's his home.'

'But you have reservations.'

'Yes, I do.'

The girls were kicking up heaps of leaves and jumping into them.

'I love Alec,' said Ellen. 'I love him so much. So why can't I just do it, tell him that of course we'll live on Seil, without thought, without regret?'

'Because it's a big step. What is it that puts you off?'

'Oh . . . the weather.' She smiled as she looked at him. 'I know that's feeble. But I'm a southern girl. And the remoteness – I'd be so far away from my family and friends. And then, as I said, my career. I would have to give up my career.'

'Hard for you, I should have thought.'

'But not unexpected. I've always known that unless I remain single, I'd probably have to stop work for a while, especially if I had a baby. And women's careers are always thought less important than men's, aren't they?' She dug her hands into her jacket pockets and walked on. 'And it's not as if I would necessarily be the only one who has to give up work. Alec will have a better chance than me of getting a part-time lectureship in Glasgow or Edinburgh because he's published more papers. But even he couldn't be sure.'

She watched Annie and Kathleen running ahead in fits

and starts, pink-cheeked, plaits flying. She said, 'But I could cope with all those things – the cold, the remoteness, and even giving up my career. What I'm not sure I can cope with is Marguerite.'

'You don't get on?'

'We're fine on the surface. We don't argue, anything like that.' She paused, finding it hard to put into words the fears that nagged at her. 'I think I can see what she's doing. She's lost her husband and she's making sure she doesn't lose her son as well.'

'Is that how she views the marriage? As losing her son?'

'I'm afraid so.'

'What does Alec think?'

'He can think no wrong of her. He won't *allow* himself to think any wrong of her.'

Spying a large Alsatian dog, Annie ran towards it. Riley loped after her, calling out her name. Ellen heard Annie grumbling, as they walked back hand in hand, 'If I had a dog, Daddy, I wouldn't have to talk to other people's dogs.'

When she had run off to play with Kathleen again, Ellen gave Riley an amused look. 'Will you buy her a dog?'

'Probably, for Christmas. She's very keen. It will make our lives more complicated, no doubt. Renée, the au pair, goes back to Switzerland in a couple of months so I shall have to find someone else.'

They parted to skirt a woman pushing a large pram, laden with twins; when they moved together again he said,

'You're concerned that if you move to the island then you'll both be under Marguerite's thumb.'

'She's manipulative. I feel very disloyal saying that, and I'd only say it to you, Riley. For instance, she likes to make out she's frail and delicate. Now and then she's unwell and poor Alec has to go dashing all the way up to Scotland. Usually it's at some crashingly inconvenient time for us, when we've been invited for dinner somewhere nice or we're planning a weekend away. And she always miraculously recovers in a couple of days. And she keeps telling us how difficult it is for her to get to the shops or to see her friends. She has everyone running around after her – Alec and Donald and Dr Campbell, all acting as her chauffeur. But she has a perfectly good car sitting in the garage. Last time we were there, I offered to teach her to drive.'

'What did she say?'

'She just laughed, as if I'd said something ridiculous. Said that she couldn't possibly. I asked her why not and she said she was afraid not all women were as strong and practically minded as I was. But she's as tough as old boots – I've seen her in the garden, hacking away at branches and clearing out streams. Oh dear.' Ellen grimaced. 'Listen to me. I sound such a bitch.'

He smiled. 'Hardly.'

'And then there's Catriona.'

'The girl next door . . .'

'Yes. If it wasn't for Catriona's . . .' again, she searched for the word, 'her history with my future husband, I'd probably

rather like her. When Marguerite's being particularly self-sacrificing, Catriona makes faces behind her back.' Ellen picked up a conker and passed it from hand to hand. 'Catriona's beautiful, Riley.'

'So are you.'

'Kind of you. But I'm not wild and devil-may-care. I can't sail a yacht single-handed because I'd probably be seasick, and I can't climb a mountain because I'm afraid of heights. Marguerite *adores* Catriona. But I can't pretend to be the sort of woman Marguerite would prefer me to be. I just can't, Riley, I've never been any good at pretending. And I can see Marguerite looking at me and comparing me to Cat and thinking, what on earth does he see in her? And with Cat – she thinks Catriona's such a sweet girl, and believe me, Riley, Cat may have many fine qualities, but sweetness certainly isn't one of them.'

'You're engaged to Alec, Catriona isn't. Alec has chosen you. What Mrs Hunter thinks doesn't matter.'

'But they used to be lovers.' She found it hard even to say. 'Alec and Cat.' She saw him frown.

'Some time ago, presumably.'

'Before he left the island to go to university.'

'Then—'

'Catriona's still in love with him, I'm sure of it.'

She stared moodily ahead of her, at the bronze-leaved trees and the green of the grass, already dulling with the coming autumn. 'Sometimes I think I'm imagining it,' she said quietly. 'I think about the things that are troubling

me and they hardly seem anything at all. Maybe Marguerite was too busy or too tired to say something nice. Or maybe she was trying to be tactful with me and ended up putting her foot in it. You know how you do, when you're trying too hard.'

Riley didn't say anything, and after a while she went on, her voice level, 'But I don't think she likes me. Alec says she does, but I don't feel it.' No: she had felt no affection or liking from Marguerite, only a mind made up, and an obdurate will. She muttered, 'I'm not having her drive us apart.'

He gave her a sharp look. 'Is there any risk of that?'

'No, of course not. We don't have to like each other, do we? It's Alec I'm marrying, not Marguerite.'

'But you may have to live with each other.'

'Exactly, Riley. The nail hit on the head.'

'Ellen, not all things are solvable. Alec may have to make a choice, and if he does, he'll choose you.'

'How do you know that?'

'Because he's in love with you.'

They walked for some time in silence. But she said suddenly, 'I sometimes think, would I ask such a thing of Alec? If it was the other way round, would I expect him to leave his home and career and bury himself in Wiltshire with my family?'

His gaze snapped round, clear-eyed. 'Would you, Ellen?'

'No, I don't think so. It would seem too much to ask. So where does that leave me?' She broke off, pressing her

fingers against her mouth. 'I can't bear to think he doesn't love me as much as I love him!'

Standing in front of her, he put his arms round her. She laid her head against his shoulder and closed her eyes, squeezing back the tears. She thought how differently she felt here in London, in Riley's company, how relieved and how free. Yes, that was it: free. Each time she went away from Kilmory House, she felt free again.

'You can't measure love,' he said gently. 'You can't weigh it up like that.'

'Can't you? Are you sure of that?'

'It's not a scientific equation, Ellen.'

She made a sound between a laugh and a sigh. 'No, I suppose not.'

'And sometimes one person has to give a little more than the other. Talk to Alec. Tell him how you feel. You'll sort it out.' He, too, laughed as they walked on, his hand lightly balanced on her shoulder. 'I don't think I'm the person to be giving you marital advice, Ellen, but there you have it, to the best of my ability.'

And yet, parting from her later that afternoon, Riley felt troubled. What Ellen was telling him was that Hunter wasn't listening. It was a measure of her loyalty and affection that she was even considering giving up her job and moving in with her future mother-in-law. Riley thought what a fool Alec Hunter was, demanding that she immure herself in the wilderness. But then, he had had Alec Hunter down

as self-absorbed years ago, when he had interviewed him at Gildersleve Hall, and the dinner at Ellen's flat had done little to alter his opinion of him. Possibly unfair, he acknowledged. He couldn't help but see Hunter through a rather cracked lens.

At home, he cooked supper while Annie sat at the table and learned her spellings. They had the dog conversation again over supper, and then Annie went to bed.

In the sitting room, he put on a record of Mozart's wind quintets, poured himself a Scotch, and took a file out of his briefcase. His visit to the Blue Duck nightclub had supplied Riley with the name of another of Bernie Perlman's spiders. The ginger-haired man – Sergeant Davies's 'spectre' – was called Lee Carter. Carter worked for Perlman as a general dogsbody, chauffeur and errand boy. A teenage delinquent with an absent father during the war years, he had graduated to a career of theft and street violence before starting to work for Perlman. A few years ago, Carter had been interviewed in connection with a murder in Battersea. The victim had had his kneecaps smashed before being tied to a pier and left to drown in the muddy tidal shallows of the Thames. Riley saw in the extreme violence and the flamboyance of the violence something in common with the death of George Clancy. Carter was a nasty piece of work.

The girl that Riley had helped up from the floor of the nightclub was called Janey Kelly. He had seen her once or twice since that evening, had bought her a coffee and

chatted to her, if she was in the mood. He thought she was a nice girl beneath the veneer of hardness, and he could tell that she was frightened of Carter and Perlman. Riley felt sorry for her, as out of her depth as a rabbit caught up in the blades of a combine harvester, and as likely to be crushed.

He was trying to establish the scope of Bernie Perlman's business interests. A lodging house here, a warehouse there, a nightclub, a casino or two. On a map of London, you could have seen how Perlman's empire had grown in a steady dark sprawl. Put together the pieces and something, eventually, would give up its secrets.

But tonight he couldn't concentrate. After a while, he put the file aside and sat, letting the music flow over him, remembering how it had felt to hold Ellen in his arms: the beat of her heart, the scent of her hair. *I'd only say it to you, Riley* – he found himself holding on to such fragments, as if he was searching for diamonds in the dust.

India and Sebastian were supposed to be going to tea with Sebastian's old headmaster, Mr Taylor, but India was late. She had arrived at work that morning almost an hour late and had gone on being late throughout the day – late to get the tables cleaned and set for lunch, late to clear away lunch, with some customers still eating their apple pie and custard while others arrived for scones and tea. Then she had to work late to make up the time lost and so wasn't able to leave the café until six. She

couldn't afford to have her wages docked: there were bills to pay.

As she walked down the street, she unbuttoned her overall and pulled out the hair clips she used to pin back her fringe while she was working. She imagined Sebastian and Mr Taylor sitting in the chintzy back room at the school, politely waiting for her, their tea going cold. Nearing the house, she saw a big black car waiting by the kerb. Lee was in the driver's seat, Bernie was sitting beside him. India's mouth went dry and she felt a mingling of anger and dread.

She considered not bothering getting changed and turning round and walking away in the other direction, but there was a smear of gravy down her jersey, and anyway, why should bloody Bernie stop her getting into her own home?

As she approached, Bernie wound down the window of the car. 'Hello, India.'

'Hello, Bernie.'

'I haven't see you for a while.'

'I've been busy.'

'Thought the two of us could go for a drink.'

'No thanks. I'm meeting someone.'

India scrabbled in her bag for her front door key. Bernie got out of the car. He said, 'I've got the feeling you've been avoiding me, India.'

Where was the bloody key? She tried to remember what had happened that morning. Sebastian had left for work

before she had got up. Had she taken her key? Had she even remembered to lock the door? Maybe she had forgotten and had just pulled it to.

'I told you,' she said to Bernie. 'I've been busy.'

'Disappointing. And after you promised me.'

'Promised you?' She looked up from her handbag. 'I've never promised you anything.'

'Oh yes, you did. All those drinks I've bought you. All those times I've treated you.'

She stared at him. She thought of his horrible parties and his stupid women and what he had done to Garrett.

She said, 'It's never a treat being with you, Bernie.'

Bernie's round, flat, walnut face altered. 'What did you say?'

India was fired up with fury and vengefulness. 'Didn't you know? People put up with you because you're rich and you think you're important, but they don't like you. Why should they? You're stupid and short and fat and ugly and you frighten people.'

Bernie grabbed hold of her ponytail and yanked her head back sharply. 'Shut up, you silly little bitch.'

He had pulled her head so far back it almost touched the roof of the car. India dropped her handbag. Tears sprang to her eyes and she gasped with pain.

Bernie gave her hair another vicious tug. 'No one talks to me like that,' he said. 'Specially not a tart like you.'

He let go of her ponytail and she staggered. Bernie's fat forefinger jabbed at her.

382

'You want to think about it. You want to think a bit more about what you say to me, India.'

The car roared away from the kerb in a screech of tyres. India put her hands to her head. She imagined chunks of hair coming out of her scalp, but when she cautiously explored it, only a few strands came away. Several passers-by were staring at her, but their faces were blurred by her tears. The contents of her handbag had scattered over the pavement; she scooped everything up and in doing so found her door key, tangled up with a bracelet and a rubber band. Wiping her eyes dry with her sleeve, she let herself into the building.

One of the girl computers stuck her head round the door of Ellen's lab and told her that there was a phone call for her. The phone was in an adjacent office. Ellen picked up the receiver and said her name.

'This is Catriona Campbell.'

A shock. She replied, 'Miss Campbell, hello. How are you?'

'I'm very well, thank you. I'm in London for a few days and I wondered whether we might meet up.'

'Alec has a lot on. I'd have to check with him.'

'I don't want to talk to Alec, I want to talk to you. I'm staying in Chelsea. Would you be able to meet me for lunch in Peter Jones?'

A mixture of curiosity and suspicion made Ellen say, 'Yes, at one o'clock.'

Catriona was already sitting at the table when Ellen arrived at the restaurant. Catriona was wearing a tailored peacock-blue jacket and a neat matching hat, trimmed with net. There was a stack of carrier bags beside her seat.

The two women exchanged the usual pleasantries while their orders were taken and served, but then Catriona said, 'I know you hate me, but there are things I need to say to you.'

'I don't hate you.'

'You should do, after that frightful dinner.' Catriona shrugged. 'In different circumstances I should probably have liked you. But we're both in love with the same man and that makes friendship impossible.'

'I don't want to know.' Ellen was unable to disguise her anger. 'Why are you telling me these things?'

'Because you should know what you're up against. You won't believe me, but I'm here out of kindness to you.'

And self-interest, Ellen thought. She said stiffly, 'Please say what you've come here to say.'

'I've always loved Alec.' Though Catriona spoke with composure her fingers crumbled the bread roll on her side plate. 'I can't remember a time when I didn't love him. Oh, I'm not going to pretend that I've never looked at another man – I'd have gone mad with boredom if that were true – but I've never *loved* another one.'

'But he doesn't love you.' Cruel, but it had to be said.

Catriona's reaction showed only in a small tightening of the mouth. 'Not now, I know that. But that can change in

384

time. I can be patient, I can wait. And anyway, I would have him even under those circumstances.'

'Alec loves me!' Ellen rose clumsily.

'*Please.*' Catriona spoke softly, and for the first time, Ellen noticed the pain in her eyes.

She gave a small shrug: well, if you must, and sat down again. 'I expect you're going to tell me that Marguerite would rather Alec married you.'

'I'm sure you've worked *that* out for yourself. She makes no attempt to hide it. Dear old Marguerite, so doggedly self-absorbed. If it's any comfort to you, I don't believe that it's out of any attachment to me. She'd rather Alec married me simply because it would mean he stayed on the island.'

'There's no reason why we can't stay on the island too, after we're married.'

'Isn't there? Do you really think you could bear it? Marguerite won't change, you know. She's far too used to having her own way. That's the awful thing about people like her, you can't change them so you end up giving in to them. Marguerite sees only what she wants to see and hears only what she wants to hear.'

There was something she had to know. 'Have you and Marguerite talked about me?'

'A little, yes.'

'I suppose she tells you when Alec and I are to visit.'

'She may have mentioned it.' For the first time, a flicker of shame crossed Catriona's face. 'Ellen, I'm not at

Marguerite's beck and call, if that's what you're saying. I wouldn't sink so low. It's just that I need to see Alec sometimes. I couldn't bear not to see him at all. I've tried that and I was miserable. Of course, it's miserable too to see him with someone else, but it's better than nothing.' She gave a thin smile. 'It's dishonourable of me, I agree, to keep coming back, keep hoping he'll change his mind, but there you are. I've often thought I should marry some rich consultant and stay away from the island, but I can't seem to make myself.'

Catriona seemed then to notice her destruction of the bread roll and wiped her hand on her napkin. She said briskly, 'I expect you're waiting for Alec to put his foot down, or for Marguerite to change her mind or to realize how torn he is. I would be, in your position. Bad enough living with Marguerite, but to have to share the house with Francis Hunter's tiresome ghost as well . . .'

'I don't know what you mean.'

'Did you know that she still keeps Francis's old clothes? They still hang in his wardrobe – she has his shirts laundered each week.' Catriona's lip curled in distaste. 'I'm going to tell you the truth about him. You'll have a different version from Marguerite, no doubt, but I think you should know. I was eleven when Francis Hunter died, so I remember him a little, though not very well. I remember finding him dislikable. He was one of those men who believe it their duty to correct any mistakes a child makes, any mispronunciation or faulty manners. My mother was

brought up on the island and she knew him well. She told me that Francis Hunter was a controlling bully. She said that he dominated Marguerite, and that Marguerite let him. Marguerite likes to play the defenceless little woman, you must have noticed that.'

'I don't see why this matters to me.'

'Well, why should you? These tedious old love affairs . . . Romeo and Juliet pale beside Marguerite and Francis.'

'All that's in the past. It's the present – and the future – Alec and I have to think about now.'

'But Marguerite's past will dictate your future, don't you see? Marguerite will never leave the island. Never. You must believe me, for your own sake. She clings on to Francis – to the myth of Francis – through the island. And she won't give up on Alec either. She's lost one of the men she loves and she'll do anything to hang on to the other. But the most important thing you need to realize is that Alec will, in the end, do as his mother wants. I've known him far longer than you have, Ellen, and I know his faults. Alec avoids emotional scenes. It's because of his mother, of course – he's had to endure her dramas all his life. And my God, can't Marguerite ladle it on when she wants to. Alec will never confront her and he'll never say no to her. I suppose the nearest he's come to standing up to her was when he became engaged to you. It was a shock to her, I can tell you. I expect he didn't tell her about it beforehand because he knew she would try to dissuade him.'

There was an unsettling ring of truth to that. There had been a recklessness about their engagement, and it occurred to her now that Alec had rushed into it so that he could present his mother with a fait accompli.

No. She would not believe that. She said, 'He didn't speak to his mother beforehand because there was no need to. It was between him and me. He's a grown man, he doesn't have to ask his mother's permission to get married.'

'Marguerite wants Alec home, and in the end, Alec will do what his mother wants.'

'You can't know that.'

'Oh, I do, I'm afraid. And I think you're beginning to know it too, Ellen.'

The small smile that had set around the corners of Catriona's mouth seemed at odds with the hurt and weariness in her eyes. She took a packet of John Player's out of her bag and waved them at Ellen. 'You don't, do you?'

'No thanks.'

'Coffee and cigarettes – how else would I keep going through a night shift? But what a fool I am, waiting for him! It ties me to nursing, which I loathe, and it means I'll never settle for anyone else. So there's another thing you should know. When Alec does, in the end, go back to the island, I mean to be there. I would do anything for him, you see. I would even submit to living with Marguerite. I'd marry him tomorrow, if he asked me, and I wouldn't so much as look back.'

'You had your chance.' Ellen's voice shook with anger and apprehension. 'Ten years ago, you had your chance.'

'Did I?' Catriona frowned. 'I'm not so sure. Alec wasn't ready to marry anyone ten years ago. It almost destroyed me to learn that. I'd thought he felt the same as I did. But you're capable of such self-deception, aren't you, when you're seventeen. It hurt so much to know that he could walk away from me. I'm afraid I wasn't very nice to him. In fact, I found myself wanting to make him hate me.' Catriona blew out a stream of smoke and, smiling, looked up at Ellen. 'I've sometimes regretted that. But then, they say that love and hate aren't always that far apart, don't they?'

Coming home from work a few days after her encounter with Bernie, India saw that the front door to the flat was open. She went inside. The room was in a terrible mess, as if a whirlwind had blown through it, throwing their possessions around anyhow. Books lay on the floor, splayed open, face down, and ornaments had been broken and plant pots upturned, smearing the carpet with earth.

Then she saw Sebastian. He was crouched on the floor by the sideboard, his head lowered and his arms wrapped round his knees. He had made himself into a small, tight ball. India knelt down beside him. When she put a hand on his shaking shoulder he flinched.

'Sebastian?' she said. She tried to keep the panicky rise out of her voice. 'Darling, what is it? What's happened?'

'Sorry,' he muttered. 'Sorry.'

As he straightened, wiping a hand over his face, India saw the pink marks round his neck.

'Who did this?' Though she had guessed.

'He was here.' Sebastian's eyes kept darting back to the front door. 'In the flat. When I came home. I just let him.'

India felt sick with fear. 'What did he want?'

'I don't know.' Sebastian's voice sounded hoarse. 'He didn't say. He knew my name, though. And yours, India!'

Looking at the angry marks on her brother's neck, India felt rage and an overwhelming guilt. 'Was he tall? Ginger hair? Stupid-looking?'

Sebastian nodded.

'If he's hurt you—'

'S'all right. I just fell against the wall.' He rubbed his head. Then he whispered, 'I didn't do anything! I didn't even try to stop him!'

'Well, thank God for that,' said India tartly. 'He'd have killed you if you had.' She rose to her feet. 'I'll make us a cup of tea.'

She went into the kitchen and stood for a moment, her hands on the edge of the sink, feeling sick. Lee had had fun in here as well, emptying tins and packets over the floor and pulling saucepans and crockery out of the cupboard. Aunt Rachel's bone-china tea set, pink flowers and gold leaf, lay in pieces on the floor. Consumed with fury, India knelt down and picked up the broken fragments.

Then she put on the kettle and went back into the other

room where Sebastian was trying to fit a geranium back in the pot.

India said, 'Seb, he won't come back. Honest. I'll make sure of it.'

They hugged, and then she made the tea, crushing three aspirins and lots of sugar into Sebastian's cup. They began to clear up the flat, putting the books back on the shelves, sweeping up the soil. Although India had resolved to make sure that Lee would not return, she knew that he was a headcase, so she wedged a chair beneath the front-door handle. The telephone rang several times but she did not answer it. Bernie had sent Lee to the flat to punish her for the things she had said to him, and as a reminder of a debt owed. She knew that they could change the locks, put up bolts, but someone like Lee would always find a way in.

When the worst of the mess was gone, she cooked supper. After they had eaten, they sat on the sofa side by side, listening to the radio. India smoked and chewed her nails, thinking, as some man talked about dahlias.

She had to work out what to do about Sebastian. The flat wasn't safe any more, would never be safe again. She must send Sebastian away somewhere where Bernie would never find him. Her only alternative was to go to Bernie. To offer herself up to him, to share his bed, to become one of his entourage.

She would sooner have died. She knew how Bernie liked his women, humiliated and submissive, the fight beaten

out of them. By the time he tired of her, there wouldn't be much left of her.

So. They could shove a few things in a bag, she could cadge some money off friends, they could get on a train and start again somewhere else. She knew, as she considered it, that it would not do. Each time they moved – and she would always be looking over her shoulder – they would become a little poorer, a little lonelier. Sebastian would hate it, moving around all the time, never having a real home. She would find friends, she always did, but what sort of friends?

There were other futures she needed to avoid. You could be too free, she had learned that a long time ago. You would always have men friends, because you were pretty and amusing, though in your emptier moments you might find yourself lying on the sofa, leafing through a magazine and letting things slide. This was a more possible future for her than one as Bernie's tart, and because of that, equally frightening. The negligence and evasion of reality that had been a part of her mother's character was a part of her too. If she was not to repeat her mother's mistakes, then she must change. She must start again.

Sebastian had fallen asleep, huddled up on one end of the sofa. The man on the radio was still talking about dahlias. All India's choices were narrowing down to only one. She went into the hall, picked up the phone and dialled Marcus Pharoah's number.

* * *

392

The weather grew wilder as Alec and Ellen drove north. Darkness fell, and as they approached the Argyll coast, rain dashed against the windscreen of the car. Sometimes a twig, blown from the trees, cracked against the bonnet, and the steering momentarily lost traction as they forded deep puddles. The black landscape was relieved only by the twin beams of the headlamps, picking out the twists and turns of the road. Though she caught mere glimpses of the sea as they drove along the coastal road from Oban, Ellen was aware of its proximity, vast and formless and powerful.

It was past eight o'clock by the time they reached the island. Over supper, she heard the bow and scrape of the trees in the wind and the ricochet of dead leaves and twigs blown against the windowpanes. As Marguerite and Alec talked, Ellen's mind drifted. She found herself watching the scene as if from the outside, noticing how each participant took their allotted role, as friends and families so often do: Marguerite, queenly, directing the course of the conversation, Donald, affable and deferential, Alec, charming his mother and pacifying her moods. It came to her that this was a role he had adopted many years ago, when he had taken on the task of compensating for the absence of his father.

She had not told Alec about her lunch with Catriona. She could have predicted the conversation that would have ensued had she told him that Catriona was in love with him. He would have repudiated it. He would have said that

Cat was playing games. *Cat likes to make mischief* — she could hear his voice. Ellen had come to see that Alec shared some of his mother's reluctance to listen.

There was a pattern to their discussions about their future. She would believe they had come to a decision about where they would live after they married, only for it to disintegrate over the ensuing days or weeks. He should start to look for a junior lectureship in Glasgow, she would say, and Alec would agree. Time would pass and nothing would happen. He did not evade, but he seemed to forget — or not even that: what she saw as a resolution, he saw as merely a suggestion. She found herself filtering their relationship through the net of Catriona's words. She wondered whether, as Catriona had implied, Alec disliked the emotional fallout of confrontation so much that he hung on, hoping for circumstances to change, even after an atmosphere had become contaminated.

Ellen went to bed early. The journey had tired her and the storm unsettled her, yet she did not, as she had hoped, quickly fall asleep. Thoughts turned and roiled through her head, troubling and unresolved.

She must have been dozing shallowly when, opening her eyes, she heard it again. She sat up, listening.

A creak, a squeak, a flurry of scratches and scrapes. Someone — something — was in the attic. Against the silence of the night, the footsteps seemed resonant and unnaturally loud. The sounds settled down to a soft, rhythmic tread that moved with purpose and direction. The boundaries of

her room – walls, ceiling – seemed fragile, and she found herself glancing in the direction of the door.

Ellen forced herself to rein in her fear. Alec or Marguerite must have gone up to the attic, that was the only explanation. But why?

Putting on her dressing gown, she left her room. She was about to switch on the light in the corridor when she saw beneath a door ahead a narrow band of illumination. As she watched, the light died, then shone again. She found herself hesitating, afraid of what she might find when she opened the door, and then she reached out and turned the handle.

Revealed by the intermittent light, she saw in front of her half a dozen stairs, leading upwards. Another flash of light from the interior of the attic showed the high roof beams above and opaque, bulky objects stowed on the floor. Nothing moved. Only the light oscillated once more, and now the oscillation seemed to Ellen to have some pattern to it. As she climbed the stairs she found herself stepping softly, as if not to forewarn whatever prowled there of her presence. She should have brought a torch, she thought. It was not Alec, this thing that walked at night, she was certain of that, and the thought that the light might go out and leave her in the darkness produced in her a visceral fear.

Through a skylight she saw, lit by the moon, the gusting outlines of the clouds. She heard another footstep, saw another flash of light. Its source came from some distance

away; she made her way in that direction, winding between dusty suitcases and tea chests. Mentally, she matched the layout of the attic to that of the house below. Alec had told her that it was possible to walk through the attics from one end of the building to the other. She knew that she was heading for Kilmory House's westernmost end, the gable closest to the sea.

A circle of light lit up an arched window that looked out over the bay. Beside it, a figure was lit up, black against the bright light, its shadow streaking across the floorboards towards her.

A moment of cold terror: then she whispered, 'Marguerite.'

Slowly, the older woman turned towards her. She was holding a torch in her hand.

'I thought it was you.' Marguerite spoke quietly. 'Alec has always been such a sound sleeper. I can never sleep when there's a storm.'

'What are you doing?'

'I like to signal out to sea.'

Ellen suppressed a shiver. 'To whom?'

'Francis, of course. I like to think it helps him find his way home. It's just a fancy of mine. Some nights, the noise of the wind seems to come into my dreams. Come here.'

Ellen approached the window. Outside, curls of moonlight glimmered on the bay. 'Look,' murmured Marguerite. 'It's just a small boat, only a day cruiser, and it has white sails. It heads back into the bay from the open sea. The sails are torn and tattered and it seems to limp a little as it

makes for the harbour. He's tired, of course, after his long battle with the storm, but he was always a fine sailor and he brings the boat safely into port.'

And for a moment Ellen found herself searching the waters of the bay, almost believing that if she tried hard enough then she might see Francis Hunter's boat coming into Ellenabeich harbour.

But the sea was empty, of course. 'There's nothing,' she murmured.

'No. He's never there, my poor darling.' Marguerite put the torch down on the windowsill.

'Marguerite, why don't we go downstairs?' Ellen spoke firmly. 'I could make us some tea.'

Marguerite shook her head. 'You go.'

'I don't like to leave you here.'

'It comforts me. Has Alec told you about that night? It was wartime, nineteen forty-one. Francis was in the Navy, guarding the Atlantic convoys. He came home on leave that autumn. He was exhausted and so thankful to return to the island. One day, he decided to go fishing. I begged him not to go to sea that day. He wasn't well, he'd had a bad cold, and the weather was on the turn. I always think I should have tried harder. I always think, if only I'd found the right thing to say.'

'You mustn't blame yourself, Marguerite.'

Again, Marguerite smiled. 'Oh, I don't. He was a man who knew his own mind. A wind got up and the storm must have swept him out to sea. The *Mairead* wasn't built

for heavy weather. I often think how it must have been for him, and how he must have fought against it. I wonder whether he felt frightened. He wasn't a fearful man, but I think how lonely he must have felt and how weary. And I wonder whether he knew that he was losing the battle.' She turned towards the window again. 'I wonder if his spirit revisits that night, if he's still there in some way, struggling against the storm, if only I could push aside the veil.'

Moonlight flickered on Marguerite's face, illuminating the curve of cheekbone and jaw, the same lines and angles that made up Alec's face.

'When he didn't come home I raised the alarm, and the fishing boats went out to look for him. But there were so few of them because of the war and it took them a long time to find him. All that night and day I watched for him from the attic. You get the best view of the bay up here. I was afraid that if I let myself sleep or rest or eat, then he'd never come home. I thought that I could bring him back by the strength of my longing. But they didn't bring him home until halfway through the next afternoon. I stayed up here until I saw the boats coming in and then I ran down to the harbour. He was still alive then – just – but his cold had turned to pneumonia. Henry Campbell did his best, but it was too late. My poor Francis was dead by nightfall.'

'I'm so sorry, Marguerite.' The words sounded thin and inadequate in the face of such grief. 'How terrible for you.'

Marguerite put a hand on the glass. 'When they brought him back to the house, he didn't speak to me. He was delirious and it was hard for him to breathe. But I knew what he wanted to say to me. He died in the house he loved and with me by his side.'

'That must be some comfort to you.'

'Do you think so? What would you know?'

There was such a fierce rage in Marguerite's eyes that Ellen stepped back, saying, 'I'm sorry – forgive me – that was a foolish thing to say.'

'No, no – you're young, how could you understand?' The rage died, the gaze dropped. 'It sometimes feels as if everything that's happened since that night has been a dream. Perhaps one night I'll look out of the window and I'll see his boat coming in, and I'll run down to the harbour again. And this time it will end differently. He'll bring the *Mairead* home and I'll take him in my arms and I'll never let him go.' A small smile. 'There's that phrase, isn't there, "mad with grief". And you think, before it happens to you, that it's just something people say. But it is a sort of madness, I think, when you lose someone you love as much as I loved Francis. It's as if you've been torn to pieces. At first, you don't even want to put them together, but I had to, for Alec's sake. You can't tear your hair out and go about in sackcloth and ashes if you have a child. But it was hard. So hard. Alec was such a comfort to me. He'd let me talk for hours. He never minded, never ran off to play like other boys would have done. Such a comfort.'

'Come downstairs, Marguerite,' Ellen said gently. 'Please.'

Marguerite's eyes focused on her. 'I daresay you think I'm an old fool, coming up here at night. I don't speak to Alec about it, he doesn't approve. But I wondered whether you thought . . .'

'What?'

'I've always believed, you see, that some events have an echo of their own.'

'An echo?'

'Do you think it's possible, Ellen?' Now, Marguerite's eyes were shining. 'Do you think that a tragedy, some great event, can mark a place? Do you think that something can remain, even after they're gone, some vestige of a soul?'

And Ellen found herself remembering something that Martin Finch had once said to her in the pub in Copfield. *But has this idea that you can explain the sighting of ghosts using quantum theory.* And for a moment her mind flew along strange and irrational paths, producing hypotheses, conjuring up mechanisms by which happiness and tragedy might imprint itself so deeply into the stones of a house that an event might recur endlessly, bouncing off time and space, implacable, relentless.

No. Nonsense, all of it.

She said, 'Isn't it our emotions, our feelings that live on? Isn't it love that remains?'

'So rational. But after Francis died, I felt his presence in this house.'

'Alec told me you'd employed a medium.'

'Did he? He told you that?'

'He was trying to explain ...' But she broke off, reddening, aware of a feeling of intrusion.

'It's a long time since I've felt Francis's presence.' Again, Marguerite's fingertips went to the glass, as if she was reaching out to touch her lost husband. 'It's as if time wears these things away.'

'Perhaps it's better that way. Kinder. We should concentrate on the living, shouldn't we?'

'Such a funny little thing. You try hard, don't you? I'm sorry if I frightened you. You must forgive me. But I can't disregard what I feel, I can't put it aside because it doesn't fit into whatever theory Alec and his friends think is right.' Marguerite's gaze swung back to Ellen. 'On all other matters our minds meet perfectly.'

Ellen said evenly, 'When you love someone so much it must be hard to let them go.'

'I had no intention of letting Francis go. I was convinced that he didn't want it either. Or perhaps you're speaking of Alec.'

Now the swords were drawn. Ellen said, 'He needs to be allowed to make his own way.'

'Alec's way is my way. He knows he must return to the island.'

'Only because he feels an obligation to you.' There, she had said it, though her heart was rattling like a small creature shaking the bars of its cage.

'Not only to me, Ellen, to his home. Alec loves his home. He loves the island.'

'You can love a place without being bound to it your entire life.'

'Can you? Is that what you think of as love?'

'Love should confer freedom. If you truly loved someone, you'd want to set them free.'

'Would you?' Marguerite's expression was scornful. 'Your generation has such a pallid idea of love. I would have followed Francis to the ends of the earth if he had told me to – and beyond, if I could. So tell me, what of duty, what of responsibility? Why break the ties that hold a family together? Why break the ties that hold a people to a place?'

'I've no wish to keep Alec away from his home.'

'His home will die without him, surely you see that. This island, too. The young will go and only the old will be left and that will be the end of it. Everything that Francis and the Hunters stood for, everything they worked so hard for would be meaningless if that were to happen. All those memories gone, all that history.'

'Why do you dislike me so?' The words flew from her throat. 'What have I done?'

Marguerite's eyes washed over her, measuring, dissatisfied. 'I don't dislike you. You're pleasant enough. But you are not the woman my son should marry.'

The phrase echoed like the toll of a bell.

'Would you prefer Catriona?'

'Catriona has her faults, but yes, I would. You,' Marguerite's lips pursed, 'you try too hard to oblige. You lack boldness. I've always despised timidity.'

'Civility, I'd call it.'

'Would you? No matter. It takes a certain sort of person to live here. It's so much harder, of course, if you're not born to the island. Do you remember when I showed you my garden and you were afraid to look over the edge of the terrace? I knew then you wouldn't do.'

'In your estimation, perhaps. Not in Alec's.'

'You would not be happy here, Ellen. I think you know that in your heart.'

'No, that's not true!'

Marguerite had moved closer to her. 'You know that I'm right. Think.' Her voice lowered, became soft and insinuating. 'Think what our winters are like. Think how alone you'd feel, cut off from everything you know. Wouldn't you long for home – for your home? Wouldn't you miss your work and your studies? Oh, you'd try not to be homesick, you'd try to make the best of it, to find new interests and new occupations, but wouldn't it always be there at the back of your mind, that regret, that suspicion that you'd made a mistake? A woman like you wouldn't be content to settle for the life of a rural Scottish housewife. Why should you be?'

'Because I love Alec!'

'But you don't belong here. Francis did. Alec does. But you never will.'

403

The torchlight illuminated Marguerite's eyes, showing them to be an implacable blue, and her words seemed to claw into Ellen's mind, voicing the questions that had tormented her for months. Because it was not only Alec who was capable of evasion, she saw that now; she was too, and it seemed to her that Marguerite was right, and that had she been a different person – a bolder person – then she might have seen the traps that lay in front of her sooner and fought harder for the man she loved.

'I only want Alec to be happy.' Marguerite's voice was gentle. 'Don't you want that too, Ellen?'

'I would make him happy!' Yet her cry sounded like a lament.

'No, you would not. You would tear him in two.' The older woman touched her hand and Ellen shuddered. 'You're cold,' said Marguerite, quite kindly. 'You must go back to bed.'

Ellen stumbled out of the attic. The torch lit her path through the old, dust-covered chattels of Kilmory House. Her footsteps, treading through the dust, weighed the building down, anchoring it to the rock of the island.

When it was light, she rose, washed and dressed and went outside. Her eyes felt gritty and her head ached. Though the wind had eased, clouds billowed across the sky, grey islands that echoed those other islands that floated weight-less on the sea. The courtyard and lawn were littered with branches torn from the trees by the wind. When Ellen

climbed up the paths behind the house, she saw a few scarlet maple leaves floating on the surface of the ponds. She had not dared hope that the fresh air might relieve her depression and fatigue; no, she knew that the events of the previous night permitted no such mercy. But she was thankful to be out of the house.

Reaching the topmost terrace, she went to stand by the low wall that separated it from the sheer drop below. Her fear of heights had gone, vanquished by another, much greater dread. She found herself remembering her dream in which she had fallen from this terrace, a dream which had echoed the death of Dr Redmond, and she wondered what it was in that event that had haunted her so long. They had not been close friends; indeed, she had hardly known him at all, but the memory of that evening had become a part of her, ingrained in her. Marguerite had spoken of certain events having an echo which oscillated for years, but the repulsion which Marguerite's obsession had effected in Ellen was deep-rooted and instinctive. Now, for the first time, she saw her reaction to Dr Redmond's death through Marcus Pharoah's eyes, and she knew that she had destroyed her own career through her neurotic imaginings and hysterical overreaction, just as Marguerite intended to destroy her future with Alec.

A rustle of leaves and then Hamish, the Scottie dog, pattered on to the terrace. He trotted towards her and she petted him, finding in his small, warm body some comfort. Far below, there was the sound of a door closing.

With Hamish cradled in her arms, Ellen looked down at Alec, crossing the lawn outside the house. Now and then as he headed through the garden, he would be consumed by the trees, but then he would emerge, climbing the hillside until he came through the wall of shrubs on to the terrace.

He came to stand beside her. 'You're up early. Are you all right? You look pale.'

'Did you know that your mother goes up to the attic at night to look for your father's boat?'

A frown. 'Still?'

'She was there last night.'

'She likes it up there, likes the view.'

She found herself searching his face for concealment and evasion. 'She goes to look for your father,' she said flatly.

'No, Ellen, that's not true.'

'She told me that she believes that something of your father remains. She called it an echo.'

'What are you saying? That my mother thinks she's seeing my father's ghost?'

She heard the anger in his voice, but persisted. 'Not that exactly, but that a part of her still hopes he'll come back.'

'And you judge her for that?'

'I'm not judging her. But Alec, the way your mother was talking to me, your father might have died six months ago, or maybe a year. Not fourteen years.'

'So we should set a time limit on grief? Miss someone

for twelve months but if it lasts any longer – what? It's a sign of madness?'

The dog, disliking perhaps the tenor of their voices, slipped out of Ellen's hold and pitter-patted away into the woodland.

'Last night,' she said slowly, 'although I knew that your father had been dead for so long, I still found myself looking out of the window and searching the sea for his boat. There was a moment when I almost believed that if you longed so passionately for someone you'd lost, you might bring them back to life. All my most deeply held beliefs sacrificed to irrationality and superstition. I'm not proud of that, and I don't want to be a part of it.'

Seeing him whiten, she could almost have postponed it, put off what she must say to him. It weighed so heavily on her heart that she found her gaze sliding away from him to the void below.

'You see, Alec, I don't think I can live here.'

'Not now, maybe. But we'll work something out.'

'No, not ever.' She looked up at him. 'So you must choose.'

'Ellen, that's not fair.'

'I'll visit the island two or three times a year and your mother can come and stay with us as often as she likes. But I can't live here. And I want you to make sure Marguerite knows that, Alec. I want you to speak to her today.'

'I can't do that. It would destroy her.'

'And me?'

'I'll do anything for you, Ellen, you know that.'

'Except this one thing.'

'Because it's unreasonable. No, it's worse than that, it's cruel.'

'I don't mean to be cruel. But your mother doesn't want me here.'

But as soon as she said it she regretted it, knowing it to be misjudged. His voice altered, becoming colder.

'I didn't know you could be like this. You seem to have taken against my mother from the start.'

'Is that how you see it?' The words shivered and she twisted her hands together. 'I'd have given up almost everything for you, Alec. I'd have given up my career and my home and my friends for you. But I won't give up my principles, my intellect, my beliefs. Not even for you.'

As she took hold of the ring on her finger, she heard him say, 'Ellen, please don't do this. You're upset. We need to talk about this calmly.'

Her hands were cold and the ring slid off easily. She held it out to him and he took a step back.

'Ellen, for God's sake.'

'I can't live in the same house as your mother, and your mother doesn't want me living in the same house as her. So I don't see a compromise, do you, Alec?'

'In time . . .'

But she did not wait to hear the rest of his sentence. It seemed to her that in those two words the point of no return had passed. That she had been teetering on the brink

and that the long fall had now begun. She took his hand and pressed the ring into it. She whispered, 'I'm so sorry, Alec,' and walked away.

There was a saying, wasn't there, about frying pans and fire, and India knew that there would be a price to pay, because there always was.

Sitting in the back of the car, which was driven by Marcus Pharoah's employee, Mr Gosse, India reflected on the events of the last twenty-four hours. The previous evening she had gone to Marcus Pharoah's flat in Belsize Park and had told him the truth. She had told him everything, about Garrett cheating Bernie out of his rent, and about her losing her temper with Bernie and about Lee hurting Sebastian. *There is this man, and I hate him so much. Have you ever had to be nice to someone you hated? It makes you feel dirty and small, like a mouse caught in a trap. Every so often he'll reach out a paw and play with me. If it suited him, he'd crush me.*

Pharoah had asked questions, gathered facts. It had reminded India of sitting an exam at school, or an awful consultation she had had a few years ago with a Harley Street consultant, when she had thought she was pregnant. She had laid open her life in all its shabby compromise for Marcus Pharoah to inspect.

Eventually, he had gone into another room to make phone calls. When he returned, he sat down beside her. 'This is what we'll do,' he said. 'A friend of mine, Matthew Sanderson, has a farm in Devon. I've spoken to Matt and

he says that Sebastian can go there. The Sandersons are good people and he'll be safe there. Sebastian can help on the farm and in return Matthew and Laura will give him board and lodging and a small wage. Gosse will drive the two of you to Devon tomorrow, India. You can settle your brother in and then you're to come back to London. You can stay here for a night or two until I find you somewhere quiet to live for the next couple of months. A seaside resort, perhaps. Yes, I know,' Marcus held up a hand, 'you're about to tell me that you'll be bored, but if you can't choose your friends more wisely then you have only yourself to blame.'

She asked about the flat and he told her that he would have it valued and put up for sale. So Aunt Rachel's flat was to be sold. Rachel who had rescued them, Rachel who had cared for them.

The journey to Devon had been long and now she was tired. India looked out of the car window, to the deep, dusky West Country lanes. The farm where she had just left Sebastian was wooded and meadowed and the Sandersons had gone out of their way to be welcoming to him. He would be fine, Sebastian had told her, when they had come to say goodbye. She had known she was leaving an important part of her life behind, and that they would never be so close again, and she had cried, her head buried in Sebastian's neck while he had hugged her.

Now, sitting in the back seat of the Jaguar, her gaze fixed on the back of Roy Gosse's neck, she thought about the

conversation she had had with Marcus Pharoah the previous evening. 'I want a nice house,' she said, and he said, 'Yes, of course.'

'And a baby.'

At that, he frowned. 'I don't think I want to go through all that again.'

This she was sure of: that if she were to lose her home and Sebastian, she needed something as well as Marcus Pharoah and his vast ambition and vanity.

'I want something of my own,' she said.

'You'll have me.'

'A baby, Marcus. Just one, if you say so. But that's what I want.'

They were in the sitting room of his flat. As she waited for his answer, she heard the distant rumble of traffic, the chime of a church bell.

And at last he said, 'Very well. One child, no more.' She put her arms round him and rested her head on his chest, and thought of doors closing in a long corridor behind her, perhaps for ever.

At Central Station in Glasgow, Ellen had half an hour before the London train left. She bought herself a cup of tea in the waiting room. Already regrets had begun to seep into her consciousness, but they came up against the barrier of her conversation with Alec on the terrace, washing like the waves against the slate jetties of Seil Island. In time, he had said to her; but time had worked against her, showing her

411

not that he loved his mother more, but that he had not loved her, Ellen, enough. The realization cut like a knife, and tears stung her eyes as she stirred her tea.

She had left Kilmory House before breakfast. She had not been able to face seeing Marguerite again and had quickly packed and asked Alec to drive her to Oban station. When he tried to stop her leaving she told him that she would walk to Oban, if necessary. In the car, he went over it all again. The hastiness of her decision, the irrationality of it. She was tired, she hadn't slept well, she had said so herself. They should go for a drive somewhere on the mainland, have a quiet chat, sort it out. The island could seem claustrophobic, he knew that. There was no need for her to rush back to London, and certainly no need to break off their engagement.

The landmarks of her journeys to Seil Island had unpeeled outside the windows of the car: the flooded quarries, the hills and marshes and the sea loch, as if her life was rushing backwards to a time before she had known him, a sparse time, as bleak as the black beaches on the island. She need say only a word, that was all, and yet her heart seemed to turn to stone a beat at a time, the cold drip-drip of her silence forming layers of disbelief and grief.

His mood, too, had changed by the time they reached Oban. As he carried her case on to the platform, he said angrily, why must she be so dramatic? And what would his mother think, her rushing off without a word?

She'll think she's won, she had thought dully.

She had gone because she had known that nothing would change. That morning would have gone on like all other mornings at Kilmory House, the routines unaltered by the conversations that had taken place in the preceding twelve hours. Had she asked too much of him? No, she did not believe so, but she felt the moment when her conviction would falter approaching, like the darkness inside a tunnel.

She left her cup of tea undrunk and went to catch her train. The red sandstone building had the melancholy of all railway stations when you are alone and unhappy, and she could almost have believed then that Marguerite had been right, and that she was sensing all the farewells that must have taken place here over the years. Waiting on the platform, her gaze went to the barrier, searching for him.

He did not come. The engine pulled in in a scream of smoke and soot and she opened a door and climbed inside. She walked along the corridor until she found an empty compartment. There was a cheap gossip magazine lying on a seat; she leafed through it as the pistons cranked and the train began to move. She longed to be back in London. She longed to be in her laboratory, working through some experiment, her mind engaged and her hands occupied with the delicate tasks she knew she did well. She needed the reassurance of measurable things.

Turning a page, she saw it. The photograph was of Marcus Pharoah and a young woman. The caption said, *Dr Pharoah, star of TV panel game 'Animal, Vegetable, Mineral', and his friend, Miss India Mayhew.* She was at first unable to take it in. This must

413

be some other India Mayhew, surely – but no, the name was uncommon, and besides, there was India, with her pale hair and that way she had of jutting out one hip as she looked up, laughing. And she remembered that she herself had introduced them, Marcus Pharoah and India Mayhew, a year ago, at the Royal Institution. *This is my friend, Miss Mayhew*, she had said, and, guessing the chain of action and reaction that must have followed that moment, a feeling of utter betrayal washed over her.

She closed the magazine and turned to the window. And she thought of Alec, and how she had left him, and pressed her forehead against the cold glass as she stared out at the passing city.

Chapter Ten

There was no answer when, the following day, Ellen rang the doorbell of the Mayhews' flat. No answer when she telephoned the next day, or the day after. No India, an apron over her frock, a cigarette in one hand and a wooden spoon in the other, stirring pots and pans on the stove.

The sense of betrayal she had felt, seeing that photograph of India with Pharoah, faltered. She knew that she had lost touch with India during her affair with Alec. Her need to be with him had been all-consuming and India had slipped down a list. She was not proud of that.

Where was India, where had she gone? Was she with Pharoah? In the shocked, bruised aftermath of her parting from Alec, when little else touched her, that thought nevertheless troubled her. India would be attracted by Pharoah's wealth and glamour. Pharoah would use her, as he had

used Andrée Fournier, and then, when he was tired of her, he would discard her.

Tuesday: Alec phoned. Hearing his voice, pleading with her to come back to him, she melted. She agreed to meet him the following evening for a meal. It was only when she saw him that she realized the depth of the emptiness she had endured over recent days. It was as if she had been hollowed out, her heart removed and put aside, raw and exhausted. He, too, looked tired and strained. As they ate an indifferent meal in a small café in the Strand, he promised to tell his mother that they would live in London after they had married. He would do whatever she wanted, if only she would come back to him.

They were together for three weeks. During that time, what began as a joyous reunion chilled. Where once, after making love, they had lain in bed together, lazily content, he now rose and dressed, saying little as he made coffee or made ready to go back to the lab. They bickered over small things – which film they would see, a difference of opinion over something they read in the newspaper. They argued about Suez: in Egypt, Nasser was buying fighter planes and reminding the British that their soldiers must leave the Suez Canal the following year.

When Ellen pointed out that Britain needed access to the canal, Alec said, 'You colonialists are all the same, you like to keep a country under your thumb.'

'Colonialists,' she echoed.

He shrugged. 'Military types, then. Always ready to send in the troops.'

One evening, there was a party to which an acquaintance had invited them.

'I can't see the point in hauling ourselves halfway across London,' said Alec.

'It would be a night out.'

'If you call warm beer and shop talk a night out.'

And so on, a low-grade, ill-tempered quarrel until he shrugged on his jacket, saying, 'OK, OK. I'd better not argue with you, had I?' and the shock of his words seemed to resonate inside her.

'What do you mean?'

His answer was cold-eyed and clear-voiced. 'You call the tune now, don't you, Ellen?'

A long silence, during which she tried to absorb the shock. She said, 'I don't think this is working, do you?'

He didn't reply. Fumbling around the room, gathering up coat and bag and gloves, her brain seemed to have lost the knack of telling her body what to do. Her buttons did not appear to fit into the holes made for them and her finger and thumb slipped on the clasp of her bag. Emerging from the flat, she stood for a moment on the pavement, unable to remember where to go.

The evenings were bad, the nights worse. She dreaded going to bed, anticipating the plummeting of her spirits that seemed to begin as soon as she put off the light, as if in the dark she was falling downstairs. She learned to

blur the empty hours with a drink or two. Sometimes she went to the pub with Joe, and sometimes, when there were bottles of beer in the kitchen, she took a couple into her room, always scrupulous about putting cash in the kitty to pay for them. It was easier to fall asleep after a drink. And a cigarette. Some nights, she padded downstairs, reinforced by alcohol, and dialled Alec's number. When he didn't pick up, she wondered where he was, who he was with. When he did answer, she put the phone down.

Just before Christmas, she found herself sitting on Riley's sofa, listening to John Coltrane and drinking whisky. Between his dashes upstairs now and then to check on Annie, who had mumps, Ellen talked about Alec. The entire affair, hardly pausing for breath, from the first moment she had seen him on the stairs at Gildersleve Hall to that final, devastating, *You call the tune now, don't you, Ellen?* She knew that she was being boring, and she knew when she started crying that she was being even more boring and that the next day she would feel mortified and humiliated. But she couldn't stop herself. Riley patted her back, gave her his handkerchief, said soothing things. While he went to have another look at Annie, she staggered to the bathroom. Her face was red and swollen, as if she, too, had mumps; she splashed cold water on it, missing and soaking her jersey because she was drunk. Returning downstairs, she curled up on one end of the sofa, her head on one of Pearl Riley's poppy-coloured cushions.

Riley woke her up and put a black coffee in her hand.

'I've called you a taxi,' he said. 'Will you be all right?' Then he made her check she had her keys and purse, helped her on with her coat and scarf and saw her into the taxi.

The next day, her pounding head and nausea was nothing compared to her sense of shame. When she remembered Riley virtually stuffing her arms into her coat, she wanted to hide in some dark corner and never come out again. How awful for him, how tedious and embarrassing. A sick child upstairs, a weeping woman downstairs. Another wave of mortification when she remembered suggesting to him that she sleep on his sofa. Perhaps he hadn't wanted her to because he had thought she might go on weeping and jabbering about Alec all night. Or perhaps he had even been afraid that she might make a drunken pass at him. *Oh God*, she thought, *never again*.

She went to Fortnums and arranged for the delivery of a bottle of malt whisky (for Riley) and a box of jelly babies (for Annie), along with a brief, apologetic note, to the Tufnell Park address. She had wanted his forgiveness; she had come to realize what a good friend he was. Then she went home for Christmas.

This was a turning point. Her mother was quietly comforting and at frequent moments produced cups of tea, boxes of chocolates and a shoulder to cry on. Her father managed to suppress his fury towards Alec some of the time, and to distract her with discussions about science and politics. The familiar routines of Christmas – carols, Christmas dinner, social occasions with friends, and long,

wintry walks – provided reassurance and a structure. Still, waking in the night, she wept, thinking of what might have been, but she was also able to acknowledge at last that passion alone had not been enough for her, and that though they could have gone on being lovers for a lifetime, she and Alec, they had lacked the day-to-day affection and mutual permission of freedom that were essential to a successful marriage.

By the time she returned to London in the New Year, Ellen had made several resolutions. No more drinking, obviously. And no more cigarettes either – she had never really liked them. And no more behaving like a madwoman, sitting on the bottom stair in the middle of the night, phoning her ex-fiancé.

And she would find her own flat. Her father had offered to help her with the money. She was twenty-six, far too old to be living like a student, and Joe would be moving out next year as soon as he finished his degree. Though it occurred to her that in doing so, she was acknowledging to herself that a chance in life had passed her by, and that she might never have the husband, children and family home that she had hoped would one day be hers, she began to look in estate agents' windows in her lunch hour.

Lastly, she resolved to try once more to find out what had happened to India. She discovered that the Mayhews' flat had been sold. None of the neighbours seemed to know where India and Sebastian had gone. When she had last seen India, she had been waitressing in a café, but

Ellen did not know which café. Sebastian had been a jobbing gardener but she had no idea where he had worked. She remembered India's boyfriend, dark-eyed Garrett, remembered dancing with him in the Mayhews' kitchen, and with a stab to the heart recalled how seeing India with Garrett had made her think with such longing of Alec.

But she hadn't a clue where Garrett lived or what his surname was or where to find him. India had had other friends, but though she recalled a name or two, Ellen recognized the impossibility of finding them among London's millions. It seemed to her, looking back, that she had hardly known India at all. India had latched on to her, and because of that, wary perhaps of a burden of unsought responsibilities, she had kept her distance.

But she did have a responsibility. It had been she who had introduced India to Marcus Pharoah. *This is what I want*, Pharoah's attitude to life had seemed to say, *and this is how I shall get it*. She wondered whether he had applied the same axiom to his courtship of India. Or whether India had made the running. Whatever, they would make a combustible pair.

She decided to try to trace India through Marcus Pharoah. She spoke to Jerry Collins, her professor. 'You know he's closed down Gildersleve Hall, don't you?' Jerry said. He hadn't mentioned it before because, well, it had seemed a sore subject. Ellen asked if Jerry knew where Pharoah had gone. 'America, apparently,' he said. 'Not sure exactly where. Not a friend of mine, you know.'

421

From further questioning of colleagues and acquaintances she discovered that Marcus Pharoah had taken up a position in a small New England college, and that he had married India. India had left England as Pharoah's wife. This Ellen at first found incredible. It was hard to imagine India marrying anyone, impossible to imagine her married to Pharoah, fulfilling the role Alison had once taken, running a household, handing round canapés before Sunday lunch. And what of Sebastian? Ellen may not have understood India much at all but she had never doubted her loyalty and love for her brother. Where was he? Had India taken him to New England with her? Did he live with the happy couple among the leafy hills and lakes of Vermont?

One day, at a conference in Manchester, she ran into Martin Finch. That evening, they ate Chinese food in the Ping Hong restaurant. Martin told her about his wife, who was expecting a child, and then Ellen nudged the conversation to the subject of Marcus Pharoah. Passing on gossip, Martin was in his element. Pharoah was a laughing stock, he told her. He'd married a girl half his age. You can get away with so much, but – Martin swept a finger across his neck – Pharoah had pretty much cut his own throat.

But on the train back to London, Ellen reflected that she had learned nothing of what had motivated India to marry Pharoah, or what had led Pharoah to marry India. Whether the match had been born out of love or greed or desperation. She only knew now that nothing ended tidily. That you could not tell what you yourself were capable of, let

alone anyone else. Little now remained of the short flare of friendship between herself and India except memories and unease. A meeting in a bookshop, debts run up and then repaid. The purchase of a coral-coloured summer dress, and a dance in a kitchen as, outside, the sap green leaves unfurled on the trees.

Part Three

1957–1959

Vermont

Chapter Eleven

The sound of Gosse's axe echoed against the trees on the far side of the pond. Looking out of the bedroom window, India saw that only the snow on the distant mountains remained, covering the rounded peaks like a dusting of icing sugar. The thaw had turned the tracks to channels of rutted mud which glistened in the weak spring sunshine. On the trails beside the house and around the pond, the mud was pitted with boot prints.

Out of a corner of the window, India made out Gosse at the shed to one side of the pond. The axe swung down in an arc, light glinting on the blade, and bit heavily into the wood. Gosse bent to pick up the cut logs and throw them into the barrow. Then he straightened, wiping the back of his hand across his forehead, and looked round.

India took a clumsy step back, away from the window. She sank on to the bed, one hand on the dome of her

belly. The baby squirmed, like an eel wriggling out of a crevice in a rock. India waited until the chopping of wood started up again. Then, hauling herself to her feet, she opened a drawer and took out gloves and a headscarf.

She was going to go out. The snow, and Dr Fisher's edict that she rest, had kept her indoors for weeks. The house, and the cold, dripping woodland that surrounded it, walled her in. She needed to feel that watery sunshine on her face; she needed to hear other voices.

Two miles away, Midhurst was the nearest town. It wasn't much of a town, just a single straight main street surrounded by a scattering of houses, garages, workshops and yards, but India imagined pottering around the shops, buying a few things and sitting in the coffeehouse, talking to people. She wouldn't stay long, an hour maybe, and would make sure to be back in time for Marcus coming home.

She did up the top two buttons of her coat, knotted her headscarf, applied lipstick and powder, then flicked a glance out of the window to check that Gosse was still at the woodshed. Then she went downstairs, holding the banister for support. The baby was due in three weeks' time and the weight she was carrying tired her.

Viola Williams only worked mornings so India was alone in the house. She plodded from room to room, collecting her things – bag, purse, car keys – then fetched her boots from the mud room and sat down on the stairs to put them on. But the zip wouldn't do up over her swollen ankles and the fur-lined leather flapped ridiculously open.

She put the boots back and heaved herself upstairs again. The problem, she thought, as she stood in the doorway, panting because of the stairs, was that she didn't own sensible shoes, such as a very pregnant woman should wear. The rows of high-heeled courts and strappy sandals looked back at her, forlorn leftovers from another life. She found a pair of lace-ups that Marcus had bought her for walking, when they had briefly imagined themselves striding out along trails together, forced her feet into them, and succeeded in tying the laces.

Chop, chop, chop. The sound of the axe reassured her. Returning downstairs, she couldn't find her bag, must have put it down somewhere, so she padded around the house, searching for it. This, she had learned, was a disadvantage of living in a big house. There were far too many places to lose things.

She found her bag in the front parlour and stood motion-less, catching her breath and planning her route out of the house as the sun washed warmly through the windowpanes. If she left the house by the front door and walked to the courtyard where the cars were parked, there would be a short stretch where she would be visible to Gosse from the woodshed. It would be safer to reach the courtyard by the road, where the trees planted along the perimeter fence would hide her.

She made her way to the small lobby at the far end of the building where they kept storm lanterns and candles, then slipped out of a side door. It was still cold but

there was a softness in the air which hinted of spring. Treading with great care over the muddy paving stones, India took the short path that led to the road. On the far side of the road were meadows dotted with bare, drably brown trees. Few vehicles came along this route, which led only to farms and small, insignificant townships, and India felt confident that she would be able to drive the few miles to Midhurst without difficulty. Marcus had taught her to drive last summer, before Rowena had visited. Their honeymoon period, she thought of it, cynically.

The meltwater had formed great puddles to the side of the road and the verges were awash with mud. India walked along a rut, one foot placed in front of the other, concentrating hard, afraid that if she slipped, something awful might happen to the baby.

Then she froze, one hand gripping the smooth, narrow trunk of a tree. She could no longer hear Gosse's axe. Perhaps the house blocked out the sound. Birds rustled in the branches; above her, crows flapped and dipped like black kites. The mud slodged round her feet, grey and viscous, and there was a green, woody smell.

She began to walk again. It was hard going, and she had to reach out now and then to the whippy branches of the saplings for support. But she was nearly there.

Peering round the edge of the thicket, she saw Gosse standing on the gravel, beside the Austin-Healey. He was leaning against the bonnet, smoking a cigarette. Silently,

and with great care, India stepped back into the trees and began to retrace her path.

They had married in the January of 1956, after Marcus's decree nisi had come through. It had been a register office wedding, with only Sebastian and a colleague of Marcus's in attendance as witnesses. India had worn a short black jacket with a white fox-fur collar over a knee-length dress of ivory satin. Marcus had looked on edge, relieved when the ceremony was over, relieved when the moment came after their lunch in a private room in the Savoy when he could shake hands with his colleague and Sebastian and see them both off in taxis.

Making love to her, he had pressed kisses all over her body, from the soles of her feet to the folds of her ears. She had sensed his utter concentration in the cocooning luxuriance of their room at the Savoy, had heard his voice whisper over and over again of his love for her. He had run a hand along the contours of her breast and hip, pausing to press a pinch of her skin between finger and thumb, and he had drawn in breath in the darkness when she had touched him.

The following morning they had flown to America via Shannon airport in Ireland and Gander in Newfoundland. Stopping for refuelling, India had watched the snowflakes dance through the foggy air. After a few days in a bitterly cold, windswept Boston they had headed north to Cape Cod. Walking along the beach, the soles of India's shoes

had crackled the frozen sand and the waves that lapped the shore had made lacy ribbons of ice. Then, north-west, through the dense, dark forests of Maine. They had kept to the routes through the valleys because of the snow, but the white bulk of the mountains had been a backdrop throughout most of their journey, disembodied above low, wispy clouds or luminous in the sunlight.

A snowstorm had forced them to spend two nights in an inn and then they had taken to the road again. Frozen opalescent lakes revealed themselves as the trees parted. Beside the road India had seen wooden shacks with logs stacked outside, a barking dog pulling on a chain and a rusty truck parked in the shadows. Covered bridges forded shallow, rushing rivers. At neat little towns they had stopped for coffee or a night's sleep.

As they drove, India had sensed Marcus's impatience. He spoke to her of his longing to start working again. He would make something new, he said, something wonderful. The Gildersleve Hall that he would create in New England would make discoveries whose significance would resound throughout the world. His voice, weighted with excitement and desire, threaded through their journey.

Now and then, India looked out of the car window. She thought of the snow in Newfoundland and the bumpy rattle of the plane through the clouds, and of the frozen sea at Cape Cod and the flare of orange light on the mountains at dusk. All these things had seemed to her to be wonders: anything was possible.

During their early months in Vermont, Marcus had still seemed to believe that he could get what he wanted. The small town of Midhurst lay in the lee of the Green Mountains; the college itself had been built three miles out of town, as if it had been feared that the main street, with its handful of old-fashioned shops, might prove a distraction to study. The college buildings, of grey granite and white clapboard, were set in a small, attractive, leafy campus.

Marcus had bought a house; they had moved in at the end of March. Fairlight House was a large, oblong building, faced with red-brown clapboard. It had formerly been a farm, and though the arable land and pasture had been sold off, there were still several acres of grounds. India had believed that was what had attracted Marcus, the thought of having grounds, of having your own pond and woods and meadows. Marcus, she had realized, liked to own things.

Their sea freight from England had arrived. There was the Healey, packaged up like an oversized Christmas present, and there were the boxes containing Marcus's notes and files and letters and certificates. India's possessions – embroidered linen pillowcases that had once belonged to Rachel, the pieces of the tea set that Lee had broken, a calendar Sebastian had made for her when she had been at boarding school, some books and gramophone records – had fitted in a single tea chest.

To begin with, Marcus had shown her off, much as he liked to show off the Austin-Healey. *This is my fast little European*

car and this is my fast little European wife. They had been invited to dinner in the houses of lecturers and deans, white wooden houses set in smooth green lawns, where kindly women had patted India's hand and asked her if she missed her home and her family. Missing Sebastian was like a nagging toothache; she noticed it most at night when there was nothing else to crowd out the thoughts – was he happy, was he lonely, would he manage without her?

When their turn came, they gave cocktail parties and lunches. After the evenings were over, Marcus listed India's mistakes. She was supposed to pay attention to the important guests instead of perching on the table, chatting to the handful of students that had been invited. You didn't dance at a cocktail party, and you didn't sit on the sofa with your legs tucked under you, screaming with laughter when someone told you jokes.

His lectures bored her; she told him that she couldn't see the point of giving a party that no one enjoyed. He grabbed hold of her hand, pulling her round to him. The point of the evening was not to give her pleasure but to reinforce his position at the college. Did she understand?

A few of the students and one or two of the faculty wives called round now and then with offerings of cake and conversation, but much of the time, while Marcus was at work, India had for company only Viola and Gosse. India liked Viola, who told her racy stories about working in a canning factory in Chicago in the war, but she loathed Gosse. He said 'Yes, Mrs Pharoah' and 'No, Mrs Pharoah'

when she asked him to take out the rubbish or fetch in logs, but India could tell that he didn't think she was the real Mrs Pharoah.

Time passed, and Marcus's satisfaction with the college waned. There was some problem with funding. The completion of the new biochemistry building had been delayed and he was having to make do with a few cramped labs in the chemistry department. He found Midhurst's smallness and isolation frustrating after London, and he disliked the Dean of Studies, a tall, thin, hollow-faced man called Lowell Crome. Mr Crome was, India conceded, very boring. He liked to steeple his hands, lean forward over his plate of pie or coffee cake, and talk for hours. When Marcus tried to interrupt, Mr Crome held up a hand and gave a little smile. 'If you would just allow me to finish, Marcus.' Mrs Crome wore her pinky-blond hair in ridges of curls, sprayed so tightly that not a single hair moved. India longed to tap them with a fingernail. When Marcus had first introduced her to Mrs Crome, the older woman's gaze had flicked between the two of them. 'My, my, you're just a little thing, aren't you?' she murmured, as her eyebrows leaped above the upswept rims of her spectacles.

In the spring, pink, white and yellow flowers had nodded in the grass. On summer's longest days, when the air was hot and humid, India liked to take out the rowing boat to the centre of the pond, from where she could see the reflections of the trees, which fractured the still surface of the water like cracks in glass. Where the narrow wooded

creeks cut into the banks, the pond was alive with the flicker of fish and darting flies. Running a hand through the water, she saw the ripples flash with light.

In August, Marcus's daughter Rowena had come to stay. Rowena Pharoah was seventeen, darkly beautiful and moody. To begin with, she had ignored India, responding to her questions with an exaggerated weariness and boredom. On the second day of her stay, Marcus had had to go into college for a couple of hours. As soon as the door closed behind her father, Rowena said to India, 'Don't expect me to talk to you. I'm here to see Daddy, not you,' and then left the house to sit by the pond and smoke cigarettes. India hadn't minded: she suspected that in Rowena's shoes she might have felt much the same, and anyway, she found Rowena as tiresome as Rowena found her. All that hanging on to Marcus's arm, all that leaning her head on his shoulder and whining, *I've missed you, Daddy*. Rowena disliked the food Viola cooked; she had nothing to wear and Marcus must take her shopping, and the house and Midhurst were boring. *My, my*, as Mrs Crome might have said. Rowena Pharoah might be a spoiled little madam, but at least it was nice to have the weight of Marcus's attention shifted to someone else for a week.

Outings with Rowena had been equally effortful. Rowena complained of car sickness and so sat in the front of the station wagon beside her father while India sat in the back. After the first couple of days, India left them to it and remained at home. This annoyed Marcus, who felt they

should get on, but there was a limit to how long anyone could put up with Rowena, and anyway, sitting in the back of the car made her feel sick. It occurred to India, when she was alone in the house, that everything was making her feel sick. Sitting on the edge of the bath, chewing her nails, trying to decide whether she was actually going to be sick, she had wondered about this.

The following morning at breakfast she had taken one look at the fried eggs on her plate and had run off to the bathroom. When she returned to the table, Marcus said perhaps she should stay in bed that day. He disliked illness, was wary of poorly people.

India said, 'I'm not unwell, I think I'm pregnant.'

And then, well. The geyser in Rachel's flat had once exploded. Watching Rowena lose her temper reminded India of that.

'Pregnant?' said Rowena.

'Yes. I'm having a baby.'

'You can't be.'

'Oh, I can, you know.' Very quiet.

'That's disgusting!'

'Do you think so?' India poured herself a cup of tea. 'But, you see, it's what happens when people get married.'

Rowena ran out of the room, sobbing. India gave a little shrug. Marcus said she could have been more tactful. India said that Rowena was behaving like a six-year-old. And so on, until he, too, lost his temper and stormed out of the room. Sitting alone at the breakfast table, running a

thumbnail along the seam of her napkin, India reflected on the fact that he hadn't said *congratulations*, or, *that's wonderful news, darling*.

Rowena insisted her father drive her back to Boston that day. She hadn't visited since. She wrote letters that Marcus read, scowling, at the breakfast table and then put in his pocket. India read them later, taking them from a shelf in his study, little masterpieces of resentment and self-pity as, outside, leaves spun from the trees and the colours of the maples on the slopes of the hills turned to fire.

The pond darkened, becoming brackish, and there was a smell of decay. Light filtered grudgingly from a bruised sky. As she walked in the woods, the dead leaves, frilled with frost, scratched underfoot. Ice crawled from the banks of the pond towards its centre, dulling the surface of the water.

She liked the differences. She liked the rhythm of the voices in drugstore and coffeehouse, the fizz of the soda fountain and the strange shapes of the pumpkins and gourds on the roadside stalls. She liked to see the mountains when she woke in the morning, and she liked not knowing the names of the trees or where the roads led to.

She had been sick for three months and then had felt quite well for three months, and then her ankles had puffed up and her fingers had turned into sausages and Dr Fisher had told her to rest. Marcus drove her once a week to Midhurst for her appointment with Dr Fisher; after the snow fell, that was her only outing.

In the coldest months, she sat with her feet up on the sofa by the window, watching the drift and speckle of the snow and the bird pecking at the peanuts. She wrote to Sebastian and to Michael and to Justine. Justine sent her a poem, Sebastian wrote back long, earnest letters about the farm and the Sandersons, and a girl he had met from a nearby village. Michael sent her picture postcards with London buses and the Tower; when India closed her eyes she could see the rows of soot-blackened houses, the people queueing at bus stops, the umbrellas jostling on the pavement, all that was familiar to her.

Boredom made her mind wander. She wondered whether her baby would be a boy or a girl. She wondered whether it would have fair hair like her or black hair like its father. She wondered whether she regretted the bargain she had made: safety for Sebastian, comfort and security for herself, in return for marriage to Marcus Pharoah.

She wondered whether Marcus regretted his side of the bargain. She suspected that though he might never have loved Alison, he might prefer to have an Alison in his life. He needed a wife who said the right things, talked to the right people. There was love and there was desire and there was usefulness. Alison had been the useful wife, India was the desired one. The only person Marcus loved – loved properly, in India's eyes – was Rowena.

She wondered whether he would love the baby. He had changed towards her since the day she had told him she was pregnant. She had thought at first that he had been

angry because the news of her pregnancy had upset Rowena; in time she had come to question whether his bad mood had been caused by the pregnancy itself. They quarrelled more: she knew how to rile him, how to give the indifferent shrug that infuriated him, how to scratch and probe at his weak spots, his hunger for status and recognition, his need to control. Marcus had wanted a wife who dedicated herself to satisfying his needs and furthering his career; what he had got was one who squirmed away from any attempt to impose authority.

Lying on the sofa, the silence seemed to enfold her like a blanket. The trees shrank back into the fog and a heavy grey pall fell over the rounded peaks of the mountains. She could lie there for hours, looking out of the window. Sounds seemed muffled, and there was an absence of echoes. She was surrounded by a wall of glass, a shell of ice; if she spoke, no one would hear her. It wouldn't have surprised her if she'd looked down at herself and discovered that she was turning invisible.

She couldn't afterwards remember exactly when it was that she had come to think that Roy Gosse was watching her. Gosse drove for Marcus, mended and cleaned the cars, cut logs and did any necessary repair work to the house. He didn't talk much and he slept and ate in the barn. He was the sort of man, India thought, who always seemed to be on the verge of losing his temper.

Go out for a walk, and when she looked back, there would be Gosse, sitting on the back porch, cleaning the

shotgun he used to kill vermin, or washing the cars and pick-up truck, hands cupped as he lit a cigarette. She might have thought he liked looking at her had she not known that he despised her. Of course, a man might despise her and still want to go to bed with her, as Bernie had done, but India did not think that this was true of Gosse, in whose glance she read only the same industriousness that he applied to replacing a tyre or trapping mice, or carrying out any other order of Marcus's. She wondered whether Marcus had been drawn to Fairlight House's isolation because, after all, it was a lot easier to keep an eye on your wife if she was marooned in the middle of nowhere.

She wasn't certain. Often she thought that the falling snow and the silence were playing tricks on her, and that her fear that she had made a mistake was only a product of those other fears that came to her when she woke in the night, her fear of having the baby, of being hurt, of something unspeakable happening.

She wondered whether, once the baby was born, she would mind less that she had come to dislike her husband. As the days passed, this question nagged at her.

She went into labour a week early. Marcus drove her to the nursing home in Midhurst, a Gothic red-brick building set in velvety green lawns. Afterwards, India could remember the daffodils in the borders by the tarmac drive, bobbing their frilled yellow heads in the wind, and she could remember the smell of the polished lino in the corridors

of the nursing home and the heavy dread that had settled on her inside the building. Schools, orphanages, hospitals: she just wasn't much good at them. But she could not remember Abigail's birth at all, could not remember her first cry. Dr Fisher told her that they had anaesthetized her, but still, it seemed negligent of her to have missed those first moments of her daughter's life.

Feverish during the days after the birth and weak from loss of blood, India dreamed of monsters with bug eyes and gaping jaws, and of gardens with acres and acres of luridly coloured flowers, stippled points of bright colour that stretched on for miles. When her temperature dropped, what remained was exhaustion. She had to lie down to recover after a visit to the bathroom or a walk to the nursery; stay on her feet too long and a hot and cold faintness washed over her.

There were days following the birth when she felt as if she was swimming underwater. Now and then she would bob to the surface and one of the nurses would put Abigail into her arms and she would study her, finding in her perfection, alternately overwhelmed with love for her and terrified by her. This persisted, this mixture of love and anxiety, an anxiety that she wouldn't be up to scratch, that she would drop Abigail in the bath or stick a nappy pin in her, as well as a deeper fear that she would make as ham-fisted a job of motherhood as her own mother had, that she would mess it up, just as she had messed up every other job she had ever taken.

But love itself was a revelation, immediate and undeniable, and by the time she left the nursing home when Abigail was a fortnight old, it had changed her chemistry, pulling her this way and that, hammering her into a different shape so that her heart and mind seemed as raw and bleeding as her post-partum body.

The baby was crying. India's eyelids fluttered open and she hauled herself up on the sofa cushions. The nurse that Marcus had engaged to help in the first six weeks must be in the yard, smoking a cigarette or making up to Gosse. India supposed that because Marcus was out, Miss Forrest thought she could get away with it. She was glad to have Abigail to herself, but she could have told Miss Forrest that she was wasting her time, that all the hair-patting and leg-crossing wouldn't get her anywhere.

Abigail was waving her limbs and squirming, making mewing little cries like a cat's. India went into the kitchen, put a pan of water to heat on the stove, took a bottle of baby milk out of the refrigerator and placed it in the pan to warm. Abigail's cries were gathering momentum, like a car engine igniting. As waves of heat and nausea washed over her, India leaned against the stove, closing her eyes. She was feeling much better now, almost well sometimes, and she had walked round the pond that morning, with lots of stops for rests, but there was still that gluey exhaustion, like fighting your way through a blanket of spiders' webs.

Opening her eyes, she folded a tea towel to take the bottle from the pan and shook a few drops of milk on to the back of her hand to test the temperature. Then she went back into the sitting room, lifted Abigail out of the Moses basket, and sat down on the sofa. Abigail latched on to the teat and began to suck, then wriggled, kicking out her legs and pulling away from the teat with a gasp and a short, high-pitched cry. India stroked her head, with its down of fine, fair hair, and the baby started to suck again.

Voices murmured beyond the window, Miss Forrest's and Roy Gosse's. India looked at the clock. It was almost three. It was so easy to lose track of time, to close her eyes and let the parts of the day, morning, afternoon and evening, blend into each other. Even now, the voices were leaching away, as though the colour had been washed out of them, and when she prised open her eyes the bottle was almost empty, and she put a hand to her forehead, wondering whether she had a temperature again.

She was dozing on the sofa when the doorbell rang. Dragging herself awake, she went to the front door and opened it.

The woman standing outside said, 'Mrs Pharoah?'

'Yes?'

'My name's Mrs Hester Devereux. We haven't met before.'

Hester Devereux was wearing a rust-coloured coat, mended at the elbows, and a cream woollen scarf and hat. Her straight dark hair was windswept and streaked with

white and a sunray of shallow lines spun out from the corners of her steel-grey eyes.

'I hope you'll forgive me for interrupting your afternoon,' Mrs Devereux said. 'I knew your husband many years ago and I wondered whether I might speak with you.'

'Marcus is at work, I'm afraid.'

'Yes, I made sure of that. It's you I wanted to speak to, Mrs Pharoah.'

India found herself glancing over her shoulder. It was a fine, sunny day and Gosse was outside, painting the back porch.

She said, 'If you're a friend of Marcus's—'

'I'm not. I was a friend of Rosanne's.'

Blurred from sleep, it took India a couple of seconds to place the name. Then she said, 'Marcus's first wife.'

'Yes.'

India showed Mrs Devereux indoors. In the mud room, Mrs Devereux took off her boots and gave her coat to India to hang on a peg. There was a front sitting room with a piano and bookcases, well away from the porch and Gosse. India invited her visitor to sit down.

'Can I get you a coffee, Mrs Devereux?'

'No, thank you. I appreciate the kind offer but I won't take up your time.'

'If you'll excuse me a moment, I just need to go and check on my baby.'

India went upstairs to the nursery. Abigail was sleeping,

arms flexed, hands fisted. In the bathroom, India splashed cold water over her face, then returned downstairs.

She closed the door behind her. Hester Devereux said, 'How old is your baby, Mrs Pharoah?'

'Abigail's almost two months old.'

'How lovely.' Hester Devereux's voice was toneless. 'Congratulations.'

'Thank you.'

'You're English, aren't you? Have you been married long?'

'A year and a half.'

'And you're happy?' Mrs Devereux leaned forward in her chair.

India heard the doubt in her voice. 'You told me you knew Rosanne. What was she like?'

Mrs Devereux's strained face relaxed. 'She was a perfect darling. Pretty as a picture. Blonde, like you. I used to tell her she was as fair as thistledown. We met at Bourchier University, in Maine, in nineteen thirty-two. We were only eighteen years old, both freshmen.'

'You were friends?'

'Best friends. But then she married Marcus Pharoah and left school. At first we kept in touch.'

'At first?'

'I had to leave Bourchier because my father was very ill. After he died, I came back to visit and I found that they'd moved out of town. I asked Marcus for the address but he wouldn't give it to me. We didn't get on, you see.'

'You didn't like him?'

'No, I'm afraid not. He was a jealous man. When he and Rosanne were courting, I could see that he didn't like her spending time with me. I've often thought since that I should have found out where she was and visited her anyway, but I didn't like to come between husband and wife.' Hester Devereux twisted her hands together. 'I'm sorry, Mrs Pharoah, you must think me very impolite, coming here and saying such things, and I don't mean to upset you. I have a friend in Midhurst, Mrs Ingalls, her husband teaches at the university, and she mentioned in a letter that she'd met you. It's such an uncommon name, isn't it, Pharoah, so I felt I had to ask Elizabeth whether it was the same Pharoah, whether he'd come back to America. And then, when she told me he'd married again . . .' Frowning, Hester Devereux cast a glance round the room. 'I remember those days so fondly, you see. Rosanne and I were firm friends from our first day at Bourchier. It was the first time I'd been away from home. Since then, I've never been so carefree. My husband died two years ago and we have three children. The two eldest have married but my youngest is still at home. It's been very hard. I don't think I'm the same person as I was then, no, not at all.'

India said gently, 'Are you sure you won't have a cup of coffee?'

'I don't want to trouble you.'

'Actually, I'm ravenous,' she said. 'I was going to have a piece of cake when you knocked at the door. May I get some for you too?'

'Then, thank you, Mrs Pharoah.'

Her visitor offered to help but India refused. In the kitchen, making coffee and cutting cake, she thought through what Hester Devereux had told her. It was easy to picture Marcus resenting the emotional bond between the two women and putting up a barrier between them. It occurred to her that she had allowed – invited – Marcus to separate her from her brother and her friends.

She took the tray back into the front room, put the side plates on occasional tables, and poured out the coffee. She said, 'You must have been awfully sad when Rosanne died.'

'I didn't know at the time. That's always troubled me. After Daddy died there was no money for me to go to college, so I had to leave. I didn't find out about Rosanne till nearly six months later. I recall every detail of that day, even though so many years have passed. It was summer and I was working in New York, in a department store. I'd met Henry, my husband, by then, and I was expecting a child of my own, though I hadn't told my employers because I was afraid I'd lose my job. Work was hard to come by back in the thirties. I remember I felt tired and sick, and then I came home and found that letter. It was from a girl I'd known at Bourchier. When I read it, I just cried.' She cut up the cake with the fork. 'You can get so caught up with your own life you neglect old friends. I've always felt bad about that. It was such a sad thing to happen. Poor Rosanne had longed for that baby.'

'Baby?' repeated India.

Hester Devereux looked up. 'Yes. Rosanne Pharoah died in childbirth. Didn't you know?'

India remembered sitting on the sofa in Marcus's flat while he told her about Rosanne. She was sure he had said that his first wife had died of an infection. *No penicillin then,* he had told her. She remembered that she had reached out and taken his hand.

India shook her head. Mrs Devereux looked stricken. 'I'm so sorry . . . So clumsy of me, I just assumed . . . It was different back then, and they were living in such a remote area. I'm sure you have wonderful physicians in Midhurst.'

'Wonderful,' echoed India. 'And the baby?'

'Well, that's the thing. That's why I thought I'd make the journey. I never knew. It's been preying on my mind since Henry died. I don't know why it should start to bother me now, but perhaps at such times you find yourself thinking of all the loose ends.' She put down her plate and turned to face India. Her expression was wounded and puzzled. 'I never found out what had happened to Rosanne's baby. Marcus had gone back to England by the time I heard of her death, but there was no mention of a child. I tried writing to a friend I knew at Bourchier, but they didn't know anything either. I thought you might be able to tell me, Mrs Pharoah, but I can see I was mistaken.'

Hester Devereux's voice had taken on a mollifying tone, but the puzzlement in her eyes remained. Shortly afterwards, the older woman got up to leave. At the door,

turning to India, she said, 'No one seemed to know what had happened to that baby. Isn't that just terrible? No one seemed to have the least idea.'

The conversation had exhausted her; India lay down on the sofa and fell asleep. When Marcus came home, he sat on the sofa arm, stroking her hair.

She said, 'Tell me what Rosanne was like.'

'Why?'

'Was she as pretty as me?'

'Yes,' he said shortly.

'Where were you living?'

'North. Far north.' He looked down at her. 'Why do you want to know?'

'I had a visitor. A Mrs Devereux. She said she was a friend of your first wife.'

The hand stilled. 'Devereux . . .'

'Hester Devereux.'

He rose and looked out of the window at the porch, where Gosse was packing up paint cans and rags. 'She was a rather sad woman, I recall. A meddler. I had to send her packing in the end. I hope you did the same, India.'

'She told me that Rosanne died in childbirth.'

'Did she now?' Slowly, he swung round to face her.

'Is it true?'

'Yes, it is.'

'You didn't tell me.'

'It was no business of yours.'

'What happened to the baby?'

450

'Leave it, India.'

She wriggled herself into a sitting position, turning to look at him. 'Did it die?'

The sun dipped through the sky, painting the pond with streaks of gold. In the distance, the summits of the mountains also caught the liquid gold light.

'It was stillborn,' he said. The anger in his voice was at odds with the heaviness in his eyes. 'There, India, does that satisfy you? I didn't want to upset you, that's all, talking about such things.'

In the middle of the night, feeding Abigail, memories of her conversation with Hester Devereux shifted uneasily.

Rosanne Pharoah . . . pretty as a picture . . . only eighteen.

No one seemed to know what had happened to that baby. Isn't that just terrible?

Why had he lied to her? Because he *had* lied to her, two years ago, in his flat in Belsize Park. He had told her that Rosanne had died of an infection when in fact she had died giving birth to a stillborn child. Rosanne could have died of an infection *after* the birth, India supposed. She herself had had an infection, after all, which had made her very ill. *No penicillin then.* Or perhaps an infection had *caused* the stillbirth. But then, why hide it? Because he couldn't bear to talk about it? Or for some other reason?

Hester Devereux's visit had cut like a knife through the weeks of drowsy disorientation that had followed Abigail's birth. India took the bottle of pills Dr Fisher had prescribed

to help her sleep and flushed them down the lavatory. Over the next couple of days she felt as if she was rising out of the mud into a sharp new clarity.

At night, she dreamed of babies. Sometimes the baby was Abigail and sometimes it was that other baby, the child of Rosanne Pharoah. In her dreams, she discovered Rosanne's baby beneath beds, in boxes, and floating beneath the frozen surface of Fairlight Pond. Always alive, though white and waxy and silent, her fingers swaying like fronds of seaweed, her mouth opening and closing as if she was trying to speak.

Marcus was at the college and Gosse had taken the pick-up truck to the garage in Midhurst, so India was alone in the house.

She opened the door to Marcus's study. There was a desk, filing cabinets, bookshelves, prints and photographs on the walls. She flicked through the compartments above the desk, where Marcus kept Rowena's letters. Then she opened the drawers. She wasn't sure what she was looking for – a letter, a diary, a birth or death certificate. When she heard a car on the road she started and hurried to the window. But it was only a lorry, logs chained to the flatbed, rattling along the road, and she went back to her searching.

A small cardboard box contained a sheaf of photographs. India snapped them one by one on to the desktop, like dealing playing cards. There was a photo of Marcus in his academic gown, and several of Rowena, in party dress or

school uniform or hard hat and hacking jacket, seated on a horse. Another snapshot was of an old house with a tower to one side of it, the jagged little teeth of crenellations notching its top. But no pretty fair-haired young wife. No baby. All those years before they had met, she thought as she put the pictures back in the box, all those years of which she knew nothing. She hardly knew him at all.

Leafing through a bundle of documents in a file, something caught her attention. The paper was the yellow-buff of milky tea, powdery and torn at the edges. The two pages both bore the same heading: Charnwood Children's Home, near Winchester, Hampshire. The date was 18 July 1942. Scanning the two sheets of paper, India saw that the information on them was divided into sections: health, educational attainment, behaviour, character, background. Typed at the top of each page was the name of a child. One of the names was Sebastian's and the other was hers.

It took her several moments to absorb the fact that Marcus had in his desk reports that the orphanage had written about her and Sebastian after they had arrived at Charnwood following the death of their mother. It took more moments before she could begin to read them.

As she read, something inside her seemed to chill and solidify. Their physical health had been satisfactory, though they had been judged ill-nourished and underweight. Her own level of education had been considered average but Sebastian had been thought backward. In the section headed 'Character', someone had written, 'India is given to violent

outbursts and appears to have little understanding of right and wrong.' The same hand noted further down the page: 'The mother was neglectful but it is believed that with proper care the children should be capable of becoming useful members of society.'

India heard the rumble of a car engine so she put the papers back into the file and returned it to the drawer. Looking out of the window she saw the pick-up truck pull off the road into the drive. She left the room.

But she must have been careless because at dinner that night, Marcus said, 'Did you find anything?' and she blinked, her nerves taut.

His knife sliced through his steak. 'I was going to get rid of Mrs Williams,' he said, 'but then I realized that it must have been you, India. If you're going to be devious and underhand, you should remember in future to take more care.'

They ate for a while. Cutlery clicked, she could hear herself chew. Then he said, 'Well, did you find what you were looking for?' and she shook her head.

'I was trying to find a bottle of gum. I wanted to mend my tea set.'

His look said, *liar*. The next day Gosse put a lock on the door of the study.

Ellen's colleague, David Shapiro, had had a paper accepted by *Nature*. They toasted him that evening in the lab with warmish beer drunk out of chemical beakers. Jerry Collins

joined them and there was some gentle ribbing by Tom MacPhee of Shapiro for the length of time it had taken him to write the paper. Then they peeled off, Shapiro and some of the others to the pub, Professor Collins to a meeting, the other female junior lecturer in the department, Freya Hawks, to meet her sister at the cinema, while Ellen stayed on to write up her notes.

She had been appointed a junior lecturer four months earlier, at the end of 1956. On hearing the news of her promotion, her parents had come up from Wiltshire and had taken her out to celebrate. She enjoyed her work, the increased contact with students and the greater responsibility, and she attended conferences in her own right now rather than as Jerry Collins's research assistant. Her colleagues were a friendly bunch; she and Freya went hiking now and then and sometimes she accompanied Tom MacPhee to concerts.

Riley had been made chief inspector at much the same time as Ellen had been promoted. They went to the Royal Opera House to see *The Firebird* and afterwards shared a bottle of champagne. When they were not working late, she and Riley talked on the phone most nights. Those conversations could flow and expand like the estuary of a river, stemmed only by the late hour and fear of the phone bill. They didn't always agree, but then neither did she ever become bored, talking to him. His opinions were neither easy nor rigid and until brought up against the solid rock of his principles, they had a fluidity. You might have

thought, if you totted up the hours they had talked together, that they must have covered every subject under the sun and yet there were always new things to say. It had become part of her routine: come home, cast off coat and brief-case, run bath, think about supper, call Riley.

Tonight, she finished her work by seven and left the building. Her flat in Earl's Court was only a short distance away so she walked home. She had moved into the flat a year ago and it never failed to give her pleasure to come home, scoop up her post from the pigeonhole in the shared hallway, then walk up the stairs and unlock her front door.

There was a kitchen, sitting room, bathroom and bedroom. No more queuing for the bath, no more breathing in other people's ashy toast over breakfast. A woman came in twice a week to clean and she sent her sheets and table-cloths to a laundry. She was twenty-eight and she had got her life in order and she didn't intend to let it ever become disordered again.

She saw that in the pile of post she had collected from the hallway, among the circulars for window cleaners, the gas bill and a postcard from a friend, was a blue airmail letter. It had been forwarded from her old address in Islington. She turned it over in her hand, then read the name and address on the back.

Frowning, Ellen reached for a paper knife, slit open the letter, and sat down. Then she flattened out the flimsy blue paper and began to read.

*   *   *

456

'What are you doing now, Riley?' She always asked him this when she phoned him. She liked to be able to picture him as if she were there.

'Sitting on the sofa, enjoying the quiet, wondering whether another drink will make my headache better or worse. Kitchen's a wreck and I don't think Annie's asleep yet.'

'How's the new au pair?'

'Hendrika? Fine.'

'That good?'

'Hmm,' said Riley.

She had him in her mind's eye now, sitting on the living-room sofa with the poppy print cushions, nursing a Scotch, listening out for Annie, aware of the latest au pair sullenly crashing pots and pans in the kitchen. He would be wearing . . . what? A white cotton shirt, top button undone, navy-blue tie loosened. His hair would be dishevelled because he had run his hand through it. His light hazel eyes, with their multitude of shades of brown, green and gold, would be drenched with ironic humour.

'How was your day, Ellen?'

She told him about India's letter. She could almost hear him frown.

'That's rather out of the blue, isn't it?'

'Nothing for nearly two years and now this.'

'How is she?'

'Well, that's the thing, I'm not sure. She's had a baby, a girl. It's rather an odd letter.' The air letter was lying open

457

on the coffee table. India's spidery handwriting, which contained a spelling mistake or two and covered only half a page, didn't really answer Riley's question. It was the sort of letter, Ellen thought, that you might write if you were in a hurry.

She said, 'She wrote to ask me whether I knew anything about Dr Pharoah's first child. I don't mean Rowena, Alison's daughter. Apparently there was another child before that, when Pharoah was in America in the thirties.'

'Excuse me a moment, Ellen . . .'

Doors opening and closing; Riley's voice, distant now, calling Annie to go to sleep. Muffled noises as he picked up the receiver again.

'Sorry about that. She had some friends round and she's still full of beans. Were you aware that Pharoah had another child?'

'No, not at all. I remember Dr Redmond telling me that Pharoah had been married before Alison but he didn't say anything about a child.'

'Two decades ago. It's a long time.'

'If there was a child, it hardly seems to have left a trace.'

'There's always a trace. It's just a question of finding it.'

'India doesn't say why she wants to know. And why doesn't she ask Marcus himself, or his family and friends?'

'Presumably she doesn't want to.'

'Exactly. Why?' There wasn't an answer to that which Ellen did not find disquieting. 'And why me, Riley? After all this time.'

'Because she trusts you. And because you knew Pharoah.'

Ellen sighed. 'I think about them sometimes,' she said. 'How India and Sebastian let me into their lives. I was lonely when I first came to London. Pretty miserable, actually. You know how usually with people it takes you a while to get to know them? They hold back till they're sure about you. But with India it was as if we'd parted only the day before. She never held back.'

'She struck me as a nice kid.'

'We had fun. I've always felt I should have warned her about Pharoah.'

'And told her what, exactly? She wouldn't have listened to you. People fall in love with people and often it doesn't make much sense to anyone else.'

He sounded tired. She said, 'You're all right, aren't you, Riley?'

'Yes, and all the better for talking to you.'

She let it go, though she didn't believe him. 'How's work?'

'Busy. Very busy. I've only just got home and I'll have to go out again shortly.'

'How's your gangster?'

'Continuing his business unimpeded by me or anyone else, I'm afraid.' He gave a short, dry laugh.

'It's odd, isn't it,' she said, 'how you can look back on a part of your life that seemed so difficult at the time, that you wouldn't have thought you'd remember with any fondness, and yet you feel nostalgic for it.'

'Are you thinking of Alec?' he said sharply.

Surprised, she said, 'Alec? No, not at all. I was thinking about when I first came to live in London. The lodging house with that awful shared kitchen, and my job at the hospital. And all the new people I met then, all the new friends. When I remember, it seems so clear, so bright. It's as if I felt more *alive*.' She made a self-conscious, exasperated sound. 'I suppose it's because I was young then.'

'You're hardly decrepit. *Annie*.'

Faintly, a child's voice, 'Daddy, I can't sleep.'

Riley said crisply into the phone, 'My love, I'm going to have to go, I'm afraid. I'll call you back tomorrow night.'

He put the phone down. In the silence, Ellen was aware of a continuing feeling of restlessness, almost dissatisfaction.

And confusion. *My love, I'm going to have to go.* 'My love'? He had never called her that before. Had he meant to use the endearment to Annie but accidentally said it to her? Tired and harassed, had he, as one sometimes did, muddled his words?

Rising, she picked up India's letter and went to the window. She glanced at the scrawled text but did not read it, her gaze flicking away to the squares of garden at the backs of the houses. A few forgotten items of washing hung limp on the lines; roses flopped heavy heads in the dusk. *My love* . . . She was rolling the edge of the thin blue paper between finger and thumb, testing those words in her mind. Strange how two words could produce such an

onrush of feelings. Or perhaps it was not that, perhaps this sudden, sharp inclination to laugh or cry was a consequence, as she had said to Riley, of remembering, of the door to the past that India's letter had unlocked.

There's always a trace, he had told her. It's just a question of finding it. The past left traces and so did the people who made it. On reflection, those early years in London seemed so vividly coloured. She was aware of a sense of loss. Are you thinking of Alec, he had asked her, but the traces were not of him.

She had achieved so much, this flat, her career, prizes that had once seemed unobtainable. Why then this nagging, disturbing feeling of regret? Carefully, analytically, she found herself inspecting the events of her early years in London. The amusement and distraction of India's company, that had helped jolt her out of the shock and loss of confidence which had followed her dismissal from Gildersleve Hall. Her gradual discovery of satisfaction in her new job. And Riley: their meeting on the hospital steps, the friendship that had begun that day.

She would do as India asked and try to find out whether another child of Marcus Pharoah's had ever existed, because that was her nature. She knew that once a question formed in her mind, she had to go on digging until she answered it.

My love . . . Did she mind that he had called her that? No, not at all. But that, too, raised questions because his words had left their own trace of absolute delight, as if

they were a magic incantation that cast an enchantment. She found that she could hardly bear to think he might have said them by mistake. She found she wanted him to have meant them with all his heart.

She was sitting at a corner table in a café in Tottenham Court Road. Catching sight of her through the window, Riley went inside.

'Hello, Janey,' he said.

As she turned her head slowly towards him, he saw the yellowing bruises down one side of her face. She was a pretty girl, very young, small and delicate-looking, her straight dark-brown hair cut in a fringe and swept up in a ponytail. Irish; beneath the cosmopolitan twang still sang an Irish lilt.

He had first met Janey Kelly in the Blue Duck nightclub two years ago. Janey was one of Bernie Perlman's girls. Riley had given her his hand to help her up after she had fallen on the floor on the night he had seen Lee Carter. Since then, he had bought her a coffee now and then, food when she looked hungry.

She said, 'What do you want, Riley?'

'Just thought I'd see how you were. Shall I get you another coffee?'

She shrugged and he went to the counter. He bought buns as well, because she looked stick thin, then carried the tray to the table and sat down opposite her.

'You look as if you've been in the wars, Janey.'

'I tripped.' She hunched her birdlike shoulders, sucked on her cigarette. 'Silly of me.'

'How's Bernie?'

'Fine.'

'And Lee?'

She tilted back her head, narrowing her eyes, letting out a thin channel of cigarette smoke. 'I hate Lee.'

'Only takes a word, Janey.'

'And I've a faceful of stitches. No thanks.' She bit at a hangnail.

'Someone like Lee doesn't know when to stop,' he said quietly. 'I think he's killed two people already. I don't want there to be a third.'

Her pretty little face creased into a scowl; she pulled down the sleeves of her yellow cardigan over her narrow blue-veined wrists and looked out of the window. 'Shove off, Riley.'

'I don't want you to get hurt.'

'Oh, how touching. Bet if I offered you a quick one round the back you wouldn't say no.' She blew smoke in his face. 'Long time since you had it, is it, copper? You're all the same. Just leave me alone.'

Driving home, Riley found himself remembering Ellen's friend, India. Another pretty girl, with her come-to-bed eyes and tousled blond hair, coupled with a jumpy, attractive, careless vivacity. Like Janey, she had that air of wildness, instability even, that some men went for. Men like Pharoah and Bernie Perlman. India Mayhew and

463

Marcus Pharoah, Janey Kelly and Bernie Perlman. Perhaps, to begin with, they were looking for protectors, these girls. Someone strong, who'd look after them.

Sometimes he thought he was getting somewhere with Janey and sometimes, like today, he suspected that he was wasting his time. During the past three years he had painstakingly built up a dossier on Bernie Perlman's business enterprises, each fragment of information contributing to the larger picture. Recently, Perlman's attention had begun to move away from gambling dens and protection rackets to the acquisition of property – houses, flats and offices in central London. Property was where Perlman thought the money was, where fortunes would be made in the second half of the twentieth century. Perhaps Bernie Perlman had decided to step aside from the violent activities of his youth in favour of a career that verged on respectability. This possibility frustrated Riley: two years, five, and it would be forgotten that Perlman's empire had been built on terror and extortion. People had short memories. He knew that he was running out of time.

He had spent the past two years patiently waiting for Janey to change her mind and help him put Bernie Perlman behind bars. He had spent those same years waiting for Ellen. It seemed to him that he had waited long enough. He wanted more than friendship. 'My love' – the term had slipped out but he would not have taken the words back even if he had been able to. He knew that he was reaching the point where he must make his feelings clear to her

even if that meant risking losing her as a friend. It was time for a decision. One way or the other. For ever, done with, for good or ill.

The first time she met him, India was hauling the carrycot out of the coffeehouse in Midhurst – the heavy door to be kept ajar with an elbow, the wheels to be lowered carefully down the steps – when he dashed across the road, held open the door for her, then lifted the pram down the steps so gently Abigail didn't stir at all.

He was young, about her own age, she guessed, and he had thick, curly brown hair and a smile that spread over his tanned face like the sun coming out. He was about a foot taller than she was and he wore dark drill trousers and a plaid shirt. When she got to know him better, she saw that round the pupils of his blue eyes was a ring of amber-brown.

The next day, he opened the door of the coffeehouse for her as she arrived. And the next, and the next. She said, 'Don't you ever work?' and he pointed across the road to the upper storey of a red-brick building.

'That's my office, ma'am. I said to myself, Linc, you go out for a coffee every afternoon and so does that lady, so why don't you go out ten minutes earlier and help her get her baby carriage up those steps.'

'Linc?' she said.

He held out a hand. 'Lincoln Strawbridge. It's a pleasure to meet you, ma'am.'

'India Pharoah,' she said. 'And this is Abigail.'

He leaned over the pram. 'May I?'

Abigail was stirring, her fat little hand dipping to the blanket, her pursed mouth opening and closing. 'Yes, of course,' she said.

Very gently, cradling Abigail's head in the palm of his big hand, he picked her up. She looked so tiny, supported against his broad chest. 'Well, aren't you a honey?' he murmured to her. 'Aren't you just a honey? She takes after you, ma'am.'

'She does, doesn't she?' India took the baby from him and stroked a silver-fair curl. 'Do you have children of your own, Mr Strawbridge?'

'No, I'm not married, but I'm the eldest of seven. My youngest brother's just eighteen months old.'

She offered to buy him a coffee but he insisted, gravely courteous, on buying one for her. He told her he had been born in Midhurst, had gone away to college to study architecture, but had come back to the town after he had qualified. 'I missed my family,' he said. 'Do you miss yours, Mrs Pharoah?'

Abigail was grizzling. India thought of Sebastian, and nodded, then unrolled the bottle from its covering of a spare nappy.

One afternoon, he told her about the houses he built. He had brought with him a long roll of paper which he flattened out on the table so that she could see the ink sketches. The houses had porches and dormer windows and long, shady verandas.

'I like to build in the vernacular style,' he said. 'It suits the landscape. If there's anything I detest, it's a house that should be in Miami or Los Angeles thrown into a town in Vermont. Vermont houses are quiet and modest. They don't like to blow their own trumpet. Same with the people. My homes are built solid to weather the winds. The walls are thick and the doors are well-fitting to keep the house warm when there's snow outside. I make my windows out of two thicknesses of glass—' He broke off. 'Aw, listen to me. You don't want to hear the technical details, do you?'

'Yes, I do,' she said. Sun was pouring through the window of the café; she adjusted Abigail's bonnet. 'Do you live in a house like this?'

He leaned back in his seat, stretching out his long legs, which struggled to fit beneath the table. 'I live in a shack a little way north out of town, where the road forks. It's not much of a place, just a couple of rooms, but I like it there. It's in a valley, and there's a fine view of the mountains and I can sit on the stoop and watch the hummingbirds. One day, I'll build a house there. I'm just starting out, Mrs Pharoah, and so far I've had only a couple of clients reckless enough to let me build them a home. Most of the work that comes to me is making a garage or adding on a sunroom. But that will change, I know it will.'

Some afternoons India sat in the café, spinning out cups of coffee, playing with Abigail. She got to know the waitresses and some of the other customers. When Linc wasn't there, she looked out of the window to where the hot

467

summer sun painted the shadows of the passers-by across the sidewalks. A convertible rolled along the street. The girl sitting in the passenger seat was wearing sunglasses and her head was covered by a flowered scarf. She leaned towards the driver, her arm along the back of his seat.

India imagined Linc standing on a building site, shading his eyes from the sun as he looked up to where the bare bones of his house rose out of the soil. She imagined him running a hand along a span of wood, testing the strength of a joist.

A letter arrived from Ellen. India waited until she was at the café to open it. It was a very Ellen sort of letter, its news presented in a factual and undramatic fashion, sent with love and best wishes, which was good of Ellen, all things considered. After she had read it, India folded it and put it back in her handbag.

Two years ago, she had sat in a nightclub in Mayfair in her stolen dress, talking to Marcus. She had asked him why Ellen disliked him and he had told her about the quarrel with his friend, his friend's death and the inquiries of the police. Now the friend had a name, Bryan Redmond. It seemed to India, after reading Ellen's letter, that Marcus had left a lot of things out.

It was so hard to know what to make of it. Marcus had a way of moulding the past into what he wanted. Suppose, after his first wife had died, Marcus hadn't wanted the baby. Suppose he had looked at Rosanne's baby with the same critical, assessing eye with which he looked at Abigail.

Suppose it had been Rosanne he had wanted, Rosanne he had longed for with all the intense possessive power of which he was capable. He might even have blamed the baby for Rosanne's death.

What might he have done? He might have put the baby in an orphanage. He might then have told anyone who asked him that it had been stillborn. He might have returned to England and hidden the baby's existence. He might have started again while his child was left stranded, alone for ever among strangers. Marcus was good at remaking himself; Marcus liked to shut doors on the past.

Chapter Twelve

A rush to finish a series of experiments which she hoped to use in a paper to be presented at a conference the following spring, and then a week's holiday, camping with Freya Hawks in Wales, had delayed Ellen from following up her promise to India to find out anything she could about the first Mrs Pharoah and her child. Returning to London in late August, she had only two more days before going back to work.

Friends and family, that's where to start, Riley had suggested when they had spoken earlier. Marcus Pharoah had a daughter, Rowena, a brother, Devlin, a nephew, Rufus, and an ex-wife, Alison. Recalling the sardonic glitter in Devlin Pharoah's brown eyes, Ellen had decided to telephone Alison Pharoah. Mrs Pharoah agreed to talk to her. After putting the phone down, Ellen remembered that Jan Kaminski, once Pharoah's right-hand man, was now a Fellow at Cambridge.

Ellen wrote to him, explaining that she would be in the area and asking whether they could meet. Kaminski had written back by return of post, inviting her to lunch.

Earlier that morning, she had called at Riley's house to borrow his car to drive to Cambridgeshire. Stopping and starting through the rush-hour city traffic before heading north on the A1, she was aware of his belongings: the notebook, Polos and I-Spy book stuffed into the glovebox, the scarf on the back seat. After Royston, she turned off the main road on to narrower country lanes, walled with hedgerows. Soon, the landmarks became familiar to her. A church spire, a village green and a shop recalled to her weekend cycle rides she had taken during the time she had worked at Gildersleve Hall.

Driving into the village of Barton, she parked on the road by the yew hedge and was assailed by memories. She remembered the night of the power cut, how the velvety darkness had seemed to press in on her as, blinded, she had made her way along the corridor. Her horror and her relief when she had encountered Alec. She remembered how the wind had whisked the frayed seedheads of the pampas grass in the Pharoahs' garden, and the confusion of her feelings that day. Yet those events seemed distant now; they had happened to a younger, different self.

Leaving the car, she walked up the gravel driveway. The house looked much as she remembered it, large, pleasant and gracious in the summer sunshine. A horsebox was parked on the courtyard; pansies and petunias spilled

from stone urns and a white rose rambled over the front door.

Alison Pharoah, her fair head bright in the morning sun, was kneeling in front of a border, a trowel on the lawn beside her, tapping a geranium from a pot. Ellen called out a greeting and Mrs Pharoah turned, then stood up. She was wearing a tweed skirt and a short-sleeved pale pink jersey.

'Miss Kingsley?'

'Yes. Thank you for agreeing to talk to me.'

Mrs Pharoah took off her leather gardening glove before shaking Ellen's hand. 'I'll get on with this, if it doesn't bother you.' Alison Pharoah's tone made it clear that she expected Ellen's agreement.

'Please. It's such a beautiful garden, Mrs Pharoah.'

Alison Pharoah surveyed the borders and lawns. 'It's a lot of work. It's so hard to get decent help these days. Marcus wanted me to sell the house but I'll be damned if I'll do that.' Her cold, pale green eyes settled on Ellen. 'You said that you had some questions for me.'

In other words, get on with it, I'm busy. Ellen asked a few anodyne questions about Marcus Pharoah's career, then said, 'You weren't Dr Pharoah's first wife, were you, Mrs Pharoah?'

'No.' A short, contemptuous outbreath. 'Nor his last.'

'His first wife was American, wasn't she?'

'From somewhere in New England. He married her when he was very young.'

'She died, didn't she?'

472

'Yes.' There was a packet of cigarettes on a nearby stone urn. Alison tipped one out and lit it.

'Do you know what of?'

Mrs Pharoah gave a quick shake of the head. 'Pneumonia or something. Marcus never talked about it. He was always very odd about illnesses. I've met you before, haven't I?'

'I came here for Sunday lunch once, about five years ago.'

'Were you one of Marcus's girls?'

'I was an employee of his.'

A sceptical smile curled the corners of Mrs Pharoah's mouth. Ellen said coolly, 'Nothing else. What did you mean when you said that Dr Pharoah is odd about illnesses?'

'He can't bear sick people.' Alison Pharoah balanced the cigarette on the edge of the urn and picked up another pot. 'Marcus likes the people around him to be good-looking, healthy and conventional. I can see now what a dull man he was. Why do you want to know? What was it you said you were doing when we spoke on the phone?'

Ellen repeated the lie that she and Riley had concocted: that she was writing a few paragraphs on Dr Pharoah, an overview of his life and work, for a scientific journal. She had never been much of a liar and she could tell that Mrs Pharoah was unconvinced. A whack on the underside of the pot with the trowel and another geranium was neatly upended, then plunged into a hole in the soil.

Ellen said, 'Did Dr Pharoah and his first wife have any children?'

473

'No, none. We only had the one child, our daughter, Rowena. Marcus didn't want any more.' Mrs Pharoah stood up again, peeled off her gloves and picked up the cigarette. 'I would have liked more.' A mixture of discontent and sadness settled over her face. 'I always wanted a son. You'd have thought Marcus would have wanted a boy, but he didn't. And yet he always loved Rowena far more than he loved me. You'd have thought that—' She broke off, pressing the back of her hand against her mouth. 'Forgive me,' she murmured. 'I haven't been well.'

'I'm sorry, Mrs Pharoah.'

Alison Pharoah's expression altered. 'I'm well rid of him. To tell the truth, I miss Gosse more than I miss Marcus. Marcus insisted on taking Gosse with him to America. Damned annoying and of course the wretched boiler broke down the day after he left. Gosse was a nasty little man, but he was good with the horses.' The cigarette stub was crushed into the urn and Mrs Pharoah glanced at her watch. 'And now, if you'll excuse me, I'm meeting my fiancé for lunch.'

Returning to her car, Ellen felt a longing to head home to London. These long ago events, these people with their skewed morality and their egotism, produced in her feelings of distaste. It was a relief to sit in the car, with its intimacy, its reminders of Riley, as she rested her hands on the steering wheel and ate a Polo.

A Rover drove at speed out of the Pharoahs' driveway. Ellen started up the car and headed for Cambridge. It was

a market day and the traffic was heavy, and she was almost ten minutes late for her lunch with Dr Kaminski.

As a senior research fellow, his rooms overlooked a garden where a fig scrambled along ancient brickwork and a handkerchief tree flailed its greenish-white pennants. Not far away, punts slid along the olivine surface of the river. Brushing off Ellen's apologies for her lateness, Dr Kaminski showed her to a small table, set for lunch, in the bay window.

'How are you, Miss Kingsley?'

'I'm very well, thank you. And thank you so much for inviting me.'

'A pleasure, a pleasure. I thought a cold lunch in this warm weather. Then we need not be interrupted.'

They discussed their work; as they spoke, Ellen thought that he had changed little since she had last seen him, only taking on, perhaps, the look of the academic, rumpled and tweedy.

They had finished the first course when he said, 'I am enjoying my life here. There is some dissension, of course – among intelligent, ambitious people that is inevitable – but only comparatively minor matters. The atmosphere at Gildersleve Hall had become poisonous by the time I left. You said that you wanted to talk to me about Pharoah, Miss Kingsley. Why is that?'

Instinctively she knew that she must tell him the truth. She said, 'A friend of mine has married him. She wrote to me, asking me to find something out for her.'

'And what was that?'

She told him about Rosanne Pharoah and the stillborn child. Jan Kaminski shook his head. 'I'm afraid I can't help you. Pharoah rarely spoke of personal matters to me. I knew Alison, of course, but . . .' He spread out his hands.

'It doesn't matter.' She smiled at him. 'It's lovely to see you anyway.'

Dr Kaminski cleared away their plates to the sideboard. His back to her, he said, 'I did, however, know poor Redmond reasonably well. I should have thought that would have been of interest to you.'

She glanced at him sharply. 'Yes, it is.'

He put a strawberry tart and a jug of cream on the table. Sitting down, he pressed his folded knuckles against his forehead and, in the squares of light that poured through the mullioned windows, she saw for the first time that he had aged after all, that he looked tired, and that the eye on the undamaged side of his face was now surrounded by deep lines. 'A headache,' he said, catching her looking at him. 'I get a lot of headaches.'

'I have some aspirins.' She made to open her bag.

'No, thank you. Let's talk. It will distract me.'

She said, 'You lived in Dr Redmond's cottage during the war, didn't you?'

'From nineteen forty-two. The three of us lived there. Pharoah and Redmond moved in first and I joined them some time later. It was Pharoah who recruited me. I had certain skills that were useful to the work of Gildersleve

Hall during the war.' He cut the tart into four, put one of the pieces on a plate, and handed it to Ellen. 'Please help yourself to cream, Miss Kingsley. I'd thought I was finished. I'd been pretty badly shot up and my nerves were wrecked. When I was well enough, I started going to scientific meetings in London. Sat at the back, so people didn't have to look at me, put my hands in my coat pockets so that no one would notice them shake. There were kind people who came to talk to me and someone must have mentioned me to Pharoah because he phoned me and we had a chat. I started work at Gildersleve Hall two days after that conversation took place. Pharoah cut through all the red tape to get me there. He was good at that sort of thing. He knew what he wanted and he got it. I was deeply grateful to him. There are few things worse than believing you'll never be of use to anyone any more, that you have no further part to play.'

Ellen found herself recalling the six months after she had left Gildersleve Hall, six months without work, during which a drab pall of isolation and futility had settled over her.

'It must have been very difficult,' she said.

'Yes, it was. For me, that was worse than the physical pain.' He nodded towards the window. 'I would have none of this now had it not been for Pharoah. I doubt if I'd have survived. I would have hoped a bomb would fall on me. So, as I said, Pharoah and Redmond were already living at the cottage by the time I went to Gildersleve Hall. After a

couple of weeks, Pharoah asked me to join them. I was relieved – my lodgings were unpleasant and my landlady was suspicious of me because I was a foreigner. We three got on well. We had certain things in common, we were all young men, uprooted from the places of our birth, and we shared an interest in science. We liked to play chess and solve crosswords and to walk in the grounds of the hall and Peddar's Wood. In the evenings one of us would cycle to the pub to fetch a jug of beer and would bring it back on the handlebars of his bike. It was a matter of honour to do so without spilling a drop, in the blackout, whatever the weather. We'd drink and talk until the early hours of the morning. I remember those conversations. I've never had conversations like them since. They were exhilarating and wonderful. We talked about everything, of the future of science, the marvellous developments the post-war years would bring, of the lives we hoped for.' He smiled. 'I was happy. Six months earlier I'd thought I'd never be happy again. We believed that we could change the world. You do when you're young.'

'Did you always get on well?'

'Not always. Sometimes we argued. I remember once telling the pair of them they were fools and walking out of the house. I sat in the wood, listening to the owls calling, and then after a couple of hours I went back.'

'What did you argue about?'

'Politics. Yes, I would say that was our main area of disagreement.'

'Dr Redmond was a communist, wasn't he?'

'I couldn't shake them out of it. It infuriated me, how two intelligent people could refuse to see what was staring them in the face. They wouldn't listen, they didn't seem to have the capacity to understand what it is to live in a country that is not free.'

Ellen's heartbeat had speeded up. 'Are you saying that Dr Pharoah was a communist too?'

'For a while, yes.' Kaminski's eyes narrowed as if he was staring back into the past. 'Communism was fashionable in the thirties, you understand, among a certain section of young people. Redmond was a card-carrying communist up to his death, so far as I know.'

'And Dr Pharoah?'

'I believe that for a short time, before the war, he may have been a party member. I'm not convinced, though, looking back, that Pharoah ever had strong political convictions. Redmond was unshakeable in his faith but I don't think it was ever as important to Pharoah. I remember feeling proud of myself, wondering whether it was my influence that had made him change his mind, but I don't suppose it had anything to do with me. I'm sure that Pharoah had by then worked out what he wanted to do and was clear-sighted enough to see that extreme left-wing politics would only be a hindrance to him.'

'Do you mean what he wanted to do after the war was over?'

'Yes.' Jan Kaminski had risen from the table. Silhouetted

blackly against the window, he looked outside. The shrieks of laughter from the punts had died down; from somewhere, Ellen heard the liquid notes of a violin.

'We had a nickname,' he said, 'the three of us, during the war. The Triumvirate, that was what our colleagues at Gildersleve Hall called us. And the Triumvirate worked it out together in those long evenings at the cottage. I think it was Redmond's idea first, that we would set up our own research institution after the war was over. Pharoah, being the only presentable one of the three of us, was to head it, to be the public face. He had that knack of inspiring loyalty in people. You wanted to please him. All Redmond cared about was having somewhere to pursue his work uninterrupted. He never wanted fame or success or money. I offered to undertake the routine work, the chasing up of funds, the bringing in of projects on time. You need someone methodical and conscientious to do that and I knew I was capable. We discussed the organization of such an institution and which branches of research we would pursue – genetics, crystallography, biochemistry. We would, of course, become world-renowned.' Jan Kaminski's mouth stretched in a shallow smile and his fingers tapped the windowsill. 'After a while, what started as a pipe dream seemed to become a possibility. Though I think that Pharoah always believed in it.' He turned back to Ellen. 'Will you have some coffee, Miss Kingsley?'

'Yes, thank you.'

'Shall we take it out to the Fellows' garden?'

Dr Kaminski made the coffee, then put on a hat over his thin blond hair and carried the tray outside. They sat in the shade of the handkerchief tree.

'Then something happened,' said Kaminski. 'In nineteen forty-four I went away for a week to oversee some tests on Salisbury Plain. When I came back to the cottage, Pharoah and Redmond were no longer speaking to each other.'

'They'd fallen out?'

'Yes.'

'Do you know why?'

The patchy shade of the tree darkened the burned skin on Jan Kaminski's face to a livid purple. 'I asked, but neither would say. Pharoah brushed it off and Redmond refused to talk to me. It was a habit of his to shut himself away for days at a time and he did so then. I wondered at the time whether Redmond had felt it a betrayal that Pharoah should alter his political allegiance so absolutely. Perhaps he'd told Pharoah so. Pharoah dislikes criticism.' He added pointedly, 'But you know that, Miss Kingsley.'

She could only say, 'Yes.'

'But I came to doubt that was the reason. It was Pharoah's attitude to Redmond that had altered rather than the other way round. Redmond remained unswervingly loyal to Pharoah for a long time after they had quarrelled. He had always admired Pharoah intensely. I suppose Pharoah could do so easily the things Redmond found impossible – talking to people, charming them, persuading them to do what he wanted. Anyway, they patched it over – Gildersleve

481

needed both of them – but it was never the same afterwards. To some extent, before that time, I had always been a little on the outside. Pharoah and Redmond had known each other for several years before I came along. When there are three of you, there'll always be two who have the deeper bond. I noticed that they began to communicate through me. I became closer to Pharoah while Redmond lived more and more apart from us. Then the war ended and all Pharoah's energy went into making his dream a reality. He was impressive. He had his plans in place – he'd got to know the right people and he and Alison were living together again, and he had persuaded her father to finance the hall. The War Office had no further use for it. It was a ramshackle old building, as you know, and they were happy enough to sell it to him.'

Jan Kaminski fell silent. Ellen said gently, 'It must have been exciting.'

'It was. So much so that I'm afraid I overlooked certain things. I've often asked myself, was that out of loyalty to Pharoah, because I owed him so much, or was it because they were good times for me, too, and I didn't want to rock the boat?'

In the silence, Ellen saw the flicker of shadows on the grass. Two men in academic gowns came out of a doorway; Dr Kaminski raised a hand in greeting as they went to sit on a bench on the far side of the garden.

He said, 'I let Pharoah pass off some of my work as his own. He had done little new research work for some time.

He claimed that the setting up of the hall had fully occupied him. Can't give a good impression without a few papers in *Nature*, he said to me, and would I mind helping him out. Gildersleve Hall would die an early death if it got round that its director was running out of ideas. When he had the chance to do some solid work, he'd pay me back.'

'And did he?' Her voice was a whisper.

'No. In fact, it happened again. And again. After a while, he didn't even ask me, he just took. We'd be at a meeting or seminar and I'd hear him come out with some theory I was working on. As if he'd thought of it himself. Perhaps by then he believed he had. So there we were, Pharoah with his growing reputation for brilliance, and me – well, I could see that my colleagues were starting to think that it was me who was burned out.'

'Did you say anything to Dr Redmond?'

'Never.'

But Redmond had known, Redmond had guessed. Ellen recalled the afternoon in Peddar's Wood, when he had called Dr Pharoah a liar and a plagiarist: the sting of snow in the air and the way that the coppiced trees had clawed at the heavy sky.

Jan Kaminski's pale blue eyes looked straight ahead. 'In nineteen thirty-nine, after the Germans and the Russians invaded Poland, I travelled to England. It was a long, arduous journey that took me almost six months, but I found my way. But once I started giving in to Pharoah's demands, I couldn't find my way back. What Pharoah did was wrong,

but what I did was equally wrong.' He smiled sadly. 'It was dishonest. There, it's a relief to admit that at last.'

'You were loyal to him,' she said gently. 'That's not such a terrible thing.'

'Do you think so? But perhaps Pharoah demanded too much loyalty.'

This, she herself had learned the hard way. Pharoah had demanded absolute allegiance and he had also demanded silence. Those who had not given him what he wanted had received summary justice.

Kaminski gave a soft sigh and said, 'In the years after the war, Redmond retreated from us. He saw me as Pharoah's man, I suspect. He'd always liked his own company, and he was an odd man, and I'm afraid he became odder over time. He changed. He was never *sociable*, but when I first knew him, he had a few close friends.'

'Dr Pharoah.'

'Yes, Pharoah, for many years. And there was a woman.'

Now she said incredulously, 'A girlfriend?'

'Yes, in London. He visited her each month. Once, Redmond and I were on the same London train. When we reached town, we found that we were both heading in a similar direction so I travelled on with him.'

'And he was visiting his girlfriend? He *said* that?'

'Not in so many words. To tell the truth, I don't think he said anything at all. But I guessed. I'm afraid I teased him a little.'

Now, Ellen felt utterly confused. But she had the

presence of mind to say, 'Where was this, Dr Kaminski? In which part of London?'

'Finsbury Park,' he said. 'Woodstock Road.'

Before she headed back to London, Ellen took the road out to Copfield. She drove past Mrs Bryant's bungalow and into the village, past the Green Man pub and the church and out along the hazel-fringed rise that led to Gildersleve. The hedge-rows were thickly leaved and she realized that she had never before seen Gildersleve Hall in summer, that her memories were of the frozen monotones of winter.

At the summit she braked, looked down and saw the hall. Parking the car, she got out and climbed on to the verge. Absently, she snapped off a twig as she peered through the branches of the hazels. The hall seemed for an instant just the same, almost as if it was waiting for Martin to run down the front steps at a clip or for Bill Farmborough to emerge from the building, briefcase in hand.

She had learned that day about the consequences of betrayal. Pharoah had betrayed Alison and her pain and bitterness remained visible. He had betrayed Dr Redmond and Jan Kaminski as well, had taken their admiration and friendship and used it for his own ends. Once, the three men had shared their excitement for the future but now Redmond was long dead, Pharoah had left the country, and only Kaminski remained, haunted by regret and disillusion.

At Gildersleve, she had been unable to see the truth, had

fumbled in the dark, stumbling against other people's desires and ambitions. She saw clearly now, and, glancing a second time, Gildersleve Hall seemed little more than a husk of a house, ivy creeping over the walls and tower, a relic from a dusty and dishonourable past.

That morning, when she had collected the car from Riley, he had sat with her in the vehicle, running through the various controls. She had been aware of him beside her, of the brush of his hand and the warmth of his skin. Touch had its own chemistry, a fierce, igniting power that filled the spaces left by words. Touch told you that you wanted someone. Touch told you they wanted you. Before they had parted, he had said to her, 'Are you sure about this? Are you sure you want to go back there?' She had reassured him, and now, as she returned to the car, she knew that she had been right to do so.

Her three months at Gildersleve had been a turning point in her life but now she was poised at another juncture. Both she and Riley had been bruised by former relationships. Neither of them, she thought, loved lightly. In law, Riley was still married to Pearl. For herself, there were all her old reservations about the difficulty of mixing marriage and career, the fear of jeopardising what had been so hard won.

And yet, as she started up the car and drove on, she was filled with a bright optimism. You could not say that anything had been easy for them. The circumstances of their first meeting, in the shocked aftermath of Dr Redmond's

death, had not been auspicious. Pearl's illness and disappearance, her own broken engagement to Alec: these events had left a long shadow. In spite of this, they had survived. Their friendship had blossomed and deepened. They would manage, she thought, she and him. No, more than manage, because she found it unbearable to imagine life without him. He was threaded into her thoughts, into her heart. A successful partnership – and here she considered her parents – was not necessarily of two people with similar characters, backgrounds and tastes, but of a couple so deeply rooted together they became different parts of the same person, like the facets of a crystal. One might sometimes look one way, one another, but they were together a whole, precious and harmonious.

Reaching the farm track, she had intended to park at the entrance to Peddar's Wood, so as not to get mud over Riley's car, but as she neared the turn-off she noticed that the rutted track was now tarmacked. Swinging on to the new road, she drove a short distance along it. The wood had been felled and not a single tree remained. In place of their enchantment, new houses, boxy in shape, their bricks a raw red, had sprung up.

Redmond always loved that woodland, Dr Kaminski had said to her as they had parted that afternoon. *Pharoah knew that. It would have been a fitting memorial to his old friend to preserve it as he had loved it, but Pharoah chose to destroy it. That was his greatest crime. Though I suppose you could say that in the end, it set me free.*

*   *   *

It was one of those rare English days when the heat lingers into the evening. Ellen was sitting in Riley's garden and they were sharing a bottle of beer.

'I know what happened now,' she said. 'I know what Dr Redmond meant when he told Pharoah he could destroy him.'

She explained to Riley about Marcus Pharoah passing off Jan Kaminski's work as his own and about his youthful communist sympathies. 'Pharoah went to America several times during the months I was at Gildersleve,' she said. 'He attended conferences and gave lectures there. He was feted in America, even more so than he was here. If Dr Redmond had made public that Pharoah had dabbled in communism then Pharoah might not have been able to travel to America any more. He might have had his visa revoked, like Professor Bernal at Birkbeck. Couple that with accusations about plagiarism – even if Dr Kaminski had refused to confirm what Redmond said, rumours can do a lot of harm. Pharoah must have known that his career might never recover.'

Riley uncapped another bottle of beer and topped up their glasses. 'It makes sense. And the child?'

Ellen shook her head. 'Nothing. Jan didn't know anything about a child. Neither did Alison Pharoah.'

'A dead end, then.'

'Yes, in some ways.'

She saw him look at her quizzically. Why couldn't she just tell him what she had come here intending to say the moment he had opened the door to her? Why instead,

after she had parked his car outside, had she talked to him about the drive, and Annie, even the *weather*, for heaven's sake? Why, now that they were alone, Annie in bed and the au pair out for the evening, did she sit on the garden bench, fidgeting and reddening like a schoolgirl, the confidence she had felt that afternoon at Gildersleve having deserted her?

They might go on in this way for ever, she thought despairingly, both aware of an attraction but unable to bring it into being, both reticent and reserved in character, the sort of people who delved into a problem, analysing it, tearing it apart, until it lay in meaningless fragments. Mutually incapable of putting it together again, of making something new.

Another thought occurred to her. What evidence had she that he was attracted to her? A brush of a hand, sitting in the car that morning. An endearment, quite possibly voiced in error. Almost nothing. There was, if you looked back critically at their history, little indication that he had anything more than a friendly affection for her. And *friend-ship* had come to have such a dull, spinsterish sound. Even back in the early days of their acquaintance, before Alec, Riley had never asked her out, never made a move. She remembered that evening in the aftermath of the break-up of her engagement when, drunk, she had suggested sleeping overnight on his sofa, and how he had bundled her out of the door and into a taxi as if she had an infectious disease. There had been numerous occasions during the

past two years when all he had to do was to reach out and take her hand. He wouldn't even have needed to *say* anything. Would she have turned him away? She knew that she would not.

But then . . . She thought of their long phone conversations, sometimes late into the night until they could hardly speak for yawning, as though neither of them could bear to be the one who ended the call. She thought of the days they had spent together, the concerts they had attended, the hours they had sat in this garden or his house, listening to music or just talking. Oh, it was all too complicated! She gave a loud sigh, wishing such things could be weighed, measured, put on a balance, total totted up, conclusion written, line drawn.

'Riley—'

'Ellen.'

They had both spoken at once. 'I'm sorry,' she said. 'You go ahead.'

'No, you first.'

'No, you. What were you going to say?'

He sat down beside her. 'It's funny, you wait, thinking one day the time will be just right but it never is. There's never a moment when there isn't risk. And you've made mistakes before, so you're wary.'

'Wary of what?' She peered hard into his eyes.

'Of speaking from the heart.'

Her own heart was racing. She whispered, 'If you were to speak from the heart, Riley, what would you say?'

490

'That I love you. That's what I was going to say. What were you?'

She felt herself teetering on the edge of great happiness. 'I was going to say that though today was a dead end in some ways, in another it was a revelation. But Riley, what did you mean when you said that you were afraid I might be a mistake? Did you mean like Pearl?'

'Never.' His voice roughened. 'Good God, no. I've been sure from the first moment I saw you. Oh, you tell yourself that it's mere attraction – and perhaps at first it is only attraction and desire, perhaps it's being in love rather than really loving. But for me none of what I first felt for you has ever diminished, it's only gathered pace. It's become a part of my life, a part of me. I love you, Ellen, and that love is as essential to me as the bones that hold me up and the blood that flows through my veins. But you may not feel the same. In fact, I can think of a number of reasons why you'd be sensible not to feel the same.'

'I can't think of any.' Her voice was small but clear.

In his eyes, a fire flared. 'Are you sure?'

'Never more so.'

'Listen, Ellen.' He gripped her hand. 'I have a child – and yes, I know you love Annie and she loves you, but nevertheless, it's a huge commitment. I have a job that can be ridiculously demanding, that takes me away at all hours, often without warning.'

'None of that matters.'

'I'm married. *That* matters. I have a failed marriage behind

me that I'm still legally tied to. I've spoken to a solicitor about a divorce but it won't be straightforward with Pearl nowhere to be found. I wonder what your family would think of that?'

'My father would dislike it.'

'Yes, I would have thought so. Quite understandably. I daresay he wouldn't be too thrilled either at the thought of you taking on another woman's child.'

'No, probably not. But he would come round.'

'Ellen—'

'And if he didn't, I'd live with it.' She was looking at him and though she knew she was smiling, she was aware also of tears aching around her eyes. Tears of joy, she thought, but also of regret for the time that they had already spent apart, those unreclaimable years.

'Joe's always liked you,' she said tremulously. 'And my mother will adore you. She loves handsome, capable men.'

A flicker of a smile. 'Even if that's so—'

'Riley, you're not going to put me off. I may as well point out to you that I'm a career woman and though I know how to bake a cake and mop a floor, I don't choose to spend much of my time doing so.'

'I've no wish to tie you to the kitchen sink.'

'Don't look so grim, darling. I love you and I'm only explaining that if we were to—'

She broke off. She had got rather ahead of herself. She felt herself go pink.

'If we were to marry? Was that what you were going to

say?' Threading his fingers through hers, he raised her hand and kissed it. 'If it was, if it's something you'd seriously consider as soon as I'm free, then you would make me indescribably happy.'

Embarrassment and uncertainty fell away, replaced by elation. She felt a deep contentment and a complete pleasure in the moment and was calm again. She was sharply aware of everything around her: of the papery rustle of a bumble bee in the trumpet of a flower, of the distant whine of traffic on the main road, and of the presence of the man sitting beside her, the pressure of his hand on the back of her neck as he drew her to him to kiss her.

'It's my life, Riley,' she said gently, breaking away for long enough to speak. 'No one else's. My decision. And anyway, what's wrong with living in sin?'

'Your father would probably shoot me.'

They kissed as the sun sank beneath the rooftops of the buildings. 'I suppose there is that,' she said. Then they kissed some more.

Once, India drove north, out of Midhurst, past Linc's place. The small wooden building was set well back from the road, halfway up the slope of the hill, among a stand of birches. India was driving the station wagon that day and Abigail was sleeping in the carrycot on the back seat. She parked and looked up at the house, and imagined Linc sitting on the raised stoop at the front, watching the hummingbirds. She pictured his strong brown hands holding a coffee mug

or a glass of beer. The sleeves of his plaid shirt would be rolled up to his elbows and the sun would throw shadows that would pick out the curve of his lip and gather round his deepset eyes.

A pick-up truck, painted a dull green, was parked on the slope. She thought she saw a movement in the meadow behind the house – a shadow, the to-and-fro of a branch – and she turned the car and drove home.

She stopped going to the coffeehouse. She knew how easily such things began, and how, the deeper you waded in, the more they clung to you. She thought of her mother and Neil dancing in the garden, how the open air had swallowed up the music of the gramophone and how her mother had rested her head against Neil's navy-blue shoulder. *Lucinda, you have to think of those children.* She, now, had a child to think of.

She applied herself to being a good wife and mother. In the afternoons, instead of driving to town, she spread a blanket on the grass and laid Abigail upon it so that she could watch the shivering leaves on the trees. She carried Abigail round the pond, showing her the fish and the sparkle of water and the pale flowers that grew in the dampest, darkest part of the woods. She wanted Abigail to be the sort of woman who knew about everything, like Ellen.

Marcus decided that they should give a summer party. He told her where she should have the invitations printed and specified the thickness of card and the wording. He dictated the guest list to her: his colleagues from Midhurst,

academics from other colleges and research institutions, a scattering of wealthy and important people from the area. India wondered who she would have invited, had Marcus asked her. The grocer's boy, the waitresses in the coffee-house. The old man she sometimes spoke to at the gate, when he was out walking his dog. Viola. Linc.

She made lists, placed orders for food and liquor, engaged maids to hand around drinks and canapés, had her nails and hair done. On the afternoon of the day of the party, she lay on the sofa in the sitting room, playing with Abigail. Her hands round her baby's middle, India lifted her up until her arms were straight and then whooshed her gently down. 'Abby's going up in an aeroplane . . . higher and higher into the sky . . . and zoom, down she goes.' Abigail chortled, her gummy mouth wide open.

The front doorbell rang. Marcus was working in his study and Viola had gone home for a couple of hours, so India laid Abigail on a blanket on the floor and went to answer it. It was the florist, with the arrangements for the party. India helped him take in the flowers, then looked for her purse. She heard Abigail start to cry and called out to Marcus to go to her. She found her purse in a coat pocket in the mud room; the baby was still crying as she fumbled urgently for notes to pay the bill.

The florist left; India went back into the sitting room. Abigail was lying on the floor, red-faced and screaming, and Marcus was standing a few yards away. It crossed India's mind that he was looking at his daughter with the same

appraising eye with which he might have regarded one of his scientific experiments.

Pushing past him, India picked Abigail up. Then she held out the infant to him. 'Hold her,' she said. It was hard to speak for fury. 'Go on, hold her. She's your daughter, Marcus. Why won't you touch her? What's wrong with you? If you really didn't want another child, then why agree to letting me have one?' The effort of not shouting made her voice shake.

'To keep you busy,' he said softly. 'So you wouldn't make a spectacle of yourself, dawdling round town and talking to strangers.'

Then he walked out of the room. As she cradled Abigail against her shoulder, India found herself fighting for breath, as if she had been running.

She went into the kitchen. Warming Abigail's bottle in a pan, staring at the tiny bubbles which set themselves free from the metal base of the pan before rising to the surface to burst, she found herself concentrating on the task because the other part of her mind flinched from closely examining the scene that had just taken place. When the bottle was ready she took Abigail upstairs to feed her. She sat down in the low chair beside the nursery window, and tucked the baby into the crook of her arm.

They had engaged a children's nurse to look after Abigail during the party, Marcus had insisted, so after feeding her, India changed Abigail's nappy and made sure that everything was ready. Viola returned to put the finishing touches

to the food. When the nurse arrived, India showed her where everything was and then went away to dress for the party. After she had bathed, she wrapped herself in a towelling robe, then searched through her wardrobe for a frock. At the end of the rail she caught sight of the white silk she had bought years ago from Berwick Street Market. She had bought it secondhand and had worn it many times. The silk ruffles round the low-cut bodice had yellowed and the edging of the slit up the front of the bell-shaped skirt had begun to fray.

She stepped into it, cranking round awkwardly to do up the zip. Then, sitting down at the dressing table, she rubbed powder into the planes and hollows of her face, painted on black wings of eyeliner, and pencilled in her eyebrows to make them dark and sooty. She chose the brightest, reddest lipstick she possessed. *Always accessorize*, she muttered to herself, and opened her jewellery box. She had lost the spray of blue waxed flowers somewhere on the long journey between the London flat and Vermont, but Marcus had bought her for her birthday a large, flashy diamond brooch in the shape of a shooting star. She pinned it on to her bosom. Satisfied, she looked in the mirror and pursed her mouth into the shape of a kiss.

She remained in the dressing room until she heard the first few cars draw up in the courtyard. There was a tap on the door; she opened it.

Viola's eyes widened, seeing her. 'Mr Pharoah says could you come downstairs, Mrs Pharoah.'

India ran her hands down her ribs, smoothing out the creases in the silk. 'Do you like it?'

Viola gave a bark of laughter. 'You're a sight for sore eyes, Mrs Pharoah. You look like Marilyn Monroe.'

India walked slowly downstairs. Half a dozen guests were in the hall, taking off summer coats and hats. She greeted them and showed them to the back veranda, where cocktails were being served. The evening sun spun a wash of apricot over the meadows and the pond.

The perfect hostess, India moved from guest to guest, enquiring after their holidays and their children, making sure everyone had a drink and a canapé. Out of the corner of her eye she saw Marcus turn to look at her.

As he drew her aside, his fingers pinched into the soft flesh of her arm. 'What do you think you're doing?' he hissed. 'You look like a tart. Go and change.'

'I like this dress, Marcus.' Where he had whispered, her voice was normal in pitch, and heads turned towards them.

The Dean of Studies was standing a few feet away. India touched his hand. 'Lowell, how delightful to see you! Let me find you a drink. It's a glorious evening, isn't it?'

After the guests had gone, after the maids and the children's nurse had been paid and sent home, he came to her in the kitchen, where she was tidying up.

'Never do that again,' he said.

Drying a glass, India held it up to the light to check for streaks. 'Do what, Marcus?'

'Try to make a fool out of me.'

'I thought it all went rather well.'

'You may be resentful of me,' he said softly, 'you may even dislike me, but you need me. You'd be nothing without me.'

'I managed perfectly well before I met you.' She put the glass away in a cupboard. 'And yes, I do dislike you. I didn't to begin with but I do now. I dislike the things you do. You've told Gosse to spy on me, haven't you? And you wrote to the children's home about me, I saw the letters in your desk. How could you do that, Marcus? How could you be so underhand?'

'I needed to find out what I was getting. Surely you can understand that.'

'I suppose if you'd found me to be inferior, you'd have got rid of me.'

'You're not inferior.' He was leaning against the door of the fridge, drinking. He pulled at the knot of his tie. 'A little shop-soiled, perhaps, but not inferior.'

'Neither is Abigail. She's a beautiful, healthy, perfect baby and you hardly even look at her.'

'I don't find small children interesting. I daresay I'll like her better as she grows older.'

India took out a cigarette, snapped her lighter. 'You mean, ignore her for the first few years of her life and then indulge her, so that she grows up as spoiled and desperate for your attention as Rowena is.'

The grip on his glass tightened. 'Stop it, India.'

'What? I can't say what I think of your darling daughter but you can ignore ours?'

Something malevolent crossed his face. 'I suppose I should have guessed that, in the end, breeding will out.'

'What do you mean?'

'Bad blood.' His voice was soft and low. 'Don't you remember asking me about it? Your mother had bad blood. Perhaps she's passed it on to you.'

'Shut up, Marcus,' she said sharply.

'She wasn't a fit person to bring up children. She was negligent. Face up to the truth, she didn't care enough about you or Sebastian to make the effort. Maybe you take after her. After tonight's little performance I'm starting to think so. I shall have to keep an eye on you. For your own sake, and for our daughter's.'

She hugged her arms round herself, as if to hold in her anger. It didn't do to lose your temper with Marcus, you didn't win. 'I'm a good mother to Abigail,' she said levelly. 'And I'll tell you something. I'll never be ashamed of my child. However she grows up, however plain or pretty she turns out to be, however clever or slow, I'll always love her and I'll always be proud of her.'

'*Ashamed?*' he repeated. 'What are you talking about?'

'You've had three children. There's the one you spoil, the one you ignore, and the one you never mention.'

In his eyes, something flickered. He said, 'I told you, the baby was stillborn.' Then he turned and walked out of the kitchen.

India's head pulsed painfully and she found that was trembling. The firestorm that had run through her that night seemed to have left her nerve endings exposed. She went outside to the veranda. As she walked slowly down the steps and along the moonlit path that led to the pond, she felt dreamy and glassy, almost beyond thought, and so light-headed she could have risen into the air like thistledown. She stood on the bank of the pond, letting the cool night air wash over her. Stars dabbed the still surface of the water and in the distance there was the cry of a bird.

Just before Marcus had left her, she had seen something that had shocked her. The expression that had passed over his face had contained an emotion she had never seen there before.

Fear.

Two days after the party, India drove to Midhurst. Parking in a vacant lot, she lifted the carrycot out of the station wagon and pushed it along the sidewalk. She bought a few odds and ends from the shops and then went to the café.

There, the waitress greeted her like an old friend and offered to warm Abigail's bottle for her. The feed was almost finished and India was wiping a dribble of milk from Abigail's chin, when she looked through the window and saw him, coming across the road.

'Hello, Linc,' she said, as he came into the café.

He smiled at her. 'I was beginning to think you'd gone back to England. It's been pretty dull, having my coffee without you.'

She settled Abigail, a round, compact little package, on her knee, and smiled at him. 'I'm sure you found someone else to talk to.'

'Not the same.'

She might have gone on with this mild flirting, as she had done on many previous afternoons, but instead she said flatly, 'I'm married, Linc.'

He sat down opposite her. 'But not happily.'

'How can you tell?'

'Happily married women talk about their husbands, but you never do. They say things like, "Do you know what John said to me last night?" or, "John took me to the most adorable restaurant."'

His voice had lifted in pitch and she knew he meant to make her laugh, but she bit her lip and stared out of the window.

'Hey,' she heard him say gently. 'I'm sorry, I've upset you.'

'You haven't.'

He stood up. 'Let's go for a walk. I'll push honeybunch and you can tell me to keep quiet when I put my foot in it.'

So they went for a walk, down the main street, past the shops and the garages, Abigail lying in the blue-grey shade, her hands reaching out to the fringes of the sun canopy.

He said, after a while, 'I missed you.'

'Linc—'

'I think you need to know. And I need to say it.'

'You shouldn't like me.'

'I do, though.'

'Not just because of Marcus. I'm not a nice person.'

He peered at her. 'Let me see . . . you shot your lover and pushed him into a creek?'

She gave a fleeting smile. 'No. But I used to steal things.'

'Ah.'

'The first time I did it I was ten years old, and the last time – oh, it was a couple of years ago.'

He whistled. 'Quite a criminal record. What are we talking about? Gold bullion, diamonds, unmarked banknotes?'

'Food, to begin with, because we were hungry, Sebastian and me.' She bit a nail. 'When I was at school, I took things that belonged to the other girls. Just little things. Nothing valuable.'

'Keepsakes.'

'Yes. I got thrown out, I had to move to another school.'

'That's tough.'

'No, not really, it was a horrible school, it was a relief. And then—'

He put his hand over hers, stopping her tearing at the piece of skin round her nail. 'You don't have to tell me. We've all done stuff, India.'

'Even you?'

'Yeah. Do you want to know? Smashed myself up on a motorbike when I was sixteen, broke my leg pretty bad. Dropped out of school the same year, travelled around for a while doing this and that, none of it very edifying, got in trouble with the police after I'd had a few drinks too many. It took me a year to realize what an idiot I was, then I stopped drinking, came home, got a job in a store, went to night school, sorted myself out. Where was your mom, while all this was going on?'

'She died when I was ten. Yes, yes, I know,' she added quickly. 'I was stealing to comfort myself for losing my mother. It's so obvious, isn't it?'

They had left the outskirts of the town and were heading along the road that led north. 'Where are we going?' she asked him.

'My place.' He grinned at her. 'I promise I make better coffee than the café.'

In the fields to either side of the road, the hay had been mown, leaving shorn, buff-coloured stalks. A veil of golden dust had settled over the grassy verges. As they walked, India told Linc about the house in the woods, about Sebastian and Neil and Mrs Day at the shop, and about the death of her mother. It struck her that it was the first time she had told anyone the whole story. Perhaps being in a different country enabled her to speak more freely. Or perhaps it was Linc that made the difference.

Reaching his home, he pushed the pram up the slope, then made coffee while India sat on the stoop, looking out

for hummingbirds. He brought out two enamel mugs and sat down beside her.

'Seems to me,' he said, 'you did rather well. You kept your little brother fed, you did your best to protect him.'

A long time ago, Rachel had said much the same thing to her. She thought how much she missed Rachel and how much she could have done now with her sensible, concerned advice.

She said, 'Marcus says that I have bad blood.'

'Helpful of Marcus. I'm taking a dislike to him.'

She wrapped her hands round her knees and leaned forward, looking down to the road. 'I don't think my blood's any different from anyone else's, not really. But I do worry that I won't be a good enough mother to Abigail.'

'India, you're a terrific mother to Abigail. You love her, you feed her, you play with her. That's all babies need. She's a credit to you.'

'But you learn from your parents, don't you? When you're a child, you think that however you live is normal, however strange or wrong it seems to everyone else. And that belief is very deep, I think, it runs right through us. What if I slip back into that? What if I'm lazy or I'm care-less, and she gets hurt? I don't suppose my mother meant to neglect us. I expect she did her best.'

He put his hand over hers. His big palm was warm where he had been holding the coffee cup, and she squeezed it. He said, 'People can change. Lives can change. If two people find each other, they help each other.'

She whispered, 'I'm afraid, Linc.'

'The best things often happen by chance. Like me being bored one afternoon at work and looking out the window and seeing you trying to get that baby carriage through the café door.'

Then he kissed her. His body was warm and resilient against hers. When, eventually, she opened her eyes, she saw that, in the shade beneath the branches of the birches, something darted and hovered, a flash of iridescent light.

She spoke to him that evening, after dinner. He was working in his study; the door was ajar.

'I want you to let me go, Marcus,' she said.

She saw him still, then swivel round in his chair. 'Let you go?' he repeated.

'Yes.'

'If you're bored, we'll have a holiday. We'll go to Cape Cod.'

'I'm not bored, it's not that. Lonely, sometimes.'

'You have the baby.'

'I'm not complaining. But I can't stay here with you.'

'No.' Softly.

'We don't make each other happy, do we?'

'Happy?' In his eyes there was bitterness and regret. 'Is that what you want, happiness?'

'Some of the time, at least. I don't mind if it's just flashes, like hummingbirds. But I'm never happy when I'm with you. And I don't think you're happy with me.'

'I've always thought it such a shallow aspiration, happiness, when there are so many other things one might have.'

'Well.' She wound her hands together. 'That's what I think. I suppose you'll say I'm running away again, but I don't think I am.'

'Who are you planning on leaving me for? That man you meet at the café?'

'I'm not leaving you for anyone but myself. You're trying to change me, I can see that you are. If you loved me, really, properly loved me, you wouldn't do that. I always think you're trying to make me into, oh,' she raised her shoulders, gave a shake of her head, 'some idea you have, some idea I don't really understand, and I hate it.'

'You're such a funny little thing. What do you expect me to say? "Very well, pack your bags, off you go?" No, India.'

'Marcus, please.'

'No.'

'You can't keep me here.'

'Perhaps not, but I shall keep the child.'

Was he taunting her? No, studying his face, she did not think so.

She said, 'But you don't love her.'

'I love you.'

'No, you don't. Whatever it is you think love is, you're mistaken. And I don't love you, I never have.'

He swung away, saying coldly, 'If you leave me, I shall keep the child. No court in the land would award you custody,

surely you see that? The neglectful mother, the mentally disturbed brother. I have the reports from the children's home and, of course, Sebastian was rejected for National Service. Written documentation, evidence, that's what counts with the law, and I have plenty of it. If you leave me, I'll make sure that you're judged an unfit mother. Custody of Abigail will be awarded to me, and you'll never see her again.'

He unscrewed the cap of his pen, and with a flourish dashed off his signature at the foot of a letter.

Climbing out of bed that night, India left Marcus sleeping beside her and walked silently out to the landing. Sebastian's letters told her that he was happy in his new home and she felt grateful to Marcus for that. They had managed, she and Sebastian, they had survived. Really, considering the circumstances, that wasn't so bad at all.

But she had to go. If she looked back, she saw that every time she found herself trapped, she had always managed to escape. The house in the woods, her first boarding school, Bernie — on each of these occasions she had, however clumsily and with however much difficulty, set herself free. And with Marcus, she could not be free.

There was not the smallest chance that she would let him take her baby from her. In threatening her, he had only reinforced her conviction that she must leave. She knew that she would have to change. No more flitting from job to job; she must find whatever work she could carry out while looking after Abigail, and she must stick to it.

And she needed to stop taking things that weren't hers: a book, a dress, someone's husband, someone's lover.

India looked out of the landing window. Threadbare clouds scurried across the face of the moon. Resting her forearms on the sill, she saw how, when the clouds moved aside, the tops of the trees turned to silver.

In the morning, Marcus drove the station wagon to college. After he had gone, India packed her bags. Viola was vacuuming downstairs and Gosse was repairing the roof of the front porch. She listened out for the tap of the hammer, footsteps on the gravel.

While Gosse was having his coffee, India went to the toolshed and took out a screwdriver. Back inside the house, she unscrewed the lock on the study door. In the study, she searched through Marcus's desk. She took out Abigail's birth certificate, her own passport, and the letters from the orphanage. In the back of a drawer she discovered a fat bundle of dollars tied up in an elastic band so she took that too, along with the keys to the Austin-Healey, Marcus's favourite car.

Then, checking that Gosse was still in the kitchen, she put the bags in the boot of the Healey. Afterwards, she fed and changed Abigail and ate her own lunch. Viola stuck her head into the dining room to say goodbye, then left the house.

India put on her mackintosh and headscarf and picked up the carrycot. The hammering at the porch started up again as she put the carrycot on the passenger seat of the

Healey. Then the car roared up the gravel drive, brushing against the hedge as India screeched on to the road. She thought she heard Gosse's yell. She drove through Midhurst, past the café and the shops and out of town. As she passed the shack by the fork on the road, she slowed and looked, but did not see Linc.

Driving north, she was soon heading along unfamiliar roads. Frequently, she looked in the mirror, checking the road behind her. She did not know at first where she was going to, but as the afternoon wore on, it became clear to her.

Chapter Thirteen

I n Woodstock Road in Finsbury Park bursts of rain swept across the street and the wind jigged at Ellen's umbrella. The tall, terraced houses, some of which had been split up into flats, contained families with small children, pensioners, and a young couple in denim jeans and checked shirts, who were knocking out the fireplace in their front room. Ellen started at one end of road, ringing doorbells, showing the people who answered a photograph.

The photograph had been taken at Gildersleve Hall during the war. Years later, she had found it in Dr Redmond's lab book, when she had taken it on the night of his death. In the snapshot, the group of young men appeared relaxed and happy. There was Jan Kaminski, standing a little apart from his colleagues, his head turned to one side so that the scarred aspect of his face was hidden. And there were Bryan Redmond and Marcus Pharoah. Pharoah was looking

at the camera but Dr Redmond had turned towards Pharoah and was smiling.

An old friend . . . lost touch during the war . . . someone thought he might live here. Some of the neighbours gave the photo a quick glance, others fetched their reading glasses and peered at it, frowning, but all shook their heads.

There she was, Ellen thought, so happy with Riley, and there was India, married to Marcus Pharoah. She didn't understand why India had married Pharoah, but it made her feel uneasy, which was why she was out in the rain, knocking on strangers' doors.

Ellen walked up another path and rang the bell to the basement flat. Rain poured from a broken gutter, splashing on to her shoes. No answer, and blinds were pulled down over the basement windows.

Next she tried the first floor flat. The man who opened the door was slight and of medium height, with a thatch of dark brown hair. His liquid dark eyes were set in a boyishly handsome face. He was wearing grey flannel trousers and a pale blue shirt.

Ellen said good morning and introduced herself. Then she held out the photograph to him. The alteration in his expression, sleepily curious before, was immediate and unmistakable.

'What do you want?' he said.

She pointed out Dr Redmond. 'Did you know him?'

'I said, what do you want?'

'To talk to you, that's all. I was a colleague of Dr

512

Redmond's. I worked at Gildersleve Hall in the autumn of nineteen fifty-two.'

'Fifty-two? Were you there when he died?' His voice, which had a gentle West Country accent, was urgent and brusque.

'Yes. It was me who found his body.'

His lips parted, then he nodded. 'You'd better come in,' he said.

'I didn't know until several weeks after his death. No one told me. He used to come here regular as clockwork, every month, and then, that December, he didn't turn up. I knew something was wrong then. Bryan was always very reliable. He'd never just not turn up.'

His name was Tony Ferrers and he was pacing around the front room as he spoke.

'Had you and Dr Redmond been friends for long?' she asked.

'A while,' he said.

'I didn't know him well,' she said. 'But we talked a few times and I liked him. I respected him.'

'He was a good man. Bryan was one of the best.'

'You were fond of him?'

'Yes, very.' A touch of defiance. He sat down on the sofa. 'I never wrote to him at the cottage. Bryan was very strong about that, said I mustn't.'

This confused Ellen. 'I don't see . . .' Though, even as she spoke, she was starting to understand.

513

As he looked up at her, his mouth twisted into a wry smile. 'I don't suppose it matters now. Bryan's been dead for years. Let's just say that ours wasn't the sort of friendship you'd want to make public, Miss Kingsley.'

'Oh. Oh.'

'Quite.'

Her gaze flicked to the photo, which was lying on the coffee table, then she looked back at Tony. 'I'm glad,' she said. 'I'm glad he had someone.'

'I've never been much of a one for reading the newspapers, just the sport in the *People*, so I didn't know what had happened. In the end, I phoned the hall. Said I was a friend. The woman who answered told me that Bryan was dead. Just came out with it, like that. I couldn't think what to say.'

'I'm sorry,' she said gently.

'Yeah. Well, I went to the library, looked up old copies of the papers. I found some articles about Bryan. "Death of a Boffin", that sort of rubbish. I cut them out when no one was looking. I wanted to know what had happened. And I wanted to remember him. Not that I'd ever forget him. The newspaper article said he'd fallen down the stairs.'

'I'm afraid so. I went to the cottage because I was concerned about him. He hadn't been into work that day and I thought he might be ill. When I got there, he was lying at the bottom of the stairs.'

'He was dead?'

514

'Yes.'

'For how long?'

She had hoped he wouldn't ask her that. 'A few hours, the police thought.'

'I hate to think of him dying alone. It used to frighten me, when I was in the desert, the thought of getting cut off from my mates and something happening.' He was looking away; he ran the back of his hand over his eyes.

'Shall I make us some tea?'

'No, I'll do it. Sorry.'

He heard him blowing his nose as he left the room. A few minutes later he returned with a tray.

She said, 'You were a soldier?'

'Yes. I was wounded at El Alamein and they sent me home. That was when I met Bryan.'

'Where did you meet?'

He gave her a look that was a mixture of shame and humour, and said, 'In some rotten little pub in Chelsea, in nineteen forty-three. Not the sort of place you'd know, Miss Kingsley. I was on my uppers, rather. I was still on sick leave from the army and I didn't have anywhere to go. I couldn't go home.' He poured out the tea. 'I come from deepest, darkest Somerset. Home life was Sundays where nothing ever happened and my dad ranting on about queers and Jews. Jesus. Anyway, Bryan was there, at the bar. Funny bloke, I thought, sort of awkward, didn't look you in the eye. We got talking and he offered to buy me something to eat, and I was lonely and I had nowhere to go,

so . . .' He shrugged. 'But I liked him. He didn't talk much, but he listened. And he was clever and he was funny and he was good to me.'

'Did he tell you about the place where he worked?'

'Not much. Said it was all very hush-hush.' Then, looking at her, he said, 'There was someone he was close to there. They shared a cottage.'

'Jan Kaminski and Marcus Pharoah.'

'That's the one, Pharoah. Do you know him?'

'He was my boss when I worked at Gildersleve Hall.' Ellen pointed out one of the figures in the photograph. 'That's him. That's Dr Pharoah.'

'Handsome devil. You can see why you'd fall for him.'

Her gaze returned to the photograph. Once more, she noticed how Dr Redmond had turned to Pharoah, and the light in his eyes.

'Had he?'

'Bryan? Oh yes, hook, line and sinker, the poor sod. He told me about him quite soon after we met. Wanted to get it straight with me, he said. I didn't need him to spell it out, though, I could tell by the way he talked about him, about Pharoah.'

Dr Redmond had remained loyal to Marcus Pharoah for a long time after their quarrel. Was it possible that what Redmond had felt had been not mere admiration, but love? Time and success had corrupted Pharoah, and yet in spite of their differences, Dr Redmond had stayed at Gildersleve. He had kept this photo, tucked into the lab book he used

each day. Could that have been because love, on his part, had never completely died?

She chose her words carefully. 'I knew they used to be friends.'

His eyes flashed, full of ironic humour. 'Just good friends,' he said. 'Dr Pharoah was a ladies' man, Bryan told me.' His tone was mocking. 'Bryan was always very careful. It's hard, that, always watching yourself.' He leaned forward in his seat, studying the snapshot, frowning. 'I always pictured him as some bluff, rugby-playing type, but he doesn't look like that, does he? Anyway, somehow he caught on that Bryan was queer. Gave him the works – disgusting, deviant, couldn't he get treatment for it, all that.' In an odd, vengeful little gesture, Tony ground a knuckle into the image of Pharoah's face. 'The poor bugger,' he muttered. 'He didn't deserve that. It wasn't as if he wanted anything from Pharoah. Just to be near him.'

'When was this?'

'It must have been a couple of months before the end of the war. After the war ended, Bryan stayed on in the cottage and the other two moved out. He came down here once a month and we had a good time. I made sure he had a good time. But you could see it, eating away at him. He changed, and in the end he wasn't the same person. He'd always been quiet but he seemed to go in on himself. Something had knocked the life out of him, you see. I think that eventually he hated Pharoah.'

'Why do you say that?'

'Last time I saw him he was spitting nails.'

'When, Mr Ferrers?'

'Autumn fifty-two. A short time before he died. November, it must have been. It was because of the woodland. Bryan thought of it as his, the cottage as well, but they weren't, not really, they belonged to Pharoah. When Bryan heard that Pharoah was thinking of selling them, he offered to buy both the house and the land. Pharoah agreed but then he told Bryan he'd had a better offer. I'd never seen Bryan so angry. He never usually lost his rag but he did then. And there's another thing.'

'What's that?'

'He was scared.'

'Of what?' But she thought she knew. 'That Pharoah would expose him?'

'Oh no, Bryan never worried about himself. He was afraid for *me*. The last time I saw him, Bryan told me he was putting this flat in my name. I told him he didn't have to do it, but he said he wanted to because that way I'd be safe.' Tony pushed the photograph back across the tabletop to her. His mouth twisted. 'A couple of years ago a friend of mine was charged with indecent behaviour. They sent him to prison for six years. He only lasted a couple of weeks – he hanged himself with a bedsheet.'

She could think of nothing adequate to say so she remained silent. Tony rose and opened the door and a golden Labrador dog ambled into the room, nails tapping on the polished wooden floor.

She said, 'Did Dr Redmond ever speak to you about Dr Pharoah's first marriage?'

Tony shook his head. 'Not that I remember. He was never one for gossip.'

Ellen thanked him for the tea and for talking to her. As she stood up, Tony spoke again.

'After Bryan went back to Cambridge that last time,' he said, 'I never heard from him again. He didn't like talking on the phone and he was never much of a letter-writer. I've a few postcards, that's all. "Tony", he'd write, "did you remember to pay the gas bill? Bryan." Never a "dear" or a "love", you see. But he *was* dear, and I did love him.' Tony bent to fondle the dog's yellow head. 'She's called Connie,' he said. 'I couldn't have a dog while Bryan was alive. He couldn't stand them.' He straightened. 'Looks like it's stopped raining. I'd better take her out for a walk, if we're finished, Miss Kingsley.'

India's progress was slow because she stopped every couple of hours at a diner to feed, change and play with Abigail. She had stayed in Montpelier on the first night, where she had bought petrol, maps and warmer clothing for the baby. The next day, she reached Bourchier College, where Marcus had met his first wife, Rosanne. But it was Hester Devereux's story of which India thought as she wheeled the carrycot through the small, pleasant campus, and of the friendship that had grown up between the two women, a friendship whose memory had lasted beyond Rosanne's lifetime, and

which had prompted Hester more than twenty years later to try to discover the truth about what had happened to her child.

At the college, a secretary in the bursar's office, charmed by Abigail and coaxed by India, unearthed old files and found out for her what she wanted to know: the address at which Marcus Pharoah had lived during the time he had been at Bourchier. A five-mile drive took India to a small town with a white clapboard church, a general store and a scattering of houses. She stopped at the general store to buy milk for Abigail and to ask directions to Rosanne Pharoah's old home at Aspen Creek.

Another drive, a few more miles north. India turned off the main highway along a narrow, tree-lined road that led up into the hills. After a short distance, she found the house. She parked, climbed out of the car, and with Abigail tucked on her shoulder, walked up the front path. The house ahead of her was small, low and white-painted, set among aspens. All around her, leaves like thousands of pale green pennies quivered in the breeze.

A middle-aged woman came out of the front door and asked her if she needed help. Abigail began to cry, and the woman, who introduced herself as Mrs Greenlaw, invited India indoors. While Mrs Greenlaw was heating up a jug of water for Abigail's bottle, India looked round. You could have fitted the entire building into Fairlight House three times over, but she saw how the late-afternoon sunshine, filtered between the branches of the trees, poured through

the picture windows at the back of the house, making liquid patterns on the polished wooden floor. When India knelt down with Abigail on the floorboards, she bobbed her head and reached out a hand, transfixed by the shifting light. Outside, a rectangle of wooden decking, strewn with leaves, looked down over a creek.

While India fed Abigail, Mrs Greenlaw drew up a small table and put a cup of coffee beside her. India asked her about the history of the house. It had been built in the early twenties, Mrs Greenlaw said, as the summer residence of a businessman from Boston, who had liked to fish and shoot in the hills. The house had changed hands frequently in the thirties and had then lain empty for several years. It was an out-of-the-way spot, Mrs Greenlaw acknowledged. She was a painter, and the moment she had set eyes on it she had known it was where she wanted to live for the rest of her life. She could have looked out of that big window for ever. She must have painted the view a hundred times.

India asked her about Rosanne Pharoah. Mrs Greenlaw frowned, pursed her mouth and shook her head. 'You should try the pastor,' she suggested. 'He's been here quite a while. He may be able to help you.'

Staying overnight at an inn in Bourchier, India thought about the house. She tried to imagine Marcus living there, sitting by the picture window perhaps, reading a book. Perhaps they had put a table on the terrace, he and Rosanne, and had breakfast there on fine summer days. Perhaps

Rosanne had paddled in the creek while Marcus had watched her from the rocks above. Perhaps they had planned their future together, a lifetime in that house of flickering light and shivering leaves. Perhaps the destruction of that future had sent Marcus off in a different direction to the one he had originally intended.

The next day, she drove back to the white Congregationalist church she had seen the previous day. The pastor's house was beside it. India knocked on the door.

Half an hour later, leaving the building, she had discovered several things. That Rosanne Pharoah was buried in the churchyard in this quiet town, and that she had been only twenty years old when she had died, a year before the pastor himself had come to live there. The pastor had known nothing of a child, but he had been able to tell India something interesting: that the midwife who had looked after Marcus's wife during her pregnancy and delivery had moved away, returning to her home town in Medway, northern Maine, shortly after Rosanne had died.

The midwife's name had been Kitty Michaud. You wonder, the pastor had said, thoughtfully stroking his beard, whether she had felt responsible – whether, even, there had been some question of negligence. Such a tragedy, after all, for a man to lose his wife and child.

A Saturday: Riley, Ellen and Annie had gone to the Natural History Museum in the morning, where they had gawped

at the dinosaurs and Ellen had attempted to explain to Annie about evolution. They had a late lunch in a restaurant in Brompton Road, then called in at a park on the way home so that Annie had the chance to run around.

Back at the house, Riley made tea and parked Ellen in the front room with the Saturday papers. He thought she worked too hard. Annie was upstairs, playing with her dolls' house. Riley carried the tray of tea things into the sitting room.

The doorbell rang as Ellen was reading out some comment Harold Macmillan had made about the testing of nuclear weapons. As he went out to the hall, Riley said over his shoulder, 'There'll be a lot of our people keeping a close eye on what the Russians are up to.'

Then he opened the door. Seeing her, recognizing her, he was for a moment unable to speak.

'Hello, John,' said Pearl.

Riley made more tea, not because any of them wanted it, but because it gave him a few moments to control his shock and anger. And at not quite five o'clock in the afternoon, it was too early for a drink.

'I want to talk to you, John,' she said. 'And I'd like to see Annie. May I come in?'

He had let her in. After all, it was her house as well. By then, Ellen had come out of the sitting room into the hallway. He did not think he would ever forget the expression on her face.

523

He introduced them. 'Pearl, this is Ellen Kingsley. Ellen, this is Pearl, my wife.' There was a bitter taste in his mouth.

Now, Pearl and Ellen were talking, Pearl with that air of lavishness that always touched her conversation, Ellen polite and composed, though Riley heard the strain in her voice. Pearl was wearing a green and white spotted summer frock with a short green jacket, black gloves and a close-fitting black hat. She looked, Riley thought, well.

Annie sat at the kitchen table, crayoning. Sometimes she looked up at Pearl. Once, catching her eye, Pearl tapped her knee and Annie came and sat on her lap for a few minutes, then slid off, left the room and went upstairs.

Riley could tell that Ellen was finding it hard to make conversation – all those questions that couldn't be voiced – so after he had put the mugs on the table and found a packet of biscuits, he said, 'Where are you living now, Pearl?'

'Cornwall,' she said. 'It's the tiniest little village, so dear, just a funny old pub and a row of dilapidated cottages. I work in a shop in St Ives. You should see me in winter, cycling through the gales.'

Ellen said, 'What sort of shop is it, Mrs Riley?' Her voice had a hollow timbre.

'We sell pottery, mostly. Beautiful pots, the most gorgeous earthy colours. I have some in my house.' Pearl laughed. 'Hardly any furniture but some wonderful pots.'

Riley said bluntly, 'Why have you come back?'

'I told you. Because I wanted to talk to you.'

He felt at that moment a rage so intense he had to look away, as if his gaze might burn.

'How long are you back for?' The question crisp, efficient.

'I haven't decided yet.' She puckered up her mouth in the way that he remembered. 'I promise I won't be too much of a nuisance.'

Was he meant to say, *you won't be a nuisance at all, Pearl?* There were things he must say to her: that she should not assume she could just walk back into their lives, and nor should she assume that she could stay here, in this house. But he had to wait. There was Annie, not knowing what the hell was going on, and there was Ellen, trying hard not to look as if she minded.

'Have you spoken to your parents?' he said.

Pearl looked down, frowning. 'Not yet.'

'You should do.'

'I know, John.' She peeled off her gloves and wrapped her hands round the teacup.

'They've been desperately worried about you. Do you realize what they've been through?'

'It's just that – Mum will cry and I just can't cope with it.' Her words were whispered.

'I'll do it, then.' Though he felt a grating despair in saying so. Because, he thought bleakly, no matter how hard you tried not to let it happen, she sucked you into her

chaotic, clamorous life. You did things for her because you felt obliged to tidy up behind her.

Ellen stood up. 'I mustn't keep you,' she said. 'You two will have so much to talk about.'

Riley saw her to the front door. 'Ellen,' he said softly.

'I have to go.'

'This makes no difference to us.'

'Doesn't it?' When she looked at him, her eyes were blank and bewildered. 'I'm sorry. I just need some time to think, Riley.'

She left the house. Pearl had gone upstairs. Riley stood, his hands fisted, breathing hard. Just as the different parts of his life had fallen miraculously into place, Pearl, with her talent for bad timing and disorder, had returned. With her, she would have brought a trail of drama and damage, because she always did.

His anger cooled. No, he thought. Not this time.

He dialled Basil and Vera's number. To Riley's relief, Basil answered the phone. There was a silence after Riley told him about Pearl, and then Basil asked, a catch in his voice, when they could come and see her. Riley told them to come round as soon as they liked.

'Thank you, John, I appreciate it. I'll tell Vera.'

Pearl came back into the sitting room. 'Annie doesn't remember me,' she said.

'It's been a long time. Three years.'

She was standing in front of him, wringing her hands

together. With an effort, he said, 'I expect she does remember you, underneath somewhere, deep in her memory.'

'I tried not to expect anything. But you can't help it, can you?'

'How are you, Pearl?'

'Better, much better.' She was looking round the room, frowning, as if she saw something wrong with it. 'I had to find a way I could live. I know that what I did was unforgivable, and I don't blame you for hating me. But you or Dad would have come after me if I'd told you where I was, and it wouldn't have worked.'

He glanced at the clock. Almost six – what the hell.

'Would you like a drink?'

'No, thanks, I don't any more.' Pearl took a packet of Player's from her handbag and tipped out a cigarette. 'Haven't managed to give up these, though.'

Riley poured himself a whisky. 'Pearl, we have to talk.'

'I know. I want a divorce, John.' She lit her cigarette and looked at him steadily. 'That's one of the reasons I came back here. I'm sorry to be so . . . so blunt.'

'It's OK.' It took a moment for him to absorb what she had said, and then he was left numb, battered, and intensely relieved.

He said, 'Why couldn't you just have written? Why the dramatic reappearance?'

'It would have been cowardly. I knew I should talk to you face to face. And I wanted to make you understand.'

'Understand what?' Fury laced his voice. 'Have you any idea what it's been like? None of us knew whether you were alive or dead. And Annie? What do you think it's been like for her? How could you do that to her? How could you leave her thinking that you just didn't love her enough?'

'Did she?' Her eyes wild, she pressed her fingers against her mouth.

With an effort, he managed to pull himself back. He let out a breath. 'I told her you loved her. I've told her that every single day.'

She whispered, 'Thank you.'

There was a silence. Pearl wiped the tears from her face with her hand; Riley pulled out a chair for her.

'Sit down. Tell me how you are.'

'I'm all right.' She smiled at him, a darting, hopeful smile. 'I'm better on my own, I've discovered. If I'm feeling angry or miserable, I don't annoy anyone else, I just go for a walk by the sea.' She was kneading the cuff of her jacket between finger and thumb. 'There's a nice doctor in St Ives, he's got me some new pills and they don't make me feel as awful as the other ones, and if I feel myself falling ill again I take some. I know that I have to. I know that horrible psychiatrist was right, that I'll always have to, and that I'll never be really well.' She let go of the crumpled cuff and looked up at him, her face blotched with tears. 'I've always been afraid that Annie would turn out like me. I couldn't face it, staying here, looking at her, always wondering, afraid my

528

beautiful girl would end up like me. I love her so much. People talk about broken hearts, don't they, and you think that's just a saying until it happens to you. I was afraid that if I stayed here, I'd poison her somehow, that I'd *make* her like me. I had to go. I've thought of her every day since, every hour of every day.'

Fleetingly, he put a hand on her shoulder. 'Annie organizes me,' he said gently. 'Tells me off if I've forgotten to iron a shirt. A year or two and she'll be checking me out before I go to work, making sure my collar's straight. She's a happy little girl.'

'And sensible, then, like you, John.'

'I suppose she is.'

'We used to have such fun, didn't we, when we were younger? Do you remember?' Her expression saddened. 'And then it all went wrong. It was my fault, of course.'

He shook his head. 'Mine too.'

'Will you let me see Annie?' Her eyes, haunted and afraid, stared at him.

'I don't know, Pearl,' he said honestly.

She didn't scream or cry, as he had been afraid she might. 'I'd like Annie to come and stay in Cornwall with me,' she said steadily. 'She'd love it there, I know she would. It's only a little house, but I could make her up a camp bed in the bedroom.' When he didn't say anything, she said, 'I've changed, John. I'm not the same as I was before. I try so hard. You wouldn't believe how I live now. I've found that I need to lead a very dull life. It's rather a chastening

discovery because I'd always thought I needed the opposite. I saw myself as someone who needed adventure and excitement. But they're not good for me, that's what I've realized. I keep an eye on myself. Three meals a day, just like you always said, and eight hours' sleep at night. I go to work and I come home and I read a book or do some sewing. If I'm having a bad time I go for a long walk over the cliffs. It's so beautiful and it's always different, so I never get bored with it.'

'Have you met anyone else?'

'One or two.' She gave her head a shake. 'Not stayers, I don't think. There's a schoolteacher who lives in Zennor, we go for walks together.' She pressed her teeth into her lower lip, then said, 'If you tell me to, I'll leave now and I won't make a fuss. If that's what you want, John. But I always tried to be a good mother to Annie. And I was, wasn't I?'

'Pearl.' Wearily, he ran a hand through his hair. 'I need to think about this.' He glanced at his watch. 'I'd better make tea. Your parents should be here within the hour.'

As he peeled potatoes and chopped carrots, he thought about what Pearl had asked of him. Annie was Pearl's daughter too. Whatever bitterness he felt he must put aside. Annie needed her mother. Yet at the same time, Annie's safety and happiness were paramount. Pearl had told him that she had changed, but he remembered too clearly her unpredictability and wildness.

Vera and Basil arrived, tears were shed and embraces

exchanged. While they were in the other room, talking to Pearl, Riley dialled Ellen's number, but there was no answer.

The serving of supper provided a welcome vestige of normality. After the meal was over, Vera and Basil tactfully took Annie into the sitting room to play a boardgame while Riley spoke to Pearl.

'Look, how about this,' he said. 'You see Annie when your parents are around as well to begin with. I'm sure they'd be delighted to take her down to Cornwall. And if that works out and Annie's happy with it, then maybe, in the future, she can visit you on her own.'

'Thank you, John. I'll make it up to her, I promise, if it takes me the rest of my life.' She kissed his cheek. 'I told my parents I'd go back home with them. I thought you'd prefer that.'

'Pearl, you'll speak to a solicitor about a divorce, won't you?' He had to get this straight.

'I promise. That girl—'

'Do you mean Ellen?'

'Yes, your lovely redhead.'

'I mean to marry her, Pearl.'

'I'm pleased for you, John.' Then her gaze wandered round the room. 'There must have been happy times here,' she said, 'but I can't remember them. That's rather sad, isn't it?'

The phone rang. *Ellen*, he thought. Riley picked up the receiver.

But it wasn't Ellen, it was Janey Kelly. Riley listened to

531

her, then gave her clear instructions and put the phone down.

Then he went into the sitting room, where Vera, Basil and Annie were playing Ludo.

'Basil, Vera, could you hold the fort for a couple of hours?'

Janey was sitting where Riley had told her to, on a bench on Well Street Common. Dusk was encroaching on the grass and trees of the common. Janey was wearing a mackintosh with the hood up, yet he could see from several yards away that she was shivering. She must have heard his footsteps because she flinched and quickly turned towards him, poised to run. He saw that her face was a mass of bruises and that one of her eyes had closed.

'Janey,' he said. He sat down on the bench beside her. 'Who did this to you?'

'Bloody Lee, who else?' She was breathing shallowly. 'Think he's broken something, Riley.'

'What happened?'

'One of the other girls saw me talking to you. The silly bitch told him.'

'I'll take you to the hospital,' he said.

She scowled. 'I don't like hospitals.'

'They'll make you better.' He spoke much as he would have spoken to Annie, had she hurt herself. 'They'll fix you up and you'll be as beautiful as ever.'

Half of her face managed a mocking grin. 'See, I always

532

knew you fancied me.' Then she blinked, looking straight ahead of her into the grass and bushes. 'I want to go home, Riley,' she whispered.

'Where's home?'

'Cork. You ever been there?'

He shook his head.

'You don't want to bother. Bloody dump of a place. I got myself into trouble, had to to come over here and sort myself out.' She gave a sour little laugh. 'I thought I was going to be a film star.'

'There's still time.'

'No.' Slowly, she shook her head. 'No, I don't think so.'

She rose and, stooping, her arms wrapped round her chest, limped beside him out of the common. As they neared his car, she said, 'I want to tell you something, Riley.'

'Leave it till you're at the hospital.'

'No, I might change my mind.' She put out a hand to the Wolseley to steady herself, then fixed him with her good eye and said, 'Bernie's got a lock-up in Brixton. It's near the station, under the railway arches. It looks like it's derelict because the door was all burned up in the war, but it isn't. You should go and have a look at it. Bernie keeps everything there.'

His heart speeded up. 'Who told you this?'

'A friend of mine.' She showed her teeth in an expression that was somewhere between a smile and a snarl. 'Pillow talk. You know. You men like to show off to girls, don't you, show us you're the big man.'

Riley helped Janey into the car, then drove her to the London Hospital. While the casualty doctor saw her, he phoned Scotland Yard. The duty officer answered his call and promised to send a WPC to the London.

Sergeant Davies had the weekend off so Riley phoned his home. Davies's wife answered the call. Riley could hear a baby howling in the background.

'Can I speak to Rob, Glenys?'

'He's just having his supper. Hold on a minute, I'll go and get him.'

Riley heard footsteps and muted conversation. Then Davies picked up the phone. Riley told him about Janey and the lock-up in Brixton.

'I'm going to have a look there now. Can you get over there, Davies?'

'I'm on my way.' Davies was chewing something. 'Wait for me, sir. Don't start without me.'

Riley put the receiver down and went back to casualty. They would be keeping Janey in overnight, a nurse told him. While he waited for the WPC to arrive, he went to the phone box and dialled Ellen's number again. Still no reply. She had gone out, perhaps.

Or perhaps she wasn't answering. Perhaps she didn't want to speak to him. What on earth had she thought, when Pearl had turned up like that? Pearl's reappearance must have spelled out to Ellen the complications involved in marriage to him. She would be taking on a daughter as well as a husband – and then there was Pearl, too. He

would never completely be able to cut Pearl out of his life because Annie would always tie them together. Might Ellen, realizing that, be having second thoughts?

The WPC arrived. Night had fallen by the time Riley left the hospital. The drive down Whitechapel Road and across Tower Bridge, then through Walworth and Camberwell to Brixton, took him half an hour. The light was going and the streets flew past, marked by the oscillation of the pools of light from the street lamps and the London skyline of terraced houses, gas storage tanks and factory buildings, black against a dirty orange sky.

He parked by the railway station, took a torch out of the glove box and a jemmy from the boot of the car, and walked down Brixton Station Road. A train dragged itself over the railway arches, smoke pluming from its funnel. Some of the arches were infilled with wooden doors, others were open black tunnels. The doors were of varying sizes and Riley saw, as he walked, that only one of them was scorched.

A gleam of headlamps at the top of the road made him sink back into the shadows, but the vehicle, some distance away, seemed to change its mind and reverse back towards the railway station. Riley shone the torch on to the burned door. An incendiary bomb, he guessed; the little that was left of the paint had blistered and much of the surface of the door had turned to charcoal, seamed and criss-crossed like the hide of a crocodile.

Riley applied himself to jemmying off the padlock. The

street was quiet and only a solitary cyclist glided past, hardly bothering to look at him. Eventually the padlock gave, Riley aimed a kick at the scorched wood, and the door opened.

He stepped inside. Shining the torch round, he saw the high brick arch above and heard the rumble of a train, magnified and echoing in the interior space. The circle of torchlight lowered, gliding over boxes and filing cabinets. All the cabinets were padlocked, like the door. As he prised open a padlock he heard a sound behind him and turned.

'Davies, is that you?'

No answer. The padlock snapped, chinking against the metal filing cabinet as it fell to the ground. Riley opened a drawer. Inside it was a row of manilla files. He took one out, and with the torch jammed under his arm, flipped through the pages of figures. Even bent accountants need to keep the books, he thought.

A footstep. Riley switched off the torch, put the file inside his jacket, and stepped behind the cabinet. As his eyes accustomed to the lack of light, he saw a bulky figure silhouetted in the doorway.

'Hello, copper!' Lee Carter's voice boomed beneath the high ceiling of the railway arch. 'Knew the stupid little cow wouldn't be able to keep her mouth shut. Should have finished her off, shouldn't I?'

Riley began to move backwards, one hand holding the torch, the other running over the shapes of the furniture to guide him. He tried to recall the layout of the archway, glimpsed when he had earlier illuminated it. How far did

the tunnel go back beneath the railway line? Might there be an exit on the other side of the bridge? And where was Davies?

Carter called out, 'Got you like a rat in a trap, copper. Used to catch rats when I was a boy. It'll be more fun with you.'

Lee Carter's torch found him. Against the curved brick wall of the arch Riley saw his own shadow, huge and black. There was a crack of gunfire, echoing against the walls. Riley began to run between the boxes and cabinets, making for the cover of the darkness at the back of the tunnel.

Carter fired again and a white-hot pain stung Riley's shoulder. He ran on, but it was like running through treacle. He could hear his lungs straining, fighting for air. Stumbling against a cardboard box, he sank to his knees.

The echoing space magnified the sound of his breathing. The light seemed suddenly to expand, filling the tunnel, and he saw Lee Carter, only a few yards away.

Riley closed his eyes.

From Bourchier, it was a drive of almost a hundred miles to Medway in northern Maine. India took her time, resting before setting off again. As she headed north, the settlements became smaller and more widely spaced apart and she stopped at every garage she came across to top up the tank with petrol. The roads narrowed and the forests thickened, the coming change of season flagged by the yellowing of the leaves, and the skies became whiter, more prone to

clouds. Now and then she saw a clearing where logs lay tumbled on the razed forest floor like a giant's spent matchsticks. Men worked in the clearings, loading up trucks, and the quiet of the Maine landscape was blotted out by the whine of the sawmill.

She had rarely been so completely on her own before. During her childhood, there had been Sebastian; even when separated from him at various institutions – school, orphanage – she had always been among other people. Then there had been the flat and Rachel, and after Rachel had died, her London friends, and eventually Marcus. She had never really been alone in Vermont, Marcus had made sure of that. Now, apart from Abigail, her days were solitary.

Always with her was the fear that she might become lost. Here, if you mistook your way or if your car broke down, you might walk for miles until you found a house. The logging tracks and the firs that grew to either side of them went on for miles; when she parked at the roadside to feed Abigail she closed her eyes for a few minutes but still saw the endless columns of trees.

A branch moved, a bird rose cawing into the air. You might drive the length and breadth of Britain and see no wild animal larger than a deer, but in these old forests in the heartland of America there were moose and bears. Were there wolves, too? She couldn't remember. Checking the map, India found her gaze drawn sideways to the dense, dark tunnels between the trees. Her hand rested on her baby's chest, feeling the rise and fall of Abigail's breath.

Take a step into those paths, she thought, walk a few paces into the wood, and you'd never find your way out. What was she doing, travelling with her child into the cold north of a foreign land to follow an old, forgotten trail?

The town of Medway was poised at the place where the East and West Penobscot Rivers met. India booked into a motel and asked the receptionist if she knew where Kitty Michaud lived. The receptionist, chewing gum as she leafed through a novel, peered out of the window to where the Austin-Healey was parked, and said, 'That yours? Cute.' Then she directed India to where a road ran alongside the river. 'There's a rusty old Ford out the front of the Michaud place. You can't miss it.'

As India drove out of town, the buildings thinned out and stretches of green dwarfed the few houses. She caught sight of the Ford, a hefty, pre-war vehicle, after a short distance. Parked at the foot of a path, it seemed to have become a part of the landscape, scoured and discoloured to a rusty brown by the Maine weather.

India drew up alongside it and looked at the house. The omnipresent fir trees stood like sentinels to either side of the small wooden single-storey building. A woman was sitting on the porch.

India lifted Abigail out of the carrycot and started up the front path. The woman on the porch stood up. She was short and plump, and she was wearing a cotton skirt and hand-knitted jersey. Her hair, a peppering of brown and grey, was tied back at the nape of her neck. Deep lines

were channelled into her broad, weatherbeaten face, and her small, dark, hooded eyes were wary.

India said, 'I'm sorry to trouble you, but I'm looking for Miss Michaud.'

'I'm Kitty Michaud. Who are you?'

'My name's India Pharoah.'

'Pharoah.' Miss Michaud's hand went to her throat.

India began to explain. Miss Michaud interrupted her, saying sharply, 'You know him, don't you? Marcus Pharoah.'

India felt a prickle of excitement. 'He's my husband,' she said.

The dark eyes darted back to the road. 'Is he here?'

'No, Miss Michaud, I travelled on my own.'

'Why have you come here?'

'I was hoping to talk to you about the baby. About Rosanne's baby.'

Kitty Michaud's body seemed to sag and she put out a hand to the porch rail. Then, straightening, she stood aside and held open the door.

'I thought everyone had forgotten him,' she said. 'I thought no one remembered him but myself.'

Tacked to the wall of the parlour were samples of colourful beadwork; on the back of the sofa and rocking chair lay pieces of quilting. 'Winters here are long,' said Miss Michaud, when India admired them. 'I like to keep myself busy.' She motioned India to sit down. 'You look a little like her,' she said.

'Rosanne?'

'The same colouring. And she was very slight, like you. How old is your baby?'

'Abigail's nearly five months old.'

'And she's well?'

'Very well, thank you, Miss Michaud.'

The older woman went to the dresser, opened a drawer and took out a book. She turned a page, then offered it to India. 'That's him. That's my Jimmy.'

India found herself looking down at a black and white photograph of a baby. It was a moment before she could say, 'This is Marcus's and Rosanne's child?'

'Yes.'

Abigail began to whimper. India adjusted her position, propping the baby against her stomach so that she could sit on her knee and look out of the window. 'Marcus told me the child was stillborn,' she said.

'Well, that was a lie. But you didn't believe him or you wouldn't be here.'

'Rosanne died, though, didn't she?'

'Yes.' Kitty Michaud closed the album and put it back on the sideboard. 'He blamed me,' she said quietly. 'He said I'd killed her. The baby was breech and she was such a little thing.'

'What happened?'

Haltingly, Miss Michaud told her story. It had been January, and there had been a snowstorm when Marcus Pharoah had come for the midwife. It had taken them more than an hour to travel the few miles to Aspen Creek. At

first, Miss Michaud had been confident that all would be well. She had delivered half a dozen breech babies before, all of them fine and healthy. By the time she had realized things were going badly and had sent Mr Pharoah off to fetch the doctor, the blizzard had worsened and he had been unable to get through to Bourchier, where the doctor lived.

'Even if he had got through it would have been too late,' said Miss Michaud sadly. 'I had to drag that little soul out of his mother or he would have died inside her. That poor girl died of a haemorrhage. There was nothing I could do for her, nothing at all.'

'And Marcus?' whispered India.

'He told me I should have saved the mother rather than the child. I tried to explain to him that I'd had no choice, that he'd have lost the pair of them, but he wouldn't listen to me. I tried to persuade him to hold his child, thinking it might give him some comfort, but he wouldn't. He said it disgusted him. That's what he called his own son. It. He wouldn't even give him a name. It was me who called him Jimmy.' Miss Michaud paused. 'That was the longest night of my life. I couldn't leave that house, you see, because of the snow and because of the baby. And you wonder, when something so dreadful happens, whether there was something else you could have done. I kept going over it in my mind, thinking should I have done this, should I have done that. I was very young, about the same age as you, I'd guess, and I'd never had much confidence in myself.' Miss

Michaud gave a raw laugh. 'My daddy always told me I'd never be up to much and I guess some of that rubs off.'

Her eyes slid back to Abigail, who was playing with the beads round India's neck. 'I got Jimmy to take a little milk,' she said, 'and I held him in my arms all night to keep him warm. I must have fallen asleep around dawn, I was so tired, and when I woke up, Mr Pharoah came to speak to me. He asked me to look after the baby while he made the funeral arrangements and I said yes, I would. The snow thawed after a couple of days and they buried that poor girl. I thought that afterwards he might come round. They say a funeral can draw a line, let you get on with the rest of your life, don't they? Though I can't say I've found it to be true. Anyway, it made no difference. He said he thought the baby looked odd, that there was something wrong with it. Jimmy was very fair, it's true, almost ghostly fair. But he had the most beautiful blue eyes.'

In the silence, India heard a car run along the road and the shriek of the gulls at the river. She said gently, 'So you went on caring for the baby?'

'It was no hardship. He was the dearest little thing. Then Mr Pharoah went away. He told me he needed time to think. He spent his time drinking, I believe. He was in a bad way when he came back a couple of weeks later. He looked like he'd aged five years. Anyway, he made me an offer. He said that he'd pay me to keep Jimmy if I agreed to move away from the area.'

'And did you?'

'Yes. He never spelt it out exactly, but he made it plain that he'd make sure I didn't work again if I didn't agree. But I'd looked after Jimmy since he was born, and I'd come to love him by then. I'd always loved babies, that was why I trained as a midwife, and it would have broken my heart to have given him up to someone else. So I came back here. I was born and brought up in Medway. I told everyone I'd adopted Jimmy, said he was a foundling. I knew that some of my neighbours thought he was my child, born out of wedlock, and I could see them looking down on me. I didn't care, though.'

'And my husband? Did he visit you at all?'

'Just the once.' Miss Michaud smoothed out the patchwork on the back of the chair. 'Jimmy was ill by then. I'll never forget the way Mr Pharoah looked at him. It was as if he should never have been born. He couldn't have stayed more than half an hour. He told me that he'd go on wiring me money each month and he said that if anything happened I was to write to his lawyer in Boston. He left me an address. That was the last I saw of him.'

'What was wrong with Jimmy?'

'I never knew.' Kitty Michaud shook her head slowly. Minutes passed before she began to speak again. 'I kept hoping it was some childhood ailment that would pass, but it never did. He was fine to begin with, but from about three months old he seemed to go downhill. He became such a restless baby. He couldn't sit and smile like your little girl, and his skin was bad, so dry. He used to get

sores, even though I did my best with calamine and zinc and castor oil. And he had a musty smell, such a strange thing. The worst thing was he didn't come on the way a child should. He just seemed to stop learning and slip backwards.'

'I'm so sorry,' said India. She found that she was holding Abigail more tightly. 'Couldn't the doctor do anything?'

'It didn't seem so. I took him to see a paediatrician in Augusta and he prescribed some medicine, but it didn't do him any good. I could comfort him when he was upset, but no one else could. We'd sit in the garden under the trees, and it would soothe him to watch the leaves move. But then he started having fits. In the end, he had such a bad fit he never came round again. He was just two years old when he died.' Miss Michaud glanced out of the window. 'I should fix us some coffee,' she said.

'Let me.' India stood up. 'I'm good at making coffee. Perhaps you'd take Abigail for me?'

India put Abigail on Kitty Michaud's lap. As she gently stroked the baby's head, Miss Michaud said, 'I pitied him. I pitied him for losing his wife and for not being able to love that child at all. He was the dearest little thing, my Jimmy. So dear.'

Ellen thought how pretty Pearl Riley had been, how elegant, well-dressed and vivacious. She thought that although Annie hadn't seemed to know Pearl, Pearl was still Annie's mother. And though Riley might not love Pearl any more, he might

545

nevertheless feel bound to her. Pearl was his wife and the mother of his child. These were ties that could not easily be brushed aside.

A couple of times that evening the phone rang, but Ellen didn't answer it. It seemed to her that Pearl's return might have changed everything. Her engagement to Alec had foundered on the rocky shores of Alec's sense of obligation to his mother. Riley was an honourable man. Could she even risk the possibility that he might feel a sense of obligation to Pearl? A part of her, remembering the grief she had endured after her broken engagement, wanted to run. Stop it now, cut it off before she got in deeper.

Before she went to bed, she drank a glass of whisky and took a couple of aspirins and, to her surprise, slept soundly for nine hours. After she had breakfasted, she read through some journal articles. But it was hard to concentrate on a complex discussion of Fourier analysis when a part of her was thinking: Pearl will only hurt him again, because people who are capable of tearing another person apart are not to be trusted. Hard to concentrate, too, while she was waiting for the phone to ring.

Why didn't he ring? The clock ticked on and she gave up all pretence of trying to read the journal. If Riley felt he had to give Pearl a second chance, even though he no longer loved her, then he was sorely mistaken. She, Ellen, must point that out to him. And as for worrying about getting in too deep, she was already in over her head — drowning, almost.

She phoned Riley's house: no answer. She tried again at intervals over the next couple of hours, but still there was nothing. At midday, she went out to buy a Sunday paper. Returning to the flat, she was sure she would hear the phone ringing as she walked up the stairs. That was what always happened, wasn't it? You waited in all morning for a call, then the minute you went out it rang, you rushed to answer it and it stopped ringing just as you picked up the receiver.

But the phone remained silent. Once again, she dialled the number of the Tufnell Park house. Could the Rileys have gone out for the day? Might they have gone to visit Pearl's parents? Yes, that must be it.

Ellen peeled potatoes and chopped runner beans. While she was waiting for them to boil, she scanned through the newspaper. A paragraph at the bottom of the front page caught her eye. *Scotland Yard Detective Shot*. Her heart made a painful squeeze and she read the paragraph through, quickly the first time, then more carefully. The detective wasn't named, but he was listed as critically ill in St Thomas's Hospital. The incident was described as a gangland shooting, which had taken place in Brixton.

The potatoes were boiling over; Ellen turned down the gas. She put a lamb chop on to cook, then dialled Riley's number again. But part of her knew as it rang that no one would answer. *Scotland Yard Detective Shot* . . . *critically ill* . . . *gangland shooting*. A great many detectives must work at Scotland Yard, she told herself; she had no reason to believe the injured detective was Riley.

Yet she couldn't eat the lunch she had cooked, and after she had scraped it into the bin, she searched through the phone directory for the number of St Thomas's Hospital. A lot of holding on and being put through ensued, during which her mouth went dry and she plaited the flex of the phone round her fingers. Then a series of inventive lies was required, and at last a staff nurse on the men's surgical ward was saying, 'Mr Riley's sister, you said? The surgeon had to operate to remove the bullet. Yes, his progress is satisfactory. Yes, visiting hours are between two and three. Only one family member at a time, Miss Riley, he mustn't be tired.'

He had woken in the night and wiggled his toes to make sure his legs were still working. It had been dark, and beside the adjacent bed a doctor and a nurse had been murmuring to each other. He had been aware of a deep, pleasurable relief in finding himself still alive. Then a doctor in a white coat shone a torch in his eyes, which reminded him of Lee Carter, in the tunnel. The doctor said, 'Where are you, Mr Riley?' and Riley thought, in what sense? In a hospital, obviously, but perhaps the question was referring to his life. He was at a crossroads, he thought of saying.

'Hospital,' he said eventually. He spied a nurse in uniform. 'St Thomas's.' Then he closed his eyes and drifted off again.

The next time he woke it was daytime. There was a clattering of trolleys and a school dinner smell. A nurse checked his pulse and temperature then pounded his pillows into

shape. There was something he needed to tell her, some message he wanted to give, but he couldn't remember what it was.

If he wasn't eating or washing or having his dressing changed, he was sleeping. Sleep kept the pain away. Surfacing, he was aware of Basil, sitting beside the bed, explaining that Annie wasn't allowed to visit, but that Vera was looking after her and that she was fine.

He must have dozed again, because he was woken by a nurse scolding someone. 'Those are for the *patient*, officer.'

Davies was sitting beside the bed, munching. 'You can spare a grape, can't you, sir?' he said, aggrieved.

Riley hauled himself into a more upright position and stifled a groan.

'You should have waited for me, sir,' said Davies. 'I was on my way.'

'Did you arrest Lee Carter?'

'Yes, sir. He's been charged with attempted murder and possession of an illegal firearm.'

'And Perlman and Rossiter?'

'They're being interviewed as we speak. And we've already rounded up some of the others. Perlman's accountant, Gerry Marks, has been telling us some interesting things about that fellow we found in the Great Dover Street warehouse.' Davies glanced at the staff nurse, who was glaring at him. 'I'd better go, sir, or I'll be told off again.'

Davies left the ward. Though Riley tried to stay awake, sleep was irresistible. He dreamed of bones, glimpsed like

pieces of broken white china beneath dead leaves. There was still something he needed to say; he struggled, and something cool and soft stroked his palm.

He opened his eyes and saw Ellen. She said, 'Hello, Riley.' Leaning forward, she touched his lips with hers. 'I only just found out. I'm afraid I haven't brought you anything.'

She sat down beside the bed. She was the only thing worth looking at in the dreary hospital ward. The clock over the door showed that there was only five minutes of visiting hour left.

He said, 'I love you, Ellen. I expect I'll forget I said it and say it all over again tomorrow. I think I'll just say it every day and then we'll know we're all right, won't we? But I love you so much, and when I've got things straight with Pearl I want you to marry me. You haven't changed your mind about that, have you?'

'No.' There were tears in her eyes, yet she was smiling. She stroked his face with the back of her fingers. 'No, I haven't changed my mind. There's one thing, though.'

'What's that?'

'Maybe, because we're to be married, I should call you John. Riley – it's starting to seem a bit formal, a bit academic. Would you like that?'

'Yes,' he said.

She smiled at him and linked her fingers through his. He was very tired, and when he tried to speak, she said softly, 'Hush, John. It can wait. Rest now.'

* * *

India stayed on in Medway, at the motel. She liked the thin light and the flat, brackish scent of the water. She liked the boats moored on the banks, with their peeling paint and phut-phutting engines, and she taught herself to like the quiet of the place, the evenings in her room with Abigail, the long walks by the river. She was testing herself by passing a winter in this remote town. She was teaching herself to tolerate boredom and loneliness, making herself into the sort of woman Abigail's mother needed to be. She kept a close eye on her daughter but Abby remained healthy, learning new things every day.

She made friends with the motel receptionist, who was called Karen. Karen mentioned that they were short-staffed in the diner, so at lunchtimes, while Karen kept an eye on Abigail in reception, India helped out, serving meatloaf and shepherd's pie to hungry loggers and truckers and the occasional hiker.

She wrote letters to Sebastian and Ellen in England. She wrote to Marcus, telling him where she was living, and recounting her conversation with Kitty Michaud.

A week later, he arrived in Medway. He wanted her to come home, he told her. He wanted her to come back with him.

'I can't,' she said. 'I'm sorry.'

They were sitting in her bedroom. Outside a full moon cast a silver light on the parked cars.

He said, 'I know you don't love me, but I can live with that. If it's because of the child,' he glanced at Abigail,

asleep in the carrycot, 'I felt the same way when Rowena was a baby. Surely, now that you know what happened, you can understand that?'

'You were afraid to love her because you were frightened she might fall ill as well.'

'I believe it to be inherited, you see. The ultimate irony, I think, is that such diseases have always been my interest, my passion. To begin with I was fascinated by the patterns they made, their symmetry and predictability, and what they tell us about inheritance. And then, after what happened to the child, I became consumed with the possibility of finding a cure.' Again, his gaze drifted to the sleeping baby. 'I could tell there was something wrong with it. I could see it wasn't right.'

'He was your son, Marcus.'

'To think that Rosanne and I could have produced such a child . . .' He pushed his fingertips against the lines on his forehead. 'I couldn't be sure. I kept hoping I was mistaken, but the infant's condition became more apparent as time went on. And if the disease is hereditary, as I believe it to be, then I may be a carrier. I've had to live with the knowledge that I could transmit this, this *curse* to the next generation. I never wanted a child with Alison but she wouldn't have married me otherwise. Thank God, Rowena was healthy.' He sighed. 'I knew it was improbable that a different marriage would result in another abnormal child. If the pattern of inheritance is as I believe, then Rosanne and I must have both been carriers. It was always unlikely

that Alison would carry the same faulty gene as well. Or you, India. But there remained the possibility.'

'So you hid it. You pretended it had never happened.'

'I buried my wife, left the child with Miss Michaud, and went home to England. All I wanted to do was to put it behind me, to start again. Only a few people knew what had happened. I threw myself into my work. I met Alison, and a year later Rowena was born. And then there was the war, of course, and Gildersleve. You forget. I made myself forget.'

'Did you?' she said. 'Did you really?'

A shadow of a smile. 'It's a part of me, inside me, written in my blood, ineradicable, unchangeable.' His eyes sought hers. 'Do you blame me for abandoning the child?'

'No, Marcus, I blame myself for marrying you.' She was sitting on the edge of the bed; she did not allow herself to turn aside from his gaze. 'I shouldn't have, I see that now.'

'I can change,' he said.

'But not enough for me. We would destroy each other, you see that, surely?'

He left that night. The way he talked, she reflected after he had gone, as if they weren't all faulty, didn't all pick up imperfections along the way.

India stayed on in Medway as the first snows fell. The motel was quieter in the winter and she helped out with the cooking and cleaning as well as in the restaurant. Abigail learned to sit and to crawl. India received a letter from

Sebastian. The girl he had been dating for months – Jenny – he was in love with her and they were thinking of getting married.

During the coldest months, the daylight limited itself to a few murky hours. The water in the Penobscot thickened, slopping against the shores. India bound Abigail to her in a papoose as she walked to the shops or headed along the river to visit Miss Michaud. Her boots sank into the snow and slabs of snow settled on the ranks of fir trees, tumbling now and then to the ground below, sending up white dust. Snowflakes rushed across the window of her room in the motel and clung to the glass.

In the New Year, she received a letter from Marcus. He was returning to England, he wrote. His position at Midhurst College had not worked out as he had hoped. He had made arrangements to pay a sum each month into an account in a bank in Montpelier, Vermont. If she did not want the money herself, he would like her to keep it towards Abigail's college fees.

Spring came. In the thaw, the river swelled and the wind fractured its surface into crescents. Abigail learned to walk round the furniture in the motel reception room, hands resting on the sofa as she sidestepped like a ballerina. One day, India was fetching a room key for a trucker who had driven in from Canada when she looked up and saw Abigail launch herself off from a table. Six steps, unsupported: India and the trucker applauded.

She wrote to Linc. She had thought of him every day

throughout that winter and spring, of the hard warmth of his body and the exploring softness of his mouth. She had thought of him standing on the stoop outside his house as the snow covered the mountains, and she had thought of him walking into the coffeehouse in the afternoons. Did he still look for her? Did he still think of her?

He wrote back to her. He had been to Medway once before, he said. A nice little town; he had liked the look of it.

The sky became bluer and the air warmed. The jukebox in the café played 'All I Have to Do Is Dream', and India looked out of the window, searching for a tall, brown-haired man with an easy smile.

Working in the diner one morning, she found herself considering a number of things. How soon she would be able to afford to go back to England to visit Sebastian. Whether it was time to move out of the motel and find a place to rent, and if so, whether she would stay on in Medway another winter or move south.

As she wiped and laid a table, she noticed a green truck draw up in the parking lot outside. A customer called out to her for more coffee; India went to fetch the pot but her gaze kept going back to the truck. She poured out the coffee and heard the door of the diner swing open.

And there he was. Denim jeans, red plaid shirt, standing in the doorway.

She put the coffee pot back on the hotplate and crossed the room to him.

'Would you like a table, sir?'

'That's why I'm here, ma'am.'

'Do you know what you want yet?' She was standing in front of him. He rested a hand on her hip.

'Yes, ma'am. Yes, I sure do. And you?'

'Yes.' She stood on tiptoe to kiss him. 'Hello, Linc,' she said.

Chapter Fourteen

Ellen was only just in time for the London train. The guard, perhaps noticing her bump, held open a door for her and waited until she had climbed inside the carriage before raising the flag and blowing his whistle. The train was busy and she murmured apologies as she made her way along the corridor, her briefcase held in front of her like a shield. All the second-class seats were taken; she was glad that John had insisted she buy a first-class ticket.

The corridor shifted and jolted as the train gathered speed. Reaching the first-class carriage, she peered through the windows of the compartments. In one, only a single seat was taken. She was about to open the door when, with a shock, she recognized that the man sitting in the window seat was Marcus Pharoah.

She could have walked away, and was tempted to, but then she opened the door and went inside.

'Good afternoon, Dr Pharoah,' she said.

He had been looking out of the window. Turning to her, he frowned. 'Miss Kingsley.'

'Are these seats free?'

'Yes, all of them.'

She sat down opposite him. She wondered whether they might travel to London in silence, nothing said, but then he spoke.

'Presumably you're not Miss Kingsley any more.'

'I'm Mrs Riley. Though I keep my maiden name at work.'

'Did you get on the train at Cambridge?'

'Yes, I was attending a conference there. And you, Dr Pharoah?'

'I was visiting my ex-wife and daughter.'

A heaviness seemed to settle over him; she thought how greatly he had changed. Though he looked older, and his hair was now almost entirely grey, it was not that which struck her, but the loss of vitality and resolution.

He said, 'And the happy event? When is it to be?'

'In two months' time. January.'

'A new decade. A child of the sixties.'

The train had reached the open countryside south of Cambridge. If she had been able to look further over the fields through the darkness and the rain, she would have been able to see as far as Gildersleve.

He must have had the same thought, because he said, 'They were good days. I miss them.'

She asked curiously, 'When were you happiest?'

'In the war, I think.'

'When you were living in the cottage with Dr Kaminski and Dr Redmond?'

'Yes.' His gaze moved back from the window to her. 'Jan told me he'd spoken to you.'

'Yes.'

'You have such a curious nature. A valuable quality in a scientist, I acknowledge.'

'I think I found out what I wanted to know.'

His smile was disbelieving, and she found herself saying, 'I think that you and Dr Redmond grew apart after the end of the war because you'd found out that he was a homosexual. I expect the division between you deepened after Dr Redmond realized that because Gildersleve was running out of money you were planning to sell the woodland. I think that he threatened to expose you, and either to make public the fact that you'd passed Dr Kaminski's work off as your own, or that you'd been a member of the Communist Party when you were young. That was what he meant when I overheard him tell you that he could destroy you.'

In the silence that lay between them there was only the clatter of the wheels on the rails and the scream of the slipstream as the train raced through a tunnel.

Dr Pharoah said, 'Both those things may be true, but the reason I sent Gosse to the cottage that evening was to find the letters I'd written to Redmond about my first wife.'

Her heart tripped; she felt the baby startle and put a hand on her belly.

'You sent Gosse to the cottage?'

'Yes.' He smiled, sadly. 'We fear most what lies inside us, don't we? And *that* was what I most feared, that he would tell Alison – and Rowena – about my son. *That* was what I thought he had meant. Afterwards, I wondered whether I'd been correct. But by then it was too late.'

'So Dr Redmond knew about the child?'

'He was one of the few people who did. I met him shortly after I returned to England, after the death of my wife. I had to talk to someone and I talked to him. He was a good listener. I'm afraid I sometimes drank too much and bored him with what had happened to me in America. No, that's not right. You couldn't *bore* him. He either listened or he walked away.' A smile flickered. 'Sometimes some bigwig would come to the hall, someone I was trying to extract money from, and Redmond would walk away while he was talking. It used to make me laugh at first, but then, as time went on, it began to annoy me. Why he couldn't *dissemble*, like other people.' Pharoah shrugged. 'I suppose I had to get it out of my system. Most people will listen to you once or twice and then you'll see them becoming impatient. Bryan never became impatient. I think,' here, Pharoah brushed a hand down the sleeve of his coat to wipe away some beads of rain, 'I think his peculiar nature allowed him to listen. He felt no need to be listened *to*. You have to give most people their

turn, don't you? But not Bryan. He wasn't a talker. You know that.'

The rain had sharpened, shooting horizontally across the window. 'My mistake was that I wrote to him,' Pharoah said. 'I poured out my heart to him in those letters. About Rosanne, about the child, about the fact that I believed the illness to be hereditary, and about the pattern I ascribed to it. Everything was there. I knew he would have kept the letters because he never threw anything away.'

'And that was what you were afraid of?'

'Yes.' His dark eyes burned. 'I was afraid for my daughter. I did not want her to be burdened with *that*.'

She wondered whether it had been only for Rowena that he had been afraid. Or whether he had taken such pride in his invulnerability, in his good health, intelligence and looks, he had found it impossible to countenance public knowledge of his imperfection.

She said, 'So you sent Gosse to the cottage to find the letters. What happened? Was there a fight? Did he lose his temper and push Dr Redmond downstairs?'

'What an imagination you have. No, nothing so sordid.' Pharoah made a short, quick sigh. 'Gosse was searching the bedroom when Redmond came home. If he hadn't taken the wretched dog with him everything would have been all right. Gosse would have hidden upstairs until Redmond went out to the garden or to Peddar's Wood, and then he would have returned to Gildersleve with the letters. But the dog got out of the room somehow. It must

have startled Redmond. He was always afraid of dogs. Perhaps he thought the creature was going for him. In his rush to get out of its way he tripped on the carpet and fell downstairs.' He met her gaze. 'It was a damnable thing to happen,' he said quietly. 'But it was an accident.'

'Then why not tell the police?'

'Don't be ridiculous, Miss Kingsley. It would have all come out – the reason I'd sent Gosse there, the letters, our quarrel. It would have been splashed across the newspapers and the inevitable questions would have been asked. And what good would it have done? None whatsoever. It would have ruined my reputation and Gildersleve's and it wouldn't have helped poor Redmond at all.'

Someone put their head round the door; Pharoah flung them a fierce glance and they retreated, shutting the door behind them. She said, 'Did Dr Redmond die instantly?'

Pharoah became motionless. Minutes seemed to pass before he said, 'No. He was still alive when Gosse left the house.'

His profile seemed to have been carved out of stone, immovable and severe. 'Did you go to him?' she said.

He shook his head. 'No.'

She whispered, 'But he was your friend!' And for the first time, a look of shame crossed his face, and he turned away, towards the window once more.

The train drew into a station. Passengers climbed off and on; this time, three men in trilbies and overcoats joined them in the carriage.

She thought they would not speak again but as they reached the outskirts of London, Pharoah leaned towards her and said, his voice low, 'If you think that I deserve to be punished for what I did, then let me assure you, I have been. My daughter, Rowena, is to marry her cousin. I went to Barton today to try to put a stop to this poisonous alliance, but it's too late. She is expecting Rufus's child.'

Ellen saw that his eyes glittered. She remembered Sunday lunch at the Pharoahs' house, all those years ago: Pharoah's dark, beautiful daughter and her saturnine cousin, huddled together in the dining room. And how Rufus had taken Rowena's plaits in his hands and pulled her towards him, and how she had let out a peal of laughter.

'I'm sorry,' she said. 'A child . . .'

'I'm sure you can work it out. If the disease is recessive, assuming I inherited the faulty gene from my parents, then it's possible that my brother Devlin has done so as well. And if so, it's also possible that we've passed it on to both Rowena and Rufus. Which would mean there's a one in four chance that Rowena's child will inherit the disease.'

There was in his eyes such an expression of horror that Ellen found herself pitying him.

He said, 'I went there today to try to tell Rowena about my son. But I couldn't. This is what I shall have to endure, Miss Kingsley, this is my punishment. This wretched and hasty wedding and a year of waiting to see whether my grandchild is healthy. And that would be the best outcome. The worst – I can hardly bear to think of it.'

He turned away. The lights of the approaching city made orange smears on the rainswept window. Ellen thought of her own child, hers and Riley's, longed-for, already beloved. She felt it move in her womb and she muttered a silent prayer for its health and survival.

He spoke to her only once again, as the train drew into King's Cross. They were rising, doing up buttons and tying scarves.

'Do you see her at all?' he said.

'India? No.' She picked up her briefcase. 'We write, though.'

'Is she happy?'

'Yes, very.'

'Please tell her – please tell her that I miss her.'

He left the carriage. Ellen waited for a few moments before also leaving, not wanting to cross his path again. But as she made her way through the crowds pouring along the platform, she was haunted by them, by Pharoah and Dr Redmond and Rowena Pharoah and her unborn child, by the cold-hearted mathematics of genetics and the way that misfortune and greed and lovelessness could write itself into future generations. And when she went through the barrier and saw Riley waiting for her, Annie at his side, she found herself rushing towards them, throwing her arms round him and burying her face in his shoulder.

'What's this?' he said, concerned. 'What's wrong?'

'Nothing,' she said. His features were blurred by her

tears; but in that moment, among her family again, her meeting with Marcus Pharoah slipped into the past and she was able to say, 'Nothing at all, love. I missed you, that's all.'

And together they walked out of the station.

JUDITH LENNOX

Catching the Tide

1933
Tessa and Frederica Nicolson enjoy one last summer at the beautiful Villa Millefiore, overlooking Florence.

Four years later, Italy is a distant memory and Tessa is revelling in the excitement of modelling in London. Unconventional and impulsive, she believes love is just a game, until a passionate affair with married author Milo Rycroft leads to tragic consequences. In the wake of disaster, Tessa flees to Florence. Following her sister to Italy, Freddie is soon swept up in adventure, danger and romance, and makes a chance encounter that will change her life.

With the outbreak of World War Two, Tessa and Freddie must fight for their own survival and happiness, unsure if they will ever see each other again . . .

Acclaim for Judith Lennox's novels:

'The beautifully written story is a compelling and emotional read' *Woman's Way*

'A compelling novel . . . a beautiful tale' *Sunday Express*

978 0 7553 4489 5

headline
review